Accession no.
36269514

D1092878

The first farmers of central Europe

Diversity in LBK lifeways

Edited by

Penny Bickle and Alasdair Whittle

With contributions by

Alexandra Anders, Rose-Marie Arbogast, R. Alexander Bentley, Penny Bickle, Christoph Blesl, Lucy Cramp, Philippa Cullen, Christopher Dale, Marta Dočkalová, László Domboróczki, Linda Fibiger, Michael Francken, Claudia Gerling, Seren Griffiths, Gisela Grupe, Julie Hamilton, Robert Hedges, Daniela Hofmann, Nándor Kalicz, Zsófia Eszter Kovács, Eva Lenneis, Tibor Marton, Inna Mateiciucová, Christine Neugebauer-Maresch, Geoff Nowell, Krisztián Oross, Ildikó Pap, Juraj Pavúk, Joachim Pechtl, Pál Raczky, Linda Reynard, Michael Schultz, Peter Stadler, Elisabeth Stephan, Maria Teschler-Nicola, Barbara Tiefenböck, Joachim Wahl, Alasdair Whittle and Carrie Wright

OXBOW BOOKS

Oxford and Oakville

Published by
Oxbow Books, Oxford, UK

ISBN 978-1-84217-530-9

Front cover: Brunn am Gebirge: anthropomorphic figurine.
Photo: Alice Schuhmacher, Naturhistorisches Museum Wien.
Back cover: Left: Reconstructed longhouse at Straubing zoo. Photo: Alasdair Whittle
Centre: Mitterndorf: burial 485 of adult male with dog. © Bundesdenkmalamt.
Right: Inside the reconstructed longhouse at Straubing zoo. Photo: Penny Bickle

This book is available direct from:

Oxbow Books, Oxford, UK
(Phone: 01865-241249; Fax: 01865-794449)

and

The David Brown Book Company
PO Box 511, Oakville, CT 06779, USA
(Phone: 860-945-9329; Fax: 860-945-9468)

or from our website

www.oxbowbooks.com

A CIP record of this book is available from the British Library

Library of Congress Cataloging-in-Publication Data

The first farmers of central Europe : diversity in LBK lifeways / edited by Penny Bickle and Alasdair Whittle ; with contributions by Alexandra Anders, Rose-Marie Arbogast, R. Alexander Bentley, Penny Bickle, Christoph Blesl, Lucy Cramp, Philippa Cullen, Christopher Dale, Marta Dočkalová, László Domboróczki, Linda Fibiger, Michael Francken, Claudia Gerling, Seren Griffiths, Gisela Grupe, Julie Hamilton, Robert Hedges, Daniela Hofmann, Nándor Kalicz, Zsófia Eszter Kovács, Eva Lenneis, Tibor Marton, Inna Mateiciucová, Christine Neugebauer-Maresch, Geoff Nowell, Krisztián Oross, Ildikó Pap, Juraj Pavúk, Joachim Pechtl, Pál Raczky, Linda Reynard, Michael Schultz, Peter Stadler, Elisabeth Stephan, Maria Teschler-Nicola, Barbara Tiefenböck, Joachim Wahl, Alasdair Whittle and Carrie Wright.
pages cm
Includes bibliographical references and index.
ISBN 978-1-84217-530-9
1. Bandkeramik culture--Europe, Central. 2. Agriculture, Prehistoric--Europe, Central. 3. Land settlement patterns, Prehistoric--Europe, Central. 4. Social archaeology--Europe, Central. 5. Human remains (Archaeology)--Europe, Central. 6. Europe, Central--Antiquities. I. Bickle, Penny.
GN776.2.B3F57 2013
930.1--dc23
2013017976

Printed and bound in Great Britain by
Berforts Information Press Ltd, Eynsham, Oxfordshire

In memory of Marek Zvelebil

Contents

3 Hungary

4 Moravia and western Slovakia

9 The supra-regional perspective

10 Performing LBK Lifeways

Authors' note

This book is about uniformity and diversity in lifeways, as approached through a study of isotopes, osteology and archaeology. Our case study is the early Neolithic of central Europe – the Linearbandkeramik *or LBK – but as an interdisciplinary study combining bioarchaeology and grave good analysis, and as a more general reflection on difference and commonality within what we term 'cultures', we hope that this work will be of wider interest to those who are thinking through similar problems in other areas and for other times.*

There are various ways in which different readers may wish to tackle this volume. Chapter 1 provides an introduction to the LBK and positions the main questions and approach of our project within the framework of current research on the European early Neolithic, and in relation to debate in anthropology about the concept of culture. Chapter 2 introduces the methods employed. Chapters 3–8 cover the six regions defined in the project, and as well as providing more general sections on the archaeological background, each gives a detailed site-by-site account of the data we have generated and how they have been interpreted; the reader coming to the LBK for the first time could take any one of these on its own. These are complemented by selected individual lifeways, presented after each regional chapter. Chapter 9 contains a more synthetic discussion of overall patterns across our study area, drawing strongly on the detailed arguments presented in the regional overviews. Finally, Chapter 10 returns to the implications of our work for wider discussion of different social scales.

Acknowledgements

A project of this size would not have been possible without the help of many people and institutions. First among these, we would like to thank our funders, the Arts and Humanities Research Council.

Much stimulating discussion and critical input were provided by our external advisors, particularly Graeme Barker (Cambridge University) in early stages of the project, and Detlef Gronenborn (Römisch-Germanisches Zentralmuseum Mainz) and Christian Jeunesse (Strasbourg University) throughout.

Access to collections for sampling and study was a cornerstone of this project, which could not have been completed without the agreement and partnership of many institutions. We owe a great debt to the museum curators, regional archaeologists and colleagues at universities and institutions who facilitated access to skeletal material and data, in some cases unpublished, granted sampling permission and assisted during the sampling process itself, among them: Alexandra Anders (ELTE Budapest), Rose-Marie Arbogast (CNRS Strasbourg), László Bartosiewicz (ELTE Budapest), Christoph Blesl (Bundesdenkmalamt Österreich), Eric Boës (INRAP, Paris), Joël Delaine (Musée Historique Mulhouse), Marta Dočkalová (Moravian Museum Brno), Lászlo Domboróczki (Dobó István Museum Eger), Bernd Engelhardt (Bayerisches Landesamt für Denkmalpflege), Michael Francken (Eberhard-Karls-Universität Tübingen), Claudia Gerling (Freie Universität Berlin), Zsuzsanna Guba (Natural History Museum Budapest), Gisela Grupe (Bayerische Staatssammlung für Anthropologie München), Gaëlle Harouard (PAIR), Christian Jeunesse (Strasbourg University), Nándor Kalicz (Archaeological Institute HAS, Budapest), Olivier Kayser (DRAC, Alsace), Corina Knipper (Mainz University), François Lambach, Eva Lenneis (Vienna University), Jutta Leskovar (Landesmuseum Linz), Tibor Marton (Archaeological Institute HAS, Budapest), Inna Mateiciucová (Brno University), George McGlynn (Bayerische Staatssammlung für Anthropologie München), Ronald Mühl (Naturhistorisches Museum Wien), Agathe Mulot (PAIR), Henriette Obermaier (Ludwig-Maximilians University Munich), Krisztián Oross (Archaeological Institute HAS, Budapest), Ildikó Pap (Natural History Museum Budapest), Juraj Pavúk (Comenius University), Michael Peters (Ludwig-Maximilians University Munich), Johannes Prammer (Gäubodenmuseum Straubing), Pál Raczky (ELTE Budapest), Martina Reitberger (Landesmuseum Linz), Sandra Schlegel (Musée de la Régence, Ensisheim), Manfred Schmitzberger (Naturhistorisches Museum Wien), Bernadette Schnitzler (Musée Archéologique Strasbourg), Michael Schultz (Zentrum Anatomie Göttingen), Joël Schweitzer (Musée Historique Mulhouse), Peter Stadler (Naturhistorisches Museum Wien), Marie Stahl (DRAC Alsace), Elisabeth Stephan (Landesamt für Denkmalpflege Baden-Württemberg), Hans-Christoph Strien (Vaihingen project), Maria Teschler-Nicola (Naturhistorisches Museum Wien), Barbara Tiefenböck (Naturhistorisches Museum Wien), Zdeněk Tvrdý (Moravian Museum Brno), Bettina Voglsinger (Naturhistorisches Museum Wien), Joachim Wahl (Landesamt für Denkmalpflege Baden-Württemberg) and Helmut Windl (Museen für Urgeschichte in Asparn/Zaya).

In addition, we are greatly indebted to László Bartosiewicz (ELTE Budapest), Zsófia Kovács (Hungarian National Museum, Budapest), Richard Madgwick (Cardiff University), Zora Mikliková (Archaeology SAV, Nitra), Elisabeth Stephan (Landesamt für Denkmalpflege Baden-Württemberg), Manfred Schmitzberger (Naturhistorisches Museum Wien) and Rose-Marie Arbogast (CNRS Strasbourg) for helping with the identification of animal bone from collections. Geoff Nowell, Christopher Dale and Fernando Laghinias (all Durham University) helped undertake some of the strontium analysis, while Thomas Higham, Fiona Brock (both Oxford Radiocarbon Accelerator Unit) and Seren Griffiths (Cardiff University) assisted with the radiocarbon dating. Panagiota Manti (Cardiff University) kindly undertook Fourier transform infrared spectroscopy (FTIR) on behalf of this project. Dan Lunn (Department of Statistics, Oxford University) helped with Appendix C, although all mistakes and misunderstandings remain of course our own. Finally, Martin Franks (Oxford University) ensured that there was always a drill for us to borrow.

The volume could not have been written without the input of the many co-authors of individual chapters and we were fortunate to work with colleagues who generously offered their time for writing, editing and working through the intricacies of the evidence. Numerous others also gave their support, hospitality, information, advice, or simply their time for discussion, among them Eszter Bánffy (Archaeological Institute HAS, Budapest), Amy Bogaard (Oxford University), Oliver Craig (University of York), Philippa Cullen (Research Laboratory for Archaeology, Oxford), Oliver Harris (Leicester University), Sarka Hladilova (Masaryk University), Corina Knipper (Mainz University), Inna Mateiciucová (Brno University), Christian Meyer (Mainz University), Janet Montgomery (Durham University), Stephen Shennan (University College London), Peter Tóth (Comenius University), Andrea Zeeb-Lanz (Generaldirektion Kulturelles Erbe Rheinland-Pfalz), and the late Marek Zvelebil (Sheffield University).

Getting a volume of this size to publication is a huge task, and we would like to extend our heartfelt thanks to the Cardiff colleagues who helped us to complete it, in particular Heather Giddens for her work on the bibliography, Daniela Hofmann for last-minute help in editing and proof-reading, Steve Mills for his support with GIS and map creation, and Ian Dennis and Kirsty Harding for help with the figures. Further assistance throughout the project and the publication process was received from Anne Brown, Aled Cooke and Sue Virgo.

The Lifeways Database

As part of the LBK Lifeways project, a relational database of existing information on all published LBK burials known to us was created (in MS Access) by Daniela Hofmann and Penny Bickle, and expanded with unpublished information from sites sampled in this project. Overall, *c*. 3000 individuals are listed. We have included basic site information (site name, site type, main references to published sources, overall date), as well as comprehensive information on the individual burials. We list age, sex and pathologies (where known), aspects of the grave rite (body position and orientation, burial location and kind of feature) and details of the grave good assemblage (including pottery, polished stone tools, chipped industry, bone tools, personal ornamentation, colouring matter, grinding stones, animal bone, any other items, and objects recovered from the grave fill). The database also contains all the isotopic data generated by the project (including information on the sample, the isotopic values and standard deviations), as well as measurements previously published by other researchers (as known to us). The isotopic data produced for this project from animal remains are available in a separate table.

We believe that the Lifeways Database currently represents the most comprehensive publicly accessible collection of data on LBK burials and provides one of the largest datasets of isotopes for a prehistoric European population.

This database will shortly be made available at the *Archaeological Data Service* (ADS) where it can be downloaded free of charge (http://archaeologydataservice.ac.uk/), along with its supporting documentation. Three important caveats should be noted. First, since we relied on published sources for many aspects and since these offer varied levels of detail, the information available is uneven. For certain traits, notably osteoarchaeological information, there were also problems in harmonising the methods used by different researchers, and the reader is referred to Chapter 2 for a fuller discussion of these issues. A comprehensive explanation of the fields used in the database, of other remaining problems, and of the decisions we made regarding the inclusion of certain kinds of information is provided in a separate document available for download with the database itself. We urge readers to study this document carefully before attempting to use the data for themselves. Secondly, as a number of sites have yet to be fully published, the information that could be included about them is restricted pending their full publication. This is the case for Polgár-Ferenci-hát (Chapter 3), Asparn, Kleinhadersdorf (Chapter 5) and Schwetzingen (Chapter 7). Thirdly, the database does not include any information published after early 2012.

Nevertheless, we hope that readers will make full use of the opportunity to explore the data for themselves.

Summary

This volume presents the results of a study of early Neolithic lifeways in central Europe. Our focus has been the interplay between uniformity and diversity. To this end, we analysed hundreds of isotopic samples of humans and animals from cemeteries and settlements of the *Linearbandkeramik* or LBK culture, dating from *c*. 5500–4900 cal BC, in Hungary, western Slovakia, Moravia (Czech Republic), Austria, southern Germany and Alsace (France). We approached questions of mobility (using strontium and oxygen isotopes), diet (investigating carbon and nitrogen isotopes, and assessing the potential of calcium), and health (based on osteoarchaeological study of selected assemblages). We incorporated the data from these varied analyses into a re-assessment of the burial evidence (including burial location, rite and grave good provision). We then identified recurrent patterns and variability at different geographical and social scales, from the individual interment to groups of burials, single sites, regions and finally the study area as a whole, and from individuals through households, clans or lineages to wider dimensions of community, network and meshwork.

LBK dietary practices were strikingly similar throughout the study area. There were also recurrent patterns in the strontium data, suggesting that the majority of the people whom we have sampled died in or close to the localities where they were born; that has made it possible to identify obvious outliers, born and raised elsewhere, and there are also recurrently detectable differences between male and female strontium ratios. The strontium data can thus be taken to suggest patrilocality as a frequent choice in post-marital residence patterns, and potentially also point to a correlation between inheritance of land and those men buried with a polished stone adze. Nevertheless, there is also variability at many social scales, from broad east–west differences in the proportion of animal protein in the diet, and regional patterning in the importance of adhering to strict body positions and orientations in the grave, right down to myriad individual ways in which people could stand out from the wider burial community around them through rite, grave good assemblage, physical condition, diet and mobility.

Chapter 1 introduces the background and rationale for the study by summarising approaches to uniformity and diversity within the LBK, set in the context of anthropological discussions of culture as performative and flexible. Dimensions of different LBK lifeways include the regionally varied input of local foragers and migrants; variability in economic strategies between settlements and households; the impact of demographic factors and regional histories; and the use of material culture (including adzes, other lithics, pottery and ornaments) to create identities at personal, household, ward, lineage or clan, site, regional and other scales. The chapter offers a detailed account of how mortuary practices have been studied, discussing especially the definition of a 'normative' burial rite and the identification of social status as two important research foci. Coming to terms with diversity, at multiple social scales, remains a significant challenge. This is the starting point for our interdisciplinary study, in which isotopic, osteological and archaeological analyses work together to tackle this issue.

Chapter 2 outlines the methodological background for the different analytical approaches (with details of the protocols for the isotopic analyses carried out at the RLAHA, Oxford, and at Durham University) and discusses important earlier work, with particular emphasis on studies of LBK material. Carbon and nitrogen measurements (obtained on 617 human individuals and 366 faunal samples) can inform on the role of animals and plants in the human diet and on livestock management strategies, but do not directly reflect either. Similarly, strontium isotopes (investigated for over 550 human individuals), which relate to the geological substrate from which diet was sourced, can reveal episodes of mobility, but not directly determine a specific origin. In both cases, our emphasis has been on exploring variation within the dataset and finding patterns between groups of burials, which could then be interpreted further. We also briefly outline the results of pilot studies of oxygen isotopes (which can track mobility by reflecting differences in groundwater) and calcium (which relates to dairy consumption). The osteoarchaeological study of 236 individuals covered the determination of age and sex, as well as the identification of dental pathologies, *cribra orbitalia*, periosteal lesions and trauma. Finally, we summarise how various aspects of the burial rite have previously been related to gender, status, ethnic identity and other avenues of diversity. For our archaeological analysis, based on over 3000 individuals, we selected burial location, body position and orientation, and grave good assemblages as the key variables. It is stressed that neither archaeological, osteological nor isotopic evidence will straightforwardly reflect identity categories or relate to only one scale of analysis, underlining the need for careful and balanced integration of the different results.

The main part of the book is formed by six regional case studies set out in Chapters 3–8. Regions were pragmatically defined in accordance with previous research foci and modern political boundaries, but further integration of all results is provided in Chapters 9 and 10. In order to maximise statistical robustness, sites within regions were selected on the basis of the number of individuals, as well as the accessibility of remains. This involved a necessary bias towards large assemblages, and therefore often towards burial grounds (although only burials from settlements were analysed for Hungary). In addition, our material mostly relates to the second half of the LBK sequence, from about 5300–5200 cal BC onwards, as earlier human remains are rare. In detail, we sampled the following sites: for Hungary (Chapter 3), Mezőkövesd-Mocsolyás, Füzesabony-Gubakút, Polgár-Ferenci-hát and Balatonszárszó-Kis-erdei-dűlő; for Moravia and western Slovakia (Chapter 4), Vedrovice (expanding on a recent study by Zvelebil and colleagues), Těšetice-Kyjovice, Brno-Starý Lískovec and Nitra; for Austria (Chapter 5), Kleinhadersdorf, Asparn a.d. Zaya, Mitterndorf and Rutzing; for Bavaria (Chapter 6), Aiterhofen and Otzing; for Baden-Württemberg (Chapter 7), Schwetzingen; and for Alsace (Chapter 8), Mulhouse-Est, Ensisheim *Les Octrois*, Souffelweyersheim and Vendenheim. Faunal samples were collected from additional sites where required.

Each of the regional chapters provides an overview of research history and of the main features of LBK archaeology, detailing in particular the arrival and development of the LBK, subsistence patterns, material culture networks and regional burial practices. After this, the results of our analyses are presented site by site, beginning with osteological data (where obtained) and leading on to the stable isotopes and strontium. These are then connected to archaeological data to provide an initial interpretation for each site. At the end of each chapter, these local narratives are compared to highlight the main conclusions from each region. This is followed by the presentation of two individual lifeways, each based on a burial selected from the regional sample, which highlight the interplay between individual biographies and wider research themes.

This approach is sensitive to regional characteristics within the evidence. Thus, although the same set of questions was brought to bear on each site, the principal focus of the discussion was adapted to the strands which emerged most strongly from the evidence. Chapter 3 (Hungary) reveals a clear sense of sex-based differences in diet, as well as outlining differences between regions of Hungary. Chapter 4 (Moravia and western Slovakia) covers the probably earliest cemetery sampled in this project (Vedrovice) and is therefore ideally placed to address questions of LBK spread and development beyond the Hungarian core regions, tracing a move towards more uniformity in burial over time as well as the continued importance of sex-based difference. This latter aspect is less emphasised in Chapter 5 (Austria), which in contrast begins to reveal the existence of groups of individuals with distinct lifeways on some sites and the use of more varied grave good assemblages in creating avenues for distinction. Both aspects remain very much at the forefront of discussion in Chapter 6 (Bavaria), which also hints at linkages between isotopic patterns (here related to diet) and the provision with polished stone tools. Polished adzes and axes are an important focus in Chapter 7 (Baden-Württemberg), where most of the previous isotopic work of the LBK had been undertaken. Our project confirmed and expanded upon these earlier conclusions regarding different patterns of male and female lifetime mobility and the existence of heterogeneous practices at the community level, perhaps down to local forager involvement. Finally, regional difference is the guiding theme for Chapter 8 (Alsace), where there is a long-running tradition of research into different practices between North and South Alsace in a range of contexts (including burial, pottery decoration and economic practices), potentially related to a greater role for local foragers in western areas of the LBK distribution.

Throughout these discussions, it is stressed that different potential avenues for distinction (for example, those revealed by isotopes and those expressed in the grave rite) do not correlate in straightforward ways. While there is a tendency for individuals who stand out in one aspect to also appear atypical in another, one can normally also find counter-examples. Instead, what we see is the creative re-combination of many potential modes of divergence in locally embedded ways.

The results for all the different regions are interpreted together in Chapter 9. The greatest part of the variation in the stable isotope measurements relates to the relative importance of Continental and Atlantic influences in the climate, and possibly also differential forest cover. This means that the LBK dataset is remarkably uniform in terms of diet, although husbandry and cultivation practices may have varied in detail. Further detailed modelling shows that our data are consistent with plausible suggestions for Neolithic diets, but also draws out a tendency for more meat/milk to be consumed in western as opposed to eastern areas of the project. In the east, sex-based differences in diet are also more marked. The strontium isotope pattern across central Europe confirms that the isotopic ranges for women are wider than those for men, interpreted as an indication of patrilocal residence. In addition, males buried with adzes fall within a tighter range than those without, and it is suggested that this reflects inheritance of land across the generations, with household or lineage heads or other such important figures marked out by polished tools. At an individual level, strontium outliers are often also distinguished through other aspects of burial treatment, for instance through a right-crouched position or a minority orientation. Residence at birth therefore had an impact on treatment in death, suggesting differentiation in LBK society along the lines both of sex and perhaps household, lineage or other membership. The former at least is also confirmed through our osteoarchaeological analysis, as females more often suffer from caries and *cribra orbitalia* than males, and gendered activity patterns existed. Nevertheless, general health did not vary much across the distribution (with the notable exception of more stress markers in the Austrian sample), and more work is needed further to fill in the gaps.

Finally, the archaeological analysis of burial location, grave rite and good assemblage (with specific reference to lithics, pottery, ornaments and ochre) showed the consistent marking out of children between seven and 13 years of age, and we suggest that this was an important threshold between childhood and a full adult identity. We confirm the special importance of males buried with adzes, who show the most formalised patterns, but also stress that other goods and practices, most notably the provision with personal ornaments, were explicitly employed in the presentation of varying identities at personal, local and regional scales. One of the strongest regional patterns concerns the stress that was variously placed on greater uniformity (in the east) or variation (in the west) in body position and orientation. Overall, the distinctions between settlement and cemetery burials, and the variation within the cemetery sample, seem connected to the scales of community which are being referenced, and which determine whether the emphasis falls on uniformity or individual difference, or on provision with grave goods as opposed to other avenues for distinction.

In Chapter 10, we use these conclusions to address the many different social scales and kinds of performance which are relevant to a consideration of LBK lifeways. As well as the individual scale, we note the importance of households and their potentially flexible composition, as also argued by recent discussions of 'house society' models in Neolithic archaeology, and the evidence for lineages or clans both in our isotopic data and in other studies; this raises the puzzle of the relative invisibility of households as such in cemeteries, and the whole question of the basis on which individual people were selected for burial in cemeteries. Widely shared patterns need not lead us to downplay the significance of diversity and flexibility, and a case is made for the importance of bilateral and cognatic or composite rather than exclusively patrilineal descent, for sodalities as one possible means of creating wide-ranging links between communities, and for the LBK as an 'imagined community', that is a system of values and practices that were shared over a vast area, albeit locally refracted. Yet these ways of relating were also historically situated, and we describe their potential trajectory from an earliest phase, dominated by a strategy of commonality in spite of the diverse origins of people and ways of doing things, via a developed phase of increasing specialisation between sites and individuals – still taking place on a background of substantially similar lifeways – to the creation of ever more tightly defined groups, which could eventually have contributed to the break-up or fundamental transformation of the LBK at its end.

There is a continued tension between practices shared over large areas on the one hand, and the potentialities for differentiation which were exploited in locally and chronologically contingent ways on the other. This pattern of 'inconsistent commonality' does not apply to the LBK only, but is evident in many other examples of geographically extensive archaeological phenomena. Our study can contribute to wider archaeological and anthropological debate about culture by suggesting ways in which conflicting theoretical foci on coherent values and contingent practice, on shared identity and individual diversity, can be bridged, through its interpretive emphasis on scale and performance.

Résumé

Ce volume présente les résultats d'une étude sur les modes de vie en Europe centrale au Néolithique ancien. Nous nous sommes concentrés sur les interactions entre uniformité et diversité. Pour cela, nous avons effectué des analyses isotopiques sur des centaines d'échantillons humains et animaux provenant de cimetières et de villages de la culture du Rubanée de 5500 à 4900 avant J.-C. calibré, en Hongrie, Slovaquie occidentale, Moravie (République Tchèque), Autriche, Allemagne du Sud et Alsace (France). Nous abordons les thèmes de la mobilité (par le biais des analyses sur les isotopes de strontium et d'oxygène), du régime alimentaire (pour lequel nous avons étudié les isotopes de carbone et d'azote et mesuré le potentiel du calcium), et de la santé (basée sur l'étude ostéo-archéologique d'assemblages sélectionnés). Nous avons intégré les résultats de toutes ces analyses dans un exercice de réévaluation des données funéraires (qui inclut le lieu de sépulture, les rites et la présence d'objets funéraires). Nous avons alors identifié des tendances et des variations récurrentes à différentes échelles géographiques ou sociales, allant des sépultures individuelles aux groupes de tombes, des sites isolés aux régions, pour enfin considérer la zone étudiée dans son ensemble, ainsi que des individus aux familles, des clans ou lignées aux communautés plus étendues, aux réseaux plus ou moins vastes.

Les habitudes alimentaires se sont montrées étonnamment similaires pour toute la zone étudiée. Nous avons également mis en évidence des récurrences dans les données du strontium, qui suggèreraient que la majorité des individus échantillonnés sont morts sur ou près de leur lieu de naissance. Ceci nous a permis d'identifier des cas particuliers évidents, qui seraient nés et auraient grandi ailleurs, ainsi que de constater des différences récurrentes décelables entre les taux de strontium des hommes et des femmes. Les données du strontium nous permettent donc d'avancer que la résidence patrilocale était habituelle comme lieu de résidence post-mariage, et semblent également indiquer un lien entre l'héritage des terres et les hommes enterrés avec une herminette en pierre polie. Toutefois, nous constatons également des variations à bon nombre d'échelles sociales, allant de la différence marquée de la proportion de viande dans le régime alimentaire entre l'est et l'ouest, aux tendances régionales concernant l'importance du positionnement du corps du défunt et son orientation dans la tombe, en passant par nombre de manières singulières permettant à des individus de se distinguer des autres défunts de par leurs rites, leurs assemblages d'objets funéraires, leur condition physique, leur régime alimentaire et leur mobilité.

Chapitre 1 présente le contexte ainsi que les raisons de l'étude et donne un aperçu de différentes approches sur l'uniformité et la diversité au Rubané à travers des discussions anthropologiques sur la culture performative et flexible. Les différents modes de vie au Rubané incluent les disparités régionales dans l'influence des chasseurs-cueilleurs locaux et des migrants, les variations de stratégies économiques entre les villages et les familles, l'impact des facteurs démographiques et de l'histoire locale, et l'utilisation de la culture matérielle (comme les herminettes, les autres outils de pierre, la poterie et les ornements) pour créer des identités à l'échelle individuelle, familiale, communautaire, de la lignée ou du clan, du site, de la région et autre. Ce chapitre donne un rapport détaillé sur la manière dont les pratiques mortuaires ont été étudiées, en se concentrant notamment sur deux aspects de la recherche : la définition d'un rite funéraire « normatif » et l'identification du statut social. Bien comprendre la diversité à des échelles sociales multiples reste un défi de taille. C'est là le point de départ de notre étude interdisciplinaire, dans laquelle nous utilisons conjointement les analyses isotopiques, ostéologiques et archéologiques pour aborder cette question.

Chapitre 2 donne le contexte méthodologique des différentes analyses (détaillant les protocoles des analyses isotopiques effectuées par le RLAHA d'Oxford et l'Université de Durham) et revient sur d'importantes études passées, en s'arrêtant plus particulièrement sur celles relatives au Rubané. Les mesures de carbone et d'azote (effectuées à partir de 617 restes humains et de 366 échantillons zoologiques) nous renseignent sur le rôle des plantes et des animaux dans le régime alimentaire humain et sur les stratégies de gestion du bétail, sans pour autant apporter toutes les réponses pour l'un ou pour l'autre. De même, les isotopes du strontium (analysés sur plus de 550 humains) qui reflètent le substrat géologique d'où provenait le régime alimentaire peuvent révéler des épisodes de mobilité, sans pour autant en déterminer un point d'origine spécifique. Dans les deux cas, nous nous sommes concentrés sur la recherche des variations dans l'ensemble des données et sur la détermination de tendances entre les groupes de sépultures, nous permettant ainsi de les interpréter davantage. Nous donnons également un aperçu des résultats des études pilotes sur les isotopes d'oxygène (qui peuvent déterminer la mobilité grâce aux différences des eaux souterraines) et du calcium (qui indique la consommation de produits laitiers). L'étude ostéo-archéologique de 236 individus a permis de déterminer leur âge et leur sexe, ainsi que d'identifier des pathologies dentaires, *cribra orbitalia,* des lésions périostées et des traumatismes. Enfin, nous avons résumé comment certains aspects des rites funéraires avaient été attribués au sexe, au statut, à l'identité ethnique et à d'autres pistes de différenciation par le passé. Pour les analyses archéologiques, qui s'appuient sur plus de 3000 individus, nous avons sélectionné le lieu de sépulture, la position du corps et son orientation, et l'assemblage d'objets funéraires comme étant les principales variables. Il est important de garder à l'esprit que ni les données archéologiques, ostéologiques ou isotopiques ne permettent d'identifier directement des catégories d'identités ou même ne se rapportent à une seule échelle d'analyse ; ce qui démontre la nécessité d'intégrer les différents résultats prudemment et systématiquement.

La partie principale du livre est constituée de six études de cas régionales réparties entre les chapitres 3 à 8. Les régions ont été déterminées de manière pragmatique, en suivant les zones définies par la recherche antérieure et les frontières politiques actuelles, tandis qu'une intégration plus approfondie de tous les résultats est disponible dans les chapitre 9 et 10. Afin d'optimiser la fiabilité des statistiques, les sites régionaux ont été sélectionnés sur la base du nombre d'individus présents, ainsi que de l'accessibilité des restes. Ceci a donc impliqué un parti-pris nécessaire en faveur de grands assemblages, et donc souvent en faveur des cimetières (bien que seules des tombes associées à des villages aient été analysées pour la Hongrie). De plus, nos données sont principalement issues de la seconde moitié du Rubané, à partir d'environ 5300–5200 av. J.-C. calibré, car les restes humains antérieurs à cette période sont rares. Voici le détail des sites d'où proviennent les échantillons : pour la Hongrie (chapitre 3), Mezőkövesd-Mocsolyás, Füzesabony-Gubakút, Polgár-Ferenci-hát et Balatonszárszó-Kis-erdei-dűlő; pour la Moravie et la Slovaquie occidentale (chapitre 4), Vedrovice (approfondissant une récente étude de Zvelebil et de ses collègues), Těšetice-Kyjovice, Brno-Starý Lískovec et Nitra; pour l'Autriche (chapitre 5), Kleinhadersdorf, Asparn a.d. Zaya, Mitterndorf et Rutzing; pour la Bavière (chapitre 6), Aiterhofen et Otzing; pour le Bade-Wurtemberg (chapitre 7), Schwetzingen; et pour l'Alsace (chapitre 8), Mulhouse-Est, Ensisheim *Les Octrois*, Souffelweyersheim et Vendenheim. Des échantillons de restes animaux ont été collectés sur des sites complémentaires quand c'était nécessaire.

Chacun des chapitres régionaux fournit un tour d'horizon de l'histoire de la recherche et des aspects principaux de l'archéologie du Rubané, en détaillant plus particulièrement l'arrivée et le développement du Rubané, les modèles de subsistance, les réseaux de culture matérielle et les rites funéraires régionaux. Ensuite, les résultats des analyses sont présentés site par site, en commençant par les données ostéologiques (quand elles ont pu être obtenues), puis viennent les résultats des isotopes stables et du strontium. Ceux-ci sont ensuite mis en corrélation avec les données archéologiques pour formuler une première interprétation pour chaque site. A la fin de chaque chapitre, ces archives locales sont comparées pour mettre en avant les conclusions principales pour chaque région. Ces conclusions sont suivies d'une présentation de deux biographies distincts, chacun basé sur une sépulture sélectionnée parmi les exemplaires régionaux, soulignant l'interaction entre les modes de vie individuelles et les thèmes de recherche plus vastes.

Cette approche prend en compte les caractéristiques régionales visibles dans les données. Ainsi, bien que chaque site soit soumis à la même série de questions, la discussion est adaptée aux aspects qui se sont très nettement dégagés des observations. Le chapitre 3 (Hongrie) indique clairement qu'il y avait des différences d'alimentation entre hommes et femmes et présente également des disparités entre régions hongroises. Chapitre 4 (Moravie et Slovaquie occidentale) traite sans doute du plus ancien cimetière étudié dans ce projet (Vedrovice), et tient donc une place stratégique pour répondre aux questions de diffusion du Rubané et de son développement en dehors des principales régions hongroises. On y voit notamment une uniformisation croissante des sépultures au fil de la période, ainsi que l'importance continue des différences entre hommes et femmes. Ce dernier point est moins marqué dans le chapitre 5 (Autriche) qui, au contraire, commence à révéler l'existence de groupes d'individus avec des modes de vie distincts sur certains sites et l'utilisation d'assemblages funéraires plus variés, créant ainsi des possibilités de distinctions. Ces deux aspects demeurent au centre de la discussion du chapitre 6 (Bavière), qui suggère également des liens entre les modèles isotopiques (en rapport avec le régime alimentaire dans ce cas-là) et la présence d'outils en pierre polie. Chapitre 7 (Bade-Wurtemberg) traite essentiellement des haches et herminettes polies dans la région où la majorité du travail préalable sur les isotopes au Rubané avait eu lieu. Notre projet confirme, tout en les étoffant, les premières conclusions sur les différents modèles de mobilité entre hommes et femmes, et l'existence de pratiques hétérogènes au niveau de la communauté, pouvant aller jusqu'au rôle local de la chasse et de la cueillette. Enfin, le thème de la différenciation régionale occupe la majeure partie du chapitre 8 (Alsace), où la recherche se penche depuis longtemps sur les différentes pratiques entre le nord et le sud de l'Alsace dans une variété de contextes (qui incluent les sépultures, la décoration des poteries et les pratiques économiques), qui sont potentiellement liées au rôle plus avéré des chasseurs-cueilleurs locaux dans la zone occidentale de la distribution du Rubané.

Tout au long de ces discussions, on insiste sur le fait que toutes les distinctions possibles (comme par exemples celles qui sont révélées par les isotopes et celles qui sont visibles dans les rites funéraires) ne sont pas nécessairement liées de manière directe. Bien qu'il y ait une tendance pour les individus qui se distinguent dans un domaine à se montrer également atypiques dans d'autres, on peut normalement aussi trouver des contrexemples. On constate plutôt un remodelage créatif de toutes les divergences potentielles au sein des pratiques locales.

Les résultats issus des différentes régions sont ensuite interprétés ensemble dans le chapitre 9. La plupart des variations enregistrées sur les isotopes stables sont liées à l'influence continentale et atlantique sur le climat, et probablement également aux différences de couverture forestière. Ceci signifie que l'ensemble des données du Rubané concernant le régime alimentaire était remarquablement uniforme, bien que les pratiques agricoles aient pu varier dans le détail. Des modélisations plus détaillées montrent que nos données concordent avec des suggestions plausibles pour l'alimentation néolithique, mais elles suggèrent aussi une tendance vers une consommation plus importante de viande dans la partie occidentale que dans la partie orientale du projet. A l'est, les différences de régime alimentaire entre hommes et femmes sont également plus marquées. Le modèle d'isotope de strontium en Europe centrale confirme que la fourchette isotopique des femmes est plus large que celle des hommes, ce qui semble être un signe de résidence patrilocale. De plus, les hommes enterrés avec des herminettes sont plus groupés que ceux retrouvés sans, ce qui pourrait représenter une transmission des terres au fil des générations. Les chefs de famille ou de lignée ou toutes autres figures clé seraient ainsi distingués par la présence d'outils en pierre polie. Au niveau individuel, les cas particuliers du strontium sont également associés à d'autres pratiques funéraires, comme par exemple une position fléchie à droite ou une orientation minoritaire. Le lieu de résidence à la naissance avait donc un impact sur le traitement funéraire du défunt, ce qui suggère qu'il y avait des différenciations dans la société du Rubané suivant le sexe, et peut-être la famille, la lignée ou d'autres appartenances. L'analyse ostéo-archéologique confirme tout au moins la différenciation suivant le sexe, car les femmes souffraient plus fréquemment de caries et de *cribra orbitalia* que les hommes, et des types d'activités selon le sexe existaient. Toutefois, la santé ne semblait pas varier drastiquement d'un bout à l'autre de la distribution (avec pour exception notoire les indicateurs de stress dans l'échantillon autrichien), mais il faudra davantage d'études pour combler les lacunes.

Et enfin, l'analyse archéologique des lieux de sépultures, des rites et des assemblages funéraires (avec des références spécifiques sur les objets en pierre, la poterie, les ornements et l'ocre) démontre que les enfants de sept à treize ans recevaient des rites spécifiques de manière consistante, ce qui nous mène à suggérer que c'était un passage important entre l'enfance et l'âge adulte. Nous confirmons l'importance particulière des sépultures d'hommes enterrés avec des herminettes, car elles étaient les plus formalisées. Mais il faut noter aussi que d'autres objets et pratiques, plus particulièrement les ornements personnels, étaient explicitement employés pour l'affirmation des identités différentes à l'échelle personnelle, locale et régionale. La pression qui était placée soit sur une plus grande uniformité (à l'est), soit sur une plus grande variation (à l'ouest) concernant la position du corps et son orientation, constituait l'un des marqueurs régionaux parmi les plus forts. De manière générale, les distinctions entre les sépultures des villages et des cimetières, et la variation au sein de l'échantillon de cimetières, semblent liées à la taille des communautés représentées. C'est elle qui détermine si l'accent est mis sur l'uniformité ou les différences individuelles, ou sur l'approvisionnement en objets funéraires plutôt que sur d'autres types de distinctions.

Dans le chapitre 10, nous utilisons ces conclusions pour aborder les questions de toutes les différentes échelles sociales et les types de performances qui sont pertinents à la considération des modes de vie au Rubané. En plus de l'échelle individuelle, on note l'importance des unités domestiques et de leur composition potentiellement flexible, comme le démontrent également les récents débats sur les modèles de « société á maison » dans l'archéologie du Néolithique, et les preuves de lignages ou de clans à la fois dans nos données isotopiques et dans d'autres études. Ceci soulève l'énigme de la relative invisibilité des familles en tant que telles dans les cimetières, ainsi que la question de la base sur laquelle des individus étaient sélectionnés pour y être enterrés. Les habitudes partagées par beaucoup de sites ne doivent pas pour autant nous conduire à minimiser l'importance de la diversité et de la flexibilité. On avance ainsi l'importance des descendances bilatérales, matrilinéaires ou composites plutôt que les transmissions patrilinéaires seules, ainsi que celle des 'sodalités' qui tissent des liens très larges entre les communautés. On fait aussi mention de l'importance du Rubané en tant que « communauté imaginée », c'est-à-dire un système de valeurs et de pratiques partagées sur une vaste zone, bien que décliné localement. Mais ces rapports aux autres trouvaient également des sources historiques, et nous décrivons leur trajectoire potentielle en commençant par une phase très ancienne, dominée par une stratégie de standardisation malgré les origines différentes de la population et les diverses manières de faire les choses, vient ensuite une phase développée de spécialisation accrue entre les sites et les individus, qui avait lieu sur un fond de modes de vie essentiellement similaires, pour enfin terminer par la création de groupes de plus en plus définis, qui pourraient avoir contribué à l'éclatement ou à la transformation fondamentale du Rubané à son terme.

Il y a une tension continue entre les pratiques partagées sur de vastes territoires d'un côté, et toutes les possibilités de différentiations exploitées de manière fortuite localement et chronologiquement de l'autre. La tendance de "standardisation inconsistante" ne s'applique pas seulement au Rubané, mais se retrouve dans bien d'autres phénomènes archéologiques très étendus géographiquement. Notre étude, grâce à sa réflexion interprétative sur l'échelle et la performance, peut contribuer à un large débat archéologique et anthropologique sur la culture, en suggérant des méthodes pour aborder la question des points théoriques conflictuels sur des données homogènes et des pratiques fortuites, et sur les identités partagées et la diversité individuelle.

Translated by Sterenn Girard-Suard

Zusammenfassung

Das Hauptaugenmerk dieser Untersuchung zu neolithischen Lebensweisen in Mitteleuropa liegt auf dem Wechselspiel zwischen Einheitlichkeit und Vielfalt. Um dieses näher zu beleuchten wurden hunderte von Isotopenproben an menschlichem und tierischem Material aus Gräberfeldern und Siedlungen der Linearbandkeramik (LBK, ca. 5500–4900 v. Chr.) entnommen. Der geographische Rahmen erstreckt sich von Ungarn über die westliche Slowakei und Mähren (Tschechische Republik) bis nach Österreich, Süddeutschland und ins Elsass (Frankreich). Unsere Fragestellungen umfassen Mobilität (gemessen mit Strontium- und Sauerstoffisotopen), Ernährungsweise (auf der Grundlage von Kohlenstoff- und Stickstoffisotopen, und mit einem Beitrag zum Potential der Kalziumisotopie) und Gesundheitszustand (basierend auf einer osteoarchäologischen Untersuchung ausgewählter Komplexe). Die Ergebnisse der verschiedenen Analysen werden in eine Neubewertung der Daten zum Bestattungswesen integriert, die unter anderem Bestattungsort, Ritus und Grabbeigaben umfasst. Wir konnten sich wiederholende Muster identifizieren, aber auch Variabilität auf verschiedenen geographischen und sozialen Ebenen herausarbeiten, vom individuellen Grab zu Grabgruppen, Fundorten, Regionen und schließlich dem gesamten Arbeitsgebiet, von Individuen über Haushalte, Clans und Lineages bis hin zu größeren sozialen Einheiten wie Gemeinschaften, Netzwerken und weiter gefassten Beziehungsgeflechten.

Bandkeramische Ernährungsgewohnheiten waren im gesamten Arbeitsgebiet erstaunlich einheitlich. Auch die Strontiumdaten bilden wiederkehrende Muster und weisen darauf hin, dass die Mehrheit der beprobten Individuen am oder in der Nähe des selben Ortes verstarben, in dem sie geboren wurden. Daher können klare Ausreißer identifiziert werden, die andernorts geboren wurden und aufwuchsen. Es zeigen sich auch systematische Unterschiede in den Werten von Männern und Frauen. Insgesamt können die Strontiumwerte im Sinne von Patrilokalität als einem wiederkehrenden postmaritalen Residenzmuster gewertet werden. Es gibt auch Zusammenhänge zwischen dem Vererben von Land und Männern mit Schuhleistenkeilen. Trotzdem zeigt sich auch Vielfalt auf mehreren gesellschaftlichen Ebenen. So unterscheidet sich der Konsum tierischer Proteine großräumig zwischen dem östlichen und westlichen Arbeitsgebiet, während Körperhaltungen und Graborientierungen regional mehr oder weniger streng eingehalten werden. Zusätzlich können sich Individuen auf sehr unterschiedliche Weise von der weiteren Bestattungsgemeinschaft abheben, zum Beispiel durch den Ritus, die Grabbeigaben, ihren Gesundheitszustand, Ernährungsgewohnheiten und Mobilität.

Kapitel 1 legt den Hintergrund und die theoretischen Grundlagen für die vorliegende Arbeit dar. Es werden zunächst unterschiedliche Herangehensweisen zu Einheitlichkeit und Vielfalt in der Bandkeramik zusammengefasst und in den Kontext sozialanthropologischer Diskussionen zu Kultur als performativ und flexibel eingebettet. Verschiedene Lebensweisen in der LBK beinhalten Aspekte wie den regional unterschiedlichen Beitrag von ortsansässigen Wildbeutern und Einwanderern; Variabilität in der Wirtschaftsweise zwischen Siedlungen und Haushalten; den Einfluss demographischer Faktoren und regionaler Entwicklungen; und die Rolle der materiellen Kultur (z.B. geschliffene Steingeräte, Silex, Keramik und Schmuck) bei der Herausbildung von Identitäten unter anderem auf persönlicher, Hofplatz-, Clan- oder Lineage-, Siedlungs- und regionaler Ebene. Ein detaillierter Überblick zur Forschungsgeschichte bandkeramischer Bestattungen kann vor allem die Definition eines 'normativen' Grabritus und das Erkennen von Statusunterschieden als zentrale Fragen bisheriger Ansätze herausarbeiten. Im Gegensatz dazu bleibt die Interpretation von Vielfalt auf verschiedenen gesellschaftlichen Ebenen eine zentrale Herausforderung. Sie bildet den Ansatzpunkt für unser interdisziplinäres Projekt, in dem sich isotopische, osteologische und archäologische Analysen gemeinsam diesem Problem stellen.

Kapitel 2 beschreibt die methodologischen Grundlagen der verschiedenen analytischen Ansätze (sowie die Analyseprotokolle für die Isotopenmessungen im RLAHA, Oxford, und an der Universität Durham) und fasst wichtige bestehende Arbeiten, vor allem zur Bandkeramik, zusammen. Kohlenstoff- und Stickstoffmessungen (die hier an 617 Menschen und 366 Tieren durchgeführt wurden) erbringen Informationen zur Rolle von tierischen und pflanzlichen Elementen in der Ernährung, sowie zu Aspekten der Tierhaltung, allerdings ohne diese direkt wiederzuspiegeln. Ebenso können Strontiumisotopen (die an mehr als 550 Menschen gemessen wurden) Migrationsepisoden nachzeichnen, da sie den geologischen Untergrund reflektieren, von dem Nahrung bezogen wurde, allerdings lässt sich kein genauer Herkunftsort bestimmen. In beiden Datensätzen haben wir uns daher darauf konzentriert, Unterschiede zu erkennen und systematische Differenzen zwischen Gräbergruppen herauszuarbeiten, die dann weiter interpretiert werden können. Die Ergebnisse unserer Teststudien zu Sauerstoffisotopen (die Migrationsepisoden dank der unterschiedlichen Zusammensetzung des Grundwassers nachzeichnen können) und Kalzium (mit seinem Zusammenhang zum Milchkonsum) werden ebenfalls zusammengefasst. Die osteoarchäologische Untersuchung von 236 Individuen identifizierte Alter und Geschlecht, sowie Zahnpathologien, *Cribra orbitalia*, periostale Läsionen und Traumata. Schließlich wird dargelegt, wie unterschiedliche Aspekte des Grabritus in bisherigen Modellen mit Geschlecht, Status, ethnischer Abstammung und anderen potentiellen Aspekten der Differenzierung verknüpft worden sind. Unsere archäologische Analyse, die sich auf eine Datenbank von über 3000 Individuen stützt, konzentriert sich vor allem auf Bestattungsort, Totenhaltung, Graborientierung und Beigaben. Es wird hervorgehoben, dass weder archäologische, noch osteologische oder isotopische Daten die in der Vorgeschichte relevanten Identitätskategorien direkt wiederspiegeln. Zusätzlich beziehen sich unsere Ergebnisse nie auf nur eine gesellschaftliche Ebene, so dass sie mit größter Sorgfalt abgewägt und integriert werden müssen.

Sechs regionale Fallstudien (Kapitel 3–8) bilden den Großteil des Buches. Die Regionen wurden pragmatisch in Anlehnung an bestehende Forschungsschwerpunkte und moderne Grenzen definiert, aber die Ergebnisse werden in Kapiteln 9 und 10 übergreifend zusammengestellt. Um die Untersuchung statistisch so robust wie möglich zu halten, wurden Fundstellen innerhalb der Regionen nach der Anzahl der Gräber und nach deren Verfügbarkeit ausgewählt. Große Serien, und daher vielerorts vor allem Gräberfelder, sind somit zwangsläufig überrepräsentiert (in Ungarn wurden allerdings nur Siedlungsbestattungen analysiert). Auch datiert unser Material größtenteils in die zweite Hälfte der Bandkeramik, ab etwa 5300–5200 v. Chr., da ältere Überreste selten sind. Die folgenden Fundorte wurden beprobt: in Ungarn (Kapitel 3), Mezőkövesd-Mocsolyás, Füzesabony-Gubakút, Polgár-Ferenci-hát und Balatonszárszó-Kis-erdei-dűlő; in Mähren und der Westslowakei (Kapitel 4), Vedrovice (wobei jüngste Untersuchungen von Zvelebil und Kollegen erweitert wurden), Těšetice-Kyjovice, Brno-Starý Lískovec und Nitra; in Österreich (Kapitel 5), Kleinhadersdorf, Asparn a.d. Zaya, Mitterndorf und Rutzing; in Bayern (Kapitel 6), Aiterhofen und Otzing; in Baden-Württemberg (Kapitel 7), Schwetzingen; und im Elsass (Kapitel 8), Mulhouse-Est, Ensisheim *Les Octrois*, Souffelweyersheim und Vendenheim. Tierknochen aus anderen Fundstellen wurden bei Bedarf mit einbezogen.

Die Regionalkapitel beginnen jeweils mit einem Überblick zur Forschungsgeschichte und den Hauptcharakteristika der Bandkeramik vor Ort, wobei besonders auf die Entstehung und weitere Entwicklung der LBK, die Wirtschaftsweise, materielle Kultur und Netzwerke und auf regionale Bestattungsbräuche eingegangen wird. Daraufhin werden die Ergebnisse unserer Analysen Fundort für Fundort vorgestellt, angefangen mit den osteoarchäologischen Daten (sofern verfügbar), gefolgt von den stabilen Isotopen und den Strontiumdaten. Zusammenhänge mit dem archäologischen Material werden untersucht, um eine erste Interpretation für jede Fundstelle zu erarbeiten. Am Ende jedes Kapitels werden diese lokalen Ergebnisse miteinander verglichen, um weitergreifende Schlussfolgerungen für jede Region zu ermöglichen. Daran anschließend werden zwei individuelle Biographien vorgestellt, die auf ausgewählten Gräbern der jeweiligen Region basieren. Sie illustrieren das Zusammenspiel zwischen Einzelschicksalen und unseren weiter gefassten Fragestellungen.

Diese Herangehensweise eignet sich besonders zur Darstellung regionaler Charakteristika. Obwohl jeder Fundort auf die gleichen Fragestellungen hin untersucht wurde, konnten daher in der Diskussion diejenigen Aspekte in den Vordergrund gerückt werden, die jeweils am stärksten aus dem Datenmaterial hervortraten. In Kapitel 3 (Ungarn) zeigen sich klare Geschlechtsunterschiede in der Ernährung, sowie Unterschiede zwischen den ungarischen Teilregionen. Kapitel 4 (Mähren und Westslowakei) behandelt die wohl älteste Fundstelle, die in diesem Projekt beprobt wurde (Vedrovice), und bildet daher eine ideale Ausgangsbasis für die Frage der Verbreitung und Entwicklung der Bandkeramik außerhalb der ungarischen Kernregionen. Es zeigt sich ein Trend zu einheitlicheren Bestattungspraktiken, sowie zur weiteren Relevanz geschlechtsbedingter Unterschiede. Letztere treten in Kapitel 5 (Österreich) weniger deutlich hervor. Statt dessen beginnen sich auf einigen Fundplätzen Gruppen mit voneinander unterscheidbaren Lebensweisen abzuzeichnen, und variationsreichere Grabbeigaben können zunehmend zur Signalisierung von Differenzen herangezogen werden. In Kapitel 6 (Bayern) spielen diese beiden Aspekte eine grundlegende Rolle, können aber um die Verbindung von bestimmten isotopischen Mustern (hier mit Bezug auf die Ernährungsweise) mit der Beigabe von geschliffenen Steingeräten erweitert werden. Steingeräte sind ein wichtiger Ansatzpunkt für Kapitel 7 (Baden-Württemberg), die Region in der die meisten bereits publizierten Untersuchungen zur Bandkeramik stattgefunden haben. Unser Projekt konnte die bestehenden Interpretationen zu unterschiedlichen Mobilitätsmustern für Männer und Frauen und zu heterogenen Verhaltensweisen innerhalb einzelner Siedlungsgemeinschaften, die vielleicht den variablen Anteil einheimischer Jäger und Sammler wiederspiegeln, bestätigen und erweitern. Regionale Differenzen bilden schließlich den Schwerpunkt der Diskussion in Kapitel 8 (Elsass), wo die Forschung seit langem eine Reihe von Unterschieden zwischen nördlichen und südlichen Gebieten herausgearbeitet hat, die sich auf die verschiedendsten Lebensbereiche beziehen (z.B. Bestattungswesen, Keramikverzierung und Wirtschaftsweise). Auch sie könnten auf eine zentralere Rolle lokaler Wildbeuter in westlichen Regionen der LBK zurückzuführen sein.

Diese Diskussionen zeigen klar, dass die verschiedenen Wege, auf denen sich Unterschiede herausarbeiten lassen (etwa über die Isotopie oder über den Grabritus), nicht direkt miteinander korrelieren. Zwar neigen Individuen, die auf eine Weise herausstechen dazu, sich in weiteren Aspekten auszuzeichnen, aber es lassen sich meist auch Gegenbeispiele finden. Wir sehen hier die kreative Neukombination der vielen verfügbaren Strategien, mit denen prähistorische Akteure sich in ihren örtlichen Kontexten voneinander differenzierten.

In Kapitel 9 werden die Ergebnisse aller Regionalstudien gemeinsam interpretiert. Der Großteil der Variabilität der stabilen Isotope kann mit der relativen Bedeutung kontinentaler und atlantischer Klimaeinflüsse und vielleicht auch mit unterschiedlicher Bewaldung erklärt werden.

Das bedeutet, dass sich die Bandkeramiker in Bezug auf ihre Ernährung erstaunlich einheitlich verhielten, wobei sich die Details von Ackerbau und Viehzucht durchaus unterschieden haben könnten. Weitere ausführliche Modelle zeigen, dass unsere Daten mit plausiblen Vorstellungen zur neolithischen Ernährung übereinstimmen, dass aber in den westlichen Regionen des Projektes tendenziell mehr tierische Proteine konsumiert wurden als weiter östlich. Im Osten treten auch geschlechtsbedingte Unterschiede in der Ernährung deutlicher hervor. Die Strontiumisotopen bestätigen, dass Frauen überall in Mitteleuropa eine größere Bandbreite an Werten aufweisen als Männer, was hier als Hinweis auf Patrilokalität interpretiert wird. Zusätzlich fallen Männer mit geschliffenen Steingeräten in eine engere Bandbreite als Individuen ohne solche Objekte, und dies könnte andeuten, dass Land über die Generationen vererbt wurde und dass wichtige Persönlichkeiten auf Haushalts- oder Lineageebene durch Beile und Äxte hervorgehoben wurden. Auf Individualebene zeichenen sich Strontium-Ausreißer oft auch durch andere Aspekte der Grablegung aus, beispielsweise durch rechte Hockerlage oder eine abweichende Orientierung. Eine Geburt in der Fremde hatte folglich Auswirkungen auf die Behandlung einer Person nach ihrem Tod, so dass die bandkeramische Gesellschaft sich sowohl nach Geschlecht, als auch nach der Zugehörigkeit zu Haushalten, Lineages oder anderen Gruppierungen differenzieren lässt. Die osteoarchäologische Analyse kann dies teilweise unterstützen, da Frauen öfter an Karies und *Cribra orbitalia* leiden als Männer, und da geschlechtsbedingte Aktivitätsmuster existierten. Trotz allem zeigte der allgemeine Gesundheitszustand im gesamten Arbeitsgebiet keine größeren Unterschiede (mit Ausnahme des vermehrten Auftretens von Stressmarkern in Österreich) und es sind dringend weitere Untersuchungen nötig, um die noch bestehenden Lücken zu füllen.

Die archäologische Analyse nach den Gesichtspunkten von Bestattungsort, Grabritus und Grabbeigaben (mit besonderem Augenmerk auf Steingeräten, Keramik, Schmuck und Farbsteinen) konnte zeigen, dass Kinder im Alter von sieben bis 13 Jahren konsistent hervorgehoben wurden, was wir dahingehend interpretieren, dass es sich hier um ein wichiges Übergangsalter zwischen Kindheit und Erwachsensein handelte. Männer, die mit geschliffenen Steingeräten bestattet wurden, zeichnen sich auch hier aus, diesmal durch die größere Formalisierung anderer Aspekte des Totenrituales. Andere Beigaben und Praktiken, so vor allem Schmuck, wurden dagegen explizit dazu verwendet, Identitäten auf persönlicher, örtlicher und regionaler Ebene zu signalisieren. Eines der klarsten überregionalen Muster bezieht sich darauf, wie streng Körperhaltungen und Orientierungen vereinheitlicht wurden, wobei sich im Westen deutlich mehr Variabilität zeigt als im Osten. Insgesamt können die Unterschiede zwischen Siedlungsbestattungen und Gräberfeldern, sowie die Variabilität innerhalb der Nekropolen, dahingehend interpretiert werden, dass jeweils unterschiedliche Ebenen der Gemeinschaftsbildung angesprochen werden, die dann einen Einfluss darauf haben, ob Einheitlichkeit oder individuelle Unterschiede im Vordergrund stehen, oder ob Grabbeigaben gegnüber anderen möglichen Aspekten der Differenzierung bevorzugt werden.

Diese Schlussfolgerungen bilden die Grundlage für eine weiterführende Diskussion der verschiedenen für die LBK relevanten gesellschaftlichen Ebenen und möglichen Lebensweisen in Kapitel 10. Neben der individuellen Ebene heben wir besonders den Haushalt und dessen potentiell flexible Zusammensetzung hervor, die auch von jüngeren Modellen zu 'Hausgesellschaften' im Neolithikum angesprochen werden, und fassen Belege für die Existenz von Lineages und Clans in unseren isotopischen Daten und in der bestehenden Literatur zusammen. Das führt uns zu der Frage, warum Haushalte auf Gräberfeldern relativ schwer zu erkennen sind, und wer überhaupt zur Beisetzung auf einem Friedhof ausgewählt wurde. Weit verbreitete Muster sollten nicht dazu führen, Variabilität und Flexibilität in den Hintergrund zu drängen, und wir argumentieren hier für die Bedeutung von bilateralen und kognatischen oder gemischten, anstatt nur patrilinearen Abstammungssystemen, sowie für die Existenz von stammesübergreifenden Verbänden als eine mögliche Strategie, weitführende Verbindungen zwischen Siedlungsgemeinschaften aufrechtzuerhalten. Wir diskutieren auch, inwiefern die LBK als eine 'imaginäre Gemeinschaft' verstanden werden kann, also als ein System von Werten und Praktiken, die über ein weitläufiges Gebiet gültig waren, aber jeweils an örtliche Gegebenheiten angepasst wurden. Diese Beziehungsgeflechte sind auch historisch eingebettet, und wir beschreiben deren möglichen Wandel von der ältesten Bandkeramik, die trotz der unterschiedlichen Herkunft ihrer Träger und Kulturgüter von einer Strategie der Einheitlichkeit geprägt bleibt, über eine entwickelte Phase zunehmender Spezialisierung zwischen Siedlungen und Individuen – noch immer vor einem Hintergrund von im Großen und Ganzen ähnlichen Lebensweisen – zur Herausbildung immer enger abgegrenzter Gruppierungen, die schließlich zur Auflösung oder grundlegenden Veränderung der LBK beitrugen.

Insgesamt lässt sich ein Spannungsfeld herausarbeiten, in dem einerseits manche Praktiken weiträumig auftreten, aber andererseits zahlreiche Differenzierungsmöglichkeiten existierten, die in örtlich unterschiedlicher und vom zeitlichen Kontext abhängiger Weise eingesetzt wurden. Dieses Muster 'inkonsistenter Gemeinsamkeit' ist nicht nur auf die LBK anwendbar, sondern findet sich in vielen anderen Beispielen geographisch weitläufiger archäologischer Erscheinungen. Unsere Untersuchung trägt zu archäologischen und sozialanthropologischen Debatten bei, indem sie zeigt wie ein interpretativer Ansatz, der sich auf das Zusammenspiel unterschiedlicher gesellschaftlicher Ebenen und auf gesellschaftliche Improvisation konzentriert, zwischen den gegensätzlichen theoretischen Schwerpunkten auf einheitlichen Wertesystemen und großräumig geteilten Identitäten einerseits und kontingenter Praxis und individueller Variation andererseits vermitteln kann.

Translated by Daniela Hofmann

Abbreviated list of figures

Abbreviated list of tables

Contributors

ALEXANDRA ANDERS
HAS-ELTE Research Group for Interdisciplinary Studies
Múzeum krt. 4/B
1088 Budapest
Hungary

ROSE-MARIE ARBOGAST
Université de Strasbourg
MISHA
5 allé du Général Rouvillois
67083 Strasbourg Cedex
France

R. ALEXANDER BENTLEY
Department of Archaeology and Anthropology
University of Bristol
43 Woodland Road
Bristol BS8 1UU
UK

PENNY BICKLE
Department of Archaeology and Conservation
Cardiff University
John Percival Building
Colum Drive
Cardiff CF10 3EU
UK

CHRISTOPH BLESL
Bundesdenkmalamt, Abteilung für Archäologie
Hofburg, Säulenstiege
1010 Wien
Austria

LUCY CRAMP
Department of Archaeology and Anthropology
University of Bristol
43 Woodland Road
Bristol BS8 1UU
UK

PHILIPPA CULLEN
Research Laboratory for Archaeology and the History of Art
Oxford University
Dyson Perrins Building
South Parks Road
Oxford OX1 3QY
UK

CHRISTOPHER DALE
Department of Earth Sciences
Durham University
Science Labs
Durham DH1 3LE
UK

MARTA DOČKALOVÁ
The Moravian Museum
Anhropos Institute
Zelný trh 6
65937 Brno
Czech Republic

LÁSZLÓ DOMBORÓCZKI
István Dobó Castle Museum
Vár út 1
3300 Eger
Hungary

LINDA FIBIGER
School of History, Classics and Archaeology
University of Edinburgh
Teviot Place
Edinburgh EH8 9AG
UK

MICHAEL FRANCKEN
Eberhard-Karls-Universität
Institut für Naturwissenschaftliche Archäologie
Rümelinstr. 23
72070 Tübingen
Germany

CLAUDIA GERLING
Exzellenzcluster Topoi
Freie Universität Berlin
Hittorfstr. 18
14195 Berlin
Germany

SEREN GRIFFITHS
Department of Archaeology and Conservation
Cardiff University
John Percival Building
Colum Drive
Cardiff CF10 3EU
UK

Gisela Grupe
Bayerische Staatssammlung für Anthropologie und Paläoanatomie
Karolinenplatz 2a
80333 München
Germany

Julie Hamilton
Research Laboratory for Archaeology and the History of Art
Oxford University
Dyson Perrins Building
South Parks Road
Oxford OX1 3QY
UK

Robert Hedges
Research Laboratory for Archaeology and the History of Art
Oxford University
Dyson Perrins Building
South Parks Road
Oxford OX1 3QY
UK

Daniela Hofmann
Department of Archaeology and Conservation
Cardiff University
John Percival Building
Colum Drive
Cardiff CF10 3EU
UK

Nándor Kalicz
Archaeological Institute
Hungarian Academy of Sciences
Úri utca 49
1014 Budapest
Hungary

Zsófia Eszter Kovács
Hungarian National Museum
National Heritage Protection Centre
Daróczi út 1–3.
1113 Budapest
Hungary

Eva Lenneis
Institut für Ur- und Frühgeschichte
Universität Wien
Franz Klein Gasse 1
1190 Wien
Austria

Tibor Marton
Archaeological Institute
Hungarian Academy of Sciences
Úri utca 49
1014 Budapest
Hungary

Inna Mateiciucová
Ústav archeologie a muzeologie
FF Masarykovy univerzity
Arne Nováka 1
602 00 Brno
Czech Republic

Christine Neugebauer-Maresch
Prähistorische Kommission
Österreichische Akademie der Wissenschaften
Fleischmarkt 22
1010 Wien
Austria

Geoff Nowell
Department of Earth Sciences
Durham University
Science Labs
Durham DH1 3LE
UK

Krisztián Oross
Archaeological Institute
Hungarian Academy of Sciences
Úri utca 49
1014 Budapest
Hungary

Ildikó Pap
Hungarian Natural History Museum
Department of Anthropology
1431 Budapest
Pf. 137
Hungary

Juraj Pavúk
Institute of Archaeology
Slovak Academy of Sciences
Akademická 2
94921 Nitra
Slovak Republic

Joachim Pechtl
Institut für Altertumswissenschaften
Lehrstuhl für Vor- und Frühgeschichtliche Archäologie
Residenzplatz 2, Tor A
97070 Würzburg
Germany

Pál Raczky
Institute of Archaeological Sciences
Eötvös Loránd University
Múzeum krt. 4/B
1088 Budapest
Hungary

Linda Reynard
Department of Human Evolutionary Biology
Harvard University
11 Divinity Avenue
Cambridge, MA 02138
USA

Michael Schultz
Zentrum Anatomie
Universität Göttingen
Kreuzbergring 36
37075 Göttingen
Germany

Peter Stadler
Naturhistorisches Museum Wien
Burgring 7
1010 Wien
Austria

Elisabeth Stephan
Regierungspräsidium Stuttgart
Landesamt für Denkmalpflege
Referat 84
Stromeyersdorfstraße 3
78467 Konstanz
Germany

Maria Teschler-Nicola
Naturhistorisches Museum Wien
Burgring 7
1010 Wien
Austria

Barbara Tiefenböck
Naturhistorisches Museum Wien
Burgring 7
1010 Wien
Austria

Joachim Wahl
Regierungspräsidium Stuttgart
Landesamt für Denkmalpflege
Osteologie
Stromeyersdorfstraße 3
78467 Konstanz
Germany

Alasdair Whittle
Department of Archaeology and Conservation
Cardiff University
John Percival Building
Colum Drive
Cardiff CF10 3EU
UK

Carrie Wright
Research Laboratory for Archaeology and the History of Art
Oxford University
Dyson Perrins Building
South Parks Road
Oxford OX1 3QY
UK

1 LBK lifeways: a search for difference

Penny Bickle and Alasdair Whittle

1.1 Introduction

From about 5500 cal BC to soon after 5000 cal BC, the lifeways of the first farmers of central Europe – the LBK, after the German labels *Linearbandkeramik* or *Linienbandkeramik* – are seen in distinctive practices of longhouse use, settlement forms and location, landscape choice, subsistence, material culture and mortuary rites. These are found across central Europe, as well as westwards of the Rhine, and eastwards into the Ukraine (Fig. 1.1). It is well known that there were a whole series of changes within the five or more centuries of LBK existence – perhaps some 20 or more generations. In bald outline,[1] the earliest phase saw a more restricted distribution and simpler houses and pottery; bigger houses and larger and more numerous settlements appeared in developed phases, from a date often given as around 5300 cal BC in most regions of central Europe; and a late phase, around the turn of the sixth millennium cal BC, is marked by increased regionalisation in pottery decoration, and in some versions, signs of stress and even crisis. Despite this awareness of a dynamic sequence, however, many of whose chronological details have yet satisfactorily to be resolved, there has been an overall tendency to see the LBK phenomenon as a whole as one characterised by uniformity (Modderman

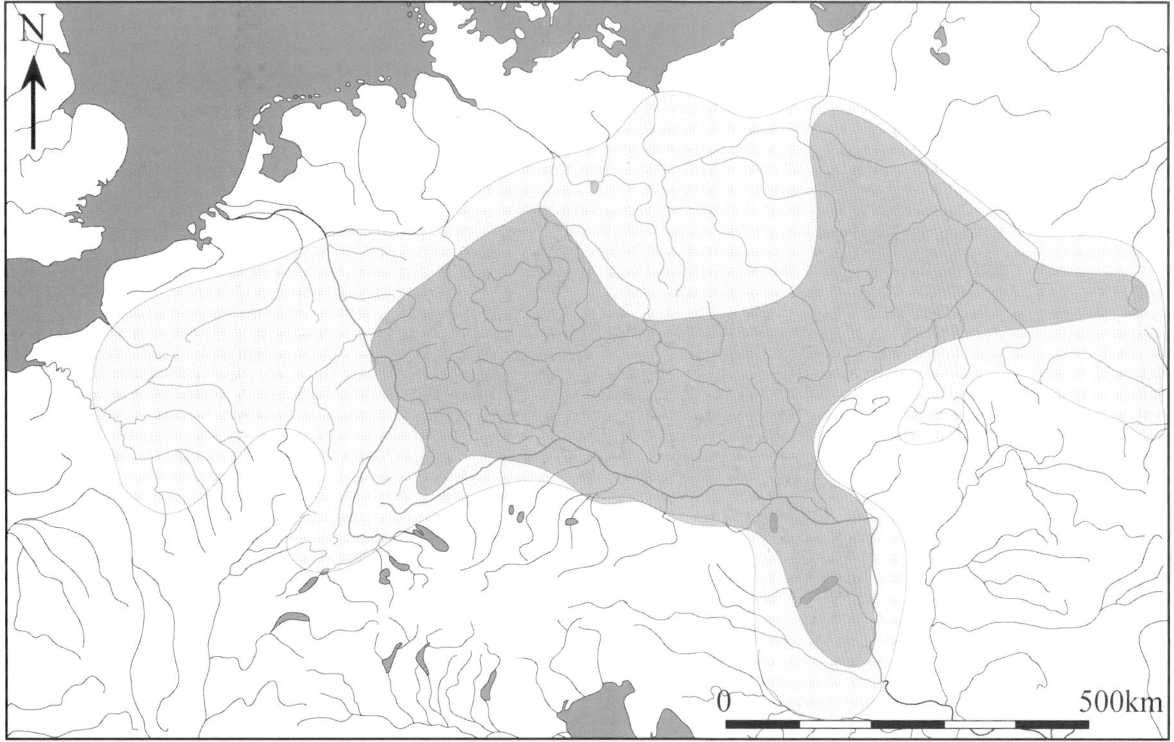

Fig. 1.1. Map of the LBK distribution showing earliest (darker) and later (lighter) phases. Base map after Jeunesse (1997, 10, fig. 1).

1988). This has been perceived at different levels, both as a summation of this period as a whole compared to subsequent Neolithic ones, and within individual aspects and phases of LBK existence; even recent debate often still revolves around the struggle to establish one or other dominant model of, for example, the arrangement of settlement space (Rück 2007; 2009), the nature of agricultural production (Lüning 2000; Bogaard 2004), the conduct of mortuary rites (Jeunesse 1997) or the conditions of social interaction towards the end of the sixth millennium cal BC and the start of the fifth (Farruggia 2002; Golitko and Keeley 2006; Gronenborn 2007a).

There may be several factors which have encouraged such a view. That the evidence for LBK existence cuts across many modern political boundaries may have helped, paradoxically, to foster a perception of uniformity among LBK people; because there is so much evidence across such a wide area, individual researchers rarely grasp the whole data set and it is thus easier for single models to prevail. That the dominant model for the emergence and spread of the LBK in the first place, at least up to the 1980s, and receiving now fresh impetus from aDNA research (Bramanti *et al.* 2009; Haak *et al.* 2005; 2010), has been that of a colonisation by outsiders has also helped to promote an idea of sameness. And for all the recent and current debates on many aspects of LBK life and death (Eckert *et al.* 2003; Lukes and Zvelebil 2004; Lüning *et al.* 2005; Hofmann and Bickle 2009; Gronenborn and Petrasch 2010; Wolfram *et al.* 2012), it is clear that much LBK research is carried out basically within a frame of reference shaped by culture history: a tendency to list traits and to seek the geographical and temporal regularities of bounded wholes. There is little surprise in this. Research on the LBK goes back to the later nineteenth century (for example in the early work of Jaroslav Palliardi in Moravia; Chapter 4.2), and was already well enough established by the 1920s for Gordon Childe to write of 'Danubian culture' (1925), at a time when anthropologists were also often concerned to list traits and delineate regularities (e.g. Haddon 1920; Benedict 1934; Kuper 1999; Bloch 2005b, 94). 'The löss lands west and north of the Danube', declared Childe (1925, 105–6), 'were first occupied by a Neolithic population whose whole culture down to the finest details remains identical from the Drave to the Baltic and from the Dniester to the Meuse'.

There have been two responses to the perception of uniformity in the LBK. The more recent one has been to take perceived uniformity at face value and to seek explicit explanations of it. Thus, Ulrike Sommer (2001) has borrowed the notion of *doxa* from Bourdieu to explore the conditions in which the agency of LBK people appears rule-bound and curtailed, while John Robb and Preston Miracle (2007) have argued for uniformity as a deliberate, if unusual, strategy of integration and social positioning at a time of extensive change, including especially among indigenous hunter-gatherers. A slightly older response has been to question the extent of uniformity in LBK existence, even if the notion of a single, bounded culture has itself been little challenged. This strand goes back to the fundamentally important paper, with its proclamation of 'diversity in uniformity', by Pieter Modderman (1988). Presented in the first place as a personal synthesis, this paper is firmly within the culture model, with emphasis on groups and networks rather than individuals, and with no discernible theoretical framework beyond a statement of general allegiance to geography with a human face (Modderman 1988, 65–6). A lot of description, of the details of house form, settlement layout, diet and the use of cemeteries, presents a somewhat generalised picture of LBK existence. Nonetheless, out of careful attention to sequence, origins, including the role of indigenous hunter-gatherers, and regional variations in physical anthropology, diet and the provision of grave goods, a rather muted case is made for some regional diversity, especially over time. This kind of strongly descriptive approach has continued to be followed in a significant number of other studies, for example prominently on mortuary rites (e.g. Jeunesse 1997) and longhouses (e.g. Coudart 1998; Rück 2009), as well as on the sequence as a whole (e.g. Gronenborn 1999; 2007b).

The project reported here has sought in the first place to contribute to the ongoing descriptive task of teasing out the extent of difference within and between LBK communities. We have taken a so far unusually large regional sample within central Europe, from northern Hungary in the east, westwards along the Danube corridor to Alsace in the upper Rhine valley. We have addressed the lifeways of LBK people through aspects of their diet, their lifetime mobility, their health and physical condition, and the presentation of their bodies in mortuary ritual. We have done this by isotopic, osteological and archaeological analysis: using extensive samples of bone and teeth for dietary and mobility isotopic analysis (carbon and nitrogen for diet, and strontium principally for mobility, with some experimental use of calcium and oxygen; Chapters 2.3, 7.7.5 and 9.2.7); a selected sample of human remains themselves for osteological examination; and the large dataset from burials in cemeteries and settlements for investigation of a wide array of funerary practices. The samples available to us come mainly from developed and late LBK sites, not the earliest.

We have also sought to combine these different lines of evidence, and many of the analyses presented later in this volume are concerned with correlating, for example, the life histories of individuals with their treatment in mortuary ritual. Going beyond this, we are interested, secondly, in teasing out the conditions in which diversity among LBK people was possible. We can follow the distinction here of Michael Carrithers (1992, 5) between variation – the range of given phenomena in specific situations – and variability, 'that set of capacities that allows us to create cultural diversity'. If we also follow his view that 'cultures are essentially mutable and labile' (Carrithers 1992, 7) and that 'change, creation, re-creation and re-interpretation, are all part of the fabric of social existence...the very stuff of human social life' (Carrithers 1992, 9), the challenge is to try to understand how lifeways in the LBK were performed.

We have used the American term 'lifeways' for several reasons. It counters, to some extent, the reliance of LBK studies on the notion of archaeological culture. It has connotations, from usage in the bioarchaeological literature, of issues of health and life histories (Larsen 1997, 86–7), but it also has a wider reach, as seen in both an early paper by Lewis Binford (1968, 12–14) and the title of a recent monograph edited by John Chapman (2010). It allows us to sidestep – or at least not take up an entrenched position in advance in respect to – some of the terminological problems which anthropologists have faced in recent debates about the relative superiority, suitability and usefulness of classic concepts such as culture and society. Thus, whereas Carrithers (1992, 34) argues that 'on balance...individuals in relationships, and the interactive character of social life, are slightly more important, more real, than those things we designate as culture', we would rather avoid such choices (though we can learn from them; Chapter 1.2 below) and prefer the idea of Renato Rosaldo (1989, 20) of a 'porous array of intersections'. Tim Ingold (2011, 162) has recently discussed the concept of a 'way of life' as a path to be followed, with keeping going involving plenty of improvisation rather than adherence to prescribed codes of conduct. Our notion of lifeways can be seen in the same spirit.

1.2 Anthropologists' culture: unbroken landscapes of variation?

To think further about the capacity for and performance of diversity, it is instructive at this stage to turn briefly to anthropological debate about culture. It is clear that, while they overlap, the archaeological and anthropological notions of 'culture' are not identical. Archaeological culture is all-embracing, whereas anthropological culture can often be separated from the concept of society or sociality. There have been intense anthropological debates about the usefulness of both terms, culture and society (Brightman 1995; Ingold 1996a; Sahlins 1999; Kuper 1999; Bloch 2005a), and these have also extended to other concepts such as identity and ethnicity (Banks 1996; Brumann 1999, 23), but it is sufficient here to see how the anthropological debate on culture can illuminate how we tend to think as archaeologists about uniformity and diversity. There is no need for us to resolve anthropological disputes, but these may help us to re-think many basic archaeological assumptions, and we return briefly in Chapter 10.5 to reflect on the shared concerns of archaeology and anthropology with the matter of culture.

Anthropological definitions of culture are many and varied. Perhaps one of the best was also one of the earliest: Tylor's nineteenth-century view (1871, 1) of 'that complex whole which includes knowledge, belief, art, morals, law, custom, and other capabilities and habits acquired by man as a member of society'. There have been many others (Kuper 1999), including the view of Rosaldo (1989, 26) that culture refers to the 'forms through which people make sense of their lives', and that of Chris Gosden (1999, 204) that 'culture is about the values that attach to people, places and things and the processes that create and change such values'.

One of the undoubted achievements of anthropology has been the documentation of worldwide cultural diversity, 'the archive of different human possibilities' as Carrithers has put it (1992, 4). What is of particular interest for us here is how such diversity has been presented. Whereas older accounts tended to parcel up the 'great arc' of cultural diversity into bounded and separable units, as followed for example by Ruth Benedict in her *Patterns of culture* (1934), a much more recent claim is for 'an unbroken landscape of variation' (Ingold 1996b, 117).[2] That view is part of the intense recent debate about both the boundaries of the culture term and its overall usefulness.[3] If there is an element of 'straw man' argumentation and a certain amount of forgetting of what earlier anthropologists actually said (Brightman 1995, 541; Sahlins 1999, 404), that is for the anthropologists to resolve. Several inter-related key points of their debate, however, are instructive for how archaeologists might approach questions of diversity.

Anthropologists have worried, first, about the presentation of culture (accepting that the term is not better abandoned altogether: see a robust defence in Brumann 1999) as an entity, a domain or a thing with an existence separate from the lives and practices which constitute it (E. Wolf 1982; Carrithers 1992; Knauft 1993, 122; Brightman 1995; Handler 2003; Bloch 2005b, 95). Carrithers has posed the challenge 'to produce a view of humans that makes them out to be something more than robots performing according to the programme of culture' (1992, 91), while Brightman (1995, 512) has noted that 'the objection to reification concerns less the ontological status of culture as an abstraction than the attribution to it of an autonomous and regulatory position relative to human agents and their conduct'. In the same vein, Abu-Lughod (1991, 153–4) has argued for taking accounts right down to the level of particular individuals. Carsten (2004, 26) has referred to the 'close, lived intimacy of life inside houses' as the everyday residential setting in which rules or concepts of kinship are actually played out. As Eric Wolf summed things up (1982, 3), 'concepts like 'nation', 'society' and 'culture' name bits and threaten to turn names into things. Only by understanding these names as bundles of relationships... can we hope to avoid misleading inferences'.

There has also been debate about whether culture, as has often been claimed, should be seen as constructed (Ingold 1996a). Geertz, for example, defined culture as 'the imposition of an arbitrary framework of symbolic meaning upon reality'[4] (1964, 39). Tim Ingold (1996b; cf. Ingold 2000; 2011) in particular has argued strongly against this view, seeing in it an unjustifiable separation of nature and culture, and urging instead what he has called the 'dwelling perspective', in which people are engaged in their environments from the outset. To the non-anthropological outsider, the papers in Ingold (1996a) may read like a high-scoring draw, since there are elements of learning and self-reflection alongside continuous engagement, and the style or character of engagement may itself derive from existing and continuously re-forming tradition (Schieffelin 1996, 136).

Few anthropologists appear now to accept the general proposition that culture is normally bounded, as was argued variously in earlier generations, for example in the work of Benedict noted above. Brightman (1995, 518–20; cf. Abu-Lughod 1991) sets out the objections to the existence of 'qualitatively distinguishable constellations of cultural forms, identifiable zones of sameness and difference', including the key observation that 'it is not that there exist *no* boundaries that could delimit cultures or collectivities but that there is a superabundance of them, no two of which segment the social or cultural field in precisely the same way'. That said, there has often been little detailed mapping of difference over wider areas; in his study of longhouses on Borneo, Metcalf (2010, 15) notes how earlier Leach had simply set aside such a challenge in his famous study of highland Burma, by ignoring cultural variation altogether. The study of Knauft (1993) of variation among south coast New Guinea people presents an unusually wide frame of spatial reference compared to most other recent ethnographies; in it he describes (1993, 39–40) how 'chain-link permutations of symbolic and political practice cross-cut south coast language-cultural areas and provided a basis for interaction across linguistic and cultural boundaries'. There is thus also a tension in studies of ethnicity as a component of culture. Barth (1969) set out one of the classic cases for ethnic difference, accepting the existence of plenty of internal variation but arguing for the importance of boundaries, seen as frequently expedient or situationalist, serving the strategies and interests of people within them. That view has been much criticised (Banks 1996; Gosden 1999), and Metcalf's longhouse study, which is focused in part on ethnicity, aims to 'show how ethnicity appeared in the thoughts of longhouse-dwelling people, and how it was constituted by, and constitutive of, their communities', through changing historical processes (2010, 4).

Given the above, it is no surprise that few anthropologists now see culture as isolated, static or internally uniform and coherent (Brightman 1995; Sahlins 1999). The whole thrust of *Europe and the people without history* was to reassert the past existence of a connected world beyond that of the west, in which things happened and changed; the definition offered of societies was 'changing alignments of social groups, segments and classes, without either fixed boundaries or stable internal constitutions' and of 'a culture' as 'a series of processes that construct, reconstruct, and dismantle cultural materials' (E. Wolf 1982, 387). Carrithers (1992, 23) has noted how the ethnographic account is often not so much in the present tense but rather a kind of freeze-frame, which suppresses all sense of change. Brightman (1995, 516–17) draws together the view that culture is normally not only internally diverse but also often contradictory. Discussing Amerindian communities in Amazonia, the papers in Overing and Passes (2000) set out subtle inflections in the preferred expression of broadly shared ideal values of peaceful social existence. Gosden (1999, 122) has suggested that 'an individual culture is more like a centre of gravity, where certain special sets of relations between people and things pertain, which are less likely to be found elsewhere'. Other studies suggest individuals as the 'loci of diverse repertoires' (Brightman 1995, 517), such as in the intersecting knowledges of men and women in the creole culture of Guyana (Drummond 1980), or in the context-dependent shifts of categorisation among Manambu men engaged in warfare (Harrison 1995).

Much more could be said on these themes, but this lets us reflect on different approaches to anthropological and archaeological culture. In brief, the evolutionary and generalising tendencies of both Morgan (1877) and Tylor (1871) were surely important, together with the succeeding fashion for tracing the diffusion of traits of culture. That was active in the early twentieth century, including in the anthropological *Kulturkreise* school in Germany (Bloch 2005b, 94). Although Sahlins trenchantly maintains (1999, 404) that '...it is astonishing from the perspective of North American cultural anthropology to claim that our intellectual ancestors constructed a notion of cultures as rigidly bounded, separated, unchanging, coherent, uniform, totalized and systematic. Talk of inventing traditions', it appears that much archaeological research on the LBK from the 1920s onwards made precisely this sort of set of assumptions. Even if, by the very criteria set out above, we have to judge the case of the LBK on its own merits, or else we deny the early Neolithic people of Europe a history, these assumptions and the language used to express them are important (Hofmann and Bickle 2011). What difference would it make if we talked routinely, for example, of the 'LBK diaspora' or the 'LBK interaction sphere' rather than of the 'LBK culture'? Not all previous assumptions are maintained today, and the next section goes on critically to review shifts in key models. But there has been a strong predisposition in past research to finding uniformity; we note how tentative Modderman's suggestion of diversity in uniformity actually was. And there remains a marked preference for single dominant models – a liking for coherence.

1.3 Trends in recent LBK research

Here we briefly review several key themes in recent research on the LBK, not as a comprehensive synthesis but as a selective introduction that provides a critical context for the contribution of our own project. Wider coverage, if not yet a complete overview, is given in a steady stream of collected papers (Eckert *et al.* 2003; Lukes and Zvelebil 2004; Lüning *et al.* 2005; Hofmann and Bickle 2009; Zeeb-Lanz 2009a; Gronenborn and Petrasch 2010; Wolfram *et al.* 2012). The regional chapters that follow provide much further specific detail and references.

1.3.1 Beginnings

The great majority of the samples analysed in this project do not come from the earliest phase of the LBK as conventionally defined; those that do come from Hungary and Moravia, in the eastern part of the area of the project (Chapters 3 and 4). Debate about the beginnings of the LBK, however, rather obviously sets the tone for models of much of the rest of the LBK, including the central themes of uniformity and diversity; the chronology of the earliest LBK phase, perhaps less obviously, is also very relevant to any view of what came after.

The human processes involved in the appearance and spread of the LBK have long been debated. Though regional chapters will note the case made by some researchers for the involvement of indigenous communities, the overwhelmingly favourite model was for a long time that of an incoming population, bringing sedentism and agriculture, ultimately from the Near East and from closer at hand Greece and the Balkans. With the better identification of the earliest style of LBK pottery (Quitta 1960), the more restricted extent of an earliest phase within the total LBK distribution came better to be defined. With the advent of radiocarbon dating, results were taken to show a very rapid initial spread of the LBK, thus reinforcing the notion of some kind of colonisation, and in due course to define an earliest phase of some two centuries in duration, *c.* 5500–5300 cal BC (Lüning 2005a). More detailed models suggested a risk-reducing economic system and settlement pattern (e.g. Bogucki 1988), and approaches in general tended to reinforce notions of a sense of uniformity, conditioned by both history and practical logic on the ground (cf. Sommer 2001, 252).

That kind of view of the beginnings of the LBK was first challenged in the 1980s. Modderman's own review (1988) called for the contribution of indigenous communities to be taken more seriously across the whole LBK distribution, and there were even more radical claims for the possibility of processes of essentially indigenous transformation (Tillmann 1993; Kind 1998; 2010; Whittle 1996), in effect substituting one clearly defined set of actors for another. It has since been commented that the more research that has been carried out on the earliest LBK, the more diversity becomes apparent (Lenneis 2005; Pavlů 2005b). The process of closer investigation began with the German-Austrian project in the 1980s on a series of settlements (e.g. Lenneis and Lüning 2001; Lüning 2005a), furthered by the recognition of the non-LBK La Hoguette pottery style in the west (Jeunesse 1987; Gronenborn 1999). From this have come a series of variations in settlement forms (e.g. Lüning 2005a; Lenneis 2008) and in the detail of earliest house forms (Stäuble 2005), both, however, within distinctive styles, as well as in preferences for crops and animals (Kreuz 1990; 2007; Pucher 1987; Uerpmann and Uerpmann 1997; Arbogast *et al.* 2001). The first studies of a possible indigenous contribution to LBK lithic production (Newell 1970) have been considerably extended (Gronenborn 1997b; Gehlen 2006; Mateiciucová 2008a), and more detailed study of earliest pottery suggests both more formal variation (Nowak 2004) and the possibility of definable groupings already within the overall earliest distribution (Kerig 2010; Strien 2009).

It is fair to claim, therefore, that the whole tenor of debate about the nature of the earliest LBK has changed over the last two to three decades, with a clear recognition now that the earliest phase already contains diversity (e.g. Gronenborn 2010a, 62; cf. Strien 2009) and may centrally involve indigenous people as well as outsiders. This sense is further reinforced by the emergence of so-called integrationist models, embracing both outsiders *and* locals in models of change (Zvelebil 2004; Lukes 2004; Lukes and Zvelebil 2008; Zvelebil and Pettitt 2008; Zvelebil *et al.* 2010; also called fusion models in Whittle 2003). That research has been principally focused on the earliest LBK cemetery at Vedrovice in Moravia (also covered in our project, in Chapter 4.7). A combination of isotopic, osteological, aDNA and archaeological research suggested considerable variation in the life histories of several individuals, in a community seen as founded by a small number of incomers from the core region of LBK origins to the south-east, in western Hungary and western Slovakia, but also as incorporating local people. Some individuals were born and lived their lives in the local area; others were born away and came in later life to the area where they died; yet others may have been born locally, moved away, but subsequently returned. Some people were argued to have been of genetic descent from the Near East, but others of much older European genetic lineages. Individual diets varied, not least as seen in the condition of their teeth, as did the provision of grave goods in their burials; though the sample is very small, there is no obvious initial correlation with genetic history.

If this begins to suggest a happy new consensus, two other considerations hint at continuing problems. The Vedrovice project drew heavily on the wider pattern of results which had emerged from previous DNA studies, principally from studies of both mitochondrial DNA and Y-chromosomes in modern populations in Europe, and the convergent (though never uniform) suggestion that incomers might have constituted not more than about 20 percent of the LBK population (Zvelebil and Pettitt 2006; 2008; summarised in Zvelebil *et al.* 2010, table 1). That view has been challenged in the most recent (and technically more reliable) aDNA studies (Haak *et al.* 2005; Bramanti *et al.* 2009; Haak *et al.* 2010; Burger and Haak 2010). These strongly suggest again difference between hunter-gatherer and early farmer (archaeologically LBK) populations.[5] Does this return us to the pre-1980s situation, or are the samples both of LBK populations in central Europe and of peripheral, mainly northern, hunter-gatherers, some of them slightly later in date than the LBK, simply too small for a definitive picture yet to have emerged? And even if the new aDNA trend were to be confirmed, where does that leave all the other arguments about the contribution of indigenous people, and for diversity in earliest LBK practice in general?

The second worry is about earliest LBK chronology.

Clearly, reliable results must be predicated on the choice of short-life, single-entity radiocarbon samples of known taphonomy in demonstrable association with the contexts they are being used to date (Bayliss *et al.* 2007), but that has often not been the case (Whittle 1990; Stäuble 2005). While the earliest dates for the LBK are still subject to discussion (e.g. Stadler and Kotova 2010a), of most relevance to the Lifeways project is the former consensus view that the earliest phase of the LBK ended *c.* 5300 cal BC. Vedrovice, noted above, can stand as a case in point. Typologically its associated pottery is of the earliest style, though not of the very earliest, but radiocarbon dating (Pettitt and Hedges 2008) suggests that the cemetery was in use principally in the 53rd century cal BC. There may then be overlap between 'earliest' LBK communities and others using subsequent pottery styles, such as the Flomborn type in more westerly regions (Cladders and Stäuble 2003; Lüning 2005a), or the developments of post-earliest, 'classical' LBK society may have to be concentrated into a shorter time period (since the dendrochronology of wood from wells appears to confirm the conventional estimates for the end of the LBK, in the earliest fifth millennium cal BC). The latter possibility would serve to accelerate the rate of change and intensify trends in the growth of settlements, at least regionally, and thus locate at least some of the samples of the Lifeways project in an even more dynamic social context, in which issues of uniformity and diversity take on ever greater significance.

1.3.2 Settlement

Settlements in the landscape

The distribution of LBK settlements across the landscape has long been correlated with lowland settings, proximity to water and the occupation of high-quality soils, classically loess. The association with loess is not exclusive, as areas like the Paris basin or Kujavia in central Poland show (Ilett *et al.* 1982; Pyzel 2009). Nor is the water-loess connection universal, as recent studies of the settlement cluster in the Graetheide region of the southern Netherlands show the use, particularly towards the end of the LBK, of other parts of the surrounding landscape with differing geologies (Amkreutz 2010). Finds of LBK material in caves and in other upland settings have been sporadic but recurrent, and have been taken to indicate seasonal use of uplands, perhaps for herding (Lüning 2000; Ramminger 2005; Knipper 2009); there are also upland lithic sources, including the likely amphibolite source at Jistebsko in the Jizera hills of northern Bohemia (Prostřednik *et al.* 2005). An initial suggestion of long-range seasonal transhumance northwards into Kujavia (Bogucki 1982) has since lapsed, as our knowledge of LBK settlement in that region, and indeed further to the north again in Chelmnoland, has expanded considerably (Bogucki 2000; Marciniak 2005; Pyzel 2009). Taking the evidence overall at face value, it seems likely that the people of LBK settlements spent much of their time in the lowlands, but were not confined to them.

Studies of settlements in the landscape were a particular feature of the 1970s (e.g. Kruk 1973; 1980; Sielmann 1972; 1976). These confirmed major trends and provided the detail of preferences for settlement location, generally in association with smaller watercourses and tributaries rather than in major valleys themselves (e.g. Kruk 1973;1980, for southern Poland); Štúrovo, on the north bank of the Danube in western Slovakia (Pavúk 1994), is an interesting exception to this pattern (Chapter 4). Recurrent kinds of location do not necessarily equate with exactly identical conditions, and Sielmann's studies suggested the possibility of different kinds of micro-climate, region by region (we will return to the issue of climate variation in Chapter 9). The number of relevant pollen diagrams has gradually increased, suggesting discernible but limited human impact on the predominantly woodland setting (e.g. Kalis and Meurers-Balke 1998; 2003; Kalis *et al.* 2003; Schweizer 2003; 2005).

Since that time, regional studies of this kind have continued, but without, perhaps, the same kind of impact. With better knowledge of the earliest LBK (chronological uncertainties notwithstanding), the identification of long-term trends in LBK settlement has become more prominent. Earliest LBK sites appear in quite varied locations (Kreuz 1990), and appear generally to be relatively scattered across the landscape, with significant distances between sites (Frirdich 2003; 2005). Nor are earliest LBK settlements particularly large (Lüning 2005a). At some point after *c.* 5300 cal BC, however, this situation changed, and conditions in the 53rd century cal BC emerge as particularly significant, even if still poorly understood in detail (Cladders and Stäuble 2003). Settlement was extended beyond the initial earliest LBK core areas, and settlements became more numerous, more closely spaced and probably more varied; cemeteries appear from this sort of date onwards (Frirdich 2003), as well as probably enclosures (Meyer 2003). Our regional chapters give further detail.

One case study elegantly modelled is that of the Mörlener Bucht in the Wetterau, in the middle basin of the Main, tributary of the middle Rhine, with a gradually intensifying density of settlements, which only slackened towards the end of the LBK (Ebersbach and Schade 2005). That modelling posited a figure of 0.3–0.5 hectares needed for cultivation per person per year; elsewhere, in a revival of interest in demography, overall figures for LBK settlement of 0.6±0.1 person per km^2 have been mooted, in a significant increase over probable Mesolithic densities (Zimmermann *et al.* 2009; Zimmermann 2010; Petrasch 2010). The biggest increases may come, judging at least by the well established sequence for the Aldenhovener Platte in north-west Germany, not at the start of occupation there, but after three or four house generations (Petrasch 2010). Elsewhere, the timing of such surges in numbers appears to vary, coming in the developed phase of the LBK in the Wetterau, as already noted, but in the earliest LBK in eastern Austria (Petrasch 2010, 355–6). Population modelling based on cemetery age profiles has also suggested that a dramatic increase in fertility rate took place at this time – by an average of two births per woman – now currently discussed as the 'Neolithic demographic transition' (Bocquet-Appel and Bar-Yosef 2008; Bocquet-Appel 2011). Such possible rates of increase may appear problematic (Robb and Miracle 2007, 111), but it is likely that some at least of the people sampled in the Lifeways project would have lived in a busy if not crowded world.

A further interest in these more recent studies has been discrimination among settlements, especially the identification of possible central places (Zimmermann 1995). The idea of networks has caught on, with larger, potentially parent settlements connected to smaller, perhaps daughter settlements and other perhaps specialised sites; Lower Austria provides one such example (Chapter 5). Apart from settlement size, control of lithic production in particular sites could be another symptom of differentiation. Thus Langweiler 8, the largest site in the Merzbachtal on the Aldenhovener Platte, seems to have a more primary role in the processing of flint blades and cores brought in from Rijckholt to the west than other neighbouring sites. Here, however, it is a moot point whether individual house clusters should be identified, rather than the ribbon of settlement along the stream valley in question (Petrasch 2003, 508). There is probably more regional diversity in the densities and groupings of LBK longhouse settlements, both large and small, than overall models have allowed. The ribbon-like nature of occupation of the Merzbachtal and the neighbouring Schlangengraben (Zimmermann *et al.* 2009, fig. 15) is not so far obviously mirrored in the dense occupation of a site like Vaihingen in Baden-Württemberg (Strien 2005; Bogaard *et al.* 2011; Bogaard 2011). Intriguingly, however, scattered longhouse settlements have been found along stream valleys, tributaries of the Tisza, on the northern edge of the Great Hungarian Plain (Domboróczki 2009; Chapter 3). Another recent important suggestion, based initially on the upper Danube but with probably wider relevance, is that settlements with very substantial longhouses and enclosures can be seen as mutually exclusive alternative forms of social display (Pechtl 2009b).

Among the longhouses

The LBK longhouse is very familiar. It and the settlements which it forms have been much studied. Certain assumptions have implicitly been made about household membership, principally that everyone belonged to a household (where else could they go?), but only to one at a time. The implications of the dominant estimate for the duration of the life of a longhouse, of some 20–30 years, have rarely been thought through, since many people must have shifted allegiance, on the one-house-at-a-time model, at least once in their lives, and some older people perhaps twice or more. Big projects, such as those on the Aldenhovener Platte, the Graetheide, and Bylany in Bohemia (Pavlů 2000b; 2010), have tended to dominate analysis, but further study has opened up the possibility of more diversity than was initially apparent, not only in house form but also in the ways houses were grouped together (Coudart 1998; Rück 2007; 2009; D. Hofmann forthcoming). The Lifeways project has not directly studied this architecture of daily life, but it was a central part of the conditions of existence.

The starting point for more recent studies of longhouses goes back to Modderman's analysis of southern Dutch sites (1970; Figs 1.2–3). That offered a now very familiar modular structure to LBK houses, with the distinction between south (or south-east), central and north (or north-west) parts, and their combinations into houses (*Bauten*: central and north-west parts), small houses (*Kleinbauten*: central part only) and large houses (*Großbauten*: all three parts together). This was initially applied to developed LBK settlements like Elsloo and Sittard, and has since been widely followed elsewhere. A related but not identical three-part structure (in some cases with the addition of a fourth component in the form of porches) has been seen in earliest LBK houses (Stäuble 2005; Lüning 2005a; 2009). A rather set way of doing things has thus appeared to be the case, ingrained in the very fabric of communal life and daily existence, even though there is no certainty about the specific role or roles of the three structural components.

Further analysis shows more variation. Coudart (1998) suggested that there were some elements which varied little, including linearity, partitioning and the liberal use of internal posts, in transverse rows, but others which differed both regionally and chronologically rather more, such as treatment of the central part, the length of buildings, and the relative size and composition of partitions. One subsequent analysis has even suggested at least 50 'types' of houses, based on such variability in combinations of structural elements (Birkenhagen 2003; D. Hofmann forthcoming). A recent view has questioned again whether these longhouses were single-storeyed or had raised platforms, at least at one end (Rück 2007; 2009).

The dominant model for the duration of a LBK house derived from the great project on the Aldenhovener Platte. The suggested normal use-life of 20–30 years was reached by estimating the overall span of the LBK occupation there, divided by 16 house generations derived by seriation of decorative motifs on pottery (Stehli 1989a; 1989b; 1994; Lüning and Stehli 1994). That model has been widely influential, for example in analysis of both Bylany and Štúrovo (Pavlů 2000b; Pavúk 1994). A variant allows *Großbauten* to have lasted up to 40 years (Louwe Kooijmans *et al.* 2003). This also has been challenged in recent years, with longer house lives mooted of 70 years or more, up to perhaps a century (Schmidt *et al.* 2005a; Rück 2007; 2009). This is frustratingly unresolved, and given the difficulties of finding short-life radiocarbon samples in direct association with the founding of individual houses, may remain so. It is worth noting, however, the seemingly characteristic struggle to impose a single model on all LBK settlements. Longer durations would also have considerable implications for the density and crowdedness of LBK settlements.

Analysis of the Aldenhovener Platte also produced the hitherto dominant model of the individual farmstead (*Hof* in German) with its attendant working space around it: of

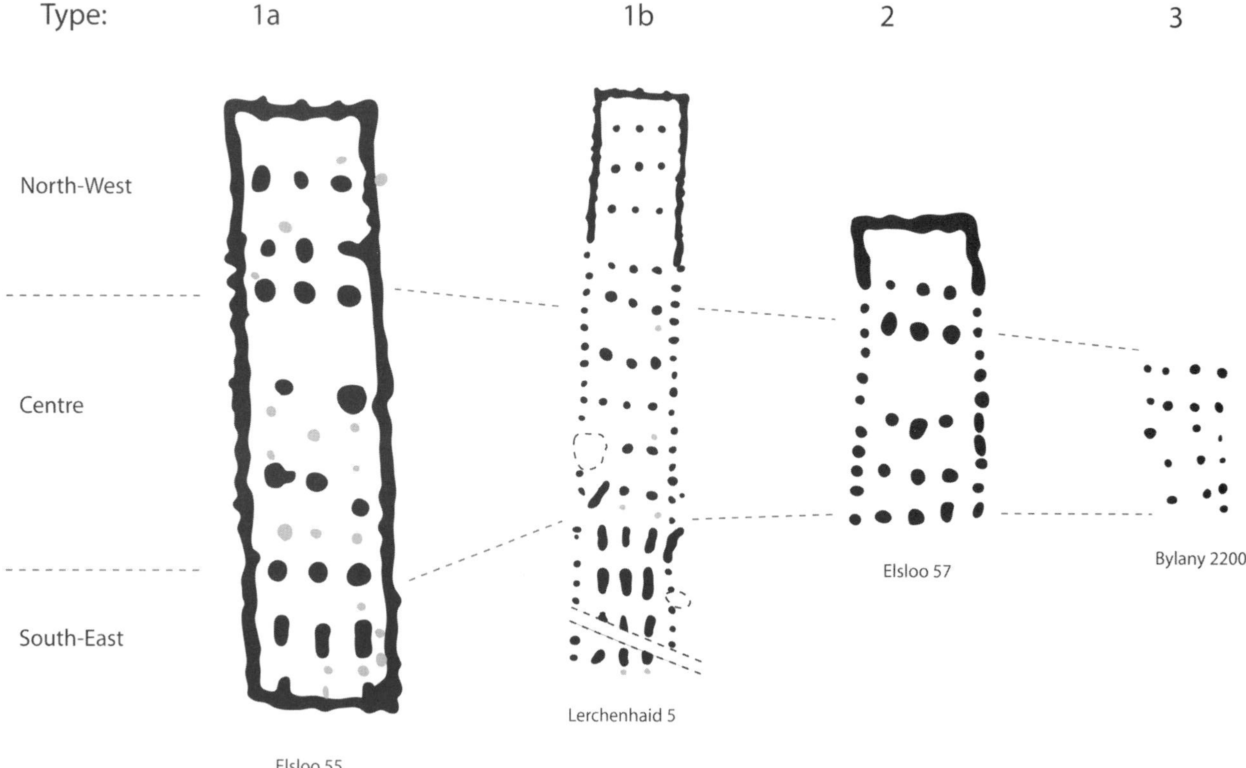

Fig. 1.2. Modderman's scheme for the partition of LBK buildings. Buildings not to scale. Elsloo 55 (c. 25 m) and 57 (c. 14 m) after Modderman 1970, plates 23 and 22; Lerchenhaid 5 (c. 37 m) after Brink-Kloke 1992, 58; Bylany 2200 (c. 9 m) after Pavlů (2000, 211).

Fig. 1.3. The recontructed longhouse from Straubing zoo. Photo: Penny Bickle.

some 25 m radius there (Boelicke 1982), though probably rather smaller in the Graetheide (Louwe Kooijmans *et al.* 2003). Successful tenure through time led, in this model, to the creation of enduring farmstead locations (*Hofplätze* in German; 'yards' in Dutch terminology: van de Velde 1979a; Louwe Kooijmans *et al.* 2003; Lüning 2005a). This has produced a picture of LBK settlements composed of a rather irregular patchwork of individual buildings (though usually sharing a common orientation), separated one from the other by working spaces, and perhaps small gardens. Analysis of Geleen-Janskamperveld in the Graetheide suggested that yards contained a central large building, an ordinary longhouse, and at least one small house (small houses tending to be placed on the periphery of the settlement as a whole), and were between 50 and 100 m in diameter (Louwe Kooijmans *et al.* 2003). Similar, but tighter, groupings have been suggested elsewhere, including for Vaihingen (Strien 2005; Bogaard *et al.* 2011). Further analysis of pottery at Geleen-Janskamperveld also suggested the existence of two 'wards' or agglomerations of yards within the settlement as a whole (Louwe Kooijmans *et al.* 2003), thus providing an overarching social framework of separate kin groups (perhaps moieties) or something similar, above the level of individual households and household clusters; the central space between the two proposed wards, where a *Großbau* is found, could have been occupied by a spiritual leader or a communal men's house.

This essentially cellular and agglomerative structure has been widely applied elsewhere, but is now itself also under challenge. An alternative model of rows of contemporary houses has been proposed (Rück 2007; 2009); once again, there is a desire to replace one dominant single model with another. The possibility of rows certainly seems convincing in some cases, especially in the eastern part of the area covered by the Lifeways project (Chapters 3 and 5), though it need not fit all settlements everywhere; some might show elements of both kinds of arrangement. Nor have the implications of row-like settlements with longer-lasting houses yet been fully considered. On the one hand, they would appear to bump up the numbers of houses in use at any one time, and thus the numbers of occupants (even with the conservative figure (Lüning and Stehli 1989; and see below) of only six people per household). On the other hand, this model might allow a kind of multiplication of the social group, with separate buildings for offspring, kin or other household members, and perhaps with building for its own sake as a sign of group prowess (as rather differently envisaged for the earliest LBK by Frirdich (2003)). This certainly offers the likelihood of considerable diversity in LBK lives on the ground, but equally makes it hard in the current state of research to pin down the residential arrangements of those LBK people, studied in the Lifeways project, who ended up in burials in the related cemeteries.

1.3.3 Subsistence

LBK people have long been identified as farmers. Childe (1929, 106) noted 'the cultivation of barley, one-corn, and perhaps emmer wheats, beans, peas, lentils, and flax, in small plots tilled with stone hoes...to hunting the Danubians made no resort'. He also saw this as the 'simplest conceivable sort of farming' and asserted that 'the peasant was free to shift his hut and break fresh ground as soon as his former fields showed signs of exhaustion' (1929, 105). This picture has changed in some ways. The spectrum of crops has been confirmed. LBK people are generally seen as sedentary agriculturalists, though there is much debate about the style and character of cultivation, and there is discussion about the range over which herding took place. Some hunting can be documented, and is one of the indications of a degree of regional diversity in subsistence. Once again, however, there is a tendency for the validity of single models to be asserted across the whole LBK distribution.

Cereal cultivation

LBK people cultivated a narrower range of plant species than is found during the Balkan Neolithic, with five main cultivated species present at LBK sites: cereals (emmer, einkorn), legumes (pea, lentil) and an oil or fibre plant (flax: but only in the second phase of the LBK; Bogaard 2004, 15; Kreuz *et al.* 2005). These are supplemented by other plants which appear less frequently in recovered assemblages (oats, naked barley, hulled barley, millet, poppy, rye, free-threshing wheat, spelt, bitter vetch and fava bean; Conolly *et al.* 2008, 2798).[6] The plant remains recovered from LBK settlements seem to have originated (directly and indirectly) from processing and only rarely from the accidental charring of storage finds (Bogaard *et al.* 2011, 397). However, crude prevalence rates should be handled carefully and, as Bakels (1991, 281) argues, the crop remains from house loam pits are unlikely to provide a direct reconstruction of frequency. For example, barley and millet are only present at the best sampled settlements (Kreuz 1990, 163; Lüning 2000, 60).

As emmer and einkorn are overwhelmingly the dominant crops, we may be fairly certain that they were the main focus of cultivation and may have been grown together in mixed fields (Lüning 2000, 60; Bogaard 2004, 14). It is usual to state that emmer dominates over einkorn (e.g. Bogucki 1988, 54; Bakels 1991, 280; Lüning 2000, 60) and this was recently found to be the case in a study of botanical remains from LBK sites in Slovakia (M. Hajnalová 2007, 301). In contrast, einkorn dominates in the Rhineland and Dutch Limburg, and is overall more frequent than emmer when both cereals are found together at a site (based on frequency of glume bases and grains which appear in similar proportions; Kreuz 2007, 271). Kreuz (2007, 271) attributes the higher prevalence of einkorn to its better suitability to the wetter conditions of the LBK climate. Two-grained einkorn became more important in cereal assemblages from the late LBK onwards (Kreuz and Boenke 2003; Kohler-Schneider 2007, 212).

Regional differences in cereal cultivation across the distribution of the LBK were suggested by Willerding (1980) and the idea was developed by Lüning (1988a; 2000). These regional groupings are mainly distinguished on the basis of the relative appearance of secondary crops (i.e. not emmer and einkorn). Overall, Lüning (1988a; 2000) divides the LBK into four cultivation zones (Fig. 1.4). In zone one, just emmer and einkorn are present; zone two has higher occurrences of barley and legumes; zone three is marked by pea cultivation and a lack of barley (particularly in Lower Bavaria; Bogaard 2004, 149); and in zone four, barley is present again, while flax and legumes are not (Lüning 2000, 60). Beyond these specific zones, poppy (perhaps illustrating western Mediterranean contacts) and flax tend to be found only in the west (Lüning 2000, 60).

There are exceptions to these regional distributions, with a charred poppy grain found at Asparn (Windl 1996), rye present in the Neckar valley (Lüning 2000, 60–1; Jacomet 2007, 233) and flax found in the later phases of the LBK in Slovakia (M. Hajnalová 2007) and Hungary (Gyulai 2007). Lüning (2000, 61) favours no particular explanation for these differences, other than a general trend to increased regionalisation throughout the LBK over time. As he states (2000, 60), these zones are defined partly qualitatively and partly quantitatively, and are therefore fairly coarse; he had to adjust the four regional growing zones when further research led to the presence of barley being demonstrated west of the Rhine: in the Moselle, the Paris basin and eastern Belgium (Lüning 2000, 60–1).

On the basis of recent evidence from Hungary, Bánffy (2004, 333–4) argues that earliest LBK cultivation in Transdanubia or western Hungary was small-scale and experimental, carried out in the spaces between houses, with einkorn, common wheat, barley and spelt. In another recent survey, Gyulai (2007, 133) found that emmer and einkorn were the most numerous species in Transdanubia, with common wheat, club wheat, spelt and millet also present. However, in this region, well sampled sites have so far been rare (see Chapter 3) and the majority of plant remains have been recovered as imprints on pottery and daub (Gyulai 2007, 133). Gyulai (2007, 131) also argues that cereal growing in the ALP (the equivalent of the LBK on the Great Plain in eastern Hungary; Chapter 3) was on a modest scale, but here barley is represented at four times the rate of wheat. Barley seems to play a more important role in the ALP than it does in the LBK, possibly even grown as a separate crop, though emmer appears to be the dominant crop (Kosse 1979, 136). The preference for barley may be associated with climatic factors such as temperature and day-length, which may be more suitable in south-east Europe (Lister *et al.* 2009, 1093). However, given the broad similarity of the climatic conditions in western and eastern Hungary, there seems to be some element of cultural choice involved.

Pulses (lentil and pea) are also thought to show regional variation with a strong preference for the eastern distribution of the LBK (Bogucki 1988, 55). However, lentil is present in the first LBK phase in Dutch Limburg (e.g. at Geleen-Janskamperveld, Elsloo-Sanderboutlaan and Beek-Kerkeveld), but not in later phases (Bakels 2003, 226, 228), and has been demonstrated to be present in low quantities in both Bavaria and the Neckar valley (Jacomet 2007, 233). Bakels (2003, 227) argues that lentil arrived on the north-western fringe of the LBK as part of a 'package' of domestic plants and subsequently fell out of use as the local Atlantic climate did not suit it. Kreuz (2007, 264, 270, 274), in contrast, argues that regional variation is rather a misnomer, as when sites have been systematically sampled all these species are present to some extent, citing two charred remains of lentil in a storage find in *jüngere* LBK contexts at the site of Eschborn, north of the Main, as evidence. The easternmost evidence for poppy certainly suggests that there may be some truth in Kreuz's (2007) argument; a lone charred poppy seed found at Asparn/Schletz came from a total of 30,000 litres of sampled soil subjected to flotation (Kohler-Schneider 2007, 212). Even here, however, flax was absent (Kohler-Schneider 2007, 212), suggesting that while the regional plant lists may not be exclusive, they do show certain preferences.

Lüning suggests (2000, 60–1) that the weed spectra might show more interesting regional connections. Forty-eight *Anthropochores*[7] have been identified for the LBK, most of which were introduced from the east and south-east of the central European area following the direction in which the LBK spread (Kreuz 2007, 276, 281). However, a small number demonstrate links with the Mediterranean and sub-Mediterranean and, as they are found from the developed phase of the LBK, may be linked with the spread of poppy, which also first appears at this time (Kreuz 2007, 281). Regional differences in weed spectra have also been demonstrated, attributed to the lack of seed corn circulation beyond regional boundaries (Küster 1992; 1995). However, weed spectra are directly influenced by cultivation methods and if these methods saw little or no regionality, lack of seed corn exchange would not create regional differences, but, rather, regionality would have developed both from differences in cereal husbandry practices *and* seed corn not travelling beyond regional boundaries (or regionally affiliated groups; Bogaard 2004, 148). In the regions studied by Bogaard (2004, 151: the lower Rhine-Meuse valleys, the Neckar valley, southern Baden-Württemberg and northern Bavaria), she identifies within-region seed corn circulation on the basis of strongly regional crop husbandry practices and weed floras, perhaps implying obligations to kin-groups living at other settlements within the same region.

The frequency of all crop species (including average concentrations of hazelnut shells) increases considerably during the developed phase of the LBK, when more charred crop remains have been recovered (Kreuz 2007, 271). Cultivated plants were supplemented by wild species, though whether wild plants were introduced to a settlement context accidentally or deliberately is more difficult to determine (Jacomet 2007, 236). As wild plants may not have been subjected to the same processing sequences as domesticated plants, it is likely that we underestimate their significance to the LBK diet (Marciniak 2005, 202). The most frequent wild plant (possibly because their shells preserve very well) that may have been a collected or additional managed food source, rather than a weed in fields of cropped plants, is hazelnut (Jacomet 2007, 236; Kreuz 2007, 268). A rare find

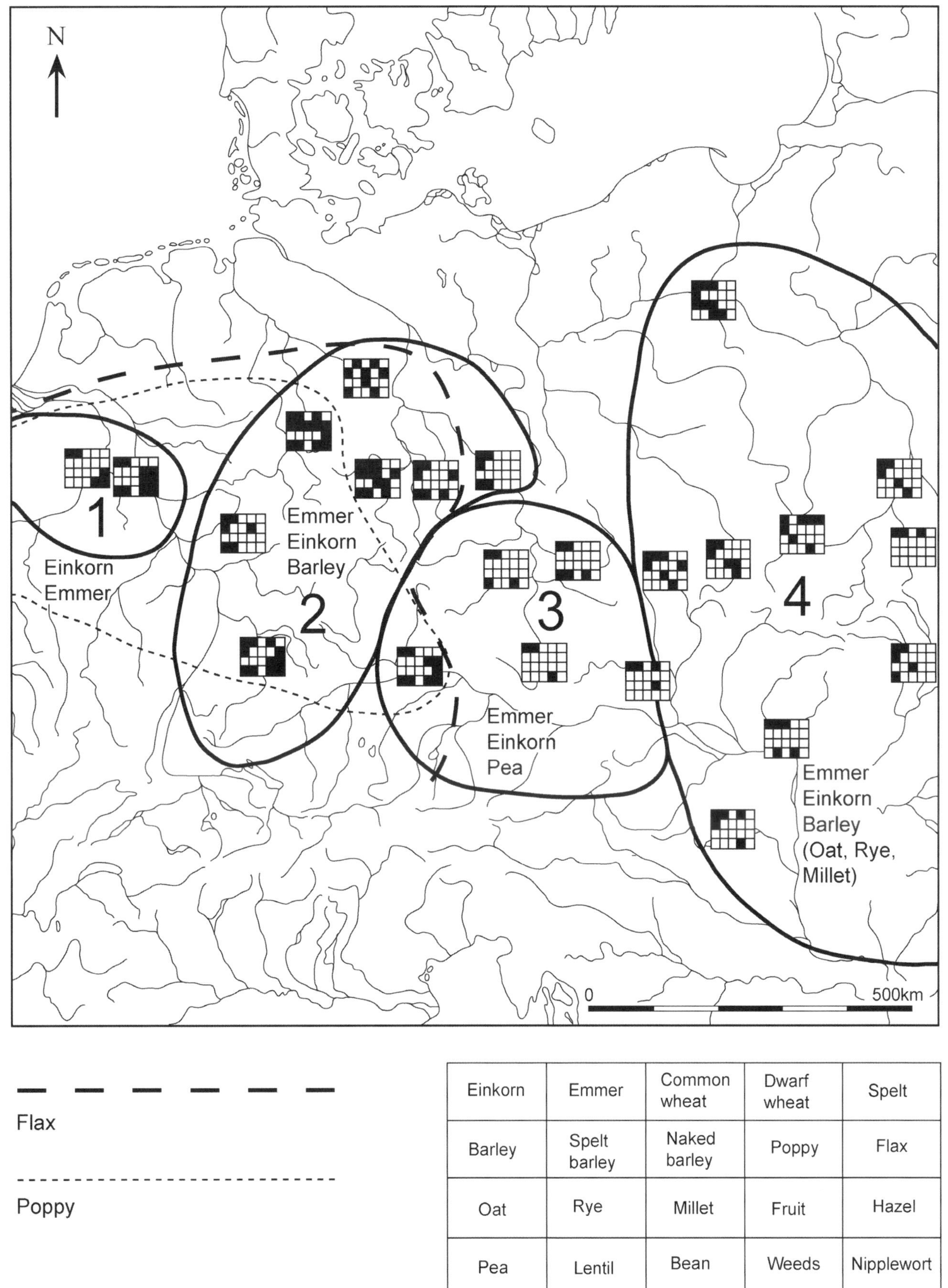

Fig. 1.4. Cereal cultivation zones. After Lüning (2000, 59).

Table 1.1. Regional subsistence patterning and crop growing conditions identified by Bogaard (2004, 149, table 6.4).

	Lower Rhine-Meuse	**Neckar valley**	**Southern Baden-Württemberg**	**Lower Bavaria**
Crop growing conditions	High productivity and moderate disturbance	Low productivity and disturbance to medium productivity and high disturbance	Medium productivity and high disturbance	Medium productivity and high disturbance to high productivity and moderate disturbance
Crop spectra	Barley virtually absent	Barley present	Barley present	Barley absent
Faunal spectra	(High cattle?)	High pig and wild	High pig and wild	High pig and wild
Regional ceramic group	Rhine-Meuse group	Württemberg group	Württemberg group (Upper Rhine group)	Bavaria-Danube group

of two charred halves of a wild apple was made at Poigen, Austria (Kohler-Schneider 2007). As well as apple, sloe is attested at LBK sites, along with mistletoe that may have been animal fodder or used for its medicinal properties (Jacomet 2007, 236). A wild cabbage or type of kale is also found (Lüning 2000, 61), as well as strawberry, rosehips and ground cherry (Kohler-Schneider and Caneppele 2010, 224; Bogaard *et al.* 2011, 396).

Methods of crop cultivation

Various models of crop cultivation have been proposed over the years for the LBK (Bogaard 2004, 21). The earliest of these was slash-and-burn or shifting cultivation, and Childe (1929, 45–6) used 'nomadic garden-culture' to explain the spread of the Neolithic. The model rests on several assumptions (soil degradation or exhaustion amongst others), which have been shown not to apply in the case of the LBK (Modderman 1970; Lüning 1979/1980; Bogucki 1988, 81–2; Bogaard 2004, 26–7). Continuous cultivation on loess soils only leads to slightly decreased yields and permanent cultivation of fields, avoiding floodplains, remains the favoured model (Rowley-Conwy 1981; Bogucki 1988; Kreuz 1990; Bogaard 2004).

Once the slash-and-burn model had been rejected, debate turned to consider extensive and intensive models of agriculture. Lüning (1979/80; 2000) supports extensive models of LBK farming, envisaging that settlements were surrounded by large fields. This is based on a calculation that each family would have required 3.75 ha, which would have been ard-ploughed at some considerable effort (Lüning 1979/80; 2000, 181; Bogaard 2004, 30). Bogaard (2004), however, has convincingly demonstrated, based on the associated weed flora, that intensive year-on-year cereal cultivation, with both autumn and spring sowing, was practised in much smaller plots or gardens; this would have provided high yields, but would have been more time-consuming.[8] 'Garden horticulture' is characterised by long-term commitment (beyond a human lifetime) to certain plots of land (Bogaard 2004, 165; Bogaard and Jones 2007) and the small-scale nature of this method of cultivation could also explain why early Neolithic farming had little impact on pollen diagrams (Kalis and Meurers-Balke 1998; 2003; Kalis *et al.* 2003; Schweizer 2003; 2005; and see above).

Although Kreuz (1990; 2007) argues for spring sowing, it seems likely that most cereal crops were both autumn- and spring-sown, continuing practices found in the preceding Neolithic cultures to the south-east (in the Carpathian basin: Bogaard 2004, 163–4; Bogaard *et al.* 2007). This would have required people to work in the fields or gardens on a year-round basis, and suggests that at least part of the population remained close to the settlement throughout the seasons. This method of crop husbandry also suggests that care for domestic animals was integrated to some extent with garden horticulture, and Bogaard (2004, 159) hypothesises that manuring of fields and grazing of stubble and cereals (to prevent lodging) were likely. However, poppy, flax and pulses would still have required spring sowing times and would have ripened later than cereals, perhaps suggesting that they were grown in fields of their own (Kreuz 2007, 273).

Within the widespread practice of garden agriculture, Bogaard (2004) was able to identify some differences between regions. These were associated with the extent of soil disturbance and the productivity of the cultivated plots (Table 1.1). Similar information appears not to be available for other regions, though intensive tillage has been identified at Mold, Lower Austria (Kohler-Schneider and Cannepele 2010). For the purposes of the Lifeways project, differences between northern Bavaria and the Neckar valley are the most salient, which suggest they were not sharing seed corn (see above).

In their intensive study of Vaihingen, in the Neckar valley, Bogaard *et al.* (2011; cf. Bogaard 2011) suggested that different 'clans' (identified through ceramic styles; Strien 2005) were growing crops at different distances from the settlement (based on inferred intensity of production, derived from differences in weed flora, and on soil pH levels). Clan A grew their crops on the land immediately around the settlement, while clan C cultivated further away, and clans D and B operated somewhere in between the two (Bogaard *et al.* 2011, 408). However, despite these differences, cultivated and wild species were well represented across the settlement, suggesting everyone had equal access to the same range of plants (Bogaard *et al.* 2011, 409). Only poppy and feathergrass showed restricted spatial distributions, and Bogaard *et al.* (2011, 413) conclude that 'restricted use of these plants contributed to differentiation' between social groups towards the end of the settlement's occupation.

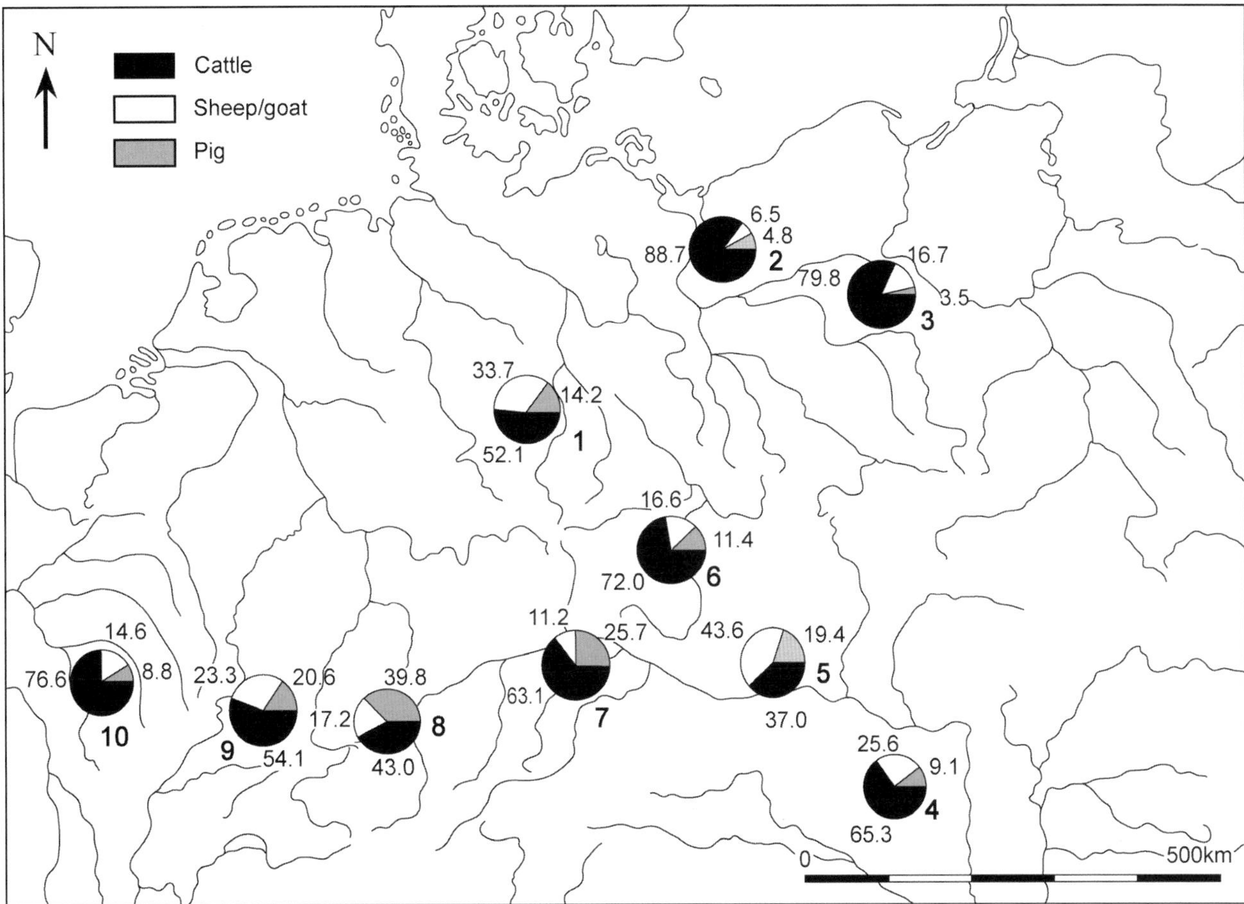

Fig. 1.5. Domestic animals by region. 1) Lower Saxony, 2) and 3) Poland, 4) Hungary, 5) Lower Austria, 6) Bohemia, 7) Bavaria, 8) Baden-Württemberg, 9) Alsace, 10) Paris basin. After Lüning (2000, 109).

1.3.4 Animal husbandry

Loess soils are not ideal for the preservation of bone, leading to a patchy and somewhat inconsistent animal bone record (Bogucki 1988, 85). Some of the biggest excavations have been carried out in areas with very poor or minimal preservation of bone (again, for example, the Aldenhovener Platte, the Graetheide in Dutch Limburg, and Bylany), but other areas have been kinder, for example the Paris basin and central Poland, and the number of better documented LBK animal bone assemblages has certainly increased over the years (Hachem 1997; 2000; Arbogast *et al.* 2001; Marciniak 2005; Bedault and Hachem 2008), but the problems associated with small assemblages, that can be easily skewed, remain relevant (Bartosiewicz 2005, 58).

Domesticated animals

The domesticated species found in LBK contexts are cattle, sheep, goat, pig and dog (Bogucki 1988; Lüning 2000; Marciniak 2005; Fig. 1.5). Sheep and goats clearly had no wild counterparts in central Europe at this time (Uerpmann 1979; Lüning 2000, 108). Cattle are now thought to have been domesticated in the Near East and introduced to central Europe, rather than being domesticated from local wild animals (Bollongino *et al.* 2006; Bollongino and Burger 2010). Based on the DNA evidence, some mixing between domesticated herds and wild animals is thought likely for pig, with possible limited local domestication, though the picture appears to be complex and is probably not yet fully resolved (Edwards *et al.* 2007; Larson *et al.* 2007). Domestic animals are often thought to have been kept in small-scale and closely managed herds (Lüning 2000; Marciniak 2005; Halstead 2006).

While sheep and goats had been the dominant species in the Neolithic of south-east Europe, cattle came to dominate in the LBK, which is usually attributed to their greater adaptability to the cooler climate and woodland vegetation of central Europe (Bogucki 1988; Halstead 1989; Benecke 1994; Lüning 2000, 108). However, at this time the landscape of south-east Europe was also much more wooded than it is today and sheep/goats dominate there (Halstead 2006, 45). It is also to be noted that some of the earliest LBK sites, including in Austria, have high numbers of sheep (Pucher 1987; Uerpmann and Uerpmann 1997; Lüning 2000, 109), so that the longer-term shift to the predominance of cattle could be as much about the social context of developed longhouse life as the basic environmental setting.

In almost all developed LBK assemblages cattle are the most frequent species, often representing more than 50% of the record (Lüning 2000, 110; Knipper 2011). For example, in central Germany cattle represent 53%, sheep/goats 34%

and pig 14% of the total assemblage, (Döhle 1993, 115; Lüning 2000, 110). Based on MNI, Milisauskas and Kruk (1989, 439) estimated that cattle frequency varied between 30% and 60% across the LBK as a whole.

Cattle are thought to have provided the greatest quantity of meat (Bogucki 1988; Lüning 2000; cf. Marciniak 2005; 2011), though Bogucki (1982; 1984; 1988, 85) argued that this was not their only use, citing milk and cheese as a significant component of the LBK diet (Salque *et al.* 2012a; 2012b; cf. Craig *et al.* 2005; Evershed *et al.* 2008). Herd composition has been analysed to assess primary use, but has so far been inconclusive. Assemblages from central Germany have been shown to be equally split between the sexes (Benecke 1994), while in Alsace bulls and cows occur at a ratio of 1:3, with 40% of the cattle from Alsace reaching only two to four years of age and older animals surviving beyond six years (Arbogast 1993; Lüning 2000, 113). For Lüning (2000, 113), this indicates the careful herd management suggested by Bogucki (1988) and perhaps hints at dairy herds. At Vaihingen, two thirds of the cattle were identified as female, though M. Schäfer (2010, 113) believes this is still too high a rate of bulls for a productive milk herd and argues that the primary reason for keeping cattle was for their meat. In contrast, ceramic sieves have also been found at LBK sites (Domboróczki 2009, 106). Ongoing lipid analysis has so far detected dairy fats from sieves in central Germany and Poland (Salque *et al.* 2012a; 2012b).

In analysis of assemblages from central Poland aimed at the social context of consumption, Marciniak has argued (2005, 210; 2011), on the basis of the parts of the animal skeleton preserved and their differential treatment, that cattle and pigs were kept for feasting, while sheep provided meat on a more daily basis, alongside a more prominent role for wild animals and plants in the diet. This approach clearly differs from those discussed above, which are mainly based on crude prevalence rates (Bartosiewicz 2005, 58). At the sites studied by Marciniak (2005, 217), cattle and sheep/goats were found in different contexts, with cattle remains placed in clay pits away from houses, which leads in part to the conclusion that they were used in communal feasting activities. This is not the case elsewhere in the LBK; even at Cuiry-lès-Chaudardes in the Aisne valley of the Paris basin, where Hachem (1997; 2000; 2011) was able to demonstrate spatial differences between the deposition of different animal species, cattle, pig and sheep/goats came from the same kind of contexts. Elsewhere, no selective deposition of different parts of the animal is yet apparent (for example, again, at Vaihingen; M. Schäfer 2010, 112).

More regional variability is seen in which species was the second most frequent. While sheep are more prevalent in Hungarian and Austrian LBK contexts, the frequency of pigs grows towards the source of the Danube (in Bavaria and Baden-Württemberg), reaching its highest rates in south-west Germany. The preference for pig in these regions appears to prevail throughout the LBK (Döhle 1993, 118; Lüning 2000, 109–10). In Alsace, although sheep/goats were the second preferred species at many sites, pigs are nonetheless more prevalent than in central Germany (as defined by Lüning 2000), this time possibly at the expense of cattle (Arbogast 1993). This tendency to prefer pigs over sheep/goats has been identified at some sites from the *älteste* LBK (Uerpmann and Uerpmann 1997; Lüning 2000, 110).

Pigs are also thought to have thrived on a wide variety of landscapes, and ecological explanations have previously been used to explain these variations, though the influence of a continued Mesolithic tradition has also been proposed in the case of Baden-Württemberg (Uerpmann and Uerpmann 1997). Overall, however, most researchers favour cultural preference rather than environment to explain the preference for pig in southern Germany and northern Alsace (e.g. Arbogast 1993; 2001; Lüning 2000, 112; cf. Döhle 1993, 121). It is also interesting to note that while sheep/goats show similar age-at-death profiles to those of cattle in Alsace, pigs seem to have been killed earlier in life, with animals over three years rarely found (Lüning 2000, 113), suggesting that pig was bred more exclusively for meat (Bedault 2009).

How the demands of horticulture and caring for domestic animals were combined has also been debated; suggestions that cattle were pastured on higher grounds during summer months, perhaps as some form of transhumance, have been long favoured, not least because Lüning's (2000) model of extensive crop husbandry envisaged little space for keeping cattle close to the settlement. This practice was demonstrated for the later Neolithic in the Black Forest Mountains (Kienlin and Valde-Nowak 2003) and by analogy seemed likely in the LBK. In Baden-Württemberg, Bentley and Knipper (2005a) had shown that non-local strontium ratios were found on cattle teeth from Vaihingen, but Corina Knipper (2011) now argues that cattle were kept close to the settlement and grazed on the open and marshy river valleys, while sheep/goats, which produce the more varied strontium and oxygen results, travelled further; though even in this case movement may not have covered vast distances. In Bogaard's (2004) model of garden agriculture, competition between animals and fields is unlikely to have been a major problem. Furthermore, cattle are often thought to have thrived in a wooded environment (Bogucki 1988) and could have relied on a large volume of leafy fodder (Marciniak 2005, 202). How far, and to what extent, cattle and other domesticated animals moved continues to be an essential question for the future.

The picture for the ALP in eastern Hungary is still fairly patchy. Kosse (1979, 133) argued that the early ALP economy was largely based on sheep/goats (60% of the domesticated animal bone recorded, while cattle and pigs only reached respective rates of 15% and 10%). At Füzesabony, which was more recently excavated (Chapter 3), the estimated ratio between cattle and sheep is 1:2 (Domboróczki 2009, 108). In the later stages of the ALP, cattle and pig grew in numbers, at the apparent expense of sheep, which Kosse (1979, 137) attributed to growing reliance on woodland resources, and Bartosiewicz (2007) to a longer-term adaptation to wetter conditions on the Plain. In contrast, at west Hungarian LBK sites, sheep/goats appear to be the second most frequent animal (after cattle: Bartosiewicz 2005, 56). Sheep/goats may have been useful for grazing cultivated land, preventing excessive growth and lodging (Bogaard 2004; Halstead 2006, 49), and this practice may be attested to in the form of dental microwear on sheep mandibles from the earlier Körös culture site of Ecsegfalva 23 on the Great Plain (Mainland 2007).

Striking evidence for within-site variation, finally, has been found in the well preserved assemblage from Cuiry-lès-Chaudardes in the Paris basin, which is one of the largest known for the LBK (Hachem 1997; 2000; 2011). Here, house assemblages showed certain species preferences between cattle, sheep/goats, wild boar and deer; wild animals were primarily associated with the smaller houses (Hachem 1997; 2000, 310). These preferences for certain animals also appeared to have a spatial dimension that was maintained across the five chronological phases of the site; bone assemblages associated with houses in the north-west of the site were dominated by wild animals, with cattle and sheep/goats also favoured by particular zones of the site (Hachem 2000, 311; 2011, figs 141–4). This kind of pattern has yet to be shown in as much detail elsewhere, though at Vaihingen there may be differences in the representation of wild and domestic animals in the settlement pits and in the enclosure ditch (M. Schäfer 2010, 114–15).

Wild animals and fish

Wild animals are present at different rates at the vast majority of LBK sites, but they generally make up less than 10% of the animal bone assemblage (Fig. 1.6; Lüning 2000, 113). As with wild plants, this may actually under-represent the contribution of wild animals to the economy of the LBK, and covers significant variation. At Vaihingen, for example, wild animals accounted for 15% of the animal bone record, a rate which remained consistent across the different phases of the LBK (M. Schäfer 2010, 109). Overall, wild boar, red and roe deer and aurochs together make up more than 90% of the wild animal bone (Döhle 2005, 276). Other species found include hare, beaver, wolf, red fox, brown bear, lynx, wildcat, polecat, marten, badger, otter, wild horse and some species of birds, which are fairly widespread across the distribution of the LBK (Döhle 2005, 280, 283). These species suggest a range of habitats from denser forest (brown bear) to lighter woodland cover (red deer), as well as patchwork grassland and forest edge (aurochs, wild boar and roe deer) and more open grassland (wild horse and hare; Döhle 2005, 284). Döhle (2005, 284) plotted the distributions of different wild animal species found at LBK settlements and suggests that southern Germany (south-west Germany around the Neckar in particular) may have had denser types of forest cover; wild horse is absent in Baden-Württemberg during the Mesolithic and early Neolithic (although it appears either side of the region, in Alsace and Bavaria).

Southern Germany also stands out because wild animals can account for much more than 10% of the animal bone record (Bavaria: 44%; Baden-Württemberg: 39%; Lüning 2000, 115). Although overall Alsace is much like the rest of the LBK, distinct differences between north and south have been identified (Arbogast 2001). On Tradition A sites (northern Alsace), the importance of hunting remains modest in all periods and wild fauna remains are uniformly rare, hardly exceeding 10% of a given bone assemblage (Arbogast 2001). On Tradition B sites (southern Alsace) however, the situation is much more diversified, as on such sites there is the highest level of variability in the percentage of wild remains, with rates reaching 20% at Wettolsheim (Arbogast 1993, 134). Similarly the regional differences identified by Döhle (1993) and Lüning (2000) cover considerable chronological and within-region variation. For example, within region 5 (Fig. 1.6; Lower Austria and Moravia) at the Austrian site of Rosenburg, between 25% and 37% of the animal bone was identified as wild, while at other Niederösterreich sites earlier LBK rates of *c.* 12–18% fell to below 10% in the later phases (Schmitzberger 2009a, 116). In Bavaria, the numbers of wild animals seem to decrease over time from rates of 54% (Wang: but note a relatively small assemblage) and 48% (Altdorf) in the earliest LBK to between 12–35% at later sites. Similarly, assemblages containing 25% or even 30% wild animals are attested in Slovakia and Hungary, against an average of *c.* 10% (Benecke 2001, 45). At Füzesabony (ALP) wild animals accounted for 20% of the animal bone assemblage (Domboróczki 2009, 106), which confirms Kosse's (1979, 137) earlier estimates and suggests a slightly higher reliance on wild animals amongst ALP communities than in the LBK of Transdanubia.

The presence of freshwater fish remains on LBK sites has also occasionally been demonstrated, and the inventory is slowly growing, but fish are not generally thought to have contributed a great deal to the diet (e.g. Asam *et al.* 2008, 124). The lack of fish may be due to poor preservation rates of fish bone and inconsistent use of flotation, though some recently well sampled sites have produced very little evidence. One fish bone (of a *Cyprinid*) was retrieved from Mold (Niederösterreich), despite an intensive sampling strategy (Schmitzberger 2010, 246). At the nearby site of Rosenburg, however, 35 fish bones were recovered, representing possibly as many as ten different species (Galik 2009, 127; Schmitzberger 2009, 116). Fish bones are said to occur in 'very small numbers' on ALP sites (Kosse 1979, 138). Freshwater resources are also present in occasional finds of pond turtle, which was found further north than its current distribution (C. Willms 2003, 190), and also of beaver, which occurs fairly regularly, though in low numbers (Döhle 2005); its pelt is considered its most useful asset (Lenneis 2009). Freshwater mussels (*Unio crassus*) also suggest that river resources were exploited, but these shellfish have received little study (Gulyái *et al.* 2007, 395).

Fish have been shown to be more regularly present at LBK sites in Belgium (including Liège Place St.-Lambert) and on a site in the Wetterau (Lüning 2000, 153; Bakels 2009, 43; Otte 1984). At the point where the upper Danube

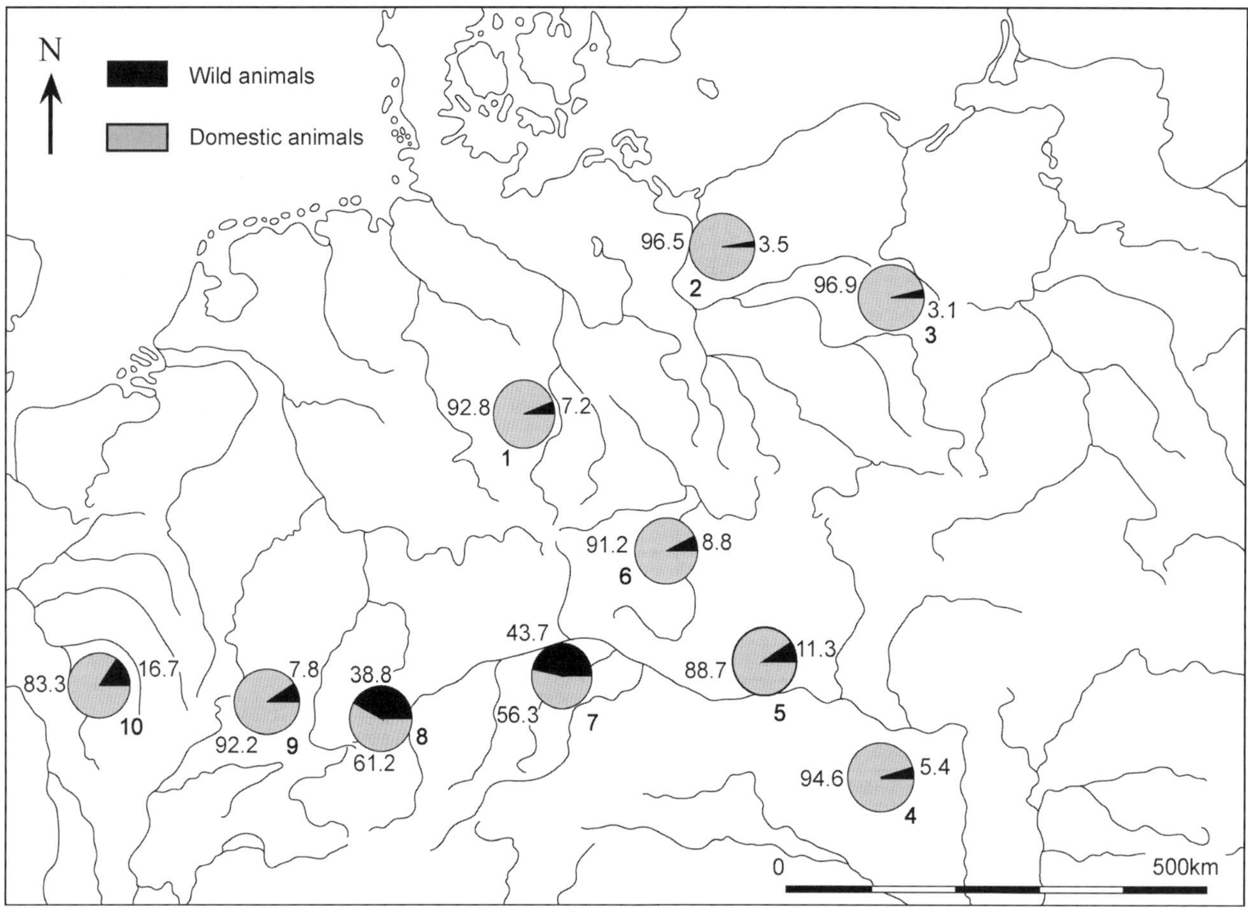

Fig. 1.6. Domestic versus wild animal frequencies by region. 1) Lower Saxony, 2) and 3) Poland, 4) Hungary, 5) Lower Austria, 6) Bohemia, 7) Bavaria, 8) Baden-Württemberg, 9) Alsace, 10) Paris basin. After Lüning (2000, 115).

valley passes the southern end of the Swabian Alb (Baden-Württemberg), the rock shelter site of Lautereck produced a context rich in fish bones, associated with earlier LBK sherds (Taute 1966, 495; Lüning 2000, 153). The fish species identified here included grayling, Danube salmon, pike, chub, lake chub, orfe, nase, barb and bream. This potential 'fishing station' may suggest that it was an activity that took place away from the settlement and makes it tempting to link the hunting focus of Rosenburg with the higher number of fish remains there. At Singen (just north of the Bodensee, in the Hegau), more than 1000 fish bones and vertebrae were found, also alongside a predominant role for hunting (Aufdermauer *et al.* 1985, 53). Here, the species found (red eye, rudd, barb, chub, tench, pike, trout and river perch) suggest that a variety of fishing techniques and water habitats were exploited (Torke 1987; Lüning 2000, 154). Interestingly, Aufdermauer *et al.* (1985, 53) suggest that wild and domestic animals at this site were found in different individual pits, perhaps echoing the case of Cuiry-lès-Chaudardes noted above.

Whether LBK people were conscious of some of the differences noted above is an open question. The recent study of Vaihingen suggests that differential land access must have been important at settlement and local level. But at a regional level, did people attach significance to the visuality of different crop preferences (cf. Evans 2003) or register difference through, say, the taste and texture of locally made bread? The other relevant unresolved question is the classic one of scale. Much of the literature implies basically autonomous, household-based activity, what has elsewhere been called the domestic mode of production (Sahlins 1974). But beyond establishing what was grown and herded, and the style in which this was carried out, there has been far less debate about the scale and goals of production. Was all household production the same? In an older terminology, was it satisfying or maximising? Did some LBK householders store more crops and accumulate larger herds than others? There are hints of this question in the discussion about the internal layout of houses, but the two spheres of debate have tended to be kept separate. Could viable herds be kept by single households or did they require the pooled resources and energies of several households? Did the inhabitants of larger sites have different goals to those of smaller ones? Were tasks separated along gender or other socially defined lines? Were those who herded also those who hunted? And what kinds of socialities did these subsistence activities produce for both individuals over their lifecourse and for how communities were bound together (Bickle 2009)? As far as the Lifeways project was concerned, it remained to be seen how far the differences in cultivation, husbandry and hunting noted above would be reflected in dietary isotopic analysis, and whether fresh evidence relevant to the issue of scale could be produced through comparison of sites and regions.

1.3.5 Mortuary practice

LBK people disposed of their dead in a variety of archaeologically visible ways (Jeunesse 1995a; 1995b; 1996; 1997). The remains of at least 3000 LBK people have been recovered (Chapter 2.4; Lifeways Database). Roughly two thirds of these have been found in burial grounds or cemeteries separate from, by varying distances, contemporary settlements. Single inhumations dominate, but there were also cremations in some regions (Trautmann 2007). A significant proportion of inhumed remains have also been found within LBK settlements, singly and sometimes in small groups, from time to time in identifiable graves but often within other features such as the ditches flanking longhouses and other pits in varying proximity to them (Veit 1996). Human remains have also been found in enclosure ditches and perimeters, as strikingly in the recent excavations at Herxheim (Zeeb-Lanz 2009b; Haack 2009; Boulestin *et al.* 2009), as well as in caves (Veit 1996).

Our ability to study LBK human remains thus rests on conditions of archaeological preservation and recovery. It appears that many inhumation graves were dug sufficiently deep, if at varying depths, to escape the erosion which has afflicted the living surfaces of longhouses and settlements. Some cremation graves and deposits were less robust, with average depths of 55 cm for cremation pits compared with 1.25 m for inhumation graves quoted for Elsloo (van de Velde 1997, 86), and the potential loss is greater. The detection of remains in features within settlements is conditioned by the extent of excavation, which has often halted as house density decreases on the periphery of sites. Some cemeteries have been discovered in their own right, usually through some form of development or initially non-archaeological intervention, without settlement remains being recorded; examples such as Nitra are given in the regional chapters. Others have been found in the wake of extensive settlement investigations, such as Elsloo in the Graetheide in Dutch Limburg (Modderman 1970) and Niedermerz across the Merzbachtal on the Aldenhovener Platte (Dohrn-Ihmig 1983), respectively some 250–300 m and 500 m from the nearest, and in each case locally largest, settlement (van de Velde 1997, 86). Other substantial settlement excavations such as those at Bylany (Pavlů 2000b) have not so far located cemeteries, though these are widespread across the LBK distribution from western Slovakia to Alsace (Jeunesse 2009, fig. 12); the map equally demonstrates the absence so far of cemeteries in the Paris basin, as well as in Hungary, Poland and parts of central Germany. It is worth noting the radical claim that the *normal* treatment of the dead in the LBK was simply exposure out in the fields or woods (van de Velde 1997). That there was selection for inclusion in both cemeteries and settlement burial seems self-evident, even on the most minimal population densities, and selection would have been even more extreme if, as could be argued, burial grounds belonged, as at Elsloo and Niedermerz, exclusively to the inhabitants of the adjacent major settlements (van de Velde 1997, 86; cf. Hoyer 2010). That question remains open, and one of the goals of the Lifeways investigation was to contribute to its examination.

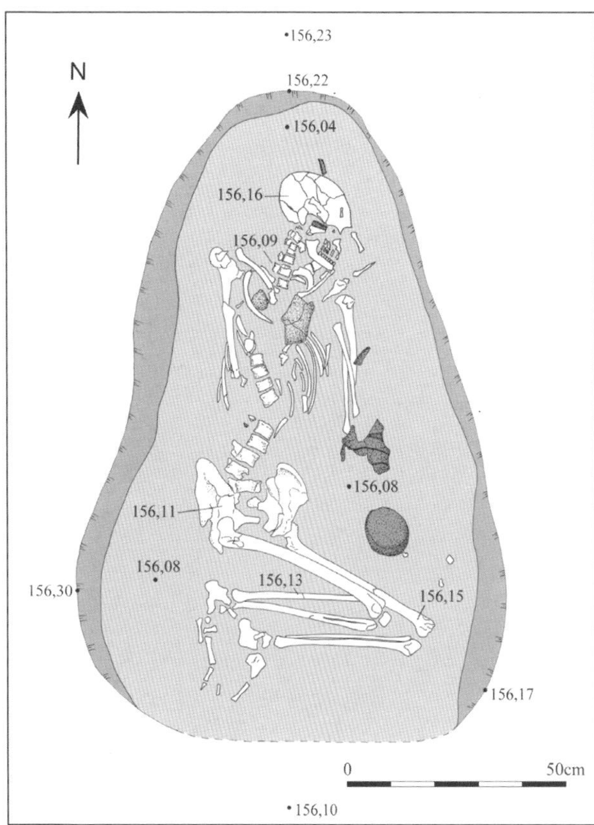

Fig. 1.7. Balatonszárszó-Kis-erdei-dűlő: burial 531.

The Lifeways project has concentrated on cemeteries, which provide our largest and statistically most robust samples, but includes some settlement burials, such as the large assemblage from Otzing, Bavaria (Chapter 6). We do not, however, imply lesser importance for settlement burials, and anyway our samples from Hungary, both in Transdanubia and from the north of the Great Plain, all come formally from settlement contexts (Chapter 3; Fig. 1.7). The Hungarian graves in question are perhaps not typical of the admittedly rather varied range of settlement burials (Veit 1996; Orschiedt 1998a). Those, in general, show less formality and repetition, with much more variety in body position, body completeness and the numbers of people in a single deposit; double or triple deposits, for example, are recorded. Accounting for such burials has proved difficult, especially in a framework which consciously or unconsciously treats formal inhumation in burial grounds as normal practice (D. Hofmann 2009); explanations have tended to resort to notions of lower or even proscribed status. An older strand of interpretation, however, sought to understand this practice in terms of different kinds of remembering and the presencing of the dead among the living (Behrens 1973, 242; Whittle 2009, 253), and this has recently been revived, in combination with notions of performance and theatralisation, the intersection between tradition and contingency, in a deliberate attempt to blur the differences between cemetery and settlement burial (D. Hofmann 2009). That is an important insight, though it does not in turn confront the separations, selections, formalities and repetitions of cemetery burial (but see D. Hofmann forthcoming). Ideally, the Lifeways project would have systematically compared these two major sets of contexts in equal numbers, across our study area. It must be clear that our sample is selective.

The mortuary dataset has steadily increased over recent decades, and several significant burial grounds (listed by Jeunesse 2003a, 21) await full publication. Mortuary practice has been at the heart of many analyses of LBK social relations (e.g. van de Velde 1979a; 1979b; Modderman 1988; Jeunesse 1995a; 1995b; 1996; 1997; 2005; 2009), and we will return to such issues below (Chapter 1.3.7). It has also been a field in which, after earlier characterisations of very uniform practice (Pavúk 1972a; compare D. Hofmann 2009a, 220), regional variation was increasingly recognised (Modderman 1988, 117–22), and now a host of both regional and chronological factors have been brought into account, especially by Jeunesse (1995a; 1995b; 1996; 1997; 2002d; 2003a; 2005; 2006; 2009).

Broadly speaking, some but not many earliest LBK burials have been found. They include the striking example of the man buried in a crouched position in one of the pits flanking a house at Schwanfeld, who has been seen as hunter or warrior or both (Gronenborn 2003; Lüning 2005a). On the basis of a single radiocarbon date, that person appears to be very early in the LBK sequence, but Vedrovice in Moravia, dated to the 53rd century cal BC, appears so far to be the earliest known cemetery, with associated pottery of earliest style (Pettitt and Hedges 2008; Zvelebil and Pettitt 2008; Zvelebil *et al.* 2010; see Chapter 4). Some of the graves from Hungarian settlements may date equally early or earlier (Chapter 3). The rest of the known cemetery distribution already noted above then appears to follow. Examples taken to be early in the developed phase of the LBK include Flomborn itself in the middle Rhineland (I. Richter 1969; Jeunesse 1997), perhaps overlapping in the 53rd century cal BC. Our regional chapters chart others, among which Nitra in western Slovakia (Pavúk 1972a) appears to be late (Chapter 4). But it is fair to comment that a more precise chronology so far eludes us. The estimates for the duration of individual cemeteries are based largely on typological analysis of associated decorated pottery, and vary; none has been extensively radiocarbon dated. That hampers our view of the wider picture. Did the fashion for separate burial grounds – the more formal embodiment of individual and group identities (Potter and Perry 2011; Wilshusen and Potter 2010) – spread quickly, or over several generations, and from where? It has no obvious precedent in indigenous Mesolithic practice in central Europe (Jeunesse 2009). It seems to coincide in general terms with the expansion and intensification of settlement normally assigned to the 53rd century cal BC onwards, but how close in time were the two processes? It has been suggested that cemeteries emerged as an alternative form of social expression when expansion was no longer viable in itself as a prime arena for claims to status (Frirdich 2005).

LBK cemeteries vary in size. Schwetzingen in the Rhineland, Aiterhofen in Bavaria (both included in this project) and Wandersleben-Gotha in central Germany appear to be the largest known, with respectively 203 graves (some of them cremations), 240 graves (including cremations) and 311 graves (of which 132 were cremations) (Gerling 2009; Nieszery 1995; Bickle *et al.* 2011; Hoffmann 1989; Jeunesse 1997). Many range into the tens up to and a little over a hundred graves. It is difficult to establish the smallest cemetery, as several with low numbers result from older and probably incomplete investigations in less than ideal circumstances, such as Quatzenheim in Alsace, now with 17 graves known (Jeunesse 2005).

Characteristically, LBK cemeteries are formed by varying concentrations of single graves. These are normally placed a little apart from one another, and there is comparatively little intercutting (though instances will be noted in regional chapters), so that the enduring marking of graves has often been inferred. Graves usually share a dominant orientation, which is normally broadly between south-east–north-west and east–west (with the head to the east/south-east) (Jeunesse 1996; 1997). It is also quite common for opposed grave orientations to occur, and although these can in some instances be confined to particular parts of cemeteries, they often appear intermingled with the more recurrent form. In some examples, graves seem to be arranged roughly in rows or lines, as at Nitra, while in others the existence of more or less distinct clusters has been discerned, as at Vedrovice (Podborský 2002b) and Aiterhofen (Nieszery 1995); Nitra in fact could be taken to show both kinds of pattern. Probable pairing of graves has also been noted at Elsloo and Niedermerz (van de Velde 1997), and could be visible elsewhere too.

Men, women and children were buried in LBK cemeteries. Men and women probably occur in more or less equal frequencies (Chapter 2.7.1), but generally with lower numbers of children. Given the expected rates of infant mortality, this suggests that children are largely under-represented in cemeteries. The recurrent rite for men, women and children alike was crouched or flexed burial, the body placed on its left side with the head to the east (and variants), facing south (and variants). There are plenty of variations in degree of flexedness, and extended burials occur (in both supine and prone positions), also with some degree of variation in flex of the legs and position of the arms; the example of Quatzenheim, probably quite late in its regional sequence, stands out for the near-total preference for the supine body position (Jeunesse 2005), which otherwise had been more common in Mesolithic contexts (discussed further throughout Chapter 8). Right-side burials also occur in the same cemeteries as left-side ones, and heads to the west – and in other positions, depending on grave orientation – are also found. Once again, it is worth noting that these alternative choices are not generally confined to particular parts of any given cemetery.

In a not insignificant number of cases, LBK people were simply laid to rest, on their own, in their graves. A very few graves have signs of internal structures or covering (but see Chapter 8.5), and some have undercut side niches (Thévenet 2004; 2009). There are finds in some upper grave fills, which can suggest a more extended process of mourning and commemoration (Whittle 1988; D. Hofmann forthcoming). In many cases, however, LBK people were buried with things, and these, in association with patterning by age and sex, have been a principal focus of LBK mortuary studies. It is worth noting that the frequency of associated things varies considerably, from the peak of 95% of the burials with grave goods at Mulhouse-Est (Chapter 8.7), to as few as *c.* 50% at Schwetzingen (Jeunesse 1997; Gerling 2009), but the average is nearer 70% (Lifeways Database). At some small cemeteries such as Entzheim, all graves were furnished, but factors of preservation are at play here (Jeunesse 1997), something that may also be an issue at cemeteries with lower frequencies of grave goods. These variations in grave good frequency are further complicated by how grave goods are classified and whether graves that only had objects within the fill of the grave are included (we will return to this in Chapter 2.7). That alone is sufficient to warn us against notions of a single typical or normative rite.

The list of things and substances which accompanied the dead is long. It includes adzes, axes, perforated maceheads (*masses perforées*), arrowheads, blades, other flint, rubbers and other stone equipment, ochre in the form of powder and nodules, whole pots and sherds, plain and decorated, *Spondylus* (from the Adriatic or Aegean) beads, armrings, pendants, perforated shell halves (occasionally referred to as medallions) and two types of buckles (including a version with a V-notch), small terrestrial, river and marine shells other than *Spondylus* (from the Mediterranean and Atlantic), very occasional perforated deer's teeth, and some animal bones presumably originally in the form of joints of meat (Jeunesse 1997) amongst others. No one grave has all these things, and the regional chapters give many specific examples of the kind of complex assemblages that do accompany the deceased in the ground.

There has been a tendency, in the search for variability and relative 'richness', to list the overall numbers of items; a more cautious approach of grouping things in categories was adopted by Modderman (1988). A general tendency is for adults to have more things than children, with some important exceptions, and in some instances at least, for men to have more things than women (Jeunesse 1995a; 1995b; 1996; 1997). It was men who were generally accompanied by adzes and arrowheads, and they were often adorned by beads, armrings and buckles, whereas women were often provided with pottery and other ornaments. Analysis at Elsloo suggested that arrowheads and adzes were predominantly associated with men, and lumps of ochre and rubbing stones with women,[9] but that plain and decorated pottery, blades and axes were found more or less equally with both (van de Velde 1997, table 1).

Exceptions and variations abound, which the regional chapters and analyses will highlight. No adzes and very few arrowheads, for example, were placed in graves in the Paris basin (Jeunesse 2009, 161). Nearly all analysis, however, has been at the level of the cemetery as a whole, thus compressing a gamut of individual biographies and contingent circumstances, potentially over both shorter and longer timescales, into one consolidated history. Little further micro-analysis of the kind suggested by Chapman (2000) for Copper Age Tiszapolgár-Basatanya has yet been attempted. Further analysis of just one cemetery, Aiterhofen, has suggested changes through the lifecourse of what it was appropriate to be given (D. Hofmann 2009a; forthcoming; Chapter 6), so that it is not just a matter of broad regional and chronological variability. The recent investigations at Vedrovice have also opened a more personalised approach to the life histories and mortuary treatment of specific individuals, though for a quite small sample of the cemetery population (Zvelebil and Pettitt 2008; Zvelebil *et al.* 2010). The Lifeways project has aimed to investigate such variability further, with a combination of isotopic, osteological and artefactual analyses.

Broader regional and chronological patterning has been emphasised many times, and progressively refined as the dataset has increased. Jeunesse in particular (1995a; 1995b; 1996; 1997; 2003a; 2009) has claimed two major regional patterns. Tradition I covers the Paris basin and Haute-Alsace. In this area, graves and bodies were mainly oriented to the east, crouched on their left sides; they were frequently covered with powdered ochre. Ornament was plentiful, in the form of shells, and especially *Spondylus*, while pots and lithics were relatively less common. Cited examples include Ensisheim, Mulhouse-Est (both analysed in the Lifeways project; Chapter 8) and Essenbach-Ammerbreite. Tradition II covers Basse-Alsace and the rest of the Rhineland, and central and southern Germany, including Bavaria. Left-crouched burials are again common, but with more oriented to the west. Bodies are less frequently ochre-powdered, and more often accompanied by fragments or lumps of ochre. Grave goods are dominated by lithics, including adzes, arrowheads and grinding equipment; ornament is less common. Cited examples include Schwetzingen, Souffelweyersheim (both investigated in the Lifeways project; Chapters 7 and 8), Sondershausen, Elsloo and Niedermerz.

How Austria, Moravia and western Slovakia fit into such a scheme has been less clear; a recent suggestion is of three broad LBK provinces, of the Great Plain and Transdanubia, central Europe, and the Paris basin (Jeunesse 2009). This is another axis of variation which was open to testing in the Lifeways project. It alerts us further to considerable diversity in mortuary practice, and also to the potential contributions from indigenous practice and possible axes of initial LBK colonisation (see also Jeunesse 1995a; 1995b; 2002a). How far it represents variability in detail, both within individual sites and between sites and regions, is perhaps another matter (D. Hofmann forthcoming). To take just one example, Essenbach-Ammerbreite was originally included in Tradition I (Jeunesse 1996), but following the full publication of Aiterhofen (Nieszery 1995) Bavaria was subsequently placed in Tradition II (Jeunesse 1997).

Jeunesse has also strongly argued for dynamic process, and against taking the picture given by Nitra, characterised as showing weak differentiation seen in the more abundant provision of goods in male graves, especially those of older men, as typical of the LBK as a whole. He has suggested more differentiation elsewhere by late stages of the LBK, with more variation in body position and the provision of weapons (*masses perforées* being taken as specialised warrior equipment), more groups within certain cemeteries with richer inventories of grave goods (often but not exclusively more marked in the case of men), and the appearance of 'rich' child burials (cutting across both Traditions I and II) (Jeunesse 1995a; 1995b; 1996; 1997; 2005; 2009). Rich child burials had higher than normal counts of grave goods, a situation argued to relate to ascribed or inherited social position. In his more restricted analyses, based only on Flomborn, Elsloo, Niedermerz, Nitra and Mulhouse-Est, Modderman (1988, 121) had also already pointed to 'social differentiation... in the final phases' of the LBK, but he cautioned, given the general spatial intermingling of 'richer' and 'poorer' graves, against exaggerating this trend. It is also a moot point whether it is quite so straightforward to read 'weak' differentiation into the situation at Nitra, as opposed to a different kind of emphasis, and the argument overall appears to rely heavily on the contrast with the one earlier case of Flomborn. Nonetheless, within the chronological framework currently available, here is another important dimension of variability to investigate, which will recur in discussion about social relations (Chapter 1.3.7) and the end of the LBK (Chapters 1.4 and 10.4).

1.3.6 Material culture patterning and regional networks

The perception of uniformity in the LBK has long implied that this was a connected world, and patterns of material culture have regularly been summoned as witnesses in support of this view. Research on material culture has tended to fall into two domains: that of pottery, with its concomitant importance for the establishment of relative chronology, and that of other things, covering a broad range of lithics, including stone adzes, *Spondylus*, and other shells. Many of the more refined and informative inferences have been derived from the study of pottery distributions through time, while other objects have served to provide a more general picture of a busily joined-up world, but without the same degree of observable trends through time.

An older view of ceramic distribution patterning is nicely captured in the synthesis of Tringham (1971), concerned with eastern and central Europe. Drawing on Quitta (1960) among others, she asserts (1971, 125) that 'in the period of initial expansion...there was a marked uniformity of pottery fabric, forms and decoration throughout the whole area', whereas 'in the middle and later periods of the Linear Pottery cultures, regional variation became apparent, in particular in the patterns of incised decoration'. Among other regional studies further west, that of Meier-Arendt (1966) on the Untermaingebiet was notably important, not least for its chronology, and its spatially tighter late LBK pottery groups were particularly striking. That kind of characterisation was followed by Modderman (1988, 69), who noted 'increasingly prominent' regional differences in the late LBK, based on the 'more compactly decorated' pottery. The same perception has lasted until recently. In his brief overview of ceramic development at a continental scale, Gheorghiu (2008, 168) refers to the LBK as a 'continental Second Temperate Neolithic Techno-complex', resulting 'from a second synthesis between agriculturalists and hunter-gatherers which spread mainly along the Danube hydrographic structure'. He goes on to assert (2008, 180) a very broad distribution for the 'music note' motif in the classical phase (with regional labels including Ačkovy in Bohemia, Zofipole in southern Poland and Flomborn in Germany), whereas Tringham (1971, 126) had observed that music-note decoration was never very popular west of Bohemia and in the Rhineland, and ends by repeating the claim (2008, 180) for a late phase 'characterised by more baroque decoration and regional variability'. Our regional chapters will provide further detail.

What this kind of patterning might mean came to be more explicitly modelled from the 1980s onwards. The general assumption seems to have been that ceramic style, especially decorative motifs and schemes, was consciously recognised. Thus in the earliest phase, and perhaps subsequently still in the developed or classical phase, material culture uniformity was part of a risk-reducing strategy which served to connect people living in relatively isolated settlement clusters (Bogucki 1988; 1995). Later on, as the landscape became more crowded and competitive, ceramic style became the conscious emblem of smaller, self-defining regional groups. A recent example is the addition to the late repertoire of the middle Rhineland of a Palatinate group, based on new research at Herxheim (Jeunesse *et al.* 2009).

There are a number of difficulties with this view of overall trends. At whatever scale proposed, internally coherent social groupings are somehow assumed. It is not clear that late LBK ceramic groups became smaller and tighter everywhere, though there is no denying the late Rhineland situation, and the quite broad distributions of the Šárka and Želiezovce styles (Chapter 4) appear to contradict that general claim. As more detailed research has been undertaken (cf. Lenneis 2005), significant regional patterning within the overall distribution of earliest pottery has in fact also been documented (Strien 2009; Kerig 2010), one suggestion being that this served to integrate incoming and indigenous people (Strien 2009, 216), and it would be interesting now to see further regional analysis of developed or classical styles (Jeunesse 1995a, fig. 2).

What can be reported is an increased interest in more individualised analysis of pottery. Lukes and Zvelebil (Lukes 2004; Lukes and Zvelebil 2008) asserted the distinction between public and private domains of meaning in the use of ceramic decoration, which seems rather mechanical, but forces us to think about whether everything has the same kind of significance. More analysis has been done of the large ceramic assemblages produced by major excavations, such that particular motifs can be tracked among the longhouses and longhouse clusters of the Aldenhovener Platte, for example (Krahn 2003; Krahn-Schigiol 2005), or within the longhouse settlements at Geleen-Janskamperveld (Louwe Kooijmans *et al.* 2003) and Vaihingen (Strien 2005; Bogaard *et al.* 2011; Bogaard 2011). In the former case, the dominant theme followed has been that of the transmission of potting knowledge, hypothetically from mother to daughter, in a virilocal residence system; in the last two cases, the emphasis has been on the identification of internal groupings: two putative 'moieties' at Geleen, and several 'clans' or 'lineages' at Vaihingen. That kind of detailed knowledge has served to break down, or perhaps better to enable connections to be found within, what had previously been treated as uniform regional groupings. Thus, the sharing of very specific links has been proposed, for example between 'clan D' (with its own locus within the settlement) at Vaihingen and sites in Alsace (Strien 2010a, 503), and a little more generally, between middle Rhineland sites and the Paris basin (Strien 2003, figs 2–4).

The general picture has been one of connection, though in many past studies without a sense of marked change through time. The idea of networks, in various guises, has come into increasingly common use (e.g. Bogucki 1988, 120; Zimmermann 1995; Krahn-Schigiol 2005; Claßen 2009; Ramminger 2009; Gronenborn 2010b). It has not been hard to demonstrate the linkages which are seemingly apparent everywhere. Thus, radiolarite from near Lake Balaton is found widely through much of the earliest LBK distribution (Mateiciucová 2008a), and sites in Bohemia, including Bylany in a developed LBK phase had Baltic erratic flint from the north-east, perhaps from the upper Oder at a distance of 180–200 km, Jurassic flint from southern Poland, some 300 km distant, quartzites from western Bohemia, up to 150 km away, and banded chert (*Hornstein*) from Bavaria, over 300 km distant (Lech 1990, fig. 4). A major source for the near-ubiquitous stone adzes made of amphibolite has now been located in the Bohemian Jizera hills (Prostředník *et al.* 2005; Ramminger 2009; and see below). As already noted, objects of *Spondylus* shell occur widely (Jeunesse 2003a, fig. 6; 2009, fig. 13), coming ultimately from the Aegean, or closer at hand, the Adriatic (E. Willms 1985; Müller *et al.* 1996; Zvelebil and Pettitt 2008). Other shells used for decoration in the Paris basin and upper Alsace included marine species imported from the (presumably west) Mediterranean or Atlantic coasts (Jeunesse 2002c). Thus the five- to six-year-old child in grave 14 at Ensisheim was wearing a necklace composed of *Spondylus* disc and cylinder beads, two perforated cowries and a perforated deer tooth (Jeunesse 2002c, fig. 3), and the many things with the man in grave 7 at Quatzenheim included shells of the Atlantic coast gastropod *Nucella lapillus* (Jeunesse 2005, 21). Gronenborn (2010b) has emphasised that the range of such connections should cause no surprise, given examples from eighteenth-century North America for individuals on the move, one literally criss-crossing the continent. And this supports the theoretical attention recently given to the significance of feet: an embodied engagement with the world through walking (Ingold 2011)!

Further analysis suggests various kinds of pattern within this web of things on the move, though these remain fully to be integrated with ceramic distributions and trends. Movement of lithics in early situations may be connected to previous indigenous networks or to relations with indigenous communities, as again in the distribution of radiolarite (Mateiciucová 2008a), or of flint from Rijckholt (Kerig 2010); it has also been suggested that the acquisition of Atlantic shells can be related back to Mesolithic traditions of ornament (Jeunesse 2002c; 2009; Lenneis 2007). Gronenborn (2010b) has listed various examples of things which appear to have come into the LBK world from the Baltic. Many discussions imply that movement of things was by hand-to-hand or down-the-line exchanges, but Gronenborn again reminds us of the ethnographic reality of direct long-range procurement, by individuals or small groups. Three further studies help to begin to analyse these situations more closely.

As part of a wider study of LBK lithic procurement in the Rhineland and surrounds, centred especially on Nordrhein-Westfalen, Hessen and Rheinland-Pfalz, Zimmermann (1995) analysed the treatment and processing of flint at sites on the Aldenhovener Platte which had been obtained from the Rijckholt source some 30 km to the west. Larger and longer-lasting sites such as Langweiler 8 were argued to be central places (Chapter 1.3.2), and the suggested model is of direct procurement from the sources by people from central-place settlements. On the Aldenhovener Platte, cores were then exchanged hand-to-hand, and blades and tools over greater distances. The wider study notes also the use of Baltic flint, Tertiary quartzite and *Kieselschiefer* (Zimmermann 1995, figs 37–40), the varying percentages perhaps reflecting as much social connections as purely logistical or other economic considerations.

The theme of varying preference is also seen in Ramminger's important study (2007; 2009) of stone adzes in north and central Hessen. Amphibolites dominate over local basalt, sedimentary rocks and lydite as the raw material preferred for adzes. In central Hessen, different amphibolites were in use, while in north Hessen (and indeed elsewhere, including at Vaihingen) only one kind of amphibolite was used. The dominant amphibolite was an actinolite-hornblende-schist, and while there are various sources of amphibolite across central Europe (Ramminger 2009, fig. 8), only the Fichtel mountains in northern Bavaria, close to the German-Czech border, and the Jizera hills of northern Bohemia match the actinolite-hornblende-schist type. An extensive area of quarrying has been identified at Jistebsko in the Jizera hills (Prostředník *et al.* 2005), with an estimated possible annual output of as many as 2000–4000 adze blades. In Hessen, imported actinolite-hornblende-schist dominates earliest and Flomborn assemblages (most of the objects are surface finds), while basalt and other local materials take over in the late LBK. On the basis of estimates of average numbers of adze per house, drawing on a wide number of settlements beyond Hessen (Ramminger 2009, fig. 12), it is suggested that demand could not have been met in the late LBK by the Jistebsko source alone (Ramminger 2009, 91). Ramminger notes (2009, 80) the variety of possible factors behind the marked preference for Jistebsko amphibolite, including distance, the production process, functional handling, aesthetics and the social connections and obligations incurred in procurement. One or two settlements, including Bylany, have very high numbers of adzes (Ramminger 2009, fig. 12; Pavlů and Rulf 1991), but the possibility of a role in adze distribution for 'central places' in Hessen is not considered. Adzes in graves were of course noted above (Chapter 1.3.5) and will be encountered frequently in the regional chapters. Beyond the Lifeways study area, adzes are not found in graves in the Paris basin (the *Rubané récent* there being late in the overall LBK sequence, and perhaps another indication of difference by this date).

Objects of *Spondylus* occur widely through the LBK distribution in central and western Europe, but closer analysis shows regional differences. The V-*Spondylus* buckle appears virtually absent from graves in the Paris basin (Jeunesse 2009, fig. 13). From west to east, deliberately broken such buckles are typical finds in the Marne and upper Alsace, while intact examples are characteristic of a broad swathe of central Europe; further east still, centrally perforated *Spondylus* shell halves dominate finds from western Slovakia (including a stray find at Nitra; Pavúk 1972a, 47) on to the Hungarian Plain (Jeunesse 2009, fig. 13). *Spondylus* armrings are less frequent than V-buckles in LBK graves, but are widely distributed along the upper Danube corridor, across central Germany and the Paris basin, though they are most frequent in lower Bavaria (Lifeways Database).

Finally, although broad patterns of varying associations of things in burials have been identified in the two claimed major traditions (Jeunesse 1995a; 1995b; 1996; 1997; Chapter 1.3.5), it appears altogether rarer for pottery and other material to be considered together. The contingent and performative nature of mortuary rites has been emphasised (D. Hofmann 2009), and details of grave assemblages given in the regional chapters will help further to support this view in many ways. One other study shows the value of combined analysis. In his investigation of the settlement cluster of the Filder in the Neckar valley, some 25 km in maximum extent, Strien (2000) observed a contrast between the general uniformity of pottery and the four or five lithic sources in use, and to some extent variations in lithic treatment; the latter suggested four or five more or less spatially separate and smaller groupings within the settlement cluster. This was explained as possibly indicating a virilocal residence system, on the basis of flint working as a male activity and potting as a female occupation (Strien 2000, 33; Eisenhauer 2003a; 2003b). Ideally, we would have a whole series of studies, combining evidence from both settlements and burials, region by region and phase by phase, and integrating information on pottery style, flint and other lithics, stone adzes, shells, and so on. The regional chapters here will make a partial contribution in this direction, but more variation can be expected with further detailed analysis. On that note, Ingold (2011, Part II) has argued for the concept of 'meshwork' in preference to the more conventional notion of network: a rhizome-like web of lines, 'a tangle of threads and pathways' (Ingold 2011, 63) necessitating movement, rather than connections between a static series of points. We will use the term at intervals throughout this volume, both as a shorthand for all manner of issues to do with scales of social interaction and to emphasise dynamic process and performance.

1.3.7 Social relations

Questions of social relations run uneasily through LBK studies, with both divergent approaches, at varied scales, and diverse models. This section provides a first look at some of the models, and we will come back to the whole issue in detail in Chapter 10. Many approaches rely on the evidence of either settlement or mortuary rites (including the treatment of things in graves); fewer combine these. It has been noted recently (D. Hofmann 2010, 34) that separate scales of analysis – from, for example, culture to household and individual via region, microregion and community – have tended to be held apart, and that coverage of these proposed scales has been uneven. The challenge of social relations has regularly been combined with the search for patterns and rules of transmission and descent, though to what extent there needs to be the kind of close relationship often envisaged could perhaps be seen as a more open question. There has also been a strong tendency to propose models that would cover the whole of the LBK, though there is plenty of evidence, some already reviewed above, for variation through time, from region to region and within given regions. There is much to question, and one goal of the Lifeways project has been to contribute to this ongoing enquiry.

One scale often invoked, seemingly unthinkingly, especially in discussions of beginnings, endings and transitions, is that of the culture as a whole (D. Hofmann 2010, 34). At the start, the culture can often be presented as an undifferentiated block of farmers, in relation to or in opposition to hunter-gatherers, or at the end of things, as a corporate though now fractured set of farmers facing a common set of social, economic and perhaps climatic tensions and difficulties. A more conscious treatment, already noted above, proposed the active operation of strongly normative *doxa* which served radically to dampen the capacity for individual agency (Sommer 2001), though it is not explained just how such a mechanism worked beyond a general appeal to the impact on a culture of its practitioners 'being newcomers in a potentially hostile and strange environment' (Sommer 2001, 257); elsewhere it has been proposed that social control was exercised by elders, especially in the earliest LBK (Frirdich 1994). Closer analysis using the concept of networks of interaction rather than culture as such, and applied at a microregional scale, has also led to the suggestion of social cohesiveness, but now in a dynamic process of change (Claßen 2009). In the lower Rhine basin, covering both the Aldenhovener Platte and the Titzer Platte to its north-east, network analysis of pottery motifs and the exchange of flint suggests an early phase of close relations and high cohesiveness, a middle phase with the emergence of distinguishable subgroups, but with strong relations between them, and a late phase in which the importance of older settlements faded and there was more separation between individual sites in settlement subgroups (Claßen 2009, 104–6, fig. 3). That this was not necessarily the same everywhere is shown by the probable existence from early in the regional sequence of a hierarchy of settlement in the Horner Becken in Lower Austria (see Chapter 5). Here, the site of Breiteneich is proposed as a central place, with secondary or lesser settlements at Mold and Mörtersdorf, a single farmstead (*Einzelhof*) at Strögen, and a specialised, task-specific site at Rosenburg (Lenneis *et al.* 2010).

At the other end of the scale, it is not the case that individuals have been neglected, because, as discussed already above, individual burials and their associated things have been closely examined (Chapter 1.3.5). Modelling of households has not only estimated possible numbers of inhabitants (Chapter 1.3.4), but recently the possible lifecourses of household members. Thus Strien (2010b), within a maximum duration of 25 years per longhouse, envisages the heir to a household (*Hof*) marrying a first wife at the age of 18, and taking over the household, subsequently acquiring further wives; sisters marry at 15 or 16 and depart for other households. But these have tended to be rather shadowy figures, and the two lines of analysis have not yet fully come together. Dead people in graves are ciphers, to which numbers of grave goods are attached, and the parents and grandparents, household heads, brothers, sisters and wives of household modelling are not yet distinguished in such mortuary analysis. On another tack, some rather general suggestions have been made about the possible kinds of individual, or personhood, that might be found in the LBK, drawing on anthropological debate about relational identity (Whittle 2003; Jones 2005; 2007). As noted above, a more specific analysis at Aiterhofen, indicating changing patterns of grave goods with increasing age for both men and women, has suggested identities that could change through the lifecourse (D. Hofmann 2009).

Much discussion has centred, on the one hand, on households within their immediate settlement context, and on the other, on cemeteries taken as a whole. Probably the kind of view the most favoured, built often from settlement analysis and not seen to be contradicted by cemetery analysis, has been that of some sort of more or less undifferentiated, egalitarian or acephalous society, with the autonomous household as the basic building block and the bastion of essential cellular independence. As noted, models for numbers of household members vary (Lüning and Stehli 1989; Rück 2009, 181; Strien 2010b; Schiesberg 2010) but many estimates do not allow an average of more than ten people. Very large houses can be assigned a special role such as cult or meeting houses (e.g. Soudský 1969), so that variation in house size is not otherwise, in this view, highly significant from the point of view of social differentiation. This kind of modelling is rarely informed by explicit reference to analogies for household variation (see Souvatzi 2008), and much of it has been framed with reference to the *Hofplatz* model. The implications of the alternative row model (Rück 2007; 2009) have hardly yet been aired.

It is worth noting in a little detail the model proposed by Bogucki (1988, 117–28), on the assumptions that land and labour would have been key factors in a context of risk and uncertainty. He followed Lüning (1982) in seeing the household as an autonomous, discrete economic unit, constrained little by availability of land but much by potential scarcity of labour; household production likewise constrained the size of herds. The risks of failure in what Bogucki saw as an uncertain environment necessitated a 'support network' or non-hierarchical social web beyond immediate microregions or settlement clusters, thus linking neighbourhood communities by exogamy and kinship bonds to much further afield; the house is seen as a 'node in an interlocking network of kinship and social ties both within the microregion and beyond' (Bogucki 1988, 121). Envisaging the widest possible definition of kin, bilateral kinship relations radiating out from each household are proposed, rather than any rigidly defined unilineal descent system. While the possibility of some difference at community level is left open, the necessity for reciprocity was seen as likely to dampen any such divergence; items such as *Spondylus* circulated as 'scarce necessities' (Bogucki 1988, 126) or perhaps bridewealth rather than as prestige items. Several of the assumptions about risk, uncertainty and the setting could be challenged, as well as the view of economic drivers, and there have of course been variations. Milisauskas (1976) explored the possibility of variation between households based on his excavations at Olszanica in southern Poland, though he too also proposed a more open system of bilateral kinship, with descent through both male and female lines (1986, 218). The case for central places has also already been noted. The Bogucki model nonetheless usefully stands for one significant strand of interpretation.

Analysis by van de Velde (1979a; 1979b; 1990; 1997) has been an important element of the other significant strand, which proposes much more social differentiation. This has been based partly on settlements and partly on cemeteries. Van de Velde's own work focused just on Elsloo (with some consideration of Hienheim in Bavaria, which van de Velde (1979a, 169) was at pains to stress was not identical to Elsloo) and Niedermerz, and more recently on Geleen-Janskamperveld (Louwe Kooijmans *et al.* 2003; van de Velde 2008); while restricted geographically, this has been an unusually integrated approach. The analysis of households, yards and wards, noted above (Chapter 1.3.4), suggested significant ranking within communities, as well as internal divisions such as the moieties proposed for Geleen-Janskamperveld; large type 1b houses at Elsloo were seen to have the largest central parts, the most adzes and decorated pottery, and the most evidence for cereal processing. Prominent figures were modelled along the lines of 'big men' or even chiefs (van de Velde 1990, 38).

Difference within a single settlement has also already been noted (Chapter 1.3.3–4) at Vaihingen (Bogaard *et al.* 2011) and at Cuiry-lès-Chaudardes (Hachem 1997; 1999; 2000; 2011). On a wider scale, the existence of lineages, defined by descent from a common ancestor, has been asserted as a key organising principle among earliest LBK communities, with the pursuit of prestige as their key social goal; this system was seen to collapse at the end of the earliest LBK and re-form in the Flomborn phase, later to change again into a series of informal interest groups (Frirdich 2003; 2005). This assertion seems to float above the data; the detailed analysis offered is of the Niedermerz cemetery (Frirdich 2003; 2005), which is not relevant to the character of the earliest LBK. But the idea of clans or lineages in general has been quite widely followed (e.g. Petrasch 2003, 511; Lüning 2005a; Strien 2005, 195).

Analysis of the cemeteries of Elsloo, and later Niedermerz, also suggested a differentiated view of LBK communities, but perhaps not identical to that seen in analysis of the Elsloo settlement (van de Velde 1979a; 1979b; 1997). The varied approaches and arguments are complex and this is not the place to rehearse them in detail, but we could summarise the outcome as the demonstration of variance in provision of grave goods by age and sex, with possible internal groupings or clusters. Some trends might suggest what van de Velde called, following neo-Marxist theory, a lineage mode of production but this is not stressed as the sole axis of explanation (van de Velde 1979a, 170). In his shorter account (van de Velde 1979b, 43–6), more is made of patterning by sex, which is interpreted in terms of matrilineal descent; this seems to rest in the appearance in female graves of either rectilinear or curvilinear motifs, but the presence of both in male graves.[10] For Elsloo both virilocal residence (based on settlement patterns) and matrilineal descent rules (based on cemetery analysis) are proposed.

We have already seen that Modderman (1988) to some extent followed this kind of analysis, which has also been taken further by Jeunesse (1995a; 1995b; 1996; 1997; Chapter 1.3.5). Jeunesse in particular has emphasised the possibilities for variation through both time and space. He has not, however, declared a preference for one or other system of descent rules, though there is perhaps an implied dominance for male status in his model (e.g. Jeunesse 1997, 87–91) that may favour patrilineal models. These have long been the subject of interpretation in LBK studies. The older view, which goes back directly, we believe, to nineteenth-century social evolutionary theory (Chapter 1.2), was of matriarchy and matrilineality. This is noted by van de Velde (1979b, 38), and can be found especially in earlier writing on central and eastern Europe (Milisauskas 1986, 218; Podborský 2002b; Chapter 4). The analysis of Nitra in particular provided a challenge to this older view (Pavúk 1972a), although Podborský (2002b) maintained that other general aspects of LBK existence, production and division of labour outweighed the significance of the patterns found there (Chapter 4).

It is against such a background that alternative suggestions have to be seen. That of bilateral kinship has already been noted, and could have much to recommend it (and see also Whittle 2009, 254). Because bilateral ties radiate outwards, specific connections dissipate through time after three or four generations (Foxhall 1995; Forbes 2007, 136–41), which would be consistent with the flux of house replacements observed in some, though not necessarily all, settlements.

The current favourite, however, is clearly that of viri- or patrilocality. As well as the earlier interpretations of van de Velde (1979b) and Pavúk (1972a), three kinds of argument have been proposed. First, the contrast, already noted, between uniform pottery style and localised traditions of flint procurement and working in one small settlement cell was used to suggest patrilocality (Strien 2000, 33). This has been quite widely cited, and counters earlier general suggestions of matrilocal residence being visible through transmission of potting skills from mother to daughter and resulting clusters of shared traits and style (Eisenhauer 2003b, 561; Deetz 1968; Hill 1970). A similar suggestion on the basis of pottery style was made for the Schlangengraben valley on the Aldenhovener Platte (Schigiol 2000, 340; Eisenhauer 2003b, 561).

Secondly, epigenetic or inherited traits on the teeth of some of the people in the mass grave at Talheim have been taken to suggest family groups, within which men appeared to have more traits in common than women; that in turn was seen as an indicator of patrilocality, within which kind of system women should be less inter-related than men (Eisenhauer 2003b). It is important to note that the Talheim sample is small, and perhaps the interpretation of such traits is open to other hypotheses. Eisenhauer (2003b, 570–2) also takes care to stress that post-marital residence rules do not unavoidably equate to descent rules, though patrilocality and patrilinearity do combine in a clear majority of observed ethnographic comparisons (Murdock 1949; Murdock and White 1969). She also notes (Eisenhauer 2003b, 570) the observation that matrilocal societies regularly have larger houses than patrilocal ones (Ember 1973), though offsets that by reference to the claims, already cited above, for relatively small family size in the LBK longhouse. The Iroquois longhouse from 900 to 1650 AD has generated a similar debate about residence and descent. One study envisages a gradual development from early patrilocal and patrilineal extended families in winter villages to a matrilocal and matrilineal system in steadily enlarging longhouses alongside the introduction of horticulture, in which women played a key role, while men were often away for hunting, raiding and trading (Warrick

1996). Homogeneity in ceramic styles within large villages is taken here to support matrilocality (Warrick 1996, 15–16), and 'pronounced variability' in longhouse size is seen to be the outcome of a growing population practising matrilocal residence (Warrick 1996). Longhouse decline in the 16th and 17th centuries, seen in sharp reductions in size, probably had many causes, and 'more flexible clan segments replaced matrilineages' (Warrick 1996, 20). It is important to stress that the Iroquois longhouse at its peak could have housed 75–100 people, in large villages which were in part a response to competition, raiding and warfare (Warrick 1996, 20). Other comparanda also support the combination of large structures, matrilocality and matrilinearity, but there does not appear to be any universal such correlation (Becuwe and Tinévez 2004).

Thirdly, the first strontium isotopic studies of LBK populations from south-west Germany (Price *et al.* 2001; 2003; Bentley 2007; Bentley *et al.* 2002; Knipper 2009) have themselves frequently been cited in support of lifetime mobility for women, which has often been taken to indicate patrilocal post-marital residence.

The Lifeways project created the opportunity to test such ideas on a much bigger sample and across a much wider area (as also called for by Price *et al.* 2012).

1.4 Project aims: investigating diversity

In covering the themes selected above, we do not wish to model LBK lifeways as conditioned only by factors of settlement, residence, subsistence, mortuary rites, materiality and descent. That is already a long list, but it perhaps leaves something out of account (Whittle 2009, 254–8). What values and beliefs motivated people to act in these centuries? We have noted suggestions such as cultural *doxa* perhaps driven by elders, the prestige-seeking aims of earliest LBK lineages, and the security-minded and risk-reducing strategies of the autonomous household. No one model yet seems to combine all these kinds of possibilities and further draw in central values and concepts. We should not be just listing similarities and differences, but thinking about the conditions in which people could act, through a dynamic historical process rather than in a static situation. So in what follows we want to bear in mind other dimensions not covered in detail above, including the role of ancestors (Lüning 2005b; 2009), the importance of the past in general beyond specific rules of descent (Bradley 1996; 2001), the possible convergence of the identities of the house and the individual human body (Whittle 2003; 2012; Hofmann and Whittle 2008), the significance of sharing and giving away, the non-accumulation of material things, and prowess demonstrated by participation in production and exchange (Whittle 1996). These kinds of considerations have not all been neglected in LBK research (see, for example, Behrens 1973; Modderman 1988, 122; Jeunesse 2002c, 60) but they could now become much more prominent alongside other research themes. We also note the debate about the conditions in which the LBK ended, though rather few of the samples examined in the Lifeways project date quite that late (see Asparn; Chapter 5.8), as possible disorder, disruption and even breakdown may be particularly revealing for the character of what went before. If there were serious conflicts at the end of the LBK (Petrasch 1999; Farruggia 2002; Golitko and Keeley 2006; Gronenborn 2007a; 2010a; Zeeb-Lanz 2009a), and all of the same date (which is not yet established), their absence from earlier in the sequence is also informative. Zeeb-Lanz (2009b) has made the intriguing suggestion of a crisis not so much of climate or resources but of the mind, spirit and belief. We also note those cases where not all the best land had been used in the LBK (e.g. Saile 2010), and the variety of regional sequences in the very early fifth millennium cal BC (e.g. Strien 2000; Kaufmann 2009; Pavlů and Květina 2009).

There is much to do. The Lifeways project fits into the wider LBK context sketched above, but was obviously not intended as a means to seek or provide solutions to all its research problems. It was designed to:

- use isotopic, osteological and archaeological analyses, wherever possible in combination, to investigate diversity in LBK lifeways;
- cover a significant part of the LBK distribution in central Europe, from northern Hungary westwards to Alsace, more or less along the axis of the upper Danube;
- provide a greatly increased number of human samples, principally from mortuary contexts, compared to previous pioneering studies, and sufficient corresponding animal samples, principally from settlement contexts;
- explore patterns and variations in human diet across the area described and through the LBK sequence (though few samples have been available from earliest LBK contexts), by means of carbon and nitrogen isotope analysis, as well as an initial investigation of calcium isotopes (Chapter 2.4);
- interrogate patterns and variations in human mobility at a lifetime scale across the area described and through the LBK sequence (though few samples have been available from earliest LBK contexts), by means of strontium, and in a few cases, oxygen isotope analysis;
- investigate patterns and variations in human health, diet, population composition and lifeways, by means of osteological analysis, on the one hand by fresh examination of selected assemblages and on the other by comparative reference to the wider available literature;
- and, finally, combine the results of such investigation with fresh analysis of mortuary rites, focusing especially on grave orientations, body positions and associated grave goods.

After the discussion of the methodology of the project in Chapter 2 (see also Appendices A and C), six main regions (Fig. 1.8) have been used in the Lifeways project for the collection and presentation of data:

- eastern and western Hungary (Chapter 3);
- Moravia and western Slovakia (Chapter 4);

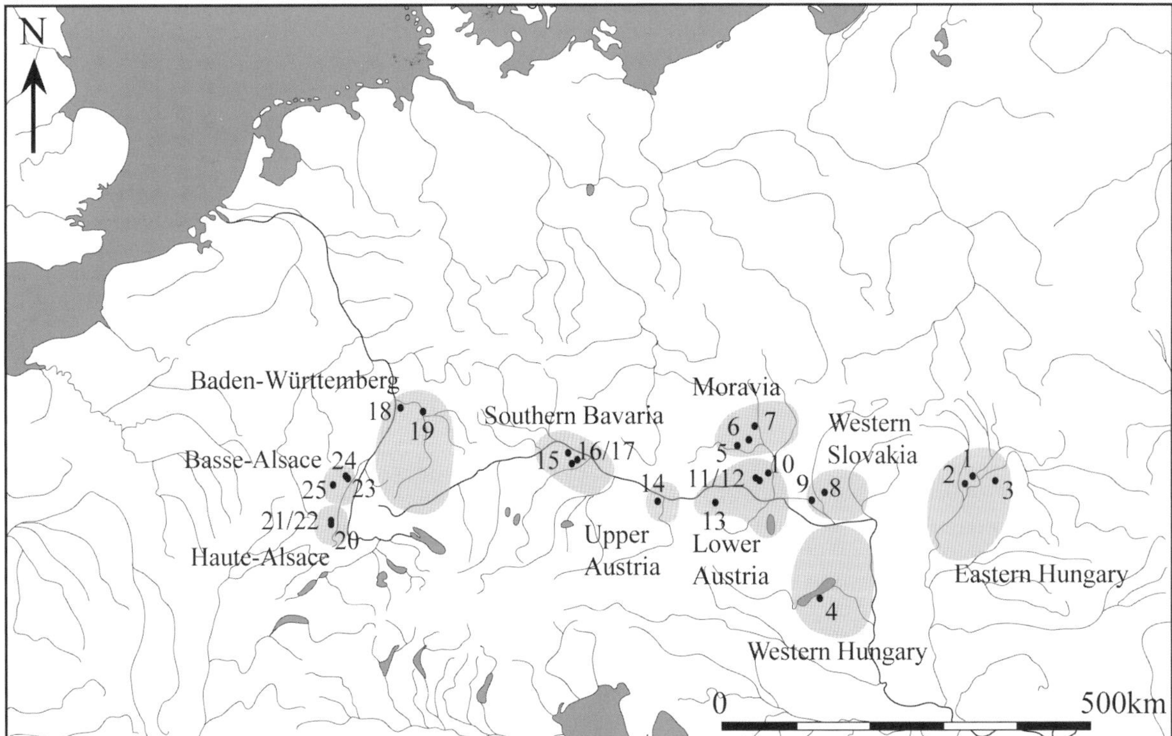

Fig. 1.8. Map of regions with sites sampled (sites are in the order that they appear in the text). 1) Mezőkövesd-Mocsolyás, 2) Füsezabony-Gubakút, 3) Polgár-Ferenci-hát, 4) Balatonszárszó-Kis-erdei-dűlő, 5) Vedrovice, 6) Těšetice-Kyjovice, 7) Brno-Starý Lískovec, 8) Nitra 'Horné Krškany', 9) Blatné, 10) Kleinhadersdorf, 11) Gnadendorf, 12) Asparn an der Zaya/Schletz, 13) Mitterndorf, 14) Rutzing/Haid, 15) Aiterhofen, 16) Otzing, 17) Lerchenhaid , 18) Schwetzingen, 19) Heilbronn-Neckargartach, 20) Mulhouse-Est (Rixheim), 21) Ensisheim les Octrois, *22) Ensisheim* Ratfeld, *23) Souffelweyersheim, 24) Vendenheim, 25) Bischoffsheim.*

- Lower and Upper Austria (Chapter 5);
- southern Bavaria (Chapter 6);
- part of Baden-Württemberg (Chapter 7);
- and Haute- and Basse-Alsace (Chapter 8).

Some new radiocarbon dates are given in Appendix B and the regional chapters are supported by the Lifeways Database (which is explained in the introductory pages). After each regional chapter, we present short accounts of the lifeways of two individuals sampled in this project.

This choice of regions was pragmatic, conditioned partly by modern political boundaries, research traditions and the practices of heritage administration. They should not, however, be taken as marking out in advance our overall perception of regional groupings within the LBK. One earlier discussion, for example, referred to the Pannonian plain, embracing western Hungary, western Slovakia, southern Moravia and north-east Austria (Tringham 1971, fig. 1). If anything, by using regions not wholly defined by the archaeology, the areas covered by the chapters often fall on either side of potential internal LBK boundaries, a fact which has proved extremely provocative and useful for discussion here (such as the north-south divide in Alsace and potential differences between Upper and Lower Austria). Each chapter provides regional research histories and the regional LBK context, before moving on to the initial presentation of analytical results. In conclusion, Chapter 9 pulls the regional data together, while Chapter 10 relates our investigations and results back to the wider framework of key LBK research problems.

Though we have discussed several issues of settlement above, most of the samples gathered for the Lifeways project come from mortuary contexts. Most of the human samples, by definition, are so derived, including our largest and statistically most significant assemblages from cemetery contexts. The major exception is the sample from northern Hungary, where graves and other human remains have so far been found in settlements, though as Chapter 3 will explore, this apparent difference may be partly a matter of definition and partly a product of the history of research so far. Animal bone samples are principally from relevant associated settlements, or the nearest accessible assemblage (Chapter 2.2.1).

The bulk of our samples belong to classical or developed and later LBK contexts, and few, mainly from northern Hungary, to the earliest phase. The regional chapters will sketch some of the major features of conventional LBK chronologies, which could be seen as more problematic than often admitted. Some new radiocarbon dates have been obtained in the course of the Lifeways project (Appendix B), but this has not in the first place been a fresh investigation of absolute chronology, desirable and urgent though that task is. The bulk of our samples probably belong, broadly, to the period between *c.* 5300 cal BC and *c.* 5000 cal BC. Given the estimates discussed above for potentially high levels of population within regions and phases of the LBK, and, following for the sake of argument the 16 house generations proposed for the Aldenhovener Platte sequence, we can reflect that the few hundred people analysed in the Lifeways project – and in related projects – still represent, despite the considerable increase in sample size, a very small proportion of those alive between 5300 and 5000 cal BC.

Though the dominant contexts available for interrogation are the grave and the cemetery, all the strands of our investigation relate also to the lives of LBK people, involving issues of diet, residence, the acquisition and use of things, and lifeways in general, so that our discussion in the regional chapters and in conclusion in Chapters 9 and 10 will not be confined solely to the mortuary sphere. We will therefore return to the wide range of themes discussed in this introduction, and we will seek to use our results not only further to establish patterns of similarity and diversity within LBK lifeways, but also to examine how the conditions of LBK existence enabled difference to flourish.

Notes

1 Further details are given by, among many others, Gronenborn 1999; Sommer 2001.

2 'The dwelt-in world is a continuous field of relationships, unfolding through time. We could think of it as an unbroken landscape of variation' (Ingold 1996b, 117).

3 This debate has broken out again in relation to notions of ontology (e.g. Alberti *et al.* 2011), and we come back to it briefly in Chapter 10.5.

4 And there is of course also the quotation from Weber used elsewhere by Geertz that people 'are suspended in webs of significance of our own construction' (cited by Rapport in Ingold 1996a, 129).

5 The designation of some haplogroups and genetic lineages as 'Palaeolithic', 'Near Eastern' and so on goes back to pioneering work by M. Richards *et al.* (1996) and Sykes (1999; cf. Renfrew 2000; Sykes and Renfrew 2000), who calculated the first appearance of various lineages in Europe based on their prevalence in *current* populations and on estimated mutation rates. As more DNA data directly from *ancient* remains is accumulating, these labels are becoming increasingly problematic. Specifically for central Europe, recent studies by Bramanti *et al.* (2009) and Haak *et al.* (2010) appear to show that several suggested 'Palaeolithic' lineages are absent from the — albeit as yet small — Mesolithic dataset (dominated by groups U and V), with their earliest actually recorded appearance now of LBK date. This means that migration at the beginning of the LBK can once again be considered as a likely scenario in some areas at least. There is also the possibility (mooted in Sykes and Renfrew 2000) that mutation rates may be less regular and predictable than previously thought, and therefore may not accurately date the branching off or diversification of haplotypes. So modern-day genetic patterning must be used very cautiously if trying to reconstruct or dismiss a specific past migration event. We must take care not to confuse the various timescales of provenance and descent which are being addressed. Genetic data are a cumulative archive of a long-term population history. At the scale of individual lives, childhood origin may be far more relevant than a migration event of many generations earlier, but the latter may still be visible genetically. Similarly, genetic data can be spatially coarse. Migration events between adjacent regions (such as Hungary and Moravia), for example, would be virtually invisible if these were settled by a genetically similar population, but the ethnic identity of the people involved could still differ. In sum, a firmer statement, either for or against migration, will only be possible when we can compare more samples of aDNA from sites dated to both the Mesolithic and Neolithic from several regions (on the importance of secure archaeological context for such samples and the importance of interdisciplinarity, see also Oliveira 2008; Bánffy *et al.* 2012). An individual's local origin should no longer be established on the basis of Sykes' (1999) suggested haplotype dates alone.

6 Conolly *et al.* (2008) class these species as part of the domestic spectrum, but Kreuz (2007, 270) argues that many of them were grown unintentionally as weeds and are more useful for demonstrating supra-regional contacts.

7 *Anthropochores* are weed species that could only have arrived in a region by direct or indirect human influences.

8 The evidence that animals were used for traction is very rare and inconsistent for LBK contexts (Bartosiewicz 2005, 57).

9 It should be noted that bone preservation was minimal at this site.

10 It should be noted that sex is attributed in this study, preservation of the human remains themselves being minimal.

2 Seeking diversity: methodology

Julie Hamilton, R. Alexander Bentley, Penny Bickle, Linda Fibiger, Robert Hedges, Linda Reynard, Carrie Wright, Philippa Cullen, Christopher Dale, Geoff Nowell and Alasdair Whittle

2.1 Introduction

The analytical techniques on offer to the archaeologist today are accelerating at an astonishing and exciting rate, providing kinds of detailed insights into past lifeways which could scarcely have been imagined just a few decades ago. Aside from radiocarbon dating, isotopic studies have been used in archaeology as far back as the mid-1960s, beginning with lead isotopes in metal and its by-products (Pollard 2011, 631). However, this form of analysis has only really become established in archaeology over the last decade and a half, reinvigorating the approach to questions of social organisation and mobility in past societies (Price *et al.* 1998; 2001; 2002; M.P. Richards *et al.* 1998; 2003a; 2003b; 2008; Schulting and Richards 2002; Budd *et al.* 2004; Bentley 2006; Bickle and Hofmann 2007; Fischer *et al.* 2007; Haak *et al.* 2008; Nehlich *et al.* 2009; Schroeder *et al.* 2009; Montgomery 2010; Tung and Knudson 2010; Müldner *et al.* 2011; Pollard 2011). Dietary isotopes and those relating to human and animal mobility provide information relating to the personal history of individuals, but these data can also be contextualised at other scales, such as at a community and population level, providing valuable insight into the extent of variation and structuring in past societies (Price *et al.* 2001; 2003; Mays *et al.* 2002; White 2004; Müldner and Richards 2007; Giblin 2009; 2011; Leach *et al.* 2009; Chenery *et al.* 2010; 2011; Montgomery 2010; Pollard 2011; Bentley *et al.* 2012; Mays and Beavan 2012).

Isotopes, however, are just part of our story here. More traditional archaeological approaches, such as osteology and burial studies, remain fundamental in producing meaningful interpretations of the isotope data. Dietary and mobility practices are embedded in the social fabric of any cultural group (Ingold 2000; Chapter 1.3). They are practised in ways meaningful to the populations under study, are relevant to how people engaged with the world around them as well as in identity formation, and are subject to change and development. With new methods, however, come novel problems which require careful attention, so that the subtleties of the different approaches are not lost as they are brought into combination with other techniques. That said, we hold that insights into past cultures are at their most powerful and rigorous when drawn from multiple sources and carried out in the spirit of collaboration between the different disciplinary streams in archaeology. This chapter outlines the methodologies used in this project and discusses the isotopes analysed (carbon, nitrogen, oxygen, calcium and strontium: Table 2.1). The results of the pilot calcium study are reported, and the osteological and archaeological approaches to the burials summarised, alongside their contribution to LBK studies to date.

2.2 Using stable isotope compositions to learn about prehistoric diets

Stable isotope measurements have been applied to the study of ancient human diet for over twenty years (e.g. Schwarcz and Schoeninger 1991; Ambrose and Katzenberg 2000). During that period measurement methods have improved greatly, especially in terms of the ease and rate of throughput of samples, and of accuracy. Such advances have been complemented by the large body of measurements that have now been accumulated. The LBK dataset, though not one of the first fields of application, is also growing. Contributions have focused on Bavarian human skeletal material (*c.* 20 individuals) as part of a longitudinal study of dietary change throughout the Neolithic (Asam *et al.* 2006; 2008). A carbon and nitrogen study on 22 individuals from the site of Herxheim has also been published (Alt *et al.* 2004; Dürrwächter *et al.* 2006). Stable isotopes also played a role in the multi-strand exploration of about 60 individuals from the Vedrovice cemetery (Smrčka *et al.* 2005; M.P. Richards *et al.* 2008a; 2008b). More results are forthcoming from regions north of the areas covered by this project, such as central Germany (including Nieder-Mörlen in Hessen; Nehlich *et al.* 2009) and Hungary (Kurt Alt, pers. comm.), and the stable isotopes from 97 individuals from three sites in Saxony-Anhalt (Derenburg-Meerenstieg II, Halberstadt Sonntagsfeld and Karsdorf) have recently been published (Oelze *et al.* 2011).

Table 2.1. The major isotopes investigated in this project and their interpretation.

Element	Expressed as	Unit	Tested on	Age at which value forms	What it tests	What variation is interpreted as demonstrating
Strontium	$^{87}Sr/^{86}Sr$	ratio	Tooth enamel (molars)	Childhood	Geology from which diet is sourced	Childhood diets were sourced from different areas/geologies in the landscape
Strontium	Sr conc.	parts per million	Tooth enamel (molars)	Childhood	Concentration of strontium in the diet	Contribution of different food types to the diet (plants = high Sr concentration, meat and milk = low Sr concentration)
Carbon	$\delta^{13}C$	‰	Bone collagen (and dentine from premolars at Schwetzingen)	Last 10–20 years of life (childhood in the case of dentine)	Source of dietary carbon	Large differences = marine vs. terrestrial resources and/or contribution of C3 and C4 plants to the diet Small differences = plants sourced from open or woodland areas (canopy effect)
Nitrogen	$\delta^{15}N$	‰	Bone collagen	Last 10–20 years of life	Source of dietary protein and proportion of protein in the diet	Differences in proportion of animal protein consumed or timing of weaning in the case of young infants
Oxygen	$\delta^{18}O$	‰	Tooth enamel (molars)	Childhood	Local drinking water	Different water sources

Our ability to relate isotopic measurements either to the diet or to the general ecosystem through understanding the processes by which isotopic ratios attain their values has also improved, but there is nevertheless a great deal more that we would wish to know; generally advances in this area happen through the interplay between theoretical (mainly physiological) ideas and appropriate sets of measurements (Hedges 2003; Sponheimer *et al.* 2003a; 2003b; Jim *et al.* 2004; 2007; Hedges and Reynard 2007; Kellner and Schoeninger 2007; Knudson and Stojanowski 2008; Froehle *et al.* 2012).

2.2.1 The principles of stable isotope analysis

Plant and animal tissue is synthesised from atoms in the local environment, which for animals originate in the food consumed. The fundamental premise of the stable isotope method, which in its simplest form is very well established, is that animal or plant tissue is composed of atoms whose isotopic composition is the same as that of the diet – except for the possibility of small offsets due to biochemical processes during metabolism. Thus a measure of the stable isotope composition of tissue, that is, the ratio of different isotopes of an element, is a direct reflection of the dietary isotopic composition. As the diet isotope composition varies, so does that of the consumer tissue.

Two sets of isotopes are of particular importance, those of carbon and of nitrogen. In each case the less common isotope is heavier by one neutron, and the isotopic composition is expressed in terms of the ratio $^{13}C/^{12}C$ and $^{15}N/^{14}N$. In absolute terms these are about 1% ($^{13}C/^{12}C$) and 0.1% ($^{15}N/^{14}N$), but are more usually expressed as the difference (in parts per thousand) from that of a convenient and internationally agreed upon standard. The official working definition is:

$$\delta = \{(Rsample - Rstandard)/Rstandard\} * 1000‰$$

where R is the measured isotopic ratio. This gives a range from −30‰ to about 0‰ for carbon relative to the PDB (carbonate) standard, and from about 0 to +20‰ for nitrogen relative to the atmospheric air standard. All values quoted here are for these standards.

Other isotopes are also of interest ($^{2}H/^{1}H$, $^{18}O/^{16}O$, $^{34}S/^{32}S$, $^{44}Ca/^{42}Ca$, $^{88}Sr/^{87}Sr$), but their application is quite specialised. The principles are similar, except that strontium isotopic variation is primarily due to geological source variation rather than physiology (Montgomery 2010; see below).

Isotopic variation in plants

The dietary 'signal' is provided by characteristic differences in isotopic composition in a given environment. These may take a number of different forms, and in any case depend on the particular ecology. For carbon ($^{13}C/^{12}C$), the biggest effect by far is due to isotopic discrimination during photosynthesis (O'Leary 1988), which varies from about 4‰ to about 20‰ from that of atmospheric CO_2, according to the photosynthetic physiology. In particular, 'C4' plants[1] (mainly tropical grasses such as maize, sugarcane, sorghum and, more relevantly here, millet), as well as marine systems, exhibit rather little discrimination between the different isotopes of carbon. Within 'C3' plants, typical of central and north-western Europe, there are rather subtle variations due to particular photosynthetic situations (for example, a plant's need to control its moisture loss through the organs which take in CO_2), so there is some response to the environment. Photosynthesis in freshwater aquatic systems may or may not show substantial discrimination different from C3 land plants and these have to be studied separately (O'Leary 1988; 1995; Heaton 1999; Dawson *et al.* 2002).

Nitrogen is also normally discriminated (from its atmospheric value) during plant protein synthesis, but nitrogen uptake depends strongly on the complex system of nitrogen cycling within the soil. Those plants with symbiotic nitrogen 'fixers' (legumes being the most important, especially in the diet) show less discrimination from its atmospheric value. If a wide range of ecological settings are being considered, it is generally possible to interpret plant nitrogen values (Handley and Raven 1992; Högberg 1997; Dawson *et al.* 2002). This is far less straightforward when applied to comparing archaeological landscapes, especially those with ancient cultivation (e.g. Lightfoot *et al.* 2011), and remains a topic for future research. In particular, for example, the role of manure in changing plant nitrogen has become a significant point of interest (Simpson *et al.* 1998; Bogaard *et al.* 2007b; Fraser *et al.* 2011).

Isotopic variation in animals

Animals eat plants, or plant detritus, or other animals which eat these. An important specialised case is ruminants whose digestive systems cultivate bacteria and other protozoa which are better able to digest less nutritious plant tissue (such as cellulose). Thus both carbon and nitrogen are transferred between organisms, and between metabolic pathways within an organism. Much of this transfer does not necessarily lead to significant change in isotopic composition (or 'fractionation') – but some certainly can. Modelling of what takes place does not yet give satisfactory detailed predictions of isotopic compositions, and semi-quantitative generalisations prevail. These are mainly observed as trophic level effects, and sometimes result from controlled feeding experiments. There is a large literature on this subject (DeNiro and Epstein 1978; 1981; Schoeninger *et al.* 1983; Minagawa and Wada 1984; Peterson and Fry 1987; Kelly 2000; McCutchan *et al.* 2003; Sponheimer *et al.* 2003a; 2003b; Hedges and Reynard 2007).

The best known effects are twofold: 1) the increase in consumer tissue $\delta^{15}N$ by about 3–5‰ (perhaps depending on animal physiology, protein content of diet, etc.) over that of the diet; 2) a similar but smaller increase in consumer tissue protein $\delta^{13}C$ by about 0.5 to 1.5‰ over that of the dietary protein. The fact that the increase is 'constant' also expresses the way in which consumer tissue reflects the diet composition.

A more subtle point for carbon is that most tissue measurements are made on carbon in protein, and it may be asked if protein carbon comes exclusively from dietary protein carbon, or dietary carbon more generally (e.g. including cellulose if considering domesticates such as cattle or sheep). This issue is particularly relevant to considering human diet, with its culturally and ecologically variable dietary mix of animal (high protein) and plant (usually lower protein but high carbohydrate) sources. In general, plant carbohydrate is not thought to contribute much carbon to tissue protein, but this can only be true up to a point. Research is continuing to explore this question (Ambrose and Norr 1993; Tieszen and Fagre 1993; Howland *et al.* 2003; Jim *et al.* 2004; 2007; Kellner and Schoeninger 2007; Warinner and Tuross 2009; Froehle *et al.* 2010).

The isotope values from bone collagen represent an averaging of dietary values over a period that reflects the rate of bone turnover. This rate is not precisely known, and is in any case variable within and between individuals and species. It varies over an animal's or human's lifetime, being faster in actively growing bone and declining with age (Geyh 2001; Ubelaker *et al.* 2006); it differs between bone of different types, e.g. trabecular or cortical (P. Hill 1998); and may also respond to physiological or dietary factors such as pregnancy, disease or starvation (e.g. Katzenberg and Lovell 1999). For humans, Hedges *et al.* (2007, 815) estimated that the bone turnover was 10–30% per year during the adolescent growth period, but about a tenth of this in adulthood, so that 'human femoral bone collagen isotopically reflects an individual's diet over a much longer period of time than 10 years, including a substantial portion of collagen synthesized during adolescence.' Ribs, with their high proportion of trabecular bone, are likely to remodel faster than dense femoral bone (Price *et al.* 2002), and this can be used to examine individual life histories (Sealy *et al.* 1995; see also Schroeder *et al.* 2009), although we have not done that in this project.[2] Rates of bone turnover in domestic mammals follow similar patterns, but are not very well characterised. They are likely to be faster than in humans, reflecting the more rapid growth and maturation, and in some cases smaller size, of animals (Pearce *et al.* 2007), and thus average the diet signal over shorter timespans. Where diets have changed on a timescale comparable to bone turnover time, this may affect interpretation and comparison between tissues, individuals and species, and probably contributes to the unexplained variation between individuals.

2.2.2 Measurement

Plant tissue does not survive well in the archaeological record, and even when it does, mainly as carbonised

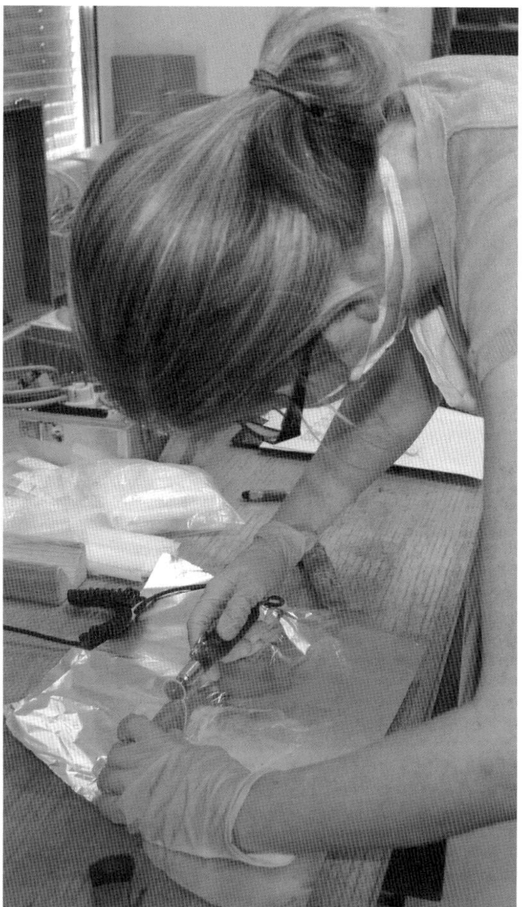

Fig. 2.1. Sampling animal bone in the Landesmuseum Linz. Photo: Linda Fibiger.

remains of crops, there are still questions about how altered the isotopic compositions have become. Plant isotopes, both carbon and nitrogen, which are such an important part of building up the isotopic picture of human palaeoecology, are now being increasingly investigated, but overwhelmingly, the main material being measured is the collagen surviving in bone or in tooth dentine (Fig. 2.1). Some work has also been done on the carbonate in bone, or – more reliably – on tooth enamel, which is believed to reflect the total dietary carbon isotopic composition (Lee-Thorp *et al.* 1989; Ambrose and Norr 1993; Koch *et al.* 1997; Balasse *et al.* 2002; Hedges 2003; Froehle *et al.* 2010; Uno *et al.* 2011). This is of some use when the dietary isotopic signal may comprise some strongly different components, although that is not the case in this project.

The survival of collagen is well studied, and depends on burial conditions (especially temperature and soil water movement). Nearly always some collagen is lost, but that which remains is usually chemically fairly unaltered, so that moderately simple procedures enable a reasonably purified form of collagen to be extracted and measured. Essentially a 50–500 mg bone sample is required (depending on preservation) which is dissolved in dilute hydrochloric acid to leave insoluble shreds of collagen. These are then dissolved in hot water and filtered. More elaborate methods can be used (e.g. selecting a certain molecular mass range). It is important to check the purity of the collagen by measuring its ratio of carbon to nitrogen, which is theoretically close to 3.17 (atomic ratio). Variation of about 5% from this ratio is acceptable. From the few milligrams of extracted collagen, an aliquot of about 2.0 mg is measured in duplicate in a continuous flow mass spectrometer. The measurement consists of an automated combustion in a flow of oxygen (to produce CO_2, NO_2, H_2O, and SO_2), followed by reduction of NO_2 to N_2, and removal of H_2O and SO_2, followed by separation of CO_2 from N_2 in a gas chromatograph. The separated gases are then transferred by flowing He sequentially to a specialised mass spectrometer, in which the ratios of ion beams from ^{13}C, ^{12}C, ^{15}N and ^{14}N are compared to each other and then with those from standards which are combusted and measured in the same way (for collagen, the amino acid alanine makes a suitable lab standard). The process is quite fast overall. About 100 bone samples can be measured in 1–2 months, depending on their preservation. The process is described in more technical detail in Jørkov *et al.* (2007, method C).

Collagen was extracted from up to 1 g of bone per sample using a modified Longin method according to a standard protocol (e.g. O'Connell and Hedges 1999). The bone was cleaned by shot-blasting, then samples were demineralised in 0.5M HCl at 4°C, rinsed with distilled water, and gelatinised in a pH 3 solution for 48 hours at 75°C. The solution was filtered, frozen and freeze-dried. Between 2.0 and 2.5 mg of dried collagen were loaded into a tin capsule for continuous flow combustion and isotopic analysis. Samples were isotopically analysed using an automated Carlo Erba carbon and nitrogen elemental analyser coupled with a continuous flow isotope ratio monitoring mass spectrometer (PDZ Europa Geo 20/20 mass spectrometer). Each sample was measured in at least duplicate and where necessary triplicate runs, using internal secondary standards (bovine liver standard, bone standard, nylon, and alanine), giving an analytical error of ±0.2‰ for both isotopes. Results are reported in unit per mil (‰) and $\delta^{13}C$ and $\delta^{15}N$ values were measured relative to the VPDB and AIR standards respectively (Mariotti 1983; Gonfiantini *et al.* 1990). Samples with C:N ratios outside the range 3.0–3.5 or with less than 1% collagen yield (weight % of whole bone) were rejected; a few accepted samples with slightly less than 1% collagen yield had an acceptable weight % of nitrogen and carbon in their collagen as well as acceptable C:N ratios (DeNiro 1985; Ambrose 1990).

Comparison between laboratories is facilitated through the use of comparable standards, and, on occasion, actual samples. We have made duplicate measurements on a set of human bones from Vedrovice (Lukes *et al.* 2008; M.P. Richards *et al.* 2008; Chapter 4.7.3). However, in fact most of the significance of the measurements here is based on internal comparisons within the Lifeways project. The statistical methodology employed in this process is detailed in Appendix C.

2.2.3 Interpretation

Ideally, palaeodietary reconstruction would consider the different classes of isotopically distinct dietary component (e.g. C4 plants, C3 plants, animals feeding from each of these, marine fish, and freshwater fish); would have available a database of isotopic compositions for each class; and would then 'model' what isotopic composition might be expected in human bone for a range of nutritionally viable combinations of the components (Phillips *et al.* 2005; Mays and Beavan 2012). We will consider these in turn, but such a reconstruction is only possible for selected human palaeoecological situations, and hardly ever applies to most archaeological questions – especially in continental Europe.

Interpretation in the context of the LBK

Referring to the list above:

a) In the context of the LBK, there are mainly C3 plants and animals. We can discount any serious consumption of marine foods, but freshwater resources may be important and could very possibly provide an additional isotopic signal, distinct from the C3 plants and animals. In general, however, we are dealing with a 'terrestrial C3 world' in which, to a first approximation, most isotopic values are rather similar, at least in $\delta^{13}C$. For $\delta^{15}N$ values, we can expect trophic differences (of 3–5‰) between animals and plants, as well as differences between plants, especially between legumes that fix atmospheric nitrogen, and other plants that do not. In any case, the different classes of isotopically distinct foods, such as they are, are subject to environmental influences (Chapter 2.2.1. and Chapter 9.2.1).

b) The only available and indubitably relevant database is the measurement set made on faunal bone from either the same site where human bones are buried, or sites believed to stand as proxies for the animals consumed by the measured humans. It is essential that a sufficient population sample of such animal bone can be measured to provide the level of information required. Animal bone tends to be isotopically at least twice as variable as human bone – needing four times as many measurements, for a given species, to achieve a comparable precision in describing a given population. Other published datasets may enable interesting comparisons, but since the isotopic distinctions within the LBK diet are rather subtle, they do not serve for direct use. Therefore this project has concentrated, as far as was feasible, on providing an adequate animal bone dataset. It is rarely possible to recover suitable plant material for isotopic analysis (but see Fraser *et al.* 2011; Lightfoot and Stevens 2012), and none has been analysed in this project.

c) Any model, defined by our data, and bearing in mind the large uncertainties in additional factors – for example, the trophic level increase in $\delta^{15}N$ in humans, or the typical value for $\delta^{15}N$ in cereals consumed by humans – is unlikely to produce an outcome that goes beyond the obvious: that of a terrestrial C3 ecosystem. However, it is worth listing the ways in which this might happen (see also Table 2.1):

1) Unexpected $\delta^{13}C$ values which signal unusually high $\delta^{13}C$ foods (e.g. C4 plants such as millet, or marine protein) or unusually low $\delta^{13}C$ foods (e.g. some possible sources of freshwater fish).

2) Unexpectedly high $\delta^{15}N$ values which would signal unusually high meat (or fish) consumption, or plant food of unusually high $\delta^{15}N$ values (for example perhaps having been treated with animal manure during its growth).

The relationship of human $\delta^{15}N$ values to that of the animal protein in human diet is both complicated and rather obscured by insufficient information (it is discussed in Bogaard *et al.* 2007b; Hedges and Reynard 2007).

Questions asked of the data

However, there are several important questions that can be addressed through comparisons within the dataset. These will be discussed in more detail in Chapter 9.2, when we consider the regional variation of stable isotope data, but to provide a context for the discussion in each of the six regional chapters these questions may be summarised as follows:

1) Are there spatial variations in faunal isotopic values over the region? If so, can they be attributed to environmental and/or to cultural (human management) causes?
2) To what extent are the human isotopic values dependent on the local faunal values, and what is the likely basis for that (e.g. whether by direct consumption, or through consumption of plants with common isotopic behaviour)?
3) How much do individual human isotopic values vary within a site, and to what extent is this connected with age at death, physiology, sex and life history?

2.3 Oxygen isotope analysis

A small number of enamel samples were also measured for the $\delta^{13}C$ and $\delta^{18}O$ values of their carbonate content. This was a pilot study to assess how informative such measurements might be in the general context of the project. Three sites were selected, separated by the Alps, in the expectation of a different meteoric signal between precipitation on the western and eastern sides. Also, the same teeth samples were measured for strontium isotopes in order to compare signals reflecting different geographical locations for food and water (Chapter 9.3).

Tooth enamel carbonate is measured by a standard protocol (Chapter 2.3.1). However, there is an important issue of sampling. Tooth enamel is formed in a spatially differentiated way as the tooth grows. The enamel composition is largely determined as it is formed, but may be subsequently modified during the enamel maturation process, which can last for a year or two (Boyde *et al.* 1988; Boyde 1989). From then on the inorganic composition is set, even including during burial. Therefore, the contribution of different spatial parts of the tooth enamel amounts to a weighting of different times of growth, albeit within a short period of the individual's lifespan (depending on the particular tooth element). For the method of sampling used here, the sample can be considered as generally comprising an average over the whole period of growth of the tooth (e.g. Montgomery 2010).

2.3.1 Methodology

The whole, or part, tooth, or fragments, were sand blasted to clean the enamel surface. Enamel powder was abraded, using a diamond bit, avoiding dentine, and sampling from the whole vertical growth as much as practicable. Typically 5 mg was collected. Where only tooth fragments were available, enamel-rich fragments were powdered in an agate mortar. The enamel powder was treated with 0.5 ml of 3% sodium hypochlorite (NaOCl) solution in 1.5 ml centrifuge tubes for 24 hours to oxidise any organic matter, then rinsed five times in deionised water in a centrifuge. It was then treated for 24 hours with 0.5 ml of 1M calcium acetate buffered with acetic acid to pH 4.9 to remove carbonate contaminants in non-carbonate lattice sites (e.g. pore filling cements), rinsed five times with distilled water and oven dried at 60°C overnight (as per Koch *et al.* 1997).

Oxygen and carbon stable isotopic results were obtained in the Oxford laboratory, using a VG Isogas Prism II mass spectrometer with an on-line VG Isocarb common acid bath preparation system. Each sample was reacted with purified phosphoric acid (H_3PO_4) at 90°C with the liberated carbon dioxide being frozen into a liquid nitrogen cooled 'cold finger' apparatus prior to admission to the mass spectrometer.

Both oxygen and carbon isotopic ratios are reported relative to the VPDB international standard. Calibration was against the in-house NOCZ Carrara Marble standard with a reproducibility of better than 0.2 per mil.

2.3.2 Interpretation

The values for $\delta^{13}C$ are listed in Chapter 9.2.6, and, as with bone carbonate $\delta^{13}C$ (but with less likelihood of diagenetic alteration), relate to the isotopic composition of the diet as a whole for the time of life relevant to the tooth formation. We have not observed a useful signal in these data.

The values for $\delta^{18}O$ are believed to relate predominantly to the local drinking water (Longinelli 1984; Luz and Kolodny 1985; Daux *et al.* 2008; Chenery *et al.* 2010). This is often close to that of the local precipitation, but, depending on how water resources are used, could come from rivers, lakes or aquifers, which can all be different (Darling 2004; Darling *et al.* 2006). The data will be discussed in more detail in Chapter 9.2.6 (rather than in the regional chapters), but each site studied has a sufficient representation to define a characteristic mean and variance. Nitra and Polgár, in western Slovakia and Hungary respectively, are indistinguishable; but they are clearly different from the western site, Schwetzingen, by an extent which accords with the expected change in precipitation $\delta^{18}O$ values (Lecolle 1985). Furthermore, Schwetzingen shows an interesting correlation between $\delta^{18}O$ and $^{87}Sr/^{86}Sr$ values (Chapters 7.5 and 9.2.6).

2.4 Calcium isotope analysis

2.4.1 Introduction and background

As part of the Lifeways project a pilot study of calcium isotopes was carried out by Carrie Wright and Linda Reynard at the Oxford laboratory. As it is not yet clear what the impact of the results are on how we understand the role of dairying in the LBK diet, the analysis and data are presented here rather than in the regional chapters.

Many of the modern human population of the world (~70%) are lactose-intolerant, like all other mammals, and do not drink milk after weaning (Tremaine *et al.* 1986). Northern Europeans and their globally scattered relations as well as a few African, southern Asian and Middle Eastern populations are the significant exception due to the presence of lactase persistence (LP) alleles, which confer the ability to produce lactase, an enzyme necessary to digest milk (Tishkoff *et al.* 2006; Itan *et al.* 2009). However, it 'is unlikely that LP would provide a selective advantage without a supply of fresh milk, and this has led to a gene-culture coevolutionary model where lactase persistence is only favoured in cultures practicing dairying, and dairying is more favoured in lactase persistent populations' (Itan *et al.* 2009, 1). The large prevalence of lactose tolerance (lactase persistence) in modern European populations, and the Neolithic domestication of animals now commonly used for dairying (Vigne and Helmer 2007), suggests that the Neolithic farmers of Europe are a good population to study for evidence of the introduction of dairy milk to the human diet.

Milk is primarily composed of calcium phosphate and water, and for lactase-persistent individuals milk and dairy foods are the easiest means of meeting critical calcium dietary requirements (Holt 1982; Guéguen and Pointillart 2000; Heaney 2009). Calcium is necessary for skeletal maturation in children post-weaning, bone maintenance in adults and reduction of osteoporotic bone loss and fracture in the elderly (Ho *et al.* 1994; Black *et al.* 2002). Additionally, bone acts as a reservoir, absorbing and releasing calcium as required and hence maintaining physiological calcium balance (Fishbein 2004). In addition there is a slow continuous remodeling or bone 'turnover' of 5% per year for cortical bone and about 10% per year for trabecular bone (Robey and Boskey 2006; Nanci and Ten Cate 2008; Heaney 2009), with calcium being part of this cycle. As a result bone can act as a record of diet for the years prior to death. The research discussed here is for a relatively new method of archaeological isotope analysis that uses the abundances or ratios of the different calcium isotopes found in the two major calcium sources in the mammal diet, plants and milk (including dairy foods for humans), to detect evidence of human dairy consumption.

Calcium has six naturally occurring stable isotopes, ^{40}Ca, ^{42}Ca, ^{43}Ca, ^{44}Ca, ^{46}Ca and ^{48}Ca (Skulan *et al.* 1997; DePaolo 2004). The main isotopes of research interest are ^{40}Ca, ^{42}Ca, ^{43}Ca and ^{44}Ca, and variations in the ratios of these isotopes are measured. Changes in isotope ratios are small and hard to detect, and are generally reported as deviations from the isotopic ratio of a standard material, as given below.

$$\delta\,^{44/42}Ca = \left(\frac{\left(\frac{^{44}Ca}{^{42}Ca}\right)_{sample} - \left(\frac{^{44}Ca}{^{42}Ca}\right)_{standard}}{\left(\frac{^{44}Ca}{^{42}Ca}\right)_{standard}} \right) \times 1000$$

In the present work we report $\delta^{44/42}Ca$ values relative to the calcium carbonate standard NIST Standard Reference Material 915a.

Modern samples of diet, milk, and bone were used to investigate changes in calcium isotope ratios (fractionation) between input (diet), reservoirs (mammal tissues, especially bone) and output (milk and urine), and suggest a potential for distinguishing different diets with calcium isotope ratios of bones (Skulan *et al.* 1997; Skulan and DePaolo 1999; Clementz *et al.* 2003; DePaolo 2004; Chu *et al.* 2006; Skulan *et al.* 2007; Hirata *et al.* 2008). Specifically, calcium isotopes undergo fractionation during mineralisation, which results in a decrease in $\delta^{44/42}Ca$ in bone relative to diet by an average of 0.64–0.65‰ (Skulan and DePaolo 1999; Chu *et al.* 2006). Milk, like bone, also shows lower $\delta^{44/42}Ca$ values compared to dietary input (Chu *et al.* 2006). In living sheep $\delta^{44/42}Ca$ values of milk are 0.54‰ and 0.6‰ lower than in the sheep's diet. Of all of the milk samples analysed, human milk has the lowest $\delta^{44/42}Ca$, with values of −0.98‰ to −1.15‰, though the diet–breast milk offset is unknown as the mothers' diet was not included in the study (Chu *et al.* 2006). It was judged therefore that calcium isotope analysis of bone had potential for dietary research through detecting isotopic differences between milk producers and milk consumers.

Milk and dairy foods, if part of the adult human diet, are a dietary source of low $\delta^{44/42}Ca$ that should be distinguishable from the other main source of calcium in the human diet, plants, which have higher $\delta^{44/42}Ca$. With milk and dairy foods having a lower $\delta^{44/42}Ca$ than plants, it is expected that human milk and dairy consumers would have a lower $\delta^{44/42}Ca$ value in their bones than non-milk and dairy consumers. It is also expected that archaeological sites from the Neolithic would be the initial period in the archaeological record where evidence of human milk and dairy food consumption would be seen.

The recently published research by Reynard *et al.* (2010; 2011) and the unpublished results discussed here used calcium isotope analysis of bone from archaeological sites to detect dairy milk consumption by ancient humans. Specifically, this work involved analysing the bone from humans and their possible milk-producing domesticates to identify a lower human $\delta^{44/42}Ca$ relative to their domesticates, which would be indicative of dairy consumption by humans. The work by Reynard *et al.* (2010; 2011) includes the European early Neolithic sites of Balatonszárszó (further details in Chapter 3.10) and Magura, as well as some Epipalaeolithic/Mesolithic and Iron Age sites. The present work was carried out on the remains from the Ensisheim sites of *les Octrois* and *Ratfeld* in southern Alsace (further details in Chapter 8.8).

2.4.2 Methodology

The laboratory methodology used in this research is based on the methods employed by Chu *et al.* (2006) and Reynard *et al.* (2010). The sample preparation involved taking a weighed powdered sample of bone (~1.5 mg) and soaking it overnight in a 2% bleach solution to remove organics. Samples were cleaned of bleach prior to dissolution in hydrochloric acid, and calcium was separated from the sample using column chromatography. A pure calcium solution is necessary for accurate mass spectrometry.

Two different column separations are needed to isolate calcium from all other elements in the sample. The first separation removes all elements other than calcium and strontium using AG50W-X12 BioRad column resin and hydrochloric acid. The second set of column chromatography separates calcium from strontium using Sr-Spec column resin and nitric acid. Chemistry and mass spectrometry were undertaken in the Department of Earth Sciences, University of Oxford. A Nu Instruments multicollector-inductively coupled plasma mass spectrometer (MC-ICPMS) was used for the measurement of calcium isotope ratios.

2.4.3 Results and conclusions

The Ensisheim mean results for cattle, sheep/goats and human males were found to have no significant difference (ANOVA, p=0.98) (Fig. 2.2; Tables 2.2–3). This was also the case when comparing the means of human males and the combined fauna of cattle and sheep/goats (t test, p=0.93). However, there was high variation between the human males, with one standard deviation of the mean being 0.13‰. A similarly high variation from the mean was seen for sheep/goats (SD=0.11‰), but this was due to one outlying data point.

These results should be interpreted in the light of the larger group of $\delta^{44/42}Ca$ and $\delta^{43/42}Ca$ archaeological human and faunal results determined by Reynard *et al.* (2010; 2011). Reynard *et al.* (2010) found that for the majority of sites they analysed, including the Epipalaeolithic site of Taforalt (Morocco), the Mesolithic/Neolithic site of Tell Abu Hureyra (Syria), the Neolithic site of Magura (Romania) and the Iron Age site of Danebury (England), in general humans had lower $\delta^{44/42}Ca$ values than the local fauna. The exception was for the LBK site of Balatonszárszó (Chapter 3.10), which like Ensisheim (Chapter 8.8), had mean human and faunal $\delta^{44/42}Ca$ results that were nearly equal to each other. As previously discussed, milk and dairy foods have lower $\delta^{44/42}Ca$ values relative to plants. If milk and dairy foods were consumed by the LBK inhabitants of Ensisheim and Balatonszárszó, we would expect an offset between dairy-consuming humans relative to the herbivorous fauna at both sites. Therefore, the data would seem to indicate that people at Ensisheim and Balatonszárszó did not consume dairy milk.

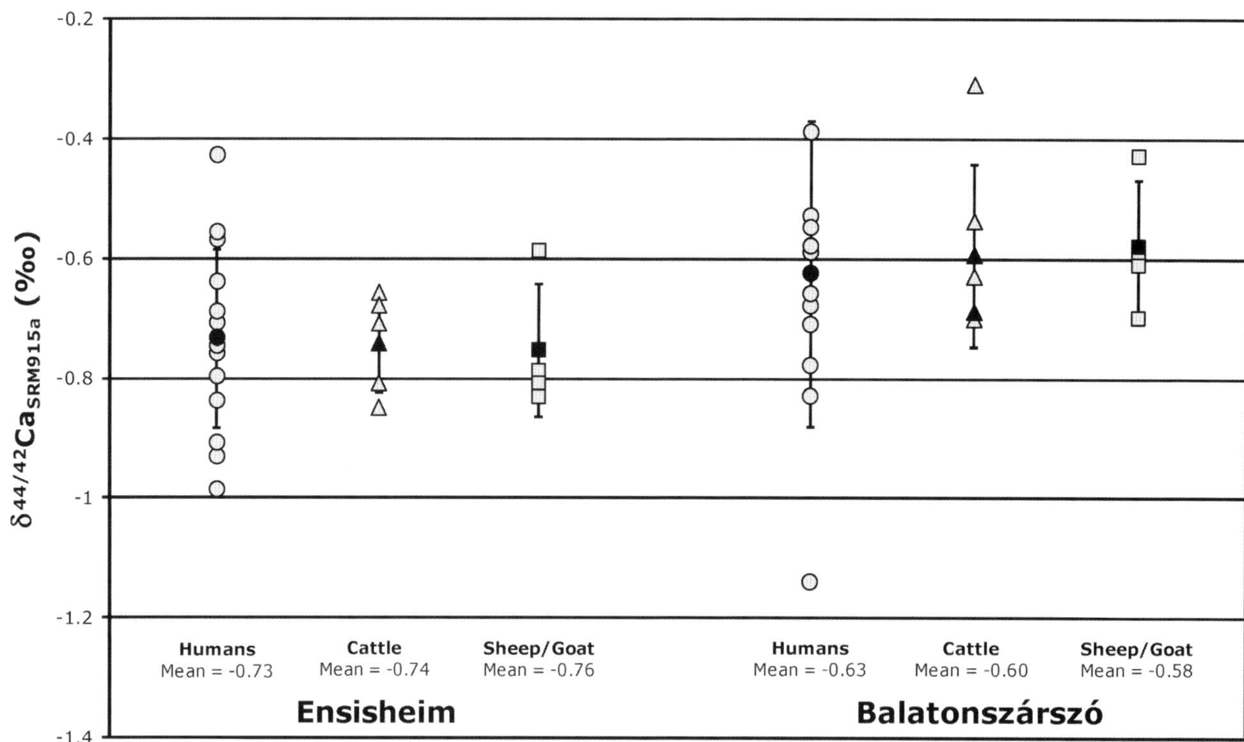

Fig. 2.2. Calcium ratios of humans, cattle and sheep/goats from Ensisheim and Balatonszárszó-Kis-erdei-dűlő.

Table 2.2. Calcium ratios of human samples, with means and standard deviations.

Human Males	$\delta^{44/42}$Ca (‰), SD	$\delta^{43/42}$Ca (‰), SD	n
LBK 303	−0.57, 0.04	−0.25, 0.06	5
LBK 308	−0.99, 0.03	−0.48, 0.07	7
LBK 310	−0.71, 0.06	−0.36, 0.08	9
LBK 311	−0.93, 0.02	−0.55, 0.05	6
LBK 313	−0.80, 0.05	−0.42, 0.05	7
LBK 317	−0.56, 0.05	−0.27, 0.08	9
LBK 318	−0.91, 0.06	−0.50, 0.03	3
LBK 320	−0.84, 0.09	-	1
LBK 330	−0.69, 0.04	−0.34, 0.07	4
LBK 331	−0.71, 0.02	−0.46, 0.00	2
LBK 332	−0.64, 0.01	−0.23, 0.06	3
LBK 333	−0.76, 0.00	−0.40, 0.04	2
LBK 335	−0.75, 0.01	−0.34, 0.07	3
LBK 336	−0.43, 0.02	−0.22, 0.09	4
LBK 338	−0.74, 0.08	−0.33, 0.06	5
	Mean (‰), SE	**Mean (‰), SE**	
	−0.73, 0.04	−0.37, 0.03	

These results cannot be accepted that simply, however, as the results from the Epipalaeolithic site of Taforalt, as well as other Mesolithic sites, showed a significantly lower $\delta^{44/42}$Ca in the human population compared to the fauna (Reynard *et al.* 2010), which fits the predicted pattern for dairy consumption by humans. As an Epipalaeolithic site, Taforalt predates the domestication of dairy animals and demonstrates that a difference in $\delta^{44/42}$Ca between humans and fauna does not necessarily indicate dairy consumption. Conversely, as in the case of Ensisheim and Balatonszárszó, a lack of calcium isotope difference cannot be straightforwardly equated to a lack of human dairy consumption.

Adding to the complexity in interpreting results is that

Table 2.3. Calcium ratios of animal samples, with means and standard deviations.

Cattle	$\delta^{44/42}$Ca (‰), SD	$\delta^{43/42}$Ca (‰), SD	n
LBK 347	-0.81, 0.05	-0.38, 0.05	8
LBK 348	-0.71, 0.05	-0.36, 0.08	8
LBK 351	-0.68, 0.06	-0.33, 0.08	3
LBK 353	-0.85, 0.09	-0.44, 0.08	3
LBK 359	-0.66, 0.09	-0.33, 0.07	3
	Mean (‰), SE	**Mean (‰), SE**	
	-0.74, 0.04	-0.37, 0.02	

Sheep/Goat	$\delta^{44/42}$Ca (‰), SD	$\delta^{43/42}$Ca (‰), SD	n
LBK 346	-0.83, 0.05	-0.41, 0.05	7
LBK 349	-0.59, 0.03	-0.33, 0.07	8
LBK 350	-0.81, 0.04	-0.39, 0.06	6
LBK 352	-0.79, 0.02	-0.41, 0.08	3
	Mean (‰), SE	**Mean (‰), SE**	
	-0.76, 0.06	-0.38, 0.02	

the humans at Ensisheim, and nearly all the humans at sites analysed by Reynard *et al.* (2010), have a greater range of values compared to the fauna. This could be due to a greater diversity of calcium sources in the human diet compared to fauna, which fits with humans being omnivores and therefore being able to acquire a wide range of foods. Individual metabolic processes could also be a factor in the wide range of human results. In the end, the human and faunal results for Ensisheim and the other sites analysed leave in doubt the usefulness of analysing calcium isotopes in bone as a means of identifying ancient human dairy consumption, at least until further fundamental investigations into calcium isotope systematics in mammals and especially humans are complete. Such work is presently under way.

2.5 Strontium isotope analysis and the local geography and geology

Primarily, strontium isotope analysis is applied to human and animal populations to determine whether an individual has moved from one geology to another over their lifetime. The methodology has been used in archaeology since the mid 1990s, originating from applications in geochemistry, where these isotopes have long been used to further understanding of geochronology (Price and Bentley 2005, 203). A substantial amount of strontium analysis has already been carried out on the LBK, with south-western Germany a particular focus (as summarised by Price and Bentley 2005; Bentley 2006; Bickle and Hofmann 2007; Knipper 2009). Results have come from the cemeteries of Flomborn (Rhineland; Price *et al.* 2001; Price and Bentley 2005; Bentley *et al.* 2002; 2003; 2004; Knipper 2009), Dillingen (Bavaria; Price *et al.* 2001; Price and Bentley 2005; Bentley *et al.* 2002; 2003; 2004; Knipper 2009), Schwetzingen (Baden-Württemberg; Price *et al.* 2001; Price and Bentley 2005; Bentley *et al.* 2002; 2003; 2004; Knipper 2009), Stuttgart-Mühlhausen (Baden-Württemberg; Price *et al.* 2003; Knipper and Price 2010) and the settlement of Vaihingen an der Enz (Baden-Württemberg; Bentley *et al.* 2003; Bentley and Knipper 2005a; 2005b; Knipper 2009), as well as the massacre site of Talheim (Baden-Württemberg; Price *et al.* 2006; Bentley *et al.* 2008) and the enclosure at Herxheim (Turck *et al.* 2012). In the eastern part of the LBK, the Vedrovice project analysed the strontium values from 22 individuals (M.P. Richards *et al.* 2008; Zvelebil *et al.* 2012). Knipper (2011) has also published a detailed study of the strontium ratios found in cattle teeth from the LBK sites in Baden-Württemberg, namely Vaihingen an der Enz, Stuttgart-Mühlhausen, Hilzingen 'Forsterbahnried'.

2.5.1 Principles behind strontium isotope analysis in archaeology

Strontium isotope analysis provides a useful geographic 'signature' from archaeological tooth enamel, indicating where a human or an animal spent its early years, when the tooth enamel mineral was forming (Figs 2.3–4). Essentially, strontium isotope ratios (^{87}Sr/^{86}Sr) are conveyed from weathering rocks, through the soil, into the food chain and ultimately into the skeleton of local organisms, without measurable fractionation (change in the ratio) during the process (Ericson 1985; Capo *et al.* 1998; Price *et al.* 2002; Bentley 2006; 2012; Montgomery 2010).

Geologically, the ^{87}Sr content of a rock is a function of how much rubidium (Rb), relative to the amount of ^{86}Sr, has been in the rock and for how long. Because of geochemical differences, the ratio of rubidium to strontium in rocks can vary by several orders of magnitude, and as a result ^{87}Sr/^{86}Sr varies from about 0.702–0.704 in typical basalts to 0.707–0.709 for most marine limestones (reflecting the composition of the ocean during their deposition) and typically above 0.710 for granites (Bentley 2006). Often, these differences in rock types roughly correspond with differences in terrain. Examples from this LBK study of central Europe include the Bavarian Forest, the Vosges Mountains and the Black Forest, each of which is underlain by granites and metamorphic rocks of extensive age, up to 500 million years old. These old granites contrast with the Jurassic and younger sandstones, evaporites and carbonates of the lowlands in their respective regions, separated by transition zones of Triassic and Jurassic sandstones, alluvial deposits, loess and marls (Knipper 2011). The highest $^{87}Sr/^{86}Sr$ ratios we recovered in this study, for example, were above 0.714, and most certainly reflect contributions from upland granites.

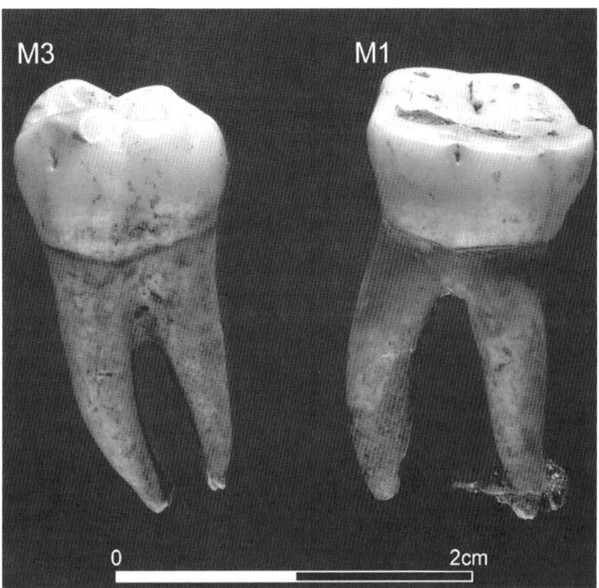

Fig. 2.3. Photo of a first and third molar from Rutzing (burial 11). Photo: John Morgan.

Because different minerals, even from the same rock, differ greatly in both their $^{87}Sr/^{86}Sr$ ratios and their Sr concentrations, their weathering will contribute unequally to the biologically available Sr. In fact, Sr isotopes in an environmental reservoir are best expressed as a mixing system of inputs and outputs, including inputs from the atmosphere and bedrock weathering, and outputs through stream- and groundwater and intermediate reservoirs that include the biosphere and soil (Bentley 2006). It has traditionally been assumed that ^{87}Sr isotopes pass from bedrock to soil into animal skeletal tissue without measurably fractionating (retaining the same ratio of $^{87}Sr/^{86}Sr$) and that any minor fractionation in any case would be corrected for through a normalisation correction routinely made in measurement to a constant $^{88}Sr/^{86}Sr$ ratio (Beard and Johnson 2000). This is an interesting frontier topic, as Knudson *et al.* (2010) have found that $^{88}Sr/^{86}Sr$ ratio actually varies slightly with trophic level, but those observed variations are less than 0.1%, and essentially confirm that fractionation of $^{87}Sr/^{86}Sr$ (which is even less, because the masses differ only by one) in skeletal tissue is negligible.

$^{87}Sr/^{86}Sr$ in environmental materials such as rocks and soils can be quite variable on even a very local scale, and hence not necessarily representative of the biologically available values (e.g. Capo *et al.* 1998; Sillen *et al.* 1998; Montgomery 2010). However, by averaging the $^{87}Sr/^{86}Sr$ differences between rocks, soils, parts of individual plants and so on, animals feeding in the same location acquire similar $^{87}Sr/^{86}Sr$ ratios in their skeletons, with a much smaller variance than in the local soils and plants (Capo *et al.* 1998; Sillen *et al.* 1998; Burton *et al.* 1999; Price *et al.* 2002; Bentley 2006; Montgomery 2010). To interpret $^{87}Sr/^{86}Sr$ ratios in geologic mixtures, mixing equations can represent the Sr concentrations of whole-rock end-

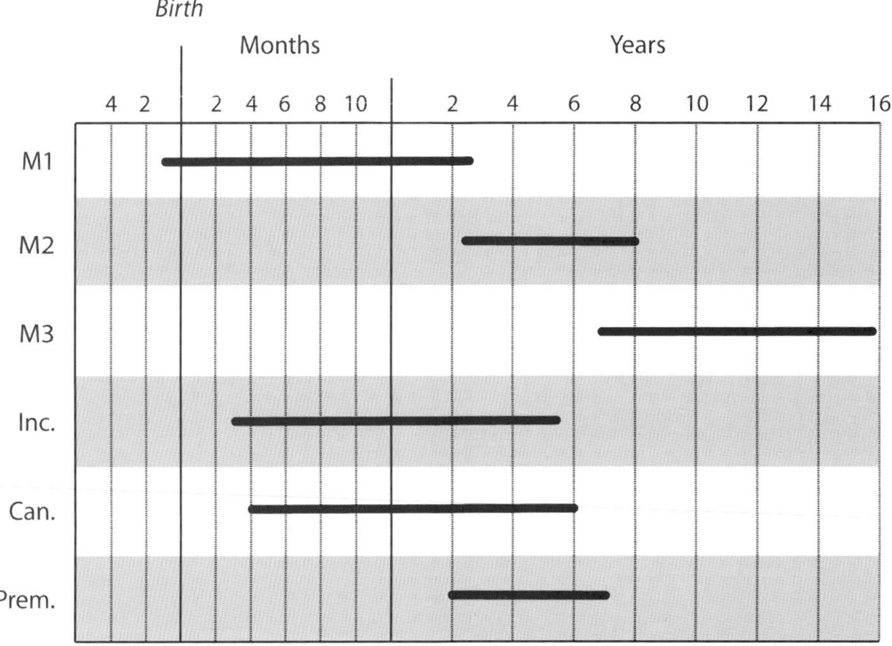

Fig. 2.4. Ages of human tooth mineralisation. After data in Knipper (2011, 132, fig. 8.3).

members, or Sr fluxes in rivers, or Sr content of the foods in an animal's diet. Mixing equations are used to predict the $^{87}Sr/^{86}Sr$ ratio in one reservoir from a mixture of its input components (Capo *et al.* 1998; Bentley 2006). Animal skeletal tissues represent mixtures of mixtures, so to speak (dietary mixtures of foods derived from soils that are mixtures), and therefore are often much less variable.

Besides mixture of environmental materials, including weathered sediments, streamwaters, and even manure added to recycled agricultural soils, there is another level of mixture seen in dietary $^{87}Sr/^{86}Sr$ ratios, which reflects the multiplicity of potential food sources accessed during the formation of the skeletal tissue. For this reason, measured human enamel $^{87}Sr/^{86}Sr$ ratios are more productively compared as pooled differences between groups. Because the $^{87}Sr/^{86}Sr$ ratio in the skeletons of animals represents a geographic average of their local, biologically available strontium, in many cases the range of the $^{87}Sr/^{86}Sr$ ratio among people from a prehistoric community can be remarkably narrow compared to the environmental variability (e.g. Giblin 2009; Cox *et al.* 2011). Considering Neolithic societies, for example, such homogeneity of strontium isotope signatures asks us to consider how intensively people farmed and worked the same agricultural soils, perhaps for generations (Bogaard 2004; Bogaard *et al.* 2011), which could effectively homogenise the $^{87}Sr/^{86}Sr$ ratio of the substrate.

Mark Pollard (2011) recently brought these issues together in a pointed critique. As he rightly maintains (Pollard 2011), strontium isotopes are rarely a magic 'signature' that pinpoints just where a person was born, as sometimes popularly portrayed. The strontium isotope ratio in tooth enamel, $^{87}Sr/^{86}Sr$, is simply a number, usually five digits (in many cases close to 0.7092, the current global average for seawater), which represents an average of the biologically available strontium taken in by a human or an animal while the sampled enamel was forming. Two people whose diets grew on similar soils would acquire similar five-digit numbers no matter how far apart they grew up. If an animal travelled while its enamel formed, then the measured $^{87}Sr/^{86}Sr$ ratio reflects a weighted average of the locations visited in the time covered by the enamel sample (Schweissing and Grupe 2003; Bentley 2006; Montgomery 2010). If it is possible to sample the enamel in very small increments along its growth axis, then the sample resolution is much improved (Nowell and Horstwood 2009), but still the $^{87}Sr/^{86}Sr$ ratio reflects an average of strontium intake for some particular time interval (Montgomery 2010).

In our study of the LBK in central Europe, we are careful to avoid these pitfalls. The fundamental starting point is that many of the uplands of our study regions in central Europe are underlain by granitic formations of higher $^{87}Sr/^{86}Sr$ ratios than the more homogeneous lowlands that are often covered in loess, the widespread aeolian sediment favoured by LBK communities. Outside Hungary, almost all the LBK sites featured in this study are located within the loess belt of Europe, where similar loess soils are the basis for biologically available $^{87}Sr/^{86}Sr$ ratios which range between 0.7085 and 0.710 (e.g. Grupe *et al.* 1997; Price *et al.* 2004; Bentley and Knipper 2005a; Knipper 2011). The exception to this are sites in Moravia (Czech Republic), which lies at the base of the Bohemian Massif, where Precambrian contributions to the loess raise the resulting $^{87}Sr/^{86}Sr$ ratios in human skeletons to between 0.7108 and 0.7105 (M.P. Richards *et al.* 2008).

Generally speaking, then, for the sites situated in central Europe, which differs substantially from the Hungarian Plain, higher than expected $^{87}Sr/^{86}Sr$ ratios should indicate subsistence off these favoured loess areas, such as (but not limited to) uplands underlain by granitic rocks and sandstones derived from their erosion, which we expect to have higher $^{87}Sr/^{86}Sr$. These non-loess areas need not be distant, since they could be as close as several kilometres from the settlement (Knipper 2011).

The focus of this project is diversity in LBK lifeways. As a means of detecting patterns of diversity, we saw it as advantageous to look within the Sr isotope data for statistically significant patterns of local versus non-local values among groups of different individuals, rather than trying to pinpoint the exact origins of a few individuals, as Pollard (2011) cautions against. For example, we might find a significantly higher proportion of non-locals among either men or women (suggestive of post-marital matrilocality or patrilocality, respectively), among those buried with a certain artefact or in a certain cardinal orientation (indicative of social or other differences between locals and non-locals), among those from a certain part of the site (characterising 'neighbourhoods' within the site), or among those whose skeletons are morphologically distinctive (showing differences in health or possibly even genetic ancestry between locals and non-locals). In this way, community diversity, subsistence specialisation and even kinship and marriage patterns may be inferred from the isotopic data, through interpretation simply of the difference between the local and non-local signatures at a particular study site.

The comparison is often enhanced by combining $^{87}Sr/^{86}Sr$ ratios with the concentration of Sr (Montgomery *et al.* 2007) and/or with other isotopes, such as oxygen and carbon or nitrogen. Even without additional isotopes, as Montgomery *et al.* (2007) describe, plotting $^{87}Sr/^{86}Sr$ versus 1/Sr can reveal distinct arrays of data points indicative of distinct human groups, even though those groups might overlap considerably in their $^{87}Sr/^{86}Sr$ ratios alone. We make liberal use of $^{87}Sr/^{86}Sr$ versus 1/Sr plots in the figures presenting our data (though the site data tables in the regional chapters report Sr ppm rather than 1/Sr).

2.5.2 Measurement

For this project, all Sr isotope analyses were conducted in the Department of Earth Sciences, Durham University. We analysed samples of enamel from the molars of over 550 LBK human skeletons from 18 sites (Fig. 1.8), ensuring a large dataset for meaningful comparison (see also Price *et al.* 2012). Based upon preservation and availability, the molar selected was typically M1 or M2, but occasionally M3 (Table 2.1). Using an established procedure, about 5 mg of tooth enamel from each individual was mechanically cleaned and dentine removed with a surgical steel scalpel, and soaked for one hour in weak (5%) acetic acid. Each sample was then dissolved in 3-N HNO_3, purified by extraction chromatography in polyethelyne columns with Sr-spec resin. With the purified Sr in 3% HNO_3 acid, $^{86}Sr/^{87}Sr$ analyses were carried out on a Thermo Electron Neptune Multi Collector Mass Spectrometer. Over all the separate analytical sessions, the average composition and reproducibility of the 212 analyses of NBS 987 Sr isotope reference material (0.71024) had a value of 0.710262±0.000001 (the ± expresses one standard error, which in the sixth digit is much smaller than the variation of the samples). Blanks were typically below 10 pg Sr and always below 30 pg Sr for all runs.

2.6 Human osteology

Human osteoarchaeology is the scientific study of human skeletal remains (Roberts 2009, 6). Their contextual analysis provides the most direct evidence of past lives, including information on age, sex, stature, population relationships and disease (palaeopathology), both at the individual and the population level (Mays 1998). Osteoarchaeological data also form the basis for successful biomolecular and archaeological investigations of human remains, including radiocarbon dating, stable isotope analysis and studies of mortuary rituals.

2.6.1 LBK osteoarchaeology: an overview

Before outlining the methodology applied for the Lifeways project, it is helpful briefly to consider the history of LBK osteology and the role which osteoarchaeological data have played in reaching wider understandings of LBK lives. While burials have been a focus of LBK research from its early stages (e.g. Heberer 1939; Kahlke 1954; Pavúk 1972a), consideration of osteological data has often been reduced to discussions of age- and sex-related differences in grave type, orientation and goods (Schweitzer and Schweitzer 1977; Höckmann 1982; Storch 1984/85; Nieszery 1995; Bulla 1998). More recently, isotopic studies have used demographic and morphological data to explore gendered patterns of migration and access to food resources, as well as questions of kinship (Price *et al.* 2001; Bentley *et al.* 2002; 2008; Oelze *et al.* 2011), again mostly focusing on age- and sex-related differences. Anthropometric studies, including measurements of crania and long bones, have taken a diachronic approach to try to distinguish between the LBK and preceding or succeeding populations (Zoffmann 2000; Meyer and Alt 2010).

While LBK skeletal remains have also been examined for evidence of disease and trauma, these studies tend to be case- or site-focused (Wahl and König 1987; Alt *et al.* 1997; Orschiedt 1997; Orschiedt *et al.* 2003; Meyer *et al.* 2004; Jacobi and Engelbrecht 2006; Lukes *et al.* 2008), form part of investigations into diachronic changes in health patterns (Haidle 1997), are based on reviews of disparate published sources rather than primary data (Peter-Röcher 2007; Wittwer-Backofen and Tomo 2008) or concentrate on select disease categories or age groups (Baum 1990; Kirchengast and Winkler 1994; Cruzeby *et al.* 2002; Dočkalová and Čižmář 2007).

Another group of palaeopathological studies include Masters theses and doctoral dissertations, and these often remain 'hidden' in the grey literature and difficult to access (Lantermann 1980), though recent practices of providing online access to dissertations is slowly changing this situation (Trautmann 2007; Tiefenböck 2010). Population-based, regional approaches to LBK osteology that consider demographic as well as metric and palaeopathological data, are virtually non-existent, with the notable exception of Bach's 1978 analysis of 189 *Linearbandkeramik* and *Stichbandkeramik* individuals from the Middle Elbe-Saale region in central Germany (Bach 1978).

All the above studies have made important contributions to increase our understanding of LBK demography, population relationships, diet and disease. However, while there have been various assumptions about the presence or degree of homogeneity in the LBK based on archaeological studies of material culture, settlement and mortuary ritual (Chapter 1.3), no attempt has been made osteoarchaeologically to try to identify either common trends or diverging patterns in LBK health and demography across the geographic distribution of LBK populations. What is more, isotopic studies have yet to move significantly beyond simple demographic analyses to a fuller integration of supporting osteological (and archaeological) data. One example is the investigation of diet without integration of dental health data as a proxy for dietary patterns (Bocherens *et al.* 2007; Oelze *et al.* 2011). This study, rather than focusing on one particular site, region or type of osteological/palaeopathological marker, applies a wider-ranging approach to the LBK burial record. Analysing a range of geographically diverse LBK assemblages, it considers multiple osteological features to investigate demography, diet/subsistence, physiological stress, deficiencies, activity, interpersonal violence, injury and infection, for integration with the archaeological and biomolecular analyses carried out for this project. In terms of the aims of the Lifeways project, this is a first attempt more fully to exploit the potential of skeletal data for helping to characterise and investigate patterns and variations in LBK lifeways, both at a population level as well as through osteobiographic studies of individuals.

2.6.2 Strength in numbers?

The osteological work carried out as part of the LBK Lifeways project has to be viewed as a pilot study. A total of 236 individuals (out of the *c.* 550 sampled for isotopic analysis) were directly analysed by Linda Fibiger, while other researchers (Chapters 3.10, 4.7, 5.7–8, 6.7–8, 7.7 and 8.9–10) contributed results on individual sites. While this total is not an insignificant sample, the regional sub-samples are of course much smaller, which has an impact on the strength of their statistically demonstrable significance and population-based inferences. The size of the sample also has to be viewed in the context of the over 3000 known LBK burials (Lifeways Database; Chapter 2.7.1). While not all of these burials are in a state of preservation that allows for a comprehensive osteological analysis (Ihmig 1971; Jeunesse 2002b; Heller 2005), a more significant problem for the population-based assessment of LBK health and lifeways is the fact that osteological results for some of the largest cemeteries, together contributing nearly a third of all known LBK individuals, remain largely unpublished. These include Schwetzingen in the Rhineland (203 graves), Stuttgart-Mühlhausen (Viesenhäuser Hof) in Baden-Württemberg (177 graves), Aiterhofen in Bavaria (240 graves) and Wandersleben-Gotha in central Germany, with 311 graves (Nieszery 1995; Price *et al.* 2003; Gerling 2009; Bickle *et al.* 2011). The same is true for the large assemblage of 138 settlement burials from Vaihingen in Baden-Württemberg (Bentley *et al.* 2003; Krause 1998). Currently available osteological information for all of these assemblages is limited to age and sex assessment, with only partial or sporadic palaeopathological assessments published to date (Lantermann 1980; Bach 1986; Carli-Thiele 1996; Welge in Krause 1998; Klingner *et al.* 2007). Undoubtedly, osteological data on such a large number of individuals have the potential not only to make a significant contribution to our understanding of LBK populations but also to challenge previous assertions based on much smaller samples – including the current study. For the moment, the Lifeways project provides the only inter-population view of the LBK, but we hope that ongoing and future research on these larger LBK skeletal assemblages will contribute to as well as expand and further challenge our perceptions of life in the *Linearbandkeramik*.

2.6.3 Lifeways osteology

The Lifeways project was carried out over three years; within that, the osteological component of the project was limited to one year. Not all burials analysed isotopically and/or archaeologically could be accessed for osteological analysis. To effectively use the limited time and resources of the project, we decided to concentrate on a number of osteological features that would best support the project aims of a population-based investigation of patterns and variations in LBK lifeways. This was achieved by recording a selective yet diverse range of osteoarchaeological features that could contribute to the investigation of population composition, diet and health (Ohio State University 2002). Recording of these features was based on clearly defined, standardised and current methodology (Buikstra and Ubelaker 1994; Brickley and McKinley 2004; Roberts 2009), outlined in more detail below. This is an important aspect to emphasise, as the failure to outline the features on which the diagnosis of age, sex and pathology is based can create a situation where results – occasionally multiple and divergent (Nieszery 1995, 91) – for a given assemblage are difficult to evaluate and compare. This can also be a problem when referring to older osteological reports as a basis for collating comparative data. Osteoarchaeology is not a static discipline, and advances in, for example, the understanding and skeletal expression of disease processes or age-related degeneration (Pinhasi and Mays 2008; Falys and Lewis 2011; Grauer 2012) necessitate caution when using data that may be based on slightly outdated approaches.

It is also important to consider and discuss preservation when reporting results, not only in terms of completeness of skeletal remains but also in terms of the surface condition of the bone. Preservation is another important factor influencing the extent and comprehensiveness of osteological analysis, and some results may have to be qualified as well as quantified, once prevalence calculations are based on preserved elements (true prevalence) rather than individuals or graves present (crude prevalence) (Henderson 1987; Fibiger and Knüsel 2005; Bello and Andrews 2006).

Osteological data recorded for the Lifeways project include the following:

Age and sex

Age and sex constitute the bases for any demographic analysis of skeletal and mortuary data. Age categories used in this report include Neonate (around the time of birth/up to one month), Infant (one month to a year), Juvenile (1–12 years), Adolescent (13–17 years), Young Adult (18–25 years), Young Middle Adult (26–35 years), Old Middle Adult (36–45 years) and Mature Adult (45+ years). Ageing of juveniles was based on observing dental calcification, growth and eruption (Ubelaker 1989, fig. 71; Smith 1991), supplemented by recording the appearance and fusion of long bone ends (epiphyses), as well as long bone length if teeth or epiphyses were not observable (Scheuer and Black 2000). For adults, morphological changes of the pubic symphysis (Brooks and Suchey 1990) and auricular surface (Lovejoy *et al.* 1985) of the pelvis were observed. Sex assessment was carried out on adult skeletal remains only by assessing up to ten morphological features of the pelvis and up to 15 morphological features of the skull (Herrmann *et al.* 1990; Buikstra and Ubelaker 1994, 19).

Where access to osteological remains was not possible age and sex has been taken from the published literature, and only rejected if sex had been applied to an individual who was a juvenile or younger. While this makes comparison difficult, it does allow broad statements about diversity in LBK populations to be made. We look to future projects to address such issues and fully expect that the application of further osteological work will significantly improve our population models of the LBK. Frequent age ranges used in LBK studies, which the reader will find in this volume, include: Infans I (0–6 years), Infans II (7–12 years) and Juvenile (13–17 years). Harmonising the different approaches to ageing skeletons is therefore inadvisable and it will be made clear in the text and tables of data who carried out the osteological analysis.

Dental caries

Caries has a complex aetiology, including genetically influenced differences in enamel formation, oral ecology and oral bacteria (Hillson 2005, 290; Lukacs 2012). The main contributing factor in its occurrence is a combination of bacterial activity and the presence of carbohydrates in the diet. During fermentation of food sugars, bacteria create acids which locally demineralise teeth and eventually result in macroscopic defects (Roberts and Manchester 2005, 65; Fig. 3.27). Increased consumption of plant-based carbohydrates is viewed as the main reason for high caries rates seen in early farming communities (Larsen *et al.* 1991; Jackes *et al.* 1997) and investigations of caries rates can provide information on access to and differential consumption of cariogenic foodstuffs (Larsen 1997, 69). For the Lifeways project, recording of caries defects was based on Hillson (2001).

Dental enamel hypoplasia

Hypoplastic enamel defects, that is, pitted or linear defects visible in the tooth crown, provide evidence for episodes of disrupted growth as a result of nutritional, pathological or general systemic physiological stress during the time of tooth formation (Goodman and Rose 1991; Hillson 2005, 169; Ogden 2008). As enamel is not remodelled during life, these defects are a record of childhood stress that is visible in the adult skeleton (Roberts and Manchester 2005, 75). While enamel development is sensitive to a whole range of physiological and metabolic factors – and enamel hypoplasia therefore often termed a non-specific indicator of stress – clinical studies indicate that under-nourishment or malnutrition play a substantial role (Goodman and Rose 1991; Roberts and Manchester 2005, 76). Enamel hypoplasia in the current study was recorded macroscopically. While it is acknowledged that this approach may miss the smallest defects (Hillson 2005, 174), it still provides a replicable benchmark as indentations can be identified and confirmed by feeling their presence with a fingernail (Ohio State University 2002).

Manipulative tooth wear

Tooth wear resulting from non-dietary use of teeth has been noted in many prehistoric as well as ethnographically documented populations. It results from the use of teeth as a 'third hand' or tool for processing materials, craft working or tool manufacture, often with strong gendered associations (Molnar *et al.* 1972; Merbs 1983, 145; Eshed *et al.* 2006; Schulting 2007). As manipulative dental wear in the form of occlusal grooves or notches of the anterior teeth (incisors and canines) had already been noted in a number of LBK assemblages (Frayer 2004; Jarošová and Dočkalová 2008), it was decided to further investigate this cultural practice for the Lifeways project (Fig. 3.27).

Cribra orbitalia *and iron deficiency anaemia*

Factors contributing to anaemia and iron deficiency are numerous and can include diet, inadequate iron resorption as a result of disease processes, excessive bleeding and gastrointestinal infections (Stuart-Macadam 1991, 105; Ortner 2003, 369; Roberts and Manchester 2005, 226). While not pathognomonic of iron deficiency anaemia (Ortner 2003, 369; Lewis 2007, 114), skeletal manifestations do include increased porosity and thinning of the outer layer of bone with a simultaneous increase in the cancellous layer of bone, evident in the roof of the orbit (*cribra orbitalia*) or the cranial vault bones (porotic hyperostosis) (Ortner 2003, 373–4). The latter is relatively rare in European populations (Roberts and Manchester 2005, 230). *Cribra orbitalia* is considered another general indicator of stress (Goodman *et al.* 1988; Jackes *et al.* 1997; Papathanasiou 2005) and in this study was recorded following the categories outlined by Stuart-Macadam (1991).

Cranial trauma and violence

It is well documented that traumatic injuries to the head are more likely to result from violence than post-cranial trauma and the head has remained a key target for assault through time (Larsen 1997, 156; Brink *et al.* 1998; Roberts and Manchester 2005, 108; Schulting and Fibiger 2012). Distinguishing conflict-related violence from accidents, falls and ritual practice may not be achievable in every case, but advances in forensic anthropology and traumatology now allow the identification of trauma patterns typical for violence and assault (Shepherd *et al.* 1990; S. Byers 2008). Analysis of the frequency of violence-related injury can reveal gendered and age-related patterns and shed light on the role and impact of violence on individuals and population groups (Martin and Frayer 1997; Walker 2001; Schulting and Fibiger 2012). A population-based study of LBK violence provides a counterpoint to the prominence of high-fatality conflict sites such as Talheim and Asparn in LBK research when exploring questions of apparent 'warfare' and 'crisis' during the period (Boulestin *et al.* 2009; Zeeb-Lanz 2009a; Teschler-Nicola 2012; Wahl and Trautmann 2012). In the current study, identification of ante- and peri-mortem cranial trauma was based on established forensic and osteological diagnostic criteria (for details see Fibiger 2012; forthcoming)

Post-cranial trauma

When considered in their sociocultural and environmental context, the analysis of post-cranial trauma patterns can shed light on past lifestyles, including differential risks of sustaining traumatic injuries associated with age, sex or status (Larsen 1997, 110; Lovell 1997; Roberts 2000). While trauma can include any injury or wound, fractures (partial or complete breaks in a bone) and dislocations (abnormal displacement of bone) present the most commonly seen types of accidental traumatic injuries in the post-cranial skeleton (Larsen 1997, 110; Judd and Roberts 1999; Roberts 2000). In some special cases, fractures may even be associated with a particular movement or activity (Knüsel *et al.* 1996). Identification and recording of post-cranial fractures in the Lifeways project were based on standard osteological and forensic criteria (Roberts 2000, 347; Brickley and McKinley 2004; Cunha and Pinheiro 2009).

Periosteal lesions

Periosteal new bone formation is a frequently recorded pathological lesion in archaeological remains, most commonly affecting the long bones (Weston 2012). The two stages of new bone formation include an initial or acute phase (woven bone) and a more remodelled phase (lamellar or compact bone) (Ortner 2003, 50), and distributed or bilateral changes are more indicative of a systemic condition. Periosteal new bone formation accompanies a variety of disease processes, including inflammation, specific and non-specific infections, metabolic diseases and trauma (Ortner 2003, 205; Kozłowski and Witas 2012; Weston 2012). For the Lifeways project, infectious and metabolic diseases were of particular interest as their prevalence can provide insights into general health and immune status as well as pathogen load and nutritional stress (Ortner *et al.* 1999; Brickley and Ives 2008, 8; Ortner 2008). Diagnosis of a particular disease category depends on the extent and distribution of the lesions but may not always be possible. Diagnosis in the Lifeways project followed established criteria (Ortner 2003; Roberts and Buikstra 2003; Brickley and Ives 2008).

2.7 Burial practices in the LBK

The history of burial studies in archaeology is intertwined with the development of the discipline itself. The study of LBK burials is no exception to this, with researchers using evidence from funerary contexts in the early Neolithic to assess, amongst other themes, social structure, individual identity and, most significantly for the project here, regional and local variation (Modderman 1970; 1988; Pavúk 1972a; van de Velde 1979a; 1979b; 1990; Veit 1993; 1996; Jeunesse 1996; 1997). These ideas have been explored in ways that pertain particularly to the context of the LBK, and wider explanations for difference and diversity are frequently linked to issues at play in Neolithic studies more broadly, specifically social structure and the nature of the Mesolithic-Neolithic transition. For a long time, however, the relationship has not been reciprocal and burial studies have in the past played a secondary role in mapping the social worlds of the LBK (D. Hofmann 2009a, 220; Chapter 1.3.5).

Identities explored through the provision of certain grave goods, therefore, have often drawn on coarse divisions between 'hunter' and 'farmer' as proxies for Mesolithic and Neolithic identities (for example, the 'hunter/warrior' at Schwanfeld: Gronenborn 2003) and have been modelled on assumptions about how high and low social status would have been portrayed in the funerary context (e.g. van de Velde 1979a; 1979b; Modderman 1988). Fortunately, this is beginning to change, in part thanks to the introduction of isotope studies. In projects such as the earlier studies in south-west Germany (Price *et al.* 2001; Bentley *et al.* 2002; 2003) and the Vedrovice Bioarchaeology project (Zvelebil and Pettitt 2008), the careful combination of biochemical data about human lifeways with the funerary context has resulted in issues of burial and death now playing a larger role in broader narratives of LBK history. Equally, a move towards exploring how burial was practised and performed – recognising funerary rites as a creative sphere for the mediation and creation of identity – has led to powerful re-imaginings of death and burial in the LBK (Frirdich 2003; 2005; D. Hofmann 2006; 2009a; forthcoming; Boulestin *et al.* 2009; Zeeb-Lanz *et al.* 2009). As there is by now a large literature on the LBK, here we focus specifically on the role which variability has played in the investigation of LBK funerary rites.

2.7.1 Previous approaches to LBK burials

The first LBK burial ground to be excavated was probably Flomborn in 1901–1903 (Jeunesse 1997, 13). Over the last 100 or so years, the corpus of LBK burials has steadily risen, particularly between the 1960s and 1980s, when large-scale excavations were taking place across Europe (Modderman 1988; Veit 1993; 1996; Nieszery 1995; Jeunesse 1997; 2003a), but also with the recognition of the variety of burial practices found in LBK contexts (Modderman 1988; Veit 1993). Modderman (1988, 117) quotes 1950 known burials, Jeunesse (1997, 25) *c.* 2500 and, most recently, Trautmann (2006, 12) argues that as many as 3500 burials of various sorts are known in the LBK (she records a total of 3481). In the database compiled for this project, 3009 burials were collected largely from published sources.[3]

As we described in the opening chapter (Chapter 1.3.5), the classic LBK burial rite has dominated our understanding of burial. 'Normal' practice is defined as a single cemetery inhumation, with the deceased placed crouched on their left-hand side, with the head oriented approximately towards the east or south-east. Although this is the most frequent combination of body position and orientation, only 37% of burials are both left-crouched and thus oriented (Lifeways Database). The idea of a regularised burial rite has dominated in LBK studies since the 1970s and the excavations at Nitra by Pavúk (1972a; Jeunesse 1996, 250). The skeletal material from Nitra had been well preserved in comparison to other cemeteries discovered about the same time, including Elsloo and Niedermerz (Jeunesse 1996, 250), and was excavated at a time when broader archaeological debate elsewhere was attempting to assess what information on social complexity, structure and organisation could be gleaned from funerary practices (Saxe 1971; Binford 1971).

Juraj Pavúk (1972a; 1972b) primarily focused on the grave goods and in whose graves they were found. At Nitra, men (4/16 graves) had fewer unfurnished graves than women (10/26 graves), and the majority of graves with goods ascribed the highest status by Pavúk (1972a, 70–3; that is, buried with *Spondylus* shell and polished stone) were those of older males and females, with a small group of very rich male graves standing out (discussed in more detail in Chapter 4.10). Thus, while Pavúk (1972a, 72) also acknowledged that LBK grave good assemblages were not static and did change through time, a model of gerontocratic communities was proposed for the LBK, in which he argued that high status was accrued only by a small group of older adult males. This argument stood out at the time, not only because a matriarchal model was favoured in the literature, but also because it was held that the LBK was formed of broadly egalitarian groups (Jeunesse 1997, 114).

The publication of Nitra was followed shortly by discussion of the cemetery at Elsloo by Pieter van de Velde (1979a; 1979b). In his studies, he retained the focus of Pavúk (1972a) on social structure and chronological change through solely considering the grave goods and their dispersal across the cemetery, and concentrated on how the mortuary rites could inform on the division of labour between the sexes by separating items that indicate a particular skill from those associated with status (or in his own terms 'dignity'; van de Velde 1979a, 113). This study was complicated by the lack of skeletal preservation at Elsloo, something van de Velde overcame by defining particular 'grave good sets' as gendered (for example, identifying the presence of polished stone and lithics as indicative of male graves, and grinding stones and ochre as female). This of course brings its own problems, not least that unfurnished graves do not play a role in this model of LBK social structure (cf. van de Velde 1997). Overall, van de Velde (1979a, 114–16; 1979b) proposed a virilocal, but matrilineal, model for LBK society because of the number of rich female graves (the rich male graves apparently not requiring explanation), and the relative distribution of kinds of decorative pot motifs in female and male graves. While van de Velde (1979a; 1979b) sought a more detailed model of LBK social structure and kinship than Pavúk (1972a), and was more explicit in acknowledging the structuralist and neo-Marxist origins of his approach, he continued in this study to treat the grave good assemblage as a direct representation of the social role of the individual interred in the grave, thus downplaying variation as meaningful in any way other than in conferring a status-based identity on the deceased.

It was not until the influential 'diversity in uniformity' essay by Pieter Modderman (1988) that variability and regional differences in the burial record were really acknowledged, but this work was more concerned with regionality rather than, for instance, the inclusion of all burial contexts or the identification of status differences. These issues only really reached prominence from the mid-1990s, on the basis of a much increased corpus (see Jeunesse 1997, 13–15 for a more detailed research history). Although some studies were concerned with other aspects (e.g. Peschel 1992; Siemoneit 1997), status distinctions now became the main focus, with Pavúk's (1972a) 'gerontocratic' Nitra model increasingly challenged by those who argued for inherited status (e.g. Jeunesse 1997; Chapter 1.3.5 for more detailed discussion).

Jeunesse (1997, 108–9) also looked back to the Mesolithic context in which the LBK appeared and argued that variation in burial rites could also be explained by the presence of indigenous hunter-gatherers at LBK cemeteries. In doing so, he significantly broadened the key identity groups thought to have been referenced in funerary rites. In the regional burial traditions identified by Jeunesse (1996; 1997; 2002c; 2005; outlined in Chapter 1.3.5) for the western LBK distribution, degree of variability also played an important role in defining the rites of different traditions. In Tradition II, the higher rates of variation in body position, orientation and grave goods are therefore related to more visible indigenous groups, while in Tradition I, the lack of variation is thought to betray a certain conservatism or desire to maintain a core LBK identity (Jeunesse 1996; 1997; 2002c; 2005). Overall, therefore, Jeunesse (2002c; 2005) argues that the variation in burial rites provides an insight into how heterogeneous different LBK groups considered themselves to be. However, on the level of the individual site the grave goods that accompanied the deceased, and the chosen orientation and position of the body, are still treated as uncomplicated representations of the individual in life.

Eva Lenneis (2007, 136) adds another dimension to the classification of 'Mesolithic' grave goods by regarding them, not necessarily as straightforward displays of a hunter-gatherer identity, but rather as indicating continuity with previous burial traditions and therefore suggestive of the involvement of an autochthonous population in the spread of the LBK, who blended Mesolithic traditions with practices brought with the LBK from the south-eastern Neolithic cultures. What constituted the burial rites of the Mesolithic populations in central Europe is not fully known as the evidence is extremely restricted (Jeunesse 1997, 32; see Grünberg 2000 for the most up-to-date corpus of Mesolithic burials, and Chapter 3.5 for the Starčevo and Körös assemblage), but the longevity of some categories of grave goods and of some funerary practices can be demonstrated (such as the use of ochre, animal teeth and snail shells; Lenneis 2007). As Lenneis (2007) has argued, while certain grave goods may speak to us of particular activities, there are not straightforward divisions between those individuals that receive only goods with a 'Mesolithic' heritage and those that receive only 'Neolithic' items (e.g. *Spondylus* shell, polished stone and pottery). Rather complex mixtures occur, undermining any assumption not only that Neolithic farmers were *de facto* high status, while those adhering to Mesolithic traditions were low status, but also that such clear-cut categorisation existed in the mortuary realm.

What the approaches taken by both Jeunesse (1997; 2002a) and Lenneis (2007) have in common is that they attempt to see LBK mortuary practice within its historical context and not as an isolated record of social identity of the living preserved without change or alteration in the burial record. This development in LBK funerary studies is part of a wider and welcome move, which is seeking to situate burial practices within the context of funerary ritual and the social presentation of death, as well as exploring what they might mean for broader questions of LBK social identity and community formation (Jeunesse 2002c; 2005; Frirdich 2003, 545; D. Hofmann 2009a, 216; forthcoming). Performance at the grave site has been foregrounded (such as smashing pottery, throwing ochre and revisiting graves; D. Hofmann 2009a; Hofmann and Bickle 2011), alongside investigating the constitution of social groupings who buried their dead together (Frirdich 2003; Jeunesse 2003a), thus viewing burial rites as active in forming and reinforcing group identity and, as such, subject to alteration over time.

For Daniela Hofmann (2009a; forthcoming), the lifecourse is paramount in the kinds of statements being made at the graveside, but this is set against broader tensions of community identity, and sub-groupings therein, in her discussion of LBK burial. At Aiterhofen, she argues that grave goods vary depending on the age as well as the sex of the deceased, pointing to the varied use of *Spondylus* between men and women. Armrings are found with males of various ages and may have been worn since childhood, but women become increasingly more likely to receive *Spondylus* if they die later into adulthood. She also stresses that it is only a subset of the community which is marked out by receiving *Spondylus* objects (D. Hofmann 2006; 2009a; forthcoming; Hofmann and Orschiedt forthcoming). The use of *Spondylus*, for example, also varies geographically and chronologically across the LBK (Jeunesse 2009) and, while such statements relating to age and sex may have been foregrounded at Aiterhofen, it is not clear whether these were widespread practices or a regionally specific emphasis on ageing, selected from a wealth of different identities connected to group identity, individual life histories, status, subsistence practices, resource access, craft specialisation and so on.

We have focused so far on research based on the large flat cemeteries. This is perhaps not surprising given that they have dominated studies of LBK death and burial. Frirdich (2003) and D. Hofmann (2009a) have both argued that cemetery burial has been prioritised for analysis because it is a practice familiar in a modern context and therefore viewed as 'normal', placing it beyond a need for explanation. Indeed, the appearance of cemeteries in the 54th or 53rd century BC is a phenomenon not yet fully understood and it is perhaps cemetery, rather than settlement, burials that should demand explanation. Modderman (1988, 118) typifies much of the attitude to LBK settlement burials, stating only that as they are 'not provided with burial gifts … their status was low'. Yet, settlement burials account for roughly a third of all known LBK burials (35%; Lifeways Database), thus representing a significant practice, and in the regions of Hungary and the Paris basin cemetery burials are entirely absent. Approximately half of all settlement burials are furnished (Lifeways Database), a rate which is overshadowed by most cemeteries, where 70% of all burials are furnished. However, not all cemeteries had such high rates of furnished burials, notably at Schwetzingen, where the rate of furnished graves drops to a rate similar to that of settlements. There may have also been additional organic goods that are not preserved.

Furthermore, clear-cut divisions in burial rites cannot be found in different burial contexts. Outside inhumations at cemeteries and settlements, human remains have also been found disarticulated at settlements, enclosure sites and caves, and cremation was also practised from the later phases of the LBK onwards. Fragmentation and revisiting grave sites have been demonstrated in a range of contexts, including cemeteries and settlements as well as enclosures (Jeunesse 1997; Orschiedt 1998a; 1999; Orschiedt and Haidle 2007; 2009; Boulestin *et al.* 2009; Thévenet 2009; Hofmann and Orschiedt forthcoming). In sum, cemetery burials do not provide a total picture of LBK funerary practice, and we should also be cautious in drawing too many stark divisions between the different treatments of the dead as many practices overlap, showing the same range of concerns with material expression and the body in death (D. Hofmann 2009a; forthcoming). Cemetery burial does imply a selection, and in this sense the burial context is important, but it remains integrated in broader concerns and ways of expression (Chapters 9.4.1. and 10.2 provide a discussion of differences between cemetery and settlement burials). Additionally, many more ways of treating the deceased may have been practised that left no trace behind (van de Velde 1997; Chapter 1.3.5) and the existence of cenotaphs (potentially furnished graves without skeletons; see Lenneis 2010d for further discussion) may be further evidence that wider practices as yet unrecorded took place.

While inhumations are the focus of study here, it is worth briefly noting the other kinds of burial practices found in the LBK, as they must surely form the context for any discussion of variability at cemeteries and the kinds of social groupings who buried their dead together. Cremations have played a rather muted role in LBK burial studies, despite accounting for approximately 10% of the burial record, with 350 mentioned in the literature (Trautmann 2007, 11). Trautmann (2007, 11) argues that this dates back to the controversy over the 'Wetterauer cremations', which were discovered in 1907 but were later shown to have been faked (see also Loewe 1958), though the presence of cremations in the LBK has been long since acknowledged (Hoffmann 1989). Thus Modderman (1988, 118–19) focused almost entirely on the cemetery inhumations, and although cremations also receive grave goods he did not suggest that cremation was the provision for a particular socio-economic (in his terms) group. There are also several cases of disarticulated remains or supernumerary bones from grave pits in cemeteries. These – and potentially also completely empty pits – may be the remains of a multi-stage funeral in which the bones of the deceased were secondarily removed or scattered (e.g. Nieszery 1995, 23–5; Gerling 2009), but have also been interpreted as graves deliberately looted in the course of inter-community conflict (Farruggia 2002).

With increasing interest taken in LBK funerary practices and a growing variety in the methodologies used, burial studies are becoming increasingly more integrated into broader considerations of the LBK (e.g. Jeunesse 2005; 2009; Zvelebil and Pettitt 2008; D. Hofmann 2009a; Zeeb-Lanz *et al.* 2009). However, studies still often remain localised to individual sites and regions, or approached as a sphere of interest separate from daily life, subsistence routine and social networks. Generally, therefore, LBK burial studies are in a good state, but questions remain that can be usefully approached by this project in an assessment of diversity in lifeways. In the chapters that follow we will consider three main aspects of burial rites:

a) whether regionally specific practices can be identified and their significance for regional cohesion distinguished (that is, whether different regions were emphasising different aspects of funerary rites at the expense of others);

b) the kinds of individual and group identities that were being expressed at cemeteries and in burial contexts (that is, whether we can identify clusters of burials which were similar, or distinct variations across cemetery and settlement burials); and

c) how the subsistence practices and life histories of individuals were recognised in the grave (that is, whether individuals whose burials were unusual in one aspect were also unusual in other ways).

Overall, therefore, the challenge taken up here is to unpick the significance of local and regional practices within the tableau of varied burial rites outlined above and to assess the salient criteria for interpreting lifeways and social organisation.

2.7.2 Determining variability in LBK burial rites

In order to develop a picture of the kinds of diversity found in LBK funerary practices between and within regions, as well as at the site level, a database was collated of published LBK burials from a range of contexts (Chapter 2.7.1). A total of 3009 burials have been added to this database at time of writing (2012). Throughout this volume, when values and trends have been determined by analysis based on the database, this is referenced as the 'Lifeways Database'. The burials were collated from the published literature where available, though the detail of information varied significantly and in some cases it has only been possible to determine that a burial was present. In other cases information varied (for instance in the case of osteological data where multiple studies have taken place, and occasionally for other aspects of burial) and had to be assessed on a case by case basis (for example the Aiterhofen osteology: Chapter 6.7.2). The main approach to the burial aspect of this project was to seek correlates between the different aspects of the funerary context and to examine how these varied on the scale of the individual, site, region and supra-region.

What was required was an understanding of how different aspects of burial relate together and whether there are significant correlations between different body positions, orientations, age, sex and particular sets of grave goods. Different aspects of burial were determined for study, which are detailed below. Age at death and sex have been left out of this list because they have just been discussed (Chapter 2.6.3), but they obviously play a large role in the analysis which follows first on a regional basis in Chapters 3–8 and then in the regional comparison and overview in Chapter 9.

Context

The burials sampled for the Lifeways project mainly came from two different contexts, settlements and cemeteries. The exception are those individuals sampled from Asparn an der Zaya, which came from the enclosure ditches and may have been buried without formal funerary rites (Chapter 5.8). There may be some ambiguity between the different categories, such as whether a small group of burials on the edge of a settlement should be counted as a cemetery (as at Těšetice: Chapter 4.8). In this case size is the defining factor, and the category of 'cemetery' has usually been reserved for those instances where large groups of people were interred in the same location, seemingly separate from settlements themselves. Similarly, many enclosure burials could also be classed as within a settlement, but those individuals found interred in the ditches themselves have been classed as 'enclosure burials'. It is also likely that the enclosure burials are vastly under-represented in the database, as they often comprise disarticulated remains and these have not been systematically included (nor are they systematically recorded for the LBK).

Orientation of the body

The orientation of the grave was recorded, with the direction of the head always named first (that is, if a burial is said to be oriented east–west, then the head would be pointing to the east). This differs from some literature on LBK burials where the grave pit orientation is noted alongside which direction the skull was facing. As the skull can be placed tightly against the edge of the pit, and given the possibility of post-burial movement of the skeleton (Chapter 2.7.1 above) and even rare missing skulls (as at at Polgár: Chapter 3.9.1), the orientation of the body was favoured. In our analysis, we treated orientation in two ways.

1) The first approach was simply by cardinal direction, where eight categories were determined (E–W, SE–NW, S–N, SW–NE, W–E, NW–SE, N–S and NE–SW, as well as a ninth, unknown, when preservation prevented orientation being determined). Just the main eight compass points were used to ensure that the numbers of burials were large enough for statistical analysis.

2) The second approach was by frequency of orientation. Häusler (1994; 2000) demonstrated that the orientation of LBK burials fell into three main categories: a dominant orientation (>60%), in which the majority of burials fell; a secondary or antipodal orientation (20–30%) which was roughly opposite to the main orientation; and rare orientations (<15%; see Fig. 9.9 and further discussion in Chapter 9.5.2). The dominant orientation varies by region (Jeunesse 1997, 63), so we divided the burials by three categories (dominant, secondary and rare orientation) and examined whether any trends could be identified.

Body position

As noted in Chapter 1.3.5 and above, LBK burials are found most frequently in the left-crouched position, but other positions are also found, including right-crouched, supine (extended on back), prone (extended on front) and in irregular positions. Occasionally, burials were noted in the literature as 'crouched', without the side on which they were placed recorded. These five different positions are very coarse categories and, for instance, the degree of 'crouched-ness' can vary enormously (Jeunesse 1997, 14, fig. 4), with some suggestions that the tightly crouched individuals were bound to keep them in this position (Kahlke 1954, 121; U. Fischer 1956, 218). Jeunesse (1997, 65) further distinguishes a category of burials that had been placed on their backs, with the legs crouched to the left or right, noting, therefore, a total of seven different body positions. We focus, however, on the five positions outlined above to maintain statistical robustness. The 'irregular' position was assigned to individuals where the body had not been disturbed after burial, and was well enough preserved to be certain that they did not fall into the other categories. In all other cases the body position was treated as unknown.

Grave goods

While in the categories above, excepting in the case of poor preservation, all graves offer a context, orientation and body position, grave goods could be absent entirely or occur in different frequencies across a range of different tools and objects, which are found broken, used or pristine. In analysing the grave goods we identified seven broad categories, following Jeunesse (1997, 70–80), each of which could then be further sub-divided and analysed by types, use (where appropriate) and frequency (number occurring in the grave). These were:

1) polished stone (adzes, flat axes, maceheads and 'double axes');

2) pottery (whole pots of various sorts, decorated and undecorated, as well as individuals sherds; occasionally there are suggestions that an entire smashed pot was included in the grave);

3) flint tools (blades, arrowheads, scrapers and cores, as well as flakes);

4) ornamentation (*Spondylus* shell, including buckles, armrings, pendants and beads, local river shells of various types, stone beads, human and animal teeth and more rarely objects made from bone and antler, such as combs and pendants);

5) bone tools and objects (needles, awls and very rarely bone figurines) and more rarely joints of meat;

6) grinding stones; and

7) colouring, such as ochre (found in lumps and sprinkled over the deceased and the soil of the grave) and more rarely graphite or iron pyrite.

As the main aim of the analysis was to determine correlations between different aspects of burial and information about the deceased (such as age at death, sex, context of burial and so on), we chose not to apply a system such as those used by Modderman (1988) and Jeunesse (1997), where grave goods were assigned points based on the rarity and the time taken to make them in order to determine the relative 'richness' of graves. We avoided this approach, partly because it had already been applied to many of the sites we sampled and would have been needless repetition (e.g. Schwetzingen; Gerling 2012), but also because we wanted to approach variation in a much more contextualising fashion, thus examining whether particular classes of objects correlated with different features of burial, rather than determining a status in an absolute sense. For this reason, we often refer to the 'complexity' of the grave good assemblage, when many different objects occur together in one grave (with further discussion in Chapter 9.5.3).

2.8 The integration of isotopes, osteology and archaeology

While it hardly needs repeating that funerary practices do far more than present an uncomplicated tableau of the identity of the deceased, it is important to remember that isotopes, although tested on the skeleton of the deceased, are created in life. This can be beneficial. If objects in the grave are thought to denote different subsistence-based identities or lifeways, then isotopic evidence can give an indication as to whether this is borne out in the diets or origins of specific individuals. However, this need for balance between the isotopes (which developed in life) and the funerary context also means that care must be taken in using the isotopic evidence. Neither burial practices nor isotopic signatures should be read as simple reflections of certain reified identities, no matter how dominant these are in archaeological interpretations (Bickle and Hofmann 2007, 1030; Knipper 2009; Bickle *et al.* 2011; Pollard 2011). For example, stable isotopes are unlikely on their own to help us distinguish between hunter-gatherers and farmers, as they reflect protein consumption rather than the use of wild or domestic resources, and we must in any case question whether such separate identity classes, based entirely on subsistence activities, were rigorously followed or recognised during the LBK (Robb and Miracle 2007; Whittle 2009; Bickle *et al.* 2011). Similarly, while strontium ratios give an indication of the geology from which childhood diet was sourced, we must resist making the jump from a suggested geographical origin to imagining that this reveals a socially recognised and unchanging identity drawn from place of birth, without first including a contextual appraisal of the available archaeological and osteological correlates (Pollard 2011; Chapter 2.5).

The isotope data will be compared with both the archaeological and osteological evidence site by site, and in relation to local and regional subsistence preferences, settlement patterns and social organisation. Table 2.1 outlines each of the isotopic elements analysed by this project and the kinds of information which they can provide, as well as an indication of how variation in the datasets is interpreted here. It is intended to be a guide to the reader through the next chapters, as we move on to present the results region by region. Each of the six regional chapters begins with an overview of the LBK archaeology from that particular region, detailing the history of studies, the arrival and development of the LBK, subsistence patterns, material networks and connections, and an outline of burial practices. Following on from this the results from each site are presented (osteology where available, stable isotopes, strontium isotopes and then archaeological reconsideration), presenting the kinds of diversity which we find on the local scale. Each regional chapter ends with a brief discussion comparing the sites sampled and highlighting first conclusions. Following each regional chapter, we explore the lifeways of two individuals in detail (taken from the region under discussion in the previous chapter). Chapter 9 then takes the inter-regional approach, looking at the dataset overall and moving to consider the patterns which we find on a larger scale. Chapter 10 offers final, general reflections on what the project has contributed to a better understanding of LBK lifeways.

Notes

1 So-called because their mechanism of photosynthesis involves four carbon atom compounds in comparison to three in C3 plants.

2 In the course of this project, human ribs were sampled where possible to ensure comparable timescales were measured for each individual.

3 The total number quoted here includes cemetery, settlement and known enclosure inhumations and cremations, but not the disarticulated remains found at Herxheim or the enclosure at Asparn/Schletz, which are included in the total quoted by Trautmann (2007, 11–12). Further sites mentioned in the literature, but not yet fully published, are thought to amount to over 1000 additional individuals.

3 Hungary

Alasdair Whittle, Alexandra Anders, R. Alexander Bentley, Penny Bickle, Lucy Cramp, László Domboróczki, Linda Fibiger, Julie Hamilton, Robert Hedges, Nándor Kalicz, Zsófia Eszter Kovács, Tibor Marton, Krisztián Oross, Ildikó Pap and Pál Raczky

3.1 Introduction

Our account of LBK lifeways begins in Hungary. That country lies, roughly rectangular, across the northern part of the Carpathian basin, framed to the west, north and east respectively by the eastern end of the Alps, the Danube and the hill ranges bordering Slovakia, and the western fringes of the Carpathian mountains, and to the south by the Drava river, western tributary of the Danube, and by the Maros, eastern tributary of the Tisza (Fig. 3.1).

In simple terms, the country is divided down the middle by the Danube and the Tisza, and those major rivers serve to define two very different settings. East of the Danube, the Alföld or Great Hungarian Plain represents the central part of the Carpathian basin as a whole. This is a tectonic depression (Pécsi 1970; Sherratt 1982a; 1982b; 1983a; 1983b), forming a flat landscape with minimal relief, drained by the Tisza running in from the north-east in Ukraine and by its west-flowing tributaries, coming from the Carpathians, the Körös system (Criş in Romanian) roughly in the middle of the Plain and the Maros more or less at the southern border. Earlier Neolithic settlement was concentrated along the watercourses of the Plain, often on the edges of terraces and ridges formed in the Pleistocene (Kosse 1979). To the north, the Plain gives way abruptly to the northern hills, the Mátra, Bükk and Zemplén, slanting away to the north-east.

West of the Danube, the landscape of the Dunántúl, or Transdanubia, is very different, alternately hilly (of varied geologies) and lowland, principally drained by small tributaries of the Drava and Danube. In the middle lies Lake Balaton, which was of larger extent in the earlier part of the Holocene, down to the start of the Neolithic sequence, with further marshes to its west (Bánffy 2004; 2008, figs 6–7). Beyond the volcanic hills north of Lake Balaton, the Rába drains north-eastwards to join the Danube near Győr, and north of its lower reaches lies the Kisalföld or Little Hungarian Plain, directly across from the western Slovakian river basin (Chapter 4.1).

LBK communities were present in both parts of Hungary, broadly in the second half of the sixth millennium cal BC: on the Alföld and in Transdanubia. They have been given separate names, variously in the east the *alföldi vonaldíszes kerámia* in Hungarian or AVK for short, or Alföld Linear Pottery culture or ALP, and in the west the Transdanubian Linear Pottery culture or TLP, or more generally, reflecting a much closer affiliation with the wider LBK phenomenon, the *Linienbandkeramik* or *Linearbandkeramik* of the region. For the sake of simplicity, this chapter will use the terms ALP and TLP. Though it shares many features with the LBK as a whole, including longhouses, an emphasis on cattle and a recurrent inhumation rite of crouched individual burials, the ALP has often been distinguished from the wider phenomenon as a kind of special case, partly because of its in many ways different pottery styles, partly because of the current view that LBK origins may best be seen to lie in Transdanubia and its immediate neighbours to the west and the north, and partly perhaps because of its southern connections, notably with the great Vinča cultural complex of Serbia and surrounds. It is also worth noting that the label 'TLP' can be rather clumsy (though we retain it here principally to differentiate between Transdanubia and the Plain), since it covers both sites in the north very close to the Austrian border (Chapter 5) and those in the south, with a different cultural sequence and open to different contacts and affiliations. This chapter will cover the two areas in succession, but will also discuss the extent of similarity and difference between and within them.

A second point of introduction is important. In Chapters 4–8 of this volume, the LBK represents the first Neolithic communities region by region across central Europe. In Hungarian terms, however, the TLP and the ALP are middle Neolithic, preceded by the early Neolithic Starčevo communities of Transdanubia and the Körös communities of the Plain, broadly of the first half of the sixth millennium cal BC (Bánffy 2004; 2008; Whittle 2007). This longer history, and the perhaps varied beginnings, as well as the connections in multiple directions, may have helped to condition some of the observable diversity in LBK lifeways in this region.

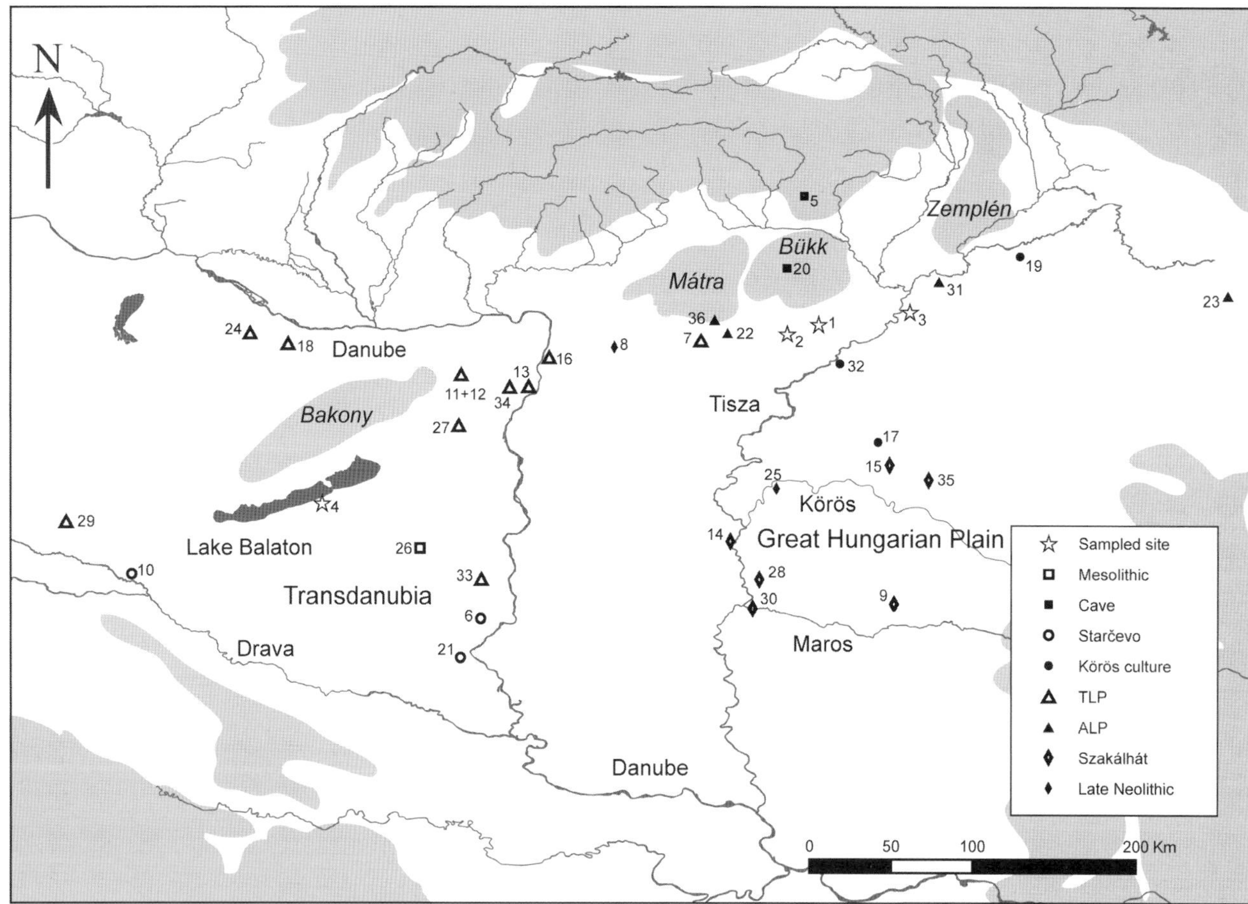

Fig. 3.1. Map of sites sampled (1–4) and others mentioned in Chapter 3. For all sites in the Polgár area see point 3. For sites in the Balaton area see point 4. Upland areas are in italics. 1) Mezőkövesd-Mocsolyás, 2) Füzesabony-Gubakút, 3) Polgár-Ferenci-hát, 4) Balatonszárszó-Kis-erdei-dűlő, 5) Aggtelek, 6) Alsónyék-Bátaszék, 7) Apc, 8) Aszód-Papi-földek, 9) Battonya-Gödrösök, 10) Becsehely I and II, 11) Bicske, 12) Bicske-Galagonyás, 13) Budapest-Kőérberek-Tóváros lakópark, 14) Csanytelek-Újhalastó, 15) Dévaványa-Sártó, 16) Dunakeszi-Székesdűlő, 17) Ecsegfalva 23, 18) Győr-Pápai vám, 19) Ibrány-Nagyerdő, 20) Istállóskő, 21) Lánycsók-Bácsfa-puszta, 22) Ludas-Varjú-dűlő, 23) Méhtelek-Nádas, 24) Mosonszentmiklós, 25) Öcsöd-Kováshalom, 26) Regöly, 27) Sukoró-Tóra dűlő, 28) Hódmezővárhey-Szakálhát, 29) Szentgyörgyvölgy-Pityerdomb, 30) Tápé-Lebő, 31) Tiszavasvári-Paptelekhát, 32) Tiszaszőlős-Domaháza-puszta, 33) Tolna-Mözs, 34) Törökbálint-Dulácska, 35) Vésztő-Mágor, 36) Visonta.

3.2 History of research

It is simplest to present the history of research in two geographical parts, though we need to examine critically the possibility that perceived regional differences are in the end the product of long-established academic traditions. As the coverage of this volume moves from east to west, we will take the Alföld first.

3.2.1 The Great Hungarian Plain

Although the wider LBK phenomenon had been recognised from the later nineteenth century and early twentieth century (see, for example, Chapter 4.1 on Moravia), and thus early Hungarian archaeologists were familiar with the idea of 'spiral meander' pottery in Transdanubia and points north and west, the story of research on the ALP is generally seen as starting with the publication of Ferenc Tompa, of the National Museum in Budapest (itself an early nineteenth-century foundation), on *Die Bandkeramik in Ungarn* (1929). Its sub-title is revealing: *Die Bükker- und Theiss-Kultur*. This was a work principally on the pottery and other finds and features of the Bükk culture, from the hills on the north-eastern fringe of the Plain (see above), and now recognised as running parallel to the later stages of the LBK (Kalicz and Makkay 1977, Tab. 1), as well as on the Tisza culture, now established as the late Neolithic of broadly the first half of the fifth millennium cal BC. What was called 'proto-Bükk' at the end of the 1920s was linked to the spiral-meander pottery of Transdanubia and central Europe: what is now recognised as the LBK. Most of the Bükk and 'proto-Bükk' finds in question came from cave sites, investigation of which had begun in the later nineteenth century, but open settlements were found after the First World War (Tompa 1929, 12–15; see also Tompa 1937). Tompa's (1929, 64) chronological table is also revealing, presenting a framework in which, over a timespan estimated as going back before 3000 BC, there are already familiar culture names including Sesklo and Dimini in Greece, Tripolye and Cucuteni in southern Russia and Galicia, and older and younger *Linearkeramik* in Moravia and Bohemia, followed by *Stichbandkeramik*; Hungary is given a single column, with *ältere Linearkeramik* followed by the Bükk culture, followed by Theiss I and II, and finally by a *Steinkupferzeit* of Bodrogkeresztúr and Bell Beaker.

Other research on open sites on the Plain expanded from the 1920s to 1930s. János Banner, of the then Ferenc József University in Szeged, excavated both Körös and Linear Pottery sites around Szarvas, in the western part of the Körös river system, and recognised them as distinct from one another (1931). By 1934, he was excavating at Szakálhát near Hódmezővásárhely, close to the Tisza north of Szeged (Banner and Bálint 1935), a site which has since come to stand for the later ALP, especially in the southern part of the Plain (Kalicz and Makkay 1977). By the 1940s the relationship between Körös and Linear Pottery was still not fully understood; though it had been defined as the first Neolithic culture of the Alföld (Banner 1937, 32), the Körös culture was still seen as some kind of local variant of the *Bandkeramik* (Banner 1942, 11–14, 19). Contributions to this phase of research by others including József Csalog can also be noted (summarised by Kalicz and Makkay 1977, 11–13; see also Kutzián 1946).

In the 1950s into the 1960s, new research and rescue investigations were undertaken more extensively on open sites on the Plain, though excavations of settlements were characteristically limited in extent, and only small houses were recognised among big pit complexes and other features (Kalicz and Makkay 1977, 13, 64–72; and see below). József Korek and Pál Patay were the first to use the phrase 'Linienbandkeramik der Tiefebene' (Korek and Patay 1958), and in a further synthesis Korek (1960) listed over 100 sites; he later carried out significant excavation on the stratified entrance to the cave site of Aggtelek, north of the Bükk hills (Korek 1970). Wider international interest can be seen in the famous paper by Quitta (1960), but still with an emphasis more on Transdanubia than the Plain, and in closer detail in papers by Lichardus (1964; 1972a; 1972b); both scholars were focused on the question of LBK origins as a whole. By the later 1960s, Ottó Trogmayer, of the Szeged museum, undertook further excavations in the south, though principally on Körös sites, and worked at the chronology of the Neolithic sequence (Trogmayer 1967; 1968); even so, some contemporaneity between classical *Linienbandkeramik* and late Körös was still envisaged (Trogmayer 1972, 75; 1982).

By this time, Nándor Kalicz and János Makkay, of the nascent Institute of Archaeology of the Hungarian Academy of Sciences in Budapest, had begun their interest in the ALP (Kalicz and Makkay 1966). Kalicz had already published (1957) a short study of Neolithic to Iron Age settlement patterns in the Tiszazug, the triangle north of Csongrád formed by the confluence of the Tisza and Körös rivers, and had clearly differentiated between Körös and ALP sites. Makkay had begun excavations in Transdanubia on the LBK site of Bicske in 1965 (Makkay 1978; and see below), and on Körös sites in the vicinity of Gyomaendrőd, north-east of Szarvas in the Körös valley, in Co. Békés from 1974 (Makkay 1992). By the time of the international conference on the LBK held at Székesfehérvár in 1970 (Fitz and Makkay 1972), still rather few Mesolithic sites had been found in Hungary as a whole, including a general absence from the Plain, except at its north-eastern fringes (Dobosi 1972).[1] The distribution of the Körös culture appeared to end in the middle of the Plain, roughly from Szolnok on the Tisza in the west, and eastwards through the northern fringe of the Körös river system (Kutzián 1944). The ALP was thus by now generally seen as the first Neolithic presence in the northern part of the Plain. Kalicz and Makkay (1972a; 1977) had already defined the Szatmár group as early within the ALP, and proposed two identifiable phases. Their 1971–2 rescue excavations at Méhtelek-Nádas (Kalicz and Makkay 1976), in the far north-east of the Plain, south of the Tisza, and close to the Romanian border, confirmed that the Szatmár I phase was a local variant of the Körös culture, and that Szatmár II was the earliest phase of the ALP.

In their landmark study of the Linear Pottery culture of the Plain (published in German) Kalicz and Makkay (1977) could list some 550 sites, documenting the steady increase in knowledge. Their first concern was with the cultural and chronological position of the *Linienbandkeramik* on the Great Plain. Taking their account back to varied Mesolithic traditions in Hungary, as well as to the Körös culture of the Plain and to Transdanubia, they traced a parallel development for the LBK in the western part of the country and the ALP in the eastern, the latter emerging via the Szatmár group and the former via the proposed Transdanubian Medina type or group (Kalicz and Makkay 1972b; 1977, 115). Nonetheless, the Transdanubian LBK went on to have strong links with central Europe, while small houses in the ALP were related to a Mediterranean tradition (Kalicz and Makkay 1977, 115). The ALP represented expansion both northwards, to the northern hills, and southwards, to the region of the Maros river, and with connections to the expanding Vinča complex (in its conventional A-B phases). The later ALP developed a series of regionalised traditions, including Szakálhát in the south and Esztár in the north, along with the Bükk group in the hills (Kalicz and Makkay 1977, 83–92), and a more or less synchronous ending was envisaged, the Tisza culture succeeding Szakálhát in the south, and Herpály-Csőszhalom replacing Esztár and Bükk in the north (parallel to Vinča B2/C) (Kalicz and Makkay 1977, 117).

These narratives of group development, contact and influence were based above all on close study of pottery, but other themes were not neglected. The dominant picture was of 'flat' sites with thin occupation layers, and a variety of larger and smaller sites; even the larger ones were envisaged as probably short-lived, with occupation coming and going (Kalicz and Makkay 1977, 64). Site details were plentifully illustrated, with examples of small, simple above-ground houses (not normally longer than 5 m), often defined more by distributions of daub than by clear arrangements of postholes; pits, often large, were recurrent (Kalicz and Makkay 1977, 64–83). In the south, however, Szakálhát settlements (of which some 100 sites could be listed) included tell-like settlements, with three levels at Tápé-Lebő and Dévaványa-Sártó, and two at Battonya-Gödrösök; some houses were larger, up to 8 m in length (Kalicz and Makkay 1977, 85). At this stage of research, generally small assemblages of animal bone were available, which suggested cattle as the dominant domesticate, followed by ovicaprids and pig, with some large and small game and fish also represented; cereals were only documented by impressions in pottery, and suggested by finds of quernstones (Kalicz and Makkay 1977, 112). In addition, from the settlement record nearly 70 graves were listed. These were all in excavated settlements, and were mostly single graves. These and others are detailed below.

A number of other related settlement studies followed quite quickly. Krisztina Kosse (1979) published her doctoral thesis, with a more detailed analysis of settlement trends in the early and middle Neolithic – the Körös and LBK – than previously attempted. This proposed that the close correlation between Körös settlements and watercourses was a floodplain adaptation in a fairly dry environment, with plenty of hunting alongside cereal cultivation and the use especially of ovicaprids (Kosse 1979, 148–9). In her ALP, broadly the same settlement pattern was proposed, with some local shifts in location but the same pattern of dispersed and water-oriented occupations; cattle were seen as coming to the fore, alongside a perhaps wider range of cereals and legumes; and some incipient settlement hierarchy was seen in the size and spacing of Szakálhát settlements in the Tiszazug (Kosse 1979, 150–4).

Shortly afterwards, the first volume of the Hungarian Archaeological Topography dealing with the Plain (for Békés County) was published (Ecsedy *et al.* 1982; cf. Jankovich *et al.* 1989; 1998; for succeeding complementary volumes). Based on archival research and walk-over survey, this covered the Szeghalom region of Co. Békés, straddling the Körös river, and its Neolithic map shows abundant red and black dots for Körös and ALP sites respectively. In turn, and building directly on this more detailed picture, the area around Dévaványa was chosen by Andrew Sherratt for further mapping and selective excavation. In the event, the project was cut short, but the published results were sufficient to reinforce the picture of dispersed ALP settlement, in a longer-term pattern of settlement nucleation by the earlier fifth millennium cal BC (Sherratt 1982a; 1982b; 1983a; 1983b).

So by the 1980s a broad picture of the development and character of the ALP had been established. Other more detailed studies followed, focused especially on refining understanding of chronology and cultural development on the one hand (Raczky 1983; 1986; 1989) and on settlement trends on the other (Makkay 1982a; 1982b; F. Horváth 1989). Interim reports on the extensive 1960s–1970s excavations on late Neolithic tells also produced important data relevant to the late ALP phase, including now more radiocarbon dates and basal levels at some sites with Szakálhát material, such as Vésztő-Mágor (Kalicz and Raczky 1987; Hegedűs and Makkay 1987; cf. Hertelendi *et al.* 1995; 1998). Much of that work was concentrated on middle and southern reaches of the Tisza, and on the easternmost parts of the Plain, and much of it has yet to come to full publication. For example, small-scale work at the Szakálhát settlement of Csanytelek-Újhalastó, west of the Tisza near Szegvár (thus again well to the south), revealed one substantial but simple post-framed house, nearly 20 m long, but with minimal internal differentiation, in one area of the site, and a further three in another (Hegedűs 1985). A northern exception was the Upper Tisza Project, geared to selective survey and selective excavation, initiated by John Chapman in the 1990s. Its recent publication includes the site of Polgár-10, radiocarbon dated to the later sixth millennium, one of a series of mainly small settlements which Chapman sees as more numerous than in the early Szatmár phase, and found now in a wide range of locations from terrace edges to floodplains to interfluves (Chapman *et al.* 2010). Other important studies have been of material culture, including the intriguing Bükk and Szakálhát face pots (Goldman 1978; Raczky and Anders 2003; Virág 2009), an unusual and potentially revealing clue to the nature of Neolithic personhood: one worth noting in an account of lifeways.

Thus far, much of the emphasis of research had been on the middle and southern parts of the Tisza valley, and on eastern parts of the Great Plain; by and large settlement excavations had opened relatively limited areas; and since the synthesis of Kalicz and Makkay it was the southern Szakálhát phase (or group) which had attracted most attention within the ALP as a whole. That was all to change dramatically with new work in the far north of the Plain.

Fresh excavation at the northernmost late Neolithic tell of Polgár-Csőszhalom resumed in 1989 (Raczky and Anders 2008, with references). The important discoveries there are another story, but excavations on the adjacent settlement in advance of the construction of the M3 motorway brought a radically new scale to field investigations from the earlier 1990s onwards. Within the framework of the M3 motorway project and in the face of other road constructions (and coinciding with the efforts of the Upper Tisza Project, noted above), an intensive field survey was carried out in the Polgár region, focused on the background from which late Neolithic settlement had emerged: and thus focused on the ALP (Raczky and Anders 2009; Nagy 2005). Large ALP houses were recognised in this Polgár work from 1994 onwards (Raczky and Anders 2009, 37, 40; Domboróczki 2009, 78).

Investigations in advance of the construction of the M3 motorway along the northern edge of the Plain were also responsible for further significant discoveries in 1994–5, at Mezőkövesd and at Füzesabony and its surrounds respectively. Samples from both settlements were obtained for the Lifeways project, and both are described in more detail below. Discoveries at Füzesabony go back to 1995 (Domboróczki 1997; 2003; 2009), initially at Füzesabony-Gubakút, where area excavation revealed large, timber-framed longhouses up to 16 m long, arranged in two rows on either side of a small stream, accompanied by pits and by a number of individual graves between the houses. Pottery and radiocarbon dates suggest beginnings by at least *c.* 5500 cal BC, if not earlier (Domboróczki 2003; further radiocarbon dating by László Domboróczki and Alasdair Whittle is underway).

So in a short space of time in the earlier 1990s appropriate excavation techniques overturned many previous assumptions about ALP settlement, and placed the north of the Plain centre-stage. Indeed, these results now raise the question of the southwards extent of longhouse use in the ALP, before the known large examples in the Szakálhát phase, and keep open the possibility of there having been local roots for the idea of LBK/ALP longhouses.

Continued research since that date has reinforced the importance of these finds in the north, not only through the work already noted at Polgár, but also through wider excavations in the immediate area, such that a number of other settlements have now been recorded; these are described further below in 3.4.

3.2.2 Transdanubia

As already noted, there was an older tradition in Hungarian research in the earlier to mid-twentieth century of linking Transdanubia to the wider world of the LBK. In essence, however, detailed knowledge was very restricted up to the 1970s, and it is especially in the last 15 to 20 years that, just as in the northern part of the Great Plain, new discoveries have been made which have radically altered understanding of the development and character of the LBK in western Hungary.

The late Mesolithic in this region is still poorly documented. That hunter-gatherers were present, even if in very small numbers, has been suggested from surveys and pollen analysis in several areas to the west of Lake Balaton, including the Kerka valley (Bánffy 2004; 2008), and the exploitation and distribution of Szentgál radiolarites from their sources north of the lake have been examined in relation to the wider Mesolithic world to their north (Mateiciucová 2008a; 2010). Closer investigation of Mesolithic occupation has been achieved by detailed survey leading to excavation of what appears to be a small base camp at Regöly, near the Kapos-Koppány confluence roughly equidistant from Lake Balaton and the Danube (Bánffy *et al.* 2007; Eichmann *et al.* 2010).

In turn, Starčevo occupation has been progressively better documented, though this does not appear to have been a dense distribution. Between the first major synthesis by Nándor Kalicz (1990), based partly on his own fieldwork at Becsehely I and Becsehely II (Kalicz 1980a; 1980b) and on further excavations such as at Lánycsók-Bácsfa-puszta (Kalicz 1978), and the surveys of Eszter Bánffy (2004; 2008), the numbers of sites known have gradually increased, almost doubling (Bánffy *et al.* 2010, 39). Little detail was available until very recently and no certain houses, for example, had been documented, although burnt daub was found in pits at Lánycsók (Kalicz 1990, 39), lending superficial support to the view from Croatia that pit-dwellings were the recurrent form of structures (e.g. Minichreiter 2001). In 2006–2009, however, large-scale rescue excavations in advance of the construction of the M6 motorway, at Alsónyék-Bátaszék, south of Szekszárd in the south-eastern part of Transdanubia, and close to the right bank of the Danube, in the valley of a small tributary, revealed a very substantial Starčevo settlement, with major pit complexes and burials, and other features including post rows, shallow ditches and ovens, which strongly suggest the former existence of above-ground houses: all now the focus of a major analysis (Bánffy *et al.* 2010; Eszter Bánffy, pers. comm.).

Szentgyörgyvölgy-Pityerdomb, where components of two houses, plausibly about 13–15 m long, were found associated with a pottery assemblage retaining many Starčevo features but suggestive too of earliest Transdanubian Linear Pottery (TLP) forms and decoration, and radiocarbon dated to just after the middle of the sixth millennium cal BC. In the surveys preceding this excavation, from the 1980s into the 1990s, only a handful of earliest TLP sites had been located, in contrast to substantially more from developed phases (Bánffy 2004).

Meanwhile, other significant research on the TLP had taken place. As far back as the early 1960s, in his analysis of the earliest LBK in central Europe as a whole, Hans Quitta (1960; 1964) had already suggested Transdanubia as a likely source area, though he could point to very few specific sites. János Makkay began excavations at Bicske-Galagonyás west of Budapest in north-east Transdanubia in 1965, on a site known since the 1930s, and the work there, carried on till 1976, revealed successive phases of the TLP (with here the *Notenkopf* style succeeded by the late Zseliz style), and some possible evidence for houses in the form of daub and post rows, though the dominant concept was of some kind of pit-house (Makkay 1978; Makkay *et al.* 1996). The earliest phase could in turn be linked to that suggested around this time for Slovakia: the Bíňa phase (Pavúk 1980a; Chapter 4). At this time Kalicz and Makkay also jointly suggested a 'Medina type' as the Transdanubian equivalent of the Szatmár group, as transitional from Starčevo to TLP (Kalicz and Makkay 1972b; 1977; Kalicz 1980c), though that has since been abandoned and the pottery in question is now seen as simply including both late Starčevo and TLP material.

Abundant TLP sites were mapped by Kosse (1979), who also emphasised the difference of their settings compared to ALP sites on the Plain. By the time of the synthesis of Roland Gläser, over 600 sites could be mapped (Gläser 1993, 42, Beilage 1), the majority across Transdanubia itself but with some extending beyond the bend of the Danube and a few on the left bank east of the Danube (see also Kalicz and Kalicz-Schreiber 2001). Much of the analysis and discussion concerns pottery and its seriation; by contrast, only relatively few houses could be recorded, including from Bicske, but with more typical longhouse

Fig. 3.2. Balatonszárszó-Kis-erdei-dűlő: excavation in progress. Top: aerial photograph. Bottom: the encircling ditch being excavated.

plans documented from Győr-Pápai vám and Sukoró-Tóra dűlő (Gläser 1993, Abb. 5), along with rather irregular ditch settings at Bicske and three other sites, and a number of individual left-side crouched inhumations.

Just as on the Plain, this picture was about to be radically changed by large-scale investigations in advance of motorway construction. First, some 20 typical longhouses, within a settlement containing at least 500 pits, were excavated on the line of the M1 motorway at Mosonszentmiklós north-west of Győr in 1993–4 (Egry 1997; 2003; Bánffy 2004, 68). Then, a major TLP settlement appeared on the line of the M7 motorway south of Lake Balaton at Balatonszárszó-Kis-erdei-dűlő, and was excavated in 2001–2003 and again in 2006 (summarised in Marton and Oross 2009; 2012; Oross *et al.* 2010; Fig. 3.2). Other similar discoveries are noted below, though none yet quite on the scale of Balatonszárszó-Kis-erdei-dűlő.

Further south, in the south-east of Transdanubia, TLP house plans have also been found in the major motorway excavations at Alsónyék-Bátaszék, and similar house plans have recently been recognised by Krisztián Oross at Tolna-Mözs from rescue excavations in advance of road construction, with pottery with many Vinča traits alongside TLP ones. This south-eastern area, including the Danube-Tisza interfluves, in general emerges as one that now needs close attention in its own right, with significant patterning between Körös and Starčevo settlements, and probably strong links between the southern TLP and the Vinča cultures (Kalicz 1994; Bánffy 2006; Bánffy and Oross 2009; 2010; Oross and Bánffy 2009; Marton and Oross 2012).

3.3 Mesolithic-Neolithic transitions and the earliest Neolithics

It can be no surprise that such a varied research history has thrown up many models for the Neolithisation of both the Great Hungarian Plain and Transdanubia. To repeat, the ALP and the TLP are not the first manifestation of Neolithic things and practices in Hungary, and both complex and extended processes can be suggested. The choice of interpretations of these possibilities is not just of historical interest, but may condition our view from the outset of this study as to whether emergent new lifeways were more or less uniform from the beginning, or, from the very varied conditions of their creation, contained many diverse strands.

The weight of opinion over the years has favoured the Körös culture as essentially an immigrant population, the northernmost extension of the Neolithic colonisation of Greece and the Balkans, though with varying allowance for contributions from the indigenous population (e.g. Raczky 1988; Starnini 2001; Kozłowski and Nowak 2010). Competing arguments (recently reviewed by Kozłowski and Raczky 2010, and Raczky *et al.* 2010) set new practices, including cultivation and animal husbandry, house building and the manufacture of fine pottery, and a general, but not complete, absence of visible Mesolithic population, against probable continuities in lithic production (Mateiciucová 2007; 2008a) and in knowledge of the landscape (Whittle 2007). The views of Ottó Trogmayer are just one example of varying interpretation. Based on his investigations around Szeged, and earlier work by Banner, which appeared to show a very diverse subsistence base, and also integrating the available skeletal evidence, he was open to seeing the acculturation and adaptations of a local population (1968; 1969). That kind of stance was also followed in wider consideration of the site of Ecsegfalva 23, though the evidence for the subsistence base had meanwhile changed (Whittle 2007).

Earlier work had appeared to establish a more or less clear northern limit to the distribution of the Körös culture, as noted above, and in recent years an influential model of some kind of climatic and ecological barrier has sought to explain this apparent pause in the extension of the Neolithic (Kertész and Sümegi 2001; cf. Halstead 1989). A variation on this, in the form of some kind of mental barrier, has recently been proposed (Raczky *et al.* 2010), but the latest evidence for the distribution of the Körös culture may cause a reformulation of these notions, as new fieldwork has located Körös settlements much further up the Tisza

Table 3.1. Eastern Hungary: the body positions and orientations of ALP burials (Lifeways Database).

	Left-crouched	Right-crouched	Crouched	Supine	Prone	Irregular	Total
E–W	30	3	4	1	0	0	38
SE–NW	55	2	1	0	1	0	59
S–N	10	0	1	0	1	0	12
SW–NE	2	0	0	0	0	0	2
W–E	1	1	1	0	0	0	3
NW–SE	0	2	0	0	0	0	2
N–S	2	0	0	0	0	0	2
NE–SW	2	0	0	0	1	0	3
Total	102	8	7	1	3	0	121

Table 3.2. Western Hungary: the body positions and orientations of LBK burials (Lifeways Database).

	Left-crouched	Right-crouched	Supine	Total
E–W	10	0	0	10
SE–NW	2	0	0	2
S–N	4	2	0	6
SW–NE	0	1	0	1
W–E	0	0	0	0
NW–SE	1	2	0	3
N–S	6	3	1	10
NE–SW	0	4	0	4
Total	23	12	1	36

valley than previously known, and radiocarbon dates from Tiszaszőlős-Domaháza-puszta and Ibrány (Domboróczki 2010a; 2010b; Domboróczki and Raczky 2010) appear to conform to an ongoing gradual spread of the Körös culture (cf. Whittle *et al.* 2002), towards the northern edge of the Plain.

Not all Körös settlements need be identical. The faunal assemblage from the northernmost site of Ibrány-Nagyerdő indicates far more hunting than in other sites to the south, though with cereal cultivation also present (Kovács *et al.* 2010; Gyulai 2010). Indeed, the Ecsegfalva project was set up partly on the basis of looking for variation in the character of Körös settlements. In the event, however, the small-scale but careful excavations revealed evidence strongly suggestive of permanent houses, and a dominant role for sheep/goat herding and cereal cultivation; previous suggestions of a major role for hunting, fishing and collecting could be shown to be based on misleading small samples (Bogaard *et al.* 2007a; Bartosiewicz 2007). Dietary isotope values for both Körös and Starčevo populations in northern Serbia appear quite similar (Whittle *et al.* 2002).

To explain the emergence of the ALP, Kalicz and Makkay (1977) looked back to what they saw as a varied Mesolithic background (also seen as an important factor by Lichardus (1972a; 1972b)), while considering what they believed were the smaller houses of the Plain as related to Mediterranean traditions. Their study established a basic contemporaneity for ALP and TLP, with pottery in Transdanubia ultimately derived from Körös traditions (Kalicz and Makkay 1977, 115), but they never fully explained the relationship of Plain and Transdanubia (at a stage in research when Starčevo sites in Transdanubia were yet to be discovered). In a later summary, Kalicz continued to refer to 'the independent Alföld-Linear Pottery Culture' (Kalicz and Koós 2001, 75). Perhaps it is now time to question this conception. Accepting the general claim that the ALP spread southwards towards the Vinča complex (Kalicz and Makkay 1977), one alternative might be to see developments in the north of the Plain as initially more closely interwoven with and spilling over from processes in Transdanubia, with a local mixture of late Mesolithic (documented recently by László Domboróczki and Róbert Kertész at the very north of the plain at Tarnaörs, as well as a while ago in the Jászság north of the Tisza (Kertész 1996)) and late Körös communities, as well as people and practices from Transdanubia, thus shifting the focus from a purely local explanation of the Szatmár group (and the individual site of Méhtelek: Kalicz and Makkay 1976). However, that kind of view is very controversial (Raczky *et al.* 2010, 162). Hard proof of any local mixture, and for the closing of a potentially long chronological gap between the local Mesolithic and the earliest Neolithic is elusive (Kozłowski 2005; but see also Mateiciucová 2007).

Subsequently, including in the Szakálhát phase, the middle and southern parts of the Plain might be seen as affiliated or related as much to the Vinča culture as to the main orbit of the LBK (cf. Kaczanowska *et al.* 2010, fig. 5; Kozłowski and Nowak 2010, fig. 18; Bánffy and Oross 2009).

That is all for the future, and large-scale excavations are now needed in that middle and southern part of the Plain. For the purposes of the Lifeways project, we can note that Mezőkövesd and early site phases at Füzesabony and Polgár-Ferenci-hát belong to an early stage of the ALP in the north of the Plain. At Mezőkövesd-Mocsolyás, a settlement some 200 m or more in diameter was found on a slight elevation, with at least three houses belonging to the Szatmár or earliest ALP phase, as well as perhaps to a slightly more developed phase, on the basis of radiocarbon dates. Rather as in the Körös culture, the rectangular structures were principally defined by spreads of burnt daub. In addition a number of individual graves (Chapter 3.7.1) were found to one side of the house group (Kalicz and Koós 1997a; 1997b; 2001).

In Transdanubia, the dominant older view has again been of immigrant Neolithic populations from the south, bringing first the Starčevo culture to the area (Kalicz 1990), and in due course the LBK culture to points north. A recent variant of this tradition is seen in the model of leapfrogging by Starčevo communities from northern Croatia to found the earliest stage of the LBK settlement at Brunn-Wolfholz on the edge of Vienna (Stadler and Kotova 2010). This may all change when new lines of research are completed. The Mesolithic presence, as at Regöly, noted above, is becoming better documented, and aDNA analysis of human remains is underway for Alsónyék-Bátaszék (Eszter Bánffy and Kurt Alt, pers. comm.). It is interesting to note, however, that in this area, as in others covered by the Lifeways project, there has been a persistent interest in the possible role of indigenous populations in the observed transformations. Roland Gläser, for example (1993, 511–12), took up earlier ideas on this theme (e.g. Lichardus 1972a; Kalicz 1980d; Pavúk 1980a) to propose that an interaction between Transdanubian late Mesolithic and Starčevo communities, in the face of some kind of resource availability crisis in the closed woodland conditions of the sixth millennium, led to the formation and rapid spread of the TLP.

Such possibilities have now been much better documented by the research at Szentgyörgyvölgy-Pityerdomb, on the basis of which Eszter Bánffy (2004, 356) has proposed that 'western Transdanubia and the Balaton region was a frontier, a contact zone between the indigenous Mesolithic population (of whom little is known) and the Balkanic Starčevo groups arriving from the south and south-east... the occupants of Pityerdomb and the other Linear Pottery settlements in the Kerka valley no doubt included members of forager groups who inhabited the mountain valleys'. This kind of model has since been further elaborated (Bánffy 2006; 2008; 2013; Bánffy and Oross 2009; 2010; Bánffy *et al.* 2007; Oross and Bánffy 2009). In essence, a series of steps for Neolithisation are proposed, rather than a single process of colonisation taking place as a 'single-event scenario' (Oross and Bánffy 2009, 175). Thus the first, 'earliest' formation of the LBK culture is attributed to Mesolithic and Starčevo interaction (from 'migrant late Starčevo groups') over a period of 4–5 generations, followed by initial, earlier LBK settlement, spread across the whole of Transdanubia but in low density and with mainly small settlements (such as the first phases of Bicske and Balatonszárszó-Kis-erdei-dűlő, though the discovery of Tolna-Mözs now begins to alter that picture), and perhaps lasting a century or more from the 55th into the 54th centuries cal BC. Only in the third 'wave' of Neolithisation did 'an economy based exclusively on farming' appear, with the classical or 'late' LBK of Transdanubia (with *Notenkopf* pottery to the north, and Keszthely to the south), represented in more numerous settlements, some of them becoming extremely large, like Balatonszárszó-Kis-erdei-dűlő as already seen, and occupying loess plateaus above and distinct from the lower-lying and marshier settings characteristic of the initial Neolithic phases. Radiocarbon dating indicates that this final transformation took place in the 53rd century cal BC. Explicit explanations of the nature of this third transition remain scarce; there seems no good reason in the light of current evidence to invoke fresh population from the south, though interaction with the Vinča culture need not be discounted. The importance of the Danube corridor itself has been recently restated (Bánffy and Oross 2010), and the distinct Körös and Starčevo populations there, and then the emerging differentiation of the area from both Transdanubia as a whole and the Great Plain, serve again to underline the potential for diversity in LBK lifeways.

3.4 The developed ALP and TLP

In describing the history of research, the dramatic increase in numbers of identified house plans in both the developed ALP of the north of the Great Plain and the TLP (the latter defined as its classical or 'late' phase) has been emphasised. Now, wider features of the emergent pattern of settlement can be noted. Since this project has sampled sites from the north of the Plain, this section will not refer again much to Szakálhát settlement in the south.

In the research focused on ALP occupation of the Polgár alluvial island within the floodplain of the upper Tisza, an area of some 66–70 km^2, excavations have now been carried out at numerous locations, including Polgár-Ferenci-hát, Polgár-Kenderföldek, Polgár-Kengyel-köz, Polgár-Király-érpart and Polgár-Nagy Kasziba (Raczky and Anders 2009; Nagy 2005). Four main phases of ALP development have been established, and radiocarbon dates obtained from several of the sites (Raczky and Anders 2009). Relatively small and dispersed sites are suggested in ALP I, close to terrace edges. The comparable site at Mezőkövesd-Mocsolyás, a little further west, has been noted above. In ALP II–III more and larger sites have been recorded, some further from water than previously. In ALP IV fewer but significantly larger sites were found, confirming the trend to nucleation by the late ALP suggested by both Sherratt and Makkay. Some of the most detailed work has been carried out at Polgár-Ferenci-hát, represented in all four phases, especially ALP IV.

In the area around Füzesabony-Gubakút, ALP settlements appear to be spaced at intervals of 1–2 km along the two small stream valleys of the area (coalescing as the Laskó and draining into the Tisza over 20 km to the south), and to be of varying size and density, but with layout in rows recurrent (Domboróczki 2009, fig. 16). Similar finds have been made a little to the east at Mezőszemere-Kismari-fenék, and in the catchment of the Tarna some 20 km to the west at Ludas-Varjú-dűlő, and in the same area but belonging to the late ALP, at Kompolt-Kígyósér, Visonta and Adács-Mancsos-rét (Domboróczki 2009, fig. 2). The latest find has come at Apc, a little further west again in the stream valley of the Zagyva, where again substantial timber-framed longhouses have been revealed by László Domboróczki, but with Linear pottery like that of Transdanubia (cf. Virág 2009). Possible impacts on woodland cover a little further north, in the hills, can also be noted (Gardner 1999).

In Transdanubia, the Balatonszárszó-Kis-erdei-dűlő site (Oross 2004; Marton and Oross 2009; Oross *et al.* 2010) lies on a low plateau to the south of the lake and this setting alone appears to differentiate it (and others like it) from the water-edge or marshy locations of Starčevo and earliest LBK occupations (Bánffy and Oross 2010). Fifty-nine substantial post-framed longhouses were revealed, variously defined by flanking ditches and post rows, along with extensive pits, the focus of occupation apparently drifting with time across the settlement area, from three widely spaced examples of early Bicske-Bíňa date, to tighter concentrations, probably arranged in rows, in the early Keszthely (belonging already to the developed LBK, equivalent to *Notenkopf* further north), classical Keszthely and Keszthely/Zseliz phases (Marton and Oross 2009, 55–7, fig. 2). An enclosure ditch belongs to the early Keszthely phase. There are also a number of individual burials, in graves and settlement pits. Further description is given below (Chapter 3.10.1), as samples were processed from the site for the Lifeways project.

Just a few kilometres from it, Balatonszemes-Szemesi-berek, also on the line of the M7, has ten reconstructable longhouses, though these were not initially recognised as such during the rescue excavations, probably of the same phase as the beginning of the developed part of Balatonszárszó (Marton and Oross 2009, 57, fig. 3). A third settlement has also been located between these two, at Balatonszemes-Bagódomb, with occupation in both the early LBK Bicske-Bíňa phase (Oross and Bánffy 2009) and the Keszthely or developed phase (Marton and Oross 2009, 58), strongly suggesting substantial growth in site numbers. Finds in and around Budapest can be noted, also with house plans, though in many cases not with areas opened on the scale of the motorway work, including at Dunakeszi-Székesdűlő, Törökbálint-Dulácska and Budapest-Kőérberek-Tóváros lakópark (L. Horváth 2002; 2004; Marton and Oross 2009, 54–5; Virág 2009, fig. 1).

With so many recent projects, especially those connected to road construction, still under post-excavation analysis, it is premature to give a fully rounded picture of either ALP or TLP subsistence, but some major trends seem clear. We can note that better recovery at Ecsegfalva 23 changed the previous general impression of very diverse Körös subsistence to a pattern focused on cereal cultivation, probably in intensive garden plots, and animal husbandry, especially of sheep/goats (Bogaard *et al.* 2007a; Bartosiewicz 2007); animal bones from one big pit feature at the new northerly site of Ibrány-Nagyerdő suggest a greater reliance on wild game, though there are also cereal remains (Domboróczki and Raczky 2010; Kovács *et al.* 2010; Gyulai 2010). A big new Starčevo culture (and LBK) sample awaits analysis from Alsónyék-Bátaszék (Bánffy *et al.* 2010). A range of cereals were recovered from Szentgyörgyvölgy-Pityerdomb, but animal bone was not preserved (Bánffy 2004, 313). The scattered evidence previously available for the ALP suggests the continuation of cereal cultivation, though more detailed analysis is awaited, and also strongly indicates a shift from sheep/goats to cattle as the dominant domesticate, and perhaps less hunting (Kalicz and Makkay 1977; Kosse 1979, 150–1; Bartosiewicz 2005). The analysis of new datasets from ALP sites in the north of the Plain, and from established TLP sites in Transdanubia is ongoing, but there is good reason at this stage to suppose that the picture of garden cultivation of cereals and the herding of cattle, with pigs and sheep/goats in supporting or complementary roles (cf. Marciniak 2005), will be confirmed as the major features of Linear Pottery subsistence in Hungary.

3.5 Burial practice and regional networks

Again it is worth briefly noting the Körös and Starčevo background. The evidence is scattered and patchy, but suggests the recurrent practice of mainly single burials, of all ages and both sexes, usually in quite small numbers, within settlements or settlement zones; it is possible, though the sample is small, that there were more female than male burials in the Körös culture (Trogmayer 1969; Chapman 1994; Whittle 2005; Paluch 2007). As with the LBK, the most frequent body position noted in a recent study is left-crouched (29%), closely followed by right-crouched (15%), with prone and supine positions occurring very rarely (the percentages represent total graves, rather than only the graves with sufficient preservation to identify body position; Paluch 2007, 247). Similarly, orientation practices of the LBK seem to have their origins in Körös practices, as east–west orientations dominate (*contra* Paluch 2007, 253), though perhaps other orientations are more equally represented than in the LBK. Another interesting parallel between LBK and Körös funerary rites is the use of ochre in graves, but otherwise, in comparison to later periods, Körös burials contain very few grave goods with only 11 furnished graves known from a total of 130 (Paluch 2007, 253). Burnt or cremated remains are also attested from settlement pits (Raczky 1988; Makkay 1992, 133).

The biggest sample of Starčevo burials so far comes from the exciting new work at Alsónyék-Bátaszék, where some 20 burials have been recovered. The mortuary rite appears varied, with recurrent contracted inhumations lying on either the right or left side of the body; some are described as 'in an extreme, twisted position' (Bánffy *et al.* 2010, 42). The burials appear to be scattered across the large settlement area, some in shallow pits and connected to former ovens (Bánffy *et al.* 2010, 42–3, fig. 10). Incomplete remains are also known, and one large pit complex contained several skulls and other bones. Therefore, while Körös and Starčevo funerary rites seem to have inspired some LBK burial rituals and practices, they are thought more varied than we find in the LBK (but see below) and it is very likely that inhumation represented just one of many possibilities for dealing with the deceased.

In contrast, a more uniform mortuary rite appears to have emerged with the Linear Pottery culture. Already in the 1970s, Kalicz and Makkay (1977) could list nearly 70 graves from their survey of the ALP settlement record, predominantly in central and southern parts of the Plain. These were all in excavated settlements, and, as earlier, were mostly single graves, though with small groups in a few instances, the largest being 13 burials at Tiszavasvári-Paptelekhát, quite close to the Tisza in the northern part of the Plain. These were still single inhumations, of both adults and children, but now predominantly in crouched positions on their left side, and variously oriented (as was the case at Alsónyék), but chiefly south-east–north-west, with head to the south-east facing west (Tables 3.1–2). A strikingly similar pattern will be seen across the other regions covered in this volume. Only about a third of burials appeared to receive grave goods (Kalicz and Makkay 1977), but the numbers of furnished graves have risen with the discovery of Füzesabony, Mezőkövesd and Polgár, and now about 45% of graves have some form of grave good (see also below). Pots, in very limited numbers, and *Spondylus* (particularly at Füzesabony and Mezőkövesd: see below) were the most common grave goods; one grave had a stone axe (Kalicz and Makkay 1977; Lifeways Database). Some of the burials appeared to be incomplete, and some human remains were also found in settlement contexts: again presaging what will be seen to be widespread practices. Burnt bones from the northern cave of Istállóskő raised the question of ritual cannibalism. Some Szakálhát burials were also noted, including 11 at Dévaványa-Sártó (Kalicz and Makkay 1977, 73–83).

In neither part of Hungary have distinctively separate cemeteries been found, unlike in all the other regions covered in this volume, very possibly simply because excavations have so far not looked in the appropriate offsite locations; the other possibility is to consider a regional variation in which burial grounds in Transdanubia were closely linked to old settlement space, perhaps going back to the traditions of the Starčevo culture.

The burials at Mezőkövesd were spread in a wide arc around the houses, with two in the area of the structures (Kalicz and Koós 1997a; 1997b; 2001; and see below: 3.7.1), seemingly suggesting an intermediate practice between settlement and cemetery burials. With 113 burials, Polgár is the biggest grouping of Linear Pottery graves found in Hungary so far, and is more redolent of the large LBK cemeteries found further west, but with the graves interspersed between the structures and features of the settlement.

In Transdanubia, a modest number of single inhumations crouched on their left sides were already known from a scatter of TLP sites before the beginning of motorway-related investigations (Gläser 1993, 76). Once again, however, it is the much larger excavations which have brought significant new discoveries. The prime example are the 43 burials found at Balatonszárszó-Kis-erdei-dűlő, mostly in the southern area of the site where houses of the established TLP phase were concentrated (Marton and Oross 2009; Oross and Marton 2012; Chapter 3.10.1). These were found both as individual graves, and also in varying deposits in pits; there is no obvious connection with particular houses. Grave goods are quite rare, but include pots, items made from *Spondylus*, blades and bone artefacts. Eighteen burials have been radiocarbon dated (along with a large number of other samples), and the results suggest, among other things, a late cluster in an area of old longhouses: perhaps the equivalent of a small separate cemetery in other regions.

More details will emerge in due course about southern TLP burials at the settlement of Tolna-Mözs (Eszter Bánffy, pers. comm.).

Finally, this had been a connected world since the Körös and Starčevo phases, when the movement of lithics including obsidian and limnoquartzites from sources to the north of the Plain, flint from the south, and radiolarite from the Szentgál source north of Lake Balaton, is particularly well documented (Mateiciucová 2007; 2008a; Bánffy 2004). Starčevo pottery in Transdanubia may well imply a network of connections of some kind to the south (Bánffy 2004; Stadler and Kotova 2010), but it is also worth noting the separations between Körös and Starčevo communities, best seen in their mutually separate distributions on either side of the Danube in southern Hungary (Kalicz 1990; 2011; Bánffy 2008; Bánffy and Oross 2010). The movement of lithics continued if not intensified in the Linear Pottery phase (Mateiciucová 2008a, 161), though it is worth noting that few classic adzes appear to have been found on Hungarian sites. A wide range of 'contact' finds of pottery have been documented between Transdanubia and the Plain, and to some extent between southern Hungary and the Vinča culture (e.g. Kalicz and Makkay 1977, 116; Gläser 1993, 336–72), but whether these are actual imports or shared motifs and decorative schemes still perhaps needs further investigation. The Linear Pottery phase also appears to be when the long-distance distribution of *Spondylus* took off, perhaps from sources on the east side of the northern Adriatic (Zvelebil and Pettitt 2008; Zvelebil *et al.* 2010), appearing from the Szatmár phase onwards on the northern part of the Plain (Siklósi and Csengeri 2011), as already noted at Mezőkövesd (Kalicz and Koós 2001).

3.6 Sites sampled

Mezőkövesd-Mocsolyás, Füzesabony-Gubakút and Polgár-Ferenci-hát on the northern part of the Great Plain, and Balatonszárszó-Kis-erdei-dűlő in Transdanubia, have been the sites in Hungary sampled for the Lifeways project.

3.7 Mezőkövesd-Mocsolyás

3.7.1 Introduction

Mezőkövesd-Mocsolyás was found during the large-scale stripping that took place in advance of motorway construction (Kalicz and Koós 2001, 46). The site is situated north of the Tisza, not far from the modern town of Mezőkövesd, and lies on the north-western edge of the known ALP distribution (Kalicz and Koós 2001, 47; Fig. 3.1). During the Neolithic, the site would have been on a low-lying hill, which stood slightly proud of the surrounding marshy areas (Kalicz and Koós 1997a, 33; 2001, 46). The site lies on an area of loess (sometimes called chernozem-brown soils; Kosse 1979, 98) some 20 km north of the Tisza river and a similar distance south from the Bükk mountains. The site is only approximately 10 km north-east of Füzesabony.

The 25 graves and a small area of settlement were found across an area about 200 by 230 m (Kalicz and Koós 1997a, 33; Fig. 3.3). In the centre of the site the burnt remains from three houses were uncovered alongside a well that unfortunately could not be excavated (Kalicz and Koós 1997a, 33; 2001, 46). Despite the lack of postholes and preserved floors, a small segment of preserved wall and the distribution of finds showed rectangular structures, approximately 9 by 12 m and 7 by 12 m (Kalicz and Koós 1997a, 33), with a linear arrangement similar to that found at Füzesabony-Gubakút (Chapter 3.8; Domboróczki 1997). The pottery from the site strongly suggests that occupation began during the formative or Szatmár phase, as the characteristic early Szatmár ceramic decoration of 'pearl-pattern' is present (Kalicz and Koós 2001, 74). Although 25 samples of animal bones and charcoal were radiocarbon dated, only 12 gave dates within the span of the ALP, covering the second half of the sixth millennium cal BC (Kalicz and Koós 2001, 74). The burials were not dated.

However, like many early ALP sites, Mezőkövesd shares many features with the late phase of the Körös culture, such as the burning of the houses (Kalicz and Koós 1997a, 33; Domboróczki 2010a, 160). The firing of the houses had been so severe that obsidian cores and grinding stones had split (Kalicz and Koós 1997a, 33). The site also produced high numbers of small clay figurines with triangular heads, over 30 in total, which appear mostly female. Many had traces of ochre on them, perhaps analogous to the spreads of ochre often found on the heads of the skeleton in LBK graves (Chapter 1.3.5 and Chapters 4–8). Other zoomorphic figurines echoed the 'bull' or 'centaur-shaped' clay object found in a grave at Polgár-Ferenci-hát (Chapter 3.9.1 below). Flat bone, shouldered spoon-like objects were

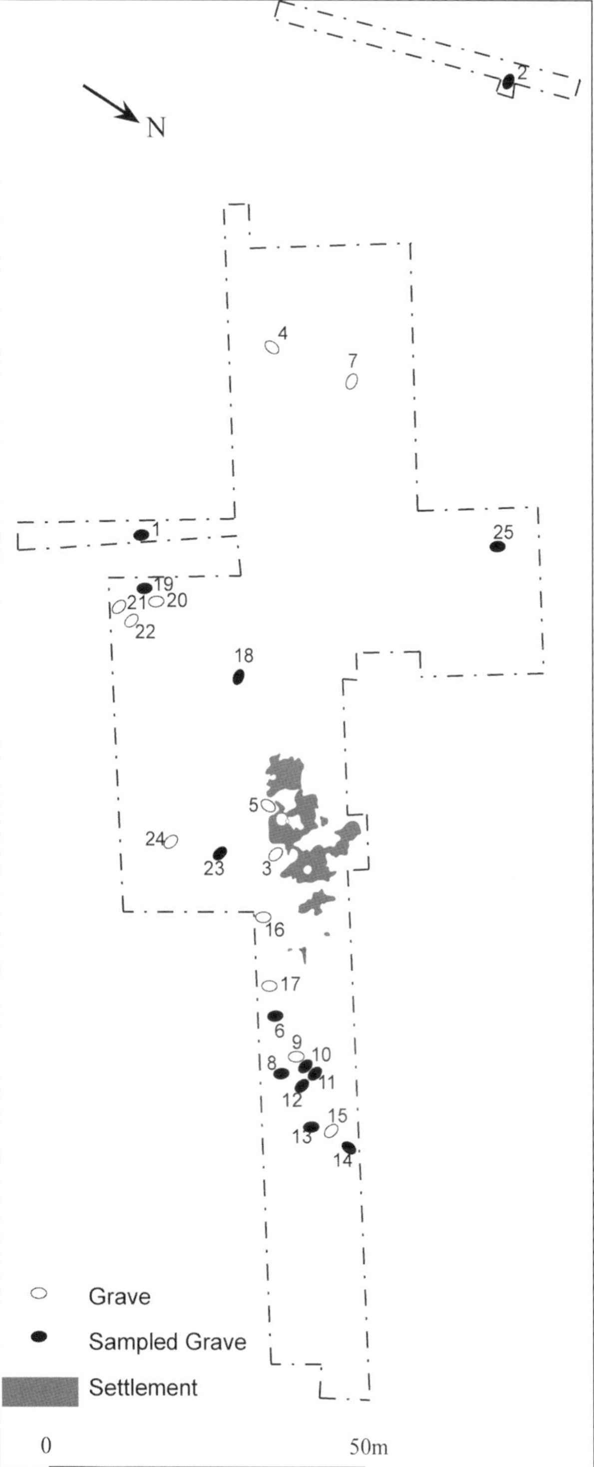

Fig. 3.3. Mezőkövesd-Mocsolyás: plan. After Kalicz and Koós (2001, 48).

also unusually numerous at the site (Kalicz and Koós 1997a, 33) and although these objects have parallels in the Körös culture, those found at Mezőkövesd are perhaps more similar to those found in the Vinča culture (Kalicz and Koós 2001, 74).

The 25 burials were found surrounding the settlement area, with only two burials (3, a neonate, and 5, described as a young child, though possibly also grave 16) associated

Table 3.3. Mezőkövesd-Mocsolyás: the isotope, osteological and archaeological data. Age and sex information from Kalicz and Koós (2001). See Chapter 2 for further definition of ages. Key for body position: LC – Left-crouched; RC – Right-crouched; C – Crouched, direction unknown; CB – Crouched on back; CF – Crouched on front; S – Supine; P – Prone; I – Irregular. Key for grave goods (number of items in brackets): U. – Unfurnished; F. – Fill only (all items listed after an F. were in the fill of the grave rather than at the level of the skeleton); Pol. – Polished stone; Cer. – Ceramics; Shd. – Sherds; Spon. – Spondylus; *She. – Other Shell; Och. – Ochre; Lit. – Chipped stone; Bon – Worked bone; Grd. – Grinding stone.*

Burial	Tooth	Sex	Age (yrs)	$^{87}Sr/^{86}Sr$	Sr ppm	$\delta^{13}C$ ‰	$\delta^{15}N$ ‰	Orient.	Body position	Grave goods
1	M1 M3	-	Adult	0.70962 0.70960	133 100	-	-	S–N	LC	U.
2	M2	M?	Adult	0.70971	177	−19.7	11.3	S–N	LC	Ochre (on skull)
3	-	-	Neonate	-	-	-	-	W–E	RC	U.
4	-	-	Adult	-	-	-	-	-	-	U.
5	-	-	Child	-	-	-	-	-	-	U.
6	M1	-	Adult	0.70984	110	−19.6	10	SE–NW	LC	Spon.(27 beads, 7 cylinder beads)
7	-	-	Adult	-	-	-	-	SE–NW	-	Cer.(1 star-shaped bead, 2 conical beads)
8	M3	M?	Adult	0.70973	183	-	-	SE–NW	LC	Spon.(5 beads)
9	-	-	Child	-	-	-	-	SE–NW	LC	Spon.(5 beads)
10	M1	-	Child	0.71012	128	-	-	E–W	LC	Spon.(8 beads, fragment of armring)
11	M3	M?	Adult	0.70965	139	-	-	SE–NW	LC	Cer.(1 miniature bowl)
12	M2	F?	Adult	0.70999	77	-	-	SE–NW	LC	Spon.(1 bead)
13	M1	M?	Adult	0.71032	207	-	-	SE–NW	LC	U.
14	M1	-	Child/Juv.	0.70954	77	-	-	SE–NW	LC	Spon.(10 beads)
15	-	-	Child	-	-	-	-	W–E	LC	U.
16	-	F?	Adult	-	-	-	-	SE–NW	LC	Spon.(4 beads)
17	-	F?	Adult	-	-	-	-	SE–NW	LC	Spon.(1 armring, 13 beads)
18	M1	F?	Adult	0.71157	83	−19.7	11.1	NW–SE	RC	U.
19	M3	F?	Adult	0.70953	159	-	-	SE–NW	LC	U.
20	-	-	Adult	-	-	-	-	SE–NW	LC	Cer.(1 miniature bowl)
21a	-	-	Adult	-	-	−19.7	10.1	-	LC	Cer.(1 miniature bowl), Spon.(1 bead)
21b	-	-	Neonate	-	-	-	-	-	-	U.
22	-	-	-	-	-	−19.8	10.4	E–W	LC	U.
23	M2	F?	Adult	0.70938	74	-	-	E–W	LC	U.
24	-	-	Child	-	-	-	-	E–W	RC	Spon.(5 beads), Lump of haematite?
25	M3	M?	Adult	0.70951	87	-	-	SE–NW	LC	U.

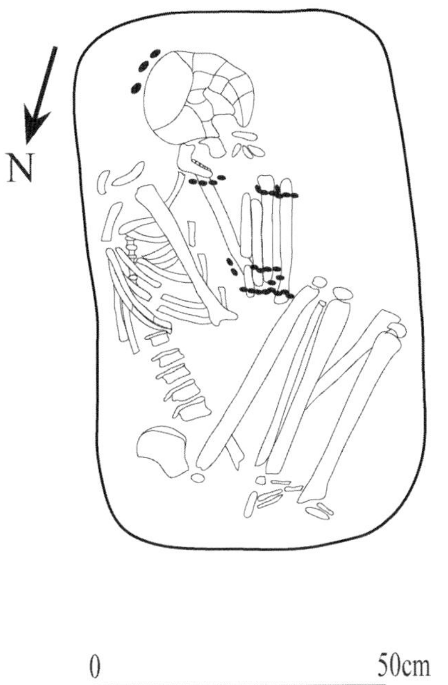

Fig. 3.4. Mezőkövesd-Mocsolyás: burial 6 (unsexed adult). After Kalicz and Koós (2001, 49).

with the houses themselves, though even these burials are on the edge of the settlement area (Kalicz and Koós 2001, 48, 60). The majority of the burials are found to the north-east of the site, though graves are also found to the south and west of the site, with grave 2 over 100 m to the west of the settlement area (Fig. 3.3). In this way the site contrasts with the other sites in this region where graves are intermingled with the settlement and its rubbish pits.

The graves appear to form clusters within the site. Kalicz and Koós (2001, 60) identify graves 8, 9, 10, 11 and 12 as one such cluster (with 13, 14 and 15, and 6 and 17, possibly also part of this cluster). It is in these graves, which lie in the north-eastern part of the site, that most of the grave goods are concentrated (Table 3.3). At the southernmost extent of the site, another group of four graves (19, 20, 21 and 22) may also form another cluster (Kalicz and Koós 2001, 60). The dominant orientation is SE–NW, with 12 of the burials placed in this direction (rising to 16 out of 20 if E–W is included). Crouched on the left side is the most frequent body position and only three burials deviate from this, being found crouched on their right-hand sides. On the whole, burials at this site are very tightly crouched (Fig. 3.4). Two of the right-crouched burials are also found in unusual orientations (W–E – only two out of 20 burials have this orientation – and NW–SE – the only example of this orientation at the site). Two burials (graves 1 and 2) have a S–N orientation; both are left-crouched. *Spondylus* beads and ceramics dominate the grave good assemblage (Kalicz and Koós 2001, 60).

3.7.2 Carbon and nitrogen analyis

Only five individuals were available for sampling, four of whom were adults, with one skeleton where the sex and age could not be determined (Fig. 3.5; Table 3.4). The mean values for the site were −19.7‰ for δ^{13}C and 10.6‰ for δ^{15}N. The animal bone assemblages from Füzesabony-Gubakút are available for comparison.

The values are tightly clustered and similar to others in the region (Chapter 3.8.3 and 3.9.3). Conclusions here are only preliminary, due to the low sample size and lack of variability, but some comments can be made. Those burials with low δ^{15}N values are accompanied by grave goods of *Spondylus*, whilst the highest δ^{15}N value of 11.3 ‰ comes from an adult, possibly male, burial, where ochre covered the skull.

3.7.3 Strontium analysis

Thirteen individuals were sampled for strontium analysis: 11 adults (five males, four females, two unknown) and two juveniles (Fig. 3.5; Table 3.5). We sampled an M1 molar and an M3 molar from grave 1, but the values were very similar for both teeth (M1=0.70962; M3=0.70960), suggesting the individual had been born and lived locally.

As Mezőkövesd lies on loess soils, the local strontium range for the vicinity is likely to fall between 0.708 and 0.710 (Bentley *et al.* 2003). The values of the community at the site may also have been influenced by the surrounding water and geologies offering a range of different values. The Tisza river ranges from 0.7089 to 0.7096 (Price *et al.* 2004) and the geology of the higher ground to the north and west of the site would have provided a very varied range of strontium values, from values less radiogenic than the loess of about 0.7077 (young volcanic rocks; Tokaj Mountains, 50 km to the north-west of the site) to those higher, about 0.71137, due to the presence of crystalline basalts (Bükk Mountains, *c.* 20 km north of the site; Seghedi *et al.* 2004; Giblin 2011). The average for the site is 0.70986±0.00055, which falls within the upper range for loess soils.

At Mezőkövesd, the mean ^{87}Sr/^{86}Sr among identified females (n=4) is 0.71012±0.00010, and among identified males (n=5) it is 0.70978±0.00031, which is a relatively large difference in comparison to other sites sampled for this project. However, the three females other than grave 18 yield ^{87}Sr/^{86}Sr ratios similar to the male mean. This is a small sample, of course, but it is interesting to note that the male Sr concentration mean (157, n=5) was higher than the female Sr concentration mean (98, n=4).

Figure 3.6 shows the strontium results graphed against 1/Sr concentration ppm. This shows that there is one outlier (grave 18) and that the rest of the individuals sampled fall into a tight cluster. The individual in grave 18 is also interesting archaeologically. This possibly female adult was not accompanied by any grave goods, but was placed in an unusual orientation of NW–SE, thus opposite to the majority of the burials at the site, as well as in a right-crouched position. There were no correlations with the stable isotope data.

3.7.4 Site summary and discussion

Mezőkövesd suggests that preferences for the orientations

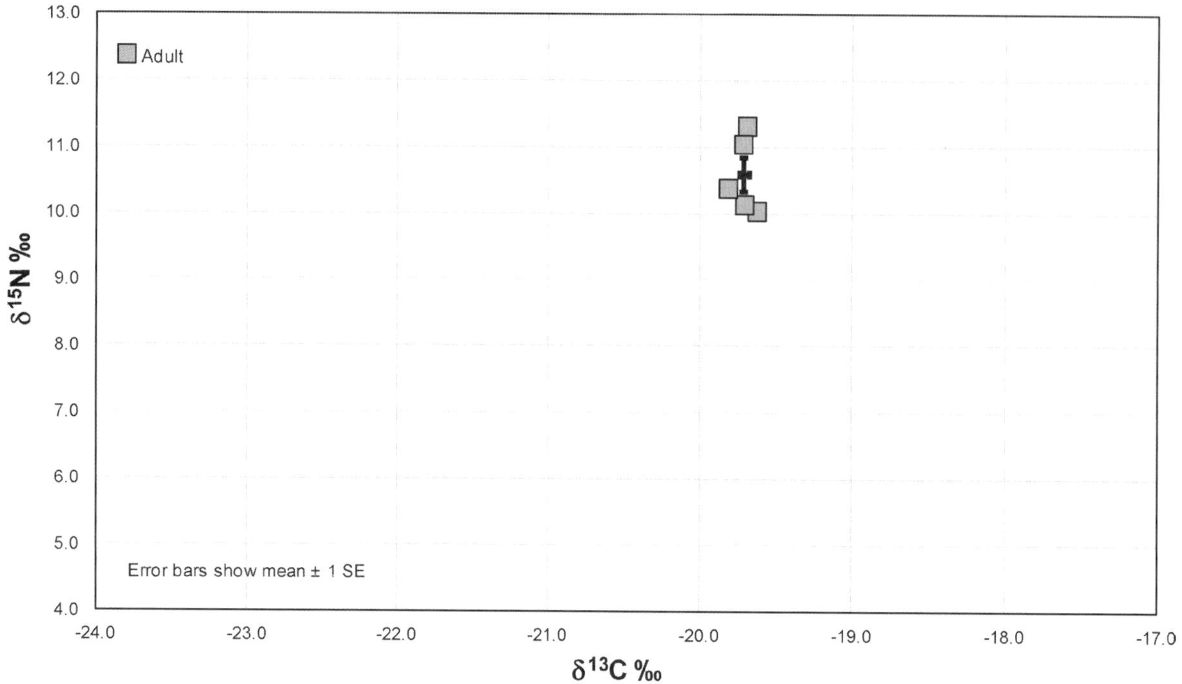

Fig. 3.5. Mezőkövesd-Mocsolyás: carbon and nitrogen isotope ratios (‰) of humans.

Table 3.4. Mezőkövesd-Mocsolyás: carbon and nitrogen isotope ratios (‰) of humans, with means and standard deviations.

Species	Age/sex	Mean $\delta^{13}C$	SD $\delta^{13}C$	Mean $\delta^{15}N$	SD $\delta^{15}N$	n
Human	All Adult	−19.7	0.04	10.6	0.64	4
Human	Unknown	−19.8	-	10.4	-	1

*Table 3.5. Mezőkövesd-Mocsolyás: strontium ratios and concentrations. 'All' includes unsexed adults. *number of analyses, not number of individuals sampled.*

Age/sex	Mean $^{87}Sr/^{86}Sr$	SD $^{87}Sr/^{86}Sr$	Mean Sr conc.	SD Sr conc.	n*
Juvenile	0.70983	0.000409	102	36	2
Male	0.70978	0.000312	159	47	5
Female	0.71012	0.001000	98	41	4
All	0.70986	0.000553	124	44	14

and body positions that were to spread across central Europe with the LBK were already in place from an early stage of the ALP, possibly borrowing from practices already frequent in the Körös culture. The provision of grave goods, however, differs from that of the majority of LBK graves, in that there were no lithics of any sort in the Mezőkövesd graves, pots were only in a handful of graves and *Spondylus* is the most frequent grave good. It is worth noting, in contrast, the large assemblage of worked obsidian cores, blades and flakes found in the settlement (Kalicz and Koós 2001, 61). Kalicz and Koós (2001, 61) suggest that Mezőkövesd was on an obsidian exchange route, specialising in the production of tools from this material. Obsidian is not unusual in northern Hungary at this time and is likely to have originated in the Zemplén hills (Kalicz and Raczky 1987; Whittle 1996, 113, 172). The site lies some 80 km from the source area in north-east Hungary and south-east Slovakia (Kaczanowska and Kozłowski 2010, fig. 2), which are likely to have had $^{87}Sr/^{86}Sr$ ratios about 0.7074 (Seghedi *et al.* 2004, 123; Giblin 2009, 493) and therefore can play no role in explaining the outlier in grave 18. Higher $^{87}Sr/^{86}Sr$ ratios (above 0.7100) are found in the Bükk Mountains (Giblin 2009, 494), through which the obsidian may have subsequently travelled, as it is found on sites in western Slovakia and Poland (Whittle 1996, 172). While it is impossible using strontium isotopes to ever give exact points of origin for individuals, this connection remains interesting.

The isotope results suggest that the majority of the individuals buried at the site shared a relatively local

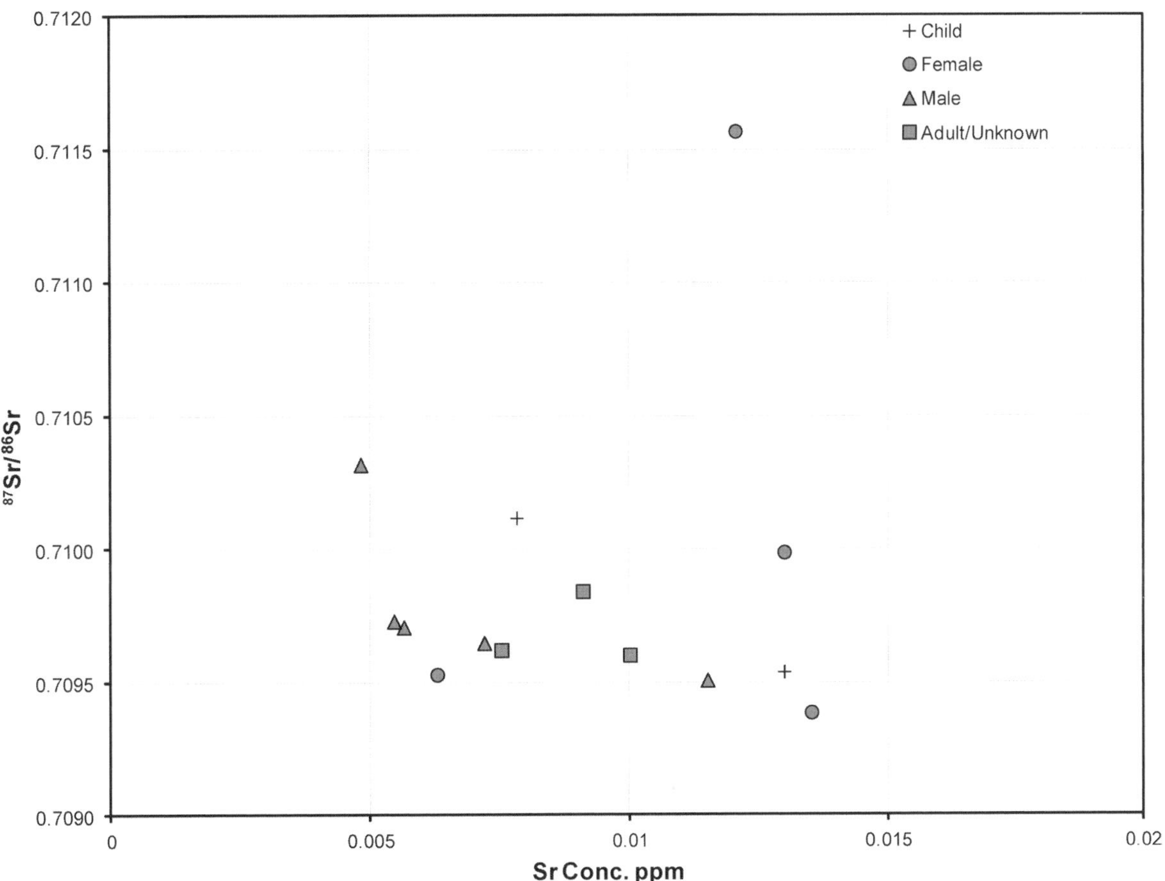

Fig. 3.6. Mezőkövesd-Mocsolyás: strontium concentration (ppm) versus ratio ($^{87}Sr/^{86}Sr$).

geographic origin. This contrasts with the amount of *Spondylus* in the graves, which is most likely to have been sourced from the northern Adriatic over 600 km away (Zvelebil and Pettitt 2008; Séfériadès 2005; 2010). This demonstrates that the community at Mezőkövesd was significantly tied into broader networks in order to access the *Spondylus*, but the role of that material in burial may not have been a straightforward demonstration of status associated with this connection. Excepting the presence of pots in three graves, the burial rites which took place at this site seem to be mainly associated with the body itself, seen in decoration, in the form of *Spondylus* beads, and in ochre, colouring and staining the body.

The suggested emphasis on the body is perhaps evidenced further by the unusual burial in grave 2. In this instance, the body had been divided into two halves at the waist and placed in two pits close to each other (Fig. 3.7; Kalicz and Koós 2001, 47). While the body was oriented in the pits as if still whole, the upper body had been placed on the back, with the hands drawn up under the chin, while the lower body was placed in a more frequent left-crouched position. The skull had been stained with ochre (Kalicz and Koós 2001, 47). One of the graves (7), found isolated in the western part of the site, contained three clay beads, which Kalicz and Koós (2001, 60) argued are copies of *Spondylus* beads in an alternative medium, made because *Spondylus* was rare and valuable (Table 3.3). The star-shaped, slightly

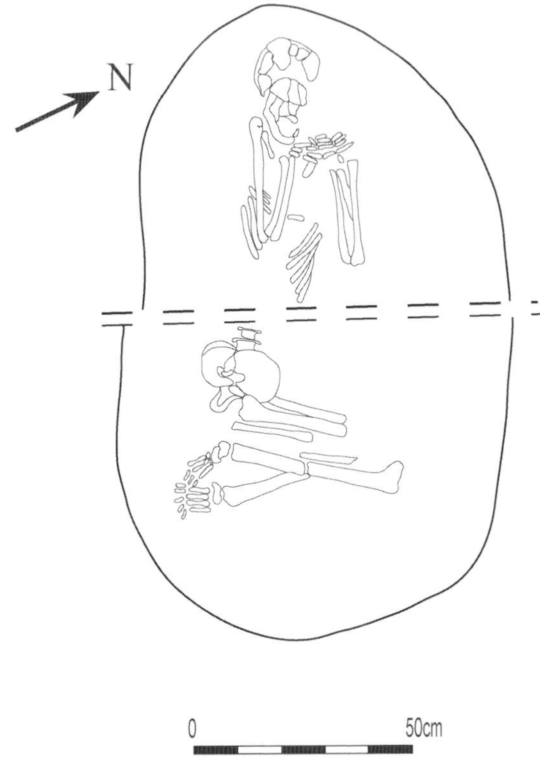

Fig. 3.7. Mezőkövesd-Mocsolyás: burial 2 (adult male). After Kalicz and Koós (2001, 49).

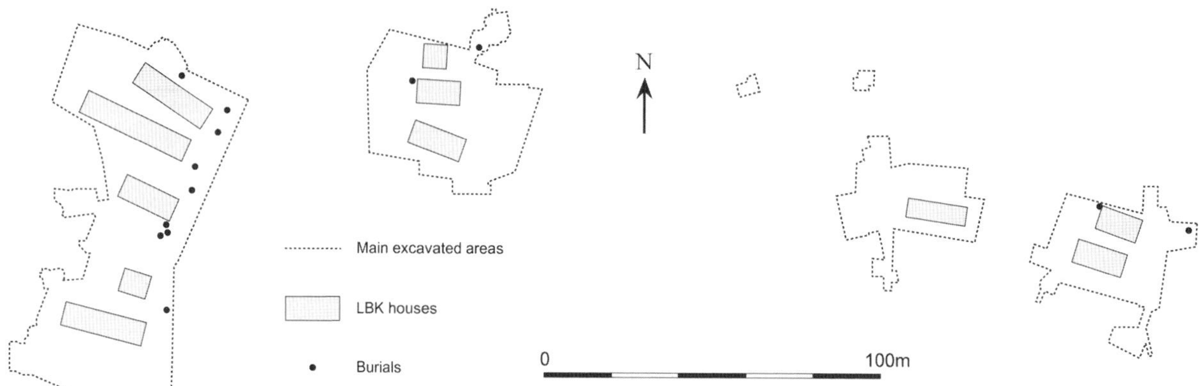

Fig. 3.8. Füzesabony-Gubakút: outline plan. After Domboróczki (1997, 20–1).

trefoil bead is, as far as we can tell, unique across the LBK distribution as a whole, and clay beads are found at only six sites across the LBK, three of which are in eastern Hungary (Lifeways Database). Perhaps they could be seen as experimentation with different material media, rather than purely as attempts to imitate *Spondylus*.

3.8 Füzesabony-Gubakút

3.8.1 Introduction (László Domboróczki)

The Füzesabony-Gubakút site is situated in more or less flat terrain, 3 km south-west of the modern village of Füzesabony and about 10 km to the south of the Mátra-Bükk foothills (Fig. 3.1). The area of LBK settlement is separated into two parts by a broad but shallow valley that was cut by a former riverbed into late Pleistocene sediment. The archaeological site extended to both banks of this streambed. Lying 10 km from Mezőkövesd, Füzesabony is situated in a similar geographical location, on loess soils and only 10 km from the foothills of the Bükk mountains, 20 km from the higher ground with its higher radiogenic $^{87}Sr/^{86}Sr$ values (Chapter 3.7.3).

After initial discovery in 1992/3, detailed research at the site was initiated in 1994 by a magnetometer survey covering an area some 320 by 80 m. The very low (maximum 3 nT) values for the magnetic maps indicated only a few features scattered over the area. This was in accordance with the surface observations, which were repeated before the beginning of the excavation in 1995. The first smaller sections of the excavation were concentrated at those points where the signals on the magnetic map were stronger. In so doing, Neolithic pits were discovered, elongated and oriented NW–SE, some of them paired and close together, but others hundreds of metres apart. A lot of interesting material came out of the pits: stone and bone tools, ceramic figurine heads, altars, miniature vessels, animal bones and pottery fragments, among them many painted ones, considered unique to the earliest phase of the ALP.

The fact that a certain regularity could be discerned among these pits, and the possibility that the discovery of further pits between them could constitute a row of such features, was a decisive factor in finding the whole settlement. Testing this idea, with the help of exploratory trenches, it was possible to find the first western row of pits. It was here where the initial pointers of sporadic, irregular occurrence of posthole-like patches in the trenches became visible and where the first graves also came to light. By opening larger sections here, further graves were found as well as traces of systematically placed postholes, in units of three in a row, clearly indicating the existence of post-framed houses. In the belief that the observations made so far could also be valid for the other parts, topsoil was removed by machine around the first western row of pits. As expected, during the course of excavation, further graves came to light, together with additional, regularly placed postholes. Once the suspicion that there was a row of pits was confirmed, other rows of pits to the east were sought by applying the same methods. By the summer of 1996, four settlement rows had been identified (Domboróczki 1997). It is important to note that the pits do not have the character of flanking loam pits, as are regularly seen on LBK sites; rather they are often situated in proximity to the shorter sides or ends of longhouses.

The most significant result of the excavation at Füzesabony-Gubakút is the discovery of the settlement layout (Domboróczki 1997; 2003; 2009). The evidence of triple-partitioned houses, 12–16 m long by 5–6 m wide, and the regular settlement structure contradicted earlier views of small, irregular ALP settlements made up principally of pit dwellings (Fig. 3.8). The houses were arranged in rows on either side of a stream. Between the houses there were pits, and at the corners of the houses there were human burials (Fig. 3.9; Table 3.6). These graves were dispersed throughout the settlement, all left-crouched and oriented with the head to the south-east or east. Seven graves were furnished with grave goods that were, bar one pot, entirely *Spondylus* ornamentation; four graves were unfurnished. The age and sex of the individual at death do not seem to

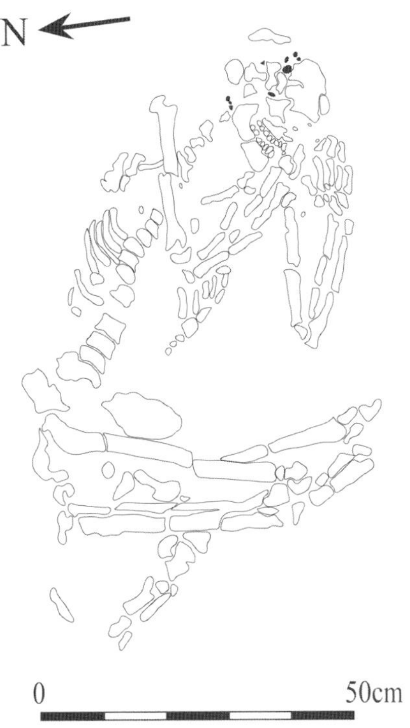

Fig. 3.9. Füzesabony-Gubakút: burial 4 (adult female). The Spondylus *beads on the skull are depicted in black.*

have influenced whether a grave was furnished, with one of the youngest individuals buried at Füzesabony (grave 13: a young infant between 2 and 3 years of age) accompanied by 116 beads of *Spondylus* (the osteology of the burials is discussed further below: Chapter 3.8.2).

The topography of Füzesabony-Gubakút and the many radiocarbon dates obtained[2] have presented an excellent opportunity to examine the chronology of the site and its internal development. Informal inspection of the radiocarbon results (based on animal bone from the pits) has suggested 12 settlement phases, each lasting 30–50 years, informally estimated as falling in the period between 5560–5000 cal BC (Domboróczki 2003; 2009; 2010b). This was supported by seriation based on 74,580 sherds derived from 18 of the 28 Neolithic pits found at the site. House-pit-grave ensembles could be identified as household areas and assigned absolute time limits. Using surface collection data gained in 2007, the whole settlement area could be modelled (Domboróczki 2009; 2010b). The working hypothesis is that the settlement began with the appearance of a pioneer family at the site around 5560 cal BC, and through a continuous history as well as a dynamic growth reached its peak with 12–14 contemporaneous houses/families in the period informally estimated as between 5325–5220 cal BC (Domboróczki 2009; 2010b).

The majority of the graves (burials 1, 2, 4–8 and 10) are located close to houses whose associated pits date to this phase (phase 4). It is in roughly this period that calibrated radiocarbon dates from the majority of burials fall, though its radiocarbon date and location may suggest that grave 9 is earlier.[3] The excavator (Domboróczki 2009, 92) attributes this burial to phase 2A (informally estimated as 5480–5470 cal BC), with graves 4 and 5 attributed to phase 4A and graves 1 and 6 to phase 4B. More formal modelling of the dates may yet resolve this sequence further, but it has to be noted that there are few chronologically diagnostic grave goods and that the relationships between the graves and the settlement pits (on which the settlement sequence has been informally based) are uncertain. However, broadly, the radiocarbon dates suggest that most of the burials at Füzesabony-Gubakút are likely to have been approximately contemporary to the settlement at Mezőkövesd.

Around Füzesabony, an interesting network of ALP settlements has been recorded, which consisted of regularly spaced larger settlements similar to Gubakút, surrounded by smaller settlements in their close vicinity, echoing the model of larger, central/mother settlements, with smaller, satellite/daughter sites around them proposed elsewhere for the LBK distribution (Domboróczki 2009; 2010b; Chapter 1.3.2). The large settlements were aligned along ancient riverbeds and located at regular intervals of some 2 km from one another. By calculating house numbers and possible population levels, and estimating the size of herds and the scale of meat consumption, it was concluded that circles of 1 km diameter probably met the requirements for the pasturage necessary for grazing 15 cattle and 30 sheep per household in a settlement of 14 families (though note differing figures in Knipper 2011). This suggests that extent of the pasturage would have been the greatest determining factor in the sustainability of a settlement during this phase of the Neolithic. Building on this model, Domboróczki (2009, 91–113; 2010b, 156–73) suggests that inter-settlement relationships may have also influenced the demographic development of the region and its settlement pattern, arguing that the individual central settlements – such as Füzesabony-Gubakút – represented different lineages or clans. Modelling the process of settlement development at different scales (by analysing different patterns and using terms such as local development, in- and outward migrations, demographic pressure, and so on) it was suggested that Neolithisation may have proceeded along similar principles for hundreds of years in the region (Domboróczki 2009, 91–113; 2010a, 156–73).

3.8.2 Osteology

Preservation

The remains of 13 individuals from Füzesabony-Gubakút were analysed. This is one of the smaller human skeletal assemblages of the Lifeways project. The remains were relatively fragmented and incomplete, with moderate to poor preservation (Fig. 3.9). Fragmentation, surface erosion and incomplete preservation of joint surfaces were widespread and limited the diagnosis of potential pathological features on affected skeletal elements.

Table 3.6. Füzesabony-Gubakút: the isotope, osteological and archaeological data. Age and sex information from Linda Fibiger (this volume). See Chapter 2 for further definition of ages.

Key for body position: LC – Left-crouched; RC – Right-crouched; C – Crouched, direction unknown; CB – Crouched on back; CF – Crouched on front; S – Supine; P – Prone; I – Irregular. Key for grave goods (number of items in brackets): U. – Unfurnished; F. – Fill only (all items listed after an F. were in the fill of the grave rather than at the level of the skeleton); Pol. – Polished stone; Cer. – Ceramics; Shd. – Sherds; Spon. – Spondylus*; She. – Other Shell; Och. – Ochre; Lit. – Chipped stone; Bon – Worked bone; Grd. – Grinding stone.*

Burial	Tooth	Sex	Age (yrs)	$^{87}Sr/^{86}Sr$	Sr ppm	$\delta^{13}C$ ‰	$\delta^{15}N$ ‰	Orientation	Body position	Grave goods	Pathologies
1	M2	F?	YA	0.71011	154	−19.9	9.9	SE–NW	LC	U.	-
2	M1 M1 M3	-	Older Adol./<20	0.71003 0.71002 0.70978	81 89 97	−20.0	10.6	E–W	LC	U.	*Cribra orbitalia*, inflammation
3	M1 M3	F	Adult<30	0.70989 0.70990	109 107	−19.8	10.5	SE–NW	LC	Spon.(51 beads)	Caries (2)
4	M1 M3	F	YMA	0.71004 0.70986	66 45	−19.8	10.2	E–W	LC	Spon.(37 beads)	-
5	M1 M3	M?	Adult>20	0.71052 0.71052	127 106	−20.3	10.5	SE–NW	LC	Spon.(4 beads)	Trauma (possible healed fracture, left radius)
6	-	-	7<	-	-	−20.5	10	-	-	Spon.(4 beads)	-
7	M1 M3	-	Adult>20	0.71075 0.71083	104 120	−20.2	10.2	SE–NW	LC	U.	-
8	M1	-	*c.* 2	0.71007	93	-	-	SE–NW	-	Spon.(49 beads)	-
9	M1 M3	M	Adult>20	0.70980 0.71005	121 108	−19.9	11.1	SE–NW	LC	Spon.(44 beads)	Enamel hypoplasia
10	M1 M3	M	0/MA>40	0.70996 0.71010	111 121	−19.8	10.5	SE–NW	LC	U.	Trauma (healed fracture, right clavicle), caries (3)
11	-	-	Juv./Adol.	-	-	−20.0	9.8	-	-	Cer.(1)	-
12	M1	-	7–8	0.71072	124	-	-	-	-	U.	Trauma (parietal fragment with 2 unhealed parallel cutmarks)
13	M1	-	2–3	0.70997	64	−19.6	13	-	-	Spon.(116 beads)	-

Demography: age and sex

The small assemblage from Füzesabony-Gubakút included seven adults, one adolescent and five juveniles. In the adult assemblage, three females, three males and one unsexed adult were present (Fig. 3.10).

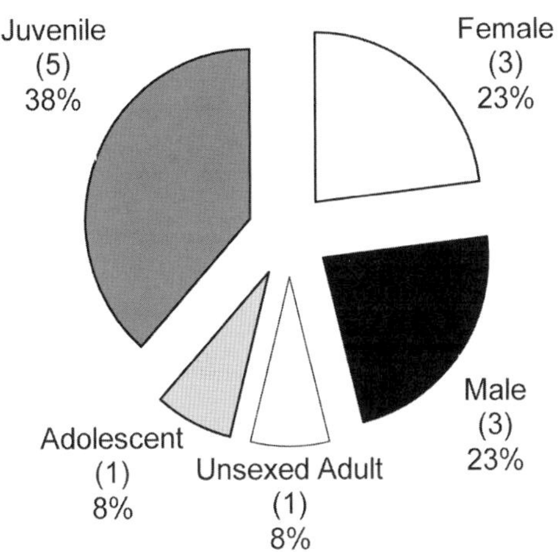

Fig. 3.10. Füzesabony-Gubakút: age and sex assessment.

The proportion of different age and sex groups, especially the large proportion of juveniles from the site (38%), presents the expected demographic profile for prehistoric early agricultural populations; however, infants were completely absent from the site. Under-representation of juveniles and infants in the burial record is not unusual and probably the result of a combination of factors, including both taphonomy and differential burial practices (Guy *et al.* 1997; Scott 1999, 30; Chamberlain 2006, 98). The sample of adults from Füzesabony-Gubakút (Fig. 3.11) was too small to make any population-based inferences, especially as two of the males could only be aged very broadly as 20+ years. In the juvenile sample, the largest number of individuals died between the ages of 1 to 8 years (Fig. 3.12). As previously noted, deaths in the earlier part of childhood are related to a variety of factors, including an increased risk of gastrointestinal infections and other diseases during weaning as well as the occurrence of childhood diseases.

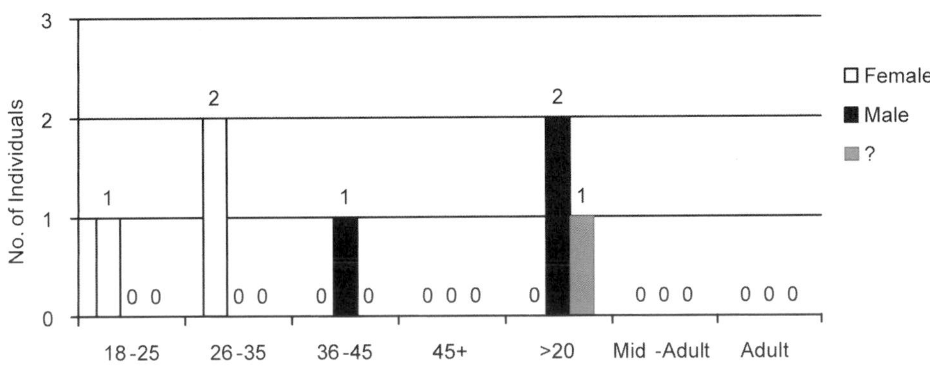

Fig. 3.11. Füzesabony-Gubakút: adult age distribution.

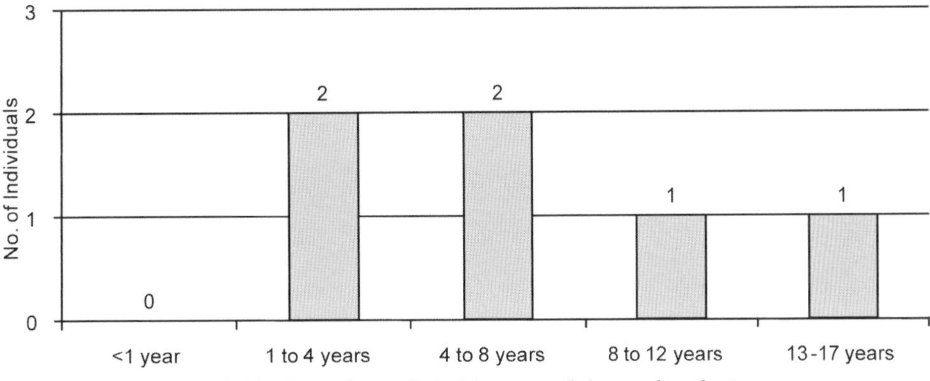

Fig. 3.12. Füzesabony-Gubakút: non-adult age distribution.

Table 3.7. Füzesabony-Gubakút: dental pathology. Individuals affected.

Group	No. of individuals with teeth	No. (%) affected by caries	No. (%) affected by enamel hypoplasia
Adult Male	3	1 (33.3)	1 (33.3)
Adult Female	3	1 (33.3)	0
Unsexed Adult	1	0	0
All Adults	7	2 (28.6)	1 (14.3)
Juvenile/Adolescent	4	0	0
Total	11	2 (18.2)	1 (9.1)

Table 3.8. Füzesabony-Gubakút: dental pathology. Teeth affected.

Group	No. of teeth	No. (%) affected by caries	No. (%) affected by enamel hypoplasia
Adult Male	85	3 (3.5)	9 (10.6)
Adult Female	79	2 (2.5)	0 (0)
Unsexed Adult	32	0 (0)	0 (0)
All Adults	196	5 (2.6)	9 (4.6)
Juvenile/Adolescent	69	0 (0)	0 (0)
Total	265	5 (1.9)	9 (3.4)

Table 3.9. Füzesabony-Gubakút: cribra orbitalia.

	No. of individuals with at least one partial eye socket preserved	No. (%) of individuals with *cribra orbitalia*
Adult Male	3	0 (0)
Adult Female	2	0 (0)
Unsexed Adult	1	0 (0)
All Adults	6	0 (0)
Adolescent	1	1 (100)
Juvenile	0	0 (0)
Infant	0	0 (0)
All Non-adults	1	0 (0)
Total	7	1 (14.3)

Adult stature

No comparison of adult male and female stature was carried out as only one individual from Füzesabony-Gubakút, an adult male, had complete enough long bones to measure the maximum length of the left femur (47.8 cm).

Dental disease

A total of 265 permanent teeth from 11 individuals could be examined. This included 196 teeth from adult and 69 teeth from juvenile and adolescent individuals (Figs 3.13–14). In the adult sample, two (28.6%) out of seven adults with preserved teeth presented with caries and one (14.3%) with enamel hypoplasia (Table 3.7). Neither condition was noted in the sub-adult sample.

Considering prevalence based on the number of teeth present, five (2.6%) out of 196 preserved teeth in the adult sample were affected by caries and nine (4.6%) by enamel hypoplasia (Table 3.8). In the sexed sample, caries rates are slightly higher in males than females, though this difference is not statistically significant. Enamel hypoplasia was noted in the male sample only, which is in line with higher enamel hypoplasia rates in adult males throughout this study.

Cribra orbitalia

At Füzesabony-Gubakút, seven individuals had at least one partially preserved orbit (Table 3.9). *Cribra orbitalia* was only noted on one individual (12.2%), an older adolescent. The sample was too small to carry out any meaningful statistical analysis.

Periosteal changes and infection

Only one individual at Füzesabony-Gubakút showed bony changes that may be indicative of an inflammatory or infectious condition. One older adolescent (burial 2) presented with vascular impressions of the endocranial surface. These may be indicating a systemic inflammatory process.

Post-cranial trauma

At Füzesabony-Gubakút, an adult male over 20 years of age

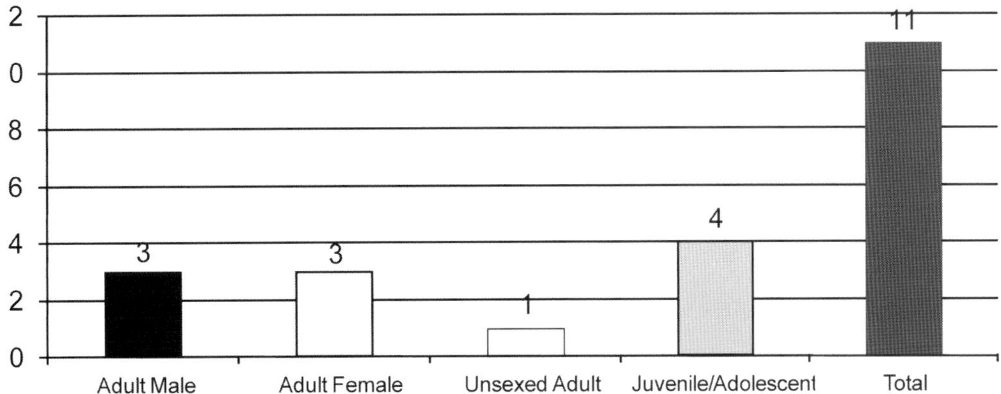

Fig. 3.13. Füzesabony-Gubakút: number of individuals with partial or complete dentitions.

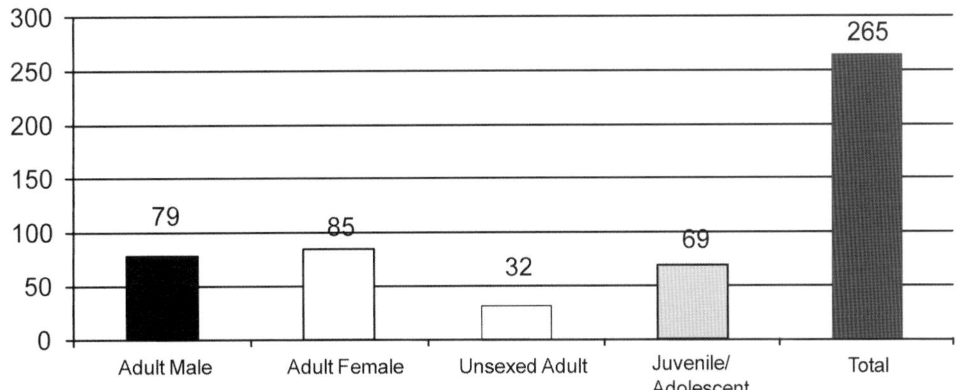

Fig. 3.14. Füzesabony-Gubakút: number of teeth present.

(burial 5) presented with a possible healed fracture of the left distal radius, whereas an older male (burial 10) had at some stage in his life suffered a fracture of the right clavicle (Fig. 3.15). The majority of clavicle fractures in a modern clinical context result from falls (Koval and Zuckermann 2006, 121). The fracture had healed, but without re-uniting the two fracture ends, resulting in a pseudoarthrosis. This individual also had a possible healed fracture of a left proximal foot phalanx. It is not possible to say whether both fractures were sustained during the same event.

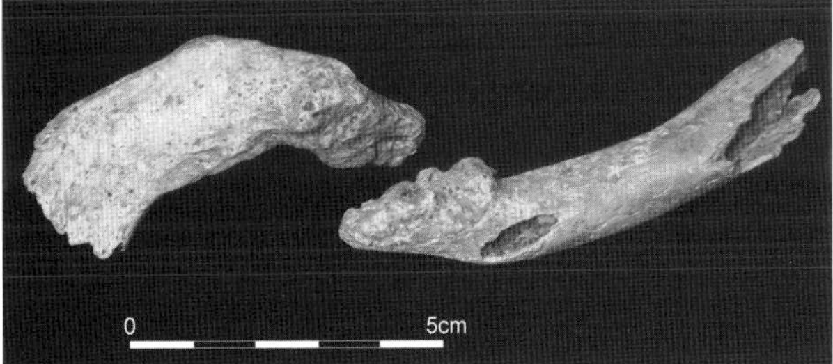

Fig. 3.15. Füzesabony-Gubakút: burial 10, fracture of right clavicle. Photo: Linda Fibiger.

Cranial trauma

A juvenile aged 7–8 years (burial 12) presented with two parallel cutmarks on a parietal fragment. The cuts appeared to have been sustained peri-mortem and may either be related to the cause of the individual's death or part of some funerary ritual (Carr and Knüsel 1997). Table 3.10 shows that crude cranial trauma prevalence in the assemblage was 2%. As the cranium of the affected individual was only represented by a few small fragments, no adjusted prevalence was calculated.

Summary

The skeletal assemblage from Füzesabony-Gubakút is too small for meaningful population-based interpretations, though the results of the analysis indicate the presence of some of the broader trends similar to those noted in the larger assemblage from Polgár-Ferenci-hát (Chapter 3.9.2). These include increased child mortality between the ages of one and ten years, as well as higher enamel hypoplasia rates in the adult male sample.

3.8.3 Carbon and nitrogen analysis

Of the 13 burials at this site, 11 provided carbon and nitrogen values, including seven adults (three males, three females and one unsexed) and four juveniles (Fig. 3.16; Table 3.11).

Age/sex differences

There were no statistically significant differences between

	No. of burials	No. (%) affected by trauma
Adult Male	3	0 (0)
Adult Female	3	0 (0)
Unsexed Adult	1	0 (0)
Adolescent	1	0 (0)
Juvenile	5	1 (20)
Infant	0	-
Total	13	1 (7.7)

Table 3.10. (left) Füzesabony-Gubakút: crude prevalence of cranial trauma.

Table 3.11. (below) Füzesabony-Gubakút: carbon and nitrogen isotope ratios (‰) of humans and animals, with means and standard deviations.

Species	Age/sex	Mean $\delta^{13}C$	SD $\delta^{13}C$	Mean $\delta^{15}N$	SD $\delta^{15}N$	n
Human	Juvenile	−20.0	0.34	10.8	1.49	4
Human	Female	−19.8	0.05	10.2	0.32	3
Human	Male	−20.0	0.29	10.7	0.33	3
Human	Unsexed adult	−20.2	-	10.2	-	1
Human	All adult	−20.0	0.21	10.4	0.37	7
Cattle		−20.3	0.50	7.0	0.91	15
Sheep/goat		−20.3	0.64	7.5	0.78	6
Pig		−20.1	0.62	7.6	1.54	7

the means of juveniles and adults, or between males and females within the human population. One juvenile aged 2–3 years at death had a $\delta^{15}N$ value of 13.0‰, 2.6‰ above the adult mean, which could reflect extended breast-feeding. Raised $\delta^{15}N$ values can also result from periods of illness and/or malnourishment where the body is effectively metabolising its own tissues (Fuller *et al.* 2005). This is a possible explanation in this case, or indeed any other case of raised $\delta^{15}N$, though such changes are more likely to be detected in bone collagen where bone turnover is fast, i.e. in growing juveniles. Most juveniles at the LBK sites studied here have $\delta^{15}N$ values indistinguishable from those of adults, except for the youngest individuals where a suckling effect is the simplest explanation, and that may well apply to this individual also. Apart from this individual, the human isotope values were tightly clustered (Fig. 3.16) and similar to those from Polgár-Ferenci-hát (Chapter 3.9.3).

Animals

The animal remains from Füzesabony-Gubakút were identified by Zsófia E. Kovács. There was much more variation in isotope values between animals of the same species than between humans, particularly in $\delta^{15}N$ (Fig. 3.17). It was not possible to select animal samples of known age and sex, so every effort was made to use bones from adult animals, to minimize age effects on isotope values (Chapter 2.2); even so, the variation within these herbivorous (or mainly herbivorous, in the case of pigs) species is striking. For example, for cattle the range in $\delta^{13}C$ values was 1.9 and in $\delta^{15}N$ values it was 3.6, equivalent to a whole trophic level. The mean $\delta^{15}C$ values were all similar, but sheep/goat and pig mean $\delta^{15}N$ was about 0.5% higher than that of cattle; there were no significant differences between species means, however, not surprisingly in view of the high variation.

Comparison of humans and animals

The difference between the adult human and cattle mean was 0.4±0.54‰ for $\delta^{13}C$ and 3.4±0.98‰ for $\delta^{15}N$; the difference in $\delta^{15}N$ was 0.5–0.6‰ less for sheep and pig. This is high compared to Polgár-Ferenci-hát, probably reflecting the difference between the two sites in faunal values, which are lower here than at Polgár, and we will return to discuss reasons for the differences between sites in Chapter 9.2.5.

Correlations with the archaeological data

With such regular orientations (seven burials are SE–NW and two, E–W) and body positions (all burials are left-crouched) there are no correlations between treatment of the body in the ground and the stable isotope results. The same is true of the relationship between grave goods and the isotope data. As *Spondylus* dominates the grave good assemblage and is not limited to any particular age or sex class this is not surprising, though it may be worth noting that the burial with the lowest $\delta^{15}N$ values (grave 11, juvenile/adolescent, $\delta^{15}N$= 9.8‰) is the only burial to be furnished with pots. There were no correlations between the stable isotope data and the palaeopathology data.

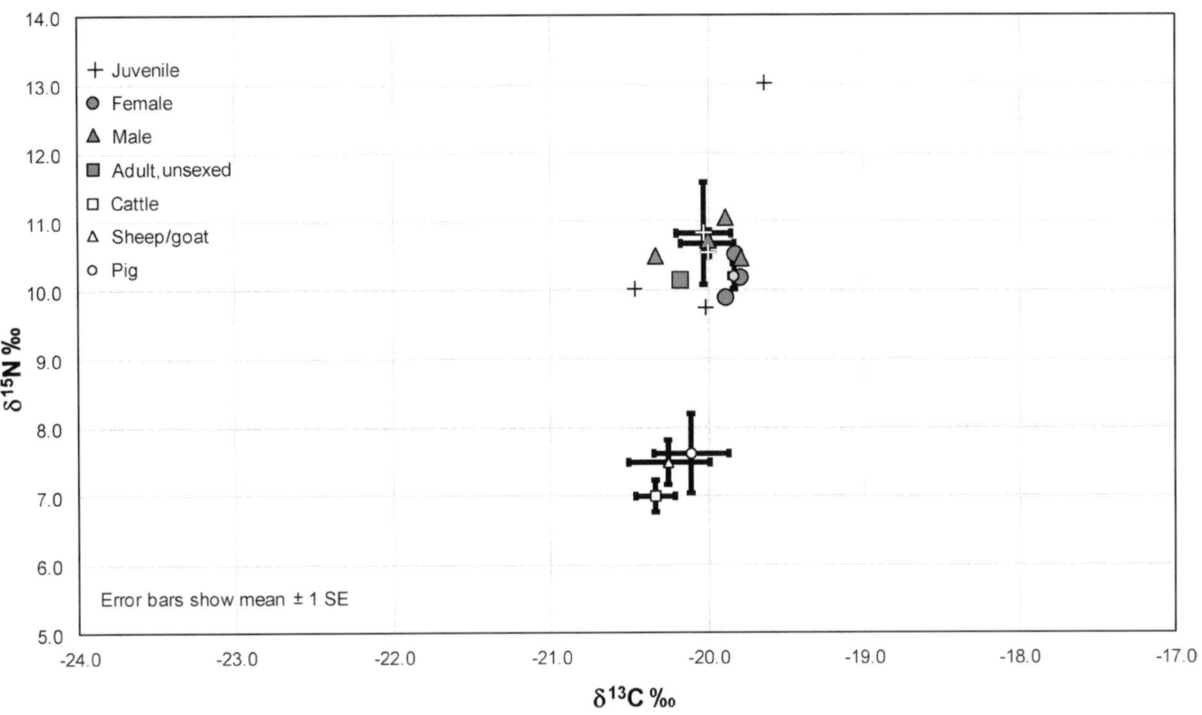

Fig. 3.16. Füzesabony-Gubakút: carbon and nitrogen isotope ratios (‰) of humans and animals.

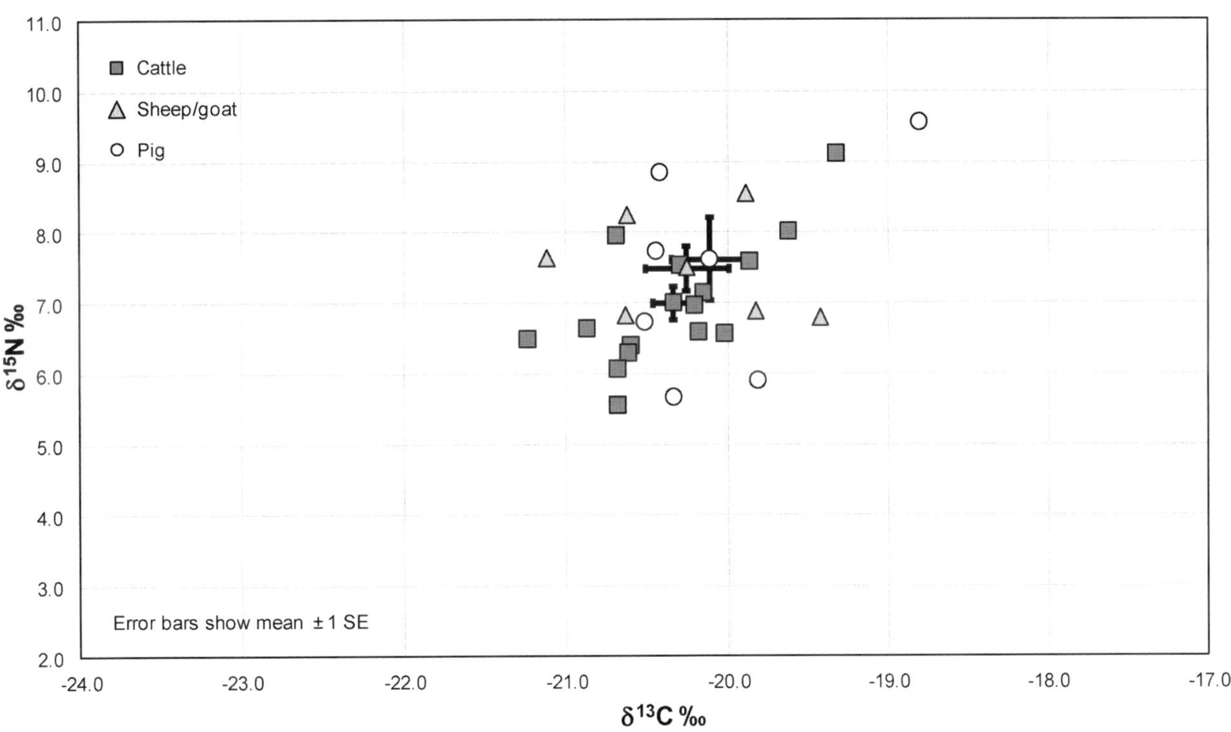

Fig. 3.17. Füzesabony-Gubakút: carbon and nitrogen isotope ratios (‰) of animals.

3.8.4 Strontium analysis

Eleven burials had sufficient enamel preservation for sampling (Fig. 3.18; Table 3.12) and in seven cases it was possible to sample both the M1 and M3 molars, making a total of 18 analyses (the M1 from burial 2 was run twice to check precision, and the two $^{87}Sr/^{86}Sr$ measurements were within 0.00002). The sample included six adults of identifiable sex (three females, three males), as well as one adult that could not be sexed. Among the juveniles, M1 molars were sampled from three children and M1 and M3 molars were sampled from an older adolescent.

At Füzesabony the mean of all individuals was 0.71021±0.00034 (accounting for the multiple ratios for several individuals). The average and standard deviation

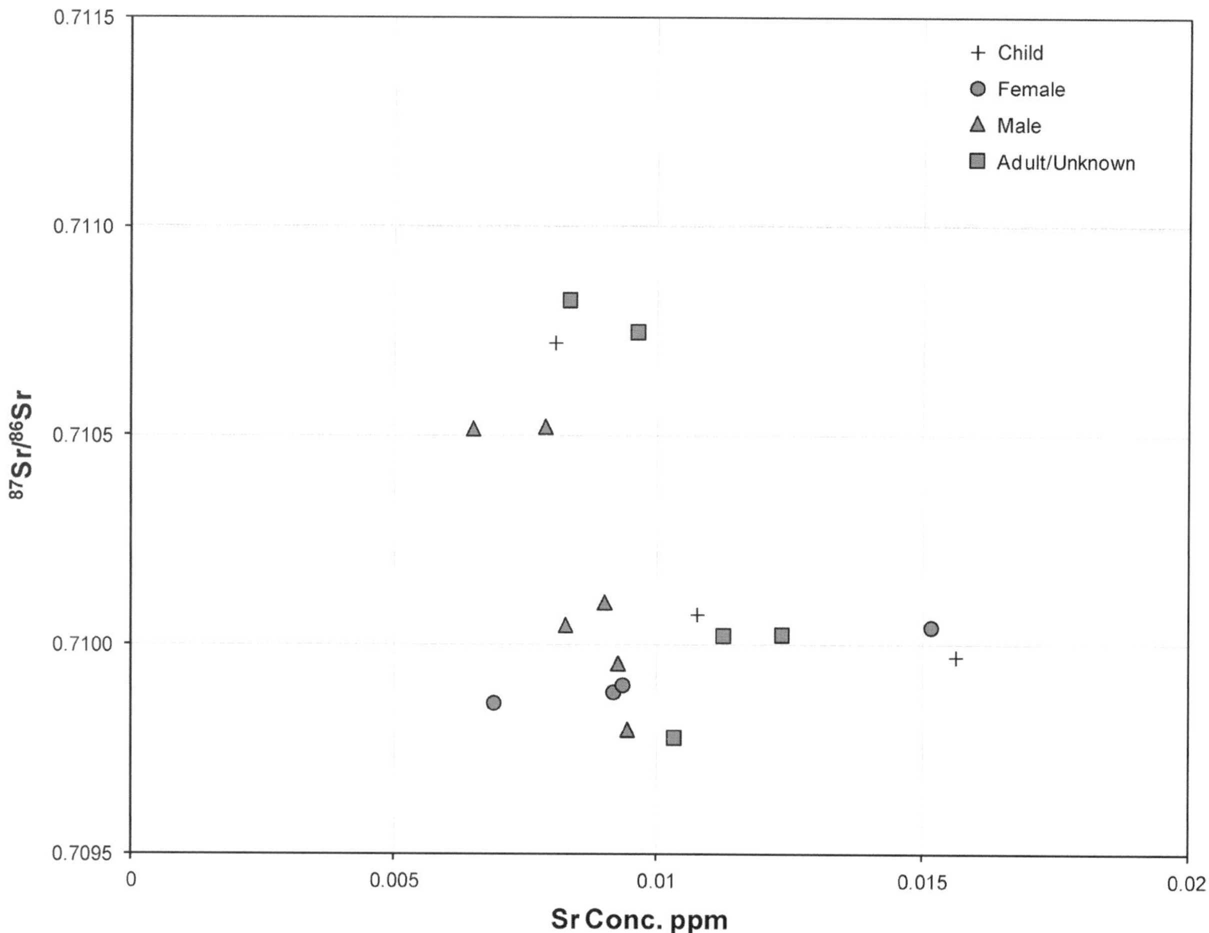

Fig. 3.18. Füzesabony-Gubakút: strontium concentration (ppm) versus ratio ($^{87}Sr/^{86}Sr$).

*Table 3.12. Füzesabony-Gubakút: strontium isotope ratios and concentrations. 'All' includes one unsexed adult. *denotes number of analyses, not number of individuals.*

Age/sex	Mean $^{87}Sr/^{86}Sr$	SD $^{87}Sr/^{86}Sr$	Mean Sr conc.	SD Sr conc.	n*
Juvenile	0.71001	0.00032	91	20	6
Male	0.71016	0.00030	116	8	6
Female	0.70996	0.00011	116	35	5
All	0.71021	0.00034	108	23	18

were almost exactly the same as the average among animals from the site (0.71019±0.00035, n=15), and the three females had similar $^{87}Sr/^{86}Sr$ ratios to the three males. There are also no significant differences between the sexes in Sr concentration values, except that those who died in childhood do have a lower average Sr concentration (91 ppm), as can be seen in Fig. 3.18.

All in all, Füzesabony yielded very similar $^{87}Sr/^{86}Sr$ ratios among humans and their animals, with sample size too small to identify any subtle differences between the sexes. We were, however, allowed to sample multiple teeth from seven individuals, thus testing whether there were any changes over individual lifetimes. The result further supports a picture of a sedentary lifestyle, as there were no $^{87}Sr/^{86}Sr$ ratio differences greater than 0.00025 for the two molars. The same is true in the case of Sr concentration, no great differences being detected between the two molars.

This homogeneity does not mean that people did not migrate, as the loess substrate of this region does not yield the $^{87}Sr/^{86}Sr$ ratio of other regions of this study. It is possible, for example, that the individuals from Füzesabony graves 5, 7 and 12 (a male, unsexed adult and child of 7–8 years respectively), with slightly higher $^{87}Sr/^{86}Sr$ ratios than the rest, could have come from (or used resources from) the region of Mezőkövesd, where the mean $^{87}Sr/^{86}Sr$ ratio is slightly higher. We cannot know for sure, but in any event there is no evidence for long-distance migration into this Füzesabony group. Furthermore, there are no correlations between the strontium, osteological and stable isotope data. In sum, the strontium isotope signatures from Füzesabony suggest a sedentary community.

3.8.5 Site summary and discussion

The isotope results from Füzesabony suggest little variation in diet and mobility patterns between the skeletons sampled, further confirmed in the similarity of strontium ratios in teeth analysed from the same individual. The higher enamel hypoplasia rates in males might suggest, however, some variation in lifeways amongst the adults sampled. The same picture of overall similarity is also strongly suggested by the burial evidence; there is little variation in orientation and body position in the grave and *Spondylus* dominates the grave good assemblage. Given that Füzesabony dates from earlier in the overall LBK sequence, we can perhaps suggest that complexity in the range of goods which accompanied the deceased grew over time in this region. As for Mezőkövesd, we have noted that the grave goods seem to be mostly associated with adorning the body.

Although the number of burials is low, it is interesting to note that the outlier (grave 5) that has been dated is assigned to settlement phase 4A. During this period of the settlement, Füzesabony-Gubakút saw the largest growth in size and in the immediate region, the number of sites in the landscape had increased in number. This poses some interesting questions about changing landscape use and how the local area became more populated. Did a group of people move into the settlement from elsewhere? Were non-loess soils increasingly cultivated as numbers at the settlement grew, or were people forced to forage, hunt or pasture their cattle at greater distances from the site?

3.9 Polgár-Ferenci-hát

3.9.1 Introduction (Pál Raczky and Alexandra Anders)

Polgár-Ferenci-hát is located just south of the Tisza towards the north of the Great Hungarian Plain, quite close to the foothills of the Bükk-Zemplén range (Fig. 3.1). Traces of the settlement were first observed along the bank of a former bed of the Tisza, over an area of 9–12 ha. Some 4 ha were investigated in rescue excavations (Raczky 2004). The site is situated on an alluvial island, above the floodplain, on favourable loess soils, though the geomorphological structure and geology of the region are quite varied (Raczky and Anders 2009, 33). The site lies some 40–60 km from Mezőkövesd and Füzesabony, and at a similar distance from the Bükk hills and Tokaj mountains, with their varied geologies.

Two phases of middle Neolithic occupation were found. The first of these can be dated to the earliest phase (Szatmár) of the ALP. It is represented by some pits and four graves. The most outstanding burial of this phase (Feature 718) contained a woman of 22–28 years of age, laid to rest on her left side, in a crouched position (Chapter 3.9.2 has further discussion of the osteology). She wore a string of *Spondylus* beads around her neck. She was buried with six regular and five miniature vessels and a centaur-shaped statuette (Raczky *et al.* 2010, fig. 6.5), similar to those found at Mezőkövesd-Mocsolyás.

The other part of the site belongs to phases II–IV of the ALP (Raczky and Anders 2009). Part of an elongated, oval double ditch system came to light in the centre of the excavated portion of the settlement (Fig. 3.19). Its pointed eastern end was closed by the segment of a third ditch. Within this enclosure, traces of intensive settlement activity were found, including the remains of two burnt houses, a layer of refuse 50–60 cm thick and several round pits. Outside the enclosure traces of a rather dispersed horizontal settlement could be identified. Combining an overall horizontal extent of 9–12 ha and a vertical accumulation of strata in its centre, the settlement of Polgár-Ferenci-hát shows contrasting site-formation processes at the end of the middle Neolithic. Characteristic pottery types identified from the settlement features are indicative of a synthesis between the Tiszadob-Bükk and Esztár-Szakálhát-Vinča ceramic styles (Raczky and Anders 2009).

In addition to settlement features, 113 graves were excavated. These represent the largest number of ALP burials in the region of the Tisza. Their relative chronological position is best characterised by the associated pottery. Forms are characteristic ALP types; semi-spherical bowls dominate and cups with globular bodies and constrained mouths also occur. Decorated vessels are ornamented with incisions. Motifs typical of the Tiszadob group, the so-called Szarvas-Érpart type and the Bükk culture are found. Unfortunately, the relative chronology cannot be fine-tuned on the basis of pottery finds. Radiocarbon dates were obtained from bone samples taken from 11 burials. They represent the time interval informally estimated as between 5300 and 5070 cal BC, largely parallel with the radiocarbon date of the settlement (informally estimated as 5310–5060 cal BC). Neither relative nor absolute dates, however, permit a more precise internal periodisation of the burials or the settlement. From a chronological point of view they are largely homogeneous, and belong to the middle Neolithic.

The graves were clustered in smaller and larger concentrations, from three to ten, within the excavated settlement area; their density is higher in the proximity of ditches and within the enclosure. In one case, it may even be hypothesised that the set of burials was arranged in relation to a former building (12 graves were excavated in the immediate proximity of feature 359). The grave pits were of oval or trapezoidal shapes. Sometimes the deceased was not placed in an ordinary grave pit, but in a storage pit. Thanks to the waterlogged deeper strata, traces of a coffin or a wooden bier could also be observed for the first time in the history of the middle Neolithic in Hungary, echoing suggestions for elsewhere in the LBK distribution (Baumann 1960; Kloiber and Kneidinger 1968; 1969; Veit 1996; Thévenet 2004; Lifeways Database). The most common orientation was SE–NW, with only minor

Fig. 3.19. Polgár-Ferenci-hát: plan. After Raczky and Anders (2012, 278).

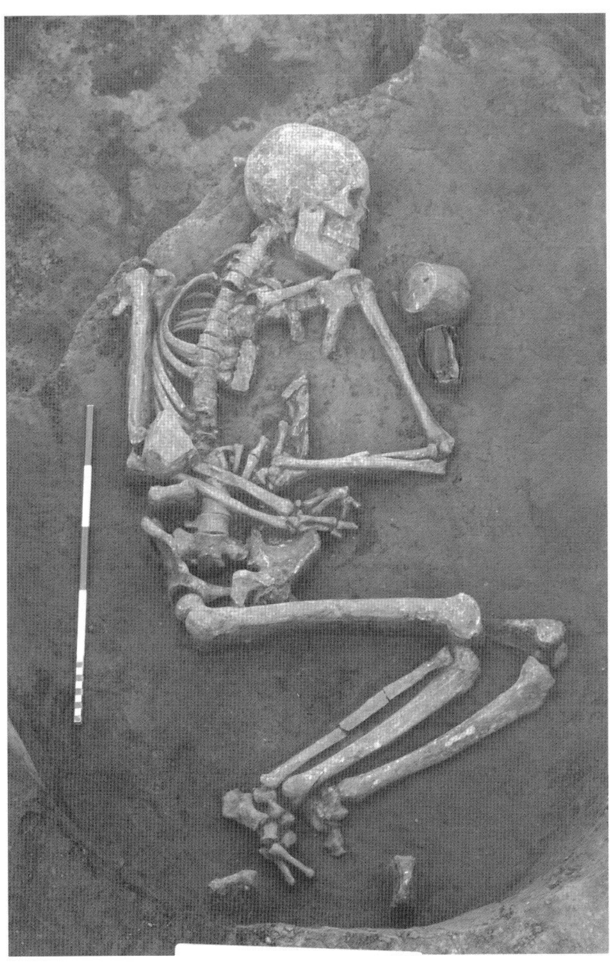

Fig. 3.20. Polgár-Ferenci-hát: selected burials. Left: burial 867/1230. Above: burial 486/687 with head missing. After Raczky and Anders (2012, 280).

variations. This type of orientation may be considered generally widespread in the distribution areas of both the ALP (Kalicz and Makkay 1977, 81; Kalicz 1998, 270) and the LBK (Peschel 1992, 188, 265).

With only three exceptions, the deceased were laid on their left sides in a crouched position (Fig. 3.20; Table 3.13). The great majority of the dead were placed in single graves, but there were two double burials. Multiple burials are also known from the ALP (Lichter 2001, 185). In four cases at Polgár-Ferenci-hát, the dead were buried without their heads. Two of these people were buried in proper graves, while the other two were placed in storage pits. All four of them were men of adultus–maturus (20–60 years) age. According to studies by Zsuzsanna K. Zoffmann, no cutmarks were present on their bones, so it seems that the deceased were not decapitated but their skulls removed some time after burial. There are innumerable ethnographic and archaeological parallels for graves containing no skulls (Zalai-Gaál 2009). Two cremation burials are of special significance. Previously, cremation in Hungary had only been known from the late Neolithic (Öcsöd-Kováshalom: Raczky 1987, 80; Aszód-Papi-földek: Kalicz 1985, 33) but is well known in the LBK of central and western Europe (Peschel 1992, 192; Nieszery 1995, 88; Jeunesse 1997).

In almost 10% of the graves at Polgár-Ferenci-hát, traces of ochre were found under the skull and the bones of the leg. This practice is well known through the entire distribution of the ALP (Kalicz and Makkay 1977, 83; Peschel 1992, 218–22). Eighty-two (72%) of the 113 excavated graves contained no grave goods. A total of 16 burials (14%) contained vessels. They usually occurred as single finds, although some of the deceased were buried with two or even three vessels. A special group of burials with vessels is represented by three graves in which vessels full of ochre were placed into the grave pit.

Another group of important grave goods is represented by stone tools, although only six graves at Polgár-Ferenci-hát contained obsidian blades or ground stone chisels, which occurred in the burials of women, men and children alike. Two additional burials of men deserve special attention. Both of them (features 697 and 867) contained a large obsidian core (exceeding 10 cm in length) placed near the head. The use of obsidian blades as grave goods is known, although they occur rarely in ALP graves (Lichter 2001, 189). Large obsidian cores, on the other hand, may be considered exceptional. Obsidian as a raw material played a key role during the middle Neolithic in the area of the ALP (Biró 1998, 33).

Signs of secondary, post-burial placement of grave goods (*Nachgaben* in German: Nieszery 1995, 103) could also be observed in five graves at Polgár-Ferenci-hát. In these cases, sherds were found at one end of the grave pit, but well above the skeleton. This practice has been interpreted as a sign of people believing that the soul of the deceased spends a certain time in the proximity of the grave and/or house and in order to break this habit, or simply as a sign of closing the period of mourning, vessels with food and drink are dug into the grave (Bertemes 1989).

In contrast to Mezőkövesd and Füzesabony, only six graves contained ornaments. Although this number may

Table 3.13. Polgár-Ferenci-hát: the isotope, osteological and archaeological data. The four Szatmár burials are marked by a star (*). Age and sex information from Linda Fibiger (this volume). See Chapter 2 for further definition of ages.
Key for body position: LC – Left-crouched; RC – Right-crouched; C – Crouched, direction unknown; CB – Crouched on back; CF – Crouched on front; S – Supine; P – Prone; I – Irregular. Grave good information is forthcoming.

Burial	Tooth	Sex	Age (yrs)	$^{87}Sr/^{86}Sr$	Sr ppm	$\delta^{13}C$ ‰	$\delta^{15}N$ ‰	Orientation	Body position	Pathology
33/42	M3	F	OMA	0.71012	137	−19.7	11	SE–NW	LC	Enamel hypoplasia
34/82	M1	F	OMA	0.70945	74	−20.2	10.6	NE–SW	I	Caries (1),
34/91	M1	-	10–11	0.70971	58	−19.7	10.3	S–N	I	*Cribra orbitalia*, enamel hypoplasia
69/133	M3	F	OA	0.7096	47	−20.3	11	SE–NW	I	Trauma (fracture radius), os acromiale, abscess or osteoma (mandible)
103/208	M2	M	OMA	0.70971	55	−19.6	9.8	SE–NW	LC	Enamel hypoplasia
134/239	-	-	Adol.	-	-	−20.3	9.5	NE–SW	LC	Enamel hypoplasia
270/432	M1	M	Mid-Adult	0.70972	56	−19.8	9.8	SE–NW	LC	Caries (1)
281/444	-	F	OMA	-	-	−20.1	10.6	E–W	LC	Tuberculosis, caries (5), enamel hypoplasia
282/445	-	M	MA	-	-	−19.8	9.1	SE–NW	LC	Trauma (healed fracture, metacarpal)
285/450	M1	M	OA	0.70962	59	−20.1	10.3	S–N	LC	Abscess or osteoma (tibia)
288/453	PM	-	1–1.5	0.70966	55	−18.7	13.6	S–N	LC	Infection, probably scurvy
289/454	-	-	10–11	-	-	−19.7	10.7	NW–SE	RC	Enamel hypoplasia
296/468	M2	F	Adult >20	0.70986	66	−19.8	9.8	E–W	LC	Caries (1)
311/486	-	F	OMA	-	-	−19.9	10.5	E–W	LC	Caries (3), enamel hypoplasia
314/489	M2	M	Mid-Adult	0.70972	99	−20.0	10.9	SE–NW	LC	Infection, enamel hypoplasia
324/499	M3	M	OMA	0.70966	85	-	-	-	-	Caries (6?), enamel hypoplasia
338/517	M2	-	10–12	0.70961	94	−20.2	9	SE–NW	LC	Enamel hypoplasia
340/519	-	F	Mid-Adult	-	-	−20.2	10.7	S–N	LC	Caries (3)
341/520	-	M	Mid-Adult	-	-	−20.0	10.1	SE–NW	LC	Caries (1), enamel hypoplasia
344/523	-	F	YA	-	-	−20.1	9.5	E–W	LC	-
347/526	M2	-	Adol.	0.70972	74	−20.0	10	E–W	LC	Enamel hypoplasia
350/529	M1	-	4–5	0.70981	48	−19.6	10.5	E–W	LC	-
353/532	M3	M	MA	0.70969	74	−20.2	9.8	SE–NW	LC	Caries (2)
356/535	M1	M	OA	0.70964	55	−19.4	10.6	E–W	LC	Enamel hypoplasia
368/562	M2	F	Mid-Adult	0.70974	55	−20.4	9.7	SE–NW	LC	Caries (6)

387/581	-	M	YMA	-	-	−19.6	10.7	E–W	LC	-
448/646	M1 (?)	-	2–3	0.70974	76	−20.0	13.2	E–W	LC	-
484/685	M2	-	Adol.	0.70972	85	−20.1	10	SE–NW	LC	-
486/687	-	M	YMA	-	-	−20.3	10.1	SE–NW	LC	-
644/944	M2	-	Adol.	0.71011	65	−19.4	10.4	SE–NW	LC	-
697/1004	M3	M	O/MA	0.70970	79	−20.3	11.6	E–W	LC	Caries (2)
698/1005	M2	M	Mid-Adult	0.71079	32	-	-	-	-	-
717/1024	M2	F	YA	0.70972	115	−20.7	9.9	SE–NW	RC	*Cribra orbitalia*
718/1025*	-	F	Adult <30	-	-	−19.8	9.9	SE–NW	LC	-
719/1026	-	-	2–3	-	-	−19.8	10.1	E–W	LC	*Cribra orbitalia*
721/1028	M1	M	O/MA	0.70957	61	−19.7	10.7	N–S	LC	Trauma (healed fracture of phalanx)
764/1079	-	M	YA	-	-	−19.7	10	SE–NW	LC, face down	-
773/1093	M1	F	OMA	0.70971	38	−20.2	10.1	SE–NW	LC	Caries (2), enamel hypoplasia
786/1109	M1	-	*c.* 1	0.70972	104	−19.5	14.2	SE–NW	-	-
805/1138	-	M	Adult	-		−20.5	10.6	E–W	LC	-
821/1168	M1	F	YMA	0.70962	64	−20.1	10.8	E–W	LC	*Cribra orbitalia*, infection
839/1198	M1	F	MA	0.70960	70	−20.0	11.4	E–W	LC	Trauma (skull, trepanation?), caries (3)
861/1222	M2	-	(Early) Adol.	0.70968 0.70967	196 128	−20.0	10.4	SE–NW	LC	Enamel hypoplasia
867/1230	-	M	OMA	-	-	−20.2	11.6	E–W	LC	-
871/1236	-	-	2–4	-	-	−19.8	12.6	E–W	S	Infection, probably scurvy
881/1252*	M1	-	3–4	0.70972	63	−19.1	10.1	SE–NW	LC	-
889/1260	M3	F	YMA <30	0.70961	95	−20.0	10.5	E–W	LC	*Cribra orbitalia, spondylolysis*
890/1261*	M3	M	OMA	0.70951	56	−19.6	9.8	E–W	RC	Caries (3), enamel hypoplasia
897/1268	M3	M	YMA	0.70964	66	−19.7	10.2	SE–NW	LC	Infection
904/1311*	-	F	Adult <30	-	-	−19.3	9.6	E–W	LC	-

seem small, as it is far from the 66% of similarly endowed burials recorded within the distribution of the ALP culture (Oravecz 1998–1999, 56–7), the six graves at Polgár-Ferenci-hát should be considered special. They yielded 13 *Spondylus* objects (beads, armrings and strings of beads around the neck and wrist). It is noteworthy that *Spondylus* artefacts came to light in the graves of children, all of whom belonged to the Infans I–II (0–12 years) age group. In summary, it may be said that the burial rite observed at Polgár-Ferenci-hát is not very different to the general mortuary practice of the ALP groups.

3.9.2 Osteology

The complete osteological analysis of the human remains from Polgár-Ferenci-hát was carried out by Zsuzsanna K. Zoffmann. The full report is forthcoming and here we present only the analysis on the burials sampled for their isotopic values.

Preservation

The remains of 50 individuals from Polgár-Ferenci-hát were analysed for the LBK Lifeways project. The skeletal remains were generally complete and in moderate to good condition, reflected in the fact that all adult remains could be sexed. A number of crania in both assemblages had been glued during post-excavation, which unfortunately involved glueing together of the mandibular and maxillary teeth along their occlusal surfaces. This prevented the detailed observation of these surfaces for pathological conditions such as caries.

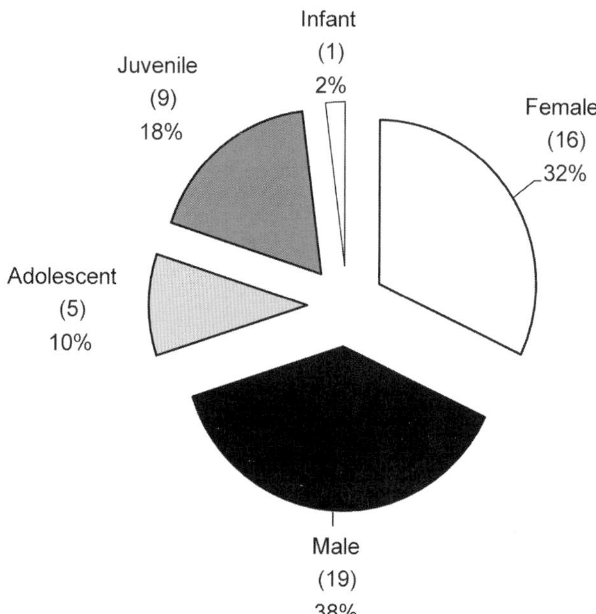

Fig. 3.21. Polgár-Ferenci-hát: age and sex assessment.

Demography: age and sex

At Polgár-Ferenci-hát, 35 adults, five adolescents, nine juveniles and one infant were analysed. The adult group consisted of 16 females and 19 males (Fig. 3.21; Table 3.13).

Only 20% of individuals at Polgár-Ferenci-hát fell into the infant and juvenile age categories. This under-representation of children is common in archaeological assemblages and probably the result of a bias in preservation of children's bones as well as of potential differences in funerary rites between adults and children (Guy *et al.* 1997; Scott 1999, 30; Chamberlain 2006, 98).

The age distribution of the adult sample from Polgár-Ferenci-hát (Fig. 3.22) shows a relatively equal distribution of females and males in the Young Adult (18–25 years) and Mid-Adult (26–45 years) age categories, though more males appeared to live beyond middle age (45+ years and older). In the juvenile sample, the largest number of individuals died between the ages of one to four years (Fig. 3.23). Mortality peaks in the earlier part of childhood are related to a variety of factors, such as an increased risk of gastrointestinal infections and other diseases during weaning as well as the occurrence of childhood diseases (Chapter 2.4).

Adult stature

Thirteen males and eight females presented with left femora that were complete enough to measure maximum length (Fig. 3.24).

Mean values for male and female left femora length showed a statistically significant difference, with significantly higher male values ($t\ (19)=5.326$; $p=0.000$). This indicates relatively robust sexual dimorphism and related differences in stature between men and women.

Dental disease and modification

A total of 1020 permanent teeth from 44 individuals could be examined. This included 775 teeth from adult and 245 teeth from juvenile and adolescent individuals (Figs 3.25–6).

In the adult sample 14 (46.7%) out of 30 adults with preserved teeth presented with caries and 11 (36.7%) with enamel hypoplasia. In the non-adult sample, five (35.7%)

Table 3.14. Polgár-Ferenci-hát: dental pathology. Individuals affected.

Group	No. of individuals with teeth	No. (%) affected by caries	No. (%) affected by enamel hypoplasia
Adult Male	14	6 (42.9)	7 (50)
Adult Female	16	8 (50)	4 (25)
All Adults	30	14 (46.7)	11 (36.7)
Juvenile/Adolescent	14	0	5 (35.7)
Total	44	14 (31.8)	16 (36.4)

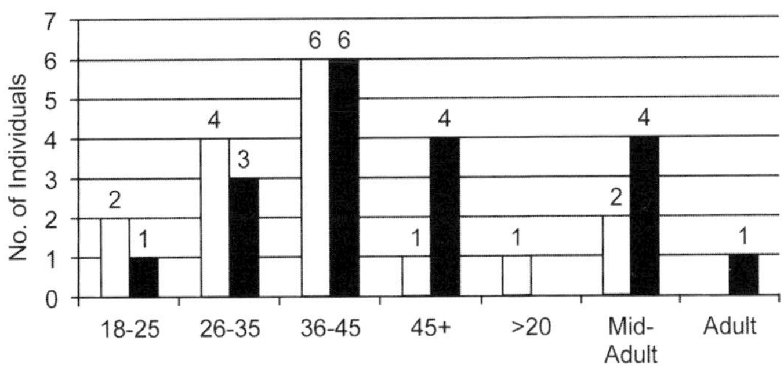

Fig. 3.22. Polgár-Ferenci-hát: adult age distribution.

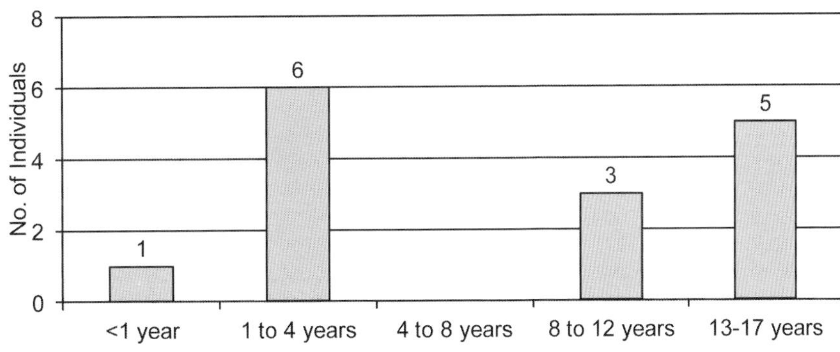

Fig. 3.23. Polgár-Ferenci-hát: non-adult age distribution.

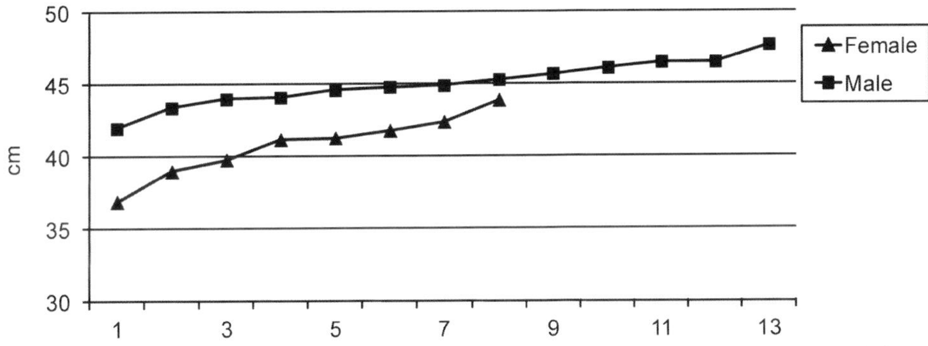

Fig. 3.24. Polgár-Ferenci-hát: comparison of the maximum length of male and female left femora.

out of 14 individuals presented with enamel hypoplasia (Table 3.14), giving an overall total of 16 (36.4%) affected individuals at Polgár-Ferenci-hát. No caries was recorded in the juvenile or adolescent sample. Cavities in the permanent dentition usually do not tend to develop until adulthood. Considering caries prevalence based on the number of teeth present, 59 (7.6%) out of 775 preserved teeth in the adult sample were affected by caries and 80 (10.3%) by enamel hypoplasia (Table 3.15). In addition, 46 (18.8%) out of 245 teeth in the non-adult sample also presented with enamel hypoplasia. This resulted in an overall total of 126 (12.4%) teeth affected by enamel hypoplasia at Polgár-Ferenci-hát.

Caries rates differed significantly between males and females when considering the number of teeth affected (χ^2=4.714, p=0.03), with more female teeth showing caries defects. Similar results were obtained for the Nitra assemblage (Chapter 4.10.2) and indicate underlying differences in diet between the sexes. One possible explanation for this result is an overall difference in health between men and women that also affected oral health and resulted in poor enamel quality and increased caries rates. The results for other pathological features examined (see below) do not appear to support substantial health differences between men and women and therefore make dietary differences the most likely explanation. Women possibly consumed a larger proportion of carbohydrates in the form of starchy plant foods (but see Chapter 3.9.3). No significant differences between the sexes were noted for the occurrence of enamel hypoplasia, though it was less frequent amongst the women investigated.

A small number of individuals at Polgár-Ferenci-hát showed signs of dental modification resulting from the use of teeth for activities other than food consumption. At least three older females had occlusal grooves on their anterior maxillary teeth (graves 281/444, 773/1093 and

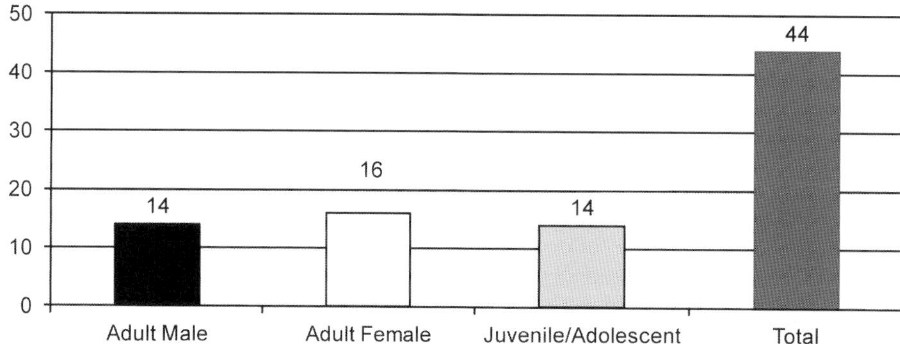

Fig. 3.25. Polgár-Ferenci-hát: number of individuals with partial or complete dentitions.

Fig. 3.26. Polgár-Ferenci-hát: number of teeth present.

Table 3.15. Polgár-Ferenci-hát: dental pathology. Teeth affected.

Group	No. of teeth	No. (%) affected by caries	No. (%) affected by enamel hypoplasia
Adult Male	366	20 (5.5)	33 (9)
Adult Female	409	39 (9.5)	47 (11.5)
All Adults	775	59 (7.6)	80 (10.3)
Juvenile/Adolescent	245	0	46 (18.8)
Total	1020	59 (5.8)	126 (12.4)

839/1198; Fig. 3.27) indicating the use of these teeth as tools, probably while producing cords or working plant fibre (Frayer 2004; Schulting 2007). This activity appears to be more strongly associated with women, indicating sexual division of particular tasks within the population (Frayer 2004; Schulting 2007). Similar changes were noted at Nitra (Chapter 4.10.2).

Cribra orbitalia

Out of 41 individuals at Polgár-Ferenci-hát who had at least one partially preserved orbit, five (12.2 %) presented with signs of *cribra orbitalia*. This included three adult women (717/1024, 821/1168 and 889/1260) and two juveniles (34/91 and 719/1026; Table 3.16). No adult men were affected. Although more women than men and more non-adults than adults were affected, neither of these differences was statistically significant.

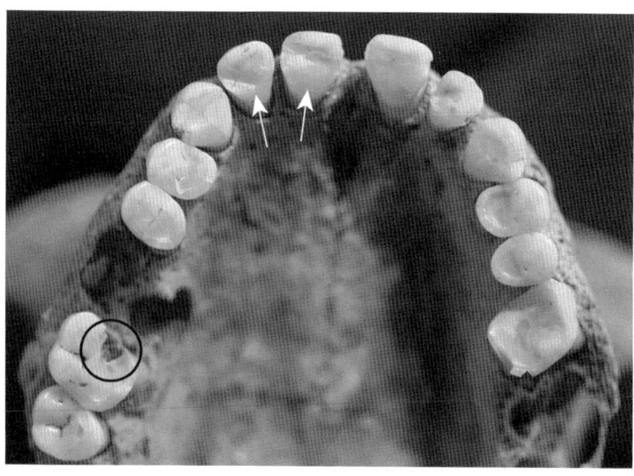

Fig. 3.27. Polgár-Ferenci-hát: occlusal maxillary grooves, burial 281/444. Arrows indicate location of the grooves. Circle indicates a carious defect on the second molar. Photo: Linda Fibiger.

	No. of individuals with at least one partial eye socket preserved	No. (%) of individuals with *cribra orbitalia*
Adult Male	13	0 (0)
Adult Female	15	3 (20)
All Adults	28	3 (10.7)
Adolescent	4	0 (0)
Juvenile	8	2 (25)
Infant	1	0 (0)
All Non-adults	13	2 (15.4)
Total	41	5 (12.2)

Table 3.16. (left) Polgár-Ferenci-hát: cribra orbitalia.

Table 3.17. (below) Polgár-Ferenci-hát: periosteal lesions and pathological changes related to inflammatory, infectious or haemorrhagic processes.

Group	ID	Age	Changes recorded	Differential diagnosis
Female	281/444	Old Mid-Adult	Periosteal new bone (mixed) on ribs and vertebrae; destructive changes on lower spine; remodelled periosteal new bone on lower legs and feet	Systemic infection – probably tuberculosis
	821/1168	Young Mid-Adult	Remodelled periosteal new bone on lower legs	Systemic infection or haemorrhagic process
Male	314/489	Old Mid-Adult	Remodelled periosteal new bone on lower legs	Systemic infection or haemorrhagic process
	897/1268	Young Mid-Adult	Periosteal new bone (mixed) on left and right leg	Systemic infection or haemorrhagic process
Juvenile	288/453	1–1.5 years	Vascular impressions and porosity of endocranium: periosteal new bone on sphenoid; porosity of right posterior-medial tibia	Metabolic condition: probably scurvy
	871/1236	2–4 years	Woven bone deposit on left mandible	Inflammation/infection or haemorrhagic process: possibly scurvy

Periosteal changes and infection

At Polgár-Ferenci-hát, six individuals presented with periosteal reactions or changes indicative of inflammatory, infectious or metabolic conditions, giving a crude prevalence of 12% (Table 3.17). Individuals affected included two adult females, two adult males and two young juveniles. It is important to note that some of the changes observed are not specific to one particular disease process and can have a variety of origins. Bilateral periosteal reactions on the lower legs, for example, may be the result of infectious conditions as well as metabolic diseases such as scurvy (vitamin C deficiency), and it may not be possible to securely ascribe the observed changes to one specific condition (Weston 2008). A number of individuals at Polgár-Ferenci-hát (821/1168, 314/489 and 697/1268), including adults of both sexes, presented with these non-specific bilateral changes.

Two possible cases of scurvy were present at Polgár-Ferenci-hát (288/453 and 871/1234). The condition is caused by prolonged deficiency in vitamin C intake, usually a dietary lack of fresh fruit and vegetables (Ortner *et al.* 2001, 343). One of its main clinical symptoms is an increased tendency to haemorrhage, either spontaneously or following minor trauma (Ortner 2003, 383), which skeletally results in increased bone surface porosity and new bone formation at the affected areas, mainly the skull, scapula and long bone ends (Geber and Murphy 2012; Ortner *et al.* 2001, 344). These changes tend to be more pronounced in children. Infants are unable to synthesise vitamin C, but generally receive adequate nutrition though breastmilk (Brickley and Ives 2008, 45). Both cases at Polgár-Ferenci-hát affect relatively young individuals (1–1.5 and 2–4 years respectively) and may be related to weaning practices and childhood diet.

One probable case of tuberculosis was present at the site. An older mid-adult female (Burial 281/444) showed changes indicative of active tuberculosis, including new bone formation on the ribs, spine and lower legs as well

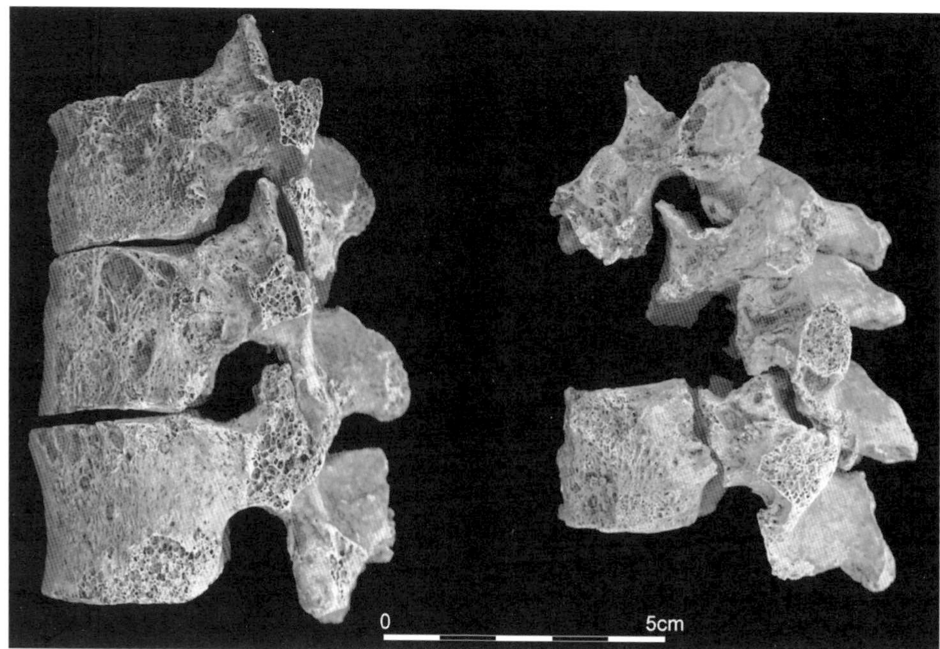

Fig. 3.28. Polgár-Ferenci-hát: Left: destructive changes to the spine. Right: vertebral collapse with kyphosis. Burial 281/444. Photo: Linda Fibiger.

as destructive changes of the ribs and spine that resulted in the collapse of one of the vertebrae and most probably a spinal bending deformity (kyphosis) (Fig. 3.28). Without further biomolecular analysis it is not possible to state whether this case is the result of infection with the human or bovine form of the disease. As only up to 5% of cases result in changes to the skeleton (Roberts and Buikstra 2003, 89), the disease is likely to have affected more than one individual at Polgár-Ferenci-hát.

Two more individuals presented with changes that include inflammatory processes in the differential diagnosis. A mature adult male (Burial 285/450) presented with a small deposit of raised compact bone on the left anterior-medial tibia, which was continuous with the cortical surface. An adult female (Burial 69/133) showed a small, compact bony protrusion continuous with the cortical surface on the right anterior-inferior mandible. Differential diagnosis includes osteoid osteoma and intracortical abscess. Osteoid osteomata are benign tumours that occur mostly between the ages of 10 and 25 years, predominantly on the bones of the lower legs. They can produce painful symptoms (Aufderheide and Rodríguez-Martín 1998, 376). Intracortical abscesses can result in very similar changes (Ortner and Putschar 1985, 376). Without radiographic examination, a secure diagnosis is difficult. Alternatively, the changes observed may be the result of a healed trauma or skin ulcer or indicate the presence of a cyst.

Post-cranial trauma

Four individuals from Polgár-Ferenci-hát showed signs of trauma to the post-cranial skeleton. A mature adult male (Burial 282/445) appeared to have suffered a fracture of the right fifth metacarpal at some stage during his life. While accidental trauma cannot be excluded, one of the common injury mechanisms for fifth metacarpal fractures is hand to hand combat (Hershkovitz *et al.* 1996). The injury may therefore be indicative of interpersonal conflict. Another male, probably aged over 40 years (Burial 721/1028), presented with possible healed fractures of a right foot phalanx and the right fifth metatarsal. Foot fractures are relatively common and usually result from direct trauma (Koval and Zuckermann 2006, 260). An older mid-adult female (Burial 69/133) presented with a healed fracture of the right distal radius. Lower arm fractures can occur as the result of direct or indirect trauma, the latter including falls on to the outstretched hand (Koval and Zuckermann 2006, 223). The individual also had *os acromiale* of the left scapula, a non-fusion of the acromion process of the scapula. This bone usually fuses by approximately 20 years (Liberson 1937; Scheuer and Black 2000, 270). Although traditionally the condition is thought to have a developmental origin, its high prevalence among the skeletal remains of soldiers recovered from the wreck of the Mary Rose as well as the combatants from the Battle of Towton has highlighted that at least in some cases its occurrence may result from a combination of developmental predisposition and mechanical strain, manifesting itself as an activity-related skeletal adaptation (Case *et al.* 2006; Knüsel 2000, 115; Stirland 2000, 121). Non-fusion of this part of the shoulder as a result of heavy use of the joint from an early age would allow for a greater range of movements of the shoulder. Finally, another female under 30 years of age (Burial 889/1260) had a bilateral vertebral arch fracture (*spondylolysis*) of the fourth lumbar vertebra. *Spondylolysis* is a stress fracture of the spine that clinically has been shown to occur in families, indicating underlying hereditary factors for its occurrence (Fredrickson *et al.* 1984; Standaert and Herring 2000, 415); however, its high

Fig. 3.29. Polgár-Ferenci-hát: possible trepanation, burial 839/1198. Photo: Linda Fibiger.

frequency among athletes points towards a significant role for habitual, strenuous movement in its occurrence, which has also been highlighted by a number of archaeological studies (Merbs 1983; Fibiger and Knüsel 2005; Molnar 2006).

Cranial trauma

One individual at Polgár-Ferenci-hát presented with bone changes that may be related to a violent episode. A mature adult female (Burial 839/1198) presented with a shallow healed depression of the right superior parietal (Fig. 3.29). A perforation in the centre of the depression appeared to be part of the original defect. The appearance of the lesion is similar to that recorded for trepanations. Trepanations may either have medicinal or ritual purposes but are common treatments for relieving pressure after head trauma and for removing and cleaning up bone fragments in cases of cranial fractures (Arnott *et al.* 2003). Table 3.18 shows that crude cranial trauma prevalence based on the total number of burials present was 2%, whereas adjusted trauma prevalence based on the number of individuals with at least 50% of the cranial vault preserved was 3% (Table 3.19).

Summary

The assemblage from Polgár-Ferenci-hát is the second largest skeletal sample analysed for the Lifeways project. Juveniles and infants are notably underrepresented, suggesting that maybe not all individuals belonging to the population group were buried at the site. While the age distribution of males and females is relatively similar, it is interesting to note that more women than men died in their 20s, while more men than women lived into their late 40s. Increased female mortality in early adulthood is most likely a result of increased mortality during childbirth at this life-stage.

Dental health differed significantly between males

Table 3.18. Polgár-Ferenci-hát: crude prevalence of cranial trauma.

	No. of burials	No. (%) affected by trauma
Adult Male	19	0 (0)
Adult Female	16	1 (6.3)
Adolescent	5	0 (0)
Juvenile	9	0 (0)
Infant	1	0 (0)
Total	50	1 (2)

Table 3.19. Polgár-Ferenci-hát: adjusted prevalence of cranial trauma.

	50+% of cranial vault present	No. (%) affected by trauma
Adult Male	13	0 (0)
Adult Female	12	1 (8.3)
Adolescent	3	0 (0)
Juvenile	5	0 (0)
Infant	0	0 (0)
Total	33	1 (3)

and females at Polgár-Ferenci-hát, indicating gendered differences in diet. Higher caries rates in females most likely result from variations in the importance of different foods consumed, particularly starchy plant foods. While biological factors, such as hormone levels and fluctuations, menstrual cycles and pregnancy-related saliva composition, diet cravings/aversions and immune suppression may also have an adverse impact on women's oral health (Lukacs 2008; Lukacs and Thompson 2009), these factors are much harder to quantify. While women might have suffered fewer early childhood stresses than men, as indicated by lower rates of enamel hypoplasia, the difference is not statistically significant. Women did show higher rates of *cribra orbitalia*, suggesting that they were more likely to suffer from iron-deficiency anaemia. In this case, biological factors (e.g. menstrual and pregnancy-related blood loss) are probably less likely to play a significant role if assuming that extended periods of breast-feeding and spaced pregnancies were the norm (Stuart-Macadam 1998). Gendered patterns are also apparent in the occurrence of non-dietary dental wear, suggesting sexual division of labour that is most likely related to the processing of plant fibres and/or production of cords. Sex-related differences were absent when considering metabolic diseases and infections. Interestingly, the only evidence for traumatic head injury at Polgár-Ferenci-hát was the possible trepanation recorded on the right parietal of a mature adult female.

In the non-adult sample, mortality rates are highest in early to mid-childhood (0–8 years), reflecting the risks of gastrointestinal infections and other diseases during weaning as well as the occurrence of childhood diseases

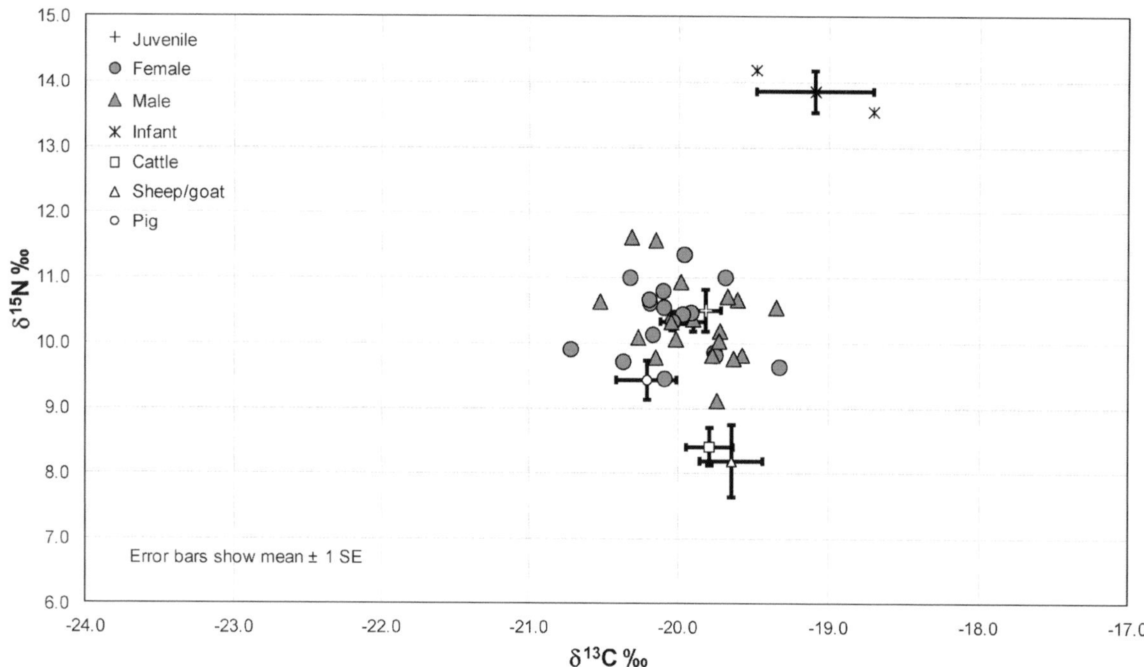

Fig. 3.30. Polgár-Ferenci-hát: carbon and nitrogen isotope ratios (‰) of humans.

Table 3.20. Polgár-Ferenci-hát: carbon and nitrogen isotope ratios (‰) of humans and animals, with means and standard deviations.

Species	Age/sex	Mean δ^{13}C	SD δ^{13}C	Mean δ^{15}N	SD δ^{15}N	n
Human	Infant	−19.1	0.55	13.9	0.45	2
Human	Juvenile	−19.8	0.34	10.5	1.15	13
Human	Female	−20.0	0.32	10.3	0.57	16
Human	Male	−19.9	0.31	10.3	0.65	17
Human	All adult	−20.0	0.32	10.3	0.60	33
Cattle		−19.8	0.54	8.4	1.04	13
Sheep/goat		−19.7	0.51	8.2	1.35	6
Pig		−20.2	0.50	9.4	0.74	6

associated with the early years of life. A quarter of juveniles also presented with *cribra orbitalia*, further illustrating the relatively poorer health status of many individuals in this age group.

3.9.3 Carbon and nitrogen analysis

In total, 33 individuals were available for sampling, representing approximately a third of the assemblage (Fig. 3.30; Table 3.20).

Age/sex differences

There was no significant difference between males and females in δ^{13}C or δ^{15}N values.

The two infants (around 1 year old) averaged 0.9‰ above the adult mean in δ^{13}C values and 3.6‰ in δ^{15}N values, presumably the result of breast-feeding. Two of the pre-adolescent juveniles (2–3 and 2–4 years old) also had distinctly high δ^{15}N values (averaging 2.6‰ above the adult mean), though another of the same age did not. This could reflect differences in the weaning age between individuals, although the precision of ageing and number of cases available here are not enough to be sure of this.

Because of the relatively full age data in the osteological report it was possible to rank individuals approximately in age order in more detail than usual. There was no clear change in δ^{13}C with age (apart from the higher values in the two infants). Overall, there was no strong relationship between δ^{15}N and age after the age of 2–4 years, and juveniles were similar to adults. Although there was no difference between males and females overall, they showed different trends with age: for females alone, δ^{15}N was significantly correlated with age (Spearman rank correlation, n=16, $p<0.001$), while males showed no correlation (though variation in male δ^{15}N increased with age). No further correlation with the osteological and palaeopathological data could be identified.

Animals

Cattle and sheep had very similar isotope values, while

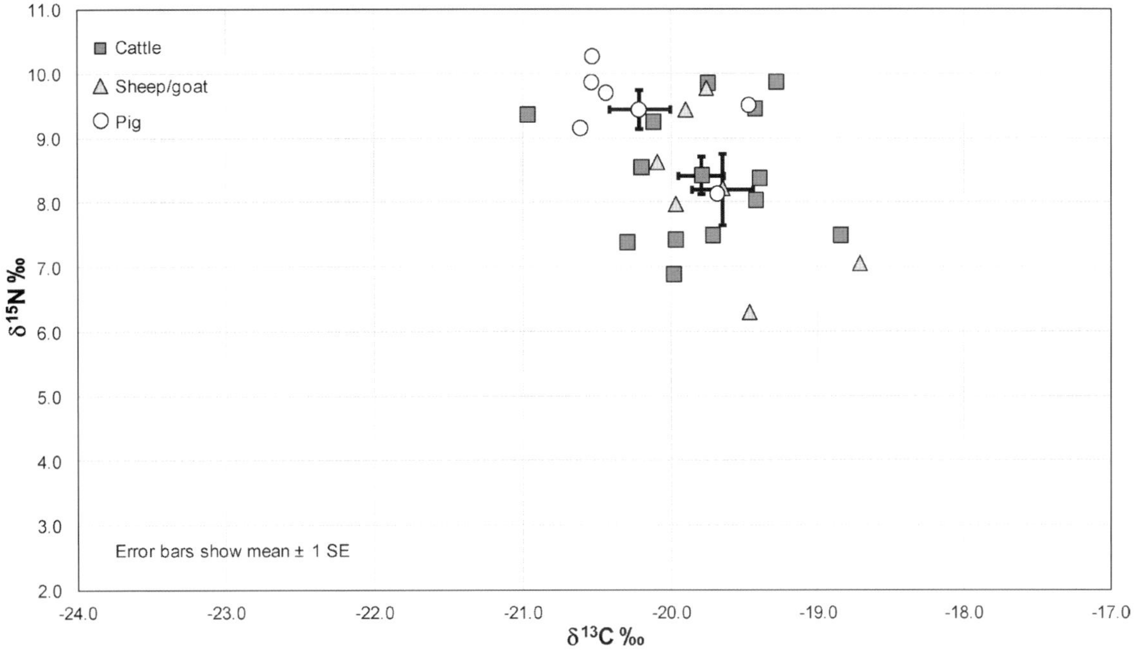

Fig. 3.31. Polgár-Ferenci-hát: carbon and nitrogen isotope ratios (‰) of animals.

Table 3.21. Polgár-Ferenci-hát: results of Tamhane's test for post hoc comparisons of means, comparing mean $\delta^{15}N$ for humans and animals. Δ is the difference between species means for each combination of species. N for fauna is as in Table 3.20, but for humans the five youngest individuals have been omitted (n=43).

Species	Cattle (n=13)		Sheep/goat (n=6)		Pig (n=6)	
	Δ‰	P	Δ‰	P	Δ‰	P
Human (n=43)	**1.9**	**<0.001**	2.1	0.057	0.8	NS
Cattle			0.2	NS	−1.0	NS
Sheep/goat					−1.2	NS

pigs had mean $\delta^{15}N$ values about 1.2‰ higher and, perhaps unexpectedly, $\delta^{13}C$ values about 0.5‰ lower, though neither of these differences were statistically significant (Fig. 3.31). The pigs appear to fall into two groups, with $\delta^{13}C$ values about 1‰ apart, possibly reflecting dietary variation or different use of landscape, perhaps on a seasonal basis; the lower $\delta^{13}C$ values could reflect greater use of woodland resources (further discussed in Chapter 9.2.6).

Comparison of humans and animals

Older juvenile and adult human mean isotope values do not differ significantly (above) and this group was used in comparisons with animals. Overall, the differences between species in mean $\delta^{13}C$ were not significant, with human means differing from faunal means by 0.1–0.3‰, but the differences between species in mean $\delta^{15}N$ were highly significant (Kruskal-Wallis ANOVA, $p<0.001$). Post hoc comparison of means shows that the difference between human and cattle mean $\delta^{15}N$, 1.9‰, is highly significant (Table 3.21) and the difference between humans and sheep/goats is close to significant.

As noted in the previous section, the difference in $\delta^{15}N$ values between humans and fauna is lower here than at Füzesabony-Gubakút. This is due to the difference in faunal values between the two sites: the human populations are not significantly different in mean isotope values, but an ANOVA on the fauna shows that the site effect is significant both for $\delta^{13}C$ ($p=0.051$) and $\delta^{15}N$ ($p<0.001$), while the species effect is not significant.

Correlations with the archaeological data

Given how close the community is in terms of the data from the stable isotope results, correlations with the archaeological data are unlikely. No patterns can be seen in the comparison between the $\delta^{13}C$ and $\delta^{15}N$ values and the treatment of the body. The burials sampled were largely oriented from E–W to S–N, with a few NE–SW and one N–S oriented burial. This makes the one NW–SE oriented burial unusual, though isotopically it does not stand out. This burial is also right-crouched. Again unusual body positions do not appear to have a relationship with the stable isotopes, though as more than two thirds of the burials are in a left-crouched position this is not surprising. The four ALBK I (Szatmár) burials also fall within the average for the site. There were also no correlations with the grave goods, though it is interesting to note that two of the neonates with breast-feeding signals (high $\delta^{15}N$) were buried with *Spondylus*. There may also be a relationship

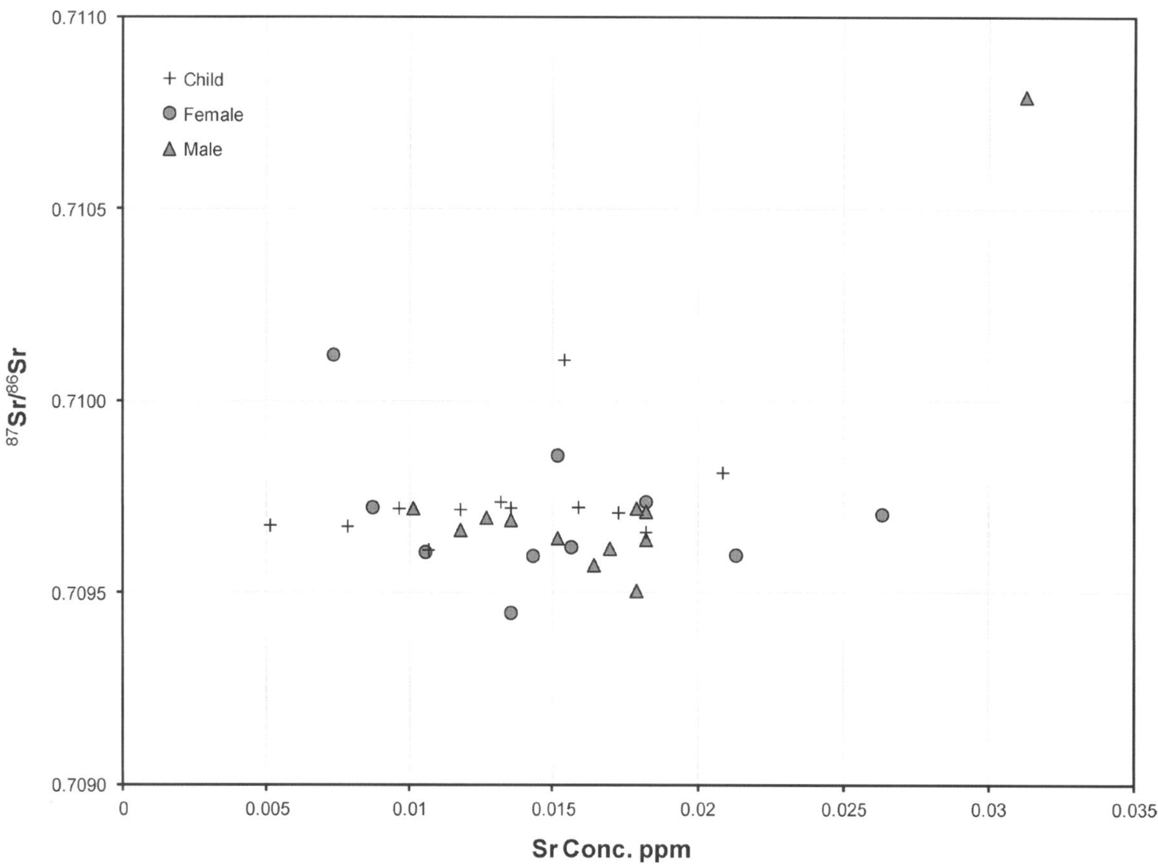

Fig. 3.32. Polgár-Ferenci-hát: strontium concentration (ppm) versus ratio ($^{87}Sr/^{86}Sr$).

*Table 3.22. Polgár-Ferenci-hát: strontium isotope ratios and concentrations. * denotes number of analyses, not number of individuals.*

Age/sex	Mean $^{87}Sr/^{86}Sr$	SD $^{87}Sr/^{86}Sr$	Mean Sr conc.	SD Sr conc.	n*
Juvenile	0.70974	0.000126	87	41	12
Male	0.70975	0.000335	65	17	12
Female	0.70970	0.000184	76	31	10
All	0.70974	0.000236	76	32	34

between *Spondylus* and high $\delta^{13}C$ values (Mann-Whitney U test, p=0.045), but only six graves are accompanied by *Spondylus*, including the graves of four infants (<5 years, including two with $\delta^{15}N$ values suggestive of a breast-feeding signature) and two adult females. No differences in the stable isotopes between the various areas of the site could be determined.

3.9.4 Strontium analysis

Thirty-three individuals were sampled from Polgár-Ferenci-hát, including ten females, 12 males and 11 sub-adults (Fig. 3.32; Table 3.22).[4] The $^{87}Sr/^{86}Sr$ mean for the site was 0.70973±0.00023 and the male (0.7975 ± 0.00032) and female (0.70974±0.00021) mean Sr ratios were the same. There was one extreme outlier in grave 698/1005 (0.71079), which was a mid-adult male, interred with no grave goods, who stands out from the rest of the settlement (Fig. 3.32). The rest of the population (ranging from 0.70945, grave 34/83, to 0.71012, grave 33/42) fall within the expected range for loess soils and the local area (see above, and Chapters 3.7.3 and 3.8.4), as well as showing a comparable range to the animals from Polgár-Piócási-dűlő (Giblin 2011, 225). As shown in Fig. 3.32, excluding the outlier, females have a greater range in strontium ratios than males, a difference which is significant in an F-test (p<0.001) but not by Levene's test (p=0.07). Since this pattern is repeated at so many other LBK sites in this study, the difference at Polgár-Ferenci-hát is well worth noting.

It is also interesting to note that the outlying samples came from second and third molars. Differences between the molars in $^{87}Sr/^{86}Sr$ ratio are just outside statistical significance (excluding the one pre-molar value; Levene's test for variance, p=0.08; different means; One-way ANOVA $F_{(2,28)}$=2.564, p=0.095). This may suggest that lifeways varied over age, with the M1 molar representing in part a breast-feeding signature from the mother's strontium intake, while the M2 and M3 molars mineralise in later childhood, when increased mobility (such as herding animals off the loess) may have been introduced. If we break this down between the sexes the numbers of samples become very low and caution must be taken with the results, but the values for male M2 molars are more variable than for M1 and M3 molars. The $^{87}Sr/^{86}Sr$ ratios are more variable (Levene's test, $p=0.001$, n=11) if the outlying value of 698/1005 is included, but the probability drops if this burial is excluded ($p=0.4$). The Sr concentrations are significantly more variable (Levene's test, $p=0.018$, n=11, with p increasing to 0.002 if 698/1005 is excluded). The reverse is true of women with M1 molars more variable in $^{87}Sr/^{86}Sr$ ratio than M2 molars, and M3 molars more variable than both the earlier mineralised teeth ($^{87}Sr/^{86}Sr$ ratio: Levene's test, $p=0.033$, n=9; Sr concentration, Levene's test, $p=0.34$, n=9).

If we compare variance in $^{87}Sr/^{86}Sr$ ratio between men and women for each molar sampled, another interesting pattern emerges. Among the four females, the range of $^{87}Sr/^{86}Sr$ ratio becomes larger from M1 molars (range=0.00026) to M2 (0.00039) to M3 molars (0.00052). Among males, however, all molars (M1, M2, M3) fall within a narrow range (0.00021), except for the M2 molar from burial 698/1005. Given the dietary differences suggested by the osteological study (Chapter 3.9.2), could this suggest that sex-based diet differences became more pronounced during early childhood (over the ages 8–12)?

Correlations with the archaeological data

There were no direct correlations between the strontium isotope data and the archaeological context of the burials, nor with the palaeopathological data. Given the overall uniformity of the grave orientations and the body positions, any patterning would be unlikely. The furnished graves (with $^{87}Sr/^{86}Sr$ ratios ranging from 0.70620 to 0.70986) are less variable than unfurnished burials (with $^{87}Sr/^{86}Sr$ ratios ranging from 0.70945 to 0.71079). The unfurnished burials include the male outlier from grave 698/1005 and the two other burials with $^{87}Sr/^{86}Sr$ ratios above 0.710 (33/42 and 644/944). There are no correlations between stable isotopes and the strontium data. The strontium ratios and concentrations did not vary across the different areas of the site, though two individuals with $^{87}Sr/^{86}Sr$ ratios above 0.7101 (graves 644/944 and 698/1005) were buried close together at the northern end of the site.

3.9.5 Site summary and discussion

It is important to note that only half the burials at Polgár-Ferenci-hát were available for sampling and the conclusions here must be seen as preliminary pending total publication of the site. $^{87}Sr/^{86}Sr$ outliers are rare and only three individuals fall outside the upper range for loess soils, but within the range of the nearby Bükk mountains ($^{87}Sr/^{86}Sr$ = 0.71137; see Chapter 3.7.3). As the human strontium ratios did not fall below the lower range for loess soils, it is therefore unlikely that the more distant Tokaj mountains or the Zemplén hills, with $^{87}Sr/^{86}Sr$ values of *c.* 0.707, were contributing to the formation of strontium in the tooth.

The isotope data and osteological analysis from Polgár-Ferenci-hát suggest some variation in lifeways, particularly in the health and diet of males and females. The osteological study identified two major differences between the sexes. The first relates to childhood health, in which males suffered more childhood stress than females. The second difference, higher rates of caries in women, suggests dietary differences – particularly that women may have been consuming more starchy foods than men. Among hunter-gatherers such as the Hadza, women, who spend more time (and therefore eat more frequently) at the camp or home-base, eat a wider variety of food, including more foraged tubers (Berbesque and Marlowe 2009; Berbesque *et al.* 2011). In a study of the dental health of present-day foragers and famers in central Africa, Walker and Hewlett (1990, 388) found that amongst the hunter-gatherers, the women had higher frequencies of missing teeth and caries rates, but amongst the farming population, while missing teeth had a higher incidence in females, caries was more frequent amongst the men. These differences are attributed primarily to dietary differences (rather than survival rates or access to dental treatment) arising in the daily practices of men and women, bringing them into contact with food sources of varied availability (Walker and Hewlett 1990; Berbesque and Marlowe 2009; Berbesque *et al.* 2011). Obviously, there are also distinct differences in the types of food which Neolithic populations in eastern Hungary were consuming and the diet of modern-day central African populations, but these studies may suggest that the observed variation between the sexes at Polgár might have related in some ways to differences in their respective mobility and daily practices.

The difference in male and female lifeways can also be identified amongst the strontium isotope data, which suggest that women had more diverse sources of strontium in their diet than males. This could be related to higher female mobility, and possibly practices of viri- and patrilocality. However, the differences between the different molars sampled may hint at sex-based dietary differences that led to some females sourcing a higher component of their diet off the loess, possibly even through continued foraging practices.

Special features in the graves recovered at Polgár–Ferenci-hát are best represented in the concentration of grave goods of unusual value or character, though in comparison to other regions in this study the range of grave goods is rather limited (*Spondylus*, pottery, four obsidian objects and one bone ring). It is possible that these goods signified unusually rich graves, possibly of people who directly owned or exchanged raw materials of high value. The obsidian is particularly interesting in relation to the strontium results as, unlike at Mezőkövesd, all $^{87}Sr/^{86}Sr$ ratios from Polgár fell above 0.7095, with no suggestion of individuals linked to the Zemplén hills – a likely source for obsidian. The occurrence of obsidian may perhaps be related to the advantageous geographical and territorial location (at the interface between three regional stylistic

Fig. 3.33. Balatonszárszó-Kis-erdei-dűlő: plan. After Oross and Marton (2012, fig. 1).

groups of the ALP) of the Polgár settlement and the as yet unclarified but possibly leading or central role of this settlement at the end of the middle Neolithic.

3.10 Balatonszárszó-Kis-erdei-dűlő

3.10.1 Introduction (Krisztián Oross and Tibor Marton)

Balatonszárszó-Kis-erdei-dűlő is in central Transdanubia on the southern shore of Lake Balaton (Fig. 3.1). It was discovered in the course of the salvage excavations carried out along the track of the planned M7 motorway when the ruins of a medieval church and a cemetery around it were investigated. The LBK settlement is located on a natural plateau[5] that slopes gently to the lake some 2–2.5 km away. The excavations of the Neolithic site were carried out between 2001 and 2006, uncovering some 10 ha.

Even though our knowledge of LBK settlements in this region has vastly expanded over the last two decades, the 48 house plans (Category A)recovered at Balatonszárszó (Fig. 3.33) are unparalleled in western Hungary (Bánffy and Oross 2009, 227–33, Tab. 2, Abb. 6; Oross and Bánffy 2009, 183–4, fig. 9). Štúrovo on the northern bank of the Danube in south-west Slovakia is so far the most comparable published site in the Carpathian basin (Pavúk 1982b; 1994; Chapter 4.4). A further 11 houses were suggested by the presence of long pits and just a few postholes between them (Category B; Marton and Oross 2009, 55–6). On the basis of that record, the three main house types of LBK architecture defined by Modderman (1970, 100–20; 1972; 1986b) could be identified, albeit in a modified form, since complete cross-rows of oval or elongated postholes could not be detected in the south-eastern part of the assumed tripartite houses. Otherwise the data reinforced Juraj Pavúk's observations from Štúrovo that the cross-rows of posts were evenly distributed in the houses (Pavúk 1994, 65). This is plausibly one of the substantial differences between the LBK architecture of the Carpathian basin and more western areas of central Europe. Alongside the house architecture, the northernmost part of an enclosure came to light in the southern periphery of the excavation (the 160 m long section of the enclosure had traces of four, or possibly five entrances) and 43 burials were discovered across the site.

Five main style groups were distinguished in the pottery. The earliest is equivalent to the pottery of the Bicske-Bíňa phase, and the second has its best parallels in the assemblages attributed by Pavúk (1980a, 45–7) to the Milanovce phase. They provide unambiguous evidence for the existence of the settlement during the early (but not earliest) LBK period. The third style group marks the beginning of the later LBK development with the pottery of the early Keszthely group, accompanied by a few sherds with *Notenkopf* decoration. Style group four is dominated by Keszthely group pottery, but with limited instances of Zseliz (Želiezovce in Slovakian) decoration. The most important characteristic of the fifth and latest style group is therefore the increase of Zseliz decorated sherds (the Keszthely and the Zseliz style decorations are often equally frequent in these assemblages) (Marton 2008). Some forty radiocarbon dates indicate that the settlement was occupied between *c.* 5350 and *c.* 5000 cal BC (Bánffy and Oross 2009; 2010; Oross *et al.* 2010).

The settlement consists of two separate but continuous occupations. Five widely separated buildings stood in the north-eastern area. Three of these were surrounded exclusively by features of the Bicske-Bíňa phase. One single building can be dated to the Milanovce phase, while the fifth one already represents early Keszthely development. In contrast, the southern part was densely built in with houses. Altogether 43 house plans with clear postholes and all the less well identified structures were located there (Fig. 3.33). The house plans of the southern settlement area can be dated by pottery of the third, fourth and fifth style groups. On this basis, the settlement was founded as a small hamlet in the Bicske-Bíňa phase of the early LBK/TLP. The residential area moved southwards and an essential change took place at the beginning of the later LBK phases when the settlement expanded and the enclosure was established. House plans of the early Keszthely phase are located in the south-eastern area, close to that of the early LBK phases. House remains associated with predominantly Keszthely style ceramics, i.e. the fourth style group, are more concentrated in the south-western part, but some of them constitute groups between the house clusters of the preceding early Keszthely phase. There are only a few house plans dated by the pottery material of the fifth and latest style group.

Most of the houses in the southern area form small groups. Each group consists of four to six house plans and gives the impression of a house row, in which the buildings shared a common long axis. Within each house row, the long pits alongside the houses and other related features yielded almost exclusively pottery of the same style group, seemingly contradicting the classical model worked out for the layout of LBK sites in the Rhineland, made up of farmstead parcels (the *Hofplatz* model; Boelicke 1982; Boelicke *et al.* 1988), but consistent with the model proposed by Oliver Rück (2007; 2009; Chapter 1.3.2). There is, however, no certain evidence that all the houses of a single row were in indisputably contemporaneous use. One possible explanation could be a version of the model suggested by Jens Lüning for the Schwanfeld settlement (Lüning 2005a), where the house plans of the early LBK were uncovered side by side in a very similar position, but without a single overlap (Stäuble 2005, 50–72, 202–4, Abb. 147, Beilage 6). Lüning argued that the successive building of these houses followed recurrent rules (Lüning 2005a, 54–61, Abb. 11).

Fig. 3.34. Balatonszárszó-Kis-erdei-dűlő: burial 780 (34–40 years at death, male).

The 43 burials were scattered over the entire excavated area of Balatonszárszó-Kis-erdei-dűlő (Figs 3.33, 3.34; Table 3.23; Oross and Marton 2012; Zoffmann 2012). Male, female and child burials occur, and are almost equally distributed. Associations could not be observed between the graves and other features like houses or long pits, with the exception of one single burial (burial 791, which was buried in its own pit just inside the enclosure ditch and its orientation followed the ditch); most of the burials were uncovered in the uppermost layers of refuse pits. Grave pits or hard-packed surfaces below the remains of the body were detected only in a limited number of cases, but the burials seem always to be separated from the pit fill. Left-crouched burials dominated (over 70% of all crouched burials). Two skeletons uncovered in a supine position appear to have been thrown into refuse pits; in another case, the representation of the skeleton was not extensive enough to determine its original position. Several variations could be detected in the orientation of the deceased, but the W–E direction was totally avoided.

Grave goods came to light in only seven burials (Oross and Marton 2012, 269–77). Pots, chipped stone tools, a stone adze, bone objects including a hairpin, two awls, a pair of *Spondylus* pendants, which appeared to have

Table 3.23. Balatonszárszó-Kis-erdei-dűlő: the isotope, osteological and archaeological data. Age and sex information from Zoffmann (2012). See Chapter 2 for further definition of ages. Key for body position: LC – Left-crouched; RC – Right-crouched; C – Crouched, direction unknown; CB – Crouched on back; CF – Crouched on front; S – Supine; P – Prone; I – Irregular. Key for grave goods (number of items in brackets): U. – Unfurnished; F. – Fill only (all items listed after an F. were in the fill of the grave rather than at the level of the skeleton); Pol. – Polished stone; Cer. – Ceramics; Shd. – Sherds; Spon. – Spondylus*; She. – Other Shell; Och. – Ochre; Ant. – Antler; Lit. – Chipped stone; Bon – Worked bone; Grd. – Grinding stone.*

Burial	Tooth	Bone	Sex	Age (yrs)	$^{87}Sr/^{86}Sr$	Sr ppm	$\delta^{13}C$ ‰	$\delta^{15}N$ ‰	Orientation	Body position	Grave goods
36	-	-	M	31–40	-	-	-	-	S–N	LC	U.
159	-	-	-	1–3	-	-	-	-	S–N	RC	U.
278	-	Long bone	-	12–14	-	-	−20.0	8.9	SE–NW	LC	U.
288	-	Long bone	-	5–6	-	-	−19.9	10.2	NE–SW	RC	Spon.(1 pair of pendants)
289	-	Femur Long bone Humerus	-	9–10	-	-	−19.5 −20.1 −20.5	9.3 9.8 9.4	NE–SW	RC	Bon.(1)
510	M1 M3	Rib Metacarpus	M	Adult	0.70918 0.70918	110 133	−19.5 −20.0	9.3 8.8	N–S	I	U.
531	M1 M3	Rib Metacarpus	M	Adult	0.70919 0.70917	77 157	−19.6 −19.9	9.5 9.5	N–S	LC	Pol.(1), Cer.(2), Lit.(2)
554	-	Long bone	F	Adult	-	-	−19.7	9.3	S–N	RC	U.
711	-	Long bone	-	13–14	-	-	−19.1	9.5	N–S	LC	U.
712	M1 M3	Long bone	M	18–19	0.70917 0.70918	150 152	−19.9	9.3	N–S	RC	U.
766	M1 M3	Long bone	M	31–40	0.70941 0.70943	87 201	−20.0	9.9	N–S	LC	Bon.(1)
767	-	Long bone	M	Adult/ Mature	-	-	−19.9	10.2	-	-	U.
768	-	Long bone	-	9–10	-	-	−20.2	9.8	S–N	LC	U.
769	-	Long bone	-	1–6	-	-	−20.2	9.8	NE–SW	LC	U.
770	M3	Rib Metacarpus	M	45–49	0.70928	157	−19.7 −20.0	10.0 9.5	N–S	LC	Spon.(1 bead)
771	M1	Rib Metacarpus	M	23–27	0.70917	115	−19.4 −19.7	10 8.9	SE–NW	S	U. [Cer.(1) ?]
772	-	Long bone	-	5–6	-	-	−19.6	8.6	-	-	U.
773	-	Rib Metacarpus	F	Adult/ Mature	-	-	−19.9 −20.0	9.8 8.4	NW–SE	LC	U.
774	-	Rib Metacarpus	F	37–46	-	-	−19.8 −20.1	9.0 8.5	-	-	U.
775	M1	Rib Scapula	-	14–16	0.70927	99	−19.3 −19.6	9.3 9.1	N–S	LC	U.
776	M3	Long bone	F	55–64	0.70948	211	−20.0	10.1	E–W	LC	U.
777	-	Long bone	F	Adult	-	-	−19.9	9.2	SW–NE	RC	U.

778	M1 M3	Long bone	F	Mature	0.70873 0.70868	143 180	−20.5	9.6	N–S	RC	U.
779	M1 dec.	Rib Pelvis	-	3–5	0.70962	73	−19.3 −19.6	11.4 11.3	S–N	LC	Cer.(1)
780	M1 M3	Rib Phalanx	M	34–40	0.70923 0.70920	107 98	−19.1 −19.7	9.6 9.3	NW–SE	LC	Bon.(2),Lit.(1)
781	-	Long bone	M	Adult/ Mature	-	-	−19.9	9.4	-	-	U.
782	M1	Rib Metacarpus	F	40–46	0.70909	88	−19.9 −19.8	10.1 9.4	N–S	S	U.
783	-	Long bone	F	56–62	-	-	−19.9	9.75	E–W	LC	U.
784	-	Long bone	M	Adult/ Mature	-	-	−20.3	10.1	-	-	U.
785	-	Long bone	M	Mature	-	-	−20.1	9.6	NE–SW	-	U.
786	-	Long bone	F	Adult	-	-	−20.2	9.6	-	-	U.
787	-	Rib Metacarpus	F	55–61	-	-	−19.6 −19.4	9.6 9.2	S–N	LC	U. [She. (1) ?]
789	M1 M3	Long bone	F	53–59	0.70872 0.70956	105 90	−20.0	9.7	S–N	-	U.
790	-	Long bone	-	5–6	-	-	−19.3	10.7	NE–SW	LC	U.
791	M1	Rib Metacarpus	F	31–40	0.70937	115	−19.7 −19.9	9.7 8.1	E–W	LC	U.
792	-	Long bone Metacarpus	M	Mature	-	-	−19.6 −19.9	9.9 9.5	E–W	LC	U.
793	M1 M3	Metacarpus Rib	M	Adult	0.70943 0.70943	106 348	−19.7 −19.6	9.7 9.6	E–W	LC	U.
794	-	Rib	F	Adult	-	-	−19.8	10.1	E–W	LC	U.
795	-	Cranium	F	Adult	-	-	−19.8	9.8	E–W	LC	U.
796	-	Patella Talus Rib	F	15–16	-	-	−19.6 −20.1 −19.5	9.6 9.7 9.5	S–N	LC	U.
797	-	Long bone		12–23	-	-	−19.9	9.3	E–W	LC	U.
798	-	Long bone	F	Mature	-	-	−20.1	9.8	E–W	LC	U.
799	-	Long bone	M	Mature	-	-	−20.3	10	-	-	U.

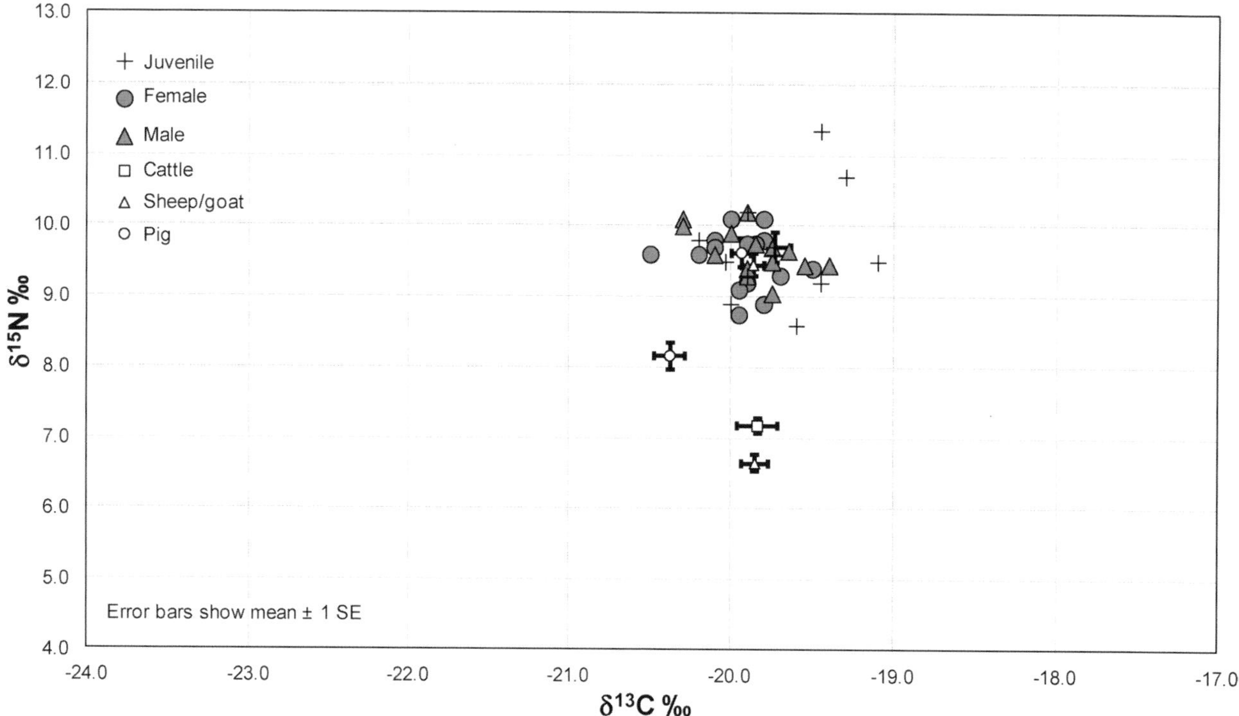

Fig. 3.35. Balatonszárszó-Kis-erdei-dűlő: carbon and nitrogen isotope ratios (‰) of humans.

been worn around the ankle, and a *Spondylus* bead were found. These grave goods belonged exclusively to men and children. Two pots, the stone adze and two chipped stone tools were discovered in burial 531 (Fábián *et al.* 2007). Another male burial (780) contained a hairpin, a bone awl and a chipped stone blade (Oross *et al.* 2004, 286–7, figs 1–2; Fig. 3.34).

On the basis of their location, stratigraphy and the radiocarbon dates, burials took place across all the phases of the settlement. It is worth noting that a larger cluster of human skeletons in the southern settlement area yielded later radiocarbon dates than the animal bone samples from pits in their environs, indicating that abandoned parts of the site were reused for interring the dead during the later phases of the site. Similarly to the settlement structure, a clear differentiation is possible between the burials discovered in the settlement area of the early LBK and those in the area with features of the later phases. All definable burials on the early LBK settlement area were left-crouched and with one single exception were oriented E–W. This unified practice altered fundamentally at the beginning of the later LBK, both concerning the position and the orientation of the bodies. Furthermore, all burials with grave goods were dated to the late period of the settlement.

Compared to the number of houses, there is no doubt that the excavated burials represent only a small portion of the population of the settlement. Agricultural activity and the removal of the uppermost soil levels directly before the excavation could have destroyed other LBK graves. Even though no LBK cemetery spatially separate from a settlement is known from western Hungary, it is unwise to write off the existence of such an arrangement entirely. The use of limited numbers of cemeteries and settlement burials could have been contemporary mortuary practices, as seen in south-west Slovakia (Farkaš 2002; Pavúk 1972b; Chapter 4.5), and the apparent absence from western Hungary might be a product of excavation history so far, though this potential difference can be noted.

3.10.2 Osteology

The osteological analysis of the human remains from Balatonszárszó was carried out by Zsuzsanna K. Zoffmann (2012).

3.10.3 Carbon and nitrogen analysis

The stable isotope values reported here were earlier analysed by Lucy Cramp, but are formally published here for the first time (Figs 3.35–6; Table 3.24). The methodology used to analyse the results was the same as is laid out in Chapter 2.2, with one sample (from burial 288) being rejected because of a discrepancy of (3‰) between two samples taken on the same bone type. Forty-one individuals from the site were sampled and in 16 cases two samples were taken from the same individual but different bones (and in two cases, three samples were taken), in order to test for consistency (Table 3.24). For the overall analysis (Chapter 9), the values from each individual were averaged to give a single mean value. In addition, δ^{15}N and δ^{13}C values were also produced from 61 cattle, 30 sheep and 21 domestic pig, whilst wild species included hare, roe deer, goat and red deer (Table 3.24).

The δ^{15}N values of the humans (from 8.1 to 11.35‰ δ^{15}N) from Balatonszárszó-Kis-erdei-dűlő suggest that some animal dietary protein was consumed, as the average

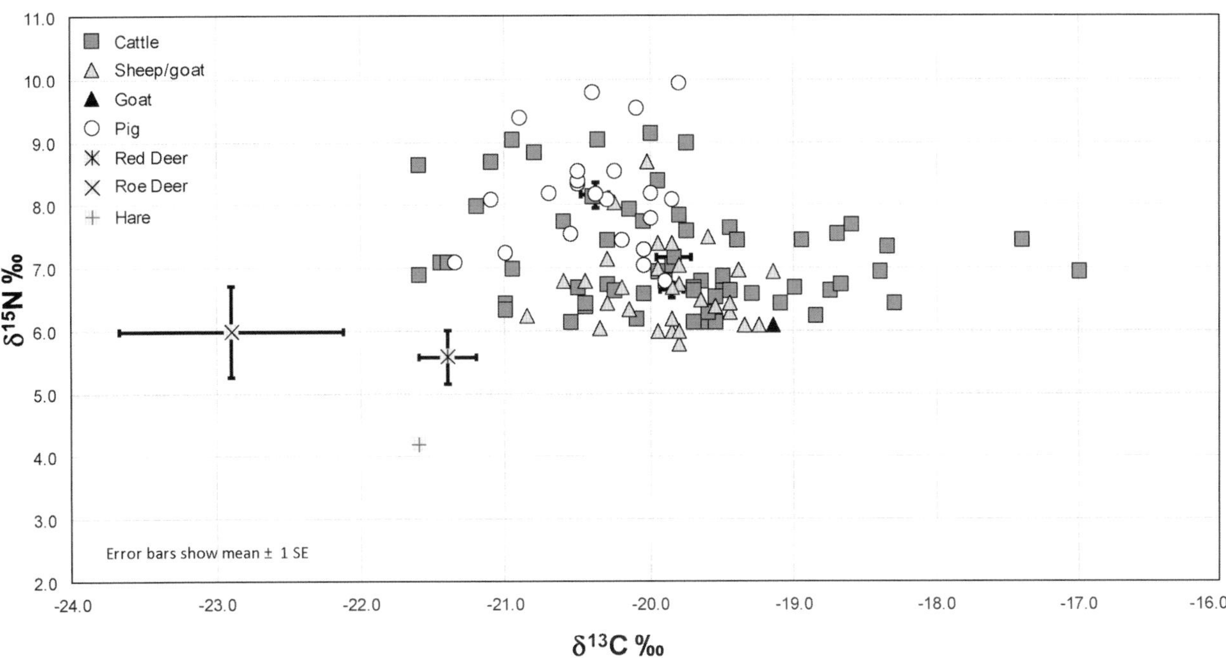

Fig. 3.36. Balatonszárszó-Kis-erdei-dűlő: carbon and nitrogen isotope ratios (‰) of animals.

*Table 3.24. Balatonszárszó-Kis-erdei-dűlő: carbon and nitrogen isotope ratios (‰) of humans and animals, with means and standard deviations. * denotes the number of analyses, not the number of individuals sampled.*

Species	Age/sex	Mean $\delta^{13}C$	SD $\delta^{13}C$	Mean $\delta^{15}N$	SD $\delta^{15}N$	n*
Human	Infant	−19.7	0.45826	10.8	0.896289	3
Human	Juvenile	−19.8	0.41887	9.5	0.569622	12
Human	Female	−19.9	0.24300	9.5	0.530148	23
Human	Male	−19.8	0.28810	9.6	0.371484	21
Human	All adult	−19.8	0.26529	9.5	0.461606	44
Cattle		−19.8	0.95883	7.2	0.834510	61
Sheep/goat		−19.9	0.41834	6.7	0.663665	30
Pig		−20.4	0.43342	8.1	0.894681	22
Hare		−21.6	-	4.2	-	1
Goat		−19.2	-	6.1	-	1
Roe deer		−22.9	1.09602	6.0	1.025305	2
Red deer		−21.4	0.28284	5.6	0.601641	2

of the human group (9.5‰) is higher than the domestic animals (2.8‰ higher than the average sheep $\delta^{15}N$ value; 2.3‰ higher than the average cattle $\delta^{15}N$; 1.4‰ higher than the average pig $\delta^{15}N$ value). The average expected enrichment of $\delta^{15}N$ values between dietary protein and consumer is in the range of 3–4‰, or higher if the consumer is a carnivore (de Niro and Epstein 1980; Schoeninger and de Niro 1984), and so the difference between human and domestic animal $\delta^{15}N$ values suggests that they were providing 40–60% of the dietary protein. Plant resources are therefore likely to have contributed significantly to the protein in the diet, with freshwater fish insignificant. The more enriched average $\delta^{15}N$ value from domestic pig (8.1) in comparison to other domesticates (cattle $\delta^{15}N$ average=7.2; sheep $\delta^{15}N$ average=6.7) is surprising and has implications for how they were managed; the $\delta^{15}N$ values suggest they were eating similar diets to humans and may have been fed on an omnivorous diet.

The $\delta^{13}C$ values of cattle are remarkably variable (−21.6‰ to −17‰). Domesticates with $\delta^{13}C$ values enriched above −19‰ are very unusual and statistical analysis of these results shows that there is a highly significant difference between the values obtained from cattle deriving from the north-eastern (mean −20.7‰, SD=0.35) and southern (mean −19.5‰, SD=0.69) parts of the settlement (*t* test=2.0, p=<0.001, n=59). This pattern is specific to cattle and is not seen in humans or other domesticates. This spatial difference suggests that different parts of the settlement were perhaps herding their animals in different locations; this is probably here largely a chronological trend, and is discussed further below (Chapter 3.10.5). The samples from wild animals (roe deer, red deer and hare) have rather depleted $\delta^{13}C$ values (−21‰ to −24‰), which are suggestive of having lived in a mainly wooded environment (and therefore influenced by the canopy effect). Given that human values have higher $\delta^{13}C$ values (mean = −19.85, 1.8–3.1‰ higher) even allowing for a ~1‰ trophic level increase, it is unlikely that these wild resources contributed significantly to the diet.

Within the population there was no distinct difference between the $\delta^{15}N$ values and $\delta^{13}C$ values of adult males and females. Overall, there were no significant differences between the $\delta^{15}N$ values and $\delta^{13}C$ values of adults and children, although three $\delta^{15}N$ analyses from children exhibit notably high $\delta^{15}N$ values (burial 779 and 790). The child in burial 779 is three to five years old and the $\delta^{15}N$ values of 11.3 and 11.4 are likely to be influenced by the nursing signal. The second child (burial 790) is thought to be five or six years old at death, but the $\delta^{15}N$ value (10.7) is determined on long bone that may have a longer turnover time than other bones (Chapter 2.2.1). However, another five- to six-year-old (in burial 772) has a very low $\delta^{15}N$ value (8.6) despite the bone analysed being a long bone. It is also surprising perhaps that the child in grave 769 (estimated between one and six years old) does not have particularly elevated $\delta^{15}N$ values (9.8), but it is still higher than the site average of 9.5. These results perhaps suggest that weaning age varied (see also above, Chapter 3.8.3). Only one of these children (779) was buried with a grave good (a half of a pot). The remaining eight children yield $\delta^{15}N$ values that are within the range of adult values.

Correlations with the archaeological data

There were no differences identifiable associated with the orientation of the graves at Balatonszárszó, but there may be a correlation between body position and $\delta^{15}N$ values. Right-crouched burials have lower average $\delta^{15}N$ values than either left-crouched or supine burials (one-way ANOVA, $F_{(3,22)}=12.417, p<0.001$, adults only), suggesting that right-crouched burials may have consumed less animal protein than those buried in other positions. With few grave goods it is difficult to distinguish any correlations between the stable isotopes and the objects which accompanied the deceased in the ground. However, no females and few adolescents were furnished, and those males that do have grave goods tend to have average or higher $\delta^{15}N$ values. There were no significant differences between the isotopic profiles of adults from the northern and southern parts of the site. Nor was there any statistical difference between the isotopic profiles of males and females both overall, or within the northern and southern areas.

3.10.4 Strontium analysis

From the settlement site of Balatonszárszó-Kis-erdei-dűlő, 15 individuals were available for sampling: eight males, five females and two juveniles (Fig. 3.37; Table 3.25). In eight cases it was possible to sample the M1 and M3 molars from the same individual, resulting in 23 analyses being carried out on the population. The settlement is situated on the shore of Lake Balaton, on loess and loess-derived soils, resulting in the local area providing strontium isotopes in the range of 0.7085–0.7105. All the values from the site fell within this range, suggesting that the inhabitants at the settlement did not practise any mobility over significant distances. However, the local geology could also be a factor in the strontium isotope values. North of lake Balaton, the Bakony mountains (the primary source for Szentgál radiolarite) principally consist of Jurassic limestone (Mateiciucová 2008a, 49), which is likely to have provided $^{87}Sr/^{86}Sr$ ratios less radiogenic than the loess (0.7070–0.7080; Price *et al.* 2004). South of lake Balaton the loess spreads across a large area of the low-lying Somogy hills (Magyari *et al.* 2005).

The mean $^{87}Sr/^{86}Sr$ ratio for men (0.70926±0.00011) was higher than the mean of females $^{87}Sr/^{86}Sr$ ratios (0.70909±0.00038). In line with the results from Polgár, female $^{87}Sr/^{86}Sr$ ratios were significantly more variable than male ratios (Levene's test, $p<0.005$). This is due to three of the female $^{87}Sr/^{86}Sr$ ratios falling below 0.7090 (two values from burial 778 and one value from the M1 molar of the female in burial 789). These results suggest that the individual in burial 778 moved to the Balaton area after her M3 molar had mineralised, but this was not the case with the female in grave 789, whose M3 molar $^{87}Sr/^{86}Sr$ ratio (0.70956) falls within the local range and who must have therefore moved before the M3 had mineralised (by age 14–16; Table 3.25). Both these individuals were found in unusual body positions. The female in burial 778, who had non-loess strontium ratios from both her M1 and M3 molars, is in a right-crouched position and the female in grave 789 was placed probably in a variant of the left-crouched position with the upper part of the torso lying on the back.

When the particular tooth sampled is examined, there is a significant difference in the means of the strontium concentrations from M1 and M3 molars (M1, mean=105, n=13; M3, mean=173, n=10; Mann-Whitney U test, p=0.004). This means that, on average, M1 molars have a lower strontium concentration than M3 molars, suggesting a switch to higher strontium concentration foods over childhood. This pattern could therefore represent a breast-feeding signature as the M1 molar is mineralising (milk is a low strontium concentration food), while the higher strontium concentrations in M3 molars could originate in a greater contribution of plant foods to the diet. Unlike the results from Polgár, no differences between the M1 and M3 molars of men and women could be distinguished.

No overall correlation between grave goods and the

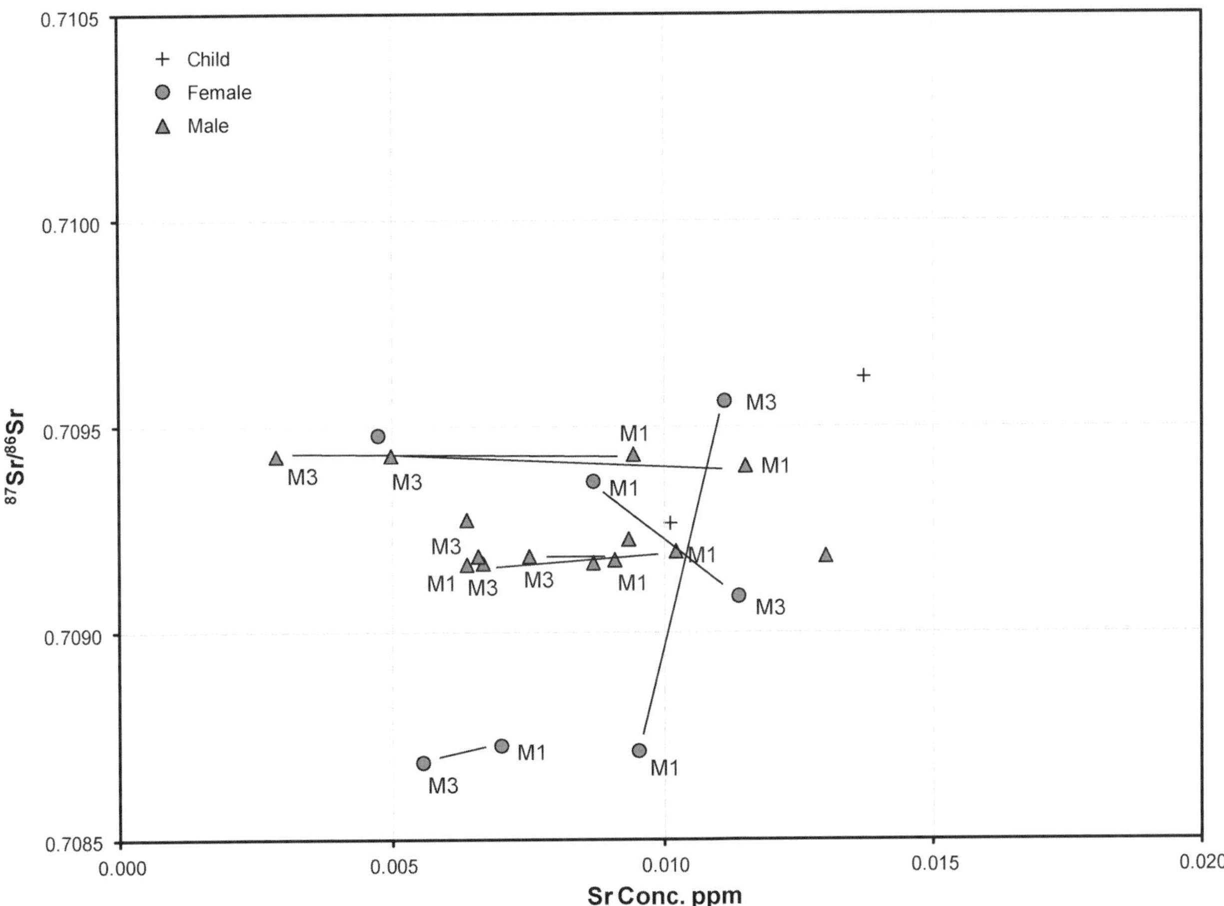

Fig. 3.37. Balatonszárszó-Kis-erdei-dűlő: strontium concentration (ppm) versus ratio ($^{87}Sr/^{86}Sr$). Lines connect teeth from the same individual.

Table 3.25. Balatonszárszó-Kis-erdei-dűlő: strontium isotope ratios and concentrations.

Age/sex	Mean $^{87}Sr/^{86}Sr$	SD $^{87}Sr/^{86}Sr$	Mean Sr conc.	SD Sr conc.	n
Juvenile	0.70944	0.00025	86	19	2
Male	0.70926	0.00011	143	68	14
Female	0.70909	0.00038	133	47	7
All	0.70923	0.00025	135	60	23

strontium isotopes could be determined, though we can note that the three of the four adult males from furnished burials that we sampled have very similar $^{87}Sr/^{86}Sr$ ratios (burial 531, with polished stone, chipped stone blades and ceramics, 0.70917 and 0.70919; burial 771, with a possible sherd (though the relationship is uncertain), 0.70917; burial 780, with hairpin, bone awl and a stone blade, 0.70923 and 0.70920), all of which fall below the site mean for males of 0.70926. One male, aged 45–49 at death (burial 770), was furnished with a *Spondylus* bead and had a slightly higher $^{87}Sr/^{86}Sr$ ratio of 0.70928. Burials which were furnished therefore have less variance in their $^{87}Sr/^{86}Sr$ ratios than unfurnished ones. This is significant (Levene's test p=0.001), but low sample numbers urge interpretive caution. This trend does suggest, however, that furnished males either had similar geographic origins or had similar dietary sources or habits in childhood.

Only one of the burials from the earliest part of the site (north-eastern area, Bicske-Bíňa phase I) was sampled. This was an adult male (burial 793), who had a relatively high $^{87}Sr/^{86}Sr$ ratio of 0.70943 on both teeth sampled. The rest of the burials fall within the later LBK/TLP phases. The two female outliers with low $^{87}Sr/^{86}Sr$ ratios are widely dispersed on either edge of the excavated area.

Correlation with $\delta^{13}C$ and $\delta^{15}N$ values

No overall correlations between the strontium data and the stable isotopes could be determined. However, the strontium outliers had unusually low $\delta^{13}C$ values. The female burial 778 had the lowest $\delta^{13}C$ value of all the burials (−20.5‰), and the other outlier (burial 789) also had a $\delta^{13}C$ value of −20.0‰, which is lower than the female mean (−19.8‰).

3.10.5 Site summary and discussion

The isotopic results from Balatonszárszó-Kis-erdei-dűlő suggest some interesting patterns of variation across both the human and animal populations. Principally the stable isotope results suggest that the community were sharing a similar diet which consisted of animal protein, but with a large contribution from plants. The $^{87}Sr/^{86}Sr$ ratios, however, do suggest that the population represented in our sample included people from geographically outlying areas, particularly the females in burials 778 and 789, who in contrast to elsewhere in this project are identified as outliers because their ratios fall below the loess $^{87}Sr/^{86}Sr$ ratio range (0.7085–0.7015). This is likely to be a result of the geology of the area and these two women need not have moved far between childhood and death. The specific molars sampled suggest that they moved at different ages. It is also interesting to note that the female who moved in after her M3 molar had mineralised, and was therefore more likely to have moved in adulthood, was buried in a right-crouched position. These two women also have low $\delta^{13}C$ values and, while these are not as low as the values from the wild animals sampled, may suggest they were consuming more foods from wooded environments (the canopy effect). Other results noted above, however, suggest generally little use of wild animals.

Throwing the results from these two women into relief are the $^{87}Sr/^{86}Sr$ ratios from males in furnished graves, which show distinctly less variation than the unfurnished males. As all furnished graves belonged to the later part of the settlement, this could indicate subsistence strategies changing to a more homogeneous diet for males over time, though it has to be noted that most burials date to the late phase of the site. A chronological change can also be seen in the $\delta^{13}C$ values of cattle with a lower average $\delta^{13}C$ value in the later south-eastern part of the site than the higher average values in the earliest north-eastern area of the settlement. This may suggest that cattle were being herded in a different location or environment, but could also relate to a change in what food sources were used for cattle. Other changes in burial practices have also been noted above, such as growing variation in body position and orientation from all burials being E–W or similar and left-crouched, to using varied orientations, as well as right-crouched and supine burial positions alongside left-crouched. Taken together these changes contribute to a picture of increasing diversity in the latter stages of the settlement.

3.11 Regional discussion

The four sites investigated in the region of Hungary come from two related but separate traditions of the LBK. Füzesabony, Mezőkövesd and Polgár, located in eastern Hungary, belong to the ALP, originating in contacts with the Körös culture, while Balatonszárszó-Kis-erdei-dűlő, in western Hungary, is part of the TLP, which is likely to have found its origins in the Starčevo culture, and it is probably from this area (and perhaps from Lower Austria as well) that the LBK spread northwards and westwards. However, this region differs in so much as the large cemeteries which we will encounter in the other regional chapters are absent, or still to be discovered, and what evidence we have comes from burials interred on settlements. Another important contrast to the rest of the sites analysed in the LBK Lifeways project is the date of the burials. At least some of the burials from Alföld sites date to the early Szatmár phase, placing them not only geographically but also chronologically at the beginning of the LBK. This strengthens connections to the Starčevo and Körös cultures in west and east Hungary respectively and suggests that some continuity in burial rites between these early Neolithic cultures and the LBK can be demonstrated.

We can usefully compare the strontium ratios and concentrations from the three Alföld sites because they lie within approximately 40 km of each other, on similar soils and at roughly equal distances from varied geologies. The individuals at Füzesabony have a higher average $^{87}Sr/^{86}Sr$ ratio (0.71015) than those buried at Mezőkövesd (0.70986), while these two sites are only 10 km apart. This difference is significant (Mann-Whitney U test, p=0.004), suggesting different mobility or food sourcing strategies. This is perhaps echoed in the average lower $\delta^{13}C$ at Füzesabony (mean = −20.0 at Füzesabony, −19.7 at Mezőkövesd), but as there were only a few samples available from Mezőkövesd for stable isotope analysis this remains an open question for future research. The $^{87}Sr/^{86}Sr$ ratios from Polgár (0.70974) are on average closer to those from Mezőkövesd, though the strontium concentrations are generally lower than those found at either Mezőkövesd or Füzesabony (Mann-Whitney U test, p<0.001). While in the results from Mezőkövesd and Polgár there is a tight cluster and one outlier, the results from Füzesabony are more variable (more widely and evenly spread; Levene's test p=0.005, excluding the outliers from Mezőkövesd and Polgár). These results suggest that the mobility and food sourcing strategies of settlements close to one another could vary.

There are also some notable differences in funerary practices between eastern and western Hungary, though as Balatonszárszó-Kis-erdei-dűlő dominates the burial assemblage from western Hungary, this may change as more burials come to light. Left-crouched burials oriented E–W and SE–NW (with the head to the east and south-east) dominated in eastern Hungary, resulting in other body positions and orientations being far rarer (Table 3.1). In contrast, the burials from Balatonszárszó are much more evenly spread across the different combinations of position and orientation (Tables 3.2 and 3.23). The greater variability in orientations and body positions at this site compared to the others discussed in the chapter perhaps illustrates connections to the greater diversity found in Starčevo and Körös burial practices (Chapter 3.5), though it must be noted that the earlier burials at this site are more uniform (E–W, left-crouched) than the later ones. It is also interesting to note that at Mezőkövesd, Polgár and Balatonszárszó outliers identified through both strontium and carbon isotopes were found in a right-crouched position. Grave goods also show interesting differences between the west and east of Hungary. In the Alföld areas *Spondylus* is frequent and emphasis appears to fall on adorning the body in the grave, while at Balatonszárszó grave goods are rare, but when they do occur a range of different objects are found.

A strong sense of sex-based diets has developed through the discussion of the osteological and isotope data gathered by this project from Hungary, alongside a shift towards a more plant-based diet in adulthood. Females from Polgár had more caries than males (Chapter 3.9.2), suggesting that they had eaten more starchy foods. We can perhaps suggest that this was because women spent more time at the settlement, but the sex-based differences certainly indicate that the lifeways of men and women were different in Hungary during the LBK.

Notes

1 Though there are several problems in this paper with the attribution of particular sites to the Mesolithic.

2 Over 40 samples have been dated so far (Domboróczki 2003); a further 36 have been submitted by László Domboróczki and Alasdair Whittle, and results are pending.

3 Radiocarbon dates are as follows: grave 1, 6295±35BP , 5350–5210 cal BC at 95% confidence (VERA-4237); grave 2, 6250±90 BP, 5466–4991 cal BC (deb-11092); grave 3, 6285±35 BP, 5350–5200 cal BC (VERA-4238); grave 4, 6325±35 BP, 5380–5210 cal BC (VERA-4236); grave 5, 6320±40 BP, 5470–5210 cal BC (VERA-4239); grave 6, 6295±35 BP, 5350–5210 cal BC (VERA-4240); grave 7, 6255±40 BP, 5320–5070 cal BC (VERA-4241); grave 9, 6489±40 BP, 5529–5367 cal BC (deb-13042); and grave 10, 6295±40 BP, 5370–5200 cal BC (VERA-4242).

4 We had intended to take as many as 50 samples for strontium analysis, but unfortunately this was not possible, as when the skulls of some individuals were reconstructed the mandibles were glued to the maxillas, often at the surface of the molars.

5 At an altitude between 149 and 160 m.

A Polgár-Ferenci-hát lifeway: burial 839/1198

On the death of this middle-aged woman, the Polgár community, perhaps her immediate relatives, chose to bury her within an area of the settlement surrounded by an enclosure. She had not lived as long as some women buried at Polgár, but her age at death was average for the community. At some point during adulthood, but before her death, she received a trepanation, following an injury or violent episode; the skull had a shallow depression, where the bone was unusually thin (Fig. 3.29). It is also possible that the trepanation was motivated by other reasons, from relieving physical symptoms such as headaches to the expulsion of evil spirits. While what encouraged the trepanation to take place is unclear, the woman in burial 839/1198 lived long enough for the bone to heal and it is unlikely that the defect is related to cause of death.

Her grave was dug at one end of an arc of burials, a short distance away from what may have been a longhouse. While we do not know how she was related to the other individuals near whom she was buried, it was appropriate that in death she should remain close to them. Those burying her chose to place her body in a left-crouched position and oriented the grave so her head was to the east, ways of treating the body that the majority of the dead received at Polgár. Her grave contained no grave goods, but this was a recurrent practice at this site. As her grave was not later disturbed, but on the edge of a spread of pits, perhaps it was marked in some way, preventing it from being cut into by settlement activities.

Her experiences in life may have also been familiar to many women who lived at Polgár. It seems that she had eaten a diet sourced mainly from loess soils in childhood (M1, $^{87}Sr/^{86}Sr$ *ratio=0.70960), as had the majority of the sampled population, suggesting she had lived locally and not travelled far during her life. Her skeleton also provided further clues as to the kind of lifeway she lived. Her teeth had been used as tools – her incisors showed evidence of wear probably caused by pulling fibrous materials across the surface of her teeth. Similar dental wear was also found on the teeth of two other older adult women at Polgár – and perhaps formed after many years of regularly repeating this activity. This would presumably have been a sedentary activity and perhaps during her life she spent many hours sitting outside a longhouse preparing fibres for making baskets or other similar objects.*

The diet of this woman was rich in starchy foods, as shown by three carious lesions. Males at Polgár were less likely to have caries, suggesting that men and women ate different diets. Caries would have been painful and can affect what food is eaten, and even in extreme cases speech, but they would have been an experience shared by many of the women at the community. The foodstuffs she consumed during the last ten or so years of her life were average in terms of dietary carbon content ($\delta^{13}C=-20.0$)*, but had elevated her nitrogen levels. In fact, she had the highest nitrogen isotope value of any female at the site* ($\delta^{15}N=11.4‰$)*, exceeded only by two males, suggesting that alongside starchy foods, she had eaten slightly more animal protein than other women. At Polgár, nitrogen values tended to increase with age. Perhaps as this individual aged her position in the community became more significant, and this was recognised through a greater access to animal protein. Overall, the daily practices of men and women, both in terms of diet and in terms of routine activities such as fibre processing, seem quite strictly defined and regulated at this site. Gendered identity, with various adjustments throughout the lifecourse, was sedimented in the body through routine experience.*

A Balatonszárszó lifeway: burial 531

Burial 531 is that of a man who died in adulthood (between 23–39 years). The strontium ratios from his first and third molars fall within the local range expected for the settlement (M1, $^{87}Sr/^{86}Sr$ ratio=0.70919, and M3, $^{87}Sr/^{86}Sr$ ratio= 0.70917, respectively), meaning that he may well have been born and lived most of his life on the soils local to Balatonszárszó. He was interred in the upper layers of a pit complex, directly between two longhouses in the southern part of the site. This pit complex incorporated the loam pits of the two houses, suggesting his burial was made after the houses had been constructed. This is supported by the pottery from the loam pits, which could be much earlier than that interred with the burial. It is unclear in how far burial 531 deliberately referenced these much earlier buildings, but if it did, then a connection was being made to a time by now quite far removed. Another burial was made further to the north in the same pit complex, again containing an adult man of a similar age at death (burial 510). That individual provided similar strontium ratios, so is also likely to have lived locally during his life.

The stable isotope measurements from burial 531 are close to the site means for males, with a carbon isotope value of −19.6‰ (local male mean −19.8‰) and a nitrogen value of 9.5‰ (local male mean 9.6‰). The stable isotope values from humans and domestic animals suggest that there was a more homogeneous diet in the later phases at the site, when this man lived, with little contribution from wild resources. It also seems that plant protein contributed significantly to his diet. He is likely, therefore, to have been engaged in farming practices, perhaps even owning and caring for his own herd of cattle or fields in the vicinity of Balatonszárszó. Both his lifeway and his burial were probably shared by other males at this site.

The legs of burial 531 were in a left-crouched position, but the upper body was slightly turned on its back, with a post-mortem dislocation of the spine at the waist. The burial was oriented north–south, as are nearly half of all male burials at Balatonszárszó. However, he was one of only seven burials to definitely receive grave goods, and in his case they stand out as unique. One of the pots in his grave had decorative motifs not found on other vessels here and his was also the only burial to receive a polished stone adze.

All furnished individuals at Balatonszárszó – these are only men and children – date to the late phases of occupation, and in this respect burial 531 illustrates a site-wide trend towards increasing diversification. In addition, the five furnished individuals with available strontium measurements exhibit a significantly reduced variance in their $^{87}Sr/^{86}Sr$ ratios compared to the unfurnished individuals. This means that people with grave goods had similar geographical origins or similar dietary habits in childhood, and this influenced the likelihood of their being marked out in death. This pattern echoes the more formalised male burials found in cemeteries across the rest of the regions analysed in this project – despite his local life, in burial he was marked out in ways that were widespread across the LBK. However, in the context of Balatonszárszó, burial 531 with his polished adze was unusual.

4 Moravia and western Slovakia

Alasdair Whittle, R. Alexander Bentley, Penny Bickle, Marta Dočkalová, Linda Fibiger, Julie Hamilton, Robert Hedges, Inna Mateiciucová and Juraj Pavúk

4.1 Introduction

The Neolithic archaeologies of Moravia and Slovakia, previously provinces first in the Austro-Hungarian monarchy and then within Czechoslovakia, and now half of an independent state and a whole state themselves, have often been treated separately. This chapter takes them together, with the sites sampled by this project standing as selected and, we hope, preliminary case studies of the numerous LBK communities which inhabited the river valleys and basins running south into the middle Danube. That geography of Danube tributaries may perhaps serve better to define this region of LBK settlement than modern and historical state boundaries (Fig. 4.1). From west to east, the major rivers in Moravia are the Dyje (Thaya in German) and the Morava (March in German), which, in turn with their tributaries including the Jihlava and the Svratka, drain from the Moravian uplands. The lower Morava forms the state boundary between Moravia and Slovakia, the Dyje (briefly the Thaya where it bends into Lower Austria) joining it more or less at the north-east corner of Lower Austria, and then the state boundary between Austria and Slovakia. The Morava runs into the Danube at Bratislava. Further description is given by Mateiciucová (2008a, 20–1). Then in Slovakia, from west to east, come a further series of Danube tributaries, principally the Váh, the Nitra, the Hron and the Ipel' (Ipoly in Hungarian), these swinging in from the north-east from the end of the Carpathian chain. More pronounced than in Moravia, there are tongues of raised ground between parts of these valleys, including the Malé Karpaty ridge between the Morava and Váh, and the Tribeč and others between the middle Nitra and Hron. The lower parts of these valleys, however, form a substantial, low-lying basin north of the Danube and west of its great bend near Esztergom, equivalent to the Kisalföld (or Little Hungarian Plain) to the south of the Danube.

The more easterly LBK communities in question in this chapter thus belong to western Slovakia, though it is worth noting that there are interesting pockets of LBK settlement in the upper reaches of the Váh, with probable connections across the Tatra mountains to LBK communities in southern Poland (Soják 2000; cf. Šiška 2002), and much further to the east, around Košice and Michalovce, there are further LBK settlements, essentially part of the LBK story in the upper Tisza and the northernmost part of the Great Hungarian Plain (Lichardus 1972a; 1972b; Šiška 1989; Chapter 3).

4.2 History of research

Research on the LBK of this region goes as far back as the late nineteenth century. At this time, an expanding interest in archaeology and a gradual increase in institutions such as museums, both national and regional, and university chairs coincided with growing urbanisation and industrialisation (Sklenář 1993). The first LBK finds came from a cave in the Moravian karst, and others followed in the 1890s, discovered and fitted into then emergent schemes of regional chronology by 'the two giants of Moravian prehistory', Jaroslav Palliardi and Inocenc Červinka (Podborský 1993, 71–3; Čižmář 2008b). Palliardi first came to prominence in the 1880s for his recognition close to Znojmo, in the basin of the Dyje, of what is now known as middle Neolithic Moravian Painted Ware (Kovárník 2008); LBK finds were included in his wider classifications of the Moravian Neolithic in the 1890s and early twentieth century (e.g. Palliardi 1914). Červinka was responsible among other work for first observations of the LBK complex, including graves, at Vedrovice, near Moravský Krumlov south-west of Brno, in the valley of a tributary of the Jihlava (Ondruš 2002), and then for his own classification of the LBK in Moravia (e.g. Červinka 1904); it was he who first developed the terminology of 'band' and 'linear' to describe LBK pottery (Podborský 1993, 72; Čižmář 2008b, 43).

Initial classification schemes were subsequently filled out by continuing investigations, including still by amateur archaeologists (Podborský 1993, 326), and wider syntheses were published in the 1930s and 1940s (e.g. Skutil 1941, on Moravian LBK graves; Eisner 1933, on Slovakia as a whole). It is revealing that a further synthesis of the Slovakian

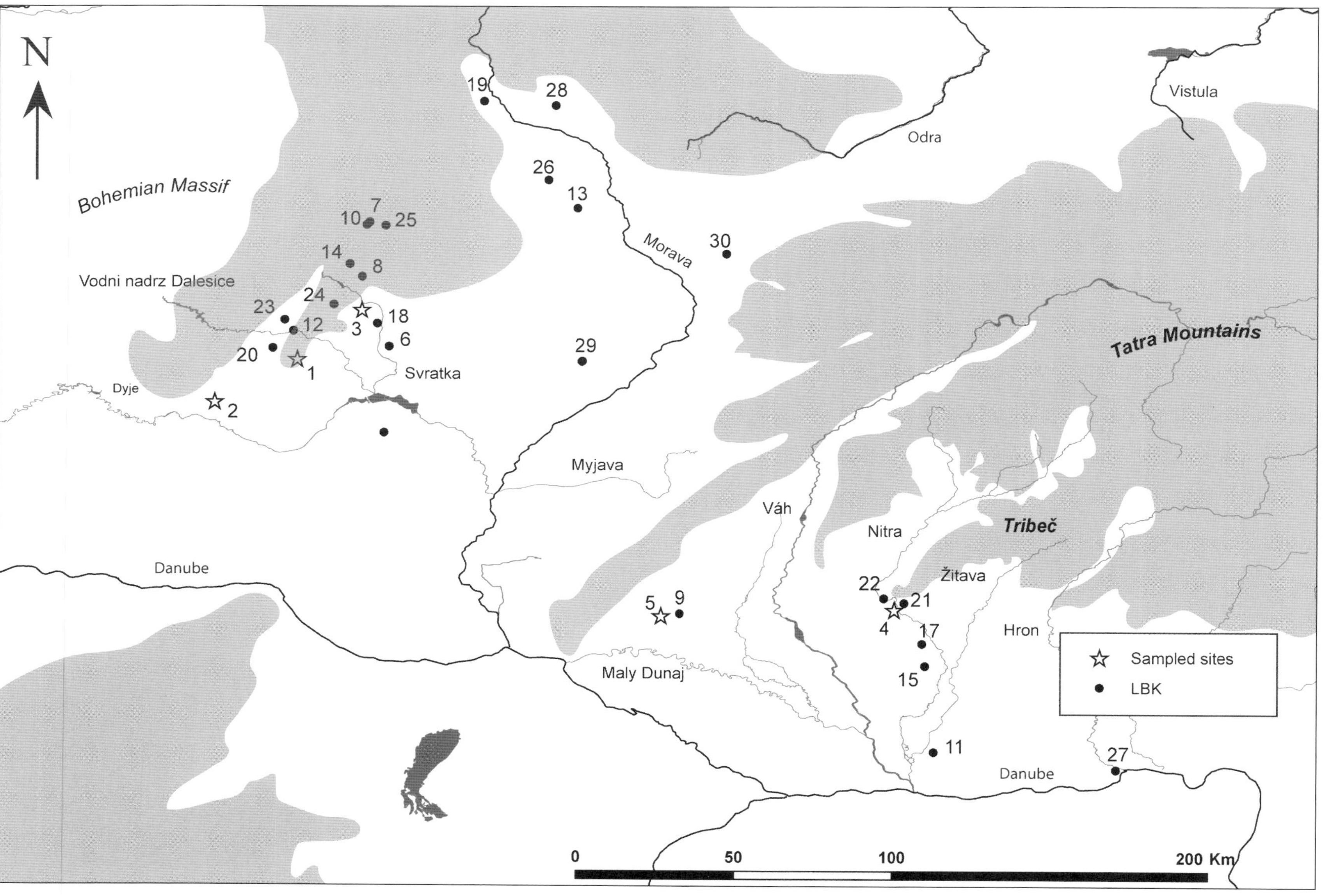

Fig. 4.1. Map of sites sampled (1–5) and others mentioned in Chapter 4. Upland areas are in italics. 1) Vedrovice, 2) Těšetice-Kyjovice, 3) Brno-Starý Lískovec, 4) Nitra 'Horné Krškany', 5) Blatné, 6) Blučina, 7) Bořitov, 8) Brno-Ivanovice, 9) Čataj, 10) Černá Hora, 11) Hurbanovo, 12) Ivančice, 13) Kralice na Hané, 14) Kuřim, 15) Lipová-Ondrochov, 16) Mikulov, 17) Milanovce, 18) Modřice, 19) Mohelnice, 20) Moravský Krumlov, 21) Nitra 'Mikov dvor', 22) Nitra-Mlynárce, 23) Padochov, 24) Popůvky, 25) Rájec-Jestřebí, 26) Slatinky, 27) Štúrovo, 28) Uničov, 29) Žádovice, 30) Žopy.

Neolithic in the 1950s still did not report the recognition of LBK houses (Novotný 1958). A recognisable change of pace, however, can be seen from that decade onwards. In Moravia, from the base of the State Archaeological Institute in Brno, later the Archaeological Institute of the Czechoslovak Academy of Sciences (Čižmář 2008b, 43), Tichý began work in the early 1950s (which was to last until the mid-1960s) on the LBK settlement at Mohelnice in the Morava valley north of Olomouc, exposing house plans and pit complexes in full, and in due course a waterlogged well (R. Tichý 1956; 1962b; 1972; Schmidt and Gruhle 2003a; 2003b; Rad. Tichý 2007). Excavation began in earnest at Těšetice-Kyjovice near Znojmo in the early 1960s (Podborský 1988; Dočkalová and Košťuřík 1996; Dreslerová 2006; Kazdová 2008), and of the settlement at Vedrovice at the same time (Podborský 2002a). In Slovakia, the Archaeological Institute was founded as an outpost within the National Museum system as far back as 1938, becoming independent in 1942 and brought into the Academy of Sciences system in 1953 (Ruttkay 1998). Notable fieldwork included graves at Nitra-Mlynárce in the early 1950s (Plesl 1952; Farkaš 2002), the rescue of the cemetery of Nitra in the mid-1960s (Pavúk 1972a), and the initiation of rescue excavations in 1965 at Štúrovo, on the north bank of the Danube just to the west of the confluence of the Hron (Pavúk 1994).

This kind of activity continued into the 1970s and 1980s, notably at Vedrovice and Těšetice in Moravia (Ondruš 2002, 12; Kazdová 2008), and Čataj in Slovakia (Pavúk 1986). In turn, this was bound up with a rigorous and persistent tradition of regional synthesis. In Moravia, Tichý was active with regional classification and periodisation of the LBK in the early to mid-1960s (R. Tichý 1960; 1961; 1962a). This approach can also be seen at a more local level in various studies, for example of settlement around Znojmo (Podborský and Vildomec 1972) and Třebíč, well up the Jihlava (Košťuřík 1986). It has continued in Moravia at a regional scale up to the present (Podborský 1993; Čižmář 1998a; 2008a; 2008b). In western Slovakia, Juraj Pavúk, excavator of Štúrovo, has contributed a fundamentally important series of syntheses on the chronology and character of the LBK, concentrating on that part of the country (Pavúk 1969; 1980a; 1982a; 1994; 2004; 2009; Pavúk and Šiška 1971; 1980).

The new conditions post-1989 led to an increase in industrial development and road-building schemes, and in turn to the founding in the early 1990s of organisations to cope with the increased demand for archaeological evaluation and excavation. A series of sites thus investigated are listed by Čižmář (2008b, 43), especially in the south around Brno and Znojmo, including Brno-Starý Lískovec (M. Přichystal 2008).[1] It appears that less of this kind of activity has so far taken place in western Slovakia (Ruttkay 1998, 139), though the situation may now slowly be changing. Other notable, research-driven investigations in the last decade have been the intensive, inter-disciplinary investigations of the two cemeteries at Vedrovice (Podborský 2002a; 2002b; Lukes *et al.* 2008; and see below), and a wide-ranging examination of the lithic sources and technologies used in the late Mesolithic and the LBK, principally in Moravia and Lower Austria (Mateiciucová 2008a).

From all this work, the presence of numerous LBK communities has been established across the river valleys and basins which drain south into the middle Danube. A figure of some 400 sites was already proposed in the 1990s for the Moravian distribution (Podborský 1993, 526), and the maps of Pavúk (1969, Abb. 57; 1980a, Abb. 1; cf. Pavúk and Šiška 1971; 1980) suggest at least another 200 or so sites, taking all phases of the LBK together, in western Slovakia. These are predominantly settlements with longhouses and pits; the possibility of pit dwellings has been considered but does not seem to be a recurrent feature (Čižmář 1998c). Some enclosures are known, as at Vedrovice and Brno-Starý Lískovec. Graves and burials within settlements are recurrent, and unlike the situation known so far in Hungary to the south (Chapter 3), Vedrovice and Nitra, among other sites, show separate cemeteries. In these, the mortuary rite was predominantly one involving single inhumations. Cremation deposits have been found more recently at Kralice na Hané, on the outskirts of Prostějov in the valley of the Valová, tributary of the Morava (Čižmář 2008b, 44; Šmíd 2008). Perhaps the LBK in Bohemia has been more widely known (e.g. Rulf 1997; Zápotocká 1998; Pavlů 2000b; 2005a; 2005b; 2010; Pavlů and Květina 2009; Končelová 2005), but the dataset from Moravia and western Slovakia has by now become formidable in its own right.

The regional chronologies and their synchronisations have been usefully set out by Mateiciucová (2008a, table 3, based on Podborský 1993 and Čižmář 1998a; Table 4.1 here). Further detail is given below, but overall the sequence is defined by changes in pottery, partly in its forms but predominantly in its decorative motifs and patterns; much reliance has been placed on detailed study of typological differences between closed (or supposedly closed) assemblages, both within and between individual sites. This has served, broadly, to define an early LBK (phase I in Moravia), with relatively simple pot forms and decoration and with relatively straightforward house plans, both of which match trends identified more widely in central Europe (Quitta 1960; Stäuble 2005), and a late LBK (phase II in Moravia), with more elaborate pottery decoration, including the 'music note' (*Notenkopf*) motif, and more numerous settlements. A latest phase is also distinguished, identified as the Želiezovce group in western Slovakia and in Moravia (phase III), followed there also by the Šárka style. In Bohemia, perhaps more in line with wider chronological distinctions within the LBK, these stages have been labelled Early, Middle, Late and Final (Pavlů and Zápotocká 1979). Relatively few radiocarbon dates have been obtained so far (e.g. Mateiciucová 2008a, 240–1, 245, for Těšetice and Vedrovice; see further below), summarised as 5450–5070 cal BC for phase I, and 5260–4900 cal BC for phases II and III (Mateiciucová 2008a, table 4); clearly much more work on refining absolute chronology needs to be done.

Table 4.1. LBK periodisation in Bohemia, Moravia and Slovakia (after Čižmář 1998a, Tab. 1).

J. Pavúk		R. Tichý		Z. Čižmář	E. Neustupný	I. Pavlů - M. Zápotocká	
Želiezovce group	III					IVb	
			Nová Ves	Šárka type (III)	V		LBK
						IVa	
	IIb	Šárka stage					
						III/IV	Final
	IIa	III	Mohelnice feature CCXX			IIIb	
					IV		
	I			Želiezovce group I IIc		IIIa	Late LBK
Late LBK						IIc	
	III	IIb		IIb	III		
						IIb	
			Vedrovice ditched enclosures				
	II			IIa$_2$			
						IIa	
		IIa			II		
	I			IIa$_1$		I/II	Middle LBK
Early LBK	Milanovce		Vedrovice cemetery		I		
						Ic	
		Ib		Ib			
	Hurbanovo					(Ib)	
	Bíňa		Žádlovice-Újezd				
	Nitra	Ia	Žopy	Ia		? (Ia)	Early LBK

4.3 The Mesolithic-Neolithic transition and the earliest LBK

Broadly speaking, the further north one comes from the Balkans and the Carpathian basin into central Europe, the more late Mesolithic sites can be identified, and so compared to Hungary (Chapter 3), a larger series of late Mesolithic occupations have been found: in western Slovakia, principally along the Váh, and also along the Žitava (parallel to the Hron) and at Bratislava, and in Moravia principally along the Jihlava, Dyje and Morava (Mateiciucová 2008a, 41–3; see also Svoboda 2008). These are mainly surface assemblages, and very few have been properly investigated; the use of caves in upland Slovakia is also known (Bárta 1990). The distinctive lithic signature is the use of trapezes (Mateiciucová 2008a, 41–3; Kozłowski and Nowak 2007).

From the outset, at whatever precise date this may prove to be, LBK sites are found on loess deposits and other good soils along the valleys already noted. Pottery forms include open and closed bowls and flasks or bottles; grooved decorative lines, including meander patterns, are typical, and there are also fingertip impressions; the details of this kind of repertoire define the phases proposed for western Slovakia and Moravia. Excavations have established the presence of simple but not insubstantial longhouses, including those of early form with outer wall trenches at Mohelnice (R. Tichý 1956; 1960; 1962b; Stäuble 2005, 126–37). A timber from a well at Mohelnice has been reported as having a dendrochronological date of 5450 BC (Pavlů 2005a, 301), but whether this relates to sapwood and therefore the date of felling was unclear; other reported dendrochronological estimates are older, while radiocarbon dates place the feature in the 53rd or 52nd century cal BC (Stäuble 2005, 134–6). A considered dendrochronological date, allowing for the absence of sapwood, has been given as 5540±5 BC (Schmidt and Gruhle 2003a; 2003b; cf. Rad. Tichý 2007). Other important sites are Brno-Ivanovice (Čižmář 1998b) and Popůvky near Brno (Bálek 2002; Čižmář 2008b). The latter is assigned to phase Ia, and has several longhouses a little short of 20 m long, apparently laid out in rows (Bálek 2002, fig. 4); rescue conditions prevented the full extent of the settlement from being established. The houses are partly defined by stretches of side ditch. Part of the settlement and the two cemeteries at Vedrovice (and see further below) have been assigned to the earlier part of phase Ib in the Moravian scheme (Podborský 2002a; 2002b, 316; Čižmář 2002, 175; Ondruš 2002); further radiocarbon dating appears to place the 'Široká u lesa' cemetery in the 53rd century cal BC, perhaps spanning some five or six generations (Pettitt and Hedges 2008). According to some general and wider models (e.g. Lüning 2005a, Abb. 23; cf. Bánffy and Oross 2010, Tab. 1), this date may appear surprisingly late, but could in fact be a better indication of the likely span of the first main phase of the LBK in central Europe (cf. Bánffy and Oross 2010, Tab. 2). Other significant Moravian phase Ib sites include Slatinky, Žádovice, Modřice and Bořitov (Čižmář 2008b). In south-west Slovakia, Pavúk (1980a; 2004; 2012) names Nitra, Hurbanovo and Bíňa as the earliest sites, which he places earlier than the LBK in Moravia.

The dominant model in the study of this region to explain the appearance of the LBK has undoubtedly been the arrival of new people from points south, with accompanying assimilation of the indigenous population (e.g. R. Tichý 1962a, 304–5; Podborský 1993, 525–6; Pavúk 1980a, 79, 84); for Bohemia, Ivan Pavlů has referred to the presence of incomers, only in small numbers, as 'missionaries or managers of Neolithisation' (2004; 2005, 301). It is worth remembering that there had been an earlier tradition in the region of thinking of indigenous development ('Substrat Theorie'), as noted by R. Tichý (1961), Quitta (1960, 23) and Pavúk (1980a, 79; see also Sherratt (2004, 53), referring back to Schuchhardt (1919)). A much more active role for indigenous people has been suggested in the 'integrationist' model proposed more recently by Marek Zvelebil and Alena Lukes (Zvelebil 2004; Rad. Tichý 2004; Zvelebil and Pettitt 2008; Zvelebil *et al.* 2010; Lukes and Zvelebil 2008; Lukes *et al.* 2008), and other comparable, if perhaps less detailed, suggestions have been noted by Mateiciucová (2008b, 36). Her own work on lithic sources and traditions identifies the strong possibility of continuity (Mateiciucová 2008a, 159): 'the LBK originated autochthonously from the local Mesolithic substrate in Transdanubia and the immediately adjacent areas (Burgenland, south-west Slovakia), under the influence of contacts with, and with a biological contribution from, Balkan early Neolithic populations, in particular from the Starčevo culture'. Thus, from an early LBK pit at Žopy near Holešov, in a tributary of the Morava (seen by its first excavators as a dwelling), there was a relatively small assemblage dominated by Kraków Jurassic flint, with some Transdanubian radiolarite, and blades and one trapeze were present (Mateiciucová 2008a, 263–7). It should be noted that other specialists maintain a different view, still radically downplaying the contribution of indigenous people, who are seen as sparse and dispersed in small enclaves (Kozłowski and Nowak 2010, 87; Kozłowski and Raczky 2010).

More genetic information is becoming available to compare with archaeological inferences, and the situation appears to be changing quite rapidly. Drawing on genetic studies (of Y chromosome haplogroups) of the modern Czech population (Kráčmarová *et al.* 2006), and other wider studies in south-east Europe as a whole of both modern and ancient DNA in male and female lines, Zvelebil and Pettitt (2006, 254–5; and references) have suggested a big picture of incoming new population in the Aegean and south-east Europe, but considerable 'cultural and genetic interaction' between Karanovo I, Starčevo, Körös and Criş communities and local hunter-gatherers, in the coastal Adriatic and the north Balkans, which 'resulted in the next generation of Neolithic communities, including the LBK'. Genetically, that is seen as including males from the local population, itself regionally diverse. The LBK consolidated in core areas of western Hungary, eastern Austria, southern Slovakia and southern Moravia, before expanding, still in its earliest phase, to Bohemia, Saxony and beyond in Germany, and southern Poland, or, according to Pavúk (2004, 78; 2012), in a more limited 'primary centre' of Transdanubia and south-west Slovakia; the LBK was not a self-aware, ethnic unit, in this view, but rather a broad social tradition and a way of doing things (Zvelebil and Pettitt 2006, 255). Initial results of aDNA studies appeared to conform to this model (e.g. Haak *et al.* 2005), including those from a minimum of three male and three female skeletons from the Vedrovice 'Široká u lesa' cemetery; haplogroups K and T2, of suggested Palaeolithic descent, were prevalent (Bramanti 2008).[2] A subsequent, wider study of LBK samples in other parts of central and western Europe, together with some late Mesolithic samples, however, has suggested a pattern of non-overlap between late Mesolithic and LBK populations (Bramanti *et al.* 2009; cf. Haak *et al.* 2010; Zvelebil *et al.* 2010, Tab. 1). We can note the low survival rate of aDNA and some problems with possible contamination at Vedrovice (Bramanti 2008, 159), and the scenario is wide open for further research.

4.4 The developed and late LBK

The sequence is structured, as noted above, predominantly by changes in pot decoration, and the developed phase

Fig. 4.2. Vedrovice: excavation in progress. Top: the ditch being excavated. Bottom: a grave from the Za Dvorem area of the site being lifted by Stanislav Šillar. Photos: Archive of the Moravian Museum, Brno.

of the LBK in Moravia and Slovakia is dominated by the *Notenkopf* motif, as an anchoring element in filled bands, at first in strongly geometric patterns. Želiezovce pottery is distinguished again by its decoration, formed by impressions made with a double-pointed tool and arranged in unbounded bands (Čižmář 2008b; Pavúk 1969). An earlier synthesis emphasised the presence of Želiezovce (the same as Zseliz: Chapter 3) pottery especially to the east of the river Morava (Podborský 1993, 527), but a more recent one notes its presence 'with greater or lesser intensity over the entire area of the Moravian LBK culture' (Čižmář 2008b). The late Šárka style is confined to Moravia, closer to its main concentration in Bohemia, and prefiguring *Stichbandkeramik*. Important though pottery has been for establishing sequence and relationships, other materials were significant. Mateiciucová (2008a, maps 7 and 8) has plotted the ongoing complexity of a very wide range of lithic materials and their distribution. Krumlovský Les chert and Olomučany chert among other materials came from Moravian sources; Jurassic flint from the region of Kraków in southern Poland was important too; and some Bakony radiolarites from the area of Lake Balaton and some Carpathian obsidian from eastern Slovakia or north-east Hungary were still being circulated. Imported *Spondylus* was present in Vedrovice in phase I (having been recorded there already in the late nineteenth century: Podborský 2002a), and remained in the inventory of the cemetery at Nitra, where it occurs in the graves of seven males and one female (Pavúk 1972a, Tab. I).

Perhaps the most important development overall in this phase is a probable increase in the number of sites, consistent with observations in other regions of the LBK distribution (Fig. 4.2). In Moravia, 'the number of settlements grows over the entire area' (Čižmář 2008b, 43), and maps of the LBK distribution in Slovakia show the same trend (Pavúk 1980a, Abb. 1; Pavúk and Šiška 1971); most of the settlements being recorded in interim reports in Moravia appear to belong to this phase (see also, among many others, Bálek *et al.* 2000; Čižmář and Geislerová 1996; 1997; Čižmář and Přichystal 2004; Geislerová 1992). It remains important, therefore, for the absolute date of the start of phase II to be better established in the future. It appears that some sites at least were larger than in phase I. The rescue excavations at Štúrovo, for example, uncovered a main area some 140 by 120 m, which had longhouses distributed across it and seemingly not confined to it. To the east a further excavated area, some 35 by 20 m in extent, and containing one substantial longhouse and its pits, suggests a minimum overall west–east extent of some 200 m (Pavúk 1994, Abb. 1, 62 and Beilage 1). The excavator has mooted a settlement area of up to 500 m along the Danube (Pavúk 1994, 240).

Ten building phases were identified at Štúrovo, from the developed (*jüngere*) LBK to the Želiezovce phase (and such continuity is at odds with the wider claims for a 'crisis' at the end of the LBK: for example, Farruggia 2002). The excavator suggests a more or less continuous occupation. Houses did not fill the whole of the main area excavated, and there is a characteristically complicated pattern of house replacement; again the excavator suggests a series of *Bauareale* or house sites, akin to the *Hofplatz* model proposed for the Aldenhovener Platte in north-west Germany (Pavúk 1994, 250). In some phases at least, however, some patterning in rows can be considered (cf. Rück 2009). The longhouses at Štúrovo with complete plans ranged from 14 m to 37 m in length. Other substantial buildings were found at Čataj north-east of Bratislava (Pavúk 1986), and the longest, at some 45 m, is recorded from Kuřim in Moravia (Bálek *et al.* 2000). At Štúrovo as elsewhere, the longhouse of the developed LBK has five rows of posts, and the excavator identified a range from very large buildings, one including a plank-walled northern end, to small, two-part or two-compartment structures; the bulk of the buildings were in a range from 20–30 m long (Pavúk 1986, Abb. 29–30). For Moravia, it has been suggested that variation in the number of storage pits accompanying longhouses may be significant for 'social stratification among the inhabitants of particular settlements' (Čižmář 2008b, 44). At a wider scale of analysis, Moravia and Slovakia have been assigned, along with Little Poland and Silesia, to an eastern zone of the LBK. With houses analysed only from Mohelnice, Vedrovice and Nitra, these regions have not figured greatly in the suggested architectural patterning (Coudart 1998), and it may be difficult anyway to fit them into typologies proposed for elsewhere to the west (D. Hofmann forthcoming).

Consistent perhaps with this broad picture of more sites forming a more populous landscape, recent investigations have taken the total number of sites in Moravia with enclosures to six (Čižmář 2008b, 44). At Vedrovice itself, south of the main identified cemetery, a very large enclosure with a flat-bottomed ditch, covering both the areas known as 'Široká u lesa' and 'Za dvorem' respectively, is some 425 by 275 m in extent (Ondruš 2002). Within this there are both substantial longhouses (Berkovec and Nývltová-Fišáková 2003, fig. 2), and further burials, perhaps part of a second cemetery. The large enclosure and associated features belong to phase IIa of the Moravian sequence, later than the start of the Široká u lesa cemetery a little to its north (Ondruš 2002; Berkovec and Humpolová 2008). At Brno-Starý Lískovec, a ditched and palisaded enclosure, from the end of phase I, is part of a much larger and long-lasting LBK settlement, with longhouses, pits, kilns, some graves and a well (M. Přichystal 2008). The enclosure has an irregular, D-shaped plan or 'half-ellipse'. It is said to belong to the 'peak of development' of the settlement (M. Přichystal 2008, 55). Other enclosures are known at Bořitov, Černá Hora, Rájec-Jestřebí and Uničov (Čižmář 2008b, 44).

No comprehensive review has been recently provided of LBK subsistence in Moravia and Slovakia, but in general terms the available evidence suggests practices and trends similar to those found elsewhere in central Europe (Chapter 1.3.3). At Štúrovo, limited flotation of pits produced carbonised cereals, with emmer dominant, and einkorn and spelt also present (Pavúk 1994, 100; E. Hajnalová 1983). Štúrovo also provided a surprisingly large assemblage of animal bones, some 3400 being identifiable from a total of some 5000 (Pavúk 1994, 101). Domesticates dominate the assemblage. Cattle provided the most bones, followed by sheep/goats, with pigs far behind, but in terms of minimum numbers of individuals, sheep/goats were more numerous than cattle; this pattern persists into the Želiezovce phase (Pavúk 1994, 101–12). Relatively small numbers of bones were found in individual features, but further details of age, sex and bone condition are not given (Pavúk 1994, 110), and although the site is by the Danube, there is no word of fishbones. Preservation was poorer in the large LBK assemblage at Těšetice-Kyjovice, where finds from the Moravian Painted Ware phase helped to provide contrasts with trends found in LBK features (Dreslerová 2006); the site has longhouses, pits and graves (see further below). Domesticates dominate again (some 95% of identifiable bones, compared with only 40–50% in the Moravian Painted Ware phase), with cattle most numerous and ovicaprines and pigs in equal numbers; cattle could be aged between 1 and 4 years, and pigs up to 4 years. Skeletal part analysis suggests that all the domesticates were being consumed in the same way, for meat (Dreslerová 2006, figs 2, 4, 6). Wild game included deer, as also at Štúrovo, but also aurochs; one fishbone, of wels (*Silurus glanis*), could be identified in a LBK context (Dreslerová 2006). A broadly comparable picture has been obtained from a sample of animal bones from the area of dense LBK occupation, with longhouses and pits, within the large enclosure at Vedrovice, excavated in the 1960s and early 1970s (Berkovec and Nývltová-Fišáková 2003). Overall, domesticates dominate again, but deer, boar, marten and beaver were also identified; cattle appear most numerous overall, but relative frequency varies in detail among the pit complexes investigated (Berkovec and Nývltová-Fišáková 2003, graphs 1–12). Domesticates were mainly of mature age, though again varying by individual context (Berkovec and Nývltová-Fišáková 2003, graphs 13–18).

4.5 Burial rites and regional networks

Burials, including those in cemeteries, have already been mentioned above, and can now be fitted into a wider overview of mortuary practice in the LBK of Moravia and Slovakia. Cemeteries have been found in both Moravia and western Slovakia. In Moravia they are found in phase I, but disappear in phase IIa, whereas in Slovakia the known examples come from the developed LBK (Čižmář 2002, 190; 2008b; Farkaš 2002), although Pavúk (forthcoming) assigns grave 12 at Nitra (see below) to the beginning of the *Notenkopf* phase in the region, which he models as contemporary to the beginning of burial at Vedrovice. Across the two regions about 200 cemetery burials are known, the numbers dominated by Nitra (75; Pavúk 1972a) and Vedrovice (97; Podborský 2002a); in comparison approximately 85 settlement burials have been found (Podborský 2002b, 323; Dočkalová and Čižmář 2007). Not all burials are published to the same extent and in some cases we can only note the number of burials present at a site (Lifeways Database).

Settlement burials appear to occur throughout the sequence in Slovakia (Farkaš 2002), but mainly in phase I in Moravia (Čižmář 2002; 2008b; Dočkalová and Čižmář 2008a; 2008b). Early examples in Slovakia probably include three skeletons from Bíňa, in the valley of a tributary of the lower Hron, and two from Čataj, none of these having grave goods (Farkaš 2002). Examples from Moravia include Ivančice, Blučina, Brno-Komín, Mikulov and Žádovice (Podborský 1993, 87–8; Dočkalová and Čižmář 2008a). A much longer list is given for the developed LBK including the Želiezovce phase in Slovakia (Farkaš 2002). Štúrovo provides several examples (Pavúk

1994; Jelínek 1975). All lack accompanying goods. A child is set in a small grave, but the rest, adults and a child, were placed in settlement pits. As we saw in Chapter 3, there appears to be some regularity in body placement, in the crouched position, but again varying from left to right side. In feature 92, the complete skeleton of an adult, possibly a woman, crouched on her right side, underlay a series of incomplete remains, many from the head, from at least two further individuals, probably younger in age and one probably female (Pavúk 1994, 96).

At Vedrovice, indications of a second cemetery have been found in the Za dvorem part of the site, with 13 inhumation graves recovered over the years (Ondruš 2002, Abb. 110); further graves, mainly of children, have also been found in ongoing excavations of the settlement to the west (Berkovec and Humpolová 2008). The principal concentration, however, is the Široká u lesa cemetery (Podborský 2002a; 2002b; Ondruš 2002). Here a total of some 97 graves have been recorded; from 95 identifiable persons, there are 25 men, 42 women and 28 children (Dočkalová 2008). The predominant burial position was crouched on the left side. A range of grave goods were deposited, though not with all the dead, from pots to polished stone adzes and axes, other worked lithics, occasional bone objects, and abundant *Spondylus* and stone ornaments. Graves identified as 'rich' were predominantly those of mature men (Podborský 2002b, 335). Much further detail is given below (Chapter 4.7.1; Table 4.2).

A range of surveys (Květina 2004; Dočkalová 2008; Dočkalová and Čižmář 2008a; 2008b; Zvelebil and Pettitt 2008; Zvelebil *et al.* 2010) have suggested wider interpretations of the Vedrovice Široká u lesa burials. Květina (2004, 389) has elaborated the proposals of Podborský (2002b) to suggest a distinction between community leaders or elders, represented by 'richer' graves, and a wider 'social identity' of the community, encompassing subdivisions based on age and kinship, seen in the proposed burial clusters. Zvelebil and Pettitt (2008, 203) conclude that locally born men and women (the great majority) tended to have more grave goods the older they were, whereas only mature or old incomers had grave goods at all (though as none of their 'non-local' individuals were 'younger' adults, it is hard to see how this claim can be substantiated). They go on to offer detailed life histories for 15 individuals,[3] which in detail illustrate surprisingly wide-ranging lifeway variations for both men and women: in origin, health, diet, age at death, and mortuary treatment including the provision and abundance of grave goods (Zvelebil and Pettitt 2008, 210–14; Zvelebil *et al.* 2010). They suggest Vedrovice as a settlement founded by incomers from western Hungary 'some time before 5300 BC', which attracted people from hunter-gatherer communities 'within the region and outside it', mainly from the Bohemian-Moravian uplands and north-east Bohemia (Zvelebil and Pettitt 2008, 213). They conclude that 'far from being a generalised signature of an ethnic group, or of a population sharing a common group identity, as the culture historical, normative concept of culture would have it, the LBK culture can now be seen to have been far more complex than its "corporate" archaeological signature at first sight suggests' (Zvelebil and Pettitt 2008, 214). A similar picture of integration at Vedrovice had also already been noted by Jeunesse (1997, 144).

We can note that there is a recurrent tendency to discuss identities at one level, despite the concurrent emphasis on varied individual biographies, in terms of a straightforward opposition between LBK and non-LBK. The wider interpretation tends to lump the whole cemetery together, although its formation may have spanned five or six generations, and implies, in its discussion of potentially both inherited and acquired statuses or social roles (Zvelebil and Pettitt 2008, 214), that burial straightforwardly reflects social position. In detail, the account, like others before it (Podborský 2002b; Květina 2004), accepts the proposed clusters (Zvelebil and Pettitt 2008, 204–5, fig. 2). As already noted, the argument goes back to the identification of a number of 'rich' burials, mainly of men, which are spaced across most of the area of the cemetery, except to its north (Podborský 2002b, Abb. 2). But there is often little clear space between the proposed clusters, and the identified 'rich' burials are both dispersed and close together within the clusters. One could as well suggest a guiding principle of lines, visible perhaps especially in the southern part of the cemetery. Given the numbers of people buried and the timespan over which the cemetery was probably in use, the mortuary population was clearly already a selection from a wider population, and it could be that this was overall more important than details of how many artefacts were either assembled or given away in funerals at the time of particular deaths.

Many of the same issues are raised by the Nitra cemetery in western Slovakia, though until this project there has not been the same range of analyses carried out as at Vedrovice (Pavúk 1972a). Excavated under rescue conditions in 1964–5, the Nitra cemetery consists of a concentration of 76 graves, predominantly of individual men, women and juveniles or children; there was one apparently triple grave (48–50: Pavúk 1972a, 30). The predominant burial position was again crouched on the left side. A similar range of grave goods were deposited, though again not with all the dead. The most abundantly furnished graves were those of older women and especially those of older men (Pavúk 1972a, 71). Much further detail is given below (Chapter 4.10.1; Table 4.15).

Others have also noted the apparently prominent position of older men within the Nitra cemetery (e.g. Sherratt 1976, fig. 8: though without much emphasis on the relative date). As already described in Chapter 1, however, a more nuanced model taking account of change through time has been stressed by Christian Jeunesse (1997, 121). He proposed a more egalitarian society earlier in the LBK and a strongly differentiated one in the later LBK, a development seen as continuing into the Lengyel culture. Nitra was considered on the cusp of change between these two broad but not universal changes (Jeunesse 1997, 118), and seen as a 'gerontocratic society weakly differentiated' (Jeunesse 1997, 114); it

Table 4.2. Vedrovice: the isotope, osteological and archaeological data. Burials 1/63–11/74 are from the settlement, 12/74–108/84 are from the cemetery and 1/85–10/89 are from Za Dvorem. Age and sex information from Dočkalová (2008, 314–15; pathologies from Dočkalová (2008) and Lillie (2008). See Chapter 2 for further definition of ages. Italics denote sampled values from M.P. Richards et al. *(2008).*
Key for body position: LC – Left-crouched; RC – Right-crouched; C – Crouched, direction unknown; CB – Crouched on back; CF – Crouched on front; S – Supine; P – Prone; I – Irregular.
Key for grave goods (number of items in brackets): U. – Unfurnished; F. – Fill only (all items listed after an F. were in the fill of the grave rather than at the level of the skeleton); Pol. – Polished stone; Cer. – Ceramics; Shd. – Sherds; Spon. – Spondylus*; She. – Other Shell; Och. – Ochre; Lit. – Chipped stone; Bon – Worked bone; Grd. – Grinding stone; n.d. – no data.*

Burial	Tooth	Sex	Age (yrs)	$^{87}Sr/^{86}Sr$	1/Sr ppm	$\delta^{13}C$ ‰	$\delta^{15}N$ ‰	Orient.	Body position	Grave goods	Pathology
1/63	-	-	6–9 mon.	-	-	-	-	-	-	*n.d.*	*Cribra orbitalia*
2/63	M1	-	5	0.71099	33	-	-	NW–SE	RC	*n.d.*	-
3/66	M1	-	9	0.71245	37	−19.9	8.7	W–E	LC	U.	Caries (1)
4/69	M1	-	8	0.71137	29	−20.1	9.9	-	-	U.	-
5/71	M1	-	6–7	0.71164	26	−19.2	8.5	-	-	*n.d.*	*Cribra orbitalia*, tibiae with Harris lines
6/72	-	-	3	-	-	-	-	-	-	*n.d.*	-
7/72	-	-	Neonat.	-	-	-	-	-	-	*n.d.*	-
8/74	-	-	Neonat.	-	-	-	-	-	-	*n.d.*	-
9/74	-	F	50–60	-	-	-	-	-	-	*n.d.*	Arthritic osteophytes on vertebral column
10/74	M1	M	40–49	0.71080	40	−19.9	9.6	-	-	*n.d.*	Caries (9), arthritic osteophytes on vertebral column
11/74	-	M	45–55	-	-	-	-	-	-	*n.d.*	Caries (3), reduced height of vertebral column, trauma (fractured humerus and tibia)
12/74	-	-	Adult	-	-	−19.6	9.3	SE–NW	-	Pol.(2), Cer.(2), Bon.(1)	-
13/75	M2	F	Adult	0.71114	68	*−19.7*	*10.1*	SE–NW	LC	Och.	Caries (5)
14/75	-	F	35–40	-	-	*−19.3*	*10.1*	NW–SE	LC	Shd.(1), Spon.(1 bead), Och., Lit.(1)	-
15/75	-	M	35–40	*0.71085*	*71*	*−19.2*	*10*	NW–SE	LC	Pol.(1), Cer.(1), Spon.(19 beads), Lit.(1), Grd.(1)	Arthritic osteophytes on vertebral column, trauma (skull, healed), tibiae with Harris lines
16/75	M1	-	3–4	*0.71115*	*77*	*−19.9*	*9.7*	SE–NW	LC	F.Shd.(1)	Enamel hypoplasia
17/75	M1	-	*c.*1	-		*−18.7*	*13.3*	SE–NW	RC	F.Shd.(2)	-
18/75	M1	-	6–7	0.71108	48	-	-	SE–NW	LC	Pol.(1), Cer.(1), Bon.(1)	Tibiae with Harris lines
19/75	M3	M	25–35	0.7108	112	-	-	NW–SE	LC	Pol.(1), Cer.(1), Spon.(24 beads), Och., Silicate pebble	Caires (1), trauma, arthritic osteophytes on vertebral column, tibiae with Harris lines
20/75	M2dec.	-	3–4	0.71125	45	−19.7	8.4	SE–NW	LC	U.	Tibiae with Harris lines
21/75	M3	F	30–40	0.71160	78	−19.6	9.2	SE–NW	LC	Cer.(1), Lit.(1)	Caries (3), *cribra orbitalia*
22/75	M2	F	35–45	0.70976	109	*−19.8*	*9.5*	SE–NW	LC	U.	Caries (5)
23/75	M3	M	17–20	0.71139	57	*−20.0*	*10.6*	SE–NW	LC	F.Cer.(1), Lit.(1)	*Cribra orbitalia*
24/75	-	-	5–7	-	-	*−19.9*	*9.2*	-	-	Cer.(1), Snail shells	Tibiae with Harris lines
25/75	-	M	Adult	-	-	*−19.5*	*10*	-	-	U.	-
27/76	-	F	>20	-	-	−20.5	9.2	SE–NW	-	Cer.(1)	-
28/76	M1	-	4–5	0.71093	67	*−19.9*	*10*	SE–NW	LC	U.	-
29/76	M3	F	18–20	0.70849	260	−20.5	9	SE–NW	LC	F.Shd.(1)	Caries (1)
30/76	M1	-	10–12	*0.71083*	*88*	*−19.5*	*9.5*	E–W	LC	Pol.(1), Cer.(1), Och.	-

										Grd.(1),	
31/76	-	F	Adult	-	-	*−20.0*	*10.3*	-	-	Pol.(1)	-
32/76	M1	-	12–14	0.71101	57	−19.9	8.5	S–N	LC	Pol.(1), Cer.(1)	-
35/76	-	-	Adult	-	-	−19.9	9.3	-	-	U.	-
36/76	M1	F	45–50	0.71183	67	−19.7	8.8	NW–SE	LC	Pol.(1), Cer.(2), Spon.(3 beads), Grd.(1)	Tibiae with Harris lines
37/76	M2	-	11–12	-	-	*−19.6*	*9.6*	S–N	LC	Pol.(1), Lit.(1)	-
38/76	M3	F	30–35	*0.71041*	*137*	*−20.3*	*9.5*	E–W	RC	U.	-
39/76	M1	-	3–4	0.71088	66	*−19.0*	*10.5*	S–N	I	Cer.(1), Spon.(11 beads), Lit.(8)	Tibiae with Harris lines
40/76	M2	-	8–10	0.71083	60	−19.6	8.8	NW–SE	LC	Lit.(1)	-
42/77	M3	F	20–30	*0.71101*	*113*	*−19.5*	*9.8*	NW–SE	CB	Spon.(2 beads)	Caries (1)
43/77	M1	-	14	*0.71124*	*78*	*−20.0*	*9.7*	W–E	LC	Lit.(1)	Tibiae with Harris lines
44/77	M1	-	10–14	0.71169	54	*−19.9*	*9.5*	-	-	F.Shd.(1)	-
45/77	M3	F	35–45	0.71048	60	-	-	SE–NW	LC	Cer.(1)	-
46/77	M3	M	20–35	0.71115	51	−19.8	9.1	SE–NW	LC	Pol.(1), Cer.(2), Spon.(2 beads), Lit.(15)	Tibiae with Harris lines
48/77	M3	F	18–25	*0.71103*	*82*	*−19.8*	*10.3*	E–W	LC	F.Shd.(4), Och.	-
50/77	-	M	Adult	-	-	*−19.8*	*9.5*	NW–SE	LC	Cer.(1)	-
51/77	M1	F	45–55	*0.70911*	*190*	*−20.7*	*9.5*	SE–NW	-	Cer.(2)	-
54/78	M3	M	20–25	*0.71109*	*58*	*−19.6*	*10.1*	SE–NW	LC	Pol.(1), Cer.(1), Spon.(2 beads), Lit.(1)	Tibiae with Harris lines
56/78	-	-	4–5	-	-	*−19.8*	*9.1*	-	-	U.	-
57/78	M3	M	40–50	0.71092	72	*−19.6*	*10.7*	NW–SE	LC	Pol.(2), Lit.(7)	Tibiae with Harris lines
59/78	M2	M	25–30	*0.71144*	*109*	*−19.4*	*10.3*	E–W	RC	Pol.(1), Cer.(1), Lit.(2)	Tibiae with Harris lines
61/78	M1	F	40–50	0.71161	81	−19.8	9.3	E–W	LC	Cer.(1), Och.	-
62/78	M1	F	30–40	*0.71129*	*127*	*−19.9*	*9.4*	SE–NW	LC	Cer.(1), Spon.(1 beads), Lit.(1)	Caries (2)
63/78	M2	M	40–45	0.71167	59	*−19.9*	*10*	SE–NW	LC	U.	-
64/78	M3	F	18–25	0.71111	57	−19.8	9.2	E–W	LC	U.	Tibiae with Harris lines
66/78	M3	M	30–35	*0.71153*	*104*	*−19.7*	*9.9*	E–W	LC	Cer.(2), Lit.(2)	-
67/78	M2	F	35–45	0.71226	53	−19.6	8.6	SE–NW	LC	U.	-
68/78	M2	F	>50	0.70959	94	−19.5	9.5	NW–SE	LC	U.	Arthritic osteophytes on vertebral column, tibiae with Harris lines
69/78	-	M	20–30	-		-	-	NW–SE	LC	Pol.(1), Cer.(5), Spon.(18 beads), Bon.(1), Grd.(1), Unworked pebble	-
70/79	M3	F	45–50	0.70995	54	−19.5	9.5	SE–NW	LC	Cer.(1), Spon.(20 beads)	Caries (2)
71/79	M3	M	35–45	0.71112	47	*−19.3*	*10.3*	E–W	LC	Pol.(1), Cer.(1), Worked antler(1)	Caries (2)

72/79	M2	F	30–40	0.71228	69	*−19.5*	*9.3*	E–W	LC	Cer.(2), She.(2), Och.	Caries (1), *cribra orbitalia*
73/79	M2	M	20–25	0.71047	47	*−19.7*	*10.2*	SE–NW	LC	Lit.(1)	-
74/79	M2	F	>50	-	-	−19.3	9.5	SE–NW	LC	Och.	-
75/79	M2	F	25–35	*0.71118*	*119*	*−19.5*	*9.3*	SE–NW	LC	Spon.(1 bead)	Tibiae with Harris lines
76/79	M2	M	30–35	0.7113	46	−19.5	9.4	E–W	LC	Pol.(1), Lit.(1), Worked antler(1)	Tibiae with Harris lines, spina bifida (on os sacrum)
77/79	M2	M	40–50	0.71113	62	*−19.3*	*10*	SE–NW	LC	Pol.(1), Cer.(1), Worked antler(1)	Caries (2), tibiae with Harris lines
78/79	M2	-	7–8	0.7115	88	−19.5	9.1	SE–NW	LC	Spon.(1 bead), She.(1)	-
79/79	M1	M	25–35	0.71112	52	*−19.6*	*10*	SE–NW	LC	Pol.(1), Cer.(1), Spon.(1 bead), Lit.(8), Bon.(1)	Arthritic osteophytes on vertebral column, tibiae with Harris lines
80/79	M1	F	35–45	-	-	−19.6	9.2	SE–NW	LC	Lit.(1)	Caries (2)
81a/79	-	F	20–30	-	-	-	-	SE–NW	LC	Cer.(2), Lit.(2), Spon.(1 bead), Unworked pebble	-
81b/79	-	-	Neonat.	-	-	*−20.1*	*10.4*	-	-	U.	-
82/79	M2	M	>50	*0.71133*	*101*	*−19.1*	*10.6*	SE–NW	LC	U.	Tibiae with Harris lines
83/80	-	F	>60	-	-	−19.5	9.2	E–W	LC	Cer.(1), Spon.(4 beads), Worked pebbles (2)	*Cribra orbitalia*
84/80	M1	-	9	*0.71097*	*100*	*−20.2*	*9.9*	E–W	LC	Marble medallion (imitation *Spondylus*?)	Tibiae with Harris lines
86/80	M3	F	25–30	0.70955	75	*−19.9*	*9.8*	E–W	LC	Cer.(1), Spon.(2 beads), Lit.(1), She.(1)	*Cribra orbitalia*
87/80	-	F	Adult	-	-	*−19.5*	*9.7*	SE–NW	LC	U.	-
88/80	M1	M	20–30	0.71118	75	−19.9	9.7	SE–NW	LC	Pol.(1), Worked antler (1)	Tibiae with Harris lines
89/80	-	F	Adult	-	-	*−20.0*	*9.3*	E–W	LC	U.	-
90/80	-	F	Adult	-	-	*−19.7*	*9.5*	-	-	Shd.(1), Spon.(1 beads), Lit.(2), Pebble with traces of ochre	-
91/80	M3	F	18–20	0.71022	100	*−19.4*	*9.8*	E–W	LC	Cer.(2), Spon.(2 beads), Lit.(3)	-
93a/80	M1 (?)	F	18–25	0.71215	27	*−19.8*	*10.2*	SE–NW	LC	Spon.(1 bead)	-
93b/80	-	-	Neonat.	-	-	-	-	-	-	U.	-
94/80	M2	F	18–25	0.71125	49	−19.7	9	SE–NW	LC	Unworked flint nodule (1)	-
95/80	-	M	50–60	-	-	*−19.6*	*9.7*	-	-	Spon.(1 bead)	Caries (1)
96/80	M1	-	3–5	0.71116	50	*−19.5*	*9.8*	SE–NW	RC	Spon.(1 bead)	-
97/80	M3	F	30–40	0.71020	82	*−19.7*	*9.5*	SE–NW	LC	Shd.(2)	-
98/81	-	-	Adult	-	-	-	-	-	-	Cer.(1)	-
99/81	M3	M	30	0.70835	101	*−20.1*	*9.5*	E–W	LC	Cer.(1)	Caries (1), tibiae with Harris lines, trauma (right tibia)
100/81	M1	F	20–30	0.71067	33	*−19.7*	*10*	NW–SE	LC	Cer. 1), Shd.(1), Spon.(1 bead)	-

101/81	M3	F	45–55	0.70944	80	*−19.7*	*9.9*	SE–NW	LC	Grd.(1), Worked pebble (1)	-
102/81	M2	F	40–45	*0.71263*	*101*	*−20.0*	*9.2*	E–W	RC	Spon.(1 bead)	-
103/81	-	F	50–60	-	-	-	-	E–W	LC	U.	-
104/81	-	F	>50	*0.71120*	*98*	*−19.9*	*9.8*	NW–SE	LC	Cer.(1), Worked flint nodule (1)	Caries (1)
105/81	M3	F	16–18	*0.71130*	*91*	*−19.7*	*9*	E–W	RC	U.	-
106/82	-	F	16–18	-	-	*−19.5*	*8.9*	SE–NW	LC	Cer.(1)	-
107/82	M1	F	18–20	*0.71137*	*49*	*−19.3*	*8.9*	W–E	LC	Cer.(2)	-
108/84	-	M	Adult-Senile	-	-	*−19.6*	*9.9*	-	-	Pol.(1)	-
1/85	M1	F	20–25	0.71102	45	−20.5	9.7	-	-	U.	-
2/85	M2	M	25–30	0.71079	49	−19.7	10.3	SE–NW	LC	Pol.(1), Spon.(12 beads), Bon.(1)	*Cribra orbitalia*
3/86	-	-	1.5–2	-	-	-	-	-	-	U.	*Cribra orbitalia*
5/88	-	-	3	-	-	-	-	SE–NW	LC	Spon.(2 beads)	-
6/88	M2	F	>50	0.70956	60	−20.2	9.6	SE–NW	LC	U.	Caries (1)
7/88	M1	F	35–45	0.71117	47	−19.8	9.6	SE–NW	LC	Shd.(1), Bon.(1)	-
8/88	M1	-	13–15	0.71094	47	−20.3	10.8	SE–NW	LC	Pol.(1), Bon.(1), Spon.(1 beads), Marble beads(68)	Tibiae with Harris lines
9/88	M2	F	18	0.71082	66	−20.2	9.7	SE–NW	LC	Spon.(30 beads), Marble beads(*c.* 506), She.(300)	-
10/89	M1	F	20–25	0.70954	66	−20.6	9.7	SE–NW	LC	Pol.(1), She.(2)	*Cribra orbitalia*

lacked, for example, the rich child graves characteristic of his proposed 'tradition II' (Chapter 1.3.5).

Though this introduction has concentrated on Vedrovice and Nitra, other cemeteries are known in both Moravia and Slovakia. For Moravia, Dočkalová (2006, 128) lists Moravský Krumlov, Padochov, Blučina-Nivky and Těšetice-Kyjovice. At the latter site, also sampled by this project, a series of LBK features including longhouses and pits have been recorded, in excavations carried on since the 1960s (Dočkalová 2005; 2006; Dočkalová and Koštuřík 1996; Dočkalová and Čižmář 2007; 2008a). Some of the graves, of children as well as of adults, appear to be isolated, and could be classed as settlement burials; one contained the incomplete remains of a woman with an estimated age of 20–25 years (Dočkalová and Čižmář 2008a, 43, fig. 6). Others, however, have been found in a more concentrated group in an area adjacent to longhouses, and could be seen as the remains of a small cemetery (Dočkalová 2005, Obr. 2; Dočkalová and Čižmář 2008a, fig. 4). The eight graves in question have varied orientations, so may not all be of the same date, though five are more or less aligned west–east, four with heads to the east and facing south. The deepest grave so far found, H20, is that of a man, crouched on his right side, with head to the south-east, facing broadly east; pots in the grave were some 60 cm above its base (Dočkalová and Čižmář 2008a, 43). For Slovakia, Farkaš (2002, 42–3, Obr. 1; cf. Plesl 1952; Jeunesse 1997) lists, alongside other possible examples, Nitra-Mlynárce (with nine graves excavated from an estimated 20, several with notable amounts of red colouring material and two burials laid out in the 'antipodal' position, of supposed Mesolithic descent: Häusler 1964), Nitra 'Mikov dvor' and Lipová-Ondrochov, to the north of Nové Zámky, in the Nitra valley.

Varied general reviews of the human remains thus provided (Dočkalová 2006; Dočkalová and Čižmář 2008a; Farkaš 2002) have been supplemented by further specialist studies, including of child burials (Dočkalová and Čižmář 2007; 2008b; Chapter 2.6).

The two most intensively studied cemeteries, Vedrovice and Nitra, also provide some of the best evidence for regional networks. Materials in the graves at Vedrovice 'Široká u lesa' (Podborský 2002b) come from a very wide area roundabout. Summarising this evidence, Zvelebil and Pettitt (2008, fig. 1) list schist from Bohemia, glacial erratic flint from Silesia, Jurassic flint from the Kraków region, radiolarite from Szentgál north of Lake Balaton, marble from western Moravia, and *Spondylus*, said by them to be from the Adriatic – at a range of some 600 km – rather than the more distant Aegean or Black Sea often inferred (Müller *et al.* 1996; Müller 1997). For *Spondylus*, Podborský (2002c) notes both sources, and Hladilová (2002, 262) simply cites 'the Mediterranean'. A new critical review keeps this issue open, though noting that the Black Sea was probably too cool in the middle Holocene for *Spondylus* to flourish, and hinting at the likely reality of movement from the Aegean into Serbia and Hungary; it also emphasises the peak of *Spondylus* distribution in the period 5400–4900 cal BC (Chapman and Gaydarska forthcoming; cf. Müller 1997; Sefériadès 1995). There was also chert at Vedrovice from the much more local Krumlovský Les and Olomučany sources (see also Mateiciucová 2008a, maps 6–8). In addition, there were shoe-last adzes and other polished stone tools made of amphibolites, seen at the time of publication as coming from north-east Bohemia (A. Přichystal 2002), but perhaps now referable specifically to the Jistebsko source in the foothills of the Jizera range (Prostředník *et al.* 2005; Ramminger 2009; Chapter 1.3.6). At Nitra, the notable *Spondylus* objects and amphibolite shoe-last adzes (Pavúk 1972a) raise the same interesting questions of provenance. There were also a few simple struck chert pieces (Pavúk 1972a, 56), as well as presumably local colouring material and graphite. The wider lithic contacts of this world, at sites beyond Vedrovice and Nitra, have been mapped by Mateiciucová (2008a, maps 6–8), and include also at sites in Moravia and Slovakia, besides the materials already noted, small quantities of Mauer radiolarites from near Vienna and Carpathian obsidian from easternmost Slovakia or north-east Hungary. Links with western Hungary have also been seen in the pottery of the early Vedrovice settlement (phase Ia/Ib) (Zvelebil and Pettitt 2008, 213), and Szentgál radiolarite was present in Vedrovice 'Za dvorem' in phase Ia (Mateiciucová 2008a, 108).

Finally, it is worth noting other aspects of the interpretive traditions of this region, in the form of bold, general social models of the nature of LBK communities, relying in large measure on the burial evidence. Thus in his summaries of the Vedrovice evidence, Podborský (2002c, 254; 2002b, 335) drew on a long established view to argue for matrilinear and matrilocal social organisation in early Neolithic society, despite the preponderance, for example, of *Spondylus* objects in the graves of men and children. Whilst acknowledging several important social roles for men and the prominence in mortuary ritual of older men (Podborský 2002b, 334–5; and see above), he maintained the importance of women in the spheres of production, subsistence and cult. In contrast, summarising the implications of the evidence from Nitra, Pavúk (1972a, 73) asserted that the dominance of men in mortuary ritual challenged the concept of matriarchy, supporting this with the view that men were also central to the tasks of clearance, cultivation, herding, house construction, and protection of the community. Both, however, as already noted above, refer to family groups and to clusters of graves within the cemeteries in question, and for the large settlement at Štúrovo, Pavúk (1994, 245) envisaged the very large house (*Großbau*) found in three of the settlement phases as communal grain store and animal stall for all inhabitants of the community, but perhaps also as the residence for some kind of acknowledged clan leader or authority (1994, 246). Finally, summarising results from the recent Vedrovice project, Zvelebil and Pettitt (2008) sidestep traditional issues of a simple choice between male or female dominance to argue for a key role for the settlement as some kind of both founder and gateway community in its wider regional context, and one in which both men and women had very varied lifecourses, as already noted above. They discuss both people who had 'gained respect and achieved high social status' (e.g. individual 79/79) and the case of individual 82/79 who 'ended up in what effectively could be seen as a pauper's grave' (Zvelebil and Pettitt 2008, 211, 212). This was a locally born man estimated at 50–60 years old, who had survived the loss of his left hand and lowermost left arm, and was buried without grave goods. But this man was significant enough to merit inclusion in the cemetery, and that fact alone is sufficient to underline the difficulties still faced in this kind of straightforward social reading of the mortuary evidence.

4.6 Sites sampled

The analyses that follow were carried out in the course of the present project on samples from Vedrovice, Těšetice-Kyjovice and Brno-Starý Lískovec in Moravia, and Nitra in western Slovakia. All fit well into the pattern of site location and development discernible for the LBK as a whole in these regions. It is worth noting that the LBK features of Těšetice-Kyjovice have been revealed in the course of long-running and still ongoing excavations around the notable *rondel* of the Moravian Painted Ware culture, belonging to the regional middle Neolithic, and that the site of Brno-Starý Lískovec is a more recent discovery, not yet fully published (M. Přichystal 2008). These regions offer considerable potential for further analyses of this kind in the future.

4.7 Vedrovice

4.7.1 Introduction

To recap, the site of Vedrovice consists of three different areas of LBK burial: the cemetery Široká u lesa, the settlement ('Sídliště') and a smaller cluster of 13 burials to the south of the cemetery on a tract of land known as Za dvorem (Dočkalová 2008, 241–2). During a series of campaigns between 1961 and 2000,[4] approximately 110 LBK burials were uncovered alongside a contemporary settlement area, represented by a large enclosure, surrounding the remains of longhouses and their accompanying pits and ovens (Lukes *et al.* 2008, 119; Figs 4.3–4).

Excavation of the Široká u lesa cemetery has perhaps not been total on its northern and eastern edges (Ondruš 2002, Abb. 7). The 97 graves are scattered over an area roughly 60 by 70 m (Fig. 4.4). On the whole no one grave is immediately adjacent to its nearest neighbour, with the exception of two intersecting or touching pairs; spacings of 1 or 2 m are quite common. Analysis of the associated pottery suggested that a series of graves in the main part of the cemetery belonged to phase Ib_1, with further additions on the northern and southern periphery in phase Ib_2, and finally further additions, mainly on the periphery but also in the centre of the cemetery, in phase IIa; significant numbers of graves could not be as precisely phased (Čižmář 2002, Abb. 8). The more recent investigations have proposed further subdivision in the form of eight clusters (Zvelebil and Pettitt 2008, fig. 2, building on Podborský 2002b, Abb. 2), incorporating two or more of the identified ceramic phases. These have some 10–15 graves each. The graves are not obviously arranged in rows, though there are hints of lines in several of them.

The Široká u lesa graves contain the inhumed skeletons, largely complete, of men, women and juveniles or children; the age and sex of some people could not be determined (Table 4.2). As noted above, there were more women and children than men (Podborský 2002b, 326; Dočkalová 2008). In several of the proposed clusters, men and women appear in roughly equal numbers, men even predominating in one or two. The graves of men were on average slightly bigger and slightly deeper than those of women. A few graves with particularly abundant grave goods have been identified (Podborský 2002b, Abb. 2, 326); these are nearly all those of men, and occur once or twice per proposed cluster (with two exceptions, in the graves of a woman and a child respectively).

The predominant burial position (Table 4.2) was crouched (to varying degrees) on the left side, in graves that were broadly aligned west–east (with variation around this), with heads to the east, facing south or south-east (Podborský 2002b, 327). Could this be a sign, as proposed for houses (Mattheußer 1991; Bradley 1996; Coudart 1998; forthcoming), of recognition of a possible direction of origin? A few are so positioned, however, that their heads face north-west (Podborský 2002b, 327). In comparison to other LBK cemeteries, there are no burials oriented with the heads to the south-west or north-east. A few other bodies lay on their right sides, heads also to the east but facing broadly therefore northwards; belonging to two men, two women and two children, these appear to be scattered through the clusters, and not to belong to a single ceramic phase. There are also five burials which Podborský (2002b, 327) describes as placed in atypical positions, though due to preservation of the skeletons in most cases it is difficult to determine what the original body position would have been, but crouched body positions appear to dominate the unusual burials also. For example, in burial 39 the body is placed with the upper body in a typical left-crouched position, while the legs are supine, but bent to the left. The reverse is true of burial 42, where the legs are in a left-crouched position and the arms bent to the left, with the torso in a supine position. In summary, burials are therefore either oriented between east–west and south–north (with their heads in an easterly direction; 65 burials) or with the head roughly to the west or north-west (13 burials). Similarly, the deceased were either placed in a right-crouched (13 burials) or left-crouched (65 burials) position, with all right-crouched burials oriented with the head to the east, south-east or south.

A not insignificant number of burials (some 26: Podborský 2002b, Taf. 2) had no accompanying grave goods at all; more of these appear to be women and children, but there are examples in male graves as well

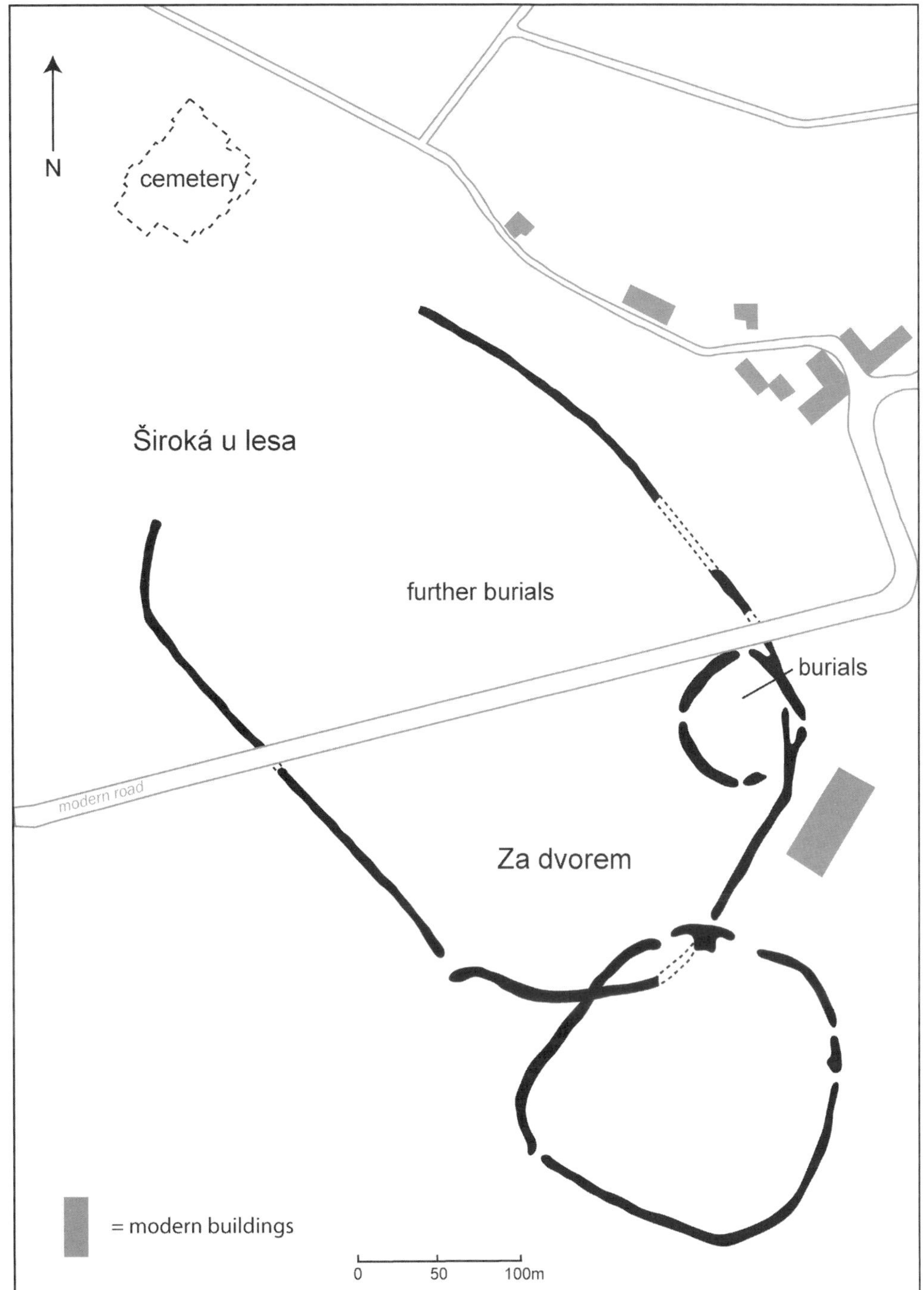

Fig. 4.3. Vedrovice: plan of the different locations. In addition to the two areas marked on the plan, further settlement burials were found in the general area north of the road. After Podborský (1998, 10).

(Table 4.2). Pots were the most recurrent grave good, occurring in about half of the graves, in roughly equal numbers with men and women, and with some child burials too (Podborský 2002b, 331). Polished stone adzes and axes, other worked lithics, occasional bone objects, and abundant *Spondylus* and stone ornaments were also deposited, and about a third of the burials had red colouring material (Fig. 4.5). Polished stone artefacts occur in 19 graves; shoe-last adzes (*Schuhleistenkeile*) were much more common than flat axes (*flache Äxte*); and 14 of these occur in 13 male graves, and two more in child graves, whereas flat axes are found with one man, one woman and one child (Podborský 2002b, 331–2). Normally these occur one by one, but in two cases (one male burial, and one uncertain but perhaps that of a child), there are two each. Other polished stone artefacts and colouring material are distributed roughly equally between the sexes, though all the 'rich' male burials have the red colouring material. More male burials are accompanied by more struck and worked lithics, of varying sources, from local chert to Hungarian radiolarite, than is the case in female burials, which had only local chert (Podborský 2002b, 333).

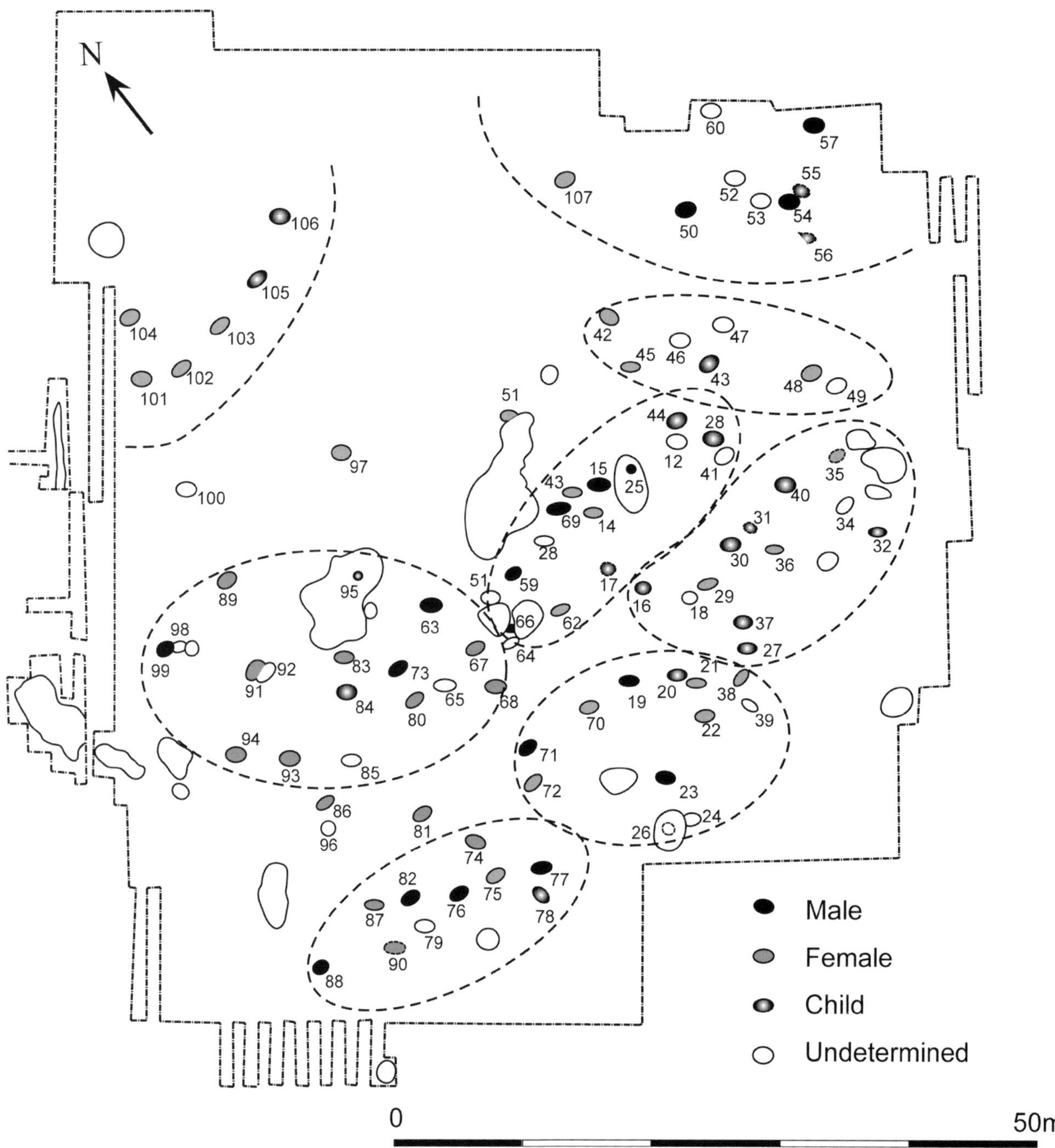

Fig. 4.4. Vedrovice: plan of cemetery, showing possible clusters of burials. After Zvelebil and Pettitt (2008, 205).

A striking and recurrent category of grave good are *Spondylus* ornaments, taking the form of pendants or near-complete shells, V-notched shells (so-called buckles, though these are only known from a couple of graves investigated in the late nineteenth century), armrings, and perforated pendants and above all beads, some found *in situ* as necklaces (Podborský 2002c). Some 129 pieces occur in 26 graves, with a few more surface finds, one of the largest assemblages in central Europe (Podborský 2002b, 333). These finds were deposited with 13 women, eight men and four children. Many of the women with *Spondylus* had just a few beads or pendants, though grave 86, belonging to an adult woman, had a medallion, a pendant and a bead, while four of the eight men so provided had more abundant assemblages. Stone, bone and antler beads and pendants are also found in these graves.

At Široká u lesa, 25 male graves contained 202 objects, 37 female graves 61 objects, and 19 child graves 37 objects. The identified 'rich' graves were predominantly those of mature men, in estimated age ranges of 30–40 and 40–50 years (Podborský 2002b, 335). These included instances with a single shoe-last adze and a *Spondylus* medallion, and another with a single shoe-last adze and a *Spondylus* armring. None of the proposed grave clusters appears to significantly outweigh the others in terms of overall numbers of grave goods. Podborský (2002b, 335) proposed that the 'rich' male graves were the burials of men with prominent social roles, including as founders of the settlement, leaders

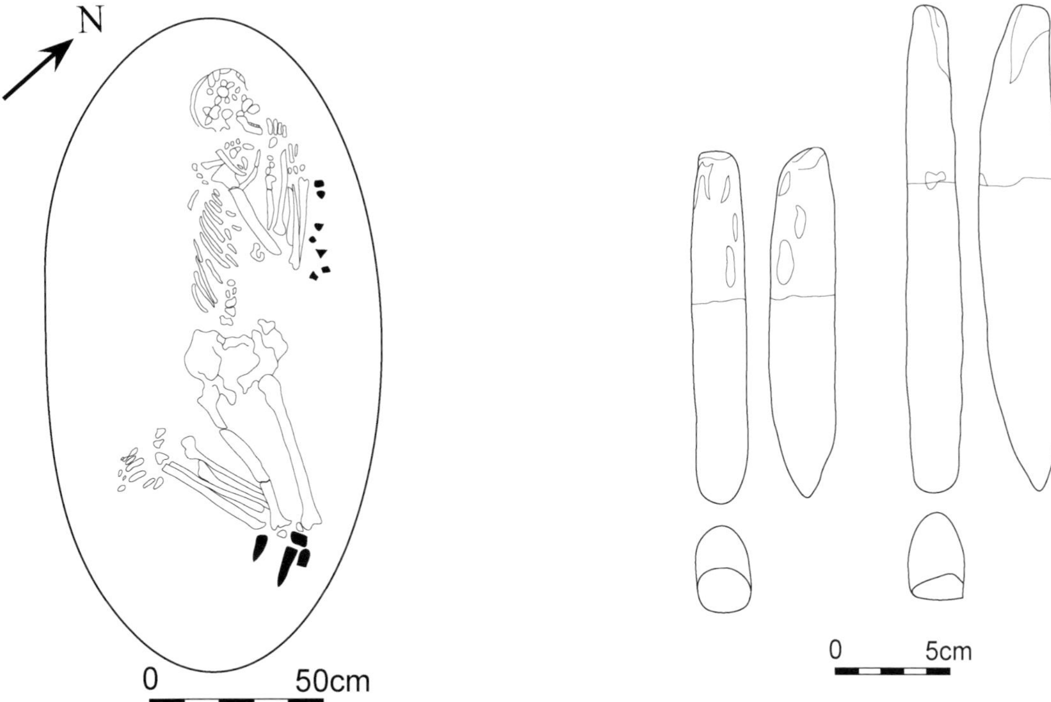

Fig. 4.5. Vedrovice: grave 57/78 (adult male) showing the location of the two broken adzes by the knees, and the adzes found in the grave. After Podborský (1998, 57).

of the first families, prominent producers of stone artefacts, organisers of exchange, fighters and hunters. Alongside this, however, he argued for matrilocality and a privileged position for women, pointing to grave 86, noted above, and one of the Za dvorem female burials.

The cemetery has recently been the focus of a major international collaborative project, which brought together a variety of bio-archaeological approaches. The recent investigations have included radiocarbon dating (Pettitt and Hedges 2008), and isotopic (Smrčka *et al.* 2005; 2008a; 2008b; Richards *et al.* 2008), osteological and dental (Dočkalová 2008; Lillie 2008; Nystrom 2008; Jarošová 2008), genetic (Bramanti 2008) and trace element (Smrčka *et al.* 2008c) analyses, coupled with contextualised interpretation (Lukes *et al.* 2008; Zvelebil and Pettitt 2008; Zvelebil *et al.* 2010).

Initial analysis of the ceramics from both the settlement and the cemetery had suggested that Vedrovice was one of the earliest cemeteries across the LBK distribution (Podborský 2002b, 336). Two samples gave calibrated dates of 5300–5000 cal BC (Podborský 2002b, 336).[5] The much larger number of dates reported by Pettitt and Hedges (2008, 126, 130) narrowed the range of the Široká u lesa cemetery to approximately 5300–5100 cal BC, over some five to six generations. The pottery from the settlement and cemetery suggests that they were contemporary (Lukes *et al.* 2008, 119), falling into three phases, from the end of the earliest LBK into the middle or late LBK (Ib_1, Ib_2 and IIa; Čižmář 2002). Combining this information with the radiocarbon dates, the probabilistic model of Pettitt and Hedges (2008, 130–1) places the Široká u lesa cemetery within the 53rd century BC, with a duration of approximately 100 years and the transition between phases I and II at the end of the 53rd or the very early part of the 52nd century BC. In total 11 graves could be phased on the basis of ceramics; eight were from Ib_1, one from Ib_2 and three from IIa. Those graves from Ib phases had lots of varied grave goods, while the three graves that could be attributed to phase IIa had far fewer, with no polished stone or *Spondylus*. This may suggest a change in funerary rites to less provision with grave goods, but given the low number of graves thus sequenced we can only speculate at the moment.

As already noted above, six individuals (of 16 sampled) from the cemetery have yielded ancient mtDNA sequences, and though a very small sample from a context with more than 80 people, may indicate a population of broadly indigenous central European genetic descent, with some admixture of ultimately Near Eastern origin (Bramanti 2008; Zvelebil and Pettitt 2008, 197). The pattern is compatible with wider studies such as by Haak *et al.* (2005). The sulphur and strontium isotope ratios of a much larger sample of individuals from Vedrovice were analysed (M.P. Richards *et al.* 2008). The sulphur isotope analyses reflect the last decade or two decades of life, and values for the 50 individuals investigated suggest largely local residence for most of the sample; five, in two groups, had values 'indicative of living elsewhere over the last 10–20 years of their lives' (Zvelebil and Pettitt 2008, 199). Strontium isotope analyses from teeth were possible for a smaller sample of 22 individuals (M.P. Richards *et al.* 2008; cf. Smrčka *et al.* 2005; 2008a; 2008b). The majority of the values suggest local origin in childhood, with five adult exceptions of both sexes, in two groups, posited as coming from uplands to both the north-west and the south-east, where at this date it is supposed that Mesolithic hunter-gatherer communities still existed (Zvelebil and Pettitt 2008, 199). Two of these 'bornaway' individuals, a woman and a man, may also have spent time in their last decades, according to sulphur analysis, away from the area of the site, but on burial, the woman was accompanied in quite normal fashion by pots, and the man (in grave 79) by an abundant assemblage, not untypical for other 'rich' graves as noted above, of pot, shoe-last adze, arrowheads of imported Polish flint, boar tusk and *Spondylus* pendant (Zvelebil and Pettitt 2008, 199, table 1). It has been debated whether the under-representation of men compared to women in the cemetery could be related to 'out-migration' (Lillie 2008; Zvelebil and Pettitt 2008, 199).

Carbon and nitrogen isotope analysis of bone collagen from 57 individuals indicates that their diet was broadly homogeneous (average δ^{13}C value of −19.7±0.4‰; average δ^{15}N value of 9.9±0.6‰), with a large component of animal protein; there is some evidence for early weaning (M.P. Richards *et al.* 2008). There are also some signs of higher δ^{15}N values in men compared to women, and a possible correlation with higher δ^{15}N values in both older men and women, possibly reflecting shifting patterns of diet through life (Zvelebil and Pettitt 2008, 208). Some correlation between higher δ^{15}N values and 'richer' (that is, numerically and categorically more abundant) grave good assemblages for both women and men exists (Zvelebil and Pettitt 2008, 208–9, fig. 6). A range of δ^{15}N values is evident for both women and men buried with *Spondylus*, and men (both younger and older) with shoe-last adzes, or shoe-last adzes and *Spondylus* (Zvelebil and Pettitt 2008, 209, fig. 7). These patterns have been tentatively interpreted in terms of access to meat being related to status; 'the hypothesis that males within LBK society acquired status as they aged, and in so doing acquired more material expressions of status and enjoyed greater access to meat remains to be eliminated' (Zvelebil and Pettitt 2008, 209). Complementary dental studies on 18–22 individuals, both men and women, suggest a diverse diet, reflecting perhaps both hard and soft foods and both wild and domesticated food sources; there is some variation by age and sex (Nystrom 2008; Jarošová 2008; Zvelebil and Pettitt 2008, 205–7, table 4).

The results presented here complement the work already achieved by this detailed study, by analysing the burials of Za dvorem and the settlement, as well as a number of individuals from the main Široká u lesa cemetery. In total, 33 individuals were analysed for carbon and nitrogen values: 22 from Široká u lesa, four from the settlement and seven from Za dvorem, in addition to the 57 studied by Richards *et al.* (2008). The tooth enamel from the molars of 72 individuals were analysed for strontium ratios; 60 from the cemetery, including the 22 analysed by M.P. Richards *et al.* (2008), seven from Za dvorem and five from the settlement.

The settlement and Za dvorem burials have not yet been radiocarbon dated, though on the basis of ceramic remains are thought to be largely contemporary with the cemetery (Čižmář 2002; Podborský 2002b). The few ceramics from the burials in the Za dvorem area could only be attributed generally to the early LBK (phase 1; Grave 2/88), but an adze showing a flat or mid-width profile was characteristic of phase $1b_2$ (Podborský 2002b, 337). Otherwise, there is little further evidence to indicate the internal chronology of burials in the settlement and Za dvorem areas. However, it seems highly likely that, along with the cemetery burials of Široká u lesa, they form some of the earliest LBK burials analysed in the Lifeways project.

4.7.2 Osteology

The human remains from Vedrovice are kept in the Moravian Museum, Brno, and have principally been studied by Marta Dočkalová, first for Podborský's (2002a) publication of the cemetery and then concurrently with Marek Zvelebil's bioarchaeological project (Dočkalová 2008). This work is also complemented by the study of Lillie (2008, 136) which differed only in a few places from the original study of by Dočkalová (2008), particularly in the ageing of the skeletons. In this project, we follow the age and sex of the skeletons published by Dočkalová (2008, 314–15) for consistency across the three different areas of the site, as Lillie (2008, 151) only analysed individuals from the cemetery and the age differences between the two studies are generally slight. Crubézy *et al.* (1997) published a comparison of Vedrovice and Nitra, but not a detailed breakdown by individual skeleton. Jarošová (2008) and Nystrom (2008) have carried out analysis of the microwear on tooth enamel.

As we noted above, females outnumber men at the cemetery and Za dvorem, and only children are found in the settlement. While the association of children and settlement burials is found more widely across the LBK, Zvelebil and Pettitt (2008) suggest that the lack of males could be due to some degree of out-migration by young males. Lillie (2008, 136) determined life expectancy as approximately 30 years, with the rate of childhood deaths dipping between the ages of five and nine, and he speculates that this may be due to deliberate non-selection of these ages for burial in the cemetery. This age range is represented at the settlement (four burials from 11).

The most frequent pathology was dental caries. These were present in five out of 17 males (*c.* 30% of all males with teeth; 2% of all teeth available for study) and 18 out of 32 females (*c.* 56% of females with teeth; *c.* 4% of all teeth available for study; Lillie 2008, 139). Given that male teeth preservation was generally better than female, this strengthens the conclusion that females suffered more from caries than males: a difference borne out in evidence for ante-mortem tooth loss (Lillie 2008, 139). While none of the children showed evidence for tooth caries, two child individuals were recorded as having enamel hypoplasia (also found in three adults; Lillie 2008, 142). The presence of wear on the incisors (unusually the maxilla), indicated sometimes by distinct grooves, suggests use of the teeth as tools (Lillie 2008, 142). This is visible to different extents on nine individuals, including two males (46/77 and 82/79) and six females (29/76, 68/78, 75/79, 93a/80, 94/80 and 97/80). Microscopic analysis of the wear patterns suggests the processing of fibrous materials (such as sinew; Frayer 2004, 98; Lillie 2008, 142).

Jarošová (2008) analysed the buccal microwear on the tooth enamel, which can indicate the composition of the diet, from 18 individuals from the cemetery. This study was complemented by Nystrom's (2008) study of occlusal microwear from 22 individuals, again from the cemetery. Occlusal microwear shows the diet in the last few weeks before death (Zvelebil and Pettitt 2008, 205). The evidence from Vedrovice suggests that the population were consuming a soft or slightly abrasive mixed diet, based largely on plants with a certain amount of cereals, with meat only a sporadic addition (Jarošová 2008, 183). The samples from Vedrovice fell within the range of gathering, fishing and hunting populations, with food staples that were tough to chew, possibly stringy vegetable matter or dried meat (Nystrom 2008, 168–9). However, there was variation, with individuals 19, 42, 46, 48 and 75 standing out as a group, differing from the rest of the cemetery, and burial 73 was a complete outlier, suggesting different food preparation methods (Nystrom 2008, 166). Nystrom (2008, 170) found no significant differences between males and females or between different age groups, but Jarošová (2008, 183) suggests that it may be possible to detect a higher intake of plants for females. Overall, however, their combined data suggest that the Vedrovice population was undergoing a transition from the 'hard' diets of hunter-gatherers to the 'softer' diets of farmers, confirmed by a reduction in the size of third molars in the population and the occasional impaction or absence of this tooth (Zvelebil and Pettitt 2008, 205).

Skeletal pathologies are more limited and are dominated by conditions such as osteoarthritis (Lillie 2008, 142, 144), which Crubézy *et al.* (2002) argue was most frequent in the region of the shoulder at both Nitra and Vedrovice, and *cribra orbitalia*, which was found on five female and two male skeletons. Beyond this, Lillie (2008, 143) identified three further individuals with skeletal pathologies. A number of vertebrae in the lower cervical, upper thoracic and upper lumbar spine of an adult female (18–20 years old, burial 64/74) had fused, involving the collapse of some thoracic and lumbar vertebrae; this would have caused the individual pain and meant that this individual had difficulty in moving (Lillie 2008, 143). The lower left arm of a mature male (burial 82/79) had been severed (or possibly amputated) about 10 cm above the wrist, possibly due to a fracture and subsequent infection (Lillie 2008, 143). Both of the burials above were unfurnished. The final pathology is the double trepanation on an adult male (35–40 years old, burial 15/75), which was one of the most richly furnished burials at the cemetery. It seems likely that the trepanation was carried out in response to an injury on the skull, which the individual survived (Crubézy 1996; Lillie 2008, 144).

4.7.3 Carbon and nitrogen analysis

All stable isotope results from Vedrovice are summarised in Figs 4.6–8 and Table 4.3. The Lifeways project sampled 33 individuals for carbon and nitrogen values: 22 from Široká u lesa, four from the settlement and seven from Za dvorem, in addition to the 57 studied by M.P. Richards *et al.* (2008). The mean δ^{13}C value for the whole site was −19.8‰, while for δ^{15}N the mean was 9.4‰. There are no significant differences between males and females within our dataset alone. However, if we combine these data with Richards *et al.* (2008), males have a significantly higher average δ^{15}N than the females across the whole site (Table 4.3; 2-tailed t test, p=0.036, n=56; based on the values from 36 females and 20 males; Mann-Whitney U test, p=0.044).

Differences between areas of the site

There are not enough burials from the settlement to make any worthwhile comparisons; mean δ^{13}C and δ^{15}N values for the juveniles are close to those of juveniles from the cemetery Široká u lesa.

The small group of humans from Za dvorem differ in both carbon and nitrogen isotope values from those from the Široká u lesa cemetery. The adult humans from Za dvorem have significantly lower δ^{13}C and higher δ^{15}N values than the adult humans from the cemetery (Fig. 4.7; Table 4.4). This is still valid for adult females only (to avoid any possibility of bias because of gender imbalance in the samples). The single male has an exceptionally high δ^{15}N value, as does the juvenile (13–15 years old at death), who unlike the male has a low δ^{13}C similar to the females at Za dvorem, but the numbers are too low to make anything of the age/sex differentiation in this population. The simplest interpretation is that they had a diet that differed isotopically from that of the people buried in the main cemetery, which could reflect chronological and/or cultural differences. Their diet could have included a higher proportion of protein from animals (or fish); the lower δ^{13}C also suggests a greater reliance on woodland resources. This is particularly interesting in the light of the strontium evidence (below) which suggests that individuals buried in different areas of the site may have had different mobility patterns.

Further variation between Za dvorem and the cemetery may also be found in their respective grave good assemblages, with two burials (8/88 and 9/88) from Za dvorem receiving 68 and 506 marble beads respectively (a highly unusual grave good across the LBK as a whole). Burial 9/88 was also furnished with 300 shells of local origin. Burial 8/88 is unusual as the δ^{15}N value (10.8‰) is very high, and is unlikely to reflect a nursing effect as the individual was approximately 13–15 years of age. The marble is likely to have been sourced from the Bohemian uplands, approximately 100 km to the north-west of Vedrovice (Zvelebil and Pettitt 2008, 201, fig. 1). Within the cemetery a young child (*c.* 9 years old; 84/80) was buried with a marble pendant, which may have been an imitation of the similar shaped *Spondylus* pendants.

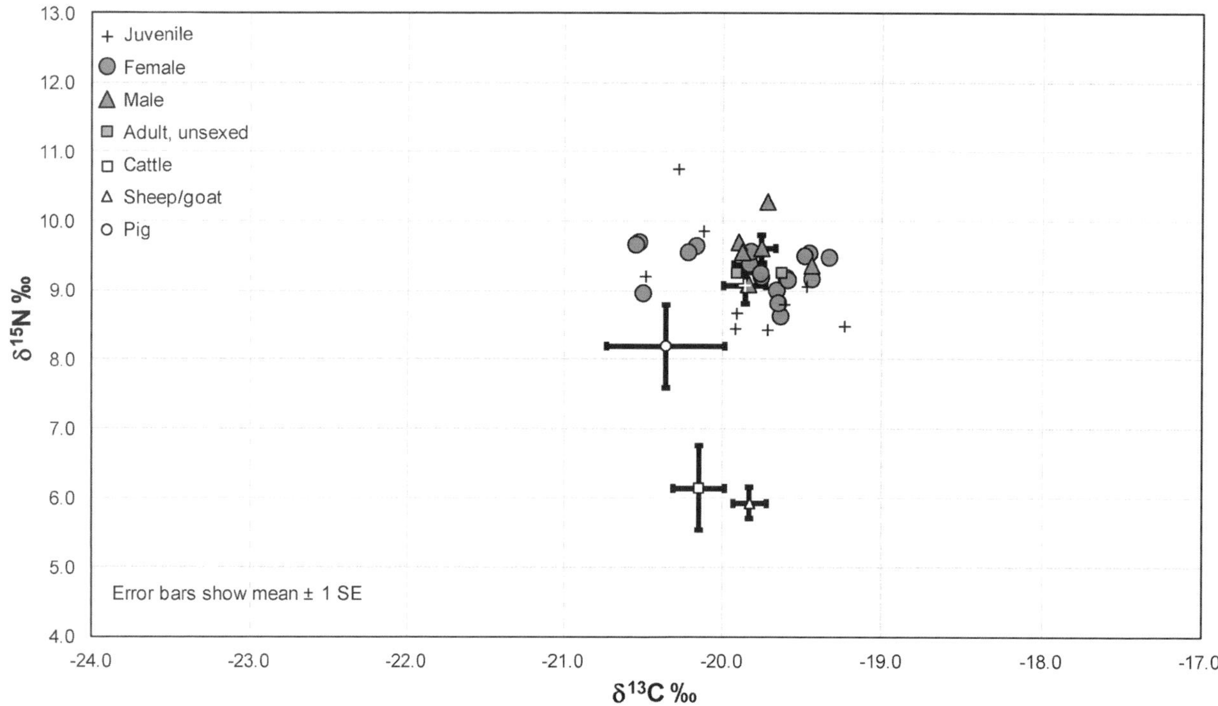

Fig. 4.6. Vedrovice: carbon and nitrogen isotope ratios (‰) of humans.

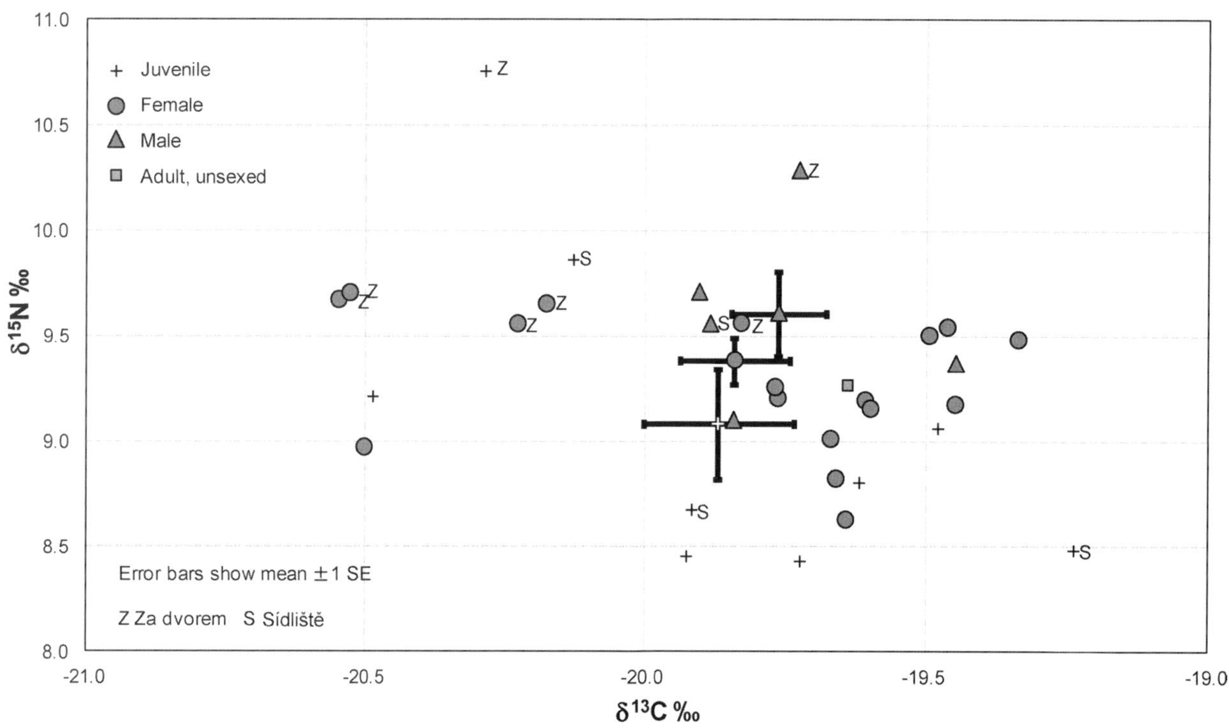

Fig. 4.7. Vedrovice: carbon and nitrogen isotope ratios (‰) of humans, shown by area.

Age/sex variation

One juvenile (grave 27/76) and one female (grave 29/76) have $\delta^{13}C$ values of −20.5‰, more than 2 SD from the respective means; both samples have good quality indicators, so this is likely to be a real difference from the general population rather than diagenesis. They are included in the statistics. There are no such clear outliers for $\delta^{15}N$.

There is no significant difference between the mean $\delta^{13}C$ values of juveniles and adults from the cemetery, or for all juveniles and adults together (no infants were sampled). At the cemetery, the mean juvenile $\delta^{15}N$ value is significantly lower than for adults (Table 4.4). This is also true for juveniles versus adults overall, but only if the juvenile from Za dvorem is omitted. While the difference in $\delta^{15}N$ values is in the direction that might be expected from

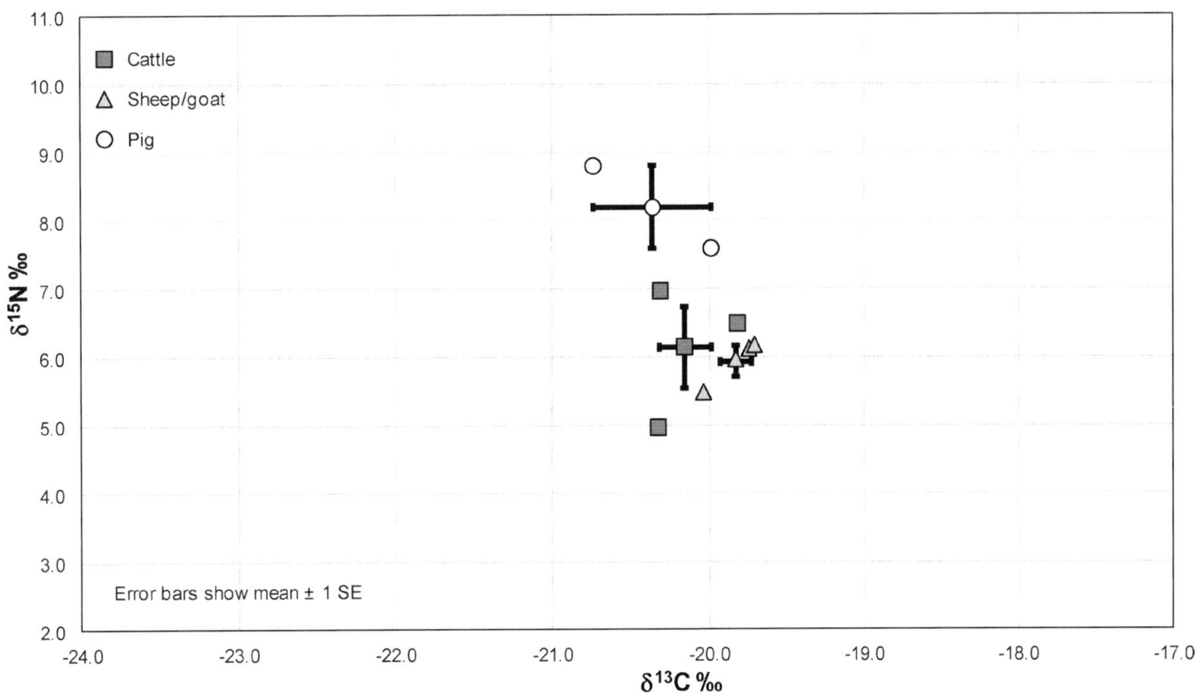

Fig. 4.8. Vedrovice: carbon and nitrogen isotope ratios (‰) of animals.

*Table 4.3. Vedrovice: carbon and nitrogen isotope ratios (‰) of humans and animals, with means and standard deviations. * includes two unsexed adults.*

Species	Age/sex	Mean $\delta^{13}C$‰	SD $\delta^{13}C$	Mean $\delta^{15}N$‰	SD $\delta^{15}N$	n	Total Human
Human	Sídliště Juvenile	−19.8	0.46	9.0	0.74	3	
Human	Sídliště Male	−20.1	-	9.9	-	1	4
Human	Široká u lesa Juvenile	−19.8	0.39	8.8	0.35	5	
Human	Široká u lesa Female	−19.7	0.29	9.2	0.27	12	
Human	Široká u lesa Male	−19.7	0.25	9.4	0.30	3	
Human	Široká u lesa Adult*	−19.8	0.20	9.3	0.00	2	
Human	Široká u lesa All Adults	−19.7	0.27	9.2	0.27	17	22
Human	Za Dvorem Juvenile	−20.3	-	10.8	-	1	
Human	Za Dvorem Female	−20.3	0.30	9.6	0.07	5	
Human	Za Dvorem Male	−19.7	-	10.3	-	1	
Human	Za Dvorem All Adult	−20.2	0.34	9.7	0.27	6	7
Human	Vedrovice Juvenile	−19.9	0.40	9.1	0.78	9	
Human	Vedrovice Female	−19.8	0.40	9.4	0.46	17	
Human	Vedrovice Male	−19.8	0.19	9.6	0.44	5	
Human	Vedrovice All Adults*	−19.8	0.35	9.4	0.35	24	33
Cattle		−20.2	0.29	6.2	1.04	3	
Sheep/goat		−19.8	0.18	5.9	0.38	3	
Pig		−20.4	0.53	8.2	0.86	2	

growing juveniles (e.g. Minagawa and Wada 1984; Ponsard and Averbuch 1999; Fuller *et al.* 2004), there are several variable metabolic processes that may affect $\delta^{15}N$ values in a growing individual, not necessarily in the same direction (reviewed by Waters-Rist and Katzenberg 2010). There are no significant differences in carbon or nitrogen isotope values between juveniles and adults overall included in the larger study of Richards *et al.* (2008), or in the combined dataset (though when the adults are separated by sex, differences do emerge; see further discussion below). It would therefore

Table 4.4. Vedrovice: results of statistical comparisons. The data are not normally distributed, so the Mann-Whitney U test has been used for significance testing.

			$\delta^{13}C$	$\delta^{15}N$
Comparison	n_1	n_2	*p*	*p*
Široká u lesa All adults × Za dvorem All adults	17	6	**<0.02**	**<0.02**
Široká u lesa Females × Za dvorem Females	12	5	**<0.02**	**<0.02**
Široká u lesa: Juveniles × All adults	5	17	NS	**0.02**
Široká u lesa: Females × Males	12	3	NS	NS
Vedrovice all areas: Juveniles × All adults	9	24	NS	NS
Vedrovice all areas: Females × Males	17	5	NS	NS

Table 4.5. Vedrovice: carbon and nitrogen values for the combined dataset (from the cemetery Široká u lesa only; results of this study in Table 4.3).

Age/sex	**Study**	**Mean $\delta^{13}C$**	**SD $\delta^{13}C$**	**Mean $\delta^{15}N$**	**SD $\delta^{15}N$**	**n**
Juvenile	M.P. Richards *et al.* 2008	−19.7	0.32	9.7	0.46	13
Female	M.P. Richards *et al.* 2008	−19.7	0.24	9.7	0.37	22
Male	M.P. Richards *et al.* 2008	−19.6	0.28	10.1	0.41	16
Juvenile	Combined data	−19.8	0.33	9.4	0.58	18
Female	Combined data	−19.7	0.26	9.5	0.43	34
Male	Combined data	−19.6	0.28	9.9	0.46	19

be unwise to make too much of this finding, based on only five juveniles. We discuss this further, in the context of the whole dataset, in Chapter 9.2.5.

There is no significant difference between the mean $\delta^{13}C$ or $\delta^{15}N$ values of males and females from the cemetery, or for all males and females together. At Za dvorem the single male (2/85) has distinctly higher $\delta^{13}C$ and $\delta^{15}N$ values than the five females, but it is hard to draw a general conclusion on this basis. His $\delta^{15}N$ value is the highest of all the adults at Vedrovice, over 2σ from the adult mean, though his $\delta^{13}C$ value is close to the overall mean.

There is thus no strong isotopic evidence in our sample from the cemetery for differentiation in diet according to age or sex, although there are exceptional individuals.

Comparison to previous analysis

Ten of the bones sampled by M.P. Richards *et al.* (2008) were re-sampled and the isotopes re-measured. There was no significant difference between our results and the original measurements for $\delta^{13}C$ or $\delta^{15}N$ (for these samples, means of $\delta^{13}C$, $\delta^{15}N$ in Richards *et al.* 2008 were −19.74±0.35‰ and 9.76±0.30‰; in this study −19.74±0.40‰ and 9.78±0.37‰, so there is no systematic difference between the studies). However, when our results (from Široká u lesa only) are compared with theirs, there is a significant difference in overall mean $\delta^{15}N$, though not in $\delta^{13}C$. This may be due to differences in age/sex distribution in the two samples; we have a much lower proportion of males, for instance, and no infants. It is difficult to formally test this because of the different numbers and proportions of individuals in the various age/sex groups in the two studies and the non-normal distribution of the data; ANOVA suggests that there may be a significant difference between males and females in $\delta^{15}N$ values, but also between the two studies when age and sex are taken into consideration. As this does not seem to reflect difference in measurement between the two studies, it seems that the two subsamples of the population at Vedrovice differ in some unknown way.

Bearing this caveat in mind, we can combine the data from the two studies (Table 4.5). To avoid the effect of location within the site, we used only data from the cemetery Široká u lesa, and we also omitted two samples with high C:N ratios from the study of M.P. Richards *et al.* 2008 (graves 51/77 and 93/80). There were no significant differences in $\delta^{13}C$ between juveniles, females and males, but differences between these groups in $\delta^{15}N$ were significant, as was the difference between adult males and females (Table 4.6). An ANOVA with post hoc comparison of means showed that male $\delta^{15}N$ was significantly higher than that of either females or juveniles (Bonferroni test, $p<0.01$). While the validity of ANOVA may be affected by the non-normal distribution of the data, this result at least indicates that the main pattern seen is the higher value of male $\delta^{15}N$, while females and juveniles do not differ significantly. Apart from the newborn (grave 81b/79) whose $\delta^{15}N$ value still mostly reflects the mother's, and the infant (grave 17/75) with the high $\delta^{15}N$ characteristic of nursing babies, there were no trends in $\delta^{15}N$ in relation to age, in contrast to the situation at Nitra (Chapter 4.10.3).

Here, as at two other sites in this project, males have significantly higher $\delta^{15}N$ values than females (see also discussion in Chapter 9.2.5).

Animals

Though the numbers of animals we could sample from Vedrovice were too low to see any statistically significant

Table 4.6. Vedrovice: results of Mann-Whitney U tests (for comparisons between two groups) or Kruskal-Wallis tests (for comparisons between three groups); individuals from the cemetery Široká u lesa only, using either data from M.P. Richards et al. *(2008) alone, or combined with data from this study.* n_J*=number of juveniles,* n_F*=number of females,* n_M*=number of males.*

					$\delta^{13}C$	$\delta^{15}N$
Comparison	**Dataset**	n_J	n_F	n_M	*p*	*p*
Juveniles×Females×Males	This study	5	12	3	NS	NS
	M.P. Richards *et al.* 2008	13	22	16	NS	**0.023**
	Combined data	18	34	19	NS	**0.005**
Females×Males	This study		12	3	NS	NS
	M.P. Richards *et al.* 2008		22	16	NS	**0.017**
	Combined data		34	19	NS	**0.004**

differences in $\delta^{13}C$ and $\delta^{15}N$ values, the pattern is similar to that at other sites (Fig. 4.8). Pigs have distinctly higher $\delta^{15}N$ values than cattle and sheep, reflecting a somewhat more omnivorous diet.

The difference between human and cattle mean $\delta^{13}C$ values is 0.5‰±0.4 (SD), and between human and cattle mean $\delta^{15}N$ values 3.5‰±1.1 (combined dataset). The difference in $\delta^{15}N$ values is higher than at the other three sites in the region, admittedly based on limited faunal data.

Correlations with the archaeological data

Overall, there were few significant direct correlations between the varied funerary rites and the stable isotope results, which given the overall similarity of the data is not suprising. No patterns with the palaeopathological data could be discerned. However, there are a few points of interest to discuss. The male (grave 57/78) with the highest $\delta^{15}N$ value (10.7‰), and with the head to the north-west, was accompanied by two polished stone tools. Both were adzes, had traces of working and had been broken approximately in the same place as if deliberately snapped in the middle. They were also placed in an unusual position, one at each knee, pointing away from the deceased. Such an arrangement may potentially be echoed at Aiterhofen, where in grave 50 two arrows were placed by the knee, though this time facing in the same direction as the face (Nieszery 1995, 339).

Those individuals with low $\delta^{15}N$ values (<9.0) are dominated by women and children, though they do not differ significantly in other ways (such as grave goods, body positions and orientation of the graves).

4.7.4 Strontium analysis

From the Vedrovice cemetery, we recovered $^{87}Sr/^{86}Sr$ ratios from 52 individuals, including five from the settlement, seven from Za dvorem and 40 from the cemetery. To this we were able to add 19 strontium ratios determined by M.P. Richards *et al.* (2008), all from the cemetery. This yields $^{87}Sr/^{86}Sr$ ratios from a combined total of 72 individuals, including 34 females, 19 males and 18 juveniles (Fig. 4.9; Tables 4.7–8). M.P. Richards *et al.* (2008), whose samples are designated in Table 4.2, used very similar sample preparation techniques (measuring a small chip of tooth whose surface was cleaned mechanically; dissolved in 3M HNO_3 and purified through columns filled with Sr-spec resin, and the purified Sr in 1 ml of Milli-Q H_2O analysed on a Thermofisher Neptune PIMMs, with seven measurements of the NBS 987 standard yielding 0.71027±0.000015). In terms of the range of values, their results are entirely consistent with ours, exhibiting no systematic shift in $^{87}Sr/^{86}Sr$ or any indications that the precision or accuracy were different between the two studies.

Vedrovice lies at the base of the Bohemian Massif, where Precambrian contributions to the loess raise the resulting $^{87}Sr/^{86}Sr$ ratios in human skeletons to between 0.7108 and 0.7105 (M.P. Richards *et al.* 2008). At Vedrovice, the mean $^{87}Sr/^{86}Sr$ among identified females (n=32) was 0.7107±0.00102, and among identified males (n=19) it was 0.71098±0.00070. These means only differ by 0.0002, but it is important to remember that it is the significance of the difference, not the size of the difference, that matters for $^{87}Sr/^{86}Sr$ signatures. If we compare each set of identified Vedrovice adults to the set of opposite sex plus unidentified sex (mainly children), the mean among the females is significantly lower than the rest of the sample (2-tailed *t* test, p=0.054), whereas the mean among males is definitely not different from the rest of the sample (p=0.8). Also the Vedrovice females have larger variance in $^{87}Sr/^{86}Sr$ than males (Levene's test, p=0.015). The mean Sr ppm at Vedrovice was not significantly different (females, 84±47 ppm; males, 69±24 ppm), although the variance in Sr concentrations is greater among females (F-test, p=0.005).

The distinction of the females is apparent also from Fig. 4.9, which shows a noticeable 'local' cluster at Vedrovice, containing men, women and children, and then outliers which are predominantly women (as always, we use the terms 'local' and 'non-local' loosely, as labels for the main cluster versus outliers). Adult females at Vedrovice make up the majority of individuals with $^{87}Sr/^{86}Sr$ ratios above 0.712 or below 0.7104, as is visible in Fig. 4.9. Considering that 30 of all 71 Vedrovice individuals are identified as females, the fact that 14 out of the 16 individuals outside this 'local' $^{87}Sr/^{86}Sr$ range are females is significant (p=0.003, χ^2=10.27, df=1). In sum, the majority of the 'non-local' signatures from Vedrovice come from adult females, who have significantly more variable $^{87}Sr/^{86}Sr$ signatures, despite the mean Sr concentrations being the same.

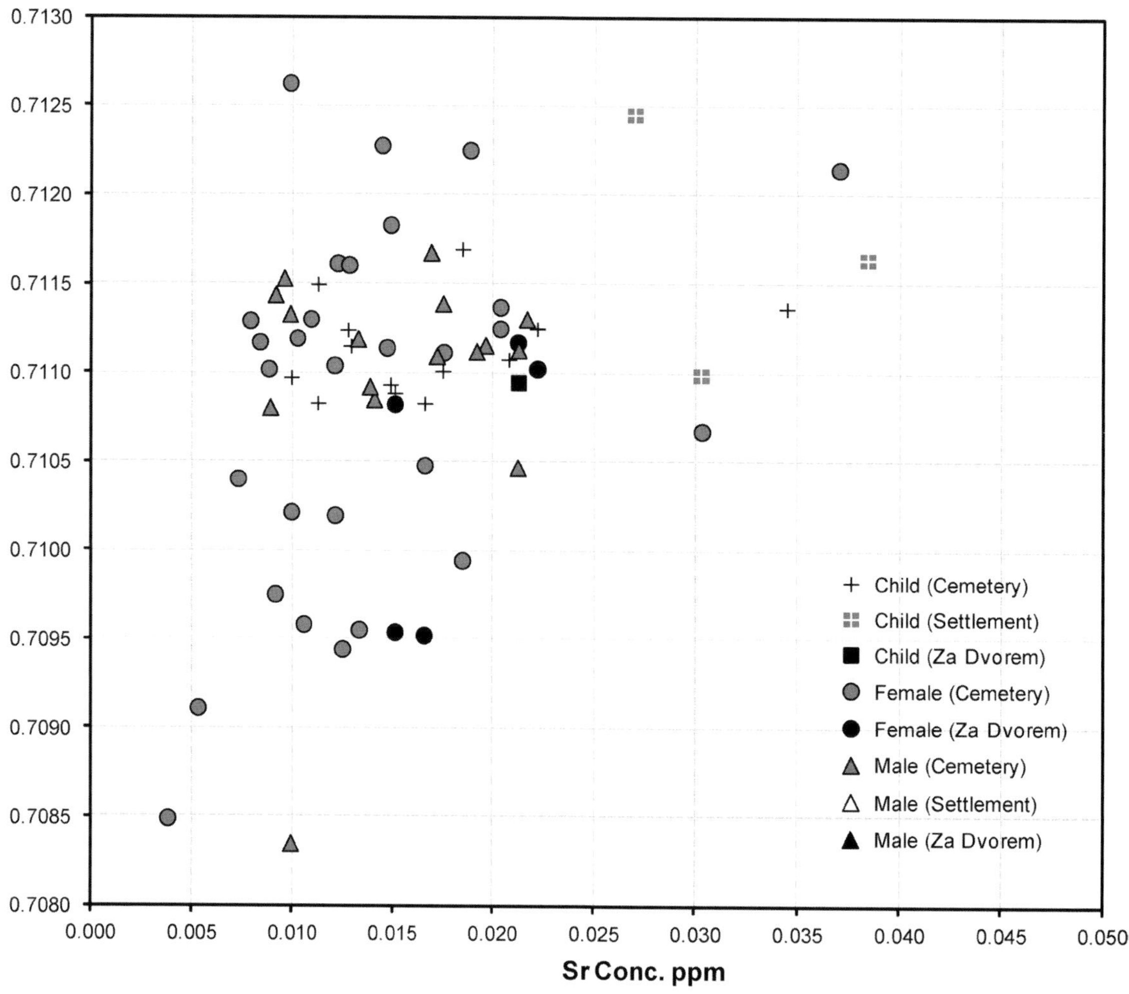

Fig. 4.9. Vedrovice: strontium concentration (ppm) versus ratio ($^{87}Sr/^{86}Sr$); all areas of the site (including data from M.P. Richards et al. *(2008).*

Table 4.7. Vedrovice: the strontium isotope ratios and concentrations summarised by molar sampled.

Molar	Mean $^{87}Sr/^{86}Sr$	SD $^{87}Sr/^{86}Sr$	Mean Sr conc.	SD Sr conc.	n
M1	0.71112	0.000649	65	34	28
M2	0.71110	0.000874	73	26	18
M3	0.71053	0.000927	89	46	21

Differences in mobility between different age groups can be investigated by analysing the strontium ratios of the molar sampled. At Vedrovice, the strontium ratios from M3 molars are on average less radiogenic than M1 and M2 molars and there is an increase in the mean strontium concentration in the tooth from M1 to M3 (Fig. 4.9; Table 4.7). The difference between M1/M2 molars and M3 molars is statistically significant (Mann-Whitney U test, p=0.017). There may also be a shift in mean strontium concentration but detecting this pattern is complicated by the settlement burials, which were dominated by juveniles, and only M1 molars were sampled. These differences suggest a dietary shift over childhood towards food sourced from a different geographic location and possibly foods with high strontium concentration (e.g. plants). This pattern may also be partly explained by the presence of a breast-feeding signature in the M1 molars sampled, which begin to mineralise about the age of two. At that age the stable isotopes suggest infants were still being nursed and milk is a food source low in strontium concentration.

It is difficult to determine whether there are sex-based differences amongst the M1 $^{87}Sr/^{86}Sr$ ratios as only three males had their M1 molars sampled (10/74, 79/79 and 88/80). However, they are very close together (0.71080, 0.71112 and 0.71118 respectively), compared with a range of 0.70911 (grave 51/77) –0.71215 (grave 93a/80) for the ten women whose M1 molars were sampled (Levene's test for variance, p=0.027). Women have significantly more variable $^{87}Sr/^{86}Sr$ ratios when the M2 molars are considered (Levene's test, p=0.015, n=16), but no difference in variance when M3 molars from males and females are compared (Levene's test, p=0.8, n=20). These results suggest that

*Table 4.8. Vedrovice: strontium isotope ratios and concentrations. * includes one unsexed adult.*

Age/sex	Mean $^{87}Sr/^{86}Sr$	SD $^{87}Sr/^{86}Sr$	Mean Sr conc.	SD Sr conc.	n
Sídliště Juvenile	0.71161	0.00062	31	5	4
Sídliště Male	0.71010	-	40	-	1
Sídliště All	0.71149	0.00060	33	9	5
Široká u lesa Juvenile	0.71112	0.00025	69	18	14
Široká u lesa Female	0.71084	0.00104	90	49	28
Široká u lesa Male	0.71099	0.00074	72	24	17
Široká u lesa All*	0.71094	0.00083	80	37	60
Za dvorem Female	0.71050	0.00076	55	10	6
Za dvorem Male	0.71079	-	49	-	1
Za dvorem All	0.71054	0.00070	54	10	7
Vedrovice Juvenile	0.71124	0.00040	61	23	18
Vedrovice Female	0.71076	0.00104	84	47	34
Vedrovice Male	0.71098	0.00070	69	24	19
Vedrovice All*	0.71094	0.00082	74	37	72

female mobility had largely taken place by the time the third molar had finished mineralising (ages 14–16).

Among the 19 identified males at Vedrovice, ten had adzes, and despite the small sample, the adze burials had smaller variance in $^{87}Sr/^{86}Sr$ (Levene's test, p=0.07) despite the mean $^{87}Sr/^{86}Sr$ not being different (2-tailed t test, p=0.35). Considering that 24 out of the total of 72 Vedrovice individuals fall outside the range from 0.7104 to 0.7115, the fact that none of the 14 adze burials fall outside this range is significant (p=0.015, χ^2=5.89, df=1). Most of the adzes were with males, of course, and if we consider the much smaller sample of 19 adult males, the clustering of adze burials (Fig. 4.4) is even tighter. Within a tighter $^{87}Sr/^{86}Sr$ range of 0.711 to 0.7115, only two of the nine males outside this range have an adze, which is just about significant (p=0.07, χ^2=3.34, df=1), given that over half (10/19) the males had adzes. Another way to look at the clustering of values among adze burials is to consider that there are only two adze burials among five highest and five lowest $^{87}Sr/^{86}Sr$ ratios among Vedrovice males (p=0.04, χ^2=4.27, df=1).

These significant patterns with the adzes at Vedrovice are all the more striking given the fact that no other significant correlations were found between $^{87}Sr/^{86}Sr$ and any other burial good, including *Spondylus*. The body configurations are so uniform that it would be unlikely to find statistically significant patterns in any case.

If the different areas of the site are compared, further differences arise (Fig. 4.9; Table 4.8). The values of settlement burials fall between $^{87}Sr/^{86}Sr$ ratios of 0.711 and 0.713, dominating amongst burials with low Sr concentrations, while burials from the cemetery and Za dvorem appear to fall in a broad mixing line running between 0.7085/0.05 and 0.7130/0.20 (Chapter 2.3 and 2.5.1 for further discussion of mixing lines). Using the Kruskal-Wallis test for variance (and therefore not assuming a normal distribution for the data) the strontium ratio and concentration are significantly different between the three areas of the site ($^{87}Sr/^{86}Sr$ ratio p=0.036; Sr conc. p<0.005), though admittedly the number of samples for the settlement (five) and Za dvorem (seven) is low. Nevertheless, this suggests that those buried in different areas of the site had different mobility patterns. The individuals from the settlement are seemingly more focused on the local area, falling within the 'local' range.

Comparisons between the nitrogen, carbon and strontium data showed only one significant correlation, between the Sr ratios and the $\delta^{15}N$ values from the sampled females. Carrying out a Kendall tau-b test (Pearson-style test, but not assuming normal distribution, which is appropriate for Sr data) the correlation coefficient is −0.375, p=0.004, n=31, which is not strong, but can also be seen in the plot (Fig. 4.10). This correlation suggests that the geographical origin of women at Vedrovice may have influenced their diet in the years leading up to their death. When the averages for the three areas of the site are plotted ($^{87}Sr/^{86}Sr$ ratios versus $\delta^{15}N$ values) the males, females and juveniles occupy different areas of the chart, which shows that the correlation between $^{87}Sr/^{86}Sr$ ratios and $\delta^{15}N$ values amongst the women may originate in the differences between the cemetery (average: $^{87}Sr/^{86}Sr$ ratio=0.71084, $\delta^{15}N$ value=9.2‰) and Za dvorem (average: $^{87}Sr/^{86}Sr$ ratio=0.71050, $\delta^{15}N$ value=9.6‰). The women buried at Za dvorem therefore had a different geographic origin to the women buried in the cemetery (Široká u lesa) and were eating a different diet. Further variation between Za dvorem and the cemetery may also be found in their respective grave good assemblages, with two burials (8/88 and 9/88) from Za dvorem receiving many imported marble beads, as noted above. Burial 9/88 was also furnished with 300 shells of local origin. Burial 8/88 is unusual as the $\delta^{15}N$ value (10.8‰) is very high for an individual of approximately 13–15 years of age.

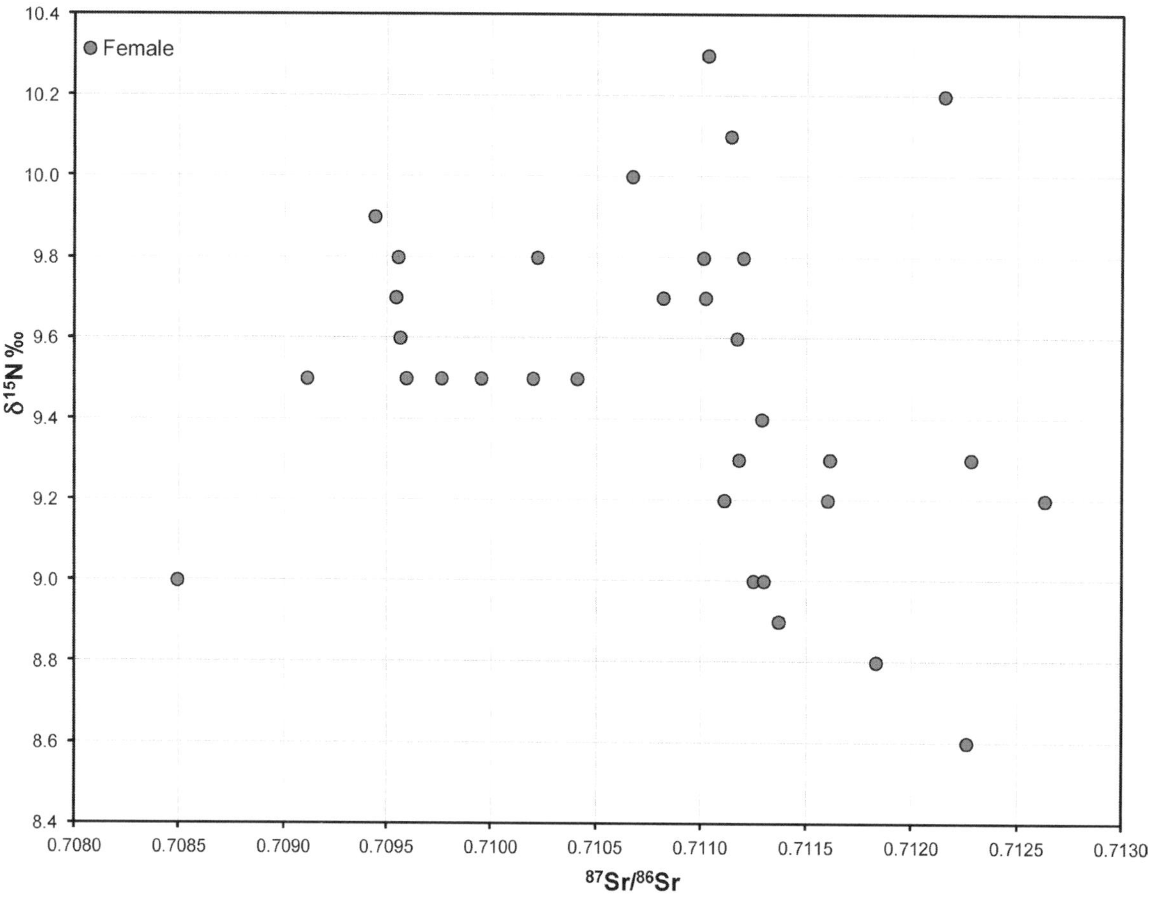

Fig. 4.10. Vedrovice: correlation between strontium ratio and $\delta^{15}N$ values for women (all areas of the site).

4.7.5 Site summary and discussion

The overall conclusions drawn from the stable isotope analysis suggest that individuals buried in different parts of the site had varied diets, but that those who were buried together were sharing a similar diet, with little evidence for variation by age and sex at the site as a whole. In contrast, the strontium analysis shows that men and women experienced different mobility patterns. We argue here that this is likely to represent virilocal or patrilocal practices, with women moving on marriage, away from the communities within which they spent their childhoods. This contributes to the picture of variability, for which Zvelebil and Pettitt (2008) argued. However, our conclusions differ in so much as we argue that the individuals sampled from the settlement are likely to have been local, with strontium values elevated out of the loess range by the local geology (Chapter 4.7.4).

The tighter range of strontium values amongst males buried with adzes, however, in many ways speaks to a certain consistency; as these strontium values were determined in childhood, yet the adze accompanied the adult in death, the pattern suggests that for some individuals their situation in childhood did determine future contexts of burial. These data therefore suggest some inter-generational transfer of potential lifeways or status, and a certain consistency over the life of the cemetery in both female patterns of mobility and access to or choice to bury male individuals with an adze.

In the analysis of Vedrovice, much emphasis has been placed on who was buried with the richest grave assemblages, particularly the occurrence of polished stone adzes and *Spondylus* in the graves of older individuals (e.g. Podborský 2002a; Květina 2004; Zvelebil and Pettitt 2008). Podborský (2002c, 335) argued on this basis that the population at Vedrovice was matrilineal or gerontocratic. However, using the new ageing of the skeletons (Dočkalová 2008; Lillie 2008), if we divide adults roughly into two age groups either side of approximately 40 years, the percentage of graves with certain grave goods drops off. Overall, lithics (ranging from present in 55% of graves to only 25%), polished stone for males (77% to 55%) and *Spondylus* shells (59% to 25%) are less frequently associated with older adults (both males and females). In contrast, while pottery remains roughly the same for males across the different age classes, it increases in the older adult females (from 30% to 52%). The 'richest' graves in terms of variety and number of grave goods (e.g. 14/75 female, 35–40 years; 15/75 male, 35–40 years; 19/75 male, 25–35 years; 46/77 male, 20–35 years; 54/78 male, 20–25 years; 69/78 male, 20–30 years; 79/79 male, 25–35 years; 81a/79 female, 20–30 years; 86/80 female, 25–30 years; 100/81 female, 20–30 years) fall between *c.* 20–40 years. Overall 23% of younger adults are unfurnished, while 41% of older adults (> 40 years) have no grave goods.

Of course, 40 years is a rather arbitrary place to draw a

divide (though osteologically ageing becomes less certain after about 45 years) and this is not to argue that there are no older adults with rich graves, but to stress that the significance of 'richer older adult' graves may have been rather over-emphasised (cf. Květina 2004, 389). Female graves (47%) are more likely to be unfurnished than males (25%). Five of the 11 child graves (*c*. <14 years) are unfurnished, and although the grave good assemblages are not comparable in complexity (in terms of varied objects and their numbers) to the adults (18–40 years), four are buried with polished stone and a different four are buried with *Spondylus* (Table 4.2). So, overall, at Vedrovice we can identify a pattern where the likelihood of receiving grave goods increases from childhood to early adulthood and then decreases again in old age, with the exception of pottery. This pattern could contrast, however, with the isotope results, which suggest shared dietary practices and some form of determination of lifecourse from birth as evidenced by the variation in the strontium isotope ratios of adult males buried with and without adzes.

The clusters proposed by Podborský (2002a) and Květina (2004) are not identifiable isotopically, nor are the possible linear arrangements running across the site from north-east to south-west, though this is not to say that the clusters are not significant to the organisation of the cemetery. As Zvelebil and Pettitt (2008, 204) note, each cluster has one or two of the very rich graves. If each of the identified clusters does represent family or kin groups, then this suggests that there was not much differentiation in status between the groups, with equal access to valued objects across the cemetery rather than concentrated in a few areas. Zvelebil and Pettitt (2008, 205) propose that cluster 7 (the north-western group; Fig. 4.4), with its poor male graves, unaccompanied by polished stone and imported lithics or shells (63/78, 73/79, 99/81), but with two rich female graves (on account of the presence of *Spondylus*: 83/80, 91/80), may represent a matrilineal group within an otherwise patrilineal community. This is an interesting proposal, given that this group is dominated by female graves (eight females to three males). However, the higher numbers of females in this group may exaggerate the importance of the 'rich' female graves; given that generally *c*. 40% of female graves in the cemetery at Vedrovice have *Spondylus*, having three burials of women that have *Spondylus* (81a/79, 83/80, 91/80) from eight in cluster 7 is nothing out of the ordinary.

The clusters do differ in orientation and in the variability of orientations (χ^2= 48.63, p=0.028, df=32, Monte Carlo exact test at 99% confidence level). Four burials of two men and two women with rare orientations form a small cluster towards the centre of the site (14/75 NW–SE; 15/75 NW–SE; 43/77 W–E; 69/78; NW–SE). All these graves are furnished, the two male graves 15/75 and 69/78 particularly so; both had adzes and impressive amounts of *Spondylus* (Table 4.2). In fact, of the four grinding stones found in graves at Vedrovice, three are in graves oriented NW–SE – though this may be as a result of NW-oriented graves generally being well furnished (only one burial from 12 is unfurnished). While there are no overall direct correlations between certain burial practices and particular grave goods, we can identify a tendency where those graves that stand out in one particular way are also unusual in other elements of the rite or accompanying objects. At Vedrovice, rather than seeing the burials that do not follow the majority as deviant, it seems more appropriate to regard them as marked out as special. Therefore, following Zvelebil and Pettitt (2008, 214), rather than treating the individual aspects of burial as signatures of particular or defined identies (e.g. high status or 'hunter'), we envisage something more fluid, in which lifeways are shaped by both inherited status and the development of a network of contacts.

4.8 *Těšetice-Kyjovice*

4.8.1 Introduction

The multi-phase site of Těšetice-Kyjovice was first discovered as part of a rescue excavation in 1956, but has since received a number of systematic explorations running from 1967 and still going, which were led principally by Vladimír Podborský (Mateiciucová 2008a, 238). Similar to Vedrovice, it is located at the point at which the Bohemian Massif meets the wider Carpathian area (Fig. 4.1), forming a sandy gravel subsoil to the loess, with granites and gneiss reaching the surface in some places (Mateiciucová 2008a, 238). This site is perhaps best known as the location of the first *rondel* to be found in central Europe, and the Moravian Painted Ware phases of the site have seen the most research to date (Podborský 1988; 2001). The area of LBK settlement, consisting of 13 longhouses and their accompanying pits situated on a gentle hillside sloping to the south-east on the left bank of the Unanovka stream (Podborský 1999), has had comparatively little consideration and has not been fully published (Fig. 4.11). The lithics, however, have recently been studied by Inna Mateiciucová (2008a).

Těšetice is located some 30 km from the sources of Krumlovský Les chert, on the eastern edge of the Krumlovian Forest, and this raw material dominates the chipped stone assemblage (66%) over nearer suitable sources (Mateiciucová 2008a, 242). Mateiciucová (2008a, 81, 243) argued that the supply to the settlement was not regular and only met the needs of the community which inhabited it. In this respect, Mateiciucová (2008a, 102) argues that the assemblage from Těšetice is typical of a consumer settlement, despite being relatively close to the raw material. In contrast, Mold, which is some 80 km away, received raw material from the Krumlovský Les chert source and redistributed it, characteristics found normally at sites close to the source – or producer settlements (Mateiciucová 2008a, 102). Exotic finds at the site are rare, but erratic silicites (*c*. 150 km from the site) and a flake and blade of Krakow Jurassic silicite (*c*. 290 km away) show contacts with areas of the LBK in southern Poland, most likely travelling through the natural corridor created by the Morava and Odra rivers (Mateiciucová 2008a, 112,

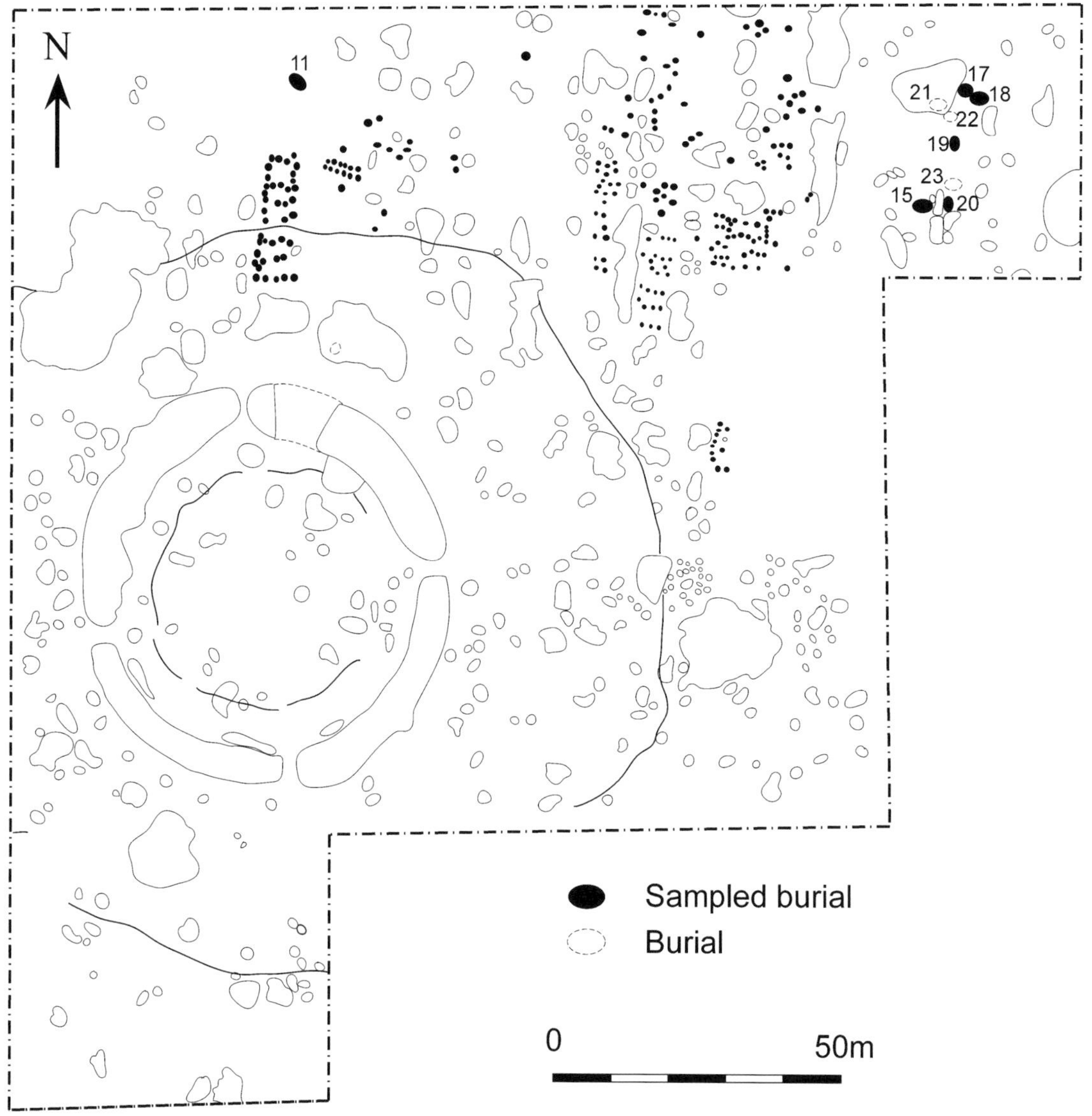

Fig. 4.11. Těšetice-Kyjovice: plan. After Dočkalová and Čižmář (2008a, 41).

242), and suggest that the site was connected into broader exchange networks.

The attention that has been given to the site has focused on the burials (Table 4.9). Eight graves were found forming a small cluster in the north-eastern part of the settlement, and consisted of seven individual graves and one double burial (Dočkalová and Koštuřik 1996). Further to the west, isolated from the main group, a single inhumation of an adult female (with an estimated age of 45–55 years) was discovered some five years earlier (1986), with a different orientation to the rest of the graves. This grave, numbered 11 by the excavators, was oriented north-west–south-east (with the head to the north-west), while the rest of the burials were oriented between east–west and south–north, perhaps echoing the pattern found at Vedrovice. Two further skeletons, not sampled by this project, have come to light more recently, of an adult female (in 2001) and a neonate (in 2006; Dočkalova and Čižmář 2007, 45). Most of the burials were associated with some form of grave goods, mainly pots and in one case a grinding stone. However, polished stone and *Spondylus* are absent in line with other settlement burials in the region.

There is strong evidence that burial may have been accompanied by further rites, including the revisiting of graves. In the cases of graves 18 and 20, pots were placed some way above the skeleton in the grave fills. For example, the globular jug (dated to Moravian phase Ib) found in grave 18 was found at the top of the grave pit, partly above the level of the pit fill (Dočkalová and Čižmář 2008a, 43). This burial had also been backfilled unusually; first the body was covered with a layer of loess and brown clay (*c.* 17 cm deep) and then with a second layer of loess and clay that had more calciferous qualities (28 cm deep; Dočkalová and Čižmář 2008a, 43). Three vessels were found in a similar position in grave 19 (Dočkalová and Čižmář 2008a, 44), perhaps echoing the *Nachgabe* found at Polgár (Chapter 3.9.1).

The pottery from the settlement suggests that it largely belongs to the middle or developed phases of the LBK in Moravia, but lack of systematic study at the site means the

Table 4.9. Těšetice-Kyjovice: the isotope, osteological and archaeological data. Age, sex and pathology information from Dočkalová and Čižmář (2007; 2008a). See Chapter 2 for further definition of ages.
Key for body position: LC – Left-crouched; RC – Right-crouched; C – Crouched, direction unknown; CB – Crouched on back; CF – Crouched on front; S – Supine; P – Prone; I – Irregular.
Key for grave goods (number of items in brackets): U. – Unfurnished; F. – Fill only (all items listed after an F. were in the fill of the grave rather than at the level of the skeleton); Pol. – Polished stone; Cer. – Ceramics; Shd. – Sherds; Spon. – Spondylus; She. – Other Shell; Och. – Ochre; Lit. – Chipped stone; Bon – Worked bone; Grd. – Grinding stone.

Burial	Tooth	Sex	Age (yrs)	$^{87}Sr/^{86}Sr$	Sr ppm	$\delta^{13}C$ ‰	$\delta^{15}N$ ‰	Orientation	Body position	Grave goods	Pathology
11/86	M1	F	45–55	0.71018	98	-19.6	9.5	NW–SE	LC	Cer.(2), Grd.(1)	-
15/91	M1	-	Inf. II	0.71145	124	-19.9	10.1	E–W	LC	U.	-
17/91	M1	-	9–10	0.71136	147	-19.5	8.8	E–W	LC	*n.d.*	-
18/92	M2	F	20–25	0.71184	157	-19.1	9.1	E–W	LC	Cer.(1), Och. on skull	*Cribra orbitalia*, enthesopathy (left knee/femur)
19/92	M3	M	16–18	0.71143	260	-19.4	8.9	S–N	RC	F.Cer.(3?)	Suggested rickets or dysplasia
20/92	M3	M	17–19	0.71166	106	-19.3	8.5	S–N	LC	Cer.(3?)	*Cribra orbitalia*, tibiae with Harris Lines
21/92	M1	M	20–22	0.71166	121	-19.5	9	-	-	*n.d.*	-
21/92	-	-	8–10	-	-	-	-	-	-	*n.d.*	-
22/92	-	-	2–2.5	-	-	-	-	E–W	-	*n.d.*	-
23/92	-	-	6	-	-	-	-	W–E	LC	*n.d.*/Cer.(1)	-

chronology is uncertain (Mateiciucová 2008a, 240). The burials present a confused picture. Ceramic styles from the graves suggest that the burials date to phase Ib_1, but three radiocarbon samples on individuals from the burial cluster gave dates likely to be contemporary with the settlement (Dočkalová and Koštuřík 1996; Dočkalová and Čižmář 2007).[6] While there is a possibility that curated pottery was placed in these graves, this could well fit into a broader picture that is developing across the LBK, which suggests that not all groups started using the developed ceramic styles of phase II at the same time. The burials could have taken place early on in the history of the settlement, before the inhabitants adopted the later LBK ceramic styles.

Fortunately, the animal bone assemblage from this site has been studied. Domestic animals dominated the faunal assemblage, accounting for about 95% of all the animal remains (NISP; Dreslerová 2006, 9). The relative frequency of the three domestic animals (cattle, pig and sheep/goat) followed the regional pattern, with cattle the most frequent species (Dreslerová 2006, 12). However, as cattle only formed *c.* 45% of the assemblage (sheep/goat: *c.* 30%; pig: just over 20%), cattle were less well represented at this site than at other studied sites in Bohemia and Moravia, where the rates reach from over 50% to above 80% (Dreslerová 2006, 12). Could there be some kind of link between the putative delay in adopting the developed LBK ceramic style and the lower percentage of cattle? Cattle were less frequent in the earlier phases of the LBK in its eastern distribution (Lüning 2000, 110; Schmitzberger 2009b; compare also Knipper 2011).

4.8.2 Osteology

The human skeletal remains from Těšetice-Kyjovice are housed in the Moravian Museum, Brno, and have principally been studied by Marta Dočkalová (Dočkalová 2005; Dočkalová and Koštuřík 1996; Dočkalová and Čižmář 2007; 2008a). Three male, two female and five child skeletons were identified, with one of the males and a child aged between nine and ten years found together in a double inhumation, though from the respective depths of the skeletons they may not have been interred in the grave at the same time. The cut of the pit could not be detected, but the child seems to have been buried first and was placed at 65–85 cm from the surface, while the adult remains were a mere 20 cm down (Dočkalová and Čižmář 2008a, 43). However, given the poor preservation of these remains, reburial and secondary rearrangement of the grave contents also remain possible.

Various pathologies presented themselves on this assemblage. *Cribra orbitalia* was visible on burial 18, as well as an enthesopathy at one of the sites of muscle attachment of the knee area of the femur (Dočkalová and Čižmář 2008a, 62). This suggests frequent use and is suffered in modern populations mainly by athletes,

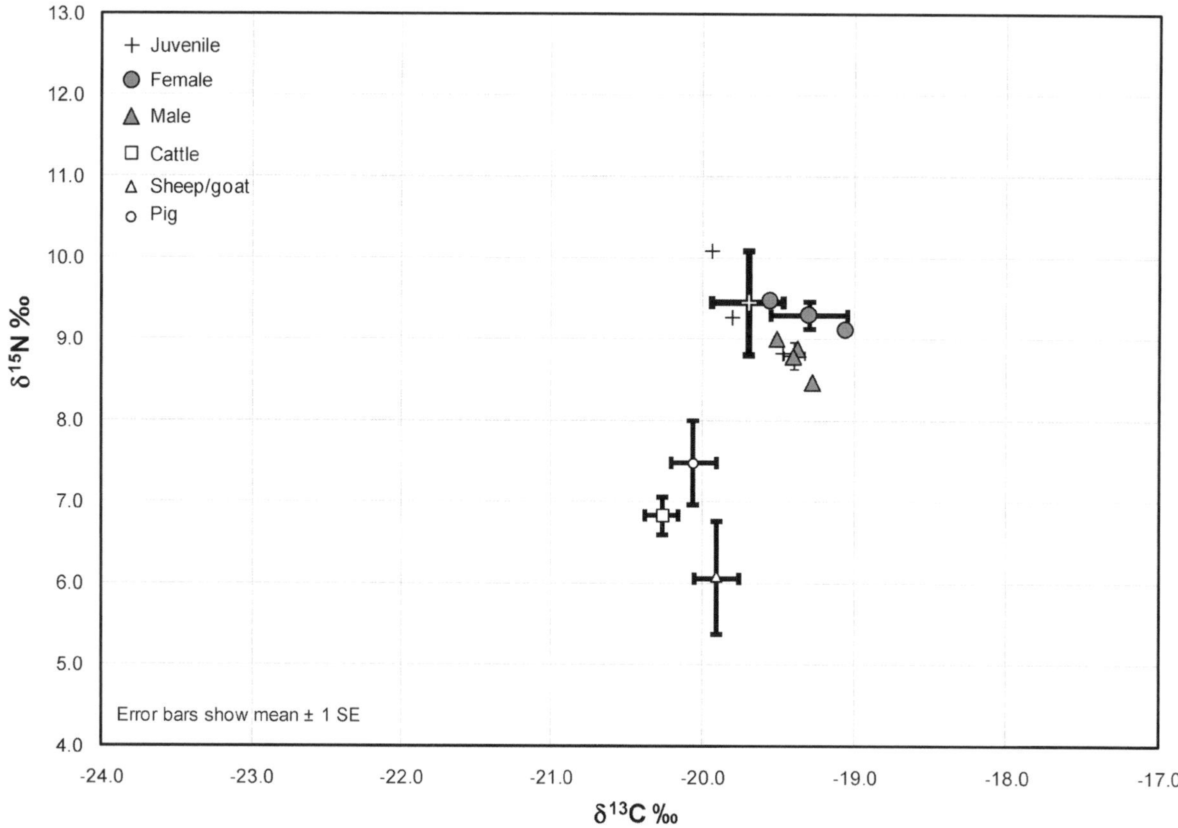

Fig. 4.12. Těšetice-Kyjovice: carbon and nitrogen isotope ratios (‰) of humans.

Table 4.10. Těšetice-Kyjovice: carbon and nitrogen isotope ratios (‰) of humans and animals, with means and standard deviations.

Species	Age/sex	Mean $\delta^{13}C$	SD $\delta^{13}C$	Mean $\delta^{15}N$	SD $\delta^{15}N$	n
Human	Juvenile	−19.7	0.33	9.4	0.91	2
Human	Male	−19.4	0.12	8.8	0.28	3
Human	Female	−19.3	0.36	9.3	0.23	2
Human	All adult	−19.4	0.20	9.0	0.36	5
Cattle		−20.3	0.30	6.8	0.65	8
Sheep/goat		−19.9	0.29	6.1	1.38	4
Pig		−20.1	0.31	7.5	1.05	4

such as skiers and long distance runners, though it may also be associated with agricultural activities. The skull of this individual had been covered in ochre.

The young male in burial 19 presented with bowing deformities of the long bones, possibly the result of rickets (Dočkalová and Čižmář 2008a, 63). These deformities are non-reversible, and depending on the degree of bowing may lead to early onset joint degeneration, but this individual was a young adult at death so may not have suffered significantly from such joint problems. If the bowing deformities are in the leg, it indicates that onset of the disease (rickets) was at a time when the individual was already walking and putting weight on these bones. This individual was the only one to be buried in a right-crouched position.

4.8.3 Carbon and nitrogen analysis

Seven burials were available for sampling and all seven produced values for carbon and nitrogen. The animal bone samples come from the LBK settlement and an archaeozoological analysis of the site was carried out by Gabriela Dreslerová (2006). The results are summarised in Figs 4.12–13 and Table 4.10. The average values for all adults at the site were −19.4‰ for $\delta^{13}C$ and 9.0‰ for $\delta^{15}N$. One of the juveniles (7–12 years old at death) has a $\delta^{15}N$ value 1.1‰ above the adult mean, but a $\delta^{13}C$ value about 0.5‰ below. The results were included even though collagen yield was only 0.9%, because all the other quality indicators and agreement between duplicate runs were good. However, poor-quality collagen tends to give $\delta^{13}C$ values that are too low, and that could be the case here.

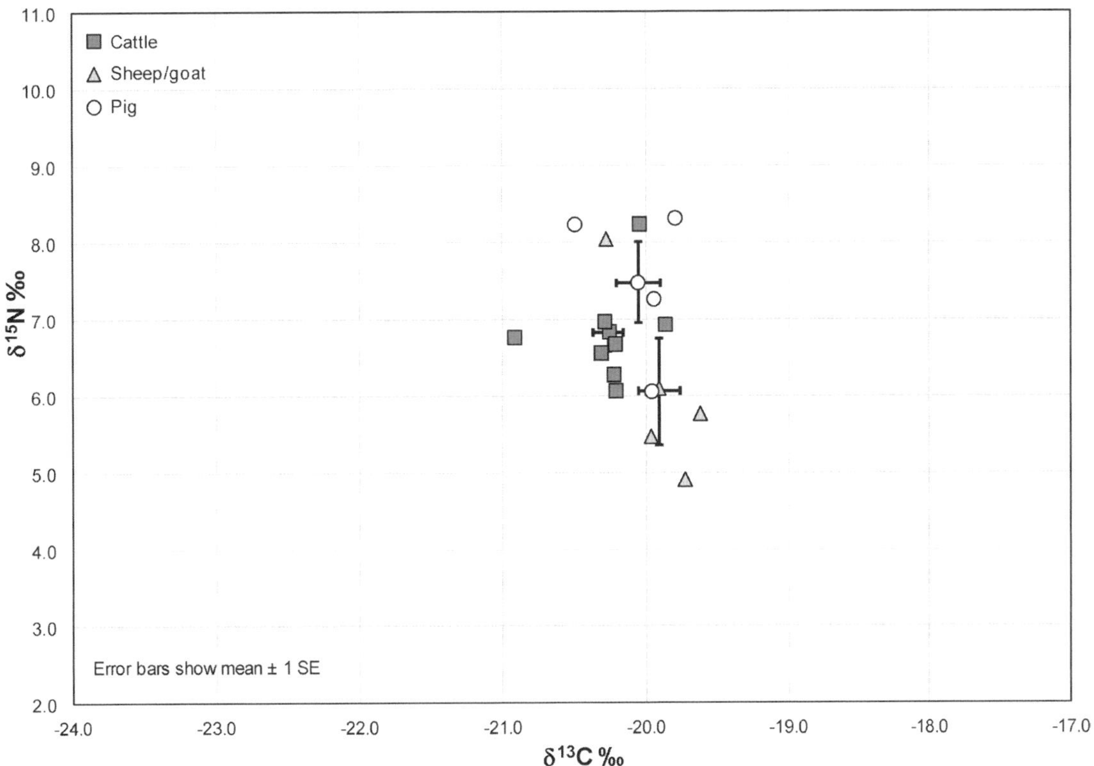

Fig. 4.13. Těšetice-Kyjovice: carbon and nitrogen isotope ratios (‰) of animals.

Table 4.11. Těšetice-Kyjovice: strontium isotope ratios and concentrations.

Age/sex	Mean $^{87}Sr/^{86}Sr$	SD $^{87}Sr/^{86}Sr$	Mean Sr conc.	SD Sr conc.	n
Juvenile	0.71140	0.00001	135	16	2
Male	0.71158	0.00014	162	85	3
Female	0.71101	0.00117	128	41	2
Těšetice all	0.71137	0.00055	145	55	7

If the measurement is accurate, the high $\delta^{15}N$ value is unlikely to reflect a suckling signal at this age, and could reflect dietary variation or a period of malnutrition or illness before death.

Numbers of humans are too low for statistical analysis by gender to be meaningful.

The difference between human and cattle mean $\delta^{13}C$ value is 0.9‰±0.4 (SD), and between human and cattle mean $\delta^{15}N$ value 2.2‰±0.7. In spite of the rather small numbers of humans, the close local and temporal association of the human and animal remains makes this a useful addition to the faunal dataset. The faunal isotopes follow a pattern like that seen at other LBK sites, with similar $\delta^{13}C$ values, and pigs having somewhat higher $\delta^{15}N$ values than the ruminants, suggesting a more omnivorous diet but not a strong concentration on woodland resources.

4.8.4 Strontium analysis

We sampled the tooth enamel from seven individuals, three males, two females and two children (Fig. 4.14; Table 4.11). The average strontium ratio for the site was 0.71137±0.00055. Most of the results cluster around this value, but there is one outlier with a much lower strontium ratio of 0.71018, which is the female in grave 11. When this individual is omitted, the average for the six tightly clustered individuals is 0.71157±0.00019 (Fig. 4.14). A similar pattern can be identified in the strontium concentration values. The cluster of results has an average Sr concentration of 152±56 ppm, while the female outlier in grave 11 has a Sr concentration of 98 ppm. The strontium data from this site follow the pattern we saw at Mezőkövesd (Chapter 3.7.3), of a tightly clustered group with one outlier.

The higher strontium ratio mean is likely to derive from the geographical situation of the site, which lies on the border between the Carpathian basin and Bohemian Massif (Mateiciucová 2008a, 238), consequently resulting in the more radiogenic ratios, and the 'local' range is likely to be similar to that of Vedrovice. Interestingly, the average at this site is closer to that for the settlement at Vedrovice than the cemetery.

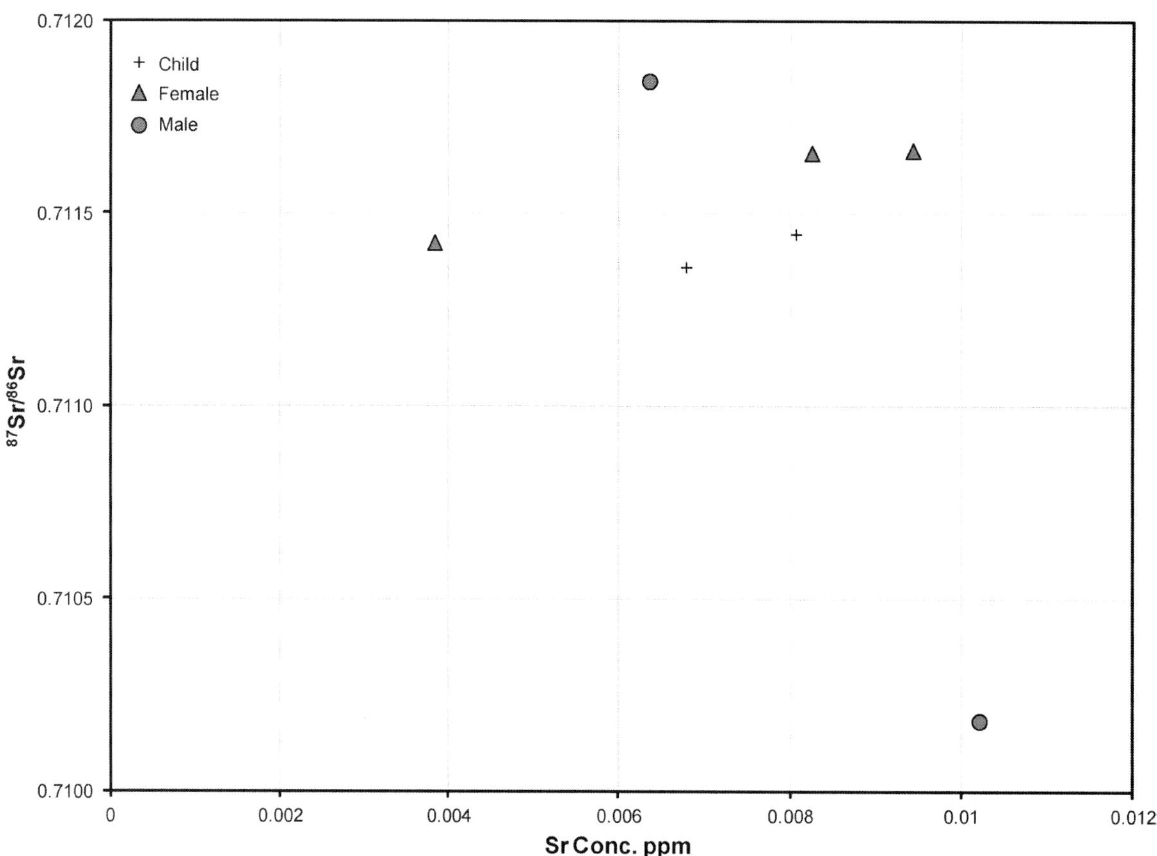

Fig. 4.14. Těšetice-Kyjovice: strontium concentration (ppm) versus ratio ($^{87}Sr/^{86}Sr$).

4.8.5 Site summary and discussion

Unsurprisingly, given the low numbers at the site, there are no statistically significant correlations between the different isotopes and the funerary rites. It may be interesting to note, however, that the female Sr outlier also had the highest $\delta^{15}N$ value of all the adults, as well as being buried in the opposite direction to the rest of the burials (grave 11). As this burial is set in another part of the site, away from the cluster from which the rest of the burials came, we cannot exclude a chronological reason for the differences, though all the evidence suggests that this individual was born away from the Těšetice area.

However, both females at this site had higher $\delta^{15}N$ values than all three of the males (though low numbers again mean that this contrast must be treated with caution). The graves had far fewer grave goods than those in the cemeteries of the region, but the clustering of the burials towards the edge of the settlement is not entirely typical of settlement burials either. The choice of location for the graves may also reflect a certain conservatism, maintaining the practices of the earlier LBK and echoed perhaps in the animal bone assemblage and pottery. The six individuals buried together, with such close strontium ratios, are likely to have spent their lives at Těšetice. However, the lithic evidence demonstrates that the settlement was connected to the broader networks of the region.

4.9 Brno-Starý Lískovec/Nový Lískovec

4.9.1 Introduction

This site is situated on the Bohunice plateau, on the southern outskirts of Brno (Fig. 4.1), and was uncovered in the course of a motorway development (Berkovec 2004, 138; Mateiciucová 2008a, 212). The site itself sits on the cadastral dividing line between the villages of Starý Lískovec and Nový Lískovec and, while both names have been attached to the site, Nový Lískovec has been the more recently favoured of the two (Berkovec 2004, 138; cf. Dočkalová and Čižmář 2007, 33–4). The change in name is partly due to the extent of the excavations which spread out over 20 ha, uncovering a large multi-phase site (Berkovec 2004, 138). Led initially by R. Tichý, campaigns took place intermittently in 1971, 1978 and 1989, and are still ongoing. A 90 m-long ditch with LBK pottery was discovered surrounding evidence for settlement occupation, with potentially up to five houses (Fig. 4.15), though the postholes are not well preserved, as well as ten inhumations (Berkovec 2004, 139; Dočkalová and Čižmář 2008a, 43).

In 2006, the grave of a neonate was discovered in a circular feature carved out of a loam pit; it was accompanied by two standing quernstones and had been laid over fragments of pottery (Dočkalová and Čižmář 2007, 34). During the same year, what was initially thought to be a

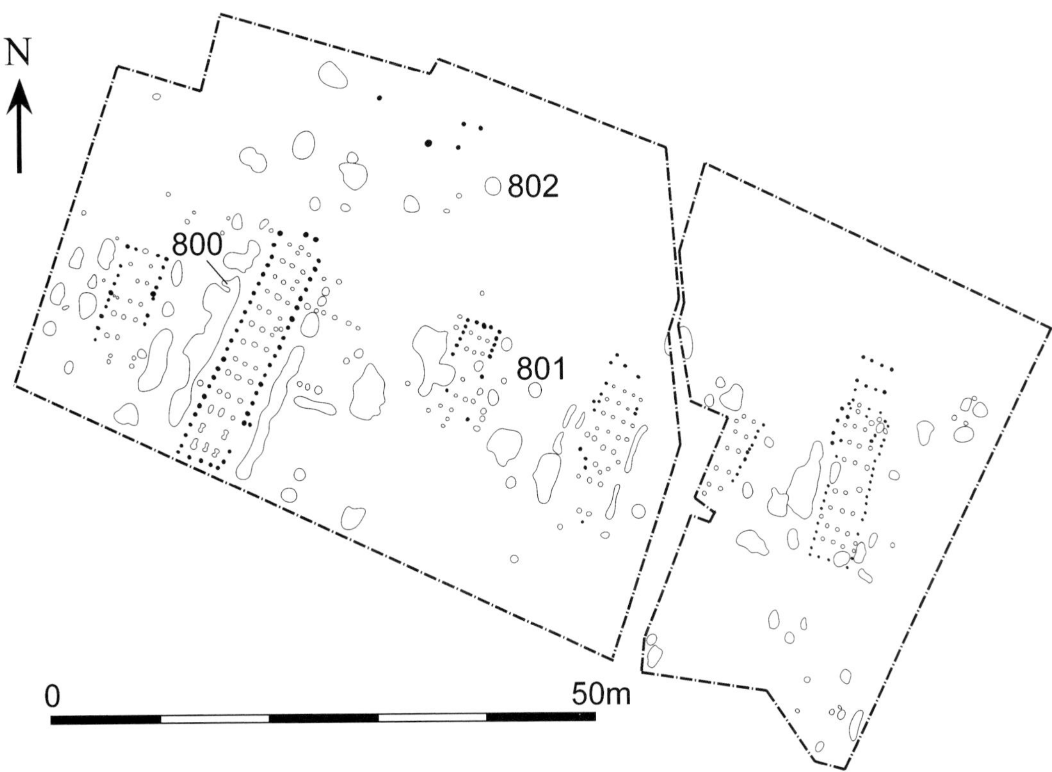

Fig. 4.15. Brno-Starý Lískovec: plan depicting the location of burials 800–802. After Čižmář and Přichystal (2004, fig. 2).

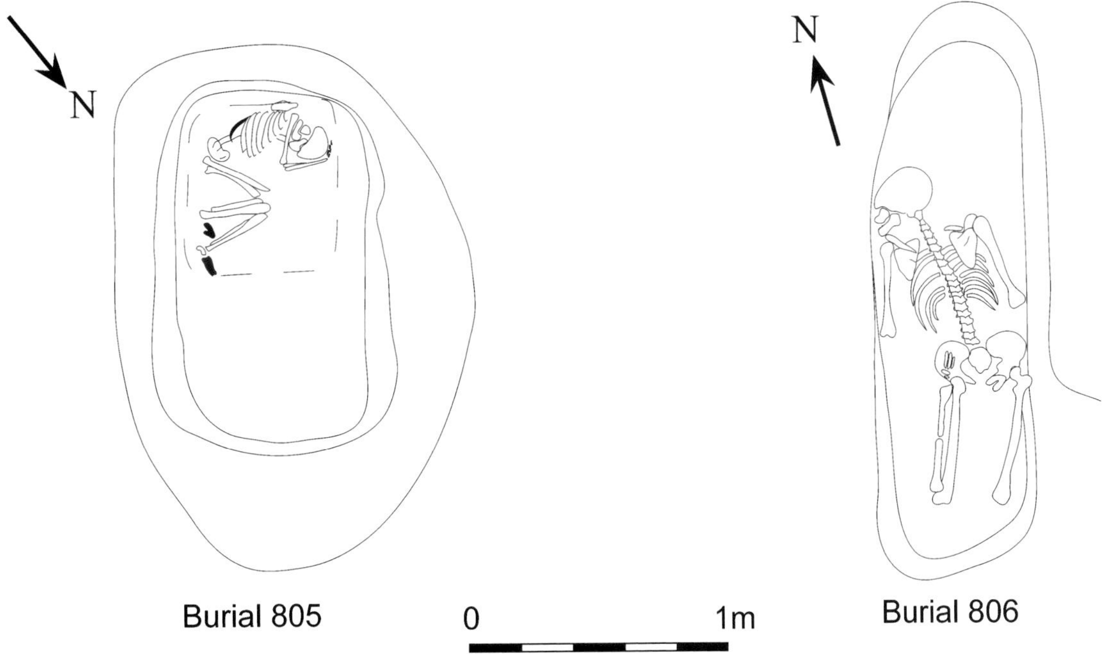

Fig. 4.16. Brno-Starý Lískovec: burials 805 and 806. After Dočkalová and Čižmář (2008a, 45).

cremation was discovered, scattered across the base of a pit, while fragments of daub, pottery and animal bones were around the edge (Dočkalová and Čižmář 2007, 34). However, on closer examination this proved to consist of fragments of an adult inhumation that had received some secondary scorching (Dočkalová and Čižmář 2008a, 52). Excavations in 2007 and 2008 brought more human remains to light, bringing the total number of individuals interred at the site to ten (Dočkalová and Čižmář 2008a, 43). Unusually, all five individuals identified as adults were sexed as male (Dočkalová and Čižmář 2008a, 43). Some of the body positions of the deceased were also unusual (Fig. 4.16; Table 4.12).

Inhabitation of the site is likely to have begun early in phase Ib, when the site was at its largest, and continued through to the end of phase II or the beginning of phase III

Table 4.12. Brno-Starý Lískovec: the isotope, osteological and archaeological data. Age, sex and pathology information from Dočkalová and Čižmář (2007; 2008a). See Chapter 2 for further definition of ages.
Key for body position: LC – Left-crouched; RC – Right-crouched; C – Crouched, direction unknown; CB – Crouched on back; CF – Crouched on front; S – Supine; P – Prone; I – Irregular.
Key for grave goods (number of items in brackets): U. – Unfurnished; F. – Fill only (all items listed after an F. were in the fill of the grave rather than at the level of the skeleton); Pol. – Polished stone; Cer. – Ceramics; Shd. – Sherds; Spon. – Spondylus; She. – Other Shell; Och. – Ochre; Lit. – Chipped stone; Bon – Worked bone; Grd. – Grinding stone.

Burial	Tooth	Sex	Age (yrs)	$^{87}Sr/^{86}Sr$	Sr ppm	$\delta^{13}C$ ‰	$\delta^{15}N$ ‰	Orienation	Body position	Grave goods	Pathology
2601/801	M2	M?	44–45	0.71043	188	-	-	NE–SW	LC	*n.d.*	-
2565/802	M1	M?	40–65	0.71071	72	−19.6	9.9	-	-	*n.d.*	-
5817/803	M3	M	20–21	0.71075	132	−19.7	10.3	-	RC	*n.d.*	*Cribra orbitalia*
7714/805	M2	M	14–19	0.70970	164	−19.9	9.8	E–W	LC	F.Cer.(1)	-
7727/806	M1	M	50–60	0.70987	150	−19.5	10.4	N–S	P	*n.d.*	*Cribra orbitalia*, fusions of cervical vertebrae, healed fracture (clavicle)
5575/534/800	-	-	6 mon.	-	-	−18.3	13.1	SE–NW	LC	Shd.,Grd.(2)	-
658/410/800	-	-	4–5 mon.	-	-	−18.0	12.9	-	-	-	-

(one feature contains Želiezovce ware), but the chronology of the site is hindered by a lack of radiocarbon dates (Berkovec 2004, 152–6; Mateiciucová 2008a, 213). We cannot yet comment on the phase, or indeed phases, to which the burials belong. Despite this, Berkovec (2004, 147) strongly suggests that the enclosure began in phase Ib, contemporary with the earliest LBK features within the settlement area. LBK finds dating to phase Ib were also found outside the enclosure area, though their character, including a far richer assemblage of stone tools, leads Berkovec (2004, 155) to suggest that this area of the site was only used for economic activities, separating them from the house structures identified within the enclosure. That would be unusual but not unprecedented in LBK contexts. The raw material used for the chipped stone industry also differed from other settlements in the Moravian region, as the assemblage was dominated by local and poor-quality raw materials, though one chert sickle blade had similarities to those produced in nearby settlements with identified specialist workshops (Mateiciucová 2008a, 216). Brno-Starý Lískovec, therefore, gives the impression of a settlement that was tied into the local settlement network, but not beyond.

4.9.2 Osteology

The osteological remains from Brno-Starý Lískovec are held at the Moravian Museum, Brno, and were analysed by Marta Dočkalová (Dočkalová and Čižmář 2008a). The ten individuals interred at the site consisted of five adult males and five juveniles/children. *Cribra orbitalia* was present on the right orbit of the well preserved skeleton of a young male (20–21 years; grave H803). This individual also had reduced height of the lumbar vertebrae, which is rare in an individual of this age (Dočkalová and Čižmář 2008a, 52). An elderly male (50–59 years, grave H806) also displayed evidence of *cribra orbitalia* (in both orbits), appeared to suffer from degenerative joint disease of the upper spine and had at some stage in his life broken his collarbone/clavicle (Dočkalová and Čižmář 2008a, 52).

4.9.3 Carbon and nitrogen analysis

Six samples were taken from the Brno graves, from two children and four adults (Fig. 4.17; Table 4.13). The infants show a trophic level effect in both $\delta^{13}C$ and $\delta^{15}N$ values, with means higher than the mean adult values by 1.6‰ and 2.9‰ respectively (both significant, t test, $p<0.001$); most likely they were exclusively or mainly breast-fed up to the time of death (4–6 months). It was possible to sample seven cattle bones, six sheep/goats and three pigs (adults, where possible; the animal bone report is not yet fully published).

The difference between human and cattle mean $\delta^{13}C$ value is 0.6‰±0.2 (SD), and between human and cattle mean $\delta^{15}N$ value 2.8‰±1.3. Cattle and sheep have similar $\delta^{13}C$ and $\delta^{15}N$ values, with considerable variation in the $\delta^{15}N$ values (Fig. 4.18; Table 4.13). Pigs have similar

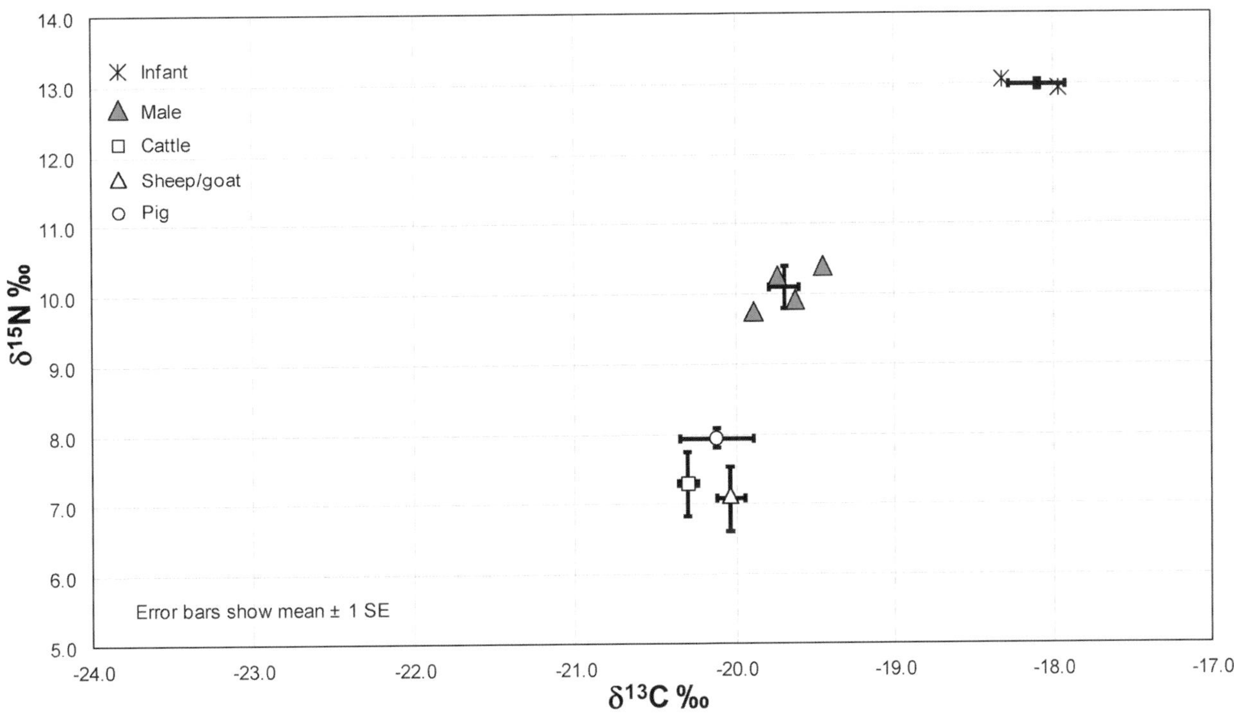

Fig. 4.17. Brno-Starý Lískovec: carbon and nitrogen isotope ratios (‰) of humans.

Table 4.13. Brno-Starý Lískovec: carbon and nitrogen isotope ratios (‰) of humans and animals, with means and standard deviations.

Species	Age/sex	Mean δ^{13}C	SD δ^{13}C	Mean δ^{15}N	SD δ^{15}N	n
Human	Infant	−18.1	0.25	13	0.09	2
Human	Male (all Adults)	−19.7	0.19	10.1	0.3	4
Cattle		−20.3	0.15	7.3	1.22	7
Sheep/goat		−20.0	0.20	7.1	1.03	5
Pig		−20.1	0.32	8.0	0.19	2

δ^{13}C values but distinctly higher δ^{15}N (though there are only two individuals and the difference is not statistically significant). This pattern is similar to that at most of the sites investigated in this project, and is consistent with the grazing of sheep and cattle on both manured and unmanured areas, with pigs obtaining a somewhat more omnivorous diet that may have included settlement waste, but there is no evidence that they made particular use of forest habitats.

4.9.4 Strontium analysis

The five males from Brno show an average that is only just within the range among males tested as part of the Lifeways project (0.7085–0.7105) and the quoted ranges for loess soils, but not as high as the mean values for Vedrovice and Těšetice (Fig. 4.19; Table 4.14). Brno-Starý Lískovec is situated like Vedrovice and Těšetice on loess soil covered by chernozem, with a complex and varied underlying geology, with a wide range of granitoids (Mateiciucová 2008a, 212). The loess in these regions derives from the late Weichselian interpleniglacial soil complex (Starkel 1977), which would have resulted in a more radiogenic local strontium ratio than that for the loess elsewhere in Europe. The strontium ratios at Brno have twice the range of those from Těšetice (Brno has a range of 0.001 in ^{87}Sr/^{86}Sr ratios, while Těšetice has a range of 0.0005), but it is likely that the individuals interred at the settlement were all from the local area. However, the two burials with the lowest and very similar ^{87}Sr/^{86}Sr ratios (805 and 806) were placed in unusual positions in their graves (Fig. 4.19).

Burial 805 was tightly crouched, the body curved to fit in a stepped section within a much larger pit and rather than the arms being placed in front of the face (as is usual in crouched LBK burials), they were bent over the skull, which in turn was drawn into the chest – as if this individual was cowering (Fig. 4.16; Table 4.12). Burial 806 was placed prone, with the head twisted to the side, facing west, the left arm extended down the side of the body and the right arm folded at the elbow. The left leg was bent at the knee, the foot resting above the pelvis, and the lower part of the right leg (below the knee) was missing, though there would

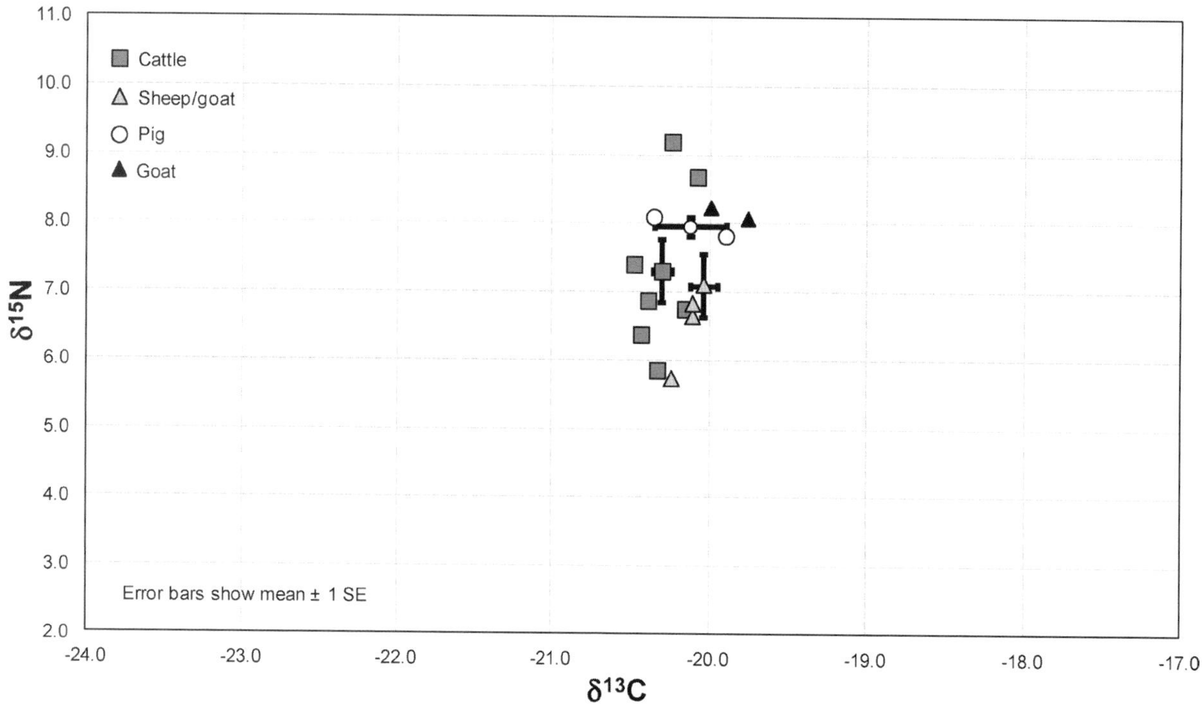

Fig. 4.18. Brno-Starý Lískovec: carbon and nitrogen isotope ratios (‰) of animals.

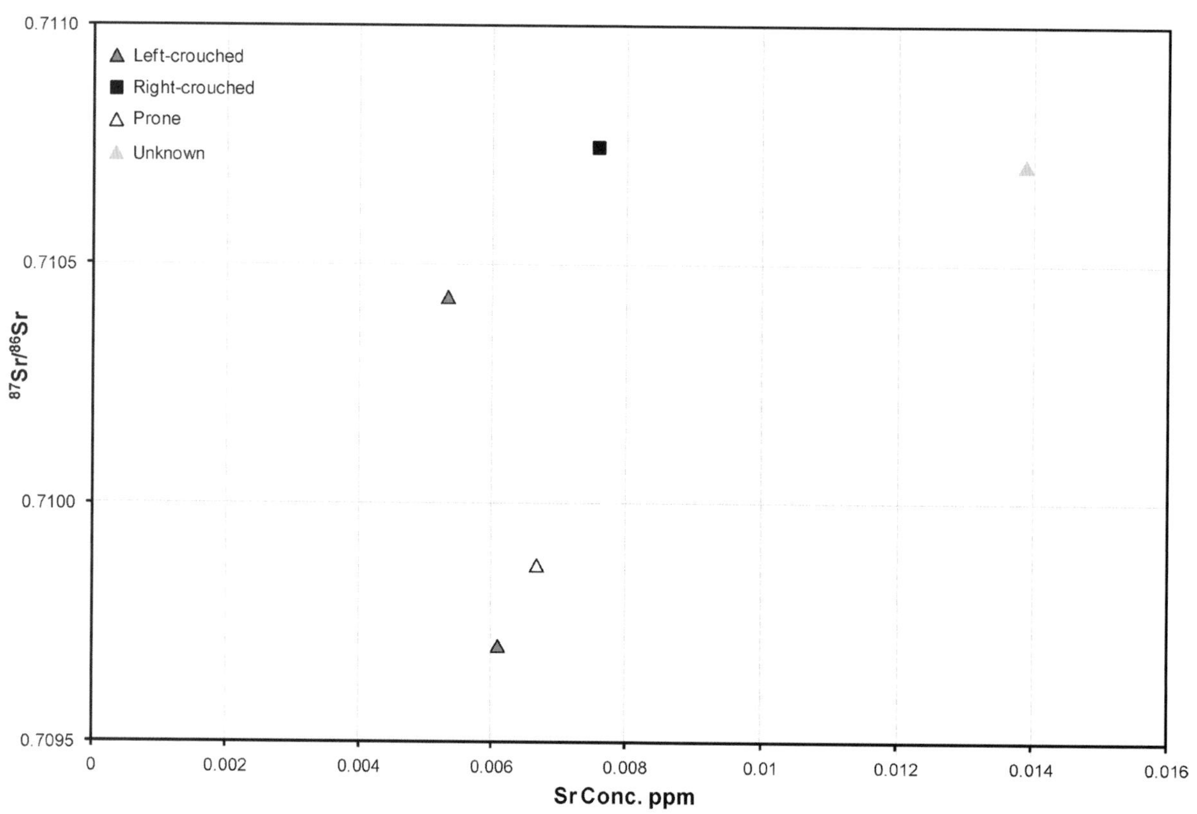

Fig. 4.19. Brno-Starý Lískovec: strontium concentration (ppm) versus ratio ($^{87}Sr/^{86}Sr$). All points are males.

Table 4.14. Brno-Starý Lískovec: strontium isotope ratios and concentrations.

Age/sex	Mean $^{87}Sr/^{86}Sr$	SD $^{87}Sr/^{86}Sr$	Mean Sr conc.	SD Sr conc.	n
Males (all Adults)	0.71029	0.00048	141	44	5

not have been space in the pit for the leg to have been lain in an extended position; it seems as if this individual was 'pushed' into the pit (Fig. 4.16). This individual (806) is also the only north–south oriented burial at this site (indeed of all our sampled sites in Moravia and Slovakia), suggesting that it may not be LBK. However, we must wait for the full publication of the site to confirm this. The positions of these two individuals in the grave could also be part of the greater variation in burial position found amongst settlement burials across the LBK.

4.9.5 Site summary and discussion

With only a few of the grave goods published and only a small number of burials, conclusions for Brno-Starý Lískovec are limited and preliminary. Overall, however, given that the strontium values are likely to be local, results appear to confirm the suggestion from the lithic analysis that the occupants at the site were focused on local rather than external contacts. The lack of females interred at the site is also worthy of comment as this is highly unusual at settlements, and this lack of female values may go some way to account for the higher than average nitrogen values.

4.10 Nitra

4.10.1 Introduction

The site of Nitra[7] dates to phase II of the LBK in western Slovakia (see below and Appendix B1). It is situated above the floodplain of the Nitra river (Fig. 4.1), on loess soils which are found intermittently along the edge of the Carpathian Mountains (Pavúk 1972a, 5). The city of Nitra sits on the border between two major geologies, with the crystalline Tribeč Mountains stretching northwards from the city and the Danubian plain to the south, east and west. However, unlike the other sites in this chapter, we would expect the local strontium ratio range for Nitra to fall within that expected for loess soils.

The 76 graves were found in two long, parallel cuttings over an area up to 50 m long by *c.* 15 m wide, with the majority of the burials concentrated at the northern end in an area some 20 m by 15 m (Fig. 4.20; Table 4.15; Pavúk 1972a, Plan 1). Further cuttings a little distance to both north-east and south-west found no further graves. A couple of the graves were empty, and the initial disturbance by building works in 1964 probably destroyed a few graves. At least eight groups of cremated human bone were also found by machine, below the surface and mostly in the area of the main concentration of graves, and these appear to be associated with the same styles of pottery as in the graves (Pavúk 1972a, 39). Although hoped for, further excavation in the vicinity proved not to be possible, so unlike at Vedrovice in this case we only have the burial ground, and no accompanying settlement.

In the main concentration, the graves were much closer to each other than at Vedrovice Široká u lesa. They are largely oriented north-west to south-east, and do not, at first sight, appear to form obvious separate clusters, but perhaps rather possible lines, as mooted above for Vedrovice; beyond the main concentration, the graves are more dispersed. The excavator, however, did suggest several possible groupings or clusters on the basis of shared orientations, depth and grave goods (Pavúk 1972a, 88): in the southern portion graves 47–52, 58, 65 and 68, perhaps also with 72, 19, 20, 27, 67, 69 and 56; on the northern edge the very similar graves 38, 40, 45, 62–3 and 76, with perhaps the child grave 42; in the same area perhaps grave 43 with 39, 42, 44 and 59; and to the east graves 2, 3 and 8, with possibly also 7 and 9, and 1, 4, 6, 10 and perhaps 74 (these two mooted clusters actually occupying the same space, but with different accompanying pottery: Pavúk 1972a, 89). In the more densely packed central concentration it is harder to pick out clusters, but the excavator suggested (Pavúk 1972a, 88) possible successions between 59 and 74 on the one hand and between 44 and 32, and other neighbouring graves, on the other; a central cluster formed by 21–5 and 34, with also perhaps 35–6, 60, 66, 41 and 53–5; and a western cluster formed by graves 37, 41, 46, 55 and 75, with the intersections, among other examples, of grave 41 over 53 and 37 over 54 indicating time-depth in this part of the cemetery. In this analysis, the detailed history of the cemetery unfolds through time by the formation of much smaller groupings of graves. The duration of this process is not known, since among other things the pottery only suggests broadly two successive or overlapping phases, with a possible correlation with the later part of the middle stage in Bohemia; a possible overall span of 200–300 years was mooted (Pavúk 1972a, 84), though that may now be rather too long. Chronological modelling of radiocarbon results obtained in the course of the Lifeways project is set out in Appendix B1.

Twenty-two graves intersect, with demonstrable superimpositions (Table 4.16); all but one of these cases lie in the main concentration.[8] In at least a further six cases neighbouring graves touch each other.[9] The superimposed graves are mainly of adults, and in only two cases are the successions between the same sex: one of men, and one of women (26/27; 41/53). The sample is small, but women follow men in four cases, while a man follows a woman in only one definite case. The intersection of graves is generally a rare occurrence in the LBK, though van de Velde (1979a) did note the 'pairing' of graves at Elsloo.

Overall, graves were found at varying depths, from 0.7–1.7 m, with the majority at a depth of 1–1.2 m (Pavúk 1972a, 26). The relative depths of the male and female graves were not noted, but almost all of the deepest graves were those of men, predominantly older individuals (2, 8, 25, 59, a young man, and 76), with only two women laid to rest at comparable depths (44, and 66, an older individual). The graves were largely sub-rectangular to oval in plan, with some small ones of less regular form; adult graves were correspondingly larger than children's, but no difference between adult male graves and adult female graves was noted. It appears that whole bodies were normally deposited, and the overwhelmingly dominant rite

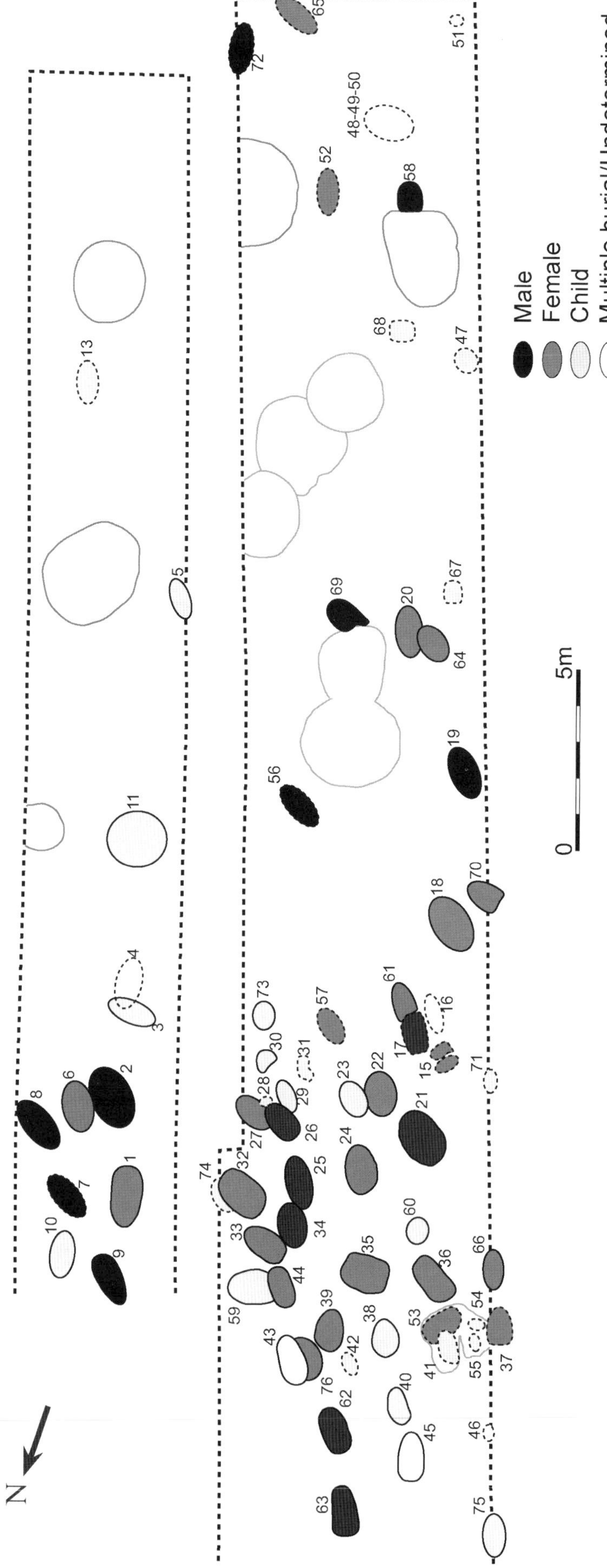

Fig. 4.20. Nitra: plan. After Pavúk (1972a).

Table 4.15. Nitra: the isotope, osteological and archaeological data. Age, sex and pathology information from Linda Fibiger (this volume). See Chapter 2 for further definition of ages. n.d. = no data.
Key for body position: LC – Left-crouched; RC – Right-crouched; C – Crouched, direction unknown; CB – Crouched on back; CF – Crouched on front; S – Supine; P – Prone; I – Irregular.
Key for grave goods (number of items in brackets): U. – Unfurnished; F. – Fill only (all items listed after an F. were in the fill of the grave rather than at the level of the skeleton); Pol. – Polished stone; Cer. – Ceramics; Shd. – Sherds; Spon. – Spondylus*; She. – Other Shell; Och. – Ochre; Lit. – Chipped stone; Bon – Worked bone; Grd. – Grinding stone; Tee. – Teeth.*

Burial	T	S	Age (yrs)	$^{87}Sr/^{86}Sr$	1/Sr ppm	$\delta^{13}C$ ‰	$\delta^{15}N$ ‰	Orientation	Body position	Grave goods	Pathology
1/64	M1	F	YA>20	0.70943	60	−20.2	9.7	S–N	LC	Cer.(1)	Caries (2), trauma (hairline fracture)
2/64	M1	M	OMA	0.70946	20	-	-	SE–NW	CF	Pol.(1), Cer.(1), Spon.(1 bead, V buckle)	-
3/64	M2	-	Adol.	*n.d.*	*n.d.*	−20.0	9.3	E–W	LC	Cer.(1)	Enamel hypoplasia
4/64	-	-	Adol.	-	-	−19.8	10.4	-	-	Cer.(2), Lit.(4), Bon.(1)	-
4/64	M3	F	YMA	0.70944	52	−19.9	10.3	-	-	*n.d*	Caries (5)
4/64	M2	M	Mid-Ad.	0.70953	115	−20.0	9.5	-	-	*n.d.*	Possible cyst on sacrum
5/64	M2	-	Adol.	0.70940	87	−20.0	9.9	SE–NW	LC	Och., Graphite pieces	*Cribra orbitalia*, possible infection
6/64	M3?	F	Mature Ad.	0.70933	109	−20.1	10.5	SE–NW	LC	Cer.(1), Spon.(6 beads)	Caries (3)
7/64	M3	M?	Adult	0.70968	109	-	-	-	-	Cer.(1), Och.	-
8/64	M1	M	Mature Ad.	0.70934	106	−19.9	11	E–W	LC	Pol.(1), Cer.(1), Spon.(1 bead)	Caries (1) and possible related infection
9/64	-	M?	Mid-Ad.	0.70945	78	−20.4	9.7	SE–NW	LC?	F.Cer.(1)	-
14/64	M1	F	Adult	0.70937	7	−20.4	9.8	SE–NW	LC	Lit.(3), Bon.(2)	-
15/65	-	F?	Adult<20	-		−21.0	10.2	SE–NW	-	F.Shd.(?)	-
15/65	M2 dec.	-	1–1.5	0.70961	39	−19.7	13	-	-	*As above*	-
16/65	-	-	Adult	-		−20.7	9.6	-	-	U.	-
17/65	M2	M	Mature Ad.	0.70949		−19.9	10.3	SE–NW	LC	Cer.(2)	Caries (2)
18/65	M2	F	Mid-Ad.	0.70931	149	−20.4	10.4	SE–NW	LC	U.	*Cribra orbitalia*, enamel hypoplasia
19/65	M2	M	OMA	0.70940	75	−19.9	10.7	SE–NW	LC	Tee.(7, human and animal)	Caries (1), enamel hypoplasia
20/65	M1	F	YMA/<30	0.70988	35	−19.9	9.9	S–N	LC	U.	*Cribra orbitalia*
21/65	PM	M	Older Ad.	0.70931	169	-	-	SE–NW	LC	Pol.(1), Cer.(1), Spon.(1 bead)	Caries (1), possible infection
22/65	M2	F	Mature Ad.	0.7086	266	−20.4	10	S–N	LC	F.Shd.(?)	Caries (1), possible infection
23/65	M1	-	11–12	0.70960	62	−20.3	9.6	SE–NW	LC	F.Shd.(?)	Enamel hypoplasia, possible infection
24/65	M2	F	YMA	0.70945	94	−20.3	10.5	S–N	LC	Cer.(1)	Caries (1)
25/65	-	M	Mature Ad.	-	-	−20.2	10.5	SE–NW	LC	Pol.(1), Cer.(1), Spon. (1 bead)	Caries (1)
26/65	M2	M	Mid-Ad.>30	0.70962	75	−20.1	10.5	SE–NW	LC	Pol.(1), Shd.(?)	Caries (4), *spondylolysis*
27/65	M3	F	Older/Mature Ad.	0.70967	85	−20.4	10	E–W	LC	Pol.(1), Cer.(1)	Caries (4), possible infection

28/65	-	-	≤6 mon.	-	-	−19.2	12.7	-	-	Cer.(1)	-
29/65	M2	-	10–12	0.70949	35	−20.5	9.6	SE–NW	LC	U.	*Cribra orbitalia*
30/65	M1	-	6–7	0.70937	55	−19.9	10.1	S–N	-	Cer.(1)	Porotic hyperostosis
31/65	M1	-	1.5–2	0.70951	47	−19.8	12.8	SE–NW	LC	Grd.(1)	*Cribra orbitalia*, infection
32/65	M1	F	YA	0.70929	58	−20.5	10.3	E–W	LC	Cer.(1)	-
33/65	M2	F?	YMA	0.70954	54	−20.3	9.8	E–W	LC	U.	*Cribra orbitalia*
34/65	M1 M3	M	Mid-Ad.	0.70950 0.70925	63	−19.8	10.5	S–N	LC	Pol.(1), Cer.(1), Spon. (frags., unworked)	Possible TB
35/65	M2	F?	Older Ad.	0.70941	67	−19.9	10.1	E–W	LC	Cer.(1), Spon.(1 bead)	Caries (1)
36/65	M2	F	Mature Ad.	0.70949	102	−20.2	10.5	SE–NW	CF	Cer.(1), Och.	Caries (3)
37/56	M2	F	YMA	0.70942	101	−20.3	9.8	SE–NW	CB	U.	Caries (4)
38/65	M1	-	6–7	0.70934	73	−20.6	10.1	S–N	LC	U.	Possible infection
39/65	M2	F?	OMA	0.71016	41	−19.8	10	S–N	LC	Shd.(?), Spon.(1 bead)	Caries (1)
40/65	M1	-	*c.* 3	0.70952	42	-	-	SE–NW	LC	Pol.(1), Cer.(1)	-
41/65	M2	-	Early Adol.	0.70940	42	−20.1	10.2	S–N	CB	Pol.(flake), Cer.(1), Lit.(1)	-
42/65	M1	-	5–7	0.70932	72	-	-	SE–NW	LC	Cer.(1)	-
43/65	-	-	Adult	-	-	-	-	SE–NW	RC	Shd.(?)	-
44/65	M2	F	Mid-Ad.	0.70979	38	−20.4	10.6	SE–NW	LC	Cer.(1)	Caries (4), trauma, (healed fracture, radius and ulna)
45/65	M1	-	Mid-Ad.	0.70952	49	-	-	S–N	LC	U.	Caries (5)
46/65	-	-	Adult or Adol.	-	-	-	-	-	C	U.	-
47/65	M1	-	1–1.5	0.70968	141	−19.4	12	SE–NW	LC	Cer.(1)	-
48/65	M1	F	YA	0.70983	43	−20.3	9.6	E–W	LC	U.	-
49/65	M1	-	5–6	0.70956	42	−20.3 −20.3	11 9.5	E–W	LC	U.	Trauma (skull, peri-mortem)
50/65	M1	-	4–5	0.70959	44	−20.2	10.6	E–W	LC	U.	Trauma (skull, peri-mortem)
52/65	-	F?	Mid-Ad.	-	-	−20.2	9.8	S–N	LC	F.Cer.(1)	Caries (2), osteomyelitis
53/65	-	F	YA	-	-	−20.1	10.6	SW–NE	LC	Cer.(1)	-
54/65	M1	-	6–7	0.70946	38	−20.3	10.7	E–W	LC	U.	Possible infection
55/65	-	-	3–6 mon.	-	-	-	-	S–N	LC	U.	Rickets
56/65	M2	M	Mature Ad.	0.70949	62	−19.9	9.7	SE–NW	LC	Cer.(1)	Caries (5), enamel hypoplasia
57/65	M2	F	YA	0.70960	55	−20.1	11.1	SE–NW	LC	Shd.(?)	*Cribra orbitalia*
58/65	M2	M	Mid-Ad.	0.70923	56	−19.8	10.6	S–N	LC?	Pol.(1), Cer.(1), Spon.(2 beads), Lit.(1), Bon.(1)	-

59/65	M2	-	Adol.	0.70946	44	-	-	E–W	LC	Cer.(1)	*Cribra orbitalia*
60/65	M2 dec.	-	*c.* 1	0.70955	45	-	-	-	-	U.	-
61/65	M2	F	Mature Ad.	0.70945	-	−19.9	10.2	SE–NW	LC	Cer.(1)	Caries (1), os acromiale
62/65	M3	M?	YMA	0.70942	54	−20.2	10.2	SE–NW	LC	U.	Caries (2), enamel hypoplasia
63/65	M2	M?	Adult>20	*n.d.*	-	-	-	SE–NW	LC	U.	Caries (2)
64/65	M1	F	OMA	0.71046	24	−20.3	9.8	SE–NW	LC	Cer.(1), Och.	Caries (2), enamel hypoplasia
65/65	M1	F	Older Ad.>40	0.70940	51		10.5	SE–NW	CB	Cer.(1), Och.	-
66/65	-	F	Older Ad.	-	-	−20.1	10	S–N	LC	Cer.(1)	-
67/65	M1	-	1.5	0.70956	79	−19.1	12.4	S–N	LC	U.	-
68/65	M1	-	8–9	0.70946	23	−20.4	9.8	-	-	Cer.(1)	Enamel hypoplasia
69/65	M1 M3	M	YA	0.70949 0.70949	75 36	−20.0	10.5	E–W	CF?	Cer.(1)	-
70/65	M2	F	YMA	0.7099	61	−19.8	10.4	E–W	CF	Cer.(1), Spon.(3 beads)	Caries (4)
71/65	M1	-	5–6	0.70936	-	−20.2	10.6	S–N	RC	Cer.(1)	Healed periostitis
72/65	M2	M	YA	0.70968	-	−20.4	10.7	S–N	CB	U.	Trauma (skull, peri-mortem), enamel hypoplasia
73/65	-	-	6–9 mon.	-	-	-	-	S–N	LC	U.	-
74/65	M2	-	2–3	0.70951	12	−20.3	10.8	S–N	LC	Cer.(1)	Periostitis
75/65	M2	-	Early Adol.	0.70949	43	-	-	S–N	LC	U.	-
76/65	M2	F?	Mid-Ad.	0.70936	40	-	-	SE–NW	LC	Pol.(1), Cer.(1), Lit.(2)	Caries (1), infection
77/65	M2	M?	Mid-Ad.	0.70920	60	−20.5	11	-	-	*n.d.*	-

*Table 4.16. Nitra: graves with direct stratigraphic relationships. Grave numbers marked with * were radiocarbon dated by this project.*

Younger grave	4	6*	17	20	26	28	37	41*	43	44	74
Older grave	3	2*	61	64	27*	26	54	53	76	59	32

Fig. 4.21. Top: Vedrovice; Spondylus *pendant/medallion from grave 78/79 (after Podborský 1998, 77). Bottom: Nitra; V-*Spondylus *buckle from grave 2 (after Pavúk 1972a, 41).*

was once more that of deposition on the left side, with head to the south-east, broadly facing south; that again could be consistent with a perception or memory embedded in mortuary practice of origins to the south; houses at Štúrovo, directly by the Danube, were largely oriented north–south (Pavúk 1994). Three right-side exceptions were found (Pavúk 1972a, 26), including the burial, in grave 43, of a mature woman on her right side, again with head to the south-east but facing broadly north or north-east. The burial position was overwhelmingly crouched, to varying degrees, with a few individuals lying on their fronts or backs, with crouched legs (Pavúk 1972a, Abb. 22).

The graves of men, women and children are distributed more or less evenly across the cemetery as a whole, though three small concentrations of adult female graves (Pavúk 1972a, 65)[10] and two possible groupings of child graves (Pavúk 1972a, 65) were noted.[11] In the original report seven burials could not be certainly aged or sexed. Of the remainder, 22 were identified as those of children or juveniles up to the age of 15, 22 as those of women, and at least 24 as those of men; there were a possible further three men amongst the uncertainly identified remains. According to the original report, children and juveniles had died at different ages, with peaks at 1 and 7–8 years, and more women died than men in the proposed adult age categories, except for 40–50 years, where male deaths predominate, and 50–60, where the two sexes are equally represented; the largest single proportion of adult female deaths fell in the 30–40 years range (Pavúk 1972a, Abb. 44).

A range of grave goods were found, including pots of various forms, shoelast adzes, flat axes, struck lithics, bone tools, bone armrings, *Spondylus* beads, pendants and 'belt buckles' (Fig. 4.21), a necklace of human and animal teeth, and mineral colouring matter and graphite (Pavúk 1972a, Abb. 46). Twenty-one of 74 graves had no goods at all (38%), which is average for LBK cemeteries (Lifeways Database). Pots, normally single vessels, were the most common grave good (found with 12 men, 19 women and eight children: 56% of graves, in line with what we would expect for LBK cemeteries), and regularly with other categories (Pavúk 1972a, 67). Pots were placed around the bodies of men, women and children in broadly similar ways, with a shared emphasis on the head; they were also placed behind both men and women, including at their feet, but only by the hands of men (and only in three cases) (Pavúk 1972a, Abb. 45). Other apparent rules determining deposition included the restriction to adult men of shoelast adzes, especially in the age range of 40–60 years, of bone armrings and the one example of a tooth necklace (grave 19, the teeth including human teeth and those of dog or fox: Pavúk 1972a, 11), and of *Spondylus* artefacts, with two exceptions in the latter category of two women (one aged 30–40, the other 50, according to the estimates of the original report), who had a single and three *Spondylus* beads respectively (Pavúk 1972a, 70).[12] Overall, the most abundantly furnished graves were those of older women and especially those of older men, in the originally estimated age ranges of 40–50 and 50–60 years (Pavúk 1972a, 71). The excavator drew attention especially to that category of older men (Pavúk 1972a, 73), and within that, noted that in the pairs of superimposed graves and others with an identifiable relationship, a polished stone tool only occurs once in the later grave (grave 26: Pavúk 1972a, 72). He interpreted that as showing change through time, rather than an unvarying reflection of relative social position (Pavúk 1972a, 72). Equally, however, this could hint at principles based on seniority, or notions of succession. And if it is legitimate to consider Vedrovice and Nitra together, as guided by a shared cultural order, the differences between them are to be noted, with the apparent shift over time to a more dominant or prominent position or at least a more showy burial rite for older men a rather striking, perhaps regionalised development.

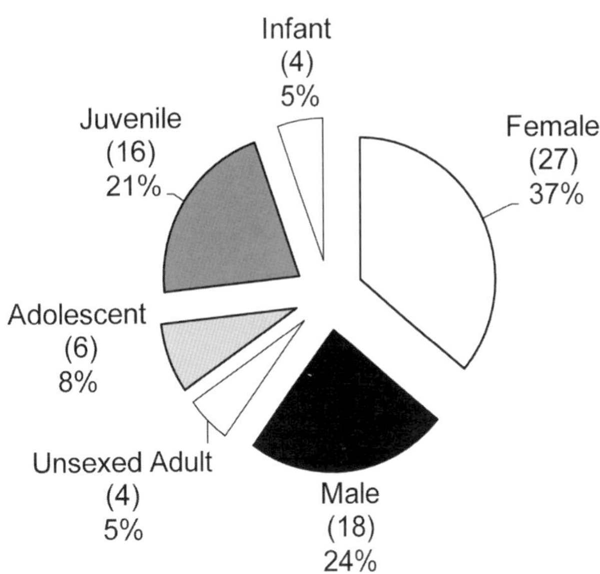

Fig. 4.22. Nitra: age and sex assessment.

4.10.2 The radiocarbon dates

The date of the cemetery has up to this point been determined from the pottery in the graves. Here we present 12 new radiocarbon dates from the cemetery (Appendix B1).

Pavúk (1972a, 76–84) assessed the ornamentation of the pottery in an attempt to produce a chronology for the cemetery, though the chronology of ceramic designs in western Slovakia during the later LBK was uncertain and only *c.* 25 graves contained pots with diagnostic traits. Overall, the cemetery falls from phase II into the early Želiezovce phase, with no interruption between the two phases, and a duration of 200–300 years was proposed (Pavúk 1972a, 84). The graves which produced the earliest pots were in graves 12 and 70, with pots from graves 3, 8, 21, 25, 40, 56 and 59 also showing characteristics of the later LBK (Pavúk 1972a, 80–4). Graves 4, 6, 17, 34, 35, 61, 71, 74 and 76 all contained pottery with early Želiezovce decoration, with 36, 47, 52 and 66 probably amongst the latest graves at the site (Pavúk 1972a, 80–1). Unusually for a cemetery, eleven pairs of graves had stratigraphic relationships. There were also other groups, such as 25, 33 and 34, where the graves inter-cut but among which the relationships were not clear (Pavúk 1972a, 81).

The graves dated by this project are 2, 5, 6, 19, 25, 27, 32, 41, 66 and 70 (Appendix B1). It was only possible to date one grave with pottery thought to be from the earliest phase of the site (grave 70), and one burial from the last phase of the site (based on the ceramic typology: grave 66 with Želiezovce decoration). So these dates must be seen as a pilot study, only offering preliminary conclusions, and it is hoped that more extensive dating of the cemetery will take place in the future. The modelling of the radiocarbon dates estimates that the cemetery started in *5370–5220 cal BC* (*95.4% probable*) or *5320–5230 cal BC* (*68.2% probable*). The end of activity at the Nitra cemetery is estimated to have occurred in *5210–4980 cal BC* (*95.4% probable*) or *5210–5090 cal BC* (*68.2% probable*). The duration of burial at the site is therefore estimated to have lasted between *20–360 years* (*95.4% probable*) or *30–220 years* (*68.2% probable*; Appendix B1 for full details).

4.10.3 Osteology

Preservation

The remains of 75 individuals were analysed, making Nitra the single largest site as well as the largest regional assemblage examined in detail for the Lifeways project. All of the Nitra skeletons are curated at the Moravian Museum, Brno. Most of the remains were in moderate or moderate to poor condition. Fragmentation, surface erosion and incomplete preservation of joint surfaces were widespread and limited the diagnosis of potential pathological features on affected skeletal elements. Some of the bones examined had also been treated with consolidant and glue during earlier post-excavation processing, resulting in a shiny, lacquered appearance of affected elements.

Demography: age and sex

The 75 burials included 49 adults, six adolescents, 16 juveniles and four infants. The adult assemblage consisted of 27 adult females, 18 adult males and four unsexed adults (Fig. 4.22).

The overall proportion of non-adults (34%), in particular the proportion of infants present (5%) is probably slightly lower than expected for prehistoric, early agricultural populations. This trend of under-representation of young individuals has already been noted for Polgár-Ferenci-hát (Chapter 3.9.2) and is probably the result of a combination of factors, including both taphonomy and differential burial practices (Guy *et al.* 1997; Scott 1999, 30; Chamberlain 2006, 98). Anthropological surveys of settlement burials in Moravia indicate that differential funerary rites for children were an important factor in their under-representation in cemeteries. Data published by Dočkalová and Čižmář (2007;

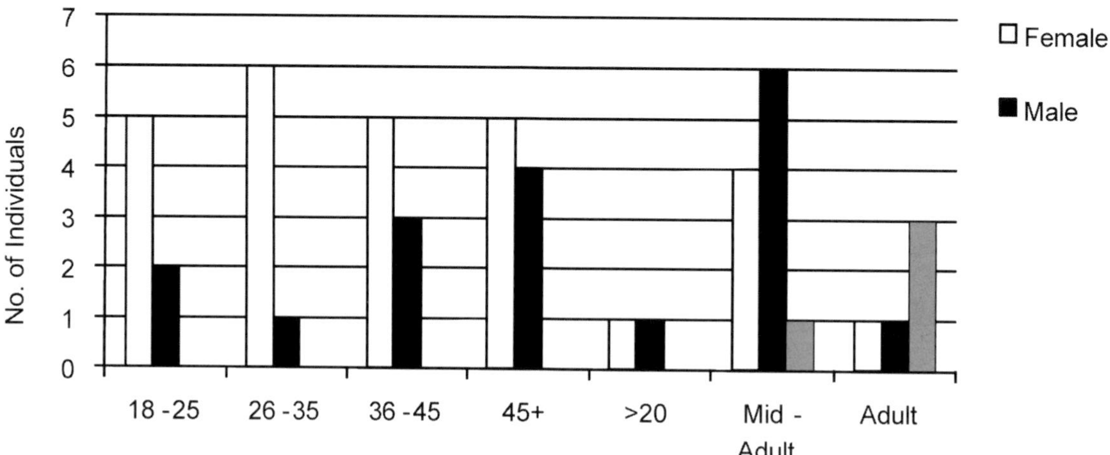

Fig. 4.23. Nitra: adult age distribution.

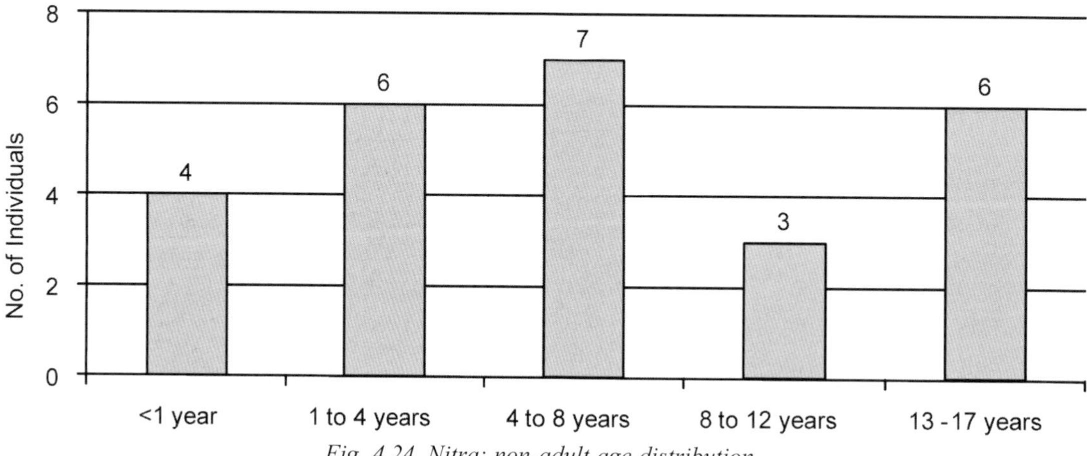

Fig. 4.24. Nitra: non-adult age distribution.

2008a) show that LBK settlement burials are dominated by children and to a lesser degree by adult women.

Looking more closely at age distribution in the adult sample at Nitra, males and females showed a very similar age distribution with the majority of individuals falling into the Mid-Adult category (26–45 years; Fig. 4.23). One notable feature was a higher number of females in the younger age groups (18–35 years), which is most likely related to increased mortality in or after childbirth.

In the non-adult sample, the largest number of individuals died between the ages of one and eight years (Fig. 4.24). This is probably due to, among other factors, the common occurrence of childhood diseases during this phase of life as well as an increased risk of gastrointestinal infections and other diseases during the important dietary change from breast milk to solid foods during early childhood (Chapter 2.4).

Adult stature

As a result of the fragmented state of preservation of much of the assemblage, only eight adult males and 11 adult females presented with left femora complete enough to measure (Fig. 4.25).

Mean values for male and female left femora maximum length showed a statistically significant difference ($t=5.060$, $p=0.02$), indicating relatively robust sexual dimorphism and related differences in stature between men and women.

Dental disease and modification

A total of 1303 permanent teeth from 71 individuals could be examined. This included 999 teeth from adult individuals and 304 teeth from adolescents and juveniles (Figs 4.26–7).

In the adult sample, 26 (57.8%) out of 45 adults with preserved teeth presented with caries and six (13.3%) with enamel hypoplasia. In the non-adult sample, three (11.5%) out of 26 individuals presented with enamel hypoplasia (Table 4.17), giving an overall total of nine (12.7%) affected individuals at Nitra. No caries was recorded in the juvenile/adolescent sample, which is not surprising as cavities in the permanent dentition do not tend to develop until well into adulthood.

When considering prevalence rates based on the number of teeth present, 70 (7%) out of 999 preserved teeth in the adult sample were affected by caries and 23 (2.3%) by enamel hypoplasia (Table 4.18). In addition, 26 (8.6%) of 304 teeth in the non-adult sample also presented with the defect. This resulted in an overall total of 49 (3.8%) teeth affected in the Nitra assemblage.

A more detailed comparison of male and female

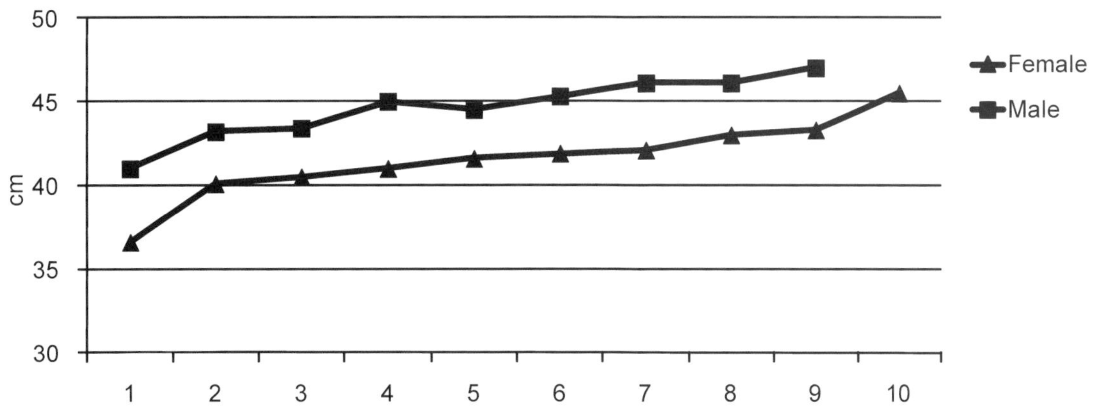

Fig. 4.25. Nitra: comparison of the maximum length of male and female left femora.

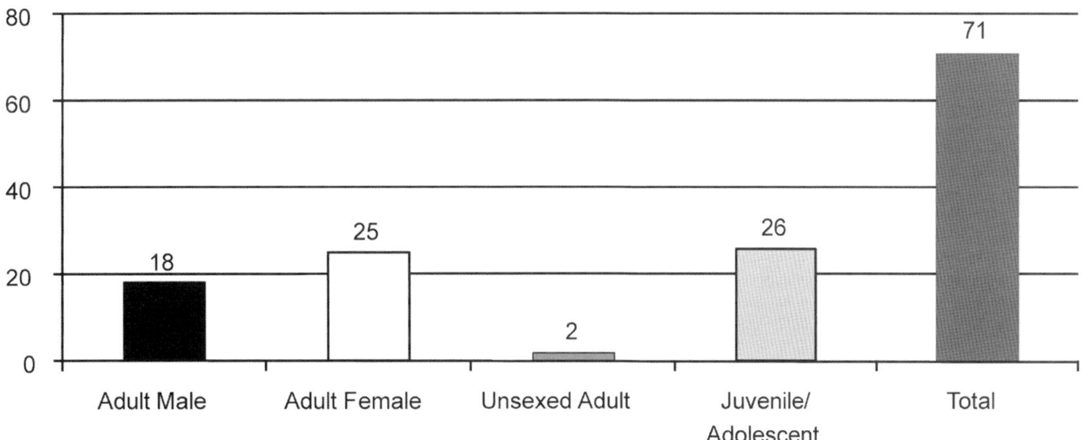

Fig. 4.26. Nitra: number of individuals with partial or complete dentitions.

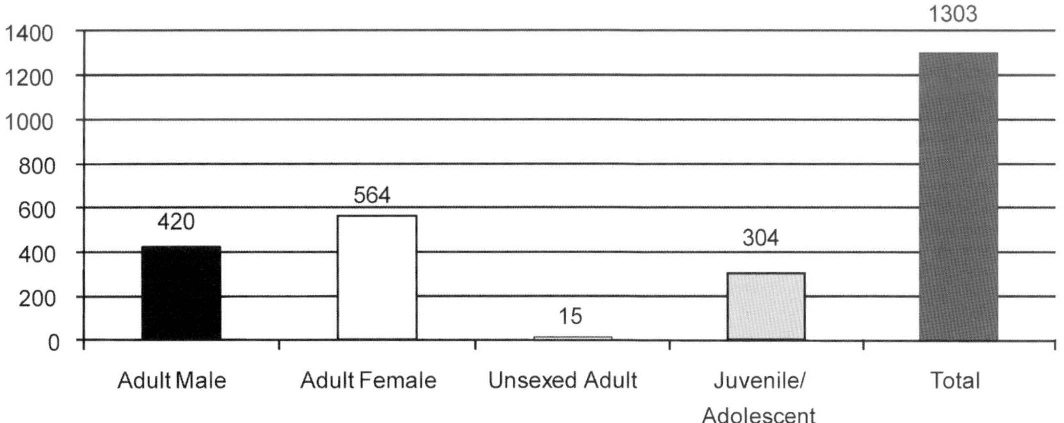

Fig. 4.27. Nitra: number of teeth present.

Table 4.17. Nitra: dental pathology. Individuals affected.

Group	No. of individuals	No. (%) affected by caries	No. (%) affected by enamel hypoplasia
Adult Male	18	7 (38.9)	4 (22.2)
Adult Female	25	18 (72)	2 (8)
Unsexed Adult	2	1 (50)	-
All Adults	45	26 (57.8)	6 (13.3)
Juvenile/Adolescent	26	-	3 (11.5)
Total	71	26 (36.6)	9 (12.7)

Table 4.18. Nitra: dental pathology. Teeth affected.

Group	No. of teeth	No. (%) affected by caries	No. (%) affected by enamel hypoplasia
Adult Male	420	15 (3.6)	14 (3.3)
Adult Female	564	50 (8.9)	9 (1.6)
Unsexed Adult	15	5 (33.3)	-
All Adults	999	70 (7)	23 (2.3)
Juvenile/Adolescent	304	-	26 (8.6)
Total	1303	70 (5.4)	49 (3.8)

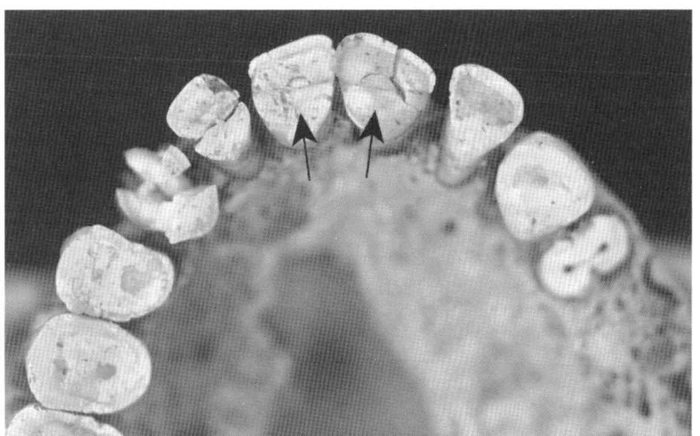

Fig. 4.28. Nitra: occlusal grooves, burial 44. Arrows indicate location of the grooves. Photo: Linda Fibiger.

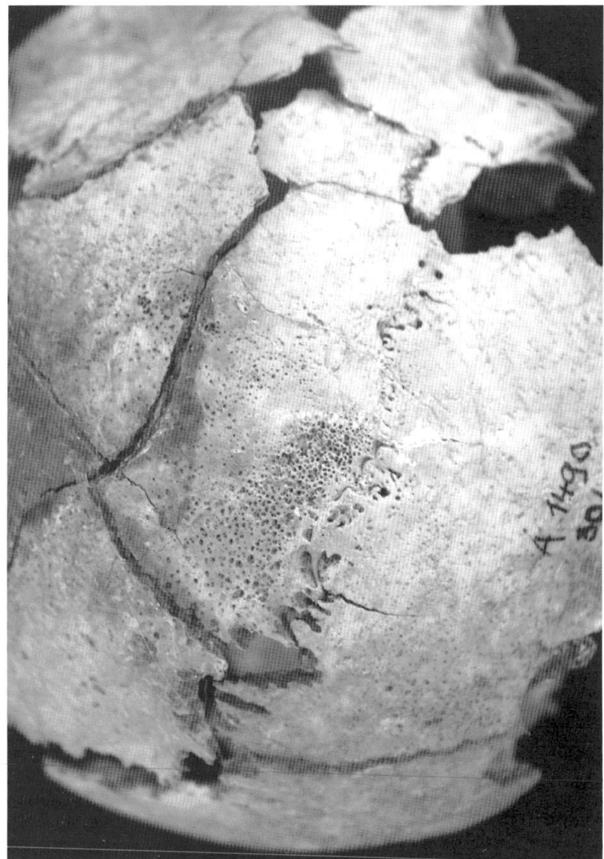

Fig. 4.29. Nitra: porotic hyperostosis, burial 30. Close-up of hypertrophic changes of the right parietal. Photo: Linda Fibiger.

prevalence rates for both pathologies shows noticeable differences between the sexes. Nearly twice as many females as males were affected by caries, and this figure is even higher when considering the number of teeth affected. This difference is statistically significant for both prevalence rates based on individuals (χ^2=4.714, p=0.03) and prevalence rates based on teeth (χ^2=10.935, p=0.001). This result is similar to that obtained for Polgár-Ferenci-hát. Overall health differences between men and women that also affected oral health seem an unlikely explanation, and dietary differences are the most likely reason for the observed differences in caries rates (which we also find in the nitrogen isotope data from Nitra; Chapter 4.10.4). No statistically significant differences were recorded for enamel hypoplasia prevalence rates, though males were more often affected than females (Table 4.17).

A number of individuals at Nitra showed signs of dental modification resulting from the use of teeth for activities other than food consumption. At least two men and four women presented with occlusal grooves of the maxillary and/or mandibular front teeth, indicating the use of the teeth as tools (Fig. 4.28). These are similar to changes noted on a number of individuals at Polgár-Ferenci-hát and again appear to be strongly associated with women and particular tasks that were carried out by them.

Cribra orbitalia

Out of 60 individuals with at least one partially preserved orbit, nine (15 %) presented with signs of *cribra orbitalia*. This included four adult women, two adolescents and three juveniles (Table 4.19). No adult men were affected. Although more women than men and more non-adults than adults were affected, neither of these differences was statistically significant. Also present was a case of porotic hyperostosis of the cranial vault (burial 30, juvenile, 6–7 years), affecting the parietals and to lesser extent the occipital (Fig. 4.29).

Periosteal changes and infection

A total of 15 individuals presented with periosteal reactions or changes indicative of inflammatory, infectious or metabolic conditions, including four women, three men, one adolescent, six juveniles and one infant (Table 4.20). With a crude prevalence of 20%, this means that at least a fifth of the population at Nitra was affected. Over twice as many non-adults (31%) as adults (14.3%) showed visible bone changes. This is not surprising in view of relatively

Table 4.19. Nitra: cribra orbitalia.

	No. of individuals with at least one partial eye socket preserved	No. (%) of individuals with *cribra orbitalia*
Adult Male	16	0 (0)
Adult Female	24	4 (16.7)
Unsexed Adult	1	0 (0)
All Adults	41	4 (9.8)
Adolescent	2	2 (100)
Juvenile	16	3 (18.8)
Infant	2	0 (0)
All Non-adults	20	5 (25)
Total	60	9 (15)

Table 4.20. Nitra: periosteal lesions and pathological changes related to inflammatory, infectious or haemorrhagic processes.

Group	Burial No.	Age	Changes recorded	Differential diagnosis
Female	22	Mature Adult	Periosteal new bone (mixed) on left and right lower legs	Systemic infection or haemorrhagic process
	27	(Older) Mid-Adult	Remodelled periosteal new bone on lower legs	Systemic infection or haemorrhagic process
	52	Mid-Adult	Osteomyelitis of right fibula	Infection
	76	Mid-Adult	Woven bone deposit on endocranial frontal and lytic defect of sphenoid	Systemic inflammatory process
Male	8	Mature Adult	Porosity of ectocranial mandible	Localised inflammatory or haemorrhagic process
	21	(Older) Mid-Adult	Periosteal new bone (mixed) on left and right lower legs	Systemic infection or haemorrhagic process
	34	Mid-Adult	Periosteal new bone (mixed) on ribs and vertebrae; destructive changes on lower spine; remodelled periosteal new bone on lower legs	Systemic infection, probably tuberculosis
Adolescent	5	13–17 years	Remodelled defect of 3rd lumbar vertebra	Localised infection?
Juvenile	23	11–12 years	Remodelled periosteal new bone on left tibia	Localised injury/ infection or haemorrhagic process
	31	1.5–2 years	Raised vascular impressions on endocranium	Systemic inflammatory process
	38	6–7 years	Remodelled periosteal new bone on right tibia	Localised injury/ infection or haemorrhagic process
	54	6–7 years	Remodelled periosteal new bone on lower legs	Systemic infection or haemorrhagic process
	71	5–6 years	Remodelled periosteal new bone on lower legs	Systemic infection or haemorrhagic process
	74	2–3 years	Remodelled periosteal new bone on lower legs	Systemic infection or haemorrhagic process
Infant	55	3–6 months	Increased medial-lateral bowing of left ulna; porous appearance of sphenoid and endocranial occipital	Metabolic disease (rickets)

high mortality rates in this age group (see above). It is important to note that some of the changes observed may have a variety of origins. Bilateral periosteal reactions on the lower legs, for example, may be the result of infectious conditions as well as metabolic diseases such as scurvy (vitamin C deficiency), and it may not be possible to securely ascribe the observed changes to either condition. Symptoms of scurvy include symmetrical haemorrhages that can result

Table 4.21. Nitra: cranial trauma.

Group	ID	Age	Trauma
Female	1	Young Adult	Peri-mortem fracture of right parietal
Male	72	Young Adult	Peri-mortem fracture of right temporal
Juvenile	49	5–6 years	Peri-mortem fractures of left and right parietal and occipital
	50	4–5 years	Peri-mortem fractures of left and right parietal and occipital

Fig. 4.30. Nitra: destructive changes of the thoracic spine as a result of tuberculosis, burial 34. Photo: Linda Fibiger.

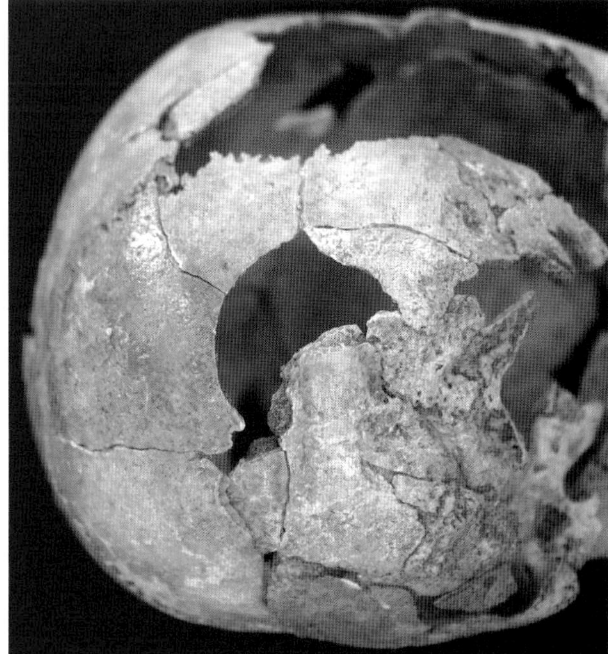

Fig. 4.31. Nitra: peri-mortem fracture of occipital, burial 49. Photo: Linda Fibiger.

in associated periosteal new bone formation (Ortner 2003, 385) as seen in the Nitra sample. One individual, a young infant (burial 55), may have suffered from rickets (vitamin D deficiency), indicated by a bowing deformity of the ulna.

One particular case at Nitra should be highlighted. Burial 34, an adult man aged between 26 and 45 years, showed skeletal changes indicative of active tuberculosis. These affected the ribs and spine and possibly the lower legs. Destruction of one of the vertebral bodies resulted in its collapse and most probably a bending deformity (kyphosis) of the spine (Fig. 4.30). Similar to the case from Polgár-Ferenci-hát, it is not possible to state whether this case is the result of infection with the human or bovine form of the disease without further biomolecular analysis. As only up to 5% of cases result in changes to the skeleton (Roberts and Buikstra 2003, 89), the disease is likely to have affected more than one individual at Nitra.

Post-cranial trauma

Post-cranial trauma rates at Nitra were relatively low. The only long-bone trauma recorded was the healed fracture of the lower arm bones of an adult female (burial 44). Another two individuals presented with signs of trauma that could be broadly termed activity-related. A female aged 45+ years (burial 61) presented with *os acromiale*, an incomplete bony fusion of the acromion process of the left shoulder blade. The origins of this condition have already been discussed in relation to the case at Polgár-Ferenci-hát (Chapter 3.9.2). While the affected individual would probably have had no symptoms, non-fusion of this part of the shoulder may have been advantageous by allowing for a greater range of movements of the shoulder. A mid-adult male (burial 26) presented with *spondylolysis* of the sixth lumbar vertebra. The possible origins of this lesion have already been reviewed (Chapter 3.9.2) and can involve both hereditary and activity-related factors. With only one case present at Nitra, it is difficult to assess the role which activity-pattern may have played in its aetiology.

Cranial trauma

Cranial trauma as an indicator for interpersonal violence was recorded on four individuals from Nitra, including one young adult male (burial 72), one young adult female (burial 1) and two children aged between four and five years (burial 50) and five and six years (burial 49) respectively (Table 4.21; Fig. 4.31). All injuries are peri-mortem and

Table 4.22. Nitra: crude prevalence of cranial trauma.

	No. of burials	No. (%) affected by trauma
Adult Male	18	1 (5.6)
Adult Female	27	1 (3.7)
Unsexed Adult	4	0 (0)
Adolescent	6	0 (0)
Juvenile	16	2 (12.5)
Infant	4	0 (0)
Total	75	4 (6.6)

Table 4.23. Nitra: adjusted prevalence of cranial trauma.

	50+% cranium present	No. (%) affected by trauma
Adult Male	16	1 (6.3)
Adult Female	24	1 (4.2)
Unsexed Adult	1	0 (0)
Adolescent	2	0 (0)
Juvenile	12	2 (16.7)
Infant	3	0 (0)
Total	58	4 (7.3)

likely to relate to the individuals' death. Tables 4.22–3 show crude trauma prevalence based on the total number of burials present and adjusted trauma prevalence based on the number of individuals with at least 50% of the cranial vault preserved.

Based on sample numbers adjusted to reflect preservation and completeness, 7.3% of individuals at Nitra were affected by cranial trauma. Figures for non-adult individuals were much higher than for adults, though this difference was not statistically significant. A higher proportion of men than women were affected, but again this result was not statistically significant.

Summary

The Nitra assemblage offers important insights into population health during the later LBK period in Slovakia. The demographic profile of the sample indicates a slight under-representation of juveniles and infants. More males than females are present. Mortality rates in the female sample peak in the 20s, which is most likely a function of increased mortality during the childbirth years. Significant differences in dental health provide indications of gendered differences in diet, with higher caries rates in females probably resulting from a diet richer in starchy plant foods. This mirrors results obtained for Polgár-Ferenci-hát. Women also appear to have suffered fewer early childhood stresses than men, indicated by lower enamel hypoplasia rates. They did, however, present with higher rates of *cribra orbitalia* as an indicator of iron deficiency anaemia. Further gendered differences were also noted in the female-weighted occurrence of non-dietary dental wear, suggesting some degree of sexual division of labour, possibly related to plant fibre processing. Considering metabolic diseases and infectious conditions, men and women appeared to be equally affected.

In the non-adult sample, mortality rates are highest in early to mid-childhood (0–8 years), reflecting the risks of gastro-intestinal infections and other diseases during the weaning phase as well as the occurrence of childhood diseases associated with the early years of life. This is further substantiated by the number of individuals in this age group who suffered from infectious and/or metabolic conditions. Although not statistically significant, it is interesting to note higher rates of violence-related trauma in the juvenile sample compared to the adults at Nitra. The affected individuals, while probably too young to have played any active role in group warfare, still provided the target for severe violence.

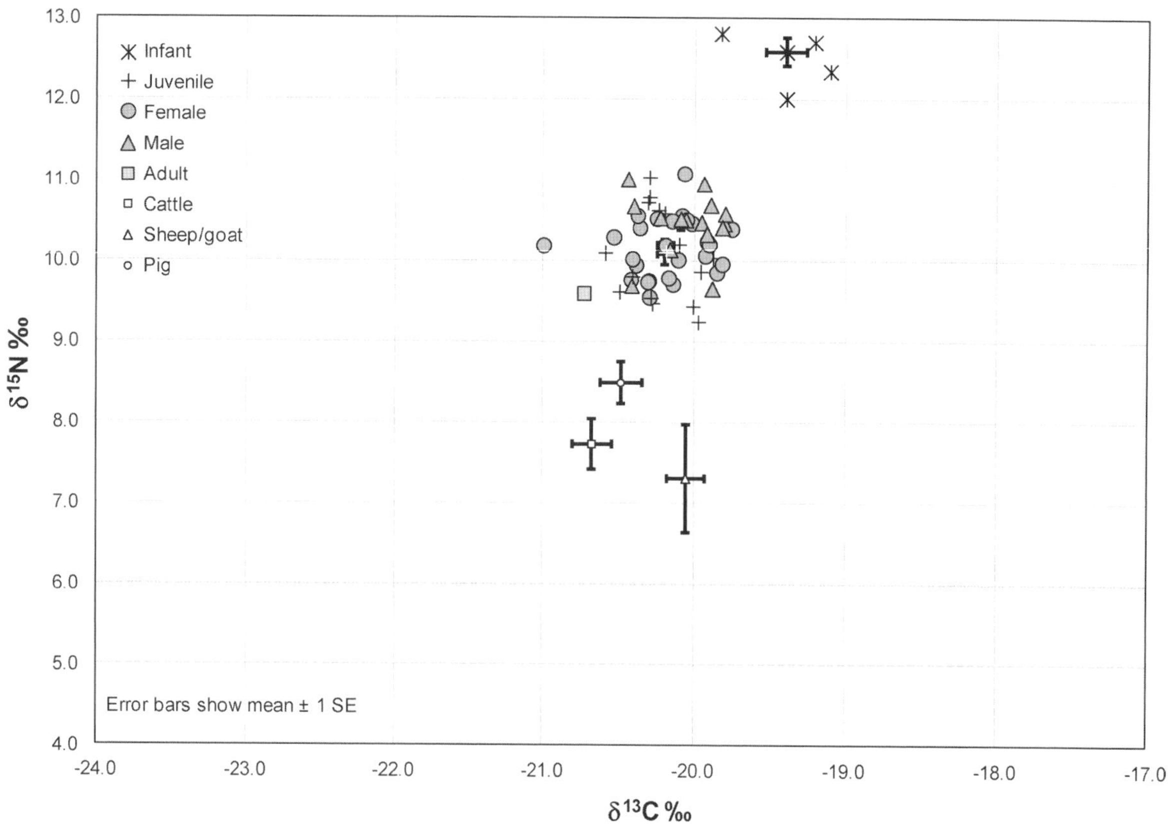

Fig. 4.32. Nitra: carbon and nitrogen isotope ratios (‰) of humans.

Table 4.24. Carbon and nitrogen isotope ratios (‰) of humans from Nitra and animals from Blatné, with means and standard deviations. 'All' includes one unsexed adult.

Species	Age/sex	Mean δ^{13}C	SD δ^{13}C	Mean δ^{15}N	SD δ^{15}N	n
Human	Infant	−19.4	0.3	12.6	0.39	5
Human	Juvenile	−20.2	0.2	10.1	0.57	15
Human	Female	−20.2	0.27	10.2	0.37	26
Human	Male	−20.1	0.24	10.5	0.39	14
Human	All adults	−20.2	0.28	10.2	0.4	41
Cattle		−20.7	0.43	7.7	1.06	11
Sheep/goat		−20.1	0.30	7.3	1.64	6
Pig		−20.5	0.37	8.5	0.68	7

4.10.4 Carbon and nitrogen analysis

Almost the entire cemetery could be sampled, thanks to the good levels of preservation. A total of 61 individuals were sampled from Nitra: five infants, 14 older children, juveniles and adolescents, as well as 14 adult males and 25 adult females (Fig. 4.32; Table 4.24).

Age/sex variation

The infants form a distinct group with elevated δ^{13}C and δ^{15}N values, the means 0.6‰ and 2.4‰ above the adult mean, respectively, typical of a nursing effect (Fig. 4.32). Apart from this, differences between the mean isotope values of other age groups are not significant (ANOVA with post hoc Bonferroni tests). However, using the detailed age information from the osteological study, there is a significant negative correlation between δ^{15}N (but not δ^{13}C) and age rank for juveniles (children and adolescents; Spearman rank correlation, r_s=−0.65, p<0.01, n=15, Fig. 4.32). This is suggestive of a physiological effect lowering δ^{15}N values during a late childhood/adolescent growth spurt, though as discussed above (Chapter 4.7.3) the subject is complex (reviewed by Waters-Rist and Katzenberg 2010; discussed in the context of the whole dataset in Chapter 9.2.5).

The difference of 0.3‰ between male and female mean δ^{15}N value, although small, is statistically significant (2-tailed t test, p=0.026), and there is no significant difference between adult age groups for either sex. In both the large cemetery groups analysed from this region, male δ^{15}N values have been slightly but significantly higher than those of females (further discussion in Chapter 9.2.5).

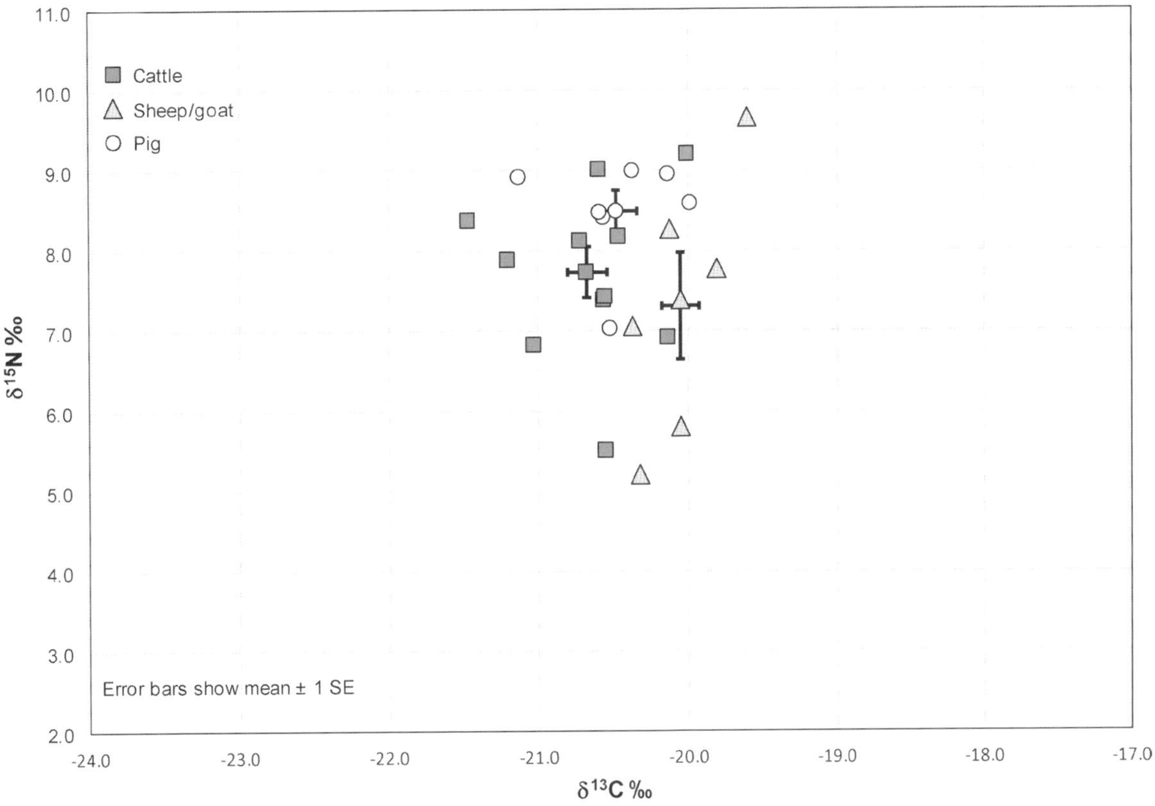

Fig. 4.33. Blatné: carbon and nitrogen isotope ratios (‰) of animals.

Animals

Finding a relevant animal bone assemblage to compare to Nitra was difficult and the site of Blatné, which is about 30 km from Nitra, was the nearest available collection (Pavúk 1978; 1980b). There is wide variation in the $\delta^{15}N$ values of both cattle and sheep at Blatné; as usual, the mean pig $\delta^{15}N$ value is slightly higher than those of the herbivores, though the difference is not statistically significant (Fig. 4.33). Sheep/goats have significantly higher $\delta^{13}C$ values than cattle (ANOVA with post hoc Bonferroni test, p=0.01). This could reflect feeding in more open or drier environments, and is in line with the pattern usually observed, though at many sites it is not statistically significant.

The difference between the mean adult human and cattle $\delta^{13}C$ and $\delta^{15}N$ values is 0.5±0.51 and 2.5±1.13‰, respectively. The difference in $\delta^{15}N$ values is rather low in comparison to Vedrovice, though in line with results from the other two sites in the region; how meaningful it is depends on the relevance of the comparison of humans from Nitra and animals from Blatné. Although overall the $\delta^{15}N$ values at Nitra are high for the region, so are those of the animals, so this probably reflects an environmental rather than a dietary difference.

Correlations with the archaeological data

As the means for men, women and children (those without a nursing signature) are very similar, correlations between burial practices and grave goods at Nitra and the stable isotopes must be discussed cautiously. No correlations could be identified between the body positions and orientations and the stable isotope results, which is not surprising given the overall uniformity of Nitra in this respect. However, some trends in the data were visible when compared to certain classes of grave good. Men buried with polished stone adzes (five graves) tend to have higher $\delta^{15}N$ values (above 10.5‰, male mean=10.5‰), but this was not statistically significant (2-tailed t test, p=0.19, n=12) and includes an outlier of a mature adult with a $\delta^{15}N$ value of 11.00‰ (burial 8/64). The only significant trend identified amongst the women (Fig. 4.34) was a relationship between high values of $\delta^{13}C$ and the presence of *Spondylus* in the grave (with *Spondylus*: mean=−19.8‰, n=3; without *Spondylus*: mean=−20.2‰, n=22, p=0.004, 2-tailed t test, n=25), but as only three female graves sampled contain *Spondylus* we should be cautious in accepting these results. However, if the infants still influenced by a nursing signal are excluded, this trend can be identified in the population as a whole (with *Spondylus*: mean=−19.9‰, n=8; without *Spondylus*: mean=−20.2‰, n=42, p=0.001, 2-tailed t test, n=50). The significance drops to p=0.002 (n=34) when unfurnished graves are excluded.

There is no apparent correlation between the stable isotope values and the spatial layout of the cemetery.

4.10.5 Strontium analysis

Strontium isotope ratios were obtained from 61 individuals from the LBK cemetery at Nitra, including one unsexed

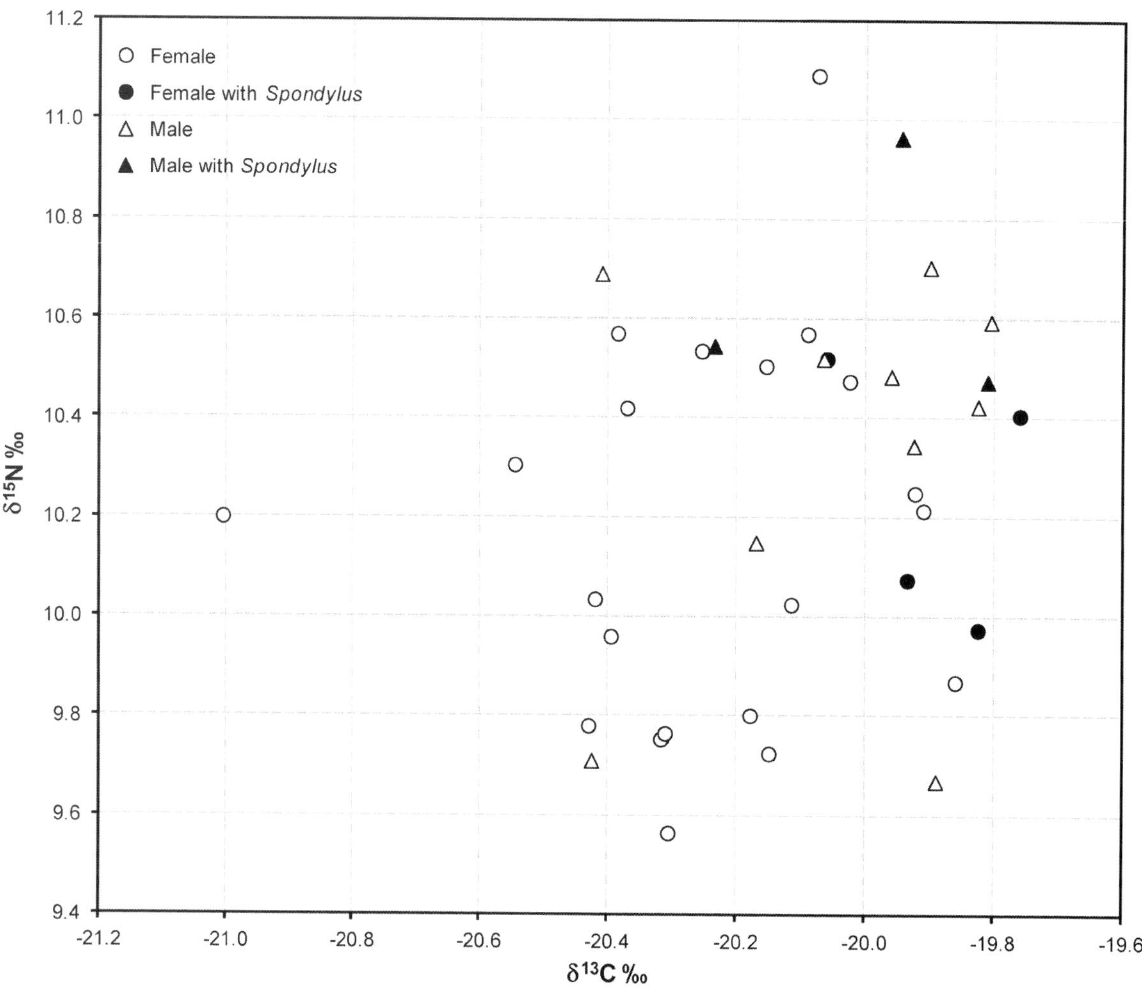

Fig. 4.34. Nitra: carbon and nitrogen isotope ratios (‰) of humans shown in relation to the presence of Spondylus.

*Table 4.25. Nitra: strontium isotope ratios and concentrations. 'All' includes one unsexed adult. * denotes number of analyses, not number of individuals.*

Age/sex	Mean $^{87}Sr/^{86}Sr$	SD $^{87}Sr/^{86}Sr$	Mean Sr conc.	SD Sr conc.	n*
Juvenile	0.70948	0.00009	42	13	15
Male	0.70944	0.00013	74	59	15
Female	0.70952	0.00039	100	106	25
All	0.70948	0.00025	72	74	61

adult, 16 males, 23 females and 21 juveniles (Fig. 4.35; Table 4.25). As discussed above, Nitra was situated on loess soils and we would expect the 'local' range to fall within the average strontium ratios for this type of soil (0.7085–0.7105). However, upland outcrops of non-loess and more radiogenic soils were not that far from the cemetery, including in the Tribeč Mountains (the westernmost extent of the Carpathian Mountain range), which are only tens of kilometres from the site. The mean $^{87}Sr/^{86}Sr$ among identified females (n=23) was 0.70953±0.00035, and among identified males (n=16) it was 0.70945±0.00014; both these values fall within the expected signatures for loess soils. These mean values are not significantly different, but an F-test indicates that the Nitra females have significantly (p=0.0004) greater variance in $^{87}Sr/^{86}Sr$ than the males (the more robust Levene's test yields p=0.07). The mean Sr concentrations at Nitra were essentially the same for females (70±51 ppm) and males (82±35 ppm). As at Vedrovice, therefore, we find a local cluster of men, women and children, contrasting with outliers that are predominantly women. As Fig. 4.35 shows, all six of the 61 sampled individuals at Nitra with $^{87}Sr/^{86}Sr$ above 0.7097 were female, which is significant (p=0.008, χ^2=7.10, df=1). Hence, as at Vedrovice, the adult females at Nitra have significantly more variable $^{87}Sr/^{86}Sr$ ratios.

Females show greater variance in their $^{87}Sr/^{86}Sr$ ratios

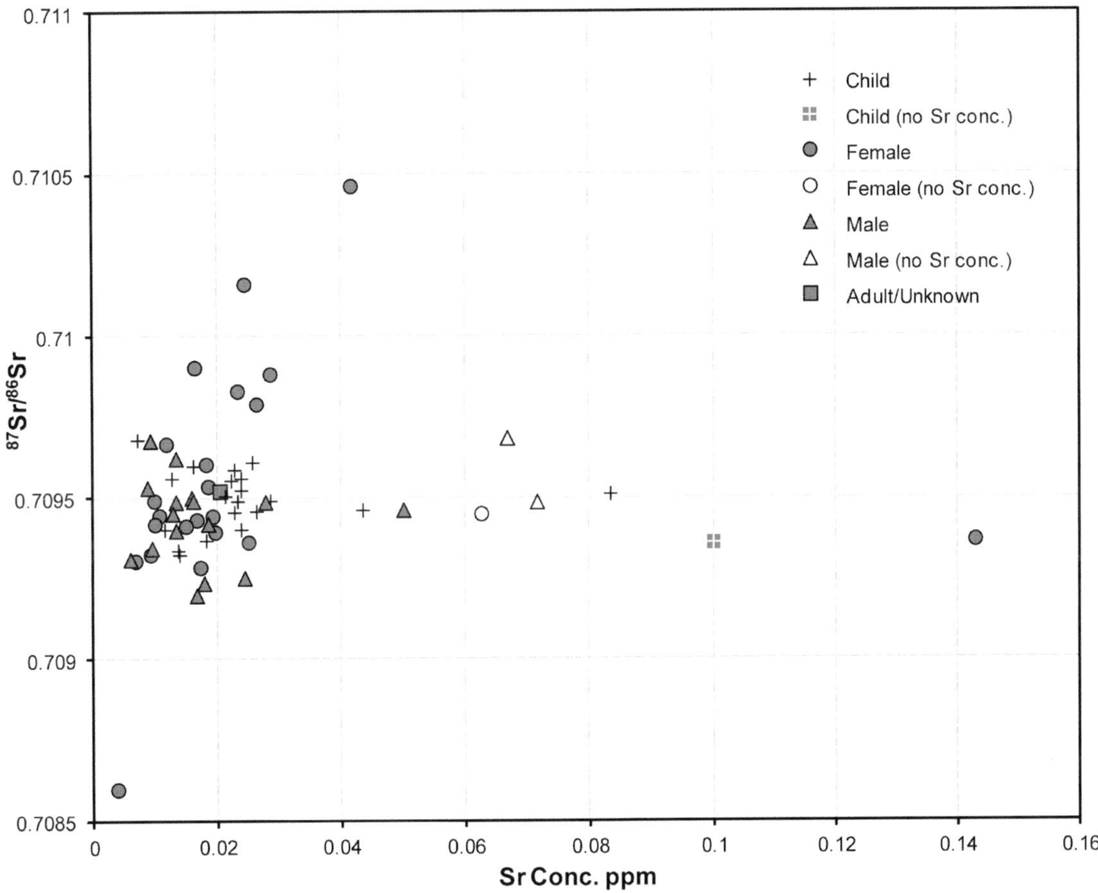

Fig. 4.35. Nitra: strontium concentration (ppm) versus ratio ($^{87}Sr/^{86}Sr$).

from M1 molars than males (Levene's test, p=0.03, n=12), but not for their M2 and M3 molars. Given the low numbers of samples available for analysis by the time the dataset from Nitra has been divided by sex and molar sampled, we would be cautious in extrapolating from these results (only seven M3 molars were sampled). However, considering that no M3 molar has a value above 0.7097, a similar trend to that at Vedrovice may be noted, where M3 molars have less variance than other teeth sampled.

Correlations with the archaeological data

Considering the Nitra males buried with ground stone adzes, the variance in ^{87}Sr/^{86}Sr is not significantly smaller for the adze burials, but the mean ^{87}Sr/^{86}Sr might be slightly lower for Nitra males with adzes (with adze, 0.70937±0.00015, n=6 versus 0.70951±0.00011, n=9 without adze; 2-tailed t test, p=0.062). When we add the unsexed burials and compare adze versus non-adze burials among all but the adult females (we do not want to add females because they are significantly different), the adze burials have significantly lower mean ^{87}Sr/^{86}Sr (2-tailed t test, p=0.030). The Sr concentrations (ppm) did not differ between adze and non-adze males at Nitra. Seven of the 17 identified males at Nitra had adzes, and four of these seven cluster as the lowest ^{87}Sr/^{86}Sr ratios of Nitra males (p=0.02, χ^2=5.71, df=1). No other trends could be identified in the data, nor were there any significant correlations to the stable isotope data.

There are three female outliers: burial 22/65, a mature adult female, with a ^{87}Sr/^{86}Sr ratio of 0.70860, burial 39/65, an older mature possible female, with a ^{87}Sr/^{86}Sr ratio of 0.71016 and burial 64/65, an older mature female, with a ^{87}Sr/^{86}Sr ratio of 0.71046. None of these values falls far from the mean for the site as a whole or far from the ^{87}Sr/^{86}Sr range of the loess. No outliers could be determined for males and children. Taking the potential clusters discussed above (Chapter 4.10.1), as well as investigating potential rows of burials (e.g. burials 63, 62, 76, 44, 33, 32 and burials 45, 40, 48, 35, 24, 23), no difference or patterning in the strontium isotopes could be found. However, four of the five individuals with the most radiogenic ^{87}Sr/^{86}Sr ratio (burials 20, 48, 64 and 70) are found in the widely spaced southern end of the site, which may hint that geographic origin may have played a role in influencing where the deceased were placed within the cemetery. Ongoing aDNA research on samples from the cemetery (Anna Szécsényi-Nagy, pers. comm.) may help to throw further light on these issues.

4.10.6 Site summary and discussion

The strontium ratios from Nitra have a very narrow range, overwhelmingly falling within the loess ^{87}Sr/^{86}Sr ratio range; these values are considerably closer than any of the other sites sampled in this region. The tightly clustered range found at Nitra is likely to have arisen in part from the geological conditions in the vicinity of the site, but given the proximity of higher radiogenic $^{87}Sr/^{86}Sr$ ratios in nearby mountain ranges it also suggests a community that did not source food from those uplands in any great quantities (and see Chapter 4.11). Despite this narrow range of values, females were still distinctly more variable than males, suggesting more varied origins for women than for men. Differences in strontium ratios could also be detected between burials with and without polished stone items and adzes in particular, with those individuals buried with adzes having $^{87}Sr/^{86}Sr$ ratios that are more concentrated.

The stable isotope values from Nitra are tightly clustered, suggesting that those buried at Nitra were sharing a very similar diet, though males may have been consuming more animal protein than females. However, both the strontium isotopes and osteological study indicate different lifeways for men and women. This suggests that while men and women had diets that were probably of similar composition, they were possibly sourcing their foods in different ways or from different locations. As teeth mineralise in childhood, this strengthens arguments for patrilocality, with female strontium values originating in a wider variety of locations in the vicinity of the site than those for males. The osteological study suggests that the daily tasks engaged in by the sexes were different, shown by the distinct wear marks on teeth. The higher rate of caries for women may suggest that they were eating more starchy foods, perhaps related to their lower animal protein intake inferred from the nitrogen values.

Following the re-analysis of the osteological collection from Nitra, we can examine whether the trends identified by Pavúk (1972a) hold true. Certainly, the older age classes remain the recipients of the most complex grave good assemblages. *Spondylus* is only found in burials with individuals aged as mature adult or above, predominantly in male graves, though neither of these facts explains the significant difference in $\delta^{13}C$ values between burials with and without *Spondylus* shell (Chapter 4.10.4). In comparison to Vedrovice, the prevalence of *Spondylus* in the graves is only slightly reduced (15% for Nitra; 18% for Vedrovice), but the amounts going into each grave at Nitra are severely restricted. There may also be a correlation between an individual receiving *Spondylus* in the grave and high carbon isotope values, which suggests they were eating foods from a more open landscape. This could well have a chronological explanation, as the landscape is thought to become progressively more open throughout the LBK.

Polished stone is similarly restricted to the older adult age classes amongst males, but is also found with a three-year-old infant (grave 40) and a flake of a polished stone tool is found with an adolescent (grave 41). The polished stone item in the grave of a mature-older adult female (grave 27) is a flat axe, though another in grave 76, with a possible female, is an adze. Pots also appear to be influenced by age and sex; 75% of male graves have pots, 58% of women have pots, with the majority of the ceramic wares associated with the older adult classes. Although infants and juveniles did receive grave goods, there are not the rich graves seen at Vedrovice and further west (as in Alsace: Chapter 8). Overall, therefore, we follow the arguments of both Pavúk (1972a) and Jeunesse (1996; 1997) that the more complex grave good assemblages were associated with older adults, and males in particular. Men buried with polished stone adzes at Nitra tend to have higher nitrogen values than those buried without and this may suggest there was some differentiation in the community, with some individuals having more restricted access to animal protein.

The orientation and position of the deceased in the grave at Nitra are overwhelmingly uniform, with almost all graves falling between E–W and S–N; the only exception is burial 53/65, which is oriented SW–NE. This grave was situated in a cluster of four graves, and was cut by burial 41/65, which was oriented approximately S–N. Burial 53/65 was accompanied by an undecorated miniature bottle (height 6.7cm; Pavúk 1972a, 18). Only two burials were in a right-crouched position, thus making this cemetery one of the most conservative cemeteries in the LBK and perhaps explaining why Pavúk (1972a; cf. Jeunesse 1996) argued that there was such a uniform burial rite in the LBK.

Of particular interest at Nitra are the inter-cutting burials. Some form clusters of graves (such as burials 26–9 and 37, 41, 53–5), for which it is tempting to suggest some form of familial relationships. For example, the cluster of burials 26–9 consists of a mature adult male (26), mid-adult female (27), both relatively well furnished with a polished stone item each and ceramics, as well as a neonate (28) and an unfurnished 10–12 year-old juvenile (29), with two further children nearby (30 and 31). In the second cluster, an adolescent (41), two young adult females (53 and 37), an infant (55) and 6–7 year-old (54) were buried together. Equally, the triple burial of individuals 48–50 seems to suggest a closely related group; the right arm of the adult female (48) is placed over the central child (49), resting against the skull of burial 50. The two children in this burial had suffered cranial injuries, which were a likely cause of their deaths, and the positioning of the female's right arm appears to draw attention to this. The inter-cutting pairs of graves may also suggest a close relationship between the individuals, but a detailed investigation of these burials shows important differences. For example, the male and female buried in graves 2 and 6 respectively both lived into older adulthood and were buried with *Spondylus*, but their graves contained different forms of ceramic (Pavúk 1972a, 81, 84). Cutting grave 76, a left-crouched burial of a possibly female mid-adult with an adze is a burial of another adult (un-sexed) who had been placed in a right-crouched position, so the two individuals were facing away from one another. Grave 53, a burial of a young adult female, is the only individual to be oriented with the head to the south-west and was cut by burial 41, which was aligned in the opposing orientation, SSE–NNW, with the head to the south.

In contrast to the strontium isotope results, external contacts are demonstrated at Nitra by the pot in grave 17, which is described by Pavúk (1972a, 84) as a *doppelkonisches Gefäß*, decorated with sharply cornered, incised zig-zag lines. Both the shape and design are unknown in later LBK contexts in western Slovakia but occur frequently in Alföld Linear Pottery contexts. However, the *Grübchen* (small depressed pits) around the middle of the pot are more characteristic of the Transdanubian LBK, and suggest a blending of different cultural or regional elements of ceramic design. The *Amphore* (a square body with rounded corners, complemented by a long neck) in grave 2 similarly speaks to wider contacts throughout the LBK milieu and perhaps suggests ties to the Tiszadob-Kapušany group (a regional variant of ALP; Kalicz and Makkay 1977). This group is found in the foothills of the Carpathian Mountains, at a higher altitude to the Alföld sites on the Great Hungarian Plain and on areas that were less suitable to the agriculture practised by LBK and ALP farmers (Kertész and Sümegi 2001, 238). If we were able to detect any individuals buried at Nitra from this area they would be likely to have higher radiogenic signatures than the loess, but the individuals in both these graves have local signatures. While this does not preclude the possibility that these two individuals were travelers or born away from Nitra, it suggests that individual mobility may not have been required in the formation of broad contacts.

4.11 Regional discussion

In this chapter, we have examined the isotopes from four contrasting sites. The large assemblages of Nitra and Vedrovice, the first true cemeteries to be discussed in this volume, suggest divergent mobility and burial practices, while the small number of samples offered by the settlements of Brno-Starý Lískovec and Těšetice-Kyjovice also add to the picture of varied burial traditions as well as raising questions about the form and scales of settlement communities.

In Moravia and western Slovakia, the arrival of the LBK signalled the earliest Neolithic in the region and, for the most part, an 'integrationist' model is favoured, in which a small number of incomers, bringing the LBK from the south and south-east, attracted the attention of and subsequently incorporated indigenous hunter-gatherers (Zvelebil 2004; Zvelebil and Pettitt 2008; Lukes and Zvelebil 2008; Lukes *et al.* 2008; Mateiciucová 2008b). The strontium isotope results from Vedrovice, probably one of the earlier cemeteries in the LBK (Hedges and Pettitt 2008), suggest a mobile and heterogeneous community (see also Zvelebil and Pettitt 2008) though no distinct 'indigenous' versus 'incomer' isotope signature could be determined, nor are there clear indications from the burial evidence that such clear oppositions were the basis on which identity was constructed. The different areas of the site appear to begin contemporaneously during phase 1b (on the basis of ceramic typologies; Podborský 2002b, 337), which makes the difference in their stable isotopes all the more stark. The place of burial for the different groups living in the Vedrovice area seems to be determined by the dietary community in which they lived, with people being buried alongside those with whom they were sharing dietary and hence in all likelihood daily routines as well.

In contrast, for the cemetery at Nitra, which perhaps began later than Vedrovice, the strontium results show less variation, with the majority of individuals falling within a tighter range of $^{87}Sr/^{86}Sr$ ratios (0.7092–0.7099; compare Figs 4.9 and 4.35). Other distinct differences between the two cemeteries can be determined. At Vedrovice the graves of young adults (under 40) received the most varied and complex grave good assemblages, while at Nitra it was the older adult and mature males that received the most complex combinations of grave goods. Nitra is more uniform than Vedrovice; the orientations of the burials all fall between E–W and S–N, with one exception (burial 53 is oriented SW–NE), while at Vedrovice 15 burials are oriented between SW–NE and W–E and therefore a small but significant number of burials were placed in the opposing direction to the majority of graves. The difference is more subtle in body positioning, but more variability can be detected at Vedrovice than Nitra (at both sites 65 burials had sufficient preservation to determine the position of the body in the grave, but at Nitra 63 are left-crouched, as opposed to 58 at Vedrovice). This contrasts with the stable isotope data, which demonstrated greater differences between the sexes in terms of diet at Nitra than at Vedrovice.

So in comparison to Hungary (Chapter 3), where the burial evidence came exclusively from settlement contexts, the burial assemblages from the sites of Vedrovice and Nitra are likely to have brought together geographically and socially wider groups of people. This is perhaps reinforced by the tightly clustered strontium ratios from Těšetice, which when taken together with their burial location (in a close cluster on the edge of the settlement), might suggest that the people in question were all from the same kin-group or closely related in life.

The osteological study at Nitra found significant differences in dental health and the rate of childhood stress between the sexes, following the results from Polgár-Ferenci-hát (Chapter 3.9.2). In combination with the evidence in female teeth for plant fibre processing and the higher nitrogen values for men at Nitra, this suggests that men and women were eating different diets that may be related to the daily activities in which men and women were engaged. The lifeways of men are likely to have differed significantly from those of women, but these differences are fairly widespread, being found across both Hungary and Moravia and western Slovakia.

However, there may have been more localised variation in how such differences in lifeways between the sexes related to how status and gendered identity were presented in the grave at death. At Vedrovice the most complex grave good assemblages are found with younger adults of both sexes, while at Nitra they accompany only older adult males. Yet, in most cases the individuals buried in these graves did not necessarily stand out as having lived significantly different lifeways to the rest of the community. In the case of the sites discussed in this chapter, status has been just one of many ways in which identity has been configured in the choice of objects that went into a grave. Indeed, whether widely shared notions of status existed during the LBK (faithfully reproduced at all cemeteries) can be questioned. There is plenty of scope in the discussions above to see gender and connections (both near and far) as just as significant, if not more so, in how the grave good assemblage came together.

Notes

1 The site lies at the intersection of three cadasters, and parts of it are also known as Brno-Nový Lískovec and Brno-Bohunice.

2 See again Chapter 1, note 4.

3 In their numbering: individuals 48/77; 23/75; 102/81; 77/79; 79/79; 59/78; 14/75; 46/77; 15/75; 91/80; 51/77; 82/79; 69/87; 70/79; and 39/76.

4 An earlier campaign (1910–11) in the Za Dvorem area of the site also uncovered a minimum of nine burials, but very little is known of these (Podborský 2002b, 336).

5 The dates are: Vera-1831 Human bone, 6220±35 BP (5300–5050 cal BC 2σ) and Vera-1832, Human bone, 6155±35 BP (5220–5000 cal BC 2σ), as quoted by Pettitt and Hedges (2008, 125).

6 The radiocarbon dates on human bone are: grave 11, 6150±35 BP, 5220–5000 cal BC (at 95% confidence) (Vera-2610); grave 18, 6210±35 BP, 5300–5050 cal BC (Vera-2609); and grave 20, 6240±35 BP, 5310–5200 cal BC (67.6% confidence) or 5180–5060 cal BC (27.8% confidence).

7 Sometimes also known in the literature by the nearby village of Horné Krškany or by the road along which it was found, Priemyslová ulica.

8 Graves 4 over 3 (4/3), 6/2, 17/61, 20/64, 26/27, 28/26, 37/54, 41/53, 43/76, 44/59 and 74/32 (Pavúk 1972a, 81).

9 Graves 33 and 34, 34 and 25, 29 and 26, 39 and 76, 22 and 23, and 16 and 17 (Pavúk 1972a, 81).

10 Graves 32, 33, 43 and 44; 24, 22, 61, 18 and 70, with 15 and 17 flanking them; and 37, 41, 53 and 66 (Pavúk 1972a, 65).

11 Graves 38, 40, 42, 54–5 and 60, and 23, 28–31 and 73 (Pavúk 1972a, 65).

12 The 30–40 year-old adult in grave 70 was uncertainly identified as female in the original report (Pavúk 1972a, 22, 70).

A Těšetice lifeway: burial 11

The strontium isotope ratio (M1, $^{87}Sr/^{86}Sr$ ratio=0.71018) of the adult woman in burial 11 at Těšetice is much lower than that of the other individuals at this site. This value falls outside that commonly recorded from loess soils in the study area, but not that of loess soils recorded elsewhere. We can speculate that she had been born into a LBK community from outside the immediate area; perhaps she even originated in a neighbouring region such as Lower Austria, which seems to have had close ties to the Moravian LBK (for example, the sites in the Horn basin are only 80 km away). This individual may have been a stranger at Těšetice, while still possibly growing up at a LBK settlement. We do not know at what age she first moved to the site, but in the light of trends in female mobility in the LBK overall, which may be connected to patrilocality, it could even be suggested that this woman only moved to Těšetice upon marriage. The Krumlovský Les chert source is not far from the site of Těšetice (c. 30 km) and her movement to the settlement could have possibly been tied up in the networks which spread raw materials such as this one. Perhaps in her late teens or in early adulthood, she set out from the settlement of her birth to move to Těšetice, travelling through a network of kin and relations that existed across the region.

On the death of this woman, her non-local origins did not prevent her from being buried with grave goods. She received two vessels and a grinding stone, which is a relatively substantial assemblage given the overall tendency for restricted grave goods at Těšetice. However, she was marked out as different in other ways. While the other individuals at the site were buried relatively close together, she was some distance apart from the main cluster, ten metres behind a LBK longhouse. Furthermore, hers is the only burial oriented NW–SE, although still placed in the most frequent, left-crouched position. The majority orientation at the site is E–W, with one antipodal burial with head due west (child burial 92), and two individuals oriented N–S.

In her case, difference in origin may have manifested itself as a lifelong habit of a slight difference in diet – perhaps consuming a little more fish, or slightly more animal protein. Her carbon isotope signature ($\delta^{13}C=-19.6‰$) falls within the range of values in this small burial community, but, in contrast, her nitrogen isotope value ($\delta^{15}N=9.5‰$) is the highest among the adults at Těšetice, higher even than the males (though we cannot exclude the possibility that she came from a different phase of the settlement to the other burials). However, the only other female identified at Těšetice (burial 18) died in early adulthood, probably in her early twenties, but still provided the second highest nitrogen signature for the site ($\delta^{15}N=9.1‰$), so there may be a gendered component.

It is also possible that, as the woman in burial 11 died in her late forties or early fifties, we are here faced with one of the relatively few females in this study to survive into mature adulthood, and who hence could have made a long-term contribution to the community in terms of labour, sociality or offspring, recognised through greater access to animal protein. She was also singled out in death, perhaps because of her non-local origin or her consistently distinct lifeway as shown by dietary isotopes.

A Nitra lifeway: burial 34

Burial 34 is of an adult man, who is likely to have died in middle age. On his death he was furnished with a polished stone adze with traces of hafting and use, as well as a decorated bottle and an unworked Spondylus *fragment. At Nitra, older adult men in general were marked out in death by receiving the most complex grave assemblages. While it is therefore tempting to suggest that the polished stone adze in this burial had been a prized tool in daily use, this individual is likely to have had restricted mobility, as during his life he contracted tuberculosis.*

It is not possible to distinguish the human from the bovine form of tuberculosis from skeletal changes alone, and so we do not know whether this individual was infected for instance by consuming infected cow's milk or by being in contact with other sufferers. The disease had affected his ribs and spine, and possibly the lower legs as well. Destruction of one the vertebral bodies resulted in its collapse and most probably a bending deformity of the spine. As well as a crouched appearance, this man would have probably had a persistent cough and suffered weight loss. Possibly he also had difficulty in walking. He is unlikely to have had the full physical capacity of other, healthier adult males, and the disease would have compromised his participation in those tasks that required walking far, or heavy lifting – in other words, herding, many of the routines of agricultural life, hunting, visits to neighbouring settlements, and many others. Largely, this man may have become restricted to sedentary activities and contact with people beyond the immediate settlement may have become difficult. Nevertheless, the fact that he survived his illness long enough for skeletal changes to manifest themselves shows that others, most likely co-residents or kin, took care of him.

The strontium isotope ratios from his first and third molars (M1, $^{87}Sr/^{86}Sr$ ratio=0.70950; M3, $^{87}Sr/^{86}Sr$ ratio=0.70925) suggest that he had lived locally all his life, falling within the average values for Nitra as a whole. While we cannot exclude the possibility that this individual did not move away from the Nitra area at some point during his life, it does seem certain that he was born and raised on loess soils and these average values place him firmly within the LBK community at Nitra. The $\delta^{15}N$ value (10.5‰) is also average for the Nitra community, while his carbon value ($\delta^{13}C=-19.8$‰) falls at the higher extremes of the population range, suggesting that he ate a diet sourced predominantly from the open landscapes that surrounded the settlement. So despite tuberculosis he was still consuming a diet similar to many of the active men buried at the cemetery.

On his death, he was placed in an extremely crouched position on his left side; deviating slightly from the dominant orientation of SE–NW, he was oriented more S–N, with his head to the south. The grave was dug amongst the central cluster of burials and, as his grave included pottery with early Želiezovce decoration, many of the burials around him may have already taken place by the time he was buried – his death is likely to have taken place after the neighbouring burial 25, also of an adult man. We can speculate that this burial position marked a relationship of some form between the two men. Like the man in burial 34, this neighbour was buried with a polished stone adze, a pottery vessel and an item of Spondylus.

In spite of his illness, then, the man in burial 34 was not marked out in death from others in the community. Quite to the contrary, he was given a recurrent token of male identity – a stone adze – although he may have struggled to carry out the full range of tasks associated with this object in the last years of his life. He was not excluded from access to exotic items often interpreted as of 'high status', although he could no longer easily have travelled to other communities to obtain them. Perhaps the giving of unshaped pieces could hint that this individual was now more engaged in making ornaments, rather than in passing them on himself. In his final years, this man's experience of life would have differed markedly from his earlier years, his activities would have reduced in number and his social network could have contracted to just immediate kin. However, in spite of these very different potentialities, he was laid to rest in accordance to what we would term a typical well furnished male grave at Nitra, and he blends perfectly with the majority of people in what may well have been the community of his birth. The broadly shared, gendered lifeway of a successful, locally grounded male life in this case took precedence over the realities of illness and loss of physical capacities.

5 Austria

Penny Bickle, R. Alexander Bentley, Christoph Blesl, Linda Fibiger, Julie Hamilton, Robert Hedges, Eva Lenneis, Christine Neugebauer-Maresch, Peter Stadler, Maria Teschler-Nicola, Barbara Tiefenböck and Alasdair Whittle

5.1 Introduction

In this chapter we move southwards from Moravia and Slovakia into Austria, rejoining the course of the Danube in the lowland areas of northern Austria. Here LBK settlements are found situated on loess soils around secondary water courses on either side of the Danube, avoiding the higher ground of the Alps to the south and most likely set in amongst patches of deciduous woodland (Kreuz *et al.* 2005; Sommerer 2005). Along the northern Austrian border, the crystalline (granite and gneiss) southern parts of the Bohemian Massif reach into Lower Austria from the north-west (Neugebauer 1993, 9; Havlíček *et al.* 1998, 53). South of the Danube, but north of the Alps, Molasse sediments are found on the Alpine foreland alongside a narrow band of sedimentary (Flysch) rocks (Neugebauer 1993, 11; Havlíček *et al.* 1998, 53), but LBK settlement concentrates on the loess soils of river terraces, which overlaid Pleistocene gravels (Händel *et al.* 2009).

The majority of LBK sites (Fig. 5.1) are found in the Burgenland and in Lower Austria (Niederösterreich), but there is also a smaller cluster of sites in Upper Austria (Oberösterreich; Lenneis 1982a; 1995; 2001; 2003; 2008). North of Vienna, sites cluster around the Kamp, Pulkau and Zaya rivers, as well as the Schmida and Göllers, while in the Burgenland (which is south of Vienna and the Danube) settlements have been found along the tributaries of the Leitha and Triesting (Lenneis 1995, 15, 25). Sites are also found south of the Danube, west of Vienna, situated in the vicinity of the Traisen and Pielach rivers (Lenneis 1995, 25; Pieler 2004; Masur 2009; Coolen 2012). In Upper Austria, far fewer clusters of settlements have been excavated, but there are hints of the earlier LBK phases at the sites of Leonding and Rutzing (Lenneis 1995; Grömer 2001; Gruber 2009, 134). Even during the later phases, LBK find-spots in Upper Austria appear to have continued their concentration in the Linzer Zentralraum (Gruber 2009, 134, 136). Further west of Linz there appears to be a small hiatus in LBK settlement, with the next cluster of sites falling in Lower Bavaria (Niederbayern; Chapter 6.1).

Two broad phases are identified for the LBK in Austria. The earliest, named *Vornotenkopf*, corresponds to phase I, known elsewhere in the LBK distribution as the *älteste* and *ältere* LBK (Ruttkay *et al.* 1976; Lenneis 1989; 1995; 2001; 2006; 2008; 2010b). The *jüngere* LBK is then known as the *Notenkopf* ('music note') after its characteristic ceramic style with impressed dots, located on and at the end of the lines. This ceramic style is regarded as the eastern counterpart to the Flomborn style, and, for the most part, LBK ceramic styles in Austria are oriented eastwards. Chronological development in Austria echoes that of Moravia (Chapter 4.4; Table 4.1), particularly in Lower Austria where the temporal schema is based on Tichý (1960; Lenneis 1995, 24). Recent excavations at the site of Brunn am Gebirge provide evidence that early Neolithic communities in Austria had a role to play in forming the LBK from its very beginning (Lenneis *et al.* 1996; Lenneis 2008; Mateiciucová 2002; Stadler 2005; Stadler and Kotova 2010), and the evidence for a violent episode at the Asparn an der Zaya enclosure suggests that they may have been equally as active in its end (Windl 1996; Teschler-Nicola *et al.* 1996; Farruggia 2002; Wild *et al.* 2004). Alongside contributing to how the LBK as a whole is characterised, recent publications of the excavations at Neckenmarkt, Burgenland (Lenneis and Lüning 2001), and at sites in the Horn basin (Pieler 2010; including the sites of Strögen: Lenneis and Lüning 2001; Rosenburg: Lenneis 2009; and Mold: Lenneis 2010a) provide insights into how some of the constituents of the micro-regional settlement clusters in Austria may have interacted.

5.2 History of research

The discovery and collection of LBK finds and sites first began early in the nineteenth century in Austria, when amateurs, mostly concerned with amassing collections of finds, took an interest in archaeology (Pieler 2010, 8). Academic archaeology similarly had an early start, with Moriz Hoernes (1852–1917) holding the first chair in Europe to be dedicated to prehistory, from 1899 in Vienna (Ruttner 2003, 11; Urban 2004, 37). With this position

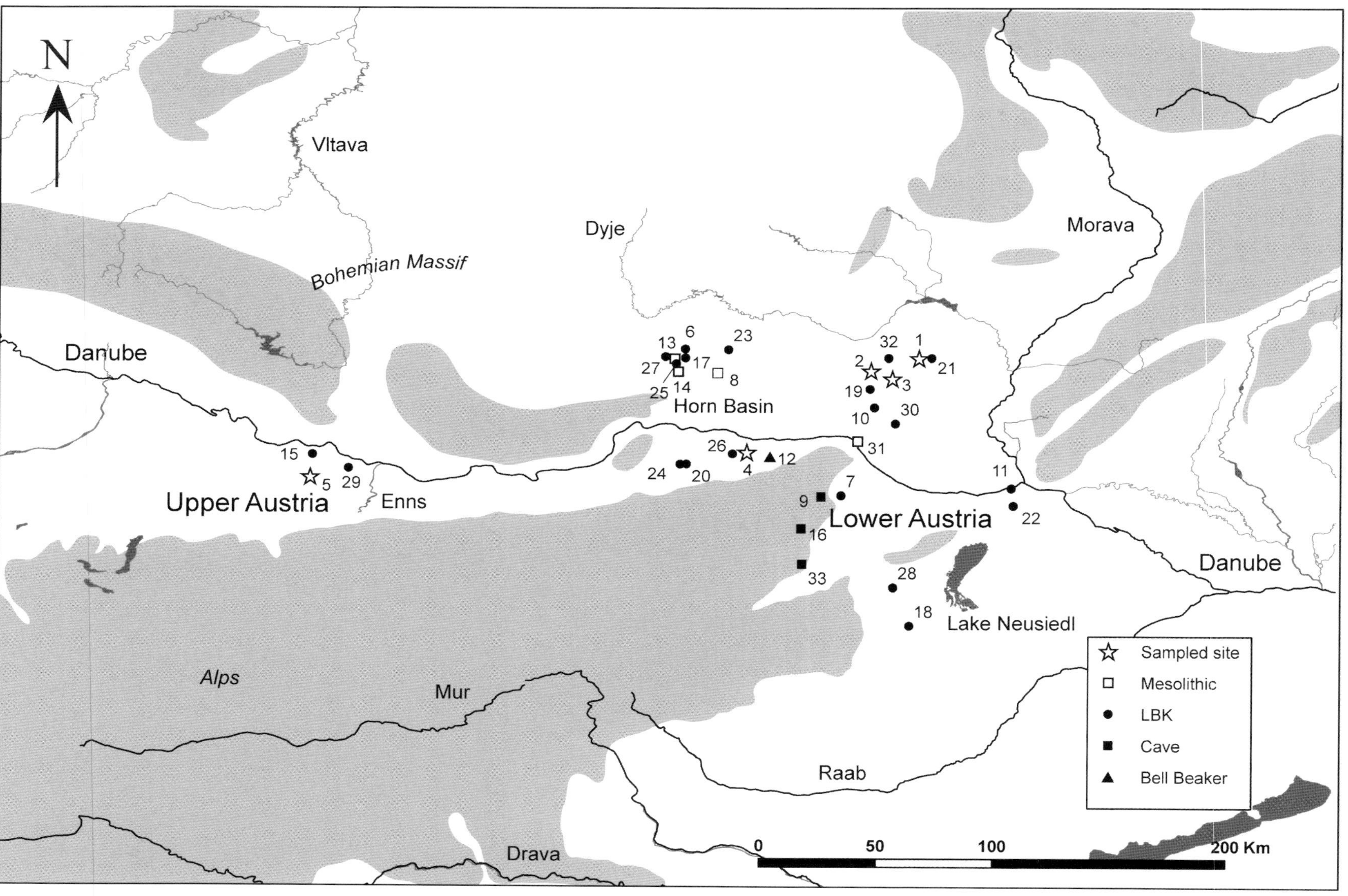

Fig. 5.1. Map of sites sampled (1–5) and others mentioned in Chapter 5. 1) Kleinhadersdorf, 2) Gnadendorf, 3) Asparn an der Zaya/Schletz, 4) Mitterndorf, 5) Rutzing/Haid, 6) Breiteneich, 7) Brunn am Gebirge, 8)Burgschleinitz, 9) Geoleshöhle, 10) Großrußbach-Weinsteig, 11) Hainburg-Teichtal, 12) Henzig, 13) Mühlfeld, 14) Kamegg, 15) Leonding, 16) Merkensteinerhöhle, 17) Mold, 18) Neckenmarkt, 19) Niederleis and Thomasl, 20) Pottenbrunn, 21) Poysdorf, 22) Prellenkirchen, 23) Pulkau, 24) Ratzersdorf, 25) Rosenburg, 26) Saladorf, 27) Strögen, 28) Taborac, 29) Tödling, 30) Ulrichskirchen, 31) Wien-Bisamberg, 32) Wultendorf, 33) Zigeunerhöhle auf der Malleiten.

the *Institut für Ur- und Frühgeschichte der Universität Wien* (1914) was also founded, which is where other early prehistorians such as Oswald Menghin and Richard Pittioni (1954, 2–3) would study and teach (Urban 1996, 4; Ruttner 2003, 11; Eibner 2006, 7). At a comparable time, the Natural History Museum in Vienna (*Naturhistorisches Museum Wien*) opened its doors (1889), and it was the director of its Anthropology department (*Anthropologische Abteilung*), Josef Bayer, who initiated rescue excavations at Kleinhadersdorf – the first Neolithic cemetery found in Austria (Bayer 1931; Lebzelter and Zimmermann 1936).[1] These developments occurred alongside the founding of numerous local or *Landesmuseen* and the continued committed work of amateurs (Pittioni 1954, 1).

Excavation and research were carried out before the Second World War, but developed more or less from chance finds and rescue excavations (Lenneis 1995, 24). In Austria, large-area excavations, which took place across Europe after 1945, focused primarily on later prehistoric periods, which left the LBK comparatively less well known (Lenneis 1995, 24). For example, the excavations which took place in the 1960s and 1970s on the Aldenhovener Platte and at Bylany remained without parallel in Austria for a long time. This did not, however, prevent debate about what role the Austrian LBK played in the development and spread of the LBK as a whole. As the hyper-diffusionist models for cultural change championed by Oswald Menghin (1931; Kohl and Pérez Gollán 2002, 562) gave way, Pittioni (1954) suggested that acculturation of the local Mesolithic populations helped to spread the LBK to Austria, though the presence of the earliest LBK was yet to be proved in Austria at this time (Pittioni 1954, 132). The vast majority of this research was, and to a certain extent remains, focused on Lower Austria, with the western half of the Danube valley in Austria attracting comparatively less interest (Gruber 2009, 133).

The 1960s brought Quitta's (1960) work on the earliest LBK, to which he attributed seven sites from Austria (Berg 1961/1965), though the chronology continued to be based on comparison to other regions, primarily that developed by Tichý (1960) for Moravia. Three phases of the LBK (*älteste, jüngere* and *jüngste*) were envisaged, developing in parallel with those that were later suggested by Meier-Arendt (1966) for the western distribution of the LBK and by Pavúk (1969) for western Slovakia and its surroundings. The chronology continues to be largely based on Moravian sequences (e.g. R. Tichý 1960; Table 4.1), but the appropriateness of this was confirmed by Eva Lenneis' (1977) doctoral thesis as well as by subsequent investigations (Pieler 2004; 2010).

The late 1970s marked the beginning of the first truly systematic research into the LBK in Austria (Pieler 2010, 5). Renewed interest in the earliest phases was ignited by Elisabeth Ruttkay's excavations at Prellenkirchen in the early 1970s (Ruttkay *et al.* 1976; Lenneis 2006) and continued into the 1980s (1983–7) by the *Ausgrabungen zum Beginn des Neolithikums in Mitteleuropa* project of Jens Lüning and Eva Lenneis (Lenneis 1989; Lenneis and Lüning 2001). At a similar time, the *Notenkopf* phase was also increasingly better understood, with the first complete *Notenkopf* house plans to be excavated in Austria found at the well known enclosure site of Asparn an der Zaya/Schletz (Windl 1983; 2005; Lenneis 1991; 1995, 28).

So, over the last 30 years rescue excavations have been complemented by a growing number of research projects targeting specific problems, such as the beginning of the LBK and the character of the *Vornotenkopf* phase. Most recently in Upper Austria, a settlement with a minimum of 11 longhouses, surrounded to the north and west by ditches, came to light in 2001 at Tödling near St. Florian (Gruber 2009, 135), while some of the seven areas of settlements at Brunn am Gebirge, Vienna (excavated 1989–2005), appear to be providing answers to long-asked questions about the very beginnings of the LBK (Stadler 2005; Stadler and Kotova 2010). Most recently the publication of a number of sites from the micro-region of the Horn basin, Lower Austria (Lenneis 2009a; 2010a), a doctoral survey of the area (Pieler 2010) and a geophysical survey[2] have delivered a detailed understanding of possible inter-settlement networks, but whether this model is applicable elsewhere in Austria remains a question for future research. An intensive microregional study in the district of Melk, south of the Danube, produced another settlement network applying new methods and models for reconstruction (Coolen 2012). The results seem to reflect stark differences in site density, even between neighbouring valleys (Coolen 2012, 119), suggesting varying systems in the two regions.

5.3 *The arrival of the LBK:* Vornotenkopf *and the earliest Linearbandkeramik*

5.3.1 The late Mesolithic

The Mesolithic which precedes the LBK in Austria is poorly known, with the majority of sites identified only from flint scatters (Leitner 1984; Antl-Weiser 1993; Lenneis 2001; Eichmann 2004; Mateiciucová 2008a; Svoboda 2008). Leitner (1984) listed 18 Mesolithic sites for the whole of Austria, some of which appear never to have been published, while Antl-Weiser (1993) specified no more than ten. These sites are situated in high-altitude rock shelters and caves (Svoboda 2008, 232) and along water courses, clustered around the river Kamp and south of Eggenburg, in Lower Austria, favouring sandy soils (Mateiciucová 2008a, 41). The only site from this lowland region which has been partly excavated is the site of Kamegg (Kamptal), which seems most likely to date to the earlier Mesolithic (Berg and Gulder 1956; Antl-Weiser 1986; Mateiciucová and Trnka 2004; Mateiciucová 2008a). Possible late Mesolithic assemblages have been identified at Mühlfeld and Burgschleinitz (both Waldviertel), as well as north of the Danube in the Weinviertel at Wien-Bisamberg, a mountain close to Vienna (Kmoch 1966; Mateiciucová 2008a, 22). These produced fairly mixed assemblages in terms of the chronological attribution of the tools and production techniques (Mateiciucová 2008a, 41).

After the discovery of the Iceman on the Schnalstal glacier (South Tyrol, northern Italy) a few metres from the Austrian border, intensive field surveys were conducted in the Alpine regions of Austria, which have added a few more Mesolithic sites to the inventory (Lenneis 2001, 99) and led to two pollen cores being taken in northern Tyrol (at Katzenloch, Seefeld, and Kirchbichl, Wörgl: Kohler-Schneider 2007, 209). The pollen cores have been taken to suggest evidence for the presence of cereals in the seventh millennium cal BC (Kohler-Schneider 2007), but whether this really indicates early cereal agriculture is much more problematic (Behre 2007a; see longer discussion in Chapter 7.3). The Alpine Mesolithic sites identified by these surveys are situated at high altitudes and are therefore likely to have been reachable only during the summer months, suggesting seasonal exploitation of upland resources (D. Schäfer *et al.* 1998; D. Schäfer 1999; Leitner 2004; Laus 2009).

The rock shelter of Zigeunerhöhle (Elsbethen near Salzburg), which dates to the second half of the Mesolithic in Austria,[3] contained a burial of a two- to three-year-old child, placed in a sitting position and facing south (Rettenbacher and Tichý 1994). Once the pit had been refilled, a charcoal layer indicates that a fire had been lit directly over the burial (Rettenbacher and Tichý 1994). The geographical location of this site would seem to suggest closer links with southern Germany (Orschiedt 1998b; Svoboda 2008, 235), while sites in the Waldviertel seem to have much in common with Mesolithic sites in Moravia, a connection which continues into the LBK (see below; Lenneis 1995; Mateiciucová 2008a, 38). As the majority of sites are known from flint scatters, finds such as Zigeunerhöhle remain rare and our understanding of the Mesolithic background must necessarily rely on what information can be gleaned from the lithic assemblages.

The raw materials used to produce lithic tools do not appear to have been transported any great distance during the Mesolithic; rather there appears to be a preference for local and regional cherts and radiolarites (Mateiciucová 2008a, 57, 140). Krumlovský Les chert appears to be the furthest travelled rock type in this region during the Mesolithic and reached the site of Bisamberg, 75 km from its source in south-western Moravia (Mateiciucová 2008a, 57; cf. Bánffy 2004, 379). A preference for local sources occurs alongside a high variety in the types of material used for the production of chipped tools (Mateiciucová 2008a, 140–1). This suggests that Mesolithic hunter-gatherers were using whatever stone was available or to hand in the course of a varied and mobile lifestyle, rather than employing specific sourcing strategies.[4] Elsewhere in Europe, this pattern changes during the Terminal Mesolithic, when higher-quality materials were selected for the production of regular blades and some raw materials began to travel much further (Kind 1992; Tillmann 1993; Gronenborn 1999; Mateiciucová 2001; 2008a). For Inna Mateiciucová (2001; 2008a) these changes laid the groundwork for the expansion of the LBK in this region of Europe, but, with few sites dated securely to this period, the character of the Austrian Terminal Mesolithic remains uncertain.

5.3.2 The earliest LBK

Early LBK sites in Austria favoured loess soils along secondary water courses, avoiding the floodplains of major rivers such as the Danube (Lenneis 1982a; 1982b; 1995; 2001; 2008, 164). This preference for high-quality soils continued throughout the LBK (Lenneis 2008, 165).[5] Other environmental considerations also appear to have influenced the locations settled by early LBK communities. From the *älteste* LBK, Austrian sites were situated in zones that today have no more than 900 mm average rainfall (Lenneis 1982a, 10; 1995, 14; 2001; 2008, 165). Regions with higher temperatures (over 9ºC) were favoured only during the earlier LBK in Austria, with a preference for slightly cooler temperatures increasing alongside the numbers of sites situated in drier zones throughout the whole of the LBK (based on modern climate data; Lenneis 2003, 282, fig. 2; 2008, 165, 176).

In contrast to the limited number of Mesolithic sites, the earliest LBK in Austria is well represented, with 80 sites or find-spots now known (Lenneis 2003, 288–9). The sites appear to cluster in Lower Austria and Burgenland, with only two sites (Leonding: Grömer 2001, and Rutzing: Lenneis 1989) known in Upper Austria. Our knowledge of these sites is thanks in large part to the *Ausgrabungen zum Beginn des Neolithikums in Mitteleuropa* project (1983–1987), for which Eva Lenneis summed up the state of knowledge (Lenneis 1989) and directed the Austrian excavations together with Jens Lüning. Prior to this project, Quitta (1960, 153) had noted the presence of a mere seven sites, as at this time early pottery was known only from surface collections and at sites with later *Notenkopf* ware as well (Lenneis 2006, 13). When Elisabeth Ruttkay (Ruttkay *et al.* 1976, 849) coined the term *Vornotenkopfkeramik* for the oldest LBK in Austria in 1976, only 19 sites were known. Her recognition of this early phase was based on excavations at the site of Prellenkirchen, situated south of the Danube on the Leitha River, where the pottery was characterised by its simple linear decoration and was tempered with plant matter (Ruttkay *et al.* 1976; Lenneis 2006, 13).

Ruttkay *et al.* (1976, 849–51, our translation) commented on the 'unequivocal analogies' that could be drawn between the early LBK pottery found at Prellenkirchen and that present on sites to the west (in Württemberg, Hessen and Moravia) and east (Slovakia and west Hungary), but the relationships between the oldest LBK in Austria and beginnings of the LBK in Moravia, Slovakia and Hungary were still not certain (Lenneis 1995; 2001; 2006, 15; Lenneis and Lüning 2001). At this time the cemetery and settlement at Rutzing had only recently been excavated (Kloiber and Kneidinger 1968; Kloiber *et al.* 1971). Since then, Neckenmarkt was fully excavated and has now reached publication, alongside Strögen (Lenneis and Lüning 2001). To this notable record of detailed publication, the early LBK sites of Rosenburg (Lenneis 2009) and Mold (Lenneis 2010a) can now be added as well. Strögen, Rosenburg and Mold are situated north of the Danube, in the Waldviertel of Lower Austria, within a cluster of sites which continue in occupation in the later

LBK phases (found in the Horn basin: Pieler 2006; 2010), while Neckenmarkt falls in central Burgenland, close to the Hungarian border (Fig. 5.1). Together these sites provide significant insights into the character of earliest LBK lifeways in Austria.

Eva Lenneis (1990; 1995, 14; 2001; 2008, 164; Lenneis and Lüning 2001, 9) distinguishes the *ältere* from the *älteste* LBK, arguing for an initial phase (*Anfangsphase*) when the LBK emerged from a Starčevo basis (Lenneis 2010b; *contra* Pavúk 1980a). The reason for this is the discovery of the Brunn am Gebirge complex, a multi-phase settlement south of Vienna. Sites IIa and IIb of Brunn produced some of the earliest radiocarbon dates for the LBK in Austria (estimated time span of 5540–5280 cal BC, but see below; Stadler 2005, 270), followed by Strögen (estimated time span of 5500/5450–5300/5250 cal BC; Lenneis and Lüning 2001, 188–9) and Neckenmarkt (estimated time span of 5380–5200 cal BC; Lenneis and Stadler 2001, 200; Lenneis and Lüning 2001, 190), the last two probably sharing the same time range. The end of the *ältere* LBK can be estimated by the dates from Rosenburg (estimated time span of 5350–5200/5150 cal BC; Lenneis 2009, 92) and the dates from Mold (estimated time span of 5300–5040 cal BC; Stadler 2010, 28 Tab. 2). The special character of the pottery of these settlements led to the definition of the *Übergangsphase* LBK I/II (a transitional phase LBK I/II; Kowarik 2010; Lenneis 2010b). While at Rosenburg the youngest dates indicate the beginning of phase IIa of the Moravian chronology, which also means the beginning of *Notenkopf* decoration, the Mold sequence ends in the fully developed phase II (IIb).

Alongside the early radiocarbon dates, Brunn am Gebirge has also produced pottery, which in the opinion of the excavator Peter Stadler and of Eva Lenneis is very similar to that found in Hungary west of Lake Balaton (Lenneis and Lüning 2001, 7; Lenneis 2010b). In the oldest parts of this site (Brunn IIa) vessels are not made in a truly LBK style, crucially missing typical LBK decoration (Stadler 2005, 270; Stadler and Kotova 2010a, 330). Stadler (2005, 270; Stadler and Kotova 2010a, 330; Stadler and Kotova 2010b) describes this pottery as fired at low temperatures with no decoration except for plastic ornamentation, which he argues has much in common with the late Starčevo culture in southern Hungary (see also Lenneis 2001, 105). Recently, such demonstrable connections to the south-east have been supplemented by the presence at Brunn IIa of pottery in a style of Starčevo ware found in Croatia (Stadler and Kotova 2010a, 345). These Starčevo connections are seemingly complemented by very early radiocarbon dates (5650–5600 cal BC; Lenneis and Stadler 2002; Stadler 2005; Stadler and Kotova 2010a, 326; supported by Gronenborn 1999, 155), suggesting contemporaneity between the final phases of the Starčevo culture and the beginning of the LBK (Bánffy 2004, 265). In this model of the earliest origins of the LBK, the settlement at Brunn IIa perhaps represents a long-range movement or colonisation by Starčevo communities (Stadler and Kotova 2010a; 2010b).

This need not mean that the LBK originated solely in the Starčevo culture and there are reasons to be very cautious in accepting these early dates. In the absence of animal bone, the dates from Brunn were produced on charcoal from oak wood and can only be accepted as *termini post quos* (Stadler and Kotova 2010a, 331). Furthermore, the model cannot currently account for chronological overlap between the settlements, which must surely be very likely. Finally, the relationship between the pit dated and the actual house (as representing a period of site occupation) is a recurrent problem across the LBK. The earliest houses in Austria (from Brunn IIa, Strögen and possibly Rosenburg) have much in common with the earliest houses identified at Bruchenbrücken (Wetteraukreis: Stäuble 1997) and Schwanfeld (Bavaria: Gronenborn 1997b). These houses had parallel internal rows of three posts, flanked on either side by linear ditches, the so-called *Mohelnice* style (Lichardus-Itten and Lichardus 2004; Stäuble 1994; 2005; Lenneis 2004a), but not the tripartite arrangements of posts seen in later houses (Cladders and Stäuble 2003). This style of architecture had no parallels in contemporary cultures (such as the Starčevo-Körös-Criş complex and the earliest Vinča), which leads Lenneis (1997; 2004a; 2004b; 2008) to argue strongly for an indigenous origin for the LBK. The poor preservation of houses currently hinders further analysis (Stäuble 2005).

Some of the long trapezes found at Brunn IIa made from Szentgál radiolarite had much in common with examples from the late Mesolithic site of Kaposhomok (*c*. 50 km south of Lake Balaton, Hungary: Mateiciucová 2003; 2008a, 75). Furthermore, Mateiciucová (2003; 2008a, 94, 159) found 'segments' of the type known at late Mesolithic sites in northern Hungary, south-west Slovakia and southern Moravia, in the assemblages at Brunn IIa and Neckenmarkt. This type of tool is also made from Szentgál radiolarite, which is sourced from the Bákony Mountains, not far north of Lake Balaton, northern Hungary (Mateiciucová 2003; 2008a, map 5; Chapter 3.1). The model of an indigenous contribution to the development of the LBK in parts of Austria is supported by Mateiciucová (2008a, 158), who argues on the basis of Mesolithic-Neolithic lithic assemblage continuities that 'the LBK originated autochthonously' (see also Chapters 3.3 and 4.3).

The animal bone assemblages from the earliest Austrian LBK show interesting regional variability, as well as distinct differences to those from later LBK contexts (Pucher 1987; 2001). Although the animal bone is poorly preserved, Kunst (2001) cautiously suggests that domestic and wild animals made up equal parts of the animal bone assemblage at Leonding, Upper Austria, thus demonstrating a similar proportion to those found at other *ältere* and (mostly) *älteste* LBK sites in Bavaria (Chapter 6.4). In Lower Austria, at Strögen and Neckenmarkt,[6] wild animals have no great significance, but the relative importance of sheep/goats is considerably higher than in later LBK contexts (Pucher 1987; 2001, 267). At Strögen, sheep/goats (*c*. 70% of the assemblage) are the dominant animal and there is no evidence for domesticated cattle, while at

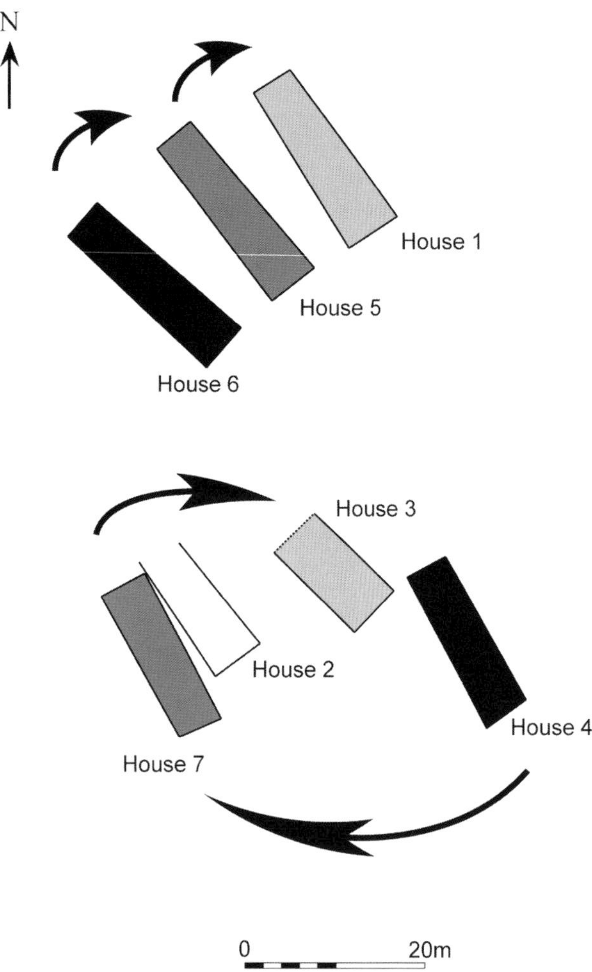

Fig. 5.2. Neckenmarkt, Lower Austria: sequence of construction. After Lenneis (2004a, 155).

Neckenmarkt cattle represent approximately 30% of the total assemblage, but still come second to sheep/goats, which account for about 40% of the identifiable animal bone assemblage (Pucher 1987; 2001, 267). Similar rates of sheep/goat prevalence are also seen at other early LBK sites in Lower Austria, which Pucher (2001, 269) attributes to the influence of the Starčevo-Körös cultures, which had higher rates of sheep/goats than cattle.

At the *ältere* LBK site of Brunn IIb, cattle represented nearly 25% of the identifiable animal bone (Pucher 2001, 267). The earlier LBK thus saw variability in the animal favoured at a particular site, which may imply diverse animal husbandry practices. Cattle and domestic pig are thought to be far more suitable than sheep/goats to the environment in which LBK communities lived and, from the end of the earlier LBK in Austria, cattle became the dominant species in the animal bone assemblages, as they do across the LBK (Uerpmann and Uerpmann 1997; Pucher 2001). Thus variability in early animal bone assemblages gives way to more uniform dominance by cattle at the point in time when more regional variability is demonstrable in the ceramic and burial record (see also Chapter 8.4).

Variability in the earlier LBK in Austria has also been demonstrated in the patterns of settlement. Although early LBK sites clustered together in loose groups or *Siedlungsverbände*, spread out along river valleys (Bánffy 2000; 2004, 33), the organisation of the settlements appears to change through time (Lenneis 2008). At Neckenmarkt, houses were found in two rows (Lenneis and Lüning 2001). In the northernmost group of houses, construction moved successively from south-west to north-east (with the latest house built in the north-east; Lenneis and Lüning 2001; Lenneis 2004a; 2008, 168).[7] This pattern was not repeated in the southern row of houses, where the sequence of building jumped from west to east and then back into the centre (Fig. 5.2; Lenneis and Lüning 2001; Lenneis 2004a; 2008, 168). This second pattern of building, in which the houses were spaced further apart, is found more frequently throughout the distribution of the early LBK (Lenneis 2008, 170). Lenneis (2008, 173) argues that from the earliest LBK 'two different patterns of settlement organisation existed side-by-side, often on the same site'.

Contrasting views of the earliest LBK in Austria are thus developing, with diversity, continuity, migration and innovation all potentially visible in the evidence. Austrian researchers largely regard the LBK in Austria as primarily an indigenous culture, but one inspired by contacts with farming communities to the south and east. However, the characteristics of these contacts remain uncertain and the evidence is not uniform across Lower Austria (Mateiciucová 2003, 100; 2008a, 160). In the absence of further evidence, marriage alliances and lithic-exchange networks remain the favoured conduits along which information could have travelled (Whittle 1996; Mateiciucová 2003; 2008a), but the degree of admixture between incomers and indigenous groups remains open to question. With a relatively uncertain Mesolithic background to the first LBK sites, it remains to be seen whether the identified variability had its origins in previous indigenous differences or in the blending of local Mesolithic practices with the influences of farming cultures around them. Conversely, such a strong emphasis on an indigenous contribution to the LBK is at odds with recent aDNA studies which suggest a strong genetic input from the Near East and the Balkans (Haak *et al*. 2010; cf. Haak *et al*. 2005; Bramanti *et al*. 2009). As we discussed in Chapter 1, aDNA is certainly proving a productive avenue of research, but the degree of admixture between local hunter-gatherers and incoming farmers and the nature of their contact remain essential research questions for the future.

5.4 The developed and late LBK

At a date informally estimated as 5300–5200 cal BC (Lenneis *et al*. 1996), the character of the LBK in Austria changed. As in other regions, the developed phase of the LBK is characterised by an increase in the number of sites and the eventual emergence of regional sub-groupings from a previously more uniform material culture (Lenneis 1995, 24–6; but see also Lenneis 2004a; 2004b). Lenneis (1995, 25) noted that some 15 years ago there were 280 find-spots, which is more than three times the number of sites known for the early LBK, and this number has expanded since. Known as the *jüngere* LBK in this region, the phase is named for its ceramic style, with *Notenkopf* decoration. The most frequent ceramic form becomes the *Kumpf*, a bowl-shaped pot (Lenneis 1995). Although during the *Notenkopf* phase the number of settlements increased, 64% of sites were still located on loess soils,[8] a higher percentage than in Hungary (40–50%) or Bohemia (*c.* 50%), but fewer than in Slovakia (88%) and on the lower Rhine (99%; Lenneis 1982a, 7).

Despite the presence of loess soils along the course of the Danube as it crosses Austria, the gap between the small cluster of sites around Linz and the more densely occupied areas of Lower Austria remains. In the western half of this gap, the absence of LBK sites might be explained by the focus of modern development, but the eastern part seems not to fulfil the climatic conditions required by LBK communities, with an annual rainfall rate today above 900 mm (Lenneis 2003, fig. 2). However, during this phase sites also began to be found across a wider range of environmental conditions, including further away from water sources and at a wider range of heights (Lenneis 1977; 1982a; 1982b; 1995; Pieler 2010). Further west a possible overlap between *älteste* and *jüngere* LBK phases has been interpreted as possible evidence for an influx of new population (Cladders and Stäuble 2003). Where Austrian LBK settlements have been studied in detail, little hiatus or re-organisation is suggested between the two phases, though changes do occur. For instance, in the well studied micro-region of the Horn basin, Pieler (2010, 252) identifies a trend from a smaller number of slightly larger sites to more frequent but significantly smaller settlements.

In the late *jüngere* phase of the LBK, further sub-groups are identified in the ceramics. Lower Austria continues its strong connections to Moravia (Šárka-style pottery; Čižmář 1998a) and to Slovakia and western Hungary (Zseliz or Želiezovce groups and Keszthely group)[9] (Lenneis 1995, 26–7; see also Chapter 4.4), but the sites around Linz, in Upper Austria, begin to demonstrate ceramic affiliations to Bavarian styles (Lenneis 1995, 26; Grömer 2001; Gruber 2009; Chapter 6.5). The Šárka style found in Austria (both Upper and Lower) is most closely related to the Moravian form, rather than demonstrating characteristics of the repertoire in Bohemia (Lenneis 1977; Gruber 2009). The most typical Šárka decoration is the *Hühnerleitermotiv*, a fine incised line densely crossed by short cutmarks, but decoration made by single impressions in lines is also common, and the main ceramic form is a slightly pear-like vessel (Lenneis 1977). At Rutzing, two motifs found in Lower Bavaria are present: incised lines paired with rows of small depressions (*Grübchenreihen*) not related to the main linear bands, and rectilinear and curvilinear bands interrupted by a secondary motif of small vertical lines (Lenneis 1995, 26). This picture of different pot decoration also includes the presence of the eastern and southern Hungarian styles of Bükk and Szakálhát in Lower Austria, possibly representing imports (Lenneis 1995, 26).

This mosaic of ceramic styles, apparently concentrated in particular locations but also found outside their immediate centres, presents a complex picture of exchange, mobility and affiliation. This increasing regionalisation, however, is not matched by a reduction in the movement of certain materials. Indeed, both Pittioni (1980) and Lenneis (1995, 26) have argued that the appearance of Želiezovce or Bükk ceramics in Austria may be in some way related to the circulation of *Spondylus* and obsidian (Chapter 3.5; Harrer and Lenneis 2001). This period also sees the beginning of the large flat cemeteries across the LBK and in Austria the cemeteries of Kleinhadersdorf, Mitterndorf and Rutzing begin about this time. The largest and earliest cemetery in Austria remains Kleinhadersdorf with 57 inhumations and some indication of cremations, though it appears to have suffered serious erosion and the original number of graves is likely to have been higher, possibly as many as around 200 in total (Bayer 1931; Neugebauer-Maresch 1992; Neugebauer-Maresch and Lenneis forthcoming).

5.4.1 Settlement networks

Variation in the different strategies which communities at particular settlements were pursuing may have also reached back into the *älteste* phase of the LBK in Austria, and the large settlement cluster of the Horner Becken (Horn basin) includes sites of a range of sizes which suggests that variability was an inherent part of the LBK from the beginning (Fig. 5.3). This group of sites began during the *ältere* LBK and then continued to be occupied into the *Notenkopf* phase (Stadler and Lenneis 2009; Pieler 2010). In this micro-region 22 *ältere* LBK settlements have been found in an area that stretches over 100 km^2 (Lenneis *et al.* 2010, 81). The site of Mold began during the transitional Phase I/II (Kowarik 2010; Lenneis 2010b), and is described by Lenneis (2009, 181–2, fig. 71; Lenneis *et al.* 2010; Pieler 2010) as a *Sekundärplatz* (secondary place) in relation to the possible central place at Breiteneich. The latter site has yet to be excavated, but a geomagnetic survey showed it had at least 40 houses and probably lasted throughout the LBK, until the late *Notenkopf* phase. If the estimated size of this site is correct, Breiteneich grew to 8 ha, four

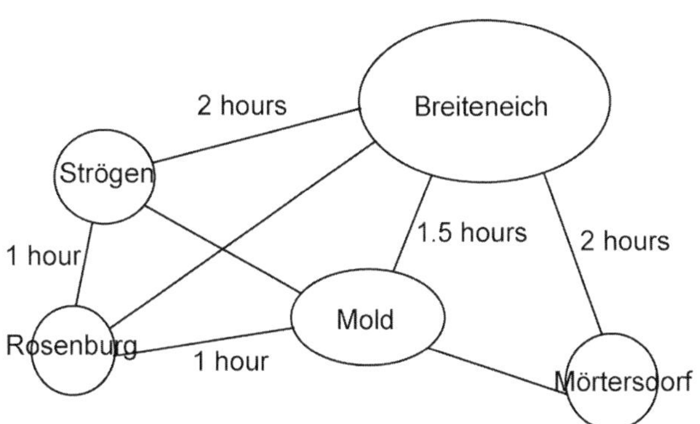

Fig. 5.3. Horn basin settlement network, Lower Austria. After Lenneis (2009, 182).

times larger than the second largest site (Pieler 2010, 252). These sites fall within an easy day's walk (Lenneis 2009; Lenneis *et al*. 2010; Pieler 2010) and suggest some interesting possibilities for discussing the variability in LBK lifeways.

Lenneis (2001; 2004b; 2009) has identified significant differences between the settlements. The large type 1 houses (as defined by Modderman 1988) are missing at the site of Rosenburg, but are present at the neighbouring sites of Strögen[10] and Mold (Lenneis 2009, 181), with more variation in house size at Mold (Coolen 2004; Lenneis 2010a). These two sites had significantly higher cereal remains and stone tools associated with cereal processing, such as sickle blades, flints with sickle gloss and fragments of quernstone, which were almost completely missing at Rosenburg (Lenneis 2009, 183).[11] The absence of sickle blades at an early LBK site is not unusual as it appears that this harvesting technique was only really exploited during the later phases (from the *Notenkopf*; Kohler-Schneider 2007; Kreuz 2007). As Lenneis (2009, 183) points out, the single fragment of quernstone probably suggests that some cereal processing did take place at Rosenburg, but that it was not a priority for the community at this settlement.

Despite this, the cereal and plant remains from Rosenburg suggested differences between individual houses, with concentrations falling around houses 2 and 3 (Brinkkemper 2009, 156–7). An area of pits to the north-west of the main settlement area had the highest number of cereal grains and hazelnut shells, which, as Brinkkemper (2009, 157) argues, suggests that this area was dedicated to specific activities. At Mold, while no direct link between house size and the concentration of finds in the pits could be discerned, agricultural production did appear to be concentrated at the largest houses (*Großbauten* 1 and 13, as well as the smallest house 11)[12] and the densities of various tools and pottery varied between contemporary houses (Lenneis 2010a, 336).

As noted above, the percentage of cattle in the animal bone assemblages rises in the *Notenkopf* phase, but some variation is maintained with settlements such as Brunn I and III, Gnadendorf and Ratzersdorf having rates that varied between 40% and 70% (Pucher 1987; 2001; Schmitzberger 2009a, 119). At Mold, cattle remains occur at a rate of 65.2% for the settlement as a whole, although in the loam pits of houses from the later phases at the settlement (*Notenkopf*) this rate reaches above 80% (Schmitzberger 2010, 250; Lenneis 2010a, 330). A contrast to this general picture is provided by the animal bone assemblage at Rosenburg, which showed distinct practices compared to other settlements, although the assemblage is very small (Schmitzberger 2009a, 111). Schmitzberger (2009a, 116–17) identified a higher presence of wild animals amongst the remains than at other sites in the vicinity (between 25% and 37%) with the remains of ten different species represented. As a result of a comprehensive sampling and sieving strategy, this site also produced rare evidence for the consumption of fish, with the remains of two different species (Galik 2009).

Rosenburg, as with other sites beginning during the later phases of the earliest LBK, has a high proportion of sheep/goats in the animal bone assemblage (Pucher 1987; 2001; Schmitzberger 2009a; 2009b). Within Rosenburg itself, however, the finds appear equally distributed between the houses (Stadler and Lenneis 2009, 177–8). Lenneis (2009, 185–6) suggests that Rosenburg found its place in the broader settlement network by specialising in hunting, collecting pelts and fishing, while people at sites such as Mold concentrated on production from farming activities. This is seemingly confirmed by the molluscan analysis, which suggests that while Rosenburg was surrounded by forest, Mold was set in a more open landscape (Frank 2009, 147). It is interesting to reflect that if a site such as Rosenburg were to be found in Upper Austria, the high proportion of wild animals *might* be explained as showing ties to Bavaria and the southern German LBK, rather than how it found its place in a broader settlement network.

Franz Pieler (2010, 240) argues that the Horner Becken could well serve as a model for Lower Austria more widely, with central places (*Zentralplätze*), secondary settlements (*Sekundärsiedlungen*), special (or specialised) places (*Sonderplätze*) and single farmsteads (*Einzelhöfe*). However, as he also notes (Pieler 2010, 240–1), there are no clear defining rules for the different categories of settlements in such models of central places and satellite settlements, and variation is highly likely. Further differences in artefact distribution around houses were also identified between smaller and larger sites (Pieler 2010, 251); small sites had a dense central zone, which was surrounded by a zone of fewer finds, though flint dominated at the edges of the scatter. Larger sites tended to have concentrations at one end of the houses, suggesting that the increased numbers of neighbours may have impacted on the deposition patterns of other houses (Pieler 2010, 251). Questions therefore remain about the nature of this network and how this influenced individual and community lifeways. Were these separate groups or settlements choosing to do things differently? Or did they envisage themselves as contributing to a wider community, distributed across the landscape? To what extent did regional preferences and local variations influence the lifeways of these communities?

Areas of communal activity within LBK settlements have in many ways been neglected, with households envisaged as largely autonomous. However, shared foci are frequently visible, such as the well found at Asparn (Windl 1994). The wooden structure was built with the same technology as that at Erkelenz-Kückhoven, North Rhine-Westphalia (Windl 1994). At Asparn/Schletz 13 'dome-like' features, which are thought to be ovens, were also found (Petrasch 1986). Structures with traces of burning were also found at Rosenburg, with the destroyed remains of a fireplace found in pit 198 (a linear feature, close to building 4, which is unlikely to be a longhouse) and the *in situ* remains of fireplaces in pits 241 and 242, all three in close proximity (Lenneis 2009, 36). The four large settlement sites with enclosure ditches known in eastern Austria (Asparn an der Zaya, Großrußbach-

Weinsteig, Pulkau and Poysdorf), also provide a further variation in settlement networks to that recorded in the Horn basin (Pieler 2010, 241). The construction of the enclosures shows considerable variability and may have had a profound effect on the experience of community at different sites. While the enclosure at Asparn surrounds the settlement area, magnetic prospection of a LBK settlement located between Niederleis and Thomasl (Mistelbach) showed two well-spaced concentric ditches (*c.* 50 m apart in places), set to the north-west of the main, densely packed *Notenkopf* settlement (Fehlmann 2011). This site lies over 10 km from Asparn/Schletz, illustrating that diverse practices could be found quite close together. A far bigger enclosure lies at Weinsteig, Großrußbach, known from aerial photographs, geomagnetic prospection and limited excavation, and consists of a single ditch forming a rectangle (Doneus *et al.* 2001).

Further variety in the types of site found in Austria may be seen in the three cave sites that have produced LBK pottery: Merkensteinerhöhle near Gainfarn, Geoleshöhle near Kaltenleutgeben and Zigeunerhöhle auf der Malleiten near Bad Fischau (Lenneis 1982a; Lenneis 1995, 27). These sites were found in the early twentieth century and no plans of these sites exist. They are thought likely to represent seasonal camps for herdsmen or hunters (Neugebauer 1993, 36; Lenneis 1995, 27). Despite the lack of information, these cave sites remain a tantalising hint that more complex settlement patterns may have existed during the LBK than is often envisaged.

5.4.2 Regional networks in the developed LBK

The Horn Basin settlement cluster provides an image of the possible nature of LBK communities in Austria on a local level, but it formed part of a larger regional grouping. Primarily, LBK regions are defined by ceramic styles and although we should be cautious in mapping networks from them directly, they do give a useful indication of possible inter-regional connections (Lenneis 2000, 79). Represented most prominently in Lower Austria is Moravian Šárka-style pottery, and strong connections to this neighbouring region are envisaged (Lenneis 1995). Šárka decorated vessels are also found at sites south of the Danube (around the Traisen, Persching and Tulln rivers; Blesl 2005, 65) and at sites around Linz (Grömer 2001; Gruber 2009).

The small group of sites found in the Linzer Zentralraum numbers only nine (Gruber 2009, 134). Leonding and Rutzing both produced pottery of the *Vornotenkopf* style (Lenneis 1995; Grömer 2001; Gruber 2009). During the *jüngere* LBK, evidence of contact between Bohemia or Moravia and Upper Austria has also been found at Leonding and Haid in the form of Šárka-style pottery (Lenneis 1995, 26). This style, however, was found alongside sherds with designs characteristic of later Lower Bavarian LBK styles (Lenneis 1995, 26; Grömer 2001, 33; Gruber 2009, 134). Interestingly, an imported Alföld LBK pot was found at Leonding (Grömer 2001, 17), some 400 km from its source. Gruber (2009, 134, our translation) suggests that during the late *Notenkopf* phase this region was 'in the position of a border area between southern Germany, and eastern Austria and Moravia', influenced by the preferences and styles of both regions. Certainly, raw materials in the form of chert from Bavaria and Krumlovský Les chert from Moravia are both found in this region (Binsteiner and Ruprechtsberger 2008; Gruber 2009, 139). However, while such finds indicate varied ties running along the course of the Danube, links into Bohemia, excepting the presence of Šárka pottery, which is also known in this region, appear limited and further research is required.

Over the comparatively short duration of occupation at Mold, Lenneis (2010a) identifies an increase in imported materials. While in the earliest phases at this site raw materials for lithics were mainly sourced from the surrounding region (up to approximately 65–75 km away), the houses from the later phases used locally sourced material in limited amounts, preferring sources in southern Poland (over 300 km north) and western Hungary (230 km south-east; Mateiciucová 2010, 171, 178). However, in some of the *jüngere* LBK houses (15 and 16), southern Moravian (230 km north) sources retained an important role alongside Polish and Hungarian sources (Lenneis 2010a, 344). This follows the trends identified by Mateiciucová (2008a, 62), which see a reorientation of lithic materials during the middle LBK away from the south-east of Lower Austria and towards importing material from the north and north-east (Moravia, Bohemia and the Kraków area of Poland), requiring travel through the Moravian region discussed in the previous chapter. Axes and adzes, which are predominantly found in cemeteries, are made from serpentinite and amphibolite most likely sourced from the Bohemian Massif (Lenneis 1995, 40). Perhaps most surprisingly, the raw material of some quernstones found at Mold and Kleinhadersdorf came from central Bohemia.

Regional differences have also been identified in the prevalence of certain species of cereals (Chapter 1.3.3; Lenneis 2000, 78). While Šárka sites appear to have focused more on the cultivation of emmer and einkorn, the west Slovakian Želiezovce groups also grew oats, spelt and barley (Lüning 1988a, 84–5, footnote 52; Lenneis 2000, 78). Cultivation practices in Austria appear to follow the Moravian Šárka groups, with a dominance of einkorn, followed by emmer, with only rare instances of barley, pea and lentil (Kreuz *et al.* 2005). Einkorn, while not producing the highest yield, is more suited to heavy rainfall, which tallies with indications that central Europe was wetter during the Atlantic period (Kreuz 2007; Kreuz *et al.* 2005). In contrast to Bogaard's (2004) argument that LBK people practised autumn and spring sowing of cereals, Kreuz (2007, 274; Kreuz *et al.* 2005; Kohler-Schneider and Caneppele 2010) suggests that only summer cultivation with spring sowing was known in the Austrian LBK.

In the Austrian animal bone assemblages the dominance of sheep and goats in the earliest phases of the LBK gives way to cattle in the later phases (Schmitzberger 2009b). This shift in focus has been explained in terms of the increased suitability of cattle for the central European environment (Lüning 2000, 110–12). In comparison to the higher rates of wild animals found in southern German settlements, their prevalence only reaches about 10% for the Austrian region as a whole (Döhle 1993; Lüning 2000, 115). Although percentages of wild animals on individual sites can vary between 2% and 25%, between the *Vornotenkopf* and *Notenkopf* the rate of wild animals in assemblages drops (Schmitzberger 2009b, 26). The decreasing presence of wild animals has been interpreted by Uerpmann and Uerpmann (1997, 577) as representative of a reduced availability of wild species due to the removal of their habitat in the course of the agricultural activities pursued by LBK farmers.

The site of Rutzing is located at a higher elevation and has more rainfall on average over the year than sites in Lower Austria, which may account for some variation between this site and others in Lower Austria (Lenneis 1982a). Rutzing does have higher rates of wild animals (42%) than settlements in Lower Austria (Schmitzberger 2009b, 149). However, given that the numbers of wild animals in assemblages rise steeply in the middle Neolithic of Austria (reaching between 50% and 90%), the high proportion of wild animals at this site may be partly due to contamination from later periods. As Schmitzberger notes (2009b, 150, our translation), 'the stratigraphic separation of the cultural horizons (LBK or Münchshöfen), is not possible from the archaeological publications'. However, the elevated numbers of wild animals could show that, along with the pottery, Rutzing may have had similarities in practice to LBK settlements in Lower Bavaria. While regional differences have thus been identified across the LBK, whether these are due to variance in practice or responses to certain limits imposed by environmental conditions will continue to be debated.

5.5 Mortuary rites

Excluding the 67 known individuals found at the Asparn/Schletz enclosure[13] and the 18 skull caps from der Taborac near Draßburg (skull caps were also found at Hainburg-Teichtal and Asparn; Lenneis 1995, 34), we recorded 167 inhumations in Austria (Lifeways Database). Of these burials, 112 are from cemeteries (Rutzing, 24 graves; Mitterndorf, 24 graves; Kleinhadersdorf, 57 inhumations, with four cremations). The remaining burials were isolated finds or came from settlement contexts (*c.* 33% of the burials), which is a similar, but slightly higher rate, to Baden-Württemberg (Chapter 7) and Moravia and western Slovakia (Chapter 4). The vast majority of dateable burials are of the *jüngere* LBK phase (*Notenkopf* pottery), though as an inhumation of a child with *ältere* (*Vornotenkopf*-like) pottery was found at Wultendorf (Neugebauer-Maresch and Neydharth 1988, 220), other early burials are also likely – for example at Kleinhadersdorf (Chapter 5.6.1). During the excavations of the earlier LBK settlements at Brunn four inhumations came to light (Stadler and Kotova 2010), including an individual who was buried with seven trapezoidal arrowheads and seems likely to also date to the earlier LBK phases (Jeunesse 1997, 154). There may also be some early LBK burials associated with the settlement at Asparn (Windl 2002, 573). However, too few early LBK burials have been dated to permit the investigation of chronological changes.

Fig. 5.4. Brunn am Gebirge: anthropomorphic figurine. Photo: Alice Schuhmacher, Naturhistorisches Museum Wien.

Often seen as connected with burial practices, figurines have been suggested to be acting as *Substitutopfer* for the deceased (Kaufmann 1989, 128). Only found in fragments, parallels have been drawn between the disarticulation of the human skeleton and the breaking apart of the figurines (Kaufmann 1989). The earliest and most remarkable figurines are known from the early Brunn settlements (Hansen 2007, 293, fig. 178, Taf. 498; Stadler and Kotova 2010a, 320, fig.10; Fig. 5.4). During the *Notenkopf* phase in Austria, when cemetery burials develop, the numbers of figurines in the settlements decrease. Conversely, anthropomorphic and zoomorphic depictions and plastic additions on pots become more frequent, particularly towards the end of the *jüngere* LBK (Lenneis 1995, 43), though examples are known from the *Vornotenkopf* phase (such as the face on the pot sherd from Ulrichskirchen, Mistelbach; Maurer and Jama 2006, 19). These objects vary from clearly anthropomorphic (such as the female figurine formed from incised lines and plastic decoration on a sherd from der Taborac near Draßburg; Lenneis 1995, 43, fig. 17) to zoomorphic (Pieler 2006, 27–8).

Table 5.1. Austria: demography of burials at cemeteries and settlements (Lifeways Database).

	Males		Females		Adults		Children		Total (inc. unknowns)	
Cemeteries	31/101	31%	24/101	24%	69/101	68%	23/101	23%	112/167	66%
Settlements	5/55	9%	3/55	5%	10/55	18%	16/55	29%	55/167	33%
In total	36/167	22%	27/167	16%	79/167	47%	39/167	23%	167/167	100%

Table 5.2. Upper Austria: the body positions and orientations of burials (Lifeways Database).

Head direction	Left-crouched	Right-crouched	Total
E–W	2	2	4
SE–NW	0	1	1
S–N	1	2	3
SW–NE	0	1	1
W–E	0	0	0
NW–SE	1	0	1
N–S	1	1	2
NE–SW	1	3	4
Total	6	10	16

Table 5.3. Lower Austria: the body positions and orientations of burials (Lifeways Database).

Head direction	Left-crouched	Right-crouched	Crouched	Supine	Irregular	Prone	Total
E–W	15	0	2	0	1	0	18
SE–NW	17	1	0	0	0	0	18
S–N	3	0	0	0	0	0	3
SW–NE	1	1	0	0	0	0	2
W–E	5	2	0	0	0	0	7
NW–SE	8	1	0	0	0	0	9
N–S	2	2	1	0	0	0	5
NE–SW	2	2	1	0	0	0	5
Total	53	9	4	0	1	0	67

As elsewhere in the LBK distribution, the majority of cemetery sites seem to have begun during the *jüngere* LBK (*Notenkopf*) phase and continued into the later phases. However, about a century after Vedrovice in Moravia (Chapter 4.4), Kleinhadersdorf begins in the transitional phase LBK I/II, continues throughout phase II, and only ends in the final phases as evidenced by the presence of Šárka and Želiezovce pottery (Neugebauer-Maresch and Neugebauer 1987; 1990; Neugebauer-Maresch and Lenneis forthcoming). The occurrence of cremations at this cemetery, a practice which is thought to have developed later in the second phase of the LBK, also appears to confirm the longevity of this site (see also Chapter 4.5). The later phases of the *jüngere* period may also be represented by the remains at Asparn with Šárka and Želiezovce pottery (Windl 1996, 19–21, figs 6–7), further supported by radiocarbon dating (Wild *et al.* 2004, 382).

Taking into account the varied problems with using older osteological analyses (where the methodology is often unknown), we can examine some of the broader patterns of burial in Austria (summarised in Tables 5.1–3). Slightly more identified males were interred at cemeteries than women and children, who have a similar rate of occurrence. Overall, the main conclusion we can draw is that children are more likely to have received burial on settlements and adults at cemeteries, as is practised across the LBK. Here, as elsewhere, inhumations are generally placed in a pit, with left-crouched body position and orientations with the head to the east or south-east dominating. This direction of burial orientation (E–W through SE–NW) accounts for 43% of all burials, though the percentage drops slightly for settlement burials (38%; Lifeways Database). However, rather than all other orientations rising in representation, the difference can be accounted for by an increase of antipodal orientations (SW–NE represents 1.9% of cemetery burials and 8.7% of settlement burials). These differences are slight, but may hint at a broader significance. Left-crouched burials account for 64% of burials overall, but are more dominant on cemeteries (left-crouched: 73%; right-crouched: 27%). Amongst settlement burials front-crouched (7%) and irregular body positions (7%) also occur (Lifeways Database). Approximately 46% of burials are unfurnished, rising to 65% among settlement burials (Lifeways Database). This is a higher rate of unfurnished settlement burials than Alsace (50%; Chapter 8.5), but as with the frequency of different orientations and body positions, burial practices in Austria are generally in line with what is found across the LBK (Lifeways Database).

The range of grave goods in LBK burials in Austria encompasses the items found across the LBK, with some notable regional practices. However, once skeletons that cannot be sexed and aged are discarded, the numbers are too small to build up a statistically reliable picture for how grave goods varied over age and between the sexes for the region as a whole. Unsurprisingly, the only exception to this are polished stone tools, which are present in 46% of male (that is, osteologically sexed as male) burials, with the majority of these burials coming from the three cemeteries. However, as this represents just 21 burials, there is not a sufficient number to determine whether provision varies with age (though they appear to occur in roughly the same proportion across the adult age classes). It is a similar case with other grave goods, though pottery appears to be less frequent with children than with adults and, while *Spondylus* objects are found associated with burials across the ages and sexes, they tend to be found more on cemetery sites and with adults (Lifeways Database). In Austria the sprinkling or spreading of ochre over the head of the deceased is also attested (seen especially at Kleinhadersdorf: Neugebauer-Maresch and Neugebauer 1990, 182; Chapter 5.7.1). Regionally specific practices can also be identified. Like in most cemeteries from Bavaria eastwards (Austrian, Bavarian and Moravian burials, but excluding Nitra), shells of species living along smaller rivers were used (*Theodoxus danubialis* and *Lithoglyphus naticoides*), seemingly in place of the marine shells (from the west Mediterranean or Atlantic) found at cemeteries further west (Lenneis 2007, 135; 2010d). In a similar vein, use of animal teeth (or fox mandibles), as well as bone and antler toggles, as grave goods may also be limited to just this region and Bavaria (Jeunesse 1997; Lenneis 2007, 135).

There are some burial rites in Austria which do not follow the pattern of cemetery or settlement burials. The multiple skull caps found at three Austrian sites (Asparn, Taborac near Draßburg and Hainburg-Teichtal: Lenneis 1995, 34) are suggestive of secondary burial rites. At the site of Hainburg-Teichtal, an adult female had been decapitated and the skull cap deposited near the remains of the skull (Neugebauer 1981a; Lenneis 1995). Hence, this practice may have been an action performed on the body of the deceased in the context of funerary rites, rather than merely carried out to obtain a useful object. This burial was accompanied by an unusual grave good of a spoon-like, hollowed out animal bone (Neugebauer 1981a; Lenneis 1995).

The individuals from Asparn present yet further variability (Chapter 5.8). The 67 individuals studied from this famous enclosure site were found in unusual positions at the bottom of the ditch, prone, and occasionally with crossed limbs, and many were incomplete, missing distal skeletal elements, seemingly having died in the course of a violent attack (Chapter 5.8; Teschler-Nicola *et al.* 1996, 48; 1999, 483). As many remains showed distinct evidence of gnawing by carnivores, it appears that Asparn does not represent formal burial rites, but rather abandonment, with the deceased exposed for possibly as long as six months (Teschler-Nicola *et al.* 1999, 447). Parallels to the burial pit at the site of Talheim, Baden-Württemberg, have obviously been drawn, though at Asparn it seems that the site was abandoned and few attempts had been made to bury the dead (Windl 1996; Teschler-Nicola *et al.* 1996; 1999; Chapter 7.5 for a discussion of Talheim). Late radiocarbon dates from Asparn mean that the site has contributed to the growing debate around whether the LBK ended in crisis and the uniqueness of the burials here must be stressed. These individuals at Asparn received no recognisably formal funerary rites.

5.6 Sites sampled

For the Lifeways project the three cemetery sites known in Austria were sampled: Rutzing/Haid, Linz, Upper Austria; Mitterndorf, south of the Danube near St. Pölten; and Kleinhadersdorf, district of Mistelbach, Lower Austria. We were also fortunate to be able to sample the human remains from Asparn, Mistelbach, for carbon and nitrogen analysis. While animal samples were available to provide context for the human data from Rutzing, we had to look slightly further afield for appropriate samples in Lower Austria. The site at Gnadendorf, Mistelbach, provided an ideal selection of domesticated animals and is situated approximately 8 km to the north-east of Asparn, and some 10 km south-west of Kleinhadersdorf.

5.7 Kleinhadersdorf

5.7.1 Introduction (Christine Neugebauer-Maresch and Eva Lenneis)

The following text is based on the final report for the site (Neugebauer-Maresch and Lenneis forthcoming) according to the state of research in March 2012.

Location and excavation

Kleinhadersdorf is a small village at the western end of the town of Poysdorf in the north-east of Lower Austria, close to the Moravian border (Fig. 5.1). The immediate surroundings have very fertile soils, mainly on a loess base, which means the area has been intensively used for agriculture including vineyards. The site of the cemetery in the Marchleiten lies on a slope with decline from east-northeast to west-southwest and had been used as a vineyard in the twentieth century, subsequently becoming a field for crops. Damage to the graves was caused by posts in the vineyards, soil erosion and ploughing. Therefore the preservation of the cemetery is highly variable and it is unlikely that the whole area of the ancient cemetery has been investigated (Fig. 5.4). The lack of graves in the highest part of the cemetery, to the north-east and east, might be due to destruction by erosion together with agricultural use. Immediately south-east of the known cemetery area, many stray finds indicate a quite extended LBK settlement area which might be (partly) contemporary. Further LBK settlements are known within a distance of 2–5 km to the north and north-east (around Poysdorf), one of which has been partly excavated (Blesl and Neugebauer 1994).

Finds and even destroyed graves are known from this site in Marchleiten since 1911. In 1931 Josef Bayer carried out the first small rescue excavations of the cemetery at weekends and holy days. After his death, Lebzelter and Zimmermann (1936) excavated some more graves. While Bayer made quite good drawings and photos of the graves, the documentation by the other two is very poor and consists only of photographs and hardly any further information. Twenty-one graves were excavated at that time (G1a-c–G19), but the recording is such that we cannot identify the location of many of them precisely. We only were able to correlate nine of the graves excavated in 1931 with pits unearthed during the later investigations.

In 1987 the *Bundesdenkmalamt* in Vienna decided to start a new excavation in the central part of the area, because a new vineyard was to be planted there. Under the direction of Johannes-Wolfgang and Christine Neugebauer, the results of the first campaign showed the need for further investigation, which was done in four more campaigns up to 1991. An area of at least 5000 m^2 was uncovered and about 100 pits excavated (Verf.1–90; Neugebauer-Maresch 1992).[14] Only about a third of these pits (36) still contained a burial or the disturbed remains of skeletons; all others were empty graves (26), burial pits nearly completely destroyed by ploughing (10), some postholes and the pits of formerly excavated graves (11). Only a small part of the latter could be identified as graves from 1931 (Fig. 5.5).

Burial practice

As far as we can observe, the 57 inhumations were single burials with only two exceptions (Table 5.4); a young woman was buried together with a new-born child (Verf. 5), and there were also two small children of the same age (G.17a,b). More than half of the dead (55%) were oriented with the head to the south-east, and another portion (19%) with the head to the north-west, but no graves were oriented with the head to the SSE, S, SW and WSW. There are some differences of orientation for individuals of different sex and age, but they are not significant. The impressive dominance of the orientation SE–NW is shared by other LBK cemeteries in east-central Europe, including Těšetice-Kyjovice (Dočkalová and Koštuřík 1996; Chapter 4.8), Vedrovice (Ondruš 2002, 126; Podborský 2002b, 327; Chapter 4.7) and Nitra (Pavúk 1972a, 32; Chapter 4.10).

Most of the deceased were placed in a more or less crouched position on their left side (85%), and much more seldom on their right side (15%). More than half of the bodies (65%) lay on their side with their hands in front of the face; quite often the upper part of the bodies lay on the back (32%), and only in few cases on the belly (3%); legs are crouched and put to one or other side. The degree to which the leg is flexed is extremely varied and seems mainly to be due to the shape and size of the grave pit. The extreme dominance of left-crouched positions is once again shared by Vedrovice (Podborský 2002b, 327; Chapter 4.7) and Nitra (Pavúk 1972a, 26; Chapter 4.10), but also by other LBK cemeteries such as Flomborn (I. Richter 1969, 158), Sengkofen and Mangolding (Nieszery 1995, 78; see also Chapter 9.5). The custom of strewing red ochre around the head is attested at Kleinhadersdorf, but only for nine individuals (Fig. 5.6). Some traces of red ochre on grinding stones indicate further use of this mineral, perhaps for painting the body, but these traces might have no connection with the grave ritual.

There are seven pits with scarce traces of burned (human?) bones; four of them might be cremation burials. The large number of empty graves (26) seems to be a speciality of the Kleinhadersdorf cemetery. Half of them contained some ceramic fragments, and only very few an axe or a fragment of a grinding plate. Flint objects or personal ornaments are not present. Eleven pits had no finds at all. The shape of the pits and the situation of the few finds give the impression that the body – perhaps enveloped in some textile or other – had been taken out carefully, while some of the grave goods may have been removed, leaving those of lesser importance. As in some other LBK cemeteries, these empty grave pits do not seem to be cenotaphs as such; that is, they are not the fully equipped graves of absent persons (for more details: Lenneis 2010c).

Grave goods

In analysing the grave goods and their position in the pits, we formed the impression in many cases that there is spare room for some items which are not preserved. So it does not seem correct to speak of 'rich' or 'poor' graves, but only of graves with varying amounts of grave goods present and as we cannot estimate the value of absent goods at all, we are wary of using the amount of goods present as indicators of the social status of the deceased. Nevertheless it is very interesting to compare the preserved situation for the individuals of different sex and age, and also with those in other LBK cemeteries.

The position of the different grave goods in the pits clearly shows a preference for the area around the head, especially for pottery, as well as around the upper body. Only few of the grave goods were placed on or beside the mostly strongly flexed legs. This phenomenon might be due more to the practical aspect of space in the grave around the legs than a 'taboo' of placing objects close to the legs, as this is seen at other LBK cemeteries (for example, grave 57/78, Vedrovice; Chapter 4.7.3). The structure of grave goods and the amount of the preserved objects differ considerably. As in most LBK burial grounds, the majority of males were equipped with the greatest variety and the largest amounts of preserved grave goods. The typical male grave goods at Kleinhadersdorf, as well as in other LBK sites, consist of adzes, flint arrowheads and a rather large amount of pottery of various kinds. The larger number of grinding stones and bone artefacts in the graves of men compared to those of women and children at Kleinhadersdorf seems to be a more local phenomenon.

*Table 5.4. Kleinhadersdorf: the isotope data. Age and sex information from Tiefenböck (2010). See Chapter 2 for further definition of ages. Key for body position: LC – Left-crouched; RC – Right-crouched; C – Crouched, direction unknown; CB – Crouched on back; CF – Crouched on front; S – Supine; P – Prone; I – Irregular. Grave good data are forthcoming (Lenneis and Neugebauer-Maresch forthcoming). * denotes graves with no information available.*

Burial	Tooth	Sex	Age (yrs)	$^{87}Sr/^{86}Sr$	Sr conc. ppm	$\delta^{13}C$ ‰	$\delta^{15}N$ ‰	Orientation	Body position
G1a	M3	M	40–60	0.70881	194	−19.5	9.3	E–W	LC
G1b	M2	F	40–60	0.70913	96	−19.6	9.4	SE–NW	LC
G1c	M2	F	35–55	0.70971	134	−20.1	9.2	NW–SE	LC
G2*	-	-	-	-	-	-	-	SE–NW	RC
G3*	-	-	-	-	-	-	-	-	-
G4	-	-	Adult	-	-	-	-	-	-
G5	-	-	3	-	-	-	-	-	-
G6	-	-	35–50	-	-	−19.8	9.5	SE–NW	LC
G7	M2	M	Adult	0.71013	47	−19.6	9.5	SE–NW	LC
G8	-	M	20–30	-	-	−19.9	8.7	-	-
G9	-	-	3–4	-	-	−19.4	9.6	W–E	LC
G10	-	-	2–2.5	-	-	-	-	SE–NW	LC
G11	-	-	Adult	-	-	-	-	W–E	-
G12	M3	M	35–55	0.71003	108	−19.7	9.6	-	-
G13*	-	-	-	-	-	-	-	-	-
G14	M1 M3	F	20–25	0.70975 0.70992	150 70	−20.2	8.9	-	LC
G15	M1 M3	F	25–35	0.71010 0.71004	102 55	−19.5	9.8	-	LC
G16	-	M	30–15	-	-	−19.6	8.8	-	LC
G17a	M1	-	3–4	0.70997	98	−19.8	8.3	W–E	LC
G17b	-	-	3–4	-	-	-	-	-	-
G18	M1 M3	-	17–22	0.70993 0.71004	47 124	−19.8	9.1	-	-
G19	M1	M	25–35	0.71035	37	−20.2	8.3	SE–NW	LC
3	M1	M	50–60	0.70907	51	−19.4	10	E–W	LC
5-1	M1 M3	F	18–25	0.70942 0.70946	55 133	−18.9	9.8	SE–NW	LC
5-2	-	-	0–6 mon.	-	-	-	-	SE–NW	LC
7	M1		6–7	0.7098	77	−20.0	9.6	SE–NW	RC
10	-	M	Adult	-	-	−19.6	9.7	-	-
11	M2	-	10–12	0.71016	60	−19.8	9.1	SE–NW	LC
13	-	-	-	-	-	-	-	-	-
17	M3	M	35–40	0.71003	37	−19.8	9.8	SE–NW	LC
22	M1	-	2 ± 8 mon.	0.70991	38	−19.0	11.9	SE–NW	
26	M2	-	1–1.5	0.71029	82	−19.0	12.4	SE–NW	LC
29	M2	M	20–30	0.70925	105	−20.0	10.2	SE–NW	LC
32	M3	F	20–30	0.71141	91	−19.9	9.2	SE–NW	LC
37	-	-	-	-	-	-	-	-	-
40	M2	M	25–35	0.70985	70	−19.9	10.4	NW–SE	LC
42	-	-	-	-	-	-	-	-	-
43	M1	-	12–17	0.70999	146	−20.3	8.9	W–E	LC
46	-	-	-	-	-	-	-	-	-
49	M2		Adult	0.71021	99	−19.7	9.6	NE–SW	RC

52	-	-	-	-	-	-	-	NW–SE	LC
53	-	-	-	-	-	-	-	-	-
54	-	-	-	-	-	-	-	-	-
55	M3	F	30–50	0.71275	51	−19.8	9.3	N–S	RC
56	M2?	F	40–50	0.70961	77	−20.0	9.8	NE–SW	LC
57	M1 M3	M	17–25	0.70993 0.70993	114 75	−20.1	9.9	SE–NW	LC
59	M1		6–8	0.70911	66	−20.2	9.3	NW–SE	LC
64	-	-	-	-	-	-	-	-	-
65	M1 M3	F	35–45	0.70899 0.70907	42 51	−20.0	9.3	SE–NW	LC
66	M1 M3	-	17–25	0.71211 0.71446	75 81	−20.1	9.7	-	-
67-1	-	-	-	-	-	-	-	SE–NW	LC
67-2	-	-	-	-	-	-	-	SE–NW	RC
69	M2	M	40–60	0.71057	115	−19.5	9.4	NW–SE	LC
70	-	-	-	-	-	-	-	-	-
79	M2	M	25–30	0.71018	159	−19.9	9.9	NW–SE	LC
80	-	-	3–4	-	-	-	-	NW–SE	LC
81	M1	M	17–25	0.70961	50	−19.6	10	SE–NW	LC
82	M3	-	25–35	0.70966	83	−20.0	9.2	-	-
89	-	-	-	-	-	-	-	-	-
90	-	M	Adult	-	-	−19.7	10	-	-
91-1	M1 M3	F	30–50	0.70953 0.70969	78 166	−19.6	10.3	-	-
91-2	M2	-	17–25	0.70961	124	-	-	-	-

The preserved grave goods of the ten female burials show less variety and smaller quantities. Four of them do not have any preserved grave goods, which is in clear contrast to the provision of others with valuable ornaments as well as to women elsewhere who were much more richly supplied with durable goods in other LBK cemeteries, for example in Thuringia (Kahlke 2004, 60) and Saxony (Fritsch *et al.* 2011, 86). The representation of children (including juveniles) at Kleinhadersdorf is unusually high (18), ten of them dying very young (Infans I: under six years old). The number of furnished child graves, especially those of the youngest, is over the mean found for the LBK (Siemoneit 1997, 28) and the percentage of children supplied with adzes (55.5%) is exceptionally high.

Pottery. The most frequent grave good is pottery; only 50% of the grave pits contained pottery and for the inhumations the percentage is slightly higher (52.6%). The pottery consists of nearly complete vessels, mostly from the bottom of the graves at the level of the inhumation, and of sherds, both from the burials and the pit fills. The sherds have been refitted and examined, using established methodologies for settlement inventories (Lenneis 2001; 2009). Typological analyses have been carried out, as well as seriation with the WinSerion 1.26 Beta Program by Peter Stadler. Typologically the oldest vessels come from the transitional phase of *ältere* to *jüngere* LBK in Austria (*Übergangsphase* LBK I/II; Lenneis 2010b). By far the most frequent ceramic decoration was characteristic of the

Fig. 5.5. Kleinhadersdorf: plan. After Stadler in Neugebauer-Maresch and Lenneis (forthcoming).

Notenkopf style and the most frequent decoration is very similar to the Moravian LBK pottery of phase IIa, with some pottery clearly showing characteristics of the sub-phases IIa$_1$ and IIa$_2$ (according to Čižmář 1998a; 2002). Fewer pots have decoration typical of Moravian phases IIb and IIc. Within the pottery of the latest LBK phase (Moravian phase III after R. Tichý 1960; Čižmář 1998a), some vessels have decorative traits of the Šárka group, and others of the Želiezovce group, indicating connections to the west and north-west (north-west Moravia, Bohemia) and to the east and north-east (Slovakia, south Poland).

Stone implements. The connections detailed above are even more impressive when the procurement patterns of the stone raw materials are considered. Inna Mateiciucová has done an extensive analysis of the 25 chipped stone artefacts, which show striking similarities to the comparable objects of the Vedrovice cemetery (Mateiciucová 2002). Most of the artefacts are Jurassic silicites of the Kraków-Czestochowa highlands, while some are Szentgál radiolarites and others cherts from Krumlovský Les in south-west Moravia (Fig. 5.7). As in Vedrovice there are two groups of artefacts: blades and blade fragments serving as all-purpose knives and trapezoid items of microlithic character, which are interpreted as arrowheads.

There are different kinds of raw materials used for the polished stone tools. The 20 adzes are all made of high-quality kinds of amphibolite, but the raw materials used for the five axes are significantly different. Neither as yet has a

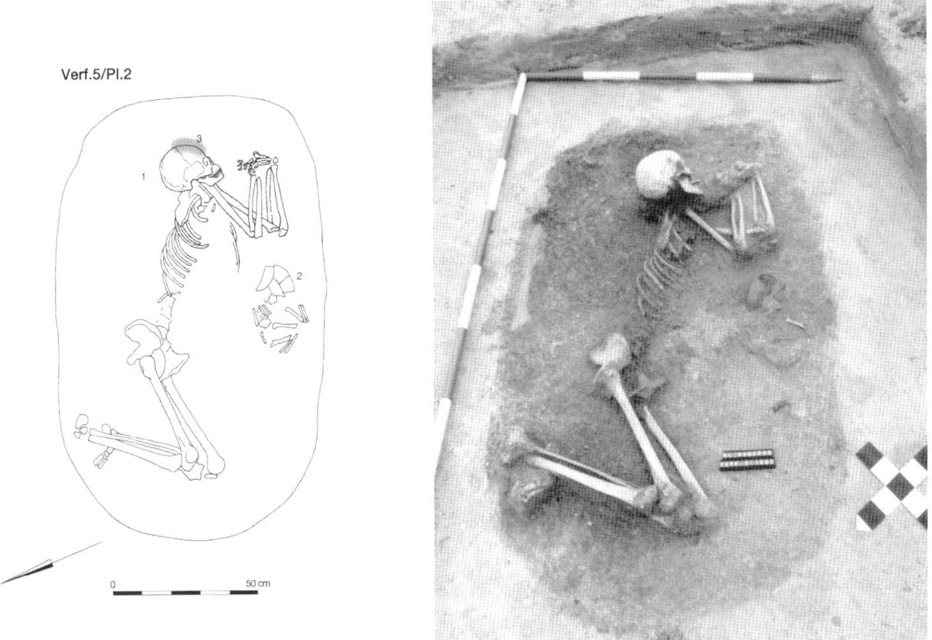

Fig. 5.6. Kleinhadersdorf: burials Verf. 5–1 and 5–2. After Neugebauer-Maresch and Lenneis (forthcoming).

Krakow Jurassic silicite
250 km
Krumlovský Les chert
250 km
Vedrovice-Gräberfeld
150 km
Kleinhadersdorf
80 km
Bakony radiolarites
80 km
Transdanubian radiolarites
Krumlovský Les chert
Krakow Jurassic silicite
Krakow Jurassic silicite ?
other
50km

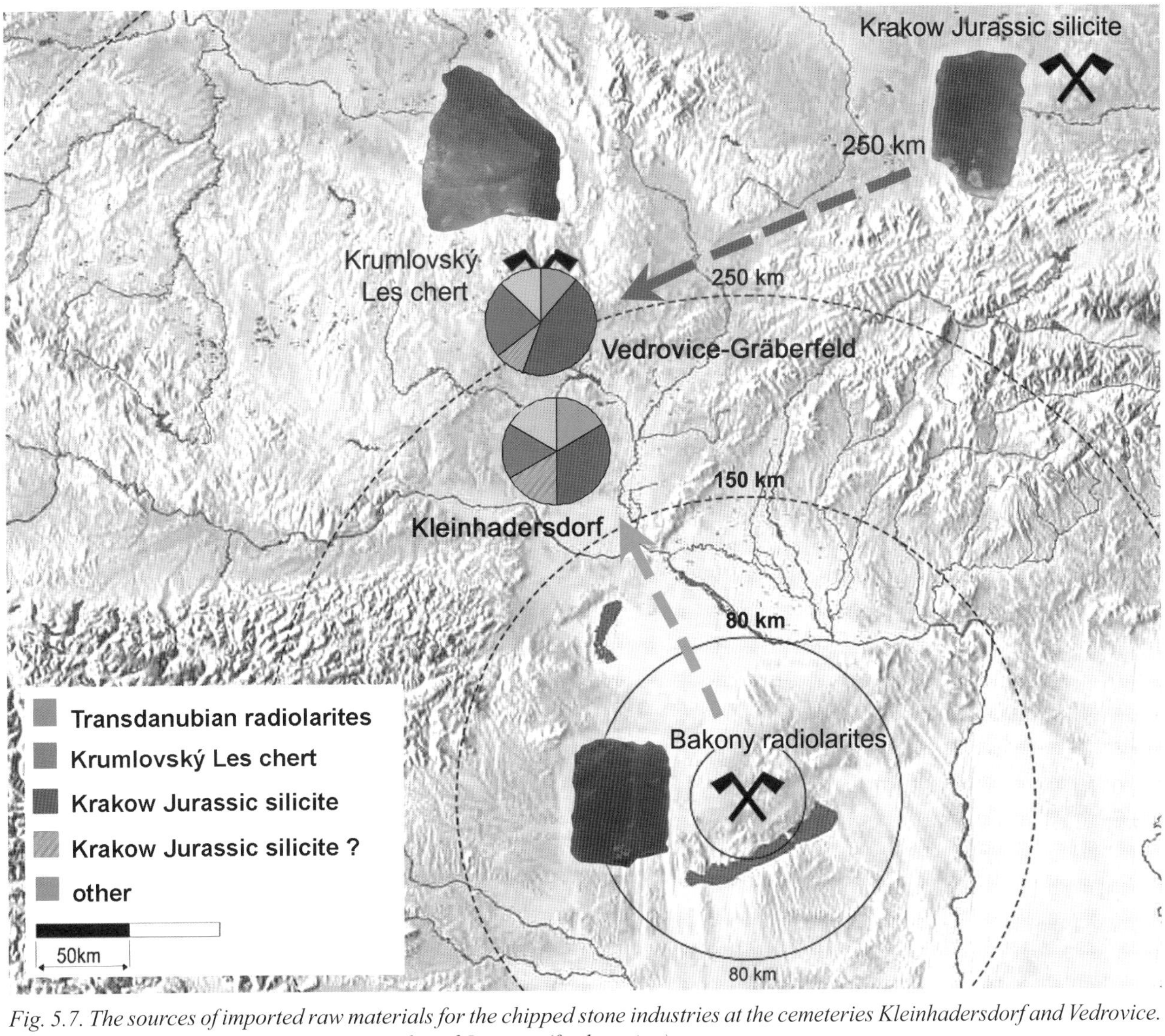

Fig. 5.7. The sources of imported raw materials for the chipped stone industries at the cemeteries Kleinhadersdorf and Vedrovice. From Mateiciucová in Neugebauer-Maresch and Lenneis (forthcoming).

precise region of origin. All adzes and axes had been used, some of them even showing evidence of intensive use.

The big quantity of twenty grinding stones seems to be a speciality of the Kleinhadersdorf cemetery. They take two different forms. There are rather thin ones (2–3 cm), which occurred as nearly complete big plates or broken halves, and which could not have served as a millstone for cereal grains. We also find the broken parts of former quernstones for grinding cereals, but no complete ones. Some of both forms show traces of ochre. Most of the thin grinding plates are of local sandstone, but the fragments of the former quernstones are made of different high-quality materials (Robert Seemann (†) and Michael Götzinger, pers. comm.). Some of them might have come from central Bohemia, as we found out for other quernstones from the LBK settlement of Mold, about 80 km west of Kleinhadersdorf (Lenneis 2010a, 343).

Bone artefacts and animal bones. There are very few bone artefacts, such as five awls, mainly made from bone and antler of roe and perhaps red deer. The most exceptional find is a pair of boar tusks (Neugebauer-Maresch 1992, 9, Abb. 8), belonging to one of the most richly equipped men (Verf. 81).

Personal ornaments. Eighteen graves (33%) contained personal ornaments, a frequency below Vedrovice (37.6%; Podborský 2002b, 333, table 2; Chapter 4.7), but higher than Nitra or Aiterhofen (25% each; Jeunesse 1997, 102; Chapters 4.10 and 6.7).

Ornaments on the head are only found in two child graves, while they are more often known from adult graves on other LBK sites. This is especially the case with the decorations made of small snail shells, which here only come from an infant grave, where they must have been sewn on a bonnet (Verf. 26; Harzhauser *et al.* 2007). Most ornaments are found in the graves of women (46%), less often in the graves of men (33%) and rather seldom in those of children (20%; Lenneis 2007; 2010d). Ornaments made of *Spondylus* shells are not very abundant. 18.5% of all inhumations had at least one piece, which is far below the situation at Vedrovice (29.4%; Podborský 2002b, 333; Chapter 4.10) or Ensisheim (24%; Jeunesse 1997, 102; Chapter 8.8) but at a higher frequency than is found in several other LBK cemeteries. 40% of the women and 30% of the children were equipped with *Spondylus* ornaments, but rather few men. An adult woman and an infant had the only big *Spondylus* necklaces. While the frequency of child graves in Kleinhadersdorf (27.8%) is just slightly over the mean in LBK graveyards (25%), their provision with personal ornaments (46.7% of neonatus, Infans I and Infans II) is remarkably high (mean 15.5%; Simoneit 1997, 30, table 8). Together with the high frequency of adzes accompanying children, this gives the impression that children had been highly esteemed by the community here, more than was usual for the time.

5.7.2 Osteology

The osteological remains from Kleinhadersdorf are held at the Natural History Museum in Vienna and have recently been analysed by Barbara Tiefenböck (2010), under the guidance of Maria Teschler-Nicola. The full results are forthcoming (Neugebauer-Maresch and Lenneis forthcoming), and only a short summary is provided here. Infants and juveniles were under-represented, which is in line with what we have found elsewhere (Chapter 3.9.3). The rate of caries is higher than the currently estimated rate for the LBK as a whole, suggesting a carbohydrate-rich diet, but more generally, the rate of stress indicators such as porotic hyperostosis and *cribra orbitalia* points towards a community with insufficient nutrition (Tiefenböck 2010, 154–62). However, the occurrence of traumas and evidence for infectious disease was low and far less frequent than has been identified amongst the population at the late LBK site of Asparn (Chapter 5.8; Tiefenböck 2010).

5.7.3 The animal remains from Gnadendorf

This *Notenkopf* pit complex was found during gravel extraction and a rescue excavation was carried out by the *Abteilung für Bodendenkmalpflege* by J.-W. Neugebauer in 1980 (Neugebauer 1981b, 334; Neugebauer-Maresch 1983; Boschin 2009, 156). The wild fauna spectrum, which made up 10.6% of the total animal bone assemblage, suggests that the site was set in a mosaic landscape of forest and parkland (Boschin 2009, 163, 167). Pigs were underrepresented in comparison to other contemporary sites in Lower Austria (just 9.7%, compared with 18.4% at Pulkau and 31.7% at Ratzersdorf), but cattle and sheep/goats had similar rates with just over 40% and 30% respectively (Boschin 2009, 168). A total of 15 samples were taken, six each from cattle and sheep/goats, but only three from pig. The stable isotope results from Gnadendorf are reported below (Table 5.5).

5.7.4 Carbon and nitrogen analysis

In total 40 individuals were originally sampled for stable isotope analysis, but one sampled failed to pass quality indicators (Appendix A) leaving 39 $\delta^{13}C$ and $\delta^{15}N$ values, from 16 males, ten females, five unsexed adults, six juveniles and two infants (Fig. 5.8; Table 5.5).

Apart from two infants with high $\delta^{13}C$ and $\delta^{15}N$ values reflecting suckling, the human isotope values at Kleinhadersdorf are tightly clustered with no significant differences between the means of the age and sex groups. The only exception is a young adult female (grave Verf. 5-1) with a $\delta^{13}C$ value of −18.9‰, more than two standard deviations higher than the mean. This could be due to inclusion of C4 plant foods in the diet, such as millet, or possibly freshwater fish, though marine foods seem unlikely, and her $\delta^{15}N$ value is normal. Grains of broomcorn millet and foxtail millet have been found at LBK sites, though not in sufficient numbers to suggest that they were a regular crop and these species may have grown as weeds (Kreuz 1990; Bakels 1992; for a recent survey of millet present at LBK sites, see Hunt *et al.* 2008), so consumption of millet is a possible explanation. While mean adult $\delta^{13}C$

Table 5.5. Carbon and nitrogen isotope ratios (‰) of humans from Kleinhadersdorf and animals from Gnadendorf, with means and standard deviations.

Species	Age/sex	Mean $\delta^{13}C$	SD $\delta^{13}C$	Mean $\delta^{15}N$	SD $\delta^{15}N$	n
Human	Infants	−19.0	0.01	12.2	0.35	2
Human	Juvenile	−19.9	0.33	9.1	0.48	6
Human	Female	−19.8	0.38	9.5	0.41	10
Human	Male	−19.8	0.23	9.6	0.57	16
Human	Unsexed adults	−19.9	0.17	9.4	0.27	5
Human	All adults	−19.8	0.27	9.5	0.47	31
Cattle		−20.4	0.35	7.2	0.61	6
Sheep/goat		−19.8	0.57	7.2	0.77	6
Pig		−20.4	0.01	7.2	0.76	3

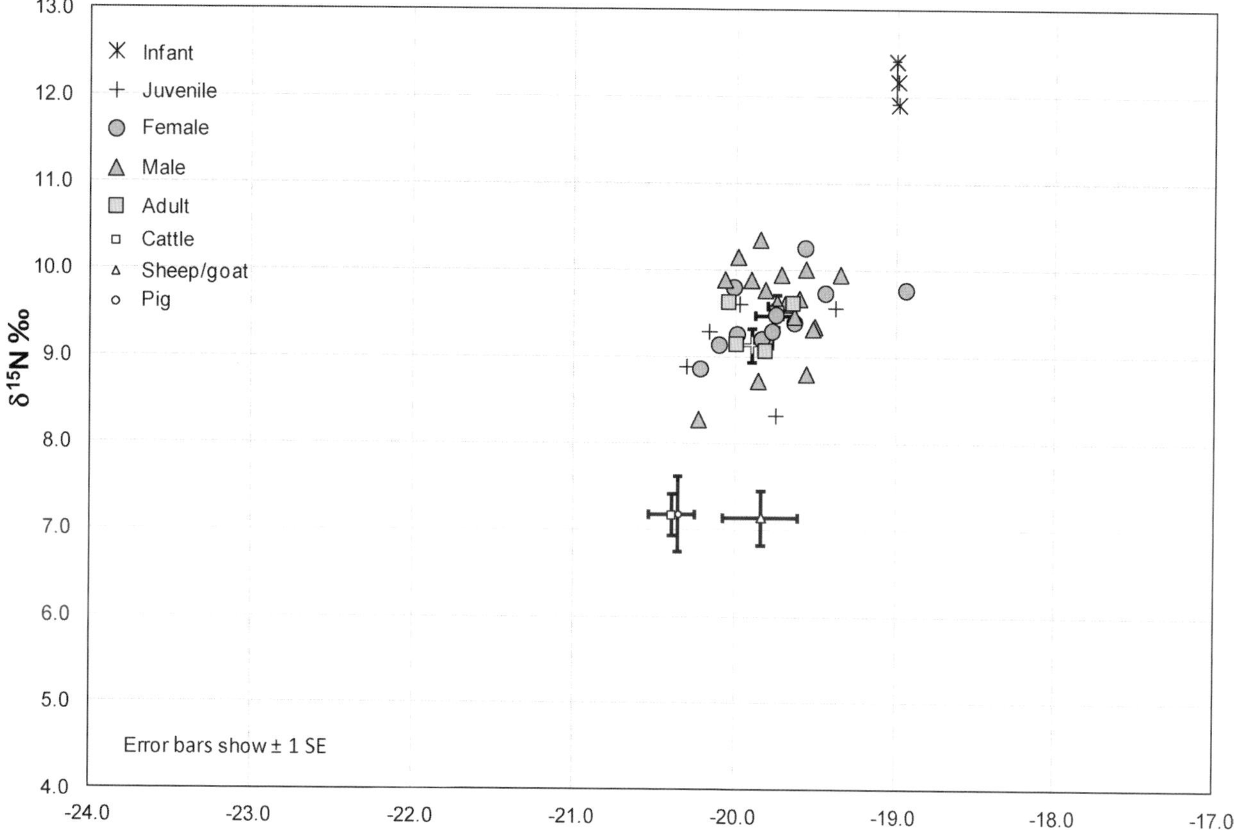

Fig. 5.8. Kleinhadersdorf: carbon and nitrogen isotope ratios (‰) of humans.

values tend to be higher at the more easterly sites, this is the highest adult value in the whole project, and would be unusual even at those sites, so a dietary difference seems a more likely (though not exclusive) explanation than simply an origin further east, and the strontium ratios from the first and third molars suggest that this individual had lived locally on the loess.

Animals

The animals from Gnadendorf (Pucher 1987; 2001; Schmitzberger 2009a) have very similar $\delta^{15}N$ values, including the pigs (Fig. 5.9; Table 5.5). The mean $\delta^{13}C$ value for sheep/goats is higher than that of cattle and pig, as often noted, but none of the differences in mean isotope values are significant (ANOVA), reflecting the rather small sample numbers.

The difference between human and cattle mean $\delta^{13}C$ and $\delta^{15}N$ values is 0.6‰±0.44 (SD) and 2.3‰±0.77, respectively, similar to those in the neighbouring region of Moravia and western Slovakia.

Correlations with the archaeological data

No correlations with the archaeological data could be determined, either by body position or orientation of the grave.

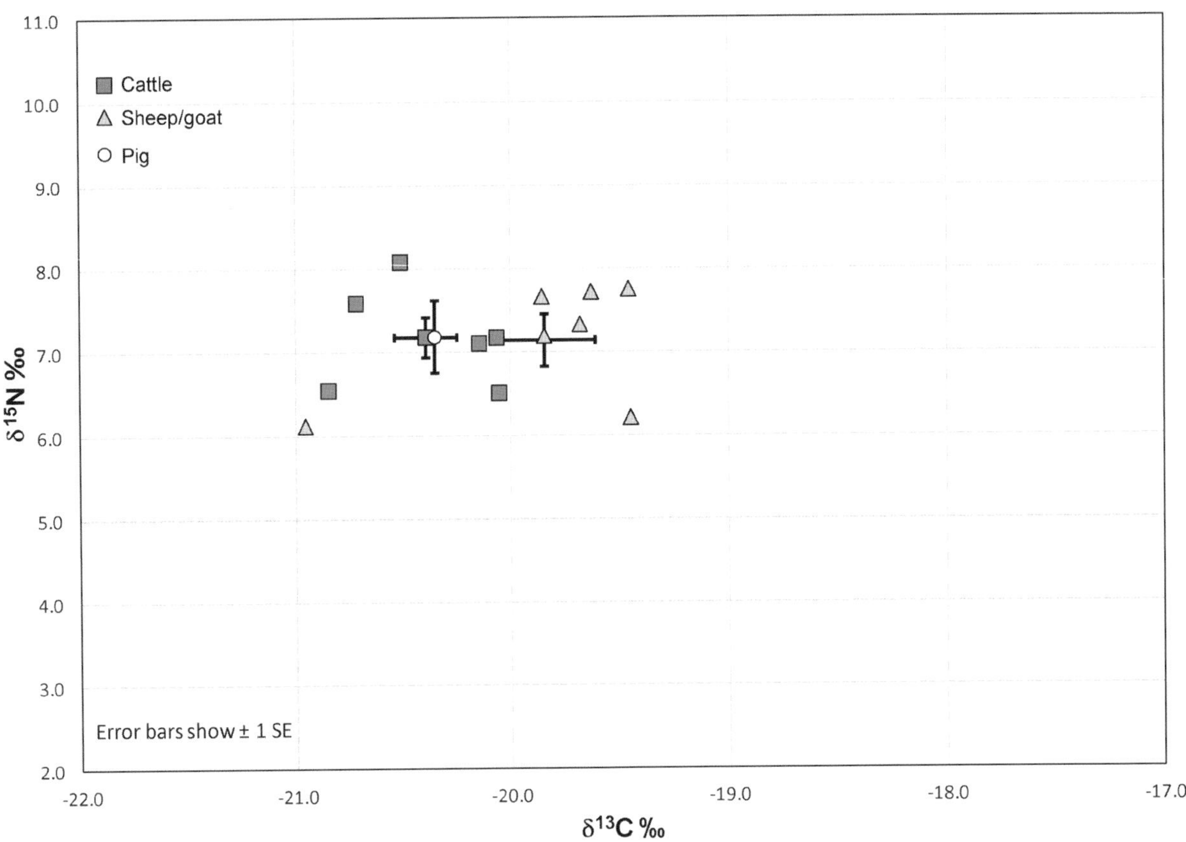

Fig. 5.9. Gnadendorf: carbon and nitrogen isotope ratios (‰) of animals.

5.7.5 Strontium analysis

We sampled the teeth from 34 individuals, including ten females, 12 males, seven children and five unsexed adults. In the case of eight individuals we were able to analyse the strontium ratio in both their first and third molars (burials 5–1, 57, 65, 66, 91–1, G14, G15 and G18), giving a total of 42 analyses (Fig. 5.10; Table 5.6).

Excluding the outlying value from burial 66, the mean $^{87}Sr/^{86}Sr$ ratio is 0.70992±0.00012 (1 SD), which is consistent with strontium values found on the loess (0.7085–0.7105; Bentley 2006). Kleinhadersdorf lies on a west-facing slope within a region of high-quality loess soils and therefore we would expect individuals living locally to fall within the loess range. However, the site is approximately 50 km east from the higher elevations of more radiogenic $^{87}Sr/^{86}Sr$ ratios of the Bohemian Massif, which has produced strontium ratios above 0.7110 (Grupe *et al.* 1997; Price *et al.* 2004, 16). Strontium ratios that fall below the loess range may have also been found nearby, originating in the Molasse basin (Grupe *et al.* 1997), which stretches along the Alpine basin into the northern part of eastern Austria. However, as none of the $^{87}Sr/^{86}Sr$ ratios from Kleinhadersdorf fall below the loess range it is unlikely that food or resources on this geological feature were exploited by the community who buried their dead at Kleinhadersdorf.

Overall, there are no significant differences in the mean values between men (0.70983±0.00051) and women (0.70991±0.00098), though the female $^{87}Sr/^{86}Sr$ ratio average is higher. There is no significant difference between the male average strontium concentration (89 Sr ppm) and the female (90 Sr ppm), nor when the ranges are compared. Though there is also no significant difference between the range of strontium ratios for males and females, two of the three strontium outliers are identified as females. The third outlier (based on $^{87}Sr/^{86}Sr$ ratio) is an unsexed adult, aged 17–25. These three outliers, grave 32 (female, 20–30 years), grave 55 (female, 30–50 years) and grave 66 (unsexed, 17–25 years), may fall along a 'mixing line', but with so few samples this must remain as a suggestion only. The $^{87}Sr/^{86}Sr$ ratios from the outliers suggest origins in, or use of, upland landscapes.

There were no overall differences in strontium data between the different teeth sampled (comparing M1, M2 and M3 molars), and where two teeth had been sampled from the same individual the $^{87}Sr/^{86}Sr$ ratios were often very close. The only exception to this were the M1 and M3 molars sampled from grave 66, where it is interesting to note that the M3 molar value is further away from the site mean than that of the M1 molar. This does not necessarily mean that this individual moved away from the local area and back again, but does suggest that the individual in question was in the late teens at least on arrival in the Kleinhadersdorf area, death following shortly afterwards. In five of the eight cases where an M1 and M3 molar were sampled, the M3 molar had a greater Sr concentration ppm than the M1; the reverse is true in the other three cases. We have no immediate explanation for this pattern.

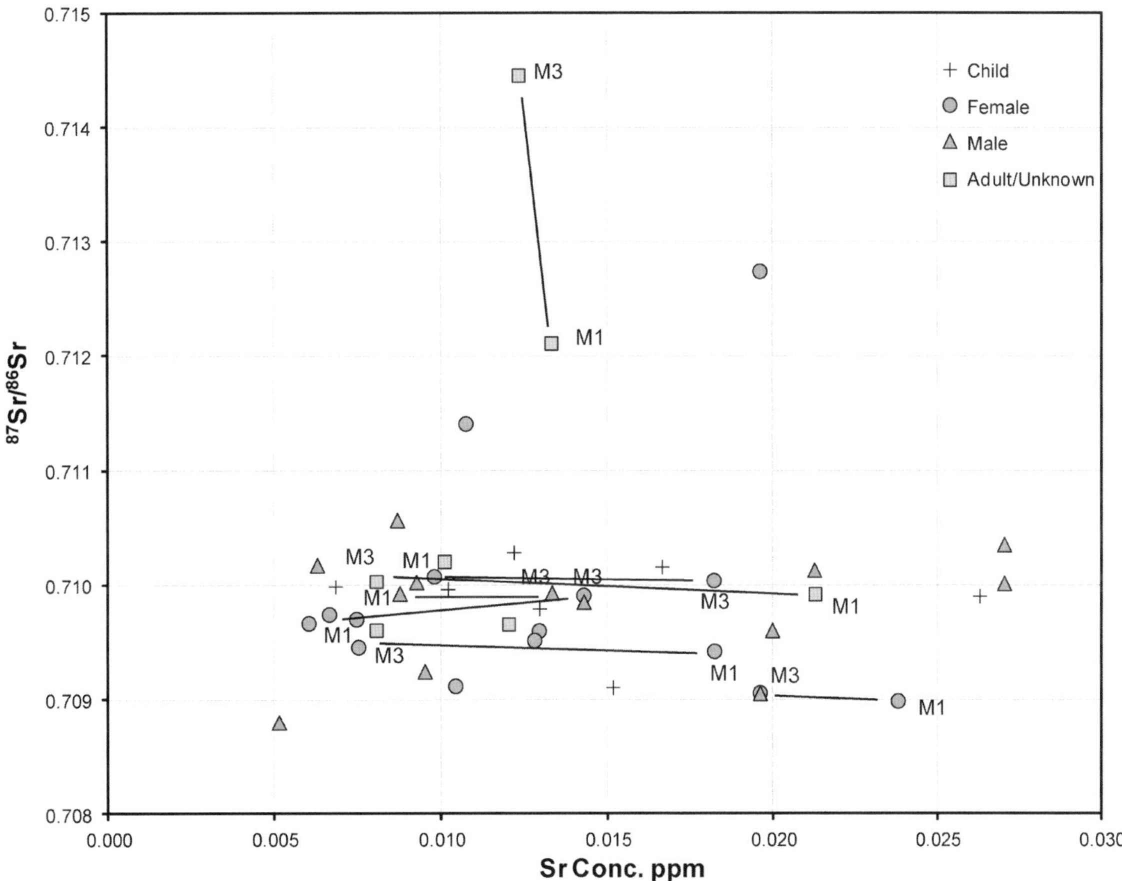

Fig. 5.10. Kleinhadersdorf: strontium concentration (ppm) versus ratio ($^{87}Sr/^{86}Sr$). Lines connect teeth from the same individual.

*Table 5.6. Kleinhadersdorf: strontium isotope ratios and concentrations. 'All' includes five unsexed adults. * denotes number of analyses, not number of individuals.*

Age/sex	Mean $^{87}Sr/^{86}Sr$	SD $^{87}Sr/^{86}Sr$	Mean Sr conc.	SD Sr conc.	n*
Juvenile	0.70989	0.00038	81	34	7
Male	0.70983	0.00051	89	49	13
Female	0.70991	0.00098	90	40	15
All	0.71004	0.00102	88	39	42

Correlations with the archaeological data

There was no correlation between $^{87}Sr/^{86}Sr$ ratios and the orientation and body position of the graves. However, burials oriented with the head to the west or north-west had a higher average strontium concentration (orientation with head to the east and south-east: Sr conc. mean=77, n=20; orientation with head to the west and north-west: Sr conc. mean=105, n=8; Mann-Whitney U test, p=0.027). This may suggest that those oriented in this secondary position (between W–E and N–S) were eating more foods with higher strontium concentration, such as cereals. However, as this pattern does not correlate with the stable isotopes, it is difficult to explain. As only five burials were placed in a right-crouched position and all the rest were left-crouched, it is not surprising that there were no overall significant patterns concerning body position. However, it is worth noting that one of the outliers in terms of $^{87}Sr/^{86}Sr$ ratio, grave 55, was placed in a right-crouched position and was one of only two burials oriented with the head to the north. At Rutzing in Austria and Polgár in Hungary, right-crouched burials are over-represented among the strontium isotope outliers. Female grave 32 is accompanied by a pot with Šárka decoration, which would have had its origins in Moravia or Bohemia. Travel across uplands between these areas and the district of Mistelbach may account for her elevated strontium value of 0.7111. There were no correlations with the stable isotope results.

5.7.6 Site summary and discussion

In general, the isotopic results from Kleinhadersdorf stress homogeneity, rather than structured difference (Table 5.4). Despite a few interesting outliers, the majority of the population lived in the area throughout their lives and sourced their food nearby. The lack of identifiable differences between men and women and across age groups suggests that any social hierarchy or differences were not reflected in diet and that access to certain types of food was not restricted for certain groups in the population. The strontium isotope ratio of burial 32 (0.71141) suggests that the Kleinhadersdorf population had connections to Moravia and Bohemia. This is particularly interesting as a small amount of the raw material for grinding stones and chipped stones, comes from there (see Chapter 5.4.2).

Some details of individual life histories at Kleinhadersdorf, finally, can be noted. The young woman in grave Verf. 5-1 with a $\delta^{13}C$ value of −18.9‰ is thought to have had a special diet (Chapter 5.6.4). The stable isotope values of bone collagen represent an average over the last several years of life (Chapter 2.2.1), so it is unlikely that this is connected solely with her pregnancy – though recent consumption of a diet with a very high proportion of C4 plants cannot be entirely excluded. If obtainable, the stable isotope values of the newborn child might throw some light on this, as they would record the mother's diet over a more recent period. She was buried together with a newborn child (Verf. 5-2) who seems to have been the cause of her early death (Fig. 5.6). Her body was placed in the left-crouched position with her head to the south-east, following the most usual burial rite of the site. She had some red ochre on her head. Her hands were unusually positioned up in front of her to give room for her baby. The large space below the child suggests once again that some perishable grave goods had been included in the grave.

One of the three outliers in terms of $^{87}Sr/^{86}Sr$ ratio, grave Verf. 66, was heavily damaged. Little can be said about the original situation of this burial of an unsexed 17–25-year-old, but this person was furnished with a pot, decorated in typical Moravian phase IIa_1 style (Table 5.4), indicating contemporaneity with the majority of inhumations at the site. The two other outliers in terms of $^{87}Sr/^{86}Sr$ ratio are both women, but of different ages. The elder one (grave Verf. 55) was between 30–50 years old at death. Her body was in the right-crouched position, rare for Kleinhadersdorf (15%). More unusual is the orientation of her body, with her head to the north, which she shares with only one other person in the cemetery. She had one of the two *Spondylus* necklaces found at this site around her neck. Among her grave goods was one of the few preserved bone awls. The radiocarbon date for her is the earliest from Kleinhadersdorf (Appendix B2). As she could have come from another region, it is tempting to suggest that she might have been one of the founders of the community who buried their dead at this place, and it could also be that case that she brought the *Spondylus* ornament with her. Her grave is in the centre of the northern group, not far from the unsexed person of grave Verf. 66.

The younger women in grave Verf. 32 was between 20 and 30 years when she died. Her skeleton was not very well preserved. However, we can determine that the upper body lay on the back, which is not unusual here, but the hands were crossed on her upper body, which is rather an unusual position. The few surviving portions of her legs indicated a crouched position, perhaps to the left. The head of the body was oriented to the south-east and therefore shares the main orientation of the site (55%). A small piece of *Spondylus* was found on the pelvic bones which might be the last remains of a shell on a belt. The only surviving grave good was a single small pot, decorated in typical Šárka style. This inhumation, therefore, clearly belongs to the last phase of the cemetery, contemporary with the Moravian LBK phase III (Table B2.1). A radiocarbon date for her broadly supports this (Appendix B2). The young woman might have come from north-west Moravia or even perhaps Bohemia, as indicated by the decoration of the pot and her strontium values. She might also have been one of the last burials to take place at the site as she was placed within the southernmost groups where most of the later inhumations were found.

5.8 Asparn an der Zaya/Schletz

5.8.1 Introduction

Asparn an der Zaya/Schletz is situated in the north-eastern corner of Austria, approximately 50 km north of Vienna, not far from the Moravian and Slovakian borders (*c.* 25 km and *c.* 35 km respectively; Fig. 5.1). Earlier stray finds had suggested that a large LBK site was present in the vicinity (Fehlmann 2011), and then this large enclosure site was discovered in the early 1980s by aerial photography and geophysical survey, and interpreted as a large settlement surrounded by a ditch system (Trnka 1982; Teschler-Nicola 2012). The site was excavated by Helmut Windl (*Niederösterreichisches Landesmuseum*) between 1983 and 2005, and to date *c.* 20% of the site has been exposed (Windl 1994; 1996; 2002; 2009; Fehlmann 2011; Teschler-Nicola 2012). A slightly trapezoidal rectangular ditch appears to be cut by two oval concentric ditches, with the majority of the human remains coming from the outer oval ditch (Teschler-Nicola *et al.* 2005).

Molluscan analysis has suggested that the site, situated on loess soils, was constructed in semi-open landscape, perhaps at the edge of the forest or surrounded by clumps of trees or bushes (Windl 1996, 24). Pine, spruce, elm, lime, birch and hazel are represented in the pollen diagram, suggesting mixed deciduous woodland (Draxler 1994, 22–3). The site itself consists of a large oval double ditch (*jüngere* LBK) and a semi-rectangular ditch (possibly *ältere* LBK), which stretches out towards the north-east of the double enclosure (Fig. 5.11). The area enclosed contains a LBK settlement with two houses associated with *Notenkopf* pottery, though as only 20% of the site has been excavated it is envisaged that far more houses would have once stood at the site (Windl 1996, 12). Pottery from the enclosure ditches suggests that these features were constructed during the later *Notenkopf* and Želiezovce phases. This is seemingly confirmed by the radiocarbon samples, which date the enclosure to an informally estimated span of 5210–4950 cal BC (Wild *et al.* 2004).

Unlike in the rest of the sites in this project, the individuals discovered in the enclosure ditches at Asparn do not appear to have received formal burial rites and there seem to be no deliberate grave goods. However, three burials in the older rectangular ditch were placed in a crouched position (Windl 2005, 453) and four burials were found within the settlement, two of which were accompanied by grave goods of pots, beads, flint, a *Spondylus* armring, a grinding stone and ochre (Windl 2002, 573). On the basis of the finds in these graves, Windl (2002, 573) suggests that they come from the *ältere* phases of the site. The rest of the human bone assemblage is constituted from the cranial and post-cranial remains of an estimated 100 individuals, found on the base of the outer ditch (Wild *et al.* 2004, 378).

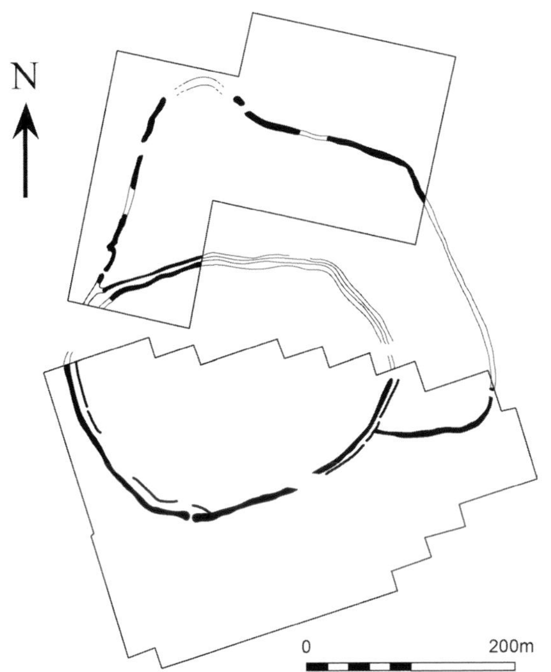

Fig. 5.11. Asparn an der Zaya/Schletz: plan of the enclosure ditches. After Wild (2004, 378).

Osteological analysis has been carried out on 67 individuals (Teschler-Nicola *et al.* 1996; 1999).

A small amount of isotopic analysis has already been carried out at Asparn. In the late 1990s, human bone (rather than tooth enamel) from the 67 individuals was subjected to strontium isotope analysis (Latkoczy *et al.* 1998). At this time the technique was very new, there was little concern about the exchange of strontium in human bone with ground water and the methodology was still being refined (Bentley 2006). The human bone selected for analysis showed a population with similar Sr isotope ratios (ranging between 0.708 and 0.715, with no outliers; Latkoczy *et al.* 1998). However, we should be very cautious in accepting these results, particularly as the standard deviations on the results are high, and must wait for further strontium isotope analysis to be conducted, as is currently planned.

5.8.2 Osteology (Maria Teschler-Nicola)

The skeletal population recovered in the enclosure ditch is of particular interest with respect to its demographic parameters, and pathological and taphonomic alterations (Teschler-Nicola 2012). By considering the radiocarbon data (Wild *et al.* 2004) and the frequency of analogue peri-mortem alterations such as fractures and animal gnaw marks, we have assumed that the individuals represent a cross-section of a contemporaneous population. Two uncommon or atypical demographic findings attracted our interest: the dearth of young females (the number of young males identified in the Asparn sample is greater by a factor of *c.* 3) and the presence of very young children in the absence of their putative mothers. With a total of 67 individuals, the number is small, and we therefore report the age at death distribution only by using age classes; 26 (38%) are immature, and 41 (62%) are adult, of whom 26 were sexed as male, and 13 as female, with only one indeterminate. The sex ratio is conspicuous. It is balanced for individuals who died between 40–60 years (ten males, nine females), but it is unbalanced for younger individuals who died between 20–40 years (17 males, five

Table 5.7. Asparn an der Zaya/Schletz: carbon and nitrogen isotope ratios (‰) of humans and animals, with means and standard deviations.

Species	Age/sex	Mean $\delta^{13}C$	SD $\delta^{13}C$	Mean $\delta^{15}N$	SD $\delta^{15}N$	n
Human	Infant	−18.8	-	12.9	-	1
Human	Juvenile	−19.8	0.36	9.4	0.50	5
Human	Female	−19.6	0.20	9.1	0.28	6
Human	Male	−19.6	0.11	9.6	0.42	17
Human	Adult	−19.6	-	9.4	-	1
Human	All Adult	−19.6	0.14	9.5	0.44	24
Human	Unknown	−19.7	0.16	9.3	0.79	5
Cattle		−19.8	-	6.9	-	1
Sheep/goat		−20.2	0.16	8.0	0.99	2
Pig		−20.2	-	6.2	-	1

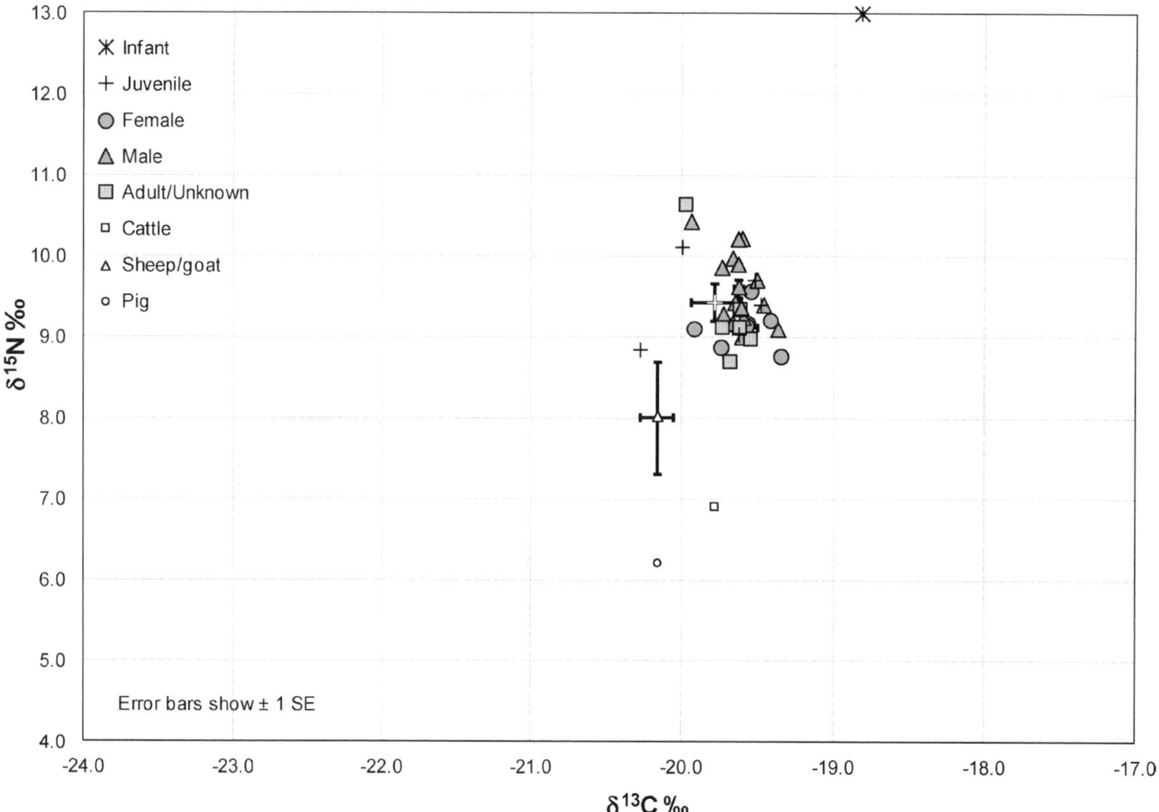

Fig. 5.12. Asparn an der Zaya/Schletz: carbon and nitrogen isotope ratios (‰) of humans.

females). Although not statistically significant, such an age and sex distribution is noteworthy. In consideration of the peri-mortem fractures observed, we have interpreted this atypical relation as result of the abduction of women by aggressors. The presence of newborns at the site seems to confirm our conclusion (see below, with the $\delta^{13}C$ and $\delta^{15}N$ values of a single infant showing a nursing effect).

With the exception of a short summary in an exhibition catalogue (Teschler-Nicola *et al.* 1996), where a few cranial and post-cranial dimensions, body height and epigenetic traits were discussed, no other morphometric data have been collected and analysed so far (though a paper using 3-D landmarks and morphometrics is in preparation). Interestingly, the male individuals of Asparn do not differ very much in their body height from the Early Bronze Age populations of the same geographical area (representing the Aunjetitz cultural group). Male individuals of the LBK sample vary between 160 cm and 173 cm, with a mean of 167.5 cm (the long bones of the Aunjetitz males are less robust and slightly longer). Females are not sufficiently well preserved in statistically significant numbers.

The initial systematic investigations of pathological changes have provided evidence for unspecific symptoms of malnutrition, such as porotic hyperostosis and structural changes at the orbital roof (*cribra orbitalia*). The latter were observed in more than 40% of the sub-adults and in 63% of the males and 75% of the females. Features implying vitamin C deficiency were also diagnosed and represented in the form of sub-periosteal newly built bone formations on the longbones (32% of subadults, 50% of males and 50% of females exhibit these structural changes). These results point to a seasonally fluctuating availability of resources. But we think it will be necessary to carry out further investigations, by also including the skeletal remains recovered during the last excavation campaigns (when the sample increased to about 100 individuals) and by using a more detailed data sheet, a prerequisite for further comparative studies.

Up to now, the osteological investigations have concentrated on and highlighted peri-mortem skeletal changes (Teschler-Nicola 2012). So initial results and their implications are only briefly summarised here. The investigated sample comprised skulls and skull fragments from 33 individuals, including all ages, and both males and females. It was striking that the entire sample revealed fractures induced peri-mortem and that nearly all parts of the skull were represented. The fractures differ in size and shape, implying the use of a variety of objects, including flat axes and shoe-last adzes. Most of the identified defects are direct fractures; a few were caused by an indirect force (they are localised at the cranial base, such as around the foramen magnum). The majority of crania show multiple traumata, and single fractures seem to be the exception. The high degree of fragmentation, which is also evident in very robust, thick-walled male crania, implies the use by the aggressors of mainly blunt weapons, with high-impact force and power. Additionally, several variable face- and tooth fractures were found. As the skeleton of the mid-

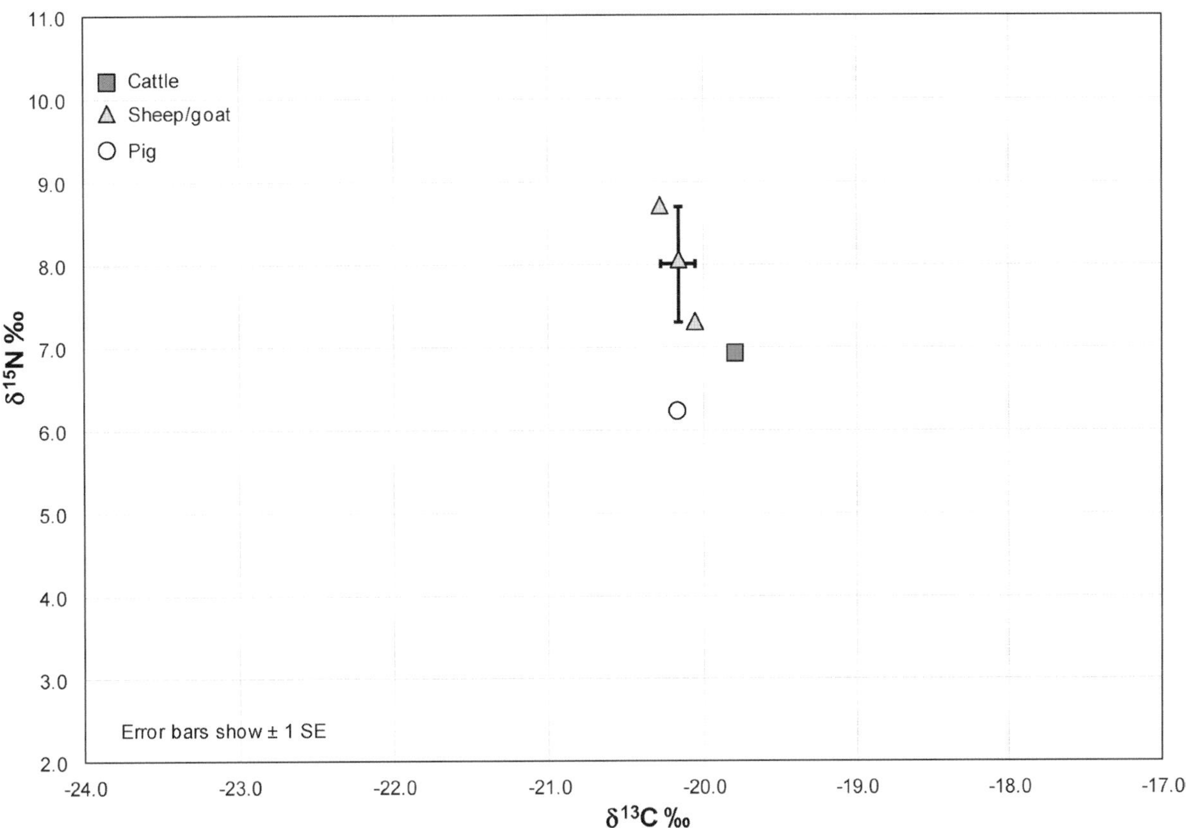

Fig. 5.13. Asparn an der Zaya/Schletz: carbon and nitrogen isotope ratios (‰) of animals.

face is relatively resistant to enormous forces (because the mandible absorbs a part of the traumatic energy; Hardt and Kuttenberger 2010), the fractures observed on the mandibles, the anterior alveolar process and other portions of the mid-face may also be seen as indicators of tremendous force, substantiating our hypothesis of a massive violent attack against the occupants of Asparn.

Besides this consistent pattern of peri-mortem trauma, the whole sample of the skeletal remains from Asparn was characterised by a particular kind of condition: a dismemberment and disarticulation of the skeletons, as mentioned above, and the presence of small ovoid depressions and crateriform crushing of the compact bone on certain parts of the skeletons. We have ascribed these features to gnawing by animals and have interpreted the bite marks as the consequence of corpses lying uncovered on the surface of the ditch fill for an extended period of time. The degree of preservation allowed us to conclude that the dead of Asparn must have remained exposed for quite some time, possibly for up to half a year.

5.8.3 Carbon and nitrogen analysis

We obtained carbon and nitrogen stable isotope measurements from 35 individuals from Asparn, but ran some repeat samples of which the averages are presented in Table 5.7. The sample is dominated by males (17) with six females, five juveniles, one infant and six unsexed individuals, one of whom was classified as adult (Fig. 5.12).

Age/sex variation

The single infant from Asparn shows a clear nursing effect, with δ^{13}C and δ^{15}N values 0.8‰ and 3.9‰ respectively above the adult female mean. Apart from that, there were no clear trends with age in δ^{13}C or δ^{15}N values. Among the adults, the mean female δ^{15}N value was 0.5‰ lower than that of males, and the difference was significant (ANOVA, p=0.021). This is quite a big difference compared with other sites, possibly because this population is unusually coherent (that is, from a single event), so what is usually a quite small and subtle effect is not being obscured by changes over time, which might well happen at a large long-lived cemetery.

A few individuals seem to have slightly lower δ^{13}C values than the main group – one of these, a young adult male (individual 8) is more than two standard deviations from the male mean in both δ^{13}C (low) and δ^{15}N (high) values. The varied values from other individuals are not technically outliers, an effect of the low number of samples and greater variability of juveniles and females; and the particularly low δ^{13}C value (individual 18) is a measurement of borderline quality – though still acceptable on our criteria – which may affect δ^{13}C (see Appendix A).

Animals

Unfortunately the faunal sample from Asparn was very small and cannot sustain detailed analysis (Fig. 5.13).

The difference between adult human and cattle means is 0.2‰±0.14 (SD) for δ^{13}C and 2.5‰±0.44 for δ^{15}N, but there is only one cattle individual, so this may not be a very reliable estimate. Using the values from Gnadendorf (about 8 km away) as a comparison (Chapter 5.7.3), the difference between adult human and cattle means is 0.8‰±0.38 (SD) for δ^{13}C and 2.2‰±0.75 for δ^{15}N. This may be a more useful comparison as the fauna at Asparn do not seem particularly different from Gnadendorf and the human values are similar to those at Kleinhadersdorf, also compared with Gnadendorf fauna.

5.8.4 Strontium analysis

For Asparn, strontium analysis is being carried out independently of the Lifeways project.

5.8.5 Site summary and discussion

Overall, the carbon and nitrogen values from the human population at Asparn show a community sharing a similar diet. Four or five individuals appeared to deviate from the main cluster of the results (individuals 8, 18, 20 and 63, as well as possibly individual 9), through having lower carbon values. However, the differences are slight and may not be significant. Unlike for the other sites in this project, Asparn allows us to see the carbon and nitrogen values from what is likely to have been a contemporary population. This may suggest that the time-depth at some cemeteries may mask subtle differences between the sexes.

5.9 Mitterndorf im Tullnerfeld

5.9.1 Introduction

This site is the most recent LBK cemetery to come to light in Austria and was excavated between 2003 and 2005 by Christoph Blesl and the *Bundesdenkmalamt*, in advance of high-speed rail development works running south of the Danube, between Vienna and St. Pölten (Blesl *et al.* 2003; 2004). This series of excavations also led to the discovery of two new settlements at Saladorf and Pottenbrunn, *c.* 3.5 km and *c.* 20 km to the west of the cemetery (Blesl and Stöckl 2004; Blesl and Kaiser 2005; Masur 2009, 17), and the burials appear to have been contemporary with the settlements, having taken place during the later part of the *Notenkopf* phase (Blesl *et al.* 2003, 23). At the site of Mitterndorf itself a shallow pit came to light, also dating to the late *Notenkopf* phase, which contained large numbers of complete and fragmentary adzes (Blesl *et al.* 2004, 28).

These sites are situated on the south banks of the Perschling, a tributary of the Danube, in an area of LBK settlement that stretches between the Tulln and Traisen rivers (Fig. 5.1; Lenneis 1995; Pieler 2004). This region was settled during the *ältere* LBK, but settlement expanded significantly during the later phases (Lenneis 1982a), including to areas off the loess, on glacial gravel deposits (Sommerer 2005, 18–19). Thus both Saladorf and Mitterndorf were found on glacial gravels and *c.* 5 km from the Molasse deposits of the northern Alpine foreland (Sommerer 2005, 18). Loess and Pleistocene marine deposits make up the rest of the surrounding geology (Price *et al.* 2004, 27).

In total, 28 graves were found (Table 5.8), including a cenotaph, two cremations and one double burial of two young infants (aged 2–3 and 6–7 years; Chapter 5.9.2). The nine adult female burials outnumbered the five adult males who were interred at the cemetery, and there were also three young children and a late juvenile/early adolescent present (Chapter 5.9.2). Fifteen of the graves (46%) were unfurnished, which included all the child burials, in contrast to Kleinhadersdorf, and the burial of the early adolescent. Polished stone was found in five graves (including the possible cenotaph), associated with male burials, while pottery was found in graves of both sexes (seven graves). *Spondylus* beads and V-shaped buckles were found in five burials and in four cases *Spondylus* also accompanied a polished stone tool. Some lithics, an antler point and possible stone beads account for the rest of the grave good assemblage. Graves are mainly east–west oriented and left-crouched, though in comparison to other burials in Lower Austria, there is a slight preference for burials with the head to the north or north-east (rather than south and south-east), perhaps suggesting more in common with Rutzing and Upper Austrian burial practices, where north-east is the dominant orientation (Chapter 5.10). The four right-crouched burials at the cemetery are oriented to the north, north-east and west – the unusual orientations for this site.

Of particular interest is grave 485. This individual has the most impressive range of finds (Fig. 5.14; Table 5.8), including the burial of a young dog (3–4 years) placed at the foot of the individual. The deposition of a whole animal is very rare in the LBK. While joints of meat are attested at sites throughout the LBK (40 cases are present in total: Lifeways Database), other examples of complete dog skeletons do exist. As well as a complete dog skeleton at the settlement burial at Złotniki, Poland, in a similar position at the feet of the deceased (Veit 1996, 118), Zalai-Gaál *et al.* (2011, 52–3) identified a further likely example in Slovakia, as well as a possible example in the Körös culture and two in the Bavarian *Stichbandkeramik* (SBK). The example from Blatné, Slovakia, was accompanied by sherds decorated in Želiezovce style (Zalai-Gaál *et al.* 2011, 52). In their survey, which mainly focuses on the Lengyel and Tiszapolgár cultures, Zalai-Gaál *et al.* (2011) argue that dog burials are something apart from the practice of putting joints of meat in the grave, though the presence of a dog's leg in a burial of an adult male (grave 113) at Aiterhofen (Nieszery 1995, 287) may suggest otherwise. The higher frequency of complete dog skeletons in the cultures that follow the LBK in these areas may point to this being a later development in LBK burial practices.

5.9.2 Osteology

Preservation

The remains of 27 individuals were analysed. Overall, the

remains were mostly in poor or moderate to poor condition. Preservation was largely incomplete, with fragmentation, surface erosion and incomplete preservation of joint surfaces limiting the diagnosis of potential pathological features on affected skeletal elements.

Demography: age and sex

Of the 27 individuals analysed, 23 were adults and four were juveniles. The adult assemblage consisted of nine adult females, five adult males and nine unsexed adults (Fig. 5.15).

The proportion of non-adults (15%), together with a total absence of infants, is much lower than expected and common in archaeological assemblages. It most probably results from a bias in preservation of children's bones as well as potential differences in funerary rites between adults and children (Guy *et al.* 1997; Scott 1999, 30; Chamberlain 2006, 98).

A more detailed look at the age distribution in the adult sample at Mitterndorf shows a similar age pattern in the male and female samples, though it should be borne in mind that the assemblage is relatively small and that a proportion of adults could not be sexed or could only be aged very broadly (Fig. 5.16).

In the non-adult sample, one individual died between the ages of 1–4 years, two died between 4–8 years and one between 8–12 years (Fig. 5.17). Unfortunately, the sample is too small to establish any meaningful child mortality patterns at Mitterndorf.

Adult stature

As a result of the fragmented state of preservation of much of the assemblage, femoral length measurements were only available for three adult males. Values ranged between 42.0 and 47.5 cm, representing the range of values obtained for other assemblages as part of this project.

Dental disease and modification

A total of 347 permanent teeth from 19 individuals could be examined. This included 291 teeth from adult individuals and 56 teeth from juveniles (Figs 5.18–19).

In the adult sample, six (40%) out of 15 adults with preserved teeth presented with caries, and four (26.7%) with enamel hypoplasia. Out of four individuals in the non-adult sample, one (25%) presented with enamel hypoplasia (Table 5.9), resulting in an overall total of five (26.3%) affected individuals at Mitterndorf. No caries was recorded in the juvenile sample.

When considering prevalence rates based on the number of teeth present, nine (3.1%) out of 291 preserved teeth in the adult sample were affected by caries and 10 (3.4%) by enamel hypoplasia (Table 5.10). In addition, one tooth (1.8%) in the non-adult sample also presented with enamel hypoplasia. This resulted in an overall total of 11 (3.2%) teeth affected by enamel hypoplasia at Mitterndorf.

A comparison of male and female prevalence for caries and enamel hypoplasia shows slightly higher rates for females; however, neither of these differences is statistically significant, contrasting with results for Nitra and Polgár-Ferenci-hát.

Cribra orbitalia

Out of eight individuals with at least one partially preserved orbit, two (25%) presented with signs of *cribra orbitalia*. Both individuals were adult females (Table 5.11).

Periosteal changes and infection

Periosteal reactions or changes indicative of inflammatory, infectious and metabolic conditions were noted on three individuals at Mitterndorf, including one adult woman, one adult man and one unsexed adult (Table 5.12), giving a crude prevalence of 11.1%. No trauma was recorded.

Summary

The relatively poor state of preservation of the Mitterndorf assemblage limited the osteological analysis and any population-based conclusions. Unlike other assemblages, no significant sex-related differences in dental health were noted. However, similarly to trends established at other sites so far, non-adults were under-represented, and more females showed signs of anaemia (*cribra orbitalia*).

5.9.3 Carbon and nitrogen analysis

Although stable isotope analysis was attempted on the human bone from Mitterndorf, unfortunately the preservation was so poor that no bone collagen could be extracted.

5.9.4 Strontium analysis

A total of 15 individuals were sampled, including five males, six females, one juvenile and three adults of indeterminate sex. In the case of the male interred in grave 91, both the M1 and M3 molars were sampled, giving a total of 16 analyses at this site (Fig. 5.20; Table 5.13).

For the nearby Bell Beaker site of Henzig, which has also been analysed for strontium isotopes, Price *et al.* (2004, 27) argue that the local range is 0.7088 to 0.7091. Henzig is located on fluvial gravels, but surrounded by loess. The average strontium $^{87}Sr/^{86}Sr$ ratio for Mitterndorf falls above this range but well within that of the loess (0.7085–0.7105). Two outliers have $^{87}Sr/^{86}Sr$ ratios that are outside this range – grave 329 (an adult female) and grave 73 (early mature adult male) – and their $^{87}Sr/^{86}Sr$ ratios suggest more radiogenic soils, the closest of which are to be found some 50 km north (in the Bohemian Massif, across the Danube).

There are no significant differences in the mean or variance of strontium concentrations or ratios between men and women at Mitterndorf, with both the outliers included and excluded in the calculations. Unusually for sites sampled in the project, there is a positive correlation between $^{87}Sr/^{86}Sr$ ratios and strontium concentration (r^2=0.437, p=0.07, n=15), which suggests that the community could have been consuming a diet from a high 1/Sr conc./low

Table 5.8. Mitterndorf: the isotope, osteological and archaeological data. Age and sex information from Linda Fibiger (this volume). See Chapter 2 for further definition of ages. As bone collagen extraction failed, there are no stable isotope results from this site. Key for body position: LC – Left-crouched; RC – Right-crouched; C – Crouched, direction unknown; CB – Crouched on back; CF – Crouched on front; S – Supine; P – Prone; I – Irregular. Key for grave goods (number of items in brackets): U. – Unfurnished; F. – Fill only (all items listed after an F. were in the fill of the grave rather than at the level of the skeleton); Pol. – Polished stone; Cer. – Ceramics; Shd. – Sherds; Spon. – Spondylus*; She. – Other Shell; Och. – Ochre; Lit. – Chipped stone; Bon – Worked bone; Grd. – Grinding stone; n.d. – no data.*
** The details from this grave were taken from Blesl 2005, 68.*

Burial	Tooth	Sex	Age	$^{87}Sr/^{86}Sr$	Sr conc. ppm	Orientation	Body position	Grave goods	Pathologies
1	-	-	-	-	-	-	-	Cenotaph: Pol.(2), Spon.(buckle)	-
8	-	F?	YMA	-	-	E–W	LC	U.	Possible infection
10	M1	F	Adult >20	0.70927	79	E–W	LC	U.	Caries (1)
13	-	-	4–5	-	-	-	-		-
17	M1	-	2–3	0.70916	69	N–S	-	U.	-
18a	-	-	6–7	-	-	-	-	U.	-
18b	-	-	Late Juv/Early Adol.	-	-	-	-	U.	-
19	M1	F?	Adult	0.70909	82	-	-	*n.d.*	Enamel hypoplasia
21	-	-	Adult/>20	-	-	-	-	*n.d*	-
27	M1	F	OMA	0.70950	63	N–S	RC	Cer.(1)	Enamel hypoplasia
28	M2	-	Mid-Adult	0.70941	79	NE–SW	RC?	She.(1)	Caries (2), enamel hypoplasia
35	-	-	Adult	-	-	E–W	I	U.	-
73	M1	M	YMA	0.71061	43	E–W	LC	U.	Caries (2)
75	-	-	Adult	-	-	E–W?	LC?	Cer.(1)	-
91	M1 M3	M	Adult/>25	0.70984 0.70954	60 58	E–W	LC?	Pol.(1), Spon.(buckle)	Possible peri-mortem trauma (spine)
92	-	-	Adult	-	-	W–E	LC	Spon.(buckle), Lit.(1)	-
93	-	F	Adult	-	-	NE–SW	LC	U.	-
156*	-	F?	Adult	-	-	-	LC	Cer., Spon.(4 beads), She.(?)	-
315	-	-	-	-	-	-	-	Cremation	-
316	-	-	-	-	-	-	-	Cremation	-
329	M1	F	Adult	0.71112	60	E–W	LC	Lit.(1)	*Cribra orbitalia*, enamel hypoplasia
358	M1	M	OMA	0.70968	85	E–W	LC	Cer.(1)	Enamel hypoplasia
420	M3	F	Adult >25	0.70952	59	E–W	LC	Cer.(1), She.(28), Stone object	*Cribra orbitalia*, caries (1)
475	-	F?	YMA	-	-	E–W?	LC?	U.	-

485	M2	-	Mid-Adult >30	0.70879	110	W–E	LC	Pol.(1), Cer.(1), Spon.(V buckle), Grd.(1), Whole dog (3-4 years), also possible stone bead	Possible infection
486	M1	-	Adult >20	0.70942	69	W–E	RC	U.	-
487	M2	F?	YA	0.70967	59	E–W	LC	U.	-
508	-	-	Mid-Adult	-	-	E–W	LC	Cer.(1)	Caries (2)
511	-	M?	YMA <30	-	-	NW–SE	-	U.	-
512	M2	M	Mid-Adult	0.70980	60	W–E	LC	Pol.(2), Spon.(3)	Caries (1), possible infection
515	M2	M	Mid-Adult	0.70909	69	N–S	RC	Pol.(1)	-

Fig. 5.14. Mitterndorf: burial 485 of adult male with dog. © Bundesdenkmalamt.

^{87}Sr/^{86}Sr ratio source and a lower 1/Sr conc./higher ^{87}Sr/^{86}Sr ratio source (Chapter 2.3 for longer discussion of mixing lines). The end-member with low strontium ratio is likely to have been sourced in the vicinity of the site, whereas the upper end-member source could perhaps have been some distance from the area. If the upper outliers are excluded, the significance of the correlation falls (r^2=0.485, p=0.08, n=13) and disappears completely if the lower outlier (grave 485; ^{87}Sr/^{86}Sr ratio=0.70879) is also excluded (r^2=0.222, p=0.122, n=12). This would leave the site at Mitterndorf with a tightly clustered group of individuals with a local origin and three outliers from varied geographic origins.

Correlations with the archaeological data

With such a small assemblage, there is no overall patterning that can be distinguished (for example, all right-crouched burials fall in the main cluster of burials), but a couple of notable trends can be identified. The individual with the lowest outlying ^{87}Sr/^{86}Sr ratio (grave 485: 0.70879) is interesting archaeologically as the grave good assemblage included a complete dog skeleton (discussed above; Fig. 5.14). This individual was also buried with a polished stone adze and a *Spondylus* V-buckle. The other two graves with both polished stone and *Spondylus* have very similar ^{87}Sr/^{86}Sr

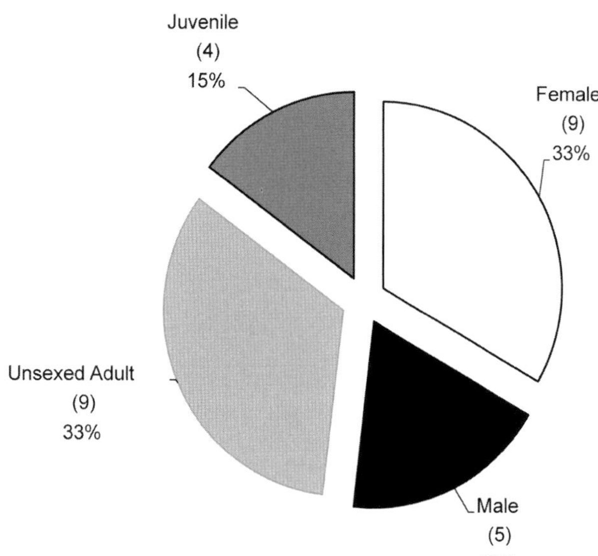

Fig. 5.15. Mitterndorf: age and sex assessment.

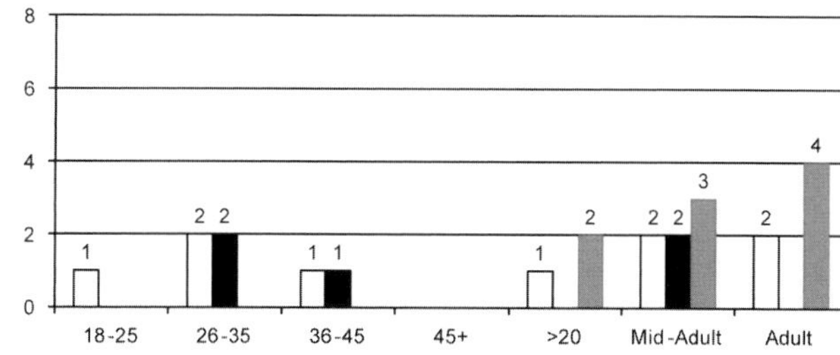

Fig. 5.16. Mitterndorf: adult age distribution.

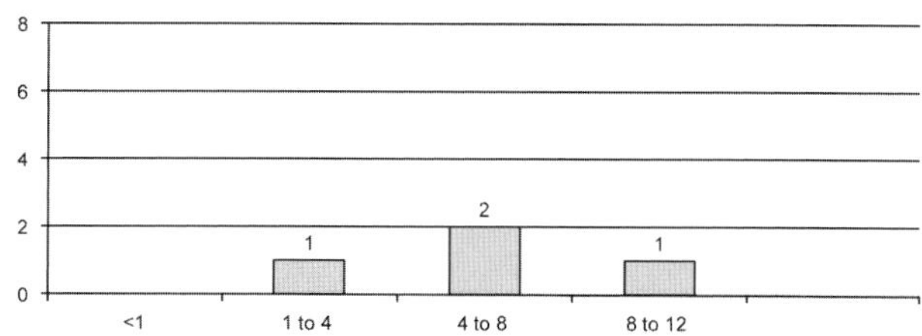

Fig. 5.17. Mitterndorf: non-adult age distribution.

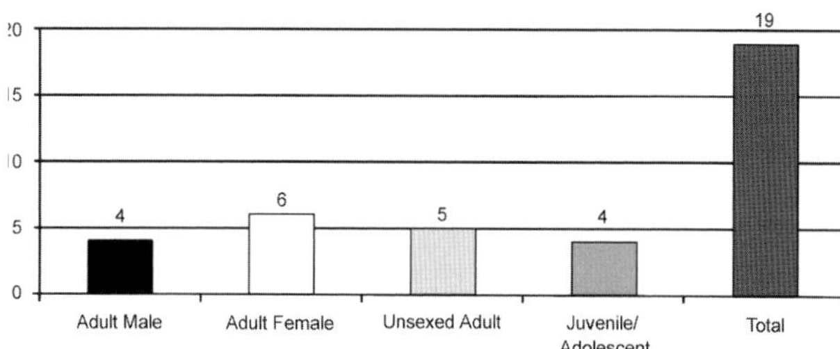

Fig. 5.18. Mitterndorf: number of individuals with partial or complete dentitions.

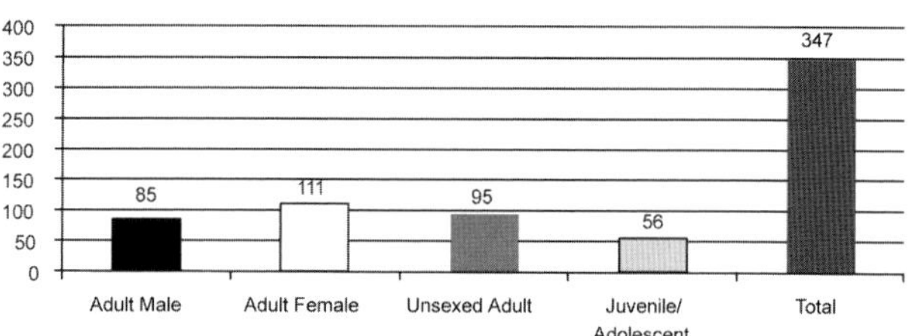

Fig. 5.19. Mitterndorf: number of teeth present.

ratios (grave 91: M1 molar=0.70984, M3 molar=0.70954; and grave 512: M2 molar=0.70980), which may suggest that they have similar geographic origins or shared diet in childhood. Neither of the outliers with $^{87}Sr/^{86}Sr$ ratios above 0.7105 was accompanied by a polished stone axe.

5.9.5 Site summary and discussion

The strontium isotope results from Mitterndorf fall into a group of tightly clustered values, with three outliers. There are few age and sex differences across the $^{87}Sr/^{86}Sr$ ratios, but the number of samples is limited. The two individuals with $^{87}Sr/^{86}Sr$ ratios above 0.7105 are unlikely to have originated in the immediate vicinity of the site and are therefore likely to have moved into the area at some point after their first molars had mineralised, but the archaeological context of their burials does not point towards any unique attributes or their identification as outsiders. However, the individual in grave 485 does seem to stand out with a number of unique features in the grave goods accompanied by the lowest $^{87}Sr/^{86}Sr$ ratio from the site. This unsexed adult, who died after the age of 30, had the most complex grave good assemblage at the cemetery including a polished stone adze, a *Spondylus* V-buckle, a grinding stone and, highly unusually, a complete dog skeleton placed at the feet of the deceased. This individual had also suffered from an injury or infection on the lower left leg, which the forelegs of the dog appear to embrace. The Mitterndorf cemetery is late in the *Notenkopf* sequence and this burial may hint at the beginning of changes to come in the *Stichbandkeramik*.

5.10 Rutzing

5.10.1 Introduction

Rutzing/Haid sits on the lower terrace of the river Traun, between Linz and Marchtrenk, in Upper Austria (Fig. 5.1). The excavations were carried out during the 1960s in rescue conditions, after the site was discovered in the course of ongoing gravel extraction (Fig. 5.21; Kloiber and Kneidinger 1968; 1969; Kloiber *et al.* 1971). They produced two areas of Neolithic settlement and two of Neolithic cemetery (not all LBK), though it seems extremely likely that these areas were once joined, before destruction by machining (Kloiber and Kneidinger 1968, 12). The cemetery itself, situated 300 m from a LBK settlement, is also likely to have once been larger than the 24 graves recovered, and a further four graves (25, 28, 29, 30) were machined away in their entirety (Kloiber and Kneidinger 1969, 24). The general preservation of the skeletons is poor (see below for demography and osteological analysis).

While the site produced *Vornotenkopf* pottery, suggesting it had some earlier LBK settlement (Lenneis 2001; 2008),

Table 5.9. Mitterndorf: dental pathology. Individuals affected.

Group	No. of individuals with partial/complete dentitions	No. (%) affected by caries	No. (%) affected by enamel hypoplasia
Adult Male	4	1 (25)	1 (25)
Adult Female	6	2 (33.3)	2 (33.3)
Unsexed Adult	5	3 (60)	1 (20)
All Adults	15	6 (40)	4 (26.7)
Juvenile	4	0	1 (25)
Total	19	6 (31.6)	5 (26.3)

Table 5.10. Mitterndorf: dental pathology. Teeth affected.

Group	No. of teeth	No. (%) affected by caries	No. (%) affected by enamel hypoplasia
Adult Male	85	1 (1.2)	2 (2.4)
Adult Female	111	2 (1.8)	3 (2.7)
Unsexed Adult	95	6 (6.3)	5 (5.3)
All Adults	291	9 (3.1)	10 (3.4)
Juvenile	56	0	1 (1.8)
Total	347	9 (2.6)	11 (3.2)

Table 5.11. Mitterndorf: cribra orbitalia.

	No. of individuals with at least one partial eye socket preserved	No. (%) of individuals with *cribra orbitalia*
Adult Male	2	0 (0)
Adult Female	3	2 (66.7)
Unsexed Adult	1	0 (0)
All Adults	6	2 (33.3)
Juvenile	2	0 (0)
Total	8	2 (25)

Table 5.12. Mitterndorf: periosteal lesions and pathological changes related to inflammatory, infectious and haemorrhagic processes.

Group	ID	Age	Changes recorded	Differential diagnosis
Female	8	Young Middle Adult	Remodelled periosteal new bone on left tibia	Localised injury/ infection or haemorrhagic process
Male	512	Mid-Adult	Remodelled periosteal new bone on right tibia and fibula	Localised injury/ infection or haemorrhagic process
Unsexed Adult	485	Adult	Remodelled periosteal new bone on left tibia and fibula	Localised injury/ infection or haemorrhagic process

most of the vessels from the settlement area of Rutzing and all the graves seem to come from the *jüngere* LBK (Phase II). The orientations of graves at Rutzing are very varied (Kloiber and Kneidinger 1969, 24), with no one direction dominating (Table 5.14). At Rutzing half the burials are oriented between N–S and E–W, with their heads to the north, north-east and east, whereas it is more common across the LBK for the orientations to fall with the head to the east, south-east and south (Lifeways Database). The frequency of different body positions at Rutzing also suggests variation from the pattern seen at other cemeteries, as over half of the individuals where

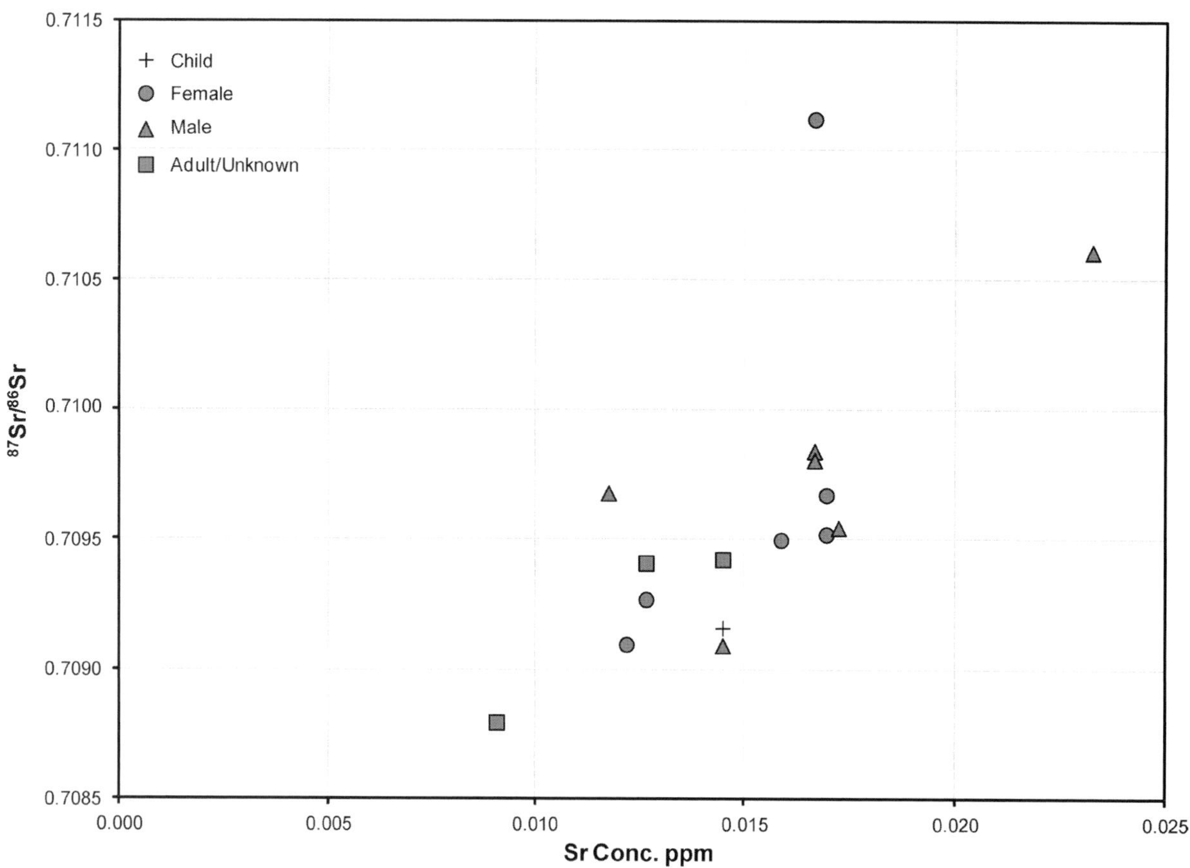

Fig. 5.20. Mitterndorf: strontium concentration (ppm) versus ratio ($^{87}Sr/^{86}Sr$).

*Table 5.13. Mitterndorf: strontium isotope ratios and concentrations. 'All' includes three unsexed adults. * denotes number of analyses, not number of individuals.*

Age/sex	Mean $^{87}Sr/^{86}Sr$	SD $^{87}Sr/^{86}Sr$	Mean Sr conc.	SD Sr conc.	n*
Juvenile	0.70916	-	69	-	1
Male	0.70946	0.00042	74	20	6
Female	0.71004	0.00079	60	13	5
All	0.70959	0.00057	69	15	16

body position is identifiable are buried right-crouched (nine are right-crouched and six are left-crouched: Kloiber and Kneidinger 1968; 1969; Lifeways Database).[15]

The right-crouched burials are concentrated in the northern half of the cemetery (nine right-crouched, three left-crouched, with five graves having insufficient preservation to determine body position), leaving a small cluster of six graves to the south that are almost all left-crouched (five left-crouched, and one grave with insufficient preservation; Fig. 5.21). In the southern cluster E–W burials dominate (graves 12, 31–33), with one SE–NW burial (grave 12) and one W–E burial (grave 13: see below), while in the northern cluster orientations are spread over N–S, through NE–SW (the most frequent orientation) to E–W, with four burials oriented to the south. Furthermore, in the northern group of burials not one grave is both E–W or SE–NW oriented and left-crouched (the dominant orientation and body position for LBK burials as a whole). No spatial patterning in the grave goods could be determined.

Nine of the 24 burials are unfurnished (37.5%), which is slightly higher than the average for all LBK cemeteries (*c.* 33%). Grave goods at the site follow the normal range of objects found in the LBK (Fig. 5.22), including two male graves with polished stone adzes (grave 8, where the adze is unusually placed beneath the head, and grave 13) and seven graves with pots (Kloiber *et al.* 1971). The eight graves with *Spondylus* are perhaps a slightly higher number than we would expect on average across the LBK, but the amount of *Spondylus* in each grave is low. Of particular interest amongst the grave goods are those that furnished burial 13, which included two fox teeth, which is suggestive of the fox mandibles found predominantly in Bavaria (Chapter 6.5), and 120 imitation deer teeth made from bone, which are very rare and only known in a couple of other instances (e.g. two such objects were in the grave of a 2–3-year-old, in the early LBK cemetery at Bruchstedt, Thuringia; Kahlke 2004; Lenneis 2007, 135–6). However, like the ceramic beads at Mezőkövesd (Chapter 3.7), there is no need to immediately assume that because the imitation teeth were made out of another material they were less valuable or fakes.

Lenneis (2007, 136) connects these objects to a 'hunter' identity that drew on earlier Mesolithic practices and makes links to deer teeth present in graves. Red deer teeth were more frequent in Mesolithic burials across Europe; they are found at the Bavarian Mesolithic skull nest at Ofnet (Orschiedt 1998b), and further afield in Denmark at the well known Mesolithic cemeteries found there (Tilley 1996, 39, 41). However, this correlation is by no means straightforward and as Lenneis (2007, 136) points out, graves containing such objects also often have 'Neolithic equipment such as adzes and ceramics besides their hunting arms'. In the case of burial 13 at Rutzing this is certainly true; the imitation deer teeth and fox teeth were present alongside *Spondylus* beads as adornment around the neck, and a polished stone adze and *Spondylus* V-buckle in the area of the pelvis, making it the 'richest' grave at the site in terms of the quantity of grave goods (Kloiber *et al.* 1971, 29). Clearly, there is no simple divide between 'Mesolithic' and 'Neolithic' grave good assemblages. It is interesting to note, however, that this burial is also the only W–E oriented burial at the cemetery.

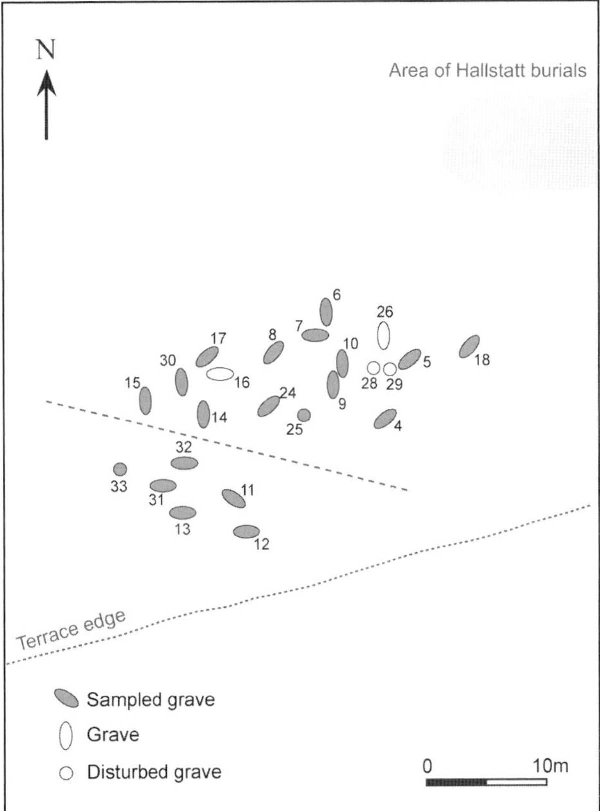

Fig. 5.21. Rutzing: plan of the cemetery. Dashed line shows the two groups of burials suggested by the carbon isotope values. After Kloiber and Kneidinger (1969, 23).

5.10.2 Osteology

Preservation

The remains of 24 individuals from Rutzing were analysed. The skeletal remains were mostly in poor or moderate to poor condition. Preservation was largely incomplete and fragmentation, surface erosion and incomplete preservation of joint surfaces were widespread, limiting the diagnosis of potential pathological features on affected skeletal elements.

Demography: age and sex

The 24 individuals analysed included 15 adults and four juveniles. The adult assemblage consisted of three females, six males and six unsexed adults (Fig. 5.23).

The proportion of non-adults (29%) and the total absence of infants indicate an under-representation of the younger section of the population in the burial record, probably resulting from a bias in preservation of children's bones as well as potential differences in funerary rites between adults and children (Chamberlain 2006, 98; Guy *et al.* 1997; Scott 1999, 30).

A more detailed look at the age distribution in the adult sample at Rutzing shows a similar age pattern for males and females, though it should be borne in mind that this sample is very small and that a proportion of adults could not be sexed or only be aged very broadly (Fig. 5.24).

In the non-adult sample, two individuals died between the ages of 1–4 years, three died between 4–8 years and three between 8–12 years. Unfortunately, the Rutzing sample is too small to establish any meaningful child mortality patterns (Fig. 5.25).

Adult stature

As a result of the fragmented state of preservation of much of the assemblage, no femoral length measurements were available.

Dental disease and modification

A total of 280 permanent teeth from 17 individuals could be examined, including 181 teeth from adult individuals and 99 teeth from juveniles and adolescents (Figs 5.26–7).

In the adult sample, four (40%) out of ten adults with preserved teeth presented with caries, and four (40%) with enamel hypoplasia. In the non-adult sample, one (14.3%) presented with enamel hypoplasia and caries (Table 5.15), resulting in an overall total of five (29.4%) individuals at Rutzing affected by caries and enamel hypoplasia respectively.

Considering prevalence rates based on the number of teeth present, ten (5.5%) out of 181 preserved teeth in the adult sample were affected by caries and nine (5%) by enamel hypoplasia (Table 5.16). In the non-adult sample,

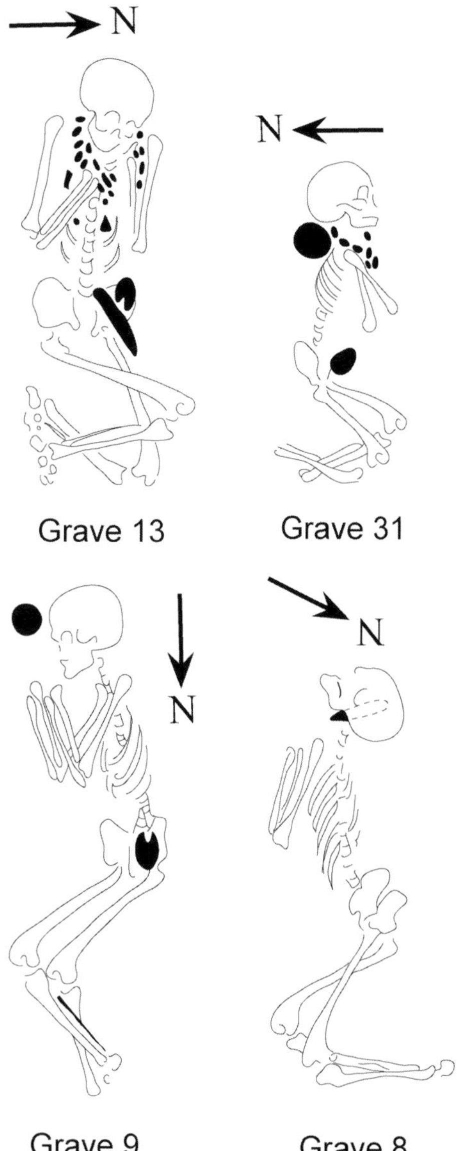

Fig. 5.22. Rutzing: four burials with grave goods. After Kloiber et al. *(1971, 29).*

two teeth (2%) presented with caries and one (1%) with enamel hypoplasia. This resulted in an overall total of 12 (4.3%) teeth affected by caries and ten (3.6%) by enamel hypoplasia.

A comparison of male and female prevalence for caries and enamel hypoplasia shows higher rates for females, both for individuals and the number of teeth affected, though this difference is not statistically significant. Enamel hypoplasia rates are very similar for both sexes.

Cribra orbitalia

Out of nine individuals with at least one partially preserved orbit, five (55.6%) presented with signs of *cribra orbitalia.* This included two adult males and three juveniles (Table 5.17). Also present was a case of porotic hyperostosis (burial 30).

Periosteal changes and infection

Periosteal reactions or changes indicative of inflammatory, infectious or metabolic conditions were noted on five individuals at Rutzing, including one adult female, two adult males and two juveniles (Table 5.18), giving a crude prevalence of 20.8%. One young adult male (burial 13) suffered from a pulmonary infection, indicated by periosteal new bone formation on the ribs (Roberts and Buikstra 2003, 101f.). Accompanying periosteal new bone on the shoulders and hips indicated the presence of a systemic condition (Fig. 5.28) and differential diagnosis includes tuberculosis.

Post-cranial trauma

A young adult male (burial 13) had suffered a vertebral arch fracture (*spondylolysis*) of the fourth lumbar vertebra. The origins of this lesion have been discussed previously (Chapter 3.9.2) and can include hereditary and activity-related factors.

A young mid-adult male (burial 14) presented with a well defined area of periosteal remodelling and thickening of the distal anterior-medial ulna shaft. There was no deviation in angulation of the bone compared to the left side. Without radiographic examination it is difficult to determine the exact origin of the changes observed, but differential diagnosis includes a healed fracture and/or a localised injury or infection. No cranial trauma was recorded at Rutzing.

Summary

The small Rutzing assemblage is characterised by similar age distributions for adult males and females and a slight under-representation of young individuals, especially infants. Dental health follows a pattern observed in other assemblages studied in the Lifeways project, with adult females showing higher caries rates. Anaemia as indicated by the presence of *cribra orbitalia* was only present in adult and juvenile individuals, though the sample of observable orbits is small and may not be representative of the population as a whole. Periosteal changes indicative of infectious and/or metabolic conditions were present in all age groups and both sexes, and included a pulmonary infection. Trauma prevalence was low.

5.10.3 Carbon and nitrogen analysis

From the individuals buried at Rutzing, 20 had sufficient preservation to be sampled for carbon and nitrogen analysis, including six males, three females, four unsexed adults and seven juveniles (Fig. 5.29; Table 5.19).

Age/sex variation

Unsurprisingly in view of the low sample numbers in each group, none of the differences between age/sex group means were statistically significant. The wide range in $\delta^{15}N$ values of the three females is noticeable, with values of 8.6‰, 9.1‰ and 10.3‰. One juvenile (grave 7, age 4–5 years) had a $\delta^{15}N$ value of 11.6‰, more than two standard

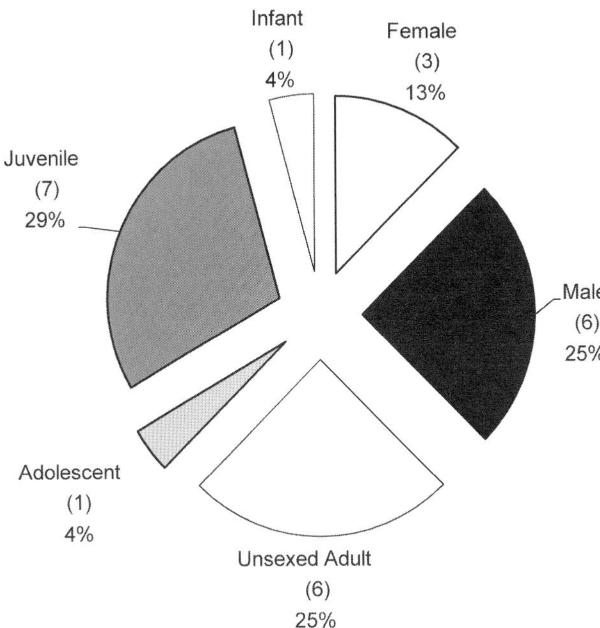

Fig. 5.23. Rutzing: age and sex assessment.

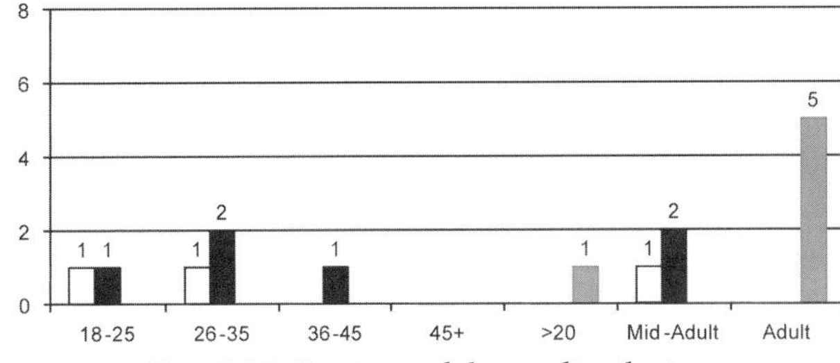

Fig. 5.24. Rutzing: adult age distribution.

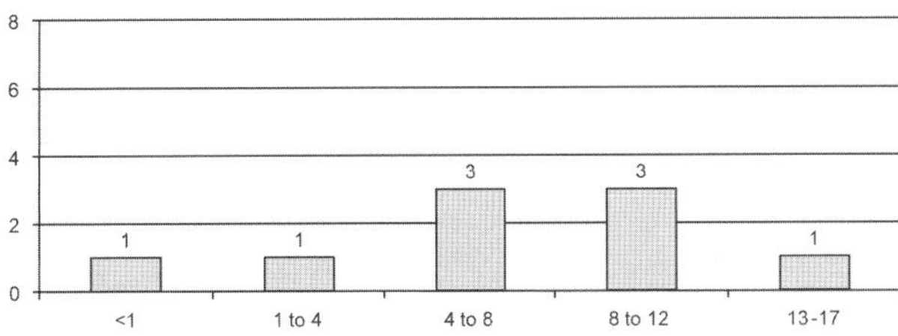

Fig. 5.25. Rutzing: non-adult age distribution.

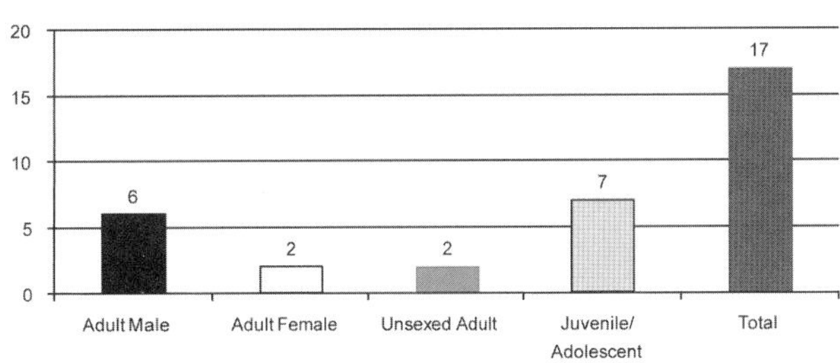

Fig. 5.26. Rutzing: number of individuals with partial or complete dentitions.

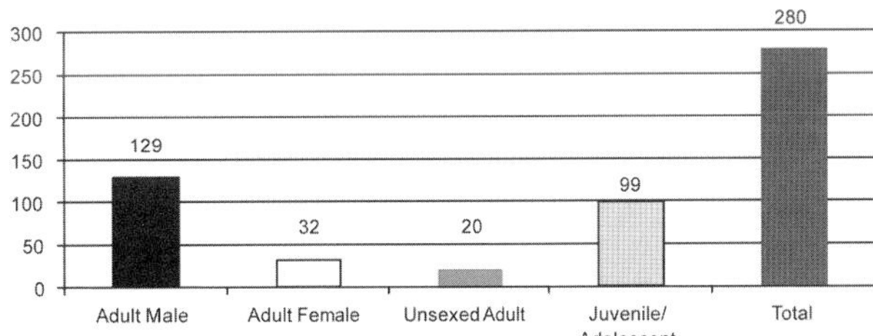

Fig. 5.27. Rutzing: number of teeth present.

deviations from the mean. This is unlikely to be a suckling signal at this age, and might reflect a dietary difference or even be the effect of illness or starvation (Waters-Rist and Katzenberg 2010).

Animals

One cattle individual has a high $\delta^{15}N$ value more than two standard deviations from the mean. Possibly this is a fragment from a juvenile animal, although we tried to avoid this in sampling.

The animals from Rutzing show an unusual pattern of $\delta^{13}C$ and $\delta^{15}N$ values (Fig. 5.30; Table 5.19). Low numbers of sheep/goats and pig urge caution in interpreting the results, though these are very suggestive of meaningful differences compared to sites to the east. There is a particularly wide range of cattle $\delta^{13}C$ values, with three individuals with two standard deviations or more lower than the mean. Pigs have higher $\delta^{13}C$ values than either cattle or sheep, but $\delta^{15}N$ values are similar to those of the herbivores. Overall the difference in $\delta^{13}C$ values is not significant (ANOVA, df=2, p=0.08), but a post hoc test showed that cattle and pig mean $\delta^{13}C$ values were significantly different (Tamhane, p=0.02). This is reminiscent of the pattern seen at sites further west (Chapter 8), and may represent a greater use of forest resources (Hamilton *et al.* 2009). On this interpretation, the cattle with the lowest $\delta^{13}C$ values would be feeding in more densely shaded habitats. The pigs would have elevated $\delta^{13}C$ values because forest fungi are contributing significantly to their diet, but $\delta^{15}N$ values similar to those of herbivores because of a lower contribution of human or settlement refuse. This implies a different form of husbandry to that seen at more eastern LBK sites for pigs, and to some extent cattle, and it may well be connected with other unusual features of this site, such as the different climate and the greater occurrence of wild animals (further discussed in Chapter 9.2.6). However, it must also be noted that the stratigraphy from this site was not clear and there may have been some mixing from later periods in the animal bone assemblage (Schmitzberger 2009b, 150; Chapter 5.4).

The single red deer sample has a $\delta^{13}C$ value similar to the low cattle values and a lower $\delta^{15}N$ value than any of the domestic animals. This is the usual pattern (Chapter 3.10.3) and probably reflects the wild animal's greater use of forest resources and exclusion from manured areas. The difference between adult human and cattle mean $\delta^{13}C$ and $\delta^{15}N$ is 1.3‰±1.01 (SD) and 3.5‰±1.18, respectively, both high relative to sites in neighbouring regions.

Correlations with the archaeological data

There are no correlations between the burial rites and

Table 5.14. Rutzing: the isotope, osteological and archaeological data. Age and sex information from Linda Fibiger (this volume). See Chapter 2 for further definition of ages. Key for body position: LC – Left-crouched; RC – Right-crouched; C – Crouched, direction unknown; CB – Crouched on back; CF – Crouched on front; S – Supine; P – Prone; I – Irregular. Key for grave goods (number of items in brackets): U. – Unfurnished; F. – Fill only (all items listed after an F. were in the fill of the grave rather than at the level of the skeleton); Pol. – Polished stone; Cer. – Ceramics; Shd. – Sherds; Spon. – Spondylus*; She. – Other Shell; Och. – Ochre; Lit. – Chipped stone; Bon – Worked bone; Grd. – Grinding stone.*

Burial	Tooth	Sex	Age (yrs)	$^{87}Sr/^{86}Sr$	Sr conc. ppm	$\delta^{13}C$ ‰	$\delta^{15}N$ ‰	Orientation	Body position	Grave goods	Pathologies
4	-	-	9–11	-	-	−20.9	9.2	NE–SW	-	Spon.(armring)	*Cribra orbitalia*
5	-	M?	(Young) Mid-Adult	-	-	−20.7	9.7	NE–SW	RC	U.	Caries (4), enamel hypoplasia
6	-	-	5–7	-	-	−20.7	9.1	S–N	-	Cer.(1)	*Cribra orbitalia*, Caries (3)
7	M1	-	4–5	0.70863	43	−20.3	11.6	E–W	RC	Cer.(2), Shd.(?), Lit.(1), Bon.(1), She.(frag.)	Possible infection
8	M2	M	YMA	0.70889	58	−20.5	10	NE–SW	RC	Pol.(1)	Caries (2)
9	M2	F	YA/>20	0.71268	66	−20.2	8.6	S–N	RC	Shd.(?), Spon.(buckle)	Caries (3), enamel hypoplasia
10	M1	-	>3	0.70870	60	−20.7	9.1	N–S	-	U.	-
11	M1 M3	-	Adult >20	0.70825 0.70838	96 126	−20.4	10.7	SE–NW	-	Lit.(3), She.(8)	-
12	-	-	Adult	-	-	−20.6	8.9	E–W	-	U.	-
13	M1 M3	M	YA	0.70909 0.70919	81 89	−20.2	9.8	W–E	LC	Pol.(1), Lit.(7), Spon.(7 beads, buckle), Tee.(2, fox), Imitation deer teeth made from bone (120)	*Cribra orbitalia*, pulmonary infection, *spondylolysis*
14	M1	M	OMA	0.70925	69	−21.1	9.6	N–S	LC	U.	*Cribra orbitalia*, fracture or infection of ulna, enamel hypoplasia
15	-	M	Mid-Adult >30	-	-	−20.5	9.4	S–N	RC	Cer.(1, Shd.s)	-
16	-	-	*c.* 1	-	-	-	-	E–W	RC	Spon. (armring/pendant?), She.(4)	-
17	M2	F	Mid-Adult	0.70954	117	−20.7	10.3	NE–SW	LC	Cer.(1)	Caries (1)
18	M1 M2	-	Adult	0.71139 0.71142	64 111	−20.4	9.1	SW–NE	RC	Spon.(2)	-
24	P1	-	9–10	0.70903	66	−20.7	9.5	NE–SW	RC	Cer.(1), Lit.(1),Spon. (2 beads), She.(2)	Possible infection
25	-	-	Adult	-	-	−20.6	9.6	-	-	U.	Possible infection
26	M1	-	6–8	0.70872	48	−20.8	8.5	S–N	LC	U.	-
27	-	-	-	-	-	-	-	-	-	-	-

28	-	-	Adult	-	-	-	-	-	-	U.	-
29	-	-	Adult	-	-	-	-	-	-	U.	-
30	-	F	YMA	-	-	−20.5	9.1	N–S	RC	U.	Infection (spine)
31	M1	-	10–12	0.70896	87	−20.6	9.7	E–W	LC	Cer.(1), Spon.(1), She.(11)	*Cribra orbitalia*
32	M1	M?	YMA	0.70924	68	−20.4	9.7	E–W	LC	U.	Possible infection, enamel hypoplasia
33	M1 M3	-	Adol.	0.70887 0.70901	46 81	-	-	-	-	Spon.(1)	Enamel hypoplasia

Table 5.15. Rutzing: dental pathology. Individuals affected.

Group	No. of individuals with partial/complete dentitions	No. (%) affected by caries	No. (%) affected by enamel hypoplasia
Adult Male	6	2 (33.3)	3 (50)
Adult Female	2	2 (100)	1 (50)
Unsexed Adult	2	0	0
All Adults	10	4 (40)	4 (40)
Juvenile/Adolescent	7	1 (14.3)	1 (14.3)
Total	17	5 (29.4)	5 (29.4)

Table 5.16. Rutzing: dental pathology. Teeth affected.

Group	No. of teeth	No. (%) affected by caries	No. (%) affected by enamel hypoplasia
Adult Male	129	6 (4.7)	7 (5.4)
Adult Female	32	4 (12.4)	2 (6.3)
Unsexed Adult	20	0	0
All Adults	181	10 (5.5)	9 (5)
Juvenile	99	2 (2)	1 (1)
Total	280	12 (4.3)	10 (3.6)

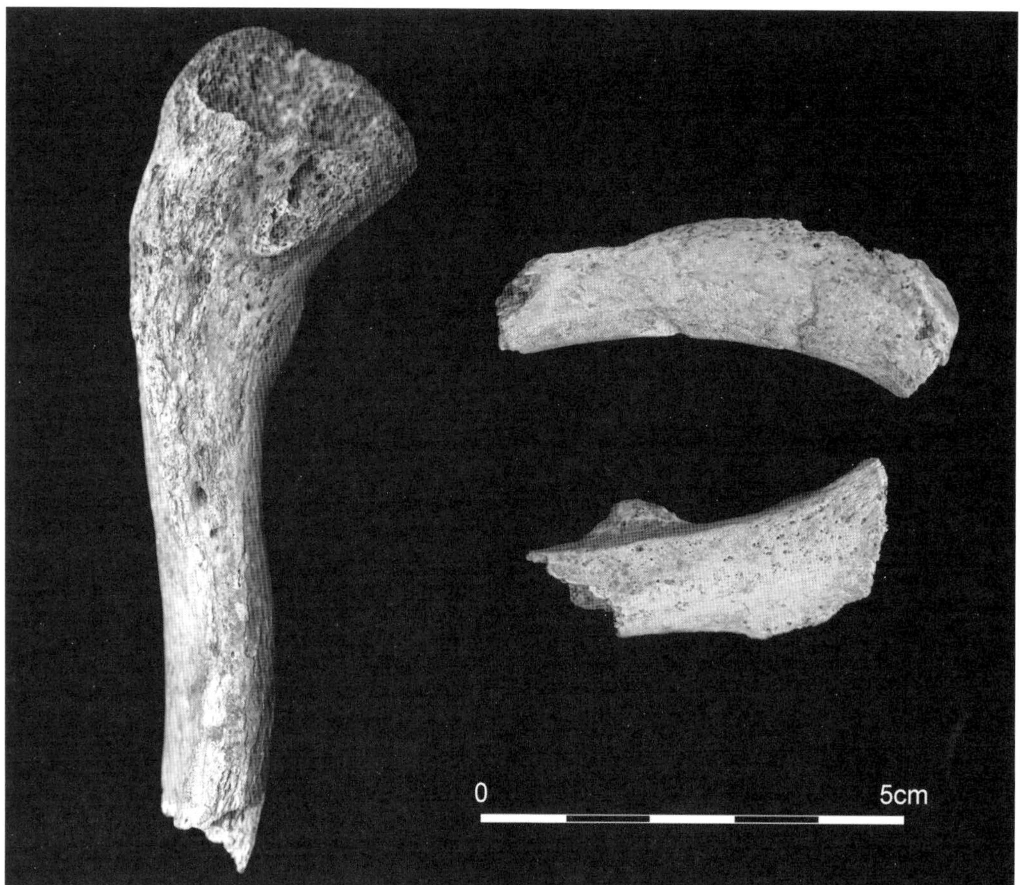

Fig. 5.28. Rutzing: new bone formation on clavicle (top) and ribs (bottom), burial 13. Photo: Linda Fibiger.

grave goods, and the stable isotope results, nor with the palaeopathological data. However, there are hints that there may be some spatial patterning in the cemetery, as those individuals with $\delta^{13}C$ values below −20.7‰ are only found in the more variable northern group of burials, while the male with the most complex grave good assemblage (burial 13) has the highest $\delta^{13}C$ value from the site as a whole (−20.2‰) and is located in the small southern cluster of burials. Overall, however, the difference in the means of the two groups is very small (northern group M=−20.6‰; southern group M=−20.4‰). This suggests that the individuals interred in the southern cluster could have been sourcing less of their food from the woodland or non-manured areas than those buried in the northern part of the cemetery, though admittedly we are on the edge of significance here (if the outliers are excluded; 2-tailed *t* test, p=0.04, n=18).

5.10.4 Strontium analysis

At Rutzing, we sampled the 14 individuals where the molars had been preserved, including four males, two females, two unsexed adults, the adolescent and five juveniles (Fig. 5.31; Table 5.20). In the case of four individuals, the M1 and M3 molars (graves 11, 13 and 33) or M1 and M2 molars (burial 18; Table 5.14) were sampled.

The area of loess (0.7085–07105) on which Rutzing sits is in the Molasse basin and is therefore surrounded by soils with expected strontium ratios between 0.7080 and 0.7090 (Price *et al.* 2004). Although Rutzing is approximately 40 km from the Flysch zone, which would supply values outside this range, the more radiogenic granites of the Bohemian Massif are just 10 km away on the northern bank of Danube. The site mean falls within the expected range for loess soils (0.70940±0.00119). As there are only two females within the sample from Rutzing, any conclusions from a comparison with the males must be handled cautiously. The female $^{87}Sr/^{86}Sr$ ratio mean falls outside the loess range (loess=0.7085–0.7105; female $^{87}Sr/^{86}Sr$ mean=0.71111±0.00222), but this is because of the outlier in grave 9.

There is a statistically significant difference between the $^{87}Sr/^{86}Sr$ ratio ranges for adults and juveniles (Levene's test, p=0.042, excluding outliers), which is difficult to explain as strontium analyses test the tooth and therefore the $^{87}Sr/^{86}Sr$ ratio represents the value at the time the tooth mineralised rather than at age of death. However, one possible explanation for this pattern could be found in who was included in cemetery burials, with inclusion in cemeteries increasing in adulthood, resulting in the greater variability seen in the strontium isotope data amongst adults. Cemeteries may not have been closed groups, with certain individuals earning the right to be buried in them throughout their lives.

Table 5.17. Rutzing: cribra orbitalia.

	No. of individuals with at least one partial eye socket preserved	No. (%) of individuals with *cribra orbitalia*
Adult Male	3	2 (66.7)
Adult Female	1	0 (0)
Unsexed Adult	1	0 (0)
All Adults	5	2 (40)
Juvenile	4	3 (75)
Total	9	5 (55.6)

Table 5.18. Rutzing: periosteal lesions and pathological changes related to inflammatory, infectious and haemorrhagic processes.

Group	ID	Age	Changes recorded	Differential diagnosis
Female	30	Young Middle Adult	Destructive changes on sacrum	Infection
Male	13	Young Adult	Periosteal new bone on clavicles, left scapula, left hip and ribs	Systemic infection, probably pulmonary origin
	32	Young Middle Adult	Remodelled periosteal new bone on lower right leg	Localised injury/infection or haemorrhagic process
Juvenile	7	4-5 years	Periosteal new bone on lower legs	Systemic infection or haemorrhagic process
	25	9-10 years	Remodelled periosteal new bone on both legs; increase endocranial porosity	Systemic infection or haemorrhagic process

Table 5.19. Rutzing: carbon and nitrogen isotope ratios (‰) of humans and animals, with means and standard deviations.

Species	Age/sex	Mean δ^{13}C	SD δ^{13}C	Mean δ^{15}N	SD δ^{15}N	n
Human	Juvenile	−20.7	0.18	9.5	1.00	7
Human	Female	−20.5	0.23	9.3	0.88	3
Human	Male	−20.5	0.31	9.7	0.21	6
Human	Unsexed adults	−20.5	0.11	9.6	0.83	4
Human	All adult	−20.5	0.23	9.6	0.58	13
Cattle		−21.8	0.98	6.1	1.03	11
Sheep/goat		−21.1	0.59	5.8	1.45	3
Pig		−20.7	0.39	5.8	0.60	4
Red deer		−22.7	-	2.8	-	1

There are two outliers with ^{87}Sr/^{86}Sr ratios that fall above the loess range (grave 18, unsexed adult, both M1 and M2 molars above 0.71113; grave 9, female young adult, M2 molar 0.71268). Both burials were right-crouched, contained *Spondylus* and were oriented towards the south (grave 18 to the south-west). Both these individuals also had low δ^{15}N values (grave 9: 8.6; grave 18: 9.1), suggesting they had a different diet to the rest of the group. Another potential outlier can be identified from grave 11. In this case, both the M1 and M3 molars from this unsexed adult fell below the loess range (0.7085–07105), with ^{87}Sr/^{86}Sr ratios of 0.70825 and 0.70838 respectively, which suggests that they originated from areas south of the loess along the Danube. This individual was buried with flint flakes (possibly an arrowhead) and eight *Dentalium* shell beads, and also has the highest δ^{15}N value (10.7‰) of all the adults from Rutzing. If all three of these individuals are excluded, then a mixing line can be identified (r^2=0.629, p=0.001), running from a high 1/Sr conc./high ^{87}Sr/^{86}Sr ratio to a low 1/Sr conc./low ^{87}Sr/^{86}Sr ratio. Generally M2

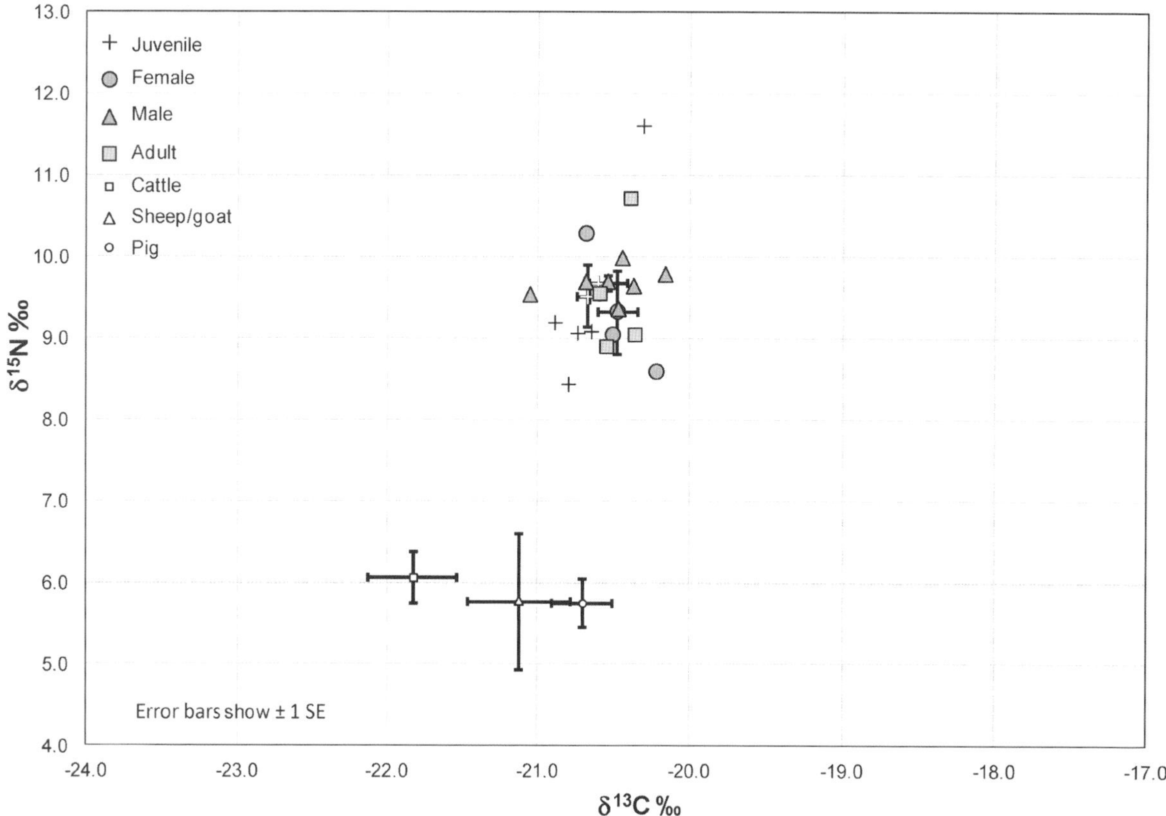

Fig. 5.29. Rutzing: carbon and nitrogen isotope ratios (‰) of humans.

and M3 molar $^{87}Sr/^{86}Sr$ ratios are higher than those from first molars, though this is not a statistically significant difference (variance or mean). In the cases where two teeth have been sampled from the same individual, the tooth that mineralised later is consistently higher in strontium concentration ppm, suggesting a shift to a higher strontium concentration food.

Correlations with the archaeological data

Overall, no particular correlations could be determined between the archaeological data, palaeopathological data and the strontium isotopes. It may be significant that the two outliers with strontium ratios above the loess range are both buried in the northern part of the site, where orientations and body positions are more varied than in the southern part of the site, where the outlier with a strontium ratio below the loess range was interred. Furthermore, the latter is the only burial at the cemetery oriented with the head to the south-east.

5.10.5 Site summary and discussion

In many ways Rutzing is a highly unusual site, in terms of both the archaeology and the isotopic results. Right-crouched body positions are more frequent than left-crouched at this cemetery and burials oriented with the head to the north and north-east dominate, in comparison to burials in the neighbouring regions of Lower Bavaria and Lower Austria, where burial orientations follow the more prevalent pattern of E–W or SE–NW and left-crouched burial positions are the most frequent. The body positions and orientations are also more varied, with no one orientation representing more than 25% of the burials. Similarly, although right-crouched burials dominate the body positions found at Rutzing, they do not have the frequency of left-crouched burials seen elsewhere. So Rutzing stands out in two ways: a different emphasis on body position and orientation, and also the occurrence of more difference within the cemetery itself.

It is interesting therefore that the stable isotope results are perhaps indicative of different animal husbandry routines and potential greater use of the forest compared to other regions in this project. A possible explanation for this pattern could lie in the more sparsely occupied nature of Upper Austria during the LBK, which may have meant that the landscape around settlements was more densely forested. The strontium isotope results also differ in so much as a potential mixing-line runs in the opposite direction to others identified in this project (such as Aiterhofen; Chapter 6.7), but the $^{87}Sr/^{86}Sr$ ratios suggest that the majority of the population originated from the loess areas around the cemetery, suggesting that it was resource use rather than the origin of the population that differed.

Given that it is the cemetery as a whole rather than particular individuals which stand out as different in this case, we can perhaps suggest that at Rutzing these statements were being made about the community as a whole rather than the identity on the scale of the individual lifeway.

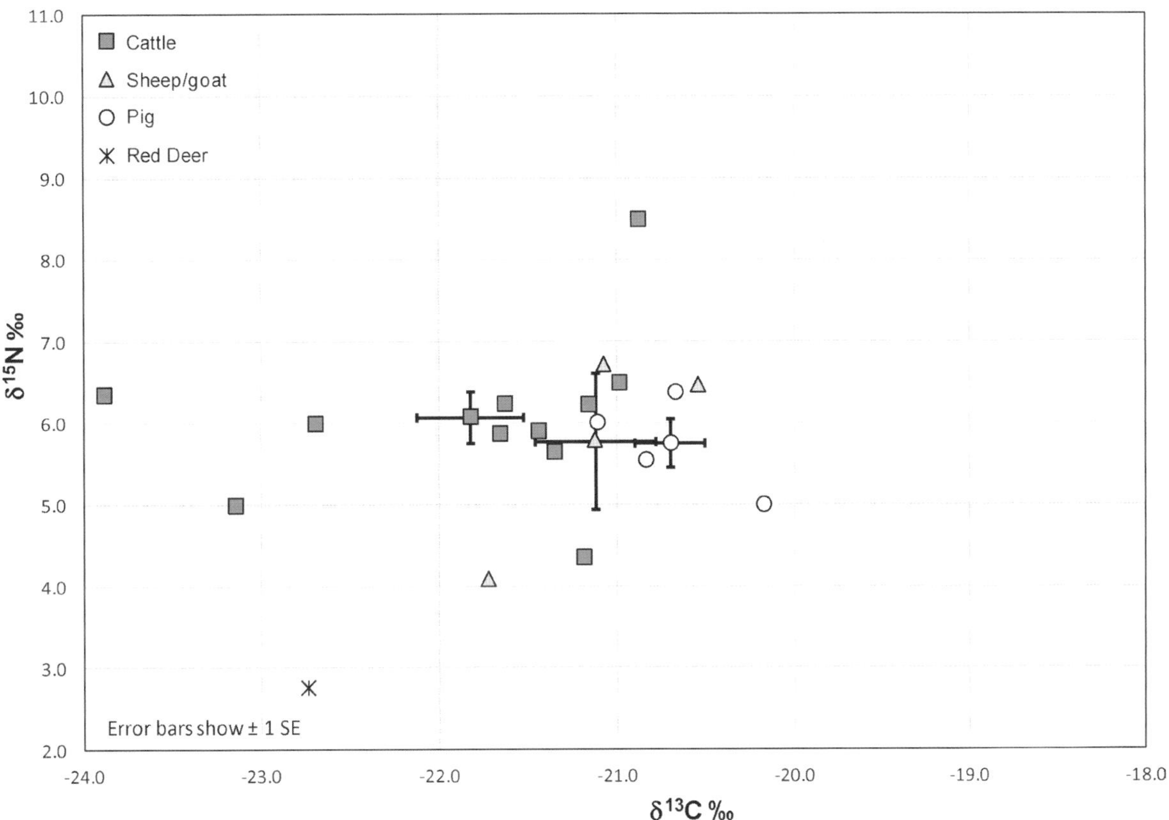

Fig. 5.30. Rutzing: carbon and nitrogen isotope ratios (‰) of animals.

*Table 5.20. Rutzing: strontium isotope ratios and concentrations. 'All' includes unsexed adults. * denotes number of analyses, not number of individuals.*

Age/sex	Mean $^{87}Sr/^{86}Sr$	SD $^{87}Sr/^{86}Sr$	Mean Sr conc.	SD Sr conc.	n*
Juvenile	0.70885	0.00017	62	17	7
Female	0.71111	0.00222	92	36	2
Male	0.70913	0.00015	73	12	5
All	0.70940	0.00119	76	24	18

Within this general pattern, however, the southern cluster of burials stands out as unusual at Rutzing, but normal for the rest of the LBK. The low $\delta^{13}C$ values are concentrated in the northern part of the cemetery, perhaps suggesting that two groups buried their dead at Rutzing; one group conformed more closely with the pattern seen in other sites in this project, concentrating on, for example, subsistence practices on the open land around the settlement, and a second larger group used a greater proportion of woodland resources. As it is unlikely that the whole cemetery is preserved, especially given the generally poor preservation of the skeletal remains, further conclusions about the relative sizes of the two groups are difficult.

Grave 13 stands out as a particularly unusual burial. In this grave was the inhumation of a young adult male, who had suffered from a pulmonary infection and was buried with a complex grave good assemblage, including *Spondylus* beads and V-buckle, a polished stone adze, seven pieces of flint, including some produced on raw material from Bavaria, and 120 imitation deer teeth. This individual was also buried with two fox teeth, which may also demonstrate connections to Bavaria, as fox mandibles appear to be a regionally specific grave good found there (D. Hofmann forthcoming). In this respect, the W–E orientation of this grave (the only grave found with this orientation at the site) is interesting as it perhaps orients this individual towards the origin of some of his grave goods. The $\delta^{13}C$ value of this individual is the highest at the site (−20.2‰), perhaps suggesting that this individual consumed fewer woodland resources than others interred at the cemetery.

5.11 Regional discussion

This chapter has focussed on the westernmost area of the *Notenkopf* LBK, found in the regions of Austria, Moravia

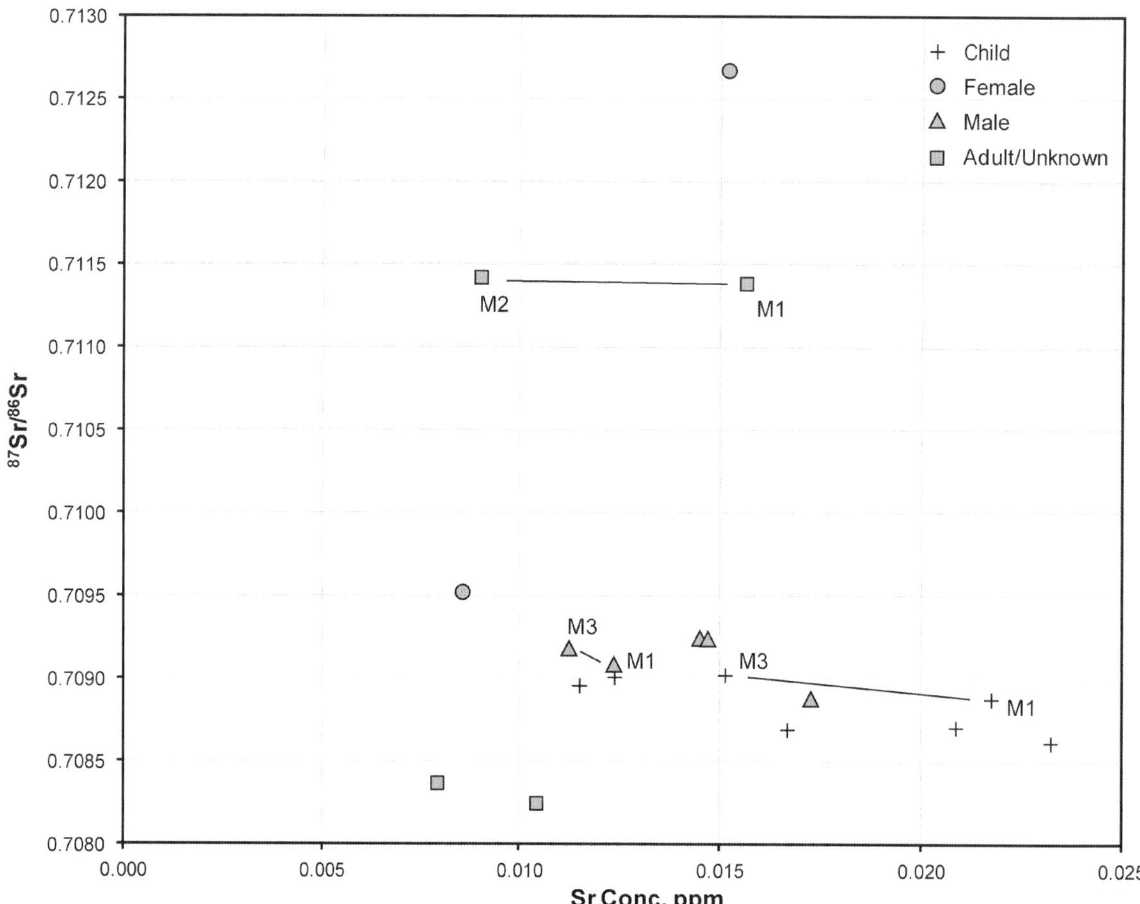

Fig. 5.31. Rutzing: strontium concentration (ppm) versus ratio ($^{87}Sr/^{86}Sr$). Lines connect teeth from the same individual.

and western Slovakia from the *jüngere* LBK (Lenneis 1995; 2000; Čižmář 1998a; Pavúk 2009). As we move into Bavaria (Chapter 6), the emphasis will change, with northern parts looking more to the west and north, rather than to the east, at least in terms of the development of ceramic styles (Gronenborn 1999; Cladders 2001). The LBK of Lower Austria, therefore, was very much connected to that found in Moravia (Lenneis 1995; 2000) but, as our strontium results from Kleinhadersdorf illustrate, this did not preclude ties further afield, such as into Bohemia. Upper Austria similarly demonstrates connections in both directions along the Danube, even possibly reaching as far as eastern Hungary as demonstrated by an imported Alföld pot at Leonding (Grömer 2001, 62–3), and certainly was not a forgotten enclave, despite lower settlement density compared to Lower Austria and the gap in LBK settlement distribution that surrounds it on both sides.

The isotope results from the four sites sampled in Austria differ only slightly from the overall pattern seen in Chapter 4, but the sex-based differences identified in the osteological collections studied in Hungary and Slovakia were not replicated in the Austrian assemblages. For the three cemetery sites where strontium isotopes have been sampled (Kleinhadersdorf, Mitterndorf and Rutzing), the results all formed a major cluster with two or three outliers with strontium ratios that fell outside the range expected for loess soils, following the pattern found at Nitra, but contrasting with the broad spread of strontium ratios found at Vedrovice (Chapter 4.11). This could relate to the varying geologies found around Vedrovice and the general uniformity of loess used by LBK communities in Austria and Slovakia (Lenneis 1982a, 7; see also Chapter 5.4). However, as most of the sites sampled from Austria, with the possible exception of some early graves from Kleinhadersdorf, do not date as early as Vedrovice, the pattern we see amongst the strontium isotope data may also relate to changing landscape use and community composition as the LBK developed.

In Chapter 3, we suggested that unusual body positions and orientations were more likely amongst the strontium outliers and, while this was less prominent in the sites under discussion in Chapter 4, we can tentatively suggest that we find this pattern again in Austria. One of the strontium outliers at Kleinhadersdorf, a female buried in grave 55, was placed in a right-crouched position and was one of two burials at the cemetery to be oriented with the head to the north. This may also be the case at Rutzing, though the situation is complicated by the dominance of right-crouched burials at the site. Both outliers were right-crouched, but were oriented with their heads to the south-west and south, which are comparatively rare orientations at Rutzing. A similar connection between unusual orientation and right-crouched burials can be seen at Mitterndorf, where right-crouched burials are oriented in the rarer directions, but at this site the outliers are oriented east–west (with the exception of burial 485) and in a left-crouched position.

In contrast, the stable isotopes are more variable than those presented in Chapter 4, with the isotope values from the Upper Austrian site of Rutzing deviating significantly from patterns found elsewhere. The $\delta^{13}C$ values suggest that differing subsistence practices took place in this region, with more use of resources from the forest, though less manuring of fields may have also produced this pattern. As Rutzing is the only site sampled from Upper Austria, it is not possible at the moment to determine whether this is a regional or site-specific pattern. Given the evidence surrounding variation in subsistence practice found at sites in the Horn basin, Lower Austria (Chapter 5.4), where the nearby settlements of Rosenburg and Mold had very different subsistence activity profiles, the carbon isotope values at Rutzing could well be illustrating very localised practices.

The differences within the stable isotope values at Rutzing may also suggest that the kinds of activities in which individuals from the same settlement or community were engaged also impacted on burial contexts. While grave goods, except adzes, do not appear to correlate in straightforward ways with the isotope values, at Rutzing the $\delta^{13}C$ values within the population did vary across the site. Body position and the orientation of the grave do not correlate with the isotope results overall. However, when the spatial layout of the site was considered alongside how differing body positions and orientations were combined in clusters or neighbouring graves, certain emphases could be determined. Woodland resources appeared to have been exploited more by those individuals buried in the more variable northern cluster of burials at Rutzing. It is tempting in this case to posit the existence of two groups using the cemetery, perhaps in the form of 'clans', such as are identified for the settlement at Vaihingen (see further discussion in Chapters 7.4 and 10).

The stable isotope values from Asparn and Kleinhadersdorf can usefully be compared because the sites are located so close together and are therefore likely to have experienced similar climatic conditions. While the $\delta^{15}N$ values are very similar at both sites, the $\delta^{13}C$ values from Asparn form a tighter cluster than those from Kleinhadersdorf. The means from both sites are fairly similar and the difference is just outside statistical significance (Asparn mean=−19.6‰, Kleinhadersdorf mean=−19.87‰, 2-tailed t test, p=0.051, but is significant by Mann-Whitney U test, p=0.015), but the variability of the carbon values is significant (Levene's test, p=0.014). The higher $\delta^{13}C$ values from Asparn suggest that the community at this site were sourcing their food from less forested areas or more manured areas, but the difference in variance also indicates less variation amongst the dietary sources of the Asparn community than the population buried at Kleinhadersdorf.

The chronological difference between these two sites could be highly significant here. The burials at Kleinhadersdorf perhaps accumulated over about two centuries Neugebauer-Maresch and Lenneis forthcoming), while Asparn is thought to represent a single event and a living population. The variance in $\delta^{13}C$ values could therefore be illustrating the opening up of the landscape through the span of the LBK or a move away from using woodland resources over time. The radiocarbon dates from the Kleinhadersdorf cemetery (Appendix B2) suggest a use of the site for about 200 years. Given that Asparn was a settlement site and Kleinhadersdorf a cemetery, potentially used by multiple groups, it is also possible the community buried at Kleinhadersdorf was more diverse than at Asparn.

Finally, in this chapter we have also explored some of the variations in grave goods and assemblages of objects found in burials across the Austrian LBK. As Lenneis (2007) has argued, the grave good assemblages do not divide in simple ways between those buried with 'Mesolithic' and those buried with 'Neolithic' objects. A prime example of this is the use of local snail shells (Lenneis 2007, 132, table 1), as all the sampled burials accompanied by this grave good had strontium signatures that suggested the people in question lived on loess soils. While the isotope data may not therefore help to resolve exact meanings behind particular configurations of grave goods, they do, perhaps, suggest that regarding grave goods as having a single, fixed or exclusive identity is simplifying a complex network of meanings.

Complex assemblages of objects, such as those that accompanied burial 13 at Rutzing, point to multiple associations (the burial brings together Bavarian flint, *Spondylus* from the Adriatic and a polished stone adze, which possibly originated in Bohemia), which may have been more associated with the connections and ties which communities had than with the particular individuals interred in the graves. These kinds of complex statements about the mixing of different contexts may be symbolised by the inclusion in this grave of 120 imitation deer teeth. They potentially echo the clay beads at Mezőkövesd, which may have been attempted copies of *Spondylus* (Chapter 3.7.1), but also demonstrate possible connections to cultures to the south-east, such as the Vinča culture where bone imitations of deer teeth are far more numerous and such copies have also been found made from stone (Selena Vitezović, pers. comm.). The reach of relationships is potentially very wide.

Notes

1 This department can trace its roots back to 1876 and the *Anthropologisch-Ethnographische Abteilung am k.u.k. Naturhistorischen Hofmuseum* (Internet ref. 1). The Anthropology department was then divided into three (anthropology, prehistory and ethnology) in 1924 (Internet ref. 1).

2 This project was called *Frühbäuerliches Leben vor 7000 Jahren – eine Rekonstruktion* and was funded by the FWF (Förderung der Wissenschaftlichen Forschung; Project no.: 18980–G02).

3 Human bone (ETH Zürich) gave a date of 8020±125 BP or 7350–6600 cal BC (Svoboda 2008, 226).
4 As we will discuss below, this changes substantially during the LBK of Austria (Mateiciucová 2008a).
5 High-quality soils are defined by Lenneis (2008, 165) as having high fertility and light arability.
6 Both sites, however, have similar rates of wild animals to other LBK settlements: Neckenmarkt: 18%; and Strögen 14% (Pucher 1987; 2001, 265).
7 The phasing of the houses is derived from ceramic seriation (Lenneis and Lüning 2001).
8 This number rises to 72% when single finds and cemeteries are also included (Lenneis 1982a, f.1, 8).
9 The Zseliz or Želiezovce group may have reached into the eastern border area of Austria as this ceramic style appears to define the assemblage found at Hainburg-Teichtal, not far from the Austrian-Slovakian border, but mostly this pottery was an import or an imitation of this style (Lenneis 1995, 27).
10 Strögen has the remains from four houses, of which only one had sufficient preservation to identify house type. This was a type 1 house or *Großbau* (Lenneis 2009, 181).
11 Flotation at Rosenburg produced only 200 plant macro-remains, which gives an exceptionally low density for the LBK of 0.05 plant remains per litre of earth (Brinkkemper 2009, 153). Strögen had twice the quantity of botanical remains as were found at Rosenburg (Kreuz 1990), while Mold had many times the concentration recorded at Rosenburg (Kohler-Schneider *et al.* 2009).
12 At Mold, *Großbau* 1 is thought to date to the beginning of the settlement (transitional phase LBK I/II), while *Großbau* 13 was most likely built during a later phase (Lenneis *et al.* 2010, 85).
13 It is sometimes estimated that as many as 200 individuals are represented at Asparn (Wild *et al.* 2004, 378).
14 *Verfärbung* or feature.
15 There appears to be some confusion over whether burial 5 is left- or right-crouched as Kloiber *et al.* (1971, 24, 28) attribute it as left-crouched in a table, while their text describes the skeleton as right-crouched. Here we follow Hahnel (1994, 117), who describes the burial as right-crouched.

A Mitterndorf lifeway: burial 329

The adult woman in burial 329 was interred in an orientation and body position that many of the dead in LBK cemeteries received. She was placed in a left-crouched position and oriented with her head to the east. Her body was tightly crouched and her grave pit was just big enough to accommodate her, with very little room for extra grave goods. Those who took on the responsibility of her burial chose to treat her body in the most frequent rite seen at this cemetery, respecting the dominant orientation and body position. However, the strontium ratio from her first molar (M1, $^{87}Sr/^{86}Sr$ ratio=0.71112) suggests that she did not originate from the local community. In her childhood, at least, she had eaten a diet that had a significant non-loess contribution. The nearest examples of soils with these values are probably found 50 km to the north, in the Bohemian Massif.

As we saw in Chapter 4, such strontium values can be seen at sites in Moravia, such as Brno, Těšetice and Vedrovice. So this woman need not have been born into a community not living a LBK way of life, but rather could have moved from sites north of the Danube at some point during her later childhood or early adulthood. Perhaps, as envisaged for the lifeway of the woman in burial 11 at Těšetice, she moved for marriage – but in this case possibly travelled in the opposite direction to that person. Unusually for a female burial, a flint object had been included in the grave of burial 329. This may have been a way of expressing her non-local origin, while the position and orientation of the body expressed that she now belonged to the community which buried her.

*Unfortunately, due to poor preservation, we do not have stable isotope values for the individuals buried at Mitterndorf. However, there are some clues to her adult diet found in her skeleton. She had suffered from iron deficiency anaemia (*cribra orbitalia*), which was possibly diet-related, though this can also be related to excessive bleeding or inhibited iron absorption due to diseases such as gastrointestinal infections or gut parasites. The presence of* cribra orbitalia *indicates that she may have suffered some level of dietary stress during her adult years. Perhaps her diet had not provided her with adequate quantities of iron or she had repeatedly had infections. Anaemia can leave sufferers lethargic, but can also weaken the immune system, perhaps leading to a greater susceptibility to illness. Her lower canines also showed evidence for enamel hypoplasia, which suggests that she may have had an inadequate diet or an illness in childhood as well. However, she was not unique in suffering from these conditions and they are also found on the skeletons of women with strontium ratios which suggest that they lived on the loess. This fits well with the general results found in this project that origin (loess and non-loess) and state of health did not necessarily correlate well and, despite not living her entire life within the local community, the health of the woman in burial 329 at Mitterndorf was similar to that of other women buried there.*

A Rutzing lifeway: burial 14

With the lowest carbon isotope value for the cemetery (−21.1‰), the diet of the man in burial 14 may have differed slightly from that of the rest of the population. He could have sourced more of his food from a wooded environment than others living in the Rutzing community. Perhaps he had eaten more wild resources. However, at Rutzing there are also some cattle with exceptionally low $\delta^{13}C$ values, and these could have contributed more protein carbon to his diet. We could even go so far as to suggest a link between a specific individual and his, or his relations', ownership of specific heads of cattle, which may have been kept in more forested areas. Perhaps the man in burial 14 even favoured cattle over pig meat (as at Rutzing the pigs have high carbon values). In any case, his nitrogen value (9.6‰) suggests he was eating an average amount or the cattle with the lower $\delta^{13}C$ values contributed more protein to his diet. It is also possible that he was consuming their milk as well.

If his low carbon value can be explained by a preference for the consumption of cattle, perhaps this was reflected in his social standing in the community. He had reached a quite advanced age at the time he died (older mid-adult) and is probably one of the longest-lived individuals to be interred at the cemetery. The strontium ratio from his first molar (M1, $^{87}Sr/^{86}Sr=0.70925$) falls within the local range for the loess, and it is likely that he had spent most of his life in the local area and was perhaps buried near the settlement of his birth. Possibly he was given access to the cattle preferentially as a mark of respect to a senior member of the community. However, like many individuals at Rutzing, his skeleton also hints at a diet which may have been poor episodically, or at periods of stress during his lifetime. Burial 14 showed evidence for iron-deficiency anaemia in the shape of cribra orbitalia, *which is generally more frequently found with women, and his teeth exhibited enamel hypoplasias, suggesting that he had suffered dietary stress or illness in childhood as well. The anaemia may have left him suffering from fatigue and increased his susceptibility to other infections. He may have also broken his left arm or suffered an infection that caused changes in his ulna.*

The suggestion that he was a high-status individual is not echoed in the grave good assemblage, since he was not provided with any grave goods. The N–S orientation of the grave is within the range of the dominant orientation at the site, though it is the E–W and W–E oriented graves which have the most grave goods. Perhaps the lack of grave goods tallies with the kinds of statements being made in the burial through the treatment of the body; burial 14 is left-crouched, which occurs in reduced frequency at this site, and is located in the northern cluster of burials. It is in the burials of this northern cluster that the most variability in orientation, body position and the lower carbon isotope values are found. Perhaps, on his death, he was buried amongst those members of the community with whom he had shared a diet, or even a cattle herd. They could have been his kin, or perhaps a broader group more like a clan, who had exploited different resources to other groups but nonetheless chose to bury their dead together.

6 Southern Bavaria

Daniela Hofmann, Joachim Pechtl, R. Alexander Bentley, Penny Bickle, Linda Fibiger, Gisela Grupe, Julie Hamilton, Robert Hedges, Michael Schultz and Alasdair Whittle

6.1 Introduction

Bavaria is Germany's largest federal state, reaching from the Rhön mountains in the north to the Alps in the south. It is dominated by two large river systems with their tributaries: in the north the Main, which eventually joins the Rhine, and in the south the Danube, which flows from its source in Baden-Württemberg through Bavaria and then on to the south-east. These axes of communication have strongly influenced the cultural affiliation of northern and southern Bavaria from prehistory onwards (Zimmermann 1995; Bück in Engelhardt 2006, 61; Roth 2008; Pechtl 2010, 42–6). The region referred to here as southern Bavaria is located largely south of the Danube, comprising – from east to west – the modern administrative regions of Lower Bavaria, a very small part of the Upper Palatinate, northern areas of Upper Bavaria, and finally Swabia, which straddles the border with Baden-Württemberg (Fig. 6.1).

Southern Bavaria is dissected by numerous rivers flowing into the Danube. Beginning from the east, the Inn and Isar run in a roughly south-west–north-east direction, while rivers further west, such as the Lech and the Iller, run more north–south, making west–east travel difficult (Küster 1995, 9). LBK sites tend to be located along the smaller streams and tributaries of these riverine axes (such as the Aiterach, Ödbach and Irlbach; K. Reinecke 1978a; 1982; Gronendijk 1992; Gerhard 2006, map 30; Pechtl 2009a, 4), although especially in the Gäuboden there are also sites on the terraces of the Danube itself, for instance at Stephansposching (Pechtl 2009a) and on the higher terraces south of Regensburg (Schier 1985, 17; Paetzold 1992, 98).

Defining clear geographical borders to this area can be difficult, especially in the west and south-east. To the north-east, the mountain range of the Bavarian Forest separates Bavaria and Bohemia, although there is evidence that this was no barrier to communication in the Neolithic (Chapter 6.4.4). North of the Danube, the ranges of the Franconian and Swabian Albs also provide reasonably clear demarcations, although they have yielded LBK finds (Bück in Engelhardt 2006, 57). However, the territory of Swabia continues westwards into Baden-Württemberg without any obvious geographical breaks. Only west of Ulm is there a break in loess cover that could form a convenient boundary with the Baden-Württemberg LBK. Similarly, there are no real physical barriers between the Danube and the Alps; the only clear limiting factor is the extent of the fertile loess soils preferred by the LBK.

A continuous loess cover exists in the eastern part of the region, in the flat, very fertile Lower Bavarian area now known as the Gäuboden, roughly between the modern towns of Regensburg and Vilshofen (Küster 1995, 9; Völkel 2006, 27). Loess patches of various sizes exist throughout the tertiary hills which extend south- and westwards towards Landshut and beyond, but the further west one goes, the stonier and less fertile the soils become (Küster 1995, 9). The southern part of southern Bavaria is dominated by sediments of glacial origin, which were not settled by agricultural communities until the latter half of the Neolithic (Uenze 1990; Nadler and Zeeb 1994; Küster 1995, 9).

The Gäuboden is a relatively warm, dry and fertile environment with a long vegetation period of over 220 days a year, corresponding to the conditions preferred by early Neolithic settlers elsewhere (e.g. Sielmann 1972; Lenneis 2008, 165). However, these conditions deteriorate as one moves into the tertiary hills (R. Hofmann 1983/84, 121–4; Sachweh and Enders 1996, maps 16 and 47; Pechtl 2009a, 5), and compared to other areas, southern Bavaria has been characterised as a rather marginal zone, where the parameters tolerable for LBK settlement only existed in restricted areas (Sielmann 1972, 28–33). Although this work has been criticised as too coarse-grained to take into account the variety of local conditions (Bakels 1978, 135; Kreuz 1990, 162), or indeed the impact of continuing fluctuations in rainfall throughout the LBK (Schmidt and Gruhle 2003a; Schmidt *et al.* 2004), parts of southern Bavaria certainly fell short of ideal LBK settlement conditions in spite of the presence of loess soils (Pechtl 2009c, 82–3).

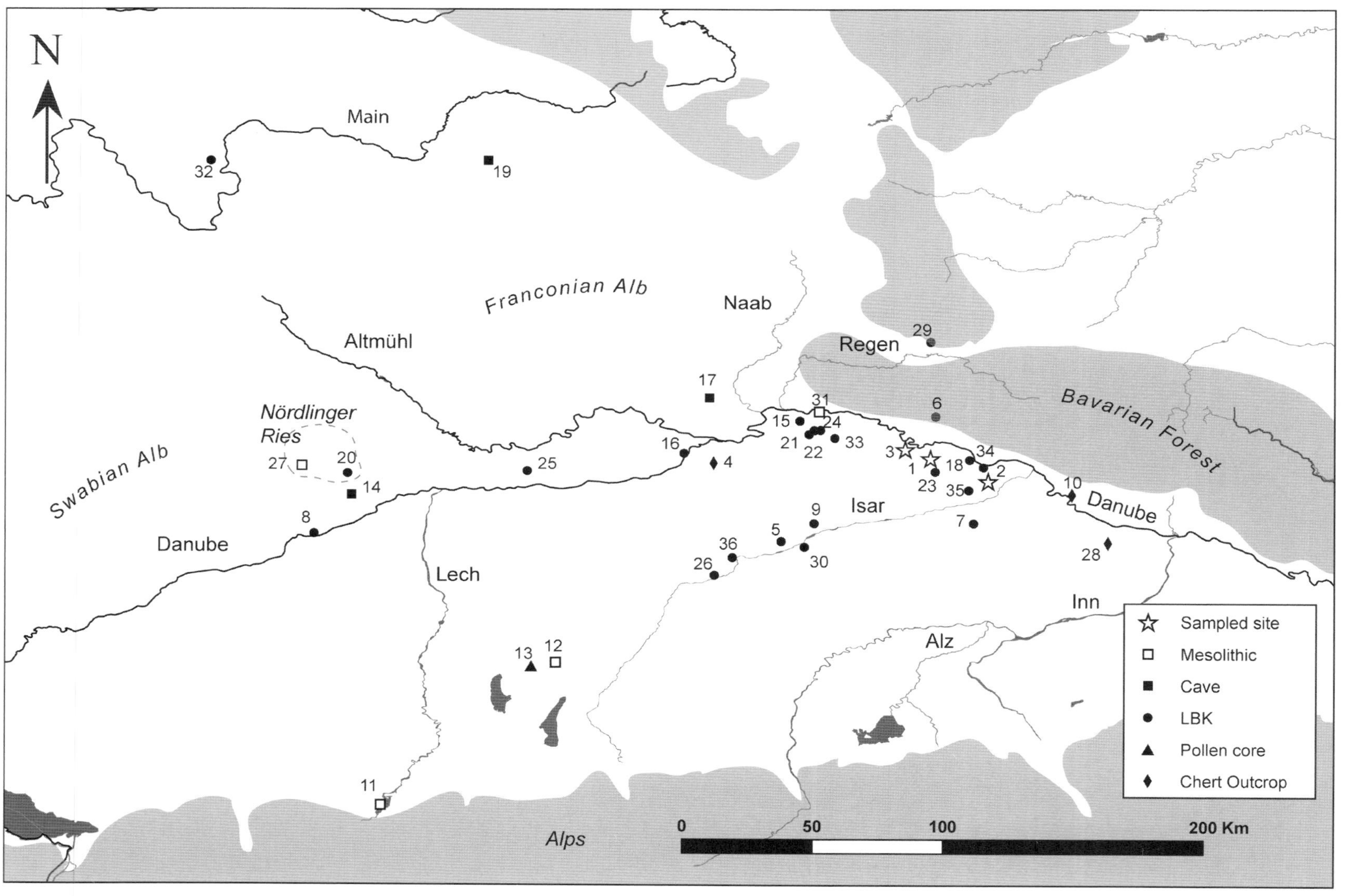

Fig. 6.1. Map of sites sampled (1–3) and others mentioned in Chapter 6. Upland areas are in italics. 1) Aiterhofen, 2) Otzing, 3) Lerchenhaid, 4) Abensberg-Arnhofen, 5) Altdorf, 6) Ascha, 7) Aufhausen, 8) Dillingen, 9) Essenbach-Ammerbreite, 10) Flintsbach-Hardt, 11) Forggensee 2, 12) Germering-Nebel, 13) Görbelmoos and Pilsensee, 14) Hanseles Hohl, 15) Harting, 16) Hienheim, 17) Hirschenstube, 18) Irlbach, 19) Jungfernhöhle, 20) Kleinsorheim, 21) Köfering, 22) Mangolding, 23) Meindling, 24) Mintraching, 25) Nassenfels, 26) Niederhummel, 27) Ofnet, 28) Ortenburg, 29) Pemfling, 30) Sallmannsberg, 31) Sarching 4, 32) Schwanfeld, 33) Sengkofen, 34) Stephansposching, 35) Wallersdorf, 36) Wang.

6.2 History of research

As elsewhere, the history of research into the Bavarian Neolithic began in the nineteenth century, when amateur societies started to collect and curate finds more systematically and carry out some limited excavations (Schmotz 2002a, 204; Zeeb-Lanz 2003, 293). In 1929, Paul Reinecke attempted a first study of Bavarian LBK pottery. Although Bavarian material also played a role in the crucial definition by Quitta of an earliest LBK phase (1960; see also Süß 1954; Chapter 6.3), interest in general somewhat languished in the middle decades of the twentieth century (Schmotz 2002a, 205), perhaps because southern Bavarian pottery decoration appeared much more conservative than, for example, that of the Rhineland (van de Velde 1979a, 155–7). The most concerted analyis was begun by Kurt Reinecke in the late 1970s and early 1980s. He drew up a still widely used distribution map of LBK sites in Lower Bavaria (K. Reinecke 1982) and proposed a rough phasing of the material (K. Reinecke 1978b), but unfortunately never completed his work. Further suggested chronologies since then (Brink-Kloke 1992; Herren 2003) have proved problematic (for extensive discussion: Pechtl 2009a, 83–91; see Chapter 6.4).

The 1980s saw the publication of various gazetteers collating available information on surface finds and excavated assemblages from a particular area. The two most important studies are those of Schier (1985) on the Danube valley south of Regensburg and Schmotz (1989) on the confluence between the Isar and Danube. Both are still invaluable today, largely also because all findspots were checked for their reliability by studying the finds and attempting to ascertain the extent of sites. Smaller-scale surveys of the same kind were for instance carried out by Schötz (1988) on the Vils valley and by Engelhardt (1995) around the village of Ergolding. The Nördlinger Ries saw an early gazetteer (Dehn and Sangmeister 1954) and a co-ordinated fieldwalking programme (e.g. Krippner 1984; 1995; 2000; Zeeb-Lanz 2003, 293), which makes the known site distribution there particularly reliable.[1]

Together, Kurt Reinecke's 1982 map, the information in the sites and monuments record, made accessible to the public for instance by Gerhard (2006, maps 30 and 37), and the more detailed studies available all confirm the clustering of LBK sites in specific areas (Fig. 6.1). This pattern is probably reliable, although there is a certain bias for regions with local historical and archaeological societies and other interested amateurs (Schmotz 2002a, 204) or with county archaeological services (Pechtl 2010, 36). In addition, most information relates to areas extensively ploughed today, part of the reason why more hilly – and generally also more forested – regions such as the tertiary hills remain relatively empty of LBK finds (Paetzold 1992, 95; Pechtl 2009a, 16). For the Vils valley at least, Schötz (1986) could show that hillier areas were indeed more sparsely settled, but this remains to be confirmed elsewhere. In the Ries, LBK sites lie west of the river Wörnitz, but seem less focused on the loess than elsewhere. Also, site catchments contain a greater proportion of river meadows and some are found at higher elevations than is generally the case (Zeeb-Lanz 2003, 296–8). In addition, the caves, especially of the southern slopes of the Ries, have been used in LBK times (Dehn and Sangmeister 1954; Weißmüller 1986; Chapter 6.4).

From the 1950s, the *Denkmalamt* expanded (Brink-Kloke 1992, 1; www.2; Petzet *et al.* 1999) and from the 1970s onwards, a parallel network of smaller town- or county-focused *Stadt-* and *Kreisarchäologien* was established (Schmotz 2007b). This resulted in a much improved monitoring of building and extraction work, a better collaboration with local amateurs, and therefore an increase in archaeological information. In recent years, a squeeze on funding means that this situation is reversing, with many posts not renewed upon the retirement of their incumbents, or replaced with part-time positions (Schmotz 1995; 1996). In addition, there is currently no coherent system of developer-funded archaeology in Bavaria (Rind 1994, 33). Many sites, while excavated under *Denkmalamt* management, are actually staffed with non-professionals, while post-excavation analysis and publication rely on finding willing postgraduate students in search of a dissertation project (Schmotz 1996, 14; 2002a, 213; Raßhofer 2001, 33). Much material remains entirely unstudied.[2]

Nevertheless, some large-scale and important excavations of LBK sites took place under state management and are now at least partly published. Most notable among these is Sallmannsberg near Landshut (Brink-Kloke 1992), a relatively small site but the only one in the region to be completely excavated. Larger interventions were also carried out at Köfering and Harting near Regensburg, at Lerchenhaid near Straubing (Brink-Kloke 1992; Herren 2003), and in the 1990s at Otzing and Stephansposching near Deggendorf (Schmotz and Weber 2000; Pechtl 2009a), as well as at Altdorf (Engelhardt *et al.* 1997; Meixner 1998; see 6.4). In addition, numerous smaller excavations provided further house plans and portions of enclosures (for lists, see Schmotz 1997; 2002a, 211; D. Hofmann 2006, appendices 1 and 2; Pechtl 2009a; 2010, 51, appendix 1; and the excavation lists in *Das Archäologische Jahr in Bayern*). The 1970s and 1980s also saw the discovery of many of the key cemetery sites in the area (such as Aiterhofen: Nieszery 1995; Chapter 6.5).

Alongside these rescue interventions, there were a limited number of university-funded excavations. Pieter Modderman was active here for over two decades, beginning with the excavation of the LBK and middle Neolithic settlement of Hienheim near Kelheim in the 1960s and 1970s (Modderman 1977; 1986a), the first systematic LBK settlement excavation in southern Bavaria (Schmotz 2002a, 205) and still the only large-scale one in the Kelheim area. A detailed survey of the Ödbach valley near Straubing was coupled with the partial excavation there of the densely settled site of Meindling (Modderman 1978; 1992). The 1980s also saw the investigation of selected earliest LBK sites under the auspices of the wider project led by Jens Lüning (Chapters 5.3.2 and 6.3.2). In the Freising area, this work is complemented by the tireless excavation activities of the local archaeological society, making this geographically marginal region of central importance in Bavarian LBK studies (Neumair 1994).

For Lower Bavaria, the Upper Palatinate and the Kelheim cluster, this sometimes directed but largely piecemeal history of excavation has yielded around 380 cemetery burials and over 100 settlement burials, many of which could be sampled (see 6.5 and 6.6), in addition to over 400 house plans (D. Hofmann 2006, appendix 6; Pechtl 2010; Lifeways Database). In the Nördlinger Ries, excavation has so far been limited (Zeeb-Lanz 2003), although houses are now known from several locations, most notably Baldingen (Krahe 1989), Herkheim (Mattheußer 2009) and Utzwingen (Rück 2001; Staude 2007). Finally, Swabia has seen the excavation of a cemetery at Dillingen (Nieszery 1995) and the discovery of an enclosure with disarticulated human remains and some houses nearby (Dietrich and Kociumaka 2001). Further house plans are known from Wittislingen (Dietrich 1994) and Langenreichen (Pechtl 2008).

Rather than an actual lack of information, the Bavarian material has thus long suffered from a lack of synthesis and of sustained interest by researchers not caught up in the day-to-day running of *Denkmalamt* services. There are signs that this is changing, with more synthetic treatment of key regions and site types and a renewed effort at creating a sound chronological framework and establishing micro-regional differences (e.g. Schmotz 2002a; Peters 2004; von den Driesch 2004; D. Hofmann 2006; Pechtl 2008; 2009a; 2009b, 2009c, 2010). This ties in well with the overall aims of the Lifeways project.

6.3 Arrival and development of the LBK in Bavaria

6.3.1 The late Mesolithic

As in many other LBK areas, the later Mesolithic of southern Bavaria remains relatively poorly known (Street *et al.* 2002, 406), although increased interest by local collectors has resulted in a steady increase in known sites (Feldmann in Züchner 2006, 52). The loess areas themselves are relatively empty of Mesolithic settlement traces, at least partly due to the substantial post-LBK erosion on these kinds of soils. By analogy with the southern slopes of the Alps and with Baden-Württemberg (Chapter 7.3; Jochim 1998; Clark 2000; Mussi 2001), one could expect a rich Alpine foreland record, but the evidence in Bavaria is much poorer, especially for the late Mesolithic. This is perhaps partly due to a geologically more active environment and the resulting reduced chances of findspots compared to the southern Alps (cf. Della Casa *et al.* 1999), as well as to a shift in late Mesolithic settlement towards areas more likely to experience severe erosion (Wischenbarth 1999, 107). However, a lack of sustained academic interest also plays a role (Wischenbarth 2000; Street *et al.* 2002, 413; A.-L. Fischer *et al.* 2009, 45).

Recently, a late Mesolithic camp was excavated at Germering-Nebel, just west of Munich (A.-L. Fischer *et al.* 2009, 53; T. Richter 2009). The site, located on the lower terrace of the Parsberg, yielded a lithic assemblage predominantly derived from well known sources near the Danube, later also exploited during the LBK; flint from the Franconian Alb, the Bavarian Forest and Abensberg is present alongside material from local gravels and a very small proportion of north Italian imports (A.-L. Fischer *et al.* 2009, 53). Although outside the area of LBK settlement, the lithic material nevertheless shows that Lower Bavaria, too, was frequented by late Mesolithic populations.

The site is close to two pollen profiles, the Görbelmoos (*c.* 7 km further west; Küster 1997) and the Pilsensee cores (less than 20 km to the south-west; A.-L. Fischer *et al.* 2009, 55). While the former suffers from bad preservation in crucial sections of the core, the Pilsensee profile could show early human impact; a marked decrease of hazel from a date estimated at *c.* 6400 cal BC may roughly coincide with the presence of cereal pollen. Although elsewhere it is the distinction between cereal and grass pollen which is proving problematic (Chapters 7.3 and 8.3), at Pilsensee these early dates are considered controversial largely due to potential radiocarbon measurement errors introduced by lakewater sediments. Yet A.-L. Fischer *et al.* (2009, 55) point out that there has been little research into how such artificially old dates should be corrected. For them, the cereal pollen may be connected with climatic deterioration around 6200 cal BC, which led to a reduction in hazel across the region (Tinner and Lotter 2001). Indeed, even the latest corrected date of *c.* 5600 cal BC would be earlier than any earliest LBK settlement so far known from southern Bavaria (A.-L. Fischer *et al.* 2009, 56; see also Chapter 6.3.2). In view of the possibility of late Mesolithic cereal cultivation in central Switzerland (Tinner *et al.* 2007) and the critical approach of Behre (2007a; 2007b), this question remains a research priority (see also longer discussion in Chapter 7.3). For now, the presence of pre-LBK cereals in the region remains doubtful (*pace* Kossack and Schmeidl 1974/75) and new analyses are urgently needed. In contrast, early human impact in the form of deliberate opening of the forest cover through burning is now suggested for several locations (e.g. Kortfunke 1992; Knipping 2001).

Areas of higher Mesolithic site density concentrate in the valleys of the low mountain ranges, with distinct clusters for instance around Regensburg (Schier 1985; Street *et al.* 2002, 408) and Kelheim (contributions in Rieder *et al.* 1989; Weißmüller 2002; see also D. Hofmann 2006, 677–82). Near the Danube, sites are often located on sandy rises (Schier 1985, 16; Kaulich 1993), with assemblages from rock shelters especially in the western extremities of the study area and just beyond (Taute 1966; Menke 1978; Street *et al.* 2002, 411). The river Lech seems to form a distinct boundary, although it is unclear to what extent this is due to a longer tradition of directed Mesolithic reasearch. West of the Lech, plentiful Mesolithic evidence is known from the Federsee, the Allgäu and upper Danube (Chapter 7.3; Gulisano 1994; 1995; Gehlen 1995; 2010), from north of the Swabian Alb, the Ries (most notably the Ofnet head burials; Frei and Krahe 1988; Grünberg 2000, 45; Orschiedt 2002) and along the Neckar. Further east, sites are fewer, and La Hoguette pottery is so far absent from the Nördlinger Ries eastwards (for a recent overview, see Gehlen 2006, 48). Perhaps the best known site in the east is Sarching 4, south-east of Regensburg, located on sandy soils near the Danube and comprising the remains of a possible building (Schönweiß and Werner 1974; Schönweiß 1988; for criticism, see A.-L. Fischer *et al.* 2009, 48–50). The flint assemblage has been typologically assigned to an early phase of the late Mesolithic (Gronenborn 1997a).

Overall, numbers of late Mesolithic sites in southern Bavaria remain low, especially in the eastern areas later densely settled by the LBK. It is unclear whether this is due to unfavourable conditions for hunter-gatherers, such as a dense forest with low biomass, the fact that early Atlantic sediments are only rarely preserved in loess areas (A.-L. Fischer *et al.* 2009, 48), or the dependence on comparatively rare diagnostic flint material for site identification (see below). Instead, Gehlen (2006, 50) suggests a cultural border of some kind separating southern Germany into an eastern and a western zone, a division that was to remain relevant for subsequent Neolithic settlement. Long-range contacts cross-cutting many such potential borders are evident from the few Mediterranean shells recovered from sites such as Ofnet (Álvarez Fernández 2003), the northern Italian flint from Germering and the occasional polished stone tools found in secure Mesolithic contexts (A.-L. Fischer *et al.* 2009, 57–63). Although the evidence remains thin on the ground for now, southern Bavaria at least shows the potential for further study into the cultural choices made by late Mesolithic groups, which may have influenced both their uptake of economic and other innovations and the way they differentiated themselves from other contemporary communities (Gehlen 2006, 52).

This renewed optimism lies at the heart of recent attempts to find a greater role for a potential hunter-gatherer population in current Neolithisation models even for south-eastern Bavaria (see also Freund 1963, 131, 161), but the obstacles remain considerable. The earliest LBK and late Mesolithic flint industries partly overlap (both, for instance, produce symmetrical trapezes), and specialists rely on the presence of diagnostic arrowheads to attribute surface material (A.-L. Fischer *et al.* 2009, 45–8). Moreover, radiocarbon dates for late Mesolithic sites are so far virtually absent, being limited to one measurement for the site of Forggensee 2 in the Allgäu (Gehlen 2010, 26), and both faunal complexes and assemblages of human bone are rare (Grünberg 2000; Street *et al.* 2002, 407; A.-L. Fischer *et al.* 2009, 46; but see contributions in Taute 1980 for rock shelters in Swabia). Furthermore, the recent overview of known late Mesolithic sites in A.-L. Fischer *et al.* (2009, 51–3) shows just how much material has been inadequately excavated or is now lost (see also Feldmann in Züchner 2006, 47). Research into the Mesolithic-Neolithic transition in southern Bavaria is still hampered by this inadequate state of research. Nevertheless, on current evidence the arrival of the earliest LBK in the region stands out as a period of profound change, with houses, pottery and most of the lithic material derived from earlier LBK practices further east. Late Mesolithic foragers may have been present, but in comparison to what is argued for other regions covered by this study their influence on the development of the local Neolithic is likely to have been comparatively restricted. Although they may well have joined LBK communities, they appear to have made little or no impact in terms of the material culture assemblage.

6.3.2 The earliest LBK in southern Bavaria

Research into the earliest LBK in southern Bavaria began as early as 1954, when Süß identified a particularly old variant of the LBK. The landmark study of Quitta (1960) also included several sites from the region. In 1979–80, the first undisturbed settlement inventories and house plans anywhere in the western area of the earliest LBK were documented at Altdorf near Landshut (K. Reinecke 1983). Further crucial stimulus was provided from 1985 onwards by the large-scale project of Lüning on the earliest LBK, in the course of which excavations were carried out at Enkingen and Kleinsorheim in the Ries (Lüning 1988b; Reuter 1991; 1994), at Mintraching near Regensburg and at Wang near Freising (Lüning 1986a; Hillemeyer 1989), alongside Schwanfeld in Franconia (Lüning 1986b). This was followed by extensive publication of the results (Kreuz 1990; Gronenborn 1997b; Cladders 2001; M. Uerpmann 2001; Hillemeyer 2003; Stäuble 2005). In addition, the *Archäologischer Verein Freising* carried out both surface survey and test excavation at Niederhummel, followed by small-scale excavation by Cardiff University[3] in 2008 (Engelhardt *et al.* 1991; D. Hofmann 2009b; Hofmann *et al.* forthcoming). Earliest LBK settlements have also been revealed at several other isolated sites, but the material has not yet been analysed.

Alongside excavations, surface finds form the second main source of information. In this context, the long-term investigations by Krippner (1995; 2000, 75) in the Ries and by Neumair (1991, 13–16) in the Freising area are particularly noteworthy, as their directed search for earliest LBK sites has significantly enlarged our material basis. Smaller regional overviews have also provided reliable data for the areas around Neuburg an der Donau, Regensburg and Landshut, the Isar confluence and the Vils valley (Davis 1975; Schötz 1984, 24; Schier 1985, 18; Schmotz 1989, 7–68; Engelhardt 1995). However, a thorough synthesis of the earliest LBK in southern Bavaria is still lacking and the proceedings of a 2008 conference can only provide a starting point (A.-L. Fischer *et al.* 2009; Pechtl 2009c; D. Hofmann 2009b).

Overall, 62 sites with definite earliest LBK material are currently known from southern Bavaria, with a further 15 uncertain identifications. This constitutes a veritable explosion of sites compared to the late Mesolithic, but the number remains modest in the context of the LBK as a whole. Twelve of these sites have seen rescue or research excavations, but most others are known exclusively through surface finds (Pechtl 2009c, 82, 112–13, appendix 1). As far as is possible to ascertain, all these sites are settlements, although house plans are preserved at only a few places and are of rather modest quality (Stäuble 2005). So far, securely dated inhumations, as well as any kind of special-purpose site, are absent from the earliest LBK in southern Bavaria. As in other regions, dating earliest LBK sites remains problematic. Relatively few vessels are decorated and the restricted typological variation of pottery motifs makes it difficult to establish a robust relative chronology. Isolated traits of the dating schemes found further east (covered in Chapters 3.3, 4.3 and 5.3) can be traced further west and can, with all due caution, be used to suggest a division of the Bavarian earliest LBK material into an earlier and a later horizon (for more detail, see Pechtl 2009c, 88–91).

Mapping the results of this analysis yields a surprising result. The only earliest LBK settlement with exclusively earlier decorative characteristics is Kleinsorheim in the Ries, where an additional three sites show an elevated number of earlier alongside some later elements. A similar ratio is otherwise only visible at two sites in the Danube valley in the western part of southern Bavaria. In contrast, in the eastern Gäuboden and along the Isar, there are almost exclusively later elements of the earliest LBK. Possibly, then, the *Bandkeramik* settlement of southern Bavaria began in the earlier phase of the earliest LBK, but remained confined to the Ries and the upper Danube, while the central Gäuboden and the Landshut area were only settled in the later earliest LBK horizon. Finally, the eastern Gäuboden has yielded only isolated finds of this later horizon, evidently already paired with material of a developed *Notenkopf* style. These assemblages are thus transitional to the *ältere* or early LBK (Pechtl 2009c, 90, figs 6–7). So far, there are only a few radiocarbon dates from Wang (Cladders and Stäuble 2003, 496) and Niederhummel (Hofmann and Whittle 2011, 59; Hofmann *et al.* 2012), and given the shape of the calibration curve, the lack of stratigraphic relationships and the weakly differentiated material, it is currently impossible to narrow these dates down. However, they seem to support the late beginning suggested by typology. This means that Niederhummel was probably founded around 5300 cal BC at the earliest, and Wang slightly later in the 53rd century cal BC. Earliest LBK sites in the Neckar valley are similarly late (Chapter 7.3; Pechtl 2009c, 84–8; see also Chapter 4.7.1 on Vedrovice).

Even more than in later phases, the spatial distribution of earliest LBK sites is restricted to small patches of the region and most sites are close to the large rivers, with the Danube forming the central axis of settlement (Pechtl 2009c, 81, fig. 1). Ecological factors play a strong role here, as loess soils are almost exclusively chosen and only particularly warm and dry areas are settled (Pechtl 2009c, 81, fig. 1, 83, fig. 2). At the micro-level, ecotones are the preferred location choice, often leading to a linear arrangement of sites along river terraces or at the transition between loess plateaus and hilly areas. In general, sites are spaced at least around 2 km apart (Pechtl 2009c, 98, fig. 12). In the Ries, as well as around Regensburg and Landshut, there are denser and more extensive settlement clusters (K. Reinecke 1983; Schier 1985, 18; A.-L. Fischer 2011), with some sites abandoning the preferred and strategically important riverine axes and reaching well into the hilly hinterland.

So far, data on earliest LBK economy and diet are limited. The excavations at Enkingen, Mintraching and Niederhummel have provided modest assemblages of botanic macro-remains dominated by einkorn and emmer, alongside barley and some millet, lentil and flax (Kreuz 1990, 91, 99–103; Küster 1991; Amy Bogaard pers. comm.; Hofmann *et al.* 2012), pointing to a fully developed agricultural system with a broad spectrum of plants. Given that only areas most suitable for agriculture were chosen at this time, cereals were probably the central dietary component. They were supplemented by gathered plants such as hazelnuts and sloe, although the spectrum could likely be extended through new analyses.

Animal bone assemblages are published for Wang, Mintraching and Altdorf (von den Driesch 2004, 333, Tab. 1). All three inventories are relatively small but have produced a relatively high proportion of wild animal bone, between 47.6% and 55.1%. Although in terms of meat weight, the domesticates – sheep/goats, pig and especially cattle (as well as dog) – dominate, hunting was evidently an integral part of the economic strategy. Whether and to what level milk was used is currently unclear (see also Salque *et al.* 2012a; 2012b). It is still impossible to reveal different economic strategies within southern Bavaria, but in terms of inter-regional comparisons Bavaria and adjacent Baden-Württemberg tend to show much higher wild animal bone percentages than all other earliest LBK areas (Lüning 1997a, 73–4; M. Uerpmann 2001). This could be the heritage of an acculturated late Mesolithic hunting population, but the elevated percentages do not actually coincide well with other 'Mesolithic' indicators, such as La Hoguette pottery. Perhaps this is a strategy of diversification through which a farming lifestyle in a climatically challenging region could be stabilised (Schibler 2001, 157–8), or simply one more indicator of LBK diversity and flexibility, in line for instance with assemblages from Austria.

Lithic material has been reported from Enkingen, Kleinsorheim, Mintraching, Altdorf and Niederhummel (K. Reinecke 1983, 57–60; Engelhardt 1991; Tillmann 1993; Gronenborn 1997b, 25–32), and all these assemblages share certain basic traits. Nodules of Jurassic chert were the preferred raw material and mostly originated in the Franconian Jura, but sometimes also the Swabian Alb and rarely the Ortenburg area. As a rule, raw materials were obtained from nearby sources. Tabular cherts and cherts from river gravels are only rarely attested. Interestingly, most of the cherts cannot actually be attributed to a specific outcrop, which probably means that sources frequently differed from those exploited in later LBK phases. Radiolarites from the Szentgál area of Hungary are definitely long-distance imports and make up between 4%

and 6% of the assemblages at Niederhummel (Tillmann 1993, 159) and Mintraching, which is a surprisingly high proportion. In smaller numbers, they are attested as far as the Ries (Mattheußer 2009, 20). Wittlingen chert from Baden-Württemberg is not definitely attested on Bavarian sites (Gronenborn 1997b, 30).

Overall, then, stone tools have some part to play in our reconstruction of communication networks. Most of the raw materials are regional, and numerous smaller outcrops appear to have been used, so that southern Bavaria can be characterised as a 'flint province' in its own right. Within this area, exchange was intensive and even sites relatively far from sources, such as Niederhummel and Altdorf, were adequately supplied with regional raw materials. However, the relatively elevated percentage of Szentgál radiolarite, especially in the eastern part of southern Bavaria as far as Regensburg, reveals the existence of an intensive and long-lasting communication system with earliest LBK regions further east (Mateiciucová 2008a, 148, map 6). In contrast, there are no contacts of comparable intensity to the west, as the lack of Wittlingen cherts shows. How far the techniques of preparation of blade cores and the presence of trapezes reflect continued contacts with Mesolithic groups is difficult to assess. These traits are already characteristic of the earliest inventories of the southern German earliest LBK, so that by the time southern Bavaria, including its more easterly areas, was extensively settled, they had presumably already been part of a Neolithic material culture for several generations.

So far, whether and to what extent earliest LBK communities in southern Bavaria were in contact with neighbouring Mesolithic groups is unclear. La Hoguette pottery, so characteristic for Württemberg, is represented by a single sherd from Nördlingen at the extreme western edge of southern Bavaria (Pechtl 2009c, 100; for a longer discussion of La Hoguette pottery, see Chapters 7.3 and 8.3). Pottery, in spite of its general typological similarity, is more fruitful for discussing questions of group formation and contact within the earliest LBK. Motifs such as crosses, 'anthropomorphs' and hooked line bundles are concentrated in the western part of southern Bavaria and the adjacent Neckar area (Pechtl 2009c, 92–5, fig. 19; Strien 2009, 215). This concentration of figurative motifs suggests the existence of a spatially coherent group, at least for the later part of the earliest LBK. In contrast, the eastern part of southern Bavaria lacks these motifs. A tentative cultural boundary can thus be drawn. Interestingly, the results of flint and pottery analyses do not match up. Pottery links western Bavaria to the Neckar area, but the Wittlingen chert so characteristic for the Neckar remains absent across all of Bavaria. At the same time, the areas around Regensburg and Landshut belong to the 'western' group defined through pottery, but have high percentages of Szentgál radiolarite from the east. This suggests a highly complex and multi-layered system of contacts within which the orientation of individuals and groups could diverge considerably.

For now, as there is currently little evidence for acculturating indigenous foragers, the migration of farmers is, for many researchers, the preferred explanation for the start of the LBK in this region (Pechtl 2009c, 99–102). As the ultimate origin of the earliest LBK probably lies in the north-western Carpathian basin (Chapters 1.3.1 and 3.3), it was long believed that southern Bavaria was colonised by groups from the Austrian-Moravian area travelling along the Danube (Quitta 1960, 164–5, fig. 3). However, both the few radiocarbon dates and ceramic typology suggest that stretches of the Danube in western Austria and eastern Bavaria were settled relatively late, much later for instance than the Main area (Pechtl 2009c, 87, fig. 4). Correspondingly, the earliest assemblages in southern Bavaria are located in its extreme west: in the Ries, which is connected to the Main via settlements in southern central Franconia, and along the upper Danube as far as Regensburg (Pechtl 2009c, 91, fig. 7).

A new model has thus been proposed (Pechtl 2009c), with an initial earliest LBK migration from Hungary via Moravia and Bohemia to central Germany and along the Main, from where it reached the Ries perhaps around 5400 cal BC. Only then did colonisation proceed along the Danube eastwards to Regensburg. A second, less dynamic phase characterised by typologically later material sees the settlement of the eastern Gäuboden and the Landshut area, where further expansion stalled. At this time, more innovative communities further west had already begun to form the Flomborn style, and the *Notenkopf* style was developing further east. Material from the formative stages of either style is absent in southern Bavaria, where people evidently preferred a conservative adherence to earliest LBK material. In this context, the development of the earliest LBK regional style current between the Neckar and the upper Danube could be interpreted as a deliberate act of cultural demarcation.

It is only from perhaps around 5300 cal BC or even later that many settlements with developed *Notenkopf* pottery suddenly appear in the eastern part of southern Bavaria, although isolated earliest LBK sherds can still occur. This may be connected with a second wave of migration, this time indeed proceeding eastwards along the Danube. The two streams met in central southern Bavaria, creating a stylistic boundary with a small zone of overlap especially around Landshut (Pechtl 2009c, 102–4). Although by this time the earliest LBK was also ending in western parts of southern Bavaria, being substituted by assemblages with mixed developed Flomborn and *Notenkopf* characteristics, this boundary remains salient for centuries. Overall, the rather partial Neolithisation of southern Bavaria emerges as a protracted process characterised by both dynamism and stagnation. Any contemporary hunter-gatherers may well have coexisted with Neolithic groups over the long term, and there was potential to establish diverse and long-lasting relations between the two groups. Yet definite archaeological data in support of such a scenario are so far lacking and foragers appear to have left little impact here on LBK material culture and practices.

Table 6.1. Chronological scheme for southern Bavaria and its relation to adjacent regions. After Pechtl (2009a, figs 43 and 44).

Lower Main (Meier-Arendt 1966)	Württemberg (Strien 2000)	Southern Bavaria		Stephans-posching	Type Inventories	Upper Austria (Grömer 2001)	Bohemia (Pavlů 1986)
GG	GG		IIa	IIa	Osterhofen-Schmiedorf	Lengyel / Bavarian MNL	SBK IVa
HST II	HST II	Middle Neolithic	Ib	Ib	Atting-Rinkam	?	SBK III
V HST I			Ia	?	Aiterhofen gr. 229		SBK II
IV	8	late	IVb	6		Šarka	IVb SBK I
	7	LBK	IVa	5	Aiterhofen gr. 33		IVa III/IV
	6				Aiterhofen		
III		mid	IIIb	4	gr. 66, 74, 81, 106, 131		IIIb
	5	LBK					
			IIIa	3			IIIa
	4			2		Notenkopf	IId
			IIc				
	3	Noten-kopf		1	Lerchenhaid enclosure		IIc
			IIb				IIb
			IIa				
	2B				Aiterhofen B20		IIa
II			Ic?			developed Vornotenkopf	I/II
	2A						Ic
		Vor-notenkopf	Ib		Altdorf		Ib
I	1		Ia		Kösching	?	(Ia)

6.4 The developed and late LBK

6.4.1 Typological development and regionalisation

In southern Bavaria, earliest LBK communities probably existed well into the 53rd century cal BC, while elsewhere developed LBK styles were already established. However, it is also possible that both more conservative and more innovative settlements existed side by side within the region, at least for a time. In spite of much continuity, the transition to the developed LBK is marked by ruptures in many spheres. A colonisation wave by members of the Austrian-Moravian *Notenkopf* communities in the east is possible (Chapter 6.3). It is so far unclear whether a similar increase in population and a further colonisation from core Flomborn regions also took place in the west.

Discontinuities are particularly noticeable in the pottery, which now clearly differs in make, shape and decoration. The material from the Aiterhofen-B20 excavation is a good example (K. Reinecke 1978a). Bands consisting of two or three lines and often filled with impressions are clearly linked to a later Flomborn tradition, but there are also *Notenkopf* motifs with easterly connections and even a typically earliest LBK vessel. Straubing-Lerchenhaid provides a similarly mixed assemblage, albeit with a stronger *Notenkopf* component (Schmotz 1997, 133–7). The *Notenkopf* style proper decreases towards the west, but is present across southern Bavaria and even as far as Ulm-Eggingen in Baden-Württemberg (Kind 1989, plate 4, 20).

Subsequent typological developments are most clearly apparent in the inventories of large and long-lasting sites, such as Köfering and Stephansposching (Brink-Kloke 1992; Pechtl 2009a). In central areas, a typical southern Bavarian regional style developed, clearly derived from the *Notenkopf* sphere and characterised especially by simple lines with superimposed structuring motifs (Pechtl 2009a, 114). Six chronological phases can be distinguished and are closely connected to the Bohemian sequence, although a correlation with Württemberg is also possible (Table 6.1; Pechtl 2009a, 754, fig. 44). Areas further west, along the upper Danube, the Lech and in the Ries, show a connected but significantly different development with both marked regional peculiarities and evident relations to Württemberg and the Main (Pechtl 2009a, 114). The main settlement foci of the Gäuboden and Isar can be further subdivided. For instance, there are noticeable differences in the spectrum and popularity of certain kinds of decoration, most clearly in the later LBK. Comb-decorated material, typical for the Rhine and Main LBK, occurs quite regularly along the upper Danube as far east as Regensburg and in the Landshut area, but is completely absent further east. Barbed-wire motifs, characteristic for the Bohemian-Moravian Šárka style, show a complementary distribution and are frequently found in eastern parts of southern Bavaria (Pechtl 2009a, 114).

An analysis of pottery decoration thus shows similarities and differences at varying scales, emphasising the differentiated nature of preferred networks (Chapter 6.4.4). Overall, the region can be divided into three areas. The western and eastern Gäuboden are clearly differentiated and are separated by a boundary roughly around modern-day Straubing, while the Landshut area shows a greater amalgamation of traits from both (Fig. 6.2). In addition, the analysis of a substantial ceramic assemblage from Stephansposching has suggested the existence of two competing styles coexisting within the settlement towards the end of the LBK, and which were increasingly strongly demarcated (Pechtl 2009a, 82).

The late LBK is generally characterised by a process of divergent stylistic developments, and inventories even from nearby sites, such as Adldorf-Kreuzäcker (Husty 1999), are again clearly different.

The investigation of architectural remains broadly supports the observations made on pottery. The size, shape and construction of buildings differ markedly compared to the earliest LBK (Stäuble 2005; Pechtl 2009a, 384, 388). Four-aisled, rectangular and tripartite houses (also known as 'Geleen-type' houses: Modderman 1970) now appear in southern Bavaria (Fig. 6.3) and remain in use until the end of the sequence with only minor modifications (D. Hofmann 2006, appendix 6; Pechtl 2010, 40–2). At least in the late LBK, however, these exist alongside buildings with clearly divergent characteristics, such as a trapezoidal ground plan and doubled wall posts. Again, a continuous development can be proposed that increases in dynamism and eventually results in the side by side existence of conservative and more novel elements.

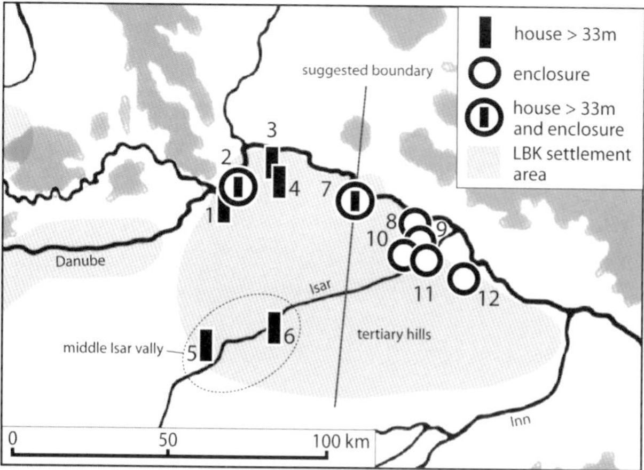

Fig. 6.2. The suggested division between western and eastern Lower Bavaria. Base map from Pechtl (2009b, fig. 5).

The spatial distribution of certain construction elements shows clear regional preferences, with the central and eastern parts of southern Bavaria characterised by more frequent 'Bavarian J' post settings, showing connections much further to the east (Pechtl 2010, 44, fig. 6; see also Coudart 1998; D. Hofmann 2006, appendix 5). Differences in building orientation once again contrast the eastern and western Gäuboden, with an overlap in the Landshut area (Pechtl 2010, 46, fig. 7), a pattern supported by the distribution of house lengths (D. Hofmann 2006, appendix 5; Pechtl 2009b, 189, 190, figs 3–4). Large longhouses occur mostly in the west, and enclosures mostly in the east, and the use of these different strategies for putative prestige accumulation may even show differences in the social organisation of LBK communities in those areas (Pechtl 2009b, 191, fig. 5).

In sum, the transition from the earliest to the developed LBK means a clear break in almost all aspects. Since a hiatus is unlikely, an initial conservative adherence to old traditions, followed by a quick and deliberate re-orientation towards the new material culture, possibly brought by new migrants from the east, is one plausible explanation. The core area of southern Bavaria – the Regensburg area, the entire Gäuboden and the settlement cells along the Isar – remains a definable cultural unit, one of the many regional groups of the LBK. Specific traits were developed, such as a ceramic decoration characterised by structuring motifs, the preference for the 'Bavarian J' post setting or the use of graphite as a black colourant in graves, opposed to the

Fig. 6.3. Unterpleichfeld (Würzburg): LBK longhouse under excavation. © Bayerisches Landesamt für Denkmalpflege-Luftbilddokumentation; *Foto: Klaus Leidorf, 4th of March 2003; Archiv-Nr. 6126/258, Dia 8774-35.*

more usual red (Pechtl and Eibl 2011, 37). The smaller settlement cells further west along the upper Danube and Lech and in the Ries are distinctly different. Influences from more easterly regions can be traced, but diminish quickly as those from Württemberg and the Franconian areas around the Main become more tangible. Thus, while the Hienheim LBK (Modderman 1977; 1986a) can still be seen as a strongly divergent variant of the south-east Bavarian LBK, the material from the Dillingen area must already be classified as south-west German, alongside the settlements near Ulm (Kind 1989) and in the Swabian Alb (Knipper *et al.* 2005).

Finally, the core area of southern Bavaria itself is far from culturally homogeneous. Characteristic pottery decoration, preferred flint raw materials and architectural peculiarities can be used to differentiate the western and eastern Gäuboden. As the region around Landshut combines elements of both zones it must be seen as an individual grouping in its own right. This kind of regionalisation is increasingly stressed in the later phases of the LBK. Nevertheless, these boundaries exist from early on and most likely go back to the initial agricultural colonisation of southern Bavaria.

6.4.2 Settlement structure

Settlements in southern Bavaria can consist of a single house, as in Langenreichen (Pechtl 2008, 32), or up to several dozen contemporary buildings, as at Stephansposching (Pechtl 2009a, 501–5). Larger sites show no planned layouts, and no 'paths' are visible even where some houses show aligned gable ends. However, there is a general trend to build as far away as possible from one's neighbours (Pechtl 2009a, 493–5). Communal installations take the form of earthworks and cemeteries, rather than paths or plazas. How far concentrations of features such as pit ovens, slit-shaped pits or settlement burials reflect communally used areas is still unclear (but see D. Hofmann 2006, chapter 4).

As elsewhere (for example, Claßen 2009), *Hof* or yard areas within settlements in southern Bavaria, such as Regensburg-Harting (Herren 2003) or Stephansposching (Pechtl 2009a), are thought to be inherited down the line for several generations. A new house was generally built in each generation, although there are rare examples of houses being inhabited for longer, or of more than one contemporary building existing in a yard at any one time.

Smaller-scale settlement patterning can at present only be discussed for the area around the Isar-Danube confluence, where more data are available (Pechtl 2009a, 526–30). Here, two zones with very different characteristics can be defined. Zone 1 comprises the strategically favourable areas along the terrace edges of the Danube and Isar. Here, few sites, generally early and long-lived foundations, are arranged at regular but relatively large distances from each other. For instance, Stephansposching was surrounded by settlements of comparable size at Otzing, Wallersdorf and Irlbach. Straubing-Lerchenhaid and Aiterhofen also belong to this zone. Small, potentially dependent sites around the large settlements are virtually absent. This could reflect a previously unrecognised LBK settlement system in which sites of similar size and comparable social rank co-operated or competed with each other over the long term, with earthworks potentially playing a part in the latter scenario (Pechtl 2009b). In contrast to what is suggested for example for the Rhineland and elsewhere (e.g. Zimmermann 1995; Lüning 1997b; Petrasch 2003), there is no central place with partly dependent satellite communities, but a far more volatile situation of equals jostling for position.

In contrast, zone 2 comprises the hinterland of the Gäuboden and the tertiary hills, where sites are much more concentrated, but are generally small or medium-sized and shorter-lived. These settlement networks could be very flexible. For instance, the directed and swift colonisation of the Lech valley was followed by an equally precipitate abandonment, perhaps in response to climatic fluctuations (Pechtl 2008). This led to a more dynamic settlement system comparable to conditions elsewhere in the LBK distribution (Claßen 2005; Pieler 2010). The Ödbach valley provides a particularly good example. Sites are located at short distances from each other on either side of the stream, with Meindling standing out in terms of building density and length of occupation (Groenendijk 1992; Modderman 1992). Here, then, hierarchically structured settlement clusters may well have existed, as was probably also the case in the area of the Lech confluence (Pechtl 2008, 29), and elsewhere (for example in Austria; Chapter 5.4).

6.4.3 Animals and plants

As elsewhere in the LBK, the main cereal crops in southern Bavaria are einkorn and emmer wheat, supplemented mainly by peas (Lüning 2000, 59). Compared to areas further west, einkorn seems to dominate more decisively (R. Hofmann 1983/84, 153). Where systematic flotation of pit fills has taken place, the spectrum of plants is more extensive. At Altdorf-Aich near Landshut, barley, poppy, lentil, flax and even a single grain of millet were identified, alongside a series of wild plants (Labes 2003). This questions the earlier idea that Bavaria was part of a south-eastern LBK zone in which barley was unknown until the later Neolithic (Bakels 1978, 63; Lüning 1997a, 45). Instead, millet, so far mostly known from eastern Germany, and poppy, originally from the western Mediterranean, highlight the range of contacts which the inhabitants of Aich had (Labes 2003, 16). Nevertheless, the quantities of plant remains recovered are small and the regionalisation of LBK crop spectra, especially from the middle of the LBK onwards, is still very much debated (Bakels 1978, 66; R. Hofmann 1983/84, 153; Kreuz 1990, 163; Lüning 2000, 59).

Regional preferences in terms of animal species have also been proposed. Although cattle would have contributed the greatest amount of meat, pigs played a much greater role than sheep/goats as secondary meat producers in Bavaria, as in neighbouring Baden-Württemberg (Chapter 7.4.4; Lüning 2000, 109; Ganslmeier 2001; von den Driesch

2004). In addition, hunting remains relatively important, especially in the earliest LBK, as noted above. In later LBK assemblages, such as from Lerchenhaid, Köfering or Sallmannsberg, wild animal remains still make up 12–35% of faunal assemblages (Ziegler 1985/86, 9; Lüning 2000, 114; Ganslmeier 2001; von den Driesch 2004, 333). As noted in Chapter 1.3.4, this is in stark contrast to eastern Germany, Slovakia, Bohemia and Transdanubia, where hunted remains generally account for less than 5%, and at most 10% (Döhle 1993, 108–10). Von den Driesch (2004, 345) has argued that these elevated percentages reflect a more varied forest composition in southern Germany, which would have offered better conditions for game to thrive. In addition, hunting may be an element of dietary diversification, potentially especially important in areas in which climatic conditions were less favourable to agriculture, such as parts of southern Germany (Sielmann 1972; Pechtl 2009c, 83–4). Lüning (1997a, 29), however, stresses that ecological factors are less important than regional dietary preferences in explaining this pattern.

In contrast to wild animals, freshwater fish were apparently not consumed on a large scale by many communities. Asam *et al.* (2008, 124) argue from isotope data that there is no indication that fish would have made a major contribution to the diet. Fish bones are rare or absent from most LBK sites in Bavaria. Even the settlement of Nassenfels in the Altmühl valley, a site on a rocky promontory at the border between a loess patch and an extensive boggy area and very close to the Schutter stream, has yielded few fish remains (Rieder and Tillmann 1989; Renner 1994), although it must be pointed out that the intervention here was very small-scale. Interestingly, however, the burial of an eight- to ten-year-old child from Aufhausen was accompanied by a belt decorated with teeth of the carp-like *Rutilus meidingeri*, a find so far unique for the LBK (Kreiner and Pscheidl 2006) and implying that some importance was accorded to fish. The lack of fish bone from settlements may partly have to do with the adverse preservation conditions in many areas, which may especially affect fragile fish remains, and with the inconsistent use of flotation to recover small bones. It cannot therefore be excluded that fishing did play some part in the diet, as attested in Baden-Württemberg at the settlements of Singen (Aufdermauer *et al.* 1986) and the specialised fishing station at the Lautereck rock shelter (Taute 1966; Chapters 1.3.4 and 7.4.4).

In this context, LBK cave occupations in Bavaria deserve mention. In areas such as the southern edge of the Nördlinger Ries and the Swabian Alb (Dehn and Sangmeister 1954; Hahn *et al.* 1985; Weißmüller 1986; Frei and Krahe 1988), the Altmühl valley (e.g. Tillmann 1989) and the Upper Palatinate (Neudert 2005), there are several examples of LBK material from caves which does not appear to be primarily funerary in nature.[4] Generally, the remains consist of a few sherds and flint tools, and the function of these cave sites is unclear. Those listed by Weißmüller (1986) can contain domesticated animal remains, but the Hirschenstube site (Neudert 2005) yielded only wild animal bone, including boar, red and roe deer, pond turtle, duck and grey goose. Neudert (2005, 29) thus suggests a possible use as short-term hunting camp, although due to disturbance by illegal excavators, stratigraphy and finds associations remain poorly understood. It is also possible that the Hirschenstube cave functioned as a temporary camp for people on their way to more northerly areas of Bavaria, perhaps prospecting for raw materials (Neudert 2005, 29).

6.4.4 Regional networks

As discussed above in terms of flint distribution and pottery decoration, networks of varying scales connected Bavaria to other LBK regions. In addition, the distribution of settlement sites can be used to suggest the location of important communication routes. For instance, the broad band of sites along the Danube confirms the importance of an east–west communication axis. Actual routeways to areas beyond Bavaria varied widely in terms of distance and difficulty. The densely settled Neckar valley is only 50 km away from the upper Danube around Ulm and the sites near Blaubeuren in the Swabian Alb, and a similar distance separates the Ries or the sites of southern central Franconia from the Main valley settlement zone. The valleys of the Wörnitz or Altmühl and of the Tauber respectively make for easy contact. While the nearest sites in Austria near Linz are already 60 km away from the confluence of the Rott with the Inn, and 90 km from the LBK sites west of Passau, the Danube still provided relatively easy access, and a further link beyond to Moravia and eastern Austria.

In contrast, reaching Bohemia was far more challenging. It is still only about 60 km as the crow flies from the Gäuboden and Straubing to the settlement clusters around Domažlice, but the landscape makes larger detours unavoidable. The most likely path through the Bavarian and Bohemian Forests led along the Cham-Furth basin, within easy reach of Straubing via the Stallwang basin. An alternative route, slightly longer but still easily passable, follows the Regen valley. Further possible cross-mountain paths to Bohemia exist, but present greater difficulties (Zápotocká 2002). Indeed, two remote settlements support the use of the Stallwang basin. Ascha in the Kinzach valley is already far within the foothills of the Bavarian Forest (Pechtl 2009a, 17–19). From here, it is only 28 km to the next site near Pemfling in the Cham-Furth basin, with the nearest Bohemian sites now only a further 40 km away. If the sites on both sides of the mountains were indeed contemporary, the way to Bohemia may have taken little more than three days.

In addition, routine use of areas off the loess must also be taken into account, although archaeological evidence is relatively sparse. For instance, the sites on the Swabian Alb may not lie on loess, but are still located on soils of comparable quality and in climatically favourable micro-environments and are hence part of 'regular' settlement activity (Knipper *et al.* 2005). In contrast, Ascha and Pemfling lie on small loess patches, but are extremely isolated and thus most likely represent exceptional communities along the transit route to Bohemia. In addition, isolated finds of shoelast adzes are known from the Bavarian Forest, but are mostly undated and hard to interpret in terms of either chance losses or hoards (Winghardt 1986; Valde-Nowak 2002). In addition, the low mountain ranges were probably used for hunting, as suggested by cave occupations, or crossed to obtain a range of raw materials attested on settlement sites, such as granite, gneiss, graphite and various sandstones from the Bavarian Forest, or flint from the outcrop at Flintsbach-Hardt (Weißmüller 1991; Pechtl 2009a, 190–254; Pechtl and Eibl 2011, 390–4). However, pollen analyses have so far failed to clearly show any LBK impact (Nelle 2002, 336).

Overall, there is direct evidence for the use of 'peripheral' landscapes away from agriculturally exploited loess soils, but such hints are rare and difficult to interpret. Reconstructions of the catchment area of large sites such as Stephansposching suggest that regular and probably quite intensive use of such areas did take place (Pechtl 2009a, 520–5). On this basis, the Bavarian Forest could have been used extensively for forest grazing, and hunting trips lasting perhaps up to several days could have reached as far as the Cham-Furth basin.

In addition, both so-called 'contact finds' (that is, objects that can be classified as imports on the basis of their raw material or typological characteristics) and general similarities in material culture, which attest to links with other areas, have been identified in Bavaria. Here again, pottery decoration provides a prime source material. In spite of intra-regional differences noted above, Bavaria is generally oriented eastwards to the *Notenkopf* style. Typological links are particularly strong with Bohemia, while those with the Austrian-Moravian area are of secondary importance (Pechtl 2009a, 116–17). Similarities to south-western Germany are most marked in the western areas of southern Bavaria, which can in fact be classed as belonging to this sphere. In contrast, similarities to the material from the Rhine or Main areas are very faint.

Given the overall similarity of material culture, it is virtually impossible to identify contact finds from Bohemia, and to a lesser extent from Austria or Moravia. However, such objects showing links to the west and north are known. Some pieces originate from Baden-Württemberg, but conversely there are no Bavarian finds from that region (Strien 2010a, 499–503). Contacts to the Franconian and Rhineland LBK are more frequent in the west, but isolated examples occur as far as Regensburg and Landshut; these are attested by comb-decorated vessels. In return, a few Bavarian finds from the Aldenhovener Platte in north-west Germany may reflect kinship relations (Strien 2010a, 502). Contacts with areas quite far to the east are exemplified by a so-called face pot and by an imitation of Želiezovce decorations from Stephansposching (Pechtl 2009a, 536). In terms of architecture, the 'Bavarian J' post setting shows stronger affinities with the east than with the west and north (Pechtl 2010, 44). Interestingly, the pattern here seems different to that of pottery, as the greatest similarities in house orientation and constructional details are to be found with Austria rather than Bohemia.

The exchange of flint raw materials is also an indicator of social relationships between regions. Southern Bavaria contains several outcrops of good quality flint, and procurement is attested at Abensberg-Arnhofen in the west and Flintsbach-Hardt in the east (Weißmüller 1991; Roth 2008). The most important flint exchange network is centred on Abensberg-Arnhofen, and a small area immediately surrounding the outcrop yields almost exclusively this type. It is surrounded by a wider area in which the amounts of Arnhofen chert in site assemblages steadily decrease to about 20% (Roth 2008, 649). Alongside the Kelheim area itself, the western Gäuboden, the tertiary hills as far as Landshut and the upper Vils valley are all part of this zone. In contrast, the eastern Gäuboden and adjacent tertiary hills as far as the lower Vils valley were provisioned with chert from around Ortenburg, and especially from Flintsbach itself. Arnhofen chert still makes up about 10% of assemblages in the Ulm area, but then falls away rapidly with only isolated pieces from Württemberg or Franconia (Roth 2008, 654–6). Interestingly, the distribution is also very extensive to the east, leaving out the Ortenburg-dominated eastern Gäuboden to reach into southern Bohemia and as far as Linz (Roth 2008, 645, 670). Western Bavaria thus enjoyed a certain level of contact with the Neckar and Main areas and Bohemia. In contrast, the distribution of Ortenburg chert in eastern-southern Bavaria reflects the area already defined through pottery decoration and architectural preferences. Ortenburg chert does not seem to have been exported, although this could be partly connected to the difficulty recognising this rather plain material. This is one of several distinctions between western and eastern parts of Lower Bavaria, a theme addressed again below (Chapter 6.9).

In addition to such regular contacts, rare imports of exotic material are also attested. These comprise Hungarian radiolarite in the earliest LBK (Gronenborn 1997b, 25–32; Mattheußer 2009, 20), and later on individual pieces of Slovakian obsidian (Schötz 1988, 8; Pechtl 2009a, 143). Northern Bohemian quartzite makes up about 1% of the chipped stone inventory at Stephansposching. This is remarkable because Bavarian flint is of much better quality, and Bohemia itself is actually rather poor in raw materials and dependent on various imports (Pechtl 2009a, 177). These few pieces are a further argument for the strong ties to Bohemia which evidently went beyond purely economic necessity. Similarly, materials of western origin, such as Wittlingen chert from the Swabian Alb or Upper Rhineland chalcedony, occur in small quantities at Stephansposching. So-called 'Pseudo-Baltic' flints, most likely from central Germany, are slightly more frequent, but comprise only 2% of the Stephansposching assemblage. These rarer raw materials in particular show a very uneven distribution within the settlement, suggesting that different households could tap into a variety of networks and occasionally achieved long-distance contacts (Pechtl 2009a, 176–81).

A very different kind of long-distance network is

reflected in the distribution of stone adzes. As elsewhere, most adzes in Bavaria were fashioned in actinolite-hornblende-schist, largely sourced in northern Bohemia (Ramminger 2009). In contrast to Hessen, where the supply of this material collapses in the later LBK, sites such as Stephansposching are regularly provisioned throughout the sequence, again reinforcing the impression of close ties with Bohemia (Ramminger 2009, 93; Pechtl 2009a, 243). Lastly, *Spondylus* shells also reached Bavaria from the east via an even more extensive network and were buried in large numbers at sites such as Aiterhofen (Nieszery 1995, 187; Chapter 6.7.1 below).

In sum, a variety of networks criss-crossed southern Bavaria and linked it with neighbouring areas. While some of these relations may have been based on personal contacts, such as occasional pieces of Wittlingen chert, others are long-distance networks which remained stable over several generations. Clearly, the closest ties of southern Bavaria were with Bohemia and along the Danube to Austria and Moravia, with links to the west and north far more restricted.

6.5 Burial rites

6.5.1 Known sites

Southern Bavaria is relatively rich in funerary remains, especially compared to other regions covered in this project, with over 400 burials recorded in the Lifeways Database – only Baden-Württemberg has more (Chapter 7.5). However, the evidence is not uniformly distributed geographically. For instance, no burials securely dated to the LBK are known from the Nördlinger Ries, in spite of its concentrations of LBK sites. The only possible example is a crouched inhumation from Nördlingen-Nürnberger Straße (Zeeb 1993; Zeeb-Lanz 2003, 298), but as only some flint tools accompanied the burial it must be considered undated. Skull fragments from a pit at Nähermemmingen (Frickinger 1934) were dated to the LBK on the strength of associated ceramic material.

The situation is better further south in Swabia. At the cave site of Hanseles Hohl (Fronhofen, Dillingen), the fragmented and partly burnt remains of ten individuals, from young children to mature adults, were discovered associated with two hearths. The dating of this site remains controversial. The human bone was associated with flint tools, polished adzes, a *Spondylus* armring and two further *Spondylus* artefacts, grinding stones and sherds of a variety of Neolithic groups; most material was late LBK, but *Stichbandkeramik*, Rössen, Münchshöfen and later pottery was also present (Dehn and Sangmeister 1954, 30; Orschiedt 1999, 152–4). Only one individual seems to show traces of violence, having suffered a blow to the head. Although many bones have been lost, Orschiedt (1999, 156) therefore argues that Hanseles Hohl is part of regular funerary practice in the late LBK or early middle Neolithic, a reading also supported by the presence of *Spondylus* shell, otherwise found mostly in cemetery graves.

Nearby, the early Neolithic cemetery at Dillingen-Steinheim was excavated in 1987. It comprises 27 inhumations (Nieszery 1995, 57–60), but the range of grave goods is very limited compared to eastern Bavaria. Polished stone tools and pottery are the most frequent goods, and some graves also receive flint tools and ochre, but personal ornamentation, including *Spondylus*, is absent with the exception of one antler toggle in grave 23.

About 300 m south-east of the burial ground, a stretch of enclosure ditch with a double internal palisade surrounding at least three longhouses was excavated in 2000 (Dietrich and Kociumaka 2001). Two groups of skeletons, one comprising eight and the other 20 individuals, were discovered here. There is as yet no further detail, although the excavators mention that about half of these individuals were buried in a left-crouched position with heads to the east, whereas the remainder were found in irregular positions. Dietrich and Kociumaka (2001, 34) reconstruct a massacre, with some victims thrown into the ditch by attackers and the others later reverentially buried by survivors; further osteological examination, planned for the coming years, is needed.

Most information for burial practice comes from the eastern half of southern Bavaria, especially from a cluster of sites near Straubing and in the southern extremity of the Upper Palatinate, but also from near Landshut, Deggendorf and, to a lesser extent, Kelheim. A total of 78 settlement burials are known from these areas, of which more than half come from the single site of Otzing (Chapter 6.8; Schmotz and Weber 2000). In addition, there are 360 individuals from cemetery sites, including 244 inhumations (of which ten are from double inhumations), 106 cremations (of which 18 are from double cremations) and ten individuals represented by partial remains. The majority (244 individuals) come from the site of Aiterhofen-Ödmühle (Chapter 6.7; Nieszery 1995), but further sites of note include Essenbach-Ammerbreite near Landshut (29 individuals; Brink-Kloke 1990), Mangolding and Sengkofen south of Regensburg (respectively 13 and 32 individuals; Nieszery 1995), and Stephansposching near Deggendorf (42 individuals; Schmotz 1992).

Overall, LBK communities in southern Bavaria had a wide range of funerary practices. As with other regions, inhumations and cremations in settlements and separate cemeteries dominate our sample, but it is likely that these represent only a part of the population (Nieszery 1995, 13–18). Remains securely dated to the earliest LBK are entirely absent; the settlement burial of an immature individual from Altdorf is among the earliest known remains, but dates to the Flomborn/*Notenkopf* horizon (Christlein 1982). However, by the developed and late LBK, a series of settlement and cemetery burials are known, comprising single and double inhumations and cremations. Finally, towards the end of the period, the burial of fragmentary remains in caves, analogous to the example from the Franconian Jungfernhöhle (Kunkel 1955; Orschiedt 1999), may also begin. It is hard at present to comment further on the remains from the Dillingen enclosure, but at least some of these may be related to 'regular' funerary behaviour as indicated by similar finds from Stephansposching (Pechtl 2009a, 301, 306) or Vaihingen (Krause 1997, 106–10).

The settlement burials from southern Bavaria generally correspond to the LBK-wide characteristics observed by Veit (1993; 1996). Compared to cemetery burials, they receive a restricted range of goods and are also more likely to go unfurnished; in contrast to the LBK overall (47% of all settlement burials are unfurnished; Lifeways Database) and areas such as Thuringia and Saxony (under 50% unfurnished), Bavarian settlement burials very often lack goods (*c.* 74% unfurnished). Where present, pottery and flint tools are the most common grave goods, with imported shell and polished tools in particular very low compared to cemetery sites. This could partly be explained by the relatively high proportion of children (over 44%, with 33% juveniles and adults). Where more in-depth osteological studies have been carried out elsewhere (e.g. Orschiedt 1998a), women tend to dominate the sample from settlements, but there is as yet no indication that this holds true for Bavaria. Body positions and orientations are variable.

In contrast, the positions and orientations of cemetery burials are often relatively standardised. In addition, cemetery burials can be lavishly furnished, with only just over 36% receiving no recognisable grave goods. Polished stone adzes and flint tools are relatively frequent, and compared to neighbouring regions such as Baden-Württemberg there is a greater emphasis on personal ornamentation. Imported shells of various kinds (*Spondylus*, *Dentalium*, *Protula*) are found alongside limestone beads and local Danubian shells (*Theodoxus*). The latter are an artefact category largely restricted to Bavarian and Austrian sites. In addition, a range of artefacts such as bone combs, small bone rods or wands and fox mandibles and teeth occur in Bavarian and Austrian cemeteries, but not elsewhere (Jeunesse 1997; Lenneis 2007). Exclusively Bavarian goods may be greenstone beads and perforated graphite pieces (Pechtl 2009a, 260–3; Pechtl and Eibl 2011, 371–9). This greater range of goods is supplemented by some unique pieces such as an ammonite fossil from Essenbach (Brink-Kloke 1990, 450). The selectively expanded ranges of goods, especially in terms of ornament provision, create a recognisably local variant within the limits of the overall LBK cemetery tradition.

6.5.2 Previous isotopic analysis

Several Bavarian sites have seen isotopic analysis. In the course of a study of Neolithic foodwebs, Asam *et al.* (2006; 2008) investigated selected individuals from the LBK sites of Essenbach, Sengkofen, Dillingen and a site referred to as 'Landshut', alongside later material. They measured carbon, nitrogen and oxygen isotopes, comparing the human values to a range of animal species from late Neolithic Pestenacker. The early and middle Neolithic remains were very uniform in terms of diet, with little difference between sites. The trophic level overall was lower than for later Neolithic humans, who also showed more inter-site variation. Sex-based differences in protein intake could only be detected from the Bell Beaker period onwards (Asam *et al.* 2006, 17; 2008, 122). Since the main goal had been to reconstruct trophic levels and the impact of climate on diet, skeletal material was selected largely on the basis of preservation, rather than archaeological questions, such as grave good provision or burial rite.

The only site to have seen previous strontium isotope analysis is Dillingen (Bentley *et al.* 2002; Price and Bentley 2005), but the skeletons sampled in these studies and those included by Asam *et al.* do not overlap. Bentley *et al.* (2002, 800) sampled 17 individuals, 12 males and five females. Of these, six males and all females were classed as 'non-local'. On this basis, a spatial clustering of locals and non-locals was proposed relying on four groups of graves identified by Nieszery (1995, 63). Group 2 is said to contain the most varied selection of grave goods and the fewest non-locals, while group 1 is particularly poor in grave goods but contains a high proportion of non-locals, as do groups 3 and 4. Finally, it was proposed that local individuals at Dillingen were significantly more likely to be buried with polished stone tools (Bentley *et al.* 2002, 801; Price and Bentley 2005, 211).

In both these studies the sample sizes were fairly small. In addition, Nieszery himself stresses that his spatial groupings for Dillingen should not be taken at face value, as large parts of the site suffered significant erosion and many graves may have been destroyed. As a more reliable partition, he proposes an eastern and western group (Nieszery 1995, 64). This would result in more 'migrants' being buried in the eastern part, where sherds at the level of the skeleton are also more frequent, but the overall differences in the range of grave goods are evened out in this alternative scheme.

Moreover, there is uncertainty as to the implications of 'non-local' individuals. On the one hand, Bentley *et al.* (2002, 802) suggested that this may relate to a wider catchment area, rather than strictly off-site origin. Indeed, Dillingen lies north of the Danube, only about 10 km south of the Swabian Alb, where post-Neolithic archaeological pig teeth have yielded surprisingly high strontium signatures (Bentley and Knipper 2005b, 639). On the other hand, Price and Bentley (2005, 212) argued that the spatial separation of non-locals at Dillingen could be chronological, with incomers starting off a new cemetery that continued to spread westwards, or alternatively could be down to status differences between 'local' and 'foreign'. These results deserve to be tested on a larger sample.

6.6 Sites sampled

Two sites, the cemetery at Aiterhofen near Straubing and the settlement burials from Otzing near Deggendorf, roughly 15 km to the south-east, were sampled in the course of this project (Fig. 6.1). Both sites are established in the *ältere* LBK and span the entire sequence, with Aiterhofen also yielding some middle Neolithic material. Some animal bone was recovered from the settlement features just to the south of the Aiterhofen cemetery, but as this was insufficient in quantity, the assemblage from one of the Lerchenhaid enclosures, roughly 8 km to the north-west of Aiterhofen, was sampled instead.

6.7 Aiterhofen-Ödmühle

6.7.1 Introduction

The cemetery of Aiterhofen is located near the modern hamlet of Ödmühle on the right bank of the Aiterach stream, which flows into the Danube *c.* 4 km further to the north (Fig. 6.1). Field survey data from the area were collected by Kurt Reinecke (1978a), who recognised a total of ten settlements, mostly located on the left bank. This profusion of evidence was part of Nieszery's (1995, 56) argument for seeing Aiterhofen as a cemetery shared by several small communities. However, it remains uncertain whether all the findspots plotted by Reinecke are in fact separate sites. At least the three surrounding the cemetery could form one large site comparable in extent to Stephansposching or Otzing further to the east (Pechtl 2009b, 527). The only excavated site, Aiterhofen B20 (K. Reinecke 1978a) on the left bank, apparently predates the establishment of the cemetery. Two badly preserved house plans were revealed, but the total extent of the site remains unknown. Four settlement burials formed a small cluster just north of house 2, with a fifth burial west of the house. Bone preservation was limited, but two children and three adults are represented, most crouched on their left sides but with a variety of orientations. Two of the adults had been buried with grave goods: pottery and a polished adze in one grave, and a selection of flint tools in another (K. Reinecke 1978a, 76–9).

The Aiterhofen cemetery was discovered in 1975 and substantially excavated, although a few graves may have been missed in the north-west and south-east corners (Fig. 6.4) and several could have been destroyed unobserved during quarrying (Hanöffner and Siftar 2007, 38). In addition, the cemetery itself and the area further south yielded settlement traces of the LBK, middle, late and final Neolithic, and the Hallstatt and La Tène periods (Hanöffner and Siftar 2007), which may have destroyed some LBK graves. The LBK settlement evidence is mostly concentrated to the south of the cemetery, with some overlap. It comprises 24 pits and pit complexes, some yielding animal bone, seven 'slit-shaped pits', 21 'grave-like' pits (see below), the possible partial remains of a house and parts of a ditch system ('ditch III') (Hanöffner and Siftar 2007, 39–47). A 25-m stretch of this ditch runs west–east and has been dated to the LBK. It seems to divide the settlement from the bulk of the graves further to the north, although there are some graves south of the ditch. While it is tempting to see the ditch as delimiting the cemetery, this would only have applied to certain phases of the site's use, and relative dating remains too coarse to establish the chronological relationships between the different features. A second linear ('ditch I') also contained a large quantity of LBK sherds. It is cut by grave 30, believed by Nieszery (1995, 270) to be middle Neolithic, but not definitely datable according to Hanöffner and Siftar (2007, 51). They nevertheless provisionally assign this ditch to the middle Neolithic.

On present evidence, the Aiterhofen cemetery contained 157 single and three double inhumations (a total of six individuals), 56 cremations, nine double cremations (18 suggested individuals) and a further nine individuals represented by isolated bones, giving a total of approximately 240 individuals. In addition, three cremations, one double cremation and one inhumation are argued to be of possible middle Neolithic date (Nieszery 1995, 89).

As no radiocarbon determinations exist, the dating of Aiterhofen hinges on three main approaches: the use of artefacts believed to be chronologically diagnostic; grave seriation; and relative dating by pottery seriation. For example, doubled adze blades (*Doppelhacken*) could date some cremations to the early middle Neolithic (Nieszery 1995, 89). However, since most other known examples are stray finds or come from late LBK graves (Nieszery 1995, 159; Czekaj-Zastawny and Zastawny 2002; Weiner 2003), this attribution remains uncertain, although the pottery in grave 229 is certainly middle Neolithic. Similarly, Nieszery (1995, 188–91), following E. Willms (1985, 373–5), uses the presence of *Spondylus* shells to assign some graves to an early horizon. Indeed, potentially primarily late LBK cemeteries such as Stephansposching[5] (Schmotz 1992) have few or no imported shells. However, elsewhere, most notably in Alsace, late LBK graves with *Spondylus* are known, and so its reliability as a chronological indicator remains to be independently established (Jeunesse 1997, 55, 94). A seriation of all Aiterhofen graves on the basis of position, orientation and grave good inventory (Farruggia 2002) must also be rejected, as every single element of the rite or goods assemblage (e.g. presence/absence of bone tools, vessel shape, body orientation, stone tool morphology etc.) was *a priori* assigned equivalent value as a chronological indicator, an assumption almost certainly wrong (for further discussion, see D. Hofmann 2006, 709–12).

Dating through ceramic seriation remains difficult, as pottery is not a particularly common grave good at Aiterhofen (a total of 49 vessels were recovered from 37 inhumation graves; 11 inhumations and 11 cremations contained sherds at the level of the skeleton) and not all vessels are suitable for a chronological study. Nieszery (1995, 131–8) devised a system based on the scheme of Brink-Kloke (1992) for Bavaria and argued for the beginning of the site at some point in the middle LBK (in what he calls a 'Flomborn' horizon) and for its continuation into the middle Neolithic. Following this scheme, the earliest burials are near the centre and in the north-west (D. Hofmann 2006, 708). Farruggia (2002) relies on the seriation for Baden-Württemberg of Strien (2000), but the few comparable motifs are those not particularly chronologically diagnostic (for example, Strien 2000, tables

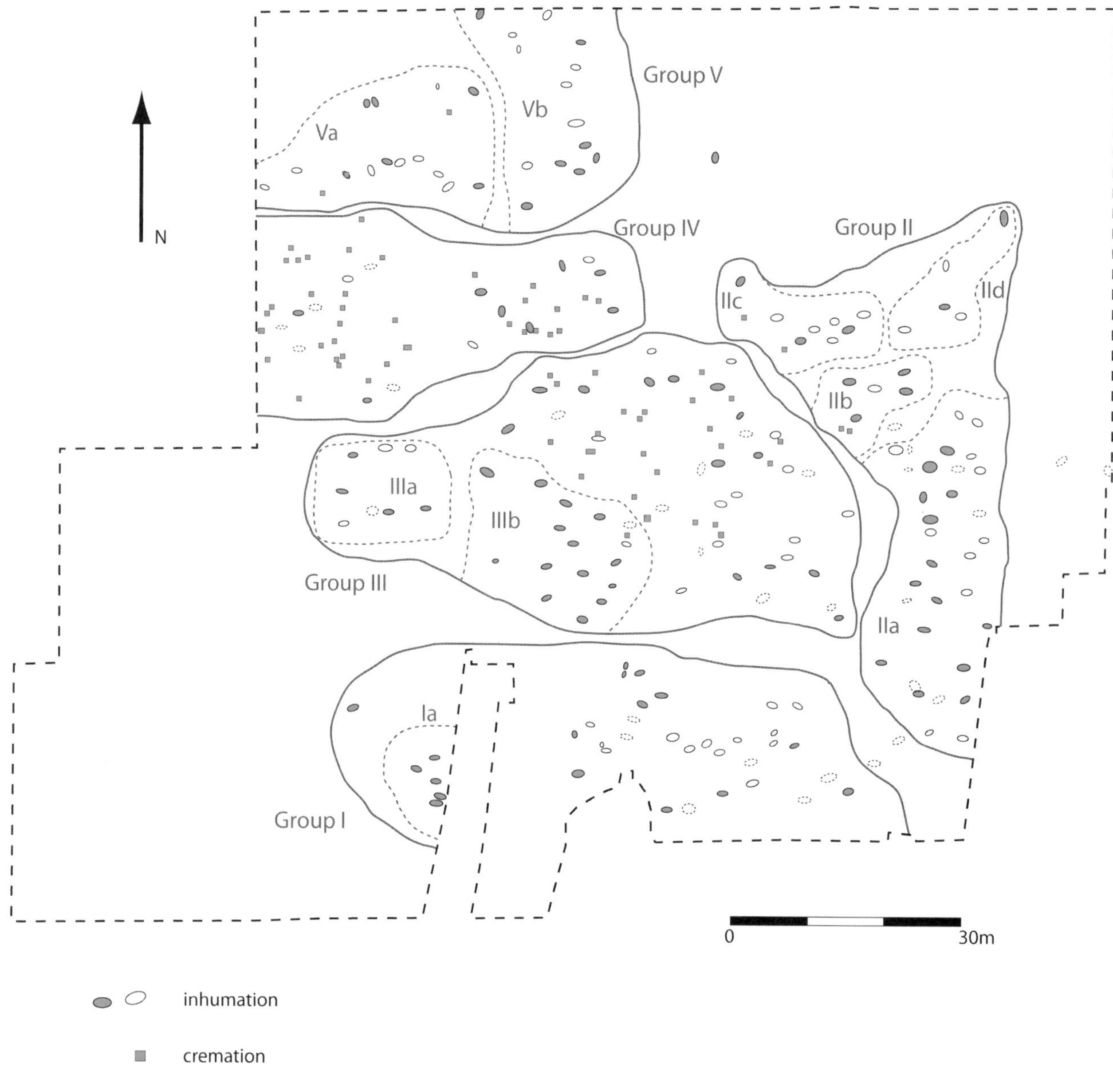

Fig. 6.4. Aiterhofen-Ödmühle: plan. After Nieszery (1995, 55, fig. 19). Sampled inhumations are shown in grey.

4.43–4). Finally, Pechtl (2009a, 94) uses six pottery-rich graves to link Aiterhofen to his chronological scheme for southern Bavaria, which includes the most assemblages so far and provides inter-regional comparisons (Table 6.1). The graves date from Stephansposching phases 3 or 4 into phase 6. This corresponds to a start in phase III in the Untermaingebiet (Meier-Arendt 1966), which in turn is equivalent to phases 5 and 6 in Baden-Württemberg (Strien 2000), phases VIII–X of the Merzbach sequence (Stehli 1994) and phase III in Bohemia (Pavlů 1986). Some single Aiterhofen vessels, however, may well be earlier. The cemetery continues to the end of the Bavarian LBK (Pechtl 2009a, figs 43–4), spanning a period of perhaps two or three centuries overall. This coincides with Hanöffner and Siftar's (2007, 50) dating of the settlement remains.

Initially, the cemetery was divided into five spatial groupings on the basis of larger empty spaces separating clusters of graves (Nieszery 1995, 64). This claim remained hard to assess until the subsequent publication of all excavated features, which shows significant encroachment by later activity within Nieszery's 'empty' areas (Hanöffner and Siftar 2007). It is hence unwise to interpret the proposed spatial groupings in too much detail, as large ditches and pit clusters may have destroyed many graves between them. In addition, the idea that these are family plots (e.g. Nieszery 1995, 66) is not supported by their demographic composition. Children up to seven years of age conspicuously cluster in group V, while males or females dominate some groups (see D. Hofmann 2006, 712–21). However, it remains the case that certain kinds of grave good or rite are particularly common in certain areas of the cemetery, regardless of whether one uses

Nieszery's (1995) groups, the seriation of Farruggia (2002) or simple distribution maps of given traits as a base line. On that basis, the sampling strategy for this project aimed at including a representative number of individuals from all areas of the cemetery.

Since only inhumation burials could be included in the present project, they are also the focus for analysis here, but the cremations can be briefly summarised. In general, fewer grave goods were recovered from them compared to inhumation burials, and almost half are unfurnished. The dominant grave good for the Aiterhofen cremations are polished stone tools or flints, all burnt and some broken, while ornaments are absent. Cremations cluster in the northern and western areas of the cemetery, and since the rite is generally thought to become more common in the later LBK (e.g. Jeunesse 1997, 59; Trautmann 2007), this may have a chronological dimension. It is even possible that several more middle Neolithic individuals remain unrecognised among the unfurnished cremations, or that the greater erosion in the south may have destroyed further cremations there (Nieszery 1995, 62). Double cremations have been suggested in nine cases, a feature which would be unique to Aiterhofen (Nieszery 1995, 297–304). This could not be confirmed by more recent analyses, as the material is lost (Trautmann 2007, 160). There is also no available information on the bone weights recovered. Nevertheless, the presence of cremations here ties in with a general trend to diversification in funerary customs and a greater emphasis on fragmenting the body in the later part of the LBK (e.g. D. Hofmann forthcoming).

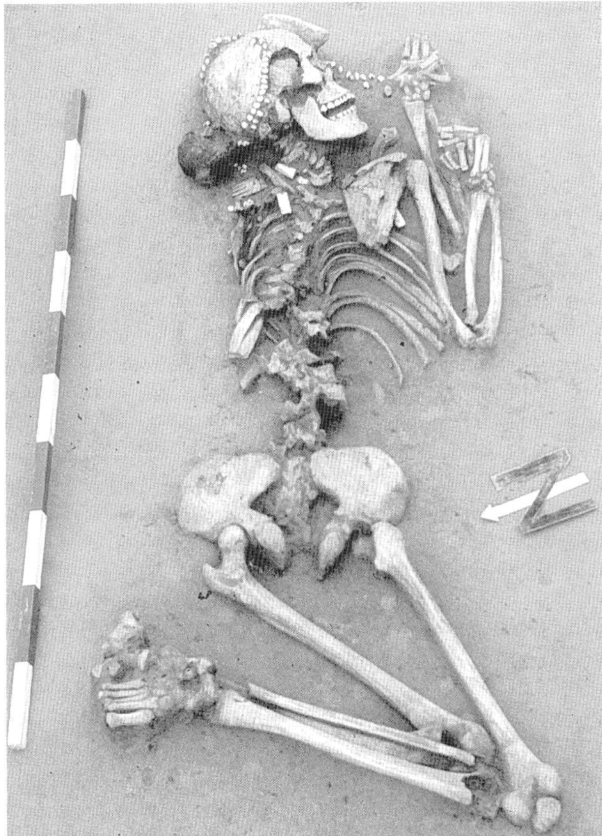

Fig. 6.5. Aiterhofen-Ödmühle: burial 60 (adult female, 40–45 years). Reproduced with the kind permission of the Bayerisches Landesamt für Denkmalpflege.

Of the 153 inhumations with available data, 124 (81%) are oriented with their head to the east or east-south-east, 14 have their heads in a general westerly direction, and 15 are positioned on a broadly north–south axis (Fig. 6.5; Table 6.2). Of the 141 individuals well enough preserved to ascertain position, 110 (78%) were crouched on their left side, 24 on their right and only three on their back or front. Two individuals were found in a supine position, and one was prone. Grave 33 contained a woman buried in an unusual position. She was placed on her back, her lower arms flipped back so that her hands touched her shoulders, and her legs drawn up in a rhomboid position. Burials in strikingly similar positions have also been recovered from Ensisheim and Vendenheim in Alsace (Jeunesse *et al.* 1996; Lefranc 2002; Chapter 8.10) and from Wittmar in Lower Saxony (Rötting 1983), suggesting that in spite of its irregularity this position held some significance. Ninety-four individuals (67%) at Aiterhofen are both left-crouched and have an east–west orientation. This comprises the majority of inhumations and contrasts with a more heterogeneous group which deviates in one or both aspects. The latter should, however, not detract from the general impression of a considerable degree of conformity in the positions and orientations of the Aiterhofen inhumations. Orientations, for instance, are more standardised here and at Sengkofen than at Essenbach or Mangolding.

The degree to which specific individuals followed this majority practice varies across the Aiterhofen cemetery and between different demographic groupings. For instance, among the women it is juveniles and younger adults who

Table 6.2 (over the next 8 pages). Aiterhofen: the isotope, osteological and archaeological data. Age and sex information from Nieszery (1995), see discussion in text.
Key for body position: LC – Left-crouched; RC – Right-crouched; C – Crouched, direction unknown; CB – Crouched on back; CF – Crouched on front; S – Supine; P – Prone; I – Irregular.
Key for grave goods (number of items follows in brackets; frag. = fragment): U. – Unfurnished; F. – Fill only (all items listed after an F. were in the fill of the grave rather than at the level of the skeleton); Pol. – Polished stone; Cer. – Ceramics; Shd. – Sherds; Spon. – Spondylus; *She. – Other Shell; Och. – Ochre; Ant. – Antler toggle; Lit. – Chipped stone; Bon – Worked bone; Grd. – Grinding stone; Firelighting kit – this includes the presence of pyrite or manganese as well as tools (such as flint or a bone awl) that could be used to start a fire (Nieszery 1995, 163–8).*

Burial	Tooth	Sex	Age (yrs)	$^{87}Sr/^{86}Sr$	Sr conc. ppm	$\delta^{13}C$ ‰	$\delta^{15}N$ ‰	Orient.	Body position	Grave goods
1	-	-	-	-	-	-	-	E–W	LC	Pol.(1)
2	-	-	-	-	-	-	-	E–W	LC	Pol.(2), Spon.(18 beads, armring), Lit.(3), Firelighting kit
3	-	F	20–30	-	-	-	-	E–W	-	U.
4	-	-	-	-	-	-	-	E–W	-	U.
5	-	-	-	-	-	-	-	E–W	LC	U.
6	-	-	10–12	-	-	-	-	NE–SW	LC	U.
7	-	-	-	-	-	-	-	E–W	-	U.
8	-	-	-	-	-	-	-	-	-	U.
9	Upper incisor	F	20–30	0.70907	66	−20.5	10.2	E–W	LC	Spon.(14), Stone beads(15)
10	M2	M	>60	0.70942	43	−20.2	10.7	E–W	LC	Pol.(3), Spon.(27 beads, armring, buckle), She.(2), Lit.(1), Firelighting kit, Bon.(1)
11	-	F	50–60	-	-	-	-	E–W	LC	Spon.(2 beads), F.Shd.(7), Daub
12	M2	M	30–35	0.70906	43	−20.4	10.4	SE–NW	LC	Pol.(2), Spon.(7 beads, armring), Stone bead(1), F.Shd.(4)
13	-	M?	20–25	-	-	−20.4	9.7	-	-	Pol.(1), Spon.(armring)
14	M3	F	20–30	0.70955	56	−20.5	9.9	E–W	LC	F.Cer.(5)
15	M2	M	30–40	0.70933	49	−20.1	10.7	-	-	Pol.(3), Shd.(4), Spon.(1 bead), Lit.(2)
16	-	-	12	-	-	-	-	-	-	Shd.(2), Animal Bone (cremated)
17a	-	-	10–12	-	-	-	-	E–W	-	Shd.(2), Animal Bone (cremated)
17b	-	-	-	-	-	-	-	-	-	*Partial burial of calcinated human longbone*
18	M1 M2	M	40–45	0.70948 0.70959	46 55	−20.1	10.2	E–W	LC	Pol.(2), Cer.(1), Spon.(6 beads, armring, buckle), Lit. (4), Bon.(1), Firelighting kit
19a	-	F	20–30	-	-	−20.4	9.6	E–W	LC	Spon.(armring), F.Shd.(8), Graphite
19b	-	-	10–12	-	-	-	-	-	-	*Partial burial of human distal humerus fragment*
20	-	M?	16–18	-	-	-	-	SW–NE	LC	U.
21	M2	M?	18–20	0.70951	50	−20.1	9	-	-	Pol.(1), Limestone plate
22	M2	F?	Adult	0.70939	42	−20.6	9.5	E–W	-	Stone bead(5), F.Shd.(5)
23a	-	-	10–12	-	-	−20.5	10	E–W	LC	F.Shd.(12), Cremation(13 frag.s of human longbone)
23b	-	-	-	-	-	-	-	-	-	*Partial burial of a calcinated human skull fragment (ochred) and 13 longbone fragments*
24a	-	M	Adult	0.70962	44	−20.6	9.8	E–W	LC	Pol.(2), Graphite, F.Shd.(2), Cremation
24b	-	-	<40	-	-	-	-	-	-	*Partial burial of 5 calcinated skull fragments and long bone fragment*

25	M3	M	45–50	0.71024	71	−20.1	9.6	E–W	LC	Pol.(1), Spon.(armring), Lit.(4), Firelighting kit
26a	M3	M	Adult	-	-	−20.2	9.7	E–W	-	U.
26b	-	-	Inf. I/II	-	-	-	-	E–W	-	U.
27	-	-	Adult	-	-	-	-	E–W	-	U.
28	M2	M	30–35	0.70935	76	−20.3	10	E–W	LC	Pol.(2), Spon.(25 beads, armring, buckle), She.(5), Lit.(2), Bon.(1), Firelighting kit
29	M1 M2	M	40–45	0.70917	51	-	-	E–W	LC	Pol.(1), Lit.(1)
30	-	-	10–14	-	-	-	-	NW–SE	I	*Non-LBK ceramics*
31	-	M	30–35	-	-	−20.3	9.5	E–W	LC	Graphite, F.Shd.(3), Lit.(1)
32	-	F	>60	-	-	-	-	E–W	RC	Spon.(Buckle), She.(238), Stone bead (4), F.Shd.(4)
33	-	F	Adult	-	-	-	-	W–E	I	Cer.(1), She.(3), Stone bead (1), Graphite, F.Shd.(9)
34	M2	M?	Adult	0.70944	45	-	-	E–W	RC	U.
35	M2	M	35–40	0.70993	63	-	-	E–W	LC	Cer.(1)
36	M2	-	25–30	0.71012	52	−20.3	9.5	E–W	LC	Pol.(1), Cer.(1), Lit.(2), Firelighting kit
37	-	-	40–45	-	-	-	-	NE–SW	LC	Shd.(12)
38	-	F	18–20	-	-	-	-	NE–SW	LC	Cer.(1)
39	M1	F?	6–10	0.70961	41	-	-	E–W	RC	Cer.(1), Lit.(1)
40	-	F?	Adult	-	-	-	-	NE–SW	LC	U.
41	M2	M?	10–12	0.70875	82	−20.7	9.2	E–W	LC	Pol.(2), Spon.(8 beads, armring), Lit.(3), Bon.(1), Ant.(1), F.Shd.(42), Firelighting kit
42	-	M	>60	-	-	−20.0	10	W–E	LC	Bon.(1), Firelighting kit, F.Pol.(1), Lit.(1)
43	-	M	Adult	-	-	−20.8	9.1	E–W	LC	Pol.(1), Stone bead (8)
44	-	-	-	-	-	-	-	E–W	LC	U.
45	-	F	30–35	-	-	-	-	E–W	LC	Grd.(1)
46	-	-	Adult	-	-	-	-	E–W	LC	F.Lit.(1)
47	-		7–13	-	-	−20.4	9.4	E–W	LC	Bone/antler comb (remains of)
48	M1	M	25–30	0.70951	36	−20.7	9.9	E–W	LC	Pol.(2), Spon.(armring), Firelighting kit
49	-	F?	40–50	-	-	-	-	E–W	LC	U.
50	M2	M	>60	0.70952	68	-	-	NE–SW	CB	Lit.(4), Bon.(2), F.Shd.(21), Calcinated bone
51	-	-	Adult	-	-	-	-	E–W	LC	U.
52	-	-	-	-	-	-	-	E–W	LC	U.
53	-	F	30–35	-	-	-	-	E–W	LC	U.
54	-	-	-	-	-	-	-	E–W	LC	U.

55	M2	F	20–30	0.70951	38	−20.2	9.9	E–W	LC	Lit.(2), Bon.(1), Firelighting kit, Grd.(1)
56	M1 M2	M	40–45	0.70917 0.70939	94 51	−20.3	10.2	W–E	LC	Pol.(2), She.(1), Lit.(1)
57	M2	M	30–35	0.71416	47	−20.2	9.7	E–W	CF	U.
58	M1	-	3–6	0.70912	42	−20.4	11.1	-	-	Pol.(2)
59	-	F?	Adult	-	-	-	-	-	-	U.
60	M2	F	40–45	0.70916	67	−20.5	9.9	E–W	LC	Cer.(1), Spon.(16 beads), She.(80), Bon./antler (1), Grd.(1), F.Shd.(4), Calcinated bone (human?)
61	M3	M	35–40	0.70960	70	-	-	E–W	LC	Pol.(3), Spon.(buckle), Lit.(3), Cattle rib
62	-	M	Adult	-	-	-	-	NE–SW	RC	U.
63	-	-	20–30	-	-	-	-	W–E	LC	Cer.(1), Lit.(1)
64	-	M	50–60	-	-	-	-	E–W	LC	Pol.(1), Bon.(1)
65	M3	M?	25–30	0.70959	40	-	-	E–W	LC	Pol.(1), Lit.(1), Firelighting kit
66	-	-	Adult	-	-	−20.8	10	N–S	CB	Pol.(1), Cer.(3)
67	-	-	Not Adult	-	-			E–W	LC	Cer.(2), F.Cer.(1)
68	M1	F	40–50	0.70954	38	−20.4	9.9	E–W	CB	Cer.(1), Spon.(22 beads, buckle), Lit.(1), Graphite
69	M2	F	20–30	0.70964	53	−20.5	9.5	E–W	LC	Cer.(1)
70	-	-	Adult	-	-	-	-	E–W	LC	Cer.(1), Graphite, Grd.(1)
71a	-	-	-	-	-	-	-	E–W	LC	U.
71b	-	M?	12–14	-	-	-	-	E–W	CB	F.Graphite
72	M2	-	Adult	-	-	-	-	E–W	LC	Lit.(1), Graphite, Bone/antler comb, F.Shd.(1)
73	-	M?	20–25	-	-	-	-	E–W	LC	U.
74	M2	M	25–35	0.70905	113	−20.6	9.4	E–W	RC	Cer.(4)
75	M2	-	25–35	0.70967	79	-	-	W–E	RC	Lit.(7)
76	M2	F?	30–39	-	-	-	-	E–W	CB	Pol.(1), Cer.(1)
77	-	-	-	-	-	-	-	W–E	RC	Cer.(2). Grd.(1)
78	M3	M	25–30	0.70951	39	−20.5	9.8	E–W	LC	Lit.(3), Och.
79	-	-	-	-	-	-	-	E–W	CB	U.
80	-	F?	Adult	-	-	-	-	E–W	RC	Cer.(1)
81	-	-	-	-	-	-	-	W–E	LC	Cer.(2)
82	-	M?	Adult	-	-	-	-	E–W	S	Grd.(1)
83	M1	F?	4–6	0.70950	48	-	-	E–W	LC	U.
84	-	-	18–20	-	-	-	-	E–W	LC	Cer.(1)
85	M1	M	60+	0.70950	40	−20.5	10.2	E–W	LC	Lit.(3), Bon.(4), Firelighting kit, F.Cer.(1), Shd.(3)
86	-	M?	20–30	-	-	-	-	E–W	LC	Pol.(1), Cer.(1), Lit.(1)

87	-	M	Adult	-	-	-	-	N–S	LC	Pol.(1), Cer.(1), Lit.(1), Firelighting kit, F.Cer.(1)
88	M2	M?	10–12	0.71007	40	−20.7	10.1	E–W	LC	Pol.(1), Cer.(1), Lit.(11), Firelighting kit, F.Cer.(1)
89	M1	F	25–35	0.70936	47	−20.1	10.1	E–W	LC	Cer.(1), Graphite
90	-	M	>60	-	-	-	-	E–W	CF	Pol.(1), Ant.(1)
91	M2	F	Adult	0.70959	76	−20.3	9.1	E–W	LC	Cer.(1)
92	M2	F	35–40	0.71437	98	-	-	E–W	LC	Cer.(1), F.Shd.(8)
93	M1 M3	M	50–55	0.70881 0.70911	94 90	-	-	E–W	LC	Pol.(1), Lit.(1), Ant.(1)
94	-	M	Adult	-	-	−20.7	9.6	E–W	LC	Pol.(1), Cer.(3), Lit.(2), Firelighting kit, Sheep leg, F.Cer.(1)
95	-	-	-	-	-	-	-	E–W	LC	Cer.(1)
96	-	-	-	-	-	-	-	E–W	LC	Pol.(1), Lit.(3),
97a	-		Adult	-	-	-	-	E–W	RC	U. *Unsure whether two individuals or one (partial cremation?)*
97b	-	F?	Adult	-	-	-	-	-	-	U.
98	-	F??	Adult	-	-	-	-	E–W	RC	Lit.(3), Graphite(2)
99	M2	F	18–20	0.70947	24	−20.6	9.7	NE–SW	LC	F.Shd.(1)
100	M2	F	40–50	0.70949	37	−20.8	9.5	NE–SW	LC	U.
101	-	-	40–50	-	-	-	-	E–W	LC	U.
102	M2	M	>60	0.70950	35	−20.5	10.5	NE–SW	LC	Pol.(3), Och., Lit.(6), Firelighting kit, Pig leg, Fox mandible
103	-	M?	Adult	-	-	-	-	E–W	LC	U.
104	-	F?	20–30	-	-	-	-	E–W	LC	Graphite
105	-	M	Adult	-	-	-	-	E–W	LC	U.
106	M1	F	50–55	0.71025	91	−20.1	9	E–W	CF	Cer.(3), Lit.(1)
107	-	F	20–30	-	-	-	-	E–W	CB	U.
108	M2	M	50–55	0.70952	35	−20.3	10	NW–SE	LC	Bone/antler comb (remains of)
109	M1	F	30–35	0.70979	46	−20.2	10.1	NW–SE	RC	Cer.(1)
110	-	M	35	-	-	-	-	W–E	CF	U.
111	M2	F	25–30	0.70952	42	−20.4	9.8	E–W	LC	She.(6)
112	-	F	40–45	-	-	-	-	E–W	LC	Pol.(1), Cer.(1), Grd.(1)
113	M2	M	30–35	0.70894	94	-	-	E–W	LC	Pol.(1), Cer.(2), Lit.(1), Firelighting kit, Bon.(1), Dog leg, F.Shd.(1)
114	-	-	Adult	-	-	-	-	E–W	LC	U.
115a	M3	M	>60	0.70912	68	−20.4	9.8	NW–SE	RC	Pol.(1), Cer.(1), Och., F.Shd.(1)
115b	-	-	Juv./ Adult	-	-	-	-	-	-	*Partial burial: 4 teeth and part of jaw*

116a	M1	F	40–45	0.70943	38	−20.5	9.9	NE–SW	LC	U.
116b	-	-	7–8 mon.	-	-	-	-	-	-	U.
117	-	M	40–45	-	-	-	-	NE–SW	CB	Pol.(1), Lit.(5), Ant.(1)
118	M1	M	40–60	0.71051	59	−20.7	9.8	W–E	RC	U.
119	M1	M	30–35	0.70921	150	−21.0	9.5	E–W	LC	Cer.(1)
120	-	-	Adult	-	-	-	-	NE–SW	LC	Pol.(1), Lit.(2), Firelighting kit
121	M2	M?	30–40	0.70962	41	-	-	E–W	RC	U.
122	-	-	Adult	-	-	-	-	N–S	RC	U.
123	-	F??	45–60	-	-	-	-	NE–SW	CB	U.
124	-	-	Adult	-	-	-	-	E–W	LC	U.
125	-	-	-	-	-	-	-	E–W	LC	U.
126	M1	M?	20–30	0.70965	28	-	-	N–S	CB	U.
127	M2	M?	20–40	0.70974	64	-	-	N–S	LC	U. *Possible wooden grave construction - not LBK?*
128	-	-	20–40	-	-	-	-	S–N	RC	U.
129	-	-	1.5–4	-	-	-	-	-	-	Cer.(1)
130	M2	M	25–35	0.70897	61	−20.9	9.5	E–W	LC	Lit.(1), Ant.(1)
131a	-	F?	6	-	-	-	-	N–S	LC	Cer.(1)
131b	-	M?	4–6	-	-	-	-	NE–SW	LC	Cer.(1)
132	-	M?	4	-	-	-	-	W–E	LC	Cer.(2)
133	-	M?	4–5	-	-	-	-	N–S	RC	U.
134	-	F?	Adult	-	-	-	-	E–W	LC	U.
135	-	-	Adult	-	-	-	-	E–W	RC	U.
136	-	F	40–50	-	-	-	-	NE–SW	CB	Cer.(1)
137	M2	F	30–40	0.71008	36	−20.5	10.2	E–W	RC	Cer.(1), Lit.(2)
138	-	-	-	-	-	-	-	E–W	LC	F.Animal bones
139a	M1	M?	15–20	0.70905	80	−20.6	9.4	E–W	LC	Pol.(1), Lit.(2), Spon.(8 beads, armring, buckle), Bone/anter comb, Bon.(1), Firelighting kit, F.Shd.(1), Animal bone
139b	-	-	Juv.	-	-	-	-	-	-	*Partial burial of human skull frgament burnt, in fill of 139a*
140	M2 M3	F	40	0.70979 0.70956	62 36	−20.3	9.7	NE–SW	P	U.
141	M3	M	35–40	0.70948	41	−20.0	10.3	E–W	LC	Pol.(1), Spon.(15 beads, armring, buckle), Stone bead (5), Fox mandible
142	M2	M	40–50	0.70962	43	−20.6	9.2	E–W	LC	Lit.(2), Bon.(1), Firelighting kit

143a	-	M??	15–18	-	-	-	-	E–W	LC	Spon.(8 beads, buckle), She.(34), Stone bead (5), Bone/antler comb, F.Shd.(1), Human bone (4)
143b	-	-	2–6	-	-	-	-	-	-	*Partial burial in fill of 134a (Pelvis and humerus)*
143c	-	-	Adult	-	-	-	-	-	-	*Partial burial in fill of 134a (Ribs)*
144	M1	F	>60	0.70917	59	−20.7	9.5	NE–SW	CB	U.
145	-	M?	12–14	-	-	-	-	E–W	RC	U.
146	-	F	50–55	-	-	-	-	E–W	LC	She.(13)
147	M2	-	10	0.70917	58	−20.6	9.8	E–W	LC	U.
148	M2	M??	15	0.70938	7	−20.6	9.4	E–W	LC	U.
149	-	M??	25–40	-	-	-	-	E–W	-	Pol.(1), Cer.(1)
150	M2 M3	F	>60	0.71084 0.71114	48 39	−20.1	9.8	E–W	S	She.(102)
151	-	M	Adult	-	-	-	-	E–W	LC	F.Lit.(1)
152	-	-	-	-	-	-	-	E–W	-	U.
153	-	M	40–50	-	-	-	-	E–W	CF	Pol.(2), Cer.(1), Lit.(5), Firelighting kit
154	-	-	Adult	-	-	-	-	W–E	LC	Cer.(1)
155	-	-	Adult	-	-	-	-	W–E	LC	Cer.(1)
156	-	M	40–50	-	-	-	-	N–S	CF	Pol.(1)
157	-	-	-	-	-	-	-	E–W	-	Cer.(1)
158	M1	F	30–40	0.70962	41	−21.0	10	S–N	CF	Pol.(1), Cer.(1), Lit.(3), Firelighting kit, Ant.(1),
159	M1	F	>60	0.70912	130	-	-	N–S	CB	Pol.(1), Lit.(5)
160	-		Adult	-	-	−20.4	9.4	E–W	LC	U.
161	-	M?	Mature	-	-	-	-	-	-	Cremation: Pol.(2)
162	-	-	Inf. II/ Juv.	-	-	-	-	-	-	Cremation: U.
163	-	F?	>Adult	-	-	-	-	-	-	Cremation: Quartz pebble
164	-	M??	>Adult	-	-	-	-	-	-	Cremation: U.
165	-	F?	>Juv.	-	-	-	-	-	-	Cremation: Pol.(1)
166	-	F	>Adult	-	-	-	-	-	-	Cremation: Cer.(1)
167	-	-	>Adult	-	-	-	-	-	-	Cremation: Pol.(1)
168	-	-	Adult	-	-	-	-	-	-	Cremation: U.
169	-	M??	Adult	-	-	-	-	-	-	Cremation: U.
170	-	M??	Adult	-	-	-	-	-	-	Cremation: U.
171	-	F??	>Adult	-	-	-	-	-	-	Cremation: U.
172a	-	M??	Mature/ Senile	-	-	-	-	-	-	Cremation: U.

172b	-	-	Inf. I/II	-	-	-	-	-	-	Cremation: U.
173a	-	-	Adult	-	-	-	-	-	-	Cremation: U.
173b	-	-	Inf.	-	-	-	-	-	-	Cremation: U.
174	-	-	Inf.II/ Juv.	-	-	-	-	-	-	Cremation: Pol. (1)
175	-	-	-	-	-	-	-	-	-	Cremation: U.
176	-	F??	>Adult	-	-	-	-	-	-	Cremation: Pol.(2)
177a	-	-	Adult	-	-	-	-	-	-	Cremation: Pol.(1)
177b	-	-	Inf.	-	-	-	-	-	-	*As above*
178	-	M??	>Late Adult	-	-	-	-	-	-	Cremation: U.
179	-	F??	>Juv.	-	-	-	-	-	-	Cremation: U.
180	-	-	Inf.II	-	-	-	-	-	-	Cremation: Graphite
181	-	-	Inf. II/Juv.	-	-	-	-	-	-	Cremation: Pol. (1)
182	-	-	Inf. II/Juv.	-	-	-	-	-	-	Cremation: Pol. (1)
183	-	-	Adult	-	-	-	-	-	-	Cremation: U.
184	-	F??	>Juv.	-	-	-	-	-	-	Cremation: Hammerstone
185	-	M??	Mature	-	-	-	-	-	-	Cremation: Pol.(4), Lit.(2), Graphite, Shd.(1), Firelighting kit
186a	-	-	Juv./ Adult	-	-	-	-	-	-	Cremation: Lit.(1), Graphite
186b	-	-	Inf.	-	-	-	-	-	-	*As above*
187	-	-	-	-	-	-	-	-	-	Cremation: Shd.(3)
188	-	M??	>Adult	-	-	-	-	-	-	Cremation: Pol.(2)
189	-		Inf. I/II	-	-	-	-	-	-	Cremation: Pol.(1), Lit.(1)
190a	-	-	Adult	-	-	-	-	-	-	Cremation: Pol.(1)
190b	-	-	<Juv.	-	-	-	-	-	-	*As above*
191	-	-	Inf. II	-	-	-	-	-	-	Cremation: Cer.(1)
192	-	-	Adult	-	-	-	-	-	-	Cremation: Pol.(1)
193	-	-	-	-	-	-	-	-	-	Cremation: U.
194	-	-	-	-	-	-	-	-	-	Cremation: U.
195	-	-	Adult	-	-	-	-	-	-	Cremation: U.
196	-	-	Inf. II?	-	-	-	-	-	-	Cremation: Pol.(1), Cer.(1), Lit.(2)
197a	-	-	Juv?	-	-	-	-	-	-	Cremation: U.
197b	-	-	Inf.	-	-	-	-	-	-	Cremation: U.
198	-	-	Mature	-	-	-	-	-	-	Cremation: U.
199	-	F??	>Adult	-	-	-	-	-	-	Cremation: U.
200	-	M??	Adult	-	-	-	-	-	-	Cremation: Shd.(2), Hammerstone (1)

201	-	-	Juv.	-	-	-	-	-	-	Cremation: U.
202	-	-	Inf.II	-	-	-	-	-	-	Cremation: Lit.(1), Quartz pebble
203	-	-	>Inf.II	-	-	-	-	-	-	Cremation: U.
204	-	M??	Juv./ Adult	-	-	-	-	-	-	Cremation: Pol.(2)
205a	-	-	Adult	-	-	-	-	-	-	Cremation: U.
205b	-	-	Inf.	-	-	-	-	-	-	Cremation: U.
206	-	-	Adult	-	-	-	-	-	-	Cremation: U.
207	-	-	Inf.II	-	-	-	-	-	-	Cremation: Pol.(1)
208	-	F??	Adult	-	-	-	-	-	-	Cremation: Shd.(1)
209	-	M??	Adult	-	-	-	-	-	-	Cremation: Pol.(1), Bon.(1)
210	-	-	Inf. I/II	-	-	-	-	-	-	Cremation: U.
211	-	-	-	-	-	-	-	-	-	Cremation: Pol.(1)
212	-	-	Inf. II/Juv.	-	-	-	-	-	-	Cremation: Pol.(1)
213	-	-	-	-	-	-	-	-	-	Cremation: Pol.(1)
214	-	F??	>Juv./ Adult	-	-	-	-	-	-	Cremation: Cer.(1)
215	-	-	-	-	-	-	-	-	-	Cremation: U.
216	-	F??	>Adult	-	-	-	-	-	-	Cremation: U.
217	-	-	Inf. I	-	-	-	-	-	-	Cremation: U.
218	-	-	>Inf. II/Juv.	-	-	-	-	-	-	Cremation: U.
219a	-	F??	Adult	-	-	-	-	-	-	Cremation: U.
219b	-	-	Inf. I	-	-	-	-	-	-	Cremation: U.
220	-	-	>Adult	-	-	-	-	-	-	Cremation: U.
221	-	-	>Inf. II/Juv.	-	-	-	-	-	-	Cremation: Shd.(1)
222	-	F??	Juv./ Adult	-	-	-	-	-	-	Cremation: Pol.(1)
223	-	M??	Adult	-	-	-	-	-	-	Cremation: U.
224	-	-	Inf. I	-	-	-	-	-	-	Cremation: Pol.(1), Lit.(2), Shd.(2)
225	-	F??	Adult/ Mature	-	-	-	-	-	-	Cremation: Pol.(1)
226	-	M??	Adult	-	-	-	-	-	-	Cremation: Cer.(1), Graphite
227a	-	-	Adult	-	-	-	-	-	-	Cremation: Shd.(5)
227b	-	-	Inf.	-	-	-	-	-	-	*As above*
228	-	-	Inf. II/Juv.	-	-	-	-	-	-	Cremation: U.
229	-	F??	Juv./ Adult	-	-	-	-	-	-	Cremation: Cer.(2)

conform most closely, with a diversification among older individuals. This picture can be broadly paralleled for the male skeletons (Table 6.2). Of the 15 children with available data (all sub-adults, excluding juveniles), a total of seven were either not left-crouched or not east–west oriented, resulting in a rather heterogeneous group. There are also spatial differences in the frequency of orientations and positions, although these partly intersect with age. In group V, most burials do not correspond to the majority orientation and position, but this group is also particularly rich in children and in mature or older adults, the very age categories most likely to show variation. To an extent, this also applies to the inhumations in group IV. In contrast, group I is very uniform; everyone is left-crouched, and only one individual shows a strongly deviating orientation.

Similarly, grave goods show strong age- and sex-related patterns (Table 6.2). Among the women, there is a clear trend from receiving, as young adults, either no goods or almost exclusively pottery, to an increasing focus on ornamentation later in life. Especially females who are mature or older can be buried with large assemblages of idiosyncratically combined items. Grave 32, for instance, contained 234 *Theodoxus* shells from the Danube, four beads of imported *Protula* shells, a *Spondylus* belt buckle and four limestone beads. Others were buried with carved bone combs or *Dentalia*. Especially the river shells are often arranged in elaborate headdresses, and together with the presence of combs this suggests an emphasis on hairstyles as an important element of personal presentation (e.g. Engelbrecht *et al.* 2003). Most of these particularly lavish female graves are found towards the centre of the site. Other artefacts occasionally found in female graves, regardless of age, are grinding tablets, ochre and flint tools.

As elsewhere, male graves contain a wider range of grave good types, some – such as polished stone tools and *Spondylus* armrings – exclusive to males (Table 6.2). It is also more difficult to identify clear age-related trends. Overall, there are slightly fewer unfurnished men (17%, or 27% including all probable men) than women (15%, or 31% including all probable women). In general, younger males are more likely to remain unfurnished than older individuals, and there are more younger men among those buried with pottery, but these trends are less pronounced than for females. Polished stone tools are a primarily, but not exclusively, male item here. Even if we exclude the piece from grave 112, secondarily re-used to grind ochre, and the two uncertain identifications (graves 21, 76), we are left with two anthropological females buried with adzes or axes (graves 158–9). There are isolated examples of females with stone tools from other cemeteries (Frirdich 2005, 95), but the additional presence of arrowheads in grave 159 would be very unusual. The reliability of this finding must await full publication of the sexing methods used. The provision with polished adzes tends to increase over the course of male lives; 60% of adults above 30 years of age compared to 45.5% of juveniles and young adults have them.

While adzes and axes are spatially quite evenly spread across the cemetery, this is not the case for either imported shells or arrowheads (Fig. 6.6). Twelve of the 64 inhumations sexed as male were buried with imported shell items, of whom four have the full set of armring, buckle and beads. These men are rarely buried with pottery or arrowheads, although all but one have polished tools, creating a recurrent, albeit not completely rigid, pattern of preferred associations. Seven individuals with imported shell fell into the 'older adult' category or older, as against one older child, one juvenile and three young adults. Most of these graves were found in the southern half of the site. Based on his study of *Spondylus* armring diameters, Nieszery (1995, 185) has suggested that these objects were worn from late childhood, but were so tight that they could not be removed from the arm of a fully grown man.

It is harder to draw up recurrent associations for the 11 men buried with arrows. All but two also have polished tools, and five have firelighter kits.[6] Pottery and ornaments also occasionally occur. The age profile is similar to that for the men with imported shells, with whom there is only a small overlap; there is one older child and one young adult, while all the others are older adult or mature, including two individuals aged at least 60 years. While both arrows and imported shells thus tend to be buried with older individuals, they often exclude each other, and most graves with arrows are in the central and northern parts of the site, where the spectrum of grave goods in general is also more diverse. Several other items with more strongly local, Bavarian or southern German associations, such as small bone wands, antler toggles (cf. Haack 2008), fox mandibles and bone combs, are too rare to discern any definite associations, but are slightly more frequently found with older individuals. Overall, and with further results pending, we can state that the younger the individual, the more likely they are to be associated with pottery or to have unfurnished burials. Older individuals, generally more lavishly provided for, fall into two groups: those with a focus on arrowheads and, to an extent, local ornaments, and those with a clearer emphasis on imported shell items. These groups have few overlaps.

Children between about three and six years of age can receive goods, most often pottery. There is even a grave good specific to children, a small closed bowl with gripping holes on either side just below the rim, potentially to help smaller children to grasp vessels properly (Siemoneit 1997, 37). Polished stone and flint tools are also occasionally present, but as elsewhere in the LBK become more frequent with older children (Siemoneit 1997, 30–5). There is a general diversification of grave goods at this stage; ornaments, firelighters, various flint and bone tools, and ochre are deposited for the first time. The burials of older children are also the least likely to go unfurnished, but most still receive no particularly gender-specific grave goods. At Aiterhofen only one individual under the age of juvenile was found with imported shells, and only one other child received arrowheads. Both are in the respective spatial groupings in which these goods are relatively more frequent. The graves of juveniles and

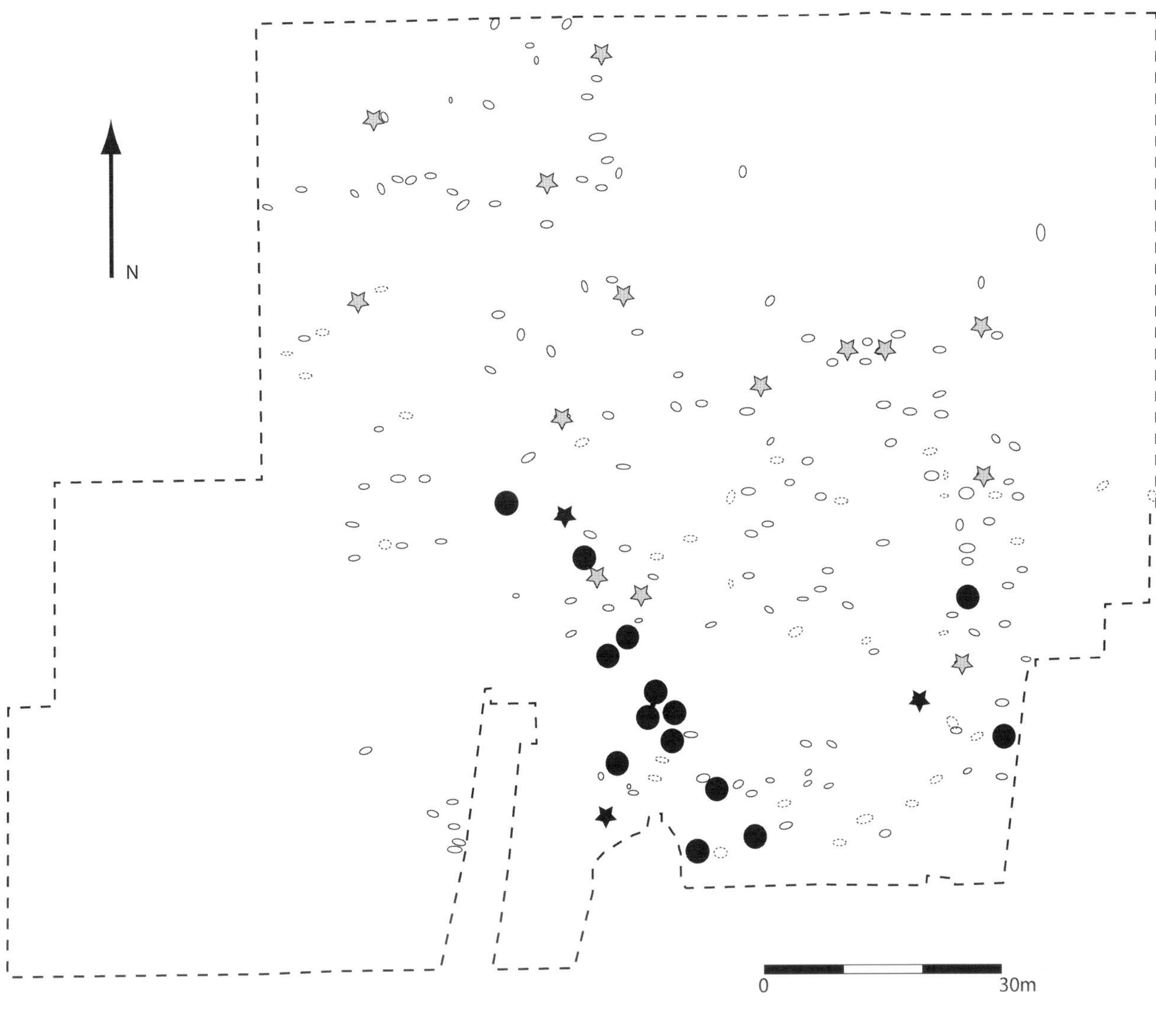

Fig. 6.6. Aiterhofen-Ödmühle: distribution of graves with arrows and graves with Spondylus. *After Nieszery (1995, 55, fig. 19).*

juveniles/young adults (eight individuals in total) can be among the most lavishly furnished in the cemetery, also receiving more ornaments, or in contrast go unfurnished. This could relate to this age group sitting on the boundary between older children – quite likely to be marked out through burial goods – and younger adults, the most likely to go unfurnished.

There are some indications that specific individuals may come from areas outside Bavaria, or in any case have particularly strong links in this direction. Thus, Strien (2010a) has identified the pottery in graves 81 and 66 as being from Baden-Württemberg and central Germany respectively. Similarly, the adzes in graves 12 and 61 are narrow and flat, falling within the preferences of the 'middle Neckar' pottery grouping defined for Baden-Württemberg. A bone arrowhead similar to those from Schwetzingen (Chapter 7.7.1) was also found at the nearby Sengkofen cemetery (grave 21), suggesting that these ties were relatively frequent. However, these individuals – generally males or adults of unknown sex – were not consistently marked out through a particular element of the burial rite, such as position or orientation.

Finally, the category of 'grave-like pits' without bodies[7] deserves some discussion. Their definition is complicated by the presence of settlement traces, and only pits both shaped and oriented like graves have been included here. Some of these features contain sherds and animal bone, and isolated examples also yielded a complete pot and a few pieces of calcined bone (both now lost; Hanöffner and Siftar 2007, 45, 116). It remains unclear whether these features relate to individual graves in their vicinity, but they apparently spread further to the north than the bulk of settlement traces and are hence likely to be associated with funerary activity. They have been interpreted as either emptied in the course of a multi-stage funeral (Nieszery 1995, 28) or looted by enemies (Farruggia 2002, 99). In either case, the total removal of all human bone seems perhaps unlikely. Given that similar features are now attested for several other sites (Chapters 5.7, 8.7 and 8.10; e.g. Schweitzer and Schweitzer 1977, 60–2; Pellett 1978; Neugebauer-Maresch and Neugebauer 1989; Walther and Schwedler 1991, 206; Kahlke 2004, 96–9), it could also be suggested that these pits contain the residue of commemorative rituals (see also D. Hofmann forthcoming).

However, the potential for the exhumation or disturbance of some individuals remains. Isolated bones of two humans have been recovered from the fill of grave 143, while additional mandible fragments and teeth were found in grave 115. Schultz has also identified the fragment of a child bone with burial 19 (Nieszery 1995, 267). Isolated cremated human bones came from the fills of five further graves (numbers 17, 23, 24, 97, 139) and may represent scattered or disturbed cremations, rather than deliberate deposits (cf. Trautmann 2007, 136). There are indications of other manipulations. Teeth may have been intentionally removed (graves 65, 145), or placed on the skull of the deceased (graves 33, 100). Grave 140 has been disturbed in antiquity, and this may also be the case for burial 159, as the tibia and fibula of one leg were found relatively far from one another (Nieszery 1995, 87).

6.7.2 Osteology

By the time of the definitive publication of the grave inventories (Nieszery 1995), the skeletal material had been studied by four different anthropologists, Lantermann, Schröter, Schultz and Baum, who occasionally reached diverging conclusions on the sex and age of the deceased (see catalogue in Nieszery 1995, 264–304). Nieszery relied mostly on Lantermann's unpublished data, which he had asked Schröter to 'check' (Nieszery 1995, 91), but it is not clear from the catalogue whether Lantermann's or Schröter's identifications are being used in any particular case. Baum's (1990) study attempted to age and sex individuals on the basis of the dental material alone and was on that basis largely disregarded, although he succeeded in recognising additional immature remains (the foetus in grave 116). Finally, those skeletons that could still be found in 1990 were sent to Professor Michael Schultz at Göttingen, who added his own identifications. A separate, detailed palaeopathological study on the Aiterhofen children has also been carried out (Carli-Thiele 1996). The surviving skeletal material is still stored at the *Zentrum Anatomie* at Göttingen University, where it was sampled in 2009, but several individuals, including all cremated remains (Trautmann 2007, 160), are missing.

For this project, sexes and ages for inhumations have been assigned where there was a consensus view amongst all anthropologists quoted in the catalogue (Table 6.2). Where this was not given, the ageing and sexing follow the majority verdict, with the sexing classed as insecure ('m?' or 'f?'). In addition, all sex identifications offered for immature individuals were classed as insecure. This is in contrast to Nieszery (1995, 91), who relied more squarely on the Lantermann/Schröter identifications, but modified these 'on archaeological grounds' where he felt that the grave good inventory did not match the anthropologically determined sex. This applies to eight graves, most of them anthropological females with 'male' goods (graves 21, 55, 76, 98, 137, 158, 159), but only one male with 'female' goods (grave 143). The age and sex identifications used in this project (inhumations only) give a total of 33 females (with a further 16 probable females) and 33 males (with a further 30 probable males). A total of 24 inhumation burials were those of immature individuals, including juveniles, but younger children still remain under-represented. The additional individuals postulated by Schultz in burials 105 and 137 were not entered, as they are not confirmed by other anthropologists and the drawings appear to show single inhumations, but further study to confirm the existence of additional skeletal material is desirable. Among the cremations, 15 have been classed as possibly female (of which four have 'male' goods according to Nieszery) and 15 as possibly male, with 49 unsexed. Twenty-nine individuals (over 36%) were classed as immature (Table 6.2). These identifications can no longer be corroborated.

Immature individuals also show some age-related patterning, although numbers remain low. Younger children (within the Infans I age range, 0–6 years; Chapter 2.4) are less likely to be included in the cemetery, older individuals (above six years) are most often present, and children under three years tend to be part of double burials. This contrasts with other, smaller Bavarian sites, such as Essenbach, where the minimum age of inclusion was as high as six (Siemoneit 1997, 18–21). Such age thresholds could relate to important stages in the physical and social development of children (M. Kohl 1978; McHugh 1999, 19; Scott 1999, 66–80). One possible scenario for Aiterhofen is that the observed age threshold of around three years could coincide with weaning, as there is a high incidence of enamel hypoplasias which formed between the ages of three and four. These could relate to nutritional stresses connected to the shift to solid food (Carli-Thiele 1996, 177; Baum 1990, 195; see also Bach and Bach 1989). Compared to the Wandersleben cemetery in Thuringia, the Aiterhofen children have more hypoplasias and caries (Carli-Thiele 1996, 165), potentially indicating protein deficiencies and an over-reliance on carbohydrates. This could be exacerbated by regional dietary preferences, as the teeth of the entire Aiterhofen population, including adults, have a relatively high caries incidence (Baum 1990, 189–91; Carli-Thiele 1996, 179–84). More data on health, nutrition and weaning are necessary to confirm this.

Among the pathologies (Tables 6.3–4), caries and enamel

Table 6.3. Aiterhofen: dental pathologies. Grave numbers in bold have been identified by several researchers. For calculus, Baum's (1990, 193) positive diagnosis on 95 out of 108 investigated individuals has not been maintained, as the discrepancy with the conclusions of other researchers, notably Carli-Thiele (1996), is great and these conclusions should ideally be verified. Inflammatory processes were diagnosed by Baum partly through measuring the distance of the margo alveolaris to the cervix.

	Graves listed in Baum (1990)	Graves listed in Carli-Thiele (1996)	Graves listed in Nieszery (1995)	Totals
Caries	10, 12, **23**, **25**, **32**, **36**, 37, 38, **48**, **50**, **56**, **57**, **61**, **64**, **68**, 74, **76**, 78, **88**, **93**, 98, **100**, **101**, 102, 106, 107, 108, 109, 113, 116, **140**, 144, **146**, **147**, 150, **151**, **153**	**23**, 71/2, **88**, **131.2**	15, **23**, **25**, **32**, 33, **36**, **48**, **50**, **56**, **57**, **61**, **64**, **68**, **76**, **88**, **93**, **100**, **101**, 112, 123, **131.2**, **140**, **146**, **147**, **151**, **153**, 158	44
Calculus	[not listed]	39, 88		[2]
Enamel hypoplasias	12, 15, 21, **23**, 25, 30, 33, 36, **39**, 53, 55, 57, 60, 65, 68, 69, **71/2**, 78, **88**, **99**, 107, 113, 115.1, 121, 141, 151	20, **23**, **39**, 41, **71/2**, 83, 84, **88**, **99**, 131.2, 133, 139, 147, 148		35
Inflammation (periodontal disease, sinusitis, abscess)	**11**, **33**, 35, **36**, 50, **56**, 61, 64, 68, 85, 93, 111, 142, 144, 146, 153	23, 41, 145	**11**, **33**, **36**, **56**	19
Ante-mortem tooth loss	11, 48, 56, 64, 68, 100, 116, 137, 150			9
Other	14, 151, 153: possible trauma, in the first two cases related to another tooth invading the tooth cavity 23, 50: hypodonty; 33, 48: supernumerary tooth (in the latter case, odontoma is also a possibility)		144 granuloma on maxilla, 153 possible granuloma on root of molar	

hypoplasias are the most frequently identified, thanks to the exhaustive study of Baum (1990, 189), who could show that, in general, women developed caries earlier than men and linked this to possible dietary differences. Alongside the pathologies described above, Carli-Thiele (1996) has also identified *cribra orbitalia* in some children, pointing to iron deficiency anaemia. There are some instances of trauma, such as a broken right femur in grave 55, while the senile male in burial 42 seems to have survived an arrow wound. Various inflammations and dental abscesses also occur. Older individuals have occasionally been diagnosed with arthritis and degenerative joint diseases. Finally, graves 33 and 48 near the south-eastern corner of the cemetery may both have had a supernumerary tooth, a condition in which heredity could play a role (Garvey *et al.* 1999).

6.7.3 The animal remains from Lerchenhaid

As the animal bone assemblage from Aiterhofen was very limited, we turned to the nearby settlement and enclosure site of Lerchenhaid for a more substantial range of samples. A LBK and middle Neolithic settlement was excavated here between 1979 and 1982 (Brink-Kloke 1992). At this time, a 70-m stretch of two intersecting ditches, one accompanied by a palisade, was also excavated just to the west of the settlement area. It was only during geophysical work in the 1990s that the full extent of the earthworks was revealed. At least three enclosures existed here, one consisting of a doubled ditch circuit (Schmotz 1997, 129–38). The pottery from the excavated portion of the ditches was initially classed as late LBK (see Schmotz 1997, 129–38), but may in fact date to early phase II of the scheme proposed by Pechtl (2009a, 93). The associated animal bones have been identified and published by Ziegler (1985/86). The stable isotope results from the animals sampled at Lerchenhaid are reported below (Table 6.5).

6.7.4 Carbon and nitrogen analysis

We sampled 74 individuals for stable isotope analysis, of whom 14 were excluded as unreliable or not returning enough collagen (Fig. 6.7; Table 6.5). The remainder includes 20 females, 27 males, one infant and seven adolescents. Of the adults, 25 were estimated as within the age range of 18 to 40 years at time of death, and 18 as over

Table 6.4. Aiterhofen: non-dental pathologies.

Grave	Condition	Reference
14	Coxa vara	Nieszery 1995
20	Cranial periostosis, possible traces of haematoma on teeth (suggested vitamin C deficiency).	Carli-Thiele 1996
23	*Cribra orbitalia*, new bone growth on bulbus superior (suggested haemorrhagic process)	Carli-Thiele 1996
25	Depression in scapula (suggested inflammatory process)	Nieszery 1995
37	Cranial atrophy	Nieszery 1995
38	Harris lines	Carli-Thiele 1996
41	*Cribra orbitalia* and porous lamina externa, possible healed trauma on right fibula	Carli-Thiele 1996
42	Depression in rib (suggested trauma caused by arrow)	Nieszery 1995
55	Fractured right femur with chronic osteomyelitis	Nieszery 1995
57	Lamina interna of occipital bone shows osteomyelitis (possible tumor). Humeri are different lengths	Nieszery 1995
68	Extended iliac crest (possible birth-related defect)	Nieszery 1995
71/2	Thinning of lamina externa	Carli-Thiele 1996
85	Degenerative changes on vertebrae and joints, first rib joined to sternum	Nieszery 1995
88	Possible haemorrhagic process or inflammation of os frontale, new bone growth on left fibula and both femurs (suggested vitamin C deficiency)	Carli-Thiele 1996
102	Possible damage to distal joint surfaces on both humeri	Nieszery 1995
113	Thinning and new bone formation on parietal and frontal bones	Nieszery 1995
139	Layered new bone growth on both fibulae (systemic disease, suggested Morbus Pierre Marie-Bamberger)	Carli-Thiele 1996
140	Degenerative changes on vertebrae	Nieszery 1995
144	Degenerative changes on vertebrae	Nieszery 1995
147	*Cribra orbitalia*	Carli-Thiele 1996

40. The infant was aged as a three- to six-year-old (grave 58; Nieszery 1995, 275), but is very badly preserved. In spite of this uncertainty, its higher nitrogen level may still be due to a breast-feeding signal.

The carbon and nitrogen stable isotope values of humans from Aiterhofen are tightly clustered (Fig. 6.7). There is no overall trend in $\delta^{13}C$ or $\delta^{15}N$ values with age, and juveniles are not significantly different from adults, or males from females (ANOVA, $p>0.05$). However, when both sex and age are taken into account, male and female mean $\delta^{15}N$ values differ significantly over their lifetime. Using a finer division of ages based on the osteological data from Nieszery (1995), males show a slight upward trend in $\delta^{15}N$ values with age which is significant (Spearman rank correlation, 2-tailed, $p<0.02$), while females show a slight downward trend which is not significant. We hesitate to make too much of this, however, because if the two old males (>60 years) with the highest $\delta^{15}N$ values are omitted, the trend is no longer significant (Spearman rank correlation, 2-tailed, $p=0.10$). Nevertheless, even without these two individuals, in the oldest age groups the male mean $\delta^{15}N$ value is higher than that of females (ANOVA, n=3 males, 4 females, $p=0.05$). Trends with sex and age for the whole dataset are further discussed in Chapter 9.2.5.

Animals

Only a few measurements were available from fauna at Aiterhofen, and none were identified as sheep/goats (Fig. 6.8; Table 6.5). One was from red deer which has lower $\delta^{13}C$ and $\delta^{15}N$ values compared to either cattle or pig, probably reflecting feeding in environments with denser forest cover and possibly away from fields. Pig and cattle means were similar, though points for both species show a range of >3‰ in $\delta^{15}N$ values, and 2‰ in cattle $\delta^{13}C$ values. With so few animals it is not possible to interpret this rigorously, but it does suggest feeding in a wide range of environments.

The difference between adult human and cattle $\delta^{13}C$ and $\delta^{15}N$ mean values was 0.4‰±0.76 (SD) and 2.7‰±1.51, respectively. There is a better sample of animals from Lerchenhaid (see above), intended to provide a baseline for Aiterhofen, but the cattle at this site had a mean $\delta^{15}N$ value of 5.5‰, significantly lower than the cattle at Aiterhofen (2-tailed t-test, $p=0.027$). It is therefore doubtful that the difference between the Aiterhofen human and Lerchenhaid cattle (or other animals) mean $\delta^{15}N$ values is meaningful.

Correlations with the archaeological data

Very few correlations between the stable isotopes and the archaeological evidence could be determined overall, but a number of significant patterns emerged. Neither body position nor orientation showed any overall patterning, but there is a potential clustering of individuals with secondary or less frequent orientations.

Spatially, there was a difference between the northern and southern halves of the cemetery in terms of $\delta^{13}C$ values. Overall, the female values in the northern half were more variable than in the south (Levene's test, $p=0.024$). This may indicate that women in the northern part of the

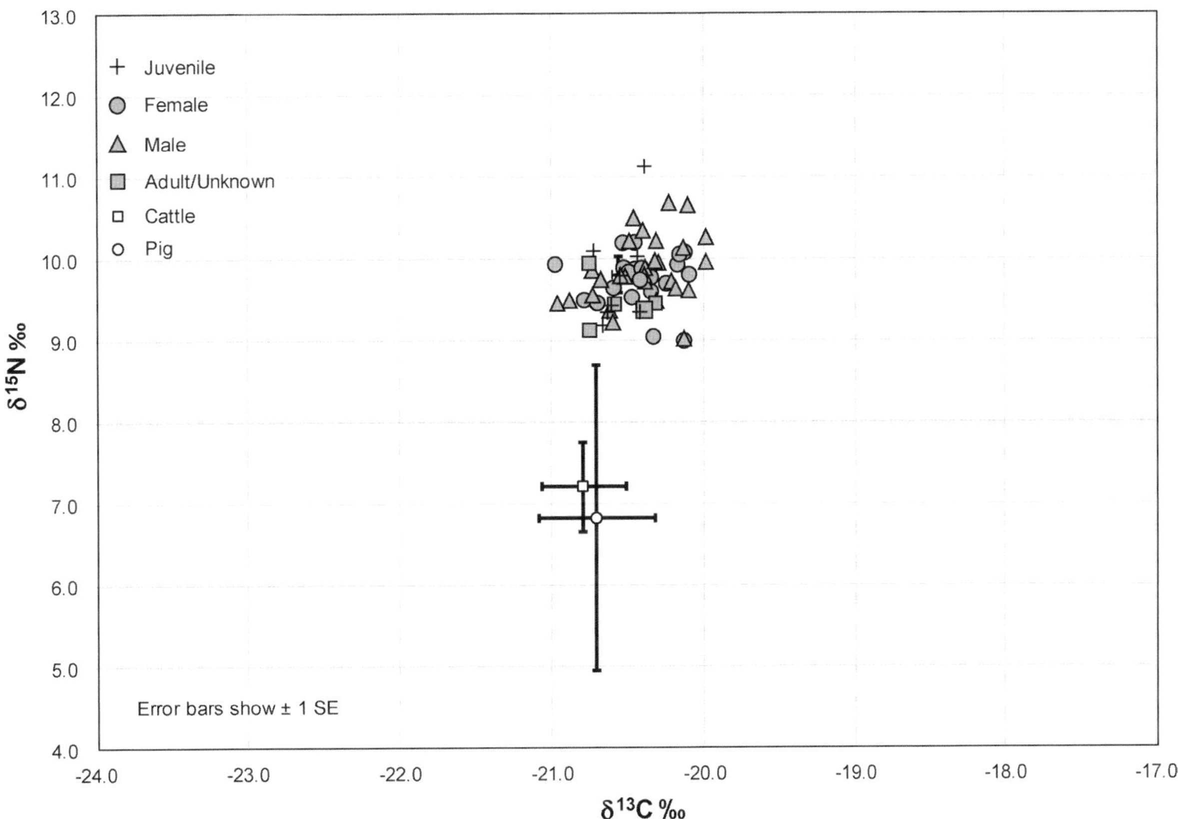

Fig. 6.7. Aiterhofen-Ödmühle: carbon and nitrogen isotope ratios (‰) of humans. Faunal means are shown for comparison.

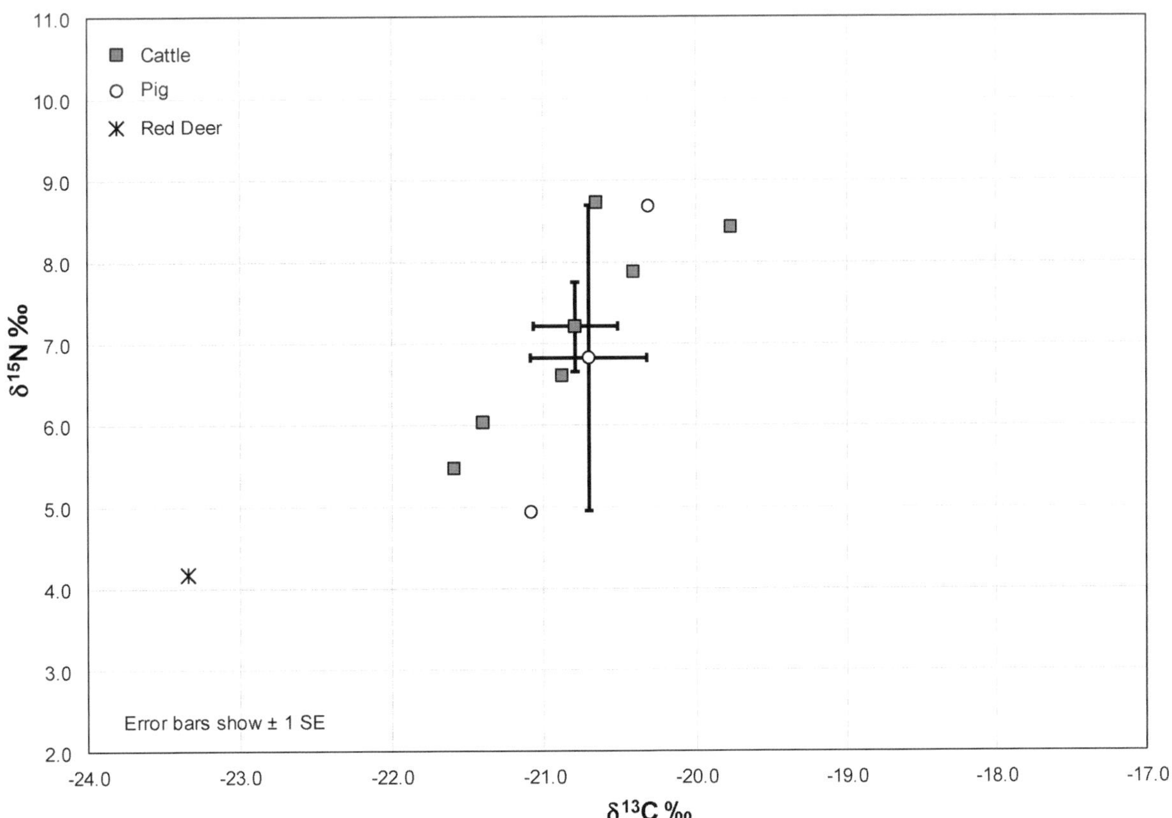

Fig. 6.8. Aiterhofen-Ödmühle: carbon and nitrogen isotope ratios (‰) of animals.

Table 6.5. Carbon and nitrogen isotope ratios (‰) of humans from Aiterhofen and animals from Lerchenhaid, with means and standard deviations.

Species	Age/sex	Mean $\delta^{13}C$	SD $\delta^{13}C$	Mean $\delta^{15}N$	SD $\delta^{15}N$	n
Human	Infant	−20.4	-	11.1	-	1
Human	Juvenile	−20.6	0.12	9.8	0.64	8
Human	Female	−20.4	0.23	9.8	0.33	20
Human	Male	−20.4	0.26	9.9	0.42	27
Human	Unsexed adult	−20.3	-	9.5	-	1
Human	All Adults	−20.4	0.25	9.8	0.38	48
Human	no data	−20.6	0.17	9.5	0.35	4
Cattle		−20.9	0.72	7.1	1.46	5
Pig		−20.7	0.54	6.8	2.66	2
Lerchenhaid						
Cattle		−21.2	0.83	5.5	1.27	16
Sheep/goat		−20.6	0.85	5.8	1.34	6
Pig		−20.8	0.22	6.8	1.31	6

cemetery had a more diverse plant protein intake than those in the south. This difference is probably largely down to the values of individuals in Nieszery's spatial group V at the north-west edge of the site (group V mean $\delta^{13}C$=−20.8‰, compared to the overall female average of $\delta^{13}C$=−20.4‰). Group V also stands out for a number of other reasons, most particularly its age profile skewed towards younger individuals (see above) and the greater number of burials not interred in the left-crouched position.

In the southern part of the cemetery, we identified a cluster of burials with similar values (graves 10, 12–15) (Fig. 6.4). These burials showed significantly elevated $\delta^{15}N$ values (an average of 10.3‰, as opposed to the overall average of 9.8‰). They also stand out because of their complex grave good assemblages. All males received *Spondylus* artefacts and two have three polished stone tools each (graves 10 and 15). On this basis, we identified a similar cluster with some complex grave good assemblages to the west (graves 139–144). Of these, grave 141 is also a male with an elevated $\delta^{15}N$ value. As reported in Bickle *et al.* (2011, 1254), the only discernible correlation of stable isotope patterns with artefacts concerned stone adzes. Males with three polished stone tools (graves 10, 15 and 102) had higher $\delta^{15}N$ values. A one-way ANOVA test ($F_{(3, 55)}=9.3$, $p<0.01$) suggested that $\delta^{15}N$ value varies with the number of stone tools throughout, with males buried without adzes having the lowest average values.

The only other possible correlation of stable isotopes and grave goods concerned *Spondylus*, where a 2-tailed *t* test ($p=0.028$, n=29) suggested that males with *Spondylus* had a significantly higher average $\delta^{15}N$ value (males without *Spondylus* had a mean of 9.7‰, those with had a mean of 10.2‰). However, we believe that this pattern is largely created by those males with *Spondylus* who also received three polished stone tools. If the three males with three stone adzes are excluded, the significance drops to $p=0.063$.

6.7.5 Strontium analysis

In total, 71 strontium ratios were determined, coming from 64 individuals: 24 adult females, 33 adult males, one unsexed adult and six juveniles (Figs 6.9–11; Table 6.6). Two molars were sampled in the case of graves 18 (M1 and M2), 56 (M1 and M2), 93 (M1 and M3), 140 (M2 and M3), 150 (M2 and M3) and two values were determined on an M3 molar from grave 78.

Local geology and expected strontium ranges

The biologically available strontium isotope range from the loess soils around Aiterhofen is 0.7086–0.7103 (Bentley and Knipper 2005b). However, the gneisses and granites of the Bavarian Forest start only 20 km away north-east of the Danube and yield a $^{87}Sr/^{86}Sr$ ratio >0.711 (Schweissing and Grupe 2003; Janz and Vennemann 2005). Other possible signatures falling just below the loess ranges can be found in the carbonate sediments of Alpine origin further to the south in the Molasse basin ($^{87}Sr/^{86}Sr$=0.708–0.710) and in the variable sedimentary lowlands to the north-west ($^{87}Sr/^{86}Sr$=0.7086–0.7103; Bentley and Knipper 2005b).

Age/sex differences

The mean $^{87}Sr/^{86}Sr$ ratio for all samples is 0.70965±0.00089. This includes two extreme outliers (graves 57, adult male, and 92, adult female) who had values above 0.7140. This suggests that their childhood diet was sourced from the more radiogenic geology characteristic of central European uplands; the Bavarian Forest is the nearest possible source area for Aiterhofen. Excluding these two outliers, the mean $^{87}Sr/^{86}Sr$ ratio for females is 0.70982±0.00107, for males 0.70960±0.00083, and for juveniles 0.70926±0.00031 (this includes multiple tooth samples per individual). This is consistent with a childhood diet derived from loess soils. There were no significant differences between the sexes and between age groups in either the mean or variance of strontium concentrations and ratios.

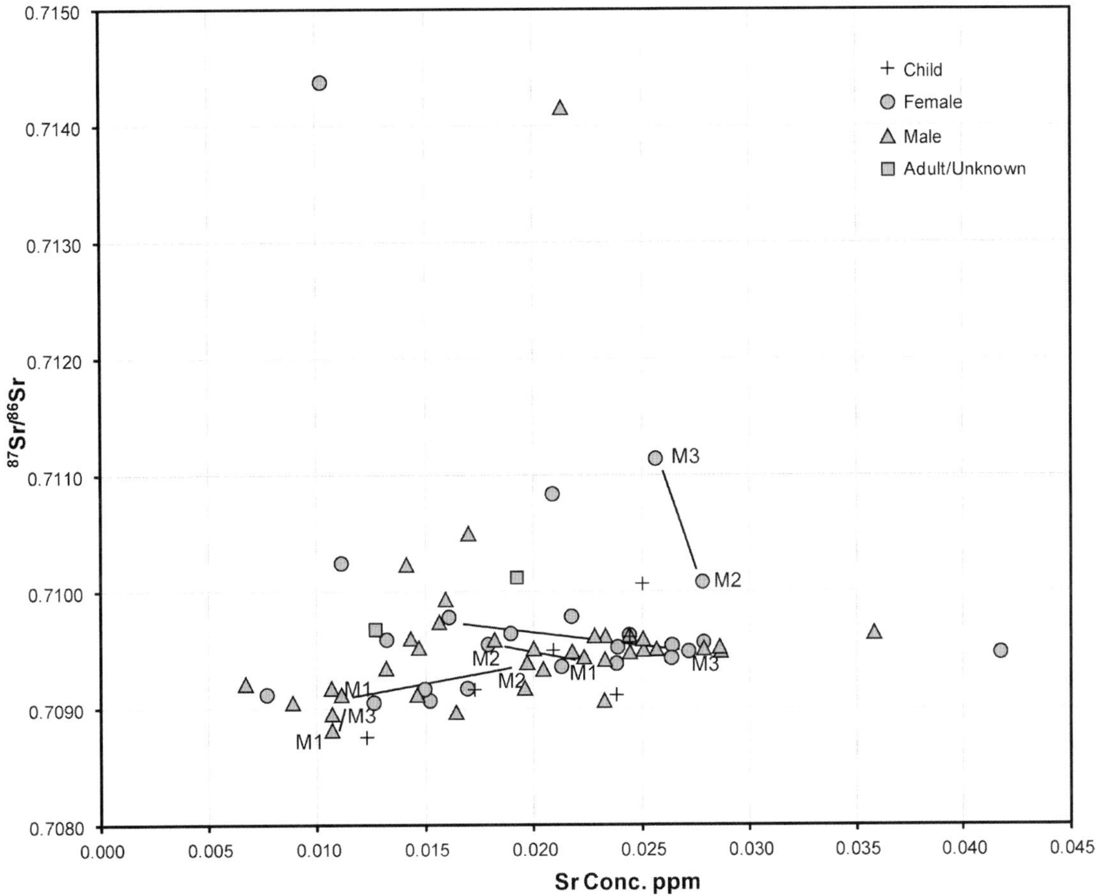

Fig. 6.9. Aiterhofen-Ödmühle: strontium concentration (ppm) versus ratio ($^{87}Sr/^{86}Sr$).

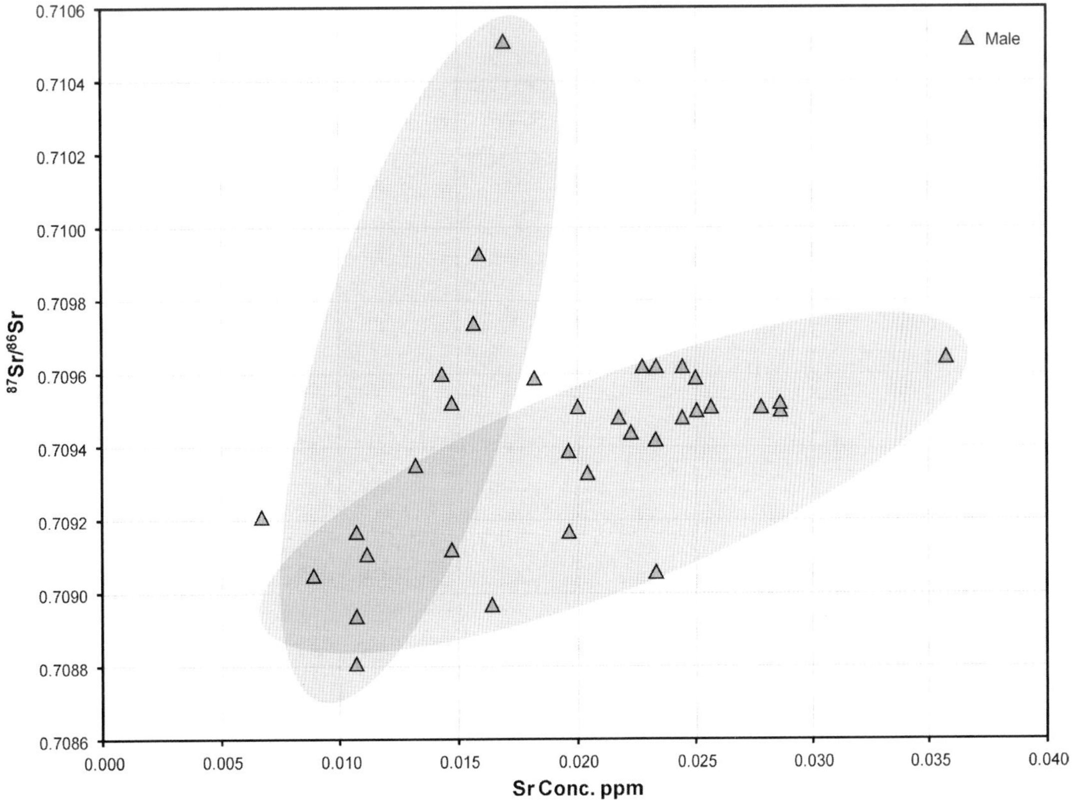

Fig. 6.10. Aiterhofen-Ödmühle: strontium ratio against 1/Sr ppm for males, showing two arrays.

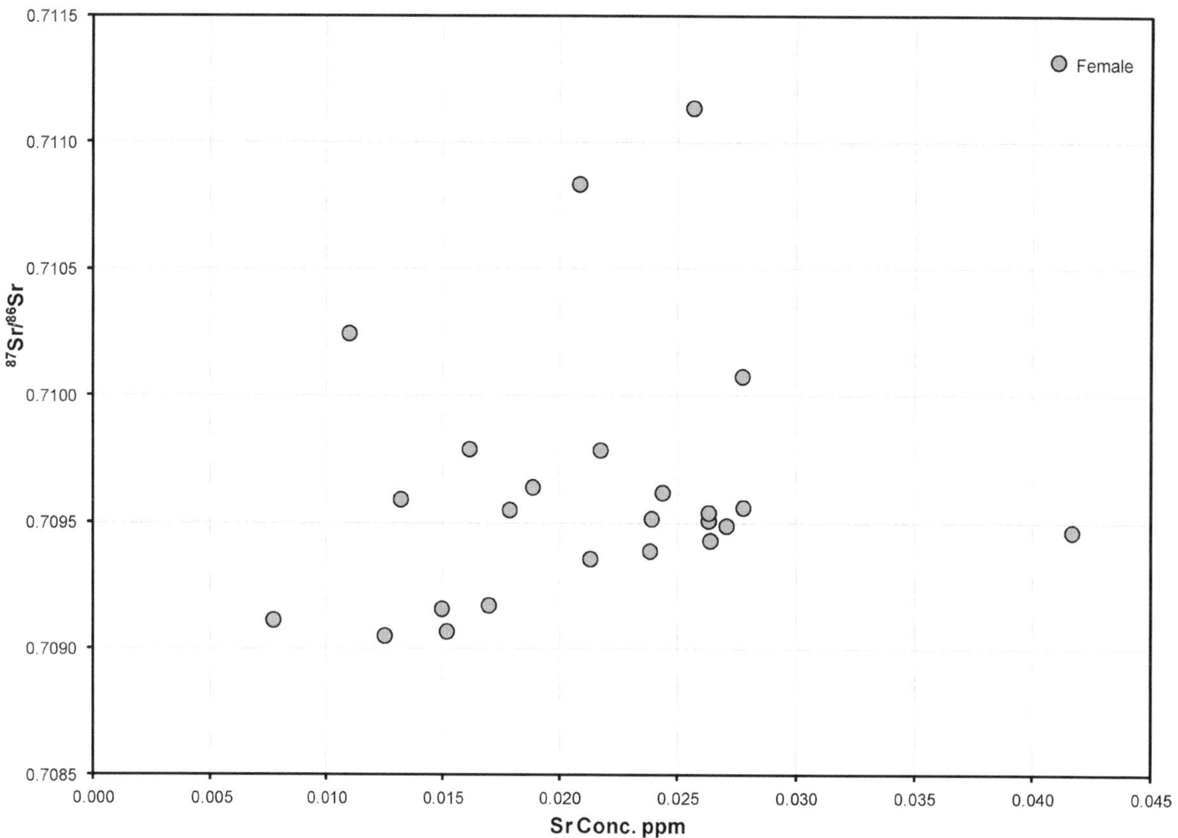

Fig. 6.11. Aiterhofen-Ödmühle: strontium ratio against 1/Sr ppm for females, showing a diffuse cluster.

*Table 6.6. Aiterhofen: strontium isotope ratios and concentrations. 'All' includes unsexed adults. * denotes number of analyses, not numbers of individuals.*

Age/sex	Mean $^{87}Sr/^{86}Sr$	SD $^{87}Sr/^{86}Sr$	Mean Sr conc.	SD Sr conc.	n*
Juvenile	0.70926	0.00031	52	31	6
Male	0.70960	0.00083	58	24	38
Female	0.70982	0.00107	56	24	25
All	0.70965	0.00089	57	24	71

However, when strontium ratio is plotted against 1/Sr ppm, two distinct arrays can be identified within the male data (Fig. 6.10; for the upper male array, r^2=0.769, n=11, p=0.01; for the lower male array, r^2=0.625, n=26, p=0.01). The lower array is consistent with a predominantly loess-derived diet, while the upper array suggests a mixture including more off-loess elements (Chapter 2.4). The two arrays share a common end-member, which falls at the lower end of the loess range. Although we cannot currently determine what these end-members are in real terms, it is possible to propose that the shared end-member reflects a common resource such as drinking water, while the higher end-members are likely to have arisen from different food sources, such as cattle grazed in different areas. These arrays cannot be explained by either chronological developments throughout the use of the cemetery or by spatial patterns. We therefore suggest that they reflect two co-existing subsistence strategies that were present long-term.

There is no overall patterning amongst the women, whose values form a diffuse cloud (Fig. 6.11). This means that their childhood diet was derived from a range of different sources which show no consistent patterning. One possible explanation is that they were coming from several different communities, all located on loess soils, and may have moved to Aiterhofen later in life.

There were no significant differences in the mean and variance of the different teeth sampled. However, a second molar, which mineralises in later childhood, was sampled in the case of both extreme outliers. Wherever two molars of the same individual were sampled, the tooth that mineralises later was closer to the overall mean strontium ratio for the site. The only exception is burial 150 (a mature female with a large assemblage of shells), whose ratios are both slightly higher than the loess range. The third molar is more radiogenic than the M2 molar (with ratios of 0.71114 and 0.71084 respectively). This means either that she moved into the Aiterhofen area after her third molar had mineralised between the ages of eight and 16 (Chapter 2.3), or that her dietary intake was becoming increasingly similar to that of the males in the upper array discussed above.

Correlations with the archaeological data

There are no overall correlations with body position or orientation. Comparing the two male arrays also yielded no discernible patterning. The two outliers are not differentiated by their grave goods in a consistent way and are both left-crouched (with the upper body of burial 57 on its front) and oriented east–west. Grave 57 was unfurnished, while grave 92 was buried with a pottery vessel and a perforated piece of graphite. They therefore fall within the expected range of LBK funerary variability and are not marked out as 'foreign' in an explicit manner. The piece of graphite is the only possible indication of this here, as graphite occurs in the Bohemian Massif, from Passau eastwards (Pechtl and Eibl 2011). However, graphite is a relatively common grave good at Aiterhofen and also occurs with many individuals analysed who fall within loess signatures. Furthermore, the use of perforated graphite pieces is largely resticted to southern Bavaria (Pechtl and Eibl 2011, 371, fig. 14). The two potential Baden-Württemberg immigrants that could be sampled (graves 12 and 61) also fall within the loess signature.

There was only one significant pattern related to grave goods. The individuals buried with polished stone tools had a significantly lower mean strontium ratio (males with stone tools: 0.70941; males without: 0.70980; Mann-Whitney U test, $p=0.03$). Even if the outlier in grave 57 is excluded, the difference remains significant, but the probability drops to $p=0.04$.

For the females (excluding the extreme outlier), there is a difference in mean strontium ratios between the northern and southern halves of the cemetery (2-tailed t test, $p=0.016$), with the northern group having a higher mean (0.70971) than the southern group (0.70938). The males showed no spatial patterning. There were no significant differences in the variance between the northern and southern groups for either males or females. This suggests that females in the northern group tended to source their diets from a different range of locations than those in the south.

Correlations between strontium ratios and the stable isotopes showed no overall pattern. The different strontium ratio for the females in the northern group is probably down to burials 106, 109 and 137, and reinforces the impression of variability already suggested by the more varied $\delta^{13}C$ values in this part of the site. Higher strontium ratios suggest the inclusion of a higher proportion of non-loess derived foods, while the more variable $\delta^{13}C$ values may indicate the exploitation of a wider range of landscapes with different densities of canopy.

6.7.6 Site summary and discussion

As we concluded in a preliminary presentation (Bickle *et al.* 2011), the isotope results from Aiterhofen suggest a community with several different exploitation strategies, probably practised concurrently. For the males, these fall into two distinct arrays, with one group making greater use of high-strontium ratio foods from childhood. The lack of such patterning among the women is consistent with patrilocality, as they may have come from several different communities, each with their own subsistence strategies, and moved to Aiterhofen later in life. The females in the northern half of the site may also have exploited a wider range of environments in the years before their death.

The distinction between a northern and southern half of the cemetery is visible in other ways. *Spondylus* shells, for example, are mostly deposited in graves in the south, while arrowheads predominantly occur with males in the north. Spatial group V as defined by Nieszery, at the north-western periphery of the site, also contains more individuals in non-left-crouched body positions than elsewhere, although numbers are small. The group also includes many children. In contrast, all the males with three polished stone tools are in the south of the cemetery, where the most complex grave good assemblages cluster.

This pattern could be interpreted in a number of ways. First, we could be seeing a chronological change from simpler grave good assemblages to more complex ones. This could tie in with a potentially less open landscape earlier on, as $\delta^{13}C$ values remain varied in the north. Over time, the landscape could have progressively opened up, leading to more similar values in the south. At the same time, there could be a trend to greater differentiation in grave goods. This is also the model suggested by Jeunesse (1997) and Farruggia (2002).

However, a straightforward chronological interpretation of the spatial patterning remains problematic. For example, cremations, generally believed to date later in the sequence, are mostly found in the northern half. The graves dated on the basis of pottery are few, but also do not seem to correspond to a straightforward north–south development. In addition, it appears that the two distinct male arrays existed throughout the use-life of the cemetery. Alternatively, then, the community at Aiterhofen could have been diverse from the beginning, with different dietary strategies and grave good preferences co-existing. As elsewhere, the only grave good to show a consistent link to isotopic patterning is the stone adze. At Aiterhofen, this remains restricted to the possession of more than two polished stone tools, which correlates with higher $\delta^{15}N$ values. Yet in contrast to other sites, males buried without stone adzes do not have a significantly wider range of strontium ratios than those buried with adzes. Consistent with other sites sampled in this project, we do not see a one-to-one correlation between clearly demarcated lifeways, specific grave goods and/or body treatments.

6.8 Otzing-Gartenäcker

6.8.1 Introduction

Otzing is located between the modern towns of Wallersdorf and Plattling, about 2 km north-west of the river Isar (Fig. 6.1). A first trial excavation was carried out in 1964 by Modderman, but remains unpublished (Schmotz and Weber 2000, 15). Extensive excavations began in 1996, when a first section of a LBK village was excavated in the 'Am Ledererfeld' area (Schmotz 1997). This revealed seven reasonably well preserved LBK house plans, several fragmentary buildings and a series of ovens. Some houses had been cut by a later LBK earthwork with internal palisade, which could be followed over a length of about 50 m and showed two clear entrances. There were also two settlement burials, but there are no further available details (Schmotz 1997, 151–4; Schmotz and Weber 2000, 15).

About 300 m further east, in the 'Gartenäcker' fields, a much larger excavation took place from 1998 to 2000, revealing at least 63 houses, 48 ovens and 45 burials (Schmotz and Weber 2000; Schmotz 2001; 2002b; Pechtl 2010, 51, appendix 1). An additional two isolated skulls are mentioned in Schmotz (2002b, 267). No trace of the earthwork came to light at Gartenäcker and at first sight the settlement density appears higher than at Am Ledererfeld (Fig. 6.12). It remains unclear whether the two areas were once part of the same LBK site, but given the size of other LBK settlements in the vicinity, most notably Stephansposching (Schmotz 1994; Pechtl 2009a), this is a distinct possibility. So far, no detailed post-excavation work has been carried out on the Otzing material. It was provisionally dated to the middle and late LBK (Schmotz and Weber 2000, 19), but a brief later inspection of parts of the material by one of the authors (J. Pechtl, unpublished) also yielded a substantial amount of older material. Given the current stage of research, it is not possible to date any of the settlement burials more precisely or to suggest a possible sequence.

The Otzing houses are mostly oriented north–south and seem to form two loose clusters separated by an empty strip of ground, although this could well be due to local erosion patterns (Schmotz 2001, 17). Both the pit ovens and the burials form small clusters scattered all over the site, and it is impossible to assign them to specific buildings without further information. Equally, there is no apparent preference for inserting burials close to a particular part of the house or at a certain point along the wall, as has been argued for the Paris basin (Thévenet 2009). Eleven of the burials are located at the northern end of the site, the only point where the edge of the settlement seems to have been reached. Seven of these are clustered quite close together and have been described as a possible small cemetery by Schmotz and Weber (2000, 22–4), but they are less well preserved than the remainder and have yielded no grave goods (Schmotz 2002b, 269). A further 16 inhumations are located in the empty strip bisecting the site, while the others are scattered between the houses (Fig. 6.12).

The presence of so many settlement burials is unique for Bavaria (Table 6.7). Such quantities are only paralleled in Hungary, where settlement burials dominate, and at Vaihingen, where a greater number of burials were placed at the then edge of the settlement (Krause 1998). There are several other peculiarities. First, the demographic composition of the sample differs from cemetery sites. Children and juveniles dominate (25 out of 45 individuals, or 55%, with 28.8% adults), and many more young children (Infans I: 0–6 years) are present than on cemeteries (12 individuals, or 48% of the immature individuals). This demographic pattern probably comes closer to actual child mortality in prehistory than is the case for other sites. Of the 13 Otzing adults, six (46.2%) are female or possible female, and only three male. It is especially notable that all individuals over 30 years of age have been classed as female. In addition, the percentage of unfurnished graves (71%) is much higher here than for cemetery sites, but generally in line with other settlement burials in Bavaria. Children especially tended to have no grave goods, although the only *Spondylus* artefact came from the grave of an Infans I. Other goods include pottery, flint and polished stone tools, graphite and bone artefacts such as needles. Although reduced when compared to cemeteries, this is a relatively varied spectrum of grave goods compared to other Bavarian settlement burials. Burial 34 contained only the skull of a juvenile or young adult; no further information is available on two further isolated skulls mentioned by Schmotz (2002b, 267). In contrast to cemetery sites, the orientations of the graves are also far more varied. Among the 37 individuals with information for body position, only 17 (45.9%) were left-crouched. There are no clear spatial patterns in terms of the distribution of age and sex groups or elements of the grave rite across the site (D. Hofmann 2006, 777–9).

To an extent, these patterns correspond to what is expected for LBK settlement burials in general (e.g. Veit 1996; Orschiedt 1998a). What sets Otzing apart is the high number of burials and especially of double burials. There are five instances of the latter, mostly either an adult and child or two children (Schmotz and Weber 2000, 22), and they appear very diverse in terms of their choreography (cf. D. Hofmann 2009a). For example, a contrast can be suggested between double burials facing away from each other – such as the woman and child in grave 10 or the two children in grave 27 – and those sharing a common orientation and position, such as the two children in grave 19, where the older child embraces the younger (Fig. 6.13). There are other interesting parallels. For instance, the two children buried on a paving of sherds in grave 27 face away from each other, but their legs are overlapping. This mirrors two sequential child interments (graves 31 and 32) from a pit complex, also facing in opposite directions but with legs towards each other. The body positions in double grave 29 and in grave 16 are very unusual and more reminiscent of the later Münchshöfen culture (Böhm and Schmotz 1991).

The presence of so many double burials, some referencing each other, suggests that although each death resulted in an interment which was to some extent unique, certain performances were recognised as particularly salient and were referenced time and again. This may well have taken precedence over the tracing of relationships and identities through grave goods (see also D. Hofmann 2009a). Similar ideas could also apply to some of the single burials (e.g.

Fig. 6.12. Otzing-Gartenäcker: plan. Burials sampled are shown in black. After Schmotz and Weber (2000, Beilage 1).

D. Hofmann 2006, 226–8). Unfortunately, drawings or photographs are not available for all burials, and further, more detailed interpretation must await full publication of the results.

6.8.2 Osteology

The human remains were studied by Peter Schröter and by Linda Fibiger as part of the 'Skeletal evidence for interpersonal violence in the Neolithic of Northwest Europe' project (Fibiger 2010; Schulting and Fibiger 2012). One individual at Otzing (burial 22), a child aged between 9 and 11 years, had suffered two fatal injuries to the left side of the head.

6.8.3 Carbon and nitrogen analysis

Measurements of carbon and nitrogen stable isotopes were obtained from 18 skeletons comprising eight infants, four juveniles/adolescents, five females ranging from young adult to late mature in age, and one individual without age/sex information (Fig. 6.14; Table 6.8).

Age/sex variation

With no male skeletons in the sample, we are unable to compare the sexes. The infants are unusual in showing no sign of a breast-feeding signal. While the anthropological ageing simply provides an age range of 0–6 years, this pattern would suggest that none of these infants fall at the younger end of the age range. The $\delta^{15}N$ values of the

Table 6.7. Otzing: the isotope, osteological and archaeological data. Age and sex information from Schmotz and Weber (2000). See Chapter 2 for further definition of ages.
Key for body position: LC – Left-crouched; RC – Right-crouched; C – Crouched, direction unknown; CB – Crouched on back; CF – Crouched on front; S – Supine; P – Prone; I – Irregular.
Key for grave goods (number of items in brackets): U. – Unfurnished; F. – Fill only (all items listed after an F. were in the fill of the grave rather than at the level of the skeleton); Pol. – Polished stone; Cer. – Ceramics; Shd. – Sherds; Spon. – Spondylus*; She. – Other Shell; Och. – Ochre; Ant. – Antler; Lit. – Chipped stone; Bon – Worked bone; Grd. – Grinding stone.*

Burial	Tooth	Sex	Age (yrs)	$^{87}Sr/^{86}Sr$	Sr conc. ppm	$\delta^{13}C$ ‰	$\delta^{15}N$ ‰	Orientation	Body position	Grave goods
1	-	-	Adult	-	-	-	-	W–E	LC	Pol.(1), Lit.(1)
2	-	-	Immature	-	-	-	-	N–S	LC	U.
3	M1	F?	Inf I	0.70935	*n.d.*	−20.4	8.1	W–E	RC	Shd.(5)
4	-	F?	Older Adult	-	-	−20.3	8.7	N–S	LC	Shd.(5), Och.
5	M3	F?	Late Mature	0.70961	*n.d.*	−19.7	8.9	NW–SE	CB	Cer.(1)
6	M1	F?	Young Adult	0.70909	*n.d.*	−20.2	8.1	E–W	CF	U.
7	-	-	Inf I	-	-	-	-	S–N	LC	U.
8	M2	M	Adult	-	-	-	-	SE–NW	LC	Lit.(1)
9	M3	M	Adult	-	-	-	-	E–W	LC	Bon.(1)
10a	M2	F?	Mature	0.71071	81	−20.2	8.2	N–S	CF	U.
10b	-	-	Inf I	-	-	-	-	E–W	LC	U.
12	M1	-	Inf I	-	-	-	-	SE–NW	RC	U.
13	-	-	Immature	-	-	-	-	W–E	LC	U.
14	M2	F	Juv.	0.70928	*n.d.*	−20.3	8.4	S–N	RC	U.
15	-	-	Inf I	-	-	-	-	SW–NE	RC	U.
16	-	-	Inf II	-	-	-	-	NW–SE	S	U.
17	M3	F?	Older Adult	0.70975	69	−20.1	8.8	SE–NW	LC	Cer.(1)
18	M1	-	Inf I	0.71419	42	−20.4	7.6	E–W	RC	U.
19	M3	M?	Inf II	-	-	-	-	NW–SE	LC	U.
19	-	-	Inf I	-	-	-	-	NW–SE	LC	U.
21	M1	M?	Inf II	-	-	-	-	S–N	RC	Cer.(1)
22a	-	-	Immature	-	-	−20.2	8.7	NE–SW	S	U.
22b	-	-	Adult	-	-	-	-	SW–NE	RC	U.

24	-	-	Adult	-	-	-	-	NW–SE	LC	U.
25	M2	F?	Late Mature	-	-	-	-	S–N	LC	Cer.(1)
26	M2	-	Inf II	0.70924	53	−20.1	7.7	SW–NE	LC	U.
27a	-	M?	Inf I	-	-	−20.1	8.3	S–N	S	Cer.(1)
27b	-	-	Inf I	-	-	-	-	NW–SE	RC	Spon.(frag.), Bon.(2)
29a	M3	-	Juv.	0.70985	37	−20.5	8.8	NW–SE	S	U.
29b	M2	-	Inf II	0.70974	49	−20.7	8.1	SW–NE	S	U.
31	-	-	Inf II	-	-	-	-	S–N	LC	U.
32	-	-	Inf II	-	-	-	-	N–S	LC	U.
33	M1	M?	Inf I	0.70915	59	−20.3	8.5	N–S	RC	U.
34	M2	M?	Juv./Young Adult	-	-	-	-	-	-	Pol.(1), Ant.(frag.)
35	-	-	Adult	-	-	-	-	E–W	LC	U.
36	M1	-	Inf I	0.7093	51	−20.6	7.7	NW–SE	RC	U.
37	M1	M?	Inf I	0.70939	38	−20.3	8.4	E–W	RC	U.
38	M1	-	Juv.	0.70945	50	−20.5	7.9	S–N	RC	Cer.(1)
39	M3	-	-	0.70995	38	−20.2	8.9	-	-	U.
40	-	-	-	-	-	-	-	-	-	U.
41	-	-	-	-	-	-	-	-	-	U.
42	M2	-	-	-	-	-	-	-	-	U.
43	-	-	-	-	-	-	-	-	-	U.
44	-	-	-	-	-	-	-	-	-	U.
45	-	-	-	-	-	-	-	-	-	U.

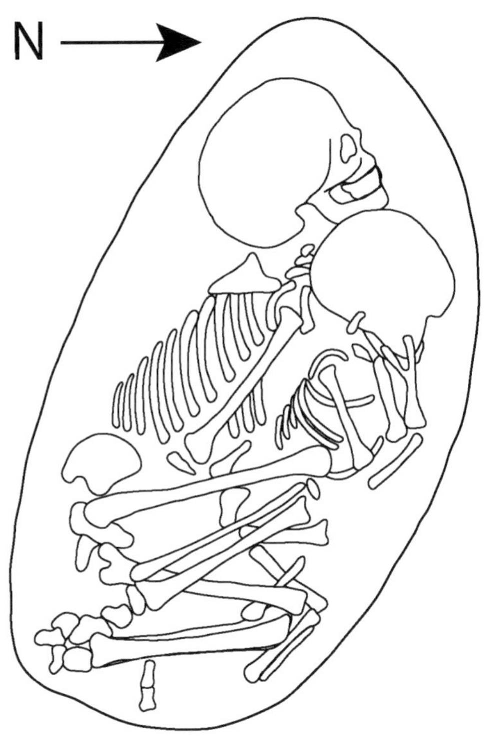

Fig. 6.13. Otzing-Gartenäcker: double burial 19. After Schmotz and Weber (2000, 29).

children are significantly lower than those of the adult females (ANOVA, p=0.04), though there is some overlap (Fig. 6.14). This could suggest a diet low in animal protein, whether meat or milk; such a diet might also have a low overall content of protein and poor protein quality, and could even be a contributory factor to the early deaths of this group. It would tie in with high caries rates at Aiterhofen revealed by Carli-Thiele (1996), indicative of a high-cereal diet. Alternatively, this could be an example of high growth rate in young children leading to lower δ^{15}N values (reviewed by Waters-Rist and Katzenberg 2010), but we have little evidence for this in the overall dataset (Chapter 9.2.5).

Animals

No animals were sampled from Otzing, but animals from Lerchenhaid (Fig. 6.15) may provide a reasonable comparison, as the two human samples from Lerchenhaid have δ^{13}C and δ^{15}N values in a similar range to those at Otzing. We should be cautious in this comparison, because Lerchenhaid is geographically closer to Aiterhofen than to Otzing, but the δ^{15}N values for both cattle and humans are clearly higher at Aiterhofen. This could have a number of explanations, but one possible reason is that cattle at Aiterhofen grazed on higher-nitrogen plants, such as manured crops. Local subsistence practices could therefore have varied at the micro-regional scale. With this caveat, the difference between adult human and cattle δ^{13}C and

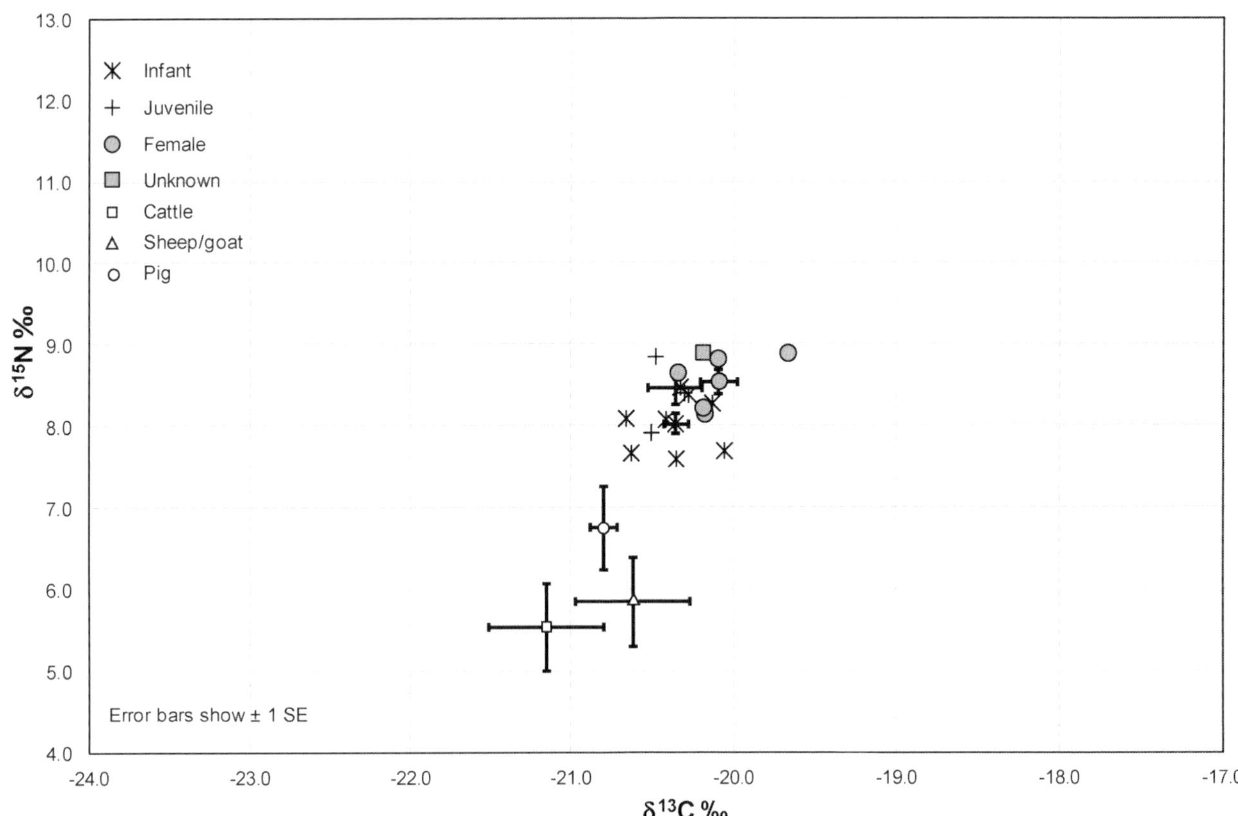

Fig. 6.14. Otzing-Gartenäcker: carbon and nitrogen isotope ratios (‰) of humans. Lerchenhaid fauna are shown for comparison.

Table 6.8. Otzing: carbon and nitrogen isotope ratios (‰) of humans, with means and standard deviations.

Species	Age/sex	Mean $\delta^{13}C$	SD $\delta^{13}C$	Mean $\delta^{15}N$	SD $\delta^{15}N$	n
Human	Infant	−20.4	0.21	8.0	0.34	8
Human	Juvenile	−20.4	0.16	8.5	0.41	4
Human	Female	−20.1	0.25	8.5	0.34	5
Human	Unknown	−20.2	-	8.9	-	1

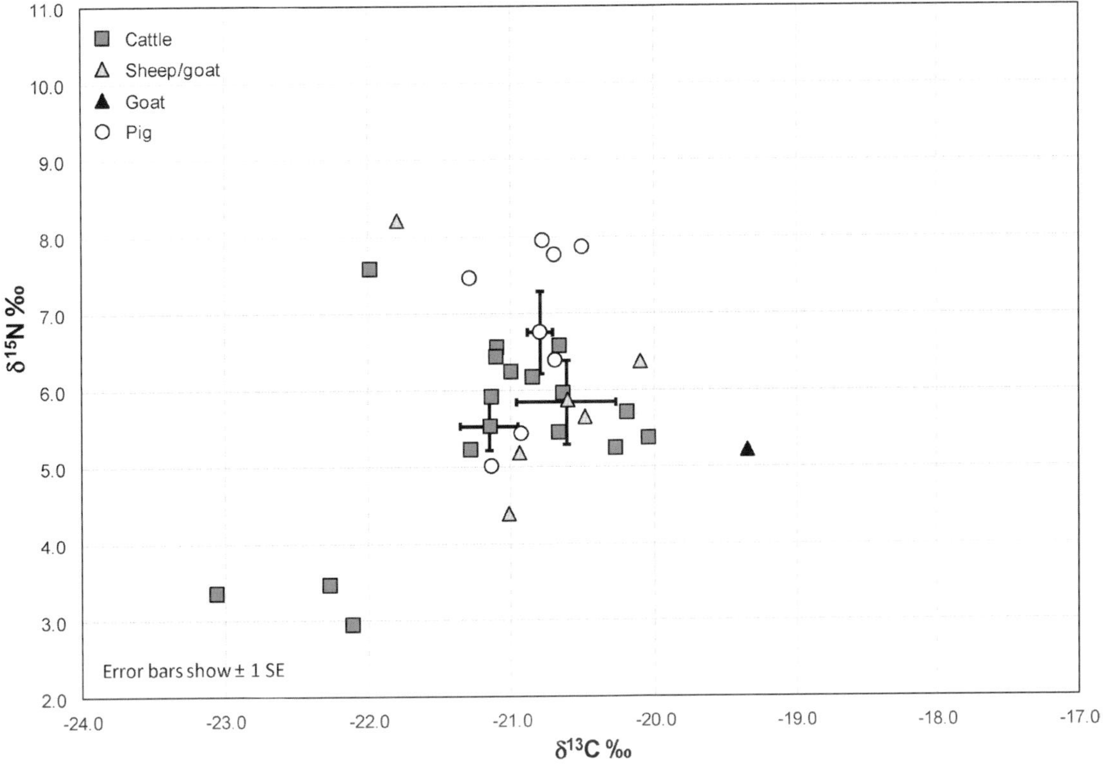

Fig. 6.15. Straubing-Lerchenhaid: carbon and nitrogen isotope ratios (‰) of animals.

$\delta^{15}N$ mean values was 1.1‰±0.87 (SD) and 3.0‰±1.32 respectively.

Correlations with the archaeological data

Left- and right-crouched burials show different variances in $\delta^{13}C$ values, with right-crouched individuals more varied (Levene's test, p=0.006, n=16). Right-crouched individuals also have a lower $\delta^{13}C$ mean value ($\delta^{13}C$=−20.4‰) than left-crouched burials ($\delta^{13}C$=−20.2‰; 2-tailed t test, p=0.009). There was no patterning relating to burial orientation. Grave goods also showed no patterning, but this is perhaps not surprising. On cemetery sites the strongest patterning was related to polished stone adzes which, given the lack of males, are absent at Otzing. Grave goods are in any case rare, in line with other settlement burials.

6.8.4 Strontium analysis

Fifteen strontium results were determined on 15 individuals (including four females, four juveniles and six infants; Fig 6.16; Table 6.9). The general geological situation is the same as for Aiterhofen.

The overall mean for Otzing (0.70987±0.00131) is consistent with a primarily loess-derived diet. There is one outlier, an Infans I (grave 18; Sr ratio 0.71419). Most children sampled in the Lifeways project have local signatures, and this individual is thus unusual. The ratio is consistent with an early childhood spent elsewhere, but could also relate to the mother moving into Otzing whilst already pregnant or breast-feeding. As for Aiterhofen, values of 0.714 are likely to have arisen from use of upland resources; the Bavarian Forest remains the nearest source at a distance of roughly 25 km. The presence of this outlier explains why the Infans I category has a higher strontium ratio mean than the females and older children and juveniles. If this outlier is excluded, there is no significant difference between the age groups. Too few samples were available to detect patterns related to different teeth.

Correlations with the archaeological data

There are no correlations between the strontium ratios or concentrations and either grave good provision or body treatment.

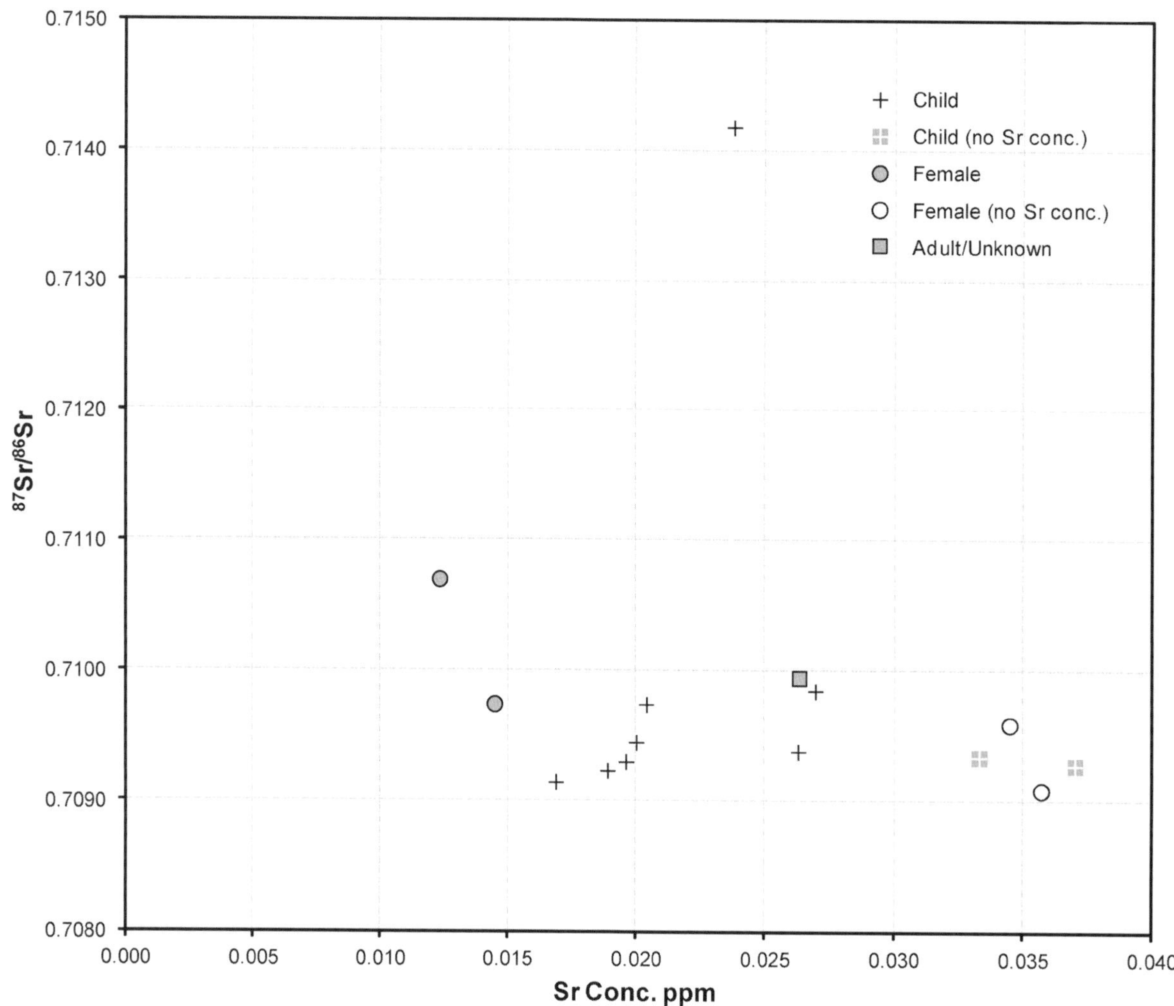

Fig. 6.16. Otzing-Gartenäcker: strontium concentration (ppm) versus ratio ($^{87}Sr/^{86}Sr$). An artificial Sr. conc. value was assigned where no measurement was available.

Table 6.9. Otzing: strontium isotope ratios and concentrations.

Age/sex	Mean $^{87}Sr/^{86}Sr$	SD $^{87}Sr/^{86}Sr$	Mean Sr conc.	SD Sr conc.	n
Infant	0.71010	0.002002	49	9	6
Juvenile	0.70949	0.000231	45	7	4
Female	0.70979	0.000676	75	8	4
Unknown	0.70995	-	38	-	1
All	0.70987	0.00131	51	14	15

6.8.5 Site summary and discussion

For Otzing, there are no correlations between the strontium ratios or concentrations and any aspect of body treatment or grave good provision, although an outlier is present. The only pattern revealed for the stable isotopes relates to a higher variability in $\delta^{13}C$ values for right-crouched inhumations.

In general terms, it is possible to split the settlement burials at Otzing into those buried relatively close to houses and those buried in more open areas of the site. This is of course only an approximation. The dating evidence is not sufficient to decide whether a given burial was interred next to a contemporary house, an already abandoned building or simply at a spot where a house was erected at some later point. Similarly, some of the open areas may be down to particularly severe erosion, and buildings may have stood here. However, accepting for the moment that this division is plausible, burials close to houses were mostly crouched on their left side (eight out of 12), while in open areas half the individuals were crouched on their right (nine out of 18). There is also more variability in the orientation of burials in open areas (with heads to the west, north-west or north) than for those next to houses (all buried with their heads to the east or south-east).

Given the caveats noted above, the pattern must be treated with caution and should be seen as a suggestion to be tested further where better evidence permits. Yet it appears that we can contrast a more 'conservative' group of burials closer to houses with a more varied group distributed in more open areas of the site. Interestingly, this does not coincide with any patterning in stable isotope values or strontium ratios. Whatever difference was being signalled here, it was not related to diet or geographical origin in a straightforward way.

6.9 Regional discussion

Southern Bavaria, where all the individuals sampled in this study were buried, has extensive contacts with other LBK areas, particularly across the Bavarian Forest to Bohemia. Individuals identified as outliers by their strontium ratios and with potential links to these areas were found at both Aiterhofen and Otzing, but were not consistently marked out through either grave rite or provision of grave goods. Similarly, individuals with links to Baden-Württemberg in their grave good assemblage do not stand out isotopically. As noted for other case studies in this volume, there is no consistent way in which 'foreignness' is marked out, and no single correlation between isotopic indicators of outside origin and grave goods or burial rites. There are also no significant differences in either the strontium ratio or concentration between the sites, and in both cases the majority of individuals derived their childhood diet from the loess.

Overall, the stable isotopes also suggest a relatively similar range of subsistence practices in the region, although given the differences in the values for the animals from both sites no close comparison can be attempted at this stage. Cattle at Aiterhofen may have grazed on manured stubble, providing an indication that herd management could differ within the region. In addition, subtle variations in subsistence strategies could be identified between individuals buried on the same site, for instance the exploitation of a greater range of environments for the females in the northern part of Aiterhofen, or the two male arrays at the site. As with other regions, there is also a link with the provision of polished stone tools, although in this case it concerns a potentially elevated consumption of animal protein by individuals with three adzes or axes, rather than a narrower range of strontium values. Otherwise, there are no consistent correlations between body treatment, grave good provision and isotopic values.

It remains hard to compare Aiterhofen and Otzing in any detail, as one is a cemetery and the other a site with settlement burials. Many of the observed differences in the complexity of grave good assemblages or the relative standardisation in body positions correspond to what is expected on this basis.

What the investigation of these sites has shown is that burial was a very flexible strategy which could be used creatively to express many subtle distinctions between individuals and groupings, which do not easily map on to absolute categories such as foreign and local. At both Aiterhofen and Otzing, we can also identify the building up of certain burial traditions. At the cemetery site, grave good assemblages as well as spatial patterns could be used to identify several groupings, while at the settlement relations among the deceased and between them and the living were perhaps more consistently expressed through location with respect to houses and through rites such as double burials.

Perhaps the most interesting pattern to emerge is the possible identification of two spatial groupings at both sites. At Otzing, those buried closer to houses appear more unified in their orientation and position than those further away from structures; these latter are more often not in a left-crouched position. Right-crouched positions also correlate with more varied $\delta^{13}C$ values. At Aiterhofen, the northern half of the site has more simple grave good assemblages, a greater number of arrowheads among men and more varied $\delta^{13}C$ values among women, which may indicate the use of at least some more forested areas for subsistence. This contrasts with the southern half where women had more similar $\delta^{13}C$ values, but where there were more complex and diverse grave good assemblages also including *Spondylus* and some men with more than two polished tools. These distinctions may have persisted throughout the use of the cemetery, and this makes an interesting parallel with other sites studied in this project, most notably Rutzing (Chapter 5.10).

Interestingly, similar subdivisions can also be suggested for two further sites in southern Bavaria (as well as at Dillingen; Chapter 6.5.2), although these could not be sampled in the course of the present project. At Essenbach, the cemetery is incompletely excavated, but it may be possible to distinguish a north-western part of more tightly clustered graves from a looser scatter in the south and east. The first group has a higher number of children and more non-standardised positions and orientations, while the scattered graves are predominantly left-crouched and east–west oriented. The latter can also receive *Spondylus*, although the assemblages remain more modest than at Aiterhofen (D. Hofmann 2006, 734–9).

At Stephansposching, the full extent of the cemetery is again unknown, but graves are more tightly clustered in the western half of the excavated area. Although the numbers of males are very similar in both groups, polished stone tools were more often buried with individuals in the west, while pottery and goods in the grave fill are more frequent in the east. Numbers are not sufficient to assess potential differences in the provision of ornaments and other goods or in orientation and position, especially given the many cremations (D. Hofmann 2006, 745–50).

It is also worth pointing out that not all cemeteries in southern Bavaria are equally richly furnished. Sites like Aiterhofen provide a clear contrast to Stephansposching, with its focus on cremations and on inhumations with fewer goods. Cemeteries are as yet few in number, so this is an indication only, but it is tempting to speculate that we are seeing different ways in which burial practices could come to be co-opted as part of a 'competition between equals' scenario in a settlement system lacking central places (see Chapter 6.4.2). At some sites, notably Aiterhofen, greater resources were channelled into provision with grave goods and the creation of large collectivities, providing opportunities for expressing distinctions between groupings, including between settlements. Therefore, the burial community, or at least the burial audience, may have been wider than just a single settlement. In contrast, at Stephansposching differences between individuals were more muted. At nearby Otzing no burial ground has yet been found, and in line with settlement burials elsewhere the distinctions between the individuals interred here are subtle and perhaps rather aimed at an audience of immediate kin and co-residents. At both Stephansposching and Otzing, collections of graves perhaps served a purpose more akin to stressing the unity of the burial community – and in the case of settlement burials perhaps predominantly of immediate kin and co-residents – rather than being aimed at a wider audience (a question taken up in Chapter 9.5). These reflections point to potential distinctions in the ways in which burial could respond to wider transformations and concerns.

In addition, and in line with the other divisions within Bavaria noted above, cemeteries only occur in the areas with the largest settlements and are entirely absent from the tertiary hills with their smaller, shorter-lived and more scattered sites. Dillingen, at the extreme western periphery, is much closer, both geographically and in terms of practice, to Baden-Württemberg than to southern Bavaria, but is again situated near a large settlement. Cemeteries as a whole emerge as part of the strategies binding larger social groups together, albeit this is achieved in different ways, by either accentuating or suppressing variability between individual graves. In western parts of southern Bavaria, the focus of competition and elaboration remains the household in its increasingly monumental building (Pechtl 2009b). This does not mean, however, that interaction spheres were more circumscribed. Indeed, the distribution of Arnhofen flint far exceeds that of varieties from eastern Bavaria and documents the far-flung networks of those who obtained and traded it. It is more difficult to establish whether this kind of exchange was dominated by specific households, as may be expected from the prominence of monumental buildings in the area. In terms of the role of mortuary practices, there is an indication that the absence of particularly large burial grounds and the prominence of households may go hand in hand. Certainly, there are no sites here comparable in longevity, burial density and sheer size to Aiterhofen, although individual graves at cemeteries such as Sengkofen and Mangolding can stand out through complex assemblages. As Chapter 10 argues, households are hard to identify in cemetery sites, and perhaps values of relative household aggrandisement were easier to reconcile with a stress on smaller burial collectivities. In the tertiary hills, there seems to have been no desire to implicate the dead in inter-community or inter-household competition, and this may tie in with a generally shallower time depth for sites there, perhaps indicating a reduced emphasis on notions of long-term descent and community stability. Social entanglements at varying scales may have called for different ways of representing ideas of community.

At an inter-regional level, Bavaria sits uneasily between the burial traditions of Jeunesse (e.g. 1995a; 1996; 1997, 101–3; 2006; outlined in Chapter 1.3.5). His Tradition I is characterised by relatively greater standardisation in position and orientation, greater emphasis on ornaments and the provision of powdered ochre. In contrast, Tradition II sees more varied body positions and orientations, a more restricted range of ornaments, more flint tools, more cremations and less ochre. In Bavaria, we witness both a relatively high proportion of flint tools and cremations, and a preference for powdered ochre, standardised positions and provision with ornaments. It thus shares elements with both Traditions I and II, as well as yielding graves which combine artefacts seen as typically 'Mesolithic' and typically 'Neolithic' by Lenneis (2007), for example river shells and *Spondylus* ornaments. In line with other regions in this project, then, the subtle variations in subsistence strategies within an overall loess-based diet, and their relation to other potential indicators such as grave good provision, do not correlate precisely with each other. There were many competing identities which could be referenced in funerary rites. Burial is revealed as a creative arena, responsive to wider trends, and embedded in a variety of negotiations at different scales which continuously transformed the kinds of roles it could play.

Notes

1 In contrast, the Bavarian sites and monuments record remains difficult to access and use (Schmotz 2002a, 205).

2 The outlook is not all dark, however. An important impetus for the more systematic study of Bavarian prehistory in general was the foundation of the *Gesellschaft für Archäologie in Bayern* (Bavarian Archaeological Society) by Rainer Christlein in 1981, which regularly publishes on Neolithic research in Bavaria.

3 Led by Alasdair Whittle.

4 For examples from other regions, see e.g. Bárta 1956; Jeunesse 1990a; Walter 1985. Interestingly, there are fewer remains from the Franconian Alb (see e.g. Stoll-Tucker 1997; Tillmann 1989; Neudert 2005, 23), where ritual use seems more prominent, as also shown by the open-air site at the Hohle Stein (Seregély and Link 2009). Cave sites in Austria are noted in Chapter 5.4.

5 Although material as early as the middle LBK may be present.

6 Nieszery (1995, 163–4) has identified portable strike-a-lights which were often deposited close together as if in a bundle. The full kit includes an *Unio* shell for supporting the kindling, a pyrite nodule and one or more flint items (a core, blade or flake) to produce a spark, and a bone awl to help kindle the flame. However, in Nieszery's definition the presence of two items from this list is already sufficient to reconstruct a firelighting kit.

7 The term 'cenotaph' is avoided here, as the pits were not well observed during excavation, and it is unclear whether the goods were actually laid out in the same manner as would be the case in a regular grave (see also Chapter 5.7.1).

An Aiterhofen lifeway: burial 57

The man in burial 57 was between 30 and 35 years of age. He had been laid to rest with his head pointing due east, and although his upper body is on its front, the legs are crouched to the left. The stable isotope values of this individual are close to the means for males at this site, with a nitrogen value of 9.7‰ (male mean 9.9‰) and a carbon value of −20.2‰ (male mean −20.4‰). A large contribution of carbohydrate from plants to his diet is also supported by the presence of caries. However, in terms of strontium isotopes, this is one of only two outliers at Aiterhofen (the second one being the woman in burial 92). The ratio of 0.71416 exhibited by a second molar from burial 57 is consistent with a childhood spent away from the loess (the isotope range around Aiterhofen is 0.7086–0.7103), perhaps in the uplands of the nearby Bavarian Forest/Bohemian Massif. This individual would only have moved to Aiterhofen in later childhood or adulthood, perhaps upon marriage.

In spite of his non-local origin, this man was not marked out through any particular grave rite, but exhibits choices commonly made at Aiterhofen. His grave is also located towards the centre of the site in an area with high burial density. On one level, a born-away person could become accepted as part of the burial community. In this case, a possible origin in the Bohemian Massif serves to reinforce the close connections between Bavaria and Bohemia which existed in the LBK. At Aiterhofen, they may be manifested in the presence of graphite as a colorant, which can be sourced in the uplands separating Bavaria and Bohemia. More generally in the region, pottery decorations and flint distribution networks also attest to the fact that these mountains must have been crossed relatively regularly. Whether the man in burial 57 could have done so towards the end of his life is uncertain. Pathological changes on the inside of his skull may indicate a brain tumour, and among the range of possible symptoms, headaches and loss of balance may have impeded his ability to travel.

However, this man also received no grave goods, along with around a quarter of all male individuals. This is interesting, as there are overall correlations between isotopic signatures and the kinds of grave good assemblages which an individual received in death. The link between polished stone axes and a tighter range of strontium values for males is just outside statistical significance at Aiterhofen, but here there is a trend for older men to have an elevated nitrogen signature and hence perhaps to have consumed more animal protein. High nitrogen values are also correlated with the possession of more than two polished stone tools. So we can suggest that the kinds of status positions which this individual held in life did not call for a display of wealth in the grave, at least not in a way connected with the deposition of grave goods. A non-local origin could be one possible contributing factor, but age may also play into this to a degree.

A lower-status position for this individual could also be suggested on the basis of stress markers on his teeth (enamel hypoplasia), which indicate the survival of an episode of illness or malnutrition in childhood. However, these indicators are very common at Aiterhofen and do not seem to correlate with the complexity of the grave good assemblage. They could be linked to stresses experienced for example during weaning. Overall, a non-local origin at Aiterhofen could be connected to a burial without grave goods, but this is an interpretation substantially influenced by the pattern found on other sites. Locally, age may be a more important factor in regulating for example access to a different diet. Indeed, in terms of the burial rite itself the man in grave 57 was perfectly integrated into his local burial community.

An Aiterhofen lifeway: burial 150

Burial 150 contained an adult female over 60 years of age, laid to rest in a supine position and with her head to the east. At −20.1‰, her carbon value is slightly higher than the site average for females (−20.4‰), while her nitrogen value of 9.8‰ corresponds exactly to the female mean. This suggests a diet that did not include large amounts of plant foods grown in a forested environment. The carious lesions identified in this individual corroborate the importance of starchy foods. Unsurprisingly for a person of this age, caries may even have led to ante-mortem tooth loss, although this can have various other causes, including gum disease or the use of teeth as tools. Two strontium measurements were obtained from this individual, one on a second molar (0.71084) and one on a third molar (0.71114). Both of these values are slightly above the local range (which for Aiterhofen is 0.7086–0.7103), but they are not incompatible with a childhood diet largely derived from loess soils elsewhere (for example in Moravia).

These strontium values fit well with the suggestion of patrilocality. Women at Aiterhofen in general show less patterning in their strontium values than men, suggesting that they could have moved here from several other communities upon marriage. At least initially, women could therefore have been newcomers and perhaps even outsiders in their post-marital communities, and for burial 150 this may be reflected in the marginal position of her grave at the western edge of the site, in an area with relatively few other burials. The change in strontium values between this woman's second and third molars is also interesting, as the values are moving further away from the Aiterhofen local range with age. This could mean that she only moved to the site once her third molar was fully mineralised, which could be as late as 16 years of age. Alternatively, her diet may have been assimilating to that of the upper array revealed for the male strontium values, which would mean that she joined a section of the Aiterhofen community who had a greater off-loess component in their diet.

This potential 'foreignness' of burial 150 was, however, not marked out in the burial rite. While a supine position is unusual for Aiterhofen, this may here be connected to this woman's high age at death, as other elderly individuals at the site are also buried in unusual positions. Age is important at Aiterhofen in other ways, especially in terms of male diet, shown by an increase in nitrogen values for older men. As far as orientation is concerned, burial 150 does not stand out from the majority of people interred here.

Neither is there any indication that this woman may have received fewer grave goods, and hence been of 'lower' social status, on account of her non-local origins. On the contrary, she was buried with an extensive assemblage of shell ornaments. Among them are six tubular beads made from the shells of Protula*, a marine worm with a distribution that overlaps that of* Spondylus *and which is sometimes found attached to the outside of* Spondylus *shells. Their presence here suggests that this woman was part of wide-ranging networks. Interestingly, however, she was also buried with 96* Theodoxus danubialis *shells, collected locally from the river Danube. These were found around the back of her head and neck, and were most probably either sewn on to a hairnet or cap, or braided directly into the hair. Ornaments like these are found in other burials in Bavaria (at Aiterhofen for example with the female in grave 32) and Austria, but not elsewhere.*

The woman in burial 150 was thus originally a stranger at Aiterhofen, having spent her childhood in another community. Yet her burial assemblage also references a strongly regional identity, and the way she was laid to rest shows that no less material investment or care were accorded to her than to many of the local females.

7 Baden-Württemberg

R. Alexander Bentley, Penny Bickle, Michael Francken, Claudia Gerling, Julie Hamilton, Robert Hedges, Elisabeth Stephan, Joachim Wahl and Alasdair Whittle

7.1 Introduction

Two major rivers characterise the landscape of Baden-Württemberg, the Rhine to the west and the Danube to the south and south-east. The curving path of the Neckar bisects the region, to join the Rhine in the north. Between the river valleys, the uplands and mountains offer contrasting geographies and geologies. Granites and gneisses shape the uplands of the Black Forest, which lies between the Neckar and Rhine rivers, and of the Odenwald, which is north of the Neckar (Fig. 7.1; Bentley and Knipper 2005a; 2005b; Knipper 2009). South of the Neckar, the Swabian Alb consists of Keuper sandstones and calcareous rocks (such as Muschelkalk and limestones), part of which are covered by loess soils, while tertiary volcanoes form the geology in the Hegau region west of Lake Constance (the Bodensee; Bentley and Knipper 2005b; Knipper 2009, 145; Knipper 2011).

This landscape can be divided into different areas of LBK occupation. We can identify settlement clusters in the Neckar valley, which has two concentrations of settlement: the Rhein-Neckar *Kreis* (Lindig 2002) and the Upper Neckar valley (Strien 2000); in the Hegau region, west of the Bodensee, where sites extend into Switzerland (Fritsch 1987; 1998; Dieckmann and Fritsch 1990; Strien 2000); in an area directly north of the upper Danube, including the settlement of Ulm-Eggingen (Kind 1989); and in the Kaiserstuhl, which is situated between the east bank of the Rhine and the river Elz (Fig. 7.1; Stöckl 1992; Strien 2000: Lefranc 2007a). More recently, a new regional group bridging the Rhine at the Rhine-Neckar confluence has been identified, in the Pfalz (Palatinate; Jeunesse *et al.* 2009).

As in other regions covered in this project, we can piece together a complex history for the LBK along the river valleys of Baden-Württemberg. Comparatively strong evidence for terminal Mesolithic groups coincides with the presence of the earliest LBK, particularly in the Neckar valley (Kind 1997; 1998; Gronenborn 1999; 2007a; Strien 2000). The region has seen the most extensive strontium isotope analysis so far carried out on LBK material (Price *et al.* 2001; Bentley and Knipper 2005a; Knipper 2009). Schwetzingen (Price and Bentley 2005), Vaihingen an der Enz (Bentley *et al.* 2003; Bentley and Knipper 2005a; 2005b; Knipper 2009), Talheim (Bentley *et al.* 2008) and Stuttgart-Mühlhausen (Price *et al.* 2003; Knipper 2009; Knipper and Price 2010) have already received differing extents of isotopic study, with the detailed and multi-faceted research at Vaihingen in particular (Krause 1998; Strien 2005; Bogaard *et al.* 2011) fast making this site essential in any broader discussion of the LBK as a whole. Most recently Corina Knipper (2011) has presented strontium and oxygen isotope ratios on cattle teeth from three LBK sites in Baden-Württemberg (Vaihingen, Stuttgart-Mühlhausen and Hilzingen), which suggest heterogeneous animal husbandry strategies. In this chapter, we focus on the extended results from the cemetery of Schwetzingen.

Despite the considerable significance of the region for LBK studies and long acknowledged regional ceramic styles (Lüning 1988a; Modderman 1988; van Berg 1990; Strien 2000), recent syntheses of the LBK in Baden-Württemberg are not numerous. As a result, a small number of principally large settlements and cemeteries dominate our understanding, but those might well be the exception rather than the norm and may correspondingly distort our view of the communities in this region. Because of its exceptional character, Talheim remains the most discussed burial site from the region, and Coudart (1998) only included one Baden-Württemberg site, the Danubian site of Ulm-Eggingen, in her study of longhouse architecture. This settlement (Kind 1989), together with Gerlingen (Neth 1999), form the major published excavations in Baden-Württemberg, with a full publication of Vaihingen eagerly anticipated (partly published by Krause 1998; Bentley *et al.* 2003; Strien 2005; Bogaard *et al.* 2011; Bogaard 2011). Our understanding of burials is similarly limited, with Stuttgart-Mühlhausen yet to receive extensive and detailed publication.

Hans-Christoph Strien (2000), however, has discussed the lithics and pottery in the south-western distribution of the LBK, and proposed a chronology for the Neckar and Alsace areas. Other regional considerations of chronology

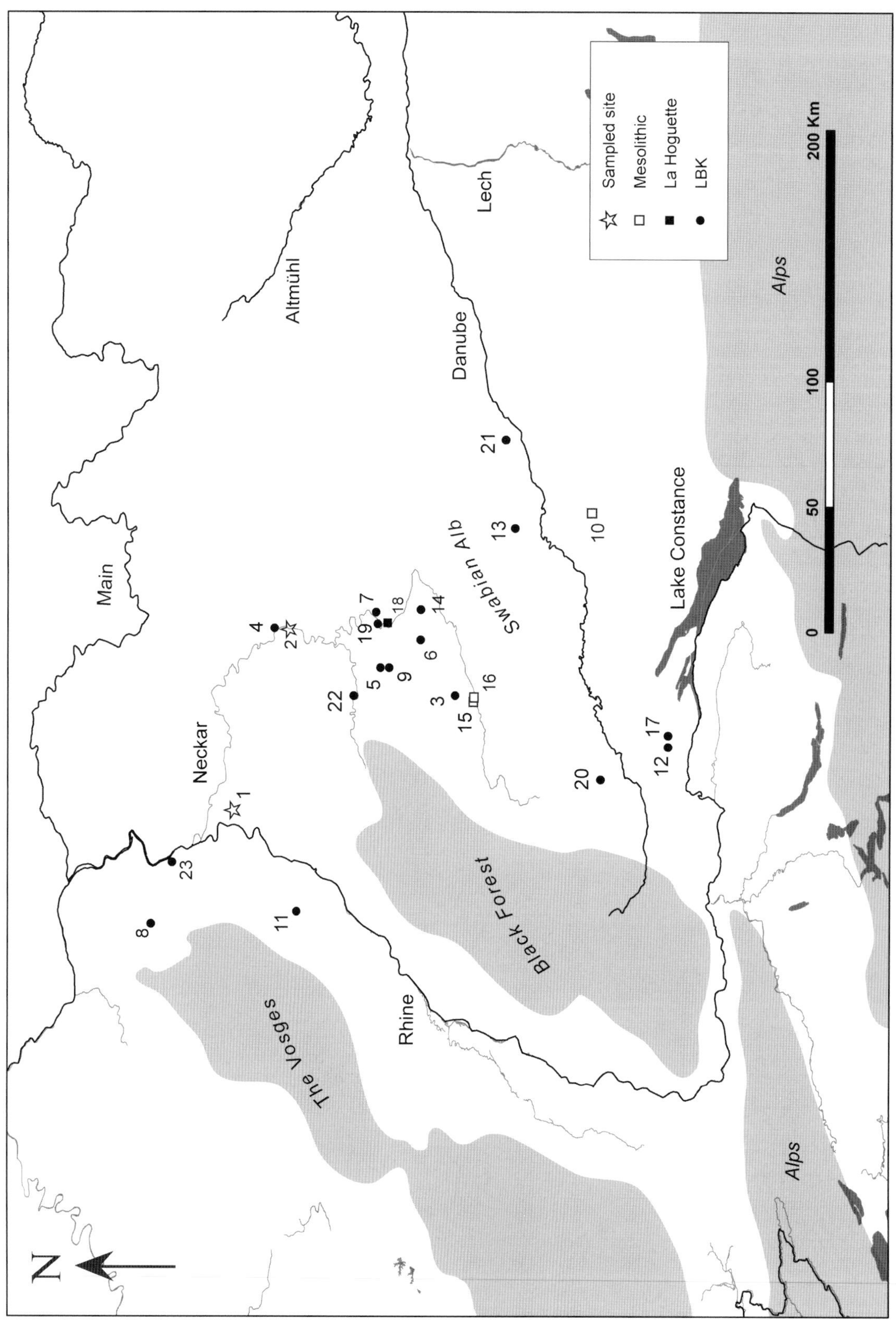

Fig. 7.1. Map of sites sampled (1–2) and others mentioned in Chapter 7. Upland areas are in italics. 1) Schwetzingen, 2) Heilbronn-Neckargartach, 3) Ammerbuch, 4) Bad Friedrichshall, 5) Ditzingen, 6) Echterdingen 7, 7) Fellbach-Oeffingen, 8) Flomborn, 9) Gerlingen, 10) Henauhof-Nord II, 11) Herxheim, 12) Hilzingen, 13) Lautereck, 14) Neuhausen auf der Filden, 15) Rottenburg-Fröbelweg, 16) Rottenburg-Siebenlinden, 17) Singen, 18) Stuttgart-Bad Cannstatt, 19) Stuttgart-Mühlhausen, 20) Talheim, 21) Ulm-Eggingen, 22) Vaihingen an der Enz, 23) Worms Unter Platt.

Table 7.1. Chronological phasing of the LBK proposed for selected parts of Baden-Württemberg and neighbouring regions (after Gerling 2012; Lefranc 2007a; and other cited sources). Note that for Strien (2000, 51) the Flomborn style appears in the Neckar valley and Alsace first in phase 2A (at Gerlingen), while he sees phase 3 as transitional between early and middle LBK.

Region	**Basse-Alsace/Haute Alsace**	**Main valley**	**Neckar valley and Alsace**	**Rhein-Neckar Kreis**	**Pfalz**
	Jeunesse (1999); Lefranc (2007a)	Meier-Arendt (1966)	Strien (2000)	Lindig (2002)	Jeunesse *et al.* (2009)
Jüngste Bandkeramik	V	V	9 (not in Neckar)	VI	V
Jüngere Bandkeramik	IVb IVa	IV	8 7 6	V IVb	IVb IVa
Flomborn/ Mittlere Bandkeramik	III	III	5 4 3	IVa IIIb IIIa	IIIb IIIa
Ältere Bandkeramik	II	II	2B 2A	II	II
Älteste Bandkeramik		I	1	I	

followed shortly afterwards, illustrating the affiliations and networks formed by the communities in the micro-regions of Baden-Württemberg (Heide 2001; Lindig 2002). More recently, Jeunesse *et al.* (2009) have indentified a further cultural group in the Pfalz, which although mainly falling beyond Baden-Württemberg is relevant for discussion here as it includes the Schwetzingen cemetery. The chronology of Strien (2000; 2005) divides the LBK into nine phases, but it is the five-phase chronology of Meier-Arendt (1966) which continues to be the basis for cultural sequencing in the absence of a significant series of radiocarbon dates.

7.2 History of research

The first LBK finds in Baden-Württemberg came to light towards the end of the nineteenth century, with the first synthesis of finds following in 1908 (Wagner 1908; 1911). Since then a number of different catalogues have been produced, such as by Albert and Schröter (1971) and Kraft (1977). These were mostly lists of all the finds attributed to the LBK but they also considered issues of chronology as well. As we saw in Chapter 6 for Bavaria, the development of archaeological studies is influenced by activities of the regional *Denkmalpflege*. After the Second World War, the first law in Baden-Württemberg ensuring the conservation of historic buildings and monuments was passed in 1949, ultimately leading to the formation of the regional *Denkmalpflege* in 1962 (www.3). State-directed excavations are recorded in various journals leading to good coverage of the sites discovered, but only a few sites received more substantial publication. The activities of the *Denkmalpflege* continue to dominate the investigation of archaeology in this region.

For a long time, the LBK of Baden-Württemberg played a rather muted role in wider studies, overshadowed by the excavations on the Aldenhovener Platte in the 1960s and 1970s. The last 40 years, however, have brought greater investigation and discussion of regional boundaries and affiliation, and, ultimately, have ignited debate on cultural identity and origin. The exceptional find of the mass grave at Talheim (Wahl and König 1987; Wahl and Trautmann 2012) has attracted significant attention to the human remains themselves, but not to their regional context. Instead, focus has been on the early part of the LBK, with the sizeable assemblage of La Hoguette ware in Baden-Württemberg resulting in significant debate throughout much of the 1990s about the beginning and nature of transmission of the LBK and farming practices (Lüning *et al.* 1989; Tillman 1993; Kind 1997; 1998). Yet, even here, there is a tendency for individual sites to be taken as examples for the LBK as a whole, rather than set within their immediate regional context.

In contrast to this approach, Strien (2000) was the first to consider the ceramic and lithic remains in Baden-Württemberg for their chronological significance in comparison with other regions of the LBK. This was followed shortly afterwards by revised chronologies for the Kraichgau (between Heilbronn and the Rhine; Heide 2001) and the Rhein-Neckar *Kreis* (also known as the Neckarmündungsgebiet; Lindig 2002). More recently Jeunesse *et al.* (2009, 76) produced a new seriation for pottery in this region, further sub-dividing the LBK around the Rhine-Neckar confluence into three groups (Rhine-Main, Neckar and Pfalz, which stretches from Worms southwards to Landau, primarily on the west bank of the Rhine). The new Pfalz group is thought to include Schwetzingen, the cemetery site sampled here. Table 7.1 shows how the various chronologies relate to each other (following Gerling 2006; 2012, 113; Lefranc 2007a). Unfortunately, there has been little consistent radiocarbon dating carried out in the region and this remains a priority for the future. To this end, 11 dates from the Schwetzingen cemetery were obtained as part of this project, the results of which are discussed below (and in more detail in Appendix B1).

Today, a lively debate continues on the beginning and end of the LBK in Baden-Württemberg. The persistence and survival of hunter-gatherers, as well as the arrival of the LBK, continue to be debated, while increasing evidence for violent events at the end of the LBK has given renewed attention to Talheim (e.g. Wahl and Trautmann 2012). Substantial and significant isotope analysis has been carried out in the region; in fact it was here that the first attempts to investigate LBK mobility through the study of strontium isotopes took place (Price *et al.* 2001; 2002; Bentley *et al.* 2002). Knipper (2004; 2009; 2011; Bentley and Knipper 2005b) has mapped the biologically available strontium values across southern Germany and consequently, for strontium isotopes at least, it is one of the best known regions under study in this project. However, many questions remain about both the social formation of LBK communities (Jeunesse 1996; 1997; Strien 2000; Bentley *et al.* 2003; Eisenhauer 2003a; 2003b) and the nature of long-distance contact and exchange (Strien 2010a).

7.3 Arrival and development of the LBK

As we have seen in previous chapters, many LBK scholars have grown comfortable with a model of Neolithic expansion into central Europe that envisages a mixture of incoming farmers and indigenous groups, the latter perhaps leading a way of life that was based predominantly on hunting and gathering but which might also have included experimentation with cereal growing and pottery (e.g. La Hoguette ware; Lüning *et al.* 1989; Gronenborn 1990; 1999; 2007a; Tillman 1993; Nielsen 1994; Whittle 1996; Kind 1992; 1997; 1998; Jeunesse 2000a; 2000b; 2001; 2003b; Jochim 2000; cf. Allard 2005; 2007; see also Chapter 6.3). Despite a broad convergence on the occurrence of 'admixture', the extent of contact and speed of change continue to challenge current models and we are still some distance from comprehending how such cultural interactions worked on the ground (although it was the mechanisms of this transition that the earliest applications of strontium isotope studies to the LBK first set out to investigate: Price *et al.* 2001). So the nature of contacts, interactions and transformations from around 5500 cal BC has been heavily contested, with, as yet, little agreement (Tillman 1993; Whittle 1996; Kind 1997; 1998; Gronenborn 1999; Gehlen 2006). Baden-Württemberg is an interesting region for tackling these problems as it forms the south-western limit of the earliest (*älteste*) phase of the LBK and La Hoguette ware is present within a supposed final Mesolithic substrate.

The end of the Mesolithic in Baden-Württemberg is characterised, as elsewhere in central Europe, by a drop in the number of known sites (Jochim 1990; 1998; Jochim *et al.* 1998). Temporarily occupied hunting-fishing camps, both open-air and in rock shelters, are found in south-west Germany during the Mesolithic, alongside longer-occupied base camps (Gronenborn 1999, 136; Kind 2006, 252). These sites illustrate highly diverse subsistence strategies based on hunting and foraging, which seem to vary in turn with the different environments of south-west Germany (Kind 2006). These sites are characterised by the presence of trapezoidal microliths and regular blades (Gehlen 2006, 42). In this region, the Late Mesolithic, the Final Mesolithic and La Hoguette groups are largely treated as separate entities, distinguished on the basis of the presence or absence of certain flint artefacts as stone tool production processes did not differ significantly (Gehlen 2006, 42). The Late Mesolithic is thought to have come to an end shortly after 5800 cal BC (roughly estimated from available radiocarbon dates of variable quality), while the Final Mesolithic and La Hoguette are then thought to co-exist until after the arrival in the region of the LBK (Gehlen 2006, 42–3). To this mix we can also potentially add the *Buchauer Gruppe*, which was proposed by Kind (1992; 1997) and is based on his excavations at the Baden-Württemberg site of Henauhof-Nord II. The Final Mesolithic, La Hoguette and LBK groups are thought to have lived alongside each other for at least 200 years from 5500 cal BC if not longer (Lüning *et al.* 1989; Kind 1997; 1998; 2006; Gronenborn 1998; 1999; Strien 2000; Manen and Mazurié de Keroualin 2003; Gehlen 2006).

7.3.1 Hunter-gatherers who farmed? The Final Mesolithic

The chronological overlap between different groups, the degree to which lithic assemblages demonstrate continuity, the evidence for early cereal growing and, ultimately, the role of indigenous groups in the arrival of the LBK, all continue to be the major points of contention in the literature for this region (Jochim 2008, 219). Although there is much overlap between the different models for the arrival of the LBK, what is at stake is the extent of adoption of domesticates and pottery before that date, and whether indigenous groups were assimilated into the LBK soon after its arrival or in a more drawn-out process. Determining the nature of human interactions which formed the social network at this time is crucial to understanding the extensive transformations of this period. The characteristics of LBK-Mesolithic exchanges are very difficult to pin down and seem to vary across different categories of evidence and sites. Kind (1992; 1997) suggests, at least on the basis of the evidence from the open-air site of Henauhof-Nord II,[1] that there was little interaction between indigenous and incoming groups during the early Neolithic and, hence, sees the LBK as responsible for the arrival of farming. However, he presents a somewhat different argument for the Mesolithic open-air sites at Rottenburg-Siebenlinden, where he argues that indigenous involvement in the transition to agriculture built up to a 'point of no return', while envisioning a reduced role for incomers (Kind 1998; 2006; 2010).

Principally, the final Mesolithic is considered to be represented by different hunter-gatherer groups, one of which produced a pottery style known as La Hoguette. La Hoguette pottery is present in the earliest phases of about ten LBK sites in the Neckar valley,[2] though more sites continue to be found, and also at a small number of non-LBK sites (Manen and Mazurié de Keroualin 2003, 118; Gehlen 2006, 44, 49).[3] Studies of La Hoguette and LBK ceramic fabrics at the LBK site of Bruchenbrücken (in the Wetterau, north of Baden-Württemberg) showed that they were both made out of local clays (Eisenhauer 2003a), while the lithic assemblage at the site appears to have elements of the Mesolithic repertoire (Gronenborn 1990, 178; Gehlen 2006, 44; Mateiciucová 2008a, 73). For Gronenborn (2007b, 80) this meant that both groups were living side-by-side in what ostensibly appear to be 'LBK villages'.

However, Strien (2000, 78, our translation) argues that La Hoguette ceramic designs are 'genetically independent' from the LBK and posits an earlier start date for this pottery. Based on ceramic styles, connections between La Hoguette ware and the southern French Cardial ceramic groups appear stronger than those to the LBK world (Constantin 1985; Manen and Mazurié de Keroualin 2003; Jeunesse and van Willigen 2010).[4] La Hoguette vessels were decorated using spatulas of two, three, four or six points (Crombé 2009, 481). Manen and Mazurié de Keroualin (2003, 138) argue that La Hoguette pottery developed through contacts between the Cardial groups and more northerly hunter-gatherers, which existed along the Rhône valley at some point between 5800 and 5600/5500 cal BC, but this has been contested (van Berg 1990; Constantin and Vachard 2004; Crombé 2009, 482). Yet La Hoguette pottery-using groups are spread out in areas around the Doubs, the upper Rhine and Neckar valleys, and therefore predominantly in areas of LBK settlement. At some point, perhaps from as early as 5500 cal BC, these hunter-gatherers came into contact with LBK groups from the east (Gehlen 2006, 49) and their chronology appears from then on to be bound up in changes within the LBK (Jeunesse 1987; Lüning *et al.* 1989; Strien 2000, 77; Manen and Mazurié de Keroualin 2003; Gehlen 2006).

Pottery, in the early Neolithic at least, appears to be very much a social medium and could have been associated, perhaps, with feasting (Robb and Miracle 2007, 113). It is, therefore, a conspicuous medium for communication, not only at the point of creation but also during use (Dobres 1995; Sommer 2001). LBK and La Hoguette wares differ in two important ways: in chosen temper (La Hoguette pots contained temper such as bone and shell, while early LBK ones employed coarse chaff; Lüning *et al.* 1989; Cladders 1997b; 2001; Sommer 2001, 252), as well as in surface design. While the chosen temper neither varies nor is found mixed, there are rare instances of La Hoguette designs on LBK fabrics (LBK designs are not found outside LBK contexts; Cladders 2001), demonstrating that innovation was possible, but not really explored by either set of users. La Hoguette ware was also possibly made for ostentatious display, particularly in the areas around the Rhine and Neckar rivers (Pétrequin *et al.* 2009, 513). If we take into consideration the contexts of production and use, this may demonstrate that the respective production techniques of LBK and La Hoguette wares were not on 'show' to the same extent as design and decoration. Aggregations of different groups could have encompassed the sharing of food and drink and consequently involved more opportunity for pottery style to be displayed to a wider group than the fabrication of the ceramic ware, which may well have been carried out in a more closed context (such as being passed on between the generations from mother to daughter: Sommer 2001).

Internal differences within La Hoguette designs have also been identified. Styles vary not only left and right of the Rhine, but within Baden-Württemberg itself (Lüning *et al.* 1989, 381–2; Manen and Mazurié de Keroualin 2003, 136, 138). Some of these differences may be chronological; La Hoguette is associated with the *älteste* LBK east of the Rhine, but with the later *Rubané ancien* in the west (Table 7.1; Jeunesse 1987, 18; Lüning *et al.* 1989, 385), and differences within Baden-Württemberg occurred between contemporary groups. While evidence for contact with LBK groups is rare, it does not follow that it was insubstantial, distant or the same across the geographical and chronological distribution of La Hoguette material. Whilst at Bruchenbrücken La Hoguette ware is found associated with six of the seven earliest phase houses (some 100 sherds in total; Lüning *et al.* 1989, 364), other sites boast no more than a couple of sherds (though the size of sherds varies enormously; Lüning *et al.* 1989, 367–70). At the site of Rottenburg-Fröbelweg (*älteste* LBK), Kind (2010, 452) describes hundreds of objects as 'belonging to La Hoguette'. While we should be wary of equating the amount of pottery found with the number of people present, it does suggest variety in contact.

Aside from the presence of this alternative ceramic ware, the different cultural traditions can also be identified in the lithic assemblages (Gehlen 2006; Mateiciucová 2008a). Gehlen (2006, 43) argues that although La Hoguette pottery has much in common with Cardial ware, the lithics associated with this group do not influence La Hoguette assemblages. Rather, it seems that La Hoguette-associated lithics share similarities with late Mesolithic groups in central and south-west France (particularly triangular arrowheads with facial retouch: Gehlen 2006, 43). However, at Rottenburg (*älteste* LBK), some of the lithic tools have been fashioned from a flint (*silex à bryozoe*) which is sourced along the Saône river (Kind 2010, 453–4). The connection between the LBK and the south/central-eastern parts of France therefore echoes the shared ceramic styles of La Hoguette and Cardial, and may suggest that the LBK was adopting or maintaining Mesolithic networks (a potential Cardial sherd was found in Alsace; Chapter 8.3).

The production techniques of regular blades (direct percussion: Mesolithic; punch technique: Neolithic) should allow us to trace whether Mesolithic groups were present on early LBK sites (Mateiciucová 2008a, 78). Such examples of Mesolithic production techniques were present at Bruchenbrücken (Wetterau), Mintranching (Bavaria) and Enkingen (Bavaria), and some possible examples are also present at Schwanfeld (near the Main river, northern Bavaria; Mateiciucová 2008a, 78), though the importance of indigenous communities in the Bavarian *älteste* LBK has been downplayed by regional specialists (Pechtl 2010; Chapter 6.3). Gehlen (2006, 44) lists two other possible LBK sites from Baden-Württemberg itself: Rottenburg-Fröbelweg (also discussed by Kind 1998; 2006; 2010) and Ammerbuch. At Rottenburg-Fröbelweg, similarities to nearby lithic assemblages occur alongside the appearance of tools novel to the region such as perforators and sickle blades (Kind 2010, 453). The production of regular blades in LBK contexts has, on the whole, been taken as evidence for the indigenous contribution to the LBK (Tillmann 1993; Gronenborn 1997b; Kind 1998; Gehlen 2006; Mateiciucová 2008a). However, their presence varies across the LBK, with Tillmann (1993) arguing that the indigenous contribution is far stronger in its southern distribution.

Other differences between the LBK and final Mesolithic groups may also be indicated by varied economic strategies. Stuttgart-Bad Cannstatt, contemporary with the earliest LBK in the region, has a small faunal assemblage but is not associated with LBK finds (Gronenborn 1999, 140; 2007b; Meurers-Balke and Kalis 2001).[5] Roe and red deer, aurochs and wild boar are present at this site alongside domesticated sheep/goat but, in contrast to the LBK, no domestic cattle were identified (Meurers-Balke and Kalis 2001; Gronenborn 2007b, 80). Consequently, Gronenborn (2007b, 80–2) refers to the La Hoguette group as 'herders' and 'pastoralists' (one assumes of sheep/goats) as well as 'hunter-gatherers', living at 'multi-tradition farming villages'. Thus he supports (Gronenborn 2007b) the naming by Jeunesse (2001) of La Hoguette as a *Néolithique initial* rather than terminal 'Mesolithic' group. However, as Gehlen (2006, 51) argues, the small domestic faunal assemblage at Stuttgart Bad-Cannstatt is not seen at other possible La Hoguette sites in the vicinity and at Stuttgart Bad-Cannstatt only four square metres were ever excavated (Crombé 2009, 483). Furthermore, the tendency to see the LBK as a unified phenomenon, caring for predominantly domesticated animals, may hide internal differences; at a nearby *älteste* LBK site, also called Rottenburg-Fröbelweg, domestic animals only formed 10% of the assemblage, which is otherwise dominated by wild species such as red deer, roe deer and wild boar (Stephan 2005; Kind 2010, 454)[6] and this may suggest that further attention to site use (what activities were taking place at a site) may be beneficial in future considerations of La Hoguette, early LBK and the Final Mesolithic.

Other hints that La Hoguette groups may have been aware of domesticates comes in the form of cereal pollen which is claimed to be present in the pollen record from early in the seventh millennium across a wide area north of the Alps (Erny-Rodmann *et al.* 1997; Meurers-Balke and Kalis 2001; cf. Behre 2007a; 2007b; Tinner *et al.* 2007). However, whether this represents even small-scale growing of cereals has been severely critiqued. Behre (2007a; 2007b) dismisses the presence of cereal pollen as direct evidence for agriculture, stresses the ambiguities still present in techniques of pollen identification (many are or could be large wild grasses) and points out contradictions in the way in which the pollen diagrams were interpreted. At Stuttgart-Bad Cannstatt, the pollen grains are regarded as illustrating threshing rather than growing, despite such processing activity generally producing much more pollen than is present at the site, something which Meurers-Balke and Kalis (2001) acknowledge themselves (Behre 2007a, 210). Behre (2007a, 215) asserts that unless securely dated macroscopic cereal remains are present at a site there is no certain evidence for agriculture. We are, on this basis, forced to throw out most, if not all, of the evidence for early cereal growing in this region (cf. Gehlen 2006; Jeunesse 2003b).[7] This leaves us with very little evidence, where the presence of independent La Hoguette groups has been suggested, that they had any involvement with a Neolithic way of life as experienced by LBK communities, beyond making and using pottery, even if cereals and domesticated animals were consumed on rare occasions. Their subsistence activities seem to be chiefly based on hunting and gathering, with domestic animals an opportunistic addition to the diet (Kind 2010, 456).

We are still left asking, therefore, what form interaction between the two groups took, and the nature of contact seems enormously varied. La Hoguette ware, when found on LBK sites, is not present in separate contexts to LBK pottery (Lüning *et al.* 1989; Reim 1992; Manen and Mazurié de Keroualin 2003; Gehlen 2006); it is not possible on LBK settlements to identify specifically 'La Hoguette' longhouses (which have only this pottery present in the associated loam pits), nor areas associated with different lithic technologies. Therefore, the evidence points towards a loosely affiliated group of hunter-gatherers, who took opportunities as they arose (Bird-David 1990; 1992; Grinker 1994; Ingold 1996a; 1996b; Robb and Miracle 2007, 112; D. Hofmann forthcoming). If a separate group of people were producing La Hoguette ware in LBK contexts, they were doing so while still being part of 'LBK' households. We have tended, therefore, to be over-reliant on the label 'La Hoguette' as standing for a homogeneous group.

The history of La Hoguette pottery suggests that when the LBK began in the region under discussion here, a 'Neolithic' way of life was not alien to indigenous groups – domesticates were known. The presence of La Hoguette pottery in LBK assemblages could signal exchange between different groups or people moving into LBK households. This explanation is reminiscent of the Mesolithic-Neolithic transition model which argues that the arrival of farming in a region populated with hunter-gatherers would result in a one-way movement of young women 'marrying' into farming groups (Zvelebil 1996; 2000; 2004; Zvelebil and Dolukhanov 1991). However, as our discussion has shown, this probably was neither a universal nor a universalising experience (cf. Zvelebil 1996; 2000; 2004). In contrast to the emphasis placed on the evidence for early farming in recent decades, the decision of indigenous people to bring pottery into their material repertoire has gone largely without comment. Similarly, changes in lithic technologies are largely viewed as a convenient second medium for archaeologists to test 'Mesolithic-ness' and 'Neolithic-ness', rather than signalling the arrival of a different range of daily tasks. This is not to say that identification with certain groups did not matter, but rather to re-formulate the question away from what *the* relationship between the 'LBK' and 'La Hoguette' was like towards considering what the visible possibilities and contexts of social relations were. In all likelihood, therefore, when the LBK arrived in this region it came into direct contact with indigenous groups, which included a scale of relations that went from inter-marriage to far more distant and infrequent interactions.

At the time when the LBK arrived in the region, clusters of longhouses may well have been the setting in which people living different ways of life were drawn closer together (Whittle 1996; 2003). The arrival of the earliest LBK in Baden-Württemberg may not therefore have been straightforward. While the homogeneity of the earliest LBK has frequently been commented on, some differences between sites on the Neckar and Lower Rhine-Meuse regions and those further east (Slovakia, Moravia, Bohemia, Lower Austria and Lower Bavaria) were noted by Modderman (1988). Gehlen argues (2006, 49–50), on the basis of the distribution of La Hoguette pottery, that a cultural border existed in the early Neolithic between Baden-Württemberg and Bavaria; La Hoguette ware certainly does not reach far into Bavaria (Manen and Mazurié de Keroualin 2003; Gehlen 2006). This boundary had previously been identified for the whole of the LBK by Modderman (1988, 69) in both ceramic techniques and styles, but Cladders (1997b) argues that such differences in the earliest LBK pottery are only visible in complex statistical analysis and may not have been obvious to the potters themselves (see also Sommer 2001). More recently, however, the notion of regional differences in pottery from the earliest LBK has gained currency again (Lenneis 2004b; Strien 2005).

When the first LBK communities moved up the Neckar valley into Baden-Württemberg, this was not necessarily just the 'Neolithic' confronting the 'Mesolithic', nor the 'LBK' meeting 'La Hoguette'. Lithics ascribed to different traditions are found together at Bruchenbrücken and Goddelau (Hessen; Tillmann 1993; Gronenborn 1997b; Mateiciucová 2008a) and certain traits remain part of the LBK lithic toolkit after La Hoguette-style pottery is no longer made (cf. Allard 2005); Final Mesolithic and La Hoguette groups leave their mark on Flomborn LBK groups in the form of triangular points and local elongated trapezes and in raw material networks of Maas valley flint and Swabian Alb cherts (Strien 2000, 74; Gronenborn 2007b, 80; though new LBK lithic exchange networks were also created). La Hoguette pottery is thought to have disappeared during the Flomborn phase east of the Rhine (Strien 2000; Gronenborn 2007b), and for Gronenborn (2007b) this represents the assimilation of the herder/hunter La Hoguette group into the LBK. This may well be the case: piecemeal adoption of new kinds of existence by opportunity-taking hunter-gatherers whose affiliations came to be caught up in LBK networks and lifeways. The speed at which this took place, however, still needs to be determined.

7.4 Regional networks and diversity: the developed and late LBK

The persistence of foragers after the *älteste* LBK continues to be contested (Tillmann 1993; Whittle 1996; Kind

1997; 1998; Strien 2000; Jeunesse 2001), though from the discussion above it seems most likely that, in Baden-Württemberg at least, the middle LBK (Table 7.1; Phase III; Meier-Arendt 1966; Phase 4; Strien 2000) developed as the last La Hoguette pottery was made. In parallel to the *Notenkopf* style (discussed in Chapters 4 and 5), the second phase of the LBK is known in western regions as the Flomborn and the process by which it developed is sometimes referred to as 'Flombornisation'. As in other regions of the LBK, this phase is characterised by increasing regionalisation across the LBK, recognised most readily in a diversification of ceramic decoration, but also in lithic technologies, animal husbandry and cereal growing, architectural styles and burial practices (Modderman 1988; Jeunesse 1997; Whittle 1996; Coudart 1998; Sommer 2001; Cladders and Stäuble 2003; Frirdich 2003; Bogaard 2004; Pechtl 2009b).

At this time the LBK expands into new areas, sites in regions already occupied increased in number, and the large cemeteries such as Flomborn and Stuttgart-Mühlhausen began. Some long-running settlements, such as Gerlingen (Neth 1999) and Vaihingen (Krause 1998; 2003; Strien 2005; Bogaard *et al.* 2011), have evidence of the earliest LBK phases but many early sites are abandoned at this time and new sites occupied nearby (Strien 2000). The apparent growth in the number of identifiable differences between regions occurs alongside greater diversification both within Baden-Württemberg and within individual settlements, such as Vaihingen. In this section, we examine some of the networks in place across Baden-Württemberg and question what the different scales of diversity mean for the formation of community relationships and individual lifeways in the LBK.

7.4.1 Settlement networks

Continuity from the end of the *älteste* LBK into the Flomborn or middle LBK is a matter of some debate (Stäuble 1995; Sommer 2001; Cladders and Stäuble 2003; Lüning 2005a; Schade-Lindig and Schade 2010). Few *älteste* sites see continuous occupation and those that do appear to be reorganised at this time (Stäuble 1995; Gronenborn 1999; Neth 1999; Strien 2000; Sommer 2001; Cladders and Stäuble 2003; Schade-Lindig and Schade 2010). At the long-running settlement of Gerlingen (*c.* 5 km west of Stuttgart), the longhouses change orientation, from approximately north–south to north-east–south-west, and there is an apparent hiatus in occupation (Neth 1999, 175–9). During phase 3, two houses are found about 100 m to the west of the rest of the settlement and then, from the beginning of phase 4, the earliest areas are occupied again (Neth 1999, 100, 170). It is at this site that Strien (2000, 51) identifies the first instances of the Flomborn style in phase 2A. A similar change in house orientation is also seen at Vaihingen, suggesting some community-wide reorganisation (Krause 1998; Cladders and Stäuble 2003, 501). The change in house orientation is also seen more widely across the LBK and this practice appears to echo the adoption of Flomborn ceramic decoration; organic tempers also decrease in use (Schade-Lindig and Schade 2010, 464).

However, at Bad Friedrichshall (10 km north of Heilbronn in the Neckar valley), no changes in settlement layout or house orientation between the *älteste* LBK and Flomborn could be determined (Cladders and Stäuble 2003, 501). With this variability in the history of different settlements, Cladders and Stäuble (2003, 502) argue that the transition to the middle LBK did not happen at the same time everywhere and, indeed, that *älteste* LBK groups may have initially lived alongside 'Flomborn' groups.[8] The Flomborn style appears to have spread quickly, suggesting strong inter-regional contacts across the LBK and possibly even another period of colonisation taking the LBK west of the Rhine (Schade-Lindig and Schade 2010). However, the continuity of site use in Baden-Württemberg may be an exception, with other areas of the LBK demonstrating a larger break between *älteste* LBK and middle LBK groups (Cladders and Stäuble 2003; Schade-Lindig and Schade 2010).

Alongside continuity in site use, Baden-Württemberg settlements show dense clustering of houses, with many overlapping house plans (Kind 1989; Krause 1998; Neth 1999, 183; Bogaard *et al.* 2011). Even at smaller settlements, such as Singen am Hohentwiel, Konstanz (Aufdermauer *et al.* 1985), houses seem to be preferentially built close together. This form of spatial organisation is also seen on settlements in Bohemia (e.g. Bylany: Pavlů 2000b) and Bavaria (e.g. Stephansposching: Pechtl 2009a), but not further north and west, on the Aldenhovener Platte (e.g. Langweiler 8: Krahn 2003), in Haute-Alsace (e.g. Sierentz: Lefranc 2001; 2007a; Lefranc and Denaire 2000; Chapter 8) and the Paris basin (e.g. Cuiry-lès-Chaudardes: Coudart 1998; Hachem 2011; comment in Bogaard *et al.* 2011). Recent excavations have shown similar dense and overlapping house plans in Basse-Alsace, at Bischoffsheim (Lefranc *et al.* 2004; Lefranc 2007c) and in the Nordrhein-Westphalia region, at the site of Erkelenz-Kückhoven (Lehmann 2004; Nockemann 2008). The similarity in settlement patterns between Basse-Alsace and Baden-Württemberg strengthens the model of Jeunesse (1995b; 1996; 1997), which connects these two areas in burial practices (burial tradition II; Chapter 8). While it is thus tempting to suggest a regional preference for intensely nucleated settlements, Erkenlenz-Kückhoven is close to sites such as those on the Aldenhovener Platte, which have more widely spaced buildings. So while some regions tend towards certain settlement densities, there are clear variations, even between nearby settlements. Furthermore, the 'yard' model developed at more widely spaced settlements on the Aldenhovener Platte may also apply to sites where longhouses are built closer together, such as Bischoffsheim (Lefranc *et al.* 2004, 63–5) and Vaihingen (Krause 1998; Strien 2005; Bogaard *et al.* 2011).

As one of the longest-lived (occupied from the *älteste* LBK through to the late phases) and most densely packed settlements in the Neckar Valley, Vaihingen an der Enz has approximately 100 longhouses partly enclosed by a ditch (Krause 1998; Bentley *et al.* 2003; Strien 2005; Bogaard

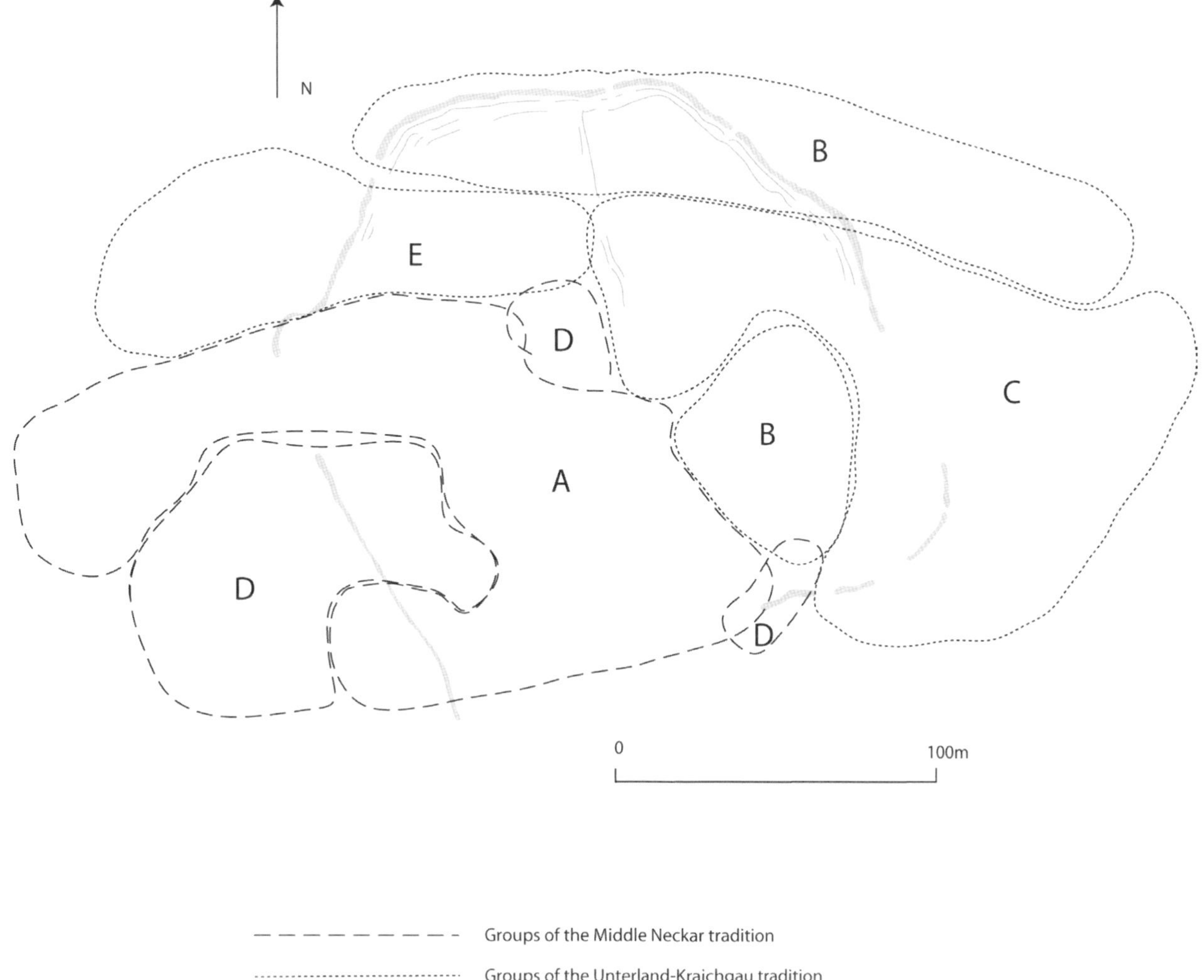

Fig. 7.2. Vaihingen: plan showing outline of enclosure and palisades and approximate extent of the clan groups and subgroupings. Compiled from data in Bogaard et al. *(2011) and Strien (2005).*

et al. 2011). Strien (2005, 189) estimates that there are 17 phases of construction at Vaihingen on the basis of ceramic seriation, with the ditch which encloses most of the settlement dating to the Flomborn period. Based on ceramic analysis across groupings of houses, Strien (2005) argues that the population at Vaihingen was made up of different 'clans' and lineages which are primarily visible in the ceramic and lithic assemblages; while one group used a type of 'Mesolithic' arrowhead (group B), another decorated their pottery with designs of Transdanubian origin (group A) and it may be possible to sub-divide these groups further (Bogaard *et al.* 2011). Differences between groups are not straightforward nor limited to single categories of evidence; instead, we see diversity in both material culture and subsistence practices (Fig. 7.2).

The botanical remains at Vaihingen varied between the 'clans' indicating that each group pursued a slightly different cultivation strategy (identified in the weed spectrum), and thus it is highly likely that house groups were using different fields (Bogaard *et al.* 2011). Bogaard *et al.* (2011) argue that this variation is due to the distance at which the fields of each group were situated away from the settlement. Intensity of soil disturbance is thought to drop off with a move away from the immediate area around Vaihingen, as the visiting of fields became more time-consuming. The connection between household groups and fields remained constant throughout the life of the settlement, suggesting that these differences were an inherent part of the structure of the settlement. The enclosure ditch also appeared to be segmented with perhaps each group responsible for a different length of the ditch (Bogaard *et al.* 2011). Despite this, Bogaard (*et al.* 2011) also stress the communal nature of life at Vaihingen as the main cereal crop does not vary across the settlement. So constituent groups within the LBK community at Vaihingen were doing the same things differently and patterns of difference were constant over time between the groups.

Similar divisions of LBK settlements have also been seen elsewhere and in other forms of evidence. At Cuiry-lès-Chaudardes, in the Paris basin, Hachem (1997; 2000; 2011) demonstrated that domesticated animal remains varied across the settlement, with different houses having

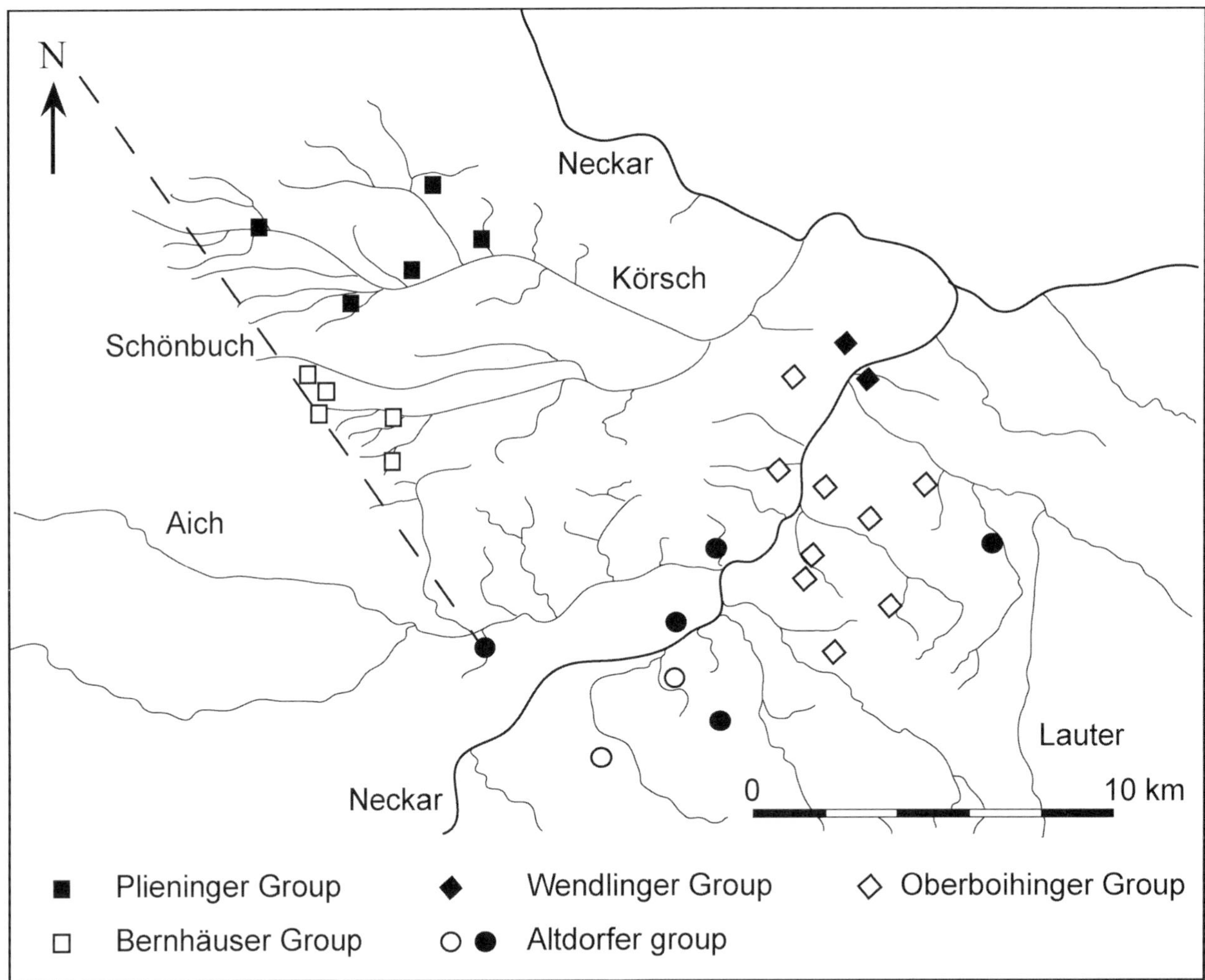

Fig. 7.3. The settlement groups of the middle Neckar valley. After Strien (2000, 33).

particular concentrations of cattle, wild boar and sheep/goats. Nockemann (2008) also identified differences within lithic technologies at Erkelenz-Kückhoven and Weisweiler (Nordrhein-Westphalia). At Erkelenz-Kückhoven the frequency of certain tools varied across the settlement, with arrowheads and borers more frequent in the north-west and blades with sickle gloss more common in the south-east (Nockemann 2008, 5). At Weisweiler the difference in raw materials used is rather stark; the house group outside the enclosure used different raw materials to those inside the enclosure (Nockemann 2008, 7). Differences in the lithic assemblages at Vaihingen can also be seen in the supply of raw materials and artefact types (Krause 2003; Strien 2005; Bogaard *et al.* 2011). Rijckholt flint (from the Maas basin) is associated with group C (Bogaard *et al.* 2011), and use of this flint declines at the end of the middle LBK (Zimmermann 1995, 16; Mateiciucová 2008a, 64). Mateiciucová (2008a, 163) and Nockemann (2008, 2) describe Rijckholt flint as high quality. On this basis, group C at Vaihingen has long-distance contacts to 'good' flint, while having 'poor' and more distant fields. A straightforward hierarchy may not have existed at Vaihingen, and difference within settlements may have been complex.

This picture of inter-related, yet autonomous, household groups, therefore, directly recalls the *Hofplatz* model (Chapter 1.3.2). Bogaard *et al.* (2011) emphasise the differences between wards at Vaihingen as unequal (some groups had access to closer fields with higher productivity), but they also stress that this did not lead to inequality or hierarchy at the settlement. Different ways of doing and being were not barriers to the creation of community. House groups with connections to the Kraichgau (north of Vaihingen, but still in Baden-Württemberg), which were possibly cultivating more distant fields, appear to leave Vaihingen at the end of the Flomborn phase, coinciding with a reduction in settlement size (Bogaard *et al.* 2011). Bogaard *et al.* (2011) infer that the group had been free to leave and suggest the relative position of their fields may have been a factor. The enclosure ditch also appears to have silted up completely by the end of the Flomborn phase, when a number of burials were deposited within it (Bentley *et al.* 2003; Bogaard *et al.* 2011), seemingly marking this change in the size of the settlement and hence the relationships between different groups. Clearly connections and networks beyond the immediate settlement impacted on specific site histories.

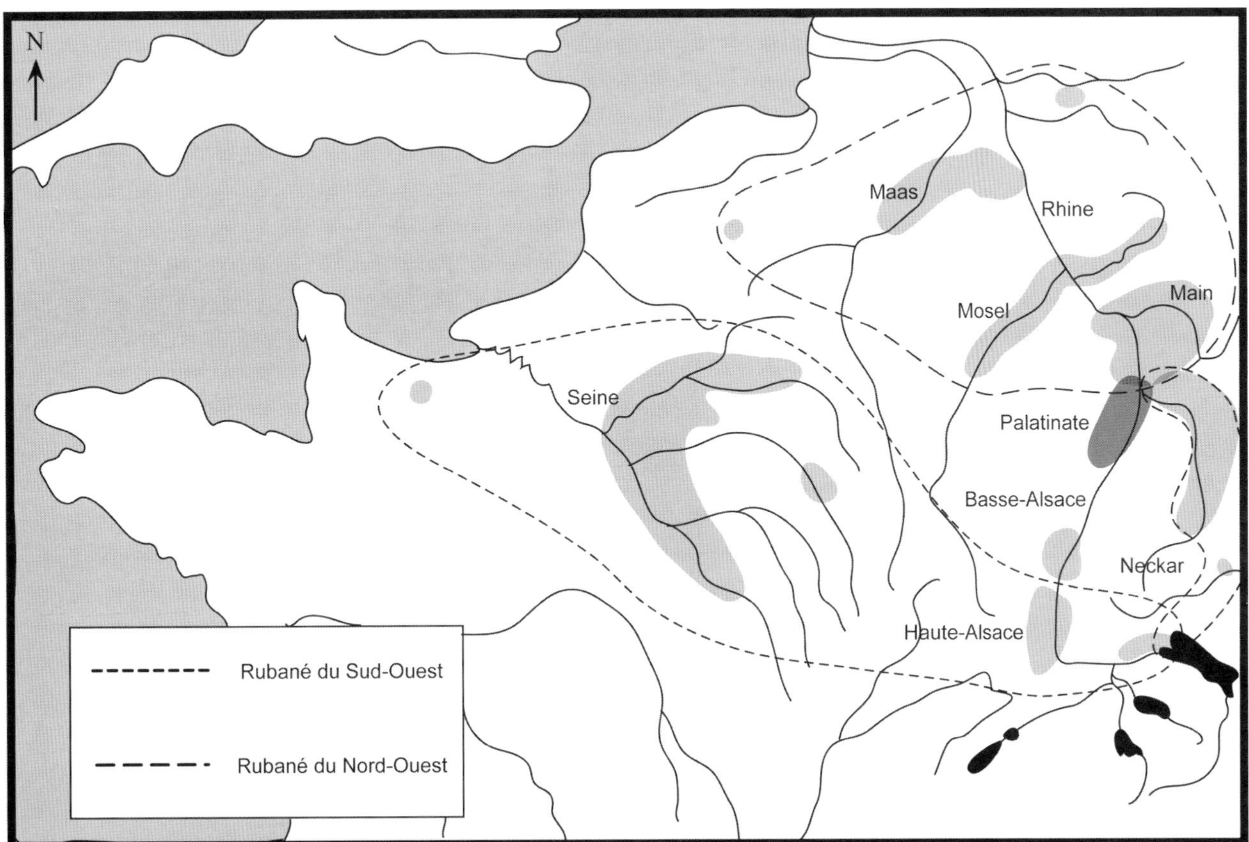

Fig. 7.4. The regional groups of the western LBK as envisaged by Jeunesse et al. *(2009, 76).*

7.4.2 Regional networks

Inter-site models of the LBK are often characterised as one central settlement surrounded by smaller 'daughter' settlements (Chapters 1.3.2 and 5.4; Whittle 1996, 144; Petrasch 2003, 510). Stehli (1989b) models this as a pioneer settlement colonising a region, with subsequent generations forming settlements nearby. Kin-based groups are widely envisioned, in which marriage relations were arranged through patrilocality (Strien 2000; Eisenhauer 2003a; 2003b; Claßen 2009; Bentley 2007). These local and regional connections are primarily recorded in similarities in ceramic and lithic styles and the movement of raw materials (Strien 2000; Lindig 2002; Blouet *et al.* 2007; Hauzeur 2007; Jeunesse *et al.* 2009), but also in architecture (Coudart 1998) and burial practices (Jeunesse 1996; 1997). The five groups which Strien (2000, chapter 4) identifies in the upper Neckar valley are not based on one single variation in their lithics, but rather on how the different forms in which raw material was transported, knapping techniques, percentages of burnt flint and its distribution across the settlement were combined (Fig. 7.3). So while the Altdorfer group combines a number of different practices, the Oberboihinger group is only recognised as a separate group in the raw materials it used (see also Chapter 1.3.6; Strien 2000, 31).

These five groups appear to be mainly geographical clusters based around the upper basins of tributaries of the Neckar river, occupying these areas over many generations and suggesting a relatively stable middle LBK period (Strien 2000, 32). Unlike the LBK in the upper Neckar valley (Strien 2000) and the group of sites in the upper Danube (Kind 1989; Jeunesse *et al.* 2009), it appears as if sites in the Pfalz began during phase IIa (from Meier-Arendt 1966; which corresponds to Strien's (2000) phases 2a and 2b; Jeunesse *et al.* 2009, 68). This is slightly earlier than sites in Alsace, which begin in phase IIb (Lefranc 2007a; Jeunesse *et al.* 2009, 69). From phase III, the Pfalz group has stronger affinities to the groups along the Neckar (Jeunesse *et al.* 2009, 73). The Rhine does not appear to be a barrier between different groups, as the cemetery at Schwetzingen and sites at the Neckar confluence show elements of the Pfalz group (Jeunesse *et al.* 2009, 73; Fig. 7.4). However, mere geographical proximity does not explain why certain characteristics should be found across some areas and not others, and, crucially, what form contact between the groups identified above took.

Regional ceramic styles appear to have been quite consistent, with mixed deposits appearing only on the boundaries between regions (Figs 7.4–5); for example, at Worms *Unter Platt*, elements of the Rhein-Main, Neckar and Pfalz group were all found together (Jeunesse *et al.* 2009, 74). This contrasts with particular decorative motifs that appear in more than one region, suggesting that the groups within a region tended to share alliances with surrounding regional groups (Chapter 1.3.6). Lines of impressed dots can be found in the upper Neckar

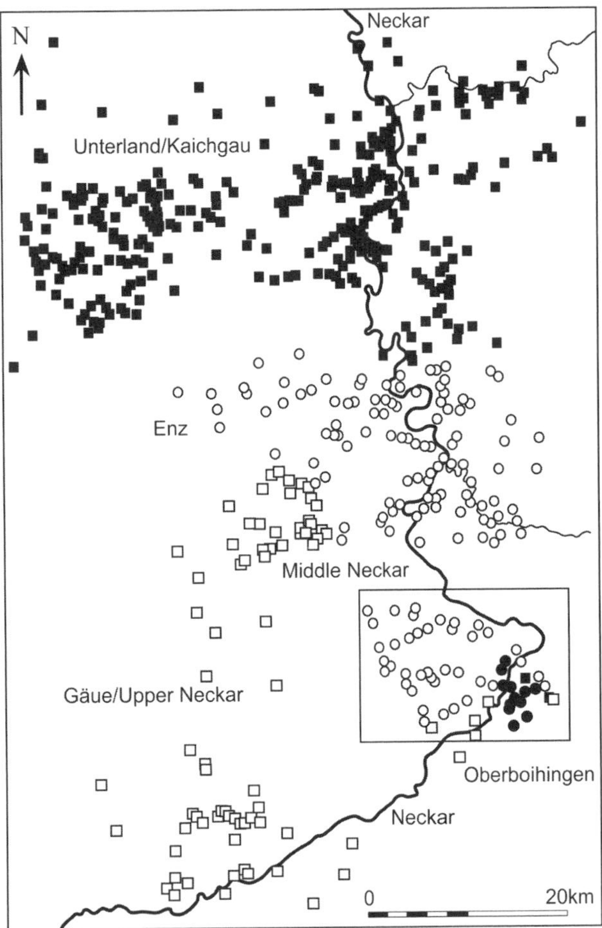

Fig. 7.5. Distribution of LBK regional groups in the Neckar valley. After Bogaard et al. *(2011, 404). Inset shown as Fig. 7.3.*

valley, Alsace, around the Moselle river, in the Paris basin (where the motif is produced using comb-technology) and possibly in the lower Main region; the rare 'grid patterns' (*Gittermuster*) are found around the Neckar, lower Main and in the Pfalz (Strien 2000, 53; Jeunesse *et al.* 2009, 73). For example, Hauzeur (2007, 77) found that groups in the Moselle valley had stronger contacts with other LBK groups in Lorraine, the Pfalz and Neckar area than elsewhere. This seems to vary over time, with sites in the French Moselle (Lorraine) apparently forming two groups in the later phases, while southern sites demonstrated continuing affiliations to the Neckar valley and northern groups concentrated on connections to the Rhine-Meuse area (Blouet *et al.* 2007, 96).

On a settlement level, pottery analysis has demonstrated that while some decorative motifs could be ascribed to specifically identified wards (as groups of 'yards; Chapter 1.3.2), *Zwickel* or secondary motifs appear to move across yards between settlement phases (Pavlů 2000; Krahn 2003; Strien 2005; Claßen 2009; Bogaard *et al.* 2011). Pechtl (forthcoming), following Sommer (2001), argues that the exchange of secondary motifs is best explained by patrilocal residence rules operating at LBK settlements. On this basis, women, who had learnt pottery production techniques from their mothers as children, had to adhere to the major or main motifs used by their husband's family but could continue to use the secondary motifs of their mothers (Pechtl 2009a; forthcoming). If this is the case, then the movement of secondary motifs between wards tracks the movement of women as they married into different groups present at the settlement. In this instance, this would mean women were not moving far from their place of birth.

For Strien (2000, 33), LBK pots were produced and decorated by women, and men controlled lithic technologies. While there was little change in how flints were processed throughout the life of a settlement, ceramic designs showed widespread similarities and frequent changes (Strien 2000, 33). Thus it has been envisaged that women were introducing decoration styles learnt from their parents' village to their husband's and over time taking on styles used by women in their new home (Kolhoff 1999, cited in Claßen 2009, 100). Strien (2000, 33, our translation) suggests that a woman 'native to Alsace had possibly married into the settlement of Echterdingen 7 [located 5 km south of Stuttgart] because of the combination of styles present on the sherds'.[9] However, as pottery from the Kaiserstuhl region shares many decorative features with Alsatian styles, from both Basse- and Haute-Alsace (Stöckl 1992, 10–12), the pottery styles used at Echterdingen 7 could have had more complex geographical origins. Marriage partners may thus have been sought in diverse regions, at some distance, and nearby. This model is, however, developed from large, multi-phase settlements such as Bylany (Pavlů 2000b), Langweiler 8 (Krahn 2003), Stephansposching (Pechtl 2009a) and Vaihingen (Strien 2005). The experience of those communities inhabiting smaller settlements may have differed.

7.4.3 Inter-regional networks

Surprisingly, Strien (2000, 53) could find little evidence, in either ceramic patterns or the lithic assemblage, that contacts had existed between Baden-Württemberg and LBK communities to the east. At the Danubian settlement of Ulm-Eggingen only two sherds could be said to have Bavarian designs (Strien 2010a, 502), and a sherd found at Neuhausen auf der Filden (10 km south-east of Stuttgart) had the only instance of a Šárka-style decoration found to date in this region (Strien 2000, 53). This is not the case in the middle Neolithic, when Großgartach and SBK pottery decorations are more similar and raw material from the Franconian Alb was a substantial part of the lithic assemblage (Strien 2000, 53). There are hints that these connections began to develop at the end of the LBK in the construction of a naviform house in the final phases of the settlement at Ulm-Eggingen (Kind 1989). This style of house is found in post-LBK cultures such as the SBK, which follows the LBK in Bavaria and elsewhere (Coudart 1998, 82; Jeunesse 2009, 158).

Conversely, however, evidence of contacts with Baden-Württemberg has been found in Bavaria in the form of ceramic motifs suggesting connections with the Unterland-

Kraichgau area of the Neckar valley (Strien 2010a, 503). A pot in grave 81 at the Bavarian cemetery of Aiterhofen has decoration in the Baden-Württemberg style and the size and shape of adzes in graves 12 and 61 suggest that they originate from the middle Neckar area (Strien 2010a, 499). Thus while finds in Baden-Württemberg indicate connections to the west, the relationship with its eastern neighbours was not reciprocated to the same extent or in the same materials (Strien 2010a). Contacts between LBK regions were therefore not simply stronger when geographically closer, dropping off as distances increased. Rather, it seems that particular relationships could be maintained over substantial distances; Strien (2010a, 502) suggests a greater exchange of pottery (in the form of decoration styles) between Bavaria and the Aldenhovener Platte, than between Bavaria and Baden-Württemberg, despite the latter pair being much closer. These long-distance contacts appear to be rather stable over the middle LBK, a period which could have lasted for as long as eleven generations (Strien 2010a), though it seems that more material was leaving Baden-Württemberg than getting in. This is particularly evident at the cemetery of Schwetzingen, where very few extra-regional contacts can be demonstrated (Gerling 2006; 2012, 122; Gerling and Francken 2007).

The site of Herxheim, a little to the north in the Pfalz, stands in rather stark contrast to other sites discussed here, as the material found at this site clearly illustrates that it was part of a much broader network (Zeeb-Lanz *et al.* 2009). Ceramic styles and lithics both point to wide networks of circulating material. It is particularly interesting to note that Wittlinger chert, which is so prevalent in the Kraichgau areas of the upper Neckar valley, is represented very poorly, while cherts originating in the more southerly uplands of the Franconian Jura or Swabian Alb appear more frequently in the assemblage (Zeeb-Lanz *et al.* 2009, 207). Given the potential number of dead who received funerary rites at this site, Herxheim clearly stands out as extraordinary in the archaeology of the LBK, but it seems firmly embedded in its social networks (Zeeb-Lanz *et al.* 2009; Boulestin *et al.* 2009).

What is not clear in any of the examples discussed above is whether finished pots were imported or exotic designs were being used to decorate locally made ceramics (Strien 2000, 53; Claßen 2009; Pechtl forthcoming). When the fabrics of pots with extra-regional designs were analysed from the settlement at Bad Nauheim-Nieder-Mörlen auf dem Hempler (Hessen), all but a few were made on local clays, but this was interpreted as population movement and a phase of colonisation at the beginning of the Flomborn phase (Schade-Lindig and Schade 2010, 471). Patterns of similarity in ceramic styles have been taken to represent either kin-based affiliation, directly related to the movement of women, or translated directly to population movement. Lithics, in contrast, are thought to relate to very different forms of movement and relationships. Claßen (2009, 101, author's emphasis) describes the exchange of raw flint as 'representative of *economic* relationships' between different settlements and regions. The raw materials used for the production of the lithic tool assemblage in Baden-Württemberg were more varied than in other regions, but were dominated by Wittlinger chert (as had been the case in the Mesolithic), which was circulated as rough cores, with the final tool produced on individual settlements (Gronenborn 1999, 165, 168; Strien 2000, 79). Wittlinger chert sources are found in the Swabian Alb and while most commonly found on sites in Baden-Württemberg, circulated material does reach to the Rhine-Main confluence (Gronenborn 1999, 165, 167–8). In contrast to the mobility suggested by pottery, this movement of lithics is frequently tied to masculine identities and to the lives of men, not least because polished stone tools occur most frequently in male graves (Jeunesse 1997; Strien 2000; Claßen 2009; D. Hofmann 2009a).

7.4.4 Animals and plants

Regional variation, as noted in Chapter 1, has also been seen in the relative frequency of different animal species and crop remains in LBK assemblages. Baden-Württemberg falls into Lüning's (2000, 59–61) zone two of cereal preferences, with emmer and einkorn dominating, but with barley and legumes also cultivated as well as some poppy. The biggest contrast to previous regions discussed in this project is the greater presence of barley and poppy in Baden-Württemberg (compare Chapters 3, 4, 5 and 6, though see Chapter 6.4.4.). Barley is often observed to cope better with poor growing conditions and on this basis Bogaard (2004, 148) suggests that this may signal higher productivity in growing conditions for glume wheats in those regions where barley is absent, but for the time being this remains speculation. However, Bogaard (2004, 149) does identify the Neckar and southern Baden-Württemberg areas as having lower productivity than sites in Bavaria, which perhaps hints at different emphases in cereal husbandry practices. However, as the evidence from Vaihingen demonstrates, there is substantial variation even on a local scale (Bogaard *et al.* 2011).

Amongst the animal bone assemblages, Baden-Württemberg shows one of the highest regional rates for pigs and sheep/goats (*c.* 40–50% of the animal bone assemblages), which is only slightly behind cattle (*c.* 43%; Döhle 1993, 115; Lüning 2000, 109; Knipper 2011, 18–20). However, the animal bone assemblages have vastly different rates of preservation and really only come from eight sites, many of which may only represent the *älteste* LBK phase (Knipper 2011, 18). As these values are crude prevalence rates, they may not give the true contribution of particular species to the diet, but differences between the regions do suggest that the emphasis on cattle did vary across the distribution of the LBK (Lüning 2000, 109). In her analysis of the animal bone assemblages from across the LBK, however, Knipper (2011, 34) emphasises the extreme variability of the data from Baden-Württemberg. If pigs were contributing a greater proportion of meat to the diet in Baden-Württemberg than in other regions, this could signal various different practices. Pigs are often kept close to the settlement and their prevalence at the expense of cattle may signal less mobility. It is also possible that the more Atlantic climate conditions found in the western distribution of the LBK were more suitable for pigs, leading to their thriving in this region. Rose-Marie Arbogast has also argued that varied rates of pig between north and south Alsace indicate openness of the landscape, with depressed rates of sheep/goats indicating a more forested landscape (Chapter 8.4.3).

About 39% of the animal bone assemblage from Baden-Württemberg has been classed as wild (Lüning 2000, 115): a rate surpassed only in Bavaria (Chapter 6.4.4). This value may conflate animal bone assemblages from both the *älteste* and *jüngere* phases and there is evidence to suggest chronological differences (Kind 1992; Knipper 2011). The rate of wild animals seems to decrease in the later phases of larger settlements and enclosures (such as the site of Heilbronn-Neckargartach, sampled for fauna here) while hunting appears to continue as significant at smaller settlements such as those in the vicinity of Ammerbuch and Hilzingen (Knipper 2011, 20). The high rates of wild animals in the region have been explained in various different ways, including with reference to climate and ecology, the continued presence of indigenous hunter-gatherers and the varying functions of different settlements (Knipper 2011, 36–8). While the reality of ecological zones proposed by Sielmann (1972) has been questioned (e.g. Kreuz 1990), when Döhle (2005, 284) plotted the distributions of different wild animal species found at LBK settlements against the types of environment exploited, he suggested that south-western Germany, and the areas around the Neckar in particular, may have had denser types of woodland cover than elsewhere during the LBK.

Though pollen diagrams from Baden-Württemberg certainly suggest that woodland was the predominant landscape cover during the LBK, it was also likely to have varied on a local scale (Knipper 2011, 81, 103). Similarly the evidence discussed in Chapter 1.3.4 for fishing in the Hegau (the settlement site of Singen) and Swabian Alb (the rock shelter site of Lautereck) may not of course reflect practices found in the immediate locality around Schwetzingen. However, these sites show that we cannot ignore the possibility that hunted and wild animals were more significant in the LBK diet in Baden-Württemberg than in other regions, with the role of indigenous groups, variation in the subsistence practices of different settlements and the ecological settings of LBK sites all likely to have played a role in producing this pattern.

7.4.5 Previous isotopic studies and models of LBK sociality

Practices of patrilocality have been suggested by previous isotopic studies in Baden-Württemberg (Price *et al.* 2001; Price and Bentley 2005; cf. Eisenhauer 2003a; 2003b; Chapter 2.3). The first strontium values for people from LBK contexts came from the large cemeteries of Flomborn (in the Pfalz) and Schwetzingen which lie some 45 km apart in the upper Rhine valley (Price *et al.* 2001; Price and Bentley 2005; Bentley 2006). Both developed within the middle period of the LBK, though Schwetzingen seems to be later (estimated as 5200–5000 cal BC; Appendix B1), and are examples of large flat cemeteries, with few overlapping burials; Flomborn has 85 burials, Schwetzingen over 200. The number of individuals initially sampled was small (Flomborn: 11 individuals; Schwetzingen: 36 individuals) compared with the number of individuals analysed in this study, but produced some interesting results. Local ranges for both these sites were defined as ±2 SDs from mean human bone values, which gave ranges of 0.70957–0.71033 for Flomborn and 0.70868–0.71013 for Schwetzingen (Price *et al.* 2001, 600). Both these ranges fall roughly within the biologically available strontium ratios identified for loess by Bentley and Knipper (2005b, 637): 0.7086–0.7103. Even if we apply this local range, which is more generous than that which Price *et al.* (2001) originally assigned for the local areas around the two cemeteries, the non-local individuals whom they identified still fall outside the range for the loess. Seven of the 11 individuals sampled at Flomborn were outliers and a further seven were also identified as non-local from the 36 burials analysed from Schwetzingen (Price *et al.* 2001, 600). The resultant conclusion from this early study was that substantial 'residential mobility' took place, in which females moved more than males (Price *et al.* 2001, 601–2).

As female adults were predominant among individuals identified as non-local, models of LBK farmers marrying hunter-gatherer women from nearby uplands were favoured, neatly fitting expectations already in place as a result of the presence of La Hoguette material and following models of patrilocality (see above). A small isotopic study of cattle at Vaihingen also showed a high incidence of non-local strontium ratios (Bentley and Knipper 2005a; Knipper 2009), fitting a possible pattern of transhumance. However, just as with the human data, this was not the case with every individual sampled. Two cattle sampled from Stuttgart-Mühlhausen *Viesenhäuser Hof* had different strontium ratios; while one had spent its life on the loess, another appeared to have spent at least 1.5 years on other soils/geologies (Knipper 2009, 154). This does not mean that the first specimen spent its entire life at Stuttgart-Mühlhausen; indeed, it is possible that it may have moved between different loess areas in the Neckar valley. Hence the distance animals moved may have varied. Moving with animals could have been a seasonal practice, with animals generally being pastured on higher ground during the summer months (Kienlin and Valde-Nowak 2003; Halstead 2005, 45). It has been suggested that such a practice took place throughout the summer months during the later Neolithic in the nearby Black Forest Mountains (Kienlin and Valde-Nowak 2003). It is, of course, also possible that cattle from other areas were introduced or exchanged into the local area from other groups.

More recently, however, Knipper (2011) has revised this model. She argues that, as Baden-Württemberg is geologically very variable, even over short distances, more extensive isotopic studies on bovine teeth show that cattle herds were more regularly kept close to settlements on loess or seasonally on river valley pasture, with limited transhumance to low mountain ranges only evidenced at Vaihingen (Knipper 2011, 361). In contrast to the limited ranges of domestic animals, different degrees of mobility are still being found in the human values (Bentley 2007; Bentley *et al.* 2008; Knipper and Price 2010; Knipper 2011, 341–2). To date, the individuals sampled from the cemeteries of Flomborn, Schwetzingen and Stuttgart-Mühlhausen *Viesenhäuser Hof* and the settlement of Vaihingen do not show clearly defined patterns of mobility based entirely on sex or age, but rather trends which are more or less prominent at the different sites. Unlike the cemeteries, the Vaihingen strontium data showed little variation in average strontium values between the sexes and males outnumber females in the non-local group (Bentley *et al.* 2003; Knipper 2009). Rather, strontium ratios at Vaihingen appear to vary with the location of the burial. Individuals at this settlement were interred in two different locations; they are either found in the ditch which surrounds the site or in pits, some interspersed in the settlement. Burials from the enclosure ditch not only had a wider range in their strontium values, but also had higher numbers of individuals classed as non-locals (Bentley *et al.* 2003, 481). Bentley *et al.* (2003) inferred status and possibly even ethnic differences between the two groups of burials, but later work by Strien (2005) suggests that the burials may belong to the same clan (at least in the case of those with grave goods, where affiliation could be identified), suggesting that the variation in strontium ratios is within one group. It is unlikely that the ditch and settlement burials are contemporary, with the ditch being filled in quickly at the end of the Flomborn phase, and there may yet be a finer chronological resolution for the burials. As noted above, at this time a number of the groups which have been identified within Vaihingen (Strien 2005; Bogaard *et al.* 2011) are proposed to have left the settlement. Did variability in mobility among some groups feature in their choice to move away?

A recent isotopic analysis of the cemetery of Stuttgart-Mühlhausen, which is only 20 km from Vaihingen, however, presents further contrasts. While Knipper and Price (2010, 60) found that males here were more likely to have a loess strontium signature, and while in its earliest phase many women had non-local signatures, the picture became significantly more complex when multiple teeth were analysed. Knipper (2009, 151) demonstrates that non-local strontium ratios in women are found in teeth which mineralise in early life, while non-local values were completely missing in similar teeth from male skeletons. High radiogenic isotope values for third molars were found in burials 30 and 47, both of whom were male and had local Sr ratios for their first molars (Knipper 2009, 150; Knipper and Price 2010, 59). As the third molar mineralises during the teens, these non-local strontium ratios have been interpreted as some form of transhumance (Bentley and Knipper 2005a; Knipper 2009; Knipper and Price 2010; cf. Knipper 2011). There are thus three possible mobility strategies suggested for LBK populations on the basis of strontium isotopes from Baden-Württemberg: limited or no mobility; one-off movements into the settlement predominantly made by women; and seasonal/temporary mobility or transhumance principally experienced by men in their teens.

Evidence that people buried at settlements did not have uniform mobility strategies has also been found in the isotopic study of the population buried at Talheim. The mass burial at Talheim (discovered and excavated 1983–4) includes 34 men, women and children who were massacred and then buried in a very short space of time (Wahl 1985; Wahl and König 1987; Wahl and Trautmann 2012). Given the special nature of this site, Talheim is often viewed as a 'living population' and the individuals are thought to have been living in a nearby, but as yet unexcavated, settlement (Wahl and König 1987; Bentley *et al.* 2008; Wahl and Trautmann 2012). When strontium, carbon and oxygen isotopes are combined, the population resolves into three groups (Bentley 2007; Bentley *et al.* 2008). The three groups include two local groups and a third whose strontium values are more radiogenic than the local range (Bentley 2007; Bentley *et al.* 2008). This local/non-local division between the three groups was also visible in some, but not all, of the epigenetic traits identified by Alt *et al.* (1995). While traits 554, 164 and 333 correlated with the isotopic groups, trait 673 was found across the population (Bentley *et al.* 2008, 298–9). Thus the mobility strategy an individual pursued seems not to have been entirely based on familial relationships but may have been in part influenced by it (Bickle and Hofmann 2007, 1035; cf. Bentley *et al.* 2008).

One of the long favoured explanations for Talheim was that the population met their deaths at the hands of a raiding party. The lack of adult females amongst the dead, though only 20 of the 34 individuals buried in the pit had been analysed, is often cited in support of this argument, as young women were argued to be desirable assets alongside cattle (Price *et al.* 2006; Bentley 2007; Bentley *et al.* 2008). However, there are four late juvenile to adult women amongst the remaining 14 individuals, thus leading to a far more balanced population being represented (Wahl and Trautmann 2012). Wahl and Trautmann (2012) question whether, in light of this, the two local groups can really be considered as different, as the main reason for separating the groups cited by Bentley (2007; Bentley *et al.* 2008) is the lack of females in group one and their presence in group two. The non-local group fall within strontium ranges from local uplands (the Black Forest and northern parts of the Swabian Alb; Wahl and Trautmann 2012). Some of the sherds found mixed in with the deceased at Talheim are decorated with designs associated with the Stuttgart area (50 km south of Talheim), and if, as Bentley *et al.* (2008) suggest, non-local strontium ratios represent herding practices then the region around Stuttgart is likely to have been passed through on journeys from Talheim to the Black Forest.

7.4.6 The end of the LBK

The events at Talheim fall late in the LBK sequence in Baden-Württemberg and are often cited as evidence for a period of violent upheaval at the end of the LBK (Gronenborn 1999; 2007a; 2007b; 2009a; Farruggia 2002; Wild *et al.* 2004; Boulestin *et al.* 2009). This model for social change at the end of the LBK is tied in with a number of other changes. The large cemeteries come to an end. Some settlements were abandoned (such as Ulm-Eggingen and Gerlingen: Neth 1999; Strien 2000), while others reduced in size (such as Vaihingen: Strien 2005). Long-distance networks associated with the circulation of lithics changed and ceramic styles underwent rapid stylistic change (Gronenborn 1999, 189).

There is also evidence from the late LBK which may prefigure such changes at its end. For instance, strontium analysis has also suggested changes in mobility by the time of the late LBK, as the number of non-local values decreased (Knipper 2009; Knipper and Price 2010). In his study of settlement networks in the lower Rhineland, Erich Claßen (2009, 104) found little change in the direction in which raw materials were travelling, for a period of approximately 200 years, only changing at the end of the middle LBK phase. Those settlements closer to the sources of raw material near Rijckholt showed greater intensity of production and distributed blanks to other settlements, but this did not lead to centralised control, and it is suggested that distributors did not have a privileged position in the network (Claßen 2009, 104). Overall, Claßen (2009, 106) argues that kinship relationships dominated a relatively stable middle LBK phase, in which close ties were maintained between settlements and sites that began earlier were more embedded in the settlement network. In the late LBK, new sites began to figure in the production and exchange of raw material and the intensity of relations decreased (Claßen 2009, 106).

We are still not certain why these changes should have occurred at the very end of the LBK, though a number of explanations have been put forward, mainly based on competition for land in changing environmental conditions (Wahl and König 1987; Strien 2000, 81; Strien and Gronenborn 2005; Gronenborn 2007a; 2009a; Zimmermann *et al.* 2009). The move towards shorter-lived, less densely occupied settlements seems to be echoed in the last settlement phases at Vaihingen (Krause 1998; Bogaard *et al.* 2011), and more generally across the upper Neckar valley (Strien 2000), which seems to suggest that different scales of community were now being formed. However, there is evidence that the scale and pace of change varied across the LBK distribution (Zimmermann 2002; D. Hofmann 2006). For example, in the Pfalz, the final phase of the LBK is only found at the site of Herxheim (Jeunesse *et al.* 2009), while in Baden-Württemberg, during the last two phases of the LBK, Hinkelstein pottery traditions (which originate in the Rhine-Hessen area) spread south into the Neckar valley (Strien 2000, 66, 81; Gronenborn 2007b, 85) and bring with them new raw material connections (Strien 2000, 53).

7.5 Burial practices

In the literature, more than 650 graves are referred to in this region (668 in the Lifeways Database; this does not include the cemetery of Flomborn, outside Baden-Württemberg in the Pfalz, nor the remains from the enclosure at Herxheim, also in the Pfalz). This number does include two large cemeteries which have yet to be published in detail: Fellbach-Oeffingen (116 burials, including cremations: Biel 1988; Nieszery 1995; Jeunesse 1997; Trautmann and Wahl 2005) and Schwetzingen (214 burials, including cremations: Gerling 2006; 2012, 10; Trautmann and Wahl 2005; Gerling and Francken 2007). To those cemeteries, we can also add Stuttgart-Mühlhausen *Viesenhäuser Hof* (*c.* 180 inhumations in two distinct areas: Kurz 1994; Nieszery 1995; Knipper and Price 2010). Burials are also found at settlement and enclosure sites and these inhumations make up about 25% of recorded burials (Lifeways Database). Approximately half of these burials come from just two sites; the 34 individuals found at Talheim and the 46 inhumations in both the ditch which surrounds the site and associated with the longhouses at Vaihingen (Bentley *et al.* 2003; 109 burials are quoted in Krause 1998, but this has yet to be confirmed). This number, however, does not include the disarticulated humans remains found at settlements and at sites such as the enclosure at Heilbronn-Neckargartach (Biel 1988; Jeunesse 1997, 46).

The Neckar valley and Pfalz cemeteries fall into Tradition II proposed by Jeunesse (1995b; 1996; 1997; Chapter 1.3.5), which he regards as demonstrating more variability (in body position, orientation and provision with grave goods) than Tradition I. As Tradition II was defined largely by cemeteries outside the Baden-Württemberg region (including Souffelweyersheim, Quatzenheim, Entzheim, Flomborn, Niedermerz and Elsloo; Jeunesse 1996, 131), this gives us the opportunity to examine whether the trends which were used to classify this group apply to the wider Neckar area. The key aspects of Tradition II are higher instances of pots and lithics, fragments of (rather than powdered) ochre and fewer shell ornaments.

The cemeteries in the Baden-Württemberg area do appear to match some of the criteria of Tradition II. Ochre is found in fragments rather than as powder at the cemetery of Stuttgart-Mühlhausen and *Spondylus* occurs very rarely in graves at Schwetzingen and Stuttgart-Mühlhausen (Jeunesse 1996; 1997; Trautmann and Wahl 2005; Gerling 2006; 2012; Gerling and Francken 2007). However, the total number of graves with pottery appears to be closer to Tradition I (52% at Schwetzingen, including graves with sherds in the fill; Gerling 2006, chapter 3; 2012, 36). Amongst the graves with pottery, those of women and children predominated and children seemed to be more likely to receive miniature vessels (Gerling 2012, 62). The frequency of lithics in the graves also seems much lower than Jeunesse (1996, 132, tab. 1) notes for cemeteries in the Tradition II regions (Lifeways Database; *c.*11% at Stuttgart-Mühlhausen and *c.* 19% at Schwetzingen; Gerling 2006; 2012). The occurrence of lithic tools in the graves across all cemeteries in Baden-Württemberg is, in fact, more in

Table 7.2. Baden-Württemberg: the body positions and orientations of burials (Lifeways Database). Only burials where orientation and body position had survived are included here.

	Left-crouched	Right-crouched	Crouched	Supine	Prone	Irregular	Totals
E–W	47	13	3	8	0	0	71
SE–NW	4	2	1	1	0	0	8
S–N	1	3	1	0	0	0	5
SW–NE	22	2	0	1	0	0	25
W–E	24	0	1	1	0	0	26
NW–SE	5	0	0	0	0	0	5
N–S	13	6	3	4	0	1	27
NE–SW	51	8	2	2	0	0	63
Totals	167	34	11	17	0	1	230

line with the values which Jeunesse (1996, 132) quotes for southern Alsace (*c*. 35%). If we add settlement burials to this, the number of graves receiving flint objects drops even further (to *c*. 15%; Lifeways Database).

Jeunesse (1996, 132) also found that Tradition II had more variability in body position and the orientation of the grave than Tradition I (in which 80% of burials were placed crouched on the left side, with the head to the north-east). In northern Alsace, he found that a significant number of burials were supine (43%; Jeunesse 1996, 134). This is not the case for cemeteries in Baden-Württemberg, where approximately 73% of burials were placed on their left sides (Table 7.2). Where Baden-Württemberg does follow Tradition II, however, is in the variety of orientations used, though the emphasis appears to fall on opposing orientations (north-east to east, 58%; and south to south-west, 22%; Table 7.2). The Schwetzingen cemetery accounts for most of the burials oriented to the north-east and may skew the distribution. In contrast to north Alsace, very few burials oriented north-west are found (Chapter 8.5). So the cemeteries of Baden-Württemberg appear to have elements of both the burial traditions identified by Jeunesse (1996); like Tradition II, ochre is used in fragments rather than as powder, there are fewer *Spondylus* ornaments included in the graves than in Tradition I, and a variety of grave orientations are used. However, the occurrence of lithics and pots in the graves is more similar to Tradition I and *c*. 73% of burials are placed in the left-crouched position.

Given that Baden-Württemberg cemeteries sit geographically between the two groups, it is perhaps unsurprising that they have characteristics of both traditions. It is more difficult to understand why fewer grave goods were used in this region than elsewhere. If Jeunesse (1995a; 1996; 1997) is correct and grave goods represent the status inherited by a small group in LBK society, then Baden-Württemberg groups did not achieve as much access to high-status goods prized elsewhere in the LBK, or possibly were adhering more strongly to certain elements of Mesolithic burial practices (see also Chapter 8.5) at the expense of LBK affiliations. It is also possible that *Spondylus* was not sought out, with other burial rites used preferentially to express identity and relations.

7.6 Sites sampled

The cemetery site of Schwetzingen was first analysed for strontium isotopes by R. Alexander Bentley and T. Douglas Price in the late 1990s, when 36 individuals were sampled for strontium isotope ratios (Bentley *et al.* 2002, 801). Here we revisit the cemetery, expanding the number of individuals sampled to above 100 and also investigating the assemblage for carbon, nitrogen and oxygen isotopes. Suitable animal bone material in the vicinity of the cemetery is not available (Knipper 2011, 18). However, as human carbon and nitrogen values already exist for Herxheim (Dürrwächter *et al.* 2006) and can act as a comparison (though the number of samples is low), we decided to look for sites further east and a suitable archaeozoological collection was identified at the enclosure of Heilbronn-Neckargartach. The assemblage has not been studied in detail, but Elisabeth Stephan identified the species and assisted with the selection of samples.

7.7 Schwetzingen

7.7.1 Introduction

The cemetery of Schwetzingen was located on the eastern bank of the Rhine, not far south of the Neckar-Rhine confluence (Fig. 7.1). Although the site is situated on coarse-grained loess sediments, above the floodplain of the Rhine, it lies less than 20 km from a variety of different geologies including granites, gneisses, Keuper sandstones and limestones (Gerling 2006; 2012, 14). Investigations in the late 1980s and early 1990s found LBK sherds in the vicinity of the cemetery, suggesting settlement areas approximately 2 km to the south-east and to the north-east, but the pottery was from earlier in the LBK sequence than the cemetery and therefore whether one or many settlements used the cemetery remains unknown (Gerling 2006, chapter 1; 2012, 15). The cemetery itself was discovered and excavated subsequently, in 1988 (Behrends 1989; 1993;

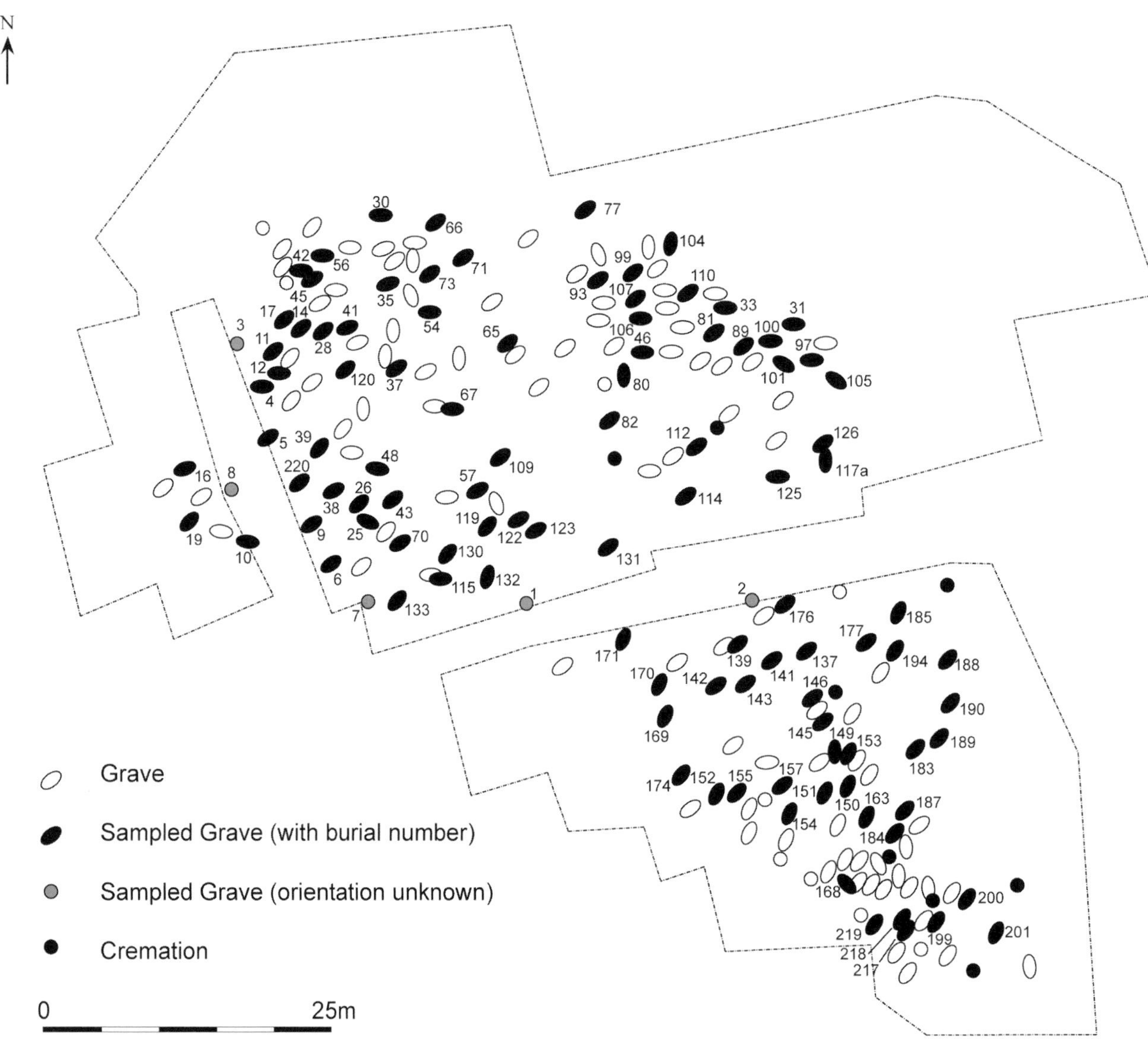

Fig. 7.6. Schwetzingen: plan. After Gerling (2012, 263). Only sampled burials are numbered.

1997a; 1997b; 1999; Trautmann and Wahl 2005; Gerling and Francken 2007), when 203 inhumations (including at least four double graves), 15 cremations and 15 graves without skeletons (possible so-called 'cenotaphs'; Lenneis 2010c) were found across an area approximately 100 m by 50 m (Gerling and Francken 2007, 43; Fig. 7.6). This makes Schwetzingen one of the largest cemeteries in the LBK, with a comparable number of burials to Stuttgart-Mühlhausen *Viesenhäuser Hof* (Kurz 1994). However, Schwetzingen appears to be somewhat later than Stuttgart-Mühlhausen, dating towards the end of the LBK (estimated at 5200–5000 cal BC; Trautmann and Wahl 2005; Price and Bentley 2005; Gerling and Francken 2007).

Stylistically, the pottery found at Schwetzingen and in the area around it (just south of Mannheim) seems to have strong relationships to the southern part of Rhine-Hessen and the Pfalz (Heide 2001; Gerling 2006; 2012; Jeunesse *et al.* 2009). Although attempts at more detailed

Table 7.3 (over the following 7 pages). Schwetzingen: the isotope, osteological and archaeological data. Age and sex information for inhumations from Joachim Wahl (unpublished), for cremations from Trautmann (2007). See Chapter 2 for further definition of ages.

Key for body position: LC – Left-crouched; RC – Right-crouched; C – Crouched, direction unknown; CB – Crouched on back; CF – Crouched on front; S – Supine; P – Prone; I – Irregular.

Key for grave goods (number of items follows in brackets; frag. = fragment): U. – Unfurnished; F. – Fill only (all items listed after an F. were in the fill of the grave rather than at the level of the skeleton); Pol. – Polished stone; Cer. – Ceramics; Shd. – Sherds; Spon. – Spondylus*; She. – Other Shell; Och. – Ochre; Lit. – Chipped stone; Bon – Worked bone; Grd. – Grinding stone.*

Key for isotopic information: Carb. – sample from bone carbonate; Dent. – sample from dentine.

Burial	Tooth	Sex	Age (yrs)	$^{87}Sr/^{86}Sr$	Sr conc. ppm	$\delta^{13}C$ ‰	$\delta^{15}N$ ‰	$\delta^{18}O$ ‰	$\delta^{13}C$ Carb.	$\delta^{13}C$ Dent.	$\delta^{15}N$ Dent.	Orient.	Body position	Grave goods
1	PM	-	-	0.71208	451	−20.1	8.5	−5.3	−12.3	-	-	-	-	U.
2	-	-	*c.*12	-	-	-	-	-	-	-	-	-	LC	Cer.(1)
3	PM	-	Senile	0.70925	71	−20.4	9.2	-	-	-	-	-	-	U.
4	PM	M?	Adult	0.70929	56	−20.2	8.9	-	-	-	-	E–W	LC	Bon.(1)
5	PM	M	Adult/ Mature	0.71031	78	−20.3	9.2	-	-	-	-	NE–SW	LC	Lit.(3)
6	-	M	Adult	-	-	−20.2	8.6	-	-	-	-	NE–SW	S	Pol.(1), Bon.(2)
7	PM	M?	Mature	0.70965	62	−20.4	9.5	-	-	-	-	-	-	U.
8	PM	M	Adult	0.71038	81	−20.1	9.6	-	-	-	-	W–E	-	Lit.(1)
9	PM	F?	Adult	0.71115	64	−20.5	9.1	−4.5	−10.9	−20.3	9.7	NE–SW	RC	U.
10	PM	M	Adult	0.70968	85	−19.9	9	-	-	-	-	NW–SE	LC	Cer.(1)
11	PM	F?	Mature	0.70995	75	−20.3	9	-	-	-	-	SW–NE	LC	U.
12	PM	F?	17–18	0.71012	64	−20.3	8.2	-	-	-	-	E–W	RC	Shd.(1)
13	-	-	*c.*6–8	-	-	-	-	-	-	-	-	SW–NE	LC	U.
14	PM	M	Adult	0.70932	62	−20.2	9	−4.7	−12.5	−20.3	9.9	NE–SW	LC	Lit.(4), Bon.(1)
15	-	-	*c.*14	-	-	-	-	-	-	-	-	NE–SW	LC	Pol.(1), Lit.(1)
16	PM	M	Adult	0.70930	74	−20.1	9.9	−4.8	−12.5	−20.2	8.8	NE–SW	CB	Pol.(1), Lit.(2), Bon.(1)
17	PM		16–17	0.71001	61	-	-	-	-	-	-	S–N	-	Pol.(1), Bon.(3)
18	PM	F?	Mature	-	-	−20.2	9.1	-	-	-	-	SW–NE	LC	U.
19	PM	F?	Mature	0.70983	143	−20.2	8.7	-	-	-	-	NE–SW	RC	U.
20	-	-	*c.*4	-	-	-	-	-	-	-	-	SW–NE	LC	Cer.(1), Shd.(3)
21	-	-	7–8	-	-	−20.1	8	-	-	-	-	NW–SE	LC	Pol.(1), Cer.(1), Lit.(1), Bon.(1)
22	-	-	*c.*4	-	-	-	-	-	-	-	-	E–W	RC	U.
23	-	-	-	-	-	-	-	-	-	-	-	-	-	Cenotaph: F.Shd.(10)
24	-	-	-	-	-	-	-	-	-	-	-	-	-	Cenotaph: F.Shd.(4)
25	PM	F?	Adult	0.70923	61	−20.0	8.1	−5.0	−12.0	−20.0	9.1	SE–NW	LC	Cer.(1), She.(2), F.Shd.(13)
26	PM	M	Adult	0.70975	74	−20.0	9.1	-	-	-	-	SW–NE	LC	Pol.(1), Lit.(4)
27	-	-	-	-	-	-	-	-	-	-	-	-	-	Cenotaph: U.
28	PM	F?	Adult/ Mature	0.70939	44	−20.2	8.6	−4.8	−12.5	−20.7	9.5	NE–SW	LC	U.
29	-	-	-	-	-	-	-	-	-	-	-	-	-	Cenotaph: U.
30	PM	F?	Mature	0.71003	75	−20.4	8	-	-	-	-	E–W	LC	F. Shd.(3)

31	PM	-	*c.*17	0.71033	58	−20.4	9.1	-	-	-	-	W–E	LC	Cer. 1)
32	-	F?	Young Adult	-	-	-	-	-	-	-	-	SE–NW	LC	Lit.(1)
33	PM	-	*c.*4	0.70984	71	−20.4	9.1	-	-	-	-	SW–NE	LC	Cer.(1), Lit.(1), Grd.(1)
34	-	-	-	-	-	-	-	-	-	-	-	-	-	Cenotaph: F.Shd.(57), Lit.
35	PM	M	Adult	0.70955	106	−20.0	9.1	-4.3	−11.7	−20.1	9.6	NE–SW	LC	Pol.(1)
36	-	-	*c.*11–12	-	-	-	-	-	-	-	-	NE–SW	LC	Cer.(1), Shd.(1), She.(35)
37	PM	F	Adult	0.70938	87	−20.1	8.7	-4.1	−11.4	−20.5	9.6	NE–SW	LC	Shd.(2), Bon.(8), She.(2)
38	PM	F?	Senile	0.70990	154	−20.1	8.3	-	-	-	-	SW–NE	LC	U.
39	PM	F?	Adult	0.70957	77	−20.3	9.1	-	-	-	-	NE–SW	LC	Cer.(1)
40	-	-	Adult	-	-	-	-	-	-	-	-	E–W	-	U.
41	PM	F?	Mature	0.71019	83	−20.2	8.6	-	-	-	-	SW–NE	LC	U.
42	PM	F?	Adult	0.71184	83	−20.4	8.7	-5.3	−12.1	−20.4	10.6	E–W	RC	F. Shd.(14)
43	PM	M	Mature	0.70964	101	−19.8	9	-	-	-	-	NE–SW	RC	Pol.(1), Cer.(1), Lit.(4), Grd.(1)
44	-	-	*c.*2–3	-	-	-	-	-	-	-	-	SW–NE	LC	U.
45	PM	-	*c.*16	0.70954	81	−20.1	8.6	-	-	-	-	SW–NE	LC	F. Shd.(19)
46	PM	-	Mature/ Senile	0.70964	194	−20.3	8.8	-	-	-	-	W–E	LC	F. Shd.(2)
47	-	-	*c.*4	-	-	-	-	-	-	-	-	N–S	LC	F. Shd.(9)
48	-	F?	Adult	-	-	−19.9	8.6	-	-	-	-	NW–SE	LC	Cer.(1), Spon.(armring, pendant), Bon.(1)
49	-	-	*c.*0–6 mon.	-	-	-	-	-	-	-	-	NW–SE	-	U.
50	-	-	-	-	-	-	-	-	-	-	-	-	-	Cenotaph: F.Shd.(10)
51	-	-	*c.*3	-	-	-	-	-	-	-	-	NW–SE	-	Cer.(2), Lit.(3), F.Shd.(11)
52	-	-	*c.*1–1.5	-	-	-	-	-	-	-	-	NW–SE	-	F.Shd.(2)
53	-	-	*c.*5–6	-	-	-	-	-	-	-	-	NE–SW	LC	U.
54	PM	F?	Mature	0.71435	192	−19.7	9.7	-4.8	−11.8	−20.5	9.7	E–W	LC	Shd.(1), Lit.(1)
55	-	F	Mature	-	-	-	-	-	-	-	-	E–W	LC	F.Shd.(2), She.(4), Bon.(1)
56	PM	M	Adult	0.70942	53	−20.1	9.1	-	-	-	-	E–W	LC	Bon.(1), Grd.(1)
57	PM	F?	Mature	0.70923	78	−20.3	8.5	-	-	-	-	NE–SW	LC	Shd.(1)
58	-	M	*c.*20	-	-	-	-	-	-	-	-	E–W	LC	Cer.(1), Lit.(1), Bon.(1)
59	-	-	-	-	-	-	-	-	-	-	-	-	-	Cenotaph: F.Shd.(1)
60	-	-	-	-	-	-	-	-	-	-	-	-	-	Cenotaph: F.Shd.(11)
61	-	F	Adult	-	-	-	-	-	-	-	-	SW–NE	LC	F. Shd.(1), She.(1)
62	-	-	*c.*10–12	-	-	-	-	-	-	-	-	W–E	LC	U.

63	-	-	*c.*7–8	-	-	-	-	-	-	-	-	NE–SW	LC	F. Shd.(1)
64	-	-	-	-	-	-	-	-	-	-	-	-	-	Cenotaph: F.Shd.(9)
65	PM	F?	Adult	0.71232	73	−20.1	9.3	−4.8	−12.2	−20.6	9.5	NE–SW	LC	Cer.(1)
66	PM	M	Adult	0.71047	71	−20.3	8.8	−4.2	−15.0	−22.0	12.8	-	-	F. Shd.(1)
67	PM	F?	Adult	0.71007	57	−20.3	9.7	-	-	-	-	E–W	LC	Cer.(1), Bon.(1), F. Shd.(26)
68	-	-	*c.*9–12	-	-	-	-	-	-	-	-	SW–NE	LC	U.
69	-	-	*c.*9–10	-	-	-	-	-	-	-	-	N–S	LC	U.
70	PM	M	Adult	0.70930	46	−20.1	8.8	−5.2	−12.3	−20.4	9.8	SW–NE	LC	Pol.(1), Lit.(2), Bon.(2), Pebbles (2)
71	PM	F?	Adult	0.70984	41	−20.5	8.4	-	-	-	-	E–W	LC	Cer.(1), Shd.(9)
72	-	-	*c.*9	-	-	-	-	-	-	-	-	NE–SW	LC	Cer.(1), F.Shd.(2)
73	PM	M	Adult	0.70937	41	−19.8	9.1	−4.1	−11.7	−20.2	9.7	NE–SW	LC	Cer.(1), Lit.(3)
74	-	-	-	-	-	-	-	-	-	-	-	-	-	Cremation: F.Shd.(33), Pol.(1)?
75	-	M?	Mature?	-	-	-	-	-	-	-	-	-	-	Pol.(1), Bon.(1), F.Shd.(38)
76	-	-	*c.*6	-	-	-	-	-	-	-	-	SW–NE	LC	U.
77	PM	M	Adult	0.71079	47	−20.1	9.1	−4.4	−12.2	-	-	NE–SW		F.Shd.(2)
78	-	-	Adult	-	-	-	-	-	-	-	-	-	-	Cremation: Pol.(1), F.Shd.(13)
79	-	-	*c.*4-9	-	-	-	-	-	-	-	-	-	-	U.
80	PM	M	Mature	0.70972	57	−20.2	9.4	-	-	-	-	N–S	LC	Pol.(1)
81	PM		Adult	0.71023	49	−20.0	9.2	-	-	-	-	NE–SW	LC	Lit.(1), Shd.(1)
82	PM	M	Mature	0.70926	220	−20.2	9.8	-	-	-	-	NE–SW	RC	Bon.(1)
83	-	-	-	-	-	-	-	-	-	-	-	-	-	F.Shd.(51)
84	-	-	-	-	-	-	-	-	-	-	-	-	-	Cenotaph: F.Cer.(1), Lit.(2)
85	-	-	*c.*4–5	-	-	-	-	-	-	-	-	W–E	LC	Cer.(1)
86	-	-	*c.*3–5	-	-	-	-	-	-	-	-	E–W	-	F.She.(1)
87	-	-	1.5	-	-	-	-	-	-	-	-	E–W	LC	U.
88	-	-	*c.*6-7	-	-	-	-	-	-	-	-	W–E	LC	U.
89	PM	F?	Adult	0.7121	163	−20.1	9.5	−4.6	−10.3	−20.4	10.7	NE–SW	LC	Shd.(3)
90	-	-	*c.*1.5–2	-	-	-	-	-	-	-	-	SW–NE	LC	U.
91	-	-	-	-	-	-	-	-	-	-	-	-	-	Cenotaph: F.Shd.(6)
92	-	-	-	-	-	-	-	-	-	-	-	-	-	Cenotaph: F.Shd.(1)
93	PM	M	Adult	0.71063	87	−20.2	9.5	−4.2	−11.5	−20.1	9.4	NE–SW	LC	Lit.(1), F.Shd.(1)
94	-	-	14–15	-	-	-	-	-	-	-	-	NE–SW	LC	F.Shd.(4)
95	-	-	*c.*1.5	-	-	-	-	-	-	-	-	SW–NE	LC	F.Shd.(2)
96	-	-	12–13	-	-	-	-	-	-	-	-	-	-	U.

97	PM	M	Mature	0.71023	86	−20.3	8.6	-	-	-	-	NW–SE	LC	Lit.(1), Bon.(1)
98	-	-	*c.*3–4	-	-	-	-	-	-	-	-	W–E	LC	Pol.(1), Lit.(1), Bon.(3), She.(19), Graphite bead, F.Shd.(2)
99	PM	F	Adult	0.71092	68	−20.2	9.5	-	-	-	-	SW–NE	LC	Cer.(1), Spon.(1 bead), F.Shd.(1)
100	PM	F?	Adult	0.71037	78	−20.1	9.4	-	-	-	-	E–W	LC	U.
101	PM	F?	Senile	0.70939	100	−20.1	10.7	-	-	-	-	SE–NW	LC	Cer.(1)
102	-	-	*c.*6	-	-	-	-	-	-	-	-	S–N	RC	Sandstone(frag.)
103	-	-	*c.*8	-	-	-	-	-	-	-	-	NE–SW	LC	F.Shd.(4)
104	PM	M	Mature	0.70988	23	−20.4	8.8	-	-	-	-	NE–SW	LC	Lit.(3), F.Shd.(6)
105	PM	F?	Adult	0.70978	64	−19.9	9.4	-	-	-	-	E–W	LC	Grd.(frag.)
106	PM	M	Mature	0.71041	65	−20.9	8.9	−3.7	−12.1	-20	9.2	W–E	LC	Lit.(1), Bon.(5), Grd.(1),Och.(2), She.(2)
107	PM	M	Adult	0.70965	69	−20.1	8.9	-	-	-	-	NE–SW	LC	Lit.(1)
108	-	-	*c.*3–4	-	-	-	-	-	-	-	-	E–W	LC	F.Shd.(5)
109	PM	F?	Adult	0.71086	130	−20.1	9.5	-	-	-	-	NE–SW	LC	Cer.(1), Bon.(1), F.Shd.(2)
110	PM	M?	Adult	0.70936	81	−20.4	8.5	-	-	-	-	SW–NE	LC	Shd.(2), She.(3)
111	-	-	*c.*13–15	-	-	-	-	-	-	-	-	SW–NE	LC?	F.Shd.(1)
112	PM		Mature?	0.70974	22	-	-	-	-	-	-	NE–SW	LC	U.
113	-	-	Adult?	-	-	-	-	-	-	-	-	-	-	U.
114	PM	F?	Adult	0.71014	73	-	-	-	-	-	-	NE–SW	LC?	U.
115	PM	-	16–19	0.70928	64	−20.4	9.2	-	-	-	-	E–W	RC	U.
116	-	-	*c.*6–7	-	-	-	-	-	-	-	-	W–E	LC	U.
117a	PM	M	Adult/ Mature	0.70971	59	-	-	-	-	-	-	S–N	RC	F.Cer.(1), Shd.(2), cremation in fill?
117b	-	-	*c.*11–12	-	-	-	-	-	-	-	-	NE–SW	LC	Shd.(1), F.Shd.(20)
118	-	M	Adult	-	-	-	-	-	-	-	-	-	-	U.
119	PM	F	Adult	0.70967	94	−20.1	8.4	-	-	-	-	NE–SW	LC	U.
120	PM	F	Adult	0.71022	56	−20.3	8.8	−4.3	−11.0	−20.4	10	E–W	LC	U.
121	-	M	Adult	-	-	−20.3	8.9	-	-	-	-	-	-	U.
122	PM	F	Adult	0.71009	81	−20.3	9.3	−5.7	−12.2	−20.3	9.3	SW–NE	LC	Cer. (1)
123	PM	F	Adult	0.70943	42	−20.3	8.3	−5.4	−12.4	−20.5	10.1	NE–SW	LC	F. hd.(2)
124	-	-	*c.*2	-	-	-	-	-	-	-	-	NE–SW	LC	U.
125	PM	F	Adult	0.71045	103	−20.5	8.8	-	-	-	-	E–W	LC	U.
126	PM	F	Adult	0.70952	49	−20.1	8.1	−4.6	−12.0	−20.3	9.4	NE–SW	P	Graphite(1)
127	-	-	-	-	-	-	-	-	-	-	-	-	-	Cremation: F. Shd. (8)

128	-	F	Mature	-	-	−20.0	9.9	-	-	-	-	E–W	LC	U.
129	-	-	6–7	-	-	−20.2	7.8	-	-	-	-	NE–SW	LC	Bon.(1)
130	PM	M	Mature/ Senile	0.70997	69	−20.0	8.4	-	-	-	-	NE–SW	LC	Bon.(1, pendant)
131	PM	F?	Adult	0.70980	56	−20.4	8.7	-	-	-	-	NE–SW	LC	Cer.(1), Manganese oxide bead?
132	PM	M	Adult	0.71335	132	−20.4	8.4	−5.0	−12.3	−20.1	10.4	NE–SW	LC	Pebble(2), F.Shd.(1)
133	PM	M	Adult	0.70962	69	−20.0	9.1	-	-	-	-	SW–NE	S	Pol.(1), Cer.(1), Lit.(10), Bon.(1), F.Shd.(3)
134	-	-	*c.*10–11	-	-	-	-	-	-	-	-	NE–SW	LC	U.
135	-	-	Adult?	-	-	-	-	-	-	-	-	-	-	Cremation: F.Shd.(14).
136	-	F	Adult	-	-	-	-	-	-	-	-	NE–SW	LC	U.
137	PM	F?	Mature	0.70924	111	−19.9	8.5	-	-	-	-	NE–SW	LC	Shd.(2)
138	-	-	*c.*6	-	-	-	-	-	-	-	-	SW–NE	LC	Pol.(1), Lit.(1), Bon.(1)
139	PM	M	Mature	0.71085	100	−20.0	9.3	-	-	-	-	NE–SW	LC	Lit.(1), F.Shd.(1)
140	-	F	Mature	-	-	−20.0	8.6	-	-	-	-	NE–SW	-	F.Shd.(5, 3 not LBK)
141	PM	F	Adult	0.70959	50	−20.4	9.4	-	-	-	-	SW–NE	LC	Cer.(1), Pebble
142	PM	M	Mature	0.7096	104	−20.2	8.4	-	-	-	-	NE–SW	LC	Bon.(3), She.(2), Shd.(1)
143	PM	M	Adult	0.70934	77	−19.9	8.6	−4.8	−11.9	−20.3	9.1	NE–SW	S	U.
144	-	M	Mature	-	-	-	-	-	-	-	-	NE–SW	LC	Shd.(1)
145	PM	F	Mature	0.71125	70	−20.5	9.2	-	-	-	-	NE–SW	LC	Cer.(1), F.Shd.(1)
146	PM	F	Adult	0.70987	46	−20.5	7.9	-	-	-	-	NE–SW	LC	Cer.(1), F.Shd.(21)
147	-	-	12–14	-	-	-	-	-	-	-	-	NE–SW	LC	Shd. (1)
148	-	-	-	-	-	-	-	-	-	-	-	-	-	Cenotaph: Cer.(1), F.Shd.(1)
149	PM	F	Adult	0.70996	137	−20.2	7.6	-	-	-	-	N–S	RC	U.
150	PM	F	Adult/ Mature	0.71215	109	−20.2	8.5	−4.5	−10.4	−20.6	10.2	N–S	LC?	U.
151	PM	F	Adult	0.71191	135	−20.4	8.3	−4.8	−12.7	−20.5	10	SW–NE	LC	Spon.(1 bead)
152	PM	M	Senile	0.70952	72	−19.9	8.9	-	-	-	-	SW–NE	LC	Pol.(1), Lit.(1), Pebble, Cremation in fill
153	PM	F	Adult	0.70996	67	−19.7	7.7	-	-	-	-	SW–NE	LC	Cer.(1)
154	PM	M	Mature	0.70974	54	−20.2	8.6	−5.7	−13.6	−21.1	11.6	NE–SW	RC	Cer.(1), Lit.(2), She.(2), F.Shd.(18), Pebble
155	-	-	*c.*11	-	-	−20.3	7.8	-	-	-	-	W–E	LC	Cer.(frag.)
156	-	-	*c.*4–5	-	-	-	-	-	-	-	-	-	-	U.
157	PM	M	Mature	0.70981	61	−19.9	8.4	-	-	-	-	NE–SW	LC	F.Shd.(2)
158	-	-	*c.*7–8	-	-	-	-	-	-	-	-	NE–SW	RC	Shd.(1), Grd.(1)

159	-	-	16–17	-	-	-	-	-	-	-	-	NE–SW	RC	F.Shd.(1)
160	-	-	Inf. II	-	-	-	-	-	-	-	-	NE–SW	S	Cer.(1)
161	-	-	*c.*2	-	-	-	-	-	-	-	-	NE–SW	LC	U.
162	-	-	Adult	-	-	-	-	-	-	-	-	SW–NE	-	U.
163	PM	F	Adult	0.71011	52	−20.2	9.7	-	-	-	-	NE–SW	LC	U.
164	-	-	-	-	-	-	-	-	-	-	-	-	-	U.
165	-	-	Juv.	-	-	-	-	-	-	-	-	NE–SW	-	U.
166	-	M	Adult	-	-	-	-	-	-	-	-	NE–SW	LC	F.Shd.(2)
167	-	-	*c.* Inf. II/Juv.	-	-	-	-	-	-	-	-	NE–SW	-	U.
168	PM	-	Adult/ Mature	0.71012	52	−19.6	9.1	-	-	-	-	NE–SW	LC	U.
169	PM	M	Adult	0.71092	82	−20.1	8.9	−4.6	−13.0	−20.3	10.1	SW–NE	CB	Frag. of limestone
170	PM	F	Adult	0.70957	75	−20.1	7.9	-	-	-	-	NE–SW	LC	Spon.(2 beads), Manganese oxide bead, F.Shd.(14)
171	PM	F	*c.*20	0.70954	58	−20.1	9.5	-	-	-	-	NE–SW	LC	F.Shd.(2)
172	-	-	Juv./ Adult	-	-	-	-	-	-	-	-	SW–NE	-	U.
173	-	-	*c.*6	-	-	-	-	-	-	-	-	SW–NE	-	U.
174	PM	M?	Adult	0.71084	49	−19.6	8.3	-	-	-	-	NE–SW	RC	Lit.(1)
175	-	-	*c.*5	-	-	-	-	-	-	-	-	W–E	LC	U.
176	PM	F?	Adult	0.70954	34	−20.1	10.1	−4.7	−12.1	−20.6	10.5	NE–SW	LC	Bon.(1), F.Och.
177	PM	M	Adult/ Mature	0.70983	39	−20.0	9.2	−5.3	−12.8	−20.4	9.6	NE–SW	LC	Pol.(1), Cer.(1), She.(1)
178	-	-	2–3	-	-	-	-	-	-	-	-	-	-	U.
179	-	-	14–15	-	-	-	-	-	-	-	-	NE–SW	LC	U.
180	-	-	5–6	-	-	-	-	-	-	-	-	SW–NE	RC	Cer.(1), F.Shd.(4)
181	-	-	3–4	-	-	-	-	-	-	-	-	N–S	RC	F.Shd.(2)
182	-	-	10–13	-	-	-	-	-	-	-	-	SW–NE	LC	Shd.(8), Lit.(1), Grd.(frag.)
183	PM	F	Mature	0.70952	85	−20.0	8.7	-	-	-	-	NE–SW	LC	Cer.(1), Shd.(1)
184	PM	F	Mature	0.70955	59	−19.9	9	-	-	-	-	NE–SW	LC	Cer.(1), Pebbles(2)
185	PM	M	Mature	0.70953	43	−20.3	9.8	-	-	-	-	SW–NE	RC	U.
186	-	F?	Late Juv./Early Adult	-	-	-	-	-	-	-	-	E–W	RC	U.
187	PM	-	Mature	0.70969	65	−19.8	9	-	-	-	-	NE–SW	LC	Pol.(1), Cer.(1), Lit.(1), Bon.(2), F.Shd.(2)

188	PM	F	Adult	-	-	−20.2	8.6	-	-	-	-	NE–SW	LC	F.Shd.(5)
189	PM	M?	*c.*18	0.71088	81	−20.1	8.9	-	-	-	-	NE–SW	RC	Lit.(1), Bon.(2), Och.
190	-	F	Mature	-	-	−20.2	9	-	-	-	-	NE–SW	LC	Shd.(2), Lit.(1)
191	-	-	*c.*5	-	-	-	-	-	-	-	-	SW–NE	LC	Cer.(1), Cremation in fill
192	-	-	>Juv.	-	-	-	-	-	-	-	-	-	-	Cremation: Lit.(1)
193	-	-	>Inf. II	-	-	-	-	-	-	-	-	-	-	Cremation: U.
194	PM	M?	Adult	0.70943	70	−19.7	8.3	-	-	-	-	SW–NE	LC	Bon.(3)
195	-	-	*c.*3	-	-	-	-	-	-	-	-	SW–NE		F.Shd.(10), Lit.(1)
196	-	-	7-9	-	-	-	-	-	-	-	-	NE–SW	LC	*F. Non-LBK Shds*
197	-	-	*c.*4	-	-	-	-	-	-	-	-	NE–SW	LC	Shd.(12)
198	-	-	Juv./ Adult	-	-	-	-	-	-	-	-	-	-	Cremation: F.Shd.(31)
199	PM	F	Adult	0.70979	*n.d.*	−20.4	9.2	-	-	-	-	NE–SW	RC	U.
200	PM	M	Mature	0.70958	64	−19.6	9.2	-	-	-	-	NE–SW	LC	Pol.(frag.), Cer.(1), Lit.(1), She.(2)
201	PM	F	Adult/ Mature	0.70937	*n.d.*	−20.2	8.7	-	-	-	-	N–S	RC	Cer.(1)
202	-	-	>Juv.	-	-	-	-	-	-	-	-	-	-	Cremation: F.Shd.(20)
203	-	-	*c.*6	-	-	-	-	-	-	-	-	N–S	RC	Cer.(2), Bon.(4)
204	-	-	6–9	-	-	-	-	-	-	-	-	N–S	LC	Grd.(1)
205	-	-	Adult	-	-	-	-	-	-	-	-	NE–SW	RC	U.
206	-	-	Adult	-	-	-	-	-	-	-	-	-	-	Cremation: Pol.(1), Shd.(40)
207	-	-	4–6	-	-	-	-	-	-	-	-	NE–SW	RC	U.
208	-	-	8–7	-	-	-	-	-	-	-	-	-	-	U.
209	-	-	Adult	-	-	-	-	-	-	-	-	-	-	Cremation: Pol.(frag.), Lit.(1), F.Shd.(9)
210	-	-	>Inf. II	-	-	-	-	-	-	-	-	-	-	Cremation: U.
211	-	F	Adult	-	-	-	-	-	-	-	-	NE–SW	S	2nd burial: Child (c.5 years)
212	-	-	Juv./ Adult	-	-	-	-	-	-	-	-	-	-	Cer.(1), Grd.(frag.), F.Shd.(4)
213	-	-	1–5	-	-	-	-	-	-	-	-	-	-	Cer.(1)
214	-	-	-	-	-	-	-	-	-	-	-	-	-	Cenotaph: Cer.(1)
215	-	-	10–12	-	-	-	-	-	-	-	-	NE–SW	LC	U.
216	-	-	*c.*20	-	-	-	-	-	-	-	-	N–S	S	U.
217	PM	F	Senile	0.70913	72	-	-	-	-	-	-	NE–SW	LC	Cer.(1)
218	PM	M	*c.*18	0.70951	70	−20.3	8.8	-	-	-	-	NE–SW	RC	Cer.(1), Lit.(2)
219	PM	F	Adult	0.71172	114	−20.1	8.8	-	-	-	-	N–S	LC	U.
220	PM	M	Adult	0.71066	*n.d.*	−19.7	8.4	-	-	-	-	SW–NE	LC	Pol.(1), F.Shd.(34)

Table 7.4. Schwetzingen: the body positions and orientations of inhumations (information from Gerling 2012).

	Left-crouched	Right-Crouched	Crouched	Supine	Prone	Irregular	Totals
E–W	13	3	0	0	0	0	16
SE–NW	3	0	0	0	0	0	3
S–N	1	1	1	0	0	0	3
SW–NE	22	2	0	1	0	0	25
W–E	10	0	0	0	0	0	10
NW–SE	3	0	0	0	0	0	3
N–S	11	6	0	2	0	1	20
NE–SW	49	8	2	2	0	0	61
Totals	112	20	3	5	0	1	141

seriation have failed (using WinBASP), a rough chronology for the cemetery can be suggested (Gerling 2012, 112). The earliest pots in the cemetery have a Flomborn-style decoration (phase III; Meier-Arendt 1966; phase 4/5; Strien 2000; phase 3b/4 Heide 2001; Phase IIIb/IVa; Lindig 2002), but most of the graves date to the later phases of the LBK (*jüngere* and perhaps *jüngste* phases; Gerling 2012, 112–15). The earliest grave in the cemetery is likely to be grave 122, in which an adult female was buried with a bottle decorated in the Flomborn style; very few other graves date to this period (Gerling 2006; 2012). The majority of the burials took place between the beginning of the *jüngere* LBK and the transition between the *jüngere* and the *jüngste* phases, with no occurrence of the very last ceramic styles of the LBK recorded (Table 7.1; Gerling 2006; 2012, 114). Gerling (2006; 2012), therefore, could only divide the burials into roughly three phases: late Flomborn/*mittlere* LBK, *jüngere* LBK and the transition between the *jüngere* and the *jüngste* LBK. Eleven radiocarbon dates were obtained in the course of the Lifeways project, and are presented in Appendix B1. This is only a limited number of burials and we must be very cautious about extrapolating further. The initial modelling of the radiocarbon dates suggests that burial could have started at Schwetzingen between *5260–5080 cal BC* (*95.4% probable*) or *5190–5100 cal BC* (*60.2% probable*), while the end of the cemetery is estimated at *5170–5010 cal BC* (*94.3% probable*) or *5140–5050 cal BC* (*68.2% probable*). The total duration of burial is estimated to be *0–160 years* (*95.4% probable*), most probably *0–80 years* (*68.2% probable*; we refer the reader again to Appendix B1 for further detail and discussion).

Using this sequence, we can see some spatial patterning at the cemetery, with the older graves in the south-east and younger graves towards the north-west (Gerling 2006, chapter 8; 2012, 117). It is interesting to note that the earliest grave is in the north-western section of the cemetery, possibly suggesting that an earlier part of the cemetery was returned to at a later date (Fig. 7.6; Table 7.3). Alternatively, the cemetery could have spread progressively westwards. Graves in the north-western area were more likely to receive arrowheads in higher numbers, while in the southern part of the cemetery when graves received arrows they were only in ones and twos (Gerling and Francken 2007, 44). Polished stone is also most frequent in the north-western part of the cemetery, with a dense cluster of burials with polished stone in the southern end of the north-western cluster (burials 6, 15, 16, 21, 26, 43, 70, 133 and 220). The relative increase in the numbers of arrowheads included in the grave may therefore have a chronological explanation and appears to replace higher numbers of bone points in the graves found in the eastern and southern parts of the site (Gerling 2006, chapter 6; 2012, 97). The site suggests fewer distinct clusters of burials than other large cemeteries discussed in this volume. However, the density of burials varies across the site, with the graves closest together at the southern, north-eastern and north-western edges of the cemetery.

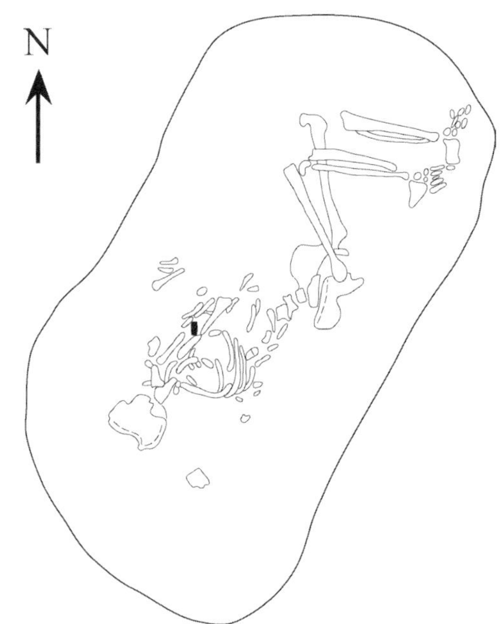

Fig. 7.7. Schwetzingen: burial 151. From Gerling (2012, 219). The Spondylus *bead is shown in black.*

The osteological examinations of the skeletal remains were carried out by Joachim Wahl (Table 7.3). Demographically the site has slightly elevated numbers of women (56.1%, compared with 43.9% men) and a higher proportion of sub-adults than other LBK cemeteries (36.5%, *c.* 30% of which were classed as Infans I, 0–6 years, and II, 6–12 years; Gerling 2006; 2012; Gerling and Francken 2007). Given the numbers of unsexed adult inhumations and cremations, we should perhaps be careful in drawing too many conclusions about the elevated numbers of women here. As noted in Chapter 2.7, there has been a tendency to argue that male burials are over-represented at this time (Jeunesse 1997, 53; Nieszery 1995; Hofmann and Orschiedt forthcoming), but it appears that males and females occur in roughly equal numbers at LBK cemeteries as a whole. However, the number of juveniles is slightly elevated from the average for cemeteries in the LBK (36.5% juveniles at Schwetzingen compared with 28% for the LBK as a whole; Lifeways Database) and is in line with what would be expected from a population at this time (Chamberlain 1997; 2000; 2006).

The orientations of burials at Schwetzingen, as noted above in Chapter 7.5, appear to fall into two major directions, to the north and north-east and to the south and south-west (Fig. 7.7; Table 7.4). This differs from the majority practice at LBK cemeteries, in which burials oriented to the east and the south-east dominate. So although there are two main orientations at the cemetery, there is actually less variation in burial orientation than is seen at other cemeteries. However, the body positions are much more similar to the average for body positions in LBK cemeteries, with left-crouched burials accounting for approximately 80% of the burials (Table 7.4). There is some variation in body position over the different age classes. Those individuals in the oldest and youngest classes adhere to the left-crouched position more strongly, while in the adolescent and early adult age groups left- and right-crouched burials are more equal (though these age classes are also the smallest).

The cemetery is unusual for the low numbers of objects which furnished the graves (50% of graves, which is approximately 10% lower than the average for LBK cemeteries) and no graves have the rich and complex assemblages seen in Moravia or Slovakia (as at Vedrovice and Nitra; Chapter 4), Bavaria (as at Aiterhofen; Chapter 6.7) and Alsace (Chapter 8). In part this is because only four graves contained *Spondylus* objects (graves 99, 151 and 170 contained one or two beads each, while grave 48 contained an armring and a pendant; Gerling 2006; 2012, 106–7). The lack of *Spondylus* at the site may also relate to how late in the LBK sequence the burials at Schwetzingen occurred. *Spondylus* is thought to decrease in frequency over the later phases of the *jüngere* and *jüngste* LBK (Nieszery 1995, 186), though the frequency of *Spondylus* may vary by region as, pending further publication of a number of cemeteries, Baden-Württemberg burials had many fewer *Spondylus* grave goods than other regions (Jeunesse 1997, 94–5). Polished stone was slightly less

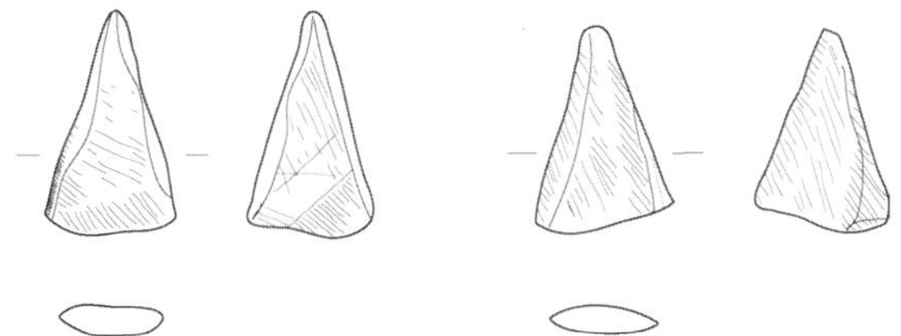

Fig. 7.8. Schwetzingen: example of bone points (burial 97). After Gerling (2012, 246).

frequent than average (about 11% of graves had polished stone compared with 15% for the LBK as a whole) and seems to have preferentially been placed by the upper part of the body in graves with older men (Gerling 2006; 2012, 77). Flint arrowheads were mainly associated with male burials, but provision of flint blades was influenced by age, with long blades found in the graves of older men, and fragments in the graves of adolescents (Gerling 2006; 2012, 90).

While very few imported goods could be identified at all at the site, pottery and stone tools (including chipped stone) suggest different affiliations (Gerling 2006; 2012). As discussed above, the pottery style belongs to the Pfalz group, which lies mainly west of Schwetzingen and the Rhine (Gerling 2006; 2012; Jeunesse *et al.* 2009), but the stone tools were most likely made of material from the uplands of Baden-Württemberg, to the south and east of the cemetery, and draw comparisons with the cemeteries at Stuttgart-Mühlhausen and Fellbach-Oeffingen in the Neckar valley (Gerling 2006; 2012, 65, 81). Gerling (2006; 2012) suggests that pots and polished stone had been made specifically for the burial context, seen in the poor quality of the pottery and lack of use-wear on the adzes and axes. In grave 129, a perforated T-shaped axe made from red deer antler accompanied the deceased, which had certainly been used. These objects are found across Europe in later Mesolithic and Neolithic contexts (Zvelebil 1994, 55, 60), including at other LBK sites such as Eilsleben, Sachsen-Anhalt (Klassen 2004, 121) and it has been suggested that tools of this type originated on the north of or on the northern margins of the LBK, supported by the finds of LBK adzes in non-LBK contexts (Gronenborn 2009b, 536). Further connections to the north have been suggested at the Baden-Württemberg sites of Vaihingen and Ditzingen (Stuttgart), where antler fragments had been decorated with 'drilled pits' which were typical of the late Mesolithic in the Baltic region (Gronenborn 2009b, 536).

Connections southwards may also be hinted at. In grave 200 the decorative designs on a bottle-style pot are very evocative of those found on Cardial ware in southern France, and were mixed with a local LBK style (Behrends 1997b, 23; Lefranc 2007a, 274). This pot was not an import, but created by a local potter, aware of the Cardial style (Lefranc 2007a, 274). Another possible explanation for these designs is that they echo basketry and rope work that could have been in widespread use at the time (Crombé 2009). The fragment of grinding stone in grave

Table 7.5. Heilbronn-Neckargartach: carbon and nitrogen isotope ratios (‰) of animals, with means and standard deviations.

Species	Mean $\delta^{13}C$	SD $\delta^{13}C$	Mean $\delta^{15}N$	SD $\delta^{15}N$	n
Cattle	−21.4	1.13	8.7	1.00	8
Sheep/goat	−20.3	0.55	8.5	0.54	4
Pig	−21.1	0.35	8.1	0.73	2

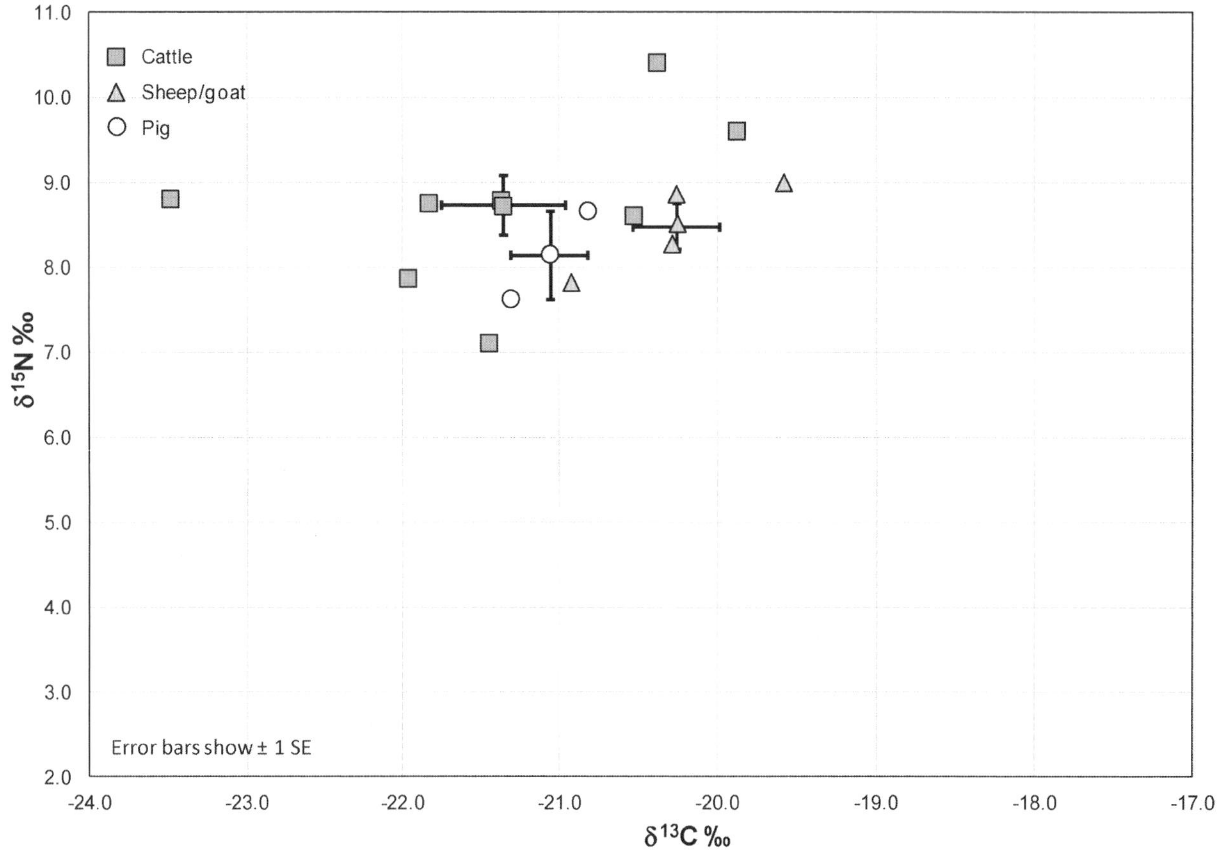

Fig. 7.9. Heilbronn-Neckargartach: carbon and nitrogen isotope ratios (‰) of animals.

43 did appear to be made of an imported sandstone and there is another in grave 56, though its origin is not stated (Gerling 2006; 2012, 102). Snail shells were present in seven graves (nos 12, 25, 36, 55, 61, 98 and 110; Gerling 2006; 2012, 104). In burial 98, 19 perforated snail shells were found around the neck, and the 35 snail shells found in burial 36 were in a similar position. The shells in grave 98 were *Nucella lapillus* (dog whelks) and therefore likely to have come from the Mediterranean (Gerling 2006; 2012, 104) or the Atlantic coast (Jeunesse 1997, 117). A further seven graves had freshwater mussels (*Pseudunio auricularis*, *Unio crassus*, *Unio pictorum*, *Anodonta cygnea* and *Ostrea edulis*) that could have been gathered locally (Gerling 2006; 2012, 104).

Objects made from bone, specifically triangular bone points that may have been used as arrowheads (Fig. 7.8), are more frequent than the average (4%) across the LBK as a whole, occurring in 13% of the graves at Schwetzingen (55 objects in 27 graves; Gerling 2006, chapter 6). The average number may be an under-representation due to preservation conditions, but this rate is only matched by the cemetery of Kleinhadersdorf (where 13% of graves have bone objects, but not bone arrowheads), which appears to have a far richer grave good assemblage than Schwetzingen. What these objects were used for is uncertain, and, unlike flint arrowheads, they are found equally in male and female graves (Behrends 1997b, 19). Bone objects were mainly made from the ribs of red deer or cattle (78%), but smaller objects were fashioned from the metapodials of smaller animals (e.g. sheep/goats, pigs and wild boar; Gerling 2006, chapter 6; 2012, 93 identification by E. Stephan). The high numbers of bone objects in the graves may have come from a shifting emphasis on what constituted high status goods towards the end of the LBK (Gerling 2006; 2012). Gerling (2006; 2012) argues that bone objects emerged as more important in *jüngere* and *jüngste* LBK burials at Schwetzingen, as items such as *Spondylus* and polished stone became less frequent.

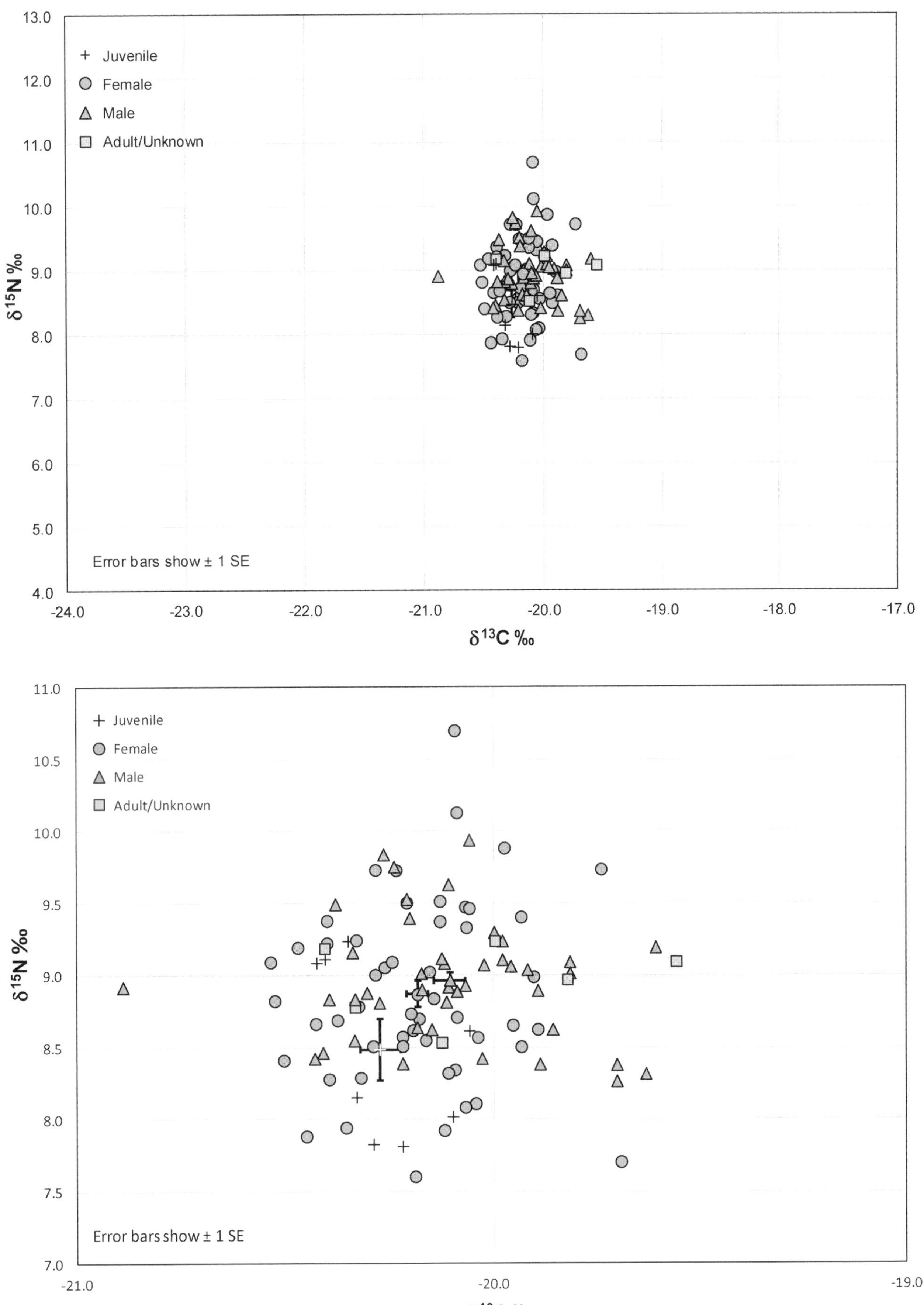

Fig. 7.10. Schwetzingen: carbon and nitrogen isotope ratios (‰) of humans. Top: usual scale, showing clustering. Bottom: close-up of data.

Table 7.6. Schwetzingen: carbon and nitrogen isotope ratios (‰) of humans, with means and standard deviations.

Species	Age/sex	Mean δ^{13}C	SD δ^{13}C	Mean δ^{15}N	SD δ^{15}N	n
Human	Juvenile	−20.3	0.14	8.5	0.60	8
Human	Female	−20.2	0.19	8.9	0.64	52
Human	Male	−20.1	0.24	9.0	0.42	43
Human	Unsexed adult	−20.0	0.35	9.1	0.18	5
Human	All adult	−20.1	0.23	8.9	0.54	100

Table 7.7. Schwetzingen: the mean of δ^{13}C values by orientation category.

Orientation category	Orientations	δ^{13}C ‰ mean	% of burials in category (where orientation could be identified)
Dominant	N–S, NE–SW and E–W	−20.14	67
Secondary	SW–NE and W–E	−20.20	24
All others	SE–NW, S–N and NW–SE	−19.95	9

7.7.2 The animal remains from Heilbronn-Neckargartach

The enclosure at Heilbronn-Neckargartach was identified from aerial photography in 1980 and subsequently excavated in 1988 (Biel 1988; Schmidgen-Hager 1992, 175). It is located *c.* 30 km from Schwetzingen and 4 km west of the Neckar river, on eroded loess soils overlying calcareous rock formations (Schmidgen-Hager 1992, 173). The pottery suggests that the site was in use from phase 4 to 8, with some hints that it may have begun in phase 2b (following Strien's 2000 chronology; Schmidgen-Hager 1992, 195; Table 7.5) and therefore contemporary with the cemetery at Schwetzingen. Within the enclosure, there are traces of longhouses but they are not well preserved (Schmidgen-Hager 1992). There was also one complete grave of a two-year-old child, as well as a possible five further fragmented adult individuals, who appeared to have peri-mortem cranial fractures (Schmidgen-Hager 1992; Orschiedt 1998a, 98; Fibiger 2010).

Carbon and nitrogen analysis

The δ^{15}N values for animals at Heilbronn-Neckargartach are unusually high (Fig. 7.9; Table 7.5). Overall analysis suggests that this cannot be solely explained by geographic or climatic factors (discussed further in Chapter 9.2.5). The differences in δ^{13}C and δ^{15}N values among species are not significant; the sheep/goats have a slightly higher mean δ^{13}C value, and the two pigs show no sign of elevated δ^{15}N or δ^{13}C values compared to the herbivores. Cattle show a wide range of δ^{13}C values, and the lowest is −23.5‰, close to 2 standard deviations from the mean, suggestive of feeding in a closed-canopy environment. The δ^{15}N value from this animal is close to the mean, so it is less likely to be a wild individual. Two wild pigs at Herxheim had a mean δ^{13}C value 2‰ below that of the domestic pig (Dürrwächter *et al.* 2006), further suggesting that the presence of aurochs (wild cattle) does not explain the range of δ^{13}C values at Heilbronn-Neckargartach.

7.7.3 Carbon and nitrogen analysis

In total, 109 individuals were sampled from Schwetzingen for carbon and nitrogen analysis. As determined by Joachim Wahl and Michael Francken, this includes 52 females, 43 males, eight juveniles, five unsexed adults and one with no age/sex data (Fig. 7.10; Table 7.6). Among the adults were three young adults, 56 adults, five classed as adult/mature, 27 mature and four senile. No infants were sampled. All but four of the samples were from rib bones and where these were not available other bones with short turnovers were sampled (phalanx: graves 7 and 37, and metapodial bones; grave 3 and 21). As well as those on bone, samples of tooth dentine from the premolars sampled for strontium isotopic study were analysed for their stable isotope values. This was carried out on 28 teeth, chosen for sufficient dentine (Chapter 7.7.7).

The isotope values are tightly clustered. There are no strong trends with age or sex. Some of the children have noticeably low δ^{15}N values, but overall they are not significantly different from males or females (ANOVA with Bonferroni post hoc comparison of means, juveniles versus adult males, p=0.071). Females show a wider range of δ^{15}N values than males, and the difference in the error variance is significant (Levene's test, p<0.01). Considering the large number of samples from Schwetzingen, the lack of variation is striking, and suggests that these people had rather similar diets, at least in terms of the proportion of protein derived from animals and the range of environments from which food was sourced.

There are a few outliers (at or more than two standard deviations from the mean), including a mature male with a

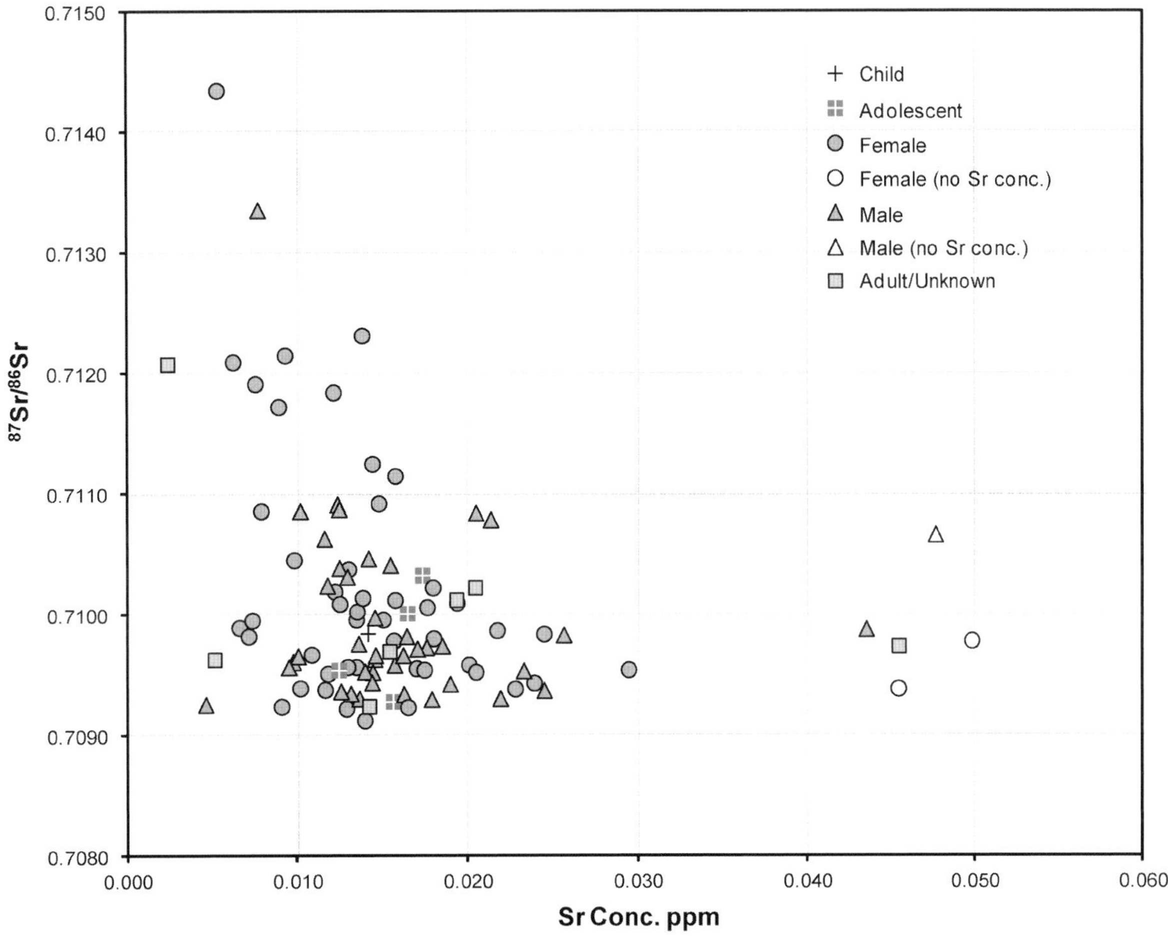

Fig. 7.11. Schwetzingen: strontium concentration (ppm) versus ratio ($^{87}Sr/^{86}Sr$).

Table 7.8. Schwetzingen: strontium isotope ratios and concentrations. 'All' includes seven unsexed adults.

Age/sex	Mean $^{87}Sr/^{86}Sr$	SD $^{87}Sr/^{86}Sr$	Mean Sr conc.	SD Sr conc.	n
Juvenile	0.70980	0.00041	67	9	5
Female	0.71022	0.00105	83	35	48
Male	0.70995	0.00075	74	31	42
All!	0.71008	0.00091	82	51	102

very low $\delta^{13}C$ value (grave 106), three adult males (graves 174, 194 and 220) with a high $\delta^{13}C$ and a low $\delta^{15}N$ value, a senile female with a high $\delta^{15}N$ value (grave 101), a mature female with high $\delta^{13}C$ and $\delta^{15}N$ values (grave 54) and an adult female with a high $\delta^{13}C$ but a low $\delta^{15}N$ value (grave 153). Of these, the female in grave 54 has a very high $^{87}Sr/^{86}Sr$ ratio (0.71435), two males with high $\delta^{13}C$ values (graves 174 and 220) have Sr values of 0.71084 and 0.71066, and the male with the low $\delta^{13}C$ value (grave 106) has an $^{87}Sr/^{86}Sr$ ratio of 0.71041, all higher than the local group; the others have typical $^{87}Sr/^{86}Sr$ ratios. The outliers are discussed further below. It is possible that the low $\delta^{13}C$ value for grave 106 reflects poor sample quality. The C:N ratio is 3.5 and the percentage of collagen 1.9%, which is within the acceptable limits but close to the boundary (Chapter 2.2; Appendix A.20). If the measurement is valid, it could reflect food sources from forest habitats, or, conceivably, freshwater fish consumption, though the $\delta^{15}N$ value is not unusually high (Keaveney and Reimer 2012; cf. Dürrwächter *et al.* 2006).

Animals

Animals from Heilbronn-Neckargartach were sampled to provide a baseline for Schwetzingen (Chapter 7.7.3). However, with mean $\delta^{15}N$ values between 8 and 9‰, very little lower than those of the humans at Schwetzingen, they seem unlikely to provide a valid comparison, so we are unable to calculate the difference between human and faunal means for this site. The range of human carbon and nitrogen values at Herxheim is similar, but from a much smaller sample. The mean values for humans at Herxheim are −20.1‰ (δ^{13}C) and 9.8‰ (δ^{15}N; Dürrwächter *et al.* 2006). There are also currently values from one cattle individual (−21.2‰ and 7.0‰) and one pig (−20.9‰ and 7.8‰), which is too few samples to be useful and perhaps also not appropriate for comparison to Schwetzingen humans as their values are still only 1‰ lower in δ^{15}N. Overall, this points to variation in environment, or use of the environment, between sites, even ones that are geographically quite close.

Correlations with the archaeological data

Overall, there are no correlations between the stable isotopes and the treatment of the body in the grave (body position and orientation), though the six sampled burials which do not fall into the dominant or secondary burial positions do have a significantly different δ^{13}C value mean to the rest of the population (2-tailed *t* test, p=0.019, n=102; Table 7.7). The low numbers of burials in this category urge caution, but this suggests that burials with unusual orientations tended to have higher δ^{13}C values. There were no differences in the δ^{13}C and δ^{15}N values of furnished and unfurnished burials, and individuals buried with pottery, flint, worked bone, local shell or *Spondylus* did not appear to stand out from the averages for the cemetery.

The only grave good that may correlate with the stable isotope results was polished stone. Males buried with polished stone adzes (13 graves, 12 of which were sampled) had a higher average mean δ^{15}N value (9.1‰) than those burials without (8.9‰) but this is not statistically significant (2-tailed *t* test, p=0.3, n=41). However, there was a significant difference in the means of the δ^{13}C values. Those males buried with a polished stone item had a higher mean (−20.0‰) than those buried without (−20.2‰; 2-tailed *t* test, p=0.011, n=41). This significance is retained if the δ^{13}C outlier in grave 106 (without a polished stone axe) is excluded (2-tailed *t* test, p=0.019, n=40). This pattern is suggestive of subtle differences in diet between the men buried with polished stone and those men buried without.

Few spatial patterns across the cemetery could be determined, but the group of burials in the north-eastern part of the site may stand out. This cluster of burials had lower average δ^{13}C values than the rest of the site, which was just outside significance (−20.2‰ compared with −20.1‰; 2-tailed *t* test, p=0.054, n=106), as well as a higher average δ^{15}N value. This difference is significant if the outlier with a high δ^{15}N value (10.7‰) is included (9.1‰ compared with 8.8‰; 2-tailed *t* test, p=0.048, n=106), but not if this individual is excluded (9.0‰ compared with 8.8%; 2-tailed *t* test, p=0.091, n=105). Demographically this group does not stand out from the rest of the cemetery, though it has fewer grave goods than other parts and none of the complex grave good assemblages found only in the western part. This trend in the stable isotope data cannot be immediately explained, though it could suggest that there were some dietary differences between the clusters at the cemetery. No significant differences in the stable isotope values could be determined between the two main phases defined for the cemetery (*mittlere* to the beginning of the *jüngere* phase and the *jüngere* to *jüngste* phase, as defined by the pottery: Chapter 7.7.1; Gerling 2006; 2012, 117). While the means and variances for δ^{13}C values for the two phases are virtually identical (*mittlere/jüngere*=−20.13‰, n=10; *jüngere/jüngste*=−20.15‰, n=6), the δ^{15}N mean value appears to drop over time (falling from 8.9‰ to 8.5‰), but this is likely to be influenced by the lower juvenile values as there are two children in the sample of graves dated to the *jüngere/jüngste* phases and none in the *mittlere/jüngere* phases.

The stable isotope outliers (graves 54, 101, 106, 153, 174, 194 and 220) are also interesting archaeologically. The senile female who had the highest δ^{15}N value (10.7‰), was buried with an undecorated pot, but in the orientation of SE–NW which in contrast to the LBK as a whole is unusual at Schwetzingen, as only three burials are found in this orientation. The elevated δ^{15}N value could have originated in the higher consumption of animal protein (meat or milk) or perhaps freshwater fish. Three of the burials with high δ^{13}C values (153, 194 and 220) are buried in the secondary orientation of SW–NE and left-crouched, though a fourth (burial 174) is buried in the dominant orientation of NE–SW, but in a right-crouched position. The mature male in grave 106 who had the very low δ^{13}C value (−20.9‰) had a highly complex grave good assemblage, including a grinding stone, bone points, local river shell and ochre. The outliers are spread across the cemetery.

7.7.4 Strontium analysis

The individuals sampled for strontium analysis totalled 102, again determined by Joachim Wahl and Michael Francken, including 48 women, 42 males, five juveniles and seven adults of indeterminate sex (Fig. 7.11; Table 7.8). Only the premolars were available for sampling, which mineralise in childhood, normally between the second and fifth year of life (Knipper 2011, 132; Fig. 2.4). Schwetzingen lies at the confluence of the Rhine and Neckar rivers, in an alluvial valley, and previously 36 individuals had been sampled for ^{87}Sr/^{86}Sr ratios, nine of which had ratios which fell outside the local ^{87}Sr/^{86}Sr ratio range and were therefore considered immigrants (Bentley *et al.* 2002, 800). Women dominated the sampled individuals with non-local signatures (five were women, three were males and one was unsexed) and a model of patrilocality was put forward (Bentley *et al.* 2002, 801). The results also suggested that males buried with polished stone were more likely to fall within a range of ^{87}Sr/^{86}Sr ratios suggesting that they had lived on the local loess (Bentley *et al.* 2002, 801).

At the time of that study, the local ^{87}Sr/^{86}Sr ratios were identified as falling between 0.7085 and 0.7103, with the loess thought to have a ^{87}Sr/^{86}Sr ratio at or below about 0.710 (Bentley *et al.* 2002; Bentley 2012). This has since been shown to be the case and the varied geology of south-west Germany is now well understood. Bentley and Knipper (2005b) mapped the biologically available ^{87}Sr/^{86}Sr signatures of the region from archaeological tooth enamel

Table 7.9. Schwetzingen: summary of the $\delta^{18}O$ and $\delta^{13}C$ carbonate values in tooth enamel. 'All' includes one unsexed adult.

Sex	$\delta^{18}O$ mean	$\delta^{18}O$ SD	$\delta^{13}C$ carbonate mean	$\delta^{13}C$ carbonate SD	n
Female	−4.8	0.4389	−11.7	0.7566	15
Male	−4.6	0.5399	−12.5	0.9207	14
All	−4.8	0.4937	−12.1	0.9016	30

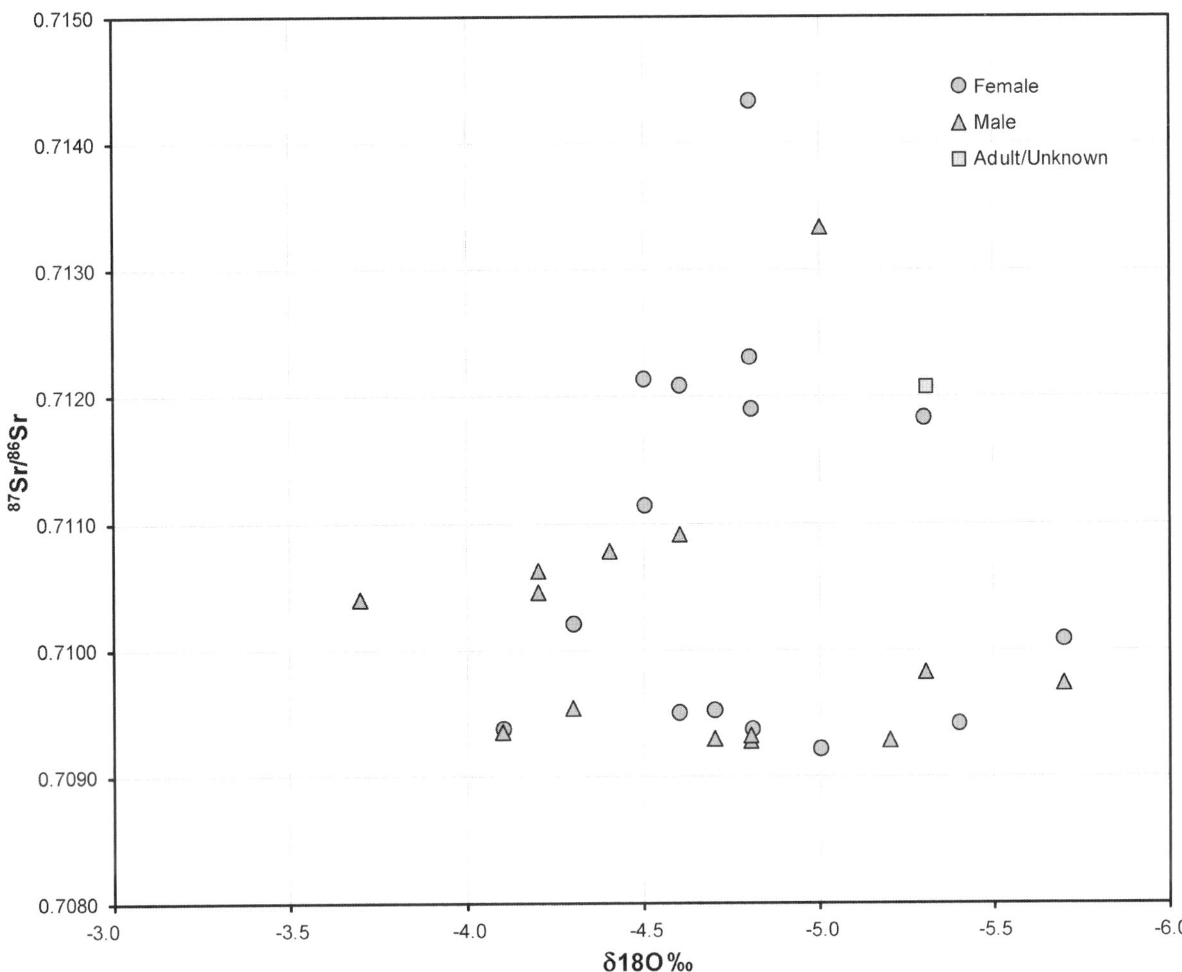

Fig. 7.12. Schwetzingen: strontium ratio ($^{87}Sr/^{86}Sr$) versus oxygen values ($\delta^{18}O$, in ‰).

samples of domestic pigs, finding ratios that varied from 0.7086 in the lowlands, to as radiogenic as 0.722 in the crystalline uplands. In general, the nearer one gets to the granitic mountainous regions of the Odenwald or the Black Forest, the higher the $^{87}Sr/^{86}Sr$ ratios (Bentley and Knipper 2005b), while the foothills and the rivers of the Rhineland plain have $^{87}Sr/^{86}Sr$ values close to 0.710, representing a mixture between highly radiogenic groundwater and weathered calcareous sediments of the Alpine Molasse, the loess and Tertiary marls (Tricca *et al.* 1999, 143). Schwetzingen itself lies at the transition zone between the uplands and the alluvial valley, and the local geology contains Triassic and Jurassic sandstones, evaporites and carbonates (Tricca *et al.* 1999).

The study undertaken for the Lifeways project confirms the earlier argument that females had the most variable $^{87}Sr/^{86}Sr$ ratios, which were influenced by values developing from non-loess soils. Overall, the majority of the population fall into a tight cluster (mean $^{87}Sr/^{86}Sr$ ratio=0.70989), with a second possible array of seven burials dominated by women (mean $^{87}Sr/^{86}Sr$ ratio=0.71168) and two extreme outliers (Fig. 7.11). If the two extreme outliers in graves 54 (a mature female with an $^{87}Sr/^{86}Sr$ ratio of 0.71435) and 132 (an adult male, with a ratio of 0.71335) are excluded, the mean female $^{87}Sr/^{86}Sr$ ratio is 0.71014±0.00086 (n=47), whilst for males, the mean is 0.70987 ± 0.00053 (n=41). The female mean is higher (1-tailed t test, p=0.04, n=88). The juveniles are noticeably similar to the male $^{87}Sr/^{86}Sr$ ratio mean and variance (Table 7.8). We carried out a 1-tailed t test as our hypothesis was that the females would have a higher mean $^{87}Sr/^{86}Sr$ ratio. The variance among females is also greater than among the males (significantly so using an F-Test, p=0.002), but not using the more robust Levene's test, p=0.09). The Schwetzingen strontium isotope ratios are

Table 7.10. Schwetzingen: summary of the carbon and nitrogen values from tooth dentine. 'All' includes one unsexed adult.

Sex	$\delta^{13}C$ dentine mean	$\delta^{13}C$ dentine SD	$\delta^{15}N$ dentine mean	$\delta^{15}N$ dentine SD	n
Female	−20.4	0.175811	9.9	0.489336	15
Male	−20.4	0.539898	10.0	1.10349	13
All	−20.4	0.383567	9.9	0.81884	29

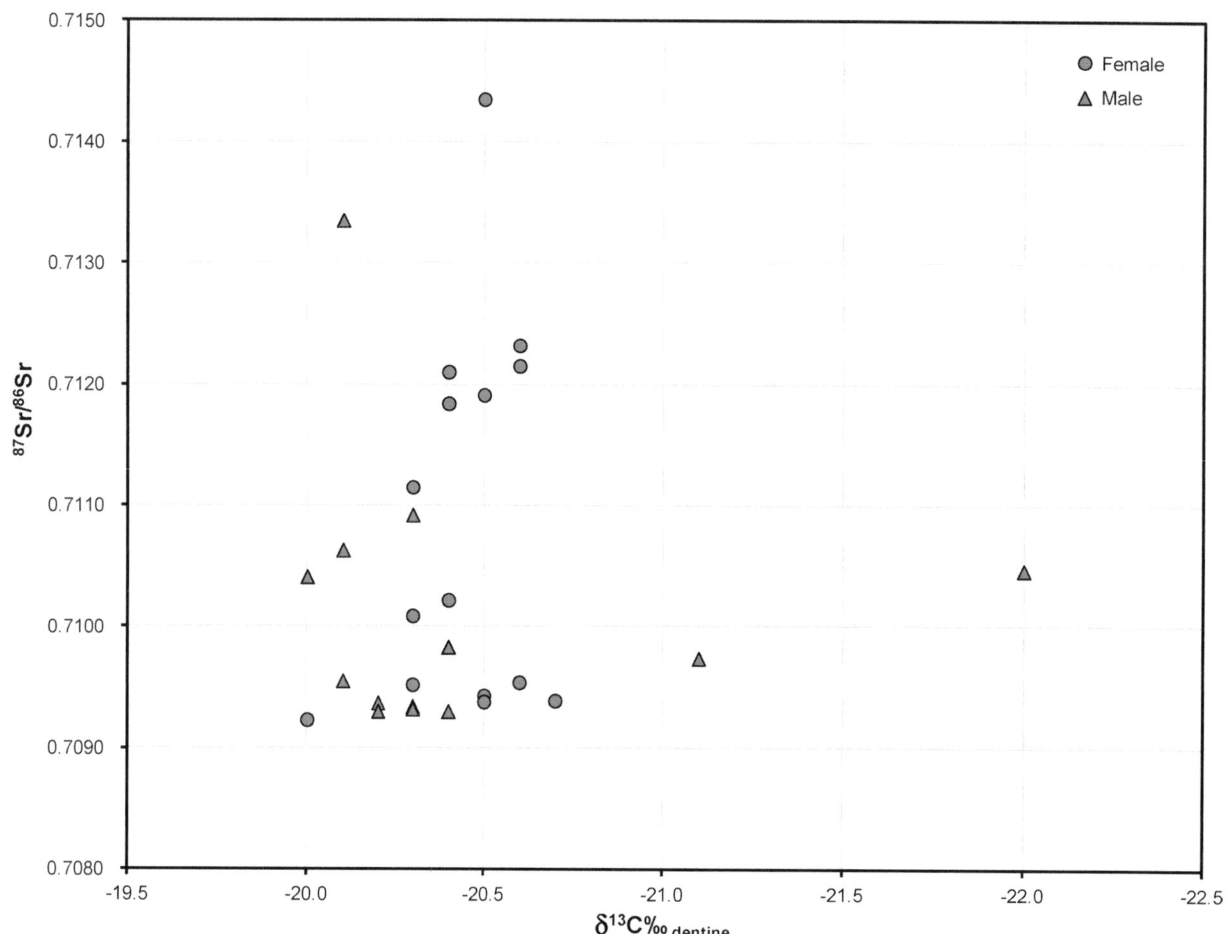

Fig. 7.13. Schwetzingen: strontium ratio ($^{87}Sr/^{86}Sr$) versus dentine carbon values ($\delta^{13}C$, in ‰).

thus in line with the results found elsewhere in this project and consistent with the earlier argument for practices of patrilocality. No differences in the strontium concentration averages or variances could be determined.

Correlations with the archaeological data

There were no overall correlations between the strontium isotopes values and body positions and orientations. Most of the individuals (graves 1, 9, 42, 54, 132, 150, 151, 169 and 219) with $^{87}Sr/^{86}Sr$ ratios above 0.7103 were oriented in the dominant orientation (N–S and NE–SW) and were left-crouched. These graves were, however, sparsely furnished; graves 9, 150 and 219 were unfurnished and the rest had one or two items at most, including sherds and flint tools. The right-crouched individual in grave 42, however, had 14 pot sherds included in the fill of the burial and a *Spondylus* bead was included with the individual in grave 151. Grave goods such as complete pots, grinding stones, bone points (Chapter 7.7.1), local river shells and, as identified by the earlier study (Bentley *et al.* 2002), polished stone adzes were all concentrated in graves falling within the main cluster of results.

While no further correlations between the strontium isotope ratios from the female graves and grave goods were found, among the male burials (n=41) a significant pattern in relation to polished stone could be discerned. The mean $^{87}Sr/^{86}Sr$ ratio among those without an adze is 0.70995±0.00057 (n=29), but for males with an adze it is 0.70968±0.00035 (n=12). Although these means are statistically the same (2-tailed t test, p=0.15, n=41), the variance among the males without an adze is significantly greater (Levene's test for variance, p=0.03). Burials with adzes show some clustering at the cemetery, with a group of nine burials close together in the western part of the

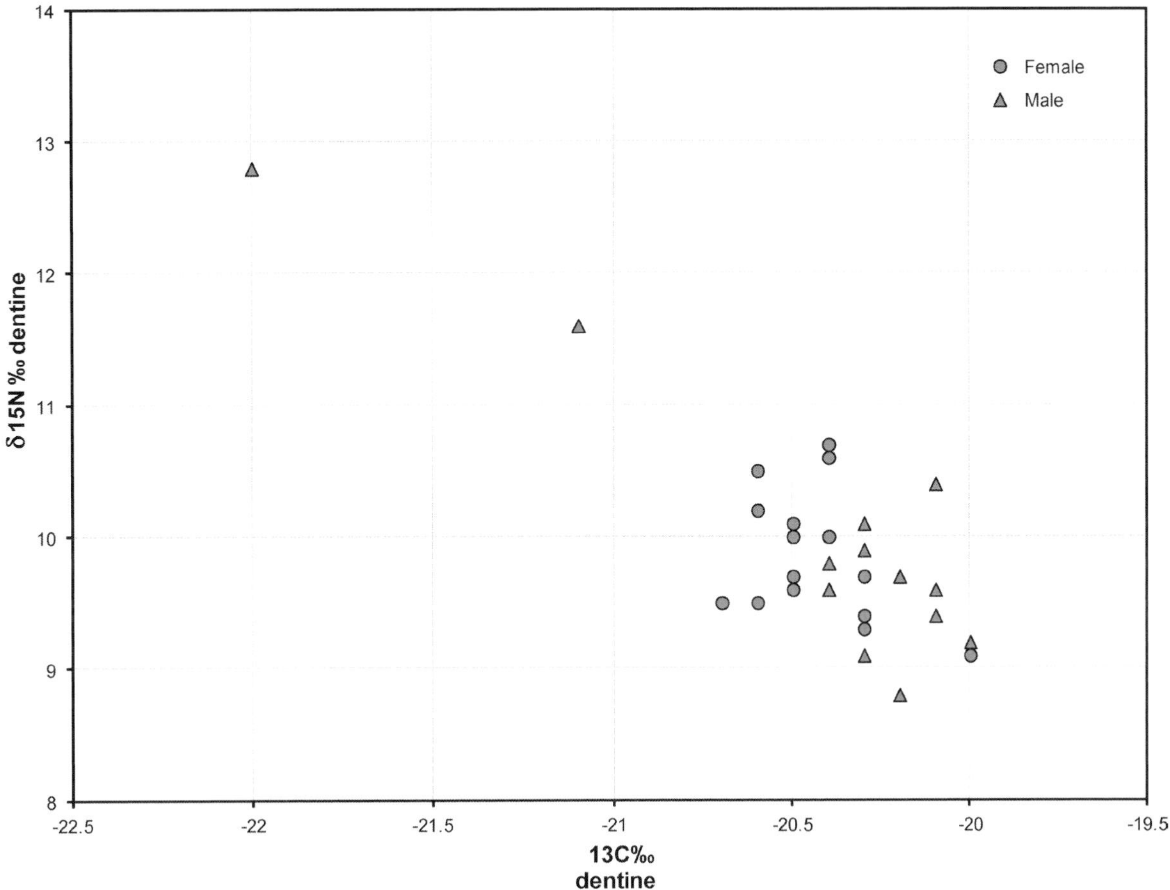

Fig. 7.14. Schwetzingen: dentine carbon ($\delta^{13}C$, in ‰) versus nitrogen ($\delta^{15}N$, in ‰) values.

cemetery (Fig. 7.6; Gerling 2006, chapter 4.3.2; 2012, 75). It is in this western area of the cemetery that most of the complex grave good assemblages are found. This concentration of the burials with the most grave goods may have a chronological explanation, as it is in this area of the cemetery that the youngest pottery is found, but as no differences could be found in the strontium data using the ceramic sequence proposed in Gerling (2006; 2012), the isotope data cannot shed light on this pattern.

Comparing the different parts of the cemetery, Bentley (2001) found that the mean $^{87}Sr/^{86}Sr$ ratio among sampled individuals from area 1 in the north-west of the cemetery (Fig. 7.6) differed from that in area 2 in the middle and from area 3 in the south-east, whereas results from areas 2 and 3 were not significantly different. The distinction of individuals from area 1 was further supported by lead isotope measurements ($^{206}Pb/^{208}Pb$ and $^{207}Pb/^{208}Pb$; Bentley 2001). From these results it was proposed that area 1 of the Schwetzingen cemetery contained the most local residents. However, with the larger sample of 102 individuals, these spatial differences no longer hold true (One way ANOVA, $F_{2,99}$=0.123, p=0.88), though both the extreme outliers identified by the Lifeways project were buried in the north-western cluster of the site. Given that there appears to be some chronological patterning behind the spatial arrangement of the cemetery, we can perhaps suggest that the varied mobility and subsistence practices that led to the $^{87}Sr/^{86}Sr$ ratios found at Schwetzingen remained fairly constant over the life of the cemetery.

7.7.5 Oxygen, carbon and nitrogen analysis of teeth

We also analysed tooth enamel at Schwetzingen for $\delta^{18}O$ and $\delta^{13}C$ isotopes. As the whole of the premolar was available for sampling, we had sufficient tooth dentine to also carry out tests for $\delta^{13}C$ and $\delta^{15}N$ values (Table 7.9). Oxygen isotopes, in combination with strontium, can help to refine the geographic origin of individuals as they provide information about drinking water sources (Chapter 2.3). The general implication of these results for our overall picture of the LBK will be discussed in Chapter 9 along with the dentine results from other sites in this project, but here we report some of the findings as they relate to Schwetzingen specifically. Thirty individuals (15 females, 14 males and one unsexed individual) were sampled including, where possible, the burials which had outlying $^{87}Sr/^{86}Sr$ ratios (9, 42, 54, 132, 150, 151 and 169).

When the 30 $\delta^{18}O$ values are plotted against the strontium ratios reported above, two arrays can be determined (Fig. 7.12). One array is horizontal with all individuals having a very similar $^{87}Sr/^{86}Sr$ ratio (mean=0.70949±0.00023, n=15), and the second array falls on the diagonal, stretching from a $^{87}Sr/^{86}Sr$ ratio above 0.713 and a $\delta^{18}O$ value of about −5 down to a $^{87}Sr/^{86}Sr$ ratio of about 0.710 and $\delta^{18}O$ value of about −4.2 (Fig. 7.12). Lower (more negative) $\delta^{18}O$ values probably originated in the uplands, and, coupled with the likelihood that more radiogenic $^{87}Sr/^{86}Sr$ ratios in Baden-Württemberg also signal upland usage, this suggests that the individuals forming the diagonal array spent their time between uplands and lowlands. Men and women are well represented across both the arrays, so they cannot be explained by different sex-based practices (Fig. 7.12) and interestingly, all the males buried with an adze that were sampled fall in the lower horizontal array, repeating the trend found above in the strontium isotope ratios alone.

A similar pattern can also be seen when $\delta^{13}C$ values from tooth dentine are plotted against the $^{87}Sr/^{86}Sr$ ratios, though this is less clear (Fig. 7.13; Table 7.10). What is also suggested by this plot is that females tended to have lower $\delta^{13}C$ values (dentine only and therefore values from childhood). The mean $\delta^{13}C$ dentine value for the females (−20.4‰±0.18) is significantly (2-tailed *t* test, p=0.002, n=26) more negative than among males (−20.2‰±0.14), if two clear outliers are excluded (Fig. 7.14). These outliers are burial 66, an adult male ($\delta^{13}C$=−22.0‰ and $\delta^{15}N$=12.8‰), and burial 154, a mature male ($\delta^{13}C$=−21.1‰ and $\delta^{15}N$=11.6‰). All the above values were determined by tooth dentine and therefore the high $\delta^{15}N$ values from the outliers probably represent a breast-feeding signature from childhood.

However, in the case of both burials 66 and 154 the dentine $\delta^{13}C$ values are consistently lower (more negative) than the value from bone collagen (burial 66, dentine $\delta^{13}C$=−22.0‰ and collagen $\delta^{13}C$=−20.3‰; burial 154 dentine $\delta^{13}C$=−21.1‰ and collagen $\delta^{13}C$=−20.2‰). Overall, the average dentine $\delta^{13}C$ value (−20.4‰) was lower than that from bone collagen (−20.1‰), while the average dentine $\delta^{15}N$ value (9.9‰) was higher than that from bone collagen (8.9‰). There were no significant differences between the stable isotope averages from dentine for men and women, in line with what was determined for the stable isotope values from bone collagen. The average difference between the $\delta^{13}C$ values (0.46‰) was lower than the average difference between $\delta^{15}N$ values (1.0‰).

7.7.6 Correlations between the different isotopes

While there are no overall correlations between the $^{87}Sr/^{86}Sr$ ratios, strontium concentration and the $\delta^{13}C$ and $\delta^{15}N$ values, the seven individuals falling outside the main $^{87}Sr/^{86}Sr$ ratio cluster (Chapter 7.7.6) have a lower mean $\delta^{13}C$ value (−20.3‰ compared with a mean of −20.1‰ for all adults at the cemetery). As females dominate this group and females, overall, tend to have lower $\delta^{13}C$ values, this result is not statistically significant, but the lower $\delta^{13}C$ values are perhaps consistent with this group sourcing more of their food from potentially more forested upland areas (Fig. 7.10). The $\delta^{15}N$ values of this group with higher $^{87}Sr/^{86}Sr$ ratios are consistent with the rest of the cemetery. When the outliers are considered, individuals with unusual $^{87}Sr/^{86}Sr$ ratios often have typical $\delta^{13}C$ and $\delta^{15}N$ values, and *vice versa*. There is no easy equation between 'diet' and 'origin' at Schwetzingen, but there are certainly hints that there was some patterning.

7.7.7 Site summary and discussion

Overall, the isotope results from Schwetzingen have demonstrated some interesting differences in lifeways across the population, primarily suggesting that there were two potential mobility patterns that may have related to how the different components of the diet were sourced (Figs 7.10–11). This is consistent with the arguments made elsewhere in this volume, and by Bogaard *et al.* (2011) for Vaihingen, that different groups within a community were exploiting varied landscapes in the vicinity of settlements. This argument is perhaps complicated by our current lack of knowledge of where the population buried at Schwetzingen lived (Gerling 2006, chapter 1; 2012, 15), as well as, of course, the distinct possibility that cemeteries were in some way selective, but the isotopes strongly suggest that different food sourcing patterns co-existed at Schwetzingen. Amongst the oxygen and strontium results, two groups could be identified: a main cluster to which most sampled individuals belonged and a smaller secondary group that were most likely using both local lowland and upland resources. In comparison to the strontium isotope ratios, where females had more variable $^{87}Sr/^{86}Sr$ ratios than males suggesting more varied origins and patrilocal practices, men and women were equally represented in both arrays, suggesting that there were two groups or communities rather than gendered dietary practices.

In contrast to the strontium and oxygen data, the stable isotope data indicate that for the most part those buried at Schwetzingen had a fairly similar dietary protein intake. This suggests that although groups may have been using different landscapes around Schwetzingen they were eating a fairly consistent diet. The varied geology of Baden-Württemberg (Bentley and Knipper 2005a) and the suggested presence of denser woodland in the region (Döhle 2005, 284) mean that the individuals in the upper array would not have have had to travel far from the Rhine-Neckar confluence to influence their isotope data (Knipper 2011). There were also a handful of outliers in the stable isotope data but they are very varied and no single explanation can be put forward to explain their presence in the data. The stable isotope value of each outlier could thus have a different origin; physiological processes such as disease, individual choice of diet and an origin outside the Schwetzingen locality could have all contributed to their deviation from the central cluster of the stable isotope values.

The strongest association between the isotope data and the burial rites was, as with other sites already discussed in this volume, provision with polished stone adzes. Males buried with adzes had far less variation in their strontium isotope ratios and on average had slightly elevated nitrogen values. This pattern is consistent with these males sourcing most of their diet from the loess and having low mobility. At Schwetzingen older males were most likely to receive polished stone items in the grave (Gerling 2006; 2012;

Gerling and Francken 2007), suggesting that the adze may have been associated with a status earned in later life. However, because the strontium isotope values come from a tooth mineralised in childhood, the correlation between burial with an adze and strontium ratios implies that burial with an adze was in some way determined by geographic origin at birth and a loess-based diet. Older males were more likely to receive complex burials at Schwetzingen and in this respect parallels can be drawn to the cemetery of Nitra.

Amongst the female graves, a trend to fewer grave goods and more unfurnished burials can be identified (Gerling 2006; 2012). Younger adult women received varied grave good assemblages, including the most ornamentation (e.g. shell beads), and 32% were unfurnished, whilst the older (mature and senile) females received pots almost exclusively and the number of unfurnished burials rose to 40% (Gerling 2006; 2012, 62). The burials of three older females stand out from this pattern (54, 55 and 190). Burials 54 and 190 are two of the three female burials which receive lithics, and grave 55 contained four shell beads and one animal bone in the fill. This overall pattern contrasts with Aiterhofen, where older females were more likely to receive ornamentation (Chapter 6.7.1). This could perhaps be explained by the lack of *Spondylus* at Schwetzingen as well as a reduced focus on personal ornamentation as grave goods more generally, which makes the cemetery appear poorer in comparison to the general patterns in the LBK. In fact, it could be that personal ornamentation was not favoured as a grave good at Schwetzingen. Perhaps in its place, the high frequency of pot sherds included in the grave fills suggests a different emphasis in burial rite.

The cemetery does have some spatial variation, with three possible clusters identified. In the northern part of the cemetery (using the break in excavation as a dividing line; Fig. 7.6), the burial orientations are more varied than in the southern part (χ^2=35.15, df=7, Monte Carlo sig. 2-sided, p<0.001), though dominant and secondary orientations are spread throughout the cemetery and there is no spatial patterning by body position. It is also in the north-western part of the cemetery where burials with the most complex grave good assemblages are concentrated (Gerling 2006; 2012, 121). Rather than envisaging the northern area of the cemetery as the location of the 'high status' graves, we could argue that it is actually more variable in comparison to the more uniform southern part. Given the possible chronological movement of the cemetery westwards, we could perhaps also argue, following Jeunesse (1997), that the later burials show more diversity. Although the isotope data showed little spatial differentiation, the southern part of the cemetery has a significantly lower δ^{13}C mean value which, if earlier than the northern burials, suggests perhaps a move towards a more open landscape over time.

7.8 Regional discussion

While the stable isotope values from Schwetzingen indicate few outliers, the strontium ratios suggest a heterogeneous community, with some individuals eating a predominantly lowland and local diet, while others sourced more of their food from the uplands and woodlands. Although this may not have translated into vastly different mobility patterns, the correlation with burial with an adze does show that it was meaningful for the lifeways of the Schwetzingen community. What we do not see at the cemetery of Schwetzingen is the clear division of groups in the isotope data into possible 'clans', as identified at the settlement of Vaihingen (*c.* 60 km away; Chapter 7.4; Bogaard *et al.* 2011). While we do not suggest that those living at Vaihingen would have buried their dead at Schwetzingen, it is interesting to note that we do not see a clear division of separate dietary groups along the lines of the different groups suggested by the settlement evidence. We could perhaps suggest that the group of seven burials with high strontium ratios which fall outside the main cluster at Schwetzingen (Fig. 7.11) does imply some variation, since the outliers all appear to be different in some manner.

The isotope results from Schwetzingen confirm what was proposed by Bentley *et al.* (2001). It is thus concluded that females demonstrate a wider range of lifetime mobility, consistent with a model of patrilocality, and that males with polished stone adzes have a tighter range of strontium ratios, suggesting that they were sourcing their diet from the fertile loess soils. In many ways, however, the strontium results contrast with recent work from Stuttgart-Mühlhausen (*c.* 80 km from Schwetzingen) on multiple teeth, which found that young men were experiencing a period of mobility away from the lowland loess areas during the time in which their second molars mineralised (at *c.* 3–8 years of age), but that otherwise the population was fairly homogeneous (Knipper and Price 2010; Knipper 2011). Knipper (2011) rejects the suggestion that these ratios could have developed through practices of transhumance with cattle into the uplands over summer months. Rather, she argues that herds were kept close to the settlement year-round and leaves the raised strontium ratios in M2 molars unexplained, pointing to the varied nature of the geology in the immediate vicinity of the sites (Knipper 2011). While multiple teeth were not available for sampling from Schwetzingen, the strontium and oxygen results from premolars (which mineralise earlier than the second molars) at this cemetery site do suggest that there was variation in mobility practices across the community, including both men and women using the uplands. The differences between the two sites are unlikely to be explained by chronological changes, as they overlap in time; rather they seem to contribute to an overall picture of variation throughout Baden-Württemberg. Thus more similarities can be drawn between the strontium and oxygen results from Schwetzingen and Talheim (Bentley *et al.* 2008) than with the cemetery of Stuttgart-Mühlhausen, despite Talheim being geographically closer to Stuttgart-Mühlhausen.

While the correlations between the isotope data and the grave goods continue to be focused on provision with polished stone adzes, Schwetzingen presents some interesting variation compared to the sites discussed in previous chapters. Following Jeunesse's (1996; 1997)

Tradition II, there is a reduced emphasis on grave goods that could be classed as personal ornamentation (that is, objects which dressed the body) at the cemetery. Jeunesse (1996; 1997) also argued for the continued presence of acculturated hunter-gatherers in Tradition II burials. As with the isotope data, the burial rites do not group together in a straightforward way that would be suggestive of exclusive identities reflected in burial practice. In its place, a multifaceted drawing together of identity, connection and performance seems to have taken place. For example, despite the lack of material imported in the Schwetzingen cemetery, evidence of wider contacts could be found in some graves (e.g. burial 200 was accompanied by a local pot with Cardial designs), and an extended burial rite may be suggested by the presence of the ceramics in the grave fills and even the possibility that some skeletons may have been removed from pits after their inhumation (Gerling 2006; 2012, 27; cf. Lenneis 2010c).

Earlier in this chapter (7.3.1) we devoted significant space to discussing the beginning of the LBK in Baden-Württemberg and the development of La Hoguette pottery. We did so partly because earlier isotopic analyses had sought to explore the possibility of a continued hunter-gather presence at LBK settlements (e.g. Price *et al.* 2001), and we wanted to present the regional context for this discussion, but also because the evidence demonstrates the complex mixture of subsistence and material practices, as well as the multitude of possible identities, present from the very earliest LBK in Baden-Württemberg. While we would perhaps question whether persistent hunter-gatherers were still around at the time when the Schwetzingen cemetery began to form, exploitation of wild animals did continue and seemingly at a higher rate in this region in comparison to others examined in this project (with the exception of Bavaria; Chapters 6.4 and 7.4.4). The isotopic data from contexts in Baden-Württemberg, however, have shown that while the population does not clearly resolve into two separate groups, there are significant differences that may relate to how the varied landscapes outside settlements were exploited. It would be problematic to assign particular broad-brush categories of identity such as 'hunter-gatherer', 'Mesolithic' or 'Neolithic' to the diversity found amongst the strontium and oxygen data, and the lack of correlation between these isotopes and the funerary practices suggests that at death more complex and nuanced statements about identity were being made.

Notes

1 This open-air site is situated on the peat of the Federsee (Kind 1992; 1997; Jochim 2006).

2 Lüning *et al.* (1989) list no more than ten sites with La Hoguette pottery for the *älteste* LBK in Baden-Württemberg, out of 20 known sites from this period at this time; Manen and Mazurié de Keroualin (2003, 118) found 12 LBK sites where La Hoguette ware was present, but argue that only four or five are from the very earliest phases.

3 Manen and Mazurié de Keroualin (2003, 118) note only two sites where La Hoguette ware has been found in isolation (without LBK pottery) in Baden-Württemberg. Gehlen (2006, 44, 49) considers there to be at least four 'La Hoguette' only sites in this region on the basis of lithic assemblages: Bad-Cannstatt, Baden-Oos, Taunhaf and Kappelberg.

4 Jeunesse and van Willigen (2010, 596) also identify instances of Cardial and Epicardial pottery at a number of LBK sites, one of which – Heidelberg-Wieblingen – is from Baden-Württemberg. In return, so to speak, two instances of LBK-related designs have been identified on Cardial and Epicardial pots (Jeunesse and van Willigen 2010, 596).

5 Stuttgart-Bad Cannstatt has a radiocarbon date of 5460–5290 cal BC (68.2% confidence; UtC-5450; 6353±45 BP: Meurers-Balke and Kalis 2001, 634). The date was produced on the organic remains from a sherd of La Hoguette pottery taken from the lowest layer of the site.

6 This animal bone assemblage consists of 1085 identifiable bones, of which 65% were red deer, 8% sheep/goats, 2% cattle and 1% domestic pig (Kind 2010, 453).

7 However, Petrequin *et al.* (2009) claim to have found such evidence in the Alpine foreland.

8 Cladders and Stäuble (2003, 501) suggest that this might be the case with the Baden-Württemberg settlement of Rottenburg. Despite being *älteste* LBK in style, this settlement produced a set of radiocarbon dates that fall during the 53rd-century plateau in the radiocarbon calibration curve and therefore within the beginning of the Flomborn phase. It is thus difficult to extrapolate the chronological relationship between this settlement and the Flomborn phase sites around it.

9 The Alsace-related pottery at Echterdingen 7 is found in three different pits and a further Haute-Alsace sherd was found about 50 km further north at Heilbronn-Klingenberg (Strien 2000, 53).

A Schwetzingen lifeway: burial 151

This adult woman, buried with a single Spondylus *bead, was laid to rest in a SW–NE orientation and crouched on her left side. Her carbon values fall in the lowest 20% of the population, which may suggest that foods sourced from a more forested environment formed a larger component of her diet than they did for other women at the site. She also stands out through a rather low nitrogen value of just 8.3‰ (female mean at the site is 8.9‰), further corroborating the idea of a diet different from that of most others. In her case at least, this difference correlates with a non-local origin, as at 0.71191 her strontium ratio is much higher than the female mean of 0.71022. The oxygen value from her tooth dentine (−4.8‰) places her in the upper array identified in Fig. 7.10, suggesting that she had eaten a combined upland and lowland diet.*

In general, the female strontium values at Schwetzingen are already higher than those of males, and throughout the volume we have used this as an indication of patrilocality. For the woman in burial 151, this non-local origin was combined with a continued divergence in terms of dietary practices throughout her lifetime. This is the case for other individuals at Schwetzingen and a group of women with similar strontium ratios form a secondary cluster away from the majority of the cemetery. Although we cannot yet judge how the women in this cluster were related, perhaps we can speculate that the woman in burial 151 followed the lifeway of other women in her birth community and, on marriage, moved into the Schwetzingen area.

She was laid to rest in the second most frequent or 'antipodal' orientation at Schwetzingen. Nevertheless, she was buried in what is the standardised position for this site, and so at this level was fully integrated in the wider burial community. This casts an interesting light on the provision with Spondylus *for burial 151. At Schwetzingen, non-local males tended to receive fewer goods, but that pattern does not hold for this woman, who instead seems particularly marked out by being one of only four burials with imported shells (or indeed any kind of personal ornament). Moreover, burial 151 lies in what is suggested to be the older portion of the Schwetzingen cemetery, in the south-east of the site, where grave good assemblages are in general less complex compared to later phases. In sum, although a single* Spondylus *bead would not be considered noteworthy on a site like Aiterhofen (Chapter 6), in the local context this burial would have stood out.*

It is always difficult directly to link the provision of particular goods with a 'higher' or 'lower' social status. In this case, a more fruitful suggestion may be that as an incomer, this woman was marked out in death through her grave goods. Indeed, given the relatively low complexity of the grave good assemblages at Schwetzingen in general, it is interesting that many of the goods that were deposited do explicitly refer to far-flung contacts. Of particular note are the antler T-axe in grave 129, an item with strong connections to the Mesolithic groups of the North European plain, and a vessel in grave 200 whose decoration evoked Cardial designs, ultimately of Mediterranean inspiration. Both these items point far beyond the confines of the LBK culture itself, as does Spondylus*. 'Foreignness' was hence more generally considered an aspect of identity worth referencing at the graveside.*

Within a patrilocal system, such as that argued for Schwetzingen, it is perhaps not surprising that burial should stress the identity of 'incomer'. On the one hand, we may expect a tension between the positive connotations of outside brides ensuring the continuity of the local group, while on the other hand suspicion or fraught relations can often form an element of affinal relations. As with burial 151, however, these associations and relations are complex and can be loaded with competing values. At once marked out through routine activities, this woman nevertheless conformed to the majority body position and her non-local origin was referenced in positive ways through her grave goods.

A Schwetzingen lifeway: burial 185

With a strontium ratio of 0.70953, the mature man in burial 185 falls well within the local range of the site and therefore could have been born and grown up in or around Schwetzingen itself. However, despite seemingly having belonged to this community throughout his life, he was laid to rest in a way unusual for this cemetery: in a right-crouched position, with his head to the south-west. His SW–NE orientation is the second most common at Schwetzingen, and is antipodal to the majority NE–SW placement. In addition, most individuals at this site are left-crouched, and this position is also the most common specifically among mature individuals, which makes his right-crouched position stand out all the more. Although quite likely a man with local origins, burial 185 is thus marked out through his placement in the grave.

His stable isotopic values also suggest that he may have differed from the majority of the community in terms of dietary composition. At −20.3‰, his carbon value falls in the bottom third of the population and may point to a greater importance of resources from more wooded areas. More striking is his high nitrogen value, which at 9.8‰ is well above the local male mean of 9.0‰. Finally, the burial is entirely unfurnished, and thus runs counter to several of the trends identified for local individuals at Schwetzingen. Local men in general are more likely to receive polished stone tools than non-locals. They also show a tendency towards higher nitrogen values and hence possibly greater consumption of animal protein. Moreover, it is often particularly older males who are marked out with the most complex grave good assemblages. His position in the more sparsely furnished south-east part of the site may have worked against burial 185 receiving a very wide range of grave goods, but certainly on the grounds of his age, diet and origin he would overall be expected to have been given a polished tool.

The absence of such an item is therefore striking. It is difficult to suggest specific reasons for why this man should have been excluded from receiving any grave goods at all, other than to note that a right-crouched position seems often to coincide with burials which have other unexpected or out of the ordinary features. Local origin and compatible dietary practices were evidently not always enough to guarantee membership of the group of males with polished tools. We must contemplate other, achieved dimensions for inclusion, and perhaps also the possibility that any status or position referenced by an axe or adze could be lost over a lifetime.

8 Alsace

Penny Bickle, Rose-Marie Arbogast, R. Alexander Bentley, Linda Fibiger, Julie Hamilton, Robert Hedges and Alasdair Whittle

8.1 Introduction

In the last of our regional considerations of the isotope results, we reach the westernmost extent of the Lifeways project, crossing the Rhine into France and the region of Alsace (Fig. 8.1). The Alsatian landscape is framed by the upper course of the Rhine, whose valley is some 40 km at its widest (Lefranc 2007a, 11), and bounded by the Vosges mountains to the west, the Alps to the south, the Black Forest to the east, and to the north, the Rhine valley continues into Germany. The variety of different geologies

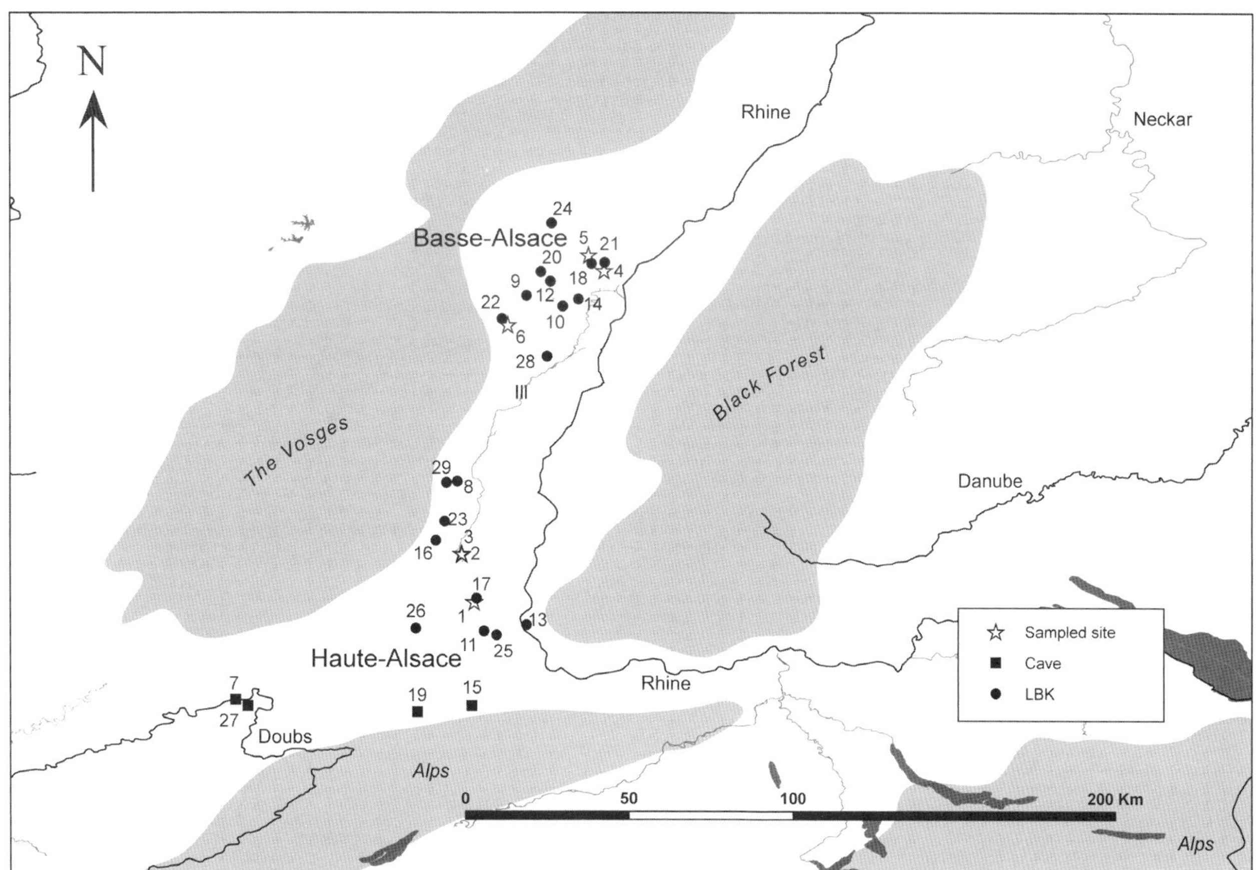

Fig. 8.1. Map of sites sampled (1–6) and others mentioned in Chapter 8. Upland areas are in italics. 1) Mulhouse-Est (Rixheim), 2) Ensisheim les Octrois*, 3) Ensisheim* Ratfeld*, 4) Souffelweyersheim, 5) Vendenheim, 6) Bischoffsheim, 7) Bavans, 8) Colmar* route de Rouffach*, 9) Dachstein, 10) Entzheim, 11) Geispitzen, 12) Ittenheim, 13) Kleinkems-Istein,14) Lingolsheim, 15) Lutter, 16) Merxheim Breitenkopf, 17) Mulhouse-Est* Île Napoléon*, 18) Mundolsheim, 19) Oberlarg, 20) Quatzenheim, 21) Reichstett, 22) Rosheim* Sainte-Odile*, 23) Rouffach* Tuilerie*, 24) Schwindratzheim, 25) Sierentz, 26) Spechbach-le-bas, 27) Voujeaucourt, 28) Westhouse* Ziegelhof*, 29) Wettolsheim* Ricoh.

in this region is very similar to that seen in the previous chapter. The Vosges mountains are formed from crystalline granites and metamorphic rocks to the south and sandstones to the north, and the transition between the plain along the Rhine and the uplands consists of the sous-vosgiennes hills (or lower Vosges) formed from limestones, which are the focus for wine growing today (Lefranc 2007a, 11). The plain is bisected by the rivers Doller and Ill, which flow into the Rhine at Strasbourg. Just beyond the alluvial soils along the banks of these rivers, terraces are formed from loess soils, which are found in intermittent patches throughout the region and form the focus for early Neolithic settlements (Jeunesse 1980; Arbogast and Jeunesse 1990, 287; C. Thévenin 1993, 77; Lefranc 2007a, 15). The climate of the upper Rhine is often thought to mark the beginning of the more Atlantic climates in the westerly part of the European continent (Sielmann 1972; Kreuz 1990), but the Vosges mountains act as a barrier to the influence of the oceans, resulting in a more continental climate with similar annual average temperatures and rainfall (700–900 mm per year) to the rest of the LBK distribution covered by this project (Lefranc 2007a, 15; Chapter 9.2).

Although Alsace forms a coherent geographical entity, the LBK[1] sites can be divided into two distinct groups (J. Schweitzer 1980; J. Wolf 1980; Jeunesse 1990; 1995a; 1995b; 1996; C. Thévenin 1993; Ilett and Constantin 1993; Arbogast 2001; Lefranc 2007a). The LBK has been separated into groups in Haute-Alsace (southern Alsace) and Basse-Alsace (northern Alsace), following the two modern *départements* of Alsace, with the boundary between these two different cultural groups lying just north of the modern town of Colmar (Jeunesse 1995b; Lefranc 2007a). This bipartite division of the Alsatian settlement pattern has previously been explained by geographical factors, such as the distribution of the loess, which is less prevalent on

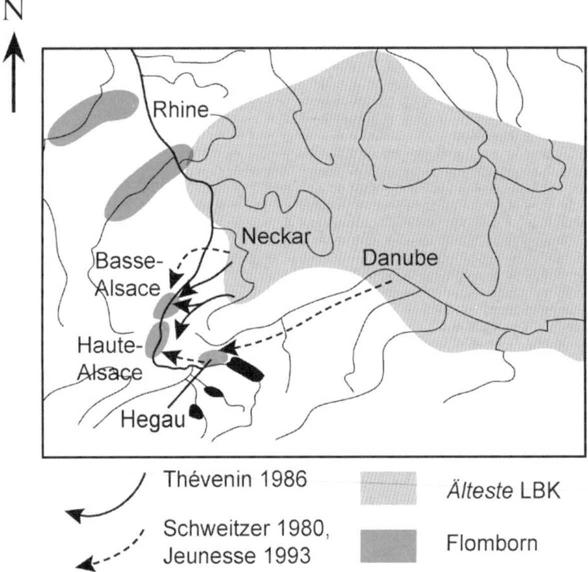

Fig. 8.2. The suggested colonisation routes along which the LBK reached Haute- and Basse-Alsace. After Lefranc (2007a, 33).

the plain between Strasbourg and Colmar (Bonnet *et al.* 1980, 116; J. Wolf 1980, 211). However, this has since been refuted as more LBK settlements have come to light (Lefranc 2007a, 22, 151) and thus the division of LBK Alsace appears to rest better on cultural differences rather than on varying environmental conditions.

One possible explanation for such differences could be found in the means by which the Neolithic arrived in this region (Fig. 8.2). By the time the LBK expands into Alsace (whether by colonisation, adoption by local hunter-gatherers or a mixture of both) there were several different regional traditions already being practised throughout the LBK distribution (see Chapter 8.2 for discussion of chronology; Jeunesse 1990b; 1996; 1997; Whittle 1996; Coudart 1998; Gronenborn 1999; Farruggia 2002; Lefranc 2007a). This suggests that the two LBK groups in Alsace could have had their origins in different LBK groups further east. Indeed, the recent re-evaluation of the pottery at two sites along the boundary north of Colmar (Wettolsheim *Ricoh* and Colmar *route de Rouffach*) indicates that the expansion into Alsace is chronologically complex, occurring in waves from Bavaria and the Neckar valley (Lefranc 2007a, 208–9). However, the presence of the possibly pre-Neolithic La Hoguette[2] pottery in the region, with its hints of Mediterranean origins, implies that we should not dismiss an indigenous contribution to the LBK in Alsace (Constantin 1985; van Berg 1990; Constantin and Blanchet 1998, 603; Manen and Mazurié de Keroualin 2003; Pétrequin *et al.* 2009).

8.2 History of research

The excavation of LBK sites in Alsace began slightly later than in other regions covered by this project, during the first half of the twentieth century, with the excavations of the cemeteries at Souffelweyersheim and Lingolsheim (Forrer 1910; 1938; Forrer and Jaenger 1918). These excavations were led by the Swiss-born Robert Forrer, who dominated archaeology in Alsace in the early twentieth century as conservator at the *Musée archéologique* in Strasbourg (1909–1939; Châtelet 2009, 9). The wartime occupation led to the formation of the *Landesamt für Ur- und Frühgeschichte*. This was transformed into the *Direction des Antiquités Nationales* in 1945, with Alsace the first region in France to benefit from a state-run service protecting archaeology and leading excavations (Châtelet 2009, 8), and the rate of excavation increased (Denaire *et al.* 2008). Although regulated by the state, the majority of excavations during the post-war period were carried out by volunteers and local societies (Lefranc 2007b, 21; Denaire *et al.* 2008, 9). From the 1980s onwards this changed, and archaeology across France saw increasing regulation and the growth of developer-funded archaeology (Denaire *et al.* 2008, 10; Châtelet 2009, 10). During this decade the *Direction des Antiquités* (renamed the *Service Régional de l'Archéologie* in 1991) undertook large-scale projects which were carried out by AFAN (*Association pour les Fouilles Archéologiques Nationales*), and volunteers continued to

Table 8.1. Alsace: the five chronological models in use. Adapted from Lefranc (2007a, 23).

Region	**Haute-Alsace**	**Haute-Alsace**	**Basse-Alsace**	**Main river valley**	**Neckar valley and Alsace**
Author of model	C. Thévenin (1988; 1993)	Lefranc (2007a)	Jeunesse (1999)	Meier-Arendt (1966)	Strien (2000)
Rubané final	V	V	V	V	9
Rubané récent	IVc IVb IVa	IVb IVa	IVb IVa	IV	8 7
Rubané moyen	IIIb IIIa	III	III	III	6 5 4
Rubané ancien	IIb IIa	II	II	II	3 2B 2A
Rubané le plus ancien				I	1

excavate in their local area (Lefranc 2007b, 21; Denaire *et al.* 2008, 10).

In 2001, the law pertaining to rescue archaeology in France changed, resulting in the creation of the national organisation INRAP (*Institut National de Recherches Archéologiques Preventives*), which subsequently replaced AFAN (Denaire *et al.* 2008, 11). However, this law left several ambiguities as regards the financing of developer-led archaeology in France and paved the way for competitive tendering, which in turn has led to a number of different organisations operating in Alsace (Denaire *et al.* 2008, 11). Today, excavations are mostly developer-funded, carried out by either INRAP, the *Pôle d'Archéologie Interdépartemental Rhénan* (PAIR) or *La Société Antéa* (Lefranc 2007b; Denaire *et al.* 2008, 11). To date, 140 LBK sites have been excavated in the Alsace region (94 in Basse-Alsace and 46 in Haute-Alsace; Lefranc 2007a, 15).

There has also been a strong tradition of research in Alsace, particularly focused on regional patterns of LBK ceramic decoration and burial practices (Jeunesse 1980; 1993; 1997; 1999; A. Thévenin 1980; 1993; J. Schweitzer 1980; C. Thévenin 1993; Lefranc 2007a). From the late 1970s onwards, sufficient evidence had been accumulated to allow researchers to investigate cultural relationships within the Alsace region and how they related to the wider LBK distribution. Gérard Bailloud (1976) first emphasised the relationships between Haute-Alsace and the Paris basin through detailed consideration of the techniques of ceramic decoration. This theme was carried through to the first synthesis of LBK research in Alsace, produced in 1980; the main problems identified concerned the definition of LBK chronology and whether the LBK arrived in Alsace from Bavaria or the Neckar valley (Thévenin and Thévenot 1980; Lefranc 2007a, 15). The 1980s also saw the formation of *L'Association pour la Promotion de la Recherche Archéologique en Alsace*, which produces an annual journal (Lefranc 2007b, 21).

Unfortunately no site in Alsace has to date received the detailed investigation seen at some of the larger sites elsewhere (such as Cuiry-lès-Chaudardes, Paris basin; Vaihingen, Baden-Württemberg; and the Merzbach and Schlangengraben valley sites, Aldenhovener Platte). This may be due to the restricted number of complete house plans found in Alsace; for example, no Alsatian sites were included in the study by Coudart (1998) of LBK architecture. However, currently more than 70 LBK houses are known in Alsace, with the majority appearing in the last 20 years (Lefranc 2007b, 73); in the last ten years, excavations at the site of Bischoffsheim have revealed some 40 well preserved house plans (Lefranc *et al.* 2004). In southern Alsace (Haute-Alsace) the sites of Colmar, Sierentz (which has imported pottery from Basse-Alsace and the Neckar valley; Mauvilly 1997; Wolf and Viroulet 1997; Jeunesse *et al.* 2007a; Lefranc 2001) and Wettolsheim have contributed to our understanding of everyday life (Jeunesse 1993). In contrast to the settlement evidence, a number of well studied cemeteries, such as Mulhouse-Est and Ensisheim, both sampled as part of this project, have been found in Alsace. These have been considered in detail and have contributed significantly to our understanding not only of LBK funerary traditions but also of the broader regionalisation of LBK communities (Jeunesse 1993; 1995a; 1995b; 1996; 1997; 1999).

Chronologies developed for elsewhere in the LBK have been influential in determining the Alsatian sequence; Meier-Arendt's (1966) five-stage periodisation of pottery from the Main has been particularly significant. Currently, the Alsatian LBK is divided into four periods: *Rubané ancien*, *Rubané moyen*, *Rubané récent* and *Rubané final* (Table 8.1). The *Rubané ancien* phase corresponds to an initial phase of LBK occupation in Alsace and not to the earliest LBK further east (that is, it is not the *älteste* LBK), but there is a general equivalence between the *ancien*, *moyen* and *récent*, and the *ältere, mittlere* and *jüngere* phases. The existence of these four periods is largely accepted by specialists, yet their relative timings remain

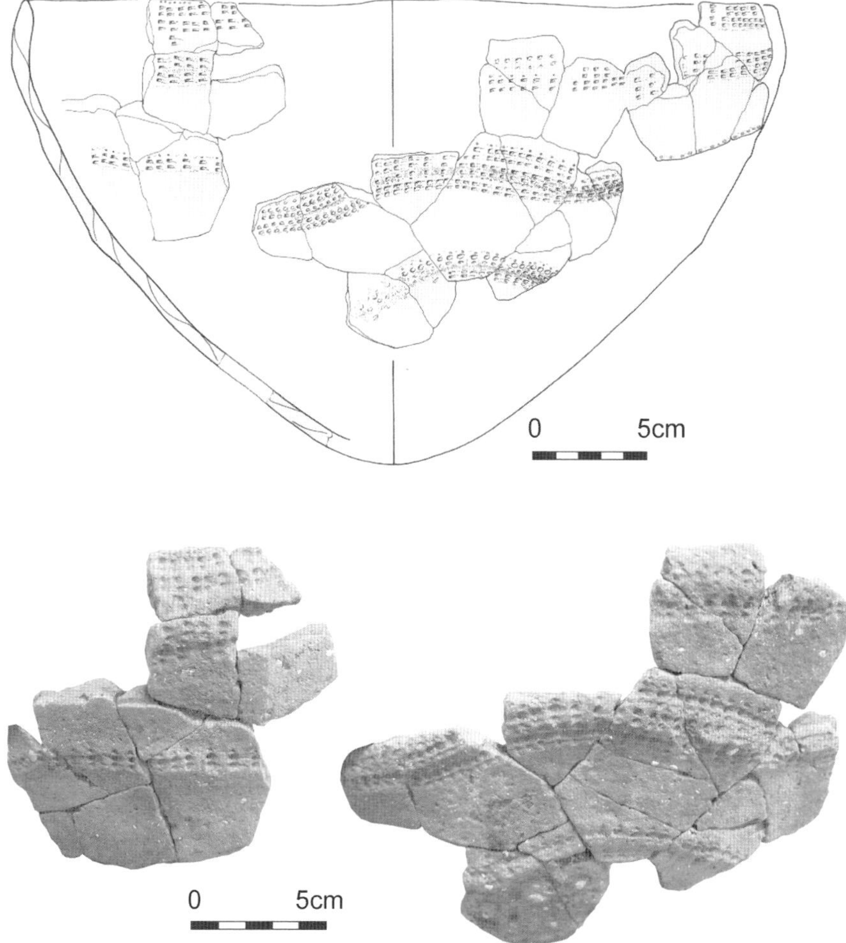

Fig. 8.3. A La Hoguette pot from Choisey (Jura). Drawing: Anne-Marie Pétrequin, CRAVA. Photo: Pierre Pétrequin, CNRS. From Pétrequin et al. *2009, 495.*

disputed (see below). This is partly due to the limited number of radiocarbon dates: Lefranc (2007a) quotes only 19 radiocarbon dates from the settlement sites of Colmar, Wettolsheim, Dachstein, Reichstett, Schwindratzheim and Mundolsheim. These dates include the measurement on the trepanned individual from the Ensisheim cemetery (Alt *et al.* 1997, 360). Relative dating has been achieved through detailed study of the ceramic assemblages, first by Jeunesse (1993) and latterly by Lefranc (2007a). So the internal development of the LBK in Alsace can fairly confidently be determined from pottery, though the phases thus constructed can only approximately be correlated with calibrated radiocarbon dates.

Today, issues of regionality and origins continue to inspire debate amongst archaeologists studying the LBK in Alsace. Both Jeunesse (1997; 2000a; 2000b) and Arbogast (1993; 2001) have demonstrated that differences exist on the regional scale. Lefranc (2007a) used a detailed ceramic seriation to refine understanding of the chronological relationship between the different phases of the LBK in Haute-Alsace and Basse-Alsace. These contributions have gone a long way to demonstrating the extent to which the different regions were in contact, but the nature of those contacts still needs to be explored. Were these groups loosely associated and heterogeneously networked, or did they have tightly controlled hierarchies, with formalised routine connections? Did regional alliances result in shared practice or did they leave scope for LBK communities to do things differently?

8.3 The arrival and development of the LBK

The pattern and strength of regional identities and networks have been long debated in Alsatian LBK archaeology. At issue, particularly during the 1980s, was whether the two LBK groups identified in Alsace originated from two different LBK groups populating the north and south of the region respectively or moved from one location, but subsequently formed different cultural groupings during the LBK. Over the last twenty years this debate has grown to include the contribution of local Mesolithic groups and has led to a more refined understanding of the regional chronology (Jeunesse 2000a; 2000b; 2001). However, despite this, colonisation remains the favoured explanation for the arrival of the LBK, and the contribution of indigenous Mesolithic groups has often been significantly marginalised (Jeunesse 2000a; 2000b). While today the model of LBK colonisation continues to be supported by researchers, it is now also accompanied by growing evidence for complex interactions between farmers and hunter-gatherers in the form of La Hoguette pottery (Fig. 8.3).

In the first volume thoroughly to consider the origins of Alsatian LBK populations (Thévenin and Thévenot 1980), two models were proposed which remain influential today. Thévenin and Sainty (1980) concluded that the LBK arrived in the region first from the Neckar valley during the early Flomborn phase (on the basis of similarities in ceramic decorative patterns), with the groups spreading out into Basse-Alsace during a second phase (the *Rubané moyen*) and influenced by the late Flomborn groups around them (in Haute-Alsace, the Neckar valley and Rhine basin). However, this was challenged in the same volume by J. Schweitzer (1980) and J. Wolf (1980, 200–1), who preferred to see two different groups populating Alsace. In this model, communities moved from the Neckar valley into Basse-Alsace, and along the Danube and across the Black Forest into Haute-Alsace (Bonnet *et al.* 1980; J. Schweitzer 1980; J. Wolf 1980). This was based on similarities in ceramic designs, geographical proximity and on the higher presence of *Spondylus* in burials in Haute-Alsace cemeteries, a feature which is also found in Bavaria (Chapter 6.5; Bonnet *et al.* 1980; J. Schweitzer 1980; J. Wolf 1980; Jeunesse 1990; 1993; 1995b; 1997; Lefranc 2007a). Christian Thévenin (1988; 1993, 76) subsequently supported the former model of André Thévenin, based on the strong evidence for contacts between the whole of Alsace and the Neckar valley during the *Rubané moyen*. This has not been substantiated by the recent work by Lefranc (2007a) on the ceramic styles throughout Alsace, who proposes that a northern route brought groups south from the lower Rhine and Neckar areas into Basse-Alsace, but that the LBK in Haute-Alsace originated from the south-east, with regionalisation demonstrable from the earliest phases (Flomborn).

We will return to the development of the LBK in Alsace below, but it is worth considering what role local Mesolithic groups played in the earliest and, indeed, later stages of the LBK in the region. More recently, an increased role for local hunter-gatherers in the Neolithic transition in Alsace has been advocated, as has been the case with other areas of the LBK (Chapters 3.3, 4.3, 5.3 and 7.3; contrast Chapter 6.3). It is possible that the start of the Neolithic in Alsace and the arrival of the LBK in the region may not have been coeval. The occurrence of La Hoguette pottery in Alsace and the possible presence of cereal pollen claimed to date to the end of the seventh millennium cal BC strongly suggest for Jeunesse (2003b, 99) the presence of a pre-LBK Neolithic/terminal Mesolithic on the western fringes of the *älteste* LBK. This has also been suggested by others (such as Erny-Rodmann *et al.* 1997 and Gronenborn 1998, 191), who see this claimed cereal pollen as evidence for experimental farming on the part of Mesolithic hunter-gatherers who were in contact with Neolithic groups (see also Chapter 7.3).

This pre-LBK period is considered by Jeunesse (2003b, 105) to have begun around 6000 cal BC in the Rhineland, approximately half a millennium before the first LBK communities arrived in central Europe at about 5500 cal BC (Gronenborn 1999; Lüning 2005a). A La Hoguette cultural horizon has been considered to develop due to initial contacts between Neolithic populations on the one hand and indigenous hunter-gatherers living around the Rhine and Neckar valleys on the other (Jeunesse 1987; 1998; Gronenborn 1990; van Berg 1990; Whittle 1996; Manen and Mazurié de Keroualin 2003; Pétrequin *et al.* 2009). Most researchers perhaps still prefer to follow the original suggestion by Constantin (1985) that La Hoguette demonstrates links with southern French farming groups belonging to the Cardial culture. Most recently, Pétrequin *et al.* (2009) have argued that La Hoguette ware developed in the Jura from contacts with Cardial ware-using groups and then spread out rapidly throughout the Rhine and Neckar valleys.

The limited evidence for sites with La Hoguette pottery is far from conclusive. As we saw in Chapter 7, while the site of Stuttgart-Bad Cannstatt (Baden-Württemberg) has undisturbed La Hoguette sherds clearly not associated with LBK ware, it also dates to the Flomborn phase (estimated as 5200–5100 cal BC; Gronenborn 1998, 191), slightly after the LBK is thought to have arrived in Alsace. Indeed, the majority of the evidence for a Final Mesolithic is found concentrated in the Neckar valley, Baden-Württemberg, rather than in Alsace (Kind 1992; 1998; Manen and Mazurié de Keroualin 2003, 124; Pétrequin *et al.* 2009). Other evidence from cave sites, such as Bavans in the Doubs valley (south-west of Alsace), where La Hoguette sherds have been found alongside domesticated sheep, suggests that La Hoguette pottery could be associated with the terminal Mesolithic (Chaix 1997, 193). This does seem to suggest that the LBK arrived at a time when local hunter-gatherers were experimenting with making pottery and consuming some domesticated animals (Gronenborn 1990, 177; 1998, 191; Chaix 1997, 193; Jeunesse 1998; 2003a; Pétrequin *et al.* 2009). Additionally, a possible sherd of Cardial ware has been found at the LBK site of Westhouse *Ziegelhof*, Basse-Alsace (Lefranc *et al.* 1998, 17–18; Lefranc 2007a, 270), suggesting possible LBK-Cardial connections of some kind (Constantin 1985; Lichardus-Itten 1986).

In contrast to possible Mediterranean influences, stylistic traits in LBK pottery that can be seen as inspired by both La Hoguette and Limburg styles arrived late in the Alsatian sequence, in the *Rubané récent* (Jeunesse 1995a), and La Hoguette and Limburg sherds continue to be found in contexts up to and including the *Rubané récent*. Jeunesse *et al.* (2007b, 66) argue that the sherds in question, which are concentrated in the Bischoffsheim-Rosheim area of Basse-Alsace, are not residual finds because they are very fragile and would not have survived out of context. This suggests that the terminal Mesolithic co-existed alongside the first LBK communities in Alsace for 200–300 years (the *Rubané ancien* and *Rubané moyen*), if not longer. The date range for La Hoguette has recently been argued to be as much as 500 years (from *c.* 5400 cal BC to *c.* 4900 cal BC;

Pétrequin *et al.* 2009, 491–3), though this requires further confirmation with more extensive radiocarbon dating and formal modelling. However, the argument for a persistent Mesolithic is supported by Mauvilly (1997, 344), who notes the presence of Mesolithic lithics at *Rubané* sites. There are three instances where Mesolithic tool-types can be distinguished from classic LBK ones, in the lithic assemblages at Bischoffsheim, Colmar and Spechbach-le-bas (Mauvilly 1997, 344).

While Bischoffsheim and Colmar are long-lived sites first occupied during the *Rubané ancien*, settlement at Spechbach-le-bas does not begin until the *Rubané récent*. Building on this discussion, Jeunesse (2000a) proposes a model which includes a *composante autochtone*, or 'indigenous element', contributing to the LBK in Alsace as well as incoming groups. As Jeunesse (2000a; 2002a; 2003a) places a great deal of significance on the evidence for pre-LBK elements of Neolithic life, the arrival of the LBK is considered as the adoption of a new cultural order and communities mixing, rather than either a wholesale change in their way of life for local communities or colonisation from the east. In these ways, both the ceramic and lithic evidence are seen as pointing to some kind of co-existence of both Mesolithic and Neolithic groups for some time after the LBK first arrived in the region (Manen and Mazurié de Keroualin 2003; Pétrequin *et al.* 2009). Lüning *et al.* (1989) also supported this model of a Final Mesolithic and argued that the communities that made La Hoguette ware in fact were responsible for bringing cereal cultivation and domesticated animals to the Neckar valley before the LBK.

This model, however, is not accepted by everyone. The occurrence of persisting Mesolithic hunter-gatherers has since been questioned for the LBK in the Paris basin by Allard (2005; 2007), who argues that going beyond the hypothesis in the case of Limburg ware is problematic. Whether either of these ceramic styles – La Hoguette or Limburg – illustrates a cultural identity separate from the LBK, let alone a surviving Mesolithic population, as yet still remains unclear. As Manen and Mazurié de Keroualin (2003, 125) argue, the association between Late Mesolithic lithic assemblages and non-LBK pottery is not consistent, and though the nature of La Hoguette ware itself is not clear, it cannot be securely dated before the arrival of the LBK. Recently Pétrequin *et al.* (2009) attempted a reconstruction of a La Hoguette pot, which led them to argue that its makers were originally skilled Cardial potters, producing ware for ostentatious display, which was later imitated by experimenting Mesolithic hunter-gatherers.

Furthermore, as noted in Chapter 7.3, whether the presence of cereal pollen in the record for central Europe at this early date during the Final Mesolithic is reliable has recently been called into question (Behre 2007a; 2007b). Difficulties in identifying domestic and wild species from *Cerealia* or *Cerealia*-type pollen and the insignificant quantities in which it has been found, led Behre (2007a; 2007b) to argue that the hypothesis that cultivation took place during the Mesolithic should be rejected (cf. Jeunesse 2003b; Petréquin *et al.* 2009). Certainly at the moment the picture remains hazy at best. The only Alsatian Mesolithic site that suggests the presence of a separate pre-LBK Neolithic community is the cave site at Oberlarg *l'abri du Mannlefelsen* (Mauvilly 1997, 343), which is located away from loess soils. The picture developed for this period is thus a complex pattern of mixture, communication and exchange, with a possible terminal Mesolithic living alongside the earliest LBK communities and only becoming assimilated during the *Rubané récent*.

Consequently, researchers have preferred to look beyond Alsace to the eastern and earlier distribution of the LBK to explain its arrival in the region and the subsequent cultural differences. Here some knowledge of the subsequent development of the LBK in Alsace is necessary. After the earliest phases (from the Flomborn period), Jeunesse (1993; 1995c, 119) argues that the western LBK can be divided into three separate geographical and cultural groups: *Rubané du Nord-Ouest* (RNO), *Rubané du Centre* (RC) and *Rubané du Sud-Ouest* (RSO), with Haute-Alsace making up part of the RSO and Basse-Alsace part of the RC. More recently, Jeunesse (1997; 2000b; Jeunesse *et al.* 2009, Abb. 15) has separated the central grouping (RC) into the *Rubané de Basse-Alsace* (RBA) and *Rubané du Neckar* on the basis of regional ceramic styles. These different groupings are also visible in burial practices, with Jeunesse (1995b; 1996; 1997) identifying two traditions of burial (Tradition I and Tradition II: noted already in Chapter 1.3.5, and discussed in Chapter 7.5 and below). Tradition I is found in Basse-Alsace and the RNO, while Tradition II is found in Haute-Alsace and hence across the RSO. While the burial evidence as well as the material culture supports some form of regional differentiation, the chronology of the LBK in Alsace is clearly significant in these debates.

Both Christian Thévenin (1988; 1993) and Hans-Christoph Strien (1993) have suggested similar chronologies for the arrival of the LBK in Alsace. Thévenin (1993, 76, 81) placed the earliest LBK in Alsace (the *Rubané ancien*) towards the middle or end of the Flomborn phase. Strien (1993, 64) likewise places the earliest LBK in Alsace during Stehli's (1973) phase 2B of the LBK, hence coinciding with its second phase of expansion and increased regionalisation (Chapter 1.3.1 and 1.3.6). The most influential chronologies in Alsace were initially developed from Meier-Arendt's (1966) scheme, omitting the earliest LBK found further east (Table 8.1), and this can be seen in the models subsequently developed by C. Thévenin (1988; 1993) and Jeunesse (1993; 1999). The main differences between the models lie in the extent to which each of the four phases is thought to be sub-divided, rather than the broader chronological development. Table 8.1 illustrates these different schemes for sub-dividing the LBK in Alsace. Lefranc (2007a) has recently reconsidered the ceramic material, using the most up-to-date corpus of evidence, and suggested a refined sequence that closely follows that of Jeunesse (1993; 1995c; 1999). Lefranc's (2007a) work illustrates how necessary understanding the chronology is to developing a more detailed appreciation

Table 8.2. Summary of the regional differences between Haute- and Basse-Alsace.

Region	Regional ceramic Tradition (Jeunesse 1995c)	Burial Tradition (Jeunesse 1996; 1997)	Main features of tradition	Animal Tradition (Arbogast 1993; 2001)	Main features of tradition	Other differences
Basse-Alsace (Northern Alsace)	*Rubané du Centre* (RC) or *Rubané de Basse-Alsace* (RBA)	II	More variation in grave goods, body position and orientations, less ornamentation, more flint *'Acculturated hunter-gatherers'*	A	Pig are second most frequent animal Fewer wild animals	Naviform houses present
Haute-Alsace (Southern Alsace)	*Rubané du Sud-Ouest* (RSO)	I	More 'equal' – fewer differences in grave goods, body positions and orientations, more ornamentation *'Traditionally LBK/Danubian'*	B	Sheep/goat are the second most frequent animal Highly varied numbers of wild animals	Prevalence of trapezoidal longhouses Higher frequency of stone bracelets More restricted areas of loess soils

of community and regional relationships within the LBK. He argues that the different ceramic styles of the *Rubané ancien* in Alsace correspond to both the Flomborn style (in Germany) and the Ačkovy style (in Bohemia; Lefranc 2007a, 151) in north and south Alsace respectively, hence suggesting Alsace was colonised by two different groups (one from the Neckar valley into Basse-Alsace and another from Bavaria via the Hegau region near Lake Constance into Haute-Alsace; Fig. 8.2).

The chronology of the later LBK was also refined by Lefranc (2007a, 277), who demonstrates that the development of the two Alsatian LBK communities was diachronic (rather than contemporary). Thus it is extremely difficult to distinguish between the two groups during the *Rubané ancien*, a feature which lasts into the *Rubané moyen*, but in the following periods regional differentiation is stronger, with *Rubané récent* and *Rubané final* starting slightly earlier in Basse-Alsace than in Haute-Alsace (Jeunesse 1993; 1995c; Lefranc 2007a, 191, 283). The most marked change in pottery is the disappearance of curvilinear designs in Basse-Alsace between the *Rubané moyen* and *Rubané récent*, while these continue to be used in Haute-Alsace through the *Rubané récent* (Jeunesse 1995c, 3). Lefranc (2007a, 188) stresses that although his analysis demonstrates a significant difference between the regions it does not explain why such differences should have developed or expanded. The sites of Colmar and Wettolsheim, at which a mixture of styles are found, certainly suggest that from the *Rubané ancien* phase a boundary developed in the Colmar district that was consolidated during the *Rubané moyen/Rubané récent*, with two geographically defined identities developed (Lefranc 2007a, 177, 284). Lefranc (2007a, 26–7, our translation and emphasis) argues that at the site of Wettolsheim *Ricoh*, the 'cohabitation of these groups can be illustrated by the finds' of a mixed 'vocabulary' of styles of ceramic decoration, which were 'strictly limited to the frontier zone' and demonstrated the presence of two separate '*ethnic groups*' in Alsace.

8.4 Regional networks and diversity

Despite the choice of the term 'ethnic' by Lefranc (2007a, 27) to describe the two different regional groups in Alsace, there have been few attempts explicitly to characterise the mechanisms by which different regional groupings in the LBK recognised and classified themselves. Jeunesse (1995c, 11) identified regional groupings in the western LBK, which he thinks develops from the Flomborn phase onwards (as discussed above: the RNO, RSO, RBA and RN). These four groups are primarily visible in decorative designs on pottery, but differences can also be identified in strategies for exploiting domesticated animals (Arbogast 2001), in house orientation (Jeunesse 1995c, 10–11), in the occurrence of ceramic and stone bracelets (Jeunesse 1995b; 1995c), in burial traditions (Jeunesse 1996; 1997) and possibly in the lithic technologies as well (Mauvilly 1997, 345; for a summary of the regional patterns, see Table 8.2). Lefranc (2007a) and Jeunesse (1995a; 1995b; 1999; 2001; 2003a) both imply that the regional groups are coherent networks, with an identity defined by shared practices as well as geographical location. However, the regional differences did not develop in isolation and locally specific styles or practices are also accompanied by evidence for contacts between regions (Jeunesse 1995a; 1995b; 1997; 2001; 2003a; Lefranc 2007a). This demonstrates that although there were dominant streams of influence along which styles and practices were shared between groups, LBK communities were also heterogeneously networked.

8.4.1 Regional connections

Overall, when contacts are identified through pottery decoration in Basse-Alsace, they predominately point to connections with south-west Germany and the Neckar valley. Numerous examples of Alsace-related ceramic designs have been found in the Neckar valley, and even as far as Ulm-Eggingen on the Danube, illustrating that contact was reciprocal (Lefranc 2007a, 254, 261, 277). In Haute-Alsace, Sierentz *Sandgrube* and *Tiergarten* and Merxheim *Breitenkopf* have sherds from the Neckar valley (Lefranc and Denaire 2000; Lefranc 2001; 2007a, 253–4), though pottery decoration in this region demonstrates stronger affiliations with the Paris basin (Aisne and Marne valleys/Plaine sous-vosgienne; Jeunesse 1993; Strien 2000). Hence, groups in the Paris basin are thought to have originated in Haute-Alsace, moving first to the Marne and then to the Aisne valley, with the connections between the regions subsequently maintained. Voegtlin *et al.* (1988) described this relationship as a *Rückstrom*, with designs and techniques which originated in the Paris basin influencing the style of ceramics found in Haute-Alsace during the *Rubané récent*. Lefranc (2007a, 235–43, 274, our translation) supports this model, arguing that the influence of Paris basin ceramic designs 'profoundly modifies' those of Haute-Alsace. However, while Jeunesse (1995a; 1995b; 1997; 2003b) and Lefranc (2007a) stress the coherence of the RSO as a region, they do not discuss the mechanisms which held these geographically spread communities together. The RSO may, in fact, date back into the Mesolithic, when ties to the Paris basin are visible in the lithic assemblage (Mauvilly 1997, 343–4).

Strong connections between Haute-Alsace and the rest of the RSO are also demonstrated through the prevalence of longhouses with trapezoidal plans,[3] which suggests that technical knowledge as well as ceramic styles were shared throughout the region (Jeunesse *et al.* 2007a, 43). In contrast, naviform house plans appear limited to the distribution of the RNO, while people in the RBA and RN continued to construct rectangular houses (Jeunesse *et al.* 2007a, 46, fig. 7). Lefranc (2007a, 243), following Jeunesse (2001), also demonstrates connections between Basse-Alsace and the Paris basin, though these are far more limited. Pottery at only one site in the Paris basin (Bucy-le-Long, Aisne valley) has affiliations to the styles present in Basse-Alsace (Lefranc 2007a, 244), suggesting that while contacts between these regions took place, they were to some extent limited or restricted. Thus, while Haute-Alsace appears to be connected strongly to the RSO and hence oriented westwards, Basse-Alsace, with its strong ties to the Neckar valley, is oriented to the east and north; despite their proximity to one another, the communities of Basse- and Haute-Alsace chose to emphasise their networks beyond the immediately neighbouring region.

These differences are also identifiable in the way in which different resources were moving across LBK networks. The presence of *Spondylus* shells in the graves of Haute-Alsace follows the ceramic connections to southern Bavaria (Chapter 6.5), while this material does not seem to have reached Basse-Alsace and the Neckar valley in as high quantities (Jeunesse 1997; 2003a; Lefranc 2007a). In contrast, the lithic raw material used in Alsace was influenced by what was available locally (Mauvilly 1997, 331). High-quality Jurassic flints decrease from south to north Alsace (from more than 80% at Ensisheim to 30% in Basse-Alsace) and are likely to have been sourced in the Jura or at Kleinkems-Istein, east of the Rhine and south of the Kaiserstuhl (Lefranc 2007a, 13). Polished stone also seems to be mainly produced on local stone from the Vosges, but flint from the Paris basin was reaching Basse-Alsace (Mauvilly 1997; 2001). So while pottery may show the dominant orientations of communities in Alsace, these were not a barrier to other contacts.

8.4.2 Settlement patterns

Such regionalisation does not mean that every community or settlement in the two Alsatian regions had the same degree of contact (represented in ceramic styles, stone tools or shell ornaments) beyond the immediate area. Within each region, settlement size and duration varied, suggesting that relationships internal to Basse- or Haute-Alsace may have also been complex. Amongst the ceramic styles of Basse-Alsace, Lefranc (2007a, 280–1) could identify some sub-groupings. For example, the 'Rosheim style' is visible throughout the *Rubané récent* (phase IVa) and *final* (Lefranc 2007a, 281), suggesting that regional groups could possibly be sub-divided into varied groups – in the same way that different 'clans' were suggested for Vaihingen (Chapter 7.4). However, as is the case for much of the LBK distribution, the extent to which sites have been excavated varies enormously, with many sites only partially investigated or identified from surface finds (Lefranc 2007a, 151; 2007b). Despite this, Jeunesse (1980) proposed two models of settlement pattern in Basse-Alsace. First, settlements were built on the loess terraces of the major river valleys clustered in groups of about 1 km in size (Jeunesse 1980). Secondly, smaller watercourses were followed into the plateaus of Alsace and settlements established in their interior (Jeunesse 1980). These models have been considered to be chronologically successive, with the initial inhabitation of the major rivers followed by further settlement inland (Jeunesse 1993).[4] In Basse-Alsace all areas of the loess are settled from the early phases (*Rubané ancien*), though Lefranc (2007a, 155) underlines the variability in density of settlement in this region. Small groups appear to cluster together alongside a number of more isolated settlements (Lefranc 2007a, 157). From the *Rubané récent* about 20 more sites develop and some sites are abandoned, though the relative density in Basse-Alsace remains the same (Lefranc 2007a, 159). This is then followed by a decrease in settlement density in the *final* phase (Lefranc 2007a, 162).

While all the sites in Basse-Alsace are situated on loess soils, this is not the case in Haute-Alsace, where the distribution of the loess is more restricted (Lefranc 2007a, 155). Despite this, the development of settlement in Haute-Alsace follows that of Basse-Alsace, with an initial occupation surviving through the *Rubané moyen*, but then, while some early sites are abandoned, overall the number of sites increased during the *Rubané récent* (Lefranc 2007a, 165). This is particularly visible in the area south of Mulhouse (the Sundgau plateau) where sites are occasionally found off the loess (Lefranc 2007a, 165–9). There is also a similar decrease in the number of sites during the *Rubané final* in Haute-Alsace (Lefranc 2007a, 168).

How the relationships between these settlement groups were articulated is as yet uncertain. For Bischoffsheim in Basse-Alsace, Lefranc *et al.* (2004) considered the suggestion of 'central places' as developed for the Aldenhovener Platte by Lüning (1998) and expanded in detail by Zimmermann (1995). In this model one site acts as a central or dominant site in a region, with the settlements nearby characterised as dependent satellites (Lüning 1998). However, despite the size of Bischoffsheim – it has some 41 houses over three hectares – the excavators describe it as 'very poor' because polished stone is rare (Lefranc *et al.* 2004). This site is not far from the smaller settlement of Rosheim *Sainte-Odile*, which has a very rich and diverse assemblage including pottery imported from the Neckar valley, Hessen and the earliest phase of the *Stichbandkeramik*, as well as an enclosure ditch (Jeunesse 1991; Jeunesse and Lefranc 1999; Mauvilly 2001, 51). This site is therefore classed as the 'high-status central place' compared to Bischoffsheim's poor and densely packed satellite settlement. Following the same theory, in Haute-Alsace one could perhaps suggest that the site of Sierentz *Sandgrube* and *Tiergarten* could have been a central location due to its large size – 12 house plans are preserved – and so-called rich assemblages (Wolf and Viroulet 1992; 1997), as well as Ensisheim, where the grave goods speak to external contacts (Lefranc 2007a, 283). However, these models remain only tentative suggestions, and Lefranc (2007a, 151) regards it as still too early to carry out a study as detailed as that of Lüning (1998) on the Aldenhovener Platte.

Clearly, those living at the different settlements in Alsace did not have the same degree of contact beyond the immediate region, but we must be cautious in equating evidence for external contacts with the relative significance of a settlement. Moreover, imposing such classifications as 'rich' and 'poor' on past communities is highly problematic. Bischoffsheim is a large and clearly long-lived site (representing the *Rubané ancien* to *récent*) and thus represents a significant commitment not only to that location but to the local community as well. It may not have the same concentration of finds exotic to Alsace as Rosheim, but its duration and size seem to speak of success in other forms. Those living at Bischoffsheim intensively exploited ochre, which was plentiful in the vicinity (Lefranc 2007a, 15). However, Rosheim only begins during the *Rubané récent* (Jeunesse and Lefranc 1999), the period during which Bischoffsheim is abandoned and so, although they may overlap by a couple of generations, the two sites may represent two different ways of living, with Rosheim signalling the development of more marked hierarchies towards the end of the LBK (Lefranc *et al.* 2004). It is also at this point in the Alsatian chronology that regionality develops more strongly.

Use of areas off the loess is also suggested by the several cave sites situated near the southern border of Alsace with Switzerland and in the Doubs valley (Jeunesse 1990a, 231, 236). At Oberlarg, a LBK occupation layer is probable, but as the pottery present was not decorated, the cultural horizon to which it belongs cannot be definitively determined (Jeunesse 1990a, 231). In the case of three other caves, Lutter, Bavans and Voujeaucourt, LBK occupation is more certainly shown by the presence of decorated pottery (Jeunesse 1990a, 231, 234–5). As was the case for the caves discussed in Austria (Chapter 5.4), these sites are known from older or minimal excavations and it is difficult to determine how they were used during the LBK. Jeunesse (1990a, 233, 236) argues that several different explanations are possible, including evidence for Mesolithic groups in contact with the LBK and seasonal exploitation through transhumance. However, unlike Jungfernhöhle, Bavaria, there is no evidence for ritual use of caves in the Doubs valley and taphonomic problems make the assemblages difficult to recover and date accurately. While further research is required to determine the role of these sites in the settlement network, their presence contributes to a growing picture of landscape use during the LBK which went beyond the restricted zone of loess soils.

8.4.3 Animals and plants

Before the *Rubané récent*, two different traditions of animal husbandry can be identified in Alsace, each defined by the second most frequent species in the bone assemblage. In Tradition A, domestic pig is the second most frequent animal in assemblages after cattle, while in Tradition B, sheep and goat remains are more frequent than domestic pig (Arbogast 2001, 79). Tradition A corresponds to the area covered by Jeunesse's RNO and RBA and Tradition B to the RSO (Arbogast 2001; Table 8.2). Arbogast (2001) prefers to see these differences as cultural rather than ecological;

the landscapes of the RSO are as varied as those of the RNO or RBA. We seem to be dealing with the preferences of certain communities, rather than economic decisions based on environmental constraints. Bedault (2009, 124) argues that as pigs have large litters, reproduce relatively frequently and reach their optimum weight quickly, their increased presence in the archaeological record could represent a search for greater productivity; she tentatively suggests that in the case of the Villeneuve-Saint-Germain culture (of the earlier fifth millennium cal BC in the Paris basin) this change may have originated in a population growth.

The B tradition could reflect a strong preference for pastoral activity, based on the exploitation of ruminants, which could have required areas of grazing or open land, and could be linked to a specific agro-pastoral economy that also requires space for cereal crops (also suggested by Lüning 2000). This may have led to competition for space between grazing and agriculture as well as the overall need to clear land. Where pigs dominate (in Tradition A), the demand for grazing land would have been lessened, as this animal can feed in forests and on waste land. This second form of rearing is therefore more flexible and provides some evident advantages. Alternatively, the choice of pigs could reflect a response by the RNO groups to specific situations such as less open land or less cultivation. The model of small garden agriculture (Bogaard 2004) suggests that competition between grazing animals and cultivated land could have been easier to balance than Lüning (2000) envisioned and this suggests that the choice of pigs or sheep/goats as the second most frequent domestic animal may have been independent of the overall subsistence strategy.

Like other aspects of the LBK culture in this region (such as decoration of pottery and longhouse styles), this variation in the representation of animal species could also be linked to the suggested different colonisation paths that introduced the LBK to Alsace, though overall such differences have not been as clearly mapped for other regions as they have for Alsace, so this is hard to substantiate. The variance could have also found its origins in the integration of local traditions, such as the hunting strategies of indigenous groups, into LBK subsistence strategies. On Tradition A sites (northern Alsace) the importance of hunting remains modest in all periods and wild fauna remains are uniformly rare, hardly exceeding 10% of the total bone assemblages. Wettolsheim, near Colmar, is the only exception, with a rate of 20% hunted animals in the assemblages during the *Rubané ancien* (Arbogast 1993, 134). On Tradition B sites, however, the situation is much more diversified and the highest levels of variability in the percentage of wild remains are recorded; the frequency of wild animals can vary between 5–30% of the assemblage (Arbogast 1993, 134; 2001, 78). It is interesting to note these differences alongside the restricted distribution of loess soils in Haute-Alsace. The major structured differences between Haute- and Basse-Alsace are summarised in Table 8.2.

While ceramic styles and burial evidence therefore suggest more regionalisation from the *Rubané récent*, the animal bone assemblages appear to homogenise during this phase (Arbogast 2001). From the beginning of the *Rubané récent*, pig comes to be the second most frequent animal across the whole of Alsace (while sheep and goats persist in this role in the Paris basin), bringing about a change in the domestic animal sphere, rather than just the wild (Arbogast 2001, 79, 88). If pot decoration was strongly characterising regional and local affiliations, demonstrating that communities were identifying with geographically defined groups, the animal bone assemblages appear to suggest that in contrast everyday activities with animals were actually fairly similar from the *Rubané récent* onwards. However, this is not to say that all the people in any given settlement or community were carrying out the same tasks, and burial evidence does suggest that social differences between people beyond age and sex were recognised (Jeunesse 1995a; 1995b; 1996; 1997).

8.5 Burial practices

To date some 300 LBK burials have been excavated in Alsace, which were overwhelmingly found in cemetery contexts and mostly date to the *Rubané récent* (Boës 2003, 34; Lifeways Database). In Haute-Alsace, Mulhouse-Est (22 burials) and Ensisheim (43 LBK burials, one non-LBK) dominate the burial assemblage, while the 110 burials from the Vendenheim cemetery (99 individuals) have recently doubled the number of known graves in Basse-Alsace, by adding to those from Entzheim (11 burials), Quatzenheim (13 burials) and Souffelweyersheim (52 burials). Focussing on the cemetery burials, Jeunesse (1997) divides the Alsatian burials by the two broad traditions of LBK inhumation, Tradition I and Tradition II, which he identified in its western distribution. These traditions follow Tradition 0, which Jeunesse (1996, 125) based on the site of Nitra (Chapter 4.10), while he identifies Tradition I in Haute-Alsace (and RSO) and Tradition II in *Rubané du Nord-Ouest, Rubané de Basse-Alsace* and *Rubané du Neckar*, and echoing the differences seen in the animal bone assemblages. These traditions are distinguished by variations in body orientation and position, and the types of grave goods used, which, as we have discussed before, Jeunesse (1995b; 1996) argues indicate the social status of the deceased (Chapters 1.3.5 and 7.5). The cemetery sites on which Tradition I is based are Mulhouse-Est and Ensisheim (both sampled by this project), with further sites on the Marne and in the Paris basin, and Tradition II is largely developed from studies of the cemetery sites of Souffelweyersheim (sampled here), Quatzenheim and Entzheim from Alsace, as well as Flomborn, Niedermerz and Elsloo to the north.

The key features of Tradition I are the sprinkling of ochre, and imported shells (including *Spondylus*), which are all but absent in Tradition II, where lumps of ochre and local shells seemingly take their place (Jeunesse 1995a, 127). However, the most significant difference between the two is the greater variation between graves in Tradition II.

Although *Spondylus* and other shell ornaments contribute to some of the graves in Tradition I being classed as rich or high-status burials, when other grave goods are considered, the graves appear far more equal. Burials from Tradition II, on the other hand, have a number of identifiable differences in body position and orientation (particularly seen at Vendenheim; Chapter 8.10.1), as well as in the varied occurrence of stone tools, including polished stone adzes and axes, and the use of local shells. Clay bracelets also appear to demonstrate regional affiliation or identity, with a higher concentration in Haute-Alsace and hence Tradition I than in Basse-Alsace (31 to 7: Jeunesse and Sainty 1992).

The different aspects of funerary tradition are seen by Jeunesse (1997) as representing varied aspects of LBK social identity. Grave goods are largely considered to demonstrate social status, with polished stone tools and exotic or imported shells, such as *Spondylus* ornaments, considered key indicators of access to earned or inherited wealth as well as being important markers of masculinity (Jeunesse 1997; 2002a). However, some aspects of the grave rite and grave goods are seen as remnants of Mesolithic burial practices, such as the sprinkling of ochre and body position. Jeunesse (2002a, 203) suggests that differences in orientation and body position may be signalling the presence of acculturated hunter-gatherers in LBK cemeteries. Hence, Tradition I burials are seen as being more 'traditionally' LBK than Tradition II, which in turn are seen to include semi- or partially 'acculturated' hunter-gatherers.

The burials of Basse-Alsace stand out amongst LBK burials because of a concentration of extended or supine burials. Although these account for only *c*. 8% of all LBK burials, in Basse-Alsace the rate of supine burials rises to 52% (Lifeways Database; Table 8.2). However, rather than being seen as a regional peculiarity, this variation in body position may also relate to the development of middle Neolithic burial traditions (Jeunesse 1997, 67; 2004; Boës 2000; 2003). In the cultures which follow the LBK in Alsace – Großgartach, followed by Rössen – burial practices are incompletely researched in comparison to the larger cemeteries found further north (Spatz 1997; Müller 2002; 2003; Denaire 2009), but extended burial in a supine position was the most frequent position at the more recently excavated cemetery at Rosheim (Boës 2003, 40). Furthermore, Boës (2003) identifies a trend through the LBK towards separating the body of the deceased from the soil of the grave. At earlier cemeteries such as Mulhouse-Est and the small group of four burials at Geispitzen (Haute-Alsace) the skeletons showed no movement, suggesting that they were surrounded by soil when they decayed, while in some burials at *Rubané récent/final* cemeteries such as Ensisheim and Vendenheim the extremities (hands and feet) and mandibles had moved and rotated in ways suggestive of decomposition in a void (Boës 2000; 2003, 35–7).

The presence of a void around the body allows the grave to be easily revisited and the skeleton manipulated, a practice that seems highly likely to have taken place in the LBK. In grave 2 at Ensisheim, the burial of an adult female, the individual had originally been placed in a left-crouched position, but the grave was revisited, when the femora and humeri were placed over the thorax, leaving the lower legs in their original position (Boës 2003, 37; Jeunesse 2003a, 23). In grave 44 at Ensisheim, as well as the dislocation of the hands and feet suggesting they had decayed in a void, the left ulna and clavicle had moved in ways suggesting human intervention (Boës 2003, 37). This type of practice may also have been seen in Basse-Alsace at Vendenheim, where Boës (2003, 37) argues that as many as eight burials could have been revisited, including the double grave 137, where the right arm of burial 137a had been placed in amongst the grave goods *c*. 20 cm to the south of the skeleton. This practice appears to be widespread across both Tradition I and II burials, as similar voids or niches have been identified in the Paris basin (Thévenet 2004).

As Jeunesse (2003a, 23) argues, this suggests burial rites which were considerably more complex from a temporal perspective than has previously been assumed. At the enclosure site of Ittenheim (Basse-Alsace), an oval pit cutting the end of a ditch contained a complex arrangement of human remains (Lefranc and Boës 2009, 203). At the base of the pit an adult male, lying on his back, was missing both lower legs (this appears to be a post-mortem intervention and the burial pit was not large enough to include them), parts of the skull and one arm; approximately 40 cm above this burial a collection of human bones had been placed, including possibly the humerus of the lower burial and the remains from at least one further individual (Lefranc and Boës 2009, 204; Lefranc *et al*. 2010). Lefranc and Boës (2009, 209) draw a comparison between the treatment of the human remains found at Herxheim and that at Ittenheim. Certainly complex manipulations of the deceased at varied stages of decay seem likely in many contexts of the LBK. The careful excavation methods employed in these cases (using the principles of *anthropologie de terrain*; Duday 2009) have not always been matched elsewhere, particularly on older excavations, and this practice may be far more recurrent across the LBK than normally envisaged.

Three other burials at Ittenheim were found associated with longhouses (Lefranc *et al*. 2010). Overall, settlement burials account for about 10–15% of the burials in Alsace, with 39 burials identified on settlements to date (11 from Basse-Alsace, 28 from Haute-Alsace; Lifeways Database). In his study of settlement burials across the LBK, Veit (1996, 193) indentifies 12 cemetery sites and 28 settlements with burials from Baden-Württemberg and Alsace (which he treats together). In Alsace, therefore, settlement burials are a small but not insignificant aspect of burial practices. In line with what has been found elsewhere, settlement burials in Alsace tend to be unfurnished (20 burials are without grave goods; Lifeways Database), though those that do have accompanying grave goods do not differ significantly from those found in cemetery burials. However, polished stone tools are rarer (only three instances in settlement burials: at

Fig. 8.4. Mulhouse-Est: plan. After Schweitzer and Schweitzer (1977, 14).

Bischoffsheim, Rouffach *Tuilerie* and Wettolsheim; Sainty *et al.* 1984; Sainty *et al.* 1988; Jeunesse and Sainty 1991; Lefranc *et al.* 2004). The numbers of children and adults are roughly equal in settlements (17 children compared with 15 adults), though too few of the adult burials are sexed to judge whether females dominate significantly (Lifeways Database).

8.6 Sites sampled

Four cemetery sites were sampled in the Lifeways project (Ensisheim, Mulhouse-Est, Souffelweyersheim and Vendenheim). Ensisheim and Mulhouse-Est are in Haute-Alsace and so form part of the RSO (*Rubané Sud-Ouest*) group of the LBK (Jeunesse 1997). Souffelweyersheim and Vendenheim are in Basse-Alsace, and thereby part of the regional grouping of the LBK found only in this region (and called by Jeunesse the *Rubané de Basse-Alsace*). Alongside the cemetery sites, two settlement sites were sampled for animal bone. These were Ensisheim *Ratfeld* for Haute-Alsace and Bischoffsheim for Basse-Alsace.

8.7 Mulhouse-Est (Rixheim), Haute-Alsace

8.7.1 Introduction

The cemetery of Mulhouse-Est was first discovered in the summer of 1964 at a gravel extraction site situated on the northern edge of the village of Rixheim (Schweitzer and Schweitzer 1977, 13; Fig. 8.1).[5] During this initial excavation 13 graves were uncovered (Schweitzer and Schweitzer 1977, 13). Excavations then continued intermittently until 1972, by which time 22 graves had been uncovered (Schweitzer and Schweitzer 1977; Gerhardt and Gerhardt-Pfannenstiel 1984/85; Jeunesse 1997). Nieszery (1995, 243) suggests that as many burials again may have been interred on the site and the area certainly experienced a substantial amount of destruction (Fig. 8.4). Roger and Joël

Schweitzer (1977)[6] then excavated Mulhouse-Est under rescue conditions. New fieldwork is plannd for 2013.

The cemetery is situated only 500 m south of a LBK settlement site, known as Mulhouse-Est *Île Napoléon* (Schweitzer and Schweitzer 1977, 12; Lefranc 2007a, 316). This site is a surface scatter of sherds dating from the *Rubané ancien* through to the later stages of the *Rubané récent* (Lefranc 2007a, 316). However, the majority of the pottery from the settlement dates to the *Rubané ancien* and *moyen* phases (Lefranc 2007a, 316). The burials themselves in the cemetery date exclusively to the *Rubané moyen* (Jeunesse 1997, 12, 27; Lefranc 2007a, 316). Not only does this mean that the cemetery was in use while the nearest identified settlement was inhabited, but it also makes Mulhouse-Est the earliest LBK cemetery in Alsace.

During the *Rubané moyen*, the number of settlements in Haute-Alsace increases by about half (six new sites were occupied in addition to the 11 which continue from the *Rubané ancien*), but the cemetery is the only new site established in the immediate area east of the river Ill (Lefranc 2007a, 165). The loess is much less abundant in the southern part of Alsace, with the majority of this soil concentrated in a strip 2–3 km wide along the Ill (Lefranc 2007a, 162–3). Lefranc (2007a, 162) describes the loess on the western bank of the Ill as less permeable and in an area of higher rainfall, suggesting drier conditions on the eastern bank, where the LBK occupation is concentrated. From the *Rubané récent* the Sundgau plateau is more extensively occupied, coinciding with another doubling in the number of identified sites (Lefranc 2007a, 165–6). It is at this point at the beginning of the *Rubané récent* that most cemeteries in Alsace start (Jeunesse 1997; Lefranc 2007a).

Kurt Gerhardt and Dora Gerhardt-Pfannenstiel carried out the original osteological study, published 12 years after the initial excavation (Gerhardt and Gerhardt-Pfannenstiel 1984/85, 55). This study concluded that more adult females were buried at the cemetery than males (9–10 skeletons were sexed as female in comparison to only five identified as male) and this was confirmed by Linda Fibiger's reanalysis as part of this project (Chapter 8.7.2). Child or juvenile burials (including a three- to four-month-old neonate) occur at an average frequency for the LBK at Mulhouse-Est. The majority of the burials share the same orientation (Table 8.3). Slightly more than half the burials are oriented NE–SW, with the head to the north-east as was also found at Ensisheim (Storch 1984/85, 29; Jeunesse 1997, 62–3). One burial deviates from this orientation and was buried in the 'antipodal' position of SW–NE (grave 20). Jeunesse (1997, 63) regards this as a regional phenomenon as antipodal burials are also rare at Ensisheim. A slight majority of burials at Mulhouse-Est are left-crouched (ten from the 19 burials where body position is known) and there appears to be no relationship between position of the body in the grave and its orientation.

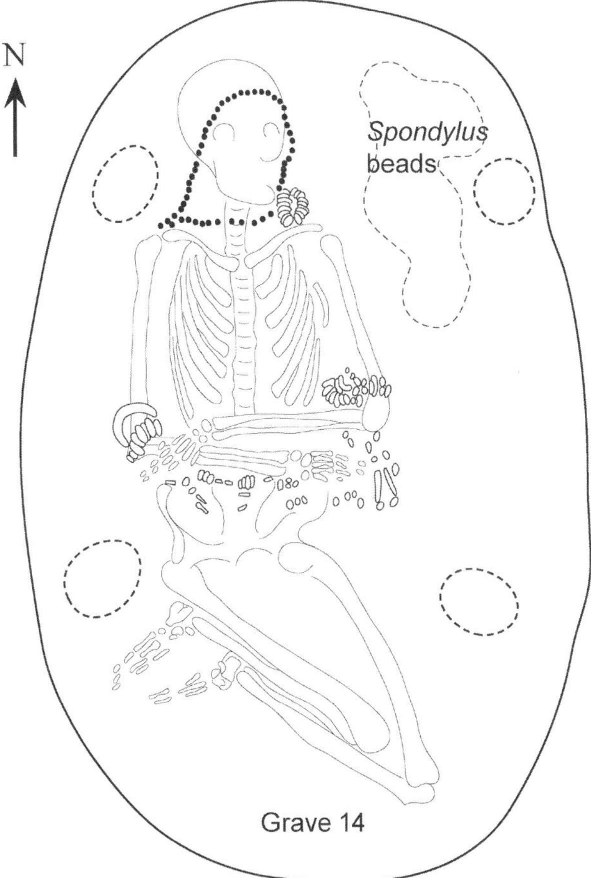

Fig. 8.5. Mulhouse-Est: burial 14. The four postholes are shown by the dotted lines. After Schweitzer and Schweitzer (1977, 42).

An unusual feature of the graves at Mulhouse-Est is the occurrence in six graves (burials 2, 11, 14, 15, 18 and 24) of stake or posthole-like[7] features around the skeleton (Fig. 8.5; J. Schweitzer 1971, 15; Schweitzer and Schweitzer 1977, 21, 44, 35; Jeunesse 1997, 60). Similar features have also been indentified at other cemeteries. Jeunesse (1997, 60) notes a similar pattern of four postholes surrounding the skeleton in two graves at Sondershausen, Thuringia (Kahlke 1954; 1957; 1958), and in one burial at the LBK cemetery of Arnstadt, also Thuringia (Neumann and

Table 8.3 (next page). Mulhouse-Est: the isotope, osteological and archaeological data. Age and sex information from Linda Fibiger (this volume). See Chapter 2 for further definition of ages. adol. = Adolescent, mon. = months.
Key for body position: LC – Left-crouched; RC – Right-crouched; C – Crouched, direction unknown; CB – Crouched on back; CF – Crouched on front; S – Supine; P – Prone; I – Irregular.
Key for grave goods (number of items in brackets): U. – Unfurnished; F. – Fill only (all items listed after an F. were in the fill of the grave rather than at the level of the skeleton); Pol. – Polished stone; Cer. – Ceramics; Shd. – Sherds; Spon. – Spondylus*; She. – Other Shell; Och. – Ochre; Lit. – Chipped stone; Bon – Worked bone; Grd. – Grinding stone.*

Burial	Tooth	Sex	Age (yrs)	$^{87}Sr/^{86}Sr$	Sr conc. ppm	$\delta^{13}C$ ‰	$\delta^{15}N$ ‰	Orientation	Body position	Grave goods	Pathologies
1	M1	-	Late Juv./Early Adol.	0.70892	37	-	-	NW–SE	LC	Spon.(1 bead), She.(220), Och.	Enamel hypoplasia
2	-	F	YA	-	-	−20.5	10.5	NW–SE	LC	Spon.(9 beads), She.(18), Och. F.Cer.(2)	-
3	-	-	-	-	-	-	-	N–S	LC	She.(23), 30 other beads, Och.	-
4	M1	-	-	-	-	-	-	NE–SW	RC	Shd.(2), She.(3), Och.	-
5	M3	-	-	*n.d.*	*n.d.*	−20.5	11.6	N–S	RC	Spon.(80 beads), She.(106), Och. Bon.(3)	-
6	M1	F	YMA	0.70880	33	−20.3 −20.2	10.6 11.2	NE–SW	LC	Cer.(1), She.(54), Och., F.Cer.(8)	-
7	-	-	-	-	-	-	-	-	-	Pol.(1, frag), Och.	-
8	M1	M?	Adult>20	0.70902	35	-	-	NE–SW	S	Och., Lit.(5)	-
9	-	-	-	-	-	-	-	-	C	Cer.(1), Shd.(3), Och. F.Pol.(1)	-
10	-	-	-	-	-	-	-	-	-	Och.	-
11	-	-	-	-	-	-	-	NE–SW	S	Pol.(1), Och. She.(1), F.Cer.(1)	-
12	-	-	Adol.	-	-	-	-	NE–SW	LC	Cer.(1), Spon.(61 beads), Bon.(1)	Possible infection
13	-	-	-	-	-	-	-	NE–SW	LC	Pol.(1, frag.), F.Cer.(2)	-
14	M1	F	Adult >25	0.70886	33	−20.1	10.8	N–S	LC	Spon.(300 beads, armring), She.(20), Och., F.Cer.(4)	-
15a	M1	F	Adult>40	0.70967	48	−20.4	11.2	NE–SW	LC	Och., Bon.(2)	Healed trauma (skull)
15b	-	-	6–9 mon.	-	-	-	-	NE–SW	I	Och.	-
16	-	-	-	-	-	-	-	NE–SW	CB	F.Shd.(1)	-
17	M3	F	Adult >20	0.70888	64	-	-	NE–SW	LC	U.	-
18	-	F	Adult	-	-	−20.2	10.3	NE–SW	RC	Cer.(1), Och., F.Cer.(3), She.(1)	-
19	Incisor	M	Mature Adult	-	-	−20.2	10.6	NE–SW	RC	Spon.(buckle, pendant), Och., F.Cer.(1)	Caries (4)
20	M1	F	YMA	0.70921	39	−20.3	9.4	SW–NE	LC	Och.	-
22	-	-	-	-	-	-	-	-	-	Cer.(1), Och.	-
24	-	-	-	-	-	-	-	NE–SW	S	Spon.(6 beads), Och.	-

Wiegand 1940; Kahlke 1954). A similar feature is also seen in Lengyel burials at Alsónyék-Bátaszék in Hungary (Zalai-Gaál *et al.* 2012). Like the *banquettes* at Berry-au-Bac, Aisne valley (Thévenet 2004, 822–3; Chapter 8.10.1), these features suggest that the process of burial was perhaps more complex than has often been envisaged. These posts may represent a small shelter placed over the deceased or perhaps marked the presence of the grave. Drawing an analogy between these posts and the posts of the longhouse is also tempting (cf. Whittle 2012). Other graves, such as 2 and 6 (Schweitzer and Schweitzer 1977), have fragmented pots that may have been deliberately smashed at the time of burial and then included in the fill of the grave.

Jeunesse (1995a; 1995b; 1996; 1997) includes Mulhouse-Est in Tradition I. As at Ensisheim, at Mulhouse-Est the presence in graves of shells and lithics seems to be mutually exclusive (though grave 11 is an exception). Lithics occur in only four graves (7, 8, 11 and 13), while shells are present in ten graves, though in varying quantities. In grave 14, more than 300 *Spondylus* shells accompanied the burial of an adult female (Schweitzer and Schweitzer 1977, 44–9). Beads formed strings around her head, waist and on both arms, where a *Spondylus* bracelet was also found, and to her east lay another collection of beads (Schweitzer and Schweitzer 1977, 42).

Although there appear to be two spatial groups (a northern and southern group), this may be largely due to preservation rather than deliberate grouping (Storch 1984/85, 24). However, six graves seem to form pairs of burials (graves 4 and 5, 15 and 17 and 18 and 20); these are either placed next to each other or, in the case of 15 and 17, intercut. Each pair seems to have opposing features; graves 4 and 5 have opposing orientations, and while graves 18 and 20 share an orientation, the heads of the deceased are facing in opposite directions. Both graves 17 and 15 stand out as unusual. Grave 15 (Fig. 8.6) is a double grave of an adult female and young child, both crouched and facing each other, with the two skulls very close and the adult's hand apparently over the child, perhaps echoing the position of the female and child in graves 48 and 49 at Nitra (Chapter 4.10). Grave 17, which is cut by grave 15, is a young adult female and is the only grave which is unfurnished; it does not even have sprinkled ochre, which is found in 19 of the 22 graves. The body position of grave 17 is also unusual as the right leg and arm/hand were both in positions not possible while the individual was living (Storch 1984/85, 24). This suggests that some form of post-mortem manipulation of the deceased may have taken place, which may also be visible in the positioning of the feet and hands in grave 20 (Storch 1984/85, 24). It is not clear from the drawings in Schweitzer and Schweitzer (1977) whether it is possible that these positions came about through the decay of the body in a void (as Boës (2003) suggested for Ensisheim and Vendenheim) or through deliberate manipulation.

Fig. 8.6. Mulhouse-Est: block-lifted remains still contained within matrix, burial 15. Photo: Linda Fibiger.

8.7.2 Osteology

Preservation

A total of 13 individuals from Mulhouse-Est were analysed.[8] The remains are curated at the *Musée historique de Mulhouse*. Together with the skeletal remains from Füzesabony-Gubakút (Chapter 3.8), this is the smallest assemblage analysed as part of the Lifeways project. Although the remains were generally in moderate or moderate to good condition, many of the burials had been block-lifted and have not been further excavated since (Fig. 8.6). As a result, not all skeletal elements could be

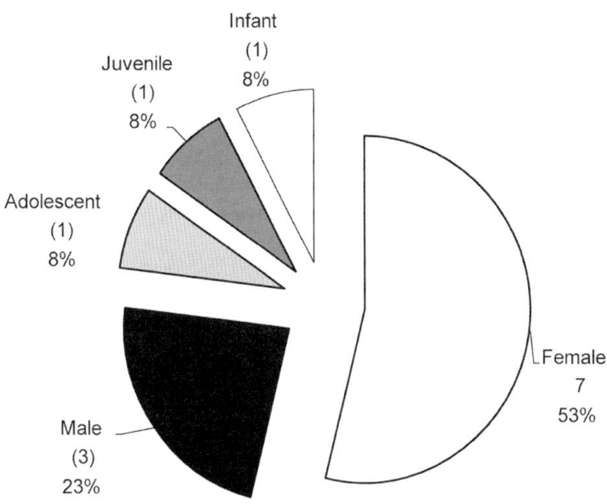

Fig. 8.7. Mulhouse-Est: age and sex assessment.

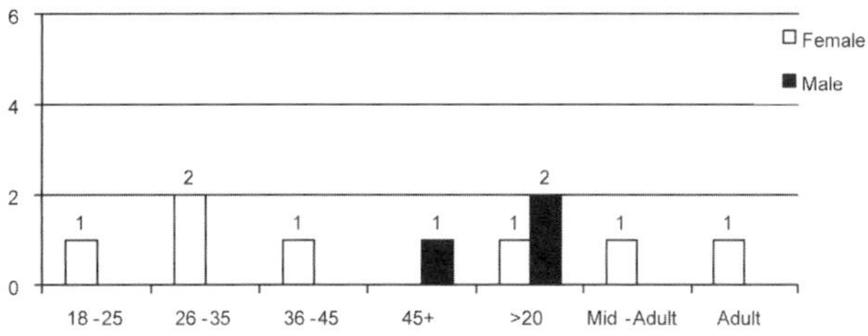

Fig. 8.8. Mulhouse-Est: adult age distribution.

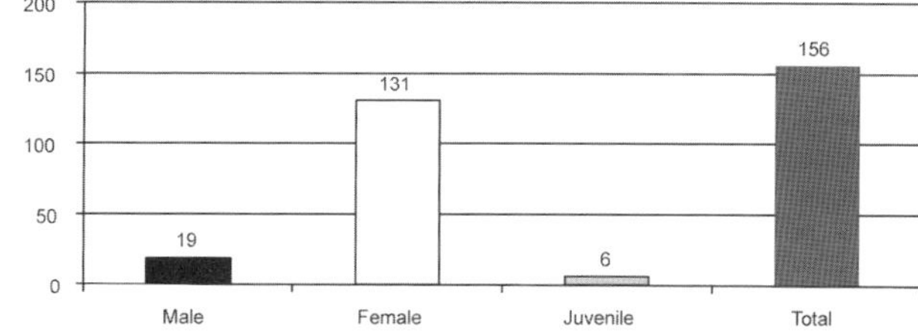

Fig. 8.10. Mulhouse-Est: number of teeth present.

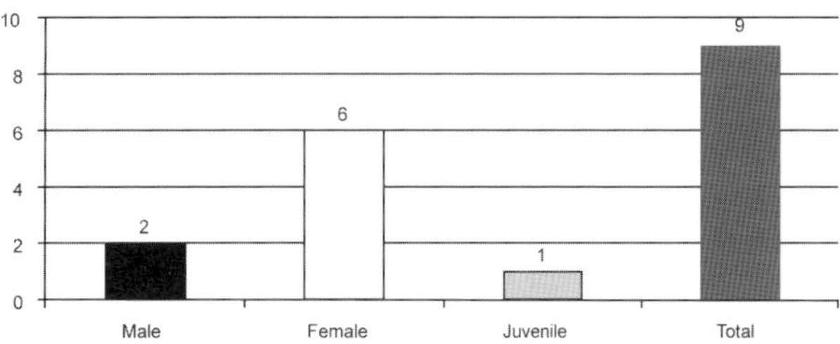

Fig. 8.9. Mulhouse-Est: number of individuals with partial or complete dentitions.

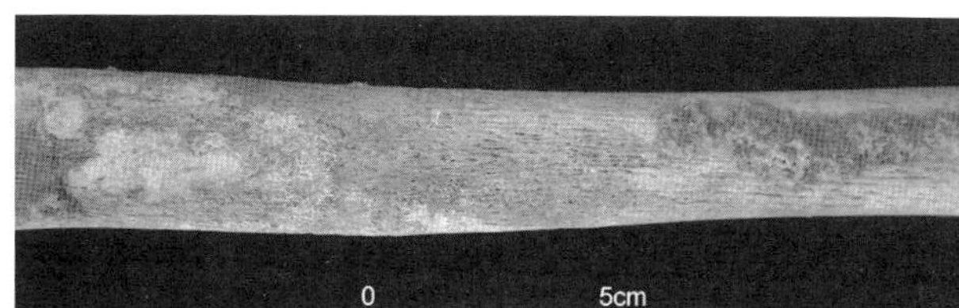

Fig. 8.11. Mulhouse-Est: medial tibia with mixed new bone deposit, burial 12. Photo: Linda Fibiger.

analysed in detail and the results presented here are based on only partially observable remains.

Demography: age and sex

The small Mulhouse-Est assemblage included 10 adults, one adolescent, one juvenile and one infant. In the adult assemblage, seven females and three males were present (Fig. 8.7).

The proportion of juveniles and infants in the assemblage is much smaller than expected for this age group, though it should be borne in mind yet again that the overall number of individuals analysed was very small. The adults in the sample were distributed across all age groups (Fig. 8.8), but again the total number was too small to make any population-based inferences. The only juvenile in the sample was probably within the upper end of this age category, whereas the infant was aged between 6 and 9 months at the time of death (Fig. 8.8).

Adult stature

No comparison of adult male and female stature was carried out at Mulhouse-Est as only one individual, an adult female, had a sufficiently preserved left femur to measure maximum long bone length (39.8 cm).

Dental disease

A total of 156 permanent teeth from nine individuals could be examined. This included 150 teeth from eight adults and one tooth from a juvenile individual (Figs 8.9–10). In the adult sample one (12.5%) out of eight adults with preserved teeth presented with caries. The juvenile individual presented with enamel hypoplasia (Tables 8.4–5).

Considering prevalence based on the number of teeth present, six (4%) out of 150 preserved teeth in the adult assemblage were affected by caries (Tables 8.4–5). In the sexed sample, caries was only noted in the male sample, which contrasts with the results obtained for other assemblages; however, the Mulhouse-Est sample is very small, does not include the whole cemetery and may not be representative. Enamel hypoplasia was noted on one (11.1%) of the six teeth in the juvenile group.

Cribra orbitalia

A total of seven adults, including three males and four females, had at least one partially preserved orbit, but no *cribra orbitalia* was noted.

Periosteal changes and infection

One individual at Mulhouse-Est, an adolescent (burial 12), presented with mixed periosteal new bone deposits on the right femur and tibia (Fig. 8.11). No other lesions were noted, making a localised injury/infection the most likely diagnosis.

Trauma

The only possibly traumatic skeletal change noted was a smooth shallow depression on the right posterior parietal of burial 15a, an older adult female, giving a crude cranial trauma prevalence of 7.7 % (Table 8.6). Adjusted trauma prevalence based on the number of individuals with at least 50% of the cranial vault preserved was 12.5% (Table 8.7).

Summary

The fact that some of the burials from Mulhouse-Est still remain to be excavated fully from their blocks and cleaned severely limited the extent of the osteoarchaeological analysis. In addition, the overall size of the sample is very small and does not really allow for wider-reaching, population-based interpretations.

Table 8.4. Mulhouse-Est: dental pathology. Individuals affected.

Group	No. of individuals with teeth	No. (%) affected by caries	No. (%) affected by enamel hypoplasia
Adult Male	2	1 (50%)	0
Adult Female	6	0	0
All Adults	8	1 (12.5%)	0
Juvenile/Adolescent	1	0	1
Total	9	1 (11.1%)	1 (11.1%)

Table 8.5. Mulhouse-Est: dental pathology. Teeth affected.

Group	No. of teeth	No. (%) affected by caries	No. (%) affected by enamel hypoplasia
Adult Male	19	6 (31.6%)	0
Adult Female	131	0	0
All Adults	150	6 (4%)	0
Juvenile/Adolescent	6	0	1 (16.7%)
Total	156	6 (3.8%)	1 (0.6%)

Table 8.6. Mulhouse-Est: crude prevalence of cranial trauma.

	No. of burials	No. (%) affected by trauma
Adult Male	3	0 (0)
Adult Female	7	1 (14.3)
Adolescent	1	0 (0)
Juvenile	1	0 (0)
Infant	1	0 (0)
Total	13	1 (7.7)

Table 8.7. Mulhouse-Est: adjusted prevalence of cranial trauma.

	50+% of cranial vault present	No. (%) affected by trauma
Adult Male	3	0 (0)
Adult Female	4	1 (25)
Adolescent	0	0 (0)
Juvenile	1	0 (0)
Infant	0	0 (0)
Total	8	1 (12.5)

8.7.3 Carbon and nitrogen analysis

Due to the poor condition of the skeletons from Mulhouse-Est (Chapter 8.7.2), only eight individuals could be sampled, including seven adults (one male and six females) and one juvenile skeleton (Fig. 8.12; Table 8.8). The burial in grave 6 was processed twice. The first value, measured on a longbone fragment, is included in the statistics; the second value, measured on a rib, is further discussed below.

Age/sex variation

The juvenile has a higher $\delta^{15}N$ value than the adults, reflecting a suckling signal, though either young enough to still retain a signal of the prenatal lower $\delta^{15}N$ value of the mother or old enough to be at least partially weaned. The single male value is very close to the female mean for both $\delta^{13}C$ and $\delta^{15}N$.

The two values measured on the female from grave 6 (longbone −20.2‰, 11.2‰; rib −20.3‰, 10.6‰) are very similar in $\delta^{13}C$ (within measurement error), but differ by 0.6‰ in $\delta^{15}N$. This value is not much greater than the measurement error (±0.2‰; Chapter 2.2), but it could reflect a change in physiology or diet over time. Tissue turnover in ribs may be more rapid than in longbones (Sealy *et al.* 1995), so that the drop of $\delta^{15}N$ value from the rib may reflect more recent nitrogen metabolism than the femur (for estimates of the difference turnover rate could make, see Hedges *et al.* 2007, 815). The difference is in the expected direction for a woman undergoing pregnancy and breast-feeding (Fuller *et al.* 2004), and indeed may provide an explanation for the overall slightly lower female $\delta^{15}N$ compared to that of males (further discussed in Chapter 9.2.5).

Animals

In the absence of animal remains from Mulhouse-Est itself, those from Ensisheim *Ratfeld* (Fig. 8.24; Chapter 8.8.3) may be a suitable comparison. It should be noted, however, that the adult human mean $\delta^{15}N$ values at Ensisheim *les Octrois* are about 1‰ lower than at Mulhouse-Est (significantly different, 2-tailed *t*-test, $p<0.001$), so it is by no means certain that this comparison is valid. Taking it at face value, the difference between adult human and cattle means is 1.4‰±0.29 (SD) for $\delta^{13}C$ and 4.2‰±0.62 for $\delta^{15}N$. This is high for both isotopes, compared to other sites in this study, and is as likely to reflect a difference in isotopic baseline between the sites as a difference in human diet or animal husbandry.

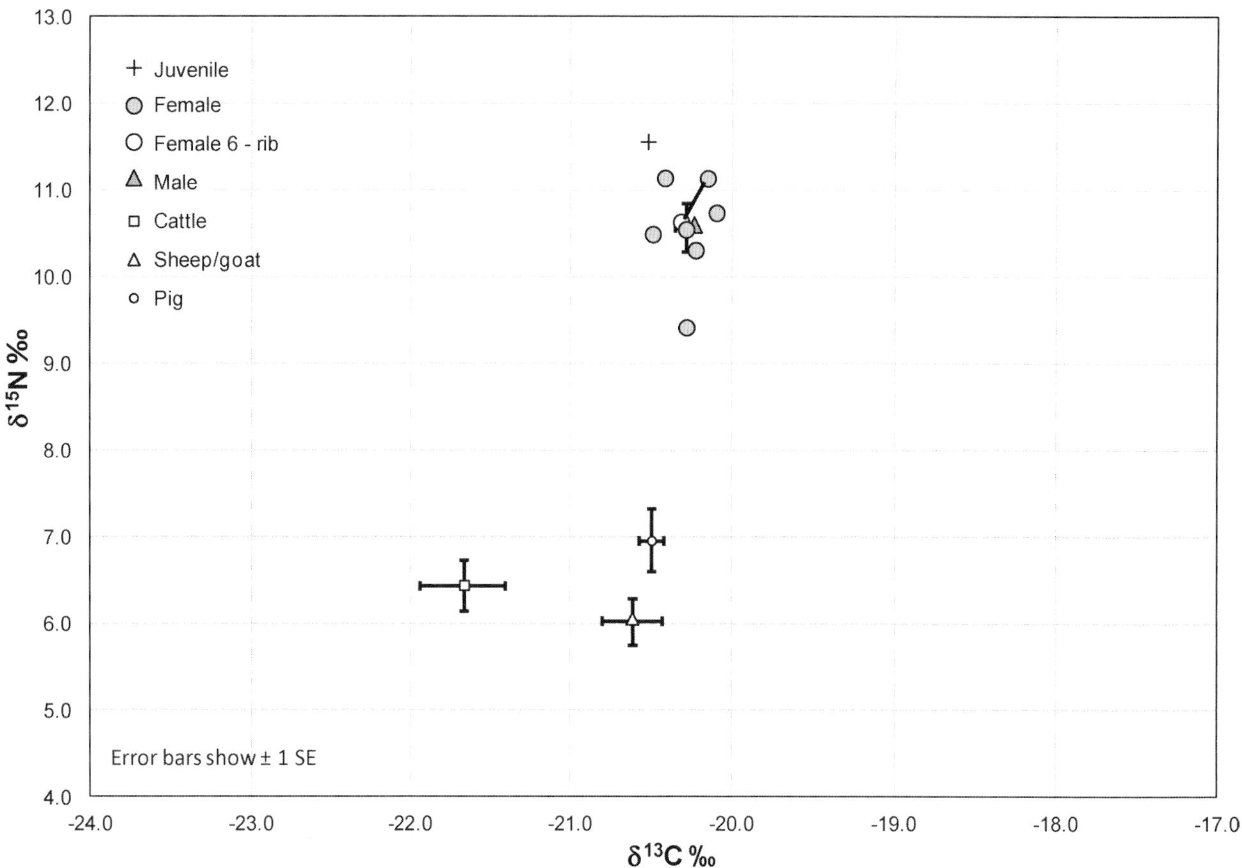

Fig. 8.12. Mulhouse-Est: carbon and nitrogen isotope ratios (‰) of humans.

Table 8.8. Mulhouse-Est: carbon and nitrogen isotope ratios (‰) of humans, with means and standard deviations.

Species	Age/sex	Mean $\delta^{13}C$	SD $\delta^{13}C$	Mean $\delta^{15}N$	SD $\delta^{15}N$	n
Human	Juvenile	−20.5	-	11.6	-	1
Human	Female	−20.3	0.15	10.6	0.68	6
Human	Male	−20.2	-	10.6	-	1
Human	All adults	−20.3	0.14	10.6	0.62	7

Correlations with the archaeological data

With only eight samples from the site, the conclusions from Mulhouse-Est are limited, but some points of interest can be raised. There was no patterning between body position and the stable isotope values. It is, however, interesting to note that the one individual buried in a secondary burial orientation (SW–NE; grave 20) had the lowest $\delta^{15}N$ value (9.4‰), which is a difference of 1.2‰ from the mean $\delta^{15}N$ value (10.6‰). This younger mid-aged female was also the only burial to receive no grave goods, excepting a layer of soil coloured with ochre. This grave was also next to the burial of adult female (grave 18), who had the next lowest $\delta^{15}N$ value (10.3‰) and, although buried in the dominant orientation of NE–SW, had been placed in a right-crouched position. No further relationships between the grave goods and the $\delta^{15}N$ and $\delta^{13}C$ values could be determined. There was also no identifiable spatial patterning in the stable isotope values, nor could any correlation to the palaeopathological data be discerned.

8.7.4 Strontium analysis

A total of ten individuals were sampled, but only seven results were returned, including results from five females, one male and one juvenile (Fig. 8.13; Table 8.9). The average $^{87}Sr/^{86}Sr$ ratio from Mulhouse-Est is 0.70905±0.00031, which falls within the expected range for loess soils (0.7085–0.7015). The loess in this region is likely to have a fairly high carbonate content (between 30–40%; Hatté *et al.* 1998), derived from calcareous Alpine sediments and the Jura, which means that the $^{87}Sr/^{86}Sr$ ratios of the loess would fall towards the lower end of the expected range and this is reflected in the average value at Mulhouse-Est.

With only seven individuals available for sampling, it is hard to compare male and female values and the data form a tight cluster (Fig. 8.13). If grave 17 is excluded, there is a significant and negative correlation between the $^{87}Sr/^{86}Sr$ ratio and 1/Sr concentration (r^2=0.93, p=0.002), which may reflect a potential mixing line, but with such low sample numbers it is hard to draw further conclusions. Grave 17

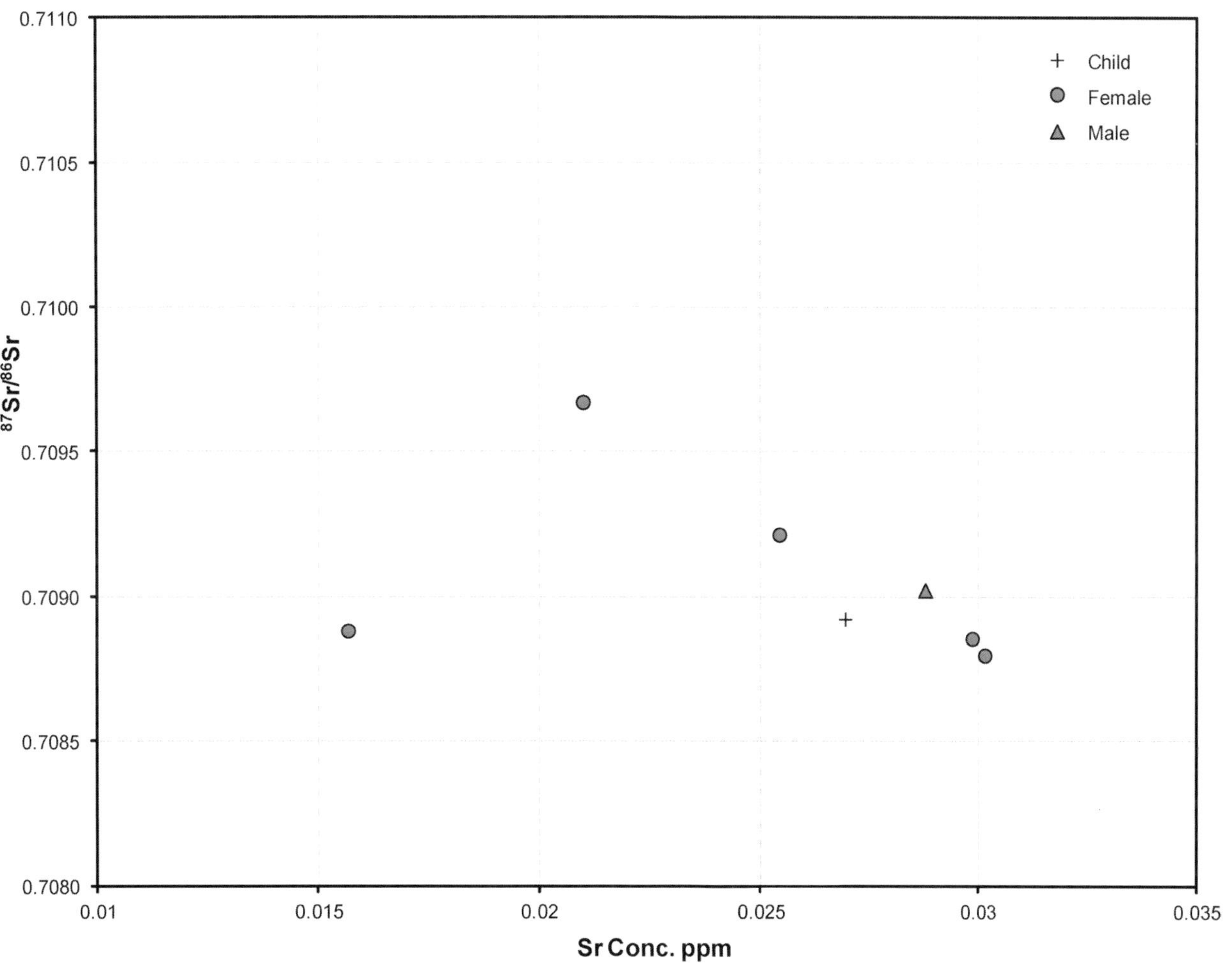

Fig. 8.13. Mulhouse-Est: strontium concentration (ppm) versus ratio ($^{87}Sr/^{86}Sr$).

Table 8.9. Mulhouse-Est: strontium isotope ratios and concentrations. 'All' includes one unsexed adult.

Age/sex	Mean $^{87}Sr/^{86}Sr$	SD $^{87}Sr/^{86}Sr$	Mean Sr conc.	SD Sr conc.	n
Juvenile	0.70892	-	37	-	1
Female	0.70908	0.00037	43	13	5
Male	0.70902	-	35	-	1
All	0.70905	0.00031	41	11	7

has a high Sr concentration value (64 Sr ppm), which falls above one SD from the mean of the site (41 Sr ppm) and stands out archaeologically, as this was the only grave sampled which had no grave goods, not even ochre.

Correlations with the archaeological data

There are no correlations between the archaeological evidence (treatment of the body in the grave and accompanying grave goods), palaeopathological data and the strontium isotope data. The individual with the highest $^{87}Sr/^{86}Sr$ ratio (burial 15a, 0.70967) was buried with two bone rings, but without shell ornamentation so frequent in the other burials. The two burials with $^{87}Sr/^{86}Sr$ ratios that stand out (burials 15a and 17) form one of the three 'pairs' of burials, otherwise there is no spatial patterning in the strontium ratios and concentration across the cemetery.

8.7.5 Site summary and discussion

Despite some potential deviation, overall the isotope data from Mulhouse-Est suggest a closely related community, sharing a similar diet and geographical origins. This is perhaps also reflected in the grave good assemblage and treatment of the body in the grave (body position and orientation), which sees little deviation across the cemetery, though it is interesting to note that the one burial (grave 20) with an opposing orientation (SW–NE, instead of NE–SW) also has the lowest $\delta^{15}N$ value. The burials at Mulhouse-Est date to the *Rubané moyen*, which places them near the beginning in the LBK sequence in Alsace, though the cemetery is not likely to be as early as Vedrovice and Těšetice-Kyjovice (Chapter 4.7–8), and this could explain the high frequency of *Spondylus* at the cemetery (Jeunesse 1997, 94). Burial at Mulhouse-Est was contemporary to the

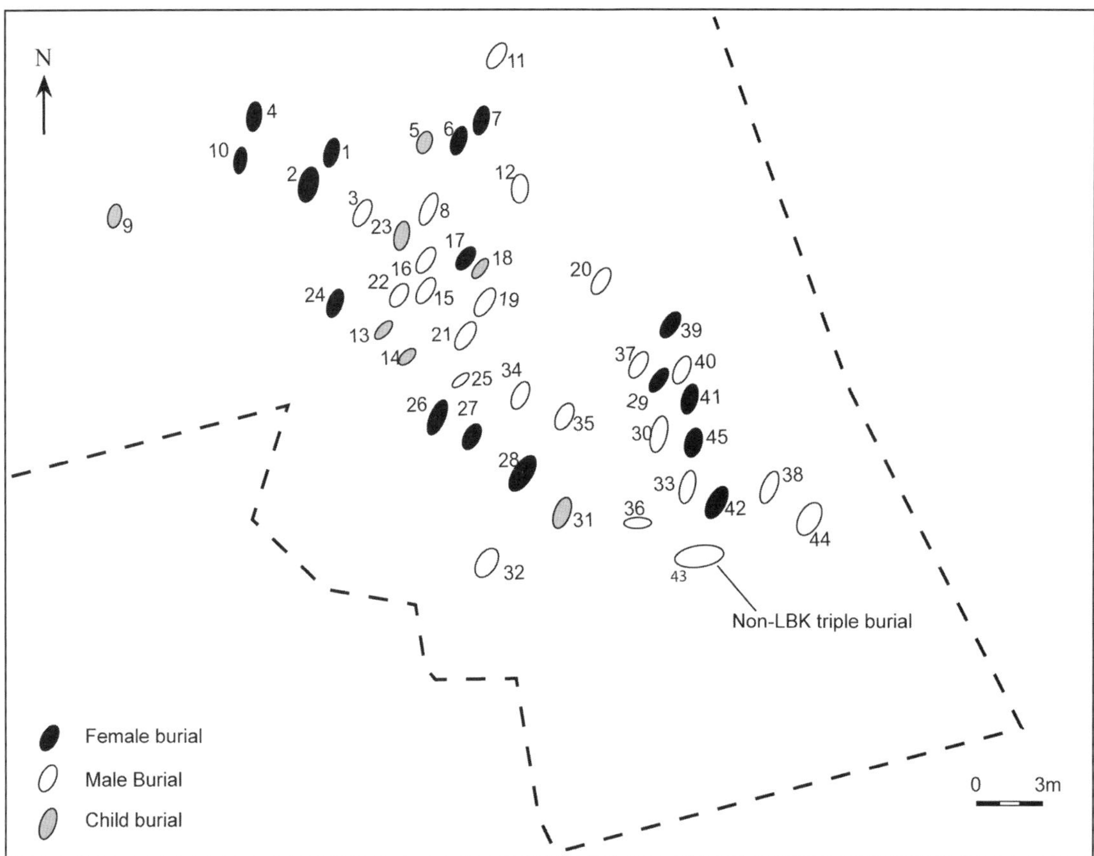

Fig. 8.14. Ensisheim les Octrois*: plan.*

as yet unexcavated nearby settlement (identified through a pottery scatter; Lefranc 2007a, 316).

In many ways, therefore, this cemetery reflects patterns identified in settlement burials in Hungary (as at Mezőkövesd-Mocsolyás and Füzesabony-Gubakút: Chapter 3.7–8), with little variation in grave orientation and body position, and grave goods that are overwhelmingly associated with adorning the body. This could suggest a trend over time away from ornaments as grave goods, represented by their reduced presence at sites such as Schwetzingen (Chapter 7.7). However, at Mulhouse-Est three burials also included polished stone adzes (13% of graves) and ten graves contained pottery of some description (*c.* 40% of graves), which are rates only slightly lower than the LBK as a whole (Lifeways Database), so this trend is by no means absolute. Jeunesse (2002c) has argued that this selection of grave goods and overall favouring of dominant orientations and body positions is part of a 'Danubian' tradition of burial practices.

The presence of bone rings (found in graves 5, 12 and 15a) is also rare for the LBK, but they have been found in an isolated burial at Emmersdorf an der Donau, Lower Austria (Seewald 1942; Lenneis 1995, 34) and one bone ring was also found in grave 103/208 at Polgár-Ferenci-hát (Table 3.13; Chapter 3.9). However, this type of grave good is more frequent in burials in the Paris basin (Bailloud 1964), and the bone rings at Mulhouse-Est may therefore be best understood as part of the RSO group, identified by Jeunesse (1995b; 1996; Chapter 8.4.1), though, unlike the Paris basin, polished stone tools are present in the graves. Burial rites, therefore, appear to be blending certain preferences at different scales of individual, community and region, while following widely found LBK traditions. Variation is found in where the emphasis falls. Those individuals identified as on the edge of the isotope distributions (burials 15a, 17, 18 and 20) could be connected to rarer burial practices (seen in orientation or lack of grave goods), but no two burials did so in the same fashion. The pairing of certain graves suggests that multiple relationships could be stressed in the spatial layout of the cemeteries. However, here at Mulhouse-Est, it is this 'pairing' of graves which is emphasised over other forms of spatial alignment.

8.8 Ensisheim les Octrois, *Haute-Alsace*

8.8.1 Introduction

The cemetery of Ensisheim *les Octrois* lies on the east bank of the river Ill in Haute-Alsace, roughly midway between Colmar and Mulhouse (Fig. 8.1). The site itself is close to the small river Quatelbach, near the commune of *les Octrois* on the loess terrace (Gallay and Mathieu 1988, 371). The cemetery was first discovered when the excavations of a long-occupied LBK settlement were extended southwards (Mathieu and Mathieu 1993, 1), and over a series of campaigns (1984, 1994 and 1996) some 45 inhumations were uncovered, including a late Neolithic triple burial (Christian Jeunesse, pers. comm.; Jeunesse *et al*. 1996). Stray surface finds of a *Spondylus* pendant and a flat axe suggest that there were once more graves that have subsequently been destroyed (Jeunesse *et al*. 1996, 21). This cemetery is one of the largest in Alsace (Fig. 8.14) and comparable in size to the Basse-Alsace site of Souffelweyersheim.

The graves appear to have been placed in amongst an earlier LBK occupation, represented by about 20 pits (Arbogast 1993; Gallay and Mathieu 1988, 372). The nearby settlement of Ensisheim *Ratfeld* is considered to have been occupied from the *Rubané ancien* to *récent*, while the cemetery is thought to begin during the *récent* phase and continue into the *final* phase (Jeunesse *et al*. 1996, 41; Lefranc 2007a, 314; cf. J. Schweitzer 1978; 1980). The cemetery thus appears to have been begun some time after the settlement was first occupied, but burial then continued after the settlement was abandoned.

Only one radiocarbon date from the LBK cemetery has been obtained, on grave 44, that of a 50-year-old male with a twice trepanned skull, which gave a result in the late sixth millennium cal BC (Alt *et al*. 1997, 360).[9] This burial is relatively isolated compared to the other burials (Jeunesse *et al*. 1996, 41). The adze type (*herminette double perforée*) in this grave is the only one which is definitely not earlier than *Rubané récent* (Christian Jeunesse, pers. comm.). Recently the triple burial in grave 43 has also been dated but this produced a late Neolithic date and can now be discounted (Christian Jeunesse, pers. comm.). The east–west orientation of these individuals is certainly unusual at this site and may suggest that grave 36, which is unfurnished but has a similar orientation, is also late Neolithic in date (Christian Jeunesse, pers. comm.).

Relatively few pots were used as grave goods, which makes secure dating of the cemetery problematic, though we can note the decreasing presence of pottery in graves as a trend identifiable in several western regions of the LBK (Alsace, Baden-Württemberg, Hessen, Bavaria) throughout its later phases, but not in the Rhine-Meuse areas (Jeunesse 1997, 94). The dating of Ensisheim also relies on the presence of lithic and shell grave goods. Significant quantities of *Spondylus* are present. Jeunesse *et al*. (1996, 47) argue that although *Spondylus* is usually characteristic of early graves elsewhere in the LBK, in its western distribution its presence in graves continues into the final stages of the LBK. Lithic types such as the double adze indicate a relatively late date (*Rubané récent*/*Rubané final*), and as those graves which do suggest a late date are not clustered but rather spread throughout the cemetery, Jeunesse *et al*. (1996, 49) suggest that the whole cemetery is late.

The demography of the cemetery is fairly balanced between men and women, but there is an under-representation of children, particularly the very young (19 males, 17 women and eight children) (Jeunesse 1997, 130). Although there is a denser concentration of graves in the centre of the cemetery, Jeunesse (1997, 130–1) does not argue for any sub-groups within the cemetery. However, he does tentatively suggest that rows of burials can be identified, but warns against relying on this too heavily (Jeunesse 1997, 131). Despite this apparent lack of order in layout of the graves, they are fairly uniform in other respects; 80% of the burials are crouched on their left side, and all but five burials have their heads to the north-east (Fig. 8.15). So, like Mulhouse-Est, the orientations of the graves and body positions show less variability than in cemeteries in Basse-Alsace. The grave goods too appear relatively homogeneous but representative of the general pattern found in Haute-Alsace. The only aspect to stand out is the low frequency of pottery in the graves (Jeunesse 1997, 134).

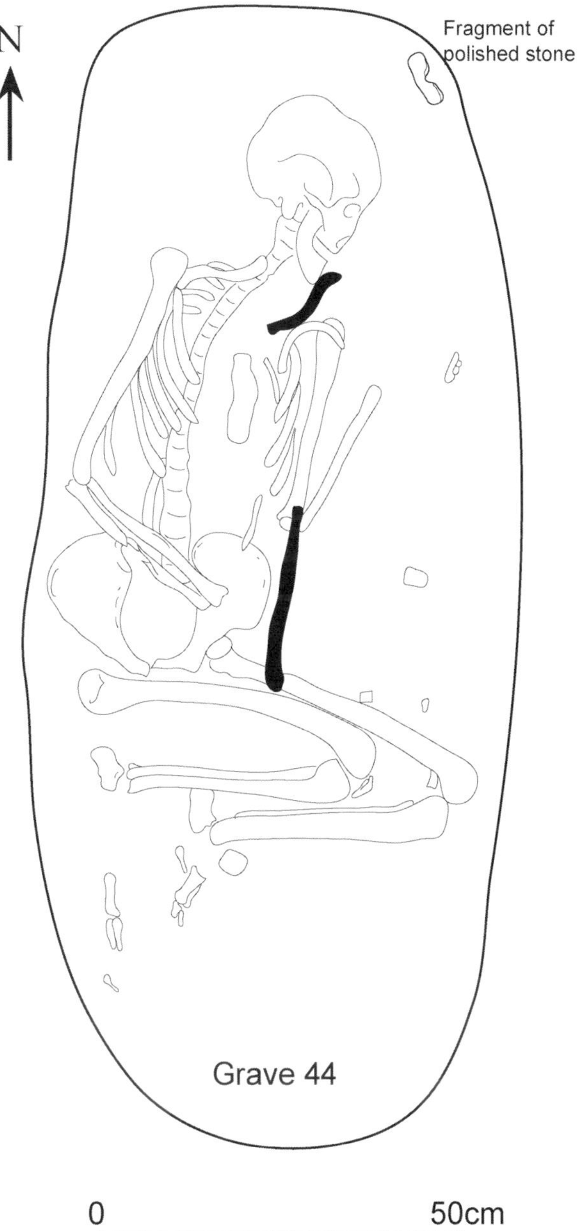

Fig. 8.15. Ensisheim les Octrois*: burial 44. The bones in black are out of their expected anatomical connection. After Boës (2000, 10).*

Only five burials have pottery vessels, only a few of which are decorated, and a further two have sherds at the level of

Table 8.10. Ensisheim les Octrois*: the isotope, osteological and archaeological data. Age and sex information from Linda Fibiger (this volume; graves 11 and 25–42, 45) and François Lambach (1993; graves 1–8, 10, 12 and 44). See Chapter 2 for further definition of ages. dec. = deciduous.*
Key for body position: LC – Left-crouched; RC – Right-crouched; C – Crouched, direction unknown; CB – Crouched on back; CF – Crouched on front; S – Supine; P – Prone; I – Irregular.
Key for grave goods (number of items follows in brackets; frag. = fragment): U. – Unfurnished; F. – Fill only (all items listed after an F. were in the fill of the grave rather than at the level of the skeleton); Pol. – Polished stone; Cer. – Ceramics; Shd. – Sherds; Spon. – Spondylus*; She. – Other Shell; Och. – Ochre; Lit. – Chipped stone; Bon – Worked bone; Grd. – Grinding stone; Firelighting kit – this includes the presence of pyrite or manganese as well as tools (such as flint or a bone awl) that could be used to start a fire (Nieszery 1995, 163–8).*

Burial	Tooth	Sex	Age (yrs)	$^{87}Sr/^{86}Sr$	Sr conc. ppm	$\delta^{13}C$ ‰	$\delta^{15}N$ ‰	Orientation	Body position	Grave goods	Pathologies
1	M2	F	44–78	0.70893	-	−20.5	8.8	NE–SW	LC	Och.	-
2	M1	F	33–65	0.70876	-	−20.3	9.9	NE–SW	LC	U.	-
3	-	M	30>	-	-	−20.2	9.9	NE–SW	LC	Och., F.Shd.(2), Lit.(1), Bead	-
4	-	F	30>	-	-	−20.2	9.1	NE–SW	LC	Och., F.Shd.(2)	-
5	-	-	9–14	-	-	−20.4	8.7	NE–SW	LC	She.(35), Och.	-
6	M1	F	25>	0.70884	83	-	-	NE–SW	LC	Shd.(1), She.(4), Och.,	-
7	M2	F	40–70	0.70899	67	−20.1	8.8	NE–SW	-	U.	-
8	M3	M	25–69	0.70928	*n.d.*	−20.1	9.4	NE–SW	LC	Pol.(1), Och., F.Shd.(3)	-
9	-	-	9–10	-	-	-	-	NE–SW	RC	Cer.(1), Bon.(1)	*Cribra orbitalia*, enamel hypoplasia
10	M3	F	30>	0.70933	43	−20.1	9.1	NE–SW	LC	Och.	-
11	M3	M?	Adult <30	0.70887	*n.d.*	−20.1	8.9	NE–SW	LC	Bon.(1)	Possible rib fracture or infection
12	M2	M	40–73	0.70925	*n.d.*	−20.1	9	NE–SW	LC	Pol.(1)	-
13	M1	-	3–4	0.70951	*n.d.*	-	-	NE–SW	LC	Cer.(1), Spon.(buckle), She.(183), Och., Lit.(1), Bon. (figurine)	-
14	M2	-	5–6	0.70968	*n.d.*	−20.0	9.3	SW–NE	LC	Cer.(1), Spon.(2 beads), She.(74), Och. Bon.(1), Tee. (1, deer), Burnt animal bone	-
15	-	M	45–76	-	-	−20.0	9.7	NE–SW	LC	Och., F.Shd. (1)	-
16	M3	F	25>	0.70987	*n.d.*	−20.5	8.8	NE–SW	LC	Och., Charred seeds	-
17	M2	F	25–60	0.71118	150	-	-	NE–SW	LC	Och.	-
18	M1	-	6–7	0.70912	*n.d.*	−20.3	9.2	NE–SW	LC	Och.	-
19	M3	M	40–69	0.70936	71	−20.0	8.8	NE–SW	LC	Pol.(1), Shd.(1), Lit. (5), Bon.(1)	-
20	M1	M	45–76	0.70884	68	−19.8	9.9	NE–SW	RC	Pol.(1), Lit.(1), F.Shd. (2)	-
21	-	M	45–73	-	-	−20.1	9.7	NE–SW	LC	Pol.(1)	-
22	M3	M	30>	0.71186	211	−19.9	10	NE–SW	LC	Och.	-
23	M2	-	11–13	0.70926	*n.d.*	−20.1	9	NE–SW	LC	She.(2), Och., F.Shd.(23)	-
24	-	F	30>	-	-	−20.0	9.5	NE–SW	LC	Lit.(1), F.She.(1)	-
25	M2 dec.	-	*c.* 3	0.70902	*n.d.*	−20.2	9.6	NE–SW	LC	U.	-

26	M3?	F	Adult >30	0.70901	*n.d.*	−20.3	9.3	NE–SW	LC	Och.	Enamel hypoplasia
27	M2	F	Adult	0.70950	78	−20.3	9.1	SW–NE	LC	U.	-
28	M3	F	Adult >20	0.70971	*n.d.*	−20.3	8.9	NE–SW	LC	U.	Caries (3)
29	M1 M3	F	Mid-Adult	0.70918 0.70893	67	−20.4	9.4	NE–SW	RC	Och.	Dental trauma
30	M3	M	Mature Adult	0.70869	*n.d.*	−19.9	8.8	NE–SW	LC	Bon.(1)	Possible infection
31	M2 dec.	-	5–6	0.70934	47	−19.7	9.8	NE–SW	RC	U.	-
32	M1 M3	M	YMA	0.70899 0.70924	41 65	−20.2	9.6	NE–SW	LC	U.	Caries (2), *spondylolysis*
33	M1	M	YMA	0.70919	52	−20.2	8.4	N–S	RC	Pol.(1)	-
34	M3	M	Mid-Adult	0.70908	55	−20.4	9.5	NE–SW	LC	Pol.(2)	-
35	M3	M	YA	0.70951	40	−20.2	9.6	NE–SW	LC	Pol.(2), Cer.(1), Spon.(buckle), She. (185), Lit.(1)	-
36	-	M?	Adult	-	-	−20.6	9.2	E–W	-	Och.	-
37	M1 M3	M	YMA	0.70918 0.70908	53 87	−20.0	9.8	NE–SW	LC	Pol.(1), Spon.(6 beads), She.(1), Lit.(9), Firelighting kit	Caries (1)
38	M2	M	YMA	0.70949	66	-	-	NE–SW	RC	Pol.(2), Lit.(1)	Caries (1)
39	-	F?	Mid-Adult	-	-	−19.8	9.4	NE–SW	LC	Cer.(1, frag.), Lit. (1, frag.)	-
40	M3	M	OMA	0.70894	71	−20.1	10.9	NE–SW	I	Spon.(buckle), Och., Lit. (7), Firelighting kit	-
41	M3	F	YMA	0.70940	74	−20.3	8.7	NE–SW	LC	Och.	Caries (1)
42	-	F	Adult	-	-	−20.4	8.9	NE–SW	LC	U.	-
44	-	M	c. 50	0.70976	78	-	-	N–S	LC	Pol.(1), Lit.(1), F.Shd. (3), Daub?, Cut through rubbish pit	-
45	M3	F	Mid-Adult	0.70905	67	−20.4	9.9	NE–SW	LC	Och.	Pulmonary infection

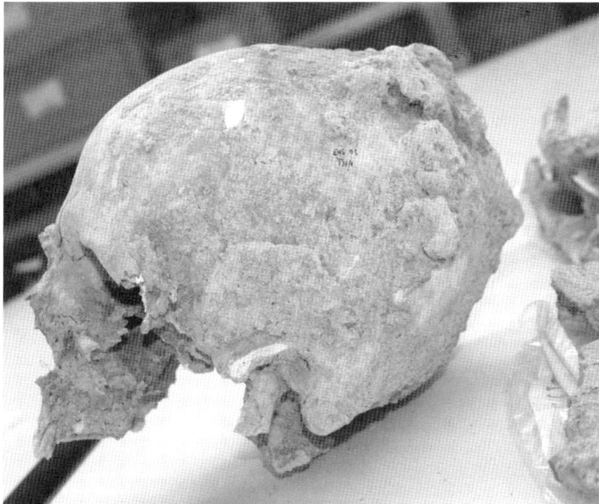

Fig. 8.16. Ensisheim les Octrois*: cranium covered in mineralised matrix, burial 28. Photo: Linda Fibiger.*

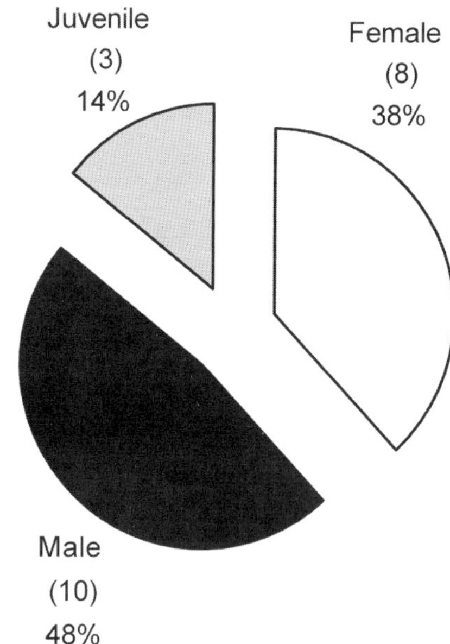

Fig. 8.17. Ensisheim les Octrois*: age and sex assessment.*

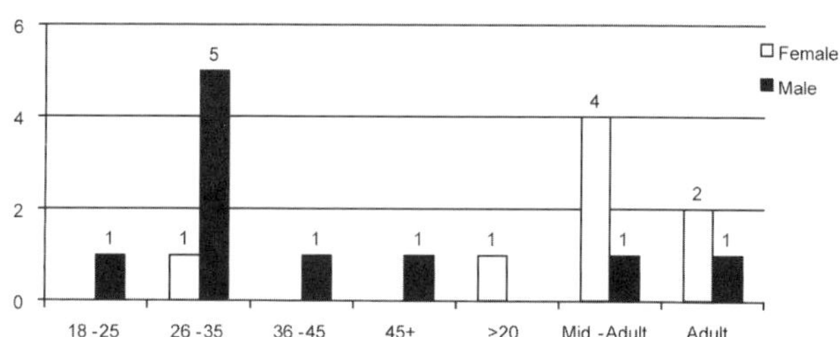

Fig. 8.18. Ensisheim les Octrois*: adult age distribution.*

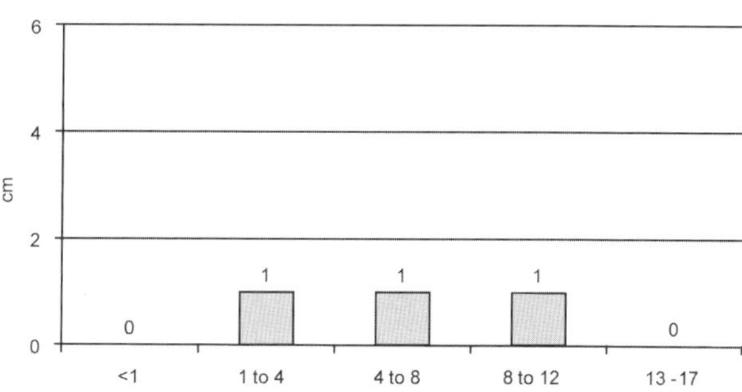

Fig. 8.19. Ensisheim les Octrois*: non-adult age distribution.*

the skeleton and eight have sherds included in the fill of the grave (Table 8.10). By contrast, the graves at Mulhouse-Est, no more than 10 km from Ensisheim, had large quantities of decorated pottery, as do other cemeteries in the broader Alsace region. Although Ensisheim contributed significantly to Jeunesse's characterisation of funerary Tradition I, it does appear to have some unique features. The key grave goods of Tradition I are sprinkled ochre and beads from small shells, both abundant at this cemetery. Jeunesse (1997) argues that the percentage of lithics is higher than average, though this occurs alongside another interesting trend, of lithics and shell ornaments appearing to be mutually exclusive (11 graves were furnished with adzes, most of which contain no shells or *Spondylus*). While each of the six individuals placed in a crouched position on the right-hand side appears to have a normal range of graves goods, only one of the graves contains sprinkled ochre.

8.8.2 Osteology

Preservation

A total of 21 individuals from Ensisheim were analysed, those curated at the *Pôle d'Archéologie Interdépartemental Rhénan* in Sélestat, Alsace. Although the remains were generally in moderate or moderate to good condition, some bones were encrusted in a mineralised matrix, which means that not all bone surfaces could be examined for pathologies (Fig. 8.16).

Demography: age and sex

The analysed Ensisheim assemblage consisted of 18 adults, including 10 males and eight females, and three juveniles (Fig. 8.17).

Similar to the other assemblages analysed for this study, the proportion of juveniles at Ensisheim, together with the total absence of infants, does not represent the expected mortality profile for the period. The adults in the sample were evenly spread across all age groups (Fig. 8.18), though unfortunately most females could only be very broadly aged as mid-adult. Similarly, the three juveniles were distributed across the juvenile age range (Fig. 8.19).

Adult stature

Only five males and two females at Ensisheim presented with left femora that were complete enough to measure maximum length (Fig. 8.20). Males and females seem to be clustered slightly closer than in other assemblages, but the sample is too small for any meaningful statistical comparison.

Dental disease

A total of 429 permanent teeth from 19 individuals could be examined, including 388 teeth from 16 adults and 41 teeth from three juveniles (Figs 8.21–2). Five individuals (31.2%) in the adult sample presented with caries and one (6.3%) with enamel hypoplasia. One juvenile individual (33.3%) was affected by enamel hypoplasia (Table 8.11). Based on the number of teeth present, ten (2.6%) out of 388 preserved teeth in the adult assemblage were affected by caries (Table 8.12) and one (0.3%) by enamel hypoplasia. In the sexed sample, caries was noted on eight (3.2%) of the male and two (1.5%) of the female teeth, whereas enamel hypoplasia occurred only on one female tooth (0.7%). In the juvenile assemblage, eight teeth (19.5%) presented with enamel hypoplasia. Overall, caries affected 2.3% of all teeth examined, whereas enamel hypoplasia rates were slightly lower with 2.1%.

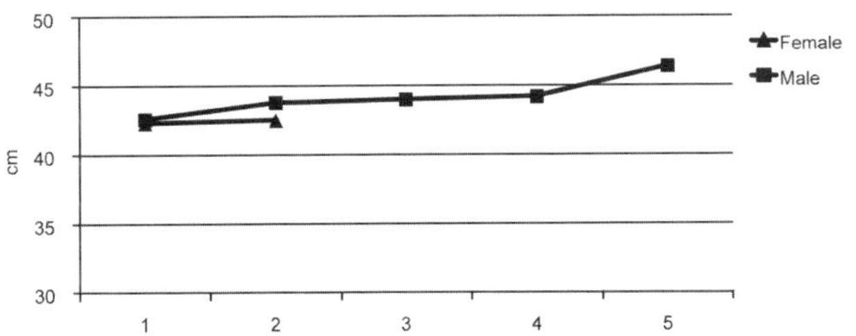

Fig. 8.20. Ensisheim les Octrois*: comparison of the maximum length of male and female left femora.*

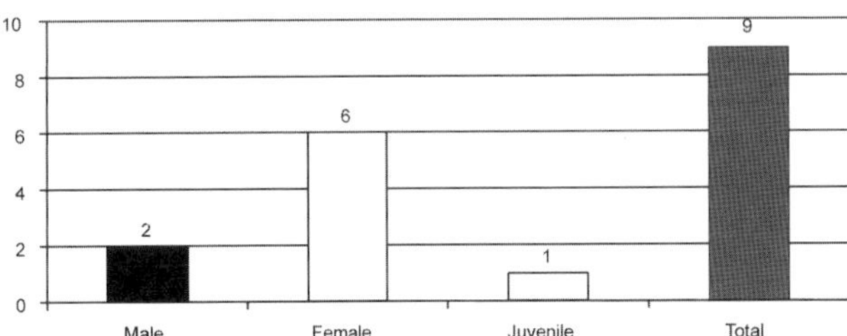

Fig. 8.21. Ensisheim les Octrois*: number of individuals with partial or complete dentitions.*

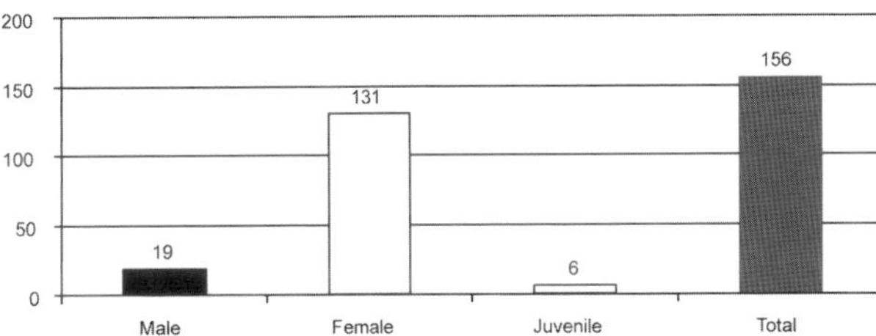

Fig. 8.22. Ensisheim les Octrois*: number of teeth present.*

Cribra orbitalia

Thirteen adults, including eight males and five females, as well as two juveniles had at least one partially preserved orbit. *Cribra orbitalia* was only noted in one individual, an older juvenile, resulting in a population prevalence of 6.7% (Table 8.13).

Periosteal changes and infection

Two individuals at Ensisheim presented with periosteal reactions or changes indicative of inflammatory, infectious or metabolic conditions, giving a crude prevalence of 9.5%. Burial 30, a mature adult male, showed healed periosteal remodelling on the left anterior-medial fibula. The unilateral, delimited nature of the changes makes a localised injury or infection the most likely diagnosis. Burial 45, a mid-adult female, presented with mixed bone deposits of the left and right ribs, concentrating in the head/neck area of the affected bones (Fig. 8.23). This is indicative of a pulmonary condition that was active at the time of death and differential diagnosis includes pleurisy and pulmonary tuberculosis (Roberts and Buikstra 2003, 101).

Table 8.11. Ensisheim les Octrois*: dental pathology. Individuals affected.*

Group	No. of individuals with teeth	No. (%) affected by caries	No. (%) affected by enamel hypoplasia
Adult Male	10	3 (30%)	0
Adult Female	6	2 (33.3%)	1 (16.7%)
All Adults	16	5 (31.2%)	1 (6.3%)
Juvenile	3	0	1 (33.3%)
Total	19	5 (26.3%)	2 (10.5%)

Table 8.12. Ensisheim les Octrois*: dental pathology. Teeth affected.*

Group	No. of teeth	No. (%) affected by caries	No. (%) affected by enamel hypoplasia
Adult Male	251	8 (3.2%)	0
Adult Female	137	2 (1.5%)	1 (0.7%)
All Adults	388	10 (2.6%)	1 (0.3%)
Juvenile	41	0	8 (19.5%)
Total	429	10 (2.3%)	9 (2.1%)

Table 8.13. Ensisheim les Octrois*:* cribra orbitalia.

	No. of individuals with at least one partial eye socket preserved	No. (%) of individuals with *cribra orbitalia*
Adult Male	8	0 (0)
Adult Female	5	0 (0)
All Adults	13	0 (0)
Juvenile	2	1 (50)
Total	15	1 (6.7)

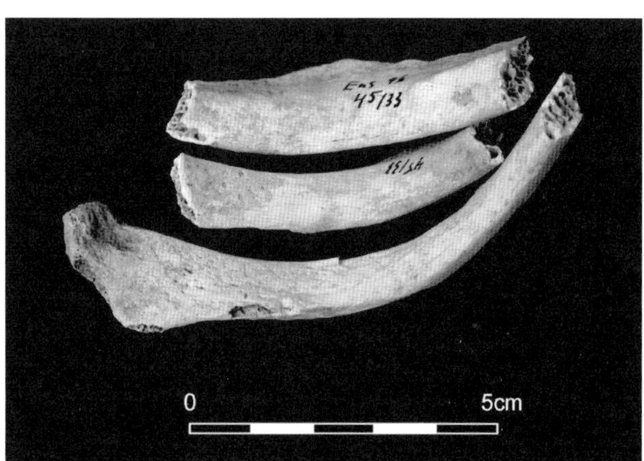

Fig. 8.23. Ensisheim les Octrois*: new bone formation on visceral surfaces of right ribs, burial 45. Photo: Linda Fibiger.*

Post-cranial trauma

Post-cranial trauma was noted on two individuals. Burial 11, a young mid-adult male, presented with a possible rib fracture. Two ribs had fused, apparently as a result of a fracture and consequent callus formation; however, without radiographic analysis this diagnosis has to remain tentative. Alternative explanations for the observed changes include new bone formation in the course of an infection. Another young mid-adult male (burial 32) presented with bilateral *spondylolysis* of the fifth lumbar vertebra. No cranial trauma was recorded.

Summary

Ensisheim is a small assemblage with some preservation issues which limited the extent of the osteological analysis. Unlike in most of the other Lifeways assemblages, caries

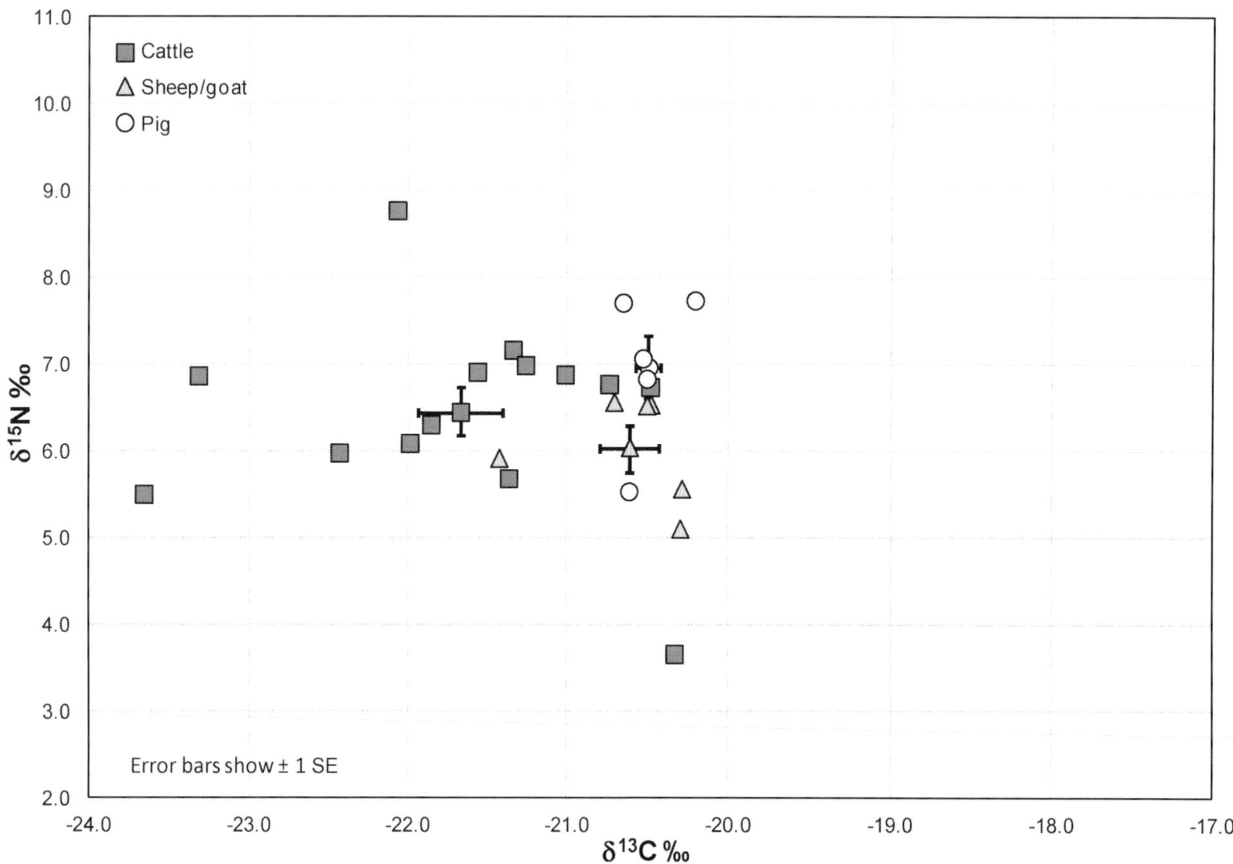

Fig. 8.24. Ensisheim Ratfeld*: carbon and nitrogen isotope ratios (‰) of animals.*

Table 8.14. Ensisheim Ratfeld*: carbon and nitrogen isotope ratios (‰) of animals, with means and standard deviations.*

Species	Mean $\delta^{13}C$	SD $\delta^{13}C$	Mean $\delta^{15}N$	SD $\delta^{15}N$	n
Cattle	−21.7	0.99	6.4	1.13	14
Sheep/goat	−20.6	0.41	6.0	0.61	5
Pig	−20.5	0.19	7.0	0.90	6

prevalence was higher in males than females and *cribra orbitalia* was only recorded in one individual. One mid-adult female was affected by a pulmonary condition, for which tuberculosis is one possible diagnosis.

8.8.3 The animal remains from Ensisheim Ratfeld*, Haute-Alsace*

The settlement at Ensisheim *Ratfeld*, located north of the cemetery *les Octrois*, was first discovered in 1981 and then excavated more fully in 1987 (Fig. 8.1; Jeunesse and Sainty 1992; Lefranc 2007a). Although no longhouses were found, pit assemblages featured pottery from all the different phases of the LBK in Alsace (from *Rubané ancien* to *Rubané final*) alongside sherds of La Hoguette ware (Jeunesse and Sainty 1992, 101). The 1987 excavations also found a burial of an adult (sex indeterminable), who was accompanied in the ground by a *Spondylus* buckle (Jeunesse and Sainty 1992, 98). The object had been broken into two halves and apparently placed on the skeleton, at the waist and sternum (Jeunesse and Sainty 1992, 101). Jeunesse and Sainty (1992, 98) argue that the burial took place during the late *Rubané ancien* and early *Rubané moyen* and therefore before inhumations started at Ensisheim *les Octrois*.

The settlement also produced abundant animal remains, with approximately 6600 bones of wild and domestic animals, birds and fish preserved, 2300 of which could be identified (Arbogast and Jeunesse 1990, 290). Domesticated animals comprised 95% of the animal bone assemblage and cattle remains were more frequent than sheep/goats and pigs (Arbogast and Jeunesse 1990, 292). The importance of these secondary animals grew over time and by the end of the settlement in the *Rubané récent* phase, the role of cattle seems to have been much reduced. This trend towards a more varied subsistence base at Ensisheim *Ratfeld* is also apparent in the wild animal bone assemblage, which is more varied in the later phases of the site (Arbogast and Jeunesse 1990, 292). One explanation of this change might be a move towards meat becoming a more consistent part of the diet in the later phases of the settlement, if cattle were reserved for feasting events. This is perhaps also represented in a change from large hunted animals (red deer and aurochs) in the *Rubané ancien* to smaller game (such as wild boar, roe deer and beaver; Arbogast and Jeunesse 1990, 292).

The difference between $\delta^{13}C$ values for cattle and those of the pigs and sheep/goats is striking (Fig. 8.24; Table 8.14). The variance is significantly different across species (Levene's test, p=0.026), reflecting the wide range in cattle $\delta^{13}C$ values. The cattle mean $\delta^{13}C$ value differs significantly from that of the other two species (ANOVA with post hoc comparison of means, Tamhane's T2, p<0.01; confirmed by non-parametric Kruskal-Wallis and Median tests showing that $\delta^{13}C$ distribution and medians are different across species). There does not seem to be a group of cattle that differs clearly from the others in $\delta^{13}C$ and $\delta^{15}N$ values, as at Rutzing in Austria (Chapter 5.10); even if the individuals with the lowest values were aurochs, the range in cattle $\delta^{13}C$ values is still wide, and the mean lower than those of sheep or pigs. There are two cattle outliers with $\delta^{15}N$ values more than two standard deviations above and below the mean, respectively. Pigs have similar mean $\delta^{13}C$ values to sheep/goats, and higher $\delta^{15}N$ values than the herbivores, but not significantly so.

The $\delta^{13}C$ values suggest that cattle were exploiting habitats with lower $\delta^{13}C$ values than sheep/goats and pigs, and the obvious candidate is forest grazing, or fodder from forest areas (Drucker *et al.* 2008; Balasse *et al.* 2012). The $\delta^{15}N$ values are not significantly lower (as we would expect with wild animals), however, so it is likely that their diet was being influenced by human activities and perhaps cattle also had access to manured areas and/or crop wastes from manured fields.

The difference between adult human and cattle means is 1.5‰±0.32 (SD) for $\delta^{13}C$ values and 2.9‰±0.60 for $\delta^{15}N$ values. The difference in $\delta^{13}C$ values seems large compared with sites further east (and see further discussion in Chapter 9.2.5).

8.8.4 Carbon and nitrogen analysis

A total of 38 individuals were sampled from Ensisheim *les Octrois*, including 32 adults (17 males and 15 females) and six juveniles (Fig. 8.25; Table 8.15).

Age/sex variation

The human $\delta^{13}C$ and $\delta^{15}N$ values from Ensisheim were tightly clustered, with no overall difference between juveniles and adults. The female mean differed significantly from the male mean for $\delta^{13}C$ (ANOVA, p=0.04) but not $\delta^{15}N$. There was also a significant trend in $\delta^{13}C$ with age rank (based on detailed osteological data) for males, but not females. Both effects reflect a relatively large group of old males with high $\delta^{13}C$ values, while there are very few old females in the oldest age rank, so it is not certain whether this effect reflects the population as a whole or is an accident of sampling. There is no trend in $\delta^{15}N$ with age among adults, or correlation between $\delta^{13}C$ and $\delta^{15}N$ values, which makes the difference in $\delta^{13}C$ hard to interpret. If lower $\delta^{13}C$ values reflected freshwater fish consumption

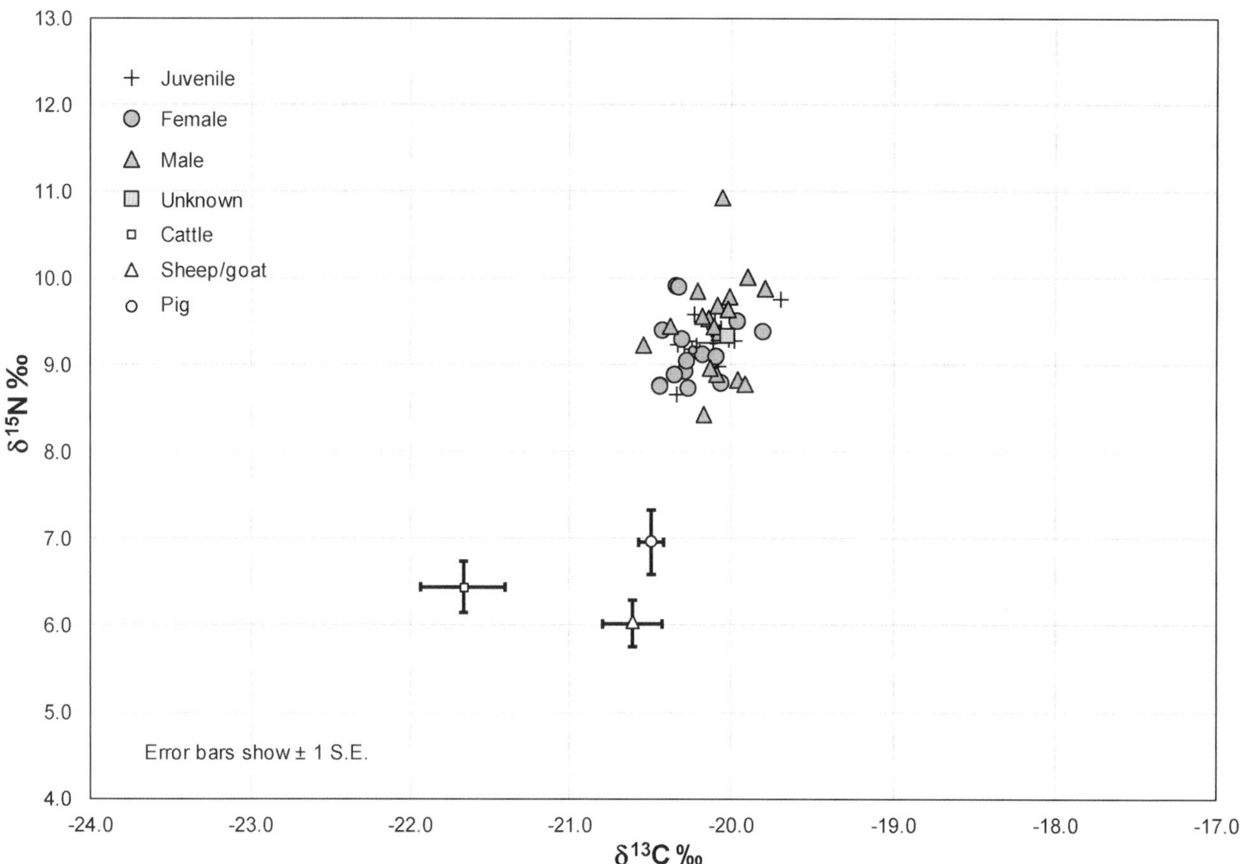

Fig. 8.25. Ensisheim les Octrois*: carbon and nitrogen isotope ratios (‰) of humans.*

Table 8.15. Ensisheim les Octrois*: carbon and nitrogen isotope ratios (‰) of humans, with means and standard deviations.*

Species	Age/sex	Mean δ^{13}C	SD δ^{13}C	Mean δ^{15}N	SD δ^{15}N	n
Human	Juvenile	−20.1	0.25	9.3	0.40	6
Human	Female	−20.3	0.18	9.2	0.39	15
Human	Male	−20.1	0.18	9.5	0.14	17
Human	All adults	−20.2	0.19	9.3	0.52	32
Human	Unknown	−20.0	-	9.4	-	1

(as suggested by the presence of fish bones at Ensisheim *Ratfeld*; Arbogast and Jeunesse 1990, 290), one would expect higher δ^{15}N values (see, for example, the results which Boesl *et al.* (2006) obtained at Pestenacker, a late fourth millennium BC site in southern Bavaria), and if they reflected more consumption of food from shaded forest habitats away from manured fields, lower δ^{15}N values (Bogaard 2011), but neither is the case. Nor is a similar effect seen at any other site examined in this project except in the data at Vedrovice when combined with that from M.P. Richards *et al.* (2008; Chapter 4.7.3). This pattern remains difficult to interpret.

The negative correlation of δ^{15}N with age rank among juveniles is very close to significant (Spearman rank correlation, r_s=−0.88, critical value for p=0.05, 2-tailed t test=0.89). The two oldest juveniles could have been undergoing an adolescent growth spurt, which would be expected to lower δ^{15}N (reviewed by Waters-Rist and Katzenberg 2010; see discussion in Chapter 9.2.5). No further correlations between the pathologies identified on the skeleton and the stable isotopes were found.

Correlations with the archaeological data

While there are no overall correlations between body position and the stable isotope results, all four of the sampled right-crouched burials fell on the edge of the central cluster: either with high δ^{13}C and high δ^{15}N values (burials 20 and 31), low δ^{13}C and low δ^{15}N values (burial 33) or just low δ^{13}C (burial 29). In grave 40, an adult male with an outlying δ^{15}N value (10.9‰) was buried in an irregular position, on his back with the legs placed in a rhomboid fashion, which echoes the 'dancer' at Aiterhofen (Chapter 6.7.1). This may suggest that the diets of individuals buried in a right-crouched position were consistently different from the main cluster but not the same as each other. In contrast, the two sampled burials with a secondary

Table 8.16. Ensisheim les Octrois*: strontium isotope ratios and concentrations (note concentration information was not available for every sample). *denotes number of analyses, not number of individuals.*

Age/sex	Mean $^{87}Sr/^{86}Sr$	SD $^{87}Sr/^{86}Sr$	n*	Mean Sr conc.	SD Sr conc.	n*
Juvenile	0.70934	0.00023	6	47	-	1
Male	0.70933	0.00063	17	79	31	8
Female	0.70933	0.00071	14	74	44	13
All	0.70933	0.00061	37	74	38	22

orientation (SW–NE in the case of Ensisheim) fell within the main cluster of the results.

When the stable isotopes are considered alongside the grave goods, further patterns can also be identified. There were no correlations when the total number of grave goods, or the complexity of the grave good assemblages, were considered. The four burials accompanied by bone objects (graves 11, 14, 19 and 30 had bone points or other objects). All had very similar high $\delta^{13}C$ and low $\delta^{15}N$ values. Their $\delta^{13}C$ (2-tailed *t* test, $p=0.007$, n=38) and $\delta^{15}N$ (2-tailed *t* test, $p=0.026$, n=8) values were significantly different from the rest of the population. The low numbers of burials with bone objects require caution in extrapolating from these results, but as three of these four burials are adult males, who on average have higher $\delta^{15}N$ values, this pattern cannot be said to have been influenced by other factors.

The individuals buried with pottery (including sherds) also had a significantly higher average $\delta^{13}C$ value than those without (2-tailed *t* test, $p=0.002$, n=37), but when males and females are analysed separately, this pattern only retains significance amongst the females (2-tailed *t* test, $p=0.004$, n=14; mean without pottery=−20.3‰, with pottery=−20.0‰). Those burials where ochre had been used had a significantly lower $\delta^{13}C$ mean (2-tailed *t* test, $p=0.037$, n=37; mean with ochre=−20.2‰, without ochre=−20.1‰) than those without, but as the difference between the means falls within the standard error, we do not place too much significance on the results. Those individuals buried with shell objects or *Spondylus* ornaments did not stand out from the rest of the samples. In comparison to other sites in this project, those males buried with polished stone adzes did not have higher $\delta^{15}N$ values than those without (buried without polished stone, $\delta^{15}N$=9.5‰, with polished stone $\delta^{15}N$=9.3‰). Those buried with two polished stone tools did have a higher average mean (9.6‰), but this was not significantly different from the rest of the population. Overall, therefore, it appears that those males buried with polished stone were not, at Ensisheim, eating a significantly different diet to those who were interred without them. Instead, it appears that provision with bone objects (males) and pottery (for females) may have marked out those eating a different diet.

8.8.5 Strontium analysis

In total, molars from 34 individuals were sampled from Ensisheim: six juveniles, 13 females and 15 males (Fig. 8.26; Table 8.16). Strontium values were not collected for the triple burial in grave 43, which dates to the late Neolithic (Christian Jeunesse, pers. comm.). In three cases, two teeth from the same individual were sampled; burial 29 (M1 and M3), burial 32 (M1 and M3) and burial 37 (M1 and M3). In each of these three cases, the $^{87}Sr/^{86}Sr$ ratios of the first and third molars were not significantly different. The cemetery and settlement at Ensisheim are on loess soils and we would expect the average values for the site to be in line with what was found at Mulhouse-Est, which lies just over 10 km away (Chapter 8.7.4). The average $^{87}Sr/^{86}Sr$ ratio for all the samples of 0.70933±0.00061 is not significantly different from the average ratio from Mulhouse-Est (Mann-Whitney U test, $p=0.11$), but is higher (more radiogenic). This perhaps reflects the greater distance of Ensisheim from the Alps and the Jura, lessening the contribution of carbonate to the loess in this region, rather than more extensive use of non-loess soils (Chapter 8.7.4). However, the presence of two outliers, with $^{87}Sr/^{86}Sr$ ratios above the loess range, may actually suggest that a different mobility pattern was present at Ensisheim.

The two outliers, graves 17 (an adult female; 0.71118) and 22 (an older adult male; 0.71186), thus suggest some use of upland resources. The concentration of strontium in the teeth sampled from both these individuals was very high in comparison to the rest of the cemetery (grave 17: 150; grave 22; 211; Fig. 8.26; Table 8.16), which may hint that the source of the diet that contributed to the values in these two teeth was significantly different to that of the rest of the cemetery population. Grave 17 was not sampled for $\delta^{13}C$ and $\delta^{15}N$, but, while the stable isotope values from grave 22 are within the main cluster of values, they are both above one SD from the mean, suggesting that the diet of this male may have varied slightly from the norm for the cemetery. There is no difference in the average $^{87}Sr/^{86}Sr$ ratios of males and females (2-tailed *t* test, $p=0.96$, n=28) or in their variance (Levene's test, $p=0.98$; outliers excluded). In fact, the male and female mean $^{87}Sr/^{86}Sr$ ratios are identical, which is highly unusual for this project. No significant differences in Sr ratio and concentration could be determined by tooth sampled (first molar, second molar, third molar).

Amongst the strontium concentration data, two clusters can be identified (Fig. 8.26; Mann-Whitney U test, $p<0.001$), which suggests that the two groups may have been consuming different food sources. However, given that some of the teeth sampled produced no Sr concentration data, these conclusions must be viewed as preliminary. These two groups cannot be identified amongst the stable isotope results ($\delta^{13}C$: 2-tailed *t* test, $p=0.52$, and $\delta^{15}N$: 2-

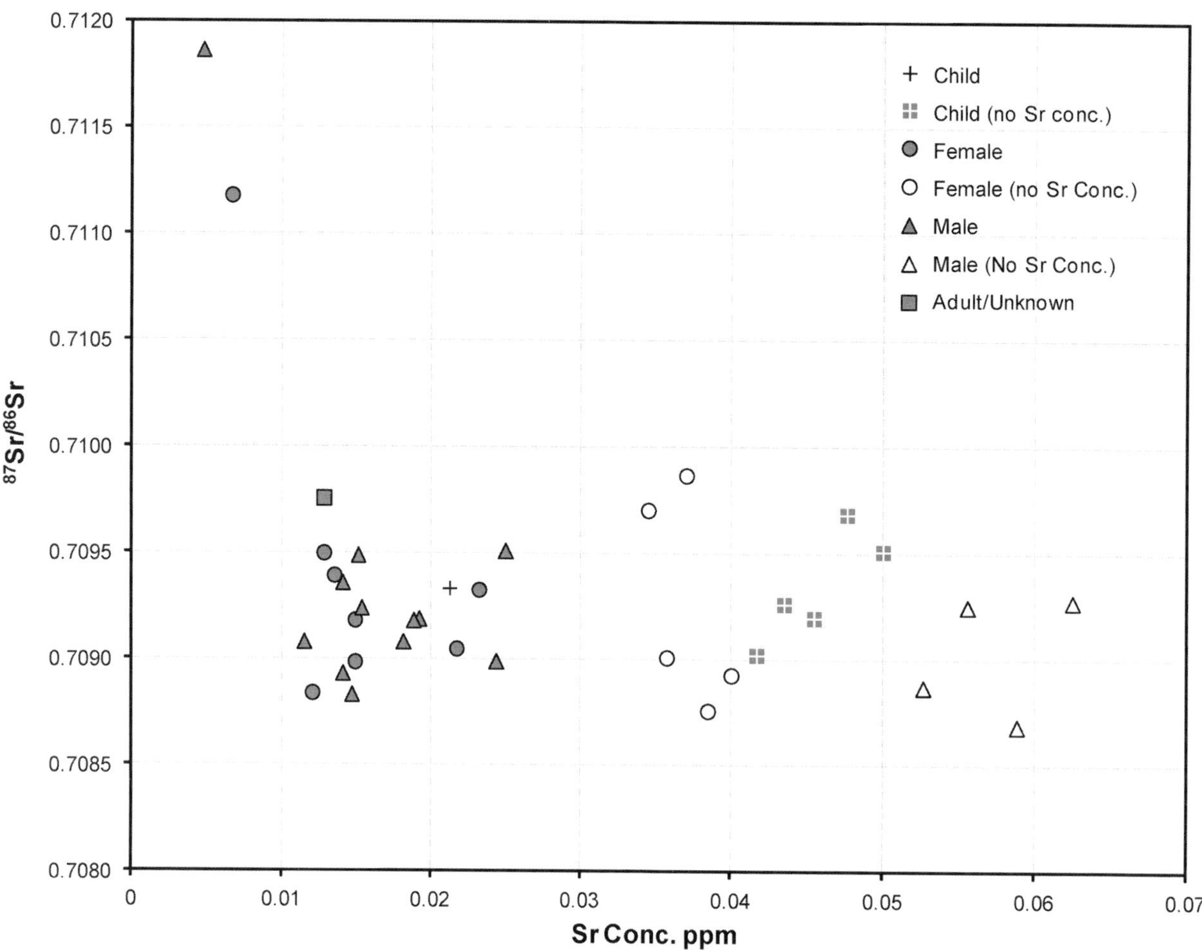

Fig. 8.26. Ensisheim les Octrois*: strontium concentration (ppm) versus ratio ($^{87}Sr/^{86}Sr$).*

tailed *t* test, $p=0.66$), so the difference between these two groups in terms of diet may not have been that great and the explanation for this difference may be found in subtle variations in how different foodstuffs were contributing to the overall diet. The group to the right of the graph (with high 1/Sr conc. ppm) consists of five males, one female and one child. Except for the female (grave 10), the rest of the individuals in this group are located together in the southern part of the cemetery (Fig. 8.26). This patterning could be explained as chronological, with a move to either higher or lower strontium concentration foods over time, or could suggest two slightly different diets co-existing throughout the life of the cemetery as we have seen at other sites, perhaps most obviously at Rutzing (Chapter 5.10). This variation may be interesting in light of the change in the animal bone assemblage, which sees a move towards the smaller domesticates (pig and sheep/goats) in the later phases of the settlement, but, admittedly, the cemetery as a whole does appear to date to the later phase of the settlement.

Correlations with the archaeological data

There were no correlations between the position of the body in the grave, its orientation or any identified pathologies and the strontium isotope results, but some patterning amongst the grave good assemblages could be identified. While there appeared to be no discernible correlations between the strontium isotope data and whether graves were furnished or unfurnished, or the total number of goods accompanying the deceased, pottery is restricted to the cluster of burials with high strontium concentration values (Fig. 8.26). There may be some overlap here with the carbon values; burials with pottery tended to have higher $\delta^{13}C$ values, they also tend to have high strontium concentrations. Understanding this pattern is, however, complicated by the lack of correlation between carbon and strontium concentration. The two Sr ratio outliers received only ochre and no further grave goods. Unusually, there were also no significant differences between those buried with polished stone and those without, following the lack of patterning found in the $\delta^{15}N$ values. Amongst the rest of the grave goods no further correlations could be seen. Overall, then, Ensisheim stands out from other cemeteries in this project as there is no correlation between polished stone and the strontium ratios.

There are no correlations between the strontium and stable isotope data, nor is there any spatial patterning amongst the strontium data. However, it is interesting to note that, as for Aiterhofen, the two strontium ratio outliers lie in the approximate centre of the known cemetery distribution.

8.8.6 Site summary and discussion

The isotope data from Ensisheim suggest some interesting intra-site variability, as well as differences to other sites discussed in this project. The stable isotope values were tightly clustered suggesting that overall the population were eating a very similar diet, but the variability in the strontium concentration may indicate some subtle differences in diet across it. As this pattern also appears to be repeated in the spatial layout of the cemetery, it could be related to changes over time. Those individuals with low strontium concentration ppm (high 1/Sr conc. ppm) still have higher strontium concentration values than most of the sampled individuals at Mulhouse-Est, and individuals buried at this cemetery are likely to have died during the *Rubané moyen*, before the start of the cemetery at Ensisheim. This may suggest a move towards foods with higher strontium concentrations over time. If this is the case, then the cemetery would have started in the south and moved northwards towards the settlement. However, in eastern Hungary, the sites sampled as part of this project were also comparatively close together and roughly contemporary, but showed distinct differences in their strontium and stable isotope data, suggesting that we might be seeing very localised differences.

At Mulhouse-Est, the individual in grave 20, who could be said to have a $\delta^{15}N$ value that stood out, also had an unusual burial orientation. However, here at Ensisheim, all sampled right-crouched burials fell on the edges of the stable isotope distributions, suggesting that alternative body positions rather than burial orientations were reflecting individuals with lifeways that varied from the norm in different ways rather than clustering together; this was not the case for some grave goods at Ensisheim which did show clustering of isotopic values. For example, the three males buried with bone tools had all had low $\delta^{15}N$ values, suggesting perhaps that this grave good had been connected with a way of life that did not involve as much consumption of animal protein as others, though admittedly sample numbers are low. Ensisheim also stands out because males buried with polished stone adzes unusually had a lower average $\delta^{15}N$ value than those without (though this was not statistically significant). Perhaps this can be connected to the greater frequency of caries in males than in females. While at other cemeteries in the LBK lifeways project, it has been the females who suffered more heavily from caries, suggesting greater consumption of plant foodstuffs, here at Ensisheim it seems that males were consuming more plants.

Females buried with pottery appeared to have higher $\delta^{13}C$ values, suggesting that their diet was more likely to have come from an open landscape than those buried without pottery. Individuals buried with pottery also appeared to have low strontium concentration values and, while there can be a fairly substantial difference in time between the mineralisation of the tooth sampled and the age which the stable isotope values represent, this pattern is interesting. High strontium concentration foods include milk and plants, while meat tends to be lower in Sr conc. (Chapter 2.3). Might we suggest that a group consuming more plants or perhaps even milk distinguished itself from the rest of the Ensisheim community through furnishing its graves with pottery?

8.9 *Souffelweyersheim* Tuilerie Reiss und Bund, *Basse-Alsace*

8.9.1 Introduction

In the same area as a large perforated axe had been discovered during the 1880s, six inhumations were found between 1917 and 1918 close to the road that ran between the villages of Souffelweyersheim and Hoenheim, north of Strasbourg (Forrer and Jaenger 1918). In the late 1930s and early 1940s, Henri Ulrich (1953, 21; Heintz 1981, 11) then uncovered a further 40 inhumations, making Souffelweyersheim the largest LBK cemetery in Alsace at the time. In 1949 and 1950, Ulrich (1953, 21–2) explored the limits of the cemetery and excavated the final six graves, bringing the total number of graves to 52 (though there are 53 skeletons as grave 1 is a double burial; Jeunesse 1997, 150; cf. Storch 1984/85, 39).[10] Today Souffelweyersheim is the second largest cemetery in Alsace after Vendenheim. Ulrich (1953, 22) also suggests that the cemetery may have extended further east or may have been associated with a possible group of isolated graves destroyed during the 1880s, so it may once have been even larger.

The cemetery itself is situated 700 m south-east of the village of Souffelweyersheim, on the very edge of the loess terrace north of a small stream named Souffel (Fig. 8.1). It covers an area of about 100 m by 80 m (Ulrich 1953, 21; Fig. 8.27). The site is part of the northernmost concentration of sites in Alsace, which focus on the loess between the rivers Bruche and Zorn (Lefranc 2007a, 155–9). Despite the relatively poor preservation of the skeletons and limited inclusion of pottery in the graves, the cemetery itself can be attributed to the *Rubané récent* (Arbogast 1983; Jeunesse 1995a, 131), a time when the number of settlements in the region increases (Lefranc 2007a, 159, 310). A number of pits which pre-date the cemetery suggest that the site was occupied as a settlement during the *Rubané ancien* and *moyen*, though no longhouses have been discovered (Ulrich 1952; 1953; Lefranc 2007a, 310). The cemetery is also not far from the settlement at Hoenheim (250 m distant), which has evidence of contemporary (*Rubané récent*) settlement activity (Ulrich 1953, 22; Lefranc 2007a, 304). The closest large settlement is that of Reichstett *Schamli, Kriegacker*, occupied from the early LBK in Alsace until the late *Rubané récent* (Lefranc 2007a, 276). In the *Rubané final* there is a dramatic drop in the number of sites on the loess around the Souffel and the cemetery also appears to have been abandoned by this phase.

The poor preservation of the site meant that almost 20 of the skeletons were not identifiable and the sex of only 18 individuals could be suggested (13 males, five females), accompanied by five children (Storch 1984/85, 35, tab. 6, 39). However, despite the lack of preservation, the size and features of the cemetery resulted in it making a significant

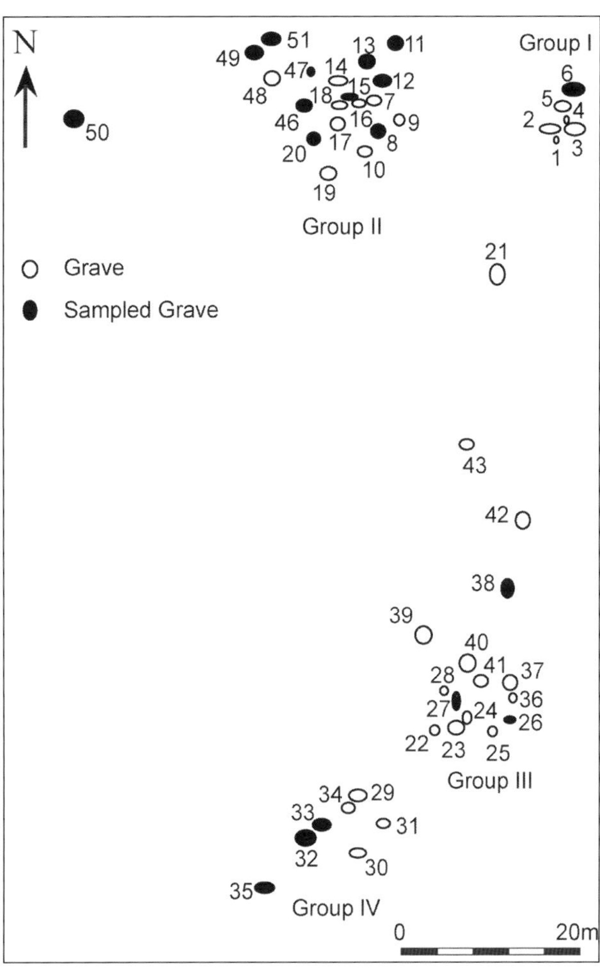

Fig. 8.27. Souffelweyersheim: plan. After Ulrich (1952, 29).

contribution to the study of LBK burials (Storch 1984/85; Jeunesse 1997).

The cemetery appears to be divided into four spatial groups of six burials (group I), 19 burials (group II), 12 burials (group III) and seven burials (group IV), with eight isolated graves (Fig. 8.27; Table 8.17). Ulrich (1953, 30, our translation) argued that these groups were 'without doubt from the same clan or family lineage' on the basis of their spatial associations. Storch (1984/85, 40) suggests that the key to understanding the groups may lie in the differing orientation of the burials, particularly as all the graves in group IV share a SE–NW orientation, with their heads exclusively to the east (Storch 1984/85, 40; Jeunesse 1997, 55; Fig. 8.27). Based on the typical grave orientation for the Rhineland (E–W, heads to the east) and body position for the LBK (left-crouched), Storch (1984/85, 51) argued that groups may be chronologically divided, with groups I and II illustrating the assimilation of indigenous peoples into the LBK and groups III and IV the development or adoption of the Großgartach tradition. Jeunesse (1997, 106) is more circumspect, certainly on the subject of chronological differences, but allows that the graves may have been grouped by familial relations.

A strong minority of burials are in secondary burial positions (either W–E or NW–SE) and those groups interring their dead in the northern group of burials (groups I and II) appear to be more variable than the southern groups (groups III and IV), which are, except for burial 27, SE–NW in orientation (Jeunesse 1995a, 135). A high percentage of burials oriented in an opposing orientation is characteristic of Tradition II cemeteries (Jeunesse 1997, 55). Taking into consideration three cemeteries from Basse-Alsace – Entzheim, Souffelweyersheim and Quatzenheim – Jeunesse (1997, 63) argued that as many as 44% of the burials in Basse-Alsace can be identified as having an antipodal orientation. He therefore preferred to argue for two distinct populations, with antipodal orientations illustrating a continued Mesolithic identity within the LBK, and used by a large proportion of the community (Jeunesse 1997, 106). However, if this explanation for antipodal graves is correct then it alone signifies a 'Mesolithic' identity, as other traditions of arranging the body of the deceased are far more variable and cross-cut previously identified groupings. Twenty-seven graves are crouched (52%), while 11 are extended (21%; Ulrich 1953, 30; Heintz 1981, 13), with no distinct differences in body position between the four spatial groups. Though the right-crouched burials do seem to cluster in group II, there is a far higher proportion of left-crouched burials in total at the cemetery (22 compared with five; Ulrich 1953, 32).

The grave goods also demonstrate variation between the spatial groups and demographic trends (Table 8.17). At Souffelweyersheim, 24 of the graves are unfurnished (Ulrich 1946; 1953), though with some 25 graves destroyed or damaged by erosion we must assume a higher number of burials would have originally been accompanied by grave goods. Seventeen graves (33% of the total, 63% of the well preserved graves) contained some form of lithics, including 14 graves with polished stone tools (Ulrich 1946; 1953). In comparison to Ensisheim and Mulhouse-Est (Haute-Alsace), shells and other ornaments are rare, occurring in only five graves, three of which are concentrated in group III. Pottery is mainly found in the form of sherds, with only two vessels in two separate graves, and could be said to cluster in group II (six of the 11 graves with pottery are found in this group). Lefranc (2007a, 250) suggests that the pottery shows affinities with assemblages from the Neckar valley. Colouring in the form of haematite and ochre is also occasionally found, but as with the lithics there appears to be no spatial patterning. With such poor preservation and so few skeletons sexed it is extremely difficult to decipher meaningful patterns tying particular grave goods to the age or sex of the deceased.

Two graves, however, do stand out. Grave 26, the burial of an eight- to nine-year-old, is among the richest in terms of range of grave goods. The child was buried with four *Nucella lapillus* (dog whelk) shells, three flint blades, a perforated polished stone axe (with remains of bone in the perforation) and a fragment of haematite (Ulrich 1953, 22–3; Jeunesse 1997, 117). This burial recalls grave 13 at Ensisheim, where a young child of three or four years was accompanied by one of the largest grave good assemblages in Haute-Alsace (Jeunesse 1997, 117). At

Table 8.17. Souffelweyersheim: the isotope, osteological and archaeological data. Age and sex information from Storch (1984/85). See Chapter 2 for further definition of ages. Key for body position: LC – Left-crouched; RC – Right-crouched; C – Crouched, direction unknown; CB – Crouched on back; CF – Crouched on front; S – Supine; P – Prone; I – Irregular. Key for grave goods (number of items in brackets): U. – Unfurnished; F. – Fill only (all items listed after an F. were in the fill of the grave rather than at the level of the skeleton); Pol. – Polished stone; Cer. – Ceramics; Shd. – Sherds; Spon. – Spondylus; *She. – Other Shell; Och. – Ochre; Lit. – Chipped stone; Bon – Worked bone; Grd. – Grinding stone.*

Burial	Tooth	Sex	Age (yrs)	$^{87}Sr/^{86}Sr$	Sr conc. ppm	$\delta^{13}C$ ‰	$\delta^{15}N$ ‰	Orientation	Body position	Grave goods
1a	-	-	-	-	-	-	-	-	-	U.
1b	-	-	Adult	-	-	-	-	-	-	Pol. (1)
2	-	-	-	-	-	-	-	-	S	Och., Lit.(1), Bon.(1), Firelighting kit
3	-	-	-	-	-	-	-	-	-	Pol.(1), Shd.(2), Och. Lit. (1)
4	-	-	-	-	-	-	-	-	LC	U.
5	-	-	-	-	-	-	-	S–N	-	Pol.(1), Lit.(2)
6	-	-	Adult	-	-	-	-	SE–NW	RC	U.
7	-	-	Juv.	-	-	−20.5	9.6	W–E	C	Pol.(1), Shd.(1), Lit.(1)
8	M2	M?	-	0.70877	99	-	-	-	RC	U.
9	-	-	-	-	-	-	-	W–E	RC	Shd.(1)
10	-	-	Late Mature	-	-	-	-	E–W	LC	U.
11	M2	M?	Adult	0.70887	46	-	-	E–W	S	U.
12	M2 M3	M?	Adult	0.70880 0.70889	128 171	-	-	-	LC	Cer.(1)
13	M1	F	Senile	0.70884	73	−20.7	11.2	NE–SW	S	U.
14	-	F?	Adult	-	-	-	-	E–W	RC	Shd.(1), Och.
15	M2	-	Senile	0.70884	146	-	-	W–E	LC	Shd.(1)
16	-	M?	Senile	-	-	-	-	E–W	LC	U.
17	-	M?	Mature	-	-	-	-	NW–SE	LC	Pol.(1), Shd.(1), Lit.(1)
18	-	M?	Mature	-	-	-	-	E–W	LC	F.Grd. (frag.)
19	-	M?	Senile	-	-	-	-	NE–SW	LC	Pol.(1), Shd.(1), She.(1), F.Shd.(3)
20	M2	-	-	0.70977	98	-	-	NE–SW	S	Lit.(1)
21	-	-	-	-	-	-	-	NW–SE	-	Pol.(1)
22	-	-	-	-	-	-	-	-	-	U.
23	-	M?	-	-	-	-	-	NW–SE	-	Animal bones (unclear if grave good)
24	-	-	-	-	-	-	-	-	-	U.
25	-	-	Inf. II	-	-	-	-	-	-	U.
26	M2	-	-	0.70905	82	−20.4	11.1	-	S	Pol.(1), Och., Lit.(3), Bon.(1), F.Shd.(1)
27	M3	-	Adult	0.70871	157	−19.7	10.9	N–S	-	Pol.(3), Shd.(2), She.(2), Lit. (3)
28	-	-	Immature	-	-	-	-	-	LC	U.
29	-	-	-	-	-	-	-	SE–NW	C	U.
30	-	-	-	-	-	-	-	NW–SE	-	Pol.(1), Grd.(1)

31	-	-	Adult	-	-	-	-	-	LC	U.
32	M2	-	Immature	0.70882	120	−19.9	10.3	SE–NW	-	U.
33	M2	-	-	0.70887	136	−20.4	11.2	-	-	U.
34	-	-	Not Child	-	-	-	-	-	S	U.
35	M1	F?	-	0.70876	47	−20.2	9.7	SE–NW	-	U.
36	-	-	-	-	-	-	-	-	LC	U.
37	-	-	Not Child	-	-	-	-	SE–NW	LC	U.
38	M2	M?	Not Child	0.70883	91	−20.1	11.2	SE–NW	S	Pol.(1), Lit.(1), Bon.(1), F.Shd.
39	-	-	-	-	-	-	-	SE–NW	LC	She.(69)
40	-	-	-	-	-	-	-	SE–NW	LC	U.
41	-	-	-	-	-	-	-	SE–NW	-	Shd.(1)
42	-	-	-	-	-	-	-	-	-	U.
43	-	-	-	-	-	-	-	-	S	U.
44	-	-	-	-	-	-	-	SE–NW	-	Shd.(1), Lit.(1)
45	-	-	Older Adult/ Early Mature	-	-	-	-	SE–NW	LC	U.
46	M2	M?	Adult	0.70878	44	−20.4	9.9	SW–NE	-	Pol.(1), Och.
47	M1	M?	-	0.70952	94	-	-	-	LC	U.
48	-	-	Adult	-	-	-	-	E–W	LC	Grd.(1)
49	M2	-	Senile	0.71277	106	−21.0	9.9	E–W	LC	Shd.(1)
50	M1	F?	Adult	0.71148	121	−20.8	10	SE–NW	S	Cer.(1)
51	M3	M?	Adult	0.70893	103	-	-	E–W	S	Pol.(1), Lit.(1)
52	-	M	Not Child	-	-	-	-	W–E	LC	Pol.(1), She.(?), Lit. (5)

Table 8.18. Souffelweyersheim: carbon and nitrogen isotope ratios (‰) of humans, with means and standard deviations.

Species	Age/sex	Mean $\delta^{13}C$	SD $\delta^{13}C$	Mean $\delta^{15}N$	SD $\delta^{15}N$	n
Human	Juvenile	−20.2	0.39	10.0	0.45	2
Human	Female	−20.6	0.37	10.3	0.77	3
Human	Male	−20.2	0.22	10.6	0.95	2
Human	Unsexed adult	−20.3	0.88	10.4	0.68	2
Human	All adults	−20.4	0.46	10.4	0.66	7
Human	Unknown	−20.4	0.05	11.1	0.04	2

Souffelweyersheim, the skull of the adult male in grave 38 had been trepanned (Ulrich 1953, 25) also recalling the burial in grave 44 at Ensisheim (Jeunesse 1997, 140). Ulrich (1953, 25) states that the trepanation was carried out on the frontal (right) part of the skull, rather than on the back of the skull (as is the case with the individual at Ensisheim). Unfortunately, Ulrich (1953, 25) does not give any further details on the trepanation.

Such parallels between cemeteries in north and south Alsace are rare and seem to go against a strong tradition of regional difference in Alsace during the *Rubané récent*. Souffelweyersheim contributed to the definition of Tradition II burial practices (Jeunesse 1995a; 1995b; 1996; 1997). As such the characteristics of Tradition II do not differ from that of the Souffelweyersheim cemetery itself. Thus, the grave goods at this site are characterised by the presence of lumps of ochre rather than a sprinkling on the body or in the grave fill (as found in Tradition I), and a greater abundance of lithics and ceramics in the graves than in southern Alsace; ornaments in the form of shell and stone beads are rarely present in the graves when compared to their prevalence in Tradition I (Jeunesse 1995a; 1995b; 1996; 1997). However, in the uniformity of orientation, presence of shells (though admittedly still rare) and lack of pottery, the burials in the southern parts of the cemetery could perhaps to be said to have more in common with Tradition I burials.

8.9.2 Carbon and nitrogen analysis

The skeletons at Souffelweyersheim were extremely poorly preserved and only 11 samples could be taken, of which two could not be assigned a sex or age. In total, therefore, three females, two males, two juveniles and two unsexed adults were sampled, alongside the two individuals for whom no age or sex data was available (Fig. 8.28; Table 8.18).

Age/sex variation

The human values are fairly tightly clustered with no clear structure by age or sex, which is not very surprising given the small size of the sample. Values are similar to those from Vendenheim (Chapter 8.10.3) and Mulhouse-Est (Chapter 8.7.3). Further comparisons on the basis of age and sex are not really possible, given the small number of individuals sampled. However, it may be worth noting that the sampled individuals fall into two $\delta^{15}N$ groups (Fig. 8.28). The upper group (burials 13, 26, 27, 33 and 38) have an average $\delta^{15}N$ value of 11.1‰, which is 1.2‰ higher than the average for the lower group (burials 7, 32, 35, 46, 49 and 50; mean=9.9‰). As the two juveniles fall in the lower group, caution must be taken in extrapolating from these results, but the significance of the difference is retained if these two individuals are excluded (2-tailed *t* test, $p<0.00$, n=9).

Animals

The nearest available faunal sample was from Bischoffsheim (about 30 km distant; Fig. 8.31; Chapter 8.10.2). The difference between adult human and cattle means is 2.5‰±1.10 (SD) for $\delta^{13}C$ and 4.2‰±1.06 for $\delta^{15}N$. This is high compared to sites east of the Rhine, and perhaps reflects low cattle values rather than a larger gap between human and faunal values overall (see Chapter 9.2.5–6).

Correlations with the archaeological data

Few significant correlations could be identified between the archaeological data and the stable isotope values, perhaps simply the result of the low number of samples. There was no patterning with body position and orientation or with the grave goods. To counter low sample numbers, the spatial groups were amalgamated into a northern group (groups I and II) and a southern group (III and IV). There was also no clear spatial patterning with the nitrogen values, though four out of six burials in the southern group came from the high $\delta^{15}N$ group and four from five of the burials in the northern group came from the low $\delta^{15}N$ group (this is not significant, 2-tailed *t* test, $p=0.13$, n=11). However, there is a spatial pattern amongst the $\delta^{13}C$ values. The southern groups (I and II) have a significantly higher $\delta^{13}C$ mean (−20.1‰) than the northern groups (III and IV; −20.7‰; 2-tailed *t* test, $p=0.006$, n=11). This could suggest that the northern group were sourcing more of their food from wooded (or covered) landscapes. However, as these two groups do not correlate directly with the two nitrogen groups, the pattern is hard to explain.

8.9.3 Strontium analysis

Sampling was again hampered by poor preservation, but tooth enamel was taken from 16 individuals, including nine males, three females and six further skeletons that could not be sexed (Fig. 8.29; Table 8.19). No juveniles were sampled, though one of the unsexed burials was possibly sub-adult. The second and third molars from the

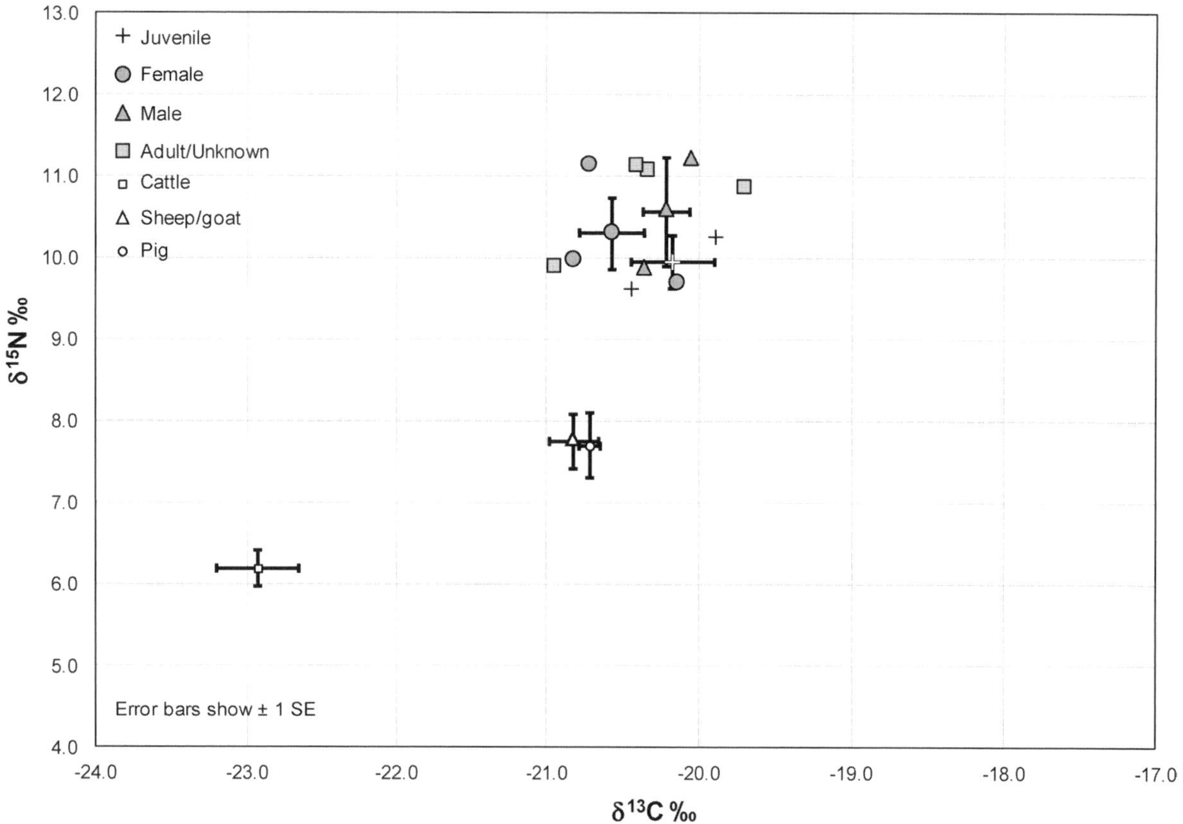

Fig. 8.28. Souffelweyersheim: carbon and nitrogen isotope ratios (‰) of humans.

adult male in grave 12 could be sampled, but there were no significant differences between the values from both teeth. Souffelweyersheim is located on a loess terrace, downstream from the sous-vosgiennes limestones, but within the upper Rhine valley, and we would therefore expect values to be similar to the sites in Haute-Alsace (Chapter 8.7.4 and 8.8.4). The mean $^{87}Sr/^{86}Sr$ ratio from all samples is 0.70930±0.0011 (n=18), which falls well within the expected loess range (0.7085–0.7105) and is close to the mean seen at Ensisheim (Chapter 8.8.4).

There were two individuals with outlying $^{87}Sr/^{86}Sr$ ratios: grave 49, an unsexed senile individual, who also had the lowest $\delta^{13}C$ (−21.0‰) and grave 50, an adult female, again with a low $\delta^{13}C$ value (−20.8‰). If these two values are excluded, the mean of the site falls to 0.70895±0.00029. Overall, the data could be said to fall into several different groups. A small cluster of three burials had low strontium concentration values (graves 11, 35 and 46; both graves 35 and 46 were in low $\delta^{15}N$ group, grave 11 was not sampled). The central cluster of graves could be possibly further sub-divided into a group with very similar $^{87}Sr/^{86}Sr$ ratios and a second group (Fig. 8.29), but we are dealing with very low sample numbers. Despite this, there might possibly be a mixing line (potentially including the two outliers) running from high $^{87}Sr/^{86}Sr$ ratio/ low 1/Sr conc. to a low $^{87}Sr/^{86}Sr$ ratio/high 1/Sr conc., but this is not significant (r^2=0.402, p=0.13). In any case, there is some variation across the results, both in strontium isotope concentration and ratio.

Correlations with the archaeological data

When body position is considered, those burials in left- and right-crouched positions are outnumbered by individuals buried in a supine or extended position. Those in a crouched position (to both the left and right) tended to have higher strontium concentrations than those in a supine position (but this is just outside the level of statistical significance, Mann-Whitney U test, p=0.07). There was no patterning associated with the different burial orientations. Amongst the grave goods, those individuals buried without polished stone adzes had more variable $^{87}Sr/^{86}Sr$ ratios than those buried with polished stone. Again this was just outside statistical significance (Levene's test, p=0.08), but as the Levene's test is very robust this pattern is worth noting. Those with pottery have significantly more variable $^{87}Sr/^{86}Sr$ ratios (Levene's test, $p<0.001$) and significantly lower strontium concentration (Mann-Whitney U test, p=0.02) than those without some form of pottery in the grave, but, again, low sample numbers require caution in interpreting the significance of these results.

There appears to be some spatial variation across the cemetery. The two outliers (burials 49 and 50) and three of the four individuals (burials 13, 20 and 47) falling along the potential mixing line belong to the southern group of burials (the fourth burial, 26, is from group III). Therefore, the north and south groups have significantly different $^{87}Sr/^{86}Sr$ ratio means (Mann-Whitney U test, p=0.025) and variances (Levene's test, $p<0.001$). The northern group also has significantly less variance in the strontium concentration

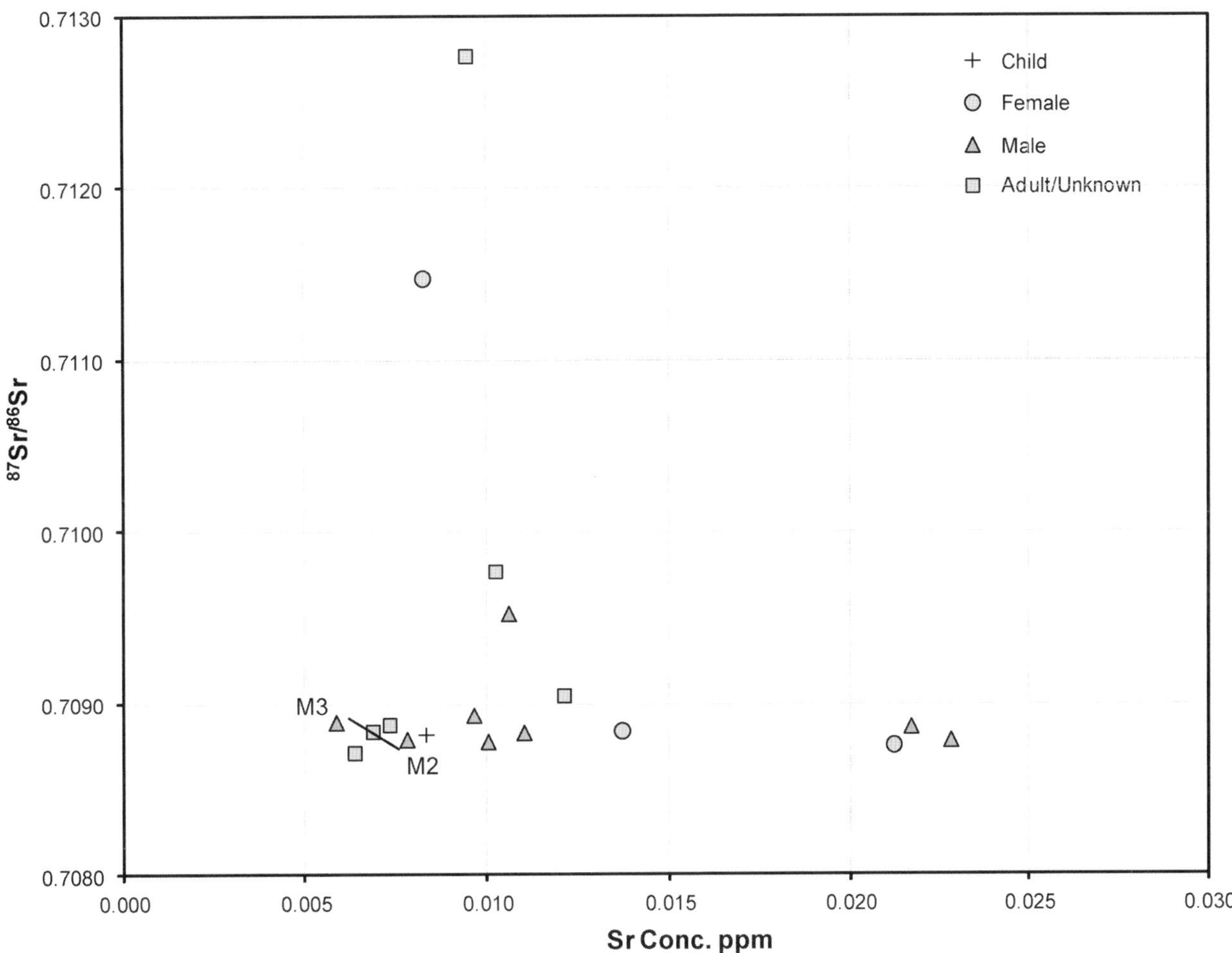

Fig. 8.29. Souffelweyersheim: strontium concentration (ppm) versus ratio ($^{87}Sr/^{86}Sr$).

*Table 8.19. Souffelweyersheim: strontium isotope ratios and concentrations. * denotes number of analyses, not number of individuals.*

Age/sex	Mean $^{87}Sr/^{86}Sr$	SD $^{87}Sr/^{86}Sr$	Mean Sr conc.	SD Sr conc.	n*
Male	0.70890	0.0002	104	44	8
Female	0.70969	0.0016	80	37	3
Unsexed	0.70969	0.0016	115	24	6
All	0.70930	0.0011	103	37	17

data, compared to the southern group (Levene's test, p=0.002). Although there is no direct correlation between body position, orientation and the strontium isotope data, it is interesting to note that the northern group is also where we see the most variation in burial orientations. There were no correlations between the stable isotopes and the strontium ratios and concentrations.

8.9.4 Site summary and discussion

The stable isotopic values from Souffelweyersheim imply that there were different dietary groups buried at the cemetery, but this variation is by no means straightforward. The two $\delta^{15}N$ groups may have merged together if more individuals could have been sampled, and the proportion of animal protein in the diet did not vary significantly between the different spatial groups at the cemetery. However, the $\delta^{13}C$ values did separate distinctively between the north and south of the cemetery. As this does not correlate with a $\delta^{15}N$ difference, the pattern is hard to explain, but the most likely conclusion to be found at the moment is associated with the canopy effect. The northern group, with their low $\delta^{13}C$ values, could therefore have sourced more of their plant protein from woodland, perhaps having a greater wild plant contribution to the diet or fields in a more forested landscape, while the southern group were perhaps eating plants sourced from a more open landscape. In some ways this can be connected to the strontium results. Low $\delta^{13}C$ values at this site could be connected to more radiogenic $^{87}Sr/^{86}Sr$ ratios and, excepting burial 26, all those falling outside the tight cluster of $^{87}Sr/^{86}Sr$ ratios were buried in the northern group of burials. Similar spatial variations could also be determined at the cemeteries of Rutzing (Chapter 5.10) and Aiterhofen (Chapter 6.8).

In their grave good assemblages and more varied body positions and orientations, the northern group of burials is perhaps therefore characteristic of a more heterogeneous group, but it certainly falls more in line with Tradition I (Jeunesse 1996; 1997). In contrast, the southern group with its less variable $^{87}Sr/^{86}Sr$ ratios and higher $\delta^{13}C$ values is also less variable in its burial rites and therefore demonstrates more of the characteristics of Tradition II, despite being located in a Tradition I region (though variability is itself one of the characteristics of Basse-Alsace funerary practices). Burials in the southern part of the cemetery also tended to have higher strontium concentrations, indicative perhaps of a diet based more on plants. The only grave good with any hint of connection with the isotopic data was pottery, which appears to correlate with the spatial patterning across the cemetery. Here, to an extent yet to be seen in any other region in this project, the clustering of burials in groups does appear to be linked to the diets and childhood origins of those buried at the cemetery. Yet, even at Souffelweyersheim, these grave clusters do not resolve clearly into two groups, but are found in the subtle combinations of different funerary rites and lifeways. Rather, and crucially so, it is the degree of difference which separates the two groups most strongly: a more homogeneous southern group and a heterogeneous northern group.

8.10 Vendenheim le Haut du Coteau, *Basse-Alsace*

8.10.1 Introduction

The cemetery of Vendenheim was found on a loess rise overlooking two small streams, the Zorn and Muhlbaechel, west of the modern town of Vendenheim, to the north of Strasbourg (Fig. 8.1; Schneikert and Lasserre 2002, 1). Discovered in 1998 and excavated by AFAN, the site covers about 3000 m² and consists of eight pits with occupation remains and 111 graves (Lefranc 2007a, 311). Two pits may have possibly been loam pits, but no postholes survived (Schneikert 2002, 13). The cemetery has 89 single burials, five double inhumations and 17 cenotaphs, though some graves were destroyed by later features and parts of the cemetery were badly decalcified, leading to poor preservation of teeth as well as bone (Schneikert and Boës 2002, 25). Thus a minimum of 99 individuals were interred at Vendenheim, making it the largest cemetery currently known in Alsace (Fig. 8.30). The earlier settlement pits, which are situated on the western edge of the cemetery, date to the *Rubané ancien/moyen*, but the graves themselves appear to date from the *moyen* and *récent* phases (Schneikert 2002, 13). The *Rubané récent* can be further divided into two phases (IVa and IVb: Table 8.1), with the oldest graves being identified as sitting on the boundary between *Rubané moyen* and *Rubané récent* (IVa) (Jeunesse *et al.* 2002, 173). The cemetery appears to last till the end of the *Rubané récent* IVb, covering the same time period as, though beginning slightly earlier than, the other cemetery sampled in Basse-Alsace, Souffelweyersheim. Due to the generally poor preservation, only 17 of the 99 skeletons could be sexed (three females, 14 males), and approximately 20 burials were determined as children. On this basis, at least 22% of the deceased at Vendenheim were under 18 (Boës and Alix 2002, 51), which is slightly below average for LBK cemetery sites (27%; Lifeways Database).

Single inhumations, double burials, cenotaphs and cremations are all found at Vendenheim (Jeunesse *et al.* 2002; Table 8.20). As Jeunesse (2002b, 167) argued that the double inhumations claimed for Aiterhofen are uncertain, since in many cases only parts of the skeleton of the second inhumation are represented, he considered Vendenheim to have the highest percentage of double burials in the LBK distribution.[11] Three of these five double burials are both children (graves 11a and 11b, 133a and 133b, and 137a and 137b) and the remaining two are of adults accompanied by children (graves 91a and 91b, and 93a and 93b). The two individuals are distinguished through opposing orientations (E–W and W–E) in the cases of graves 93, 133 and 137 or in the grave goods associated with particular individuals (one burial is unfurnished, while the other skeleton is associated with a complex grave good assemblage; graves 11, 91 and 137). Jeunesse (2002b, 168) summarises these double burials as a microcosm of the two sets of tensions which seem to be played out across the cemetery: variations in how rich the grave good assemblages are and the 'antipodal' orientations of some skeletons.

The graves can be divided into three rough spatial groups: the eastern extent of the site, where the graves are very clustered, and then two further sections to the west and south, where the graves are rather more spaced out (Fig. 8.30). It is unclear whether the spatial arrangement is due to the growth of the cemetery through time or marks different social groupings, but there is a loose correlation between grave orientation and spatial location (Lefranc 2002, 40). Furthermore, the excavators argue that it is most likely that each of the groups existed from the very beginning of the cemetery. The three double burials with opposing orientations are part of Lefranc's (2002) orientation group A. Three groups are identified (Lefranc 2002, 37); group A has SE–NW (or ESE–WNW, as Lefranc (2002) expresses the orientations) as the dominant orientation, group B is oriented mainly NE–SW and group C, E–W. Groups A and B correspond to the eastern and western sectors of the site respectively, while group C is on the periphery of the eastern area (Fig. 8.30; Lefranc 2002, 37). If we compare group A to group B, group A is mainly SE–NW or NW–SE oriented and group B is mixed between NE–SW and SE–NW (Boës *et al.* 2007, 280). Looking at the cemetery from this perspective, lines of burials sharing the same orientations can be seen (Fig. 8.30).

Cenotaph graves, in contrast to the double burials, are more frequent in group B (Jeunesse 2002b, 168). The identification of the so-called cenotaph graves, however,

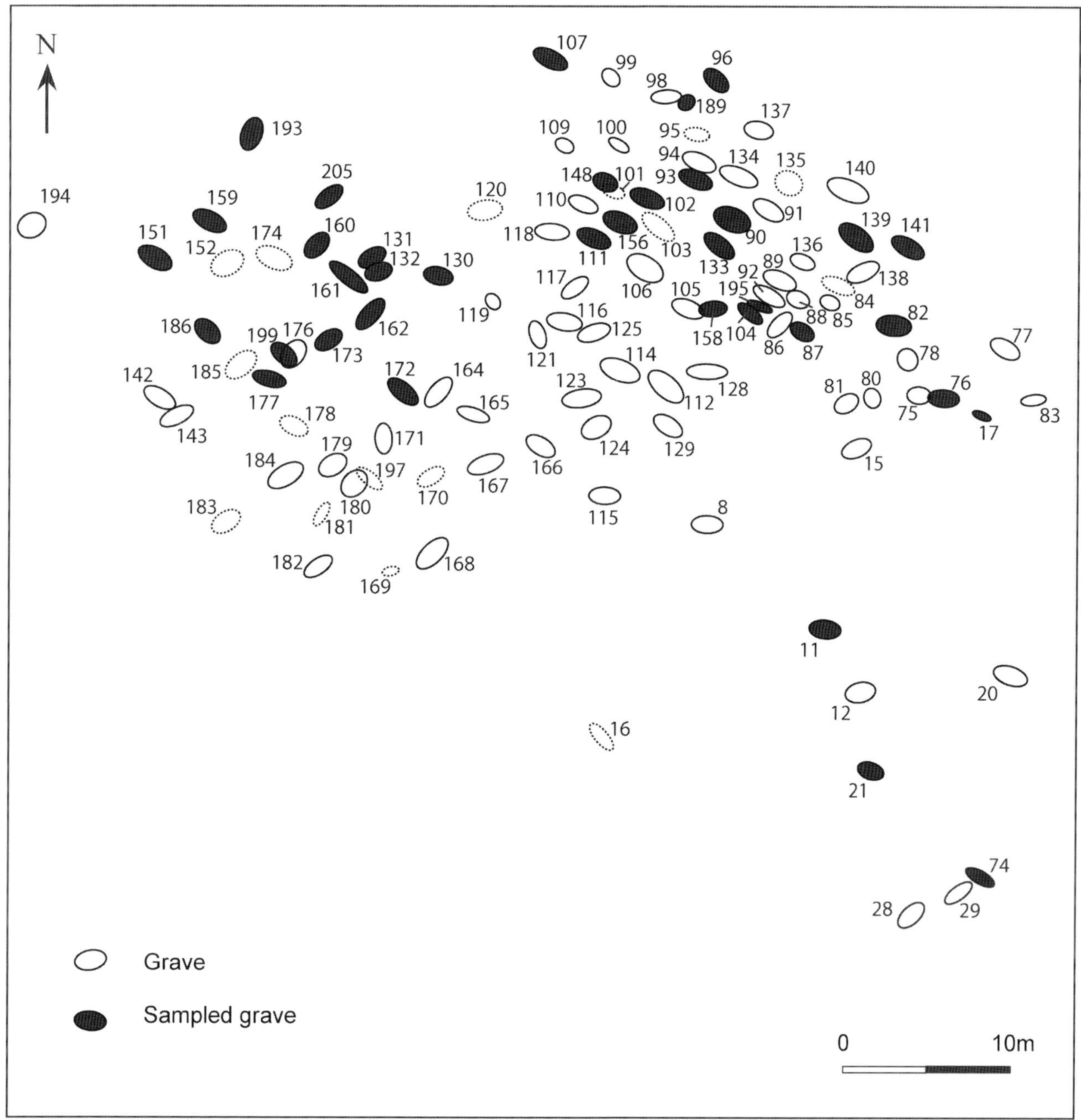

Fig. 8.30. Vendenheim: plan. After Jeunesse (2002d, fig. 10).

is not straightforward. Jeunesse (2002b, 169) argued that once the sherds included in the fill have been discounted, there are only two grave pits with goods in them (135, with one polished axe, and 180, with a grinder fragment). Jeunesse (2002a, 169) follows the suggestion of Nieszery (1995) that some LBK burial rites consisted of a number of stages. This is also part of the explanation for the *banquettes* that Thévenet (2004, 822–3) identified at the

Table 8.20 (over the next four pages). Vendenheim: the isotope, osteological and archaeological data. Age and sex information from Schneikert and Boës (2002). See Chapter 2 for further definition of ages.
Key for body position: LC – Left-crouched; RC – Right-crouched; C – Crouched, direction unknown; CB – Crouched on back; CF – Crouched on front; S – Supine; P – Prone; I – Irregular.
Key for grave goods (number of items follows in brackets; frag. = fragment): U. – Unfurnished; F. – Fill only (all items listed after an F. were in the fill of the grave rather than at the level of the skeleton); Pol. – Polished stone; Cer. – Ceramics; Shd. – Sherds; Spon. – Spondylus*; She. – Other Shell; Och. – Ochre; Lit. – Chipped stone; Bon – Worked bone; Tee. – Animal Teeth; Grd. – Grinding stone; Firelighting kit – this includes the presence of pyrite or manganese as well as tools (such as flint or a bone awl) that could be used to start a fire (Nieszery 1995, 163–8).*

Burial	Tooth	Sex	Age (yrs)	$^{87}Sr/^{86}Sr$	Sr conc. ppm	$\delta^{13}C$ ‰	$\delta^{15}N$ ‰	Orientation	Body position	Grave goods
8	-	-	Not Child	-	-	-	-	E–W	LC	Cer.(1), F.Shd.(2)
11a	M1	-	Inf. I/II	0.70913	82	−20.1	10	E–W	S	Pol.(2), Lit.(1), F.Cer.(14), Animal bones (?)
11b	M1	-	Inf. I	0.70916	74	−20.0	10.1	E–W	S	U.
12	-	-	Adult	-	-	-	-	E–W	LC	U.
15	-	-	Not Child	-	-	-	-	E–W	LC	U.
16	-	-	-	-	-	-	-	NW–SE	-	F.Cer.(3)
17	M1	M	Adult	0.70879	104	−20.2	10.4	SE–NW	S	F.Shd.(7)
20	-	-	Not Child	-	-	-	-	E–W	S	Pol.(1), Bon.(1), F.Cer.(2)
21	-	-	Inf. I/II	-	-	−20.2	10.6	W–E	LC	F. Burnt animal bones (?)
28	-	M?	Adult	-	-	-	-	E–W	LC	F.Shd.(1)
29	-	-	Adult	-	-	-	-	W–E	S	F.Shd.(1)
74	M3	M	Adult	0.70900	124	−19.9	11	W–E	S	Cer.(1), Lit.(1), F.Cer.(5)
75	-	-	Not Child	-	-	-	-	E–W	-	U.
76	M1 M3	-	Not Child	0.70878 0.70893	130 77	−20.4	11.1	E–W	-	F.Shd.(1)
77	-	-	Not Child	-	-	-	-	E–W	-	U.
78	-	-	Inf. II/Juv.	-	-	-	-	E–W	LC	F.Cer.(2)
80	-	-	Not Child	-	-	-	-	E–W	LC	U.
81	-	-	Not Child	-	-	-	-	W–E	S	U.
82	M2		Not Child	0.70881	124	−20.1	11.7	SE–NW	S	Pol.(2), F.Shd.(6)
83	-	-	Inf. I	-	-	-	-	E–W	S	Pol.(1), F.Shd.(26)
84	-	-	-	-	-	-	-	E–W	-	F.Cer.(6)
85	-	-	Not Child	-	-	-	-	SE–NW	-	Pol.(1), Och., Lit.(1), Grd.(frag.), F.Shd. (4)
86	-	F	Adult	-	-	-	-	E–W	LC	U.
87	M1	-	Inf. I/II	0.70916	77	−20.1	11.1	SE–NW	S	F.Shd.(38), Grd.
88	-	-	Not Child	-	-	-	-	E–W	-	F.Cer.(5), Lit.(1), Bon.(1)
89	-	-	Not Child	-	-	-	-	E–W	S	Grd.(1)
90	M1 M3	-	Adult	0.70918 0.70926	128 88	-	-	E–W	S	Pol.(1), Lit.(1), Animal bone, Bon.(1), F Shd. (8)
91a	-	-	Adult	-	-	-	-	E–W	S	Pol.(1), F.Shd.(39)
91b	-	-	Juv.	-	-	-	-	E–W	S	Shares F.Shd.(39) with individual 91a
92	-	-	Not Child	-	-	-	-	E–W	S	Lit.(2)

93a	M1	-	Adult	0.70919	86	-	-	E–W	S	Grd.(frag.), Firelighting kit, F. Burnt animal bone?
93b	-	-	Immature	-	-	-	-	W–E	LC	Lit.(2)
94	-	M	Adult	-	-	-	-	E–W	S	Pol.(2), She.(?), Lit.(2), Firelighting kit, Animal bone, Bon.(1), F.Shd.(8)
95	-	-	-	-	-	-	-	E–W	-	U.
96	-	-	Adult	-	-	−20.5	10.3	E–W	S	F.Shd.(27)
98	-	-	Not Child	-	-	-	-	E–W	I	Lit.(2), F.Cer.(29)
99	-	-	Inf. I	-	-	-	-	E–W	S	Perforated graphite
100	-	-	Adult	-	-	-	-	E–W	S	Shd.(1)
101	-	-	-	-	-	-	-	SE–NW	-	F.Cer.(2)
102	M1	-	Adult	0.70904	92	−20.5	10.5	W–E	S	Lit.(4), F.Shd.(6)
103	-	-	-	-	-	-	-	E–W	-	F.Shd.(6), Burnt animal bone, Daub fragments (2)
104	M1 M2	M	Adult	0.70904 0.70922	61 102	−20.2	11	E–W	S	F.Cer.(6)
105	-	-	Not Child	-	-	-	-	E–W	RC	F.Shd.(67), Grd.(frag.)
106	-	-	Not Child	-	-	-	-	E–W	S	Pol.(1), Cer.(1), F.Cer.(10)
107	M2	-	Inf. II/Juv.	0.70907	156	−20.3	11.4	W–E	S	U.
109	-	-	Not Child	-	-	-	-	E–W	S	U.
110	-	-	Not Child	-	-	-	-	E–W	S	Cer.(1)
111	M1	-	Not Child	0.70925	161	-	-	W–E	S	U.
112	-	-	Not Child	-	-	-	-	SE–NW	-	F.Shd.(15), Burnt animal bone
114	-	-	Adult	-	-	-	-	W–E	P	Pol.(1), Och., Lit.(8), Firelighting kit, F.Shd.(10), Lit.(?)
115	-	-	Not Child	-	-	-	-	W–E	CB	Pol.(1), Shd.(1), Lit.(4), F.Shd.(5)
116	-	-	Not Child	-	-	-	-	E–W	S	U.
117	-	-	Not Child	-	-	-	-	W–E	-	Pol.(1), Lit.(1)
118	-	-	Not Child	-	-	-	-	E–W	S	U.
119	-	-	Not Child	-	-	-	-	E–W	RC	U.
120	-	-	-	-	-	-	-	E–W	-	U.
121	-	-	-	-	-	-	-	SE–NW	-	U.
123	-	-	Not Child	-	-	-	-	W–E	-	Lit.(10), Firelighting kit
124	-	M	Adult	-	-	-	-	E–W	LC	F.Shd.(46)
125	-	-	Not Child	-	-	-	-	E–W	P	Pol.(1), Lit.(1)
128	-	-	Adult	-	-	-	-	E–W	S	Lit.(1), Firelighting kit, F.Shd.(1)

129	-	-	Not Child	-	-	-	-	E–W	-	Shd.(2)
130	M3	-	Adult	0.70889	106	−20.1	10.7	E–W	LC	Cer.(1)
131	M2	F	Adult	0.70874	149	−20.1	8.9	E–W	LC	U.
132	M1	-	Adult	0.71031	77	−19.9	8.8	E–W	LC	La Hoguette sherd in mouth
133a	M1	-	Inf. II	0.70893	91	−20.2	10.2	E–W	S	Pol.(2), Lit.(4), Bon.(1), F.Shd.(2)
133b	M2	-	Inf. II	0.70917	118	−20.2	10.3	W–E	LC	Pol.(1)
134	-	-	Not Child	-	-	-	-	E–W	LC	Pol.(1), Animal bone (?)
135	-	-	-	-	-	-	-	SE–NW	-	Pol.(1)
136	-	-	Not Child	-	-	-	-	E–W	-	F.Cer.(20)
137a	-	-	Inf. II/Juv.	-	-	-	-	W–E	P	Cer.(1), Shd.(1), Lit.(1) Firelighting kit
137b	-	-	Inf. II/Juv.	-	-	-	-	E–W	LC	U. (but see above)
138	-	M	Young Adult	-	-	-	-	E–W	P	Pol.(1), F.Cer.(2)
139	M2	M	Adult	0.70894	118	−19.8	11.1	E–W	S	Pol.(1), Lit.(3), F.Cer,(2)
140	-	-	Not Child	-	-	-	-	E–W	P	F.Shd.(1)
141	M1	-	Inf. II/Juv.	0.7089	78	−20.1	9.3	E–W	LC	Pol.(1), Lit.(5)
142	-	-	Inf. I/II	-	-	-	-	E–W	-	Pol.(1), Shd.(1), Animal bone, F.Lit.(1)
143	-	-	Not Child	-	-	-	-	E–W	S	F.Cer.(3)
148	M1 M3	M	Adult	0.70887 0.70902	66 97	−20.1	11.2	E–W	CF	Pol.(2), Lit.(5), Bon.(2)
151	M2	M	Adult	0.71031	147	−20.4	11	E–W	P	Pol.(1), Lit.(2), Firelighting kit, Bon.(2), F.Shd.(1)
152	-	-	-	-	-	-	-	E–W	-	F.Shd.(1)
156	M2 M3	M	Adult	0.70892 0.70898	116 84	-	-	W–E	S	Pol.(1), Lit.(1), Bon.(1)
158	M2	-	Adult	0.70912	83	-	-	E–W	S	Pol.(1), F.Shd.(2)
159	M1	-	Inf. I/II	0.71078	70	−20.3	9.9	E–W	S	F.Shd.(5)
160	M1	M	Adult	0.70894	86	-	-	E–W	CB	Pol.(1)
161	M2	F	Adult	0.70889	102	−20.3	11.1	E–W	S	U.
162	M2	-	Not Child	0.70950	101	-	-	E–W	-	Pol.(1)
164	-	-	Inf. I	-	-	-	-	E–W	-	Shd.(1)
165	-	-	Adult	-	-	-	-	E–W	S	Lit.(3), F.Shd.(2)
166	-	-	Not Child	-	-	-	-	W–E	S	Grd.(frag.)
167	-	-	Not Child	-	-	-	-	E–W	RC	Pol.(1), Cer.(1), Och., Lit.(5), Fire lighting kit,

										F.Shd.(6), Animal bone
168	-	-	Not Child	-	-	-	-	W–E	LC	Pol.(1), Och., Lit.(1), Firelighting kit
169	-	-	-	-	-	-	-	E–W	-	U.
170	-	-	-	-	-	-	-	E–W	-	U.
171	-	-	Inf. I/II	-	-	-	-	NW–SE	-	U.
172	M1	-	Inf. II/Juv.	0.70901	74	−20.3	10.5	E–W	S	Pol.(1), Shd.(1), She.(2), Och., Lit.(2), Fire lighting kit, F.Cer.(12)
173	M1	-	Adult	0.70889	102	−20.5	9.4	W–E	CF	F.Shd.(1)
174	-	-	-	-	-	-	-	E–W	-	F.Shd.(14)
175	-	-	Inf. I/II	-	-	-	-	E–W	LC	Cer.(1), Tee.(3, deer), F.Cer.(4), Animal bones
177	M1	M	Adult	0.70884	113	-	-	E–W	S	F.Shd.(5), Burnt animal bone
178	-	-	-	-	-	-	-	E–W	-	F.Shd.(38), Lit.(1)
179	-	-	Not Child	-	-	-	-	E–W	LC	F.Shd.(6), Burnt animal bone
180	-	-	Not Child	-	-	-	-	E–W	-	F.Shd.(26), Grd.(frag.), Pol.(1)
181	-	-	-	-	-	-	-	E–W	-	U.
182	-	-	Not Child	-	-	-	-	E–W	S	Och., Lit.(1), Grd.(1)
183	-	-	-	-	-	-	-	NE–SW	-	U.
184	-	-	Not Child	-	-	-	-	E–W	LC	F.Shd.(1)
185	-	-	-	-	-	-	-	NE–SW	-	F.Cer.(1)
186	M1	M	Adult	0.70884	141	−20.1	10.5	E–W	P	Och., Bon.(1)., F.Shd.(1), Burnt animal bone
189	M1	-	Adult	0.70909	127	−19.8	10.6	E–W	S	Pol.(2), Cer.(1), Shd.(4), Lit.(3)
193	M1	-	Adult	0.70877	121	-	-	E–W	LC	Pol.(1), Lit.(1)
194	-	-	Not Child	-	-	-	-	E–W	LC	U.
195	M1	-	Inf. II	0.70906	91	−20.6	10.7	E–W	S	Pol.(2)
197	-	-	-	-	-	-	-	SE–NW	-	F.Shd.(2)
199	M1	-	Inf. II	0.70881	171	−20.1	9.6	E–W	LC	F.Shd.(8), Burnt animal bone
205	M2	-	Adult	0.70885	169	-	-	E–W	-	Pol.(frag.)

Aisne valley site of Berry-au-Bac, in which the body was accompanied by a place for grave goods and the grave perhaps had an organic cover (such as of wood), which could have meant that the burial contents were revisited after inhumation. Indeed, Schneikert (2002, 35) identified a similar feature in grave 137 (one of the double burials) at Vendenheim, though in this case a second individual was placed directly above an earlier inhumation. The percentage of the graves which are pits without skeletons (15%) is comparable to the situation at Aiterhofen, though it must be recognised that this is the minimum number of empty graves. At Schwetzingen, Gerling (2006; 2012) has mooted the possibility that empty graves, were originally burials, but that the body was removed at a later date (cf. Lenneis 2010c). Cremations may well also be present at Vendenheim, though the handful of bones found in each case could equally be animal (Jeunesse 2002b, 170). However, burials 88 and 178 also contain burnt arrows, suggesting that these instances of burnt bone may well be the remains of funerary pyres. Jeunesse (2002b, 171) argues that this is likely, especially as Vendenheim has relatively poor rates of preservation. A further point of interest at Vendenheim is the presence of joints of meat in four or five of the graves. Arbogast (2002, 142) argues that these were offerings, often of the choicest cuts from young animals, placed above the head.

Being situated in northern Alsace, we would expect Vendenheim to follow the patterns of burial found in Tradition II, as identified by Jeunesse (1995a; 1995b; 1996; 1997). As noted above, we would expect lumps of ochre, rather than the powdered form, and few instances of shell or *Spondylus* accompanying the deceased, while lithics should occur more regularly. Approximately half of the graves contained grave goods (45 in total; Lefranc 2007a, 311). In line with Tradition II (Jeunesse 1993; 1995a; 1995b; 1996; 1997), there were more pottery and flint tools (particularly grinding tools), ochre fragments (rather than sprinkled), and very limited deposition of shell ornaments (overall in Basse-Alsace only 14% of graves, compared with 50% for Haute-Alsace). As is typical for Basse-Alsace sites and if sherds in the grave fills are not counted (many of which appear intrusive and date to before the beginning of the cemetery), Vendenheim has less pottery included as grave goods than sites in other regions of Tradition II (Lefranc 2002, 121). Sherds in the grave fill comprise a significant proportion of the pottery, and when pots are found in the grave they are often not complete (Lefranc 2002). The pottery also includes two interesting instances of Limburg or La Hoguette sherds in graves 105 and 132 (Lefranc 2002, 120). In the case of burial 132, the sherd was possibly placed in the mouth of an adult, oriented E–W (Lefranc 2002, 120).

As Vendenheim is part of Tradition II, Jeunesse (2002b) also identified a tendency towards more social stratification being visible in the burials there. He argued that while early cemeteries demonstrate an egalitarian distribution of grave goods, over the span of the LBK status became hereditary, with men and children having the richest graves. Two thirds of males have an adze (though only 10% have more than one) and have the long blades made of western (Champagne) flint, typical for Alsace. These blades are clearly an aspect of the western LBK, as are the *Scheibenkeulen* (maces) in the graves, but despite this there do appear to be two different dominant burial rites taking place at Vendenheim, which were contemporary. There is also a slight spatial distinction between groups A and B, with more of the very complex graves being in group A. This could reflect different social groups, but still choosing to bury their dead together. One important suggestion by Jeunesse (2002b) is that the individuals placed in extended body positions are acculturated hunter-gatherers, and indeed he regards Vendenheim as a cemetery where certain differences from the main LBK funerary practices were expressed by minimising such traditions as the inclusion of *Spondylus* in the grave. In place of more widely repeated aspects of LBK burial practices, the community who buried their dead at Vendenheim chose other categories to express themselves. This is an interesting suggestion, especially given that extended burials account for about half the burials (between 46% and 62% of the cemetery are extended, depending on whether a slight crouching of the legs is counted as a non-extended burial; Boës *et al.* 2007, 281) and therefore have a large variation within them in terms of grave goods and orientation.

It may not be appropriate to interpret one aspect of burial on its own as representing an acculturated hunter-gatherer identity; such a theory also rests heavily on the continued presence of hunter-gatherers in the region beyond the *Rubané ancien*. This may well be the case, as there are two instances of La Hoguette sherds in graves at Vendenheim, including the instance where the sherd was apparently placed in the mouth of the deceased (Jeunesse 2002b). If individuals who had adopted the Neolithic or LBK way of life during their lifetime had this expressed in their funerary rite, they did so alongside other cross-cutting identities such as those based on sex and age.

8.10.2 The animal remains from Bischoffsheim AFUA du Stade, *Basse-Alsace*

Although the existence of a LBK settlement at Bischoffsheim has been acknowledged since 1965, it was not extensively excavated until 2002 (Lefranc 2007a, 302). During the later excavations approximately 41 generally well preserved house plans were discovered (Lefranc *et al.* 2004). The site appears to have lasted from the *Rubané ancien* through to the *Rubané récent*, with nearly half the houses built during the middle and later phases of the *Rubané ancien* (Lefranc *et al.* 2004). Bischoffsheim, although situated on the loess, is not far the Vosges uplands (Fig. 8.1).

As at Ensisheim *Ratfeld*, the cattle at Bischoffsheim *AFUA du Stade* are isotopically distinct from the sheep/goats and pigs (Fig. 8.31; Table 8.21). The species effect is highly significant for both isotopes (ANOVA, $p \leq 0.001$), and cattle differ significantly from pigs and sheep/goats in

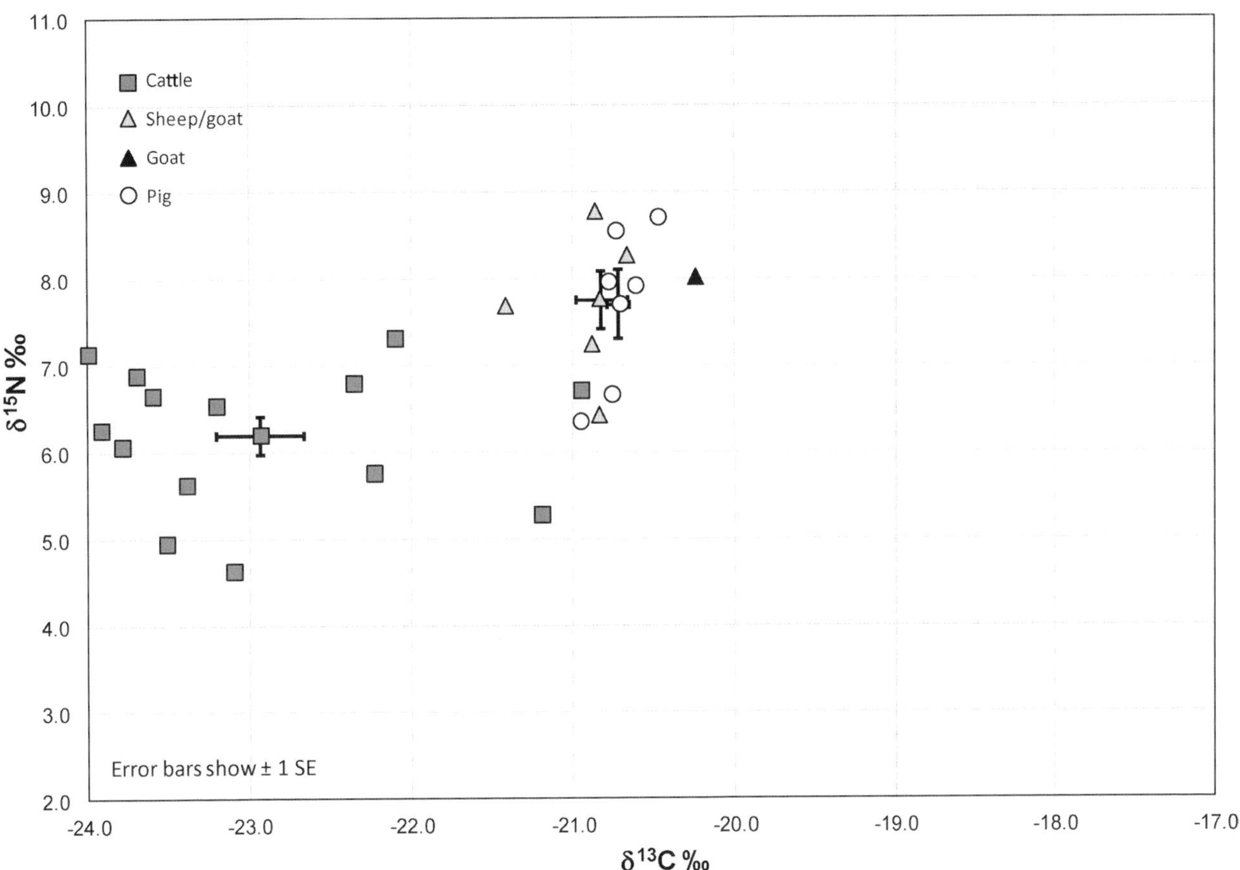

Fig. 8.31. Bischoffsheim AFUA du Stade*: carbon and nitrogen isotope ratios (‰) of animals.*

Table 8.21. Bischoffsheim AFUA du Stade*: carbon and nitrogen isotope ratios (‰) of animals, with means and standard deviations.*

Species	Mean δ^{13}C	SD δ^{13}C	Mean δ^{15}N	SD δ^{15}N	n
Cattle	−22.9	1.00	6.2	0.83	14
Sheep/goat	−20.8	0.38	7.8	0.82	6
Pig	−20.7	0.16	7.7	0.97	6

both δ^{13}C and δ^{15}N values (post hoc comparison of means, Tamhane, $p<0.001$ and $p<0.05$, respectively; sheep/goats and pigs did not differ from each other). Levene's test showed that δ^{13}C error variances were not equal across groups, so non-parametric tests were also run. The distributions of δ^{13}C and δ^{15}N values across species were significantly different ($p<0.001$, 0.005, respectively) and an independent-samples Median test showed that δ^{13}C medians were also significantly different ($p<0.001$) and δ^{15}N medians nearly so ($p=0.052$).

To summarise, cattle have much lower δ^{13}C values, and also lower δ^{15}N values, than the other domestic animals. This is compatible with greater use of forest habitats by cattle, while sheep/goats and pig would be using plant resources from more open habitats with higher δ^{15}N values, possibly due to manuring of cultivated land or proximity to human habitation. The wide spread in cattle δ^{13}C values reflects variety in the habitats used, from very low values suggestive of dense cover to higher values characteristic of more open habitats. There is no correlation between δ^{13}C and δ^{15}N values, however, as might be expected if the plants from more open areas came from manured soils. It is possible that some of the animals identified as domestic cattle are in fact aurochs, but it seems unlikely that all or many of them are; wild animals make up a low overall proportion of fauna at Tradition A settlements (Chapter 8.4.3). Bischoffsheim, though on the loess, is not far from the Vosges uplands and their extensive forest resources.

One of the sheep/goats was positively identified as a goat. This has a slightly higher δ^{13}C value than the others, with a similar δ^{15}N value, like the goat at Lerchenhaid in southern Bavaria (Chapter 6.7.3; Table 6.5). It has been included in the statistics as sheep/goat, because an unknown number of the others could also be unrecognised goats. If goats differ from sheep in their diet, this could contribute to variation in 'sheep/goat' values, but we would need

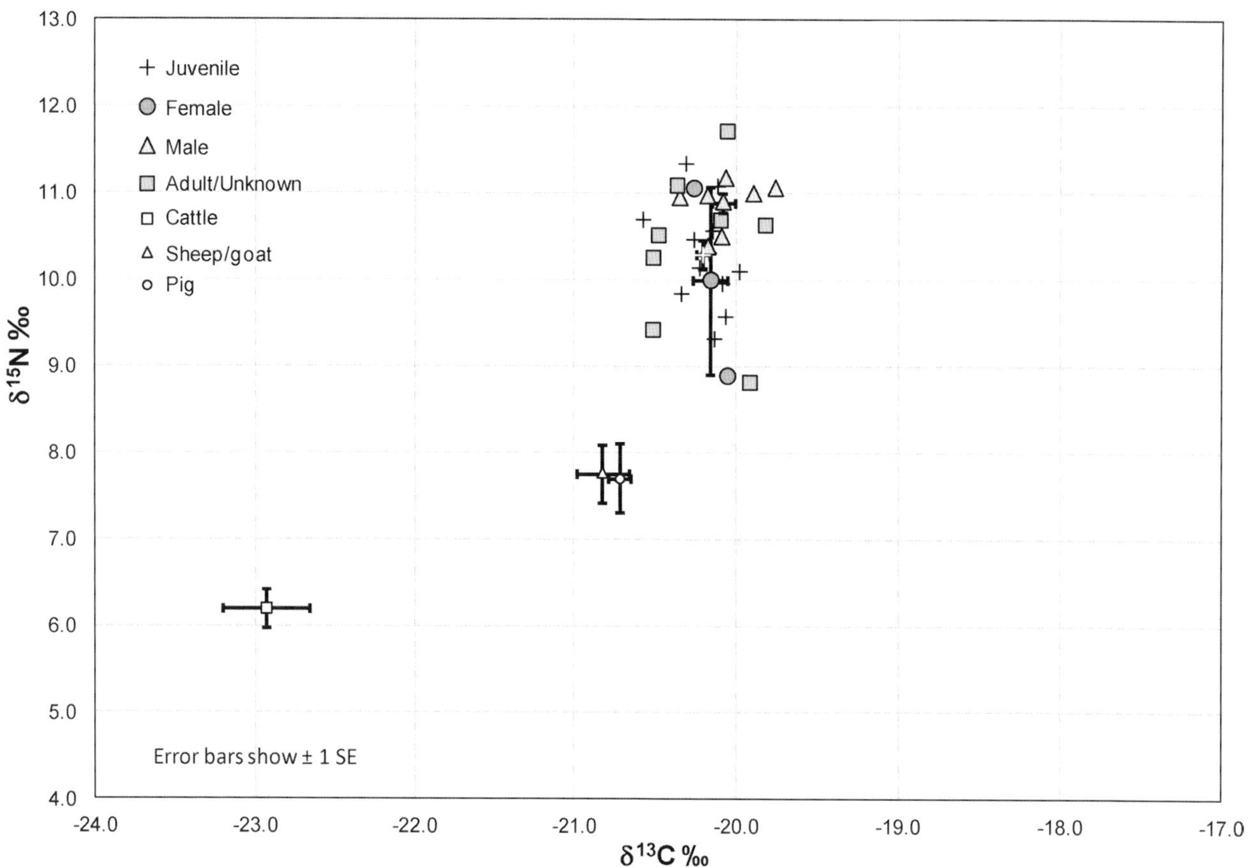

Fig. 8.32. Vendenheim: carbon and nitrogen isotope ratios (‰) of humans.

Table 8.22. Vendenheim: carbon and nitrogen isotope ratios (‰) of humans, with means and standard deviations.

Species	Age/sex	Mean δ^{13}C	SD δ^{13}C	Mean δ^{15}N	SD δ^{15}N	n
Human	Juvenile	−20.2	0.16	10.3	0.59	12
Human	Female	−20.2	0.15	10.0	1.53	2
Human	Male	−20.1	0.20	10.9	0.30	7
Human	Adult	−20.2	0.28	10.4	0.91	8
Human	All adult	−20.2	0.24	10.6	0.80	17

isotopic measurements on individuals positively identified as sheep or goat for this to be determined.

8.10.3 Carbon and nitrogen analysis

In total 29 individuals were sampled from Vendenheim (Fig 8.32; Table 8.22). The low number of individuals sampled in comparison to the 99 burials found at the site was due to the poor preservation of the skeletal material. The sampled burials included nine children, three juveniles/adolescents and 17 adults (two females, seven males and eight unsexed individuals).

Age/sex variation

Though δ^{13}C values are tightly clustered, there is a greater range than usual in δ^{15}N values. Because of the high proportion of unsexed individuals it is not possible to say whether this is related to sex. It seems to apply to the juveniles as well, but here variation could also reflect weaning. In many cases the preservation was not sufficient to distinguish infants from older children. The variation could reflect dietary differences in terms of protein source: animal (or even fish – though we might expect more variation in δ^{13}C) versus plant protein, or consumption of plants from manured versus unmanured areas. There are two adult burials with low δ^{15}N that stand out as possible outliers. While the adult female in grave 131 (8.9‰) does not seem unusual (E–W, left-crouched, unfurnished), the unsexed adult in grave 132 (8.8‰) does, as this was the individual who had a La Hoguette sherd in the mouth, possibly deliberately placed. This individual also has a relatively high δ^{13}C value (−19.9‰) and was one of three individuals at Vendenheim that have a ^{87}Sr/^{86}Sr ratio above 0.710. There were no identifiable δ^{13}C outliers.

*Table 8.23. Vendenheim: strontium isotope ratios and concentrations. * denotes number of analyses, not number of individuals.*

Age/sex	Mean $^{87}Sr/^{86}Sr$	SD $^{87}Sr/^{86}Sr$	Mean Sr conc.	SD Sr conc.	n*
Juveniles	0.70920	0.00052	97	34	11
Female	0.70881	0.00010	126	33	2
Males	0.70906	0.00039	104	26	13
Unsexed adult	0.70908	0.00039	113	29	16
All	0.70911	0.00042	106	29	42

Animals

The animals from Bischoffsheim are used for comparison. The difference between adult human and cattle means is 2.8‰±1.03 (SD) for $\delta^{13}C$ and 4.3‰±1.15 for $\delta^{15}N$. As at Souffelweyersheim, this is high compared to sites east of the Rhine, and perhaps reflects low cattle values, especially in $\delta^{13}C$, rather than a larger gap between human and faunal values overall.

Correlations with the archaeological data

At Vendenheim, as at Souffelweyersheim, supine burials outnumber crouched burials and they do appear to have slightly different average stable isotope results ($\delta^{13}C$: supine=−20.5‰, left-crouched=−20.22‰; $\delta^{15}N$: supine=10.5‰, left-crouched=10.1‰; Table 8.20), but this is only significant for the carbon values ($\delta^{13}C$ 2-tailed *t* test, p=0.039; $\delta^{15}N$, 2-tailed *t* test p=0.25, n=25). No correlations with the burial orientations could be determined. Unfurnished graves were not significantly different from furnished burials, though they had a lower $\delta^{15}N$ mean (10.2‰ compared with a site average of 10.6‰), nor were there any significant differences relating to the complexity of the grave good assemblages. A possible correlation can be identified with polished stone adzes, as the average $\delta^{15}N$ value increases as the number of polished stone tools in the grave increases (no polished stone=10.3, n=19; one polished stone item=10.4, n=6; two polished stone items=10.9, n=5). This, however, was not statistically significant (ANOVA, p=0.3). When this trend has been identified at other cemeteries it is amongst the males only, but there are too few sexed graves at Vendenheim to carry this test out on males alone. On the basis of simple presence or absence amongst the male graves, the graves with polished stone tools (mean=11.1‰, SD=0.1) are far less variable than those without (mean=10.7‰, SD=0.3; Levene's test, p=0.002). No further associations between the stable isotope data and the grave goods could be determined.

There is no obvious spatial patterning in the $\delta^{13}C$ values, but the eastern part of the cemetery (Lefranc's (2002) group A) has a higher average $\delta^{15}N$ value (10.7‰) than the western cluster (group B of Lefranc 2002) (10.0‰; 2-tailed *t* test, p=0.025, n=25). This possibly suggests that the group to the east of the cemetery were eating a diet that raised their nitrogen values without influencing their $\delta^{13}C$ values. However, this pattern may be unduly influenced by the dominance of males in the group of samples from the eastern part of the cemetery. If the males and infants are excluded, the distinction remains significant (2-tailed *t* test, p=0.034, n=19; western group mean=9.9‰; eastern group mean=10.7‰) and this suggests that the two groups may have been eating different diets.

8.10.4 Strontium analysis

Sampling was again hampered by poor preservation, but tooth enamel could be taken from 37 individuals, including 11 infants or juveniles, ten males, two females and 14 further skeletons that could not be sexed (Fig. 8.33; Table 8.23). In the case of graves 76, 90 and 148 the first and third molars were sampled, the first and second molars were sampled from burial 104, and second and third molars from burial 156, bringing the total number of samples to 42. Vendenheim is located on the loess and we would therefore expect strontium ratios similar to Souffelweyersheim and the sites in Haute-Alsace (Chapter 8.7.4 and 8.8.4). The mean $^{87}Sr/^{86}Sr$ ratio from all samples is 0.70911±0.00042 (n=42), which falls within the expected loess range (0.7085–0.7105) and is close to the mean of Souffelweyersheim (Chapter 8.9.4).

There are three outliers at Vendenheim, with $^{87}Sr/^{86}Sr$ ratios above 0.710, which are an unsexed adult in grave 132, the burial with a La Hoguette sherd found in the mouth, a male adult in grave 151, buried with a complex grave good assemblage and placed in the very unusual prone position, and a child (Infans I/II) accompanied by five sherds in the fill of the grave. The male $^{87}Sr/^{86}Sr$ ratios (mean 0.70906±0.00039) are not significantly different from the female (mean 0.70881±0.00010), either in mean (Mann-Whitney U test, p=0.27) or variance (Levene's test, p=0.52), but low numbers of sexed graves mean that deciphering any pattern would be difficult. There are also no significant differences between the male and female strontium concentration means (Mann-Whitney U test, p=0.49) or variance (Levene's test, p=0.9).

There were also no significant differences between the different molars sampled (ANOVA, $^{87}Sr/^{86}Sr$ ratio p=0.8, Sr conc. p=0.1), but in the cases where two teeth were sampled from the same individual, the tooth which mineralised later (third molar in four cases, second molar in one case) was consistently more radiogenic than the earlier tooth, though admittedly the differences are fairly small. This perhaps suggests that in the early teenage years more of the diet was sourced from upland areas. There was

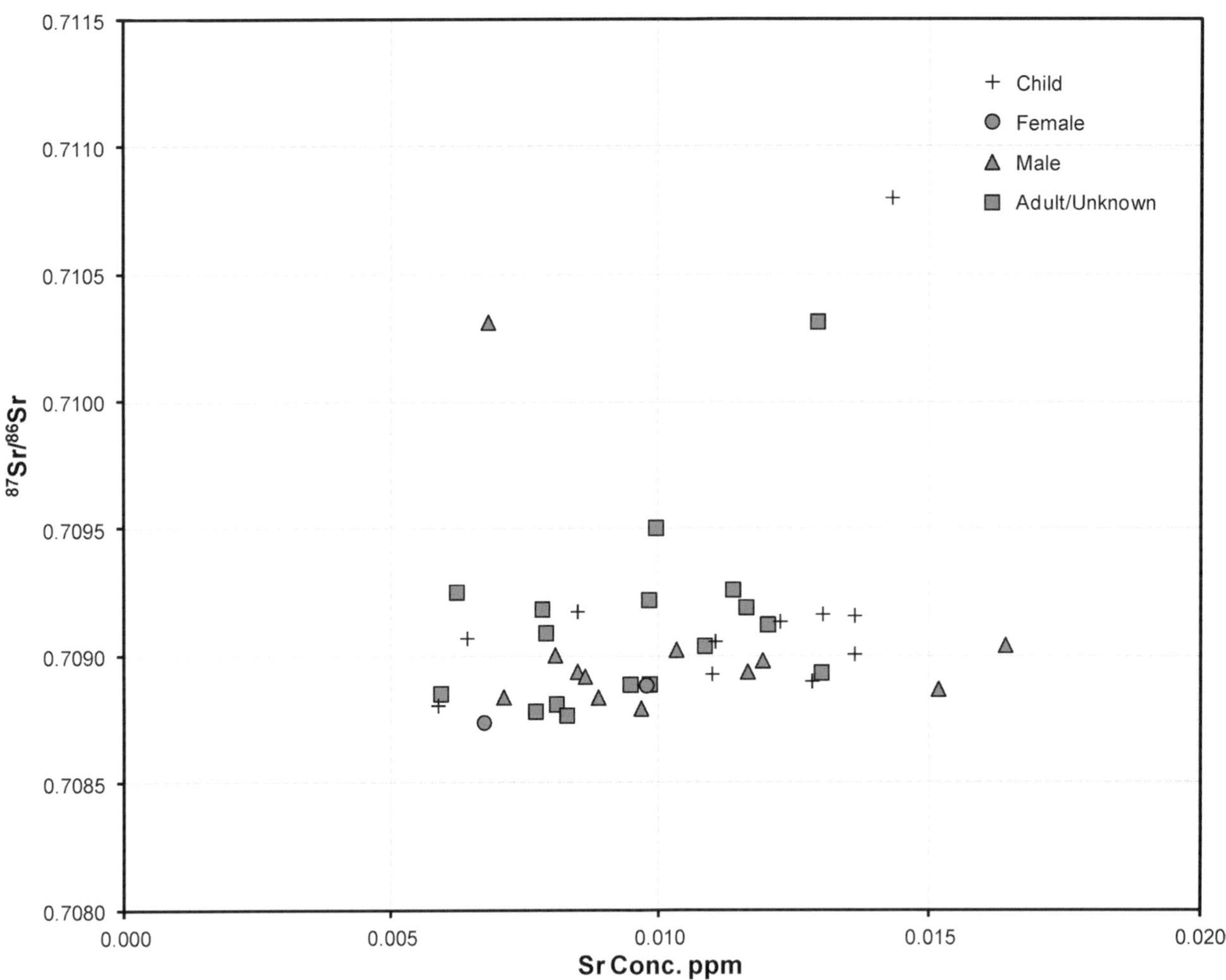

Fig. 8.33. Vendenheim: strontium concentration (ppm) versus ratio ($^{87}Sr/^{86}Sr$).

no consistency in how the strontium concentration varied between different teeth.

Correlations with the archaeological data

When the three outliers are excluded, burials in a left-crouched position have a significantly lower average $^{87}Sr/^{86}Sr$ ratio (0.70880±0.00006) to the $^{87}Sr/^{86}Sr$ ratio mean for supine burials (0.70903±0.00013; Mann-Whitney U test, p=0.01), and this also applies to variances (Levene's test, p=0.046). This suggests that those buried in a left-crouched position had very similar diets, or sourced their food from a circumscribed location. No correlations between orientation and the strontium isotope data could be determined. As noted above, there are three individuals with outlying $^{87}Sr/^{86}Sr$ ratios, these were all E–W oriented, and represent all three of the body positions found at Vendenheim (left-crouched, supine and prone).

Amongst the grave goods, unfurnished burials had a lower $^{87}Sr/^{86}Sr$ ratio mean (0.70899±0.00022) than furnished burials (0.70915±0.00050; Mann-Whitney U test, p=0.034), but no further patterns could be seen with grave goods, even when broken down by sex. No patterning in the strontium isotope data on the basis of the spatial layout of the cemetery could be discerned and there were no correlations between the stable and strontium isotopes. However, if the three individuals with outlying $^{87}Sr/^{86}Sr$ ratios are excluded, then three of the four individuals not buried in a supine position (left-crouched and prone) have the same $\delta^{13}C$ value of −20.1‰ and the fourth has a $\delta^{13}C$ value of −20.2‰, though their $\delta^{15}N$ values are very varied.

8.10.5 Site summary and discussion

In summary, the isotopic results from Vendenheim suggest a community sharing a very similar diet and similar origins, though in certain ways the isotope values vary with different funerary rites. As at other sites, such as Ensisheim, there are no true outliers amongst the stable isotope data, but those individuals that fall on the edge of the distribution can be connected to rarer or unusual burial rites. Most noticeably at Vendenheim, this is true in the case of burial 132, which has a low $\delta^{15}N$ value and a high $\delta^{13}C$ value. This burial also stands out because of the highly unusual placing of a La Hoguette sherd in the grave and possibly within the mouth of the deceased. It is tempting here, especially given the wider issues of how diets changed on the introduction of the Neolithic to the region, to draw on notions of how consumption may have related to broader constructions of identity (specifically identity as created and presented at death and in funerary rites). That this individual also has an outlying $^{87}Sr/^{86}Sr$ ratio does give strength to arguments about the maintenance of indigenous identities after the arrival of the LBK. However, the body was in a left-crouched position and oriented E–W, and was next to burial 131, an adult female who also had a low $\delta^{15}N$ value. As Jeunesse (2002b) argued, the cemetery appears to be negotiating the wider tensions between broader LBK identities and regional or indigenous lifeways, and individual burials also bring together elements of funerary practices from diverging or contrasting traditions within the LBK.

Further diversity could be identified amongst burial positions found at Vendenheim. As discussed above (Chapter 8.5), supine burials become the most frequent body position in Basse-Alsace and represent at least half of the body position at Vendenheim (Lefranc 2002; Boës *et al.* 2007). Left-crouched burials formed a fairly tight cluster within the $^{87}Sr/^{86}Sr$ ratios, while supine burials were more variable and had a higher mean, suggesting a greater inclusion of food sourced off the loess in childhood. Overall, a correlation between the strontium isotope data and body position suggests that certain lifeways in childhood influenced identity in later life, which may give some support to the arguments of Jeunesse (1997; 2002c; 2005) that status could be inherited. The practice of supine burials became more frequent in the middle Neolithic of the Rhineland, though as it is used by Hinkelstein groups (thought to be contemporary with the *Rubané final* in Hessen) we cannot be certain in which direction the influenced travelled (Jeunesse 2002c, 199). However, as already noted, Jeunesse (2002c, 203) suggests that supine burials could be acculturated hunter-gatherers. This is an interesting proposition given that, as we find at Vendenheim, we would expect indigenous groups adopting a LBK way of life not to display different stable isotope values, but there to be hints of a difference in their teeth (and hence their strontium values from childhood).

Differences in diet do not resolve into two groups that can be said to represent a community of 'farmers' in comparison to 'hunter-gatherers'. Although the cemetery does appear to have developed from two different burial groups respectively occupying the eastern and western areas, the stable isotope variations are more subtle, suggesting different emphases on particular resources rather than different diets wholesale. The individuals in the eastern group (like the southern group at Souffelweyersheim; Chapter 8.9.1) appear to be more regular and are more tightly clustered, while the western group have the most varied grave orientations and the graves are more widely spaced. As the two groups are thought to co-exist throughout the life of the cemetery, any differences identified are likely to be between groups living alongside each other, rather than changes over time. In a reverse to what was found at Souffelweyersheim, the two groups had different average $\delta^{15}N$ values, rather than $\delta^{13}C$ ones, suggesting that varied consumption of animal proteins, rather than where plant protein was sourced, distinguished the two groups. As Vendenheim and Souffelweyersheim, like Ensisheim and Mulhouse-Est, are some 10 km apart, this fits well into the pattern developing across all six regions of even nearby communities doing things differently.

8.11 Regional discussion

In this chapter, we have discussed the westernmost sites of our study and the only area in this project where the earliest LBK present in the region dates to its second expansion with the Flomborn and subsequent *jüngere* LBK phases. So the LBK entered the region at the same time as increased regionalisation was taking place across its wider distribution (Chapter 1.3.6), and this is reflected in the variability in practices found between Haute- and Basse-Alsace. The origins of the ways in which the groups in north and south Alsace vary, however, is less clear, although, as we discussed above, a combination of the different LBK influences outside Alsace to the east and the presence of indigenous groups remains the favoured explanation. Jeunesse (2002c; 2005) argued that this is the context for the variation seen in the burial rites, with the more 'Danubian' features in the funerary practices of Haute-Alsace, demonstrated by *Spondylus* in the cemeteries and more regular body positions and orientations; this contrasts with northern Alsace, where the emphasis seems to fall on deliberately shunning more traditional LBK burial practices, seen in the use of the extended body position and greater emphasis on 'antipodal' grave orientations, as well as favouring certain types of grave goods over others. However, whether this implies a certain conservatism operating in southern Alsace or that northern groups were using burials to alter or even subvert 'Danubian' LBK rites is perhaps less certain.

Such contrasts between adherence to the wider LBK norm and stronger adoption of variation can be found at other scales as well in Basse-Alsace. At Vendenheim and Souffelweyersheim significant spatial differences can be identified across the cemeteries, some of which appeared also to have a corresponding and meaningful patterning in the isotope data. This suggests that some larger groupings based on diet or mobility practices can be inferred for these cemeteries, though the social relations behind such differences are less clear. As discussed in Chapter 8.4, models of central places and satellite settlements have been favoured in the Alsace region, and such relationships between different sites could have translated into the variation seen in burial rites (Jeunesse 2002c, 210). This could explain subtle differences in the stable isotope values across the two Basse-Alsace cemeteries, with groups sourcing their foods from different locations in the wider landscape. In contrast, spatial variation in the cemeteries analysed in Haute-Alsace is not so pronounced in either the burial rites or the isotopic data, though there are hints that there may be a logic behind the pairing of burials (for example at Mulhouse-Est). The placing of two individuals next to each other is perhaps only a short step away from double burials contained in the same pit as seen at Vendenheim.

On the level of the individual, however, the different influences were combined in very varied ways, and we cannot identify straightforward correlations between different facets of burial rites. At both Mulhouse-Est and Ensisheim, those burials in rarer orientations or body positions tended to fall on the edge of the isotope distributions (this was not really the case with the Basse-Alsace sites), suggesting that the people in question were leading lifeways that took their isotopic values away from the norm, but in varied ways. Clearly, there was variation in lifeways in both north and south Alsace, but the scale on which it was experienced, and perhaps by extension recognised in the funerary assemblages, differed. In contrast to other regions in this project, males buried with polished stone in Haute-Alsace, and to a certain extent in Basse-Alsace as well, did not stand out as having significantly higher nitrogen values than those who were not furnished with these items. Rather, at Ensisheim and Souffelweyersheim, it was pottery which appeared to correlate more strongly with the isotope data. Could this represent a subtle shift in how foodways contributed to forming identity and social relations as the LBK moved into Alsace? However, associations between isotope values and strontium isotope data show that experience and origins in childhood were, as elsewhere in the LBK, contributing in some as yet undefined way to how funerary assemblages were put together, and once again raise the issue of whether identities and social relations could have been inherited.

Notes

1 The LBK is known in French as the *Rubané*, but, unless we are referring to a particular chronological subdivision of the Alsatian sequence, for consistency we will use the more general label of LBK in this chapter.

2 La Hoguette pottery was first identified by Christian Jeunesse (1986), and is named after the site in Normandy where it was first discovered (Gronenborn 1999, 138).

3 The trapezoidal house (house 11) at Sierentz (Haute-Alsace) is considered by Jeunesse *et al.* (2007a) to be the earliest longhouse to be constructed with this form as it dates to the end of the *Rubané moyen* phase.

4 This may then be followed by a decrease in settlement in the interior of the plateaus and a repeated focus on the major rivers in the final phases of the LBK in Alsace (*Rubané final*; Meier-Arendt 1966; Stehli 1989b; Jeunesse 1993; Lefranc 2007a).

5 The cemetery of Mulhouse-Est is sometimes referred to by the name of Rixheim (a nearby village), as the location of the site was first wrongly attributed to this *commune* (Jeunesse 1997, 14). Both names have been used since the site was first excavated in the sixties and early seventies, with the excavators Roger and Joël Schweitzer (1977; J. Schweitzer 1971) referring to the cemetery as Mulhouse-Est. Recently, however, the site name Rixheim seems to have fallen out of use and Lefranc (2007a, 316) does not use it.

6 Roger and Joël Schweitzer have been part of the strong tradition of amateurs who have excavated in Alsace and their work has contributed significantly to our understanding of LBK sites found in the southern part of Haute-Alsace (J. Schweitzer 1980; Lefranc 2007b, 21).

7 J. Schweitzer (1971, 15) refers to these structures as *trous de poteaux* or postholes, while Jeunesse (1997, 60) prefers to describe them as *trous de piquets*, which implies something smaller and more slight than a post. Jeunesse (1997, 60) only mentions two graves at Mulhouse-Est with these features, but in the original publication as many as six burials can be indentified with posthole structures around the deceased.

8 During analysis, an additional male skull was identified as belonging to grave 8. This is included in the osteological figures, but not the isotope tables, as its attribution is uncertain.

9 Utrecht C14 laboratory sample UtC–5406: 6155±39 BP, 5215–4999 cal BC (95.4% confidence).

10 Heintz (1981, 11) published the 52nd tomb, excavated in 1943, from Ulrich's notes. The air raids on Strasbourg and conditions in Alsace during the Second World War meant, of course, that the site was not excavated in the easiest of circumstances, and Ulrich's notes were only discovered some time later (Heintz 1981, 11).

11 There are five suggested double burials at Aiterhofen, but Jeunesse (2002b, 167) argues that alternative explanations can be found for four of them. The second burial in grave 26 is only a few ribs of a child; in grave 115 one skeleton is known only from some teeth and mandible fragments; double burial 116 is a foetus (7–8 months) and an adult female, so could be explained as a woman who died during pregnancy or childbirth; and grave 71 could be a re-cut. This leaves only grave 131 as a definite double burial in the sense that the inhumations are contemporary.

An Ensisheim lifeway: burial 13

The child in burial 13 at Ensisheim was only three or four years old at death and was one of relatively few children interred at the cemetery. The child was probably born locally, as the strontium ratio of 0.70951 fits within the local range (here falling between 0.70872 and 0.70994). There are no stable isotope values for this individual, but in line with results seen across the regions sampled in this project it is likely that they would present a breast-feeding signal. While it remains difficult to assess weaning ages, we rarely find children older than three years showing elevated nitrogen values. The weaning and post-weaning period can be a risky time for small children and potential associated problems, such as gastro-intestinal infections, may put the body under considerable strain.

Like most people at Ensisheim, the body was placed in the grave crouched on its left-hand side and with the head pointing north-east. However, in terms of general patterns at the site, it can be noted that isotopically, left-crouched individuals fell into a tighter cluster, while right-crouched burials were more likely to stand out through different dietary practices. So it is possible that a majority identity, referencing dietary routines, was consciously signalled through position and orientation here, and this was broadly equivalent to LBK-wide majority practices. Burial 13 corresponded with this stress on a wider LBK identity, here shown in grave goods, as the child was buried with a pottery vessel and flint flake. More specifically, it falls in line with what has been defined as Tradition I burials typical for Haute-Alsace by receiving a wide variety and large number of personal ornaments. A Spondylus *belt buckle and bead were combined with a local river shell, 132 discoidal beads made of a species of* Cardium, *51 beads from the shell* Columbella rustica *and one pendant made of a fossil* Venericardia *shell. The body had also been sprinkled with ochre powder.*

The shell species represented here reference a very wide network of contacts that reach well beyond Ensisheim: Spondylus *and* Columbella *from the Mediterranean,* Cardium *from the Atlantic shore, and fossil* Venericardia *most likely from the Paris basin. It is unlikely that a locally born infant of this age would have personally travelled to all these locations, or would have been actively engaged in obtaining these goods through trade or exchange. Moreover, such an extensive grave good assemblage is unusual for someone so young, and perhaps in line with models for inherited status developing in the later stages of the LBK, the kin of this individual chose to mark the child's death by furnishing his or her grave in an elaborate demonstration of their or their lineage's connections.*

However, there is an added dimension here. In addition to all the ornaments, burial 13 also received an item that is unique in the LBK. This is a sheep metapodial, its shaft polished smooth from handling, and with eyes made of white shell discs and dark resin inserted at one end, combining into a bone figurine with a rather striking expression. It is tempting to suggest an artefact made specifically for this child, perhaps a favourite toy. The life of the child in burial 13 was short, but did not go unmarked.

On the one hand, then, the burial rite fits in with wider LBK traditions and histories, while on the other it may have been used as an occasion to display the abundance of things available to the burying collectivity by including many exotic ornaments. Yet beyond all this, we are still faced with a specific death, which in this case occasioned the inclusion of an unusual item. In general, archaeologists are not comfortable with evoking emotions in their writing, and if these are accorded any place at all it is often with reference to the truly idiosyncratic, for which other explanations seem insufficient. Yet we should not lose sight of the fact that each burial, whether or not it stood out from the others, was a specific occasion, marked by a group of people who were affected by it.

A Vendenheim lifeway: burial 132

Like most of the individuals at Vendenheim, burial 132 could not be sexed, but had reached adulthood at the time of death. Isotopically, this person is remarkable in a number of ways. With a strontium isotope value of 0.71031, burial 132 falls outside the site mean of between 0.70869 and 0.70953. In addition, the carbon value of −19.9‰ is quite high compared to the adult mean of −20.2‰, while in contrast the nitrogen value is very low (8.8‰, compared to an adult mean of 10.6‰). In terms of both origin and dietary practices, this person therefore stood out from the community, and we may suggest that he or she sourced their diet from a rather open landscape and consumed animal protein less regularly than others.

At Vendenheim, different dietary habits are inevitably bound up in the discussion surrounding the representation of local hunter-gatherer identities in LBK cemeteries. Burial 132 is especially pertinent here, as the only grave good to be recovered was a sherd with La Hoguette decoration, a style of pottery often linked to the survival and cultural expression of indigenous foragers in LBK communities. The sherd was found in the mouth of the deceased, and if it had been placed there deliberately (rather than being due to post-depositional factors) would constitute a unique rite in a LBK context.

Yet in other respects, burial 132 does not correspond to suggested 'Mesolithic' practices at Vendenheim. To begin with, a diet low in animal protein and containing many foods from open areas is not what one would expect from a hunting and gathering subsistence, so that upon joining the Vendenheim community this person would have had to entirely change their lifeway (albeit in a way also not corresponding to the majority practice). Furthermore, the supine body position so popular at Vendenheim has been closely linked with a potential forager identity, as it is explicitly set against the LBK norm of left-crouched inhumation. This is corroborated by the fact that supine burials tend to have more varied strontium ratios than others, confirming the link between childhood origin and treatment in death. In contrast, burial 132 is non-local in origin, but actually very classically LBK, being buried in a left-crouched position and with head due east.

The correlation between isotopic patterning and provisioning with grave goods is also worth noting here. While some other strontium outliers, notably burial 151, have very complex assemblages, in general those of a non-local origin are more modestly furnished, and this is also the case for burial 132. Moreover, high nitrogen values at this site are particularly associated with individuals buried with polished stone tools, and here again the low nitrogen value of the person in burial 132 and the absence of an adze or axe suggest that at some levels this person retained an explicitly 'non-local' identity. Burial 132 was located in the western part of the cemetery, directly next to burial 131 which was similarly oriented E–W and placed in a left-crouched position. Burial 131 was of an adult woman, who also had a low nitrogen value (8.9‰). Perhaps these two individuals shared a diet, setting them apart from the rest of the community.

At Vendenheim, two distinct long-term histories intersected, and both were marked in the graves of individuals. On the one hand, through broad correspondence with Tradition II, this site referenced much wider and longer-term notions of appropriate LBK ways of burial. On the other hand, distinct body positions and the inclusion of fewer goods may signal a still actively experienced hunter-gatherer identity, albeit adapted to the new circumstance of farming communities and the new practice of cemetery burial. Yet this duality does not result in neat and mutually exclusive groups. Burial 132 is a case in point here, although the significance of the individual's dietary routines remains hard to grasp. A non-loess childhood diet, a sparse grave good assemblage, an exotic pottery style and the potential placing of a sherd in the mouth mean that this person did not correspond to majority LBK ways of doing things – and yet these were referenced in body position and orientation. For each specific death, there were multiple and often unique ways in which the deceased could be positioned within the trajectories of broader, traditional currents.

9 The supra-regional perspective

Robert Hedges, R. Alexander Bentley, Penny Bickle, Philippa Cullen, Christopher Dale, Linda Fibiger, Julie Hamilton, Daniela Hofmann, Geoff Nowell and Alasdair Whittle

9.1 Introduction

The evidence described in previous chapters covers a representative transect from the southern distribution of the LBK, stretching over 1200 km from the middle Danube in Hungary to the upper Rhine valley in Alsace, France (Fig. 9.1). In this chapter we move from considering the data on the local and regional scale to look for general spatial trends – the supra-regional approach – and to consider their possible underlying causes. Furthermore, where such trends are prominent, they provide the context in which the significance of variation between sites can be addressed. Of the different kinds of evidence collected here, it is the stable isotope collagen data for which a region-wide analysis is most useful (Chapter 9.2). This is partly because (a) there is a reasonably adequately sampled coverage of comparable data throughout the region, and (b) the changes in isotope value due to diet are not large when compared to the differences in isotope value between individuals, so that a large number of sites in a geographical setting provide the best chance to determine significant patterns. Stable isotope values of dietary items (especially of plants) arise from physiological processes, and also, for $\delta^{15}N$, from soil

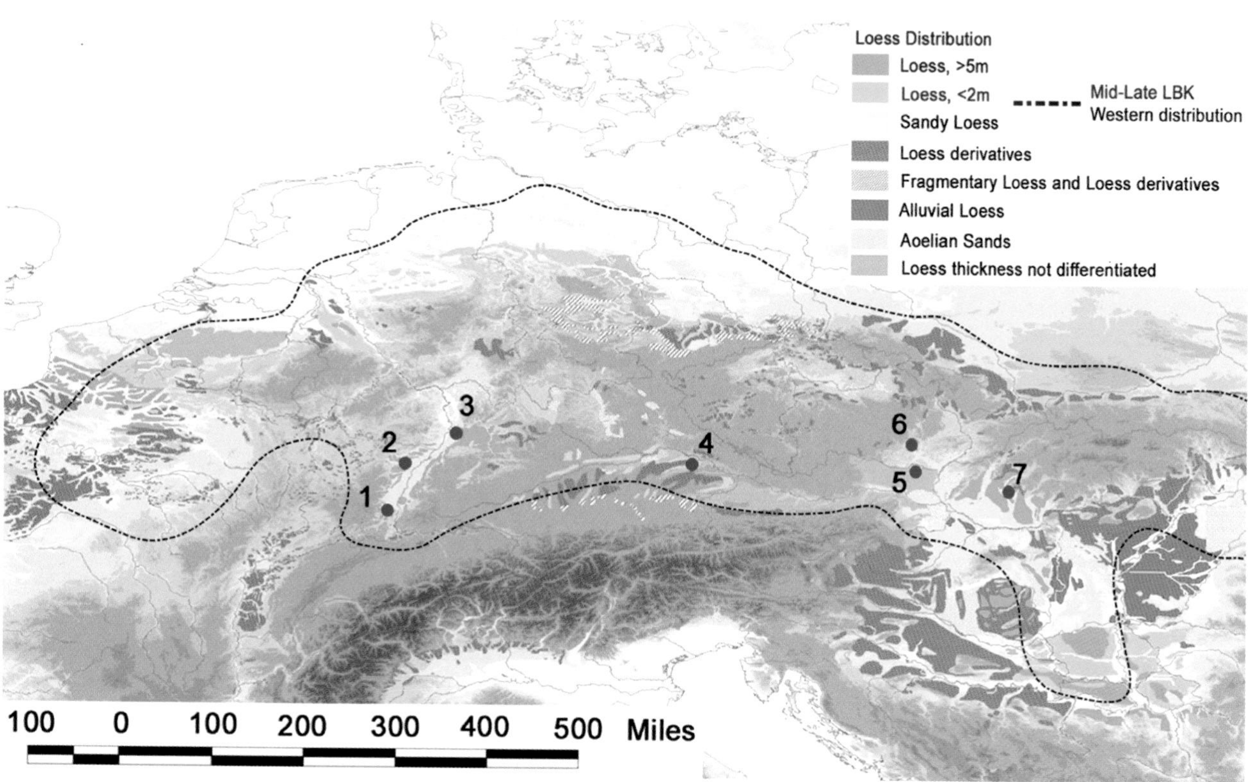

Fig. 9.1. Map showing the main distribution of loess soils in central Europe and main sites discussed in strontium section (chapter 9.3). 1) Ensisheim, 2) Souffelweyersheim, 3) Schwetzingen, 4) Aiterhofen, 5) Kleinhadersdorf, 6) Vedrovice, 7) Nitra. From Bentley et al. *(2012, 9327).*

chemistry. Both of these are influenced by local climate, soils and ecological history.

We also include here a region-wide perspective of the tooth enamel strontium isotope analyses (Chapter 9.3, noting that local geochemistry is bound to influence strontium values); of the osteological evidence (Chapter 9.4, bearing in mind that the necessarily limited sampling restricts what can be said at this level of generality); and of the funerary context (Chapter 9.5), reflecting on how the isotopic studies have helped to inform analysis of LBK burial practices.

9.2 Carbon and nitrogen analysis

This section is devoted to collagen $\delta^{13}C$ and $\delta^{15}N$ analysis (see Chapter 2.2.2 for a description of the methodology). Additional data were collected on tooth dentine (not discussed here, see Chapter 7.7), and on tooth enamel $\delta^{18}O$ (Chapter 9.2.7; see also Chapter 7.7). Individual values, site averages and intra-site patterns are described in the regional sections. Ideally, each site would have provided human and faunal samples for comparison, but this was only occasionally possible as many of the sites where human bone was sampled were cemeteries rather than settlements, with relatively few faunal specimens. Furthermore, the quantity needed for faunal samples is easily underestimated; fauna typically have at least twice the variance in their stable isotope values when compared to humans, and, as we found in this project, the three faunal species commonly encountered on sites cannot meaningfully substitute for each other. This implies an ideal sample of about twelve times as many faunal analyses as humans (i.e. four times for each species, for comparable standard errors), whereas this project has managed closer to equal numbers: 617 humans in total, of which 462 adults; and 366 fauna comprising 194 cattle, 92 sheep/goats, and 80 pigs. In several cases human-faunal comparisons had to be made using data from different sites, and in one or two cases it became apparent that the geographic/climatic disparity was probably too great to be useful. This is discussed where it occurs. When comparing sites, we have used combined adult, sexed and non-sexed data, omitting infants, children and adolescents.

It is worth saying that the dataset discussed here is by far the largest generated so far that is applicable to a relatively homogeneous population, and so provides an unprecedented opportunity for defining baselines and discerning trends over a region. In this section, we first give an overview of the pattern of the isotopic data we have found. We then consider and analyse the results in more depth. Finally, we attempt to interpret our findings.

9.2.1 The geographic and climate data

The sites are generally considered as belonging to roughly the same chronological period of the LBK, that is, the developed phase after 5300 cal BC. Spatially they are defined in terms of latitude and longitude; there is so little change in latitude that it can be disregarded. The sites also differ in altitude (from 90 to 330 m above sea level), much of this correlating closely with longitude (predominantly for east of 10°E; i.e. the Danube basin). Associated with this basic coordination of sites are changes of climate, of ecology, and possibly of cultural history and behaviour. Such differences may influence isotope values, and the dataset gives us an opportunity to investigate possible influences through the correlations found. However, there is also an inherent degree of correlation between climate, location and ecology (as well, perhaps, as settlement history), and we cannot expect variation in just two isotopes to be able to discriminate very clearly between various effects which themselves are entangled.

LBK climate data

The LBK dates of course to the Holocene, which is sub-divided on the basis of climatic fluctuations into five periods, with the early Neolithic falling within the Atlantic phase. Reconstructions of climate from this period are based on climate proxies, such as glacial ice cores (including glacier advance), $\delta^{14}C$ and $\delta^{18}O$ isotope variations, pollen records in fluvial and lake sediments and tree-ring widths, which are combined to build up a picture of fluctuations in temperature and rainfall (Schmidt and Gruhle 2003; Schmidt *et al.* 2004; 2005b; Kalis *et al.* 2003; Strien and Gronenborn 2005; Gronenborn 2009b). It should be noted that such proxies tend to react to climate changes at different temporal scales (Strien and Gronenborn 2005, 133) and that, when viewed on a geological timescale, the Holocene has experienced a rather stable climate (Wirtz and Lemmen 2003, 360).

The LBK developed during a period sometimes known as the 'climatic optimum' of the Holocene, which lasted about 4000 years, between 9000 and 5000 cal BP (*c.* 7000–3000 cal BC; Kalis *et al.* 2003). The beginning of the LBK (*c.* 5500 cal BC) is said to come after a relatively cooler period lasting from 8000–7500 cal BP (6000–5500 cal BC; Kalis *et al.* 2003, 61). During the LBK, the climate is considered to have been generally wetter and warmer than today, with average yearly temperatures 1–3°C warmer (Kreuz 1990, 7; Jacomet and Kreuz 1999, 235; Davis *et al.* 2003, 1710; Kalis *et al.* 2003). Lüning (2000, 20) qualifies this further, stating that while summer average temperatures were 2°C higher, they were only 0.5°C higher during the winter months (also Bakels 2009, 32). Rainfall is likely to have been similar to or greater than today, though perhaps concentrated more in the winter (Bakels 2009, 32). Lang (1994) estimates that the rainfall would have been 55 mm higher than today. The milder, shorter winters with longer periods of rainfall would have meant LBK communities experienced greater humidity annually and probably had a longer growing season than today (Kreuz 1990, 7–8). The warmer climate of the Atlantic period ends at the beginning of the Subboreal phase (*c.* 6000 cal BP/4000 cal BC; Davis *et al.* 2003; Kalis *et al.* 2003).

Recently, Strien and Gronenborn (2005; Gronenborn 2007a; 2009b), have turned to a wider range of climate proxies to model the intersection of climatic variation and change during the LBK. Although the dating and regional applicability of such data remain imprecise, hindering robust conclusions (Gronenborn 2009b; 2010a, 70), they find the climatic changes from 5100 cal BC the most convincing (Strien and Gronenborn 2005; Gronenborn 2009b; 2010a). Based on the tree-ring width from the well at Erkelenz-Kückhoven, Strien and Gronenborn (2005, 133) argue that cooling begins at 5145 den BC[1] and amplifies at 5112 and 5098 den BC (cf. Dubouloz 2008, 230). Gronenborn (2010c, 70) estimates that this phase ended about 5040 den BC on the basis of bog oak population dynamics in north-west Germany and Holland. 'Germination and drying-off events' (GDO) show a period of rising groundwater and the GDO at 5040 den BC is taken to represent a return to wetter conditions. Gronenborn (2010c, 68) argues that the effects of climate change could have been highly regional, with the destabilising influence of crop failure in one region sending waves spreading cultural turmoil into other regions as people were forced to turn to raiding and/or migrations to feed themselves.

Throughout the LBK a number of further fluctuations in the climate have been demonstrated which suggest phases of cooling and/or drying took place in the years between 5300 and 5100 cal BC (Davis *et al.* 2003; Kalis *et al.* 2003; Schmidt and Gruhle 2003; Schmidt *et al.* 2004; Strien and Gronenborn 2005; Gronenborn 2007a; 2009b; 2010c; Dubouloz 2008). These fluctuations are also thought to have impacted on the ecology and environment of LBK farmers. On the basis of the same tree-ring data from the Erkelenz-Kückhoven well, Schmidt *et al.* (2004, 304) identified two major drier phases at approximately 5360 den BC and 5020 den BC that sandwiched a relatively wetter period, which also saw minor fluctuations. They connect slight increases in rainfall and humidity during this period (5360–5020 cal BC) with times of increased building activity at the settlement (Schmidt *et al.* 2004, 305), suggesting that wetter phases were times of enhanced production (such as of crop growth). From 5050 cal BC, Schmidt *et al.* (2005b, 307–8) estimate a 35% drop in humidity, resulting in a cooler and drier phase, also cited as having an extremely detrimental effect on crop production at the end of the LBK.

Aside from the problems of correlating such variations with the archaeological data from the LBK, which is often poorly radiocarbon dated or sequenced on the basis of relative rather than absolute chronology (Bogaard 2011, 26), the impact of such climate variations on farming practices, food sources and population structures remains unclear, with opinions differing on what constitutes ideal conditions for agriculture. Severe periods of drought lasting several decades or the sudden onset of aridification may have catastrophic effects on society and population levels (deMenocal 2001, 667), but these extremes are not demonstrable for the time of the LBK. Davis *et al.* (2003, 1710) suggest that average temperature fluctuations since 8000 BP (6000 cal BC) have only been in the range of 0.7–0.9°C. Most likely LBK farmers were productive within a range of climatic conditions (Bogaard 2004, 5) and until the extremes of this range are a) substantially better identified and b) shown to have been exceeded, we should be most cautious in accepting this model of climate-driven social change; we do not yet fully understand what impact these fluctuations had on the LBK. Furthermore, both Hajnalová and Dreslerová (2010, 170) and Connolly *et al.* (2008, 2803) describe the dominant crops of the LBK (emmer and einkorn) as robust and as having adaptability to harsher climates.

For the purposes of this project, however, it is the presence of any regional variation in climate and ecology which is significant. The widespread applicability of some climate proxies has been questioned, with researchers arguing that the Holocene was a time when climate change progressively happened on a more regional basis (O'Brian *et al.* 1995, 1963). Broadly, the LBK appears to cover land that falls in both the Continental and Atlantic climate zones (not to be confused with the Atlantic period) of Europe, with climate becoming increasingly continental towards the south-east (Kreuz 1990, 11–12). On the basis of modern climate data and related to certain ceramic groups, Sielmann (1972; 1976) identified two *Ökologiekreise* (ecological zones) that were settled by the earliest LBK communities. *Ökologiekreis* A (mainly central and northern Germany) had less rain (500–600 mm total annual precipitation) and lower average yearly temperatures (8–9°C) than zone B (Sielmann 1972, 20). *Ökologiekreis* B (Bavaria, along the Danube, and the Neckar valley through to Heidelberg), on the other hand, had more rain (650–800 mm total annual precipitation) and higher average yearly temperatures (*c.* 9°C), resulting in a more humid climate which was less suitable to agriculture. The reality of these regions has since been questioned (Kreuz 1990, 162; Lüning 2000, 61). Kreuz (1990, 162) argues that all *älteste* LBK sites, even those in Bavaria, fall within *Ökologiekreis* A and that it is only when the *jüngere* LBK spreads into the Lower Rhine (such as the Aldenhovener Platte), the Netherlands and central France that the more Atlantic-style climate zones were experienced. The notion of the *Ökologiekreise* is not generally used today and, although Continental and Atlantic climate zones are thought significant, the Vosges shelter Alsace from the Atlantic climate (thus making its climate more Continental; Lefranc 2007a, 15) and all the regions under study here fall into the Continental zone.

Modelling the climate changes over the geographical spread of our study here is therefore better attempted using quantitative data, which on the scale we require are currently only available from modern climate measurements. While actual, absolute values may not apply well to the LBK period, given changes in both climate and vegetation cover over the past 7000 years, we believe that the geographical relationships between the values will be applicable, at least back to the mid-Holocene. The most useful dataset proved to be the International Water Management Institute World Water and Climate Atlas (Internet ref. 4), based on the data available from the Climatic Research Unit, University of East Anglia, England (Internet ref. 5). This is spatially smoothed and processed at a 10-minute resolution, allowing values to be closely linked to specific sites. Of the available climate parameters (Table 9.1), we eventually included mean monthly temperature, rainfall, number of days with rain, and Moisture Availability Index (Hargreaves 1977), each averaged over 'winter' (November–April) and 'summer' (May–September) months. Other parameters did not improve model fits (Appendix C for more details). These parameters can be fairly directly related to the physiology of plant-water relationships, important in the theory of isotope fractionation during photosynthesis. Averaging parameters over 'winter' and 'summer' reduced the number of variables while retaining a seasonal signal.

Effect of climate on isotopic variation

This huge and interesting subject is not currently well reviewed in a form suitable for archaeological application and is discussed only briefly here. In any case, most of the literature considers environments which hardly relate to our region, and generally concerns itself with far greater extremes of climate. We do not here consider $\delta^{15}N$, in part because our data do not make a convincing case for climate as the driver of the $\delta^{15}N$ variation which we see. In any case, the literature on $\delta^{15}N$ and climate, while demonstrating some clear relationships, also shows that they are frequently not replicable in other apparently similar situations.

For $\delta^{13}C$ values, despite the relationship to climate being clearer and better based theoretically, comparison between datasets is nevertheless not easy. As well as a lack of reported measurements on directly relevant environments and climates, the correlating climate parameters considered vary from publication to publication, making quantitative comparison difficult. Van Klinken *et al.* (1994) compare bone collagen values across Europe throughout the Holocene. In that paper, $\delta^{13}C$ is shown to correlate with some climate parameters, the biggest effect being July sunshine hours. Our data correlate better with different (if related) parameters, but are in general agreement. That is, the overall trend which Van Klinken *et al.* (1994) found was of about 2‰ from west to east (Britain to Greece), and we find a change of a little more than 1‰ over part of this range. Murphy and Bowman (2009) consider $\delta^{13}C$ and $\delta^{15}N$ in Australian grasses in relation to climate. Taking their data, and assuming the change is linear with summer moisture, they show a change of about 2.5‰ (in the plants) for a Moisture Availability Index change from 0.8‰ to 0.3‰, whereas we see a change of about half this amount (in herbivore collagen; Chapter 9.2.6). Hartman and Danin (2010) made a very careful study of plants in the eastern Mediterranean. The effects depend strongly on the type of plant and its season of growth; the east Mediterranean has a much more arid summer climate than the LBK region. Hartman and Danin's (2010) extensive datasets are analysed in terms of logarithmic relationships (which make comparison difficult, although represent the real world better). For a precipitation change of 500 to 1000 mm (moisture availability was not considered), the most relevant plants show an average change of 1–2‰, while, for a similar precipitation range (but different temperature regime), our values change by 1–1.2‰.

Thus overall, the change we see in $\delta^{13}C$ is in line with, but perhaps tending to be smaller than, the most recent work on climatic effects on plants.

9.2.2 Regional variation in the ecology of the LBK

Palynological records are the most ready source of data for reconstructing the environment and for appreciating the impact farming communities had on the landscape (Kalis *et al.* 2003, 38). However, these data cannot give a direct reconstruction of the landscape, with pollen records coming from 'off-site' locations such as lake deposits unlikely to show up the true extent of farming in the vicinity (Kalis *et al.* 2003, 39). Nevertheless, woodland was the dominant plant coverage during the Neolithic, though its composition would have varied across different ecological settings (Bakels 1978; Bogucki 1988, 27; Kreuz 1990; Kalis *et al.* 2003). Within the fertile river valleys, where LBK communities settled, oak, ash, lime and elm are likely to have dominated deciduous woodlands with hazel at forest edges, while the uplands and drier/sandier soils would have supported pine forests (Kalis *et al.* 2003, 40, 64). However, as Lüning (2000, 26–7) stresses, the actual composition of the woodland is likely to have varied from region to region and the density of these forests (in terms of light permitted to travel to the forest floor) has been a matter of some debate (Bogucki 1988, 30). The extent of woodland clearance by early farmers has also been debated, though the pollen evidence provides a far from conclusive story (Bogucki 1988; Kreuz 1990). Based on the pollen records of lowland southern and central Germany, Kalis *et al.* (2003, 74) downplay the impact of human activity on early Neolithic woodlands in Europe, arguing rather that 'Early Neolithic life seems to have remained strongly adapted to the forest ecosystem and evidently remained part of it'.

Some broad regional differences between areas with more Atlantic or more Continental climate have been identified on the basis of pollen analysis (Lüning 2000, 27). Bakels (1978) argued that within the wetter and low-lying Lower Rhine-Maas river system, river valleys were covered in shrub (e.g. alder), the drier watershed areas promoted mixed deciduous forests (lime, ash, elm and oak), and the vegetation found on the loess was most likely to be lime or oak-lime forest. In Bavaria, Bakels (1983/4) argued that a more Continental forest was found on the loess, with oak dominating woodland composition with some element of lime. In these drier conditions, the alluvial deposits of the river floodplains may have supported mixed deciduous forests rather than carr-shrub (Bakels 1983/84; Bogucki 1988, 32). On the uplands, such as the Bavarian Forest and towards the Alps, pine woodland would have been more prominent as the average number of days with frost per year increases (Küster 1995, 19). However, these differences are difficult to quantify and vegetation cover is likely to have varied on a highly regional level (Bakels 1983/4). The existence of open grassland/parkland has also been demonstrated (e.g. Lüning 2000, 25; Frank 2009). Indeed, the amount of open (non-forested) land in the Neolithic

*Table 9.1. Correlations between the geographical and climate factors tested for inclusion in models explaining variance in $\delta^{13}C$ and $\delta^{15}N$ values. Values of the correlation coefficient, Pearson's r, are given in the upper half of the table (note minus signs for negative correlations), and the coefficient of determination, r^2, in the lower half. Statistically significant r values are indicated by asterisks: *$p \leq 0.05$, **$p \leq 0.01$; n=23 for each comparison. Climate factors were derived from the International Water Management Institute World Water and Climate Atlas (Internet ref. 4), based on data from the Climatic Research Unit, University of East Anglia. 'Summer' and 'winter' values are means of monthly means from April to September and October to March respectively. Geographical factor abbreviations: LAT – latitude (decimal degrees); LONG – longitude (decimal degrees); ELE – elevation (m above sea level). Climate factor abbreviations: PMS – mean monthly precipitation summer (mm); PMW – mean monthly precipitation winter (mm); PDMA –mean number of days with rain per month annual average; TMS – mean monthly temperature summer (°C); TMW – mean monthly temperature winter (°C); TDRMS – mean daily temperature range maximum-minimum (°C); DFMA – mean number of days with ground frost per month annual average; RHMS – mean relative humidity summer (%); RHMW – mean relative humidity winter (%); SMS – mean sunshine hours summer (% maximum); SMW – mean sunshine hours winter (% maximum); WMA – mean monthly wind run annual average (km/h); WR – wind run range maximum-minimum (km/h); MAIS – mean moisture availability index summer; MAIW – mean moisture availability index winter (the moisture availability index MAI is defined as 'the 75% probability of precipitation occurrence, PD, divided by potential evapotranspiration, ETP' (Hargreaves and Samani 1983, 7), parameters which themselves are calculated from local temperature and precipitation data).*

Factor	LAT	LONG	ELE	PMS	PMW	PDMA	TMS	TMW	TDRMS	DFMA	RHMS	RHMW	SMS	SMW	WMA	WR	MAIS	MAIW
LAT	1	−0.31	0.34	0.03	0.01	0.39	−0.48*	−0.12	−0.40	−0.21	−0.28	−0.02	−0.56**	−0.59**	0.28	−0.12	0.11	0.09
LONG	0.09	1	−0.21	−0.51*	−0.62**	−0.92**	0.61**	−0.57**	0.53**	0.62**	−0.49*	−0.61**	0.8**	0.62**	0.43*	0.12	−0.62**	−0.66**
ELE	0.12	0.04	1	0.59**	0.29	0.50*	−0.80**	−0.59**	−0.54**	0.07	0.36	-0.12	−0.64**	-0.19	0.05	−0.61**	0.55**	0.24
PMS	0	0.26	0.35	1	0.88**	0.70**	−0.70**	−0.15	−0.17	0.11	0.87**	0.46*	−0.62**	−0.13	−0.62**	−0.77**	0.99**	0.86**
PMW	0	0.39	0.08	0.77	1	0.69**	−0.54**	0.17	−0.16	−0.02	0.74**	0.51*	−0.57**	−0.10	−0.60**	−0.48*	0.90**	0.93**
PDMA	0.15	0.85	0.25	0.49	0.48	1	−0.78**	0.28	−0.52*	−0.40	0.61**	0.62**	−0.89**	−0.66**	−0.48*	−0.39	0.79**	0.76**
TMS	0.23	0.37	0.64	0.48	0.29	0.61	1	0.29	0.65**	0.13	−0.48*	-0.16	0.92**	0.40	0.08	0.50*	−0.73**	−0.53**
TMW	0.02	0.33	0.35	0.02	0.03	0.08	0.08	1	−0.03	−0.65**	0.05	0.50*	−0.02	−0.28	−0.35	0.43*	−0.05	0.20
TDRMS	0.16	0.28	0.29	0.03	0.03	0.27	0.42	0	1	0.60**	0.04	0.23	0.68**	0.20	−0.39	0.01	−0.19	−0.03
DFMA	0.05	0.38	0	0.01	0	0.16	0.02	0.42	0.36	1	0.10	−0.04	0.36	0.40	−0.13	−0.34	0.04	0.07
RHMS	0.08	0.24	0.13	0.76	0.55	0.38	0.23	0	0	0.01	1	0.65**	−0.42*	−0.08	−0.81**	−0.62**	0.88**	0.80**
RHMW	0	0.37	0.02	0.21	0.26	0.39	0.03	0.25	0.05	0	0.43	1	−0.27	−0.49*	−0.87**	−0.23	0.56**	0.76**
SMS	0.31	0.64	0.41	0.38	0.32	0.78	0.85	0	0.46	0.13	0.17	0.07	1	0.59**	0.12	0.36	−0.68**	−0.55**
SMW	0.35	0.38	0.03	0.02	0.01	0.43	0.16	0.08	0.04	0.16	0.01	0.24	0.35	1	0.21	0.03	−0.24	−0.28
WMA	0.08	0.18	0	0.38	0.36	0.23	0.01	0.12	0.16	0.02	0.65	0.75	0.02	0.05	1	0.44*	−0.66**	−0.78**
WR	0.01	0.02	0.37	0.59	0.23	0.15	0.25	0.18	0	0.11	0.39	0.05	0.13	0	0.19	1	−0.72**	−0.52**
MAIS	0.01	0.39	0.30	0.97	0.80	0.62	0.53	0	0.04	0	0.77	0.31	0.47	0.06	0.43	0.52	1	0.91**
MAIW	0.01	0.44	0.06	0.73	0.86	0.58	0.28	0.04	0	0	0.63	0.57	0.31	0.08	0.6	0.27	0.83	1

may well have been underestimated (Vera 2000; cf. Mitchell 2005). Charcoal analysis has also suggested the presence of managed hedges in the landscape (Kreuz 1992; 2007), which may have acted as barriers decreasing the appearance of cereals by preventing cereal pollen from travelling far and thus causing the landscape to look more wooded than it was (Kreuz 1990; Bogaard 2011, 29).

In the most south-eastern parts of central Europe studied by this project, Kosse (1979, 35) found 35% of sites in eastern Hungary (Alföld Linear Pottery Culture or ALP) were on drier forested landscapes (higher oak component), while only 2% in the west were found in these conditions. However, the northern parts of the Hungarian Plain (where our ALP sites are located) are likely to have seen the same or to have had similar forest coverage to the western parts of the country (Kosse 1979, 37). The settlements clustered around Füzesabony were surrounded by a 5–6 km band of grasslands that appear to have been devoid of ALP sites (Domboróczki 2009, 102). At the southern border of the distribution of LBK and ALP sites, the Great Hungarian Plain is said to be divided by an 'agroecological barrier', which is thought to have marked a boundary between the marshy-mosaic steppe in the south and the forested-mosaic lands which the ALP and LBK settled (Raczky *et al.* 2010, 148–9, 159).

Kreuz's (1990, 17, 158) examination of ten earliest LBK sites found that the differences between sites lay not only in climatic conditions, but in distance from different ecological settings such as river meadows, uplands and more sandy soils, which would have supported very different vegetation. These differences would be specific to each site, arising from factors such as distance from water source and higher ground, as well as the different soil substrates in the vicinity of the settlement (i.e. how close the settlement was to the edge of the loess soil, on which the vast majority of sites are located). These did not vary most significantly on a regional basis but between individual sites (Kreuz 1990, 155–8). For example, Lüning (2000, 26) argued that lime dominated the south Wetterau (north of Frankfurt am Main) at the expense of oak, while in the drier northern and eastern parts of the Wetterau pine forest was more prevalent than elsewhere. Further south, in the middle Neckar, areas of mixed deciduous forest (oak, elm, lime, ash and maple) are suggested (Lüning 2000, 26). Bogaard *et al.* (2011) were able to demonstrate that these varied landscapes around settlements may have even led to differences within the settlement community itself, and not just between different settlements, on the basis of weed spectra found on the settlement of Vaihingen (Neckar valley, Baden-Württemberg), but this remains an isolated study so far.

Given this diversity we have not been able to include ecological data at the level of statistical modelling, but some differences in forest cover between the Upper Rhineland and Danube valley are thought significant; we have considered the degree to which ecological descriptions may account for some of the regional variation, especially in the fauna.

9.2.3 Overview of the carbon and nitrogen results

Here we summarise the main conclusions from the stable isotope data. The main pattern in the isotopic data is an east–west trend ($\delta^{13}C$ and, less clearly, $\delta^{15}N$, values increase to the east), which is true for all fauna (whose isotopic variations correlate well with each other), and also, although less distinctly, for humans. We discuss why we believe this trend to be climate-driven (rather than culturally driven) below, and show that when the differences due to climate are statistically removed, there is comparatively little variation left. The climate-corrected site data have become rather homogeneous, but some sites do show (in this context) anomalous values, often for just one species, and they are considered on their own (discussed below in Chapter 9.2.5). There are some comparable data for humans from other LBK sites (listed in Chapter 2.2), and these fall within the range of our dataset, but detailed comparison is limited by the rather small amount of faunal data. There is no dataset of comparable size with which to compare these LBK results as a whole, except perhaps for the UK.

Further analysis is essentially 'second order' – that is, it is looking for differences within the climate-corrected data – and is at the limits of what can be detected with the statistical resolution that our sampling provides. One important measure is the human-faunal difference in $\delta^{15}N$ or $\delta^{13}C$, which is closely related to the trophic level difference between the two species (Hedges and Reynard 2007). Its magnitude varies, again with an east–west trend, and provides important information on human dietary behaviour. There is also evidence of increasing differences in livestock management on the western side of the region (i.e. the Rhine basin; Chapter 9.2.6). A second finding, which applies to the dataset as a whole, is the isotopic difference (essentially, higher $\delta^{15}N$ for males) between adult males and females. For each of three sites (Asparn, Nitra, Vedrovice), there is a small but statistically very significant difference. For the remaining sites, taken together, there is also a smaller (on average) but still significant difference. However, for some other sites (such as Schwetzingen), although the sampling and low variance are more than adequate to reveal such small differences, none are observed.

9.2.4 Analysis of the dataset as a whole

Our main approach has been to analyse the variance in the isotope dataset in terms of a general linear model that takes the hierarchical nature of the data into account. That is, individual values can be grouped into sites. In this way, the local variances at site level are preserved. However, for making plots, it is more convenient to plot site averages.

The geographical characteristics of the sites

Figure 9.2a shows the relationship between longitude and altitude for the sites, and brings out well the two separate river catchments. Figure 9.2b superimposes the average summer temperature at the sites and shows how this is related to both altitude and longitude. These figures give a sense of the spatial structure of the supra-region, and how

*Table 9.2. Correlations between $\delta^{13}C$ and $\delta^{15}N$ values for humans and fauna. Values of the correlation coefficient, Pearson's r, are given in the upper half of the table, and the coefficient of determination, r^2, in the lower half. Statistically significant r values are indicated by asterisks: *$p \leq 0.05$, **$p \leq 0.01$; n=8 for humans, 14 for cattle and pig, 13 for sheep/goat.*

$\delta^{13}C$	Human	Cattle	Sheep/goat	Pig
Human	1	0.70*	0.81*	0.78*
Cattle	0.48	1	0.87**	0.67**
Sheep/goat	0.66	0.76	1	0.60*
Pig	0.61	0.44	0.36	1
$\delta^{15}N$	**Human**	**Cattle**	**Sheep/goat**	**Pig**
Human	1	0.55	0.80*	0.41
Cattle	0.30	1	0.81**	0.67**
Sheep/goat	0.65	0.65	1	0.67*
Pig	0.17	0.44	0.44	1

that relates to climatic variation (summer temperature being a typical example). The overall structure of correlations between climate and geography is represented in Table 9.1, from which it is clear that there is a very large amount of co-variation. This implies that it will be difficult to recognise any particular climatic measure as being uniquely responsible for variation in isotope values.

Correlation of isotopic values between the fauna

These results document our contention that the additional inter-site variability is consistent between the domesticated animals, and presumably arises from a common set of 'drivers'. The inter-site isotopic pattern found in cattle, sheep and pigs is likely to originate from a common isotopic pattern in the plants they eat. There are also differences between species which tend to be evident at particular sites, and which could be explained by the differences in their diets (which may reflect differences in management of livestock and use of landscape).

Figure 9.3 shows biplots of $\delta^{13}C$ and $\delta^{15}N$ for the site means of selected pairs of species plotted against each other, and Table 9.2 shows the values of the correlation coefficients between all pairs of species (and humans). All the plots show a significant correlation, generally with a slope of about unity. This is to be expected if the different species are registering the isotopic differences between sites in the same way. Particularly notable is the deviation from the 1:1 slope of cattle compared to sheep $\delta^{13}C$ (Fig. 9.3a); the points for most sites are below the line, i.e. cattle tend to have lower $\delta^{13}C$ values than sheep, more so at more western sites. At Bischoffsheim the difference reaches 2‰. The same pattern is seen when comparing pig and cattle (Fig. 9.3c), suggesting that it reflects a change in the isotopic relationships of cattle rather than sheep or pig. For the $\delta^{15}N$ values, pigs appear mainly above the 1:1 line compared to cattle and sheep, suggesting an offset in $\delta^{15}N$ of up to about 1‰ at most sites, as would be expected if pigs had a more omnivorous diet. This will be discussed further in Chapter 9.2.6.

Species isotopic variation with climate

We have searched for the combination of climate measures which can best account for the greatest degree of inter-site variance. Because of the already mentioned high correlation between climate measures, inter-site variance is significantly reduced by several different measures, including temperature and precipitation effects. Further inter-site variance reduction can be achieved by taking combinations of these measures, but the effect is not dramatic, and we do not think it meaningful to select a particular combination over a choice of single variables.

The outcome is summarised in Table 9.3, which documents the effects of incorporating one climate measure at a time (including longitude and altitude data for comparison) into the linear model (detailed examples of the 2-level model on which this table is based are given in Appendix C). The models describe the linear relationship between the average $\delta^{13}C$ or $\delta^{15}N$ value of a particular species and each of various climate factors that vary across sites. Longitude and elevation are also given, for comparison. The factors were entered singly into the model, combinations of factors produced little improvement in fit. Factors which significantly reduced inter-site variance compared to the null model are indicated, and the shaded cells indicate the factor that gave the greatest reduction in inter-site variance for that species and isotope (for pigs, most variation was within rather than between sites, and a number of factors were equally good at accounting for all of the inter-site variance). The figures refer to the percentage of total variance that is inter-site variance. Since the geographic and climatic factors are measured at the site level, there is very little change in intra-site (inter-individual) variance when different factors are entered into the model, and variance reduction ('explanation') can only take place at site level. For example, in the null 2-level model, with no explanatory factors entered, 55% of the variance in human $\delta^{13}C$ is inter-site variance and 45% is intra-site (inter-individual) variance. With the best explanatory factor, MAIW (Moisture Availability Index

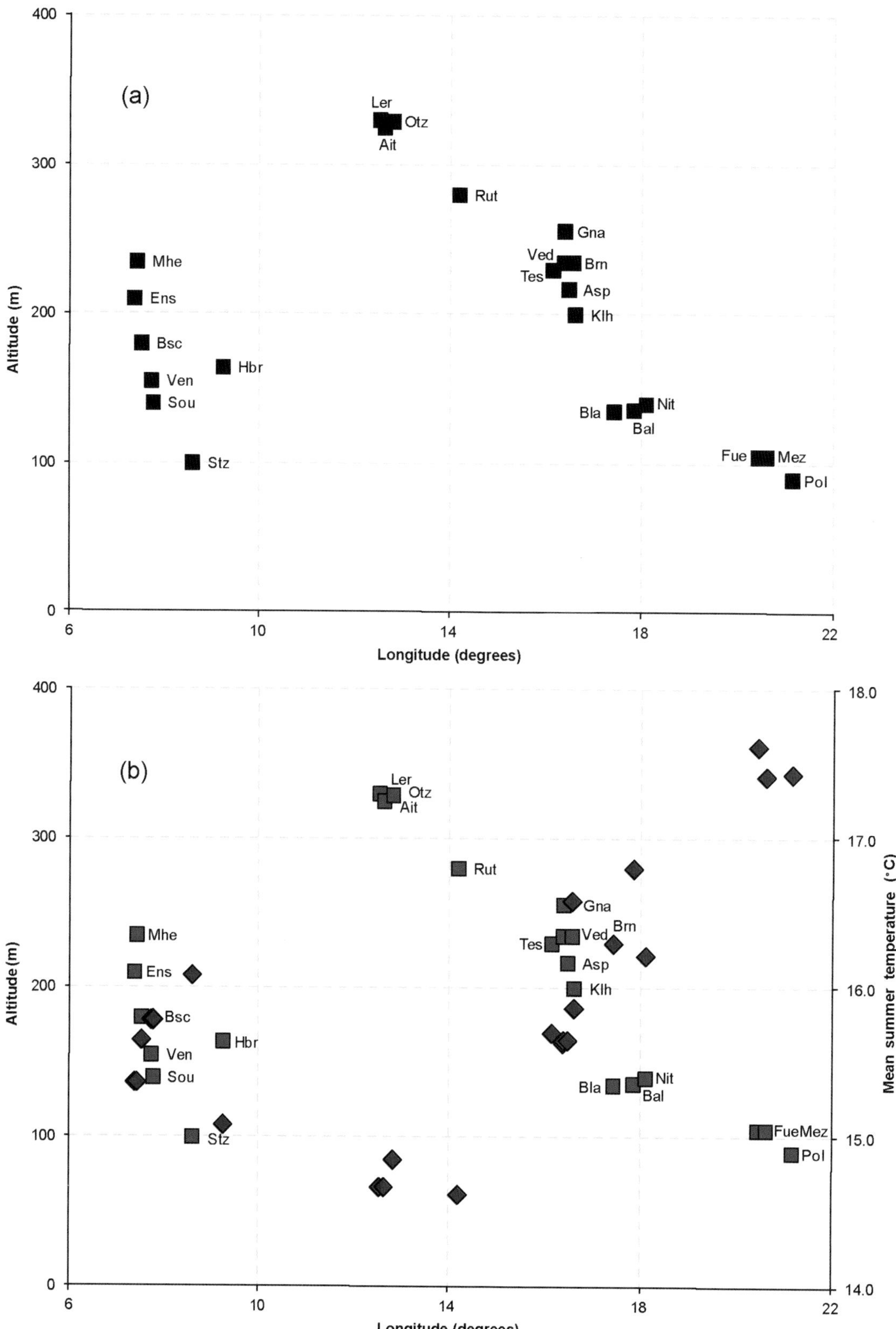

Fig. 9.2. Relationship between (a) longitude (°) and altitude (m) and (b) mean summer temperature for sites with carbon and nitrogen stable isotope data. Mean summer temperature is the average of the mean monthly temperatures from May to September. Site abbreviations: Ait – Aiterhofen; Asp – Asparn; Bal – Balatonszárszó; Bla – Blatné; Brn – Brno; Bsc – Bischoffsheim; Ens – Ensisheim; Fue – Füzesabony; Gna – Gnadendorf; Hbr – Heilbronn-Neckargartach; Klh – Kleinhadersdorf; Ler – Lerchenhaid; Mez – Mezőkövesd; Mhe – Mulhouse-Est; Nit – Nitra; Otz – Otzing; Pol – Polgár-Ferenci-hát; Rut – Rutzing; Sou – Souffelweyersheim; Stz – Schwetzingen; Tes – Těšetice; Ved – Vedrovice; Ven – Vendenheim.

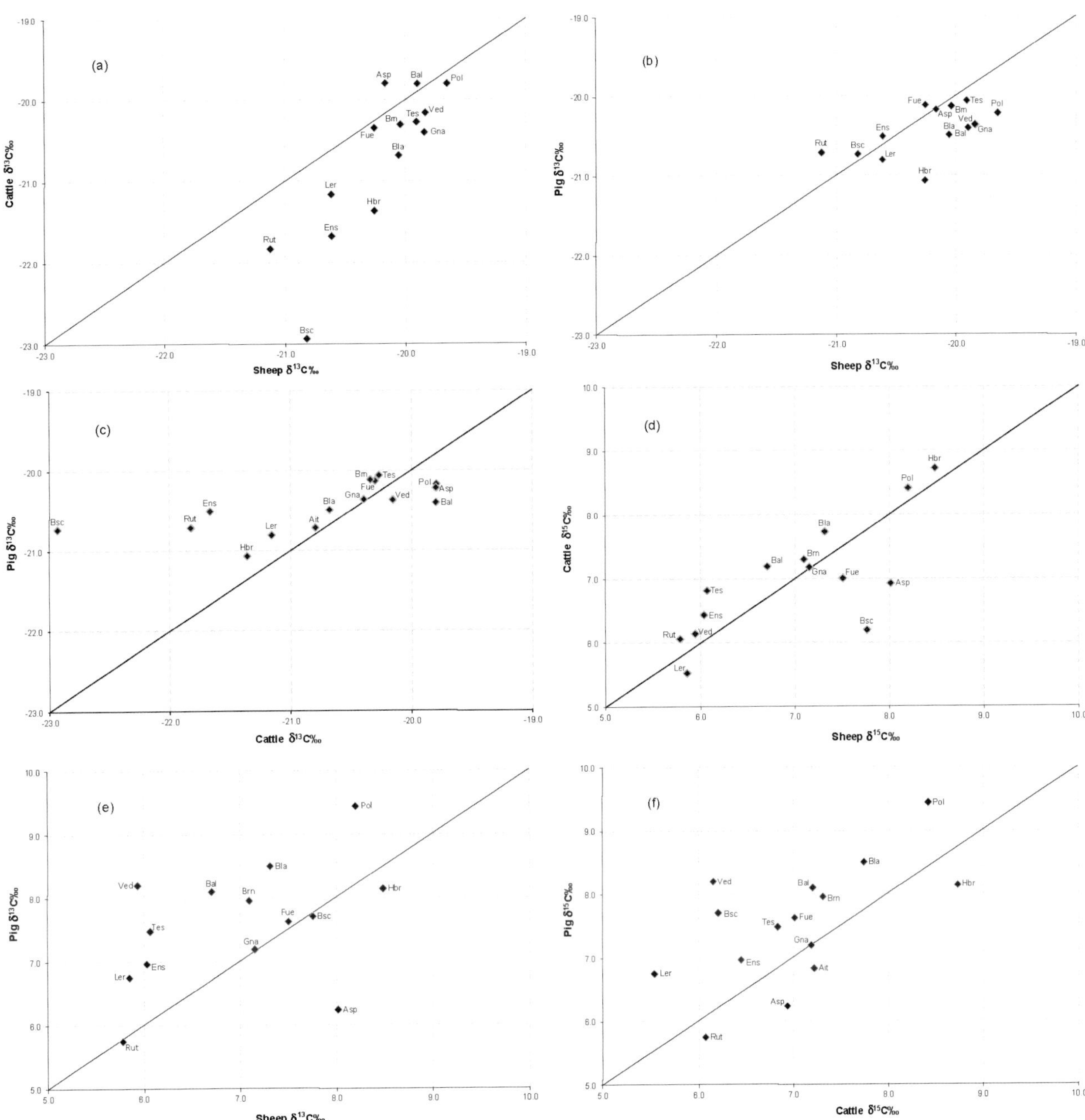

Fig. 9.3. Relationship between (a–c) δ^{13}C and (d–f) δ^{15}N for pairs of domestic species at each site. 1:1 line shown for comparison. Site abbreviations as in Fig. 9.2.

averaged over the 'winter' months November–March), included, only 20% of overall variance is inter-site variance: the intra-site variance is the same as before, and the overall variance in δ^{13}C is reduced ('explained' by the model); 35/55=64% of inter-site variance is now accounted for by MAIW. Table 9.3 can be summarised as follows.

For carbon (δ^{13}C):

a) For fauna, most of the inter-site variance can be best accounted for by precipitation measures, and there is an overall agreement between the species over which effects are the most significant.

b) For humans, distinctly less of the inter-site variance is accounted for by climatic effects, which in any case differ somewhat from the fauna – although they do still mainly involve moisture rather than temperature.

From our data, we can therefore summarise that the effect of climate on δ^{13}C is as follows: δ^{13}C increases by 1‰ as the average summer Moisture Availability Index decreases 0.7‰ to 0.3‰, or, alternatively, δ^{13}C increases by 1‰ for an increase in average summer temperature of 3°C.

For nitrogen (δ^{15}N):

c) For fauna, climate is altogether less successful in accounting for inter-site variance, with pigs less similar to sheep and cattle than was the case for δ^{13}C. This is perhaps not surprising if pigs were living

*Table 9.3. Effect of climate factors on inter-site variance in $\delta^{13}C$ and $\delta^{15}N$ for humans and fauna. The details of the 2-level models on which this table is based are given in Appendix C. Cattle at Bischoffsheim (anomalously low $\delta^{13}C$) and cattle and sheep/goat at Heilbronn-Neckargartach (anomalously high $\delta^{15}N$) have been omitted. The factors were entered singly into the model, and those that significantly reduced inter-site variance compared to the null model are indicated by asterisks: *$p \leq 0.05$, **$p \leq 0.01$, ***$p \leq 0.001$. The shaded cells indicate the factor that gave the greatest reduction in inter-site variance for that species and isotope (geographic and climatic factors considered separately). The numbers refer to the percentage of total variance that is inter-site variance.*

	$\delta^{13}C$				$\delta^{15}N$			
Factor	**Human**	**Cattle**	**Sheep/goat**	**Pig**	**Human**	**Cattle**	**Sheep/goat**	**Pig**
Longitude	**	***	**	***		**		
Elevation	*			*	*	**	**	***
PMS	***	**	***	**		*	*	**
PMW	***	***	***	***				*
PDMA	**	***	***	***		**		*
TMS	*	**	**	***		**	**	**
TMW				***				
MAIS	***	***	***	***		*	*	**
MAIW	***	***	***	***				
Between-site variance in the null model (%)	55	36	34	17	55	33	32	36
Between-site variance in the best model (%)	20	10	0	0	48	17	16	11

close to the settlement and eating more domestic refuse. However, those climate measures which are significant are associated with summer temperature and precipitation, and clearly differ from those related to $\delta^{13}C$ variation. This perhaps explains why elevation rather than longitude is a better correlating parameter for nitrogen, whereas the opposite is true for carbon.

d) For $\delta^{15}N$ for humans, we could find no climate measure that can account for the inter-site variance and the only significant correlating variable is that of altitude.

The interpretation of the results is considered in Chapter 9.2.5.

Sites which lie outside these geographic and climate trends could also be identified. Sites may be compared for their average values for each species, taking account of both the within-site and between-site variance. The 2-level models allow us to include data from sites with very different numbers of observations and hence different reliabilities, and allow the calculation of confidence limits and statistical significance testing. An example of such a comparison is shown in Fig. 9.4a. Climate factors are measured at the site level (level 2), so the plot (sometimes called a caterpillar plot) shows the level-2 residuals for each site, i.e. the site difference from the grand mean (represented by the horizontal dashed line at 0) with error bars representing ± 1.96 standard deviations. Thus, if the error bars do not cross the horizontal dashed line, the 95% confidence limits for the site mean do not include the grand mean, and the site mean is significantly different from the grand mean at the 5% level. The sites are ranked by the value of the residual, so that sites on the left of the plot have relatively low $\delta^{13}C$ values and those at the right have relatively high $\delta^{13}C$ values; as expected, most sites fall close to the grand mean (the residuals are normally distributed). In this way, it is easy to pick out sites that differ significantly from the overall mean. However, such an outlying point might be explained as due to an extreme climate, and it is therefore useful to account for some of the inter-site variance through climate, as described above. In Fig. 9.4b MAIW (Moisture Availability Index averaged over the 'winter' months November–March), the single climatic factor that best 'explains' site-to-site variation in human $\delta^{13}C$, has been included in the model. All the residuals, and their confidence limits, are now smaller, and only three sites, marked in red, differ significantly from the grand mean. While Nitra and Schwetzingen do not stand out as unusual in Fig. 9.4a, it appears from Fig. 9.4b that when the effect of MAIW is taken into account, the humans there have unusually low or high $\delta^{13}C$ values (respectively) compared to other sites with similar climates. The fauna from Nitra (actually from Blatné) are not unusual on this measure, but before we conclude that this represents a dietary difference in the Nitra humans, we should check whether differences at the intra-site (individual) level, such as age or sex distribution, make a difference, or whether contemporary fauna from closer to Nitra also had lower $\delta^{13}C$ values, which might suggest an environmental effect.

We have also examined sites which, while not being highly significant outliers, nevertheless consistently lie on the extremes of the distribution, regardless of which particular factor is chosen to reduce overall inter-site variance.

Only two sites can be regarded as very clear outliers (after climatic effects are taken into account), and then only for two species (from a total of over 100 possibilities overall). They are Bischoffsheim (for cattle $\delta^{13}C$, see Chapter 8.9), and Heilbronn-Neckargartach (for cattle and sheep $\delta^{15}N$, see Chapter 7.7). The Bischoffsheim result is actually an extreme example of the geographical trend to low $\delta^{13}C$ values for cattle in the west, and is perhaps explicable in terms of this particular trend. The Heilbronn result, which is clear for the two herbivores which usually show similar isotope trends, does not apply to pigs, and seems unrelated to any isotopic trend or other influence that we can discern. The other sites which show consistent unusual behaviour, even if not at the very high significance level, are listed in Table 9.4, for the purposes of stimulating a careful look at local site issues. For example, both Balatonszárszó (Chapter 3.10) and Polgár (Chapter 3.9) show unusually high $\delta^{13}C$ in cattle; but at Balatonszárszó, not Polgár, a small proportion of cattle with such unusually high values of $\delta^{13}C$ account for the high average, for which one suspects there must be a special reason (e.g. perhaps a small contribution from C4 plants, not given to other cattle at the site, and not seen elsewhere).

As a result of this analysis we have excluded Bischoffsheim cattle $\delta^{13}C$ data, and Heilbronn cattle and sheep $\delta^{15}N$ data, from consideration in evaluating the within-site human-faunal difference. As a consequence, the Schwetzingen human data have had to be excluded from any human-faunal comparison.

The human-fauna $\delta^{15}N$ and $\delta^{13}C$ isotopic difference

Humans would be expected to be enriched in $\delta^{15}N$ compared to the fauna, and the plants, which they consume (see discussion in Chapter 2.2.1). A smaller enrichment in $\delta^{13}C$ is also expected, but the situation is more complicated because human collagen carbon can come from both protein carbon and carbohydrate carbon (whereas human collagen nitrogen only comes from consumed protein). This enrichment, namely the difference between human $\delta^{15}N$ and animal $\delta^{15}N$, is given the symbol $\Delta^{15}N$, and similarly for $\Delta^{13}C$. Actually, the carbon comparison is rarely, if at all, made, because of insufficient resolution in the measurement of Δ. In any case, a measurement of this difference is closely related to the proportion of animal protein (in the total protein) in the human diet. We discuss the isotopes separately below, first nitrogen and then carbon.

Nitrogen. Figure 9.5 and Table 9.5 show the Δ values for each site (or pair of compared sites), for each species. Unfortunately, because the Heilbronn faunal $\delta^{15}N$ values appear so anomalous, the excellent human dataset from Schwetzingen now has no useful comparison faunal dataset for $\delta^{15}N$, and finding such a dataset would be a valuable specific aim for future work. Δ is evaluated as the difference between site means for humans and the faunal species in

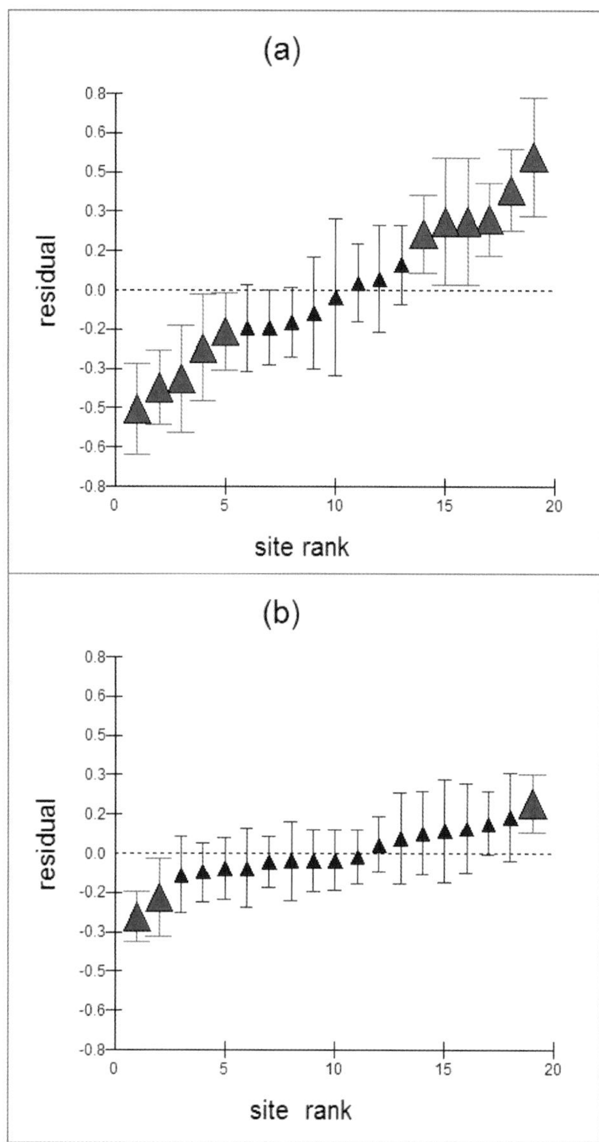

Fig. 9.4. The effect of including climatic factors in the model, using the effect of MAIW (Moisture Availability Index averaged over the 'winter' months November-March) on human $\delta^{13}C$ values as an example. (a) plot of site residuals for the null 2-level model (b) plot of site residuals when MAIW is included as an explanatory factor. Model details are given in Appendix C. The plot shows the level-2 residuals for each site, i.e. the difference from the grand mean (represented by the horizontal dashed line at 0) with error bars representing ±1.96 standard deviations. If the error bars do not cross the horizontal dashed line, the site mean is significantly different from the grand mean at the 5% level. The sites are ranked by the value of the residual, so that sites on the left have relatively lower $\delta^{13}C$ values than those on the right. (a) shows the residuals from the null model; the sites marked in red differ significantly from the grand mean (left to right: Rutzing, Aiterhofen, Souffelweyersheim, Mulhouse-Est, Ensisheim, Kleinhadersdorf, Mezőkövesd, Brno, Vedrovice, Asparn, Těšetice). (b) shows inclusion of MAIW in the model. All the residuals and their confidence limits are now smaller, and only three sites (in red) differ significantly from the grand mean (left to right: Nitra, Souffelweyersheim, Schwetzingen).

question, and the errors are the quadratically combined standard errors for the human and faunal averages – in practice these are dominated by the faunal data. Note that these are not climate-adjusted values, because comparisons are intra-site and therefore the same climate applies to both human and faunal data.

It is clear that the eastern sites (within the Danube catchment) have smaller $\Delta^{15}N$ values than the western sites (within the Rhine catchment), and this is perhaps the most significant supra-regional finding within the whole isotope dataset. The actual values are also important as there is clearly much variation, and a great deal of this is due to the rather imprecise faunal averages. The data also suggest the notion that not all sites conform to the trend. The large set of values measured here span the published range, but also help to establish a definitive set of Δ values for future comparisons, both within and beyond the LBK. Interpretation of the values is reserved for Chapter 9.2.6.
Carbon. Table 9.5 shows $\Delta^{13}C$ values for carbon. The difference between the cattle and the other fauna is striking. This is really a reflection of how much cattle change in $\delta^{13}C$ at the western end of the region, compared to all other species. This has already been mentioned as probably reflecting a specific environmental situation specific to cattle – for which the putative canopy effect in forested environments (Drucker *et al.* 2008; Lynch *et al.* 2008; Balasse *et al.* 2012) would be a strong candidate. Although the human values do not track this change ($\Delta^{13}C$ for human-cattle becomes quite large), simple models (Chapter 9.6) of reasonable diets are consistent with this.

Within-site differences: the supra-regional pattern
Here we discuss sex and age of human skeletons in relation to isotopic values in the larger perspective.
Human sex differences. Of the 632 measurements made on human bone, some 433 come from sexed individuals (we have included f? and m? along with f and m, see Chapter 2.6.3a) and these form a good statistical basis for comparison (although, of course, these are distributed over sites which differ in their average human values). (Note that these figures include results for Vedrovice published by M.P. Richards *et al.* 2008; Chapter 4.7.3.) Table 9.6 summarises the statistical analysis of each site separately (no statistical analysis was attempted for sites with fewer than five of each sex, but means are given for comparison). Of these, three sites (Asparn, Nitra and Vedrovice) show significant differences in $\delta^{15}N$ between the sexes, in each case males being enriched in $\delta^{15}N$ by 0.3–0.5‰. The table also shows sites in which no significant difference at this level was found, notably, Schwetzingen, Aiterhofen, Kleinhadersdorf, Balatonszárszó and Polgár-Ferenci-hát. Thus there are interesting geographical differences here, and it is suggestive that the three sites with a clear difference are in relatively close geographical proximity.

Other researchers have occasionally reported a statistically significant difference between the sexes, always with males having higher $\delta^{15}N$ values than females (usually by about 0.5‰; Nitsch *et al.* 2010), and this has been interpreted as either due to a dietary difference (essentially more meat for males), or a physiological difference (frequent pregnancy and lactation in females changing nitrogen balance). This dataset provides definitive evidence that a physiological explanation is not really viable, because the difference between the sexes is not significant (and is less than 0.3‰) at several sites where means can be estimated with high precision, where we would expect to see such a difference if it existed. There is nevertheless a tendency for males to be slightly enriched in $\delta^{15}N$ throughout – at all sites studied, as is seen in Table 9.6, male $\delta^{15}N$ values are either the same as or greater than those of females. Overall (taking all sites together) the difference is highly significant, and remains significant even when omitting Asparn, Nitra and Vedrovice (Appendix C). Conceivably this could reflect a very small physiological signal of, say, 0.1–0.2‰; this would have little chance of being detected against the 'noise' of analytical error and dietary variation (but see below Chapter 9.2.5).

The only site with a significant difference in $\delta^{13}C$ between males and females is Ensisheim. There is no overall difference in $\delta^{15}N$. There is perhaps a group of older males with higher $\delta^{13}C$ (though not necessarily $\delta^{15}N$) values (Chapter 8.8.3). Unfortunately we do not have enough data from other sites in the region to see whether this is an isolated instance, and it would be an interesting avenue for future research.

Human age differences. Comparisons between age categories are severely limited by sample size, once sex is accounted for. At a few sites (Polgár-Ferenci-hát, Vedrovice, Nitra and Ensisheim) we observed possible differences in isotope values between age groups or trends with age. These patterns are not widely repeated, and we are reluctant to assign much meaning to them – some patterns might appear merely by chance in such a large dataset. The humans in this study have been aged by several different workers using several different ageing schemes (Chapter 2.5) and this makes combining the age data from different sites problematic. Using data from all the sites and broad age categories (infant, child, adolescent, adult, old adult >45–50 years), the 2-level model (see Appendix C) shows that infants (<2 years) have $\delta^{15}N$ values elevated by 2–3‰ compared to adults, as would be expected because of the higher trophic level of breast-feeding infants, while the other age groups do not differ significantly. To look for more subtle post-infancy effects (e.g. a possible reduction in $\delta^{15}N$ during periods of rapid growth: reviewed by Waters-Rist and Katzenberg 2010) we used data from a subset of sites where it was possible to refine the age groupings consistently (child, adolescent, and four adult age categories). The 2-level model (Appendix C) shows that including age significantly improved the fit of the model; $\delta^{15}N$ of adolescents was 0.34% lower than the mean ($p<0.01$). However, the effect was no longer significant if Vedrovice was omitted, so, even more than the possible physiological effect of pregnancy/lactation on $\delta^{15}N$, the growth effect has proved elusive in the overall data.

We were also able to check for the effect of age and sex together. There were small but statistically significant differences of 0.20‰ in $\delta^{15}N$ between males and females, as discussed above, and of 0.08‰ in $\delta^{13}C$ (Appendix C). This is well within analytical error, and only detectable here because of the large amount of data and the ability to separate inter- and intra-site variances, but is of the right size and direction for a trophic-level effect – one would expect a change of about 1‰ in $\delta^{13}C$ for a change of 3–4‰ in $\delta^{15}N$, other things being equal. To put this in proportion, the effect is about one-tenth the size of the 'suckling effect' seen in infants. The result is consistent with the idea that

Table 9.4. Sites with isotope values that are unusual, even when overall geographic or climatic trends are accounted for.

Site	Species	Isotope value	Description
Mulhouse-Est	Human	$\delta^{15}N$	High after elevation accounted for
Bischoffsheim	Cattle	$\delta^{13}C$	Very low after climate accounted for; omitted from Δ calculation
		$\delta^{15}N$	Low after elevation accounted for
Vendenheim	Human	$\delta^{15}N$	High after elevation accounted for
Schwetzingen	Human	$\delta^{13}C$	High after climate accounted for; no fauna available for comparison
		$\delta^{15}N$	Low after elevation accounted for; no fauna available for comparison
Heilbronn-Neckargartach	Cattle, Sheep	$\delta^{15}N$	Very high after climate accounted for; omitted from Δ calculation
Rutzing	Cattle, Sheep	$\delta^{13}C$	Low in relation to longitude, but generally accounted for by climatic (rainfall) factors
Balatonszárszó	Cattle	$\delta^{13}C$	High after climate accounted for. One group of cattle particularly high, possibly reflecting a small contribution of C4 grazing
Nitra	Human	$\delta^{13}C$	Low after climate accounted for
Polgár	Cattle, Sheep	$\delta^{13}C$	Not unusual for longitude, but consistently high in relation to climatic factors
		$\delta^{15}N$	Consistently high when geographic/climate factors taken into account, though not always statistically significant (also for pig)

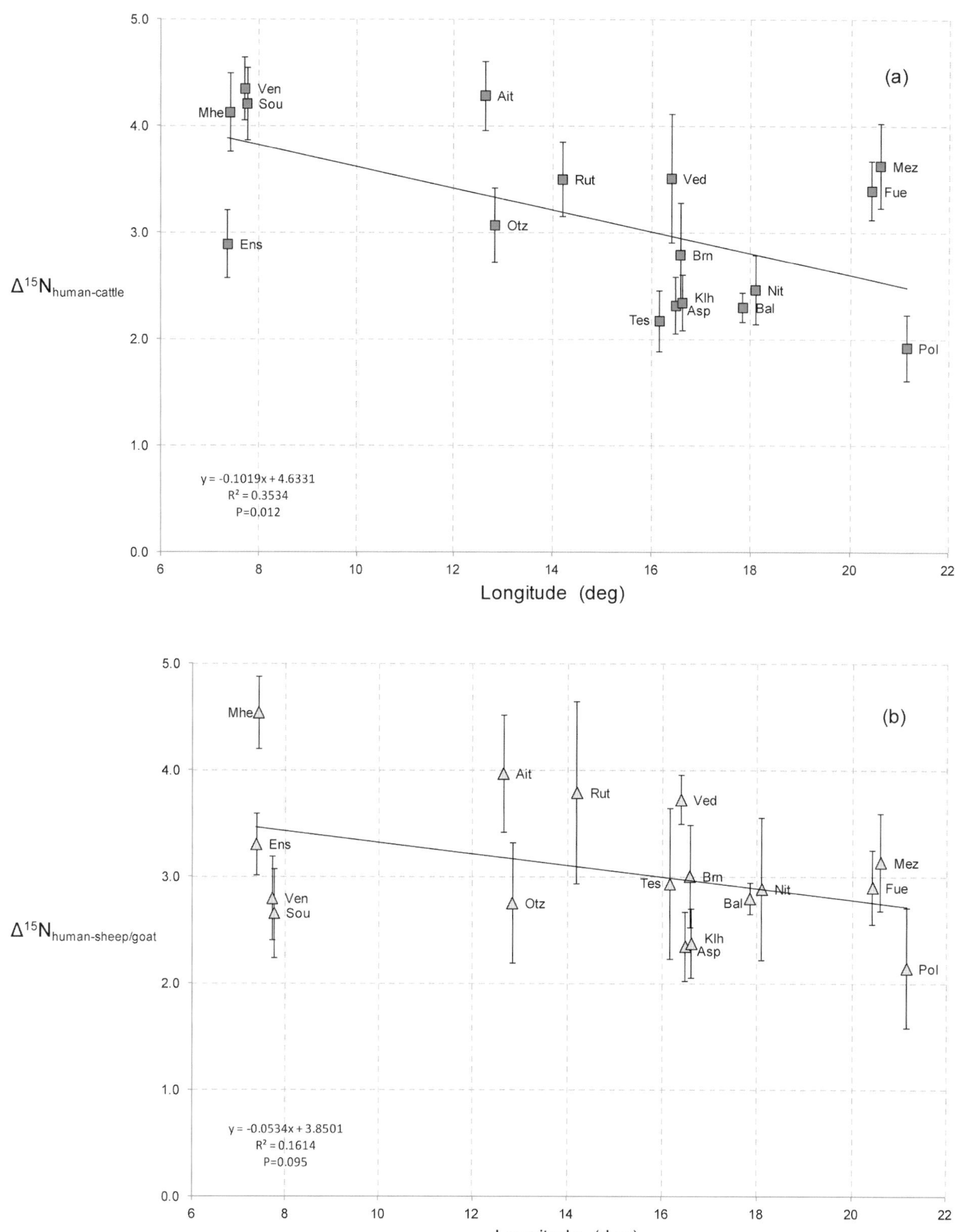

Fig. 9.5. (continued over next page) Difference between human and faunal $\delta^{15}N$ ($\Delta^{15}N_{human\text{-}faunal\ species}$) for a) cattle, b) sheep/goat and c) pig, at each site. The error bars show the quadratically combined standard errors for the human and faunal averages. Where faunal data were not available or insufficient for a particular site, faunal data from a comparable nearby site were used to calculate Δ; this applies to Mulhouse-Est, Vendenheim, Souffelweyersheim, Aiterhofen, Otzing, Kleinhadersdorf, Asparn, Nitra and Mezőkövesd; details are given in relevant regional chapters. There were too few human values from Lerchenhaid to make the comparison worthwhile, and no sufficiently comparable faunal data to calculate $\Delta^{15}N_{human\text{-}faunal\ species}$ for Schwetzingen. Site abbreviations as in Fig. 9.2.

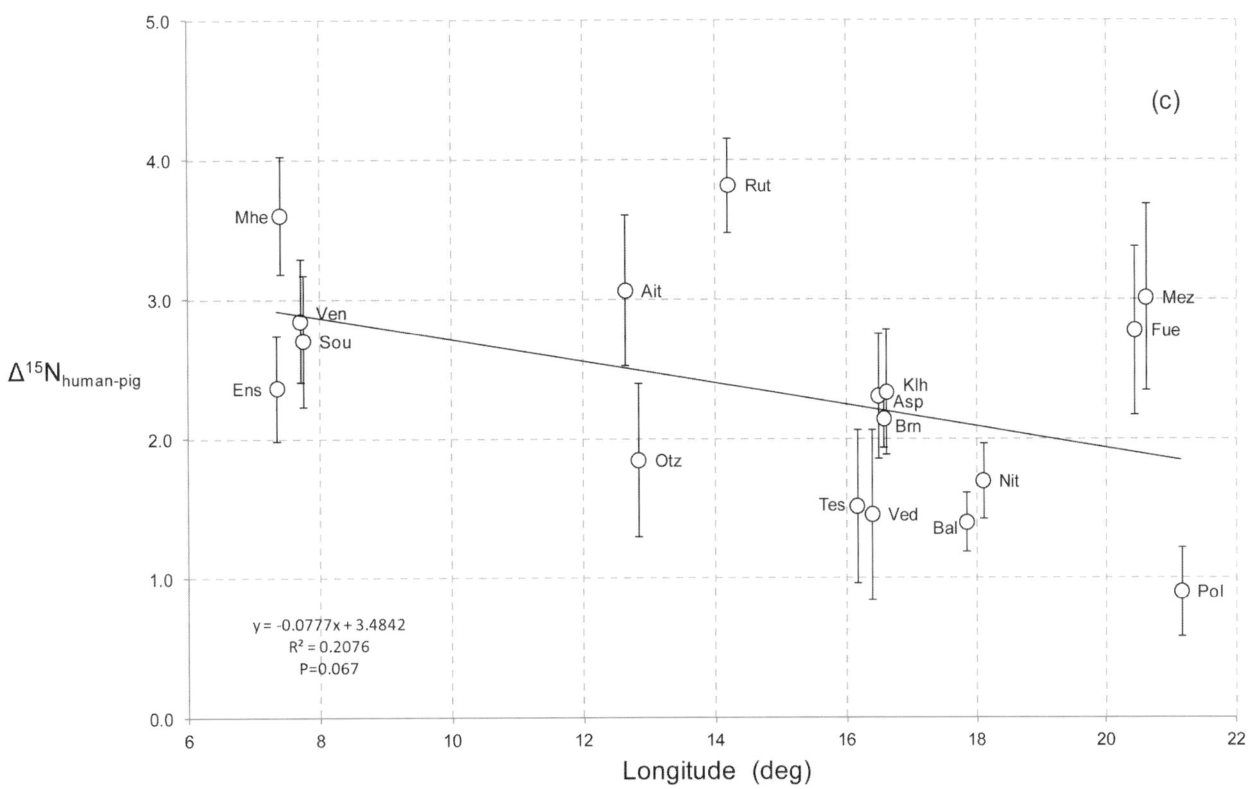

males had, on average, a slightly higher proportion of animal protein in their diets than females.

Using the whole adult dataset and two broad age categories (approximately 20–45 and over 45 years), there was no significant effect of age on $\delta^{15}N$, but $\delta^{13}C$ was very slightly higher in the older age category, by 0.06‰ (this is not a result of co-variation of age with sex, which is already accounted for in this model). With the smaller dataset and more refined age groups (young, middle, older adults, and >45 years), there was again no significant effect of age on $\delta^{15}N$, and $\delta^{13}C$ of the oldest age group was significantly higher than that of young adults by 0.11‰ in the oldest age group. This is hard to account for in terms of a dietary difference, because there is no consistent change in $\delta^{15}N$, but could perhaps reflect sourcing of dietary protein from more open areas – either from crops or from animals grazing or receiving fodder from these areas. While one would not wish to make too much of such small differences unless they are confirmed by further research, such effects could reflect the social patterning of landscape use as discussed by Bogaard (2011).

9.2.5 Interpretation of the collagen stable isotope patterns

First, we discuss the trends in isotope variation we have found. We assume that the trends for fauna simply reflect the trends for the plants they eat (while humans, of course, eat the animals as well as the plants) and note that different domesticated species may feed in different places or habitats (reflecting husbandry/human control), thus including different (proportions of) habitat components in the diet (for example meadow, forest or upland areas). This may tend to isotopically different diets – and so would tend to work against a perfect inter-species correlation.

For carbon, the biggest isotope fractionation is during C3 photosynthesis, which affects all subsequent products. The consumption of starch and protein will register more subtle isotopic redistributions which may occur as different resources within the plant are mobilised during the seasons, but these are unlikely to be manifested in the bulk collagen measurements made here. On the other hand, photosynthetic variation is well understood theoretically, and confirmed by numerous experiments and observations (Chapter 2.2.1; Farquhar *et al.* 1982; Körner *et al.* 1991). The main influences are water stress (in controlling both water loss and CO_2 uptake through stomatal performance), and the level of photosynthesis and atmospheric CO_2 provision. Reconciling field observations with specific climatic change is not straightforward; there is an abundant literature generally focusing on drier agronomic regimes where effects are more noticeable, which is not very relevant to the climate regimes encountered here. This issue is expanded above (Chapter 9.2.1). Actually it has become apparent that isotopic signals from animals can show reduced biological noise compared to direct observations on plants (Bump *et al.* 2007).

It is quite difficult to compare our results with published measurements; we give an account of this comparison above (Chapter 9.2.1). Essentially, for carbon, the differences we find are similar to, but perhaps a little smaller, than those

Table 9.5. The human-faunal difference in (a) $\delta^{15}N$ ($\Delta^{15}N_{human-faunal\ species}$) and (b) $\delta^{13}C$ ($\Delta^{13}C_{human-faunal\ species}$) for each site (or pair of compared sites), for each species.
Because of low numbers of humans or fauna, the comparisons between sites in italics were considered unreliable and were not included in the analysis. The errors (SE) were calculated as e.g. $\sqrt{((\text{Standard Error}_{\delta 15N\ human})^2 + (\text{Standard Error}_{\delta 15N\ faunal\ species})^2)}$ for each comparison. Sites are in order of longitude from west to east.

Mulhouse-Est	Ensisheim	4.1	0.37	4.5	0.34	3.6	0.42
Vendenheim	Bischoffsheim	4.3	0.29	2.8	0.39	2.8	0.44
Souffelweyersheim	Bischoffsheim	4.2	0.33	2.7	0.42	2.7	0.47
Aiterhofen	*Aiterhofen*	2.6	0.55			3.0	1.88
Aiterhofen	Lerchenhaid	4.3	0.32	4.0	0.55	3.1	0.54
Otzing	Lerchenhaid	3.1	0.35	2.8	0.56	1.8	0.55
Rutzing	Rutzing	3.5	0.35	3.8	0.85	3.8	0.34
Těšetice	Těšetice	2.2	0.28	2.9	0.71	1.5	0.55
Vedrovice	Vedrovice	3.5	0.61	3.7	0.23	1.5	0.61
Asparn	*Asparn*	2.6	0.09	1.5	0.70	3.3	0.09
Asparn	Gnadendorf	2.3	0.26	2.3	0.33	2.3	0.45
Brno	Brno	2.8	0.48	3.0	0.48	2.1	0.20
Kleinhadersdorf	Gnadendorf	2.3	0.26	2.4	0.32	2.3	0.45
Balatonszárszó	Balatonszárszó	2.3	0.14	2.8	0.15	1.4	0.21
Nitra	Blatné	2.5	0.33	2.9	0.67	1.7	0.27
Füzesabony	Füzesabony	3.4	0.27	2.9	0.35	2.8	0.60
Mezőkövesd	Füzesabony	3.6	0.40	3.1	0.45	3.0	0.67
Polgár-Ferenci-hát	Polgár-Ferenci-hát	1.9	0.31	2.1	0.56	0.9	0.32
(b) $\delta^{13}C$		$\Delta^{13}C$	SE	$\Delta^{13}C$	SE	$\Delta^{13}C$	SE
Ensisheim	Ensisheim	1.5	0.26	0.4	0.19	0.3	0.08
Mulhouse-Est	Ensisheim	1.4	0.27	0.3	0.20	0.2	0.09
Vendenheim	Bischoffsheim	2.8	0.27	0.7	0.17	0.6	0.09
Souffelweyersheim	Bischoffsheim	2.5	0.32	0.4	0.23	0.3	0.19
Aiterhofen	*Aiterhofen*	0.4	0.27			0.3	0.39
Aiterhofen	Lerchenhaid	0.7	0.21	0.2	0.35	0.4	0.10
Otzing	Lerchenhaid	1.0	0.23	0.5	0.36	0.7	0.13
Rutzing	Rutzing	1.3	0.30	0.6	0.35	0.2	0.21
Těšetice	Těšetice	0.9	0.14	0.5	0.17	0.7	0.18
(a) $\delta^{15}N$		**Human-Cattle**		**Human-Sheep/goat**		**Human-Pig**	
Humans from:	**Fauna from:**	$\Delta^{15}N$	SE	$\Delta^{15}N$	SE	$\Delta^{15}N$	SE
Ensisheim	Ensisheim	2.9	0.32	3.3	0.29	2.4	0.38
Mulhouse-Est	Ensisheim	4.1	0.37	4.5	0.34	3.6	0.42
Vendenheim	Bischoffsheim	4.3	0.29	2.8	0.39	2.8	0.44
Souffelweyersheim	Bischoffsheim	4.2	0.33	2.7	0.42	2.7	0.47
Aiterhofen	*Aiterhofen*	2.6	0.55			3.0	1.88
Aiterhofen	Lerchenhaid	4.3	0.32	4.0	0.55	3.1	0.54
Otzing	Lerchenhaid	3.1	0.35	2.8	0.56	1.8	0.55
Rutzing	Rutzing	3.5	0.35	3.8	0.85	3.8	0.34
Těšetice	Těšetice	2.2	0.28	2.9	0.71	1.5	0.55
Vedrovice	Vedrovice	3.5	0.61	3.7	0.23	1.5	0.61
Asparn	*Asparn*	2.6	0.09	1.5	0.70	3.3	0.09
Asparn	Gnadendorf	2.3	0.26	2.3	0.33	2.3	0.45
Brno	Brno	2.8	0.48	3.0	0.48	2.1	0.20
Kleinhadersdorf	Gnadendorf	2.3	0.26	2.4	0.32	2.3	0.45
Balatonszárszó	Balatonszárszó	2.3	0.14	2.8	0.15	1.4	0.21
Nitra	Blatné	2.5	0.33	2.9	0.67	1.7	0.27
Füzesabony	Füzesabony	3.4	0.27	2.9	0.35	2.8	0.60
Mezőkövesd	Füzesabony	3.6	0.40	3.1	0.45	3.0	0.67
Polgár-Ferenci-hát	Polgár-Ferenci-hát	1.9	0.31	2.1	0.56	0.9	0.32
(b) $\delta^{13}C$		$\Delta^{13}C$	SE	$\Delta^{13}C$	SE	$\Delta^{13}C$	SE

Table 9.6. Comparison of δ¹⁵N and δ¹³C of males and females at the sites in this study. The sites in italics yielded too few sexed individuals for statistical comparison to be meaningful. Mezőkövesd has been omitted because there were no sexed individuals. Data from Vedrovice includes the individuals from the Široká u lesa cemetery only. Sites are in order of longitude from west to east.

δ^{15}N	**Female**			**Male**			
Site	**δ^{15}N**	**SD**	**n**	**δ^{15}N**	**SD**	**n**	**P**
Ensisheim	9.2	0.39	15	9.5	0.59	17	NS
Mulhouse-Est	10.6	0.59	6	10.6		1	
Vendenheim	10.0	1.53	2	10.9	0.30	7	
Souffelweyersheim	10.3	0.77	3	10.6	0.95	2	
Schwetzingen	8.9	0.64	52	9.0	0.42	43	NS
Aiterhofen	9.8	0.33	20	9.9	0.42	27	NS
Otzing	8.5	0.34	5			0	
Rutzing	9.3	0.88	3	9.7	0.21	6	
Těšetice	9.3	0.23	2	8.8	0.28	3	
Vedrovice (this study)	9.2	0.27	12	9.4	0.30	3	NS
Vedrovice (combined with data from M.P. Richards *et al.* 2008)	9.5	0.43	34	9.9	0.46	19	0.001***
Asparn	9.1	0.28	6	9.6	0.42	17	0.021*
Brno			0	10.1	0.30	4	
Kleinhadersdorf	9.5	0.41	10	9.6	0.57	16	NS
Balatonszárszó	9.5	0.53	16	9.6	0.37	14	NS
Nitra	10.2	0.37	26	10.5	0.39	14	0.025*
Füzesabony	10.2	0.32	3	10.7	0.33	3	
Polgár-Ferenci-hát	10.3	0.57	16	10.3	0.65	17	NS
δ^{13}C	**Female**			**Male**			
Site	**δ^{13}C**	**SD**	**n**	**δ^{13}C**	**SD**	**n**	**P**
Ensisheim	−20.3	0.19	15	−20.1	0.19	17	0.036*
Mulhouse-Est	−20.3	0.14	6	−20.2		1	
Vendenheim	−20.2	0.15	2	−20.1	0.20	7	
Souffelweyersheim	−20.6	0.37	3	−20.2	0.22	2	
Schwetzingen	−20.2	0.19	52	−20.1	0.25	43	NS
Aiterhofen	−20.4	0.23	20	−20.4	0.27	27	
Otzing	−20.1	0.25	5			0	
Rutzing	−20.5	0.23	3	−20.5	0.31	6	
Těšetice	−19.3	0.36	2	−19.4	0.12	3	
Vedrovice (this study)	−19.7	0.29	12	−19.7	0.25	3	
Vedrovice (combined with data from M.P. Richards *et al.* 2008)	−19.7	0.26	34	−19.6	0.28	19	NS
Asparn	−19.6	0.20	6	−19.6	0.11	17	
Brno			0	−19.7	0.19	4	
Kleinhadersdorf	−19.8	0.38	10	−19.8	0.23	16	NS
Balatonszárszó	−19.9	0.24	16	−19.9	0.26	14	NS
Nitra	−20.2	0.26	26	−20.1	0.23	14	
Füzesabony	−19.8	0.05	3	−20.0	0.29	3	
Polgár-Ferenci-hát	−20.0	0.32	16	−19.9	0.31	17	NS

reported on plants and attributed to climatic effects. The magnitude of the effects which we see are consistent with relevant observations. Therefore, we believe the overall geographical trend which we see for carbon is adequately explained as a reasonably well understood response of plants to climate. However, the trend for cattle is about twice as large, and presumably reflects some specific aspect of the isotopes of plants eaten by cattle. An obvious, but untested, hypothesis is that such plants show an additional depletion in $\delta^{13}C$ due to a 'canopy effect', potentially suggesting a more forested environment in the Alsace region, or perhaps even a different composition of the forest (Kreuz 1990, 196–7), with tree species which let less light through to the forest floor.

We see a far less clear correlation between climate and nitrogen isotopes. This is not surprising, in that plant nitrogen isotope values depend on many more factors than is the case for carbon. Hot dry environments are conducive to ammonia loss (increasing the soil $\delta^{15}N$ content), while wet environments are liable to promote bacterially produced denitrification, which also leads to higher $\delta^{15}N$ values. The more nitrogen is recycled in soils, the more likely it is to increase in $\delta^{15}N$ as ^{14}N-rich small molecules are lost from the immediate system, so that agronomic history is also an important influence. We note that there is nevertheless a good correlation of all the faunal $\delta^{15}N$ values both between species (Fig. 9.2; Table 9.2) and with altitude (altitude is at least as good a predictor as climate), so there is presumably some over-riding environmental influence. As far as climate goes, summer temperature and precipitation seem to be more important than winter temperature and precipitation. Possibly, whatever processes go on in soils that affect plant $\delta^{15}N$ values, they are more active in summer and hence are more influenced by summer climate.

The domesticated fauna and their husbandry

The fact that the faunal carbon isotopic differences between sites can be accounted for almost entirely in terms of climatic influences on the plants which they consume implies a general uniformity of biological environment. This view is reinforced by the similar, if weaker, uniformity of response for nitrogen isotopes – even if there is no clear explanation. However, a 'uniform approach' is only meaningful when compared to alternatives; within our dataset we do have indications that not everything was managed in the same way (relative to the plant isotopic background). For example, the Heilbronn faunal $\delta^{15}N$ values suggest that the cattle and sheep there were being treated quite differently from other sites (the two pigs analysed were 'normal'), even if we cannot presently suggest in what way, or were exploiting a local environment with considerably higher $\delta^{15}N$ values than usual. We have already mentioned the Rhine catchment cattle, which may plausibly have enjoyed a more forested environment, whose ^{13}C-depleted values may have been incorporated through leaf fodder, or summer grazing.

We note that the extreme case of Bischoffsheim, which is some 30 km from the comparison cemeteries of Vendenheim and Souffelweyersheim, is at the western edge of the Rhine valley, with access to major forested areas in the Vosges. In any case, sheep were certainly not sharing the same environment. The cattle at Balatonszárszó have an unusual spread in $\delta^{13}C$, including quite enriched values. This may be due to the proximity of Lake Balaton (and, for example, water-based forage), or possibly to the presence of wild C4 plants in the herbage. In fact, as the discussion of outliers suggests, several sites which differ from the main body of data can now be considered in much more detail for possible underlying causes. But this serves to underline our view, based on the relationships between the faunal measurements, that the management of domestic animals was strikingly similar across the LBK sites studied here.

The occurrence of animals at LBK sites is discussed in Chapter 1. Cattle were usually the most common domestic animal and as they were also the largest were probably the major suppliers of animal protein in human diets. Age profiles suggest that they were not managed as specialised dairy herds, though they were likely to have supplied milk (Salque *et al.* 2012a; 2012b) as well as meat, and this most likely applies to sheep/goats also. Pigs differ from cattle and sheep/goats in their more omnivorous diet, and in being managed essentially for meat production. Cattle are generally thought of as more suited to woodland than sheep, and pigs might either range extensively, using woodland and other 'outfield' resources, or be more closely associated with settlements, feeding on anthropogenic waste. As Bogaard (2011) states, all three species would be important in maintaining fertility in intensively cultivated garden plots via manuring, effectively importing nutrients (especially nitrogen) from uncultivated areas, as well as recycling crop, food and other waste. They would also be important in preventing forest regeneration, maintaining open areas and possibly contributing to clearance. Sheep may also have played a role in cereal cultivation, helping to prevent tillering and lodging. Thus, the three species might use the landscape around a farming settlement in different ways, potentially reflected in their $\delta^{13}C$ and $\delta^{15}N$ values.

Grazing or browsing in shaded areas, particularly closed-canopy woodland, or fodder derived from such areas, would be likely to lower $\delta^{13}C$ values compared to more open environments (Drucker *et al.* 2008). Feeding (or foddering) on crop wastes, or on land close to or within intensively manured plots or the settlement area would be likely to raise $\delta^{15}N$ values in comparison to the wider environment. Complicating factors might be feeding on fungi, which have higher $\delta^{13}C$ values than plants (this might apply to pigs; Hamilton *et al.* 2009), or on legumes which have lower $\delta^{15}N$ than other plants (Fraser *et al.* 2011). There may well also have been different patterns of animal husbandry used within a settlement, either over time or contemporaneously (as shown for crop management at Vaihingen; Bogaard *et al.* 2011), which could obscure isotope patterning or show up as groupings within the results.

Overall, cattle consistently have similar $\delta^{15}N$ values to sheep/goats but lower $\delta^{13}C$ values, particularly towards the west (Fig. 9.3a, d; model in Appendix C). This fits well with a similar exposure to agricultural/settlement environments, but a greater emphasis on feeding in (or fodder from) shadier woodland environments for cattle. The occasional measurements from red deer (*Cervus elaphus*) at Aiterhofen, Rutzing and Balatonszárszó support this interpretation, being lower in both $\delta^{13}C$ and $\delta^{15}N$, presumably using more resources from the forest and fewer from the agricultural landscape than cattle. At Bischoffsheim, Ensisheim, Lerchenhaid and Rutzing there seems to be a distinct group of cattle with particularly low $\delta^{13}C$ values, suggesting different husbandry regimes within these sites, including greater or lesser use of woodland resources. Balasse *et al.* (2012) have shown that further north-west, at Neolithic Bercy (France), both cattle and sheep (but only some individuals) fed on a ^{13}C-depleted resource in winter, potentially leafy fodder. It is noticeable that this tendency to greater use of forest resources is commoner towards the west. There might be an ecological explanation in terms of a more forested landscape, or a milder, more 'Atlantic' climate with correspondingly greater availability of winter graze or browse. Equally, it could reflect a different attitude towards the use of forests and a greater willingness to exploit them; in this context, the higher percentages of wild game seen at some sites in Bavaria and Alsace (Chapter 1) are interesting. At Balatonszárszó there is a distinct group of cattle with high $\delta^{13}C$ values, discussed above.

Pig $\delta^{13}C$ values are overall slightly lower than those of sheep/goats (Fig. 9.3b, e; model in Appendix C), with no particular east–west patterning. This could suggest slightly more emphasis on forest resources (though less than for cattle), but this interpretation is complicated by the possibility that for pigs these would include fungi. At British Neolithic sites, pigs typically have high $\delta^{13}C$ and low $\delta^{15}N$ values compared to the herbivores, which has been attributed to free-range feeding in woodland and the consumption of large quantities of fungi (Hamilton *et al.* 2009). This is the opposite of the pattern seen in the LBK, where pig $\delta^{15}N$ values are on average distinctly higher (by 0.8–0.9‰) than those of the herbivores, particularly towards the east. This strongly suggests that the LBK pigs were more closely linked to settlements and that the 'village pig' model of feeding is more appropriate. While there is a greater difference between pig and cattle $\delta^{13}C$ towards the west (Fig. 9.3c), this seems to be more because of low cattle $\delta^{13}C$ values than any change in pig values; whatever reasons led to greater use of forest by cattle do not seem to apply to pigs – unless feeding on fungi was to some extent acting in the opposite direction to the canopy effect for pigs. It should be noted, however, that far fewer pigs than cattle were sampled for this study, and this may reduce our ability to detect subtle changes, particularly for a species like the pig with a potentially variable diet. It would be very interesting to look at sites further to the west and north to see where and when the pattern seen in the British Neolithic appears, and whether there is any relationship with the genetic changes that seem to have occurred around the same time (Larson *et al.* 2007).

The patterning of faunal isotopes reflects local ecological relationships between agriculture, animal husbandry and the environment, and is not necessarily constant over space and time. This also implies that faunal species cannot be treated as equivalent and interchangeable when deriving a baseline for human dietary studies. Comparisons between sites need to take account of geographic variation as well as the relatively large within-site variation (as discussed above). For all these reasons, larger and more comprehensive faunal samples should be a priority in future isotopic work.

The rather consistent pattern of relationships between the isotopes of the major domestic species underlines a general uniformity in animal husbandry regimes and use of the environment over this 1200 km range. The animals were integrated into crop management regimes (Bogaard 2011) and major changes in animal husbandry would affect the system as a whole. There is nevertheless an east–west trend towards greater use of forest resources, seen particularly in cattle, and hints of variation in management both within and between sites.

Human diet

If humans ate the meat (and/or milk, as isotopically milk and its products are indistinguishable from meat) from the sampled fauna, as well as plants isotopically similar to those consumed by the fauna, then we would expect a very close correlation with the faunal isotopic values. In fact the correlation is not as close as between the domesticated animals (Table 9.2), which suggests elements of human diet outside that of the domesticated fauna, and so outside what we have been able to measure. We therefore have had to speculate as systematically as possible as to what differences in the diet may account for human-faunal differences. We have done this through devising explicit models and comparing their outputs with what we do measure (see below).

But before trying to 'explain' human isotopic values through diet, we re-emphasise how similar the human isotopic values are throughout the LBK sites. Half of the variability observed can be attributed to climatic differences which have influenced the values of the meat/milk (and presumably plants), leaving very little scope for local differences. The one major regional difference, which we believe to be a trend (from west to east, or, what is closely similar, between the Rhine and Danube catchments) is the difference in $\delta^{13}C$ and $\delta^{15}N$ between humans and fauna at the same (or proximate) site. Our modelling addresses this in terms of different dietary proportions and/or different agricultural practices between the two regional extremes. Nevertheless, the differences are small and trend over a large area, and the overall impression remains one of dietary consistency throughout the LBK territory.

Within each site there is also a remarkable consistency of isotopic values, exemplified with average standard deviations of 0.23‰ and 0.48‰ for $\delta^{13}C$ and $\delta^{15}N$ respectively. As with the occasional outlying site, there are occasional outlying individuals (documented in the

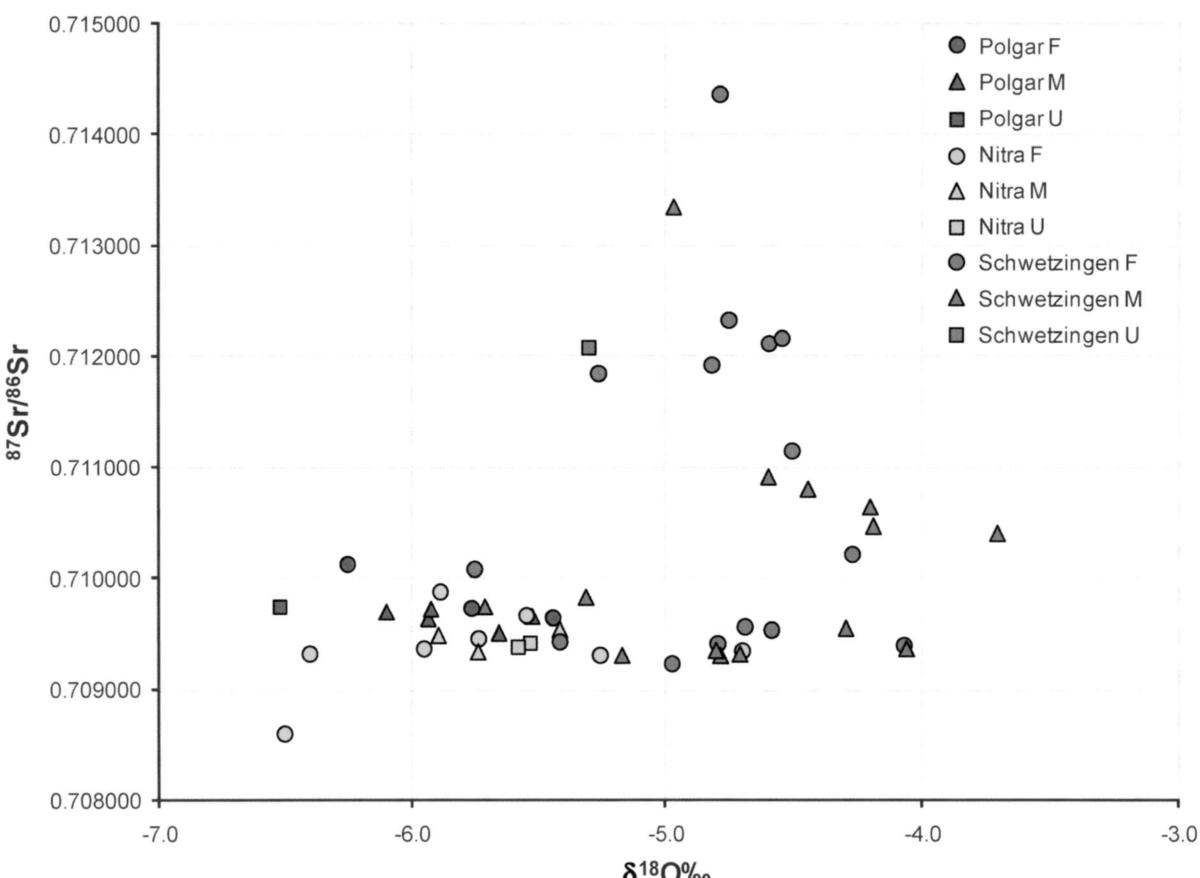

Fig. 9.6. The $^{87}Sr/^{86}Sr$ ratios in dental enamel of humans from Polgár-Ferenci-hát, Nitra and Schwetzingen plotted against their $\delta^{18}O$ values. Circles show females, triangles show males and squares show unsexed individuals.

Table 9.7. Evaluation of human collagen $\delta^{13}C$ and $\delta^{15}N$ for a range of putative diets. Figures in bold are the primary variables to generate modelled values. The isotope enrichments in the bottom section of the table were used to derive table values and calculate human values.

Diet fraction	Diet item	$\delta^{13}C$ value	$\delta^{15}N$ value	
WEST				
-	[human	−20.25	10]	
?	cattle	−22	6.5	
?	sheep	−20.7	6	
?	pig	−21	7	
?	fish	*−19*	*11*	*= estimate (local)*
?	pulses	*−23*	*1*	*= estimate (local)*
?	cereal	−24.5	4.5	= derived from 'forage'
-	[forage	−24	3.5]	= derived from faunal collagen
EAST				
-	[human	−19.7	10.5]	
?	cattle	−19.9	8	
?	sheep	−19.8	8	
?	pig	−20.2	8.5	
?	fish	*−19*	*11*	*= estimate (local)*
?	pulses	*−23*	*1*	*= estimate (local)*
?	cereal	−24	5	= derived from 'forage'
-	[forage	−23	4.5]	= derived from faunal collagen
Isotope enrichments (Δs)				
collagen human – fauna		**1.5**	**4 or 4.5**	estimates in literature
human – cereal		**4–5**	**4 or 4.5**	estimates in literature
animal – forage		3	3	estimates in literature
cereal – forage		**−1–1**	**1,0.5, 0**	estimates in literature
manured cereal – cereal		0	**0, 0.5, 1**	estimates in literature

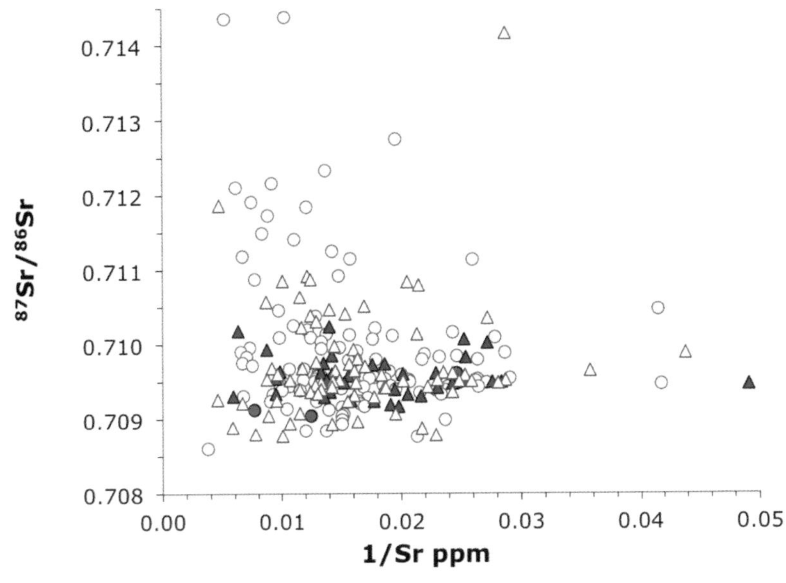

Fig. 9.7. $^{87}Sr/^{86}Sr$ versus 1/Sr ppm from adult individuals at Schwetzingen, Nitra, Aiterhofen, Kleinhadersdorf, Ensisheim and Souffelweyersheim. Circles show adult females, triangles show adult males. Filled symbols denote burial with an adze. From Bentley et al. *(2012, 9329).*

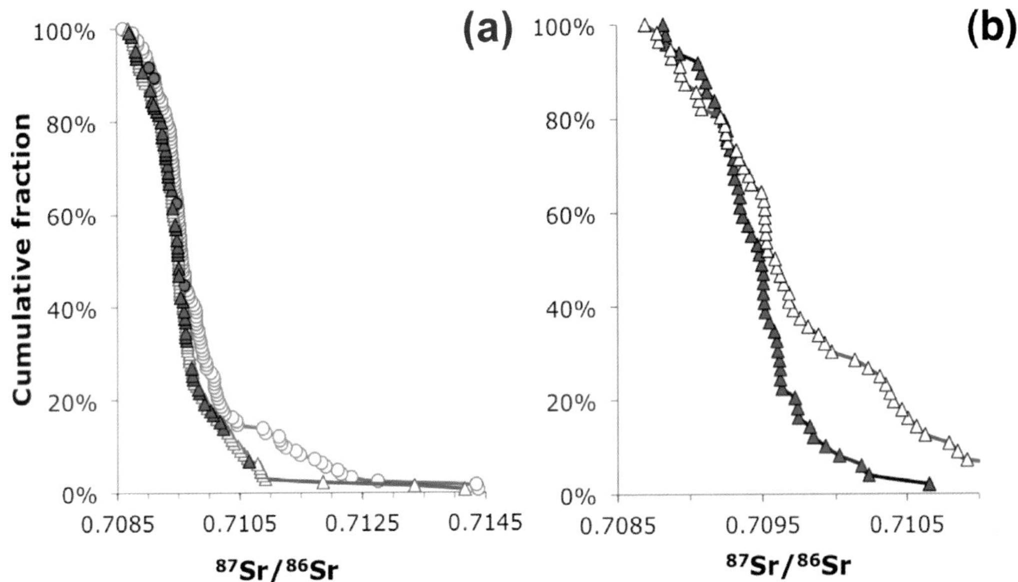

Fig. 9.8. Cumulative distribution plots of $^{87}Sr/^{86}Sr$ in human enamel from sampled LBK individuals at Schwetzingen, Nitra, Aiterhofen, Kleinhadersdorf, Ensisheim and Souffelweyersheim. a) Comparison of male (blue triangles) and female (red circles) ratios. b) Comparison of ratios for males with polished stone tools (blue triangles) and those without (white triangles). From Bentley et al. *(2012, 9329).*

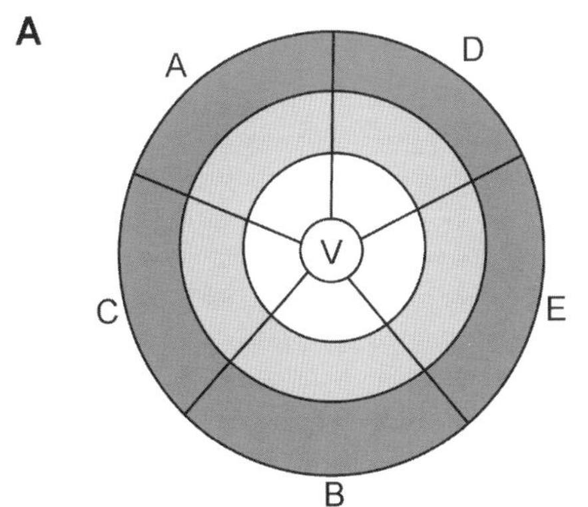

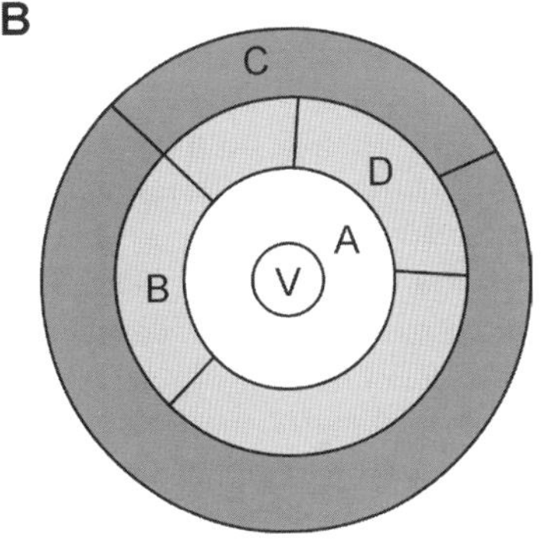

Fig. 9.9. Models of arable land distribution around Vaihingen. Left: with each clan having comparable access to all areas. Right: with some clans having preferential access to the more intensively managed 'infield' zone. After Bogaard et al. *(2011, 408).*

regional chapters), whose occurrence serves to emphasise the overall consistency. Where potential food items seem to have differed significantly in isotope value (e.g. fish, pig, and plants in nitrogen; cattle, and maybe fish, in carbon), there does not seem to have been much habitual dietary difference between the individuals of each community as represented by the sampled cemeteries. One difference is that between males and females, which for three sites is about 0.4‰ in δ^{15}N, and for another three sites is less than 0.2‰. We have already shown that there is a general small difference throughout the sampled LBK sites and the larger male-female difference is interpreted as a dietary difference, which is most simply explained as a substantially greater (rather than different) animal protein proportion in the diet of males. (Quantitatively, modelling suggests an increase of about 10%; the figures are consistent with the slight overall difference between males and females discussed in Chapter 9.2.5). The fact that the sites of Nitra, Asparn and Vedrovice are comparatively close to each other (while no other nearby site has provided an adequate sample for testing for statistical significance) is suggestive of a specifically, though not uniquely, local practice, with the diet of adult males containing a higher proportion of meat. We note that other sites, to both west and east, provide evidence of no such distinction.

Modelling the human diet. It is simple to construct a spreadsheet to evaluate the expected human δ^{13}C and δ^{15}N values, based on (a) selected isotope values of the diet (of which many have to be estimated); and (b) a set of assumed values for the various isotope enrichments involved in the food chain and subsequent metabolism. This amounts to taking a closer look at the 'trophic level effect', i.e. the isotopic enrichment between consumer and consumed. Given the uncertainties in the variables, there is a wide range of inter-dependent values which can predict (or rather retrodict) human values as measured. However, the exercise is worthwhile for several reasons. First, it clarifies the relative importance of different diets and the different isotopic relationships involved in understanding how isotopic values are achieved. Secondly, there are two consistency demands, which are relatively unusual in such modelling, which help to define matters. These are, that the same dietary composition can be applied equally to carbon as well as nitrogen (we believe we have adequately precise data for carbon to do this); and that we can compare the diets between the western (Rhine basin) and eastern (Danube basin) parts of our study area. Thirdly, it is useful to identify what dietary regimes are incompatible with the data.

The model used. This is a spreadsheet model where human collagen δ^{13}C and δ^{15}N for a range of putative diets are evaluated from measured data and assumed constants. The evaluation assumes the 'you are what you eat +X‰', as weighted for each dietary item. None of the dietary item values are exactly known; animal flesh and milk can, however, be estimated from our measurements, as can the animal forage, which is related to that of cereals. An additional set of unknowns is the degree of isotopic increase ('enrichment') at trophic levels, as well as between manured and unmanured crops. These are approximately known, so that only a small range needs to be investigated. Altogether there are far too many variables to explore the complete space thoroughly, but it is nevertheless possible to establish whether certain reasonable combinations of dietary composition and isotopic variable are consistent with what we observe. In fact the model is more constrained than might appear at first, or from experience of other models, since here we simultaneously aim for consistency with both δ^{13}C and δ^{15}N (and in many ways the δ^{13}C data appear rather more limiting for the model); also, we model both the western and eastern data sets, for which many of the variables logically should be chosen to be the same.

The input data are illustrated in Table 9.7; the figures in bold are the primary variables to generate modelled values. The model is 'run' by choosing a given dietary composition and selecting a choice of enrichment values. From this the human δ^{13}C and δ^{15}N can be calculated and compared with the measured values, aiming for agreement within 0.2‰.

Diets (or rather dietary ranges) can be found which are simultaneously compatible for δ^{13}C and δ^{15}N, for both east and west, using acceptable enrichment values. A main limit to the range of possible diet-enrichment combinations is due to δ^{13}C values; in the west, which apparently consumes more meat, based on δ^{15}N, the cattle collagen δ^{13}C is substantially less than that of humans, while in the east, with an apparent consumption of less meat, cattle collagen is almost equal to that of humans. The difference between collagen δ^{13}C of predator and prey (for an approximately 100% meat diet) is considered to be 1–1.5‰, although this value is not much discussed in the literature. The second main sensitivity is in the human δ^{15}N 'enrichment' value (Δ) selected; we examine models with Δ=4 and 4.5‰, the two values inevitably leading to fairly different diets, or similar diets but with different compensating effects (such as the enrichment due to manuring).

The main issues to be addressed are the following (and including an east–west comparison):

a) The percentage of meat/dairy consumed. We assume for the purposes here that cattle make up 50–75% of 'meat' in the diet (note that we are unable to distinguish meat from milk isotopically). While this may be an overestimation (Marciniak 2005), the alteration of the cattle/sheep/pig ratio would not make a large difference.
b) Whether we can say anything about the consumption of freshwater fish.
c) Whether we can say anything about the consumption of pulses.
d) Whether a manuring enrichment of cereal is necessary for the data to be consistent.

These questions are interwoven, nevertheless some tendencies are apparent.

Summarised results of modelling. a) West: The percentage of dietary protein which is animal-based is in the region of 50% (assuming a small manuring enrichment). This could be reduced to 40% or so by the inclusion of 5% fish, but a higher fish contribution is hard to accommodate. Pulses are difficult to reconcile with both $\delta^{13}C$ and $\delta^{15}N$, even with more fish to compensate. If the human Δ for a full trophic level is taken to be 4 rather than 4.5‰, it is necessary to invoke greater levels of cereal manuring enrichment, but even so the percentage of meat protein tends to move towards 50–55%.

b) East: The diet which fits most comfortably with the data (if Δ=4.5 ‰) is meat protein=25%, pulse protein=5–10 %, no fish, and a modest level of manuring enrichment. Higher levels of enrichment would reduce the percentage of meat in the diet still further. For Δ=4‰, it is quite difficult to find a consistent model, due to the relatively low $\delta^{13}C$ of the humans; animal protein contribution is constrained by the $\delta^{13}C$ values, but a higher manuring enrichment, with animal protein still <35%, would be consistent.

These outcomes should be treated with caution – we have not considered errors in measurement and small differences may lead to different constraints; nor have we explored anything close to all possible combinations of diet and enrichment factor. There are a large number of estimated isotopic values. Therefore we cannot claim to have identified the diet. But the modelling exercise shows that a range of realistic Neolithic diet is consistent with both human and animal collagen, for both stable isotopes, for both eastern (the Danube basin) and western (the Rhine basin) regions, very likely most prominently in the proportion of animal-based resources consumed.

9.2.6 Oxygen stable isotopes

We carried out human enamel carbonate oxygen isotope analyses on a sample of teeth from three sites, Schwetzingen, Nitra and Polgár. The aim here was to observe the degree of homogeneity within each site, and to report the difference in $\delta^{18}O$ expected between sites receiving precipitation on either side of the Alps. These data are therefore useful primarily for exploring the potential of the method to provide additional information on human movement between areas characterised by different regimes.

The results are depicted in Fig. 9.6, as a plot of $\delta^{18}O$ versus $^{87}Sr/^{86}Sr$. The eastern sites are clearly distinct, with a difference of about 1‰. This is approximately expected from considerations of isotope fractionation during precipitation out of moving air masses, although such data have not, to our knowledge, been reported in archaeological humans for these regions. Schwetzingen has a larger spread in $\delta^{18}O$ values, and, as well, a large spread in $^{87}Sr/^{86}Sr$ ratios; evidently the assemblage contains numerous individuals with non-local (non-loessic) $^{87}Sr/^{86}Sr$ ratios, who probably had a non-loess-based contribution to the diet in childhood. Our results suggest that further $\delta^{18}O$ measurements might help resolve this. For example, spatially resolved enamel measurements within a tooth would help to reduce the variance in the population and emphasize signals due to geographic water differences. It might then be possible to tell if the non-loessic $^{87}Sr/^{86}Sr$ signals are associated with high altitude $\delta^{18}O$ signals. There is, perhaps, a hint of this in the plot, in that lower $\delta^{18}O$ values tend to have higher $^{87}Sr/^{86}Sr$ ratios (for correlation with the archaeological evidence see Chapter 7.7).

9.3 Strontium isotope analysis

In this monograph, our approach has been to view the $^{87}Sr/^{86}Sr$ data collectively, in order to group individuals into meaningful analytical units, and to look next for other corroborating evidence within those groups. In particular we have looked for significantly different sex ratios within isotopic groupings, and for whether different isotope groupings corresponded with individuals buried with a certain artefact, in a certain cardinal orientation or by body position. Our identification of potential distinct groups has been enhanced by plotting $^{87}Sr/^{86}Sr$ versus 1/Sr (Montgomery *et al.* 2007; 2010), and in combination with the carbon and nitrogen isotope data. In this respect, the data are fully integrated into their archaeological context.

Overall, the fact that we found meaningful diversity in strontium isotope signatures seems fortunate, given that our study region across Europe consists primarily of fairly homogeneous lowlands covered in loess, the widespread aeolian sediment favoured by LBK farmers (Fig. 9.1). Most of our sampled LBK sites from eastern France to southern Austria are in the loess belt, where similar soils are the basis for biologically-available $^{87}Sr/^{86}Sr$ ratios that range between 0.7085 and 0.710. Vedrovice, Těšetice and Brno (Chapter 4) are among the exceptions, as they each lie at the base of granitic mountain formations (the Bohemian Massif), where Precambrian contributions to the loess raise the resulting $^{87}Sr/^{86}Sr$ ratios in human skeletons.

$^{87}Sr/^{86}Sr$ ratios outside the range of 0.7085–0.710 suggest subsistence off these favoured loess areas. These non-loess areas could be in the lowlands as close as several kilometres from the settlement (Knipper 2012) but probably at least included uplands underlain by high-$^{87}Sr/^{86}Sr$ granitic rocks and associated sandstones. We stress, however, that we are not seeking the exact 'origin' of each individual, as what concerns us is community diversity, that is, to determine whether some individuals or groups used different soils than others for their subsistence activities or to source their diet.

These group-level patterns are more relevant than pinpointing 'origins' also because dietary $^{87}Sr/^{86}Sr$ ratios in Neolithic human enamel reflect a mixture of sources, including weathered sediments, streamwaters, and possibly manure added to recycled agricultural soils. The $^{87}Sr/^{86}Sr$ ratios which we have measured reflect bio-purification, the trophic level process whereby mammals reduce the variance of $^{87}Sr/^{86}Sr$ ratios through averaging effects. Neolithic farmers would have reduced this variance even further through cultivation practices, and early agricultural communities often yield a group-specific range of $^{87}Sr/^{86}Sr$ ratios much narrower than for their environmental sources (Chapter 2.4).

If, as we suspect, LBK subsistence took place upon specific plots of land that might have been used over

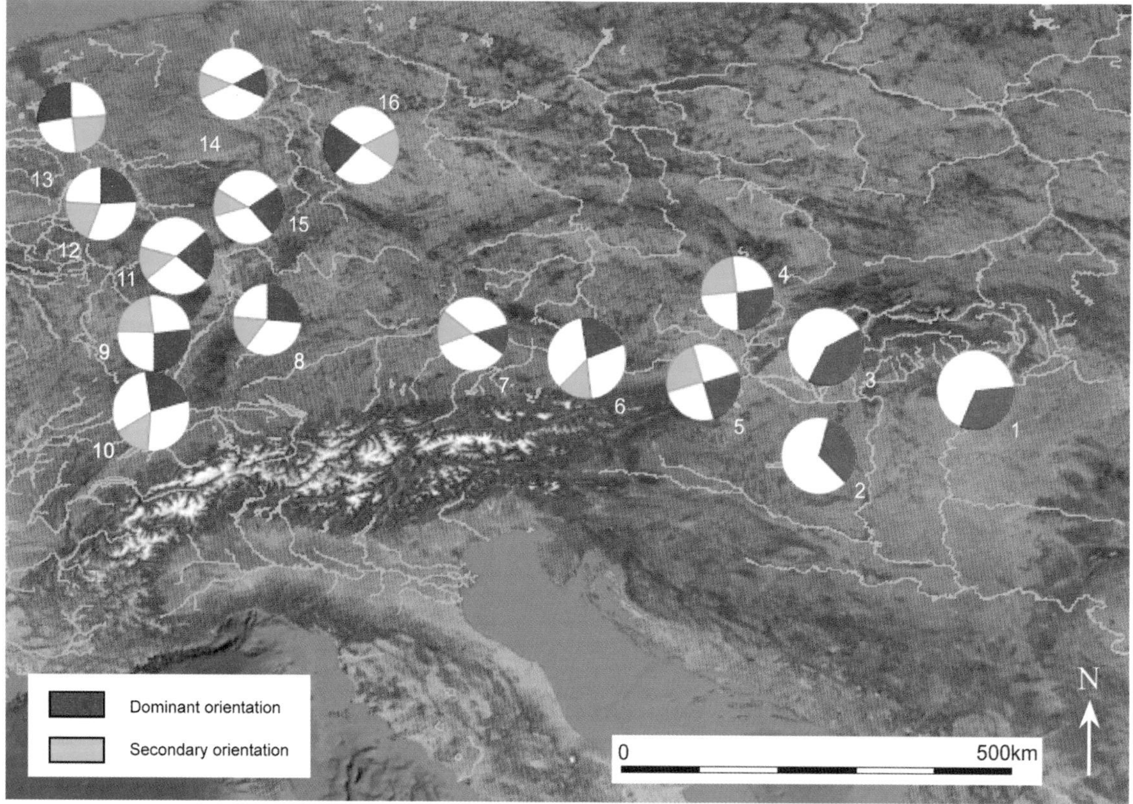

Fig. 9.10. Dominant and secondary (or 'antipodal') orientations of burials by region. 1) Eastern Hungary, 2) Western Hungary, 3) Slovakia, 4) Moravia, 5) Lower Austria, 6) Upper Austria, 7) Lower Bavaria, 8) Baden-Württemberg, 9) Basse-Alsace, 10) Haute-Alsace, 11) Palatinate, 12) Lower Rhine, 13) Netherlands, 14) Lower Saxony, 15) Thuringia, 16) Saxony-Anhalt.

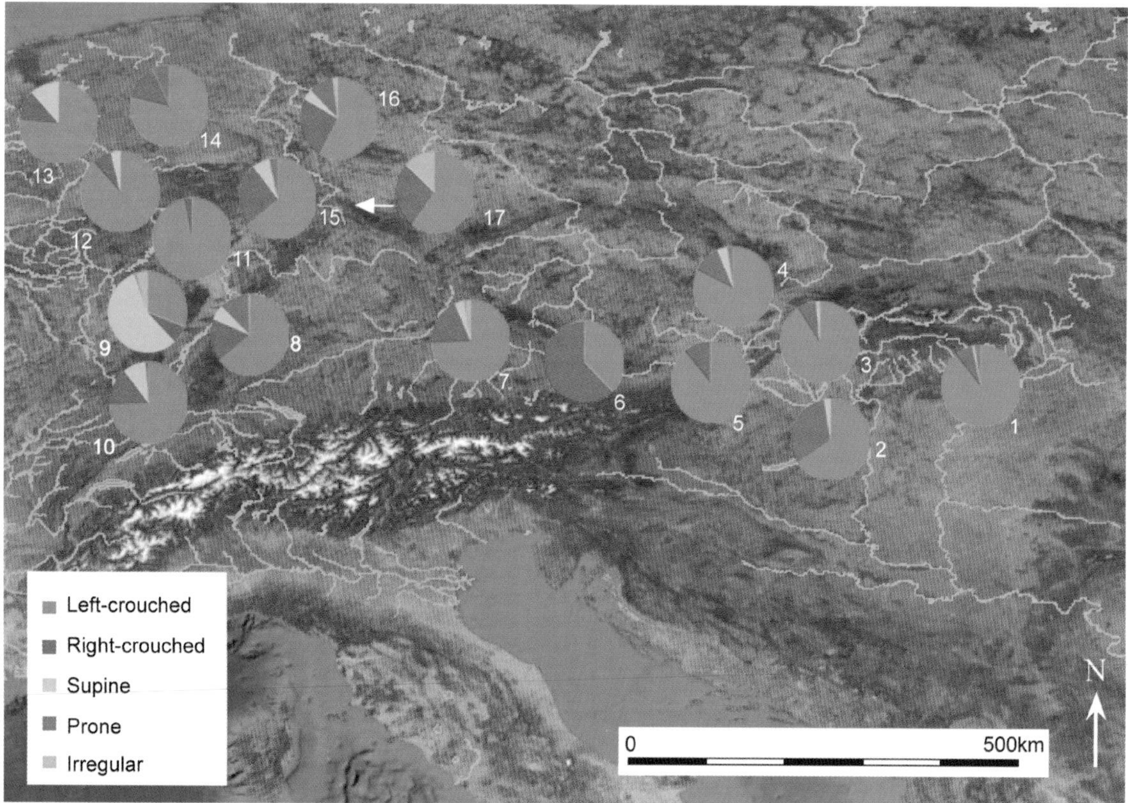

Fig. 9.11. Frequency of body positions by region. 1) Eastern Hungary, 2) Western Hungary, 3) Slovakia, 4) Moravia, 5) Lower Austria, 6) Upper Austria, 7) Lower Bavaria, 8) Baden-Württemberg, 9) Basse-Alsace, 10) Haute-Alsace, 11) Palatinate, 12) Lower Rhine, 13) Netherlands, 14) Lower Saxony, 15) Hessen, 16) Thuringia, 17) Saxony-Anhalt.

generations (e.g. Bogaard 2004; 2011; Bogaard *et al.* 2011), for example, then this soil would have been re-worked over decades, possibly manured, effectively until the group acquired a potentially quite specific, narrow range of $^{87}Sr/^{86}Sr$ ratios. Similarly, rates of domestic and wild animals have some variance across the LBK regions under study here (Chapter 1.3.5), which implies varied strategies of landscape use with potentially different underlying geologies. With their different cultural practices, other LBK groups should be distinguishable because they homogenised their soils slightly differently, or perhaps they included a greater amount of additional subsistence sources, such as livestock herding, dairying, supplemental hunting or fishing – all of which could impart a greater degree of variance to the $^{87}Sr/^{86}Sr$ ratios beyond the cultivation of specific land plots. Thus comparing the variance of $^{87}Sr/^{86}Sr$ ratios between groups has been one of our most effective tools for characterising diversity in the LBK from the strontium isotope data.

Despite the overall homogeneity of the loess soils there are still some differences (for example, in Moravia, discussed above). For this reason, in order to effectively investigate the data as a whole we have normalised the $^{87}Sr/^{86}Sr$ ratio for each human individual from each site, subtracted the mean $^{87}Sr/^{86}Sr$ ratio at the site from each individual's value, and then divided by the site standard deviation. This gets us closer to what we are after – a measure of how different the individual is from the group mean. By measuring, in units of standard deviation, the distance of each individual's strontium isotope ratio from the site mean, we can then pool all the sites together to examine patterns of variance among individuals across all the sampled LBK sites.

By viewing the dataset on the supra-regional scale, and considering broad archaeological evidence that already exists, three themes of community diversity could be investigated. We believe that, in conjunction with anthropological theory, the strontium data can inform on gender differences in lifeways, on social organisation, subsistence and status, and on other kinds of diversity through investigating the strontium isotope outliers.

9.3.1 Gendered differences in lifeways: residence and descent

A fundamental form of social heterogeneity lies in different mobility histories of males and females, which has been borne out by our strontium isotope evidence. Overall, the strontium isotope analyses of human skeletons from LBK cemeteries across central Europe show a greater proportion of females among the $^{87}Sr/^{86}Sr$ ratios above 0.7104 (Fig. 9.7). Pooling the data from Schwetzingen, Nitra, Aiterhofen, Kleinhadersdorf, Ensisheim and Souffelweyersheim, females and males show similar Gaussian distributions of $^{87}Sr/^{86}Sr$ ratios up to a cut-off of 0.711, but above 0.711 there are 15 females and only three males, a significant difference (p=0.002, χ^2=9.44, df =1; Fig. 9.8a). When we normalise the data, as just described, at each of these seven sites, and then pool the normalised data together, the variance in $^{87}Sr/^{86}Sr$ is significantly larger for females (n=152) than for males (n=147), by an F-test (p<0.001 without outliers; p<0.01 adding the four outliers) and by the more robust Levene's test (p<0.001 with or without outliers).

The larger variance of $^{87}Sr/^{86}Sr$ among females is significant at individual sites, too, especially the larger cemetery samples of Nitra, Schwetzingen and Vedrovice. The difference is clear among those of identifiable sex at Schwetzingen (n=89), where the mean $^{87}Sr/^{86}Sr$ ratio among females is 0.71014±0.00086 (n=48) and among males is 0.70987±0.00053 (n=41). At Schwetzingen, all eight individuals of identified sex with $^{87}Sr/^{86}Sr$ ratios above 0.711 are female (one was of unidentified sex). The female mean at Schwetzingen is higher (p=0.04) according to a 1-tailed t-test, and the variance among females at Schwetzingen is also greater than among the males (p=0.002 by F-test, p=0.09 by Levene's test).

The differences between sexes are similarly visible at both Nitra and Vedrovice. At Nitra, all six of the 60 sampled individuals with $^{87}Sr/^{86}Sr$ above 0.7097 were female, which is significant (p=0.008, χ^2=7.10, df=1). Similarly, the majority of the 'non-local' signatures from Vedrovice come from females, which is significant even with the more robust Levene's test (p=0.015). At Vedrovice, adult females make up the majority (14 out of 16) of individuals with $^{87}Sr/^{86}Sr$ ratios above 0.712 or below 0.7104, which is significant even when accounting for the larger number of females in the overall sample (p=0.003, χ^2=10.27, df = 1). If we compare each set of identified Vedrovice adults to the set of opposite sex plus unidentified sex (mainly children), the mean among the females is significantly lower than the rest of the sample (p=0.054, 2-tailed *t*-test), whereas the mean among males is definitely not different from the rest of the sample (p=0.8).

As at Nitra, the Vedrovice females have larger variance in $^{87}Sr/^{86}Sr$ than males (p=0.015, Levene's test). Considering that 30 of all 71 Vedrovice individuals are identified as females, the fact that 14 out of the 16 individuals outside this 'local' $^{87}Sr/^{86}Sr$ range are females is significant (p=0.003, χ^2=10.27, df=1). Ensisheim is the only site where the $^{87}Sr/^{86}Sr$ variance was not larger among females. Taken together, these patterns indicate that women and men are likely to have originated from, or obtained their subsistence from, different areas around LBK settlements. Although the specific circumstances certainly differed from site to site, the simplest explanation is that the kinship system was broadly patrilocal, that is, it was the women who relocated within an exogamous marriage network (Bentley *et al.* 2008; 2012).

Multiple lines of very different evidence support this hypothesis of patrilocality in the LBK, which has already been hypothesised based on archaeological remains (Eisenhauer 2003; Bentley *et al.* 2002), human genetic data (Lacan *et al.* 2011; Seielstad *et al.* 1998) and genetic models (Rasteiro *et al.* 2012). Using cross-cultural data in a phylogenetic comparative framework of Indo-European speaking cultures, past and present, Fortunato (2011) finds 'evidence in support of prevailing virilocality' for Proto-Indo-European language speakers. Ethnographically, patrilocality is also often strongly associated with cattle herds and ownership of livestock (Holden 2002; Holden and Mace 2003; Holden *et al.* 2003).

The identification of viri- or patrilocality for the LBK suggests that gender strongly influenced the lifeways of men and women. This argument is supported, albeit not as robustly, by the carbon and nitrogen isotope data from Alsace. At Ensisheim, for example, the sexes do not differ in their strontium and carbon isotope results, but the variance in $\delta^{15}N$ values is significantly larger among females (F-test, p=0.01). At nearby Souffelweyersheim and at Vendenheim, the sample includes only three identified females at each site, but when we pool the data from Vendenheim, Souffelweyersheim and Ensisheim together, we find differences between the sexes only in $\delta^{13}C$ (p=0.02). The mean $\delta^{13}C$ values among females are on average 40% of a standard deviation lower than the mean for each site, whereas the $\delta^{13}C$ among males averages 28% of a standard deviation higher than the site mean. In conjunction with the evidence from the analysis of dental caries (Chapter 9.4.1), this suggests that male-female dietary differences were widespread across the LBK.

Patrilocality is not necessarily exclusively associated with a patrilineal tradition, but there is good reason to suspect that this may have been practised during the LBK. Drawing upon an earlier study from the later LBK, isotopic analyses from the site of Talheim (Chapter 7.5) support the patrilineal hypothesis in rather dramatic fashion, as osteological analyses of the 34 individuals recovered from this mass grave indicate that the local adult females are missing, suggesting that the women of the community under attack were selectively spared (captured) by the attackers (Bentley *et al.* 2008; cf. Wahl and Trautmann 2012). This raises the question of the kinds of kinship bonds which existed between LBK communities and, in the case of the Talheim evidence, Bentley *et al.* (2008) favour the nuclear family as the basic foundation of the kinship structure. An analogy for a nuclear family has been made for the much later (*c.* 2700 BC) Corded Ware site of Eulau, in the Saxony-Anhalt region of Germany, by combining ancient DNA and strontium isotope analyses from a unique human burial of what may be a 'mother' over 35 years old, a 'father' over 40 years old and two boys between four and eight years old (Haak *et al.* 2008). Haak *et al.* (2008) concluded that the kinship was patrilocal, which is consistent with evidence for patrilocality earlier in the Neolithic (Eisenhauer 2003; Bentley *et al.* 2008; 2012).

9.3.2 Social organisation, subsistence and inherited status

In an elegant, focused investigation at the LBK village site of Vaihingen, Bogaard *et al.* (2011) discovered that archaeobotanical remains correlated spatially with the pottery styles across the settlement, confirming Strien's (2000) hypothesis regarding the existence of wards or clans within the village with specific access to cultivatable land in the surrounding area (Fig. 9.9). Bogaard *et al.* (2011, 412–13) concluded 'that plant husbandry and use played central roles in the construction of social identities' in the LBK community of Vaihingen, where those house groups which 'did not have equal access to the most valuable 'infield' land … had the option of abandoning the nucleated village to establish a new community elsewhere and/or to join another settlement'. In other words, Bogaard *et al.* (2011) postulate an essential link between mobility and land access. In this section we discuss the possible indicators for differences in social status within the strontium isotopes dataset.

The notion of differential land access is supported by the strontium isotope analysis of human skeletons, particularly concerning patterning between $^{87}Sr/^{86}Sr$ and the inclusion of a shoe-last adze (*Schuhleistenkeil*), the ground-stone adze which is often found in male LBK burials. Our evidence, from hundreds of LBK skeletons at sites from Slovakia to France, shows that adze burials regularly have less variance in $^{87}Sr/^{86}Sr$ ratios across the LBK distribution (Bentley *et al.* 2012; Fig. 9.8b). If we assume that loess areas do not often yield $^{87}Sr/^{86}Sr$ ratios above 0.7103, then we infer that males buried with adzes derived more of their subsistence from loess areas than males buried without an adze. Among over 300 sampled individuals pooled from Vedrovice (including data from M.P. Richards *et al.* 2008), Schwetzingen, Nitra, Aiterhofen, Kleinhadersdorf, Ensisheim and Souffelweyersheim, which included 62 adze burials from these seven sites, only one of the 41 individuals with $^{87}Sr/^{86}Sr$ ratios above 0.7103 is an adze burial (p<0.01, χ^2=7.38).

LBK adzes are disproportionately found with males, so we need to consider the sample of males on their own. If we pool together the normalised data from all seven of the sites listed above, and look at just the males, we find that the variance in $^{87}Sr/^{86}Sr$ ratio is significantly smaller for males with adzes (n=59) than for males without adzes (n=88) – this is significant by an F-test (p<0.001, with or without outliers) and by a Levene's test (p=0.014 without outliers; p=0.037 adding the three male outliers). Because there may be a bias in the sexing of adze burials (i.e., if an adze tended to be used as a clue that a skeleton was male), we can restrict ourselves just to the males sexed definitely in this project (n=59 with adzes; n=63 without), and this still yields a significant Levene's test (p<0.01 without outliers; p=0.024 adding the three male outliers) and F-test (p<0.0001, with or without outliers). Alternatively, if we look at just the raw $^{87}Sr/^{86}Sr$ data from 128 definitely sexed males from the six sites of Schwetzingen, Nitra, Aiterhofen, Kleinhadersdorf, Ensisheim and Souffelweyersheim, the $^{87}Sr/^{86}Sr$ ratios from both males-with-adze and males-without-adze follow a similar normal distribution below 0.7103, but above this value only one of the 15 definite males has an adze (p<0.005, χ^2=7.71).

We will not find a significant adze pattern at all sites individually, as sample sizes become too small at many sites. At larger sites, however, we find the same significant pattern, namely at Vedrovice (F-test, $p<0.01$; Levene's test, $p=0.07$; n=19) and Schwetzingen (Levene's test, $p=0.03$; n=41). In Alsace, at Ensisheim, Souffelweyersheim and Vendenheim, the standard deviation in $^{87}Sr/^{86}Sr$ ratio among individuals without adzes was at least twice that of the adze burials and even four times larger at Ensisheim. Furthermore, at Ensisheim, both $\delta^{13}C$ and $\delta^{15}N$ values are higher among males without adze than males with adze or females. At Vendenheim, males without an adze have slightly higher $\delta^{15}N$ values than males with an adze.

The adze pattern which we find indicates a certain measure of differentiation among males in LBK society. It may well indicate inequality rather than merely differentiation, if males buried with adzes had preferential access to loess areas for subsistence. This would be consistent with independent archaeological evidence at Vaihingen, where palaeobotanical indicators of cereal husbandry practices similarly suggest differential, inter-generational transfer of access to the most productive growing areas (Bogaard *et al.* 2011). By the later LBK, hereditary social inequality (ascribed status) is indicated by the grave goods of juveniles in Alsace (Jeunesse 1997). In contrast, the considerable variation between individuals (of both sexes) buried at settlements such as Füzesabony and Balatonszárszó further highlights the remarkable homogeneity among the LBK adze-males in central Europe.

These patterns also remind us that, although cemeteries account for the majority of LBK burials discovered archaeologically, they do not necessarily reflect the majority of LBK society. Given that we detect status differentiation within cemeteries, it seems likely that they may disproportionately represent a certain stratum of LBK society. Besides the cemeteries, another category of LBK burials are those isolated within a settlement, often in a pit next to a structure, as at Vaihingen, for example (Bogaard *et al.* 2011). These isolated settlement burials tend to include more women and children and fewer grave goods (Chapter 9.5.1). Also found are small groups of burials (usually fewer than eight graves) closely associated with a settlement, often at the side of a structure, and Jeunesse (1997) attributes their small size to the short-lived nature of LBK sites. Enclosure sites also offer a potential route for further analysis, which may yet capture another element of LBK lifeways (e.g. Turck *et al.* 2012), and future research could benefit from further comparison between burials from different contexts.

The largest proportion of the settlement strontium isotope values in this project come from the settlements in Hungary, and sites in this region show both similarities and differences to the results from cemeteries. At Polgár-Ferenci-hát, we see that the females are slightly more variable than the males, but not significantly, and furthermore the two most notable outliers are males, in contrast to the pattern found at most cemeteries. However, the nine children from Polgár-Ferenci-hát have a narrow range of $^{87}Sr/^{86}Sr$ ratios, contrasting with the significantly larger range among adults, but consistent with results found at cemeteries. The variation between teeth of the same individual at Füzesabony was not enormous but notable, with $^{87}Sr/^{86}Sr$ ratios in two different molars differing by as much as 0.0002 or so, while at Balatonszárszó one female had the quite large difference of 0.001 between molars. This is a large variation compared to the pigs which Giblin (2009) analysed from the Copper Age Hungarian Plain, which clustered very tightly around discrete values, all within 0.0001 of each other. This suggests that mobility was restricted over the centuries from the LBK to the Copper Age, and future studies could explore this temporal change, which may well reveal a growing evidence for private ownership of livestock herds with their own distinct feeding sources.

The isotopic evidence is also consistent with specialisation in subsistence activities, such as livestock herding and crop farming, organised along hereditary lines (Bogucki and Grygiel 1993; Shennan 2011). From their Talheim results, Bentley *et al.* (2008) proposed that economic specialisation could explain two group clusters in the isotopic data plotted as $^{87}Sr/^{86}Sr$ versus $\delta^{13}C$, with one group of specialised crop cultivators having similar strontium isotope signatures consistent with loess soils, and another group plotting along a diagonal array towards more upland Sr values, and less negative $\delta^{13}C$ values, potentially consistent with livestock herding (Bentley *et al.* 2008). This hypothesis has been independently proposed to explain time-sequenced strontium isotope signatures from cattle teeth at Vaihingen (Bentley and Knipper 2005). Knipper (2009; 2012), although finding that the majority of animals were herded close to the site, also sees the Vaihingen isotopic evidence as fitting well with Bogaard's (2004) model of intensive garden cultivation and with archaeozoological evidence for small livestock herds and local slaughtering and processing of the animals (M. Schäfer 2010). From strontium isotope evidence at the early Neolithic (Flomborn phase) settlement of Nieder-Mörlen in Germany (near Frankfurt), Nehlich *et al.* (2009) found that some juveniles moved from non-local upland locations in early childhood, which they determined to be consistent with transhumance societies in which children herd the animals, and the adults cultivate the crops.

These hypotheses are supported by our data from the LBK cemetery of Aiterhofen in Bavaria, where the sampled male individuals fell into two arrays. Because the carbon and nitrogen isotope evidence did not differ substantially among males, it appears that men and women at Aiterhofen had access to similar diets irrespective of origin, but that their mobility patterns differed. Bickle *et al.* (2011) suggested that men were sharing one high Sr ppm diet source (such as cultivated plants) from the local loess soils, but had two different lower Sr ppm end-members (such as meat) from somewhere off the cultivated loess soils (see Chapter 6.7).

9.3.3 Diversity: the strontium outliers

We now consider other possible markers of identity, in the body positions and cardinal orientations of the burials. Right-crouched burials are more likely to have an outlying strontium value than left-crouched burials (Chapter 9.5.2). At Schwetzingen, the right-crouched burials are at least consistent with an 'outsider' pattern. The two right-crouched female burials at Schwetzingen had $^{87}Sr/^{86}Sr$ above 0.711, well above the main modal value, whereas the two right-crouched males are well within the mode for $^{87}Sr/^{86}Sr$ but have the lowest and highest $\delta^{15}N$ values of the sample (8.9‰ and 11.6‰) and are among the bottom fifth of the sample in terms of smallest $\delta^{13}C$ carbonate-dentine spacing (7.5‰ and 7.7‰). With only a handful of right-crouched burials among the majority of left-crouched burials sampled at Schwetzingen, it is impossible to be certain of this pattern, but we can at least observe that the right-crouched burials lie at the margins of various isotope ranges. This provides a hypothesis for other LBK cemeteries.

At almost every site where we find right-crouched burials in the minority, these burials yield isotope results which plot at the margins of the main group cluster for the site. This is never statistically significant, but their presence on the margins of the isotope clusters became more convincing as it was repeated at multiple sites. If we look closely at the local cluster at Polgár-Ferenci-hát, we find that all burials are left-crouched, and that the two right-crouched burials are at the outside of the cluster, plotted as $^{87}Sr/^{86}Sr$ versus 1/Sr ppm, with the right-crouched female having among the highest Sr ppm values. These right-crouched burials also lie at the edges of the cluster of Polgár-Ferenci-hát values on a plot of $\delta^{13}C$ versus $^{87}Sr/^{86}Sr$, with the same right-crouched female having the lowest $\delta^{13}C$ of the Polgár-Ferenci-hát sample. This was also particularly visible at Ensisheim, where right-crouched burials are also more variable in terms of $\delta^{15}N$ and $\delta^{13}C$ in collagen.

Perhaps even more revealing is to simply consider the dichotomy between the predominant burial position at each site versus minority body positions, whatever they happen to be. At Vendenheim, for example, where supine was the predominant body position, the non-supine inhumations have a larger variance in $\delta^{15}N$. Looking at the normalised $\delta^{15}N$ and $\delta^{13}C$ data pooled together from Ensisheim, Souffelweyersheim and Vendenheim, we find that non-dominant burial positions have more variable $\delta^{15}N$ signatures than the dominant ones (both F-test and Levene's test, $p<0.0003$), as well as a significantly greater $\delta^{15}N$ among the dominant position (2-tailed t-test, $p<0.03$).

Cardinal orientation of the burial also revealed patterned diversity in our isotopic study. Bradley (2001) suggested that these orientations were related to LBK group identity, partly because LBK longhouses also often are oriented south–north and Gronenborn (1999, 175) suggested this position may have been representative of high status. If alignment of the head toward the east pointed to an understood origin for established members of LBK communities, it is notable that the normal eastward alignment is less common at cemeteries on the western margin of the LBK distribution. At Flomborn and Schwetzingen cemeteries, for example, many burials are aligned toward southerly or westerly directions. Could this have reflected a greater diversity of origins along the LBK frontier? And if so, could those from more diverse origins have had poorer access to land that those who were buried in the predominant NE–SW orientation?

9.3.4 Discussion

In general, then, our results show that the content and geographic provenience of human diet were correlated by sex (presumably gender) and reflected by patterns of burial including orientation and body position. Our results confirm that $^{87}Sr/^{86}Sr$ signatures are more variable among females than among males and less variable for males buried with adzes. We interpret the former as consistent with patrilocality, and the latter as consistent with better access to preferred loess soils for males with adzes. The range of $^{87}Sr/^{86}Sr$ signatures among adze-males is extraordinarily narrow, and we suggest this is more than just loess consistency but due to a within-LBK cultural habit of cultivating, working, and possibly manuring such soils repeatedly for generations, such that they attained a similar homogeneity across the LBK distribution of central Europe.

Taken together, these multiple lines of new evidence suggest that cultural groups were diversifying right from the start of the Neolithic (e.g. Shennan 2011), and that these groups had discernible differences in land access or land-use preferences. These new results support a broader picture of differential land access in the LBK within a recurrently patrilocal kinship system on the large scale, but on the smaller scale they serve also as evidence for diversity between and within early LBK communities, including different social and economic roles (e.g. Bickle and Hofmann 2007; Gronenborn 2007a; Bickle *et al.* 2011; see further discussion in Chapter 10.2.3), and domestic animals and plants being tailored to local environments (Colledge *et al.* 2004; Kreuz *et al.* 2005; Larson *et al.* 2005; 2007; Connolly *et al.* 2008). This picture of social differentiation in the LBK is further supported by new palaeobotanical evidence combined with detailed pottery analysis, together indicating differential access to tracts of cultivated land, each corresponding to different neighbourhoods of a LBK village (Bogaard 2004; Bogaard *et al.* 2011).

9.4 Osteological study

While demographic data for age and sex have played a central role in identifying some of the patterns and variances in isotopic and burial data, no significant correlations could be established between isotopic values and the occurrence of particular pathologies. The same appears to be true for mortuary data and pathology, though in some cases, for example, individuals with particular conditions such as tuberculosis appear to have had very complex burial assemblages (e.g. burial 281/444, Polgár-Ferenci-hát, Chapter 3.9; burial 34, Nitra, Chapter 4.10; and burial 13, Rutzing, Chapter 5.10). However, some cross-regional patterns and variations for pathologies do emerge. These contribute to a more comprehensive view of LBK lifeways by assessing general health against the background of dietary, mobility and mortuary studies which were the main focus of the Lifeways project. Here we discuss the evidence relating to differences between the sexes, variations relating to the east and west of the project, and broader cross-regional patterns.

9.4.1 Differences between the sexes

The rate of caries and *cribra orbitalia* in particular differed between the sexes. Caries rates for females are higher than for males at Mitterndorf and Rutzing (Chapter 5), and significantly so at Polgár-Ferenci-hát (Chapter 3) and Nitra (Chapter 4). As has already been discussed, this does not appear to be related to an overall difference in health between the sexes. While hormones can influence oral health (Lukacs 2008), the extent of their effect is still under debate. For the moment, dietary differences (such as larger proportions of starchy, cariogenic carbohydrates consumed) present the best explanation for the patterns observed, suggesting gendered practices in food distribution and/or consumption. In terms of assemblages which did not show male-female differences (Füzesabony-Gubakút, Ensisheim, Mulhouse-Est), small sample size and preservation may be contributing factors.

Cribra orbitalia, a stress indicator pointing towards iron deficiency and anaemia, affected mostly adult females, adolescents and juveniles, with only Rutzing including adult male cases. Excessive bleeding, both during menstruation and birthing, is one possible factor leading to higher numbers of adult females affected. In all cases, increasing consumption of cereals and legumes may also have an effect. Both groups of plants contain phytic acid, which inhibits iron absorption (Hurrell *et al.* 2003). This strengthens the suggestion from the stable isotope results that men and women may have been consuming different diets. Enamel hypoplasia, another stress indicator – pointing towards childhood stress during the time of tooth formation – was relatively evenly distributed between the sexes, suggesting that any contributing factors applied to children of both sexes alike and that any differences between the sexes, as reflected in *cribra orbitalia* and caries rates, may have developed from adolescence onwards.

Post-cranial trauma also indicates potential differences in male and female lifeways and was present at Polgár-Ferenci-hát, Füzesabony-Gubakút, Nitra, Rutzing and Ensisheim. It included fractures of the lower arm, rib, hand, foot and lower back, as well as cases of developmental non-fusion of part of the shoulder. More than twice as many males are affected. While it is not possible to attribute any of these injuries to a particular activity or task (with the possible exception of a metacarpal fracture of the hand; see below), high levels of physical activity in general, as well as – in view of Neolithic lifeways – a range of building-, craft- and subsistence-related tasks, potentially increased the risk of injury. This has been successfully shown for later periods, such as in the higher fracture rates of rural versus urban medieval populations (Judd and Roberts 1999). The higher fracture rate in LBK males may therefore be seen as indicative of sexual division of labour, where LBK males – through the activities they carried out – were at a higher risk of sustaining injuries. Further sex-based or gendered patterning is indicated at Polgár-Ferenci-hát and Nitra by the distribution of occlusal grooving of the anterior teeth, most likely the result of fibre or string working which appears to have been a predominantly female task (Chapters 3 and 4).

In terms of violence-related trauma, it is predominantly adult females and juveniles who were affected, with only one adult male head trauma, recorded at Nitra. The impact of violence on women and children in Neolithic societies mirrors results from other early Neolithic as well as post-LBK assemblages (Fibiger 2010; 2012; forthcoming). The paucity of male injuries is slightly surprising, though one of the post-cranial trauma cases may also be interpreted as violence-related. An adult male from Polgár-Ferenci-hát presented with a metacarpal fracture of the right hand. Clinically, this type of injury is the result of striking a hard surface and is most frequently seen in hand-to-hand combat (Hershkovitz *et al.* 1996). The cases recorded in the Lifeways project sample certainly indicate that physical violence was a recurring feature of LBK life.

The current results clearly indicate that men and women were not only likely to be engaged in different tasks and to be consuming slightly different diets, but that they also experienced different levels of physiological stress during particular life stages and were subjected to different risks of sustaining – often fatal – violence-related injuries. This strongly gendered pattern should inform our investigation and understanding of LBK lifeways and life experiences.

9.4.2 Regional variation

The current skeletal sample presents a limited survey, but preliminary conclusions can be drawn and some regional differences can be highlighted.

Currently, occlusal grooving as the result of the use of teeth as tools is found predominantly in the more easterly distribution of the LBK. In terms of indicators of stress, *cribra orbitalia* rates – as indicative of iron deficiency and anaemia – were much higher at Füzesabony-Gubakút, Polgár-Ferenci-hát and Nitra (between 12.2% and 15.0% of observable individuals) than in Alsace (between 0 and 6.7% of observable orbits affected). Population rates varied between 6.7% and 15.0% in the samples from Hungary, Slovakia and Alsace, with much higher rates of 25.0% and 55.6% respectively at Mitterndorf and Rutzing. Population rates (by individual with partial/complete dentitions) for enamel hypoplasia were highest at Polgár-Ferenci-hát (36.4%), followed by Rutzing (29.4%) and Mitterndorf (26.3%), while rates at Nitra (12.7%), Füzesabony-Gubakút (9.1%), Mulhouse-Est (11.1%) and Ensisheim (10.5%) were much lower. At present it is not possible to pinpoint the exact origins of these regional differences, though it is interesting to note the high prevalence for both stress indicators – *cribra orbitalia* and enamel hypoplasia – at the Austrian sites. While no carbon and nitrogen isotope data were available for Mitterndorf, some of the Rutzing $\delta^{15}N$ values hint at either dietary differences within the group or illness and starvation (Chapter 5). If starvation presented a recurring experience for individuals buried at these sites, this may account for the high prevalence of stress indicators observed.

Inter-regional comparisons of violence-related injuries also show some interesting variations. Healed and unhealed cranial trauma as an indicator of interpersonal violence was not recorded at all the sites, being limited to Füzesabony-Gubakút, Polgár-Ferenci-hát, Nitra and Mulhouse-Est. Within this group of assemblages, population prevalence ranged between 3.0% at Polgár-Ferenci-hát and 12.5% at Mulhouse-Est, suggesting that the frequency of violent encounters varied noticeably across the LBK distribution.

Although there are some clear regional differences, there are also similarities in the pathologies observed. One cross-regionally recorded condition is tuberculosis. Pulmonary tuberculosis, as indicated by changes to the spine and ribs, was recorded at Polgár-Ferenci-hát (Chapter 2) and Nitra (Chapter 3). Two other sites, Rutzing (Chapter 4) and Ensisheim (Chapter 5), included individuals with signs of pulmonary infection which may also be tuberculous in origin. These are among the earliest cases of tuberculosis recorded in the region. Recent DNA studies have shown *Mycobacterium tuberculosis* (i.e. the human form) rather than *Mycobacterium bovis* to be the predominant causative agent for the disease in humans, suggesting that denser, close-contact living rather than the use and proximity to animals facilitated transmission (Hershkovitz *et al.* 2008; Mays *et al.* 2001). Future DNA analysis of the Lifeways project cases may be able to further examine this hypothesis for early Neolithic central Europe. Most importantly in terms of lifeways is the fact that illness, including severe and debilitating conditions, was part of everyday life and the overall life experience was shared by all LBK communities.

9.4.3 Outlook

In terms of placing the LBK data in its wider context, it is difficult to assess to what degree the advent of agriculture-based subsistence involved a decline in general health, as the Mesolithic skeletal record is limited and a comparative, population-based dataset largely absent (Grünberg 2000; Larsen 2002). In terms of the impact of disease and impairment it is important to consider the potential clinical symptoms of some of the conditions recorded. On a micro-level, the lifeway biographies at the end of each regional chapter highlight the effect of certain conditions on the individual. In view of the relatively small dataset of 236 individuals considered for this study (compared to over 3000 LBK burials recorded by the Lifeways project) they may at present be one of the more fruitful ways to consider diversity in LBK lifeways – in terms of functional health and the effect which illness or impairment could have on the individual and on the wider community. This relates to questions of productivity, division and distribution of labour, independence and care. Symptoms of tuberculosis, for example, can include a persistent and often bloody cough, breathing difficulties, fever, chest pains, weakness and lethargy, worsening over time (Roberts and Buikstra 2003, 20); a fracture of the clavicle not only involves pain and functional impairment immediately after the event, but in cases of mal- or non-union can result in pain, loss of strength, rapid fatigability and tingling or numbness of the arm and hand (Hillen *et al.* 2010); post-traumatic symptoms of head trauma can include poor concentration, irritability, anxiety, depression, vertigo, inability to return to and carry out work effectively, chronic headache and fatigue (Couch *et al.* 2007; Gronwall and Wrightson 1974; Schafter 1997); anaemia may be accompanied by dizziness, palpitations, depression and severe impairment of cognitive function, or even lead to heart failure (Ludwig and Strasser 2001). These are just some examples of the potential symptoms which many of the individuals examined in this study may have suffered, both in the short and longer term, affecting their overall quality of life and basic functioning in everyday situations. Temporarily or long-term impaired individuals had to be helped, supported and cared for by their kin or community, depending on their expected responsibilities (such as with regard to labour and productivity) and the time of year (in terms of resource availability) among other factors, and they may therefore have put a certain degree of strain and stress on the group.

Even this limited pilot study has shown the potential of sound osteoarchaeological and palaeopathological analyses for understanding LBK lifeways and life experiences, both at the individual and population level. The next crucial step is an expansion of this sample to further test some of the patterns and variations observed, and to answer questions about the frequency of pathologies and impairment at a wider population level. In this regard the sheer numbers of the substantial and well preserved LBK assemblages from southern and south-eastern Germany (Chapter 2.6.1) offer exciting possibilities for exploring LBK health and lifestyle at a population level. In the meantime, the osteological component of the Lifeways project has provided an insight into levels of stress, impairment, conflict and pathogen-load experienced by the early farmers of central Europe.

9.5 Funerary practices at the large scale

The previous three sections have evaluated the degree of variability in LBK lifeways suggested by the stable isotopic, strontium and osteological studies at the regional and supra-regional scale. In Chapter 10, we will return to explore the impact of these data on how we envisage variability in the scales of LBK life and the kinds of diversity with which its communities lived, across a broad range of archaeological contexts. Here, we turn to think again about the funerary rites of the LBK. The following discussion has two aims: first, to examine the supra-

Table 9.8. Sex profile of LBK settlement and cemetery burials (based on Lifeways Database).

Site type	f	f?	f??	m	m?	m??	Total
Cemetery	237	118	12	279	76	12	734
Settlement	120	26	3	118	26	1	294
Totals	357	144	15	397	102	13	1028

regional and regional diversity in inhumations across the study area; and secondly, to reflect on how the isotopic and osteological analyses have informed on variation in the funerary sphere. So, the scale of approach broadens in comparison to the regional chapters, which dealt with the diversity within individual sites and between sites from the same region. The different aspects of burial rite analysed follow those laid out in Chapter 2.7.2 (in summary: age at death, sex, context of burial, orientation, body position and grave goods). Overall comments about LBK burial practices are based on the Lifeways Database with its *c.* 3000 burials, while the discussion of regional variation focuses on those regions discussed in this volume. This reduces the number of burials to 1875, and once they are broken down by categories (e.g. sex, age classes and individual grave goods), the number of burials available for analysis is even smaller.

The aim here is not to explore the entire corpus of funerary rites from the LBK (for this we point the reader to, amongst others, van de Velde 1979a; 1979b; Modderman 1988; Nieszery 1995; Veit 1996; Jeunesse 1996; 1997; 2003; Siemoneit 1997; D. Hofmann forthcoming), but rather to focus on three selected aspects, drawn out through the regional chapters (3–8). First, variation in burial context is considered, focussing particularly on any discernible diversity between cemetery and settlement burials (the two main site contexts of our sample assemblage) and any spatial patterning within the cemeteries themselves. Secondly, we tackle the variability in treatment of the body in the grave (burial orientation and body position). Thirdly, we investigate how grave goods vary regionally and by the age and sex of the deceased. We conclude this section with a discussion of funerary rites in the LBK by exploring patterns of diversity and similarity in practice across the regions sampled here.

9.5.1 Context of burial: settlement and cemetery

With the exception of Asparn (which may not be relevant for a discussion of burial practices; Chapter 5.5 and 5.9; Teschler-Nicola *et al.* 1996; 2006), this project has primarily focused on settlement and cemetery burials. As we noted in Chapter 2.7.1, settlement burials have tended previously to play a secondary role in the investigation of LBK funerary practices. In this project, we attempted to redress the balance (and a discussion of the differences between settlements and cemeteries in terms of funerary rite follows below), but the nature of the isotopic study imposed several restrictions. As this is the first large-scale project of its type, burial assemblages had to be large (to provide a significant number of burials for analysis) and settlement burials tend to occur at a rate of only a few a site, this severely limited our choice. In the western regions of the study area, Otzing, southern Bavaria, was the only available settlement with a large enough sample to be analysed (Chapter 6.8), while the absence of cemeteries in eastern and western Hungary resulted in burials from this region dominating the settlement burials numerically. Thus it would, in any case, be difficult to discern whether differences between the isotope results from cemeteries and settlements were influenced by regional variability or a real difference between the lifeways of those buried at cemeteries and at other kinds of sites. Cemeteries appear first in the 53rd century cal BC, perhaps with the beginning of burials at Vedrovice, Moravia (Chapter 4.4, Appendix B1), and they remain, to date, absent in both Hungary (Chapter 3.5) and the Paris basin. Therefore, burial in cemeteries appears to have developed with the second phase of expansion and the end of the *ältere* LBK (Modderman 1988; Jeunesse 1997; 2003a; 2009; Gronenborn 1998; Zvelebil and Pettitt 2008), while in contrast, burial in settlement contexts is a practice found throughout the duration of the LBK. Within the isotopic data, however, no specific patterns pertaining solely to settlements or cemeteries could be discerned, nor were there any distinct differences between the two contexts.

It has often been assumed that the age and sex profiles of settlement and cemetery burials differed somewhat, with men more frequent at cemeteries and women and children dominating the settlement burial record (Modderman 1988; Veit 1993; 1996, 188–9; Jeunesse 1997, 53). If only the most reliably sexed burials are included (those described as 'f' or 'm' rather than 'f?' or 'm?') then women are slightly under-represented at cemeteries, but not significantly so (p=0.25, χ^2=1.317, df=1) and there are virtually no differences in the rates of men and women found at settlements (Lifeways Database). Besides, if only a small proportion of the less reliably sexed female burials at cemeteries were included (Table 9.8), the values would be far closer. The similar rates of male and female settlement burials are maintained if the Paris basin and Hungary are excluded. On this basis, we argue that sex was not a significant aspect of defining choice of burial location. The age profiles at cemeteries and settlements, however, are significantly different (p<0.01, χ^2=58.259, df=5; ages divided into six categories: 0–6, 7–13, 14–19, 20–30, 31–44, 45+)[2] suggesting that some selection on the basis of age was being made. At both kinds of site, the adult age profiles are approximately similar, the youngest age group (category 1) is under-represented (we would expect high infant mortality) and slightly older children (7–12; category 2) are over-represented. However, the youngest age group is more frequent at settlements than at cemeteries, suggesting that settlement burials more closely fit a realistic mortality profile for the period (Chapter 2.6.1). Siemoneit (1997, 35) argued that an important age threshold was reached around the age of seven, when the grave good assemblages accompanying the child could become more complex. The age profile seen at both cemeteries and settlements suggests that passing these life-stages also influenced the likelihood of being buried at all, but specifically increased the chances of being included in a cemetery. This alone strongly suggests that some form of selection was involved in determining who was buried at a cemetery.

When the treatments of the body in settlement and cemetery burials are compared, some differences in practice can be identified. There are significant differences in the orientations found at settlements and cemeteries ($p<0.01$, $\chi^2=120.932$, df=7; Veit 1996, 184), with a greater evenness of spread across the different orientations at settlements. While 74% of all cemetery burials are left-crouched, this rate drops to 58% for settlements, and right-crouched and irregular body positions are better represented at settlements than they are at cemeteries (Lifeways Database). The supine or extended body position does not follow this pattern, but this is due to the regionally specific practice found in Basse-Alsace (Chapter 9.4.2). While the same range of body positions and orientations is found in both contexts, cemetery graves concentrate more heavily on the left-crouched position and dominant orientations (Veit 1993, 184; Lifeways Database).[3] This general pattern of more variability at settlements holds true across the LBK, with some small variations. The main exception is Upper Austria, where right-crouched burials outnumber left-crouched at the cemetery of Rutzing (Chapter 5.10).

The rate of furnished graves is far higher at cemeteries than at settlements, with an average of *c.* 50% of graves at settlements furnished compared with nearly 70% at cemeteries (Modderman 1988, 118; Veit 1996, 185; Jeunesse 1997; D. Hofmann 2009a; Lifeways Database). Men, however, are more likely to be furnished than women at cemeteries ($p=0.001$, $\chi^2=11.128$, df=1). This is not the case at settlements, where approximately 50% of male and female graves are unfurnished. There are no significant differences in furnished graves across the six different age categories, though the younger children (category 1) are less well furnished than other age groups at cemeteries (Lifeways Database). The reverse is true at settlements, with the youngest and oldest child age classes having a high frequency of furnished graves, but it must be emphasised that these differences are relatively small and not statistically significant (Lifeways Database).

Amongst the different types of grave good, only some show a higher frequency at cemeteries compared to settlements. Most notably, polished stone occurs roughly twice as frequently at cemeteries as it does at settlements (in 30% of furnished burials at cemeteries (*c.* 50% of male graves) and 14% of furnished settlement graves; Lifeways Database). An even larger difference in prevalence rate is seen in flint artefacts (25% of furnished graves at cemeteries; 8% at settlements; Lifeways Database). For other categories of grave good, and once unfurnished graves are discounted, frequency rates are similar. Pottery is present in roughly half of all furnished graves in both contexts[4] and personal ornamentation, including *Spondylus*, occurs in approximately 12% of graves (Lifeways Database). The strongest differences between cemetery and settlement grave good assemblages are rather in their complexity. For example, 25% of furnished cemetery graves have more than one grave good type, while the same is true of only 10% of settlement burials with grave goods (Lifeways Database).[5] Similarly, large numbers of sherds (e.g. >10 in a single grave) tend to occur only in cemetery graves – perhaps associated with deliberate fragmentation of pots at the graveside in cemeteries (Modderman 1985; Nieszery 1995; D. Hofmann 2009a; forthcoming) or the possibility that grave pits were left open for some time after the initial burial (Bonnabel *et al.* 2003; Thévenet 2004; 2009; D. Hofmann 2009a, 227; forthcoming).[6] So, while there may have been more variability in how the body was treated at settlements, grave good assemblages were more varied at cemeteries.

In summary, there are notable differences between cemetery and settlement burials. Age at death had a stronger impact on context of burial than sex and graves are more likely to be furnished in cemeteries than at settlements. The body positions and orientations at settlements and cemeteries cover the same range of possibilities (Veit 1996), but settlement burials are more heterogeneous in this respect. Amongst the grave goods, pottery and personal ornamentation are found at the same frequency at both cemeteries and settlements, while polished stone and flint tools are more frequent at cemeteries than settlements. The explanations for these differences could be chronological; as settlement burials account for the entire duration of the LBK and cemeteries probably develop from the 53rd century cal BC, the patterns could show a trend towards less variability in how the body is treated and changing emphases in the selection of grave goods (Jeunesse 2009, 162–3). While this remains a distinct possibility, the scale of community influencing the burial could also have had a strong influence on how different aspects of the possible burial rites were selected and combined. At settlements, the emphasis fell on individually chosen orientations and body positions, while there appears to have been more formalisation at cemeteries.

Turning now to isotopes, at some sites it was possible to show that the stable isotopes correlated to some extent with the spatial layout of the graves (e.g. Rutzing, Chapter 5.10; Aiterhofen, Chapter 6.7; Otzing, Chapter 6.8; Souffelweyersheim, Chapter 8.9; Vendenheim, Chapter 8.10). Except for Vendenheim (where the average $\delta^{15}N$ value differs), it is the average $\delta^{13}C$ values which differed between certain clusters or groups of graves. Such variation was interpreted as arising from the sourcing of food from areas of different landscape cover (such as through the canopy effect; Chapter 9.2.4). Thus one group may have been sourcing more of their food from a wooded environment than others at the cemetery. This correlates well overall with the suggestion from the strontium evidence that within a single cemetery people would have sourced their food from varied soils (particularly so at Souffelweyersheim, Chapter 8.9.5). However, strontium, location in the cemetery and carbon values do not correspond on the scale of the individual, but rather when groups of burials are considered. Comparing the higher $\delta^{13}C$ values found at the late LBK site of Asparn to the lower average $\delta^{13}C$ value from Kleinhadersdorf, a cemetery that probably ranges over several centuries (Appendix B2), we can suggest that $\delta^{13}C$ values may vary with time (Chapter 5.11). This variation may correspond to a gradual opening up of the landscape during the *jüngere* phase, when settlement density increases (Gronenborn 1998; Lüning 2000; Zimmerman *et al.* 2011; but see Chapter 9.2.2). This may suggest that in the case of Aiterhofen, Rutzing and Souffelweyersheim, differences in $\delta^{13}C$ values track the chronological development of the cemetery. However, there remains the possibility that these differences existed amongst contemporary groups. For example, the difference in $\delta^{13}C$ at Aiterhofen appears to be influenced by a small cluster at the north-west edge of the cemetery and the pattern is not easily explained chronologically (see longer discussion in Chapter 6.7.6). At Souffelweyersheim a lack of pottery in the graves and an absence of radiocarbon dating means that chronological differences are hard to explore. It is to be hoped that in the future more consistent application of radiocarbon dating will be able to resolve these issues.

At Rutzing (Chapter 5.10), Otzing (Chapter 6.8), Souffelweyersheim (Chapter 8.9) and Vendenheim (Chapter 8.10), the amount of variation in body position, range of grave goods and orientations differed between certain clusters of graves. Occasionally, this correlated with the isotopic data, and suggests that some form of shared dietary pattern was influencing where certain individuals were interred at the site, as well as the degree of similarity or diversity in practice. However, at other sites the pairing of graves was seemingly preferred (e.g. Nitra, Chapter 4.10; Mulhouse-Est, Chapter 8.7; Ensisheim, Chapter 8.8). Aiterhofen (Chapter 6.7) may fall somewhere between these two extremes, along with Vedrovice (Chapter 4.7), where both pairs and clusters of various sizes have been identified. This is not to say that potential pairs cannot be identified elsewhere (e.g. graves 131 and 132, Vendenheim), but rather that there is a different emphasis in preferred patterns of spatial arrangement. It is tempting to connect the kinds of spatial arrangement with the kind of community or identity scales being preferentially drawn out through burial rites. At Vendenheim and Rutzing, for example, broader group identities may have been stressed at the expense of others, while at Aiterhofen and Vedrovice varied kinds of relationships were expressed, resulting in pairs and clusters of different sizes.

This inference can help us to reflect on some of the differences in the frequencies of grave goods noted above. Pottery decorations often vary over quite small distances, suggesting they were subject to very local traditions (Brink-Kloke 1992; Strien 2000; 2005; Lefranc 2007a; Pechtl forthcoming) and therefore made and used within a fairly localised range (but see Boulestin *et al.* 2009; Zeeb-Lanz 2009b). This is not to say that pottery in graves was necessarily only in the local design, and the reverse has been demonstrated (Strien 2010a, 501–3), but it may often have carried with it a rather localised and small-scale sense of identity. Personal ornamentation may have been similarly close to the biographies of those with whom it was buried. *Spondylus* armrings are often found on the upper arm and due to their small diameter, it is thought that they could not have been removed without breaking them, suggesting that such items were worn continuously from later childhood with the arm growing around them (Nieszery 1995, 185). Similarly, Bonnardin (2003) has shown how the shell and stone necklaces found in the Paris basin and upper Rhine were often composed of beads with different degrees and patterns of wear, suggesting that the ornamentation was worn for a period of some duration, with certain beads replaced over time. These objects were, therefore, localised and in daily use, and probably had histories well known to the mourners at the graveside, despite varied origins (Allard and Bonnardin 2007).

Polished stone and flint tools, in contrast, may have been sourced at some distance from where the deceased lived (Zimmermann 1995; Allard 2005; Allard and Bonnardin 2007; Ramminger 2007; 2009; Mateiciucová 2008a) and while used in the same everyday settings as other grave goods, perhaps were not subjected to localised traditions to the same degree. That is not to say that polished stone and flint could not have had biographies tied to individual life or regional histories (e.g. D. Hofmann forthcoming; Chapter 9.4.3), nor to deny that both pottery and personal ornaments could have travelled some distance, with types or styles which were widely shared across the LBK networks, but rather to argue that the context in which an individual was buried influenced what was going into the grave through the scale of community enacted at the graveside. Settlement burials, therefore, may have been informed by identities on a smaller scale, such as immediate patterns of descent (and perhaps conveyed through reconstituted shell bead necklaces) or local kinship groups (e.g. perhaps echoed in local ceramic styles). Such presentations were equally valid at cemeteries, but were coupled with widely shared and more regularised and formalised funerary rites. While the differences between settlements and cemeteries are of degree rather than absolute, there were varying emphases influencing how the grave site was constituted.

9.5.2 Treatment of the body

While in this project we have chosen to focus on the position and orientation of the body in the grave, the body of the deceased could be subjected to a far wider range of actions. Apart from the intentional (or unintentional) forms of fragmentation recorded in disarticulated remains at settlements (Pariat 2007), enclosures (Farruggia *et al.* 1996; Orschiedt 1999; Boulestin *et al.* 2009) and cave sites (Orschiedt 1999), such practices can also be found in the context of inhumation. For example, the degree to which the body is crouched varies (Kahlke 1954; Jeunesse 1997), indicating that some bodies may have been wrapped or tied (Kahlke 1954, 121; U. Fischer 1956, 218; Lenneis 2010c, 164), while recent excavations in Alsace suggest that the grave site could have been revisited and the skeleton manipulated (Boës 2003; Jeunesse 2003a; see discussion in Chapter 8.5) or even removed entirely (Gerling 2006; 2012, 27). Parts of the body could be removed, either before burial, as with the individuals lacking skulls at Polgár (and where there is no space in the grave pit to accommodate a head; Chapter 3.9), or afterwards (Boës 2003; Gerling 2006; 2012; Lefranc and Boës 2009; Chapter 8.5). Similarly temporally drawn out rites may also have applied to grave goods (Thévenet 2004; D. Hofmann forthcoming; see below) and there is no reason to suppose that all bodies, or indeed deaths, were treated with identical rites, limited to a regularised orientation and crouched body position.

The dominant orientation of all inhumations in the LBK is east–west, but as we have noted throughout the volume it actually varies strongly by region (Häusler 1994; 2000; Jeunesse 1996; 1997; 2003a). As Alexander Häusler (1994, 28; 2000) noted, this is also coupled with the presence of an 'antipodal' orientation (see also Jeunesse 1997, 63), which is less frequent than the dominant one. Figure 9.10 illustrates the regional variation across the LBK as a whole; the dominant orientation is defined here as that in which 60% or more of the burials in a region fall and the secondary or 'antipodal' orientation is defined as more than 20% of the burials. Aside from the lack of 'antipodal' orientations in the eastern part of the LBK (no distinct secondary position can be identified), there are clear regional differences. No explanation for why one direction was favoured over another can currently be offered, as there is no broader geographical pattern such as exists for the direction of house orientation (Bradley 2001; see also Whittle 2012). However, the dominant direction of orientation can be connected to the degree of variability within the region.

While there was little correlation at a site level between the isotopes and treatment of the body in the grave, some overall variation can be noted in the strontium ratios (see above). Right-crouched burials have more variable $^{87}Sr/^{86}Sr$ ratios than left-crouched burials overall (Levene's test, p=0.006) and account for *c.* 10% more of the outliers than other positions (this is not significant, p=0.109, χ^2=7.551, df=4, and the numbers are low, outlying right-crouched burials numbering only 15). The frequency is maintained when Rutzing, with its high number of right-crouched burials, is excluded. Similarly, when analysed by dominant and secondary orientation (see below, and Chapter 2.7.1), outliers are more frequently in an antipodal position (30% of burials, n=20) than within the main orientation (18% of burials, n=71; p=0.031, χ^2=4.674, df=1). In this case, however, the spread of $^{87}Sr/^{86}Sr$ ratios is approximately equal for burials in a dominant and secondary orientation (Levene's test, p=0.6). These patterns suggest that a) those placed in a right-crouched position had gained their strontium ratios from more variable sources than left-crouched individuals, and b) burials with antipodal orientations were more likely to have had a larger non-loess component in their childhood diets.

Again, the patterns identified above are not absolute and we can point to plenty of examples on the local level where the trends identified above are demonstrably *not* the case. However, these correlations do suggest that the position of the body in the grave (left-crouched or right-crouched) and burial orientation (dominant and secondary/antipodal) were in some way connected to the lifeway of the deceased. We are not in the position to assess what such differences were in real terms and it would be premature to extrapolate from this that body position and orientation were directly reflecting origin. Yet these findings do illustrate that there was a relationship between an individual's life history and how their body was treated in the grave. Due to the low numbers of outliers it is difficult to assess whether these patterns are regionally variable, but they appear recurrent across the regions sampled here. However, both orientation and body position demonstrate strong variation by region and this may suggest some change in their role in the funerary rite across the LBK.

Examining the LBK as a whole, in those regions where east is the dominant orientation (Hessen, southern Bavaria, Palatinate, Lower Saxony), burials strongly adhere to the dominant and antipodal pattern, with very few burials appearing in other directions (less than 1%) and the dominant position accounting for 70% or more of the burials. In the regions where the dominant orientation is with the head to the south-east there is slightly more variation, with a wider spread across the different directions including the dominant orientation (Moravia, Lower Austria and Basse-Alsace; approximately 10% of burials fall outside the dominant and secondary orientations). Where the head to the north-east or north-west is favoured (Baden-Württemberg, Thuringia and Upper Austria), approximately 20% of burials are found in non-dominant or secondary orientations, and different orientations are more equally represented. The only exceptions to this pattern are Saxony-Anhalt (where the west dominates) and Haute-Alsace, where, although the dominant orientation is to the north, north-east and east, only 5% of burials fall in an antipodal orientation. This high frequency of the dominant orientation echoes the lack of a secondary orientation in Hungary and western Slovakia.

If we analyse the pattern of dominant and secondary orientation further, we find no significant differences between men and women, but there is variation with age at death (p=0.04, χ^2=11.65, df=5). This arises because in age category 2 (ages 7–13) more burials are from the regionally defined secondary orientation rather than the dominant orientation (dominant orientation: 112 burials; secondary orientation: 143). If there was no patterning, we

Table 9.9. Correlation between orientation and body position. For variability in body position, Low=0–20%; Medium=20–50%; High=50%+ of burials not left-crouched. For variability in orientation, Low=1–10%; Medium=10–20%; High=20%+ of burials not in either the dominant or secondary orientation.

Region	Dominant orientation	Variability in orientation	Variability in body position
Eastern Hungary	East and south-east	Low	Low
Western Hungary	North-east	Low	Medium
Slovakia	East, south-east and south	Low	Low
Moravia	East and south-east	Medium	Low
Lower Austria	East and south-east	Medium	Low
Upper Austria	North-east	High	High
Southern Bavaria	East	Low	Low
Baden-Württemberg	East and north-east	High	Medium
Basse-Alsace	East and south-east	Medium	High
Haute-Alsace	North-east	Low	Medium

would expect approximately two thirds of any age group to fall into the dominant category and a third into the secondary category (see above and Chapter 2.7.1) as we do for the adult classes, so the higher frequency of burials in a secondary orientation is noteworthy. Surprisingly, this is not due to settlement burials (where age category 2 burials are fairly frequent and orientations are more varied). Rather, the largest difference between dominant and secondary burial orientation in age category 2 is at cemeteries (dominant orientation: 62 burials or 40%; secondary orientation: 92 or 60%) – where they show roughly the reverse rate of what we would expect given overall patterns in other age groups. That an entire age group is more likely to be buried in an antipodal (rather than dominant) orientation further suggests that a direct tie between origin (or lifeway) and direction of burial is unlikely.

The position of the body in the grave also varies by region, but not to the same extent as orientation (Fig. 9.11). Left-crouched burials clearly dominate throughout most of the regions of the LBK, only Upper Austria (where right-crouched burials are more numerous) and Basse-Alsace (where supine burials dominate) differing from the pattern significantly. While some explanation for the pattern in Basse-Alsace can be offered (see below), the reasons for a right-crouched preference in Upper Austria are not readily apparent, but the number of burials is low and the assemblage is dominated by the Rutzing cemetery. The frequency of other positions, however, does vary across the different regions. Broadly, in the regions under study here, body position variability is higher in the west than in the east. This does not correlate directly with variability in orientations, but there is again a tendency in the east for lower variability, resulting in a dominance of left-crouched burials in an eastern or south-eastern direction (Table 9.9). Body position does not vary significantly with sex nor across the age categories (that is, the overall relative frequency is maintained), though child burials are more evenly distributed across the different body positions than adults at settlements (this is not significant, p=0.2, χ^2=29.01, df=25). Once this is broken down by region, the numbers become too low to analyse for significant patterns.

Grave goods do not vary significantly with the orientation of the burial (either by cardinal direction or dominant/secondary category), but there is some patterning associated with body position. Right-crouched burials are more likely to be unfurnished than left-crouched ones (59% furnished compared with 72% of left-crouched burials), receive less pottery than other positions (*c.* 10% less) and fewer objects of personal ornamentation (*c.* 5% less), but not polished stone and flint. In comparison, supine burials have a high frequency of furnished graves (60% of female graves, 85% of male graves). They also have relatively high rates of polished stone (10% higher), flint tools (10% higher) and possibly also grinding stones (3% higher). The supine pattern can be explained regionally and is due to the high numbers of well furnished supine graves in Basse-Alsace. This pattern is perhaps associated with the transition to the middle Neolithic in this region, where supine burials become more frequent and the nature of the grave good assemblage changes (Jeunesse 1997, 67; 2004).

Overall, the patterning between direction of dominant orientation and degree of variability in orientations and positions is interesting. We can perhaps propose that the eastern direction was meaningful in terms of a broader tradition of regularised funerary rites, so that in some areas the importance of tradition was comparatively downplayed. Above, we argued that differences in variability between cemeteries and settlements originated in the scale of community being emphasised in, or drawn out from, particular contexts of burial. By extension, regional orientation patterns could illustrate differences in how funerary practices were caught up in larger-scale community relationships. In southern Bavaria, for example, there could have been greater emphasis on expressing community cohesion through the treatment of the body in the grave, while in the more varied regions, such as Baden-Württemberg and Basse-Alsace, more local scales of community were being negotiated.

9.5.3 Grave goods

In this section, we re-examine the patterns associated with grave goods by age at death, sex and regional differences, as well as consider how the isotopic data correlate with certain

Table 9.10. The difference in grave good frequency between the sexes. The most reliably sexed graves are noted first and the less reliably sexed second (i.e. f then f?, and m then m?).

Difference in frequency	Male	Female
Strongly sexed grave goods (>20%)	Polished stone tools (+33%; 29%) Flint tools (+24%; 20%)	
Weakly sexed grave goods (between 20% and 5%)	Firelighting kits (+5%; 3%) Bone tools (+7%; 3%)	Ceramics (+11%; 9%)
Very weakly sexed grave goods (between 2 and 5%)		Personal ornamentation (+3%; 3%) *Spondylus* (overall; +4%; 3%) Colour (e.g. Ochre; +2%)
No differences (<2% difference)	Grinding stones River and Atlantic shell *Dentalium*	Grinding stones River and Atlantic shell *Dentalium*

object types. The discussion below picks out the objects identified in Chapter 2.7.2 as those previously thought to be significant for interpreting LBK funerary rites, because they occur at varied rates either by the age at death or sex of the deceased, or regionally. We also reflect on how the correlation between polished stone tools and strontium isotopes helps us to re-characterise the role of polished stone in the grave. As noted above, when overall patterns are discussed these are based on the Lifeways Database as a whole, but when regional variation is considered this relates to the regions under study in this volume.

Polished stone and other tools

Polished stone has most frequently been thought to denote the high status conferred on some male burials (Modderman 1988, 119; van de Velde 1990; Farruggia 1992; Nieszery 1995; Jeunesse 1997; Zvelebil and Pettitt 2008). However, its presence in the grave does not lead to a higher prevalence of other grave good types, which appear to vary independently of each other (the co-occurrence rate of different grave good types varies between 0 and 30%), with the exception of flint tools (*c.* 45% of graves with flint have polished stone) and the firelighter 'kit' (76% of graves with this item also have polished stone; Chapter 6.5 for description of this grave good item). These are the grave good classes that have the strongest difference in frequency between the sexes (polished stone is present in 34% of male and 5% of female graves; Table 9.10), so this patterning may also be associated with how maleness was expressed through grave goods, rather than solely operating as status markers. The tendency to receive polished stone increases with age at death, dropping slightly in the oldest age category (45+) for men (p<0.01, χ^2=50.408, df=5; Table 9.10), suggesting that provision with polished stone was partly influenced by how identity was characterised at different life stages. When multiple polished stone items are present in a burial, they are rarely of the same type (Modderman 1988, 119; Ramminger 2007). The examples found in graves often show evidence for wear and could have been used for as long as 8–15 years (Ramminger 2007, 264). Some polished stone tools were made on materials exchanged or brought from some distance (Ramminger 2007; Strien 2010), carrying with them a biography of their own (D. Hofmann forthcoming). Rather than a status marker alone, therefore, polished stone may have been integral to the social constitution of the individual in the grave, including their gender identity and perhaps also their commitment to obtaining, caring for and maintaining a polished stone item.

Yet, despite such potential personal histories associated with polished stone tools, the strontium isotope data implies that individuals buried with such objects were on the whole living similar lifeways. The strontium ratios of adze burials are remarkably consistent (see Chapter 9.3.2), suggesting that eating a loess-based diet in childhood, perhaps further homogenised by the effects of manuring (Chapter 9.3.2; Bentley *et al.* 2012), meant that an adult male had an increased likelihood of being buried with an item of polished stone. In Chapter 9.3.2, we suggested that this pattern may have been tied to the passing on of fields, which are thought to have been cultivated over several generations (Bogaard 2004; 2011; Bogaard *et al.* 2011). This conclusion could be reinforced by a tentative pattern between the number of polished stone items in the grave and the nitrogen isotope value of the deceased. At some sites, the average δ^{15}N value increased with the number of polished stone tools in the grave (including at Aiterhofen, Nitra, Rutzing, Schwetzingen, Souffelweyersheim, Vedrovice and Vendenheim), but low numbers on a site-by-site basis make the significance of this pattern difficult to judge (and at Ensisheim the reverse pattern is found). One potential explanation for this pattern is summarised briefly above (Chapter 9.3.2), but intake of cereals from manured soils would also tie in well with the pattern suggested from the strontium isotopes.

Polished stone tools are primarily thought to have been used for working wood (Modderman 1988, 113; Ramminger 2007) and are not, therefore, likely to directly relate to the practices of cultivation (though they could perhaps have been used for clearing woodland in the preparation of fields). Furthermore, male burials without polished stone do not cluster together isotopically (which would suggest that they shared a similar diet in childhood), but rather have more variable strontium ratios, indicating various possible routes from childhood diet to burial context and grave good assemblage. Therefore, it seems more probable that provision with a polished stone tool at death, notions of male identity (and their presentation at death) and a diet

Table 9.11. Changes in grave goods over the lifecourse (all regions). Items in italics decrease in the oldest age class (45 years and older).

Frequency of grave goods	Male	Female
Increase with age	Atlantic shell ornaments Firelighting kits Bone tools and toggles Flint tools *Pottery* *Polished stone*	Atlantic shell ornaments Ochre and other colours *Pottery* *Polished stone* *Flint tools*
Do not change	*Dentalium* beads River shell ornaments Stone ornaments	*Dentalium* beads River shell ornaments Stone ornaments Grinding stones Bone tools and ornaments
Decrease with age	*Spondylus* ornamentation Shell ornamentation (overall) Ochre Grinding stones	*Spondylus* ornamentation Shell ornamentation (overall)

consistent with use of loess soils in the vicinity of settlements were associated with how descent was organised – a central tendency amongst a range of different possibilities.

There is also very little regional variation in the frequency of polished stone in the cemeteries studied in this project (all regions only deviate slightly from a rate of *c.* 50% in male graves at cemeteries; Chapter 9.5.1), and all regions tend to show the increase in frequency over age and then a drop in the oldest age class. Polished stone remains rare at settlements (and the lack of cemeteries in Hungary may explain why there are so few polished stone items in graves in this region), except in southern Bavaria, where it occurs in 20% of settlement graves (Lifeways Database). Polished stone tools, therefore, are seemingly associated with a relative lack of variability in funerary rites; they are mostly found in cemeteries, which see the most regularised treatment of the body, are the grave good most strongly determined by the sex of the deceased and have a strong correlation with a restricted range of strontium ratios.

Flint tools are also predominantly found in male graves (24%; Table 9.10), but in some female graves as well (7%). Overall, flint tools increase in frequency across the age groups, with the same drop in the oldest age category for women, but not for the oldest men, who have the highest frequency of flint tools (33% of male age category 6 burials have flint, compared with an average of 24% for all male graves). While there is some variation in the frequency of flint tools in burials across the regions of the LBK, it is negligible. However, arrowheads appear more regularly in graves in the western part of the distribution (Basse- and Haute-Alsace, Baden-Württemberg, southern Bavaria and Upper Austria, and are very frequent in the Rhineland; Lifeways Database; Jeunesse 1997; 2009, 162).

Bone tools are slightly more frequent to appear in male (7.5% of graves) than female graves (3% of graves), and appear in increasing frequency for males. They do not show the drop-off in older age categories seen with polished stone tools. Regionally, bone tools are more frequent in the western distribution, and Baden-Württemberg stands out for its higher number of graves with more than one bone tool or object. Grinding stones, although originally considered to be a female grave good by van de Velde (1979a; 1979b; Zvelebil and Pettitt 2008, 202), are fairly equally distributed across the sexes (*c.* 5% of graves irrespective of sex; Table 9.10). Such items are very rare as grave goods in settlement burials and occur in about 6% of cemetery graves. As the numbers are low, it is difficult to distinguish whether there is any patterning by age at death or by region, though Lower Austria stands out with nearly 20% of graves containing grinding stones.

Pottery

Pottery (of all types) appears in approximately a third of all graves, and complete or mostly complete vessels occur in about 20% of burials (or 45% of furnished burials). Whole pots tend to be found more frequently with women than men, but the association is much weaker than that between men and polished stone and flint tools (Table 9.10). This suggests that pottery was not a female grave good *per se*. The rate of pottery in the grave spikes at ages 7–13 (age category 2) and then again in middle age, dropping off with the oldest age class ($p=0.04$, $\chi^2=11.688$, $df=5$), with both sexes following this pattern (Table 9.11). However, regionally, these changes over the lifecourse are only maintained at cemeteries, with settlements much more variable (Lifeways Database). In contrast to the lack of variation associated with polished stone, there are also some interesting regional differences in how pottery is distributed between the sexes. In the western regions (Haute-Alsace across to Upper Austria) women receive pottery more frequently than men, while in Lower Austria, Moravia and eastern Hungary the rates are approximately equal (or vary only by a few per cent) and in Slovakia men receive more pottery than women (though this assemblage is dominated by the cemetery of Nitra). Western Hungary had to be excluded, as the rate of pottery is low.

Personal ornaments

Personal ornamentation appears in 10–12% of graves (depending on whether items such as boar tusks and animal teeth are included as ornamentation) and is slightly more frequent with women than it is with men. The only exception is Slovakia, where shell and other ornamentation are more frequent with men than women. However, this may be due to low numbers of graves in this region (11 out of 67 reliably sexed graves contained personal ornamentation). With *Spondylus*, it appears that different types of ornament vary by sex; beads are found twice as frequently with women than men, while the reverse is true for armrings (Nieszery 1995; Müller *et al.* 1996; Jeunesse 1997; John 2011; Lifeways Database). Frequency of personal ornamentation varies across the different regions, with certain items of *Spondylus* having more restricted distributions (Jeunesse 2009, 162). It constitutes nearly the entire burial assemblage in eastern Hungary and remains highly frequent in Moravia and Slovakia, while rates drop slightly in Lower Austria, Upper Austria, southern Bavaria and Haute-Alsace. However, the presence of shell ornaments and other forms of jewellery or items worn on the body become extremely low in Baden-Württemberg and Basse-Alsace (present in >5% of graves).

The presence of personal ornamentation does not seem to vary significantly across the age classes (p=0.3, χ^2=6.023, df=5), and similar patterns are echoed by *Spondylus* and other forms of ornamentation (though the numbers of burials adequately aged become low). While any variation is not statistically significant, there is a consistent decrease over the adult age classes of a couple of per cent per category (Table 9.11). When only the burials adequately aged are included, the numbers become very low and extrapolating from regional differences is therefore difficult. However, southern Bavaria seems to go against this trend, with the frequency of furnished graves increasing with age. This appears to be due mainly to older women receiving higher rates of shell and other ornaments (Chapter 6.9 for longer discussion). It is also in this region that we find a particular range of grave goods which seem strongly regionally specific: bone combs (limited to Bavaria, with a couple of exceptions), bone and antler toggles (also found in more limited numbers in Baden-Württemberg, and regions in central Germany) and fox mandibles (Nieszery 1995; Jeunesse 1997). So, while in southern Bavaria there appears to be close attention to regularised burial traditions (such as orientation and body position), more variation is found in personal ornamentation.

Of course, objects that decorate the body could be categorised in other ways (for example by material, by manufacturing technique and by distance travelled from source) and LBK communities could well have distinguished between objects through their location in the grave or on the body, rather than material (see, for example, John 2005). However, when compared to 'tools', ornaments are the category with most variation in terms of one-off or very rare examples (e.g. imitation deer teeth at Rutzing (Chapter 5.10), boar tusks, the clay beads at Mezőkövesd (Chapter 3.7), bone rings (Alsace, Chapter 8), stone beads and stone armrings). We can perhaps suggest that personal ornamentation was a sphere in which innovation was explored.

Ochre

Ochre occurs in *c.* 10% of all graves on both cemeteries and settlements and is about twice as frequent in its powdered form than in lumps. Men are slightly less likely than women to receive ochre (Table 9.11) and, although there is not much variation across the different age classes, ochre is found in about a quarter of adult women's graves (some 15% higher than the average) and shows a slight increase with age. However, in contrast to other forms of grave good there is distinct regional variation in the frequency. Haute-Alsace and the Paris basin have a very high rate of graves with ochre (predominantly in its powdered form; 44% and 28% respectively). Jeunesse (1996; 1997, 80) identified the distinction between powdered or solid ochre as one of the key differences between his burial Traditions I and II, with lumps of ochre limited to Tradition II. This correlates approximately with the area where personal ornamentation is more limited (Baden-Württemberg and Basse-Alsace). While there is no direct correlation between receiving personal ornamentation and colour in the form of ochre, it is thus tempting to suggest that ochre had been used as a further decorative element on the deceased, perhaps coating the skin where powdered forms were found (for example, the head of burial G1c at Kleinhadersdorf had been so heavily ochred that it had dyed the skull; Tiefenböck 2010; Neugebauer-Maresch and Lenneis forthcoming). In Basse-Alsace and Baden-Württemberg, perhaps the 'lump' form was favoured as it fitted better with the reduced expectation of bodily adornment in the grave, but still allowed ochre to be used as a grave good, though this may not have been the case everywhere.

Complex mixtures

So far discussion has treated grave goods as individual categories, but just under half of all furnished cemetery graves have more than one grave good (46%; Lifeways Database). This is more likely for men than women, especially if objects such as *Spondylus* beads are counted as one object (i.e. as a necklace; Lifeways Database), and for older rather than younger individuals. About a third of furnished graves in age categories 1 (0–6) and 2 (7–13) have more than one good, but this increases to approximately 50% in age groups 3–5 and two thirds of burials in the oldest age class (category 6, 45+; Lifeways Database). Given that polished stone and pottery (two of the most frequent grave goods) drop in frequency in the graves of older adults (Table 9.11), grave good assemblages in this age category are more likely to be mixtures of rarer and less frequent grave goods. Overall, graves with three or more grave goods are more frequent in the adult age categories, particularly in Lower Austria, Moravia and western Slovakia (influenced in this region by the older adult male burials at Nitra).

The analysis of the child grave good assemblages broadly confirms Siemoneit's (1997) conclusions. Children who died between the ages of seven and 13 (age category 2) appear to be more likely to receive grave goods and more complex grave good assemblages than those under the age of seven (Siemoneit 1997; Lifeways Database). Children receive the same range of grave goods as adults, but also some more idiosyncratic objects, such as the 'figurine' at Ensisheim made from a sheep metacarpus with shell and birch tar 'eyes' and miniature pots or 'beakers', occasionally with holes punched through the rims to aid use (Siemoneit 1997, 27, 37, 72). Such objects suggest that personal use influenced inclusion of goods in the grave and there is no reason that the occasional tools in child graves were not for use (Siemoneit 1997, 78). Rather it seems that a particular life stage was passed around the age of seven, which distinguished early infanthood from later childhood. Amongst those who died in their teens or as adults, such thresholds are more difficult to distinguish, as they appear to have been marked by a more gradual increase in certain grave goods alongside a reduction in others (Table 9.11).

It has been suggested that certain grave goods form recurrent 'packages', often correlating with the sex and age of the deceased (Nieszery 1995; Jeunesse 1997; Zvelebil and Pettitt 2008; D. Hofmann 2009a; John 2011). Using factor analysis on the largest cemetery assemblages from Bavaria, John (2011, 41) argues that there was a strong co-occurrence between *Spondylus* bracelets, buckles and polished stone in male graves. However, this is a pattern recorded in only seven graves in Bavaria (at Aiterhofen and Sengkofen; Nieszery 1995) and it is not repeated in other regions. Similarly, other suggested packages (such as bone combs, freshwater shell and *Spondylus* beads with women; John 2011, 41) are found only in Bavaria and then only in six graves, again mostly from Aiterhofen (four graves). If the bone combs (a grave good of limited regional distribution) are excluded, there are a handful of graves in Haute-Alsace and the Paris basin which could be included in this category (Lifeways Database). So, the existence of definitive patterns of sexed grave goods can be questioned and, while there may have been frequent co-occurrences of certain grave goods in Bavaria, this is dominated by the assemblage at Aiterhofen. Rather, it seems that grave goods were largely independent of each other (except the 'firelighter kits' and polished stone, noted above).

There is thus a danger of placing too much emphasis on the grave goods as complete packages. Further goods made from organic remains may have been included in the grave, but not been preserved (Lenneis 2010c) and, as discussed above, objects may have been removed from the grave at a later date, or fragmented and taken away (D. Hofmann forthcoming). Furthermore, items could also be included in the fill of the grave and about 10% of all cemetery graves have objects of this sort (Lifeways Database). Pottery sherds dominate here, but the whole range of objects found at the level of the skeleton can also be found in the grave fill (Lifeways Database). Polished stone and flint remain more frequent in the fills of male graves than female graves and follow the same changes over age at death as pottery (though this may be influenced by the dominance of sherds as fill objects). In the regions under study here, objects in grave fills are most frequent in Basse-Alsace (13% of graves) and Baden-Württemberg (16% of graves), suggesting a greater emphasis on how the grave was filled after burial. Perhaps we can connect this to the possible removal of bodies seen at Schwetzingen (Gerling 2006; 2012, 27) and to the subsequent manipulation of skeletons suggested in the Alsace context (Lefranc and Boës 2009; Chapter 8.5). In these regions, perhaps graves were slightly more likely to receive attention after the initial placing of the body in the grave pit, though specific instances of *Nachgaben* at Polgár-Ferenci-hát (Chapter 3.9) suggest that revisiting of graves may have been fairly common elsewhere as well.

9.5.4 Diversity in practices

Overall, the discussion above has identified that certain variations in burial rites are stronger at different scales. On the whole, sex played a greater role in the selection of grave goods than age, while age had more impact on the location of burial and on variation in body position and orientation. The latter were more variable at settlements than cemeteries, but how much they varied also differed by region. The objects in burials could also vary regionally, with different emphases in different areas (Jeunesse 1996; 1997), but this variation also operated at the scale of settlement and cemetery burials across the LBK. As the same range of expressions can be co-opted into performances at different scales, it is not easy to tell which one was at the forefront of people's minds at any particular point and which was just a taken-for-granted aspect of the funerary rite. On a general level, the strength of formalised rites at cemeteries, with more variation at settlements, is repeated across the LBK. The boundaries between different regions themselves vary in strength. In some areas, different practices overlap, while stark boundaries are maintained in others (Fig. 9.12). For example, what appears to be emphasised in the burial rites of Basse-Alsace differs significantly from Haute-Alsace, but has much in common with Baden-Württemberg. Similarly, while western Hungary currently lacks cemetery burials, the variation of body positions and orientations suggests that it has more in common with regions further west. LBK funerary rites are often seen as strongly subjected to tradition, adhering fairly rigidly to expected norms of behaviour (Pavúk 1972a; 1972b; van de Velde 1979a; 1979b; Modderman 1988; Veit 1996). This view has been rightly criticised and regional variation has been emphasised (Jeunesse 1996; 1997; 2003; 2009; D. Hofmann 2009a; Bickle *et al.* 2011). However, the discussion above suggests that there remain some areas of funerary rites where more regularised traditions were widely adhered to. In this respect, we can point to the grave goods associated almost exclusively with males at cemeteries (such as adzes, firelighter kits, arrowheads and other flint tools). This is not to say that during the LBK a regularised gender identity existed only for males and not females, rather that cemeteries were a place where masculine identities were presented in more closely regularised, perhaps formalised, ways. We suggested above that cemeteries were places where group membership (enacted through shared diets in life, for example; see Chapter 9.2.5) was more strongly

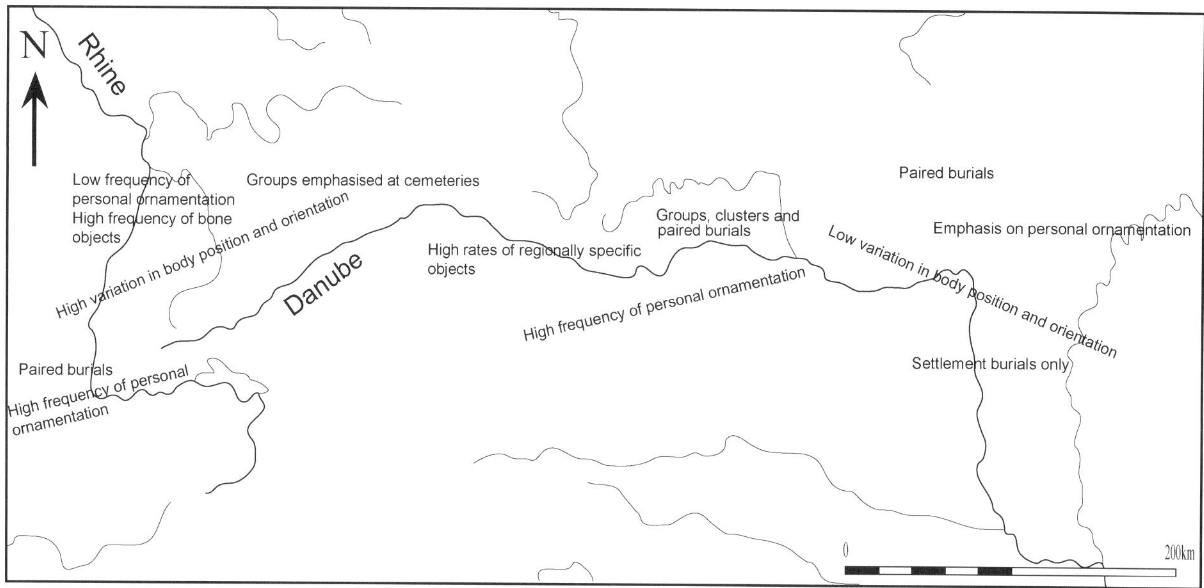

Fig. 9.12. Map of selected regional variations in funerary practices across the study area.

influencing the funerary rituals than other forms of relationships. Following on from this, it is tempting to argue that a regularised male identity was associated with the presentation of group identities and therefore more likely to be emphasised in cemetery contexts. This fits well with the suggestion from the strontium isotopes that patrilocality was widely practised, as inclusion in cemeteries may have been influenced by belonging to male lineages (see longer discussion in Chapter 10.2.4).

However, variation in other spheres can be demonstrated, and there were clearly areas in which innovation was encouraged. In southern Bavaria, a restricted range of orientations and body positions were used, but personal ornamentation was more open for experimentation. The reverse is true in Basse-Alsace and Baden-Württemberg, with their highly varied body positions and orientations. Here, following Jeunesse (1996; 1997), there was a starker contrast between the 'rich' and 'poor' graves, but the grave goods used to make these statements are polished stone and other tool types, which are not subject to high degrees of innovation. Rather than seeing regional variation in terms of how closely burials adhered to an imagined ideal LBK 'tradition', a more subtle picture can be built up in which the associations between different practices can be compared (Hofmann and Bickle 2011). In regions where body position and orientation are more variable (Basse-Alsace, Baden-Württemberg and Upper Austria) larger groups appear to be emphasised at cemeteries, whereas personal ornamentation is found in higher frequencies where smaller-scale relationships between graves were present, and orientations and body positions are more uniform (Haute-Alsace, southern Bavaria, Moravia and western Slovakia). These regional variations need not directly indicate varied social structures, but we can perhaps envisage a situation where across the LBK co-residential groups used a range of shared practices to accommodate the differences that mattered most to them.

On the level of the individual burial some age patterning could also be discerned. Two particular age classes stood out: children who died between the ages of seven and 13, and older adults who died after the age of 45. While child burials are overall more varied than adults, the second age category (7–13) was more likely to be buried in a secondary rather than the dominant orientation (defined by region), to be included in a cemetery and to receive pottery as a grave good. Siemoneit (1997) has previously argued that a particular threshold was passed about the age of seven, and after the age of 13 the funerary rites echo those of the adult age classes. Perhaps this period was a time of more ambiguity for the status of the individual within the broader group, between infancy or childhood and fully fledged adulthood, when they were more than capable of contributing to daily tasks and activities (Siemoneit 1997), but not yet fully recognised as an adult member of a community. Death in older age, in comparison, was marked not in variation in body position or orientation, but in a change in grave goods. Grave good assemblages at this time of life become more idiosyncratic (see Chapter 9.4.3), and perhaps less subject to group expectations, leaving mourners freer to create more personal and intimate experiences at the grave.

Discussion here has focused on variation across the funerary sphere. However, funerary rites did not take place in isolation from other experiences of community and were not separate from the ongoing work of daily life. The correlation between the isotope and archaeological data shows this to be the case. The varied possible lifeways experienced during the LBK did impact on the funerary sphere and fed into the diversity explored above. If patterns in isotopic data are taken as evidence of lifeways, then this operated at varied scales. At the level of the individual, right-crouched positions were used to express more varied lifeways and personal ornamentation or pottery were included in the grave because they were caught up with the individual's personal life history and kin relations. The pairs

Table 9.12. Summary of the main isotopic, osteological and archaeological patterns identified and discussed in Chapter 9. Please see Chapter 9 passim *for qualifications and exceptions to the conclusions listed in this table.*

Data source	Co-variant	Tested on	Variation	Interpretation
Carbon ($\delta^{13}C$)	Rainfall	All fauna	$\delta^{13}C$ values vary with longitude and with climate	Similarity in animal husbandry practices/feeding across the sample area; possible difference in cattle husbandry in Rhine catchment (greater use of forest resources)
Carbon ($\delta^{13}C$)	Moisture Availability Index (Winter months)	All humans	$\delta^{13}C$ values vary with longitude and with climate	Similarity in diets across the sample area
Nitrogen ($\delta^{15}N$)	Summer average temperature and rainfall	All fauna	$\delta^{15}N$ values vary with altitude and with climate	Similarity in animal husbandry practices/feeding across the sample area
Nitrogen ($\delta^{15}N$)	Altitude	All humans	$\delta^{15}N$ values vary with altitude, but it is difficult to identify one particular climatic parameter	Similarity in diets across the sample area
Nitrogen ($\delta^{15}N$)	Sex	All sexed adults	Men had higher average $\delta^{15}N$ values than women	Physiological or dietary differences between men and women. However, sites with large sample numbers where no significant difference is seen suggest dietary rather physiological differences
Nitrogen ($\Delta^{15}N$)	Geographic location	Human-cattle difference	Bigger $\Delta^{15}N$ values seen in the Rhine catchment sites	Possible differences in human diet between sites in the Rhine and Danube catchment areas
Strontium ($^{87}Sr/^{86}Sr$)	Sex	All sexed adults	Women are better represented amongst sampled individuals with non-loess $^{87}Sr/^{86}Sr$ ratios	Widespread practice of viri- or patrilocality
Strontium ($^{87}Sr/^{86}Sr$)	Male adze burials	All male burials	Men buried with adzes had a very narrow range of $^{87}Sr/^{86}Sr$ ratios	Preferential access to loess around the settlement was inherited by subsequent generations
Dental caries and *cribra orbitalia*	Sex	Sexed adults	Women had higher rates of caries than men at Mitterndorf, Rutzing, Polgár-Ferenci-hát and Nitra; *cribra orbitalia* was more frequent amongst females overall	Dietary differences between men and women
Burial context	Grave good type, body position and orientation	All burials	Cemeteries had more uniform frequencies of grave goods. Settlement burials showed greater variation in body position and orientation	Cemetery burials expressed a wider group identity, while local and individual identities rose to the fore at settlements
Treatment of the body in the grave	Region	All burials	The variability of body positions and orientations differed by region, with reduced variation associated with a dominant orientation of east–west	Traditions in funerary rites were more strongly adhered to in some (mainly eastern) regions
Grave goods	Sex	Sexed adults	Male burials showed more strongly sexed grave goods than females	Presentation of male identity in death was more closely monitored (there was greater uniformity in burial rites), as it was tied up with the expression of group-wide identities

of burials, clusters and cemeteries were perhaps above all stressing belonging to certain kin groups through a more formalised and shared burial rite, including the degree of variation in how the body was treated. Regionally specific practices (favouring or rejecting certain grave goods, degree of variation, favoured orientations) illustrate that even formalised burial practices were situated in the local context and perhaps stress the importance of connections within each region. Finally, larger groups cross-cutting different communities perhaps drew on these formalised rites to emphasise networks (involving for example masculine identities at cemeteries, patrilocal practices, and standardisation in orientation and body position).

9.6 Conclusions

Although a central aim of the LBK Lifeways project was to examine diversity through isotope analysis, we must not downplay the degree of homogeneity demonstrated in all aspects of the evidence. Table 9.12 summarises the main conclusions from this chapter. The stable isotope values suggest that there were widespread similar diets and recurrent subsistence practices, while the strontium analysis, osteological study and discussion of the funerary evidence found many cross-regional similarities which held true across the sites sampled in this project. For example, practices associated with patrilocality appear widespread across the cemeteries analysed for strontium isotopes in this project. Taken together, the results indicate that there was a shared way of doing things throughout the LBK. This highlights again the issue of what held the LBK together and in this chapter we have posited that kinship and descent were important factors in community networks. We will return to this discussion in Chapter 10. However, there are two important caveats which remain substantial questions for future research. First, the focus here on cemeteries may have limited the evidence to a particular sub-group of the broader LBK community, and secondly, the earliest phase of the LBK is largely missing from this study. We were necessarily limited to the sites where large numbers of samples were available, but as the dataset increases the ability to interpret smaller assemblages or to combine data from different areas grows.

Yet, despite such homogeneity, we have been able to identify significant patterns of difference that suggest diversity on both the large and small scale. At Aiterhofen, in the strontium data, and at Schwetzingen, in the strontium and oxygen data, two arrays could be distinguished, suggesting that those burying their dead at the cemeteries were drawn from two different groups, with different dietary practices in childhood. At a regional level, the analysis of the stable isotopes found variation in animal husbandry between the Rhine and Danube valleys and the osteological study was able to note variation in the prevalence of stress indicators, with the Austrian sites of Mitterndorf and Rutzing showing the highest frequencies. Across the funerary evidence regional differences are also present, such as the lack of cemetery burials in Hungary or the decreased rate of personal ornamentation seen in Basse-Alsace and Baden-Württemberg. However, no exact correlations between the different aspects of the evidence are readily apparent. This conclusion is similarly found in the isotopic outliers, which do not form a cluster in themselves but seem to point to significant variation at the margins of dominant practices. Thus at Kleinhadersdorf (Chapter 5.7), there is a young adult female with a very high $\delta^{13}C$ value of −18.9‰, which sets her apart from the rest of the individuals buried at this cemetery, but her circumstances are not reproduced elsewhere.

We argue, therefore, that a central group of widely shared practices formed the foundation for much of the LBK lifeway, in which many communities were caught up in maintaining the use of particular areas around settlements and passing them on over generations. Our evidence has provided no clear reasons for envisaging that those individuals who fall at the extremes of our dataset had reduced health or were of low status, and alternative ways of life, including the use of woodlands and uplands, are part of the range of potential LBK lifeways which we must make space for in our models of the LBK trajectory.

Notes

1 den=dendrochronological date.

2 The age classes are defined by the distribution of burials across the ages and the child classes are divided following Siemoneit (1997). It was reasoned that this gives a clearer picture of how grave goods and other features of the burials changed as the age at death increased.

3 There is a significant differences between the body positions and orientations of settlement and cemetery burials (p<0.01, χ^2=198.925, df=5), that is, settlement burials are more evenly spread across the different combinations of orientation and body position, while cemeteries tend to concentrate on an orientation and particular body position.

4 Rates of decorated pottery do not appear to differ between settlements and cemeteries (approximately 40% of ceramics are decorated; Lifeways Database). However, this is more complicated to judge because whether ceramics are decorated or not has not been consistently recorded in the literature and graves with decorated pottery are probably more likely to be counted as 'LBK'. Furthermore, there may be some differences in decorated pottery itself, with the quality of decoration varying significantly (Modderman 1970), but this is very hard to quantify, especially if the decoration acted as guide for other materials wrapped around pots or covering their surface (Modderman 1988, 112).

5 Only graves where it is certain that the whole grave good assemblage had been recorded are included in these figures. Therefore, it is possible that settlement burials are under-represented because graves with uncertain grave good assemblages (i.e. those where there was the possibility that certain items were not deliberately accompanying the deceased) were excluded from the analysis.

6 However, this pattern could also be explained by sherds being more readily recognised as a 'grave good' in cemetery contexts, or more easily disregarded as general 'rubbish' at settlements.

10 Performing LBK lifeways

Alasdair Whittle and Penny Bickle

10.1 Over and over: 'inconsistent commonality'

Again and again throughout this volume, we have presented evidence for shared practice and common ways of doing things, in the distinctive material and cultural frame of the LBK. At one level, the arguments for uniformity in LBK lifeways remain very strong. People built timber longhouses, cultivated cereals and husbanded domesticated animals, especially cattle, made pots and stone adzes, and buried their dead, in ways and styles that would have been familiar and instantly recognisable right across the LBK distribution in central Europe and beyond. Whether or not users of LBK material culture all spoke the same language or dialects, anyone on the move in the LBK world would surely have felt, at one level, continuously at home in settings fashioned over and over in the same kind of manner.

At the same time, both in the regional chapters and in the isotopic analyses, we have pointed again and again throughout this volume to a wealth of diversity. There were different regional histories within the overall narrative of LBK development; though relatively few of our analyses have contributed to new understanding of the earliest phases of the LBK, the varying regional trajectories are important from the beginning. They continue to be significant in later phases too, seen in the kaleidoscope of connections and differently oriented networks that are now being sketched in increasing detail. We have noted some of the evidence for variation in longhouse architecture, and the debate about settlement layout, one resolution of which (or at least a partial one) could lie in regional diversity. The opening sections in Chapters 3–8 have stressed the varying combinations of cereals and animals found across the LBK distribution in central Europe, and the following isotopic, osteological and archaeological analyses have presented a wide range of evidence for shared principal elements of diet, as well as for subtle variations in diet, general physical condition and lifetime movement by sex of the deceased, and perhaps also by social position.

There were plenty of variations on the most common way of interring the LBK individual as a left-crouched inhumation, and a very considerable range of things deposited with the dead; there is some diversity in the presence and absence of separate burial grounds or cemeteries, and perhaps in the criteria by which people were selected for interment in cemeteries. And while our analyses have strengthened the case for recurrent patterning in the diets and life histories of men and women, especially in the reduced strontium isotopic ranges seen in men buried with stone adzes, these only ever constitute part of the mortuary populations represented in cemeteries and on settlements. The arguments for diversity in LBK lifeways are therefore also strong. Some variation can be attributed to change through time or regional practices, but even within the same settlement or the mortuary population interred in a single cemetery, subtle differences can normally be found. So, in the terms of Pieter Modderman (1988), there certainly is diversity in uniformity, or in the striking phrase of Robert Carter and Graham Philip (2010, 5), from another context (of which more below), an 'inconsistent commonality'. From this perspective, the aims of this final chapter are to explore how this was made possible, to reflect on why it matters to the kinds of histories we write about the LBK and to consider what this may contribute to the wider understanding of cultural order. Two ideas are central to illuminating the impact of such diversity: scales and performance.

10.2 Practising scales

We have already noted in Chapter 1 how LBK research has tended to emphasise one particular scale of social interaction at the expense of others. LBK culture as a whole has been one favourite perspective; the idea of the region has also been a recurrent unit of analysis; and much debate of course in the last three decades has focused on the role of the house and household within the layout and functioning of individual settlements. The picture has not been static, and we have noted the addition of models of lineages and clans; a specific example of the latter, which we have quoted frequently in this volume, comes from Vaihingen in Baden-Württemberg (Bogaard *et al.* 2011; Bogaard 2012; Chapter

7.4). It is our view, however, that LBK research has not been consistently multi-scalar, and we mooted already in Chapter 1 the potential value of other terms such as 'meshwork' and 'interaction sphere'. The challenge is to go on now first to review the full potential range of relevant scales of social interaction, and then to reflect on how these might contribute to a fuller understanding of the ways in which LBK lifeways were performed.

10.2.1 Individuals and individual lifecourses: open questions?

Instead of simply highlighting a number of rather obvious scales, there is the opportunity to think about other possible dimensions and forms of association and allegiance. It is probably dangerous to use terms like starting from the bottom up or the top down, because that already begins to privilege one scale over others, so we will simply start with individual people within the LBK meshwork. As was shown in the analyses carried out by the late Marek Zvelebil and colleagues at Vedrovice in Moravia (Zvelebil and Pettitt 2008; Zvelebil *et al.* 2010; Chapter 4), individual lifeways could be strikingly varied, from those who lived their whole lives in a given locality, to those who came into a community from the outside, and Vedrovice lives also included those born locally who then moved away, only to return later in life. Further examples from the Lifeways project have been noted in our regional chapters, and a brief selection presented after each regional chapter. It is clear that, whatever the overarching tenets and norms of LBK culture may have been, individual people would have had distinctive lifecourses and been distinguishable by their varying treatment in death. This encourages us to think of individuals in the LBK not as predetermined or repetitive entities, but rather, as Debbora Battaglia has put it (1999, 115), open questions, 'subject to the constraints and manipulations of cultural forces, on the one hand, and on the other hand capable, upon reflection, of breaking with and transforming the situations in which they are formed'.

'Outliers' picked out in the isotopic analyses could sometimes be further distinguished by visibly different mortuary treatment, but were just as likely not to be differentiated from their neighbours in the mortuary populations by special interment or provision of unusual grave goods. For example, we can point to those seven burials that clustered away from the strontium average at Schwetzingen, the majority of whom were buried in the dominant orientation, with their heads to the north or north-east, and in a left-crouched position (Chapter 7.7.6). Alongside men buried with stone adzes, with the least variance in their strontium ratios (Bentley *et al.* 2012), were other men with different life histories; there were two male arrays or mixing lines, for example, in the Aiterhofen data (Bickle *et al.* 2011; Chapter 6). Equally, as well as those women whose isotopic patterns suggest more mixed diets or perhaps non-local localities in childhood, there were plenty of others who fit firmly within probable local signatures.

Although strongly sexed patterns were found in the isotopic and osteological data, variability within each sex could also be a matter of degree. Even those males buried with stone adzes were not always treated at death in identical ways. The strontium ratios of the three right-crouched males buried with polished stone at Ensisheim (Chapter 8.8) suggest that this lifeway may have been a widely shared experience. Likewise, while patrilocality could have tempered the lifeways of many women, we can point to many instances in the funerary and osteological data where diversity is present. For instance, we can compare burials 9 and 17 at Rutzing (Chapter 5.10). Burial 9 was a young adult female who had moved from a non-loess location and by her death had suffered caries in three of her third molars, while burial 17 was in middle-age when she died and in childhood had eaten a predominantly loess-based diet. Their respective carbon isotope values, however, fall at the extremes of the population. The diet of the woman in burial 9 in the years before her death is likely to have come from more open areas than that of the woman in burial 17. We can perhaps suggest that the lives of these two women took them in opposite directions; burial 9 moved from a childhood with a substantial non-loess component in the diet to eating foods sourced mainly in the open areas around the settlement, while burial 17 went from consuming a mainly loess-based diet from open areas when young to having more food sourced from woodland in adulthood (though here we cannot say from what geology the diet was sourced).

While there is recurrent evidence for different childhood diets and perhaps localities for men and women, which in turn underpins the claim for recurrent patrilocality or virilocality across the central European LBK, it is important not to construct rigid monolithic identities defined solely by gender. People were not only guided by gendered practices, but also transformed as they aged. A sense of the changing lifecourse has been noted in several studies, including again Vedrovice (Zvelebil and Pettitt 2008; Zvelebil *et al.* 2010) and Aiterhofen (D. Hofmann 2009a; Chapter 6), as well as in the funerary record more broadly (Chapter 9.5.4). In the largest sampled assemblages, we were able to show that stable isotopes point to trends with age (nitrogen values increased for men, and decreased for women) which may relate to different dietary composition. Similarly age at death seems to have had an impact on funerary rite, with the loss of a child between the ages of seven and 13 particularly marked (Chapter 9.5.3–4).

Individuals could also be defined by any number of other groupings, networks or affiliations. At several of the cemeteries we have discussed, 'paired' burials – as well as perhaps the more strictly defined double burials (as at Otzing; Chapter 6.8) – and clusters of graves (Chapters 4.7, 4.10, 5.10, 6.7, 8.7, 8.10 and 9.5.2) could be identified, suggesting ties in life between those interred. In many of these cases a mother-child relationship is strongly suggested, such as in the case of burials 48, 49 and 50 at Nitra where the arm of the young adult female is resting over one child, with the hand curving around the skull of the second (Pavúk 1972a, 17). In others, such as the graves of two mature women (18 and 20) at Mulhouse-Est, other relationships could be envisaged (Chapter 8.7). These two women had been placed in mirror images of each other; burial 18 was right-crouched but in the dominant regional orientation of north-east–south-west, while burial 20 was left-crouched and oriented in the opposite direction. The grave pits thus shared an orientation, but the individual in burial 20 was facing away from burial 18. We can perhaps imagine other relations were being stressed here – between sisters, cousins, or aunts, say, as well as possible ties by marriage among others.

For men, we can think not only of household heads, but also of fathers, brothers, uncles, sons, cousins and so on (cf. Strien 2010b), and it would be wise to think beyond purely kinship relations, and to bring in affines and other residents. Relationships between and across this mix of people might be what is being played out in, for example, the intersecting graves in the lines and small clusters at Nitra (Chapter 4). Yet it is striking how, in all the burial grounds considered in the Lifeways project, there is not more evidence for clear-cut structure in the patterning within the observable clusters. These certainly do contain some richly furnished graves, but these are both male and female, and it is hard to maintain that such clusters are only to do with the commemoration of dominant and locally-based men. Men and women, of varying ages, along with juveniles and children, occur in these contexts together, and it is perhaps at one level such togetherness or co-occurrence that is of fundamental importance, alongside or beyond the significance of potential different statuses, positions or life histories.

10.2.2 Households and house societies

What was the source of such togetherness? Here some of the traditional scales preferred in LBK research come into play. One of the dominant social facts of LBK existence was that people lived in longhouses, even though they may not have spent all their lives rooted to longhouse settlements. Depending on the outcome of ongoing debate about the duration of houses, they very possibly belonged to more than one household in the course of their lives (Whittle 2009, 256–7). If the short household duration model is right, all household members presumably had to shift their allegiance to a particular structure (though not necessarily, in the *Hofplatz* or yard model, their allegiance to a particular place within any given settlement) at least once in their lives, and perhaps twice in the case of longer-lived individuals. We also do not know whether people were only, at any one time, members of a single household. But it is instantly striking that across the burial grounds covered in this project in central Europe, and indeed beyond in the wider LBK distribution, the household as such does not show up in any easily recognisable or obvious way among the mortuary populations. The cemeteries are not just about the personae and memories of male household heads, even though there may have been a recurrent and perhaps even dominant practice of patrilocality, and their spatial layouts do not suggest the same kind of emphasis on relative separation, distance and independence that so strongly characterises longhouses on the ground as lived-in structures – at least in the dominant *Hofplatz* or yard model. So a fluctuating mix of shifting household composition, co-residence, marriage, other alliances, and other connections could be mooted as one source of diversity in LBK lifeways, at the local and intimate scale.

Could a new kid on the block also help to take this further? As is becoming increasingly well known in archaeology, the late Claude Lévi-Strauss (1982; 1987) suggested the concept of *sociétés à maison* or house societies in the 1970s. This developed from studies of situations where traditional anthropological concepts of kinship and descent did not seem to work adequately (Lévi-Strauss 1982, 163–70), using earlier observations by Boas and Kroeber among others on Northwest Coast and Californian societies. Boas, for example, found it hard to classify Kwakiutl descent groups as either matrilineal or patrilineal (Beck 2007, 5; cf. Jordan and O'Neill 2010). Lévi-Strauss therefore argued that a concept of the house itself was a key organising principle in this kind of situation (with examples extending as far as Polynesia, feudal Japan, and the noble houses of Europe), existing alongside other concepts and forms of relationship (Lévi-Strauss 1982, 176–87; 1987, 151–2; Borić 2007, 99). It is worth repeating the definition of Lévi-Strauss himself (1987, 152) of the house in this context as a:

> moral person, keeper of a domain composed altogether of material and immaterial property, which perpetuates itself by the transmission of its name, of its fortune and of its titles in a real or fictive line, held as legitimate on the sole condition that this continuity can express itself in the language of kinship or of affinity, and most often, of both together.

This has been discussed much further in a series of anthropological studies (e.g. Boon 1990; Waterson 1990; Carsten and Hugh-Jones 1995), and then taken up enthusiastically by an increasing number of archaeologists (e.g. Joyce and Gillespie 2000; Kuijt 2000; Chesson 2003; Hodder and Cessford 2004; Beck 2007; Borić 2007; 2008; J. Thomas forthcoming). What Dušan Borić (2008, 111) has called the 'frequent reification in a physical building' of the bundle of ideas represented by the concept of *sociétés à maison* has obviously been of much interest to archaeologists, and this concept has resonated productively across a number of contexts, from Neolithic south-east Europe (Borić 2008) to Neolithic Britain (J. Thomas forthcoming). But if wide applicability has been a strength, it could also be seen as a weakness, and there is a danger that all situations with houses are going to be pressed into the mould of a new and fashionable model. The distinction between house societies and societies with houses is rather ambiguous (Waterson 1995, 49, 52), and as described by Borić (2008, 111), there are other, even more general anthropological accounts (including in Bourdieu

1990; Carsten and Hugh-Jones 1995) in which the house is seen as 'an active social agent whose existence does not necessarily need to lead to the formation of the type of house society social institution with hierarchical structure that Lévi-Strauss often described...The house is seen as a microcosm that reflects and objectifies the structuring of cosmological orders'.

Given that LBK lifeways centrally involved the construction and use of substantial longhouses, does that make this specifically a *société à maison*? Does this provide a better understanding of LBK social relations than other concepts discussed above in this chapter? We can be cautious and sceptical, but there is one possibility worth noting, and if accepted this might serve further to deepen our sense of the diversity of ideas and practices within LBK society.

One of us (Whittle 2012) has recently discussed, building on earlier brief suggestions (Whittle 2003, 140; Jones 2007, 103–4), possible homologies between house and grave in the LBK, but without linking that discussion explicitly to the model of *sociétés à maison*. The argument runs as follows. Whether or not the longhouse had relatively few inhabitants in structures full of posts, and presumably screens; whether or not the longhouse always stood on its own, its *Hofplatz* space symbolising and actively signalling household independence; whether or not each and every longhouse cluster or ribbon was of equal social standing; whether or not all longhouses were kept in active use for the same length of time, since we can envisage, within overall regional chronologies, varying and overlapping durations – the longhouse was the point around which the LBK social kaleidoscope shifted. It could also be seen as a shifting assemblage of people, things and even places (cf. Harris 2012). It brought together people who were constituted by relations across a wide social landscape, and many more people than the eventual inhabitants were presumably necessary for construction in the first place, the collective effort clearly implied serving to spread the house beyond its mere location.[1] The house both concentrated and distributed identities in the LBK landscape.

On the other hand, the oriented, crouched, probably clothed body of the recurrent LBK cemetery grave could be seen as still engaged, or ready to be engaged, with ongoing activity in the world. Those that do have grave goods with them are accompanied by the things of everyday existence, from pots to tools to ornaments, distributed around (when not literally on) their bodies, ready to hand. These LBK cemetery graves often (but of course not universally so, as we have stressed throughout) present to survivors and mourners a last image of individual, intact, complete, clothed, sleeping or resting bodies, looking, perhaps expectantly, in particular, shared directions, and ready for continued action in the world. In many ways, this kind of presentation and performance could be seen as a key facet (though once again, of course not the only one) of this mortuary rite. LBK mortuary practice collects and concentrates identities.

Now, although they have often been kept apart in recent discussions, we can think about putting the two together. In the *Hofplatz* model, houses stood in their own space; graves regularly have space around them. Houses also form either yards, wards or rows, and sometimes perhaps all such elements in a single settlement; graves can be laid out in a general scatter, but also in tighter or more easily identifiable clusters, and sometimes also rows. In the *Hofplatz* model, there is continuity of building in a more or less tightly defined place, and successive buildings are repetitions. In many cemeteries, graves may have been added one by one, gradually creating the total space of the burial ground, though clusters might be seen to echo *Hofplätze*, and the same could be argued for rows of graves in comparison to rows of houses. Houses normally share a common orientation within individual settlements and regions; graves too share orientations, though there is considerably more variation in this feature of them than is the case for houses (Chapter 9.5.3). The overall north–south orientation of houses (trending to north-west–south-east as one moves north-west in the LBK distribution: Coudart 1998; Bradley 2001) is different to that of the overall regional diversity in the orientation of graves, though bodies recurrently face southwards like one end of the longhouse. Could there be both difference and linkage here, rather as Edmund Leach (1976) noted the complementary qualities of white at weddings and black at funerals? Houses, whether in *Hofplätze* or rows, represented a succession of buildings, many perhaps abandoned before they had to be, and left to decay into mounds, with protruding posts, in amongst and close to the fresh buildings occupied by former or new inhabitants (Bradley 1996); it is not normally possible to backfill a dug feature like a deep grave so that the original surface is left level, and a LBK cemetery could have consisted of a series of small oval or rectangular mounds with protruding markers, mimicking the look of one aspect of the continuing settlement.[2]

Could, therefore, at least in part, the grave, or grave and body, have been seen as a house, and conversely, could the house have been conceptualised as a body? There are sufficient ethnographic analogies to allow the latter proposition (e.g. S. Hugh-Jones 1995; C. Hugh-Jones 1996; cf. Tilley 1999; Borić and Robb 2008; Borić 2010), though the rich symbolisms of the house need not be confined to the metaphor of the body alone. Could Modderman's analysis of house parts also be recruited to the argument here? Could the modular nature of the house, in Modderman's view, be mapped on to the body? To the arguments that the north-west part of the house was special (Bradley 2001; Lüning 2009), we could add the proposition that it and the head of the body were in some ways equivalent, and the arms and hands in some ways equivalent to the middle of the house. This view would have the north-west part of the house as the head or spirit, and conversely the head region of the body, often in LBK graves with a sprinkling of red ochre, as encapsulating the inner sanctum of the house. The lived-in middle part of the house, in Modderman's view, could be sought in the middle part of the body, where hands and arms have things ready to hand. This in turn could generate a novel interpretation of the central Y- and J- post settings of earlier LBK longhouses, at least in buildings more to the north-west of the LBK distribution.

This kind of view might work best for tripartite houses, or perhaps bipartite houses, as it says little about the feet of the body and the southern/south-east parts of the house, often taken as one of the principal entrances. It probably also tramples over a lot of detail for the use of different parts of the house and the zones immediately outside it, gleaned from close study of artefacts (e.g. D. Hofmann 2010, Abb. 2). But if this view of possible homologies were to be followed, then cemetery grave and house were reworkings of each other, though not necessarily identical. In their graves, the cemetery dead lived on, but they lived in or under graves which at ground level recreated, in miniature, the look of decaying longhouses. The grave became another moment on the line of existence, or another point around which a differently configured kaleidoscope turned.

Perhaps this possible homology does open up interesting possibilities for thinking about the LBK as a *société à maison*, though we do not insist upon this point. Perhaps at best it serves to underline the scope for thinking about differing scales and kinds of social interaction within the LBK – potentially significant dimensions of diversity.

10.2.3 Lineages or clans

Whatever one's view of the possibilities discussed above, the more recent suggestions that particular lineages or clans are visible within settlements, as in the particular case of Vaihingen (Strien 2005; Bogaard *et al.* 2011; Chapter 7), and indeed that competition between such groupings drove LBK expansion and development in the first place (Frirdich 2005), introduce another important scale. On the ground, the model of clan or lineage areas within the Vaihingen settlement could be roughly equated with the wards proposed in Dutch settlement research (Chapter 1.3.2), though we make no claim that LBK settlements everywhere show the same kind of structure. Proponents of the row hypothesis, however, have so far not gone beyond identification of lines of houses, to suggest for example any commonality in row membership.[3] These various new suggestions highlight the fundamental issue of what the mortuary populations found in LBK burial grounds represent.

There is a strong general case for selection. Pieter van de Velde has made the simple but important point (1997, 87; also Nieszery 1995; Lüning 1988a) that even on the most conservative estimates of population densities in the LBK (and see Zimmermann *et al.* 2009 for more radical possibilities; Chapter 1.3.2), all the archaeologically visible and varied means of treating the dead in the LBK must under-represent the original living population. His proposal is that the normal means of disposal must therefore have been by exposure out in the landscape. This is obviously hard to evaluate and quantify, and a counter-suggestion might be that cremation was much more widely practised, though it does seem to be more visible in particular contexts than others (for example later in the Moravian sequence: Čižmář 2008b; Chapter 4.2 and 4.9). Cemetery populations could therefore plausibly be seen as a selection. This general claim too must be examined and qualified. Beyond the area of the Lifeways project, van de Velde also argues (1997, 86) that the cemetery at Elsloo is placed on the far side of the adjacent settlement, away from other local sites, and therefore belongs only to it. He estimated a settlement size of 8–11 houses, with five or six occupants each, 'together some 40 to 60 people' at any one time. Given the further estimate that the cemetery was in use for only three generations, over that span the village would have seen 120–80 deaths, compared with the 113 burials in the cemetery. We would like to know a lot more about the duration of LBK cemeteries, formally modelled in a robust Bayesian chronological framework (Bayliss 2009; Appendix B), and not all cemeteries need have had the same character, but selection in many is a plausible and attractive model.

The implications of this possibility are extensive. On this basis, the Lifeways sample, dominated by cemetery burials, cannot stand for the whole of the LBK population, and the overall extent of uniformity and diversity in lifeways thus revealed would thereby be confined to a portion of it. Some check on this could be provided by the settlement burials from Hungary, and the cases of Asparn in Austria and Otzing in Bavaria. However, as already discussed (Chapters 1.3.5 and 3.11), these settlement burials are no more representative of the population as a whole than cemeteries, as there seem in turn to have been selection processes and criteria behind them as well. While isotopic and osteological study could identify no distinct differences in lifeways between the two contexts, the discussion of funerary rites in Chapter 9.5.2 could point to varied burial practices. If many of the mortuary populations in LBK cemeteries are, as a working hypothesis, a selection from the wider population, a further plausible hypothesis is that they could represent groups within the community, such as the lineages, clans or wards already mooted above.

How far can this idea be taken, and need only a single model apply? Are we to envisage burials in cemeteries as those of the dominant clans, such as A at Vaihingen with its presumed preferential access to the best local soils (Bogaard *et al.* 2011, 405), or as drawn from across all the internal groupings – five suggested in this case – of a substantial settlement like Vaihingen? Could clan-like groupings be behind the two male arrays seen at Aiterhofen or explain the spatial variation linking isotopes and funerary rites seen at cemeteries such as Rutzing or Souffelweyersheim? Or is this allowing what may be itself an unusual settlement to dictate models that were more fluid on the ground? It is also important to remember here the debate about whether burial grounds served major or dominant settlements only, or the wider settlement pattern. Despite the suggestions of 'central places' in the LBK (Chapter 1.3.2), important lineages or clans, or some of their members, could well have been resident in smaller settlements. While the cemetery at Elsloo in Dutch Limburg can be argued, from its location, to belong only to the nearby large settlement (van de Velde 1997), that need not be the case elsewhere. Pottery studies suggest that more than one settlement may have contributed to the Niedermerz cemetery on the Aldenhovener Platte (Hoyer 2010; cf. Krahn 2003; Krahn-Schigiol 2005; Chapter 1.3.5). Elsewhere varied settlement-cemetery relations are suggested: Aiterhofen may have been surrounded by several settlements (Chapter 6.7) and the burials at Ensisheim may have been set within an older or abandoned settlement (which may also have been the case at Souffelweyersheim; Chapter 8.9), but not far from one contemporary with the cemetery (Chapter 8.8). However, the details of the surrounding settlement contexts are not available in many of the Lifeways case studies, such as Nitra (Chapter 4.10).

These considerations obviously underline the limits of present knowledge, but they also open another potential source of diversity. We do not have to impose a single model, but a general hypothesis can be that competition among and between dominant groups within local and regional LBK settlement areas would be a potent source of diversity. Allied to that were all manner of local and regional histories of beginnings, assimilations, alliances, and connections and orientations to elsewhere, which could have affected both the process of selection for cemetery burial and the details of mortuary treatment at any one funeral. It is worth remembering the observation that the amount of effort invested in mortuary ritual will often depend on the social context of succession and the situation – from success and security to ambition to stress and threat – in which particular mourners found themselves (Hodder 1982, chapter 9).

The hypothesis of patrilocality would fit the model of lineages or clans especially being represented in LBK burial grounds, and patrilineal systems of descent are an obvious possibility. We do not want to downplay what is one of the major results from our project – in the form of the recurrent and widespread lesser variance of strontium ratios for men buried with stone adzes (Bentley *et al.* 2012) – nor earlier suggestions of inherited position for children (Jeunesse 1996), but there are once again interesting other possibilities for considering further diversity and its sources.

10.2.4 Descent systems

One of the social contexts in which LBK mourners found themselves was surely the history of relations through previous generations. The discussion of the strontium data throughout the regional chapters and in Chapter 9 has reinforced the possibility that descent mattered keenly to LBK lifeways. Yet the modelling of descent systems in archaeology has had a very chequered history. In many writings on prehistory, descent systems have been largely absent until later periods, for example the third millennium cal BC when several scholars (e.g. Kristiansen 2012) see the initial emergence of 'modern' European closed systems of descent and inheritable property. By contrast, while social evolutionary models were commonplace in processual archaeology, with progression from tribal or segmentary society to chiefdoms, for example (Renfrew 1973), there has frequently been little or no emphasis placed on descent as such, even with the theoretical attention given to 'corporate descent groups' in the famous Saxe-Goldstein hypothesis No. 8 (reviewed in Morris 1991), or with the emphasis devoted to descent in classic formulations of social evolution, for example by Elman Service (1962).

Even when the idea has been present, little has normally been done with it. Post-processual archaeologists have paid even less attention, and no individual or dividual – with partible or permeable personhood – yet seems to have relations other than with very generalised or remote ancestors (cf. Whitley 2002; Whittle 2003). Perhaps in part this is because social anthropologists themselves have been at pains to deconstruct the prominence and dominance of kinship in social relations, beginning with the influential work of David Schneider (1968) and continuing in the assertion of the importance of other relationships, including co-residence, made by Janet Carsten and others (Carsten 2004). An interesting strand in this debate has been the move away from single, dominant models, seen for example in the history of the rise and decline of the model of unilineal descent (A. Kuper 1988). Real-life situations seem to offer a multiplicity of stated ideals and varied practice; bilateral descent is one interesting and relevant variant (Scheffler 1966; Milisauskas 1986; Forbes 2007). Historical analogies too offer diversity and change. It has been suggested that Iroquois longhouse communities may have begun as patrilineal, only to become matrilineal through time (Warrick 1996; Creese 2011); and indeed matrilineal kinship was combined here with clan segmentation, hereditary leadership and 'strong prohibitions against acquisitiveness, individual wealth accumulation and coercive political authority' (Creese 2011, 3–4). And on the Northwest Coast of America, there were longhouse communities with contrasting descent reckoning: matrilineal and avunculocal in one area, on the one hand, and patrilineal and patrililocal in another, on the other hand (Drucker 1955; Jordan and O'Neill 2010, 3885–6).

In LBK studies, there has in fact been an enduring interest in descent systems (Chapter 1.3.7), though those were never fully integrated with other traditional scales of analysis of LBK culture; the discussion here has already engaged with house societies and clans. The older preference in the literature, mirroring older social evolutionary theory (see also Service 1962), was for matrilineal descent. The idea of patrilineal descent goes back especially to the interpretations by Juraj Pavúk (1972a) of the cemetery at Nitra, and has been reinforced by recent research including consideration of Talheim (Eisenhauer 2003a; 2003b) and of course strontium ratios (e.g. Bentley 2007; Bentley *et al.* 2008). Perhaps it is time to revive the possibility that the older model is still relevant, not as necessarily dominant or exclusive, but as part of diverse practice within LBK communities.

Elman Service (1962, 120–40) set out a simple but thoughtful contrast between patrilineal and matrilineal systems of descent, both unilineal, and what he called cognatic and composite arrangements, which is useful as a further guide at this point. For him, virilocal residence and patrilineal descent were not surprising features of tribal society, but the widespread occurrence of matriliny was (Service 1962, 120). He noted, in a similar way to Podborský (2002b), the importance of the collaborative work of women in gardens, storage and cooking, these together encouraging uxorilocal residence (Service 1962, 121). In both these kinds of unilineal descent system, the prevailing concept seems to be of common rather than genealogical descent (Service 1962, 122), though common ancestors could be remembered some four or five generations back (Service 1962, 123). Male roles are still important in matrilineal groups; Service (1962, 125) notes that '"husbandness" and familial authority remain male roles even though males reside in wife's lineage in uxorilocal-matrilineal societies rather than in their own'. In contrast, nonlineal or cognatic groups are composed 'simply of descendants traced through either or both mother's and father's relatives' (Service 1962, 133). Now post-marital residence is expedient; even when exogamy is practised, 'newly-weds might live with whatever group of relatives they find most receptive' (Service 1962, 134). Interestingly again, he sees such flexibility as a highly useful strategy in situations of flux and change, and, again strikingly, notes the existence of residential groups with 'a mixture of lineal and cognatic principles' (Service 1962, 134–5). In this kind of case, a core of lineally related permanent inhabitants can be joined by relatives as circumstances demand and permit (Service 1962, 135).

Now this is a generalising account, and more recent discussions, post-Schneider, have sought to stress the situational, fluid and flexible nature of sociality, including co-residence (A. Kuper 1988; Carsten 2004). Nonetheless, it seems to us to reinforce the possibility of rather diverse arrangements in the LBK, especially when this culture is seen not as static, but dynamic and changing. Several choices, rather than a single model, could perhaps be considered. In line with much recent thinking, there could have been a recurrent, strong preference for patrilocality, and, given the indications from our analyses of lifeways which were determined from childhood onwards, this might have been most pertinent within dominant lineages or clans, which, following Service, could have shared common descent. Furthermore, arguing that patrilocal practices were most frequent need not preclude variation in descent practices as a whole; relatedness as lived is necessarily also contingent on who survives, who dies and how relations can fragment (Van Vleet 2008). As alternative or overlapping arrangements, arguments for matriliny can be maintained, and cognative, nonlineal groups can also be proposed.

It would be stretching interpretation of the diversity in the ethnographic record too far to propose all such variations in operation in a single settlement or regional group of settlements at any one time, but flexibility at the regional or inter-regional level could be plausible. Might this be a way to see the apparent preference in Hungary, on the evidence available so far, for settlement burials as opposed to separate cemeteries, or the diversity within a burial ground like Aiterhofen in Bavaria, or the differences between the two parts of Alsace? Could the debate about settlement layout contribute to our understanding of such possible arrangements, with for example the more common row-like layouts of the eastern parts of the distribution covered by the Lifeways project contrasting with the *Hofplatz* or yard model still supported by many LBK researchers in the more westerly LBK distribution? Can even the differences between left-crouched and right-crouched burials, or between different burial orientations, be thought of in relation to these social strategies?

Perhaps it is unhelpful to expect clear-cut signals in any of these dimensions for one or other system of post-marital residence or descent system, but it is worthwhile exploring some of the possibilities, if only because past debate on the LBK has never quite taken things this far. Thus, one way to read the evidence might be to see the existence further east of matrilineal descent groups, where the settlement row might signal the corporate nature of collective labour and shared social activities including the preparation and consumption of food, in contrast to a more westerly emphasis on individual yards or groups of yards, which might signal a more patrilocal and patrilineal system. But even within such a tentative model, allowance would have to be made for change through time, and Nitra, as often suggested (e.g. Sherratt 1976; Jeunesse 1996), could be seen as a burial ground of later LBK date with a principal emphasis on older males, suggestive of patriliny. Yet another way to interpret the data overall would be to refuse the choice of one or other clear-cut and dominant arrangement, and to open up the possibility of considerable diversity in residence and descent practice, as well as of change through time. In this model, people, households and household and other groupings would literally come and go, perhaps better fitted to the kind of cognatic, nonlineal groups briefly noted above.

10.2.5 Sodalities

This leads on to other less familiar possibilities. Much of the above discussion has focused on different kinds and sizes of self-contained or self-containing social groups, but so far mostly of relatively limited extent or scale. The concept of sodality, by contrast, offers links that cross-cut others. Originally suggested by Lowie (1948), it was defined by Service (1962, 21) as a 'nonresidential association that has some corporate functions or purposes'. In contrast to residential groups which can be located and seen on the ground, 'sodalities are not groups at all for they are never consistently or even necessarily frequently agglomerated', with 'cultural inventions such as a name, ceremony, mythology, insignia of membership and so on' being common (Service 1962, 22). In cross-cutting residential groups, they also serve, in differing ways, to integrate them (Service 1962, 22). Further, what Service calls 'pan-tribal sodalities' are what 'make a tribe a tribe, for if they did not exist then there is nothing but a series of bands, more affluent than hunters and gatherers but still bands, with only intermarriage between certain ones providing any unity' (1962, 115). Service goes on (1962, 116) to distinguish between sodalities derived from kinship (such as the clan, the kindred and the segmentary lineage) and those which are not (such as age-grades and warrior and ceremonial societies). It is the latter which could be of most interest in the LBK context.

As an analogy, the concept of sodalities has been used with considerable effect in study of the Hopewellian communities of eastern North America, particularly in the Scioto region (Carr 2006a; 2006b; Carr *et al.* 2006). This identified three local symbolic communities in adjacent valleys, which among many other features buried some of their dead together. By this means,

> ...the three communities wedded together their ancestors in an essentially permanent afterlife existence and, by implication, gave strong reason for the living members of those communities to uphold the principle of social unity they were attempting to construct (Carr 2006a, 99).

It is argued that the three communities did not 'conceive of themselves as one integrated "society" or "tribe"' but rather were held together by negotiated alliance (Carr 2006a, 99). Burial of the dead from multiple communities in a common cemetery was a key element in this kind of arrangement (Carr 2006a, 99–100). Within this practice, at least two sodalities are claimed, materially marked by copper breastplates and earspools respectively, found in burials (Carr 2006a, 100); other sodalities could be marked by copper headplates and axes ('celts') (Carr 2006b, 285–6). On the whole, these objects are not regarded as indicators of rank, because of their accompanying a wide range of ages in mortuary ritual (Carr 2006b, 282), though the latter two categories have been suggested as badges of leadership of a community, society or sodality (Carr 2006b, 285; Carr *et al.* 2006, 492–3). Such suggested sodalities would have provided the means for 'the flow of subsistence and other goods across localized kinship and localized residence groups' (Carr 2006b, 328).

Further information on sodalities is provided by analogies from Puebloan societies of the American Southwest (Carr 2006b, 284–5). Sodality membership within a community can range from low to high. It was largely confined to adult members, conferred at initiation. It is interesting to note that 'Puebloan sodality membership was most commonly restricted to males, males with the support of their wives, or males and females but with males holding positions of leadership or levels of achievement' (Carr 2006b, 284). It was possible for individuals to belong to more than one ceremonial society simultaneously. Ceremonial societies in some Puebloan groups varied in prestige and power (Carr 2006b, 284). The historic Central Algonkians also had 'sacred pack' organisations for such varied purposes as warfare, hunting, sorcery, healing the whole tribe, epidemics and drought; as in other societies, membership of these organisations was voluntary and non-hereditary, and cross-cut clans, lineages and each other (Carr *et al.* 2006b, 496).

Another vision of the importance and role of Hopewellian sodalities has been set out by Martin Byers (2011). He too has argued that Hopewell ritual and mortuary sites were the concern of much more than purely local kin groups, and that autonomous sodalities were a key but neglected dimension (A.M. Byers 2011, 11–12). Specifically, however, he has proposed that the social formations involved in the construction and use of Hopewell earthworks were more than just the outcome of alliances across multiple communities (A.M. Byers 2011, 43), and that a series of sodalities were particularly concerned with cult matters of central concern, particularly rites of soul release and world renewal (A.M. Byers 2011, 84–7). The mortuary rites in which such proposed Hopewellian 'world renewal cult heterarchies' (A.M. Byers 2011, 87) were involved were radically different to those of the LBK, involving amongst other things secondary burials, the formation of collective deposits associated with earthworks, and perhaps notions of multiple souls (A.M. Byers 2011, 88, 91–2).

There is no intention here simply to import one or other of the competing Middle Woodland hypotheses straight into the social landscape of the central European LBK. But the idea that LBK cemeteries could have formed from multiple communities, or from people drawn from across multiple communities, both local and non-local, is powerful and could be informative. Perhaps some of the many inter-regional material connections noted in the introductions to Chapters 3–8 could be interpreted within a framework of sodalities, alongside possible kinship links and those provided by other forms of alliance. Could stone adzes mark a very widespread, predominantly male sodality, and various forms of *Spondylus* ornaments, which are more regionalised within the LBK of central and western Europe (Jeunesse 2009, fig. 13) other sodalities, with both male and female membership? Alternatively, we could argue that the position of the body in the grave and the orientation of the deceased were not exhibiting variation from the norm of burial practices (i.e. right-crouched deviant burials *versus* 'normal' left-crouched ones), but rather recast each position or orientation as signalling belonging or alliance at scales beyond the immediate community. The advent of supine burials in northern Alsace, could, in this model, have been a search to express belonging to newer networks developing in the later phases of the LBK.

The suggestion of sodalities is not inconsistent with previous modelling of LBK networks. For example, as already noted in Chapter 1.7, the risks of failure in what he saw as an uncertain environment necessitated in the view of Peter Bogucki a 'support network' or non-hierarchical social web beyond immediate microregions or settlement clusters, thus linking neighbourhood communities by exogamy and kinship bonds to much further afield; the house in particular is seen as a 'node in an interlocking network of kinship and social ties both within the microregion and beyond' (Bogucki 1988, 121). Envisaging the widest possible definition of kin, bilateral kinship relations radiating out from each household are proposed, rather than any rigidly defined unilineal descent system. While the possibility of some difference at community level is left open, the necessity for reciprocity was seen as likely to dampen any such divergence; items such as *Spondylus* circulated as 'scarce necessities' (Bogucki 1988, 126) or perhaps bridewealth rather than as prestige items. But with sodalities, a further range and kind of connections, beside or beyond projections about status or position alone, could have been made within networks and meshworks, at closer and longer range.

10.2.6 Imagined communities and contingent assemblages

While the discussion so far privileges particular kinds and scales of social interaction, there are of course still others, at the wider if vaguer scale constituted by ideas of community, network or meshwork. This again offers under-explored opportunities to think about affiliations which create links and ties across such a scale. If the arguments for a narrow and exclusive selection from particular kinds of LBK social groupings as the basis for the formation of burial grounds seem too generalised to cover all cases – given the probable range in size, duration, internal groupings and clusters seen in the cemeteries across the distribution of the Lifeways project and beyond – then the next model to consider could be that of the wider community. That has some attractions. The dietary analyses emphasised again and again a general and repeated commonality of diet, over and above the evidence of variation in detail. The strontium analyses also indicated the prevalent recurrence of predominantly locally raised people in the mortuary populations of the burial grounds. So perhaps it is simply over-complicating matters to seek too much internal difference within them, and more preferable to see the LBK cemetery – again with suitable allowance for variation from region to region and through time – as emblematic of the marking in mortuary ritual of a dominant social practice of sharing and connection across community, network or meshwork.

While the notion of community continues to provide a useful terminology for certain collective actions, as a social concept it presents both advantages and disadvantages. It is hard to find a single definition, since usage can imply both some unproblematic, bounded, finite, self-identifying and locally residential group, and a much wider sense of participation, as far as the idea of 'moral community' described by Johnson (1994) in an account of the modern Nuer. Affective and performed community is often fragile, and its values have to be worked at (Canuto and Yaeger 2000; Overing and Passes 2000; Amit 2002; the topic has been usefully reviewed by Harris 2012). Such ambiguities and shifting temporalities could fit well with the model proposed above for LBK mortuary populations, but they also result in an analytically very vague and open-ended definition. Perhaps that too can be turned to advantage, and we might not need to worry about where community begins and ends within a wider notion of network or meshwork. It scarcely seems credible to see LBK culture as a whole as a single, interactive system (Chapter 1.3.6), more than the sum of its parts.

The regions which we have used in this volume have in part been pragmatically defined, but we can nonetheless argue for meaningful regional distinctions, on the one hand within modern regions, such as Basse-Alsace and Haute-Alsace (Chapter 8), and on the other between and across them, such as Bavaria compared with Lower Austria, Moravia and western Slovakia (Chapters 4–6), and in turn those compared to northern Hungary, which has its own nested differences between Transdanubia and the Alföld (Chapter 3). It could be worth noting what Service (1962, 111) had to say about the tribe, a term currently neglected in LBK and other Neolithic studies, but which points to the gap between thinking about community and thinking about the wider culture:

> A tribe is an association of a much larger number of kinship segments which are each composed of families. They are tied more firmly together than are the bands, which use mostly marriage ties alone. A tribe is of the order of a large collection of bands, but it is not *simply* a collection of bands.

The term 'tribe' is unfashionable not only in British interpretive discourse but also in current LBK scholarship, but whether or not it is to be retained, this definition can help us to think about the wider scales of social interaction within LBK culture – or the LBK interaction sphere. What were the ties that bound people and groups together, at wider scales? This too has been a neglected question, apart from the implicit assumption in culture historical approaches that members of a given archaeological culture would necessarily all share the same values. One significant attempt to address this can be mentioned again. Ulrike Sommer (2001) has explored whether a notion of conservative and strongly normative *doxa*, following Bourdieu, could explain the apparent uniformity and limited scope for individual agency in the LBK. That too runs into the difficulty of conceiving a single, coherent and enforceable or sanctioned system that extended over such a geographical scale, as well as tending to downplay the evidence for local or regional differences as noted throughout this volume.

Perhaps a better way to come to terms with this extended dimension of the LBK is to borrow, from a much quoted study of recent and historical nationalism, the notion of 'imagined communities' (Anderson 1991). Just as with community, Anderson notes (1991, 3) that notions of nation, nationality and nationalism have all proved very hard to define. Treating them as 'cultural artefacts of a particular kind' (Anderson 1991, 4), formed in particular combinations of circumstances, but compatible with other values and capable of being transplanted, he defines the nation in particular as an imagined political community (Anderson 1991, 6). It is worth quoting this more fully:

> It is *imagined* because the members of even the smallest nation will never know most of their fellow-members, meet them, or even hear of them, yet in the minds of each lives the image of their communion...Communities are to be distinguished, not by their falsity/genuineness, but by the style in which they are imagined (Anderson 1991, 6).

If this borrowing is justified,[4] what were the styles in which the LBK was imagined? Beyond the scales and concerns of particular individuals, households, descent groups and even perhaps sodalities, what were the further values, ideals and dreams that constituted part of the fabric of LBK lifeways? In the case of the nation, Anderson (1991, 7) has proposed 'finite, if elastic, boundaries', because 'no nation imagines itself as coterminous with mankind'. In the case of the LBK, perhaps the reverse was the case. The areas studied by the Lifeways project have not on the whole taken us to the variable and shifting boundaries of the LBK, and we need not propose that the LBK sphere was cut off from the even wider world; there is good evidence for contact with the beyonds of north, west and south (Chapter 1.3.6). But the area covered by the LBK is indeed vast; the scholars of at least a dozen modern nation states contribute to its study. Was there then a shared, ideal vision of peaceful, settled community, independent but connected, and capable of endless replication, more or less to the edge of the relevant world? Could something like that, alongside the hard practicalities of the local interests of colonisers and indigenous people, and of the press or push of more and more people on the ground, have helped to fuel the spread and then long-enduring maintenance of LBK lifeways? In turn, could the demise of this putative vision have been connected, alongside many other factors, with the ending of the LBK?

At this scale we also find the concept of assemblages, as well as imagined community, useful in getting at the 'inconsistent commonalities' of the LBK. The concept of assemblages is defined by Manuel DeLanda (2006; see also Borić and Miracle forthcoming; Harris 2012) as historically contingent actual entities, not instances of ideal forms, and not as seamless totalities but collections of heterogeneous components that should be analysed as such.[5] Following Gilles Deleuze, DeLanda stresses that assemblages are characterised by 'relations of exteriority': 'a component part of an assemblage may be detached from it and plugged into a different assemblage in which its interactions are different' (DeLanda 2006, 10). In order to avoid the production of 'reified generalities', 'we must instead focus on the historical processes that produce these products' since 'the identity of any assemblage at any level of scale is always a product of a process... and it is always precarious, since other processes...can destabilize it' (DeLanda 2006, 28). The ontological status of assemblages is that of 'individual singularities', which are 'historically contingent' (DeLanda 2006, 40; Borić and Miracle forthcoming).

The concept of assemblage has, at its heart, the insistence by Deleuze (1994; Deleuze and Guattari 2004) that 'becoming' (that is, that assemblages are caught up in an ongoing process of coming into existence) is a continual process of repetition and differentiation. This is to argue that social phenomena cannot be explained either in terms of norm or of deviation, but rather in how diversity operated at varied scales. Expressed plainly, if we seek to define and explain only the dominant pattern (for example of kinship), we will fail to grapple with the history in which that pattern was created and maintained (or, rather, repeated). Things are also central to the notion of assemblages (Harris forthcoming), and in the context of the LBK that of course opens up a powerful range of materiality of all kinds for further consideration.

So, as already argued, it could be attractive to see LBK cemeteries as contingent and shifting assemblages drawn from the wider community. Oliver Harris has recently referred to 'affective assemblages' (2012). Cemeteries present a range of men, women and children, and abundant variation in the ways in which their social personae were marked by funerary ritual and provision of grave goods. Who ended up in cemeteries, as opposed to elsewhere in the landscape (van de Velde 1997), could rather simply be seen in this model as the result of circumstance, dependent on particular individual life histories, contingent events, household trajectories or community formations. While we need not trouble ourselves here with expounding further the often difficult work of Deleuze and DeLanda, we do envisage that a sense of repeated diversity was integral to how LBK traditions were maintained and in the next section, we move on to present a narrative of LBK history drawing on the multiple scales at which the LBK was performed.

10.3 Repeat performances: a narrative of LBK lifeways

From an analytical point of view, the Lifeways project has indicated both commonalities, in diet, residence and lifeways, and divergences, in lifecourses, mortuary practice and positioning in the networks. From a broadly interpretive point of view, we have indicated a whole series of scales at which LBK people may have operated. That has taken us from the individual lifecourse and household to the imagined communities of endless connection. No one scale seems to suffice on its own, and there is no sense in which, from this perspective at least, the LBK was fractal. It is important at this point, therefore, to try to see how these putative scales – which we argue were more than our own analytical constructs – may have interrelated. We need to see how LBK lifeways were performed, and that is perhaps best done within a temporal perspective, covering the beginning, development and ending of the LBK.

As preliminary observation, it is worth underlining the varied temporalities of our suggested scales. There are no commonly agreed life tables for LBK populations (cf. Robb 2007, 40–3), but our own data (Lifeways Database; Chapter 9.4), based admittedly on our currently rather broad-brush adult ageing techniques, suggest that a lifespan of 50 years or more would have been relatively unusual; the bulk of the population may have died at an earlier age. The so far conventional model for house duration is roughly half that span, with the implication already noted that individuals would have belonged to more than one physical house in the course of their lives; the now competing house row model may offer a duration in line with or greater than long human lifespans. In both models, current chronologies offer many examples of long-lasting settlements: for example, 12 or 14 house generations in the models for the Aldenhovener Platte, or 17 or 18 in that for Vaihingen (Bogaard *et al.* 2011; Bogaard 2012). Not just the house plot or household may have endured, but also tenure of land (Bogaard *et al.* 2011; D. Hofmann forthcoming). Whatever the selections involved in their formation, burial grounds may also have lasted for many generations, though we are seriously hampered by the current imprecision in the date estimates for their duration of use. Ceramic styles and regional groupings also seem, on conventional interpretations of current evidence, to have developed over a timescale of at least several generations.

Such temporal variation is a potent but neglected source in its own right of diversity in practice. But we need to go further, to inject the sense of how these putative varying scales were performed and made sense. We could quote again the dictum of Bruno Latour (1993, 117) that the network is always local, but we need to try to understand the connection between local practice and other dimensions of the assemblage or network (or whatever other term might be preferred). Shared values and individual strategies, the circumstance of commonality and the room for manoeuvre, repeated practice and contingent performances, enduring norms and the flux of individual lives, houses and graves, can all make best sense within a situated history of LBK development and change.

10.3.1 Beginnings

So we can pull all this into a brief narrative, at the same time assessing how this project has helped to make a difference to our understanding of the performance of LBK lifeways.

There is currently broad consensus that the LBK began in Transdanubia in western Hungary, if not also in adjacent areas including southern Slovakia. The finger points at interaction between scattered late Starčevo communities and elusive late Mesolithic inhabitants. It remains unclear whether on the Great Hungarian Plain and indeed in parts of the Danube valley late Körös communities were also involved in the transformations out of which the LBK way of life came into existence, and in turn interaction between such communities and indigenous groups to their north can also be noted as a possibility. In both western and eastern Hungary, it need not necessarily be a case of setting incomers against indigenous people, since both Starčevo and Körös communities may already have had members of quite diverse origins and descent. It is only fair to note that some would still prefer to think of LBK beginnings in terms of incomers alone, for example as seen in the model of Starčevo communities leapfrogging from Croatia to beyond the bend of the Danube (Stadler and Kotova 2010a). But taking the more complicated view of mixed origins, something happened to transform social practice and interaction in the middle of the sixth millennium cal BC, and that sets the tone in terms of the theme of performance, right from the beginning.

We do not yet understand what the key elements were which triggered this transformation, and apart from anything else the still imprecise chronology continues to hamper us. Was this event-like, with one community somewhere, in a specific place and at a specific time, creating the idea of larger houses (as at Szentgyörgyvölgy-Pityerdomb) or responding to the fact of larger social groups by coming up with such buildings, and did the success of this experiment spread rapidly through the existing social networks? Or was it a more extended process, with a gradual increase in numbers of people on the ground, leading to both bigger and longer-lasting social aggregations for which the longhouse solution eventually emerged? In that scenario, the seemingly greater and certainly more visible number of Körös communities is still worth keeping in the frame, though they have often been left out of recent modelling of LBK beginnings.

Whatever model is to be preferred, existing practices were involved but were extended and transformed. Decisions were made to enlarge houses, either by people already habituated to dwelling in smaller versions, or by people committing to house life for the first time. Other existing material culture was changed, including new forms for pottery compared to both Starčevo and Körös styles, though there are also strong arguments for considerable continuity in lithic technology and in the distribution of lithics along pre-existing networks (Mateiciucová 2008a). If indigenous people were involved in these transformations, as we would argue is extremely likely, the adoption of both cereal garden cultivation and of animal husbandry was a further major transformation, though it is less clear at this stage in research whether or how much the nature of gardens or the composition of flocks and herds changed over the early generations of the LBK. Burial practice also shows some continuity on Hungarian territory at least. There had been burials in and around Körös settlements, though we know less about late Starčevo practice in Transdanubia, and the apparent lack of separate LBK (TLP and ALP) burial grounds on both sides of the Danube in Hungary was emphasised repeatedly in Chapter 3. But going on the evidence of sites like Füzesabony, Polgár-Ferenci-hát and Mezőkövesd-Mocsolyás in the north of the Plain, with time more burials accumulated in and around ALP settlements, compared with practice in the Körös culture, and much more consistent choices of body position and orientation emerged.

In general, though we had access to relatively few samples relevant to the earliest LBK, especially further west into central Europe, the Lifeways project has contributed new relevant analyses from those sites in the north of the

Great Hungarian Plain. Not all need be of earliest date, as detailed in Chapter 3, but the impression overall is of a commonality of diet on the one hand, as seen in the stable isotope values, and of life histories on the other, as seen in strontium ratios, which had probably been established early in the LBK. Variation in the lifeways of the sexes, which was perhaps to become a fixture of descent patterns seen in the strontium data from the cemeteries further west, may too have been part of these recurrent histories, with higher prevalence of caries amongst women suggesting they consumed a more starchy diet than men (Chapters 3.9 and 9.4).

An emphasis on commonality is also the case as we follow the further spread of the earliest LBK into Moravia, at the site of Vedrovice, through the combined analyses of the previous investigations led by the late Marek Zvelebil and of the Lifeways project itself. Marek had already set out a convincing scenario of Vedrovice as a gateway community, involving people of both outside and local descent (Zvelebil and Pettitt 2008; Zvelebil *et al.* 2010), which we would argue is still compatible with the newer aDNA studies which have appeared alongside it and since (though, as noted throughout this volume, those have tended to re-emphasise the role of incomers). Again the combined analyses suggest shared diet and predominantly local lives, but with the presence too of the 'born-aways' and wanderers whom Zvelebil has already emphasised. Perhaps one of the most surprising aspects of the study so far of Vedrovice, with its earliest LBK material culture, is its chronological position, established by formally modelled radiocarbon dates as belonging predominantly to the 53rd century cal BC. This may be telling us, though much more precise dating has yet to be achieved elsewhere, that the initial spread of the LBK was much slower and also much more patchy than has often been modelled. Might that better fit a model of complex and diverse composition for earliest LBK communities in general, rather than that of a single stream of uniform colonisers? If the evidence suggests the variety in backgrounds and individual life histories which we have hinted at throughout this volume, a more gradual spread of transformed lifeways would have given more time for the integration of people of differing descent.

Part of the success of LBK lifeways presumably lay in the fact that people of diverse origins could be accommodated within its shared value system and its shared material languages, and we would not make such a clear-cut distinction between public and private material styles as Marek Zvelebil and Alena Lukes (Zvelebil 2004; Lukes 2004; Lukes and Zvelebil 2004). Presumably there was no predetermined outcome or guiding pre-existing template of behaviour, and LBK lifeways may have emerged more or less contingently out of the mix of traditions and circumstances in which it was formed and performed. Did it 'make sense', in the context of the times, for all sorts of people to commit to doing things in broadly similar ways – 'uniformity' – while still retaining the capacity for independent agency – 'diversity'? Rather than a universal pre-formed strategy, an emergent commonality may have served the ends of sufficient individuals and communities to create the interaction sphere or assemblage or meshwork which we recognise as the earliest LBK.

Our analyses further west have not included the earliest LBK. Process may not have been uniform, and there remain considerable challenges in constructing a more robust and more precise chronology of developments. The arguments for complicated histories of first appearances have been set out through the regional chapters, and in the example of Bavaria, also the case for colonisation (Chapter 6). Further west again, in Alsace, we come to an area where there has been sustained discussion of the likely contribution to the formation and composition of the regional LBK from indigenous La Hoguette communities, even though those remain hard to characterise with much certainty. Imprecise chronology hampers us yet again. But the many differences between Haute-Alsace and Basse-Alsace set out in Chapter 8, in terms of both settlement, diet and lifeways, and mortuary practices, can be set against a potentially complicated background of strong contributions from indigenous traditions. Perhaps, in this region, more was at stake in terms of performing an 'LBK' identity, but such a challenge was responded to in different ways. Thus we could argue that in Haute-Alsace, the mortuary sphere was the place to reinforce norms of tradition and shared values, while in Basse-Alsace, funerary rites were subjected to greater innovation. Given that this kind of interpretation of the evidence across the LBK regions covered by the Lifeways project, the early stages of the establishment and performance of LBK lifeways were likely to have been quite diverse in detail, region by region, while at the same time belonging to a broadly similar interaction sphere or meshwork.

On that note, finally, questions of post-marital residence, descent and social differentiation in the earliest LBK remain open. The Hungarian and Moravian strontium ratios suggest a majority of more or less locally resident population, and the pattern of males buried with adzes who had had geographically more restricted childhoods or diets does not seem so prominent here. The apparent absence of formal cemeteries in Hungary could perhaps be compatible with matrilocal rather than patrilocal post-marital residence, or indeed with a less well defined system altogether. There are women as well as men in the clusters within the Vedrovice cemetery. A wider argument has been made for the existence of defined clans or lineages in the earliest LBK as a whole, which drove both expansion and change (Frirdich 2005), but neither the size of individual settlements nor their density need require this differentiation at this stage, and this may rather emerge in the developed LBK.

10.3.2 The developed LBK

As we have seen, many narratives of the LBK place the end of the earliest LBK at around 5300 cal BC, and subsequent changes are then seen as following thick and fast. While this may be true for some regions, the situation seems at present more complicated, with transition or overlap in the following century at least. That model would imply more gradual change at first, but then even faster acceleration subsequently, and it is worth keeping both scenarios in mind.

From this Flomborn/*Notenkopf* phase onwards, there were more people on the ground. The LBK continued to expand to the west, beyond the Rhine into north-west Germany, the southern Netherlands and eastern Belgium, and ultimately into northern France. Interaction with indigenous communities in the upper Rhine seems to be behind many of the variations visible in LBK practices in Alsace. Without arguing for universal similarities, in any given region, including those already settled in the earliest LBK, more sites can be found, with greater differentiation in size and in some cases probably character. A good example out of many is the settlement 'cell' of the Horn basin in Lower Austria, with the large, possibly central, site of Breiteneich, smaller but still substantial sites such as Mold and Strögen, and the smaller still and probably specialised site of Rosenburg (Chapter 5.4.1; Lenneis 2009; Pieler 2010). Another good example is Balatonszárszó-Kis-erdei-dűlő in Transdanubia, where the settlement appears in a location not preferred in the previous earliest phase (Oross and Bánffy 2009), and visibly develops from a small scatter of houses to the north of the site to a series of much larger concentrations in its southern part, seemingly arranged in rows, and bounded at some point by a ditch (Marton and Oross 2009; 2012; Oross *et al.* 2011). There is much variation, as Chapters 3–8 have emphasised, and changing local sequences have to be taken into account, some areas probably filling up faster than others.

This is the time when the size range of longhouses became much more varied, some getting much larger than before, with a corresponding greater division of internal space, notably in the bigger structures. As noted above for Balatonszárszó, rows of houses were probably more of a feature in the eastern part of the LBK distribution covered by this project, though again there is variation (Lenneis 2008), and the presumably stark difference between rows of houses (Rück 2007; 2009) and the individual *Hofplatz* or yard needs to be taken into account in modelling the nature of LBK communities. Developed LBK longhouses are distinctive, and hardly to be confused with other Neolithic or later architectures; there was a common way of building, with comparatively little regional variation across the LBK distribution as a whole (Coudart 1998; forthcoming; D. Hofmann forthcoming). But these three dimensions alone of longhouse size, internal arrangements and layout within settlements remind us of the potential for difference at the lived, local scale.

This is also the time when separate or formal burial grounds appear across much of the LBK distribution, as seen in the great majority of cemeteries sampled in this project. These too vary considerably in size, and appear not to have formed quickly, but to have developed grave by grave, although neither the tempo nor the duration of individual cemeteries is well understood. Nor do we fully understand the social relations presented and played out in LBK burial grounds. It is our view that they must represent a selection of the total population, and one possibility is that it was prominent or pre-eminent households, clans or lineages that dominated the formal funerals of this kind; many of these people may have been predominantly local, but we have also mooted the contribution of multiple communities, for example through sodalities of various possible kinds. Many funerals were carried out in a broadly similar way, individual bodies being placed at the base of pits prepared on the whole in such a way as not to intersect with existing, and presumably marked, graves, with a recurrent left-crouched body position and shared orientation. But again there is plenty of variation. We have consistently noted right-crouched burials across the distribution, and supine burials were a notable feature in Alsace. The Lifeways Database shows variation by region in the percentages of body position and orientation (Figs 9.10–11), and others before us have drawn attention to variation in the provision of grave goods. Following Jeunesse's (1996; 1997) Tradition I and II, we noted in Chapter 9.5.4 that the amount of variation itself could differ region to region and site to site. All this, just as with settlements and longhouses, reminds us again of the potential for difference at local and individual scales, within widely shared and broadly similar mortuary practices.

A further generalisation about the developed LBK can be risked, that this was also the time when regional networks of connection and interaction, and especially their directionality, intensified. Perhaps we need to be more cautious here, since studies have shown the extent and variety of lithic distribution already present in the late Mesolithic and earliest LBK (Mateiciucová 2008a), and because statements about the nature of the situation in the earliest LBK may simply reflect the current progress of research rather than the actual state of affairs (Lenneis 2005; Kerig 2010). Nonetheless, the regional chapters have noted a mass of connections seen both in shared pot styles and decorative motifs, which presumably reflect movements and interactions of people, and in distributed lithics, which may in many cases reflect a wider set of movements including hand-to-hand exchanges. The regional chapters have frequently noted a directionality in these links; this was a connected world, but not randomly so, and connections (or assemblages) may speak for all manner of origins, group and individual histories, and alliances. It is hard to think of LBK communities which were not linked to elsewhere, but the ways in which this was achieved and maintained appear to have varied in detail.

Finally, it hardly needs repeating that LBK communities remained committed in the developed phase to their choice of loess and other high-quality soils, for the location of their settlements. The evidence also suggests a broadly similar economy across the LBK distribution, with cattle husbandry and garden cultivation of cereals to the fore, with relatively few wild animals hunted, though again the introduction (Chapter 1.3.3) and the regional chapters have underlined plenty of broad variation by region and by individual site.

The main or developed period in which LBK lifeways were played out is thus a comparatively short one on current date estimates: some three centuries, or twelve generations (at 25 years per generation, for sake of argument). Nor was this a static situation, as the evidence for expanding regional settlement distributions indicates, as well as the signs of change at the turn of the millennium. How then has the Lifeways project contributed to our understanding of how LBK lifeways were performed? Together with the insights provided by other recent research, our answers rest in a sense of differing scales.

There was much common practice that must have helped to bind LBK communities together. From many a geographical perspective, and for the individual on the move, this could have seemed a world more or less without end, with what lay beyond not necessarily unknown but broadly speaking irrelevant to the central concerns of LBK existence. In the developed phase, no major lithic material, for example, came from outside the LBK orbit taken as a whole, and the crucial resources of herds and gardens lay close to hand, probably constantly under observation. To the individual away from his or her home settlement, whether engaged in long-range herding, raw material procurement or exchange, alliance building or matchmaking, material culture, architecture and funerals would all surely have seemed familiar, even if details varied. The same ailments, illnesses, aches and pains, and the same risks of inter-personal violence, were perhaps encountered more or less everywhere, though Linda Fibiger has drawn out some regional variation; much wider study of the human osteology than this project was able to achieve would be highly desirable in the future.

Commonality of lifeways has been reinforced in the results of this project, as set out site by site and region by region, and discussed in Chapter 9. The stable isotope analyses underline broadly similar values across the distribution studied, with comparatively few outliers. A broadly shared kind of diet appears to have been a fact of life in the LBK distribution studied here, and may have helped to foster a sense of solidarity and community. The strontium ratios also reveal repeating patterns of predominantly local residence; though the details vary interestingly from site to site and from region to region, over and over again the signatures formed in childhood seem to indicate largely local populations. The dead found in the formal cemeteries were also treated in broadly similar ways, in terms of both the manner in which burial grounds were laid out and the nature of the performance of individual funerals. The strontium ratios have also strongly suggested the operation of a widely distributed practice – right across the distribution studied in this project – of burying adult men with stone adzes who had had more restricted mobility or dietary sources in childhood, which in turn has been taken to support post-marital patrilocality, possibly some form of unequal access to land, and forms of inherited social position.

The latter possibilities can also be inferred from the recent combined chronological, material and archaeobotanical study of Vaihingen in Baden-Württemberg (Bogaard *et al.* 2011; Bogaard 2012). That remains a single site, of distinctive character, and we have to be cautious in generalising from it. It also serves as a useful example of how apparent uniformity can be broken down at differing scales. Like many another LBK settlement, larger or smaller, Vaihingen persisted through many generations (its occupation going back to the earliest LBK); we can surely think of it as a successful community. Yet the recent study has convincingly indicated the operation of household groupings within such a community, and in detail a varied history for these possible clans or lineages. In the same way, though the stable isotope analyses have picked out few dietary differences overall, hints of variation do exist, for example, between men and women, between clusters within cemeteries or in the mixing lines or arrays evident at Aiterhofen and Schwetzingen. So under the mantle of superficial uniformity, it becomes clearer with more detailed and more extensive analysis that differences existed within LBK communities, at the scale of both households and individuals. That sense of difference can be extended further into the landscape, for example in the recent detailed studies of Corina Knipper (2011; cf. Bentley and Knipper 2005a) in the Neckar valley, who has convincingly shown varying use of local loess, river valleys and uplands for the grazing of individual cattle, even though the dominant pattern here appears to have been that cattle were on the whole kept close to settlements.

With reference to households, our combined studies also throw up puzzles. While the household is such a prominent feature of life in LBK settlements, it is not easily detectable in cemeteries. One possibility is that, within the selection from wider populations which we argue the cemeteries must represent, the individual grave could stand for the individual household (Whittle 2012). But in this case the household as such is also masked, and we have also suggested, by analogy, the possibility of multiple communities being represented in given burial grounds, not just locally pre-eminent household members. It is also striking that it is not just adult men with stone adzes and distinctive strontium ratios who are to be found in the cemeteries, but other men, women and children, all with a range of mortuary treatments as set out in the regional chapters and discussed in Chapter 9. So, while accepting the likelihood of structured and recurrent difference within LBK communities in the selection implied by the cemeteries, we can envisage a fluid and perhaps dynamic negotiation and representation of social position in the mortuary sphere. Perhaps for much of the developed phase of the LBK, no single principle based on residence, descent, gender or age dominated LBK lifeways, and perhaps it was the plurality of affiliations and allegiances which made this way of life possible.

The individual life histories which we have sought to emphasise throughout this volume, together with others highlighted by the previous Vedrovice project, also appear to bear out this dimension of diversity within the frame of LBK lifeways as a whole. Collectively, they indicate that the LBK world encompassed people with varying descent, childhood origins, lifetime mobility, health, access to land and resources, and social position as marked by mortuary treatment. This plethora of life histories and experiences appears to exist right across the LBK distribution studied by this project; no one region has an obviously greater or lesser range of such biographies, though there is a case for a greater input from indigenous backgrounds in the western part studied here. Uniformity and diversity are to be found everywhere, and at many different scales.

10.3.3 Endings

At the turn of the sixth millennium cal BC, though the detailed chronology remains to be established precisely, the LBK world underwent a series of transformations. Pottery styles in many instances had by now become more regionalised. Some regional settlement sequences apparently come to an end, and new styles of pottery, other material culture, longhouse architecture, mortuary treatment and enclosure emerge – with broad regional variations – in the earlier part of the fifth millennium cal BC. There is the newer evidence of inter-group violence at sites like Talheim, Asparn and elsewhere, and of the dramatic mortuary treatment of Herxheim, which several scholars have used to suggest a crisis at the end of the LBK. How then can the perspectives developed in this volume contribute to better understanding of this important horizon?

In general, there is much still to establish in more precise detail. It is not clear that every regional settlement sequence ends with a significant increase in numbers of sites, and conversely it does seem clear that some regions saw even bigger concentrations of population in the earlier fifth millennium cal BC, for example in the orbit of the Lengyel culture in Transdanubia (Kozłowski and Raczky 2007). If there was some kind of crisis caused by population levels, it was not necessarily universal, and recovery was evidently swift in many areas. Nor is the sequence of climatic change sufficiently well established for it to be precisely and causally correlated with the archaeological sequence.

Our analyses of late stages of the LBK have been no more plentiful than for its early phase. In general, there is little sign in the stable isotope, strontium and osteological analyses from cemeteries which should span the latter stages of the LBK of marked change in diet, residence or life histories. Some contrasts, however, between the condition of the people at Kleinhadersdorf and Asparn might indicate at least regionally a decline in health at the end of the LBK (Maria Teschler-Nicola, pers. comm.). Yet again we need to point out the imprecision of the available chronological evidence. It is perhaps the archaeological and interpretive dimensions of the Lifeways project which might contribute in more general ways. Material regionalisation does seem significant. If the developed LBK world was characterised by the integration of multiple and varying identities, perhaps it was at a point when categories began to be more rigidly defined that lifeways could no longer be performed in the same ways. Perhaps through time the dominance of particular household groupings acted adversely on the successful maintenance of community; there may be some suggestions in the Vaihingen sequence for just that (Bogaard *et al.* 2011). Perhaps too patrilocality and hypothetically patrilineal descent began to bear down too heavily on other choices and practices; the apparent dominance of older men in the funerals at Nitra (though yet again we have to be cautious about the chronology: Appendix B) might be linkable to the apparent desire to raid for younger women, which has been claimed at Asparn, as part of a trend to a tighter control of marriage and descent. There could therefore have been causes of jealousies and tensions both between and within communities in ways that had not existed before, though on current evidence these were probably not to be found evenly across the LBK distribution. Perhaps it was as the possibilities of belonging (to certain communities and not others, for example, or to sodalities, or to more exclusive lineages – and so on) multiplied, that uniformity began to be restrictive, and diversity opened up, and the nature of LBK lifeways had inevitably to change.

10.4 Elsewheres

We have now set out our view of the LBK as a process, as a set of performances within a shared cultural framework, in which it made sense for many things to be done in the same broad way, but for others to be practised in different fashions, depending on scale and context. If this was so, our final reflections are on the uniqueness of this situation. How distinctive is the case of the LBK, and what does it bring to wider studies of uniformity and diversity?

One model could be that the supposed uniformity of the LBK was indeed unique, and that the LBK should stand out as a special case within European prehistory as a whole. The practice of doing so many things in similar ways would then be seen, if not as the inevitable outcome of pre-programmed culture, then as a strategy with which to get by in a novel situation combining the expansion of settlement into new areas and the establishment of forms of subsistence new to those areas. Only in this horizon of extensive cultural transformation was there such a premium on pulling together.

Our own view, however, is rather different. We can indeed see LBK material traditions as the outcome of situated practice, but as a strategy for complex integrations of different people with differing histories. From this perspective, there is scope for thinking of plenty of other Neolithic and later situations where there were similar goals of integration by means of widely shared practice and identity, even if not, of course, in the unique conditions of the initial spread of the Neolithic across central and western Europe. The rest of the European Neolithic sequence in fact provides several good examples, from the widely found continuation of longhouse life into the fifth millennium cal BC, the broad patterns of Chasséen,

Michelsberg and TRB pottery from the later fifth into the earlier fourth millennium cal BC, and in their different ways both the Corded Ware and Bell Beaker distributions of the third millennium cal BC (Badisches Landesmuseum 2010; Anthony 2010; Prescott and Glørstad 2012). We make no claim that these situations were identical to that of the LBK, and among other differences there was probably more regional variation in those situations than in the major part of the LBK sequence. Nor need such comparisons be confined to the Neolithic in Europe, and the case of the Urnfield culture in the later Bronze Age springs to mind. We could continue the discussion further afield still, in North America, through the examples of both the Hopewell interaction sphere (Carr and Case 2006) and the Mississippian 'transregional spatio-cultural phenomenon' or 'ethnoscape' (Pauketat 2007, 85).

To take just one example here in more detail, the terms in which the sixth- to fifth-millennium Ubaid phenomenon in the Near East has been discussed recently (Carter and Philip 2010) resonate very strongly with debate about the nature of the LBK, and it is worth quoting that analysis in order to underline this congruence. The Ubaid phenomenon denotes a 'vast Near Eastern interaction sphere' of the sixth and fifth millennia cal BC, which stretched over 2000 km from the eastern Mediterranean to the Straits of Hormuz (Carter and Philip 2010, 1). Variously defined by its pottery, and equated with both a people and a period, it is clear that the Ubaid is not a monolithic entity; older views of some kind of southern Mesopotamian ethnic core with subsequent expansion have been challenged by perspectives which stress the sharing of relatively restricted material practice over a diverse set of regions (Carter and Philip 2010, 4). As Robert Carter and Graham Philip put it (2010, 5):

> How then do we understand a prehistoric phenomenon of vast geographical and chronological extent, in which material culture similarities are displayed across different classes of artefact, but which has attenuated boundaries, or none at all and no undisputed core?

Reference is also made to the PPNB phenomenon in the same terms. It is clear in the matters of boundaries, core (if taken as likely zone of origin) and duration that the Ubaid was not identical to the LBK, but the similar way in which provisional answers are framed is fascinating. Carter and Philip go on, among other things (2010, 5–15), to discuss individual sites as 'nodes in a series of overlapping networks' (2010, 5), 'contacts between communities of broadly comparable scale' (2010, 5), and multiple emergent identities and scales of identity within a very extensive interaction sphere (2010, 6–7). Interestingly, while they concede the potential importance of post-marital patrilocality, they argue that 'it would be a major assumption to regard the exchange of women as the driving mechanism for the propagation of a ceramic style of this spatial and temporal duration' (2010, 7).

Carter and Philip (2010, 8) suggest 'a reality that might best be understood as continuous incremental change, largely effected at the level of local communities'. That might recall the dictum of Bruno Latour that the 'network is always local' (1993, 117), and we have already commented that this is in danger of underplaying the nature and effect of connections themselves, since the question must be asked of the way in which any network is made local within a wider or connected frame of reference. But like the present volume, Carter and Philip do go on to discuss both long- and short-range interactions, including matrimonial exchange, with repeated contacts and 'routinized modes of action' acting as 'webs linking individuals, households, and communities' (Carter and Philip 2010, 9). Among other things, the adoption of what are described as 'communal cemeteries' is noted, as well as a lack of consensus on the identification of marked social hierarchy (Carter and Philip 2010, 12). Again, clearly, there are potential differences between the Ubaid and LBK phenomena as well as similarities, though it is not our intention to explore these in detail here. What we have tried to stress in quoting the Ubaid case is the parallel 'recognition of the discursive and contingent natures of interaction, cultural transmission, and societal change' (Carter and Philip 2010, 13).

In this perspective, the case of the LBK does stand out for its geographical scale, but the Corded Ware, Bell Beaker, Ubaid, Hopewell and Mississippian examples all rival that scope. Nor are any of these and other examples which we have cited to be thought of as completely uniform, as the 'inconsistent commonality' of the Ubaid horizon (Carter and Philip 2010, 5) reminds us. Each case would need to be looked at in detail (cf. Shennan 2002; Mace *et al.* 2005; Jordan and O'Neill 2010), encompassing the varying scales which we have advocated in this chapter. But that the same tensions between shared and varying practice can be found in debates about other cases elsewhere reassures us in seeing LBK material practice as process, as the outcome of situated performances, and as a strategy which worked well, at least for a definable period of time, at a significant number of scales, from the communities and assemblages of the wider network or meshwork through to households and individual people.

10.5 Back to culture

In a striking ethnographic account of the realities of life in a Dayak longhouse, Christine Helliwell (1996) has described how family and other groups occupied a series of partitioned and screened compartments down the length of the building (cf. Metcalf 2010), but were nonetheless constantly and actively aware of each other's co-presence, connected by the 'community of voices' that permeated the whole structure. The partitions between each compartment in a Dayak longhouse are constructed with deliberate gaps, some of which are big enough to permit the movement of small children or animals, offering entrances and passageways between each family's space (Helliwell 1996, 137–8). Rather than fixed boundaries, used to separate apartments, these are permeable partitions or crossable borders.

These are apt metaphors for the differing scales of social interaction within the LBK as a whole.

We began our discussion of diversity in the LBK by deliberately looking at the wider debate about culture (Chapter 1.2). It troubled us that uniformity and diversity should be equally taken for granted, without discussion of the kinds of social relationships that underpinned and created them. Much debate on culture has been dominated by anthropology, as well as more recently by cultural studies (Battaglia 1999; N. Thomas 1999). In the end, anthropological discussion has concentrated on values and diversity, and much effort has been given to worrying about avoiding seeing culture as some kind of independent or autonomous regulator, as artificially constructed, and as neatly bounded. It is useful to quote again the definition of culture offered by Eric Wolf (1982, 387) as 'a series of processes that construct, reconstruct and dismantle cultural materials', and to note again the freeze-frame of many ethnographic accounts (Carrithers 1992, 23).

This volume has dissected a whole series of cultural materials and social practices across a significant swathe of the LBK distribution, with attention to development through a span of some five centuries, even if the chronology remains frustratingly less precise than we could wish. The LBK situation is archaeologically distinctive, but we have argued that it was not unique. As such, the LBK case study and other archaeological situations referred to very briefly above surely have much to contribute to the wider study of culture, and could help to bridge or break down current disciplinary boundaries and separate practices, as an alternative to archaeology simply being the recipient of theory imported from anthropology. Other current approaches, including the 'return to things' or the 'ontological turn', also involve archaeology and anthropology in a joint enterprise (Alberti *et al.* 2011). From that perspective, the LBK offers a long list of things to integrate into interpretive narratives, from houses, graves and bodies, garden plots and animals, to adzes, pottery and *Spondylus*. We believe that what the anthropologist Michael Carrithers (1992, 36) wrote of 'actual social life with all its fluidity, uncertainty, construals and misconstruals, its laboriously achieved continuity, its planned and its inadvertent innovations' resonates strongly with our approaches to the LBK in this volume. We hope in turn that the emphasis on scales and performance, which we have played through the case study of the LBK, will find wider echoes elsewhere.

Notes

1 We owe much here to discussion with John Robb and Oliver Harris.

2 In a few cases in Alsace, such as Mulhouse Est/Rixheim, there are post settings within the grave cut (Schweitzer and Schweitzer 1977; Jeunesse 1997, 60).

3 Though note Lüning (2005a) on the development of rows within Schwanfeld, in the earliest LBK.

4 One reservation might be the implied distinction between material and imagined community (discussed critically in Yaeger 2000), a point we owe to Oliver Harris.

5 We are grateful to Dušan Borić and Oliver Harris for discussion of this theme.

Appendix A
Stable isotope data and collagen quality indicators

In this appendix the stable isotope data are presented, alongside the collagen quality indicators, by site (in alphabetical order). Please refer to Chapter 2.2.2 for the methodology of collagen extraction.

Table A1. Aiterhofen (discussed in Chapter 6.7).

Grave/ Sample No.	Species	Sex	Age	$\delta^{13}C$‰	$\delta^{15}N$‰	%C	%N	C:N	%Collagen
9	Human	F	20–30	−20.5	10.2	41.2	14.6	3.3	6.4
10	Human	M	60<	−20.2	10.7	39.1	14.0	3.3	10.3
12	Human	M	30–35	−20.4	10.4	40.5	14.6	3.2	8.2
13	Human	M?	20–25	−20.4	9.7	31.1	11.2	3.3	4.1
14	Human	F	20–30	−20.5	9.9	38.0	13.6	3.3	7.7
15	Human	M	30–40	−20.1	10.7	39.2	14.3	3.2	9.6
18	Human	M	40–45	−20.1	10.2	35.9	13.0	3.2	1.1
19a	Human	F	20–30	−20.4	9.6	35.9	12.9	3.3	2.7
21	Human	M?	18–20	−20.1	9.0	38.4	13.8	3.3	3.9
22	Human	F?		−20.6	9.5	37.5	13.5	3.3	4.4
23a	Human		10–12	−20.5	10.0	38.0	13.5	3.3	6.1
24a	Human	M	adult	−20.6	9.8	37.7	13.6	3.2	4.2
25	Human	M	45–50	−20.1	9.6	38.5	14.0	3.2	5.9
26a	Human	M	adult	−20.2	9.7	33.0	11.8	3.3	3.6
28	Human	M	30–35	−20.3	10.0	37.4	13.4	3.3	5.3
31	Human	M	30–35	−20.3	9.5	27.9	9.9	3.3	1.6
36	Human		25–30	−20.3	9.5	33.7	12.0	3.3	2.9
41	Human		10–12	−20.7	9.2	38.7	14.0	3.2	5.8
42	Human	M	60<	−20.0	10.0	35.1	12.5	3.3	4.8
43	Human	M		−20.8	9.1	32.4	11.5	3.3	2.9
47	Human		7–13	−20.4	9.4	32.9	11.5	3.3	4.2
48	Human	M	25–30	−20.7	9.9	32.8	11.2	3.4	3.5
55	Human	F	20–30	−20.2	9.9	38.2	13.6	3.3	0.9
56	Human	M	40–45	−20.3	10.2	27.5	9.7	3.3	1.7
57	Human	M	30–35	−20.2	9.7	26.1	9.4	3.3	3.5
58	Human		3–6	−20.4	11.1	24.0	8.7	3.2	2.4
60	Human	F	40–45	−20.5	9.9	29.6	10.7	3.2	3.8
66	Human		adult	−20.8	10.0	35.0	12.8	3.2	8.0
68	Human	F	40–50	−20.4	9.9	33.9	12.2	3.2	4.8

69	Human	F	20–30	−20.5	9.5	32.6	11.6	3.3	2.6
74	Human	M	25–35	−20.6	9.4	28.0	10.1	3.2	3.1
78	Human	M	25–30	−20.5	9.8	24.9	9.0	3.2	2.5
85	Human	M	60<	−20.5	10.2	27.4	9.8	3.3	3.4
88	Human		10–12	−20.7	10.1	24.0	8.7	3.2	3.2
89	Human	F	25–35	−20.1	10.1	27.7	10.0	3.2	1.8
91	Human	F	adult	−20.3	9.1	25.1	9.0	3.3	1.2
94	Human	M	adult	−20.7	9.6	20.1	7.1	3.3	1.1
99	Human	F	18–20	−20.6	9.7	19.8	7.0	3.3	1.2
100	Human	F	40–50	−20.8	9.5	27.0	9.5	3.3	2.2
102	Human	M	60<	−20.5	10.5	28.9	10.3	3.3	1.5
106	Human	F	50–55	−20.1	9.0	28.9	10.5	3.2	2.4
108	Human	M	50–55	−20.3	10.0	34.2	12.4	3.2	3.5
109	Human	F	30–35	−20.2	10.1	38.1	13.6	3.3	5.6
111	Human	F	25–30	−20.4	9.8	36.8	13.2	3.2	5.1
115a	Human	M	60<	−20.4	9.8	32.9	11.9	3.2	3.7
116a	Human	F	40–45	−20.5	9.9	31.8	11.6	3.2	3.9
118	Human	M	40–60	−20.7	9.8	36.0	13.1	3.2	6.7
119	Human	M	30–35	−21.0	9.5	28.6	10.1	3.3	2.2
130	Human	M	25–35	−20.9	9.5	25.4	9.2	3.2	1.8
137	Human	F	30–40	−20.5	10.2	40.0	14.7	3.2	9.4
139a	Human	F?	15–20	−20.6	9.4	36.3	13.2	3.2	6.3
140	Human	F	40	−20.3	9.7	41.4	15.2	3.2	8.7
141	Human	M	35–40	−20.0	10.3	41.6	15.0	3.2	7.7
142	Human	M	40–50	−20.6	9.2	29.0	10.5	3.2	2.3
144	Human	F	60<	−20.7	9.5	40.1	13.3	3.5	3.7
147	Human		10	−20.6	9.8	35.2	12.6	3.3	3.2
148	Human	M??	15	−20.6	9.4	28.7	10.6	3.2	2.3
150	Human	F	60<	−20.1	9.8	39.7	14.3	3.3	4.6
158	Human	F	30–40	−21.0	10.0	18.1	6.3	3.3	1.0
160	Human		adult	−20.4	9.4	37.8	13.8	3.2	5.7
Ai-300	Pig			−20.3	8.7	40.0	14.3	3.3	12.0
Ai-301	Cattle			−19.8	8.5	31.0	10.8	3.4	5.8
Ai-302	Pig			−21.1	5.0	22.9	7.8	3.4	3.0
Ai-303	Cattle			−21.6	5.5	35.7	12.8	3.2	3.9
Ai-304	Cattle			−21.4	6.1	38.1	13.6	3.3	4.7
Ai-306	Cattle			−20.9	6.6	39.7	14.3	3.2	6.7
Ai-307	Cattle/ Red deer?			−20.4	7.9	30.8	10.7	3.4	3.5
Ai-308	Cattle/ Red deer?			−23.4	4.2	29.2	10.0	3.4	3.8
Ai-309	Cattle			−20.7	8.8	30.7	10.6	3.4	6.5

Table A2. Asparn a.d. Zaya/Schletz (discussed in Chapter 5.8).

Individual/ Sample no.	Skeleton no.	Location at the site	Species	Sex	Age	$\delta^{13}C$‰	$\delta^{15}N$‰	%C	%N	C:N	% Collagen
47	281	Outer ditch	Human	M	20–25	−19.7	9.4	33.9	12.1	3.3	4.7
7	4223	Trench 22	Human			−19.7	9.2	35.8	13.0	3.2	3.9
8	4464	Trench 22	Human			−19.6	9.3	31.1	10.4	3.5	2.0
41	685	Outer ditch S11	Human	M	45–50	−19.6	10.2	33.4	11.5	3.4	2.6
37	573	Outer ditch W-Half	Human	M	20–24	−19.6	9.4	27.0	9.2	3.4	3.1
14	119, 79a	Outer ditch S2	Human	M	18–20	−19.6	9.0	37.0	13.1	3.3	5.0
	2879	Outer ditch S20	Human			-20.0	10.7	31.6	11.1	3.3	4.0
12a	4476	Trench 22	Human			−19.4	9.2	37.2	13.2	3.3	4.4
1993/18	4475	Trench 22	Human			−19.5	9.7	31.5	10.8	3.4	2.4
6	75a, 77	Outer ditch S2	Human	M	20–30	−19.5	10.4	32.4	11.0	3.4	1.8
9		Trench 22	Human			−19.8	8.9	29.2	10.0	3.4	1.8
		Trench 22	Human			-19.6	9.0	32.2	11.0	3.4	3.6
12	649	Outer ditch S10	Human		Infans I	−19.5	9.4	29.3	9.8	3.5	1.5
1993/5	4518	Trench 22	Human	M?	30–50	−19.5	9.4	33.2	11.6	3.4	3.2
1993	4318	Trench 22	Human			−19.6	9.4	32.5	11.0	3.4	3.2
20	2873	Outer ditch	Human		Infans II	-20.0	10.1	31.1	10.9	3.3	5.8
18	558, 572	Outer ditch S9	Human		*c.* 3–4	-20.3	8.9	28.8	9.6	3.5	1.9
1997/4	5839	Trench 27.002	Human	M	25–35	−19.6	9.4	30.4	10.3	3.4	2.6
50	601	Pit 164	Human		*c.* 4	−19.6	9.1	40.4	14.3	3.3	9.0
47		Outer ditch	Human	M	20–25	−19.7	9.4	33.3	11.4	3.4	3.1

63	345	Outer ditch S7	Human		Infans I	−19.9	9.1	38.8	13.9	3.3	4.7
16	655	Outer ditch S10	Human		Infans II	−19.5	9.7	35.0	12.3	3.3	3.9
23	285	Enclosure	Human		18 mons	−18.8	12.9	38.8	13.9	3.3	7.6
1996 2		Trench 22	Human	M	30–50	−19.4	9.1	26.6	8.8	3.5	7.6
1996 1		Trench 22	Human	M	30–50	−19.7	9.5	34.1	11.9	3.3	3.4
1996 4		Trench 25.002 u.a.	Human	M	60–65	−19.6	9.9	37.7	13.6	3.2	5.9
1996 7		Trench 25.002 u.a.	Human		*c.* 5–6	−19.7	8.7	31.7	11.0	3.4	2.8
	6051	Trench 27	Human			−19.7	9.9	29.8	10.4	3.4	1.9
	5838	Trench 27	Human			−19.6	9.4	30.3	10.5	3.4	2.2
6	6		Human	M	20–30	−19.6	10.1	33.2	11.2	3.5	2.3
7	2490	Outer ditch S9	Human	F	40–50	−19.4	8.8	37.4	13.0	3.4	6.6
68	360	Outer ditch	Human	M?	20–40	−19.7	10.0	32.9	11.2	3.4	2.4
65		Outer ditch	Human	F	40–60	−19.6	9.6	34.7	11.9	3.4	2.3
24		Outer ditch S7	Human	F	20–30	−19.6	9.2	36.2	12.4	3.4	2.0
	6574	29.002.29001	Human			−19.6	9.1	36.6	13.1	3.3	4.0
8	2526		Human	M	20–25	−19.9	10.4	37.0	13.2	3.3	5.8
	295		Human			−19.7	9.1	35.1	12.6	3.3	11.0
Asp-045			Pig			−20.2	6.2	23.0	7.8	3.5	1.0
Asp-046			Sheep/ goat			−20.3	8.7	28.8	9.9	3.4	5.2
Asp-048			Cattle			−19.8	6.9	33.2	11.8	3.3	2.8
Asp-049			Sheep/ goat			−20.1	7.3	35.0	12.6	3.2	3.2

Table A3. Balatonszárszó-Kis-erdei-dűlő (discussed in Chapter 3.10).

Grave/ Sample No.	Species	Sex	Age	Bone	$\delta^{13}C$‰	$\delta^{15}N$‰	%C	%N	C:N	%Collagen
278	Human		12–14	Long bone	−20.0	8.9	31.46	11.53	3.2	6.32
288	Human		5–6	Long bone	−19.9	10.2	31.96	11.62	3.2	5.06
289	Human		9–10	Femur	−19.5	9.3	29.31	10.52	3.3	3.66
289	Human		9–10	Long bone	−20.1	9.8	20.70	7.09	3.2	1.04
289	Human		9–10	Humerus	−20.5	9.4	27.72	10.07	3.2	3.65
510	Human	M	Adult	Costa	−19.5	9.3	40.37	14.67	3.2	1.75
510	Human	M	Adult	Metacarpus	−20.0	8.8	19.81	7.09	3.3	3.09
531	Human	M	Adult	Costa	−19.6	9.5	41.03	14.85	3.3	3.76
531	Human	M	Adult	Metacarpus	−19.9	9.5	17.61	6.37	3.2	3.87
554	Human	F	Adult	Long bone	−19.7	9.3	25.86	9.43	3.2	4.37
711	Human		13–14	Long bone	−19.1	9.5	27.67	10.14	3.2	6.69
712	Human	M	18–19	Long bone	−19.9	9.3	38.56	19.58	3.2	10
766	Human	M	31–40	Long bone	−20.0	9.9	36.40	13.17	3.2	7.28
767	Human	M	Adult/Mature	Long bone	−19.9	10.2	32.11	11.80	3.3	8.89
768	Human		9–10	Long bone	−20.2	9.8	37.89	13.71	3.2	6.77
769	Human		1–6	Long bone	−20.2	9.8	36.65	13.15	3.3	7.36
770	Human	M	45–49	Costa	−19.7	10	43.93	15.52	3.2	4.39
770	Human	M	45–49	Metacarpus	−20.0	9.5	31.89	6.12	3.2	6.9
771	Human	M	23–27	Costa	−19.4	10	44.15	15.25	3.2	5.34
771	Human	M	23–27	Metacarpus	−19.7	8.9	35.36	12.84	3.2	7.93
772	Human		5–6	Long bone	−19.6	8.6	35.56	12.96	3.2	5.28
773	Human	F	Adult/Mature	Costa	−19.9	9.8	40.63	14.55	3.3	2.97
773	Human	F	Adult/Mature	Metacarpus	−20.0	8.4	37.74	13.58	3.3	4.95
774	Human	F	37–46	Costa	−19.8	9	44.82	16.45	3.2	5.12
774	Human	F	37–46	Metacarpus	−20.1	8.5	34.78	12.52	3.3	4.68
775	Human		14–16	Costa	−19.3	9.3	42.47	15.07	3.2	3.81
775	Human		14–16	Scapula	−19.6	9.1	41.48	14.73	3.3	6.15
776	Human	F	55–64	Long bone	−20.0	10.1	32.23	11.72	3.2	5.74
777	Human	F	Adult	Long bone	−19.9	9.2	31.38	11.15	3.3	4.34
778	Human	F	Mature	Long bone	−20.5	9.6	27.27	9.57	3.3	3.73

2/B	Sheep				−20	8.7	48.40	17.35	3.3	3.23
3/A	Sheep				−19.8	6.9	45.76	16.37	3.3	6.75
3/B	Cattle				−18.9	6.4	40.13	14.51	3.2	3.99
4/A	Sheep				−19.4	7.15	47.29	16.97	3.3	2.59
5/A	Sheep				−19.7	7.5	42.84	10.36	3.3	3.06
5/B	Cattle				−18.9	6.9	45.49	16.16	3.3	4.52
6/A	Cattle				−19.7	7.9	36.43	13.16	3.2	8.30
6/B	Cattle									**Fail**
7/A	Pig				−19.9	7.8	44.06	16.19	3.2	1.54
7/B	Cattle				−20	7	32.75	11.90	3.3	3.91
8/A	Cattle				−19.7	7.7	47.73	17.00	3.3	2.16
8/B	Pig									**Fail**
8/C	Sheep				−20.1	6.2	18.93	6.78	3.2	1.27
9/A	Cattle				−20.2	8	42.74	15.22	3.3	8.42
9/B	Cattle				−19.5	7.7	44.96	16.32	3.2	7.98
16/A	Cattle				−19.7	6.7	42.95	15.69	3.2	7.35
16/B	Cattle				−20.11	7.7	40.16	14.71	3.2	10.40
17/A	Cattle				−19.9	6.6	25.06	9.08	3.2	1.87
17/B	Cattle				−19.9	8.4	33.38	12.62	3.2	4.50
18/A	Cattle				−19.9	7.2	42.97	15.37	3.2	1.93
18/B	Cattle				−20.4	7.1	37.95	13.45	3.3	4.30
19/A	Cattle				−19.7	6.3	38.30	13.98	3.2	13.59
19/B	Cattle				−18.5	6.6	43.28	15.79	3.2	8.38
20/A	Cattle				−20.4	6.9	37.27	13.38	3.3	4.39
20/B	Cattle				−20.7	6.8	29.37	10.32	3.2	1.37
21/A	Sheep				−19.6	6.6	44.02	15.63	3.2	3.80
21/B	Cattle				−19.5	6.7	45.16	15.71	3.3	1.41
22/A	Cattle				−20.4	9	40.76	14.63	3.3	5.38
22/B	Cattle				−17.5	7.9	42.74	15.47	3.2	5.05
23/A	Cattle				−19.4	6.8	43.32	15.30	3.2	1.85
24/A	Cattle				−19.6	7	42.43	14.92	3.3	1.99
24/B	Sheep				−20.5	6.6	32.64	11.57	3.3	3.72

779	Human		3–5	Costa	−19.3	11.4	43.75	15.75	3.1	2.24
779	Human		3–5	Ox coxae	−19.6	11.3	41.28	14.37	3.4	2.89
780	Human	M	34–40	Costa	−19.1	9.6	44.30	15.93	3.1	5.83
780	Human	M	34–40	Phalanx	−19.7	9.3	20.04	7.16	3.3	2.98
781	Human	M	Adult/Mature	Long bone	−19.9	9.4	24.72	9.08	3.3	6.97
782	Human	F	40–46	Costa	−19.9	10.1	22.12	8.02	3.3	2.62
782	Human	F	40–46	Metacarpus	−19.8	9.4	23.24	8.27	3.3	5.46
783	Human	F	56–62	Long bone	−19.9	9.75	34.89	12.67	3.2	6
784	Human	M	Adult/Mature	Long bone	−20.3	10.1	24.52	8.66	3.3	1.33
785	Human	M	Mature	Long bone	−20.1	9.6	24.78	9.06	3.2	3.43
786	Human	F	Adult	Long bone	−20.2	9.6	27.00	9.92	3.2	5.46
787	Human	F	55–61	Costa	−19.6	9.6	29.78	10.87	3.2	2.31
787	Human	F	55–61	Metacarpus	−19.4	9.2	43.20	15.55	3.2	6.05
789	Human	F	53–59	Long bone	−20.0	9.7	29.80	10.76	3.2	3.54
790	Human		5–6	Long bone	−19.3	10.7	40.82	14.67	3.2	5.67
791	Human	F	31–40	Costa	−19.7	9.7	21.55	7.76	3.2	3.58
791	Human	F	31–40	Metacarpus	−19.9	8.1	15.31	5.50	3.3	1.62
792	Human	M	Mature	Long bone	−19.6	9.9	43.11	15.43	3.2	2.1
792	Human	M	Mature	Metacarpus	−19.9	9.5	32.00	11.38	3.3	4.48
793	Human	M	Adult	Metacarpus	−19.7	9.7	43.85	15.67	3.2	5.08
793	Human	M	Adult	Costa	−19.6	9.6	19.37	6.91	3.3	3.03
794	Human	F	Adult	Rib	−19.8	10.1	32.11	11.34	3.3	3.05
795	Human	F	Adult	Cranium	−19.8	9.8	35.8	12.9	3.24	3.6
796	Human	F	15–16	Patella	−19.6	9.6	38.05	13.57	3.3	5.84
796	Human	F	15–16	Talus	−20.1	9.7	41.77	14.36	3.4	4.43
796	Human	F	15–16	Costa	−19.5	9.5	43.92	16.04	3.2	3.42
797	Human		12–13	Long bone	−19.9	9.3	30.69	11.22	3.2	4.17
798	Human	F	Mature	Long bone	−20.1	9.8	33.58	12.15	3.2	4.2
799	Human	M	Mature	Long bone	−20.3	10	17.53	6.26	3.3	1.59
1/A	Cattle				−19.7	9	28.88	10.25	3.2	4.72
1/B	Pig				−20.4	9.9	44.52	16.17	3.2	2.22
2/A	Cattle				−20.8	9.3	15.15	4.93	3.6	0.56

25/A	Cattle					7.7	43.85	15.96	3.2	1.62
25/B	Cattle				−19.8	6.8	42.94	14.88	3.4	2.88
26/A	Cattle				−20.9	7	41.27	15.11	3.2	10.91
26/B	Sheep				−19.4	6.7	43.10	15.50	3.1	4.48
27/A	Cattle				−21.5	8.6	44.57	15.73	3.3	6.21
27/B	Cattle				−21.6	6.8	43.16	15.37	3.2	5.89
39/A	Sheep				−19.8	6.6	45.46	15.80	3.2	3.38
39/B	Cattle				−20.2	7.2	30.32	10.77	3.3	5.56
40/A	Pig				−21	7.1	29.79	10.59	3.3	3.30
40/B	Cattle				−20.4	6.6	43.17	15.83	3.2	5.92
41/A	Cattle				−21.6	7.3	43.52	15.79	3.3	3.72
41/B	Sheep				−20.4	5.9	43.37	15.52	3.2	8.05
42/A	Cattle				−20.4	6.9	67.38	22.25	3.2	1.56
42/B	Cattle				−20.4	8	45.60	16.70	3.3	5.56
42/C	Sheep				−19.9	6	39.42	14.07	3.3	6.57
43/A	Pig				−19.8	9.8	45.83	16.83	3.2	6.89
44	Cattle				−21.1	8.7	36.35	13.50	3.1	7.20
45	Cattle				−19.5	7.7	30.92	11.32	3.2	3.86
46	Cattle				−19.1	6.8	38.46	14.14	3.2	15.62
47	Cattle				−20.1	6.2	33.26	12.28	3.2	8.10
48	Cattle				−19.9	6.6	38.05	14.05	3.2	10.59
49	Cattle				−19.6	6.3	32.38	11.94	3.2	7.34
50	Cattle				−18.6	7.6	35.59	13.09	3.2	5.53
51	Cattle				−19.7	6.8	39.73	14.63	3.2	1.66
52	Cattle				−18.8	6.6	29.12	10.81	3.2	6.43
53	Cattle				−17	7	39.96	14.73	3.2	10.45
54	Cattle				−18.4	6.9	39.09	14.13	3.2	5.28
55	Cattle				−19.3	6.8	39.23	14.28	3.2	13.24
56	Cattle				−19.5	6.6	31.29	11.33	3.2	6.05
57	Cattle				−19.7	6.5	33.89	12.57	3.2	2.86
58	Cattle				−20	9.1	15.84	5.24	3.5	0.86
59	Cattle				−21	6.4	33.42	12.46	3.1	6.55

60	Cattle				−20.4	6.5	29.44	10.82	3.2	3.40
61	Cattle				−21	6.4	35.05	13.00	3.1	9.96
62	Cattle				−21.2	8.1	32.51	64.56	3.2	5.42
63	Cattle				−21.4	7.2	36.04	13.28	3.2	13.65
64	Cattle				−20.8	8.9	40.57	14.68	3.2	4.03
65	Cattle				−20.6	6.2	33.27	12.02	3.2	2.88
66	Sheep				−19.5	7.5	24.23	8.25	3.4	1.06
67	Sheep				−20.3	7.2	40.33	14.94	3.1	12.69
68	Sheep				−20.3	8.1	32.37	11.90	3.2	3.74
69	Sheep				−19.4	6	36.31	13.13	3.2	4.95
70	Sheep				−19.9	6.3	35.32	12.96	3.2	4.27
71	Sheep				−20.9	6.3	37.66	13.71	3.2	3.46
72	Sheep				−19.2	6.1	41.60	15.12	3.2	2.00
73	Sheep				−20	7.4	39.66	14.57	3.2	10.47
74	Sheep				−20	6.9	33.07	11.93	3.2	1.43
75	Sheep				−19.6	6.3	39.10	14.24	3.2	9.41
76	Sheep				−19.1	6.9	36.39	13.11	3.2	5.20
77	Sheep				−20.2	6.7	33.83	12.41	3.2	7.67
78	Sheep				−19.8	5.8	37.50	13.50	3.2	4.48
79	Sheep				−19.9	6.1	24.53	8.95	3.2	3.56
80	Sheep				−19.9	7.1	32.07	11.73	3.2	4.58
81	Sheep				−20.4	6.4	37.75	13.93	3.2	6.61
82	Sheep									**Fail**
83	Sheep				−19.3	6	23.80	8.65	3.2	4.08
84	Sheep				−20.6	6.8	41.87	15.35	3.2	10.24
85	Sheep				−20.3	6.4	36.61	13.19	3.2	3.09
86	Pig				−20.9	9.3	37.91	13.45	3.3	2.37
87	Pig				−20	8.2	30.60	11.30	3.2	4.09
88	Pig									**Fail**
89	Pig				−19.9	6.7	38.54	13.80	3.2	6.19
90	Pig				−20.1	7.3	34.94	12.89	3.2	7.10
91	Pig				−20.5	8.4	36.35	13.33	3.2	10.65

92	Pig				−20.7	7.5	14.82	4.76	3.7	0.52
93	Pig				−20.1	7.1	40.56	14.87	3.2	11.46
94	Pig				−20.5	8.4	33.47	12.30	3.2	6.54
95	Pig				−20.6	7.6	27.60	10.04	3.2	1.63
96	Pig				−20.6	8.5	36.36	13.33	3.2	11.42
97	Pig				−20.1	7.5	33.16	12.16	3.2	1.90
98	Pig				−20.6	8.2	37.98	13.98	3.2	10.04
99	Pig									**Fail**
100	Pig				−21	8	44.00	15.65	3.3	3.50
101	Pig				−20.1	9.6	36.56	13.44	3.2	4.57
102	Pig				−21.3	7.1	34.47	12.26	3.3	6.93
103	Pig				−19.9	8.1	34.68	12.61	3.2	1.49
104	Pig				−20.3	8.1	33.87	12.55	3.2	7.76
105	Pig				−20.2	8.5	29.16	10.69	3.2	4.56
106	Pig									**Fail**
107	Goat				−19.2	6.1	33.18	12.18	3.2	8.79
108	Hare				−21.6	4.2	44.50	16.36	3.2	18.84
109	Roe deer									**Fail**
110	Roe deer				−23.7	6.8	26.08	9.55	3.2	4.02
111	Roe deer				−22.2	5.2	30.02	11.02	3.2	5.39
112	Red deer				−21.6	6	41.81	15.23	3.2	8.46
113	Red deer				−20.9	5.2	35.86	12.80	3.2	4.48
114	Hare									**Fail**
143	Cattle				−18.4	7.2	46.50	17.04	3.2	4.51
144	Cattle				−19	7.1	44.54	16.43	3.2	5.87
145	Cattle				−19.7	5.9	45.80	16.80	3.2	4.02
146	Cattle				−19.1	6.5	37.31	13.82	3.1	9.78
147	Cattle				−20.4	7.7	45.52	16.48	3.3	2.10

Table A4. Bischoffsheim AFUA du Stade *(discussed in Chapter 8.10.2).*

Sample no.	Species	$\delta^{13}C$‰	$\delta^{15}N$‰	%C	%N	C:N	%Collagen
Bsc-004	Cattle	−23.6	6.7	39.5	14.3	3.2	2.8
Bsc-005	Cattle	−23.7	6.9	37.3	13.7	3.2	2.9
Bsc-007	Cattle	−22.1	7.3	37.9	13.7	3.2	3.4
Bsc-013	Cattle	−22.4	6.8	43.0	15.5	3.2	5.4
Bsc-014	Cattle	−21.0	6.7	32.5	11.8	3.2	2.2
Bsc-016	Pig	−20.8	6.7	40.9	15.0	3.2	5.7
Bsc-017	Sheep/goat	−21.4	7.7	42.7	15.6	3.2	7.3
Bsc-018	Cattle	−24.0	7.2	30.0	11.0	3.2	5.3
Bsc-019	Pig	−21.0	6.4	41.5	15.1	3.2	7.2
Bsc-020	Sheep/goat	−20.8	6.4	42.0	15.0	3.3	6.6
Bsc-021	Pig	−20.7	8.6	42.2	15.2	3.2	9.7
Bsc-022	Sheep/goat	−20.7	8.3	40.9	14.9	3.2	6.1
Bsc-023	Sheep/goat	−20.9	8.8	41.0	15.0	3.2	9.1
Bsc-024	Goat	−20.3	8.0	27.0	10.0	3.2	5.2
Bsc-025	Sheep/goat	−20.9	7.3	43.1	15.6	3.2	9.1
Bsc-027	Pig	−20.5	8.7	38.4	13.8	3.2	3.1
Bsc-028	Pig	−20.8	8.0	37.0	13.4	3.2	3.5
Bsc-031	Cattle	−23.4	5.6	32.5	11.2	3.4	2.2
Bsc-033	Cattle	−23.2	6.6	34.4	11.6	3.4	2.0
Bsc-034	Cattle	−23.9	6.3	36.0	12.2	3.4	8.5
Bsc-035	Cattle	−21.2	5.3	31.9	10.8	3.5	1.5
Bsc-036	Cattle	−22.2	5.8	39.7	14.7	3.2	7.3
Bsc-037	Cattle	−23.8	6.1	40.5	15.2	3.1	9.6
Bsc-039	Cattle	−23.5	5.0	39.0	14.2	3.2	4.8
Bsc-040	Cattle	−23.1	4.7	36.4	13.2	3.2	2.9
Bsc-046	Pig	−20.6	7.9	42.0	15.4	3.2	5.7

Table A5. Blatné (discussed in Chapter 4.10.4).

Sample No.	Species	Bone	δ13C‰	δ15N‰	%C	%N	C:N	%Collagen
Bla-001	Pig	Long bone	−20.6	8.4	35.3	12.6	3.3	8.3
Bla-002	Sheep/goat	Long bone	−19.6	9.7	34.7	12.4	3.3	9.3
Bla-003	Cattle	Bone	−21.0	6.9	35.4	12.6	3.3	10.0
Bla-005	Pig	Scapula	−20.0	8.6	43.0	15.8	3.2	5.4
Bla-008	Cattle	Rib	−20.6	7.4	35.8	12.8	3.3	2.9
Bla-009	Pig	Skull	−21.1	8.9	30.1	10.6	3.3	3.4
Bla-011	Cattle	Rib	−20.6	5.5	34.6	12.6	3.2	9.5
Bla-013	Cattle	Phalanx	−21.5	8.4	35.6	12.4	3.3	7.0
Bla-014	Cattle	Rib	−20.5	8.2	28.3	9.8	3.4	1.0
Bla-015	Sheep/goat	Scapula	−20.1	5.8	38.7	14.0	3.2	10.6
Bla-017	Sheep/goat	Long bone	−20.1	8.3	39.0	13.9	3.3	10.7
Bla-018	Pig	Long bone	−20.6	8.5	36.6	13.1	3.3	10.8
Bla-019	Pig	Scapula	−20.2	9.0	28.9	10.0	3.4	3.9
Bla-021	Cattle	Rib	−20.6	9.0	28.3	9.8	3.4	2.3
Bla-022	Cattle	Long bone	−20.7	8.1	30.8	10.7	3.4	4.3
Bla-023	Pig	Long bone	−20.5	7.1	33.3	11.7	3.3	5.7
Bla-024	Cattle	Scapula	−20.0	9.2	30.1	10.5	3.4	3.0
Bla-025	Cattle	Phalanx?	−20.6	7.5	24.4	8.3	3.4	3.2
Bla-026	Pig	Long bone	−20.4	9.0	35.0	12.3	3.3	8.0
Bla-027	Cattle	Long bone	−21.2	7.9	26.1	8.8	3.5	3.1
Bla-029	Sheep/goat	Long bone	−19.8	7.8	36.2	13.0	3.3	8.5
Bla-030	Sheep/goat	Bone	−20.4	7.1	27.6	9.4	3.4	4.3
Bla-031	Sheep/goat	Long bone	−20.3	5.2	32.0	11.5	3.3	7.1
Bla-033	Cattle	Long bone	−20.2	6.9	27.9	9.7	3.4	4.7

Table A6. Brno-Starý Lískovec/Nový Lískovec (discussed in Chapter 4.9).

Grave/Sample No.	Species	Sex	Age	Bone	δ13C‰	δ15N‰	%C	%N	C:N	%Collagen
1	Human	F	44–78	Rib	−20.5	8.8	30.2	10.8	3.3	2.5
2	Human	F	33–65	Rib	−20.3	9.9	25.9	9.2	3.3	1.1
3	Human	M	30+	Rib	−20.2	9.9	26.1	9.2	3.3	1.6
4	Human	F	30+	Rib	−20.2	9.1	37.5	13.5	3.2	7.8
5	Human		9–14	Rib	−20.4	8.7	37.9	13.7	3.2	4.2
7	Human	F	40–70	Rib	−20.1	8.8	36.4	13.2	3.2	5.1
8	Human	M	25–69	Rib	−20.1	9.4	39.3	14.3	3.2	11.8
10	Human	F	30+	Rib	−20.1	9.1	40.7	14.6	3.3	8.6
11	Human	M	Adult <30	Rib	−20.1	8.9	26.3	9.5	3.2	1.7
12	Human	M	40–73	Rib	−20.1	9.0	33.3	11.8	3.3	2.0
14	Human		5–6	Rib	−20.0	9.3	40.4	14.5	3.3	5.9
15	Human	M	45–76	Rib	−20.0	9.7	37.1	13.4	3.2	1.2
16	Human	F	25+	Rib	−20.5	8.8	32.4	11.3	3.3	2.0
18	Human		6–7	Rib	−20.3	9.2	30.6	10.8	3.3	2.2
19	Human	M	40–69	Rib	−20.0	8.8	38.5	14.0	3.2	8.0
20	Human	M	45–76	Rib	−19.8	9.9	38.7	13.9	3.3	3.5
21	Human	M	45–73	Rib	−20.1	9.7	43.8	15.4	3.3	8.3
22	Human	M	30+	Rib	−19.9	10.0	39.5	14.2	3.3	3.9
23	Human		11–13	Rib	−20.1	9.0	41.4	14.8	3.3	11.9
24	Human	F	30+	Rib	−20.0	9.5	36.1	13.0	3.2	6.7
25	Human		approx. 3 years	tibia	−20.2	9.6	39.0	14.1	3.2	5.2
26	Human	F	Adult >30	Rib	−20.3	9.3	42.5	15.5	3.2	17.1
27	Human	F	Adult	Rib	−20.3	9.1	38.0	13.6	3.2	4.0
28	Human	F	Adult >20	Rib	−20.3	8.9	33.0	11.3	3.4	3.1
29	Human	F	Mid-Adult	Rib	−20.4	9.4	39.8	14.2	3.3	12.6
30	Human	M	Mature Adult	Rib	−19.9	8.8	40.1	14.5	3.2	10.0
31	Human		5–6	Rib	−19.7	9.8	43.6	15.7	3.2	12.7
32	Human	M	YMA	Rib	−20.2	9.6	38.7	14.2	3.2	5.1

33	Human	M	YMA	Rib	−20.2	8.4	36.3	13.2	3.2	6.2
34	Human	M	Mid-Adult	Rib	−20.4	9.5	38.7	14.0	3.2	8.7
35	Human	M	YA	Rib	−20.2	9.6	36.7	13.2	3.3	3.6
36	Human	M	Adult	Rib	−20.6	9.2	25.9	9.2	3.3	2.0
37	Human	M	YMA	Rib	−20.0	9.8	37.6	13.6	3.2	8.2
39	Human	F	Mid-Adult	Rib	−19.8	9.4	42.6	15.5	3.2	9.1
40	Human	M	OMA	Rib	−20.1	10.9	40.4	14.6	3.2	12.5
41	Human	F	YMA	Rib	−20.3	8.7	38.3	14.0	3.2	9.2
42	Human	F	Adult	Rib	−20.4	8.9	36.5	12.7	3.4	7.2
44	Human	M	c.50	Rib	−20.0	9.4	35.8	12.6	3.3	5.7
45	Human	F	adult	Metatarsal	−20.4	9.9	38.4	13.8	3.2	9.6

Table A7. Ensisheim les Octrois *(discussed in Chapter 8.8).*

Grave/Sample No.	Species	Sex	Age	Bone	δ13C‰	δ15N‰	%C	%N	C:N	%Collagen
1	Human	F	44–78	Rib	−20.5	8.8	30.2	10.8	3.3	2.5
2	Human	F	33–65	Rib	−20.3	9.9	25.9	9.2	3.3	1.1
3	Human	M	30+	Rib	−20.2	9.9	26.1	9.2	3.3	1.6
4	Human	F	30+	Rib	−20.2	9.1	37.5	13.5	3.2	7.8
5	Human		9–14	Rib	−20.4	8.7	37.9	13.7	3.2	4.2
7	Human	F	40–70	Rib	−20.1	8.8	36.4	13.2	3.2	5.1
8	Human	M	25–69	Rib	−20.1	9.4	39.3	14.3	3.2	11.8
10	Human	F	30+	Rib	−20.1	9.1	40.7	14.6	3.3	8.6
11	Human	M	Adult <30	Rib	−20.1	8.9	26.3	9.5	3.2	1.7
12	Human	M	40–73	Rib	−20.1	9.0	33.3	11.8	3.3	2.0
14	Human		5–6	Rib	−20.0	9.3	40.4	14.5	3.3	5.9
15	Human	M	45–76	Rib	−20.0	9.7	37.1	13.4	3.2	1.2
16	Human	F	25+	Rib	−20.5	8.8	32.4	11.3	3.3	2.0
18	Human		6–7	Rib	−20.3	9.2	30.6	10.8	3.3	2.2
19	Human	M	40–69	Rib	−20.0	8.8	38.5	14.0	3.2	8.0
20	Human	M	45–76	Rib	−19.8	9.9	38.7	13.9	3.3	3.5
21	Human	M	45–73	Rib	−20.1	9.7	43.8	15.4	3.3	8.3
22	Human	M	30+	Rib	−19.9	10.0	39.5	14.2	3.3	3.9
23	Human		11–13	Rib	−20.1	9.0	41.4	14.8	3.3	11.9
24	Human	F	30+	Rib	−20.0	9.5	36.1	13.0	3.2	6.7
25	Human		approx. 3 years	tibia	−20.2	9.6	39.0	14.1	3.2	5.2
26	Human	F	Adult >30	Rib	−20.3	9.3	42.5	15.5	3.2	17.1
27	Human	F	Adult	Rib	−20.3	9.1	38.0	13.6	3.2	4.0
28	Human	F	Adult >20	Rib	−20.3	8.9	33.0	11.3	3.4	3.1
29	Human	F	Mid-Adult	Rib	−20.4	9.4	39.8	14.2	3.3	12.6
30	Human	M	Mature Adult	Rib	−19.9	8.8	40.1	14.5	3.2	10.0
31	Human		5–6	Rib	−19.7	9.8	43.6	15.7	3.2	12.7
32	Human	M	YMA	Rib	−20.2	9.6	38.7	14.2	3.2	5.1

33	Human	M	YMA	Rib	−20.2	8.4	36.3	13.2	3.2	6.2
34	Human	M	Mid-Adult	Rib	-20.4	9.5	38.7	14.0	3.2	8.7
35	Human	M	YA	Rib	-20.2	9.6	36.7	13.2	3.3	3.6
36	Human	M	Adult	Rib	-20.6	9.2	25.9	9.2	3.3	2.0
37	Human	M	YMA	Rib	-20.0	9.8	37.6	13.6	3.2	8.2
39	Human	F	Mid-Adult	Rib	-19.8	9.4	42.6	15.5	3.2	9.1
40	Human	M	OMA	Rib	-20.1	10.9	40.4	14.6	3.2	12.5
41	Human	F	YMA	Rib	-20.3	8.7	38.3	14.0	3.2	9.2
42	Human	F	Adult	Rib	-20.4	8.9	36.5	12.7	3.4	7.2
44	Human	M	c.50	Rib	-20.0	9.4	35.8	12.6	3.3	5.7
45	Human	F	adult	Metatarsal	-20.4	9.9	38.4	13.8	3.2	9.6

Table A8. Ensisheim Ratfeld *(discussed in Chapter 8.8.3).*

Sample No.	Species	Bone	$\delta^{13}C‰$	$\delta^{15}N‰$	%C	%N	C:N	%Collagen
EnR-001	Sheep/goat	Long bone	−20.3	5.6	21.5	8.1	3.09	2.3
EnR-002	Cattle	Long bone	−21.0	6.9	19.8	7.5	3.08	1.2
EnR-003	Cattle	Long bone	−22.4	6.0	35.2	13.0	3.15	7.3
EnR-004	Sheep/goat	Long bone	−20.3	5.1	34.7	12.7	3.19	6.1
EnR-005	Sheep/goat	Long bone	−20.5	6.5	32.6	11.9	3.19	6.0
EnR-006	Cattle	Long bone	−21.4	5.7	30.1	11.1	3.16	5.1
EnR-007	Sheep/goat	Long bone	−21.4	5.9	32.0	11.7	3.19	10.1
EnR-008	Cattle	Long bone	−20.5	6.7	23.2	8.6	3.15	2.8
EnR-009	Pig	Long bone	−20.6	5.5	27.7	10.3	3.16	5.5
EnR-010	Pig	Long bone	−20.5	6.8	34.0	12.3	3.21	7.2
EnR-011	Sheep/goat	Long bone	−20.7	6.6	28.0	10.5	3.13	3.3
EnR-012	Sheep/goat	Long bone	−20.5	6.5	35.8	13.0	3.19	14.9
EnR-013	Pig	Long bone	−20.5	7.1	32.1	11.9	3.16	6.0
EnR-014	Cattle	Long bone	−23.3	6.9	34.7	12.7	3.18	6.3
EnR-015	Pig	Long bone	−20.7	7.7	27.0	9.8	3.21	3.1
EnR-016	Pig	Long bone	−20.2	7.7	32.5	11.9	3.18	6.1
EnR-042	Cattle	Long bone	−20.3	3.7	34.4	12.6	3.18	6.1
EnR-043	Cattle	Long bone	−21.6	6.9	27.2	9.8	3.24	4.1
EnR-044	Cattle	Long bone	−21.9	6.3	30.4	11.0	3.21	4.3
EnR-045	Cattle	Long bone	−22.0	6.1	41.3	15.0	3.21	9.0
EnR-046	Cattle	Long bone	−21.3	7.2	39.4	14.3	3.21	9.4
EnR-047	Cattle	Metacarpal	−22.1	8.8	33.3	12.2	3.19	4.4
EnR-048	Cattle	Long bone	−20.7	6.8	36.5	13.1	3.25	6.5
EnR-050	Cattle	Long bone	−23.7	5.5	37.3	13.5	3.21	7.4
EnR-051	Cattle	Long bone	−21.3	7.0	39.1	14.2	3.21	7.7

Table A9. Füzesabony-Gubakút (discussed in Chapter 3.8).

Grave/Sample No.	Species	Sex	Age	Bone	δ13C‰	δ15N‰	%C	%N	C:N	%Collagen
1	Human	F	YA	Long bone	−19.9	9.9	31.5	11.4	3.24	3.5
2	Human		Older Adolescent/<20	Long bone	−20.0	10.6	30.5	11.1	3.22	4.1
3	Human	F	Adult <30	Long bone	−19.8	10.5	28.5	10.3	3.24	4.2
4	Human	F	YMA	Rib	−19.8	10.2	31.8	11.5	3.25	4.1
5	Human	M	Adult >20	Rib	−20.3	10.5	24.5	8.4	3.41	2.1
6	Human		7+	Skull	−20.5	10.0	22.1	7.4	3.42	1.5
7	Human		Adult >20	Long bone	−20.2	10.2	31.4	11.4	3.23	2.6
9	Human	M	Adult >20	Long bone	−19.9	11.1	29.0	10.4	3.25	1.4
10	Human	M	Older/Mature Adult >40	Rib	−19.8	10.5	41.3	14.8	3.24	7.7
11	Human		Juvenile/Adolescent	Long bone	−20.0	9.8	27.2	9.6	3.29	1.4
13	Human		2–3	Skull	−19.6	13.0	23.3	8.0	3.39	1.1
Fus-100	Cattle			Long bone	−19.6	8.0	38.0	13.8	3.23	5.2
Fus-101	Sheep/goat			Long bone	−20.6	6.8	42.1	15.4	3.19	7.7
Fus-102	Pig			Long bone	−20.4	8.9	40.1	14.6	3.21	5.5
Fus-103	Sheep/goat			Long bone	−19.4	6.8	29.0	10.6	3.20	5.0
Fus-104	Cattle			Long bone	−19.9	7.6	37.7	13.7	3.21	4.7
Fus-105	Sheep/goat			Long bone	−19.8	6.9	40.9	15.0	3.19	12.4
Fus-108	Pig			Long bone	−19.8	5.9	42.0	15.4	3.19	13.0
Fus-110	Sheep/goat			Long bone	−21.1	7.7	24.1	8.6	3.25	7.0
Fus-112	Cattle			Long bone	−20.7	8.0	26.1	9.4	3.23	4.9
Fus-113	Pig			Long bone	−18.8	9.6	28.8	10.4	3.23	8.1
Fus-114	Pig			Long bone	−20.3	5.7	31.7	11.4	3.24	
Fus-116	Pig			Long bone	−20.5	7.8	28.8	10.4	3.25	4.8
Fus-117	Pig			Long bone	−20.5	6.7	36.6	13.4	3.18	12.0
Fus-119	Sheep/goat			Long bone	−19.9	8.6	36.1	13.2	3.20	11.1
Fus-121	Sheep/goat			Long bone	−20.6	8.3	25.9	9.2	3.31	5.2
Fus-125	Cattle			Long bone	−21.2	6.5	30.6	11.1	3.22	9.1
Fus-127	Cattle			Long bone	−20.6	6.4	21.7	7.8	3.26	3.5

Fus-131	Cattle			Long bone	−20.0	6.6	35.4	12.9	3.20	11.0
Fus-133	Cattle			Long bone	−20.3	7.6	34.6	12.6	3.19	3.5
Fus-135	Cattle			Long bone	−20.7	5.6	17.0	6.2	3.23	2.6
Fus-136	Cattle			Long bone	−20.6	6.3	42.3	15.3	3.22	6.3
Fus-137	Cattle			Long bone	−20.9	6.7	35.4	12.8	3.23	5.7
Fus-138	Cattle			Long bone	−20.2	7.2	27.7	9.6	3.36	1.3
Fus-139	Cattle			Long bone	−19.3	9.1	42.3	15.4	3.20	8.7
Fus-140	Cattle			Long bone	−20.7	6.1	37.7	13.8	3.20	9.4
Fus-141	Cattle			Long bone	−20.2	6.6	21.6	7.8	3.22	3.0
Fus-142	Cattle			Long bone	−20.2	7.0	33.4	12.2	3.20	7.2

Table A10. Gnadendorf (discussed in Chapter 5.7.3).

Sample No.	Species	Bone	δ^{13}C‰	δ^{15}N‰	%C	%N	C:N	%Collagen
Gna-001	Cattle	Rib	−20.5	8.1	30.5	10.7	3.33	5.8
Gna-002	Cattle	Rib	−20.2	7.1	38.2	13.6	3.28	4.8
Gna-003	Cattle	Rib	−20.7	7.6	21.2	7.3	3.38	1.7
Gna-007	Cattle	Radius	−20.1	6.5	38.7	13.7	3.31	6.6
Gna-008	Cattle	Ulna	−20.1	7.2	35.5	12.5	3.31	10.6
Gna-009	Cattle	Ulna	−20.9	6.6	27.2	9.6	3.30	4.3
Gna-010	Pig	Metacarpus	−20.4	8.1	32.5	11.4	3.33	3.1
Gna-011	Pig	Tibia	−20.4	6.8	29.8	10.4	3.34	2.8
Gna-012	Pig	Scapula	−20.3	6.7	30.4	10.6	3.35	3.9
Gna-013	Sheep/goat	Rib	−19.5	6.2	41.9	14.7	3.33	7.4
Gna-014	Sheep/goat	Rib	−19.9	7.7	37.6	13.1	3.34	7.8
Gna-015	Sheep/goat	Radius	−19.7	7.3	40.2	14.4	3.26	9.6
Gna-016	Sheep/goat	Tibia	−19.6	7.7	34.9	12.4	3.28	6.3
Gna-017	Sheep/goat	Tibia	−19.5	7.8	33.9	11.9	3.33	4.4
Gna-018	Sheep/goat	Tibia	−21.0	6.1	36.7	13.5	3.17	7.1

Table A11. Table A11. Heilbronn-Neckargartach (discussed in Chapter 7.7.2).

Sample No.	Species	Bone	δ^{13}C‰	δ^{15}N‰	%C	%N	C:N	%Collagen
HBr-001	Sheep/goat	Metatarsus	−20.9	7.8	40.7	14.9	3.20	3.8
HBr-002	Cattle	Long bone	−22.0	7.9	36.4	13.2	3.22	4.3
HBr-003	Sheep/goat	Long bone	−20.3	8.3	36.1	13.3	3.17	9.3
HBr-004	Cattle	Long bone	−23.5	8.8	38.5	14.1	3.19	4.1
HBr-005	Sheep/goat	Long bone	−19.6	9.0	35.6	13.1	3.17	2.9
HBr-007	Sheep/goat	Long bone	−20.3	8.9	41.3	15.1	3.18	8.8
HBr-009	Cattle	Long bone	−21.4	7.1	33.0	12.1	3.19	5.6
HBr-011	Pig	Cranium	−21.3	7.6	31.4	11.4	3.20	2.3
HBr-013	Pig	Long bone	−20.8	8.7	38.9	14.3	3.18	4.7
HBr-016	Cattle	Rib	−20.4	10.4	35.3	13.0	3.16	2.4
HBr-018	Cattle	Rib	−21.8	8.7	36.1	13.3	3.17	11.5
HBr-019	Cattle	Rib	−21.4	8.8	32.2	11.9	3.15	4.9
HBr-020	Cattle	Long bone	−20.5	8.6	37.3	13.6	3.19	12.6
HBr-021	Cattle	Tibia	−19.9	9.6	37.9	13.9	3.19	11.6

Table A12. Kleinhadersdorf (discussed in Chapter 5.7).

Grave no.	Species	Sex	Age	Bone	$\delta^{13}C$‰	$\delta^{15}N$‰	%C	%N	C:N	%Collagen
G1a	Human	M	40–60	Rib	−19.5	9.3	39.0	14.1	3.23	9.0
G1b	Human	F	40–60	Rib	−19.6	9.4	38.2	13.7	3.26	5.2
G1c	Human	F	35–55	Rib	−20.1	9.2	41.9	15.0	3.24	10.1
G6	Human		35–50	Rib	−19.8	9.5	38.7	13.9	3.26	5.5
G7	Human	M	20–30	Rib	−19.6	9.5	41.7	15.0	3.24	10.9
G8	Human	M	Adult	Rib	−19.9	8.7	37.9	13.7	3.22	4.7
G9	Human		3-4	Long bone	−19.4	9.6	35.5	12.6	3.28	4.4
G12	Human	M	35–55	Rib	−19.7	9.6	31.5	11.3	3.25	2.1
G14	Human	F	20–25	Rib	−20.2	8.9	38.8	13.7	3.31	5.5
G15	Human	F	25–35	Rib	−19.5	9.8	41.3	15.0	3.23	8.8
G16	Human	M	30–15	Rib	−19.6	8.8	39.6	14.2	3.25	6.5
G17	Human		3–4	Rib	−19.8	8.3	38.4	13.8	3.25	5.5
G18	Human		17–22	Rib	−19.8	9.1	39.8	14.3	3.26	4.9
G19	Human	M	25–35	Rib	−20.2	8.3	36.4	12.7	3.35	2.9
3	Human	M	50–60	Long bone	−19.4	10.0	41.9	15.3	3.20	14.2
5a	Human	F	18–25	Rib	−18.9	9.8	39.0	14.1	3.22	5.9
7	Human		6–7	Long bone	−20.0	9.6	36.8	13.4	3.22	5.8
10	Human	M	Adult	Long bone	−19.6	9.7	40.7	14.8	3.21	10.8
11	Human		10–12	Long bone	−19.8	9.1	42.0	15.0	3.27	8.9
17	Human	M	35–40	Rib	−19.8	9.8	30.6	11.0	3.25	4.8
22	Human		2 ± 8 months	Rib	−19.0	11.9	40.7	14.7	3.24	12.0
26	Human		1–1.5	Cranium	−19.0	12.4	30.6	10.9	3.29	4.5
29	Human	M	20–30	Rib	−20.0	10.2	37.4	13.6	3.21	8.3
32	Human	F	20–30	Rib	−19.9	9.2	30.4	11.1	3.20	4.4
40	Human	M	25–35	Long bone	−19.9	10.4	32.7	11.8	3.23	5.2
43	Human		12–17	Long bone	−20.3	8.9	29.5	10.8	3.19	5.8
49	Human		Adult	Rib	−19.7	9.6	38.2	13.8	3.23	10.2
55	Human	F	30–50	Rib	−19.8	9.3	38.3	14.0	3.20	12.0
56	Human	F	40–50	Long bone	−20.0	9.8	34.7	12.6	3.22	6.2
57	Human	M	17–25	Long bone	−20.1	9.9	26.0	9.5	3.21	2.3
59	Human		6–8	Long bone	−20.2	9.3	37.9	13.7	3.23	9.9
65	Human	F	35–45	Long bone	−20.0	9.3	38.6	13.8	3.28	6.4

66	Human		17–25	Long bone	−20.1	9.7	29.3	10.7	3.20	3.2
69	Human	M	40–60	Long bone	−19.5	9.4	37.3	13.5	3.23	14.1
79	Human	M	25–30	Long bone	−19.9	9.9	36.2	13.2	3.21	8.4
81a	Human	M	17–25	Long bone	−19.6	10.0	30.2	10.9	3.23	4.9
82	Human		25–35	Rib	−20.0	9.2	35.2	12.4	3.31	3.8
90	Human	M	Adult	Rib	−19.7	10.0	41.0	14.8	3.24	10.8
91a	Human	F	30–50	Long bone	−19.6	10.3	41.1	14.8	3.23	14.3

Table A13. Lerchenhaid (discussed in Chapter 6.7.3).

Sample No.	Species	Bone	$\delta^{13}C$‰	$\delta^{15}N$‰	%C	%N	C:N	%Collagen
Ler-001	Cattle	Humerus	−21.1	6.6	38.9	14.0	3.24	4.9
Ler-002	Sheep/goat	Mandible	−21.0	5.2	34.0	12.0	3.31	2.1
Ler-004	Cattle	Radius	−21.3	5.2	25.5	8.4	3.53	1.4
Ler-005	Sheep/goat	Tibia	−20.5	5.7	38.3	14.0	3.19	6.4
Ler-007	Pig	Ulna	−20.8	8.0	41.7	15.3	3.19	7.8
Ler-008	Sheep/goat	Humerus	−20.1	6.4	38.3	13.7	3.26	3.2
Ler-009	Cattle	Humerus	−22.1	3.0	34.9	12.3	3.29	2.1
Ler-010	Cattle	Femur	−22.3	3.5	33.9	12.0	3.28	7.8
Ler-012	Cattle	Femur	−23.1	3.4	31.6	11.4	3.23	7.5
Ler-013	Pig	Metacarpal	−20.5	7.9	42.1	15.6	3.16	11.1
Ler-014	Cattle	Ulna	−20.7	6.6	33.0	11.7	3.29	4.1
Ler-016	Goat	Radius	−19.3	5.2	40.0	14.4	3.24	5.2
Ler-018	Pig	Ulna	−21.2	5.0	37.7	13.7	3.22	4.8
Ler-020	Pig	Metacarpal	−20.9	5.5	24.0	8.0	3.52	1.2
Ler-022	Pig	Mandible	−20.7	6.4	38.4	13.7	3.28	5.0
Ler-023	Sheep/goat	Tibia	−21.8	8.2	39.0	14.1	3.22	9.5
Ler-024	Cattle	Metatarsal	−20.7	5.5	36.8	13.5	3.18	6.4
Ler-026	Cattle	Mandible	−21.2	5.9	28.7	10.0	3.33	1.9
Ler-029	Cattle	Humerus	−20.1	5.4	30.1	10.6	3.30	1.8
Ler-030	Cattle	Metacarpal	−22.0	7.6	39.9	14.3	3.25	7.7
Ler-031	Pig	Humerus	−20.7	7.8	35.7	12.7	3.29	3.4
Ler-032	Cattle	Metatarsal	−20.9	6.2	39.6	14.5	3.18	10.6
Ler-036	Cattle	Mandible	−20.3	5.3	29.9	10.4	3.36	1.7
Ler-037	Cattle	Metatarsal	−21.1	6.5	21.6	7.2	3.50	2.4
Ler-041	Cattle	Metatarsal	−21.0	6.3	35.7	12.7	3.27	3.2
Ler-042	Cattle	Metacarpal	−20.7	6.0	30.4	10.7	3.31	4.7
Ler-043	Cattle	Metacarpal	−20.2	5.7	41.2	15.0	3.21	13.5
Ler-045	Sheep/goat	Metacarpal	−21.0	4.4	41.3	15.1	3.18	6.6

Table A14. Mezőkövesd-Mocsolyás (discussed in Chapter 3.7).

Grave/Sample No.	Species	Sex	Age	Bone	$\delta^{13}C$‰	$\delta^{15}N$‰	%C	%N	C:N	%Collagen
2	Human	M	Adult	Long bone	−19.7	11.3	35.2	12.8	3.21	14.8
6	Human	A	Adult	Long bone	−19.6	10.0	35.9	13.0	3.22	12.7
18	Human	F	Adult	Metacarpal	−19.7	11.1	41.5	15.2	3.18	14.9
21a	Human	A	Adult	Metacarpal	−19.7	10.1	31.5	11.4	3.23	8.0
22	Human		Neonate	Long bone	−19.8	10.4	32.6	11.8	3.24	4.7

Table A15. Mulhouse-Est (Rixheim; discussed in Chapter 8.7).

Grave No.	Species	Sex	Age	Bone	$\delta^{13}C$‰	$\delta^{15}N$‰	%C	%N	C:N	%Collagen
2	Human	F	YA	Rib	−20.5	10.5	38.1	13.5	3.30	7.7
5	Human		Immature	Long bone	−20.5	11.6	23.9	8.6	3.23	1.9
6	Human	F	YMA	Long bone	−20.2	11.2	31.6	11.4	3.22	1.8
T6	Human	F	YMA	Rib	−20.3	10.6	35.7	12.2	3.40	3.1
14	Human	F	Adult >25	Phalanx	−20.1	10.8	41.0	14.8	3.23	16.1
15a	Human	F	Adult>40	Rib	−20.4	11.2	38.3	13.6	3.28	3.9
18	Human	F	Adult	Rib	−20.2	10.3	38.7	13.8	3.27	5.3
19	Human	M	Mature Adult	Long bone	−20.2	10.6	23.7	8.6	3.23	2.5
20	Human	F	YMA	Phalanx	−20.3	9.4	41.8	15.0	3.24	9.4

Table A16. Nitra (discussed in Chapter 4.10).

Grave No.	Species	Sex	Age	Bone	$\delta^{13}C$‰	$\delta^{15}N$‰	%C	%N	C:N	%Collagen
1/64	Human	F	YA>20	Rib	−20.2	9.7	35.1	12.6	3.26	3.6
3/64	Human		Adol.	Rib	−20.0	9.3	32.0	11.5	3.25	3.5
4/64	Human		Adol.	Rib	−19.8	10.4	38.3	13.7	3.26	4.2
4/64	Human	F	YMA	Rib	−19.9	10.3	42.4	15.3	3.24	11.6
4/64	Human	M	Mid-Ad.	Rib	−20.0	9.5	36.9	12.8	3.37	2.4
5/64	Human		Adol.	Metacarpal	−20.0	9.9	36.5	13.1	3.26	4.2
6/64	Human	F	Mature Ad.	Rib	−20.1	10.5	38.5	13.8	3.26	5.1
8/64	Human	M	Mature Ad.	Rib	−19.9	11.0	36.7	13.0	3.28	3.2
9/64	Human	M?	Mid-Ad.	Long bone	−20.4	9.7	20.0	7.2	3.26	1.6
14/64	Human	F	Adult>20	Rib	−20.4	9.8	23.5	8.4	3.29	1.3
15/65	Human	F?	Adult	Rib	−19.7	13.0	39.2	14.0	3.26	5.2
15/65	Human		1–1.5	Rib	−21.0	10.2	37.0	12.9	3.35	3.5
16/65	Human		Adult	Rib	−20.7	9.6	31.1	11.1	3.26	4.5
17/64	Human	M	Mature Ad.	Rib	−19.9	10.3	38.2	13.5	3.29	3.4
18/65	Human	F	Mid-Ad.	Rib	−20.4	10.4	24.1	8.4	3.37	1.6
19/64	Human	M	OMA	Rib	−19.9	10.7	40.7	14.7	3.23	7.0
20/64	Human	F	YMA/<30	Rib	−19.9	9.9	39.9	14.3	3.24	8.2
22/65	Human	F	Mature Ad.	Rib	−20.4	10.0	33.9	11.9	3.32	7.8
23/65	Human		11–12	Rib	−20.3	9.6	43.9	15.5	3.30	8.3
24/65	Human	F	YMA	Rib	−20.3	10.5	42.1	14.8	3.33	8.7
25/65	Human	M	Mature Ad.	Rib	−20.2	10.5	36.3	12.7	3.33	5.3
26/65	Human	M	Mid.-Ad>30	Rib	−20.1	10.5	37.2	13.0	3.33	7.1
27/65	Human	F	Older/Mature Ad.	Rib	−20.4	10.0	39.0	13.6	3.35	6.9
28/65	Human		≤6 months	Cranium	−19.2	12.7	41.0	14.2	3.38	6.8
29/65	Human		10–12	Rib	−20.5	9.6	27.9	9.3	3.50	2.2
30/65	Human		6–7	Rib	−19.9	10.1	38.0	13.5	3.28	12.4
31/65	Human		1.5–2	Rib	−19.8	12.8	38.7	13.2	3.42	7.8
32/65	Human	F	YA	Rib	−20.5	10.3	39.9	14.1	3.31	5.3
33/65	Human	F?	YMA	Rib	−20.3	9.8	43.1	15.3	3.28	12.9
34/65	Human	M	Mid-Ad.	Rib	−19.8	10.5	37.4	13.3	3.27	5.5
35/65	Human	F?	Older Ad.	Rib	−19.9	10.1	36.1	12.7	3.32	8.0
36/65	Human	F	Mature Ad.	Rib	−20.2	10.5	33.3	11.8	3.29	10.0
37/65	Human	F	YMA	Rib	−20.3	9.8	27.4	9.3	3.42	4.2

38/65	Human		6–7	Rib	−20.6	10.1	18.7	6.4	3.41	2.5
39/65	Human	F?	OMA	Rib	−19.8	10.0	33.7	11.7	3.36	4.7
41/65	Human		Early Adol.	Rib	−20.1	10.2	33.4	11.8	3.31	5.9
44/65	Human	F	Mid-Ad.	Rib	−20.4	10.6	38.3	12.8	3.50	2.6
47/65	Human		1–1.5	Cranium	−19.4	12.0	29.4	10.5	3.27	1.7
48/65	Human	F	YA	Rib	−20.3	9.6	39.0	13.1	3.48	2.5
49/65	Human		5–6	Rib	−20.3	9.5	38.9	13.7	3.31	4.4
49/66	Human		5–6	Cranium	−20.3	11.0	28.0	10.1	3.22	2.4
50/65	Human		4–5	Cranium	−20.2	10.6	32.9	12.0	3.20	2.3
52/65	Human	F?	Mid-Ad.	Rib	−20.2	9.8	31.0	10.5	3.42	2.5
53/65	Human	F	YA	Rib	−20.1	10.6	42.0	14.7	3.34	5.6
54/65	Human		6–7	Rib	−20.3	10.7	42.8	14.8	3.38	5.3
56/65	Human	M	Mature Ad.	Rib	−19.9	9.7	41.3	14.7	3.27	3.7
57/65	Human	F	YA	Rib	−20.1	11.1	43.2	15.3	3.29	7.1
58/65	Human	M	Mid-Ad.	Rib	−19.8	10.6	42.0	14.7	3.34	4.6
61/65	Human	F	Mature Ad.	Rib	−19.9	10.2	41.2	14.7	3.28	5.9
62/65	Human	M?	YMA	Rib	−20.2	10.2	41.1	14.5	3.31	10.1
64/65	Human	F	OMA	Rib	−20.3	9.8	39.5	13.9	3.32	6.2
65/65	Human	F	Older Ad.>40	Rib	−20.0	10.5	36.9	13.0	3.32	8.8
66/65	Human	F	Older Ad.	Long bone	−20.1	10.0	28.2	10.4	3.16	2.4
67/65	Human		1.5	Rib	−19.1	12.4	39.0	13.8	3.29	13.7
68/65	Human		8–9	Cranium	−20.4	9.8	21.5	7.4	3.40	1.0
69/65	Human	M	YA	Rib	−20.0	10.5	37.5	13.3	3.30	6.9
70/65	Human	F	YMA	Rib	−19.8	10.4	39.1	13.7	3.32	5.6
71/65	Human		5–6	Rib	−20.2	10.6	43.5	15.4	3.31	8.5
72/65	Human	M	YA	Rib	−20.4	10.7	41.6	14.5	3.34	10.4
74/65	Human		2–3	Rib	−20.3	10.8	32.6	11.1	3.43	3.9
77/65	Human	M?	Mid-Ad.	Long bone	−20.5	11.0	27.2	9.6	3.30	2.2

Table A17. Otzing (discussed in Chapter 6.8).

Grave No.	Species	Sex	Age	Bone	δ13C‰	δ15N‰	%C	%N	C:N	%Collagen
3	Human		inf I	Rib	−20.4	8.1	36.7	13.5	3.17	3.8
4	Human	F	older adult	Rib	−20.3	8.7	37.3	13.6	3.20	2.6
5	Human	F	late mature	Rib	−19.7	8.9	35.0	12.3	3.33	2.5
6	Human	F	young adult	Rib	−20.2	8.1	24.3	8.1	3.50	1.3
10a	Human	F	mature	Rib	−20.2	8.2	31.9	11.2	3.31	2.5
14	Human		juv	Rib	−20.3	8.4	27.0	9.2	3.45	1.3
17	Human	F	older adult	Rib	−20.1	8.8	31.3	10.8	3.40	1.8
18	Human		inf I	Rib	−20.4	7.6	26.2	8.8	3.48	1.4
22a	Human		immature	Rib	−20.2	8.7	29.8	10.3	3.39	2.4
26	Human		inf II	Rib	−20.1	7.7	40.4	14.7	3.22	5.7
27a	Human		inf I	Rib	−20.1	8.3	29.8	10.2	3.41	1.8
29a	Human		juv	Rib	−20.5	8.8	21.6	7.3	3.44	1.6
29b	Human		inf II	Rib	−20.7	8.1	32.0	11.2	3.33	2.1
33	Human		inf I	Rib	−20.3	8.5	31.2	10.7	3.40	2.1
36	Human		inf I	Rib	−20.6	7.7	25.4	8.8	3.39	1.2
37	Human		inf I	Rib	−20.3	8.4	24.7	8.4	3.44	1.0
38	Human		juv	Rib	−20.5	7.9	31.5	11.0	3.36	2.0
39	Human			Rib	−20.2	8.9	28.5	9.8	3.40	1.5

Table A18. Polgár-Ferenci-hát (discussed in Chapter 3.9).

Grave No.	Species	Sex	Age	Bone	δ13C‰	δ15N‰	%C	%N	C:N	%Collagen
033/42	Human	F	OMA	Rib	−19.7	11.0	34.2	12.2	3.27	2.1
034/82	Human	F	OMA	Rib	−20.2	10.6	38.0	14.0	3.16	6.3
034/91	Human		10–11	Rib	−19.7	10.3	39.6	14.5	3.19	7.2
069/133	Human	F	Older Adult	Rib	−20.3	11.0	29.8	10.6	3.27	2.6
103/208	Human	M	OMA	Rib	−19.6	9.8	35.8	13.0	3.20	5.9
134/239	Human		Adolescent	Rib	−20.3	9.5	20.4	7.2	3.29	1.4
270/432	Human	M	Mid-Adult	Rib	−19.8	9.8	41.6	15.2	3.19	12.5
281/444	Human	F	OMA	Rib	−20.1	10.6	38.2	13.8	3.22	9.2
282/445	Human	M	Mature Adult	Rib	−19.8	9.1	30.9	11.2	3.21	2.9
285/450	Human	M	Older Adult	Rib	−20.1	10.3	39.8	14.5	3.21	13.5
288/453	Human		1–1.5 years	Rib	−18.7	13.6	39.7	14.5	3.20	10.7
289/454	Human		10–12	Rib	−19.7	10.7	39.6	14.5	3.20	9.5
296/468	Human	F	Adult >20	Rib	−19.8	9.8	40.4	14.8	3.19	11.0
311/486	Human	F	OMA	Skull	−19.9	10.5	39.0	14.2	3.20	8.9
314/489	Human	M	OMA	Rib	−20.0	10.9	37.0	13.4	3.22	3.9
338/517	Human		10–12	Rib	−20.2	9.0	39.6	14.4	3.21	9.6
340/519	Human	F	Mid-Adult	Rib	−20.2	10.7	38.1	13.9	3.19	13.3
341/520	Human	M	Mid-Adult	Rib	−20.0	10.1	41.8	15.3	3.18	9.2
344/523	Human	F	YA	Skull	−20.1	9.5	41.8	15.2	3.20	11.1
347/526	Human		Adolescent	Rib	−20.0	10.0	42.5	15.6	3.18	8.1
350/529	Human		4–5	Skull	−19.6	10.5	41.0	15.0	3.19	10.3
353/532	Human	M	Mature Adult	Rib	−20.2	9.8	36.4	13.2	3.22	5.4
356/535	Human	M	Older Adult	Rib	−19.4	10.6	36.7	13.4	3.19	9.9
368/562	Human	F	Mid-Adult	Rib	−20.4	9.7	27.4	9.7	3.31	1.7
387/581	Human	M	YMA	Rib	−19.6	10.7	32.0	11.8	3.18	5.9
448/646	Human		2–3	Long bone	−20.0	13.2	35.3	12.8	3.22	7.7
484/685	Human		Adolescent	Rib	−20.1	10.0	38.2	14.0	3.18	10.0
486/687	Human	M	YMA	Rib	−20.3	10.1	31.5	11.5	3.21	3.7
644/944	Human		Adolescent	Rib	−19.4	10.4	34.6	12.6	3.20	4.2
697/1004	Human	M	Older/Mature Adult	Long bone	−20.3	11.6	39.1	14.2	3.21	11.9
717/1024	Human	F	YA	Rib	−20.7	9.9	20.0	7.2	3.24	2.5

718/1025	Human	F	Adult <30	Rib	−19.8	9.9	39.2	14.3	3.19	7.7
719/1026	Human		2–3	Rib	−19.8	10.1	40.4	14.8	3.19	9.6
721/1028	Human	M	Older/Mature Adult	Rib	−19.7	10.7	38.8	14.2	3.19	7.8
764/1079	Human	M	YA	Rib	−19.7	10.0	40.5	14.9	3.18	12.9
773/1093	Human	F	OMA	Rib	−20.2	10.1	37.1	13.6	3.20	10.8
786/1109	Human		approx. 1 year	Rib	−19.5	14.2	39.6	14.4	3.21	7.6
805/1138	Human	M	Adult	Rib	−20.5	10.6	34.4	12.5	3.20	9.7
821/1168	Human	F	YMA	Rib	−20.1	10.8	39.5	14.5	3.19	10.9
839/1198	Human	F	Mature Adult	Rib	−20.0	11.4	38.7	14.1	3.21	12.2
861/1222	Human		(Early) Adolescent	Rib	−20.0	10.4	40.8	15.0	3.18	12.1
867/1230	Human	M	OMA	Rib	−20.2	11.6	36.1	13.2	3.18	10.5
871/1236	Human		2–4 years	Rib	−19.8	12.6	37.0	13.5	3.20	11.8
881/1252	Human		3–4 years	Long bone	−19.1	10.1	42.6	15.5	3.20	13.0
889/1260	Human	F	YMA <30	Rib	−20.0	10.5	27.5	10.0	3.21	1.8
890/1262	Human	M	OMA	Rib	−19.6	9.8	41.7	15.3	3.18	11.4
897/1268	Human	M	YMA	Rib	−19.7	10.2	35.7	13.0	3.20	1.7
904/1311	Human	F	Adult <30	Rib	−19.3	9.6	43.6	16.0	3.17	10.9
Pol-056	Cattle				−20.0	7.4	34.2	12.1	3.29	3.1
Pol-057	Cattle				−21.0	9.4	34.8	12.1	3.35	3.1
Pol-058	Cattle				−19.4	9.5	37.4	13.3	3.29	7.5
Pol-059	Cattle				−20.2	8.6	39.1	14.4	3.17	12.9
Pol-061	Cattle				−19.3	9.9	40.2	14.8	3.16	15.5
Pol-062	Cattle				−19.4	8.0	39.5	14.3	3.22	14.2
Pol-063	Cattle				−19.8	9.9	37.8	13.6	3.25	6.1
Pol-064	Cattle				−20.0	6.9	42.5	16.0	3.10	11.2
Pol-065	Cattle				−19.7	7.5	38.2	14.1	3.17	9.6
Pol-066	Cattle				−20.3	7.4	33.7	12.0	3.27	3.5
Pol-067	Cattle				−20.1	9.3	27.6	9.7	3.34	3.6
Pol-068	Cattle				−18.8	7.5	36.9	13.5	3.20	12.2
Pol-069	Cattle				−19.4	8.4	30.0	10.3	3.40	4.7
Pol-070	Pig				−19.7	8.1	37.0	13.4	3.22	10.9
Pol-071	Pig				−20.4	9.7	38.0	13.6	3.25	9.7
Pol-072	Pig				−19.5	9.5	36.2	12.9	3.28	10.3

Pol-073	Pig				−20.5	10.3	40.0	14.4	3.25	13.4
Pol-074	Pig				−20.5	9.9	37.8	13.9	3.18	11.0
Pol-075	Pig				−20.6	9.2	34.8	12.2	3.33	6.5
Pol-076	Sheep/goat				−20.0	8.0	37.5	13.7	3.21	11.7
Pol-077	Sheep/goat				−19.5	6.3	38.0	13.8	3.21	10.1
Pol-078	Sheep/goat				−18.7	7.1	38.8	14.1	3.21	14.4
Pol-079	Sheep/goat				−20.1	8.6	37.5	13.4	3.26	10.0
Pol-080	Sheep/goat				−19.9	9.4	39.2	14.3	3.20	10.4
Pol-081	Sheep/goat				−19.8	9.8	29.0	10.0	3.37	3.7

Table A19. Rutzing (discussed in Chapter 5.10).

Grave/Sample No.	Species	Sex	Age	Bone	δ13C‰	δ15N‰	%C	%N	C:N	%Collagen
4	Human		9–11	Skull	−20.9	9.2	33.3	11.3	3.44	5.4
5	Human	M	(Young)Mid-Adult	Long bone	−20.7	9.7	35.7	12.0	3.45	4.0
6	Human		5–7	Skull	−20.7	9.1	34.0	11.3	3.51	4.6
7	Human		4–5	Skull	−20.3	11.6	29.5	10.3	3.37	3.5
8	Human	M	YMA	Rib	−20.5	10.0	30.3	10.5	3.37	3.2
9	Human	F	YA/>20	Long bone	−20.2	8.6	28.2	9.7	3.39	3.8
10	Human		>3	Long bone	−20.7	9.1	31.2	10.6	3.43	4.9
11	Human		Adult >20	Long bone	−20.4	10.7	30.7	10.7	3.34	4.3
12	Human		Adult	Long bone	−20.6	8.9	29.7	10.4	3.33	4.2
13	Human	M	YA	Rib	−20.2	9.8	36.2	13.0	3.25	10.0
14	Human	M	OMA	Rib	−21.1	9.6	30.2	10.4	3.40	4.2
15	Human	M	Mid-Adult >30	Long bone	−20.5	9.4	31.1	10.9	3.33	2.0
17	Human	F	Mid-Adult	Long bone	−20.7	10.3	27.8	9.6	3.38	4.2
18	Human		Adult	Long bone	−20.4	9.1	26.9	9.6	3.28	4.6
24	Human		9–10	Rib	−20.7	9.5	33.4	11.5	3.38	7.3
25	Human		Adult	Long bone	−20.6	9.6	28.6	10.0	3.33	1.7
26	Human		6–8	Long bone	−20.8	8.5	31.3	11.0	3.34	2.4
30	Human	F	YMA	Long bone	−20.5	9.1	34.9	12.3	3.31	2.8
31	Human		10–12	Rib	−20.6	9.7	24.1	8.3	3.39	4.6
32	Human	M	YMA	Rib	−20.4	9.7	31.9	11.3	3.30	6.4
Ru-102	Cattle			Long bone	−21.4	5.7	25.1	9.1	3.21	4.5
Ru-103	Cattle			Long bone	−21.2	6.2	16.8	6.0	3.24	2.2
Ru-104	Cattle			Rib	−21.4	5.9	15.3	5.4	3.28	2.0
Ru-105	Cattle			Rib	−21.6	6.3	14.5	5.1	3.31	1.5
Ru-106	RedDeer			Long bone	−22.7	2.8	26.2	9.3	3.27	2.0
Ru-108	Pig			Long bone	−20.2	5.0	46.4	16.5	3.29	10.2
Ru-109	Cattle			Long bone	−22.7	6.0	41.7	15.2	3.21	9.0
Ru-111	Pig			Long bone	−20.8	5.6	41.8	15.2	3.21	12.7
Ru-113	Cattle			Long bone	−21.7	5.9	45.2	16.1	3.27	9.3
Ru-115	Cattle			Long bone	−21.0	6.5	40.5	14.6	3.23	5.7
Ru-116	Sheep/goat			Long bone	−21.1	6.7	42.7	15.3	3.25	8.8

Ru-117	Sheep/goat			Skull	−21.7	4.1	38.7	14.0	3.22	6.0
Ru-120	Pig			Long bone	−20.7	6.4	42.7	15.4	3.23	12.2
Ru-121	Sheep/goat			Long bone	−20.6	6.5	40.8	14.8	3.21	7.1
Ru-123	Cattle			Long bone	−21.2	4.4	43.2	15.6	3.22	7.4
Ru-124	Cattle			Long bone	−23.9	6.4	31.3	11.0	3.34	1.7
Ru-125	Pig			Long bone	−21.1	6.0	42.7	15.5	3.22	9.1
Ru-130	Cattle			Long bone	−23.1	5.0	29.0	10.3	3.27	1.9
Ru-131	Cattle			Long bone	−20.9	8.5	36.0	13.0	3.23	3.1

Table A20. Schwetzingen (discussed in Chapter 7.7).

Grave/Sample No.	Species	Sex	Age	Bone	$\delta^{13}C$‰	$\delta^{15}N$‰	%C	%N	C:N	%Collagen
1	Human			Rib	−20.1	8.5	41.8	15.2	3.21	6.3
3	Human		Senile	Metacarpal	−20.4	9.2	33.0	12.0	3.21	2.7
4	Human	M	Adult	Rib	−20.2	8.9	38.2	13.8	3.23	5.2
5	Human	M	Adult/mature	Rib	−20.3	9.2	36.7	13.5	3.17	4.0
6	Human	M	Adult	Rib	−20.2	8.6	25.3	8.5	3.49	0.8
7	Human	M	Mature	Phalanx	−20.4	9.5	30.0	10.6	3.28	4.4
8	Human	M	Adult	Rib	−20.1	9.6	37.4	13.4	3.26	7.0
9	Human	F	Adult	Rib	−20.5	9.1	33.2	11.6	3.35	4.6
10	Human	M	Adult	Rib	−19.9	9.0	40.2	14.3	3.27	11.0
11	Human	F	Mature	Rib	−20.3	9.0	35.0	12.4	3.29	3.6
12	Human		17–18	Rib	−20.3	8.2	42.5	15.4	3.23	12.9
14	Human	M	Adult	Rib	−20.2	9.0	33.7	12.1	3.26	4.3
16	Human	M	Adult	Rib	−20.1	9.9	37.0	13.0	3.33	1.7
18	Human	F	Mature	Rib	−20.2	9.1	30.4	10.9	3.26	2.8
19	Human	F	Mature	Rib	−20.2	8.7	34.3	12.1	3.31	1.8
21	Human		7–8	Metatarsus	−20.1	8.0	38.8	13.3	3.39	3.5
25	Human	F	Adult	Rib	−20.0	8.1	38.4	13.2	3.39	8.0
26	Human	M	Adult	Rib	−20.0	9.1	42.8	15.0	3.32	3.7
28	Human	F	Adult/mature	Rib	−20.2	8.6	39.5	14.1	3.27	3.0
30	Human	F	Mature	Rib	−20.4	8.0	40.4	14.3	3.29	4.4
31	Human		*c.*17	Rib	−20.4	9.1	37.0	13.1	3.28	5.1
33	Human		*c.*4	Rib	−20.4	9.1	38.5	13.9	3.24	11.2
35	Human	M	Adult	Rib	−20.0	9.1	36.6	13.0	3.29	5.0
37	Human	F	Adult	Phalanx	−20.1	8.7	40.2	14.6	3.22	7.1
38	Human	F	Senile	Rib	−20.1	8.3	40.1	14.5	3.23	14.6
39	Human	F	Adult	Rib	−20.3	9.1	33.8	12.1	3.25	1.7
41	Human	F	Mature	Rib	−20.2	8.6	40.0	14.4	3.23	6.1
42	Human	F	Adult	Rib	−20.4	8.7	40.5	14.7	3.22	4.6

43	Human	M	Mature	Rib	−19.8	9.0	42.0	15.3	3.22	8.1
45	Human		*c.*16	Rib	−20.1	8.6	36.6	12.9	3.31	3.8
46	Human		Mature/senile	Rib	−20.3	8.8	38.4	14.0	3.21	4.7
48	Human	F	Adult	Rib	−19.9	8.6	37.8	13.5	3.25	7.3
54	Human	F	Mature	Rib	−19.7	9.7	36.5	13.1	3.24	2.9
56	Human	M	Adult	Rib	−20.1	9.1	39.3	14.3	3.21	5.6
57	Human	F	Mature	Rib	−20.3	8.5	28.3	10.2	3.23	1.5
65	Human	F	Adult	Rib	−20.1	9.3	35.1	13.1	3.13	6.7
66	Human	M	Adult	Rib	−20.3	8.8	32.0	11.7	3.21	2.4
67	Human	F	Adult	Rib	−20.3	9.7	35.8	12.9	3.24	3.6
70	Human	M	Adult	Rib	−20.1	8.8	42.9	15.6	3.22	12.4
71	Human	F	Adult	Rib	−20.5	8.4	27.8	9.8	3.30	1.1
73	Human	M	Adult	Rib	−19.8	9.1	33.0	11.9	3.23	1.0
77	Human	M	Adult	Rib	−20.1	9.1	33.2	12.1	3.21	2.3
80	Human	M	Mature	Rib	−20.2	9.4	37.2	13.6	3.19	4.1
81	Human		Adult	Rib	−20.0	9.2	37.0	13.5	3.20	4.3
82	Human	M	Mature	Rib	−20.2	9.8	38.9	14.1	3.21	8.8
89	Human	F	Adult	Rib	−20.1	9.5	39.9	14.5	3.21	7.1
93	Human	M	Adult	Rib	−20.2	9.5	39.3	13.9	3.30	7.3
97	Human	M	Mature	Rib	−20.3	8.6	39.3	14.0	3.26	7.9
99	Human	F	Adult	Rib	−20.2	9.5	39.0	14.0	3.24	4.9
100	Human	F	Adult	Rib	−20.1	9.4	39.1	13.8	3.30	3.1
101	Human	F	Senile	Rib	−20.1	10.7	42.7	15.4	3.23	12.5
104	Human	M	Mature	Rib	−20.4	8.8	36.1	12.9	3.28	6.3
105	Human	F	Adult	Rib	−19.9	9.4	42.6	15.3	3.26	9.9
106	Human	M	Mature	Rib	−20.9	8.9	33.9	11.4	3.47	1.9
107	Human	M	Adult	Rib	−20.1	8.9	39.3	14.2	3.24	6.0
109	Human	F	Adult	Rib	−20.1	9.5	39.4	14.1	3.26	9.1
110	Human	M	Adult	Rib	−20.4	8.5	38.9	14.0	3.25	5.4

115	Human		16–19	Rib	−20.4	9.2	29.3	10.5	3.26	1.7
119	Human	F	Adult	Rib	−20.1	8.4	38.8	13.8	3.28	7.5
120	Human	F	Adult	Rib	−20.3	8.8	39.3	14.2	3.23	10.1
121	Human	M	Adult	Rib	−20.3	8.9	37.4	13.3	3.29	4.1
122	Human	F	Adult	Rib	−20.3	9.3	39.8	14.4	3.22	6.6
123	Human	F	Adult	Rib	−20.3	8.3	41.5	15.0	3.23	12.8
125	Human	F	Adult	Rib	−20.5	8.8	35.1	12.7	3.23	7.1
126	Human	F	Adult	Rib	−20.1	8.1	30.4	11.4	3.12	2.4
128	Human	F	Mature	Rib	−20.0	9.9	39.4	14.2	3.24	6.2
129	Human		6–7	Rib	−20.2	7.8	37.7	13.1	3.35	2.5
130	Human	M	Mature/senile	Rib	−20.0	8.4	41.9	15.0	3.25	7.7
131	Human	F	Adult	Rib	−20.4	8.7	40.6	14.9	3.17	5.4
132	Human	M	Adult	Rib	−20.4	8.4	43.8	15.9	3.21	8.2
133	Human	M	Adult	Rib	−20.0	9.1	42.3	15.3	3.23	9.9
137	Human	F	Mature	Rib	−19.9	8.5	35.6	13.0	3.20	3.1
139	Human	M	Mature	Rib	−20.0	9.3	38.8	14.1	3.22	4.1
140	Human	F	Mature	Rib	−20.0	8.6	38.6	13.9	3.24	4.6
141	Human	F	Adult	Rib	−20.4	9.4	37.3	13.1	3.31	2.2
142	Human	M	Mature	Rib	−20.2	8.4	41.1	14.5	3.31	3.3
143	Human	M	Adult	Rib	−19.9	8.6	40.9	14.7	3.26	6.4
145	Human	F	mature	Rib	−20.5	9.2	42.1	15.3	3.21	5.7
146	Human	F	Adult	Rib	−20.5	7.9	35.4	12.7	3.24	3.9
149	Human	F	Adult	Rib	−20.2	7.6	30.3	10.9	3.24	1.8
150	Human	F	Adult/mature	Rib	−20.2	8.5	29.5	10.5	3.30	1.2
151	Human	F	Adult	Rib	−20.4	8.3	39.4	14.0	3.27	5.1
152	Human	M	Senile	Rib	−19.9	8.9	38.7	14.0	3.23	5.2
153	Human	F	Adult	Rib	−19.7	7.7	38.6	13.8	3.27	3.6
154	Human	M	Mature	Rib	−20.2	8.6	40.5	14.6	3.23	9.3

157	Human	M	Mature	Rib	−19.9	8.4	38.4	13.5	3.33	9.6
163	Human	F	Adult	Rib	−20.2	9.7	40.5	14.2	3.32	4.5
168	Human		Adult/mature	Rib	−19.6	9.1	36.9	13.2	3.27	7.0
169	Human	M	Adult	Rib	−20.1	8.9	39.5	14.1	3.27	4.4
170	Human	F	Adult	Rib	−20.1	7.9	36.0	12.5	3.36	4.9
171	Human	F	*c.*20	Rib	−20.1	9.5	35.8	12.5	3.32	5.6
174	Human	M	Adult	Rib	−19.6	8.3	35.3	11.9	3.46	4.9
176	Human	F	Adult	Rib	−20.1	10.1	39.0	13.9	3.27	5.3
177	Human	M	Adult/mature	Rib	−20.0	9.2	39.1	14.0	3.28	2.4
183	Human	F	Mature	Rib	−20.0	8.7	39.7	14.2	3.27	6.6
184	Human	F	Mature	Rib	−19.9	9.0	37.8	14.0	3.15	10.2
185	Human	M	Mature	Rib	−20.3	9.8	42.1	15.0	3.27	4.1
187	Human		Mature	Rib	−19.8	9.0	40.7	14.1	3.37	6.0
188	Human	F	Adult	Rib	−20.2	8.6	35.0	11.8	3.46	6.1
189	Human	M	*c.*18	Rib	−20.1	8.9	30.0	10.1	3.48	5.1
190	Human	F	Mature	Rib	−20.2	9.0	35.8	12.7	3.28	8.0
194	Human	M	Adult	Rib	−19.7	8.3	41.6	14.9	3.26	8.2
199	Human	F	Adult	Rib	−20.4	9.2	39.5	13.8	3.33	8.8
200	Human	M	Mature	Rib	−19.6	9.2	38.7	13.6	3.33	6.1
201	Human	F	Adult/mature	Rib	−20.2	8.7	34.6	12.4	3.26	1.7
218	Human	M	*c.*18	Rib	−20.3	8.8	39.7	14.4	3.22	3.6
219	Human	F	Adult	Rib	−20.1	8.8	38.4	14.1	3.18	4.6
220	Human	M	Adult	Rib	−19.7	8.4	37.9	13.6	3.24	7.1

Table A21. Souffelweyersheim Tuilerie Reiss und Bund *(discussed in Chaper 8.9).*

Grave No.	Species	Sex	Age	Bone	$\delta^{13}C$‰	$\delta^{15}N$‰	%C	%N	C:N	%Collagen
7	Human		Juv.	Rib	−20.5	9.6	28.4	10.2	3.25	2.7
13	Human	F	Senile	Cranium	−20.7	11.2	19.1	6.6	3.34	1.0
26	Human		Unknown	Cranium	−20.4	11.1	23.0	8.2	3.28	2.1
27	Human		Adult	Rib	−19.7	10.9	33.0	11.9	3.25	2.0
32	Human		Immature	Rib	−19.9	10.3	40.0	14.5	3.20	1.8
33	Human		Unknown	Rib	−20.4	11.2	39.1	14.3	3.21	6.4
35	Human	F	Unknown	Rib	−20.2	9.7	29.8	10.7	3.24	2.4
38	Human	M	Not child	Rib	−20.1	11.2	36.1	12.9	3.23	3.9
46	Human	M	Adult	Phalanx	−20.4	9.9	28.2	10.1	3.24	2.2
49	Human		Senile	Cranium	−21.0	9.9	33.0	11.9	3.21	2.7
50	Human	F	Adult	Rib	−20.8	10.0	30.9	11.1	3.24	1.4

Table A22. Těšetice-Kyjovice (discussed in Chapter 4.8).

Grave/Sample No.	Species	Sex	Age	Bone	$\delta^{13}C$‰	$\delta^{15}N$‰	%C	%N	C:N	%Collagen
11/86	Human	F	45–55	Rib	−19.6	9.5	42.4	15.3	3.23	8.3
15/91	Human		Inf. II	Rib	−19.9	10.1	28.0	9.8	3.34	0.9
17/91	Human		9–10	Long bone	−19.5	8.8	36.9	13.4	3.20	4.5
18/92	Human	F	20–25	Rib	−19.1	9.1	41.1	15.0	3.20	9.5
19/92	Human	M	16–18	Rib	−19.4	8.9	34.8	12.5	3.24	2.6
20/92	Human	M	17–19	Rib	−19.3	8.5	36.7	13.4	3.21	3.6
21/92	Human	M	20–22	Rib	−19.5	9.0	32.9	11.8	3.27	1.3
Tes-100	Pig			Long bone	−19.8	8.3	41.4	15.2	3.18	8.6
Tes-103	Sheep/goat			Long bone	−19.6	5.8	39.0	14.2	3.20	5.0
Tes-104	Sheep/goat			Long bone	−20.0	5.5	38.2	13.8	3.25	4.9
Tes-105	Sheep/goat			Long bone	−19.7	4.9	37.1	13.4	3.22	5.1
Tes-106	Cattle			Long bone	−20.2	6.1	39.7	14.0	3.31	4.9
Tes-108	Sheep/goat			Long bone	−20.3	8.1	41.2	15.2	3.17	4.6
Tes-109	Cattle			Metacarpal	−20.9	6.8	40.0	14.4	3.24	6.4
Tes-111	Pig			Humerus	−20.0	7.3	37.6	13.6	3.23	4.3
Tes-113	Cattle			Long bone	−20.3	7.0	40.4	14.7	3.20	6.5
Tes-115	Cattle			Long bone	−20.2	6.7	40.1	14.3	3.27	5.2
Tes-116	Cattle			Long bone	−20.1	8.3	38.4	13.6	3.30	3.8
Tes-117	Cattle			Long bone	−20.2	6.3	38.6	13.8	3.27	5.7
Tes-119	Pig			Humerus	−20.0	6.1	39.1	14.0	3.26	9.1
Tes-120	Pig			Ulna	−20.5	8.3	41.2	14.9	3.23	4.6
Tes-121	Cattle			Tibia	−20.3	6.6	38.2	13.9	3.22	6.1
Tes-123	Cattle			Metapodium	−19.9	6.9	34.3	12.0	3.34	3.4

Table A23. Vedrovice (discussed in Chapter 4.7).

Grave/Sample No.	Location	Species	Sex	Age	Bone	δ13C‰	δ15N‰	%C	%N	C:N	%Collagen
12/74	Siroká u lesa	Human		Adult	Long bone	−19.6	9.3	35.2	12.5	3.28	1.7
20/75	Siroká u lesa	Human		3–4	Rib	−19.7	8.4	40.2	14.5	3.24	4.4
21/75	Siroká u lesa	Human	F	30–40	Long bone	−19.6	9.2	30.9	10.8	3.32	1.4
27/76	Siroká u lesa	Human	F	20+	Rib	−20.5	9.2	34.9	12.1	3.37	2.3
29/76	Siroká u lesa	Human	F	18–20	Rib	−20.5	9.0	42.4	15.0	3.31	4.5
32/76	Siroká u lesa	Human		12–14	Rib	−19.9	8.5	36.3	12.9	3.28	2.1
35/76	Siroká u lesa	Human		Adult	Long bone	−19.9	9.3	42.4	15.3	3.24	4.8
36/76	Siroká u lesa	Human	F	45–50	Rib	−19.7	8.8	37.8	13.3	3.33	2.0
40/76	Siroká u lesa	Human		8–10	Long bone	−19.6	8.8	40.0	14.3	3.28	2.5
46/77	Siroká u lesa	Human	M	20–35	Rib	−19.8	9.1	39.6	14.0	3.30	3.5
61/78	Siroká u lesa	Human	F	40–50	Rib	−19.8	9.3	38.7	13.9	3.25	3.1
64/78	Siroká u lesa	Human	F	18–25	Rib	−19.8	9.2	39.1	13.8	3.30	2.3
67/78	Siroká u lesa	Human	F	35–45	Rib	−19.6	8.6	39.4	13.9	3.31	2.4
68/78	Siroká u lesa	Human	F	50+	Rib	−19.5	9.5	41.8	15.1	3.23	4.0
70/79	Siroká u lesa	Human	F	45–50	Rib	−19.5	9.5	37.1	12.9	3.36	2.3
74/79	Siroká u lesa	Human	F	50+	Rib	−19.3	9.5	37.7	13.4	3.27	1.7
76/79	Siroká u lesa	Human	M	30–35	Rib	−19.5	9.4	43.2	15.5	3.25	7.3
78/79	Siroká u lesa	Human		7–8	Rib	−19.5	9.1	40.1	14.2	3.30	5.4
80/79	Siroká u lesa	Human	F	35–45	Rib	−19.6	9.2	42.0	14.9	3.28	6.2
83/80	Siroká u lesa	Human	F	60+	Rib	−19.5	9.2	36.4	12.8	3.32	1.8
88/80	Siroká u lesa	Human	M	20–30	Rib	−19.9	9.7	35.5	12.2	3.39	1.7
94/80	Siroká u lesa	Human	F	18–25	Rib	−19.7	9.0	40.5	14.4	3.29	6.8
3/66	Sídliště	Human		9	Rib	−19.9	8.7	30.9	10.9	3.30	1.9
5/71	Sídliště	Human		6–7	Rib	−19.2	8.5	31.3	11.1	3.29	2.0
4/69	Sídliště	Human		8	Rib	−20.1	9.9	32.4	11.6	3.26	2.1
10/74	Sídliště	Human	M	40–49	Rib	−19.9	9.6	25.6	9.1	3.28	1.7
1/85	Za Dvorem	Human	F	20–25	Rib	−20.5	9.7	21.2	7.3	3.39	1.1
2/85	Za Dvorem	Human	M	25–30	Rib	−19.7	10.3	38.0	13.3	3.34	6.4
6/88	Za Dvorem	Human	F	50+	Rib	−20.2	9.6	27.4	9.6	3.32	1.1
7/88	Za Dvorem	Human	F	35–45	Rib	−19.8	9.6	38.6	13.7	3.28	3.7
8/88	Za Dvorem	Human		13–15	Rib	−20.3	10.8	44.0	15.4	3.33	10.1
9/88	Za Dvorem	Human	F	18	Rib	−20.2	9.7	20.7	7.0	3.45	1.2

10/89	Za Dvorem	Human	F	20–25	Rib	−20.6	9.7	42.5	15.2	3.25	13.2
Ved-101	Sídliště	Cattle			Tibia	−19.8	6.5	29.0	9.6	3.51	4.3
Ved-103	Sídliště	Sheep/goat			Long bone	−19.8	6.1	36.7	12.7	3.36	7.9
Ved-104	Sídliště	Cattle			Rib	−20.3	7.0	34.7	12.6	3.20	7.7
Ved-105	Sídliště	Pig			Long bone	−20.0	7.6	39.3	14.2	3.23	11.8
Ved-107	Sídliště	Sheep/goat			Long bone	−20.0	5.5	39.6	14.4	3.21	11.4
Ved-109	Sídliště	Sheep/goat			Long bone	−19.7	6.2	37.3	13.2	3.30	10.2
Ved-111	Sídliště	Pig			Long bone	−20.7	8.8	34.7	12.0	3.39	7.3
Ved-113	Sídliště	Cattle			Long bone	−20.3	5.0	36.7	13.1	3.27	10.9

Table A24. Vendenheim le Haut du Coteau *(discussed in Chapter 8.10).*

Grave No.	Species	Sex	Age	Bone	$\delta^{13}C$‰	$\delta^{15}N$‰	%C	%N	C:N	%Collagen
11a	Human		Inf. I/II	Rib	-20.1	10.0	35.1	12.8	3.20	4.8
11b	Human		Inf. I	Rib	-20.0	10.1	33.5	12.4	3.15	2.1
17	Human	M	Adult	Long bone	-20.2	10.4	28.8	10.5	3.19	2.0
21	Human		Inf. I/II	Rib	-20.2	10.6	35.4	12.8	3.23	3.7
74	Human	M	Adult	Rib	-19.9	11.0	31.8	11.2	3.30	2.0
76	Human		Not child	Femur	-20.4	11.1	26.9	9.7	3.23	1.2
82	Human		Not child	Rib	-20.1	11.7	25.3	9.0	3.28	1.3
87	Human		Inf. I/II	Tibia	-20.1	11.1	38.5	14.1	3.18	13.0
96	Human		Adult	Rib	-20.5	10.3	32.8	12.0	3.20	4.4
102	Human		Adult	Rib	-20.5	10.5	30.3	10.6	3.33	2.0
104	Human	M	Adult	Rib	-20.2	11.0	30.6	11.0	3.26	2.5
107	Human		Inf. II/juv.	Rib	-20.3	11.4	37.5	13.6	3.22	6.3
130	Human		Adult	Humerus	-20.1	10.7	33.4	12.2	3.19	3.9
131	Human	F	Adult	Rib	-20.1	8.9	35.8	12.8	3.25	3.8
132	Human		Adult	Ulna	-19.9	8.8	28.6	10.5	3.17	2.0
133a	Human		Inf. II	Rib	-20.2	10.2	34.4	12.3	3.28	4.2
133b	Human		Inf. II	Rib	-20.2	10.3	33.2	11.9	3.25	3.9
139	Human	M	Adult	Rib	-19.8	11.1	29.1	10.7	3.16	2.3
141	Human		Inf. II/juv.	Rib	-20.1	9.3	27.2	9.5	3.34	1.8
148	Human	M	Adult	Rib	-20.1	11.2	37.9	13.8	3.19	9.0
151	Human	M	Adult	Rib	-20.4	11.0	30.7	11.2	3.21	2.9
159	Human		Inf. I/II	Rib	-20.3	9.9	30.9	11.3	3.18	3.1
161	Human	F	Adult	Rib	-20.3	11.1	37.1	13.5	3.21	3.5
172	Human		Inf. II/juv.	Rib	-20.3	10.5	38.7	14.0	3.23	6.7
173	Human		Adult	Rib	-20.5	9.4	28.4	10.0	3.31	1.6
186	Human	M	Adult	Rib	-20.1	10.5	32.4	11.3	3.33	2.3
189	Human		Adult	Long bone	-19.8	10.6	32.9	12.0	3.19	2.6
195	Human		Inf. II	Rib	-20.6	10.7	34.0	12.1	3.27	2.8
199	Human		Inf. II	Long bone	-20.1	9.6	29.0	10.4	3.27	1.9

Appendix B
Selected radiocarbon dates

This appendix should be viewed as a small contribution to furthering our understanding of the chronology of LBK cemeteries. Radiocarbon dating has not consistently been carried out on the LBK, partly due to a plateau in the calibration curve which coincides with much of its duration, resulting in a large scatter of dates (Stäuble 1995). Even though LBK cemeteries generally have very little vertical or horizontal stratigraphy, Bayesian modelling offers a way to produce more precise chronologies when radiocarbon dates on short-life material of known taphonomy and in reliable contexts are combined with prior archaeological knowledge (Bayliss 2009; Bayliss *et al.* 2007; 2011). Although not intended to be a major part of the LBK Lifeways project, it was possible to obtain a number of radiocarbon dates from the cemeteries of Nitra (Chapter 4.10), Schwetzingen (Chapter 7.7) and Kleinhadersdorf (Chapter 5.7), the latter contributing to a wider analysis being carried out by Peter Stadler as part of the forthcoming publication (Neugebauer-Maresch and Lenneis forthcoming). Modelled results were also compared to those from the cemetery at Vedrovice (Chapter 4.7; Pettitt and Hedges 2008).

B1 Radiocarbon dates from Nitra, Schwetzingen and Vedrovice

Seren Griffiths

B1.1 Radiocarbon methods

Sample pretreatment and measurement

Samples from three sites are discussed here. Radiocarbon measurements on samples from Schwetzingen and Nitra were commissioned for the LBK Lifeways project, while results measured at Oxford on samples from Vedrovice are reported in detail in Pettitt and Hedges (2008). Two samples measured at the Vienna laboratory are also reported in Pettitt and Hedges (2008).

Samples measured at the University of Oxford Radiocarbon Accelerator Unit (ORAU) were pretreated as outlined in Bronk Ramsey *et al.* (2004; see also Brock *et al.* 2007; 2010a); combustion to carbon dioxide followed the protocol in Brock *et al.* (2010b); graphitisation followed the protocol of Dee and Bronk Ramsey (2000). Accelerator Mass Spectrometry (AMS) measurement is detailed in Bronk Ramsey *et al.* (2004b; compare details in Pettitt and Hedges (2008) for Vedrovice samples measured at Oxford).

Two radiocarbon dates on bone from the Vedrovice cemetery were measured at the Laboratorium Institut für Isotopenforschung und Kernphysik, Universität Wien, using an AAA pretreatment, followed by gelatinisation, and combustion to AMS targets (Eva Maria Wild, pers. comm. 2012).

Stable isotope data

The interpretation of dietary evidence from $\delta^{15}N$ and $\delta^{13}C$ data from Vedrovice and Nitra is discussed fully in Chapter 4.7.3 and 4.10.3, while the results from Schwetzingen are discussed in Chapter 7.7.2. These data do not show evidence of a major marine or freshwater fish dietary component, and no diet-derived radiocarbon offset is inferred (Chapter 9.2; Pettitt and Hedges 2008).

B1.2 Radiocarbon calibration

Calibrated radiocarbon results are shown in Tables B1–3. Results are conventional radiocarbon ages (Stuiver and Polach 1977), calculated using the calibration curve of Reimer *et al.* (2009) and the computer program OxCal 4.1 (Buck *et al.* 1992; 1996; Bronk Ramsey 1995; 1998; 2001; 2009a; 2009b). Ranges in plain text are maximum intercepts at 95.4% confidence (Stuiver and Reimer 1986). Ranges are quoted in accordance with Stuiver and Polach (1977; but adapted for the increased precision available in later datasets – rounding out by 10 years when the error term is equal to or greater than 25 years). Calibrated radiocarbon dates are shown in outline in the figures; black distributions in the figures are posterior density estimates calculated as part of the Bayesian analysis.

Table B1. Nitra: radiocarbon dates. Posterior density estimates derive from the model shown in Fig. B1.

Lab number	Sample no. Grave no.	Material	Radiocar-bon age	$\delta^{13}C$	$\delta^{15}N$	C:N	Calibrated date range (95.4% confide-nce; cal BC)	Posterior density estimate (95.4% probability; cal BC)	Radiocarbon sample comment
OxA-24574	Ni-005 5/64	Human tibia	6222±37	−20.0	9.9	3.26	5310–5050	*5300–5090*	
P-27804	Ni-008 8/64	Human fibula	–	−19.9	11.0	3.28	–	–	Sample failed due to low collagen yield
OxA-24575	Ni-011 6/64 Stratigraphically later than grave 2	Human tibia	6226±36	−20.1	10.5	3.26	5310–5050	*5280–5080*	
OxA-24095	Ni-012 2/64 Stratigraphically earlier than grave 6	Human tibia	6298±33	−19.7	11.0	3.3	5330–5210	*5310–5210*	Low yield, passes other quality parameters
OxA-24576	Ni-014 19/64	Human scapula	6196±36	−19.9	10.7	3.23	5300–5040	*5290–5070*	
P-27806	Ni-016 21/64	Human humerus	–				–	–	Sample failed due to low collagen yield
OxA-24577	Ni-024 25/65	Human radius	6216±36	−20.2	10.5	3.33	5310–5050	*5300–5080*	
OxA-23793	Ni-025 27/65	Human fibula	6221±35	−20.4	10.0	3.35	5310–5050	*5300–5080*	
P-27808	Ni-027 26/65	Human ulna	–	−20.1	10.5	3.33	–	–	Sample withdrawn due to possible contamination
OxA-24578	Ni-031 32/65	Human radius	6138±34	−20.5	10.3	3.31	5220–4980	*5220–5050*	
OxA-24579	Ni-033 35/65	Human humerus	6317±34	−19.9	10.1	3.32	5370–5210	*5320–5210*	
OxA-24580/ P-27819	Ni-034 36/65	Human tibia	6227±35	−20.2	10.5	3.29	5310–5060	*5300–5080*	P-27819 sample note dated
P-27811	Ni-036 34/65	Human tibia	–	−19.8	10.5	3.27	–	–	Sample failed due to low collagen yield
P-27814	Ni-039 39/65	Human tibia	–	−19.8	10.0	3.36	–	–	Sample withdrawn due to possible contamination
OxA-23794	Ni-040 41/65	Human tibia	6219±35	−20.1	10.2	3.31	5310–5050	*5300–5080*	

OxA-24581	Ni-046 66/65	Human tibia	6083±35	−20.1	10.0	3.16		*5220–5100 (86.4%)* Poor individual agreement index *(A=34.2%)*	
OxA-24582	Ni-071 70/65	Human tibia	6328±36	−19.8	10.4	3.32	5380–5220	*5320–5210*	
P-27818	Ni-075 76/65	Human tibia	–				–	–	Sample withdrawn due to possible contamination

Table B2. Schwetzingen: radiocarbon dates. Posterior density estimates derive from the model shown in Fig. B3.

Lab number	**Sample no.**	**Material**	**Radiocarbon age**	δ^{13}**C**	**Calibrated date range (95.4% confidence cal BC)**	**Posterior density estimate (95.4% probability; cal BC)**
OxA-23200	Stz-006	Human bone	6142±37	−19.9	5220–4980	*5210–5060*
OxA-23201	Stz-021	Human bone	6228±37	−19.8	5310–5050	*5230–5060*
OxA-23202	Stz-026	Human bone	6233±37	−19.7	5310–5060	*5230–5060*
OxA-23203	Stz-037	Human bone	6133±37	−19.9	5220–4950	*5210–5060*
OxA-23204	Stz-048	Human bone	6243±38	−19.7	5320–5060	*5180–5060 (87.8% probability)* Poor individual agreement index *(A=54.7%)*
OxA-23205	Stz-129	Human bone	6162±36	−20.0	5220–4990	*5210–5060*
OxA-23206	Stz-133	Human bone	6202±36	−19.7	5300–5040	*5220–5060*
OxA-23207	Stz-145	Human bone	6183±36	−20.2	5290–5010	*5220–5060*
OxA-23208	Stz-155	Human bone	6187±37	−20.1	5290–5020	*5220–5060*
OxA-23209	Stz-200	Human bone	6208±34	−19.6	Weighted mean 6190±25 (T'=0.6; T'5%=3.8; ν=1) 5220–5050	*5220–5060*
OxA-23210			6171±35	−19.5		
OxA-23211	Stz-220	Human bone	6141±37	−19.6	5220–4980	*5210–5060*

Table B3. Vedrovice: radiocarbon dates. Posterior density estimates derive from the model shown in Figs B5 and B7 Sample details are taken from Pettitt and Hedges (2008).

Lab number	Sample no.	Material	Radiocarbon age	Site phasing	$\delta^{13}C$	Calibrated date range (95.4% confidence cal BC)	Posterior density estimate (95.4% probability; cal BC) Model 1	Posterior density estimate (95.4% probability; cal BC) Model 2
OxA-16650	15/75	Human bone	6299±35	1B1	−18.8	5350–5210	*5310–5220*	*5310–5210*
OxA-15367	30/76	Human bone	6219±35	1B1	−18.7	5310–5050	*5300–5220*	*5300–5130*
OxA-15385	37/76	Human bone	6332±37	1B1	−18.9	5380–5220	*5310–5220*	*5320–5210*
OxA-16617	54/78	Human bone	6240±45	1B1	−18.9	5320–5050	*5300–5220*	*5310–5140*
OxA-15131	62/78	Human bone	6266±36	1B1	−19.2	5320–5200	*5300–5220*	*5310–5200*
OxA-16621	79/79	Human bone	6244±40	1B1	−19.2	5320–5060	*5300–5220*	*5310–5140*
OxA-15363	91/80	Human bone	6305±40	1B1	−19.1	5370–5210	*5310–5220*	*5320–5210*
OxA-15425	77/79	Human bone	6298±34	1B2	−18.6	5340–5210	*5250–5210*	*5310–5210*
OxA-15429	72/79	Human bone	6268±37	1B	−18.5	5320–5200	*5300–5210*	*5310–5200*
OxA-15426	99/81	Human bone	6272±37	1B	−19.4	5320–5200	*5310–5210*	*5310–5200*
–	100/81	Human bone	–	–	–	–	–	–
OxA-15432	50/77	Human bone	6108±36	2A	−19.1	Weighted mean 6089±26 (T'=0.6; T'5%=3.8; ν=1) 5200–4930	*5210–5160 (90.2%)*	*5220–5150* Poor individual agreement index (A=19.4%)
OxA-15433			6069±36		−19.0			
OxA-16618	66/78	Human bone	6251±39	2A	−19.0	5320–5070	*5250–5070*	*5310–5150*
OxA-15365	106/82	Human bone	6141±34	2A	−19.2	5220–4980	*5220–5070*	*5220–5120*
OxA-16651	16/75	Human bone	6164±35	–	−19.4	5220–4990	*5230–5060*	*5230–5100*
OxA-15427	22/75	Human bone	6280±38	–	−19.1	5330–5210	*5310–5210*	*5310–5210*
OxA-15384	23/75	Human bone	6199±37	–	−19.0	5300–5040	*5300–5070*	*5300–5120*
OxA-15366	28/76	Human bone	6159±35	–	−19.2	5220–4990	*5230–5060*	*5230–5100*
OxA-15428	31/76	Human bone	6253±36	–	−19.4	5220–5070	*5310–5140*	*5310–5190 (94.6%)*
OxA-15386	38/76	Human bone	6300±36	–	−19.6	5360–5210	*5310–5210*	*5310–5210*
–	42/77	Human bone	Fail	–	–	–	–	–
–	51/77	Human bone	Fail	–	–	–	–	–

OxA-15368	43/77	Human bone	6146±34	–	−19.6	5220–4990	*5220–5060*	*5220–5110*
OxA-15369	44/77	Human bone	6216±36	–	−19.3	5310–5050	*5300–5080*	*5300–5130*
OxA-16653	48/77	Human bone	6290±37	–	−19.3	Weighted mean 6268±26 (T'=0.7; T'5%=3.8; ν=1) 5320–5210	*5300–5210*	*5300–5210*
OxA-16652			6248±35		−19.3			
OxA-15387	57/78	Human bone	6160±35	–	−18.9	5220–4990	*5230–5060 (95.0%)*	*5230–5100*
OxA-15388	59/78	Human bone	6246±36	–	−18.6	5320–5070	*5310–5190 (93.9%)*	*5310–5140*
OxA-15424	66/78	Human bone	6263±34	–	−18.5	5320–5200	*5310–5200*	*5310–5200*
OxA-16619	73/79	Human bone	6169±38	–	−19.3	5230–4990	*5230–5060 (91.6%)*	*5290–5110*
OxA-16620	75/79	Human bone	6289±37	–	−18.9	5330–5210	*5310–5210*	*5310–5210*
OxA-15370	81b/79	Human bone	6234±36	–	−19.1	5310–5060	*5310–5120 (93.8%)*	*5310–5130*
OxA-16622	82/79	Human bone	6250±40	–	−18.6	5320-5070	*5310–5080*	*5310–5140*
–	86/80	Human bone	Failed	–	–	–	–	–
OxA-16623	84/80	Human bone	6297±38	–	−19.4	5360–5210	*5300–5210*	*5310–5210*
OxA-15430	90/80	Human bone	6407±37	–	−19.5	Weighted mean 6396±30 (T'=0.3; T'5%=3.8; ν=1) 5480–5310	*5340–5220* Poor individual agreement index *(A=13.5%)*	*5340–5290 (33.4% probability)* or *5270–5220 (62.0% probability)* Poor individual agreement index *(A=17.1%)*
OxA-15362			6375±50	–	−19.2			
–	89/80	Human bone	Failed	–	–	–	–	–
OxA-16624	93a/80	Human bone	6226±37	–	−19.1	5310–5050	*5310–5080*	*5310–5130*
OxA-15431	96/80	Human bone	6224±36	–	−19.2	5010–5050	*5310–5070*	*5310–5130*
OxA-15364	101/81	Human bone	6182±35-	–	−18.9	5230–5010	*5290–5070*	*5290–5110*
OxA-16625	102/81	Human bone	6195±35	–	−19.4	5300–5040	*5300–5080*	*5300–5120*
OxA-16626	104/81	Human bone	6249±36	–	−19.1	5320–5070	*5310–5190 (94.1%)*	*5310–5190 (93.5%)*
OxA-16627	105/81	Human bone	6220±36	–	−19.3	5010–5050	*5300–5070*	*5300–5130*
OxA-16629	107/82	Human bone	6175±37	–	−19.3	Weighted mean (T'=0.9; T'5%=3.8; ν=1) 5220–5000	*5220–5060*	*5220–5120*
OxA-16628			6125±37		−19.3			
VERA-1831	?	Human bone	6220±35	–	–	5310–5050	*5300–5080*	*5300–5130*
VERA-1832	?	Human bone	6155±35	–	–	5220–4990	*5220–5060*	*5230–5110*
OxA-15553	179/3	Animal bone	6410±65	Settlement	−20.2	5490–5220	–	–

B1.3 Bayesian analysis and sample selection

The Bayesian modelling presented here uses Markov Chain Monte Carlo sampling. Modelling was applied using OxCal 4.1 (details of which can be found in the online manual http://c14.arch.ox.ac.uk/; Bronk Ramsey 1995; 1998; 2001; 2009a; 2009b). In the text, OxCal command query language (CQL2) parameters (Bronk Ramsey 2009b) are quoted in the `Courier` font to differentiate them from similar archaeologically meaningful terms (e.g. '`Phase`' refers to the OxCal 4.1 group command). In the figures, the model structure (including the algorithms used) can be extrapolated from the OxCal CQL2 keywords and brackets. Ranges quoted in the text in italics are posterior density estimates produced from the Bayesian statistical model.

The Bayesian models presented here use both 'uninformative' prior information, which addresses some of the statistical scatter inherent in any assemblage of measurements (Bayliss *et al.* 2007; Bronk Ramsey 2000; Buck *et al.* 1992; 1996), and 'informative' prior information (Bayliss *et al.* 2007; Buck *et al.* 1992; 1996; Bronk Ramsey 1995; Steier and Rom 2000).

In all the models for the cemeteries discussed below, the dated samples derived from articulated inhumations. Because the samples derive from articulated skeletons we can suggest that there probably are not significant offsets between the dates of death of the individuals and their burials; the remains were buried while still 'fleshed', probably less than six months after death (Mant 1987), and therefore are not residual from earlier activity on the site.

For the radiocarbon dates submitted for this project, burials were selected to represent an initial sample of the Nitra and Schwetzingen cemeteries (Figs 4.20 and 7.6). There may be further chronological structure to the development of the cemeteries.

Because the inhumations from each of the cemeteries appear to represent related archaeological phases of activity, the radiocarbon results from each individual cemetery are not independent likelihoods, but are related. It is this interpretation of relatedness that has been used to provide statistical distributions and is part of the Bayesian model structure for each cemetery.

In the case of Nitra, some additional prior information for the Bayesian model derives from the site stratigraphy. For Vedrovice, the first model presented below uses informative prior information derived from an interpretation of the site pottery phasing (Pettitt and Hedges 2008). A more neutral interpretation of the Vedrovice data is presented in a second model as a form of sensitivity analysis.

B1.4 Radiocarbon dates from Nitra

Introduction

Samples from 19 inhumations from the Nitra cemetery were submitted to ORAU. Unfortunately, due to conservation methods applied to the skeletal collection since their excavation in the 1970s, not all samples could be dated. Three samples initially submitted for radiocarbon dating (P-27808, grave 26; P-27814, grave 39; P-27818, grave 76) were withdrawn, because FTIR (Fourier transform infrared spectroscopy) analysis suggested contamination of the bone collagen in these samples with conservation products (see below; Table B1), and only one sample from grave 36 was measured, as we were uncertain of success (two samples were initially submitted to the laboratory, but only P-27819; OxA-24581 was dated). A further three samples (P-27804, grave 8; P-27806, grave 21; P-27811, grave 34) failed due to low collagen yields (Bronk Ramsey *et al.* 2004; Table B1).

Twelve samples were successfully dated (Table B1). Of these, OxA-24095 was produced on collagen which was just below the laboratory minimum of 1% weight; all other parameters were acceptable (see below). The radiocarbon dates on Nitra must therefore be regarded as a pilot study, and future work is anticipated.

Radiocarbon sample selection

The submitted radiocarbon samples from Nitra represent an initial attempt to investigate the chronology of the cemetery. Further radiocarbon dates sampling other use of the cemetery – to include the cremations, and to investigate the tradition of other material culture evidence – would develop understanding of the site. In addition to the interpretation of relatedness between all the radiocarbon dates from the cemetery, more structured chronological relationships can be identified between two inhumations dated by radiocarbon. Grave 2 (OxA-24095) is recorded as being cut by grave 6 (OxA-24575). This relationship is reflected in the model presented below.

Comment on PVA and FTIR analysis

As was common practice at the time of its excavation, PVA glue had been applied to the Nitra skeletal assemblage as a consolidant to preserve the bone. PVA had been consistently applied to the majority of each skeleton, even on heavily fragmented sections. The collagen was extracted using the procedure (O'Connell and Hedges 1999) set out in Chapter 2.2.2 (including shot-blasting the bone surface) on the samples selected for stable isotope analysis. In order to ascertain the degree of contamination, FTIR analysis was carried out at Cardiff University by Panagiota Manti and Penny Bickle. Sample data were recorded using a Perkin Elmer Spectrum One spectrometer with Attenuated Total Reflectance set-up (ATR; the software was Spectrum One) and ten scans were collected for each sample from 4000-450–cm^{-1}.

Spectra collected from the suspected contaminated bone collagen were compared to those taken from a BDH modern reference sample of polyvinyl acetate and the collagen sample from a known uncontaminated bone from the Bornish Bronze Age site. A very small infrared band at 1722 cm^{-1} by the major collagen band (1632 cm^{-1}) observed on samples P-27808, P-27814 and P-27818 could be due to the presence of polyvinyl acetate (PVAC), which has a major absorption band at 1725 cm^{-1}. Other characteristic bands from PVAC (at at 1119.80, 1370.22 cm^{-1}) overlap with collagen bands and are not clear to distinguish in

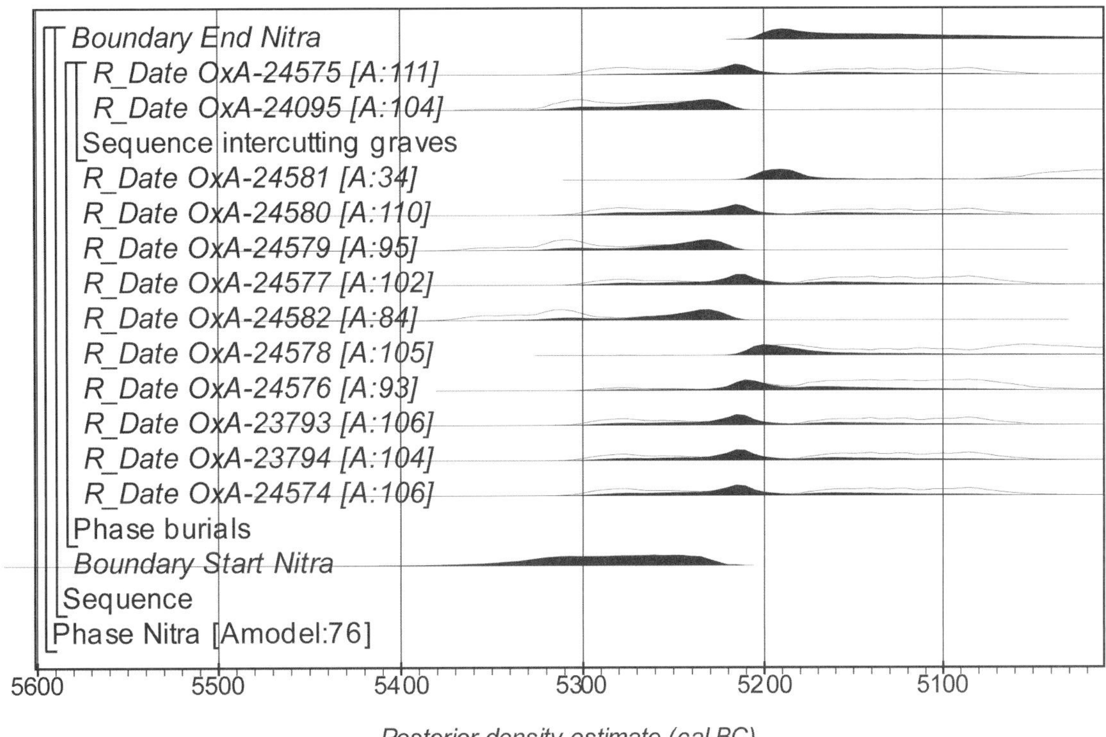

Fig. B1. Nitra: probability distributions of the radiocarbon dates. Each distribution represents the relative probability that an event occurred at a particular time. Two ranges have been plotted for each distribution. The range in outline represents the calibrated radiocarbon result, and the solid distribution represents the posterior density estimate – the output from the Bayesian statistical model illustrated in the figure. The large square brackets and CQL2 OxCal keywords define the model exactly. `Boundary` *parameters estimate the start and end of activity.*

the data. On this basis these samples were rejected from further isotopic analysis.

Results

The radiocarbon results from Nitra are not statistically consistent (T'=44.0; T'(5%)=19.7; ν=11), indicating that they probably represent individuals who died over a period of some time (Ward and Wilson 1978).

A model reflecting the prior information outlined above is shown in Fig. B1. This model has good overall agreement ($A_{overall}$=75.7%). One result (OxA-24581) shown in Fig. B1 has a poor individual agreement index (A=34.2%; Table B1). The agreement index of this result indicates a tension between this, and the model and the other data. This result could be an example of the one in 20 radiocarbon measurements when the actual age of a sample lies outside the quoted date range. Alternatively, OxA-24581 could represent a burial tradition at the cemetery from a significantly different period than the majority of the activity sampled by the other radiocarbon results.

OxA-24095 (which was produced on bone which had a slightly low collagen yield) shows good agreement (A=103.9%) with the other results and site model, and probably provides an accurate age estimate for the sample.

If the available chronometric data are representative of the cemetery use at Nitra, this activity first began in *5370–5220 cal BC* (*95.4% probable*) or *5320–5230 cal BC* (*68.2% probable; Start Nitra*; Fig. B1). The end of activity at the Nitra cemetery, as indicated by the currently available data, occurred in *5210–4980 cal BC (95.4% probable*) or *5210–5090 cal BC* (*68.2% probable; End Nitra;* Fig. B1). The activity represented by samples included in the model shown in Fig. B1 occurred over *20–360 years* (*95.4% probable*) or *30–220 years* (*68.2% probable; Duration all Nitra*; Fig. B1).

The individual in grave 2 died in *5310–5210 cal BC* (*95.4% probable*) or *5270–5210 cal BC* (*68.2% probable; OxA-24095;* Fig. B1). The individual in grave 6 died in *5280–5080 cal BC* (*95.4% probable*) or *5250–5130 cal BC* (*68.2% probable; OxA-24575;* Fig. B1). There was an interval of *0–170 years* (*95.4% probable*) or *0–80 years* (*68.2% probable; Interval_intercutting;* Fig. B2) between the deaths of these two individuals. It is possible that the individuals buried in these graves were known to each other. Using an estimate of 25 years for a human generation (Whittle *et al.* 2011), the individuals in these graves were separated by, at most, just over three generations (at *68.2% probability*). The proximity of the graves and the potential that the individuals were known to each other could indicate a familial or other close relationship between the female (>60 years at death) buried in grave 6 and the male (40–45 years at death) buried in grave 2. Alternatively these individuals could be part of the same

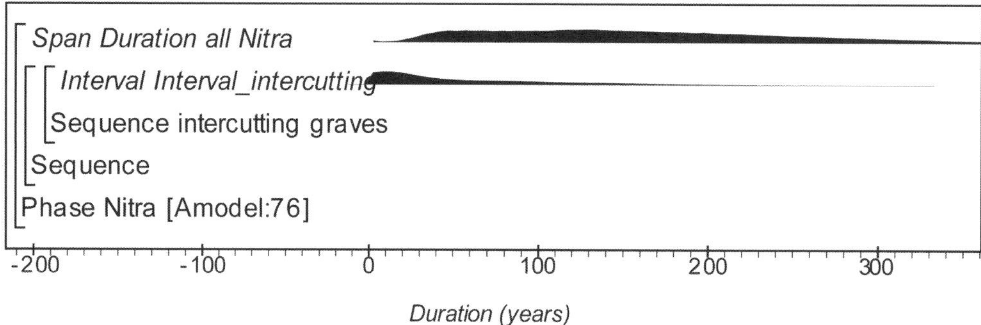

Fig. B2. Nitra: intervals between different events, and the duration of activity calculated from the model shown in Fig. B1. The large square brackets and CQL2 OxCal keywords show the model structure from which the parameters are estimated.

descent group or buried in proximity for prosaic reasons of cemetery maintenance or management.

B1.5 Radiocarbon dates from Schwetzingen

Introduction

Samples representing 11 inhumations from the Schwetzingen cemetery were submitted to ORAU.

Two true replicate measurements were produced on material from skeleton Stz-200 (OxA-23209 and OxA-23210).

Radiocarbon sample selection

Samples from the Schwetzingen cemetery were selected to provide an initial attempt to investigate the chronology of the cemetery. Further radiocarbon dates would develop understanding of the site; fewer samples were dated from graves in the north-west and north of the cemetery and none of the cremations were dated. It is also possible that some burial practices are of varying date, for example the practice of placing the body in a supine position in the grave. Jeunesse (1997, 67; 2005) has hypothesised that this practice was a later development in the western LBK regions (particularly Basse-Alsace; Chapter 8.5), where the supine body position was carried into middle Neolithic burial practices, while the crouched position was abandoned. This is an interesting suggestion given the geographical closeness of Schwetzingen (in Baden-Württemberg) to Basse-Alsace. However, only five graves at Schwetzingen (Chapter 7.7.1) were in a supine position, a rate in line with what we found across the LBK as a whole (Chapters 2.5.1 and 9.5), perhaps suggesting that this pattern was not chronological but rather part of the variation found in body position at LBK cemeteries. In any case the only grave in an extended or supine position to be dated was burial 133 (OxA-23206).

Dated inhumations from Schwetzingen represented adult and mature females and males. A range of material culture was recovered from the radiocarbon dated graves, but information about the relative chronologies of material culture from the dated graves was not available for analysis of the scientific dates, and attempts at seriation have failed (Gerling 2006).

All the dated graves were discrete features, without stratigraphic relationships with other negative features.

Results

The radiocarbon results from Schwetzingen are statistically consistent (T'=11.4; T' (5%)=19.7; ν=11), indicating that they could represent individuals who died at the same time (Table B2).

A model reflecting the prior information outlined above is shown in Fig. B3; this model has good overall agreement ($A_{overall}$=84.5%; Table B2). An estimate for the start of activity at the cemetery is *5260–5080 cal BC* (*95.4% probable*) or *5190–5100 cal BC* (*60.2% probable; Start Schwetzingen;* Fig. B3). The end of the phase as shown in Fig. B3 is estimated as *5170–5010 cal BC* (*94.3% probable*) or *5140–5050 cal BC* (*68.2% probable; End Schwetzingen;* Fig. B3). The total duration of activity represented by the phase of inhumations is estimated as *0–160 years* (*95.4% probable*), most probably *0–80 years (68.2% probable; Duration Schwetzingen*; Fig. B4).

B1.6 Further modelling of radiocarbon dates from Vedrovice

Introduction

Forty-five radiocarbon results are available from the site and settlement of Vedrovice. Forty-three of the results were produced at ORAU as part of the Vedrovice Bioarchaeology Project (Zvelebil and Pettitt 2008) and reported in Pettitt and Hedges (2008); two other results were produced at the Laboratorium Institut für Isotopenforschung und Kernphysik, Universität Wien. OxA-15553 was produced on a sample identified as 'animal bone' from the Vedrovice settlement (Pettitt and Hedges 2008, 127). All the other results were produced on human bone from the cemetery.

True replicate measurements were produced on samples as part of the ORAU quality control protocols from burials 48/77, 50/77, 90/80 and 107/82. Each of the other results was a measurement on material from a different individual.

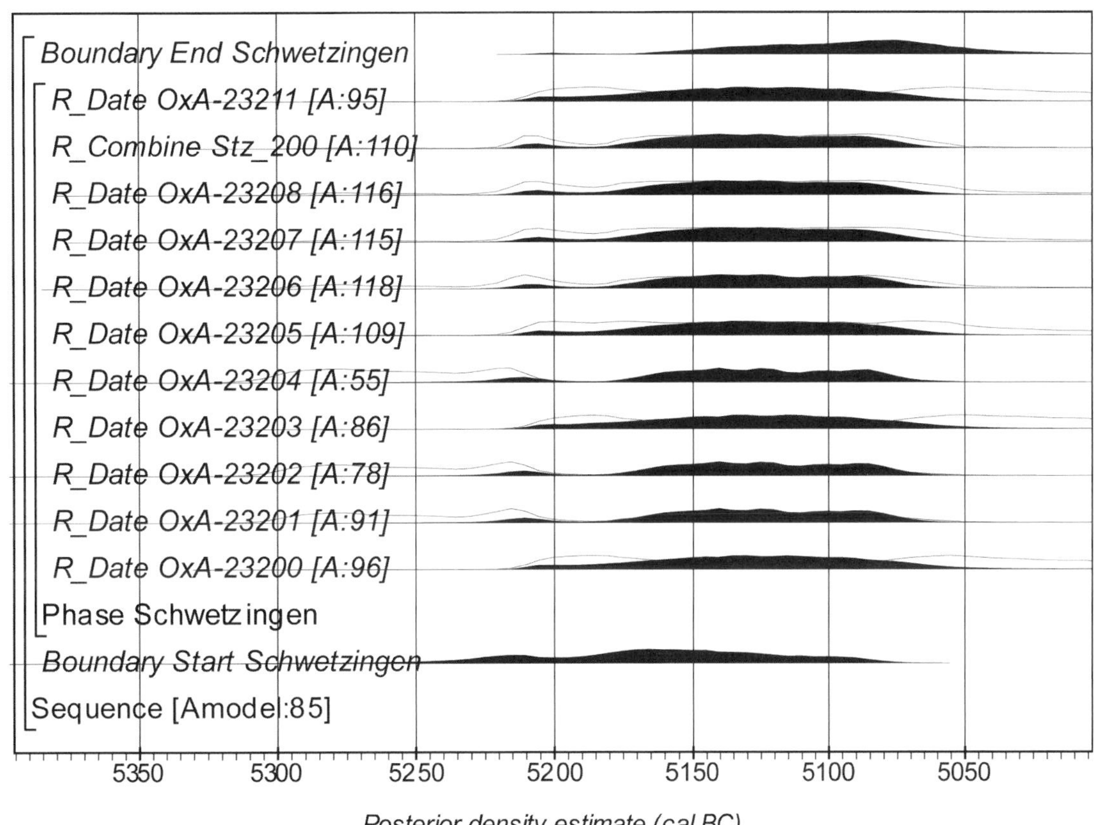

Fig. B3. Schwetzingen: probability distributions of the radiocarbon dates. Each distribution represents the relative probability that an event occurred at a particular time. Two ranges have been plotted for each distribution. The range in outline represents the calibrated radiocarbon result, and the solid distribution represents the posterior density estimate – the output from the Bayesian statistical model illustrated in the figure. The large square brackets and CQL2 OxCal keywords define the model exactly. `Boundary` *parameters estimate the start and end of activity.*

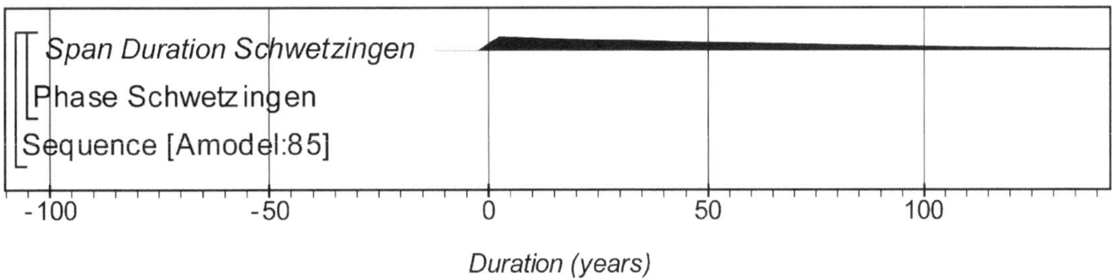

Fig. B4. Schwetzingen: the duration of activity calculated from the model shown in Fig. B3. The large square brackets and CQL2 OxCal keywords show the model structure from which the parameter is estimated.

Radiocarbon sample selection

Radiocarbon measurements from the Vedrovice cemetery represent 47% of the excavated burials.

Two models are presented here. A number of the dated burials were associated with diagnostic pottery. One model develops that presented by Pettitt and Hedges (2008). It employs one interpretation of the relative chronological information from the ceramic types to refine the radiocarbon dates. The other model employs a more neutral interpretation that the cemetery results represent a uniform `Phase` of activity, an interpretation that allows different pottery forms to exist at different points in the history of the site.

Results

The radiocarbon results presented in Table B3 from Vedrovice are not statistically consistent (T'=155.6; T'(5%)=59.6; ν=44), indicating that they do not measure the same point in time.

The details of the site pottery phases associated with different burials are shown in Table B3 (Pettitt and Hedges 2008, 127). Thirteen burials dated by radiocarbon produced

Table B4. Vedrovice: parameters from the two different models calculated in Figs B5 and B7.

Parameter name	**Model**	**Posterior density estimate (95.4% probable)**
Start Vedrovice cemetery	1 (with pottery phasing; fig. B1.5)	*5340–5230*
Start Vedrovice cemetery	2 (no pottery phasing; fig. B1.7)	*5340–5230*
End Vedrovice cemetery	1 (with pottery phasing; fig. B1.5)	*5210–5090*
End Vedrovice cemetery	2 (no pottery phasing; fig. B1.7)	*5210–5070*
FirstPotteryPhase1B	1 (with pottery phasing; fig. B1.5)	*5330–5230*
FirstPotteryPhase2A		*5240–5180*
Duration pottery phase 1B		*10–100 years*
Duration pottery phase 2A		*0–80 years*
DurationVedroviceCemetery		*20–220 years*
DurationVedroviceCemetery	2 (no pottery phasing; fig. B1.7)	*20–240 years*

pottery that could be fitted into the typological framework (Pettitt and Hedges 2008, 130). The other burials could only be attributed to the phase of inhumation burial at the site. The high percentage of burials dated by radiocarbon may suggest that we have a representative sample of the use of the site (Buck *et al.* 1992; 1996; Bayliss *et al.* 2011).

The first Bayesian model of the Vedrovice cemetery presented here includes the relative chronological information provided by the pottery. This model has been adapted from that described by Pettit and Hedges (2008, 130), which uses the archaeological evidence that pottery phase 1 predates pottery phase 2, and that pottery phase 1b$_1$ predates pottery phase 1b$_2$ (phasing based on the pottery study of Čižmář 2002). The result OxA-15553, on an animal bone from a 'settlement pit', is not included in the chronological model for the cemetery.

The model shown in Fig. B5 has good overall agreement ($A_{overall}$=73%). Selected posterior density estimates from this model are shown in Table B4. An estimate for the start of activity at the cemetery is *5340–5230 cal BC* (*95.4% probable*) or *5330–5260 cal BC* (*68.2% probable; Start Vedrovice cemetery;* Fig. B5). The end of the phase as sampled in Fig. B5 is estimated as *5210–5090 cal BC* (*95.4% probable; End Vedrovice cemetery*) or *5200–5150 cal BC* (*68.2% probable;* Fig. B5). The total duration of activity represented by the phase of inhumations is estimated as *20–220 years* (*95.4% probable*), most probably *50–160 years* (*68.2% probable; Duration Vedrovice Cemetery*; Fig. B6).

The first dated event from the pottery phase 1b is estimated as *5330–5230 cal BC* (*95.4% probable*) or *5320–5260 cal BC* (*68.2% probable; first pottery phase1b*; Fig. B5). The duration of burials associated with pottery phase 1B is estimated as *10–100 years* (*95.4% probable*) or *30–90 years* (*68.2% probable; duration pottery phase 1B*; Fig. B6).

The first dated event associated with pottery phase 2a is estimated as *5240–5180 cal BC* (*95.4% probable*) or *5230–5200 cal BC* (*68.2% probable; first pottery phase 2a*; Fig. B5). The duration of burials associated with pottery phase 2A is estimated as *0–80 years* (*95.4% probable*) or *10–50 years* (*68.2% probable; duration pottery phase 2A;* Fig. B6). Only three burials included in the model in Fig. B5 were associated with pottery type 2a. Of these, statistically consistent duplicate radiocarbon measurements on burial 50/77 have poor agreement with their position in the model; the calibrated radiocarbon results from burial 50/77 may indicate that this burial reflects later activity at the site. There are fewer radiocarbon dates associated with pottery phase 1b$_2$ and 1b than with pottery phase 1b$_1$. The limited samples for pottery phases 1b$_2$ and 2a may mean that the output from these models is less robust than the output from the model for pottery phase 1b$_1$. All the radiocarbon dates from graves associated with pottery type 1b$_1$ are statistically consistent (T'=7.2; T'(5%)=12.6; ν=6); in terms of the radiocarbon dates, the people who were buried with pottery type 1b$_1$ could have all died at the same time.

The weighted mean on the statistically consistent (T'=0.3; T'(5%)=3.8; ν=1) results on burial 90/80 have poor agreement with its position in the model presented in Fig. B5 (A=13.5%). The results from burial 90/80 are statistically consistent with the only extant result from the settlement (OxA-15553; Table B3; T'=0.3; T'(5%)=6.0; ν=2). Though the taphonomy of the dated material from the settlement is not apparent from the details provided in Pettitt and Hedges (2008), it is possible that this result and the results from burial 90/80 represent some form of earlier activity at the settlement and the cemetery. Further radiocarbon results would be needed to explore this possibility.

The second Bayesian model of the Vedrovice cemetery presented here makes no use of the relative chronology provided by the pottery assemblages. Selected posterior density estimates from this model are shown in Table B4.

The model shown in Fig. B7 has good overall agreement ($A_{overall}$=78.9%). An estimate for the start of activity at the cemetery is *5340–5230 cal BC* (*95.4% probable*) or *5340–5260* (*68.2% probable; start Vedrovice cemetery;*

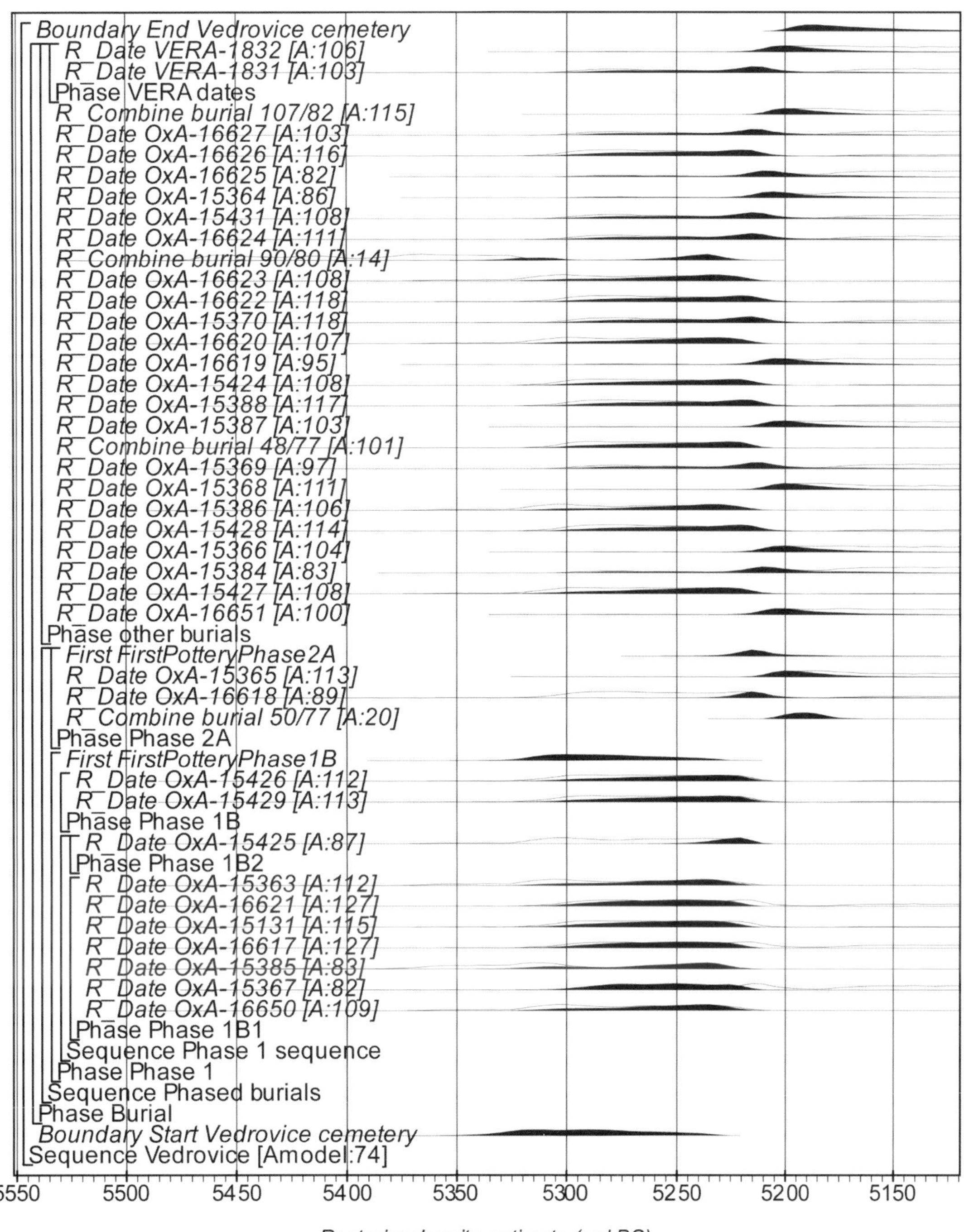

Fig. B5. Vedrovice: probability distributions of the radiocarbon dates. Each distribution represents the relative probability that an event occurred at a particular time. Two ranges have been plotted for each distribution. The range in outline represents the calibrated radiocarbon result, and the solid distribution represents the posterior density estimate – the output from the Bayesian statistical model illustrated in the figure. The large square brackets and CQL2 OxCal keywords define the model exactly. `Boundary` *parameters estimate the start and end of activity. The model structure illustrated in this figure has been adapted from that used in Pettitt and Hedges (2008, 130), which is based on the site pottery phasing.*

Fig. B7). The end of the phase as sampled in Fig. B7 is estimated as *5210–5070 cal BC* (*95.4% probable*) or *5210–5140 cal BC* (*68.2% probable; end Vedrovice cemetery;* Fig. B7). The total duration of activity represented by the phase of inhumations is estimated as *20–240 years* (*95.4% probable*), most probably *40–170 years* (*68.2% probable; duration Vedrovice cemetery;* Fig. B8).

There is little difference between the ranges for parameters calculated in the two models for Vedrovice (Table B4; Fig. B9); these posteriors are not sensitive to the highly informative prior information represented by the site pottery phasing (Pettitt and Hedges 2008), which may give us confidence in the robustness of the posterior density estimates quoted from both models.

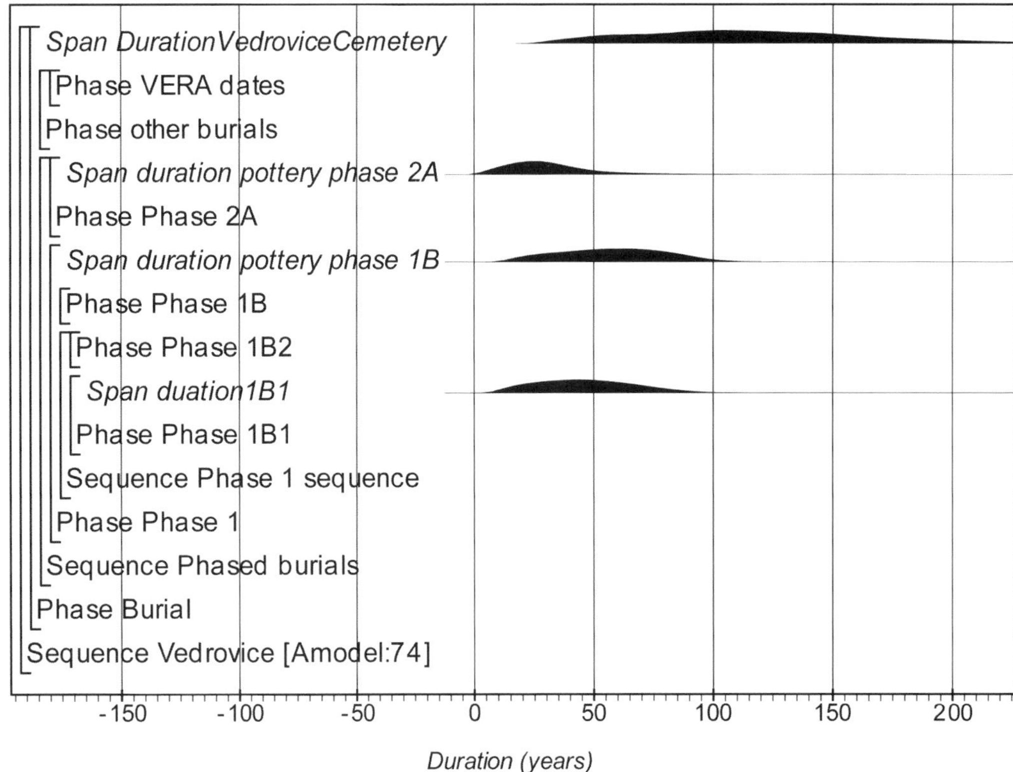

Fig. B6. Vedrovice: the duration of activity calculated from the model shown in Fig. B5. The large square brackets and CQL2 OxCal keywords show the model structure from which the parameter is estimated.

B1.7 Summary of main results produced by the LBK Lifeways project

The available data

The evidence presented here provides initial indications of the chronology of Nitra and Schwetzingen cemetery sites, and a comparative review of the chronology of Vedrovice. Radiocarbon dates produced for Kleinhadersdorf are presented in the following section (Appendix B2). There may be further chronological structure in the development or use of the cemetery sites and associated traditions; additional radiocarbon dates would be required to confirm that the initial conclusions presented here robustly characterise the chronologies of the use of these cemeteries.

The assemblage from Vedrovice, which represents a much greater proportion of the excavated graves, arguably presents a more robust sample of the chronological development of that site than at Nitra and Schwetzingen. However, even at Vedrovice, there are potential indications of a more complex picture of cemetery development. One of the individuals from the cemetery, burial 90, may have died slightly earlier than the rest of the population (though there are aspects of the radiocarbon sampling, processing, and measurement processes which could also account for this pattern). Further work on the settlement chronology and the results from burial 90 may augment our understanding of the development of the cemetery and the settlement.

Though it is suggested that the FTIR analysis undertaken for this project successfully identified significantly contaminated material from the Nitra samples, the site would benefit from further radiocarbon measurements using the appropriate pretreatment protocol for samples suspected to have been contaminated with PVA.

Chronology of cemetery use

From the limited currently available data, which may not be representative of cemetery use as a whole at these sites (and given the specific concerns with the Nitra dataset), it is possible to make some initial suggestions about the chronology of these sites. It is *61.2% probable* that the start of the Vedrovice cemetery occurred in the 53rd century BC (Fig. B10; Table B5). It is *63.8% probable* that the start of cemetery burial at Nitra occurred in the 53rd century BC (Fig. B10; Table B5). It is 69.9% *probable* that the first activity at Schwetzingen occurred in the 52nd century BC (Fig. B11). It is most probable that both of the cemeteries at Vedrovice and Nitra went out of use in the 52nd century BC; it is *93.5% probable* that the last burials at Vedrovice occurred in the 52nd century BC (Fig. B11). It is *63.7% probable* that the phase of use of the Nitra cemetery ended in the 52nd century BC (Fig. B11). The estimate for the end of the Schwetzingen cemetery is less constrained, but it is *57.6% probable* that the activity here ended in the 51st century BC (Fig. B12).

Relative order of the sites

From the available data, it is *55.2% probable* that the start of the phase of cemetery use at Vedrovice began before the phase of cemetery use at Nitra (Table B6). It is *97.4%*

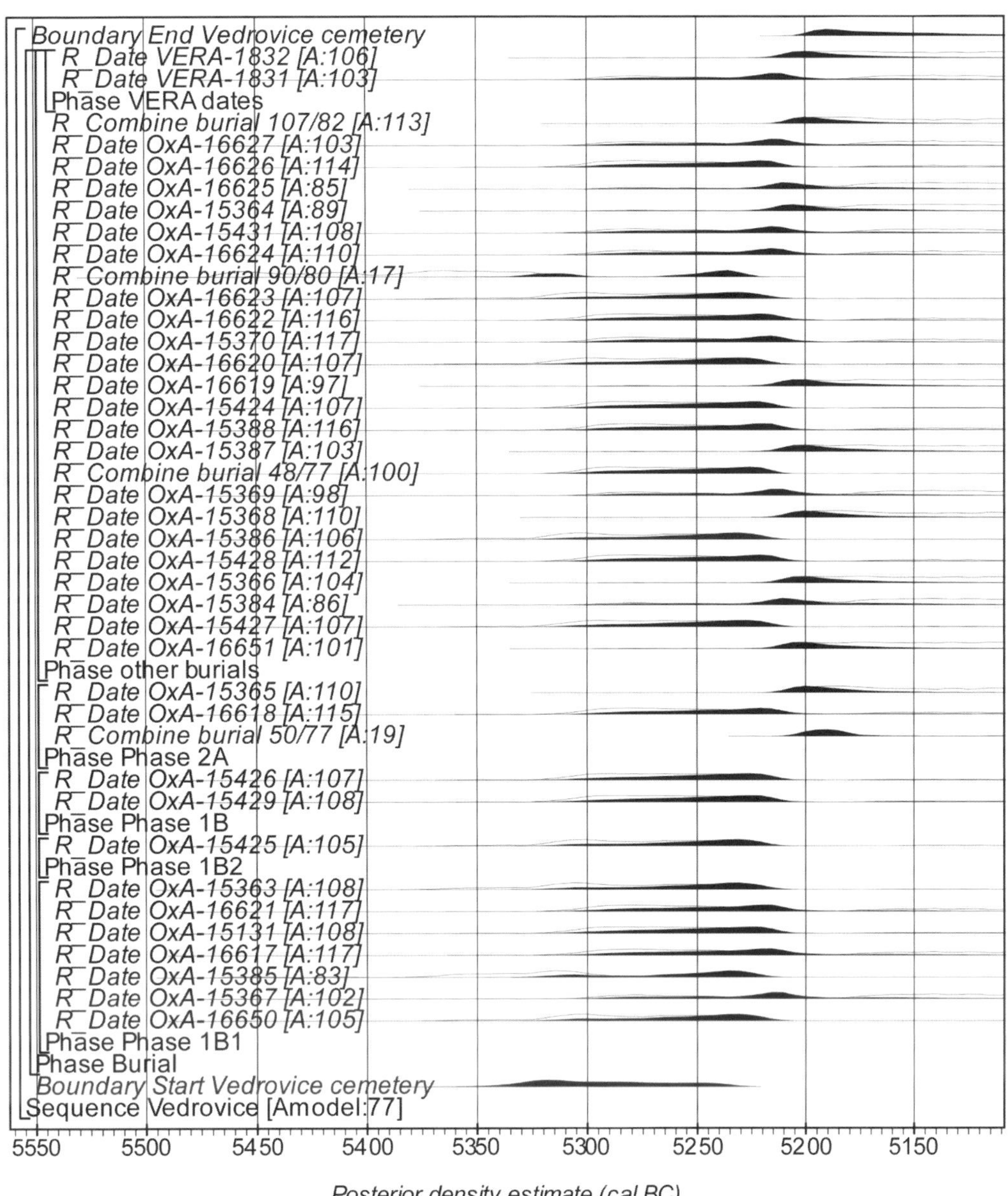

Fig. B7. Vedrovice: probability distributions of the radiocarbon dates calculated without the 'informative' prior information from the pottery phasing shown in Fig. B5. Each distribution represents the relative probability that an event occurred at a particular time. Two ranges have been plotted for each distribution. The range in outline represents the calibrated radiocarbon result, and the solid distribution represents the posterior density estimate – or Bayesian statistical model output. The large square brackets and CQL2 OxCal keywords define the model exactly. `Boundary` *parameters estimate the start and end of activity.*

probable that the start of the cemetery at Nitra occurred before the start of the cemetery at Schwetzingen (Table B6). Especially for the estimate for the start of use of the Nitra cemetery, the caution expressed above should be repeated. It is also highly probable (*98.1%*) that the start of the cemetery at Vedrovice occurred before the cemetery at Schwetzingen started to be used.

From the current data it is probable (*69.3%*) that the end of use of the Vedrovice cemetery occurred before the end of use of the Nitra cemetery (Table B6). In turn, it is probable that both the cemeteries at Vedrovice and at Nitra went out of use before the cemetery at Schwetzingen; it is *91.2% probable* that use of the Vedrovice cemetery ended before the end of the Schwetzingen cemetery. It is *67.5% probable* that the use of the Nitra cemetery ended before the end of the Schwetzingen cemetery. If the current data are representative of the use of the sites, the sites at Vedrovice and Nitra may have overlapped chronologically; both could have first been used in the 53rd century BC (Fig. B10), and both could have gone out of use at some point in the 52nd century BC (Fig. B11).

There may have been some overlap between the earlier sites and Schwetzingen; it is slightly more probable (*53.8%*) that the cemetery at Vedrovice went out of use before the

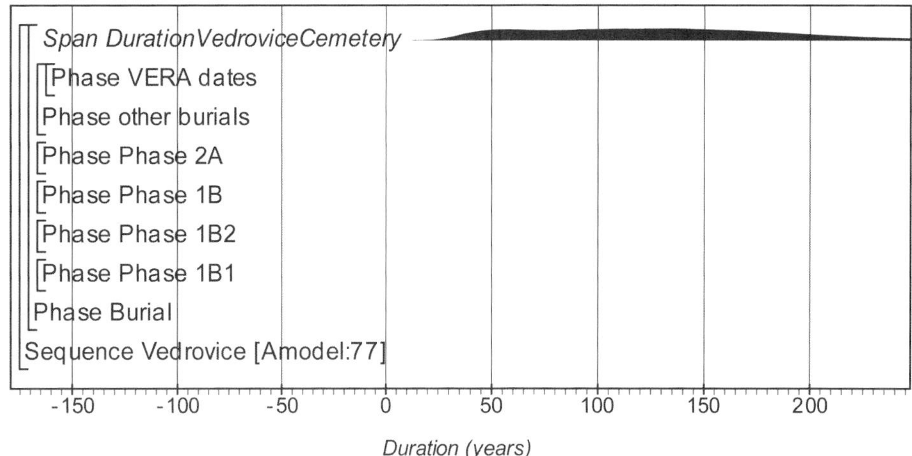

Fig. B8. Vedrovice: the duration of activity calculated from the model shown in Fig. B7. The large square brackets and CQL2 OxCal keywords show the model structure from which the parameter is estimated.

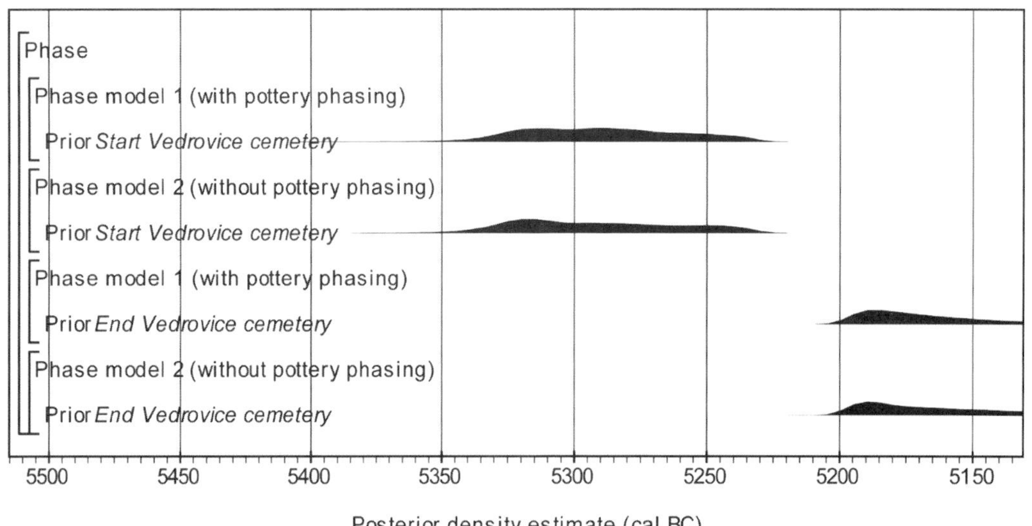

Fig. B9. Vedrovice: posterior density estimates calculated in the models shown in Figs B5 and B7 (see also Table B4).

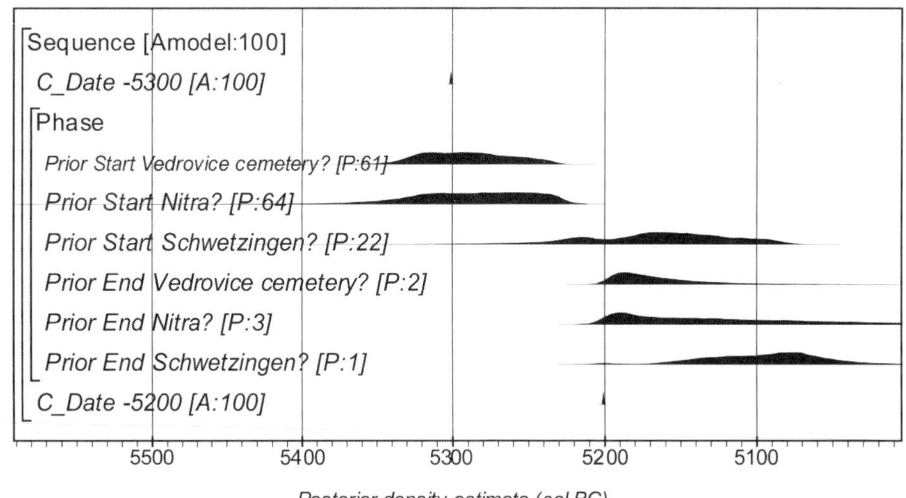

Fig. B10. The probability that different key parameters for activity from the three cemetery sites occurred in the 53rd century BC. For each posterior density estimate shown, the probability has been calculated that the posterior occurred after 5300 BC and before 5200 BC. The large square brackets and CQL2 OxCal keywords define the model exactly. The distributions shown in this model are calculated in the models shown in Figs B1, B3 and B5.

Table B5. Probability that each parameter (as calculated in Figs B1, B3 and B5) occurred in a particular century (as calculated in Figs B10–12). For example, it is 63.8% probable that the parameter Start Nitra *(as calculated in Fig. B1) occurred after 5300 BC and before 5200 BC – i.e. in the 53rd century BC (as calculated in Fig. B10).*

Parameter name	Century date range and calculation	The probability the parameter occurred in the century date range
Start Nitra	53rd century BC (fig. B10)	*63.8%*
End Nitra		*3.1%*
Start Schwetzingen		*21.5%*
End Schwetzingen		*0.7%*
Start Vedrovice cemetery		*61.2%*
End Vedrovice cemetery		*1.7%*
Start Nitra	52nd century BC (fig. B11)	*0*
End Nitra		*63.7%*
Start Schwetzingen		*69.9%*
End Schwetzingen		*40.0%*
Start Vedrovice cemetery		*0%*
End Vedrovice cemetery		*93.5%*
Start Nitra	51st century BC (fig. B12)	*0%*
End Nitra		*27.3%*
Start Schwetzingen		*7.9%*
End Schwetzingen		*57.6%*
Start Vedrovice cemetery		*0%*
End Vedrovice cemetery		*4.9%*

Table B6. Percentage probability that different parameters (calculated in Figs B1, B3 and B5) from each cemetery occurred one before the other. In each case, the percentage is the probability that the parameter in the first column is earlier than the parameter in the header row; e.g. it is 44.7% probable that the parameter Start Nitra *occurred before the parameter* Start Vedrovice *cemetery.*

	Start Vedrovice cemetery	Start Nitra	Start Schwetzingen	End Vedrovice cemetery	End Nitra	End Schwetzingen
Start Vedrovice cemetery	0%	55.2%	98.1%	100%	100%	100%
Start Nitra	44.7%	0%	97.4%	100%	100%	100%
Start Schwetzingen	1.9%	2.7%	0%	46.2%	66.9%	88.1%
End Vedrovice cemetery	0%	0%	53.8%	0%	69.3%	91.2%
End Nitra	0%	0%	33.1%	30.7%	0%	67.5%
End Schwetzingen	0%	0%	11.9%	8.8%	32.6%	0%

cemetery at Schwetzingen started to be used. It is more probable (*66.9% probable*) that the start of the cemetery at Schwetzingen occurred before the end of cemetery use at Nitra.

Further data are essential to explore these patterns more robustly. It is unclear whether the data provided by this project provide a full sample for the use of Schwetzingen or Nitra (as presented here), or Kleinhadersdorf (see B2 below and Neugebauer-Maresch and Lenneis forthcoming). This is especially pertinent as potentially temporally transgressive phases of archaeological activity at these sites may not have been sampled by the extant radiocarbon dates. For example, this could include phased development represented by the use of cremation burials, which were not sampled here, as well as possible spatial development of these cemeteries, which may not have been adequately accounted for by the density of data presented here. These data show the possibilities of Bayesian modelling in LBK burial contexts, but much remains to be done.

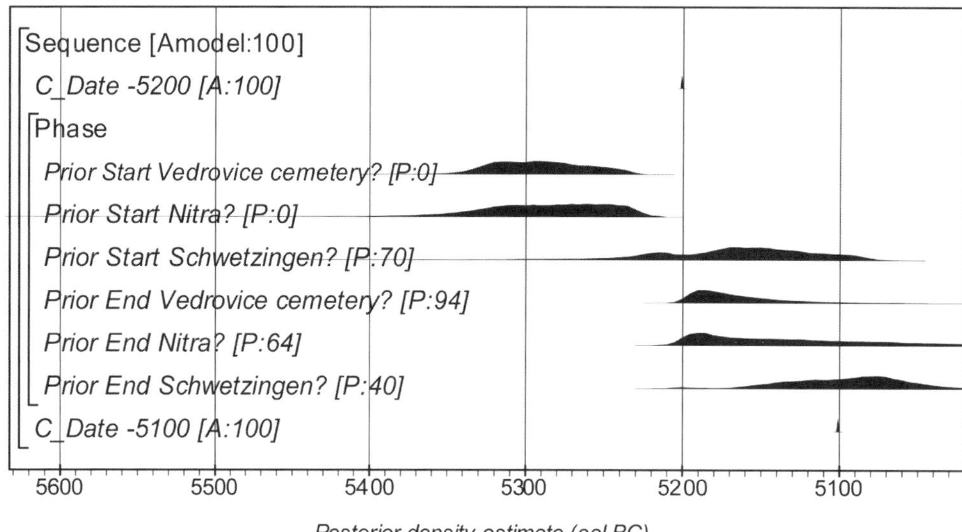

Fig. B11. The probability that different key parameters for activity from the three cemetery sites occurred in the 52nd century BC. For each posterior density estimate shown, the probability has been calculated that the posterior occurred after 5200 BC and before 5100 BC. The large square brackets and CQL2 OxCal keywords define the model exactly. The distributions shown in this model are calculated in the models shown in Figs B1, B3 and B5.

Table B7. Kleinhadersdorf: radiocarbon dates.

Grave N°	Sample code	Sex	Age	Ceramic phase	Lab. sample N°	BP	σ
55	KL-055	F	Adult	-	OxA 22936	6228	34
69	KL-069	M	Mature	Phase I b	VERA 2170	6135	35
81	KL-81.1	M	Adult	Phase I b/III	VERA 2173	6215	35
40	KL-040	M	Adult	Phase I b/III	VERA 2166	6090	35
56	KL-056	F	Mature	Phase II a	VERA 2167	6090	50
57	KL-057	M	Adult	Phase II b	OxA 22940	6215	32
79	KL-079	M	Adult	Phase II c	VERA 2171	6060	35
29	KL-029	M	Adult	Phase II/III	VERA 2164	6120	40
67/1	KL-067	-	Infans I	Phase II a/III	VERA 2169	6015	45
G. 1C	KL-117	F	Mature	Phase IIa2	OxA 22943	6118	32
80	KL-080	-	Infans I	Phase III	VERA 2172	6155	35
32	KL-032	F	Adult	Phase III	VERA 2165	6030	45
17	KL-017	M	Mature	-	OxA 22937	6156	33
17	KL-017	M	Mature	-	OxA 22938	6148	32
59	KL-059	-	Infans II	-	VERA 2168	6130	45
26	KL-026	-	Infans I	-	OxA 22939	6117	34
G. 7	KL-114	M	Adult	-	OxA 23220	6027	36
G. 1A	KL-115	M	Mature	-	OxA 22941	6214	32
G. 1B	KL-116	F	Mature	-	OxA 22942	5910	33

B2 Radiocarbon dates from Kleinhadersdorf

Peter Stadler

These data have been measured in two labs. The first group has been measured at VERA[1] within the radiocarbon project *Absolute Chronology for Early Civilisations in Austria and Central Europe using ^{14}C Dating with Accelerator Mass Spectrometry* (Peter Stadler, Susanne Draxler, Herwig Friesinger, Walter Kutschera, Alfred Priller, Werner Rom, Peter Steier and Eva Maria Wild). This project has been performed at the Vienna AMS lab at the institute of isotopic research at Vienna University.[2] The other samples were submitted to the Oxford laboratory by the Lifeways project, and will be assessed in full in the Kleinhadersdorf publication (Neugebauer-Maresch and

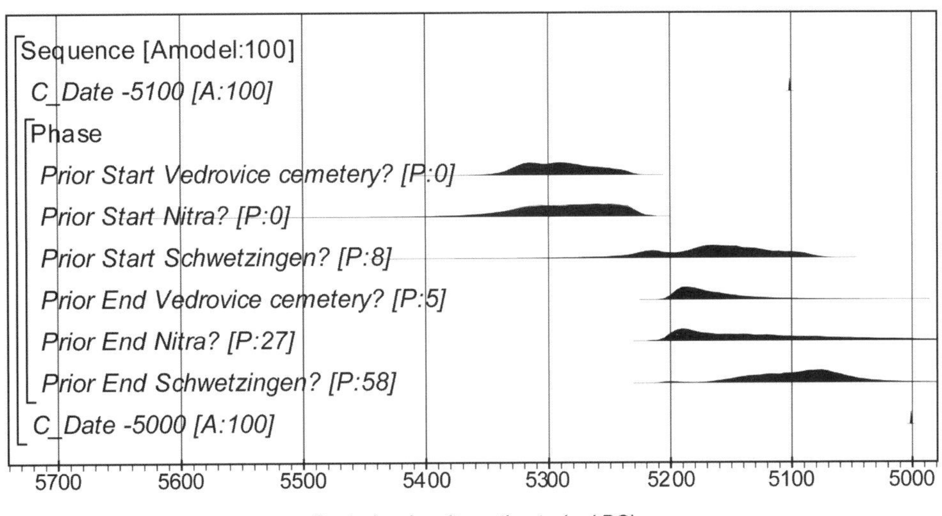

Fig. B12. The probability that different key parameters for activity from the three cemetery sites occurred in the 51st century BC. For each posterior density estimate shown, the probability has been calculated that the posterior occurred after 5100 BC and before 5000 BC. The large square brackets and CQL2 OxCal keywords define the model exactly. The distributions shown in this model are calculated in the models shown in Figs B1, B3 and B5.

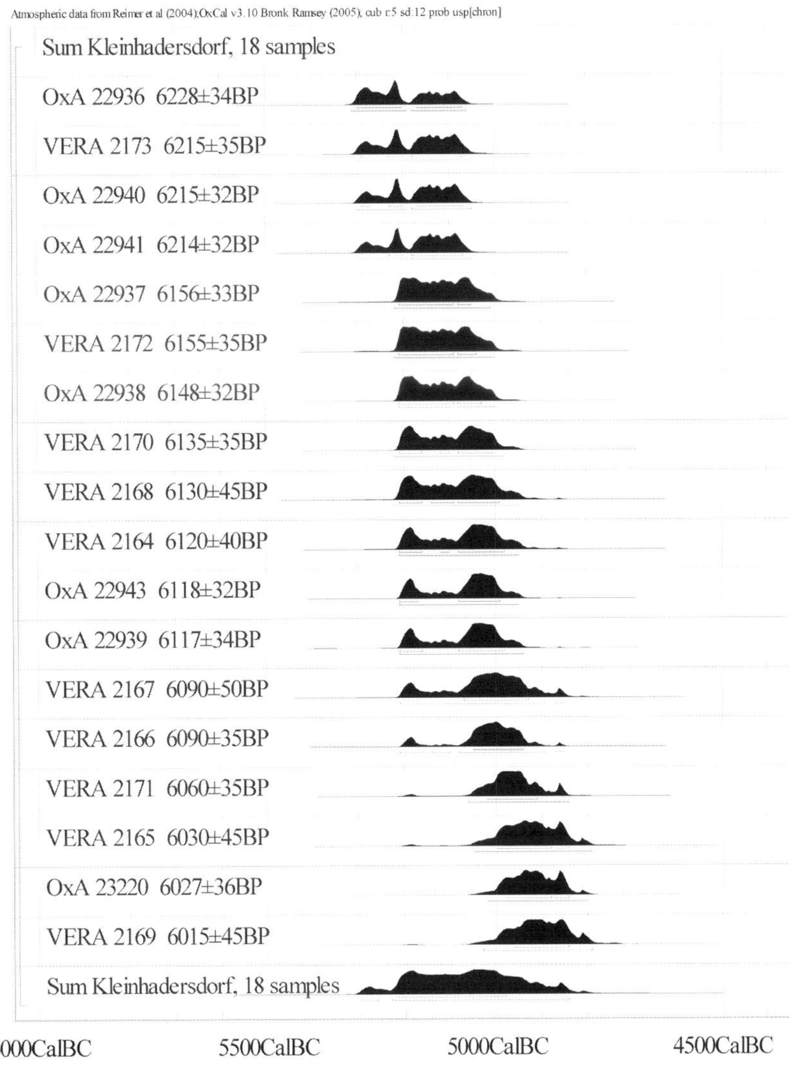

Fig. B13. Kleinhadersdorf: the radiocarbon samples, omitting the outlier OxA 22942.

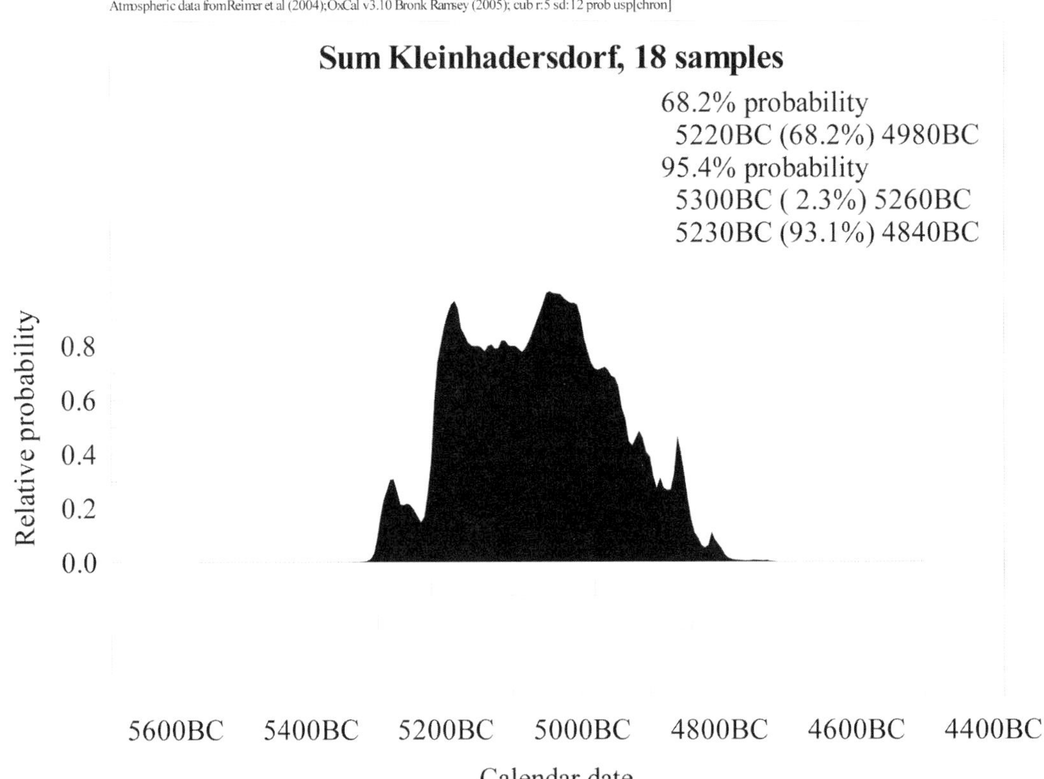

Fig. B14. Kleinhadersdorf: sum-calibration of samples, omitting the outlier OxA 22942.

Lenneis forthcoming). Evaluations have been made with OxCal, which has been developed by Christopher Bronk Ramsey (1995) at Oxford. The calibration curve of Paula Reimer *et al.* (2004) was used.

Table B7 lists the archaeological context for each of the samples and their radiocarbon dates. Further details of context will be provided in the final monograph (Neugebauer-Maresch and Lenneis forthcoming). All samples were taken from human bones, so that all dates stem from the dating of human collagen in the bone.

A sum calibration is presented (Fig. B13). All data were arranged in a sequence by descending BP values and then they were calibrated. Only one date has been omitted, because it must be an outlier, as it dates to the middle Neolithic period. As a result it can be shown that the Oxford measurements give very similar dates in comparison to the VERA samples. In Fig. B14 the sum calibration result is shown. At the 1 sigma level we obtain a time span from 5220–4980 cal BC. This might be in agreement with the absolute chronology, although with Bayesian modeling this could be refined.

In Fig. B15 the archaeological information (that is the attribution to archaeological phases by Eva Lenneis) is combined with radiocarbon dates. The agreement coefficient for this sequencing gives only a value of 37.6% and so it stays much below the agreement border of 60%, above which one could say that archaeological information coincides with the radiocarbon dates. In other words, the relative archaeological chronology of our seven samples is in contradiction to the radiocarbon results. Taking the single radiocarbon dates we can suggest some further patterns. There are no graves for phase Ia in Kleinhadersdorf, so the cemetery is likely to have started in phase Ib. In phase Ib there are two dates, which seem to be in good correlation to the overall sequence, because the singular correlation coefficients obtain values of 96.9% and 93.0%. In phase IIa, VERA 2167 gives a coefficient of only 56.1%, because the date would be young for this phase, thus questioning the assignment of this sample to phase IIa. Phases IIb and IIc give sufficient correlation, although we have only one sample per phase. For phase III, VERA 2165 would be in good correlation, but VERA 2172 is much too old and yields only a coefficient of 38.5%.

Table B8 presents the absolute chronology for the Kleinhadersdorf cemetery. This result must be considered with caution as it comes from a sequence with insufficient correlation. It seems that the problems we have seen here between archaeological attribution of phases and radiocarbon dates are similar if we use larger datasets of radiocarbon dates. Thus it is to be discussed whether archaeological phasing or relative chronology might not be improved by applying quantitative methods such as seriation or correspondence analysis, which should be done in future. The length of the phases seems to be too short, with the exception of phase IIb. Here it would be helpful to have more radiocarbon samples than one or two samples per phase. An increase in samples per phase would hopefully lead to a sequence without contradictions.

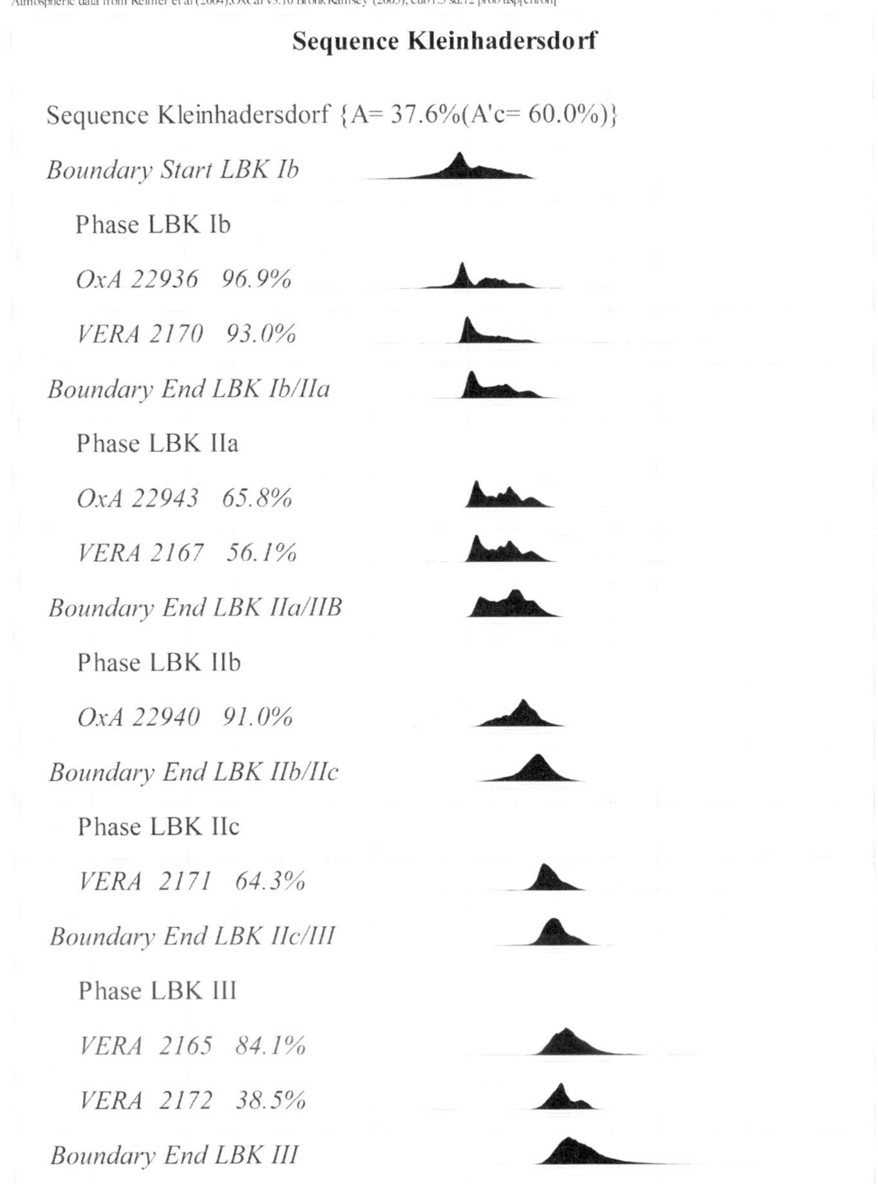

Fig. B15. Kleinhadersdorf: attempt at sequencing the eight samples attributed to phases.

Notes

1 VERA is the Vienna Environmental Research Accelerator.

2 Austrian Science Fund Project P-12253-PHY: Absolute Chronology for Early Civilisations in Austria and Central Europe using ^{14}C Dating with Accelerator Mass Spectrometry. Projektbericht an den FWF als Manuskript, 35 Seiten, 28 Tabellen, 61 Abbildungen.

Table B8. Kleinhadersdorf: absolute chronology derived from sequencing different phases.

Data on 1 σ level, years BC	Samples	Time span start with highest probability			Time span end with highest probability			Duration		
Phase	number	Min.	Max.	Mean	Min.	Max.	Mean	Min.	Max.	Mean
Ib	2	5250	5120	5185	5210	5110	5160	90	140	25
IIa	2	5210	5110	5160	5190	5060	5125	80	150	35
IIb	1	5190	5060	5125	5090	5020	5055	30	170	70
IIc	1	5090	5020	5055	5050	4995	5023	30	95	33
III	2	5050	4995	5023	5020	4930	4975	25	120	48
	7									**210**

Appendix C Carbon and nitrogen stable isotopes: statistical methods

Julie Hamilton

General approach

This project yielded $\delta^{13}C$ and $\delta^{15}N$ results from 617 humans, of whom 426 are adults, and 366 domestic fauna comprising 194 cattle, 92 sheep/goats, and 80 pigs, from 24 sites. There were also one hare, two roe deer and two red deer from Balatonszárszó, one red deer from Aiterhofen and one from Rutzing. This gives us an unprecedented opportunity to investigate variation within sites, within and between species, and between sites. At the same time, this amount of data is somewhat overwhelming, and the 'usual methods' are not really adequate to do it justice.

In Chapters 3–8, statistical results are presented conventionally, with means and standard deviations. Comparisons between groups were carried out by ANOVA, or, if more appropriate, Mann-Whitney U tests (SPSS v.17, SPSS Inc., Chicago).[1] This enables direct comparisons with other published results. Virtually all graphs have been presented at the same scale, for easy visual comparison, and as far as possible on identical axes.

For each site, values for $\Delta^{13}C_{human\text{-}cattle}$ and $\Delta^{15}N_{human\text{-}cattle}$ are also given. The cattle value is reported because the majority of animal-derived protein in the human diet is likely to come from cattle, either as milk or meat. Cattle are usually the most common domesticate and being larger than sheep/goats or pigs provide proportionally more meat/milk per individual. The Δ value was calculated as human mean $\delta^{13}C$−cattle mean $\delta^{13}C$, and the errors around each mean were calculated as $\sqrt{((SE_{human})^2 + (SE_{cattle})^2)}$. There is thus a degree of uncertainty around each calculated Δ value, which should be taken into account when interpreting Fig. 9.4. Table 9.5 gives the Δ values for humans compared with each domestic species, and the errors calculated as described here.

For analysis at a larger scale, we used a multivariate statistical approach based on general linear modelling. We need to allow for the fact that the data are hierarchically clustered – individuals within species, species within sites, and sites within regions. There is clearly variation between sites in mean $\delta^{13}C$ and $\delta^{15}N$ values, so that for example animals of a given species from the same site are, on average, likely to be more similar than animals of that species from different sites. This hierarchical structure needs to be explicitly recognised during statistical analysis. One possible route is to investigate variation only at the site level, for instance by looking at the effect of rainfall on mean human $\delta^{15}N$ calculated for each site, but it would be difficult to interpret the results without also accounting for individual variables such as sex and age, which may also differ from site to site. Alternatively, we could analyse the relationship between rainfall and the individual $\delta^{15}N$ values and add in a term for each site to adjust for the different site means, but this is computationally clumsy and we would not be able to interpret differences between sites. We therefore used a technique called multilevel modelling (also variously referred to as hierarchical linear models, nested models, mixed models, random coefficient, random-effects models, random parameter models, or split-plot designs), implemented in the MLwiN software (Rasbash *et al.* 2005, 2009a; 2009b; 2009c). These allowed us to explore the data more effectively, as well as to quantify and statistically test effects at different levels. We used 2-level models with individual $\delta^{13}C$ or $\delta^{15}N$ values as the first level and the site as the second level. Models were fitted using the Iterative Generalised Least Squares (IGLS) procedure in MLwiN.

We tested for significant differences between models using a likelihood ratio test, where the deviance (reduction in -2 × likelihood ratio) was compared to a chi-squared distribution with degrees of freedom depending on the number of parameters added to the model. Specific coefficients can also be examined. If they are normally distributed, they will be statistically different from 0 (no effect) if the *Z*-ratio (ratio of the absolute effect of an estimated coefficient to its standard error, SE) is greater than approximately 2. When sample numbers are low and/or variance is high, SE will also be high and values of coefficients will be imprecisely estimated, but these data can still be included in the overall model (so long as the residuals are normally distributed), one of the advantages of this technique.

Different subsets of the data were used for different models, depending on the questions being asked. There were no missing values, in the sense that each δ^{13}C measurement had a paired δ^{15}N measurement, and each site had a full range of climatic and geographic variables. However, individual age and sex data were only available for humans, and not for all of them. For human-faunal comparisons we included adult humans only, to avoid possible effects of including younger age groups and uneven age distribution across sites. For statistical comparisons to be valid it was simpler to use the subset of (adult) humans of known age and sex, or of humans with reasonably well defined ages, when these were being investigated.

Descriptions and explanations of models draw heavily on Steele (2008). The tables here are based on those used by Fielding (2011) to display details of models. For simplicity, many of the variables tested have been omitted, particularly if they were non-significant. Geographic and climatic variables were standardised to the grand mean (Fielding 2011, 21). The assumption that residuals were normally distributed was valid.

Geographic and climatic effects

As an example, we will start by investigating the effects of geographic and climatic variables on human δ^{13}C. The dataset comprises results from 475 adult humans at 19 sites (including data for Vedrovice from M.P. Richards *et al.* 2008).

A basic single-level model is:

$$y_i = \beta_0 + e_i$$

where y_i is the value of y (in this case, δ^{13}C) for the ith individual, β_0 is the mean of y for the population, and e_i is the residual for the ith individual, i.e. the difference between y_i and the population mean. The residuals are assumed to follow a normal distribution with mean 0 and variance σ^2. The variance summarises the variability around the mean, so if this were 0 all the points would have the same y value and lie on the $y = \beta_0$ line (see Fig. 9.3). In such a model, the site-level structure would be ignored, and the standard errors would be underestimated, leading to a high risk of Type 1 error (i.e. of concluding that effects that might be ascribed to chance were 'real'). In a 2-level model with individual results grouped by site, i.e. with site as the second level, standard errors would be correct and we could also estimate between-group variance.

A basic 2-level variance components model with no explanatory variables is:

$$y_{ij} = \beta_0 + u_j + e_{ij}$$

where y_{ij} is the value of y for the ith individual at the jth site and β_0 ('intercept' in Table C1) is the mean of y for the population. The residuals are now split into two parts: u_j is the difference between the group mean (mean at site j) and the grand mean, and e_{ij} is the difference between the ith individual and that individual's group mean. Again, the residuals are assumed to follow a normal distribution

Table C1. The results of fitting a basic 2-level variance components model with no explanatory variables for δ^{13}C of human adults.

	Estimate	Standard error
Intercept	−20.01	0.069
Random effects variances		
Site level	0.082	0.029
Individual level	0.067	0.004
Variance partition (%)		
Site level	55.0	
Individual level	45.0	

with mean 0 and variance σ^2. The total variance is now partitioned into two components: the between-group (in this case, inter-site) variance σ_u^2 ('site level' variance in Table C1), and the within-group, between-individual variance σ_e^2 ('individual level' variance in Table C1). This can be described by the variance partition coefficient (VPC), which measures the proportion of total variance that is due to differences between groups. If the VPC is 0, there is no difference between groups, and the data could be described by a single-level model at the individual level. If it is 1, there are no within-group differences, and the data could be described by a single-level model at the group level. In simple multi-level models, VPC is equivalent to the intra-class correlation coefficient, i.e. the correlation between the y values of two individuals from the same group.

Table C1 shows the results of fitting a basic 2-level variance components model with no explanatory variables. Figure 9.3a shows the site-level residuals u_j with their 95% confidence intervals, ranked by the size of the residual; the variation in size of the confidence intervals reflects the different numbers of individuals at different sites. The intercept is −20.01, with a standard error of 0.069, and has been allowed to vary randomly by site. Total variance is 0.149, with a VPC of 0.55, i.e. 55% of the total variance is between-site variance and there is considerable correlation of individual values within sites. Variance at both levels is significant (a useful rule of thumb is that the estimate should be at least twice the size of its standard error). This model is highly significantly different from a single-level model of the same data (P<0.001) and is used as the basis for further analysis.

Tables C2 and C3 summarise the effects of adding selected geographic and climatic variables into the model. The basic model is:

$$y_{ij} = \beta_0 + \beta_2 x_{2j} + u_j + e_{ij}$$

Here, β_2 represents the coefficient of the 2nd-level explanatory variable x_{2j}, the value of x at the jth site, and this is the 'estimate' given in Table C2 with its standard error. $\beta_2 x_{2j}$ gives the difference between the overall mean of human δ^{13}C and human δ^{13}C at the jth site that is accounted for in the model, and if that is sufficiently large should reduce the inter-site variance σ_u^2. Note that level

Table C2. 2-level model of $\delta^{13}C$ of human adults, with geographic explanatory variables (standardised to the grand mean and entered singly). Significant effects are shown in bold.

	M0: variance components		M1: M0+Longitude		M2: M0+Latitude		M3: M0+Elevation	
	Estimate	SE	Estimate	SE	Estimate	SE	Estimate	SE
Intercept	−20.010	0.069	−20.030	0.058	−20.005	0.071	−20.000	0.069
Geographic factors			**0.036**	**0.012**	0.023	0.104	−0.001	0.001
Random effects variances								
Site level	0.082	0.029	0.055	0.020	0.082	0.029	0.080	0.028
Individual level	0.067	0.004	0.067	0.004	0.067	0.004	0.067	0.004
Variance partition (%)								
Site level	55.0		45.1		55.0		54.4	
Individual level	45.0		54.9		45.0		45.6	
Significance testing								
−2×Log-likelihood	118.8		111.7		118.8		118.4	
Deviance			7.1		0.05		0.45	
P			<0.01		NS		NS	

Table C3. 2-level model of $\delta^{13}C$ of human adults with climatic explanatory variables (standardised to the grand mean and entered singly). Null model M0 is same as in Table C2. Climatic variables are abbreviated as in Table 9.1. [1]Deviance from M0; [2]Deviance from M1; [3] Deviance from M4; [4]Deviance from M5. Significant effects are shown in bold.

	M4: M0+PMS		M5:M0+PMW		M6:M0+TMS		M7:M0+TMW		M8:M0+MAIW	
	Estimate	SE	Estimate	SE	Estimate	SE	Estimate	SE	Estimate	SE
Intercept	−19.983	0.045	−20.028	0.036	−20.014	0.062	−20.017	0.068	−20.042	0.034
Climatic factors	**−0.017**	**0.003**	**−0.032**	**0.005**	**0.145**	**0.071**	−0.072	0.085	**−0.600**	**0.082**
Random effects variances										
Site level	0.031	0.012	0.019	0.008	0.066	0.023	0.079	0.028	0.017	0.007
Individual level	0.067	0.004	0.067	0.004	0.067	0.004	0.067	0.004	0.067	0.004
Variance partition (%)										
Site level	31.6		22.1		49.6		54.1		20.2	
Individual level	68.4		77.9		50.4		45.9		79.8	
Significance testing										
−2×Log-likelihood	103.2		95.2		115.0		118.1		93.5	
Deviance	15.6[1]	8.5[2]	23.6[1]	8.0[3]	3.8[1]		0.7[1]		25.3[1]	1.7[4]
P	<0.001	<0.01	<0.001	<0.01	0.05		NS		<0.001	NS

1 effects such as sex have been ignored here in order to treat humans in the same way as fauna, for which we do not have that information (see below for models including level 1 effects).

The model from Table C1 is repeated in the first pair of columns for reference. Neither latitude nor elevation have any significant effect, but including longitude in the model significantly improves the fit, reducing the total variance from 0.082+0.067=0.149 to 0.055+0.067=0.122. It has no effect on within-site (individual-level) variance, as it is the same for all individuals at a given site, but reduces between-site variance by (55.0-45.1)/55.0 = 22%, and the log-likelihood test (which compares the deviance, i.e. the difference between −2×log-likelihood of the null model M0 and the model being tested, against a chi-squared distribution) shows that this is significant at the 0.01 level. Note also that the coefficient for longitude is much larger than its standard error, i.e. it does not include a value of 0 within the 95% confidence limits, but this is not so for latitude or elevation.

Longitude is not in itself an explanation; most likely human $\delta^{13}C$ values are varying with an east–west climatic trend. Therefore, in the next modelling exercise we entered the climatic variables one by one. Table C3 shows

Table C4. 2-level model for δ¹⁵N of human adults, with level 1 (sex and age) and level 2 factors (longitude and elevation, standardised to the grand mean and entered singly). Sex has two categories, male and female; the reference category is female. Age has two categories, adult (up to c. *45 years) and old adult (over* c. *45 years); the reference category is adult.* [1]*Deviance from M0;* [2] *Deviance from M1.*

	M0: variance components		M1: M0+sex		M2: M1+age		M3: M1+longitude		M4: M2+elevation	
	Estimate	SE	Estimate	SE	Estimate	SE	Estimate	SE	Estimate	SE
Intercept	9.844	0.151	9.740	0.152	9.829	0.153	9.728	0.150	9.782	0.139
Sex			**0.204**	**0.048**	**0.202**	**0.048**	**0.204**	**0.048**	**0.204**	**0.048**
Age					0.049	0.054				
Longitude							0.023	0.032		
Elevation									**−0.004**	**0.002**
Random effect variances										
Site level	0.383	0.136	0.378	0.134	0.383	0.136	0.367	0.131	0.302	0.108
Individual level	0.239	0.017	0.229	0.016	0.229	0.016	0.229	0.016	0.229	0.016
Variance partition %										
Site level	61.6		62.3		62.6		61.6		56.9	
Individual level	38.4		37.7		37.4		38.4		43.1	
Significance testing										
−2×Log-likelihood	672.6		654.5		653.7		654.0		650.2[2]	
Deviance from M0/M1			18.1[1]		0.8[2]		0.5[2]		4.3[2]	
P			<0.001		NS		NS		P<0.05	

Table C5. 2-level model for human δ^{15}N with level 1 (sex and age) and a level 2 factor (elevation, standardised to the grand mean). Sex has three categories (male, female, unknown); the reference category is female. Age has five categories (infant, child, adolescent, adult, old adult); the reference category is adult. [1]Deviance from M0; [2]Deviance from M1. Significant effects are shown in bold.

	M0: Variance components		M1: M0+sex+age		M2: M1+elevation	
	Estimate	SE	Estimate	SE	Estimate	SE
Intercept	9.841	0.161	9.702	0.152	9.759	0.135
Sex male			**0.188**	**0.054**	**0.188**	**0.054**
Sex unknown			−0.024	0.106	−0.016	0.106
Age 1 Infant			**2.693**	**0.153**	**2.697**	**0.153**
Age 2 Child			−0.012	0.070	−0.011	0.070
Age 3 Adolescent			−0.094	0.107	−0.096	0.107
Age 5 Old adult			0.050	0.060	0.049	0.060
Elevation					**−0.004**	**0.002**
Random effect variances						
Site level	0.458	0.160	0.390	0.134	0.287	0.100
Individual level	0.467	0.027	0.304	0.017	0.303	0.017
Variance partition %						
Site level	49.5		56.2		48.6	
Individual level	50.5		43.8		51.4	
Significance testing						
−2×Log-likelihood	1354.1		1090.5		1084.5	
Deviance from M0/M1			263.8[1]		6.0[2]	
P			<0.001		<0.05	

some selected results in detail for human δ^{13}C; Table 9.3 summarises the overall results for humans and fauna. We also tested combinations of variables, but in practice there was little improvement in model fits, so for ease of interpretation we have based discussion on the simpler models.

Both summer and winter rainfall (PMS and PMW) provide significantly better fits than longitude alone, and winter rainfall is significantly better than summer rainfall. Summer temperature (TMS) is just significant but winter temperature (TMS) is not. The moisture availability index for the winter months (MAIW) is the best single factor, accounting for ((55.0-20.2)/55.0) = 63% of inter-site variance, though it is not significantly different from PMW.

In Fig. 9.4, the residuals (u_j) for each site are shown in order of size, based on this set of models; we have shown the null model, M0, and the model which best accounts for inter-site variance, M8. The vertical bars represent 1.96×Standard Error of the estimate, i.e. 95% confidence intervals, and if they do not include 0 – represented in the figure by the horizontal line, where there is no difference from the overall mean – we can conclude that the site mean is significantly different from the overall mean at the 5% level.

Individual effects: human sex and age

In this example we investigate the effects of individual sex and age on human δ^{15}N. The dataset comprises results from 439 sexed adult humans at 19 sites (including data for Vedrovice from M.P. Richards *et al.* 2008).

The basic 2-level model (M0 in Table C4) is similar to that in Table C3, but for human δ^{15}N. When sex is included as an explanatory variable, the model becomes:

$$y_{ij} = \beta_0 + \beta_1 x_{ij} + u_j + e_{ij}$$

Here, β_0 ('Intercept') is the overall mean of y for individuals of the reference category, in this case females, $\beta_0 + u_j$ is the mean for females at site j, and β_1 (the coefficient of which the estimate is given in Table C4) is the difference from the female mean in x (δ^{15}N) for the other category, males, at any site.

The model including sex (M1) is significantly different from the null model (M0): the overall variance is slightly reduced, mainly at the individual level as would be expected for an individual-level factor (the difference at site level reflects different sex distributions at sites). Overall, male δ^{15}N is 0.204‰ higher than that of females, and this is significantly different from 0. Including age (M2) – again, there are two categories, adults under 45 years and older

Table C6. 2-level model for human $\delta^{13}C$ with two level 1 factors (sex and age; categories as in Table C5) and a level 2 factor (MAIW; see Table 9.1). 1Deviance from M0; 2 Deviance from model with age alone (not shown); 3 Deviance from M1. Significant effects are shown in bold.

	M0: Variance components		M1: M0+sex+age		M2: M1+MAIW	
	Estimate	SE	Estimate	SE	Estimate	SE
Intercept	−19.994	0.079	−20.049	0.074	−20.071	0.039
Sex male			**0.074**	**0.026**	**0.075**	**0.026**
Sex unknown			0.014	0.051	0.027	0.050
Age 1 Infant			**0.785**	**0.074**	**0.788**	**0.073**
Age 2 Child			0.012	0.034	0.011	0.034
Age3 Adolescent			−0.058	0.051	−0.058	0.051
Age5 Old Adult			0.040	0.029	0.041	0.029
MAIW					**−0.631**	**0.083**
Random effect variances						
Site level	0.112	0.038	0.092	0.032	0.018	0.007
Individual level	0.085	0.005	0.071	0.004	0.071	0.004
Variance partition %						
Site level	56.9		56.4		20.2	
Individual level	43.1		43.6		79.8	
Significance testing						
−2×Log-likelihood	292.8		179.8		153.7	
Deviance from M0/M1			113.0[1]	8.1[2]	26.1[3]	
P			<0.001	<0.05	<0.001	

adults – makes no significant difference, so it is not included in further models. We can also include 2nd-level variables such as geographic or climatic factors, as in the previous section. This allows us to check that the conclusions from analyses such as those in Tables C2 and C3 have not been affected by ignoring human sex and age – theoretically there could be confoundment between, say, human age and sex distribution and climatic variables, both varying with longitude but for different reasons. That is clearly not so here (M3). Only one variable, elevation, affected human $\delta^{15}N$ in the simpler models (Table 9.3), and that is still significant in this set of models, significantly reducing level-2 (and thereby total) variance (M4; the coefficient β_1 is the same). In this case, where the explanatory factor is a continuous variable, β_1 is the slope of the relationship between elevation and $\delta^{15}N$, as in a simple regression. Finally, we wished to check that the overall effect was not being driven by the sites at which we identified a significant difference between males and females, so we removed Asparn, Nitra and Vedrovice from the dataset (leaving 314 sexed adults at 16 sites) and ran the models again. The effect of sex was still significant ($P<0.05$), although the coefficient β_1 was smaller (0.142).

Until now models have been described in some detail in order to clarify the statistical methodology, though we have not attempted to document each investigation comprehensively here. The remaining tables are based on similar models using both categorical variables (age, sex, species) and continuous variables (climatic and geographic factors) as explanatory variables, and provide the background to statements made in Chapter 9.

We investigated the effects of age on human $\delta^{13}C$ and $\delta^{15}N$ values in another set of models using broad age categories (infant, child, adolescent, adult, old adult >45 years). The dataset comprises results from 624 humans with estimated ages, from 19 sites (including data for Vedrovice from M.P. Richards *et al.* 2008). Selected results are shown in Table C5.

Note that overall the results are very similar to those shown in Table C4, based on adults only. In addition, overall $\delta^{15}N$ of infants is 2.7‰ higher than that of the reference category (adults), with no other categories showing significant differences.

Possible trends in $\delta^{15}N$ with age were noted at a few sites, and we wanted to see if, like the effect of sex, they were detectable in the whole dataset. We were only able to produce refined, comparable age categories for a subset of sites, and we omitted infants because the magnitude of the suckling effect was likely to obscure other trends. The dataset comprised results from 341 humans from seven

Table C7. 2-level model for faunal $\delta^{13}C$ with a level 1 variable (species) and level 2 geographic and climatic variables (standardised to the grand mean and entered singly). Climatic variables abbreviated as in Table 9.1. Species has three categories: cattle, sheep/goat and pig; the reference category is sheep/goat. [1] Deviance from M0; [2] Deviance from M1: significant effects are shown in bold.

	M0: Variance components		M1: M0+Species		M2: M1+Longitude		M3: M1+PDMA		M4: M1+MAIW	
	Estimate	SE	Estimate	SE	Estimate	SE	Estimate	SE	Estimate	SE
Intercept	−20.580	0.158	−20.288	0.167	−20.212	0.311	−20.163	0.114	−20.282	0.130
Cattle			**−0.461**	**0.094**	**−0.464**	**0.094**	**−0.456**	**0.094**	**−0.448**	**0.094**
Pig			**−0.245**	**0.115**	**−0.252**	**0.115**	**−0.244**	**0.115**	**−0.237**	**0.115**
Geographic factors					**0.120**	**0.020**				
Climate factors							**−0.355**	**0.066**	**−0.984**	**0.264**
Random effect variances										
Site level	0.337	0.138	0.317	0.129	0.072	0.038	0.088	0.044	0.153	0.068
Individual level	0.590	0.045	0.553	0.042	0.552	0.042	0.553	0.042	0.552	0.042
Variance partition %										
Site level	36.4		36.4		11.5		13.7		21.7	
Individual level	63.6		63.6		88.5		86.3		78.3	
Significance testing										
−2×Log-likelihood	877.7		854.1		835.9		838.5		844.2	
Deviance from M0/M1			23.5[1]		18.2[2]		15.6[2]		9.9[2]	
P			<0.001		<0.001		<0.001		<0.01	

Table C8. 2-level model for faunal $\delta^{15}N$ with a level 1 variable (species) and level 2 geographic and climatic variables (standardised to the grand mean and entered singly). Climatic variables abbreviated as in Table 9.1. Species has three categories, cattle, sheep/goat and pig; the reference category is sheep/goat. [1]Deviance from M0; [2] Deviance from M1.

	M0: Variance components		M1: M0+Species		M2: M1+Longitude		M3: M1+Elevation		M4: M1+MAIS	
	Estimate	**SE**	**Estimate**	**SE**	**Estimate**	**SE**	**Estimate**	**SE**	**Estimate**	**SE**
Intercept	7.135	0.203	6.861	0.223	6.899	0.216	7.033	0.178	6.900	0.197
Cattle			0.155	0.127	0.157	0.127	0.157	0.127	0.166	0.127
Pig			**0.886**	**0.155**	**0.886**	**0.155**	**0.885**	**0.155**	**0.892**	**0.155**
Geographic factors							**−0.008**	**0.002**	**−2.934**	**1.296**
Climate factors										
Random effect variances										
Site level	0.546	0.225	0.560	0.228	0.501	0.207	0.260	0.117	0.394	0.167
Individual level	1.112	0.084	1.002	0.076	1.002	0.076	1.003	0.076	1.003	0.076
Variance partition %										
Site level	32.9		35.9		33.3		20.6		28.2	
Individual level	67.1		64.1		66.7		79.4		71.8	
Significance testing										
−2×Log-likelihood	1106.4		1070.1		1068.8		1060.6		1065.8	
Deviance from M0			36.3[1]		1.4[2]		9.5[2]		4.3[2]	
P			<0.001		NS		<0.01		<0.05	

sites (including data for Vedrovice from M.P. Richards *et al.* 2008). The 2-level model showed that including age significantly improved the fit of the model; $\delta^{15}N$ of adolescents was 0.34% lower than the reference category ($P<0.05$; no other categories differed significantly). However, the effect was no longer significant if sex was included as a factor or the data from Vedrovice were omitted (273 humans from six sites). If such effects exist, large datasets with compatible age categories will be needed to detect them.

Finally, since we know that both sex and age affect $\delta^{15}N$ (Table C5), we used similar sets of models to investigate $\delta^{13}C$. If the effect in males reflects a trophic level effect, as is likely for infants, they should also have slightly higher $\delta^{13}C$ than females, by a very small amount. This appears to be the case (Table C6).

Fauna

The examples given here are based on the total results from 366 domestic fauna comprising 194 cattle, 92 sheep/goats, and 80 pigs from 15 sites, and include sites identified as outliers on various criteria (notably Bischoffsheim and Heilbronn-Neckargartach). They show the overall patterning of faunal $\delta^{13}C$ (Table C7) and $\delta^{15}N$ (Table C8) values by species, and effects of selected geographical and climatic factors.

In Table C7, the intercept β_0 in the null model M0 is the overall mean of y ($\delta^{13}C$) for all fauna, while in M1, with species as an explanatory variable, it is the mean for individuals of the reference category, in this case sheep/goats – note that the difference between the two is about 0.3‰. Model fit is significantly improved when the species are entered as separate categories. Overall, cattle and pig $\delta^{13}C$ values are each significantly lower than those of sheep/goats, by about 0.5‰ for cattle and 0.25‰ for pigs. This implies that when using faunal values to calculate a baseline for human diet, the values of different species are not simply interchangeable, but need to be considered separately (though the emphasis is usually on $\delta^{15}N$ rather than $\delta^{13}C$). Inter-site variance is considerably reduced by including longitude or climatic variables related to rainfall (see Tables 9.3, C2 and C3). A 'random slope' model (not shown here; see Steele 2008, 22–34), where the relationship between y and an explanatory factor is allowed to vary by site, as well as the intercept, was significant for cattle but not the other species, confirming the tendency for cattle $\delta^{13}C$ values to be lower than expected towards the west.

In Table C8, the difference between the overall faunal mean $\delta^{15}N$ value and that of sheep/goats is about 0.2‰. Model fit is significantly improved when the species are entered as separate categories. Overall, cattle $\delta^{15}N$ values are not significantly different from sheep/goats, but pig $\delta^{15}N$ values are significantly higher than those of sheep/goats by about 0.9‰ – enough to make a considerable difference when using fauna to provide a baseline for human diets. Inter-site variance is not significantly reduced by including longitude – the basis for our statement in Chapter 9 that the evidence for a geographic trend in $\delta^{15}N$ is less clear than for $\delta^{13}C$. Climatic variables such as MAIS do have a significant effect (see Tables 9.3, C2 and C3). Random slope models were not significantly different from the basic random intercept models shown here.

Note

1 This package of SPSS was also used for the analysis of the strontium isotopes, the osteological dataset and the examination of the burial data.

Bibliography

Abu-Lughod, L. 1991. Writing against culture. In R.G. Fox (ed.), *Recapturing anthropology: working in the present*, 137–62. Santa Fe: School of American Research Press.

Albert, S. and Schöter, P. 1971. Die ersten Belege der ältesten Bandkeramik im Oberen Gäu (Pfäffingen und Haifingen, Landkreis Tübingen). *Der Sülchgau* 15, 63–76.

Alberti, B., Fowles, S., Holbraad, M., Marshall, Y. and Witmore, C. 2011. "Worlds otherwise": archaeology, anthropology, and ontological difference. *Current Anthropology* 52, 896–912.

Allard, P. 2005. *L'industrie lithique des populations rubanées du nord-est de la France et de la Belgique*. Rahden: Marie Leidorf.

Allard, P. 2007. The Mesolithic-Neolithic transition in the Paris Basin: a review. In A. Whittle and V. Cummings (eds), *Going over: the Mesolithic-Neolithic transition in north-west Europe*, 211–23. London: Oxford University Press for the British Academy.

Allard, P. and Bonnardin, S. 2007. Modalités d'acquisition des éléments lithiques et de la parure au Néolithique ancien danubien. In M. Besse (ed.), *Sociétés Néolithiques: des faits archéologiques aux fonctionnements socio-économiques*, 23–42. Lausanne: Cahiers d'Archéologie Romande 108.

Alt, K.W., Arbogast, R.M., Jeunesse, C. and van Willigen, S. (eds) 2004. *Grab- und Bestattungssitten des donauländischen Neolithikums: neue Fragen, neue Strategien.* Zimmersheim: Cahiers de l'Association de la Promotion de la Recherche Archéologique en Alsace.

Alt, K.W., Jeunesse, C., Buitrago-Téllez, C.H., Wächter, R., Boës, E. and Pichler, S.L. 1997. Evidence for Stone Age cranial surgery. *Nature* 387, 360.

Alt, K.W., Vach, W. and Wahl, J. 1995. Verwandtschaftsanalyse der Skelettreste aus dem bandkeramischen Massengrab von Talheim, Kreis Heilbronn. *Fundberichte aus Baden-Württemberg* 20, 195–217.

Álvarez Fernández, E. 2003. Die Reise der Schnecke *Columbella rustica* während des Mesolithikums und zu Beginn des Neolithikums in Europa. *Archäologisches Korrespondenzblatt* 33, 157–66.

Ambrose, S.H. 1990. Preparation and characterization of bone and tooth collagen for isotopic analysis. *Journal of Archaeological Science* 17, 431–51.

Ambrose, S.H. and Katzenberg, M.A. (eds) 2000. *Biogeochemical approaches to paleodietary analysis.* New York: Kluwer Academic.

Ambrose, S.H. and Norr, L. 1993. Experimental evidence for the relationship of the carbon isotope ratios of whole diet and dietary protein to those of bone collagen and carbonate. In J.B. Lambert and G. Grupe (eds), *Prehistoric human bone: archaeology at the molecular level,* 1–37. Berlin: Springer.

Amit, V. 2002. Reconceptualizing community. In V. Amit (ed.), *Realizing community: concepts, social relationships and sentiments,* 1–20. London: Routledge.

Amkreutz, L.W.S.W. 2010. "All quiet on the northwestern front?" An overview and preliminary analysis of the past decade of LBK-research in the Netherlands. In D. Gronenborn and J. Petrasch (eds), *Die Neolithisierung Mitteleuropas (The spread of the Neolithic to central Europe)*, 535–50. Mainz: Römisch-Germanisches Zentralmuseum.

Anderson, B.R.O'G. 1991. *Imagined communities: reflections on the origins and spread of nationalism* (revised edition). London: Verso.

Anonymous 2000. Fundchronik für das Jahr 1999. *Bayerische Vorgeschichtsblätter Beiheft* 15, 1–250.

Antl-Weiser, W. 1986. *Das Fundmaterial von Horn-Galgenberg und seine Stellung am Übergang vom Paläolithikum zum Mesolithikum.* Unpublished PhD thesis, University of Vienna.

Antl-Weiser, W. 1993. Spätpaläolithikum und Mesolithikum. In C. Neugebauer-Maresch (ed.), *Altsteinzeit im Osten Österreichs*, 81–90. St. Pölten: Niederösterreichisches Pressehaus.

Anthony, D. 2010. *The horse, the wheel and language.* Princeton: Princeton University Press.

Arbogast, R.-M. 1983. *Les sépultures rubanées d'Alsace.* Unpublished Masters dissertation, University of Strasbourg.

Arbogast, R.-M. 1993. Restes osseux d'animaux du Rubané du nord-est de la France. In J.-C. Blanchet, A. Bulard, C. Constantin, D. Mordant and J. Tarrête (eds), *Le Néolithique au quotidien: actes du XVIème colloque inter-régional sur le Néolithique, Paris 5 et 6 novembre 1989*, 133–48. Paris: Éditions de la Maison des Sciences de l'Homme.

Arbogast, R.-M. 2001. Variabilité de la représentation des animaux sauvages et statut de la chasse sur les sites du Rubané du Nord de la France. In R.-M. Arbogast, C. Jeunesse and J. Schibler (eds), *Rôle et statut de la chasse dans le Néolithique ancien danubien (5500–4900 av. J.-C.)/Rolle und Bedeutung der Jagd während des Frühneolithikums Mitteleuropas (Linearbandkeramik 5500–4900 v. Chr.)*, 77–90. Rahden: Marie Leidorf.

Arbogast, R.-M. 2002. Les dépôts alimentaires de la nécropole rubanée de Vendenheim (Bas-Rhin). In C. Jeunesse (ed.), *Vendenheim 'Le Haut du Coteau': une nécropole du Néolithique ancien. Document final de synthèse. Tome 1: texte*, 141–2. Strasbourg: Service Régional de l'Archéologie d'Alsace, unpublished document.

Arbogast, R.-M. and Jeunesse, C. 1990. Ensisheim 'Ratfeld': quelques données sur la chasse et l'élevage au Néolithique rubané en Alsace. In D. Cahen and M. Otte (eds), *Rubané et Cardial: actes du colloque de Liège, novembre 1988*, 287–98. Liège: University of Liège.

Arbogast, R.-M., Jeunesse, C. and Schibler, J. (eds) 2001. *Rôle et statut de la chasse dans le Néolithique ancien danubien (5500–4900 av. J.-C.)/Rolle und Bedeutung der Jagd während des Frühneolithikums Mitteleuropas (Linearbandkeramik 5500–4900 v. Chr.)*. Rahden: Marie Leidorf.

Arnott, R., Fingers, S. and Smith, C.U.M. 2003. *Trepanation: history, discovery, theory*. Lisse: Swets and Zeitlinger.

Asam, T., Bösl, C., Grupe, G., Lösch, S., Manhart, H., Mekota, A.-M. and Peters, J. 2008. Palaeoecosystem reconstruction and the Neolithic transition in temperate climates. In G. Grupe and J. Peters (eds), *Conservation policy and current research*, 97–137. Rahden: Marie Leidorf.

Asam, T., Grupe, G. and Peters, J. 2006. Menschliche Subsistenzstrategien im Neolithikum: eine Isotopenanalyse bayerischer Skelettfunde. *Anthropologischer Anzeiger* 64, 1–23.

Aufderheide, A.C. and Rodríguez-Martin, C. 1998. *The Cambridge encyclopedia of human paleopathology*. Cambridge: Cambridge University Press.

Aufdermauer, J., Dieckmann, B. and Fritsch, B. 1986. Die Untersuchungen in einer bandkeramischen Siedlung bei Singen am Hohentwiel, Kreis Konstanz. *Archäologische Ausgrabungen in Baden-Württemberg 1985*, 51–4.

Bach, A. 1978. *Neolithische Populationen im Mittelelbe-Saale-Gebiet*. Weimar: Museum für Ur- und Frühgeschichte Thüringens.

Bach, A. 1986. Einige Befunde an den Skeletten aus den Körpergräbern des linearbandkeramischen Gräberfeldes von Wandersleben, Kreis Gotha. *Anthropologie* 24, 111–14.

Bach, A. and Bach, H. 1989. *Paläoanthropologie im Mittelelbe-Saale-Werra-Gebiet: Beiträge zur Rekonstruktion der biologischen Situation ur- und frühgeschichtlicher Bevölkerungen*. Weimar: Museum für Ur- und Frühgeschichte Thüringens.

Badisches Landesmuseum 2010. *Jungsteinzeit in Umbruch: die Michelsberger Kultur und Mitteleuropa vor 6000 Jahren*. Stuttgart: Primus.

Bailloud, G. 1964. *Le Néolithique dans le Bassin parisien*. Paris: Centre National de la Recherche Scientifique.

Bailloud, G. 1976. Le Néolithique en Picardie. *Revue Archéologique de l'Oise* 7, 10–28.

Bakels, C.C. 1978. Four Linearbandkeramik settlements and their environment: a paleoecological study of Sittard, Stein, Elsloo and Hienheim. *Analecta Praehistorica Leidensia* 11, 1–245.

Bakels, C.C. 1983/4. Pflanzenreste aus Niederbayern – Beobachtungen in rezenten Ausgrabungen. *Jahresbericht der Bayerischen Bodendenkmalpflege* 24/25, 157–66.

Bakels, C.C. 1991. Tracing crop processing in the Bandkeramik culture. In J. Renfrew (ed.), *New light on early farming: recent developments in palaeoethnobotany*, 281–8. Edinburgh: Edinburgh University Press.

Bakels, C.C. 1992. Fruits and seeds from the Linearbandkeramik settlement at Meindling, Germany, with special reference to *Papaver somniferum*. *Analecta Praehistorica Leidensia* 25, 55–68.

Bakels, C.C. 2003. Die neolithischen Weizenarten des südlimburgischen Lössgebiets in den Niederlanden. In J. Eckert, U. Eisenhauer and A. Zimmermann (eds), *Archäologische Perspektiven: Analysen und Interpretationen im Wandel. Festschrift für Jens Lüning zum 65. Geburtstag*, 225–32. Rahden: Marie Leidorf.

Bakels, C.C. 2007. Nature or culture? Cereal crops raised by Neolithic farmers on Dutch *loess* soils. In S. Colledge and J. Conolly (eds), *The origins and spread of domestic plants in south-west Asia*, 343–7. Walnut Creek: Left Coast Press.

Bakels, C.C. 2009. *The western European loess belt: agrarian history 5300 BC–1000 AD*. New York: Springer.

Balasse, M., Ambrose, S.H., Smith, A.B. and Price, T.D. 2002. The seasonal mobility model for prehistoric herders in the south-western cape of South Africa assessed by isotopic analysis of sheep tooth enamel. *Journal of Archaeological Science* 29, 917–32.

Balasse, M., Boury, L., Ughetto-Monfrin, J. and Tresset, A. 2012. Stable isotope insights ($\delta^{18}O$, $\delta^{13}C$) into cattle and sheep husbandry at Bercy (Paris, France, 4th millennium BC): birth seasonality and winter leaf foddering. *Environmental Archaeology* 17, 29–44.

Bálek, M. 2002. Neolitické sídliště u Popůvek, okr. Brno-venkov. *Otázky neolitu a neolitu našich krajín 2001*, 21–33.

Bálek, M., Čižmář, Z. and Geislerová, K. 2000. Předběžná zpráva o záchranném archeologickém výzkumu neolitického sídliště u Kuřimi. *Památky archeologické, Supplementum* 13, 8–19.

Bánffy, E. 2000. The late Starčevo and the earliest Linear Pottery groups in Western Transdanubia. *Documenta Praehistorica* 27, 173–85.

Bánffy, E. 2004. *The 6th millennium BC boundary in western Transdanubia and its role in the central European Neolithic transition*. Budapest: Institute of Archaeology, Hungarian Academy of Sciences.

Bánffy, E. 2006. Eastern, central and western Hungary – variations of Neolithisation models. *Documenta Praehistorica* 33, 125–42.

Bánffy, E. 2008. The boundary in western Transdanubia: variations of migration and adaptation. In D. Bailey, A. Whittle and D. Hofmann (eds), *Living well together? Settlement and materiality in the Neolithic of south-east and central Europe*, 152–65. Oxford: Oxbow Books.

Bánffy, E. 2013. On Neolithic frontiers in the Carpathian basin. In A. Anders and G. Kulcsár (eds), *Moments in time: papers presented to Pál Raczky on his 60th birthday*, 35–45. Budapest: L'Harmattan.

Bánffy, E. and Oross, K. 2009. Entwicklung und Dynamik der Linearbandkeramik in Transdanubien. In A. Zeeb-Lanz (ed.), *Krisen – Kulturwandel – Kontinuitäten: zum Ende der Bandkeramik in Mitteleuropa*, 219–40. Rahden: Marie Leidorf.

Bánffy, E. and Oross, K. 2010. The earliest and earlier phase of the LBK in Transdanubia. In D. Gronenborn and J. Petrasch (eds), *Die Neolithisierung Mitteleuropas (The spread of the Neolithic to central Europe)*, 255–72. Mainz: Römisch-Germanisches Zentralmuseum.

Bánffy, E., Brandt, G. and Alt, K. 2012. 'Early Neolithic' graves of the Carpathian Basin are in fact 6000 years younger: appeal for real interdisciplinarity between archaeology and ancient DNA research. *Journal of Human Genetics* 2012, 1–3.

Bánffy, E., Eichmann, W.J. and Marton, T. 2007. Mesolithic foragers and the spread of agriculture in western Hungary.

In J.K. Kozłowski and M. Novak (eds), *Mesolithic/Neolithic interactions in the Balkans and in the Middle Danube basin*, 53–62. Oxford: Archaeopress.

Bánffy, E., Marton, T. and Osztás, A. 2010. Early Neolithic settlement and burials at Alsónyék-Bátaszék. In J.K. Kozłowski and P. Raczky (eds), *Neolithization of the Carpathian basin: northernmost distribution of the Starčevo/Körös culture*, 37–51. Kraków and Budapest: Polish Academy of Sciences and Institute of Archaeological Sciences of the Eötvös Loránd University.

Banks, M. 1996. *Ethnicity: anthropological constructions*. London: Routledge.

Banner, J. 1931. A neolithikum Szarvason (Das Neolithikum in Szarvas). *Dolgozatok a Szegedi Tudományegyetem Archaeologiai Intézetéből* 7, 61–73.

Banner, J. 1937. Die Ethnologie der Kőrös-Kultur. *Dolgozatok* 13, 32–49.

Banner, J. 1940. *Hódmezővásárhely tötenete a honfoglalás koraig, 1. rész: a legrégibb időktől a bronzkor kialakulásáig (Geschichte der Stadt Hódmezővásárhely bis zur Landnahmzeit. 1. Teil: von den ältesten Zeiten bis zum Übergang in die Bronzezeit)*. Hódmezővásárhely: A Városi Múzeum Kiadása.

Banner, J. 1942. *Das Tisza-, Maros-, und Körös-Gebiet bis zur Entwicklung der Bronzezeit*. Szeged: Archäologisches Institut der Miklós Horthy-Universität.

Banner, J. and Bálint, A. 1935. A szakálháti őskori telep (Die prähistorische Ansiedlung in Szakálhát). *Dolgozatok* 11, 76–96.

Bárta, J. 1956. Neolitické osídlenie jaskýň pri Poráči na Slovensku. *Archeologické rozhledy* 8, 633–39.

Bárta, J. 1990. Mezolitickí lovci v Medvedej jaskyni pri Ružíne (Chasseurs mésolithiques de la Grotte des Ours (Medvedia jaskyňa), près de Ružín. (dist. Košice)). *Slovenská archeológia* 38, 5–30.

Barth, F. 1969. Introduction. In F. Barth (ed.), *Ethnic groups and boundaries: the social organisation of cultural difference*, 9–38. Bergen/London: Universitets Forlaget/George Allen and Unwin.

Bartosiewicz, L. 2005. Plain talk: animals, environment and culture in the Neolithic of the Great Hungarian Plain. In D. Bailey, A. Whittle and V. Cummings (eds), *(un)settling the Neolithic*, 51–70. Oxford: Oxbow Books.

Bartosiewicz, L. 2007. Mammalian bone. In A. Whittle (ed.), *The Early Neolithic on the Great Hungarian Plain: investigations of the Körös culture site of Ecsegfalva 23, Co. Békés*, 287–325. Budapest: Institute of Archaeology, Hungarian Academy of Sciences.

Battaglia, D. 1999. Towards an ethics of the open subject: writing culture in good conscience. In H.L. Moore (ed.), *Anthropological theory today*, 114–50. Oxford: Polity.

Baum, N. 1990. Aiterhofen-Ödmühle. Paläodontologie eines bandkeramischen Gräberfeldes in Niederbayern. *Prähistorische Zeitschrift* 65, 157–203.

Baumann, W. 1960. Körpergräber und Siedlung der Bandkeramik in Dresden-Nickern. *Arbeits- und Forschungsberichte zur Sächsischen Bodendenkmalpflege* 7, 95–138.

Bayer, J. 1931. Das erste neolithische Gräberfeld in Österreich. *Forschung und Fortschritte* 7, 233–4.

Bayliss, A. 2009. Rolling out revolution: using radiocarbon dating in archaeology. *Radiocarbon* 51, 123–47.

Bayliss, A., Bronk Ramsey, C., van der Plicht, J. and Whittle, A. 2007. Bradshaw and Bayes: towards a timetable for the Neolithic. *Cambridge Journal of Archaeology* 17.1, supplement, 1–28.

Bayliss, A., van der Plicht, J., Bronk Ramsey, C., McCormac, G., Healy, F. and Whittle, A. 2011. Towards generational time-scales: the quantitative interpretation of archaeological chronologies. In A. Whittle, F. Healy and A. Bayliss, *Gathering time: dating the early Neolithic enclosures of southern Britain and Ireland*, 17–59. Oxford: Oxbow Books.

Beard, B.L. and Johnson, C.M. 2000. Strontium isotope composition of skeletal material can determine the birth place and geographic mobility of humans and animals. *Journal of Forensic Sciences* 45, 1049–61.

Beck, R.A. 2007. The durable house: material, metaphor and structure. In R.A. Beck (ed.), *The durable house: house society models in archaeology*, 3–24. Carbondale: Southern Illinois University.

Becuwe, A. and Tinévez, J.-Y. 2004. Quelques références ethnologiques de maisons longues communautaires. In J.-Y. Tinévez, *Le site de La Hersonnais à Pléchâtel (Ille-et-Vilaine): un ensemble de bâtiments collectives du Néolithique final*, 157–64. Paris: Société Préhistorique Française.

Bedault, L. 2009. First reflections on the exploitation of animals in Villeneuve-Saint-Germain society at the end of the early Neolithic in the Paris Basin (France). In D. Hofmann and P. Bickle (eds), *Creating communities: new advances in central European Neolithic research*, 111–31. Oxford: Oxbow Books.

Bedault, L. and Hachem, L. 2008. Recherches sur les sociétés du Néolithique danubien à partir du Bassin parisien: approche structurelle des données archéozoologiques. In L. Burnez-Lanotte, M. Ilett and P. Allard (eds), *Fin des traditions danubiennes dans le Néolithique du Bassin parisien et de la Belgique (5100–4700 av. J.-C.): autour des recherches de Claude Constantin*, 221–43. Namur: Société Préhistorique Française and Presses Universitaires de Namur.

Behre, K.-E. 2007a. Evidence for Mesolithic agriculture in and around central Europe? *Vegetation History and Archaeobotany* 16, 203–19.

Behre, K.-E. 2007b. Wo sind die Nachweise für mesolithischen Ackerbau in Mitteleuropa? *Archäologische Informationen* 30, 53–7.

Behrends, R.-H. 1989. Ein Gräberfeld der Linienbandkeramik in Schwetzingen, Rhein-Neckar-Kreis. *Archäologie in Deutschland* 3, 39.

Behrends, R.-H. 1990. Ein Gräberfeld der Bandkeramik von Schwetzingen, Rhein-Neckar-Kreis. *Archäologische Ausgrabungen in Baden-Württemberg 1989*, 45–8.

Behrends, R.-H. 1993. Gräber der ersten Bauern. *Archäologische Nachrichten aus Baden* 50, 38–9.

Behrends, R.-H. 1997a. Ein bandkeramisches Gräberfeld von Schwetzingen. *Archäologische Informationen aus Baden-Württemberg* 34, 9–15.

Behrends, R.-H. 1997b. La nécropole rubanée de Schwetzingen. In C. Jeunesse (ed.), *Néolithique danubien et ses marges entre Rhin et Seine. Actes du 22ème Colloque Interrégional sur le Néolithique, Strasbourg 27–29 octobre 1995*, 17–29. Strasbourg: Cahiers de l'Association pour la Promotion de la Recherche Archéologique en Alsace.

Behrends, R.-H. 1999. Das bandkeramische Gräberfeld von Schwetzingen. *Führer zu Archäologischen Denkmälern in Deutschland* 36, 221–3.

Behrens, H. 1973. *Die Jungsteinzeit im Mittelelbe-Saale-Gebiet*. Berlin: VEB Deutscher Verlag der Wissenschaften.

Bello, S. and Andrews, P. 2006. The intrinsic pattern of preservation of human skeletons and its influence on the interpretation of funerary behaviours. In R. Gowland and C. Knüsel (eds),

Social archaeology of funerary remains, 1–13. Oxford: Oxbow Books.

Bender, H. 2006. Die Gesellschaft für Archäologie in Bayern e.V. In Gesellschaft für Archäologie in Bayern (eds), *Archäologie: Fenster zur Vergangenheit in Bayern*, 12–23. Regensburg: Friedrich Pustet.

Benecke, N. 1994. *Der Mensch und seine Haustiere: die Geschichte einer jahrtausendealten Beziehung*. Stuttgart: Theiss.

Benecke, N. 2001. Zur Bedeutung der Jagd während der Linienbandkeramik im südöstlichen Mitteleuropa und in Osteuropa. In R.-M. Arbogast, C. Jeunesse and J. Schibler (eds), *Rôle et statut de la chasse dans le Néolithique ancien danubien (5500–4900 av. J.-C.)/Rolle und Bedeutung der Jagd während des Frühneolithikums Mitteleuropas (Linearbandkeramik 5500–4900 v. Chr.)*, 39–56. Rahden: Marie Leidorf.

Benedict, R. 1934. *Patterns of culture*. Boston: Houghton-Miflin.

Bentley, R.A. 2001. *Human migration in early Neolithic Europe: a study by strontium and lead isotope analysis of archaeological skeletons*. Unpublished PhD thesis, Department of Anthropology, University of Wisconsin.

Bentley, R.A. 2006. Strontium isotopes from the earth to the archaeological skeleton: a review. *Journal of Archaeological Method and Theory* 13, 135–87.

Bentley, R.A. 2007. Mobility, specialisation and community diversity in the Linearbandkeramik: isotopic evidence from the skeletons. In A. Whittle and V. Cummings (eds), *Going over: the Mesolithic-Neolithic transition in north-west Europe*, 117–40. Oxford: Oxford University Press for the British Academy.

Bentley, R.A. 2012. Mobility and the diversity of Early Neolithic lives: isotopic evidence from skeletons. *Journal of Anthropological Archaeology* DOI: 10.1016/j.jaa.2012.01.009.

Bentley, R.A. and Knipper, C. 2005a. Transhumance at the early Neolithic settlement at Vaihingen, Germany. *Antiquity* 79 http://antiquity.ac.uk/ProjGall/bentley/index.html.

Bentley, R.A. and Knipper, C. 2005b. Geographical patterns in biologically available strontium, carbon and oxygen isotope signatures in prehistoric SW Germany. *Archaeometry* 47, 629–44.

Bentley, R.A., Bickle, P., Fibiger, L., Nowell, G., Dale, C., Hedges, R., Hamilton, J., Wahl, J., Francken, M., Grupe, G., Lenneis, E., Teschler-Nicola, M., Arbogast, R.-M., Hofmann, D. and Whittle, A. 2012. Community differentiation and kinship among Europe's first farmers. *Proceedings of the National Academy of Sciences of the United States of America* 109, 9326–30.

Bentley, R.A., Krause, R., Price, T.D. and Kaufmann, D. 2003. Human mobility at the early Neolithic settlement of Vaihingen, Germany: evidence from strontium isotope analysis. *Archaeometry* 45, 481–96.

Bentley, R.A., Price, T.D. and Stephan, E. 2004. Determining the 'local' $^{87}Sr/^{86}Sr$ range for archaeological skeletons: a case study from Neolithic Europe. *Journal of Archaeological Science* 31, 365–75.

Bentley, R.A., Price, T.D., Lüning, J., Gronenborn, D. and Fullager, P.D. 2002. Prehistoric migration in Europe: strontium isotope analysis of early Neolithic skeletons. *Current Anthropology* 43, 799–804.

Bentley, R.A., Wahl, J., Price, T.D. and Atkinson, T.C. 2008. Isotopic signatures and hereditary traits: snapshot of a Neolithic community in Germany. *Antiquity* 82, 290–304.

Berbesque, J.C. and Marlowe, F.W. 2009. Sex differences in food preferences of Hadza hunter-gatherers. *Evolutionary Psychology* 7, 601–16.

Berbesque, J.C., Marlowe, F.W. and Crittenden, A.N. 2011. Sex differences in Hadza eating frequency by food type. *American Journal of Human Biology* 23, 339–45.

Berg, F. 1961/1965. Jüngere Steinzeit. *Fundberichte aus Österreich* 8, 6–35.

Berg, F. and Gulder, A. 1956. Vorläufiger Bericht über eine neue niederösterreichische Mesolithstation aus Kamegg im Kamptal. *Archaeologia Austriaca* 19–20, 49–62.

Berkovec, T. 2004. *Ohrazené areály kultury s lineární keramikou na Moravě (I). Brno-Nový Liskovec „Pod kamenným vrchem"*. Olomouc: Archeologické centrum Olomouc.

Berkovec, T. and Humpolová, A. 2008. Vedrovice (okr. Znojmo). In Z. Čižmář (ed.), *Život a smrt v mladší době kamenné*, 45–9. Brno: Ústav archeologické památkové péče Brno.

Berkovec, T. and Nývltová-Fišáková, M. 2003. Analýza osteologického materiálu z vybraných objektů sídliště kultury s lineární keramikou ve Vedrovicích "Široká u lesa" (Osteological analysis of the selected units from the Linear Band Ceramic culture site: Vedrovice – "Široká u lesa"). *Přehled výzkumů* 44, 17–39.

Bertemes, F. 1989. *Das frühbronzezeitliche Gräberfeld von Gemeinlebarn*. Bonn: Habelt.

Bickle, P. 2009. Scene by the brook: early Neolithic landscape perspectives in the Paris Basin. In D. Hofmann and P. Bickle (eds), *Creating communities: new advances in central European Neolithic research*, 132–41. Oxford: Oxbow Books.

Bickle, P. and Hofmann, D. 2007. Moving on: the contribution of isotope studies to the early Neolithic of Central Europe. *Antiquity* 81, 1029–41.

Bickle, P., Hofmann, D., Bentley, R.A., Hedges, R., Hamilton, J., Laiginhas, F., Nowell, G., Pearson, D.G., Grupe, G. and Whittle, A. 2011. Roots of diversity in a *Linearbandkeramik* community: isotope evidence at Aiterhofen (Bavaria, Germany). *Antiquity* 85, 1243–58.

Biel, J. 1983. Ein bandkeramischer Friedhof beim Viesenhäuser Hof, Stuttgart-Mühlhausen. *Archäologische Ausgrabungen in Baden-Württemberg 1982*, 29–32.

Biel, J. 1988. Ein bandkeramischer Friedhof in Fellbach-Oeffingen, Rems-Murr-Kreis. *Archäologische Ausgrabungen in Baden-Württemberg* 1987, 38–40.

Binford, L.R. 1968. Archeological perspectives. In S.R. and L.R. Binford (eds), *New perspectives in archeology*, 5–32. New York: Aldine.

Binford, L. 1971. Mortuary practices: their study and their potential. In J.A. Brown (ed.), *Approaches to the social dimensions of mortuary practices*, 6–29. Washington: Society of American Anthropology.

Binsteiner, A. and Ruprechtsberger, E.M. 2008. *Jungsteinzeitliche Silexartefakte und Keramik im Raum Linz und in Oberösterreich*. Linz: Nordico.

Bird-David, N. 1990. The giving environment: another perspective on the economic system of gatherer-hunters. *Current Anthropology* 31, 189–96.

Bird-David, N. 1992. Beyond 'the hunting and gathering mode of subsistence': culture-sensitive observations on the Nayaka and other modern hunter-gatherers. *Man* 27, 19–44.

Birkenhagen, B. 2003. *Studien zum Siedlungswesen der westlichen Linearbandkeramik*. Bonn: Habelt.

Biró, K.T. 1998. *Lithic implements and circulation of raw materials in the Great Hungarian Plain during the Late Neolithic Period*. Budapest: Hungarian National Museum.

Black, R.E., Williams, S.M., Jones, I.E. and Goulding, A. 2002. Children who avoid drinking cow milk have low dietary calcium intakes and poor bone health. *American Journal of Clinical Nutrition* 76, 675–80.

Blesl, C. 2005. Das Altneolithikum – Linearbandkeramik. In Bundesdenkmalamt Wien (ed.), *Zeitschienen: vom Tullnerfeld ins Traisental. Archäologische Funde aus 20.000 Jahren*, 64–8. Horn: Ferdinand Berger and Söhne.

Blesl, C. and Kalser, K. 2005. Stadt St. Pölten, K.G. Pottenbrunn. *Fundberichte aus Österreich* 44, 31.

Blesl, C. and Neugebauer, J.-W. 1994. Poysdorf, Laaerstrasse. *Fundberichte aus Österreich* 33, 579–82.

Blesl, C. and Stöckl, C. 2004. Saladorf. *Fundberichte aus Österreich* 43, 36.

Blesl, C., Kalser, K. and Spatzier, A. 2004. Michelhausen und Mitterndorf. *Fundberichte aus Österreich* 43, 28.

Blesl, C., Nönnig, K. and Spatzier, A. 2003. Mitterndorf und Michelhausen. *Fundberichte aus Österreich* 42, 23.

Bloch, M. 2005a. Where did anthropology go? Or the need for 'human nature'. In M. Bloch, *Essays on cultural transmission,* 1–19. Oxford: Berg.

Bloch, M. 2005b. A well-disposed anthropologist's problems with memes. In M. Bloch, *Essays on cultural transmission,* 87–101. Oxford: Berg.

Blouet, V., Decker, E., Petitdidier, M.-P. and Thomashausen, L. 2007. L'approvisionnement en matériaux siliceux du Rubané lorrain. In F. Le Brun-Ricalens, F. Valotteau and A. Hauzeur (eds), *Relations interrégionales au Néolithique entre Bassin parisien et Bassin rhénan*, 89–97. Luxembourg: Faber.

Bocherens, H., Polet, C. and Toussaint, M. 2007. Palaeodiet of Mesolithic and Neolithic populations of Meuse Basin (Belgium): evidence from stable isotopes. *Journal of Archaeological Science* 34, 10–27.

Bocquet-Appel, J.-P. 2011. When the world's population took off: the springboard of the Neolithic demographic transition. *Science* 333, 560–1.

Bocquet-Appel, J.-P. and Bar-Yosef, O. (eds) 2008. *The Neolithic demographic transition and its consequences*. New York: Springer.

Boelicke, U. 1982. Gruben und Häuser: Untersuchungen zur Struktur bandkeramischer Hofplätze. In J. Pavúk (ed.), *Siedlungen der Kultur mit Bandkeramik in Europa. Internationales Kolloquium Nové Vozokany 17.–20. November 1981*, 17–28. Nitra: Archäologisches Institut der Slovakischen Akademie der Wissenschaften.

Boelicke, U., von Brandt, D., Lüning, J., Stehli, P. and Zimmermann, A. 1988. Struktur und Entwicklung des Siedlungsplatzes. In U. Boelicke, D. von Brandt, J. Lüning, P. Stehli and A. Zimmermann (eds), *Der bandkeramische Siedlungsplatz Langweiler 8, Gemeinde Aldenhoven, Kreis Düren*, 891–931. Köln: Rheinland-Verlag.

Boës, E. 2000. Evolution des comportements funéraires entre les VIe et Ve millénaires avant J.-C. en Alsace. *Cahiers Alsaciens d'Archéologie, d'Art et d'Histoire* 43, 5–18.

Boës, E. 2003.Comportements funéraires, modifications sociales et mentalités aux VIe et Ve millénaires avant J.C. en Alsace. In P. Chambon and J. Leclerc (eds), *Les pratiques funéraires néolithiques avant 3500 av. J.-C. en France et dans les régions limitrophes. Saint-Germain-en-Laye 15–17 juin 2001*, 33–43. Paris: Société Préhistorique Française.

Boës, E. and Alix, G. 2002. Anthropologie. In C. Jeunesse (ed.), *Vendenheim 'Le Haut du Coteau': une nécropole du Néolithique ancien. Document final de synthèse. Tome 1: texte*, 49–61. Strasbourg: Service Régional de l'Archéologie d'Alsace, unpublished document.

Boës, E., Jeunesse, C., Arbogast, R.-C., Lefranc, P., Mauvilly, M., Schniekert, F. and Sidéra, I. 2007. Vendenheim 'Le Haut de Coteau' (Bas-Rhin): remarques sur l'organisation interne d'une nécropole du Néolithique ancien danubien. In M. Besse (ed.), *Sociétés Néolithiques: des faits archéologiques aux fonctionnements socio-économiques*, 279–83. Lausanne: Cahiers d'Archéologie Romande.

Boesl, C., Grupe, G. and Peters, J. 2006. A Late Neolithic vertebrate food web based on stable isotope analyses. *International Journal of Osteoarchaeology* 16, 296–315.

Bogaard, A. 2004. *Neolithic farming in central Europe: an archaeobotanical study of crop husbandry practices*. London: Routledge.

Bogaard, A. 2011. *Plant use and crop husbandry in an early Neolithic village: Vaihingen an der Enz, Baden-Württemberg*. Bonn: Habelt.

Bogaard, A. and Jones, G. 2007. Neolithic farming in Britain and central Europe: contrast or continuity? In A. Whittle and V. Cummings (eds), *Going over: the Mesolithic-Neolithic transition in north-west Europe*, 357–75. Oxford: Oxford University Press for the British Academy.

Bogaard, A., Bending, J. and Jones, G. 2007a. Archaeobotanical evidence for plant husbandry and use. In A. Whittle (ed.), *The early Neolithic on the Great Hungarian Plain: investigations of the Körös culture site of Ecsegfalva 23, County Békés*, 421–45. Budapest: Institute of Archaeology, Hungarian Academy of Sciences.

Bogaard, A., Heaton, T.H.E., Poulton, P. and Merbach, I. 2007b. The impact of manuring on nitrogen isotope ratios in cereals: archaeological implications for reconstruction of diet and crop management practices. *Journal of Archaeological Science* 34, 335–43.

Bogaard, A., Krause, R. and Strien, H.-C. 2011. Towards a social geography of cultivation and plant use in an early farming community: Vaihingen an der Enz, south-west Germany. *Antiquity* 85, 395–416.

Bogucki, P. 1982. *Early Neolithic subsistence and settlement in the Polish lowland.* Oxford: British Archaeological Reports.

Bogucki, P. 1984. Ceramic sieves of the Linear Pottery Culture and their economic implications. *Oxford Journal of Archaeology* 3, 15–31.

Bogucki, P. 1988. *Forest farmers and stockherders: early agriculture and its consequences in north-central Europe*. Cambridge: Cambridge University Press.

Bogucki, P. 1995. The Linear Pottery culture of central Europe: conservative colonists? In W.K. Barnett and J.W. Hoopes (eds), *The emergence of pottery: technology and innovation in ancient societies*, 89–97. Washington: Smithsonian Institution Press.

Bogucki, P. 2000. How agriculture came to north-central Europe. In T.D. Price (ed.), *Europe's first farmers*, 197–218. Cambridge: Cambridge University Press.

Bogucki, P. and Grygiel, R. 1993. The first farmers of central Europe: a survey article. *Journal of Field Archaeology* 20, 399–426.

Böhm, K. and Schmotz, K. 1991. *Bestattungen der jungsteinzeitlichen Münchshöfener Gruppe*. Deggendorf: Ebner.

Bollongino, R. and Burger, J. 2010. Phylogeny and population genetics of Neolithic wild and domestic cattle. In D. Gronenborn and J. Petrasch (eds), *Die Neolithisierung Mitteleuropas (The spread of the Neolithic to central Europe)*, 81–5. Mainz: Römisch-Germanisches Zentralmuseum.

Bollongino, R., Edwards, C.J., Alt, K.W., Burger, J. and Bradley, D.G. 2006. Early history of European domestic cattle as revealed by ancient DNA. *Biology Letters* 22, 155–9.

Bonnabel, L., Paresys, C. and Thomasausen, L. 2003. Un groupe de tombes en contexte d'habitat néolithique rubané á Écriennes 'La Folie' (Marne): approche des gestes funéraires. In P. Chambon and J. Leclerc (eds), *Les pratiques funéraires néolithiques avant 3500 av. J.-C. en France et dans les régions limitrophes. Saint-Germain-en-Laye 15–17 juin 2001*, 45–53. Paris: Société Préhistorique Française.

Bonnardin, S. 2003. La parure funéraire des 6ème et 5ème millénaires avant J.-C. dans le Bassin parisien et la plaine du Rhin supérieur: traces d'usure, fonctionnement et fonction des objects de parure. In P. Chambon and J. Leclerc (eds), *Les pratiques funéraires néolithiques avant 3500 av. J.-C. en France et dans les régions limitrophes. Saint-Germain-en-Laye 15–17 juin 2001*, 99–113. Paris: Société Préhistorique Française.

Bonnett, C., Plouin-Mantzer, S. and Lambach, F. 1980. Le Rubané de la région colmarienne. In A. Thévenin and J.-P. Thévenot (eds), *Le Rubané d'Alsace et de Lorraine: état des recherches 1979*, 103–28. Strasbourg: Association d'Études Préhistoriques et Protohistoriques d'Alsace.

Boon, J.A. 1990. *Affinities and extremes: crisscrossing the bittersweet ethnology of East Indies history, Hindu-Balinese culture, and Indo-European allure*. Chicago: Chicago University Press.

Borić, D. 2007. The house between grand narrative and microhistory: a house society in the Balkans. In R.A. Beck (ed.), *The durable house: house society models in archaeology*, 97–129. Caarbondale: Southern Illinois University.

Borić, D. 2008. First households and 'house societies' in European prehistory. In A. Jones (ed.), *Prehistoric Europe: theory and practice*, 109–42. Oxford: Wiley-Blackwell.

Borić, D. 2010. Happy forgetting? Remembering and dismembering dead bodies at Vlasac. In D. Borić (ed.), *Archaeology and memory*, 48–67. Oxford: Oxbow Books.

Borić, D. and Miracle, P. forthcoming. Corporeal politics of agricultural transformations. In D. Borić and O. Harris (eds), *Body histories*. Cambridge: McDonald Institute for Archaeological Research.

Borić, D. and Robb, J. (eds) 2008. *Past bodies: body-centred research in archaeology.*Oxford: Oxbow Books.

Boschin, F. 2009. Der Tierknochenfundkomplex von Gnadendorf (VB Mistelbach, Niederösterreich). *Annalen des Naturhistorischen Museums Wien, Serie A* 110, 155–81.

Boulestin, B., Zeeb-Lanz, A., Jeunesse, C., Haack, F., Arbogast, R.-M. and Denaire, A. 2009. Mass cannibalism in the Linear Pottery Culture at Herxheim (Palatinate, Germany). *Antiquity* 83, 968–82.

Bourdieu, P. 1990. *The logic of practice.* Cambridge: Polity Press.

Boyde, A. 1989. Enamel. In B.K.B. Berkovitz (ed.), *Handbook of microscopic anatomy: teeth*, 309–473. Berlin: Springer.

Boyde, A., Fortelius, M., Lester, K.S. and Martin, L.B. 1988. Basis of the structure and development of mammalian enamel as seen by scanning electron microscopy. *Scanning Microscopy* 2, 1479–90.

Bradley, R. 1996. Long houses, long mounds and Neolithic enclosures. *Journal of Material Culture* 1, 239–56.

Bradley, R. 2001. Orientations and origins: a symbolic dimension to the longhouse in Neolithic Europe. *Antiquity* 75, 50–6.

Bramanti, B. 2008. Ancient DNA: genetic evidence of aDNA from sixteen skeletons of the Vedrovice collection. *Anthropologie* 46, 153–60.

Bramanti, B., Thomas, M.G., Haak, W., Unterlaender, M., Jores, P., Tambets, K., Antanaitis-Jacobs, I., Haidle, M.N., Jankauskas, K., Kind, C.-J., Lueth, F., Terberger, T., Hiller, J., Matsumura, S., Forster, P. and Burger, J. 2009. Genetic discontinuity between local hunter-gatherers and central Europe's first farmers. *Science* 326, 137–40.

Brickley, M. and Ives, R. 2008. *The bioarchaeology of metabolic bone disease.* London: Elsevier.

Brickley, M. and McKinley, J.I. 2004. *Guidelines to the standards for recording human remains*. Southampton and Reading: BABAO and IFA.

Brightman, R. 1995. Forget culture: replacement, transcendence, relexification. *Cultural Anthropology* 10, 509–46.

Brink, O., Vesterby, A. and Jensen, J. 1998. Pattern of injuries due to interpersonal violence. *Injury – International Journal of the Care of the Injured* 29, 705–9.

Brinkkemper, O. 2009. Die pflanzlichen Großreste. In E. Lenneis, *Rosenburg im Kamptal, Niederösterreich: ein Sonderplatz der älteren Linearbandkeramik*, 151–61. Bonn: Habelt.

Brink-Kloke, H. 1990. Das linienbandkeramische Gräberfeld von Essenbach-Ammerbreite, Ldkr. Landshut, Niederbayern. *Germania* 68, 427–81.

Brink-Kloke, H. 1992. *Drei Siedlungen der Linienbandkeramik in Niederbayern. Studien zu den Befunden und zur Keramik von Alteglofsheim-Köfering, Landshut-Sallmannsberg und Straubing-Lerchenhaid.* Buch am Erlbach: Marie Leidorf.

Brock, F., Bronk Ramsey, C. and Higham, T. 2007. Quality assurance of ultrafiltered bone dating. *Radiocarbon* 49, 187–92.

Brock, F., Higham, T., Ditchfield, P. and Bronk Ramsey, C. 2010a. Current pretreatment methods for AMS radiocarbon dating at the Oxford Radiocarbon Accelerator Unit (ORAU). *Radiocarbon* 52, 103–12.

Brock, F., Higham, T. and Bronk Ramsey, C. 2010b. Pre-screening techniques for identification of samples suitable for radiocarbon dating of poorly preserved bones. *Journal of Archaeological Science* 37, 855–65.

Bronk Ramsey, C. 1995. Radiocarbon calibration and analysis of stratigraphy: the OxCal program. *Radiocarbon* 37, 425–30.

Bronk Ramsey, C. 1998. Probability and dating. *Radiocarbon* 40, 461–74.

Bronk Ramsey, C. 2000. Comment on 'The use of Bayesian statistics for ^{14}C dates of chronologically ordered samples: a critical analysis'. *Radiocarbon* 42, 199–202.

Bronk Ramsey, C. 2001. Development of the radiocarbon calibration program OxCal. *Radiocarbon* 43, 355–63.

Bronk Ramsey, C. 2009a. OxCal 4.1b3 release note. *http://www.rlaha.ox.ac.uk/.*

Bronk Ramsey, C. 2009b. Bayesian analysis of radiocarbon dates. *Radiocarbon* 51, 337–60.

Bronk Ramsey, C., Higham, T., Bowles, A. and Hedges, R.E.M. 2004. Improvements to the pre-treatment of bone at Oxford. *Radiocarbon* 46, 155–63.

Brooks, S. and Suchey, J.M. 1990. Skeletal age determination based on the os pubis: a comparison of the Acsádi-Nemeskéri and Suchey-Brooks methods. *Journal of Human Evolution* 5, 227–38.

Brumann, C. 1999. Writing for culture: why a successful concept should not be discarded. *Current Anthropology* 40, supplement, S1–27.

Buck, C.E., Cavanagh, W.G. and Litton, C.D. 1996. *Bayesian approach to interpreting archaeological data*. Chichester: John Wiley and Sons.

Buck, C.E., Litton, C.D. and Smith, A.F.M. 1992. Calibration of radiocarbon results pertaining to related archaeological events. *Journal of Archaeological Science* 19, 487–512.

Budd, P., Millard, A., Chenery, C., Lucy, S. and Roberts, C. 2004. Investigating population movement by stable isotope analysis: a report from Britain. *Antiquity* 78, 127–41.

Buikstra, J.E. and Uberlaker, D.H. 1994. *Standards for data collection from human skeletal remains*. Fayetteville: Arkansas Archaeologial Survey.

Bulla, A. 1998. *Untersuchungen zur Frage der geschlechtsspezifischen Beigabenausstattungen bandkeramischer Gräberfelder Mitteleuropas*. Aachen: Shaker.

Bump, J.K., Fox-Dobbs, K., Bada, J.L., Koch, P.L., Peterson, R.O. and Vucetich, J.A. 2007. Stable isotopes, ecological integration and environmental change: wolves record atmospheric carbon isotope trend better than tree rings. *Proceedings of the Royal Society B* 274, 2471–80.

Burger, J. and Haak, W. 2010. Mitochondriale Haplotypen aus humanen neolitischen Skeletten der LBK bzw AVK. In D. Gronenborn and J. Petrasch (eds), *Die Neolithisierung Mitteleuropas (The spread of the Neolithic to central Europe)*, 141–6. Mainz: Römisch-Germanisches Zentralmuseum.

Burton, J.H., Price, T.D. and Middleton, W.D. 1999. Correlation of bone Ba/Ca and Sr/Ca due to biological purification of calcium. *Journal of Archaeological Science* 26, 609–16.

Byers, A.M. 2011. *Sacred games, death, and renewal in the ancient Eastern Woodlands: the Ohio Hopewell system of cult sodality heterarchies*. Lanham: Altamira Press.

Byers, S.N. (ed.) 2008. *Introduction to forensic anthropology*. London: Pearson/Allyn and Bacon.

Canuto, M.A. and Yaeger, J. (eds) 2000. *The archaeology of communities: a New World perspective*. London: Routledge.

Capo, R.C., Stewart, B.W. and Chadwick, O.A. 1998. Strontium isotopes as tracers of ecosystem processes: theory and methods. *Geoderma* 82, 197–225.

Carli-Thiele, P. 1996. *Spuren von Mangelerkrankungen an steinzeitlichen Kinderskeleten (Vestiges of deficiency diseases in stone age child skeletons)*. Göttingen: Erich Götze.

Carr, C. 2006a. Salient issues in the social and political organizations of northern Hopewellian peoples: contextualizing, personalizing, and generating Hopewell. In C. Carr and D.T. Case (eds), *Gathering Hopewell: society, ritual and ritual interaction,* 73–118. New York: Springer.

Carr, C. 2006b. The tripartite ceremonial alliance among Scioto Hopewellian communities and the question of social ranking. In C. Carr and D.T. Case (eds), *Gathering Hopewell: society, ritual and ritual interaction,* 258–338. New York: Springer.

Carr, C. and Case, D.T. (eds) 2006. *Gathering Hopewell: society, ritual and ritual interaction*. New York: Springer.

Carr, C., Goldstein, B.J. and Weets, J. 2006. Estimating the sizes and social compositions of mortuary-related gatherings at Scioto Hopewell earthwork-mound sites. In C. Carr and D.T. Case (eds), *Gathering Hopewell: society, ritual and ritual interaction,* 480–532. New York: Springer.

Carr, G. and Knüsel, C. 1997. The ritual framework of excarnation by exposure as the mortuary practice of the early and middle Iron Ages of central southern Britain. In A. Gwilt and C. Haselgrove (eds), *Reconstructing Iron Age societies*, 167–73. Oxford: Oxbow Books.

Carrithers, M. 1992. *Why humans have cultures: explaining anthropology and social diversity*. Oxford: Oxford University Press.

Carsten, J. 2004. *After kinship*. Cambridge: Cambridge University Press.

Carsten, J.and Hugh-Jones, S. (eds) 1995. *About the house: Lévi-Strauss and beyond*. Cambridge: Cambridge University Press.

Carter, R.A. and Philip, G. 2010. Deconstructing the Ubaid. In R.A. Carter and G. Philip (eds), *Beyond the Ubaid: transformation and integration in the late prehistoric societies of the Middle East*, 1–22. Chicago: Oriental Institute of the University of Chicago.

Case, D.T., Burnett, S.E. and Nielsen, T. 2006. Os acromiale: population differences and their etiological significance. *Homo* 57, 1–18.

Čermáková, E. 2002. Problémy dětství v neolitu střední Evropy (Probleme der Kindheit im Neolithikum Mitteleuropas). *Pravěk – Nová řada* 12, 7–45.

Červinka, I.L. 1904. O keramice neolitické na Moravě. *Pravěk* 2, 17–20.

Chaix, L. 1997. La transition Mésolithique-Néolithique: quelques données de l'archéozoologie dans les Alpes du Nord et le Jura. In C. Jeunesse (ed.), *Le Néolithique danubien et ses marges entre Rhin et Seine*, 191–6. Strasbourg: Cahiers de l'Association pour la Promotion de la Recherche Archéologique en Alsace.

Chaix, L. and Bridault, A. 1992. Nouvelles données sur l'exploitation des animaux sauvages de l'Epipaléolithique au Mésolithique final dans les Alpes du Nord et le Jura. *Preistoria Alpina* 28, 115–27.

Chamberlain, A. 1997. Commentary: missing stages of life – towards the perception of children in archaeology. In J. Moore and E. Scott (eds), *Invisible people and processes: writing gender and childhood into European archaeology*, 248–50. London: Leicester University Press.

Chamberlain, A. 2000. Minor concerns: a demographic perspective on children in past societies. In J. Sofaer Derevenski (ed.), *Children and material culture*, 206–12. London: Routledge.

Chamberlain, A. 2006. *Demography in archaeology*. Cambridge: Cambridge University Press.

Chapman, J. 1994. The living,the dead and the ancestors: time, life cycles and the mortuary domain in later European prehistory. In J. Davies (ed.), *Ritual and remembrance: responses to death in human societies*, 40–85. Sheffield: Sheffield Academic Press.

Chapman, J. 2000. *Tensions at funerals: mortuary archaeology in later Hungarian prehistory*. Budapest: Archaeolingua.

Chapman, J. (ed.) 2010. *From surface collection to prehistoric lifeways: making sense of the multi-period site of Orlovo, south east Bulgaria*. Oxford: Oxbow Books.

Chapman, J. and Gaydarska, B. forthcoming. *Spondylus gaederopus/glycemeris* exchange networks in the European Neolithic and Chalcolithic. In C. Fowler, J. Harding and D. Hofmann (eds), *The Oxford Handbook of Neolithic Europe*. Oxford: Oxford University Press.

Chapman, J., Gillings, M., Shiel, R., Gaydarska, B. and Bond, C. 2010. *The Upper Tisza Project. Studies in Hungarian landscape archaeology. Book 4: lowland settlement in north-east Hungary: excavations at the Neolithic settlement site of Polgár-10*. Oxford: Archaeopress.

Châtelet, M. 2009. *Fouilles et découvertes en Alsace*. Rennes: Éditions Ouest-France.

Chenery, C., Eckardt, H. and Müldner, G. 2011. Cosmopolitan Catterick? Isotopic evidence for population mobility on Rome's northern frontier. *Journal of Archaeological Science* 38, 1525–36.

Chenery, C., Müldner, G., Evans, J., Eckardt, H. and Lewis, M. 2010. Strontium and stable isotope evidence for diet and mobility in Roman Gloucester, UK. *Journal of Archaeological Science* 37, 150–63.

Chesson, M. 2003. Households, houses, neighbourhoods and corporate villages: modelling the Early Bronze Age as a house society. *Journal of Mediterranean Archaeology* 16, 79–102.

Childe, V.G. 1925. *The dawn of European civilization*. London: Routledge and Kegan Paul.

Childe, V.G. 1929. *The Danube in prehistory*. Oxford: Clarendon Press.

Chu, N.-C., Henderson, G.M., Belshaw, N.S. and Hedges, R.E.M. 2006. Establishing the potential of Ca isotopes as proxy for consumption of dairy products. *Applied Geochemistry* 21, 1656–67.

Christlein, R. 1982. Landesarchäologie in Bayern 1981 – ein Überblick. *Das Archäologische Jahr in Bayern 1981*, 13–38.

Čižmář, Z. 1998a. Nástin relativní chronologie lineární keramiky na Moravě (Poznámky k vývoji výzdobného stylu). *Acta Musei Moraviae Scientiae Sociales* 83, 105–39.

Čižmář, Z. 1998b. Osídlení Lysické sníženiny kulturou s lineární keramikou. *Otázky neolitu a eneolitou našich zemí*, Turnov – Hradec Králové, 23–46.

Čižmář, Z. 1998c. Několik poznámek k existenci polozemnic v kultuře s lineární keramikou (Einige Bemerkungen zur Existenz von Halbwohngruben in der Kultur mit Linearkeramik). *Pravěk – Nová řada* 8, 103–13.

Čižmář, Z. 2002. Keramika z pohřebiště v "Široká u lesa" (Keramik aus dem Gräberfeld in der Flur "Široká u lesa"). In V. Podborský, *Dvě pohřebiště neolitického lidu s lineární keramikou ve Vedrovicích na Moravě*, 151–90. Brno: Ústav archeologie a muzeologie, Filozofická fakulta Masarykovy univerzity.

Čižmář, Z. (ed.) 2008a. *Život a smrt v mladší době kamenné* (*Life and death in the New Stone Age*). Brno: Ústav archeologické památkové péče Brno.

Čižmář, Z. 2008b. Kultura s lineární keramikou (The Linear Pottery culture). In Z. Čižmář (ed.), *Život a smrt v mladší době kamenné*, 38–44. Brno: Ústav archeologické památkové péče Brno.

Čižmář, Z. and Geislerová, K. 1996. Sídliště kultury s lineární keramikou ve Slavíkovicích, okr. Vyškov (Siedlung der Kultur mit Linearbandkeramik in Slavíkovice, Bez. Vyškov). *Pravěk – Nová řada* 6, 51–74.

Čižmář, Z. and Geislerová, K. 1997. Pohřby v jamách na sídlišti kultury s lineární keramikou v Žádovicích, okr. Hodonín. *Pravěk – Nová řada* 7, 39–64.

Čižmář, Z. and Přichystal, M. 2004. Kostrové hroby na sídlišti kultury s lineární keramikou v Modřicích, okr. Brno-venkov (Körpergräber auf der Siedlung der Kultur mit Linearbandkeramik in Modřice, Bez. Brno-venkov). *Pravěk – Nová řada* 14, 7–37.

Cladders, M. 1997a. Befunde und Keramik des bandkeramischen Siedlungsplatzes Hambach 21, Gemeinde Jülich, Kreis Düren. In J. Lüning (ed.), *Studien zur neolithischen Besiedlung der Aldenhovener Platte und ihrer Umgebung*, 131–228. Bonn: Habelt.

Cladders, M. 1997b. Die Tonware der Ältesten Bandkeramik: Untersuchungen zur zeitlichen und räumlichen Gliederung. *Archäologisches Nachrichtenblatt* 2, 298–300.

Cladders, M. 2001. *Die Tonware der ältesten Bandkeramik: Untersuchung zur zeitlichen und räumlichen Gliederung*. Bonn: Habelt.

Cladders, M. and Stäuble, H. 2003. Das 53. Jahrhundert v. Chr.: Aufbruch und Wandel. In J. Eckert, U. Eisenhauer and A. Zimmermann (eds), *Archäologische Perspektiven: Analysen und Interpretationen im Wandel. Festschrift für Jens Lüning zum 65. Geburtstag*, 491–503. Rahden: Marie Leidorf.

Clark, R. 2000. *The Mesolithic hunters of the Trentino: a case study in hunter-gatherer settlement and subsistence from northern Italy*. Oxford: British Achaeological Reports.

Claßen, E. 2005. Siedlungsstrukturen der Bandkeramik im Rheinland. In J. Lüning, C. Frirdich and A. Zimmermann (eds), *Die Bandkeramik im 21. Jahrhundert. Symposium in der Abtei Brauweiler bei Köln vom 16.9.–19.9.2002*, 113–24. Rahden: Marie Leidorf.

Claßen, E. 2009. Settlement history, land use and social networks of early Neolithic communities in western Germany. In D. Hofmann and P. Bickle (eds), *Creating communities: new advances in central European Neolithic research*, 95–110. Oxford: Oxbow Books.

Clementz, M.T., Holden, P. and Koch, P.L. 2003. Are calcium isotopes a reliable monitor of trophic level in marine settings? *International Journal of Osteoarchaeology* 13, 29–36.

Colledge, S., Conolly, J. and Shennan, S. 2004. Archaeobotanical evidence for the spread of farming in the eastern Mediterranean. *Current Anthropology* 45, supplement, S35–58.

Conolly, J., Colledge, S. and Shennan, S. 2008. Founder effect, drift, and adaptive change in domestic crop use in early Neolithic Europe. *Journal of Archaeological Science* 35, 2797–804.

Constantin, C. 1985. *Fin du Rubané, céramique du Limbourg et post-Rubané: le Néolithique le plus ancien en Bassin parisien et en Hainaut*. Oxford: British Archaeological Reports.

Constantin, C. and Blanchet, J.-C. 1998. Le nord de la France (Bassin parisien). In J. Guilaine (ed.), *Atlas du Néolithique Européen: l'Europe occidentale*, 585–651. Liège: University of Liège.

Constantin, C. and Vachard, D. 2004. Anneaux d'origine méridionale dans le Rubané récent du Bassin parisien. *Bulletin de la Société Préhistorique Française* 101, 75–84.

Coolen, J. 2004. Das Haus 11 von Mold, Niederösterreich, und andere Kleinbauten der Linearbandkeramik. *Archaeologia Austriaca* 88, 67–102.

Coolen, J. 2012. Early Neolithic settlement in the area of Melk, Lower Austria: the survey of an LBK "Siedlungskammer". In J. Kolář and F. Trampota (eds), *Theoretical and methodological considerations in central European Neolithic archaeology, Conference Mikulov 26th–28th of October 2010*, 111–22. Oxford: Archaeopress.

Couch, J.R., Lipton, R.B., Stewart, W.F. and Scher, A.I. 2007. Head or neck injury increases the risk of chronic daily headache: a population-based study. *Neurology* 69, 1169–77.

Coudart, A. 1998. *Architecture et société néolithique: l'unité et la variance de la maison danubienne*. Paris: Éditions de la Maison des Sciences de l'Homme.

Coudart, A. forthcoming. The Bandkeramik longhouses: a material, social and mental metaphor for small-scale societies. In C. Fowler, J. Harding and D. Hofmann (eds), *The Oxford Handbook of Neolithic Europe*. Oxford: Oxford University Press.

Cox, K.J., Bentley, R.A., Tayles, N., Buckley, H.R., Macpherson, C.G. and Cooper M.J. 2011. Intrinsic or extrinsic population growth in Iron Age northeast Thailand? *Journal of Archaeological Science* 38, 665–71.

Craig, O.E., Chapman, J., Heron, C., Willis, L.H., Bartosiewicz, L., Taylor, G., Whittle, A. and Collins, M. 2005. Did the first farmers of central and eastern Europe produce dairy foods? *Antiquity* 79, 882–94.

Creese, J.L. 2011. *Deyughnyonkwarakda – "at the wood's edge": the development of the Iroquoian village in southern Ontario, A.D. 900–1500.* Unpublished PhD thesis, University of Toronto.

Crombé, P. 2009. Early pottery in hunter-gatherer societies of western Europe. In P. Jordan and M. Zvelebil (eds), *Ceramics before farming: the dispersal of pottery among prehistoric Eurasian hunter-gatherers*, 477–98. London: Institute of Archaeology, University College London Publications.

Cronk, L. and Gerkey, D. 2007. Kinship and descent. In R.I.M. Dunbar and L. Barrett (eds), *Oxford Handbook of evolutionary psychology*, 463–78. Oxford: Oxford University Press.

Crubézy, E. 1996. Surgery at the origins of agriculture: the case of central Europe. *Anthropologie* 34, 329–32.

Crubézy, E., Murail, P., Bruzek, J., Jelínek, J., Ondruš, V., Pavúk, P. and Teschler-Nicola, M. 1997. Sample characterisation of Danubian cemeteries in central Europe: the examples of Vedrovice (Moravia) and Nitra-Horné Krškany (Slovakia). In C. Jeunesse (ed.), *Le Néolithique danubien et ses marges entre Rhin et Seine*, 9–16. Strasbourg: Cahiers de l'Association pour la Promotion de la Recherche Archéologique en Alsace.

Crubézy, E., Goulet, J., Bruzek, J., Jelínek, J., Rougé, D. and Ludes, B. 2002. Epidemiology of osteoarthritis and anthesopathies in a European population dating back 7700 years. *Joint Bone Spine* 69, 580–8.

Cunha, E. and Pinheiro, J. 2009. Antemortem trauma. In D.H. Ubelaker and S. Blau (eds), *Handbook of forensic anthropology and archaeology*, 246–62. Walnut Creek: Left Coast Press.

Currie, M. 2004. *Difference*. London: Routledge.

Czekaj-Zastawny, A. and Zastawny, A. 2002. Wczesnoneolityczny czekan kamienny z Krakowa Woli Justowskiej. *Materiały Archeologiczne* 33, 201–11.

Darling, W.G. 2004. Hydrological factors in the interpretation of stable isotopic proxy data present and past: a European perspective. *Quaternary Science Reviews* 23, 743–70.

Darling, W.G., Bath, A.H., Gibson, J.J. and Rozanski, K. 2006. Isotopes in water. In M.J. Leng, (ed.), *Isotopes in palaeoenvironmental research 10*, 1–52. London: Springer.

Daux, V., Lécuyer, C., Héran, M., Amiot, R., Simon, L., Fourel, F., Martineau, F., Lynnerup, N., Reychler, H. and Escarguel, G. 2008. Oxygen isotope fractionation between human phosphate and water revisited. *Journal of Human Evolution* 55, 1138–47.

Davis, B.A.S., Brewer, S., Stevenson, A.C., Guiot, J. and Data Contributors. 2003. The temperature of Europe during the Holocene reconstructed from pollen data. *Quaternary Science Reviews* 22, 1701–16.

Davis, F.D. 1975. *Die Hornsteingeräte des älteren und mittleren Neolithikums im Donauraum zwischen Neuburg und Regensburg*. Bonn: Universität Bonn.

Dawson, T.E., Mambelli, S., Plamboeck, A.H., Templar, P.K. and Tu, K.P. 2002. Stable isotopes in plant ecology. *Annual Review of Ecology and Systematics* 33, 507–59.

Dee, M. and Bronk Ramsey, C. 2000. Refinement of the graphite target production at ORAU. *Nuclear Instruments and Methods in Physics Research B* 172, 449–53.

Deetz, J. 1968. The inference of residence and descent rules from archeological data. In S.R. and L.R. Binford (eds), *New perspectives in archeology*, 41–8. New York: Aldine.

Dehn, W. and Sangmeister, E. 1954. *Die Steinzeit im Ries: Katalog der steinzeitlichen Altertümer im Museum Nördlingen*. Kallmünz: Michael Lassleben.

DeLanda, M. 2006. *A new philosophy of society: assemblage theory and social complexity.* London: Continuum.

Della Casa, P., Bass, B. and Fedele, F. 1999. The Grisons Alpine Valleys Survey 1995–97: methods, results and prospects of an interdisciplinary research program. In P. Della Casa (ed.), *Prehistoric alpine environment, society and economy. Papers of the international colloquium PAESE '97 in Zurich*, 151–72. Bonn: Habelt.

Deleuze, G. 1994. *Difference and repetition* (translated by P. Patton). London: Athlone Press.

Deleuze, G. and Guattari, F. 2004. *A thousand plateaus: capitalism and schizophrenia.* London: Continuum.

deMenocal, P.B. 2001. Cultural responses to climate change during the Late Holocene. *Science* 292, 667–73.

Denaire, A. 2009. *Le Néolithique moyen du sud de la plaine du Rhin supérieur et du nord de la Franche-Comté: les cultures de Hinkelstein, Grossgartach et Roessen au travers de leur production céramique.* Strasbourg: Université de Strasbourg.

Denaire, A., Jeunesse, C., Voegtlin, C. and Voegtlin, M. 2008. *L'Alsace archéologique: un guide pratique pour découvrir toutes les facettes de l'archéologie régionale.* Strasbourg: Association pour la Promotion de la Recherche Archéologique en Alsace.

DeNiro, M.J. 1985. Postmortem preservation and alteration of in vivo bone collagen isotope ratios in relation to palaeodietary reconstruction. *Nature* 317, 806–9.

DeNiro, M.J. and Epstein, S. 1978. Influence of diet on the distribution of carbon isotopes in animals. *Geochimica et Cosmochimica Acta* 42, 495–506.

DeNiro, M.J. and Epstein, S. 1981. Influence of diet on the distribution of nitrogen isotopes in animals. *Geochimica et Cosmochimica Acta* 45, 341–51.

DePaolo, D.J. 2004. Calcium isotopic variation produced by biological, kinetic, radiogenic and nucleosynthetic processes. *Reviews in Mineralogy and Geochemistry* 55, 255–88.

Dieckmann, B. 1978. Neue neolithische Funde bei Oberbergen im Kaiserstuhl. *Archäologische Nachrichten aus Baden* 21, 11–17.

Dieckmann, B. and Fritsch, B. 1990. Linearbandkeramische Siedlungsbefunde im Hegau. *Archäologisches Korrespondenzblatt* 20, 25–39.

Dietrich, H. 1994. Ausgrabungen in einer linearbandkeramischen Siedlung in Wittislingen, Landkreis Dillingen a.d. Donau, Schwaben. *Das Archäologische Jahr in Bayern 1993*, 32–3.

Dietrich, H. and Kociumaka, C. 2001. Jungsteinzeitliche Befunde aus Steinheim. *Das Archäologische Jahr in Bayern 2000*, 32–5.

Dobosi, V.T. 1972. Mesolithische Fundorte in Ungarn. In J. Fitz and J. Makkay (eds), *Die aktuellen Fragen der Bandkeramik,* 39–60. Székesfehérvár: A Féjer Megyei Múzeumok Igazgatósága.

Dobres, M.-A. 1995. Gender and prehistoric technology: on the social agency of technical strategies. *World Archaeology* 27, 25–49.

Dočkalová, M. 2005. Nálezy neolitických koster z Těšetic (okr. Znojmo) (Funde von neolithischen Skeletten aus Těšetice, Bez. Znojmo). *Otázky neolitu a eneolitu našich krajín 2004,* Nitra, 21–32.

Dočkalová, M. 2006. Two skeleton graves from Neolithic settlements in Moravia (Czech Republic). *Anthropologie* 44, 127–37.

Dočkalová, M. 2008. Anthropology of the Neolithic population from Vedrovice (Czech Republic). *Anthropologie* 46, 239–315.

Dočkalová, M. and Čižmář, Z. 2007. Neolithic children burials at Moravian settlements in the Czech Republic. *Anthropologie* 45, 31–59.

Dočkalová, M. and Čižmář, Z. 2008a. Neolithic settlement burials of adult and juvenile individuals in Moravia, Czech Republic. *Anthropologie* 46, 37–76.

Dočkalová, M. and Čižmář, Z. 2008b. Antropologie a pohřbívání v moravském neolitu (Anthropology and Neolithic burials in Moravia). In Z. Čižmář (ed.), *Život a smrt v mladší době kamenné*, 236–47. Brno: Ústav archeologické památkové péče Brno.

Dočkalová, M. and Košturík, P. 1996. Seskupení hrobů nositelů kultury s lineární keramikou na neolitickém sídlišti v Těšeticích-Kyjovicích, okr. Znojmo (Eine Gräbergruppe der Träger der Linearbandkeramik auf dem neolithischen Siedlungsplatz in Těšetice-Kyjovice, Bez. Znojmo). *Sborník prací filozofické fakulty brněnské univerzity* M1, 5–30.

Döhle, H.-J. 1993. Haustierhaltung und Jagd in der Linienbandkeramik – ein Überblick. *Zeitschrift für Archäologie* 27, 105–24.

Döhle, H.-J. 2005. Nachweise wildlebender Säugetiere und Vögel aus bandkeramischen Siedlungen und ihre Eignung als Umweltindikatoren. In J. Lüning, C. Frirdich and A. Zimmermann (eds), *Die Bandkeramik im 21. Jahrhundert. Symposium in der Abtei Brauweiler bei Köln vom 16.9.–19.9.2002*, 275–88. Rahden: Marie Leidorf.

Dohrn-Ihmig, M. 1983. Das bandkeramische Gräberfeld von Aldenhoven-Niedermerz, Kreis Düren. In G. Bauchhenß (ed.), *Archäologie in den rheinischen Lössbörden. Beiträge zur Siedlungsgeschichte im Rheinland*, 47–190. Köln: Rheinland-Verlag.

Domboróczki, L. 1997. Füzesabony-Gubakút. In P. Raczky, T. Kovács and A. Anders (eds), *Utak a múltba: az M3-as autópálya régészeti leletmentései*, 19–27. Budapest: Magyar Nemzeti Múzeum and Eötvös Loránd Tudományegyetem Régészettudományi Intézet.

Domboróczki, L. 2003. Radiocarbon data from Neolithic archaeological sites in Heves county (north-eastern Hungary). *Agria* 39, 5–71.

Domboróczki, L. 2009. Settlement structures of the Alföld Linear Pottery Culture (ALPC) in Heves County (north-eastern Hungary): development models and historical reconstructions on micro, meso and macro levels. In J.K. Kozłowski (ed.), *Interactions between different models of Neolithization north of the central European agro-ecological barrier*, 75–127. Kraków: Polska Akademiai Umiejętności.

Domboróczki, L. 2010a. Report on the excavation at Tiszaszőlős-Domaháza-puszta and a new model for the spread of the Körös culture. In J.K. Kozłowski and P. Raczky (eds), *Neolithization of the Carpathian basin: northernmost distribution of the Starčevo/Körös culture*, 137–76. Kraków and Budapest: Polish Academy of Sciences and Institute of Archaeological Sciences of the Eötvös Loránd University.

Domboróczki, L. 2010b. Neolithisation in northeastern Hungary: old theories and new perspectives. In D. Gronenborn and J. Petrasch (eds), *Die Neolithisierung Mitteleuropas (The spread of the Neolithic to central Europe)*, 175–87. Mainz: Römisch-Germanisches Zentralmuseum.

Domboróczki, L. and Raczky, P. 2010. Excavations at Ibrány-Nagyerdő and the northernmost distribution of the Körös culture in Hungary. In J.K. Kozłowski and P. Raczky (eds), *Neolithization of the Carpathian basin: northernmost distribution of the Starčevo/Körös culture*, 191–218. Kraków and Budapest: Polish Academy of Sciences and Institute of Archaeological Sciences of the Eötvös Loránd University.

Doneus, M., Neubauer, W. and Trnka, G. 2001. Das jüngerlinearbandkeramische Grabenwerk von Großrußbach-Weinsteig in Niederösterreich – das größte Erdwerk der Linearbandkeramik? *Preistoria Alpina* 37, 13–26.

Draxler, I. 1994. Palynologische Untersuchung der Sedimente aus dem neolithischen Brunnen von Schletz, NÖ. *Archäologie Österreichs* 5, 22–3.

Dreslerová, G. 2006. Vyhodnocení zvířecích kostí z neolitického sídliště Těšetice-Kyjovice (Okr. Znojmo, Česká republika) (Die Auswertung der Tierknochen aus einer neolithischen Siedlung in Těšetice-Kyjovice (Bez. Znojmo, Tschechische Republik). *Archeologické rozhledy* 58, 3–32.

Driver, H.E. and Massey, W.C. 1957. *Comparative studies of North American Indians*. Philadelphia: American Philosophical Society.

Drucker, D.G., Bridault, A., Hobson, K.A., Szuma, E. and Bocherens, H. 2008. Can carbon-13 in large herbivores reflect the canopy effect in temperate and boreal ecosystems? Evidence from modern and ancient ungulates. *Palaeogeography, Palaeoclimatology, Palaeoecology* 266, 69–82.

Drucker, P. 1955. *Indians of the Northwest Coast*. New York: The American Museum of Natural History.

Drummond, L. 1980. The cultural continuum: a theory of intersystems. *Man* 15, 352–74.

Dubouloz, J. 2008. Impacts of the Neolithic demographic transition on Linear Pottery Culture settlement. In J.-P. Bocquet-Appel and O. Bar-Yosef (eds), *The Neolithic demographic transition and its consequences*, 207–35. New York: Springer.

Duday, H. 2009. *The archaeology of the dead: lectures in archaeothanatology*. Oxford: Oxbow Books.

Dunne, J., Evershed, R.P., Salque, M., Cramp, L., Bruni, S., Ryan, K., Biagetti S. and di Lernia S. 2012. First dairying in green Saharan Africa in the fifth millennium BC. *Nature* 486, 390–4.

Dürrwächter, C., Craig, O.E., Collins, M.J., Burger, J. and Alt, K.W. 2006. Beyond the grave: variability in Neolithic diets in southern Germany. *Journal of Archaeological Science* 33, 39–48.

Ebersbach, R. and Schade, C. 2005. Modelle zur Intensität der bandkeramischen Landnutzung am Beispiel der Altsiedellandschaft Mörlener Bucht/Wetterau. In J. Lüning, C. Frirdich and A. Zimmermann (eds), *Die Bandkeramik im 21. Jahrhundert. Symposium in der Abtei Brauweiler bei Köln vom 16.9.–19.9.2002*, 259–73. Rahden: Marie Leidorf.

Eckert, J., Eisenhauer, U. and Zimmermann, A. (eds) 2003. *Archäologische Perspektiven: Analysen und Interpretationen im Wandel. Festschrift für Jens Lüning zum 65. Geburtstag*. Rahden: Marie Leidorf.

Ecsedy, I., Kovács, L., Maráz, B. and Torma, I. 1982. *Magyarország Régészeti Topográfiája: a Szeghalmi járás IV/1*. Budapest: Akadémiai Kiadó.

Edwards, C.J., Bollongino, R., Scheu, A., Chamberlain, A., Tresset, A., Vigne, J.D., Baird, J.F., Larson, G., Ho, S.Y.W., Heupink, T.H., Shapiro, B., Freeman, A.R., Thomas, M.G., Arbogast, R.-M., Arndt, B., Bartosiewicz, L., Benecke, N., Budja, M., Chaix, L., Choyke, A.M., Coqueugniot, E., Döhle, H.J., Göldner, H., Hartz, S., Helmer, D., Herzig, B., Hongo, H., Mashkour, M., Özdoğan, M., Pucher, E., Roth, G., Schade-Lindig, S., Schmölcke, U., Schulting, R.J., Stephan, E., Uerpmann, H.-P., Vörös, I., Voytek, B., Bradley, D.G. and

Burger, J. 2007. Mitochondrial DNA analysis shows a Near Eastern Neolithic origin for domestic cattle and no indication of domestication of European aurochs. *Proceedings of the Royal Society B* 274, 1377–85.

Egry, I. 1997. Mosonszentmiklós-Egyéni földek. *Régészeti Füzetek* 48, 18–19.

Egry, I. 2003. Mosonszentmiklós–Egyéni földek: a Neolithic village in Transdanubia. In Z. Visy (ed.), *Hungarian archaeology at the turn of the millennium*, 104–6. Budapest: Ministry of National Cultural Heritage and Teleki László Foundation.

Eibner, C. 2006. Richard Pittioni zwischen Montan- und Industriearchäologie. *Archaeologia Austriaca* 90, 7–16.

Eichmann, W.J. 2004. Mesolithic hunter-gatherers in the Carpathian Basin and the spread of agriculture in Europe. In I. Hauszár (ed.), *Fullbright Student Conference Papers*, 161–202. Budapest: Hungarian-American Commission for Education Exchange.

Eichmann, W.J., Kertész, R. and Marton, T. 2010. Mesolithic in the LBK heartland of Transdanubia, western Hungary. In D. Gronenborn and J. Petrasch (eds), *Die Neolithisierung Mitteleuropas (The spread of the Neolithic to central Europe)*, 211–33. Mainz: Römisch-Germanisches Zentralmuseum.

Eisenhauer, U. 2003a. Matrilokalität in der Bandkeramik? Ein ethnologisches Modell und seine Implikationen. *Archäologische Informationen* 26, 321–31.

Eisenhauer, U. 2003b. Jüngerbandkeramische Residenzregeln: Patrilokalität in Talheim. In J. Eckert, U. Eisenhauer and A. Zimmermann (eds), *Archäologische Perspektiven: Analysen und Interpretationen im Wandel. Festschrift für Jens Lüning zum 65. Geburtstag*, 561–73. Rahden: Marie Leidorf.

Eisner, J. 1933. *Slovensko v pravěku*. Bratislava: Práce Ucené spolecnosti Safaríkovy v Bratislavě.

Ember, M. 1973. An archaeological indicator of matrilocal versus patrilocal residence. *American Antiquity* 38, 177–82.

Engelbrecht, T., Kühltrunk, P. and Ramminger, B. 2003. Neolithische Haartracht – alte Zöpfe? Rekonstruktionsversuch einer ältestbandkeramischen Frauenfrisur. *Archäologisches Korrespondenzblatt* 33, 317–23.

Engelhardt, B. 1991. Die Steinartefakte der Siedlung der ältesten Linienbandkeramik von Langenbach-Niederhummel. *Archäologie im Landkreis Freising* 2, 63–76.

Engelhardt, B. 1992. Eine Siedlung des älteren Neolithikums im Rottal bei Untergaiching, Stadt Pfarrkirchen. In K. Schmotz (ed.), *Vorträge des 10. Niederbayerischen Archäologentages*, 15–24. Buch am Erlbach: Marie Leidorf.

Engelhardt, B. 1995. Die Altheimer Feuchtbodensiedlung Ergolding-Fischergasse bei Landshut und ihr Hinterland. Die Entwicklung eines Kleinraumes von der Linienbandkeramik bis zum mittleren Spätneolithikum. In A. Aspes (ed.), *Settlement patterns between the Alps and the Black Sea, 5th to 2nd millennium B.C.: symposium Verona-Lazise 1992*, 233–49. Verona: Memorie del Museo Civico di Storia Naturale di Verona.

Engelhardt, B. 2006. Wie die Bayern Bauern wurden – Das Neolithikum (with contributions by S. Bück, J. Pechtl, K. Riedhammer, M. Rind, S. Scharl, W. Schier, S. Suhrbier and A. Tillmann). In Gesellschaft für Archäologie in Bayern (eds), *Archäologie: Fenster zur Vergangenheit in Bayern*, 54–75. Regensburg: Friedrich Pustet.

Engelhardt, B., Küster, H.-J. and Neumair, E. 1991. Letzte Nomaden und erste Siedler bei Langenbach/Niederhummel. *Archäologie im Landkreis Freising* 2, 43–63.

Engelhardt, B., Meixner, G. and Schaich, M. 1997. Linearbandkeramische Siedlung und Paläoböden von Aich, Gemeinde Altdorf, Landkreis Landshut, Niederbayern. *Das Archäologische Jahr in Bayern 1997*, 32–5.

Erny-Rodmann, C., Gross-Klee, E., Haas, J.N., Jacomet, S. and Zoller, H. 1997. Früher "human impact" und Ackerbau im Übergangsbereich Spätmesolithikum-Frühneolithikum im schweizerischen Mitteland. *Jahrbuch der Schweizerischen Gesellschaft für Ur- und Frühgeschichte* 80, 27–56.

Ericson, J.E. 1985. Strontium isotope characterization in the study of prehistoric human ecology. *Journal of Human Evolution* 14, 503–14.

Eshed, V., Gopher, A. and Hershkovitz, I. 2006. Tooth wear and dental pathology at the advent of agriculture: new evidence from the Levant. *American Journal of Physical Anthropology* 130, 145–59.

Evans, J.G. 2003. *Environmental archaeology and the social order.* London: Routledge.

Evershed, R.P., Payne, S., Sherratt, A.G., Copley, M.S., Coolidge, J., Urem-Kotsu, D., Kotsakis, K., Özdoğan, M., Nieuwenhuyse, O., Akkermans, P.M.M.G., Bailey, D.W., Andreescu, R.-R., Campbell, S., Farid, S., Hodder, I., Yalman, N., Özbaşaran, M., Biçakci, E., Garfinkel, Y., Levy, T. and Burton, M.M. 2008. Earliest date for milk use in the Near East and southeastern Europe linked to cattle herding. *Nature* 455, 528–31.

Fábián, S., Marton, T. and Oross, K. 2007. Újkőkori temetkezés Balatonszárszóról. In K. Belényesy, S. Honti and V. Kiss (eds), *Gördülő idő: Régészeti feltárások az M7-es autópálya Somogy megyei szakaszán Zamárdi és Ordacsehi között*, 90–2. Kaposvár and Budapest: Somogy Megyei Múzeumok Igazgatósága and MTA Régészeti Intézete.

Falys, C.G. and Lewis, M.E. 2011. Proposing a way forward: a review of standardisation in the use of age categories and ageing techniques in osteological analysis (2004–2009). *International Journal of Osteoarchaeology* 21, 704–16.

Farkaš, Z. 2002. Nálezy ľudských pozostatkov v prostredí kultúry ľudu s lineárnou keramikou na Slovensku (Human remains from the Linear Pottery culture area in Slovakia). *Archeologické rozhledy* 54, 23–43.

Farquhar, G.D., O'Leary, M.H. and Berry, J.A. 1982. On the relationship between carbon isotope discrimination and the intercellular carbon dioxide concentration in leaves. *Australian Journal of Plant Physiology* 9, 121–37.

Farruggia, J.-P. 1992. *Les outils et les armes en pierre dans le rituel funéraire du Néolithique danubien*. Oxford: Archaeopress.

Farruggia, J.-P. 2002. Une crise majeure de la civilisation du Néolithique danubien des années 5100 avant notre ère. *Archeologické rozhledy* 54, 44–98.

Farruggia, J.-P., Guichard, Y. and Hachem, L. 1996. Les ensembles funéraires rubanés de Menneville 'Derrière le village' (Aisne). *Revue Archéologique de l'Est*, supplément 14, 119–74.

Farruggia, J.-P., Kuper, R., Lüning, J. and Stehli, P. 1973. *Der bandkeramische Siedlungsplatz Langweiler 2, Gemeinde Aldenhoven, Kreis Düren*. Bonn: Habelt.

Fehlmann, D. 2011. *Die Knochen-, Zahn- und Geweihartefakte der linearbandkeramischen Siedlung Asparn an der Zaya-Schletz, Niederösterreich*. St. Pölten: NÖ Institut für Landeskunde.

Fibiger, L. 2010. *Heading for trouble: skeletal evidence for interpersonal violence in the Neolithic of northwestern Europe*. Unpublished DPhil thesis, University of Oxford.

Fibiger, L. 2012. Investigating cranial trauma in the German Wartberg culture. In R. Schulting and L. Fibiger (eds), *Sticks, stones, and broken bones: Neolithic violence in a European perspective*, 175–89. Oxford: Oxford University Press.

Fibiger, L. forthcoming. Misplaced childhood? Interpersonal

violence and children in Neolithic Europe. In M. Smith and C. Knüsel (eds), *A history of human conflict: osteology and 'traumatized bodies' from earliest prehistory to the present*. London: Routledge.

Fibiger, L. and Knüsel, C.J. 2005. Prevalence rates of *spondylolysis* in British skeletal populations. *International Journal of Osteoarchaeology* 15, 164–74.

Fielding, A. 2011. *Module 8: Multilevel modelling in practice: research questions, data preparation and analysis*. Bristol: ESRC National Centre for Research Methods, Learning Environment for Multilevel Methodology and Applications (http://www.cmm.bris.ac.uk/lemma/).

Fischer, A., Olsen, J., Richards, M., Heinemeier, J., Sveinbjörnsdóttir, Á.E. and Bennike, P. 2007. Coast-inland mobility and diet in the Danish Mesolithic and Neolithic: evidence from stable isotope values of humans and dogs. *Journal of Archaeological Science* 34, 2125–50.

Fischer, A.-L. 2011. Das Potential im Ries. *Bayerische Archäologie 2011*, Heft 1, 42–3.

Fischer, A.-L., Gehlen, B. and Richter, T. 2009. Zum Stand der Neolithisierungsforschung im östlichen Bayern: Fragestellungen, Fundstellen, Perspektiven. In M. Chytráček, H. Gruber, J. Michálek, R. Sandner and K. Schmotz (eds), *Fines Transire 18*, 45–78. Rahden: Marie Leidorf.

Fischer, U. 1956. *Die Gräber der Steinzeit im Saalegebiet*. Berlin: Walter De Gruyter.

Fishbein, L. 2004. Multiple sources of dietary calcium – some aspects of its essentiality. *Regulatory Toxicology and Pharmacology* 39, 67–80.

Fitz, J. and Makkay, J. (eds) 1972. *Die aktuellen Fragen der Bandkeramik*. Székesfehérvár: A Féjer Megyei Múzeumok Igazgatósága.

Forbes, H. 2007. *Meaning and identity in a Greek landscape: an archaeological ethnography*. Cambridge: Cambridge University Press.

Forrer, R. 1910. Neolithisches Dorf bei Hönheim-Souffelweyersheim. *Anzeiger für Elsässische Altertumskunde* 3–4, 45–50.

Forrer, R. 1938. Le cimetière néolithique de Lingolsheim à poterie poinçonnée, au crâne trépané et aux tombes de la zone rubanée. *Cahiers d'Archéologie et d'Histoire de l'Alsace* 11–16, 191–206.

Forrer, R. and Jaenger, F. 1918. Neolithisches Gräberfeld bei Hoenheim-Souffelweyersheim. *Anzeiger für Elsässische Altertumskunde* 33–6, 875–86.

Fortunato, L. 2011. Reconstructing the history of residence strategies in Indo-European-speaking societies: neo-, uxori-, and virilocality. *Human Biology* 83, 107–28.

Foxhall, L. 1995. Monumental ambitions: the significance of posterity. In N. Spencer (ed.), *Time, tradition and society in Greek archaeology: bridging the 'Great Divide'*, 132–49. London: Routledge.

Frank, C. 2009. Die Molluskenfunde. In E. Lenneis, *Rosenburg im Kamptal, Niederösterreich: ein Sonderplatz der älteren Linearbandkeramik*, 129–50. Bonn: Habelt.

Fraser, R.A., Bogaard, A., Heaton, T., Charles, M., Jones, G., Christensen, B.T., Halstead, P., Merbach, I., Poulton, P.R., Sparkes, D. and Styring, A.K. 2011. Manuring and stable nitrogen isotope ratios in cereals and pulses: towards a new archaeobotanical approach to the inference of land use and dietary practices. *Journal of Archaeological Science* 38, 2790–804.

Frayer, D.W. 2004. The dental remains from Krškany (Slovakia) and Vedrovice (Czech Republic). *Anthropologie* 42, 71–103.

Fredrickson, B.E., Baker, D., McHolick, W.J., Yuan, H.A. and Lubicky, J.P. 1984. The natural history of *spondylolysis* and *spondylolisthesis*. *Journal of Bone and Joint Surgery* 66A, 699–707.

Frei, H. and Krahe, G. 1988. *Archäologische Wanderungen im Ries. Führer zu archäologischen Denkmälern in Bayern. Schwaben. Band 2*. Stuttgart: Theiss.

Frenzel, B. 2002. Holocene climatic optimum: climates at about 7,000 to 6,500 YR BP. In B. Frenzel, M. Pécsi and A. Velichko (eds), *Atlas of paleoclimates and paleoenvironments of the northern hemisphere: late Pleistocene – Holocene*, 134–6. Budapest: Geographical Research Institute, Hungarian Academy of Sciences.

Freund, G. 1963. Die ältere und die mittlere Steinzeit in Bayern. *Jahresbericht der Bayerischen Bodendenkmalpflege* 4, 9–167.

Frickinger, E. 1934. Spiralkeramische Siedlung bei Nähermemmingen, B.A. Nördlingen. *Germania* 18, 252–7.

Frirdich, C. 1994. Kulturgeschichtliche Betrachtungen zur Bandkeramik im Merzbachtal. In. J. Lüning and P. Stehli (eds), *Die Bandkeramik im Merzbachtal auf der Aldenhovener Platte*, 207–393. Bonn: Habelt.

Frirdich, C. 2003. Strukturen im Wandel: ein bandkeramisches Gräberfeld entsteht. In J. Eckert, U. Eisenhauer and A. Zimmermann (eds), *Archäologische Perspektiven: Analysen und Interpretationen im Wandel. Festschrift für Jens Lüning zum 65. Geburtstag*, 545–59. Rahden: Marie Leidorf.

Frirdich, C. 2005. Struktur und Dynamik der bandkeramischen Landnahme. In J. Lüning, C. Frirdich and A. Zimmermann (eds), *Die Bandkeramik im 21. Jahrhundert. Symposium in der Abtei Brauweiler bei Köln vom 16.9.–19.9.2002*, 81–109. Rahden: Marie Leidorf.

Fritsch, B. 1987. Zwei bandkeramische Siedlungen im Hegau. *Archäologische Nachrichten aus Baden* 38/39, 10–17.

Fritsch, B. 1998. *Die linearbandkeramische Siedlung Hilzingen-Forsterbahnried und die altneolithische Besiedlung des Hegaus*. Rahden: Marie Leidorf.

Fritsch, B., Claßen, E., Müller, U. and Dresely, V. 2011. Die linienbandkeramischen Gräberfelder von Derenburg "Meerenstieg II" und Halberstadt "Sonntagsfeld", Ldkr. Harz. *Jahresschrift für Mitteldeutsche Vorgeschichte* 92, 25–229.

Froehle, A.W., Kellner, C.M. and Schoeninger, M.J. 2010. FOCUS: effect of diet and protein source on carbon stable isotope ratios in collagen: follow up to Warinner and Tuross (2009). *Journal of Archaeological Science* 37, 2662–70.

Froehle, A.W., Kellner, C.M. and Schoeninger, M.J. 2012. Multivariate carbon and nitrogen stable isotope model for the reconstruction of prehistoric human diet. *American Journal of Physical Anthropology* 147, 352–69.

Fuller, B., Fuller, J., Sage, N., Harris, D., O'Connell, T. and Hedges, R.E.M. 2004. Nitrogen balance and $\delta^{15}N$: why you're not what you eat during pregnancy. *Rapid Communications in Mass Spectrometry* 18, 2889–96.

Fuller, B., Fuller, J.L., Sage, N.E., Harris, D.A., O'Connell, T.C. and Hedges, R.E.M. 2005. Nitrogen balance and $\delta^{15}N$: why you're not what you eat during nutritional stress. *Rapid Communications in Mass Spectrometry* 19, 2497–506.

Galik, A. 2009. Die Fischreste. In E. Lenneis, *Rosenburg im Kamptal, Niederösterreich: ein Sonderplatz der älteren Linearbandkeramik*, 127. Bonn: Habelt.

Gallay, V.G. and Mathieu, G. 1988. Grabbeigaben der Bandkeramik von Ensisheim, Dép. Haut-Rhin (Elsaß). *Germania* 66, 371–89.

Ganslmeier, R. 2001. *Tierknochen aus jungsteinzeitlichen*

Siedlungen in Niederbayern (Altdorf, Sallmannsberg, Kirchamper, Köfering und Tiefbrunn) – Tiergräber und Tieropfer: ein Bericht zum gegenwärtigen Forschungsstand unter Benutzung neuerer Untersuchungen. Büchenbach: Dr. Faustus.

Gardner, A. 1999. The ecology of Neolithic environmental impacts – re-evaluation of existing theory using case studies from Hungary and Slovenia. *Documenta Praehistorica* 26, 163–83.

Garvey, M.T., Barry, H.J. and Blake, M. 1999. Supernumerary teeth – an overview of classification, diagnosis and management. *Journal of the Canadian Dental Association* 65, 612–16.

Geber, J. and Murphy, E. 2012. Scurvy in the great Irish famine: evidence of vitamin C deficiency from a mid-19th century skeletal population. *American Journal of Physical Anthropology* 148, 512–24.

Geertz, C. 1964. The transition to humanity. In S. Tax (ed.), *Horizons of anthropology*, 37–48. Chicago: Aldine.

Gehlen, B. 1995. Épipaléolithique, Mésolithique et Néolithique ancien dans les Basses-Alpes entre l'Iller et le Lech (sud-ouest de la Bavière). In A. Thévenin (ed.), *L'Europe des derniers chasseurs : Épipaléolithique et Mésolithique. Peuplement et paléoenvironnement de l'Épipaléolithique et du Mésolithique*, 489–97. Paris: CTHS.

Gehlen, B. 2006. Late Mesolithic – Proto-Neolithic – Initial Neolithic? Cultural and economic complexity in southwestern central Europe between 7000 and 5300 cal BC. In C.-J. Kind (ed.), *After the Ice Age: settlements, subsistence and social development in the Mesolithic of Central Europe*, 41–57. Stuttgart: Theiss.

Gehlen, B. 2010. *Innovationen und Netzwerke. Das Spätmesolithikum vom Forggensee (Südbayern) im Kontext des ausgehenden Mesolithikums und des Altneolithikums in der Südhälfte Europas*. Kerpen-Loogh: Welt und Erde.

Geislerová, K. 1992. Sídliště kultury s lineární keramikou v Drysicích, okr. Vyškov (Siedlung der Kultur mit Linearkeramik in Drysice, Bez. Vyškov). *Pravěk – Nová řada* 2, 5–21.

Gerhard, S. 2006. *Beiträge zur archäologischen Quellenkritik an Beispielen aus dem Neolithikum und der Frühbronzezeit Südbayerns*. Büchenbach: Faustus.

Gerhard, S. and Gohlisch, T. 1993. Altneolithische Fundplätze bei Landsberg a. Lech, Landkreis Landsberg a. Lech, Oberbayern. *Das Archäologische Jahr in Bayern 1992*, 34–5.

Gerhardt, K. and Gerhardt-Pfannenstiel, D. 1984/85. Schädel und Skelette der Linearbandkeramik von Mulhouse-Est (Rixheim) im Elsaß. *Acta Praehistorica et Archaeologica* 16/17, 55–90.

Gerling, C. 2006. *Das linienbandkeramische Gräberfeld von Schwetzingen, Rhein-Neckar-Kreis*. Unpublished M.A. dissertation, University of Würzburg.

Gerling, C. 2009. Schwetzingen, ein "reguläres" Gräberfeld der jüngeren Linearbandkeramik. In A. Zeeb-Lanz (ed.), *Krisen – Kulturwandel – Kontinuitäten: zum Ende der Bandkeramik in Mitteleuropa*, 103–10. Rahden: Marie Leidorf.

Gerling, C. 2012. Das linearbandkeramisches Gräberfeld von Schwetzingen, Rhein-Neckar-Kreis. *Fundberichte aus Baden-Württemberg* 32, 8–263.

Gerling, C. and Francken, M. 2007. Das linearbandkeramische Gräberfeld von Schwetzingen. *Archäologische Informationen* 30, 43–50.

Geyh, M.A. 2001. Bomb radiocarbon dating of animal tissue and hair. *Radiocarbon* 43, 723–30.

Gheorgiu, D. 2008. The emergence of pottery. In A. Jones (ed.), *Prehistoric Europe: theory and practice*, 164–92. Oxford: Blackwell.

Giblin, J. 2009. Strontium isotope analysis of Neolithic and Copper Age populations on the Great Hungarian Plain. *Journal of Archaeological Science* 36, 491–7.

Giblin, J. 2011. *Isotope analysis on the Great Hungarian Plain: an exploration of mobility and subsistence strategies from the Neolithic to the Copper Age*. Unpublished PhD thesis, Ohio State University.

Gläser, R. 1991. Bemerkungen zur absoluten Datierung des Beginns der westlichen Linienbandkeramik. *Banatica* 11, 53–64.

Gläser, R. 1993. *Die Linienbandkeramik in Transdanubien: Beiträge zu ihrer Chronologie und Entstehung*. Unpublished PhD dissertation, Ruprecht-Karls-Universität Heidelberg.

Goldman, G. 1978. Gesichtsgefässe und andere Menschendarstellungen aus Battonya. *A Békés Megyei Múzeumok Közleményei* 5, 13–60.

Golitko, M. and Keeley, L. 2006. Beating ploughshares back into swords: warfare in the Linearbandkeramik. *Antiquity* 81, 332–42.

Gonfiantini, R., Rozanski, K. and Stichler, W. 1990. Intercalibration of environmental isotope measurements: the program of the International Atomic Energy Agency. *Radiocarbon* 32, 369–74.

Goodman, A.H. and Rose, J.C. 1991. Dental enamel hypoplasias as indicators of nutritional status. In M.A. Kelley and C.S. Larsen (eds), *Advances in dental anthropology*, 279–93. New York: Wiley-Liss.

Goodman, A.H., Thomas, R.B., Swedlund, A.C. and Armelagos, G.J. 1988. Biocultural perspectives on stress in prehistoric, historic and contemporary population research. *Yearbook of Physical Anthropology* 31, 169–202.

Gosden, C. 1999. *Anthropology and archaeology: a changing relationship*. London: Routledge.

Gramsch, A. 2010. Different languages. An interview on archaeology in Germany with Friedrich Lüth. *Archaeological Dialogues* 17, 199–214.

Grauer, A.L. (ed.) 2012. *A companion to palaeopathology*. Chichester: Wiley-Blackwell.

Grinker, R.R. 1994. *Houses in the rainforest: ethnicity and inequality among farmers and foragers in central Africa*. Berkeley: University of California Press.

Groenendijk, H. 1992. Das Ödbachtal im niederbayerischen Gäuboden als Siedlungsraum im Alt-, Mittel- und beginnenden Jungneolithikum. *Analecta Praehistorica Leidensia* 25, 79–90.

Grömer, K. 2001. Neolithische Siedlung mit Lengyel-Grab in Leonding. Die Stellung Oberösterreichs im Früh- und Mittelneolithikum. *Jahrbuch des Oberösterreichischen Musealvereines* 146, 9–41.

Gronenborn, D. 1990. Mesolithic-Neolithic interactions – the lithic industry of the earliest Bandkeramik culture site at Friedberg-Bruchenbrücken, Wetteraukreis (west Germany). In P. M. Vermeersch (ed.), *Contributions to the Mesolithic in Europe*, 173–82. Leuven: Leuven University Press.

Gronenborn, D. 1997a. Sarching 4 und der Übergang vom Früh- zum Spätmesolithikum im südlichen Mitteleuropa. *Archäologisches Korrespondenzblatt* 27, 387–402.

Gronenborn, D. 1997b. *Silexartefakte der ältestbandkeramischen Kultur*. Bonn: Habelt.

Gronenborn, D. 1998. Ältestbandkeramische Kultur, La Hoguette, Limburg and ... what else? Contemplating the Mesolithic-

Neolithic transition in southern Central Europe. *Documenta Praehistorica* 25, 189–98.

Gronenborn, D. 1999. Variations on a basic theme: the transition to farming in southern central Europe. *Journal of World Prehistory* 13, 123–210.

Gronenborn, D. 2003. Der 'Jäger/Krieger' aus Schwanfeld. Einige Aspekte der politisch-sozialen Geschichte des mitteleuropäischen Altneolithikums. In J. Eckert, U. Eisenhauer and A. Zimmermann (eds), *Archäologische Perspektiven: Analysen und Interpretationen im Wandel. Festschrift für Jens Lüning zum 65. Geburtstag*, 35–48. Rahden: Marie Leidorf.

Gronenborn, D. 2007a. Climate change and sociopolitical crises: some cases from Neolithic central Europe. In T. Pollard and I. Banks (eds), *War and sacrifice: studies in the archaeology of conflict*, 13–32. Leiden and Boston: Brill.

Gronenborn, D. 2007b. Beyond the models: 'Neolithisation' in central Europe. In A. Whittle and V. Cummings (eds), *Going over: the Mesolithic-Neolithic transition in north-west Europe*, 73–98. Oxford: Oxford University Press for the British Academy.

Gronenborn, D. 2009a. Climate fluctuations and trajectories to complexity in the Neolithic: towards a theory. *Documenta Praehistorica* 36, 97–110.

Gronenborn, D. 2009b. Transregional culture contacts and the Neolithization process in northern central Europe. In P. Jordan and M. Zvelebil (eds), *Ceramics before farming: the dispersal of pottery among prehistoric Eurasian hunter-gatherers*, 527–50.Walnut Creek: Left Coast Press.

Gronenborn, D. 2010a. Climate, crises and the "neolithisation" of central Europe between IRD-events 6 and 4. In D. Gronenborn and J. Petrasch (eds), *Die Neolithisierung Mitteleuropas (The spread of the Neolithic to central Europe)*, 61–80. Mainz: Römisch-Germanisches Zentralmuseum.

Gronenborn, D. 2010b. Fernkontakte aus dem nördlichen Europa während der bandkeramischen Kultur. In P. Kalábková, B. Kovár, P. Pavúk and J. Šuteková (eds), *PANTA RHEI: studies in chronology and cultural development of South-Eastern and Central Europe in earlier prehistory presented to Juraj Pavúk on the occasion of his 75th birthday*, 561–74. Bratislava: Comenius University.

Gronenborn, D. and Petrasch, J. (eds) 2010. *Die Neolithisierung Mitteleuropas (The spread of the Neolithic to central Europe)*. Mainz: Römisch-Germanisches Zentralmuseum.

Gronwall, D. and Wrightson, P. 1974. Delayed recovery of intellectual function after minor head injury. *The Lancet* 304, 605–9.

Gruber, H. 2009. Das Neolithikum in Oberösterreich – ein Überblick zum Forschungsstand. In M. Chytráček, H. Gruber, J. Michálek, R. Sandner and K. Schmotz (eds), *Fines Transire 18*, 133–43. Rahden: Marie Leidorf.

Grupe, G., Price, T.D., Schröter, P., Söllner, F., Johnson, C. and Beard, B. 1997. Mobility of Bell Beaker people revealed by strontium isotope ratios of tooth and bone: a study of southern Bavarian skeletal remains. *Applied Geochemistry* 12, 517–25.

Grünberg, J. 2000. *Mesolithische Bestattungen in Europa: ein Beitrag zur vergleichenden Gräberkunde*. Rahden: Marie Leidorf.

Guéguen, L. and Pointillart, A. 2000. The bioavailability of dietary calcium. *Journal of the American College of Nutrition* 19, 119S–36S.

Gulder, A. 1953. Beitrage zur Kenntnis des niederösterreichischen Mesolithikums. *Archaeologia Austriaca* 12, 5–32.

Gulisano, G. 1994. Neue mittelsteinzeitliche Fundplätze im oberen Illertal und im Kleinwalsertal. *Archäologische Informationen* 17, 79–84.

Gulisano, G. 1995. Die Besiedlung des Kleinwalsertales und seiner angrenzenden Gebiete in Bayern und Voralberg von der Steinzeit bis zur Einwanderung der Walser. *Archäologische Informationen* 18, 53–65.

Gulyás, S., Tóth, A. and Sümegi, P. 2007. The zooarchaeological analysis of freshwater bivalve shells and their relevance regarding the life of a Neolithic community. In A. Whittle (ed.), *The early Neolithic on the Great Hungarian Plain: investigations of the Körös culture site of Ecsegfalva 23, County Békés*, 395–411. Budapest: Varia Archaeologica Hungarica.

Guy, H., Masset, C. and Baud, C.-A. 1997. Infant taphonomy. *International Journal of Osteoarchaeology* 7, 221–9.

Gyulai, F. 2007. Seed and fruit remains associated with Neolithic origins in the Carpathian Basin. In S. Colledge and J. Conolly (eds), *The origins and spread of domestic plants in south-west Asia*, 125–39. Walnut Creek: Left Coast Press.

Gyulai, F. 2010. Archaeobotanical research at the Körös culture site of Ibrány-Nagyerdő and its relationship to plant remains from contemporaneous sites in Hungary. In J.K. Kozłowski and P. Raczky (eds), *Neolithization of the Carpathian basin: northernmost distribution of the Starčevo/Körös culture*, 219–37. Kraków and Budapest: Polish Academy of Sciences and Institute of Archaeological Sciences of the Eötvös Loránd University.

Haack, F. 2008. Gewandknebel, Geweihknebel, Knochenknebel, Spondylusknebel – Zur Technologie, Typologie und Chronologie linienbandkeramischer Grabbeigaben. In F. Falkenstein, S. Schade-Lindig and A. Zeeb-Lanz (eds), *Kumpf, Kalotte, Pfeilschaftglätter: zwei Leben für die Archäologie. Gedenkschrift für Annemarie Häusser und Helmut Spatz*, 117–28. Rahden: Marie Leidorf.

Haack, F. 2009. Zur Komplexität der Verfüllungsprozesse der Grubenanlage von Herxheim: zwei Konzentrationen aus Menschenknochen, Keramik, Tierknochen und Steingeräten der Grabungen 2005 bis 2008. In A. Zeeb-Lanz (ed.), *Krisen – Kulturwandel – Kontinuitäten: zum Ende der Bandkeramik in Mitteleuropa*, 27–40. Rahden: Marie Leidorf.

Haak, W., Balanovsky, O., Sanchez, J.J., Koshel, S., Zaporozhchenko, V., Adler, C.J., Der Sarkissian, C.S.I., Brandt, G., Schwarz, C., Nicklisch, N., Dresely, V., Fritsch, B., Balanovska, E., Villems, R., Meller, H., Alt, K.W., Cooper, A. and the Genographic Consortium. 2010. Ancient DNA from European early Neolithic farmers reveals their Near Eastern affinities. *Public Library of Science Biology* 8:e1000536.

Haak, W., Brandt, G., de Jong, H.N., Meyer, C., Ganslmeier, R., Heyd, V., Hawkesworth, C., Pike, A.W.G, Meller, H. and Alt, K.W. 2008. Ancient DNA, strontium isotopes, and osteological analyses shed light on social and kinship organization of the Later Stone Age. *Proceedings of the National Academy of Sciences of the United States of America* 105, 18226 –31.

Haak, W., Forster, P., Bramanti, B., Matsumura, S., Brandt, G., Tänzer, M., Villems, R., Renfrew, C., Gronenborn, D., Alt, K.W. and Burger, J. 2005. Ancient DNA from the first European farmers in 7500-year-old Neolithic sites. *Science* 310, 1016–18.

Hachem, L. 1997. Structuration spatiale d'un village du Rubané récent, Cuiry-lès-Chaudardes (Aisne). Analyse d'une catégorie de rejets domestiques: la faune. In A. Bocquet (ed.), *Espaces physiques, espaces sociaux dans l'analyse interne des sites du Néolithique à l'Âge du Fer*, 245–61. Amiens: Centre des Travaux Historiques et Scientifiques.

Hachem, L. 1999. Apport de l'archéozoologie à la connaissance de l'organisation villageoise rubanée. In F. Braemer, S. Cleuziou and A. Coudart (eds), *Habitat et société. XIX Rencontres Internationales d'Archéologie et d'Histoire d'Antibes*, 325–38. Antibes: Éditions APDCA.

Hachem, L. 2000. New observations on the Bandkeramik house and social organization. *Antiquity* 74, 308–12.

Hachem, L. 2011. *Le site néolithique de Cuiry-lès-Chaudardes – I: de l'analyse de la faune à la structuration sociale.* Rahden: Marie Leidorf.

Haddon, A.C. 1920. Migrations of cultures in British New Guinea. *Journal of the Royal Anthropological Institute of Great Britain and Ireland* 50, 237–80.

Hagland, W.D. and Sorg, M.H. (eds) 2002. *Advances in forensic taphonomy: method, theory, and archaeological perspectives*. Boca Raton: CRC Press.

Hahn, J., Müller-Beck, H. and Taute, W. 1985. *Eiszeithöhlen im Lonetal. Archäologie einer Landschaft auf der Schwäbischen Alb.* Stuttgart: Theiss.

Hahnel, B. 1994. Frühneolithische Gräber in Österreich. *Fundberichte aus Österreich* 32, 107–28.

Haidle, M.N. 1997. *Mangel – Krisen – Hungersnöte? Ernährungszustände in Südwestdeutschland und der Nordschweiz vom Neolithikum bis ins 19. Jahrhundert.* Tübingen: Mo Vince.

Hajnalová, E. 1983. Paleobotanické neolitické nálezy zo Štúrova. *Slovenská archeológia* 30, 119–218.

Hajnalová, M. 2007. Early farming in Slovakia: an archaeobotanical perspective. In S. Colledge and J. Conolly (eds), *The origins and spread of domestic plants in south-west Asia*, 295–313. Walnut Creek: Left Coast Press.

Hajnalová, M. and Dreslerová, D. 2010. Ethnobotany of einkorn and emmer in Romania and Slovakia: towards interpretation of archaeological evidence. *Památky archeologické* 101, 169–202.

Halstead, P. 1989. Like rising damp? An ecological approach to the spread of farming in south-east and central Europe. In A. Milles, D. Williams and N. Gardner (eds), *The beginnings of agriculture*, 23–53. Oxford: Archaeopress.

Halstead, P. 2005. Resettling the Neolithic: faunal evidence for seasons of consumption and residence at Neolithic sites in Greece. In D. Bailey, A. Whittle and V. Cummings (eds), *(un)settling the Neolithic*, 38–50. Oxford: Oxbow Books.

Halstead, P. 2006. Sheep in the garden: the integration of crop and livestock husbandry in early farming regimes of Greece and southern Europe. In D. Serjeantson and D. Field (eds), *Animals in the Neolithic of Britain and Europe*, 42–55. Oxford: Oxbow Books.

Hamilton, J., Hedges, R.E.M. and Robinson, M.A. 2009. Rooting for pigfruit: pig feeding in Neolithic and Iron Age Britain compared. *Antiquity* 83, 998–1011.

Händel, M., Simon, U., Einwögerer, T. and Neugebauer-Maresch, C. 2009. Loess deposits and the conservation of the archaeological record – The Krems-Wachtberg example. *Quarternary International* 198, 46–50.

Handler, R. 2003. Cultural property and culture theory. *Journal of Social Archaeology* 3, 353–65.

Handley, L.L. and Raven, J.A. 1992. The use of natural abundance of nitrogen isotopes in plant physiology and ecology. *Plant, Cell and Environment* 15, 965–85.

Hanöffner, A. and Siftar, L. 2007. Die Ausgrabungen in Ödmühle, Gemeinde Aiterhofen, Lkr. Straubing-Bogen 1975–1980. *Historischer Verein für Straubing und Umgebung, Jahresbericht* 108, 31–277.

Hansen, S. 2007. *Bilder vom Menschen der Steinzeit: Untersuchungen zur anthropomorphen Plastik der Jungsteinzeit und Kupferzeit in Südosteuropa.* Mainz: Philipp von Zabern.

Hardt, N. and Kuttenberger, J. 2010. *Craniofacial trauma: diagnosis and management.* New York: Springer.

Hargreaves, G. and Samani, Z. 1983. *Rainfed agriculture in Haiti (a practical manual).* Logan (Utah): International Irrigation Centre, Department of Agricultural and Irrigation Engineering.

Harrer, A. and Lenneis, E. 2001. Die ersten Nachweise der älteren Linearbandkeramik und andere wichtige Neufunde des Frühneolithikums aus dem Raum Melk, Niederösterreich. *Archäologie Österreichs* 12, 31–8.

Harris, O.J.T. 2012. (Re)assembling communities. *Journal of Archaeological Method and Theory* online 26 June 2012, DOI 10.1007/s10816-012-9138-3.

Harris, O.J.T. forthcoming. Relational communities in prehistoric Britain. In C. Watts (ed.), *Relational archaeologies*. London: Routledge.

Harrison, S. 1995. Transformations of identity in Sepik warfare. In M. Strathern (ed.), *Shifting contexts: transformations in anthroplogical knowledge*, 81–97. London: Routledge.

Hartman, G. and Danin, A. 2010. Isotopic values of plants in relation to water availability in the Eastern Mediterranean region. *Oecologia* 162, 837–52.

Harzhauser, M., Lenneis, E. and Neugebauer-Maresch, C. 2007. Freshwater gastropods as Neolithic adornment: size selectiveness and perforation morphology as a result of grinding techniques. *Annalen des Naturhistorischen Museums Wien, Serie A* 109, 73–85.

Hatté, C., Fontugne, M., Rousseau, D.-D., Antoine, P., Zöller, L., Tisnérat-Laborde, N. and Bentaleb, I. 1998. $\delta^{13}C$ variations of loess organic matter as a record of the vegetation response to climatic changes during the Weichselian. *Geology* 26, 583–6.

Häusler, A. 1964. Übereinstimmungen zwischen den Bestattungssitten von Jäger- und Fischergruppen und der Kulturen des donauländischen Kreises. *Arbeits- und Forschungsberichte zur Sächsischen Bodendenkmalpflege* 13, 51–72.

Häusler, A. 1994. Grab- und Bestattungssitten des Neolithikums und der frühen Bronzezeit in Mitteleuropa. *Zeitschrift für Archäologie* 28, 23–61.

Häusler, A. 2000. Zu den Kulturbeziehungen Südosteuropas im Neolithikum und Äneolithikum im Lichte der Bestattungssitten. *Germania* 78, 319–54.

Hauzeur, A. 2007. Matières premières et styles céramiques: déconnexions entre réseaux économiques et culturels au Rubané: le cas de la Moselle luxembourgeoise. In F. Le Brun-Ricalens, F. Valotteau and A. Hauzeur (eds), *Relations interrégionales au Néolithique entre Bassin parisien et Bassin rhénan*, 65–78. Luxembourg: Faber.

Havlíček, P., Holásek, O., Smolíková, L. and Roetzel, R. 1998. Zur Entwicklung der Quartärsedimente am Südostrand der Böhmischen Masse in Niederösterreich. *Jahrbuch des Geologischen Bundesanstalt* 141, 51–71.

Heaney, R.P. 2009. Dairy and bone health. *Journal of the American College of Nutrition* 28, 82S–90S.

Heaton, T.H.E. 1999. Spatial, species, and temporal variations in the $^{13}C/^{12}C$ ratios of C3 plants: implications for palaeodiet studies. *Journal of Archaeological Science* 26, 637–49.

Heberer, G. 1939. Die mitteldeutschen Bandkeramiker. *Mitteldeutsche Volkheit* 6, 98–107.

Hedges, R.E.M. 2003. On bone collagen – apatite–

carbonate isotopic relationships. *International Journal of Osteoarchaeology* 13, 66–79.

Hedges, R.E.M. and Reynard, L.M. 2007. Nitrogen isotopes and the trophic level of humans in archaeology. *Journal of Archaeological Science* 34, 1240–51.

Hedges, R.E.M. and van Klinken, G.J. 1992. A review of current approaches in the pretreatment of bone for radiocarbon dating by AMS. *Radiocarbon* 34, 279–91.

Hedges, R.E.M., Clement, J.G.C., Thomas, D.L. and O'Connell, T.C. 2007. Collagen turnover in the adult femoral mid-shaft: modeled from anthropogenic radiocarbon tracer measurements. *American Journal of Physical Anthropology* 133, 808–16.

Hegedűs, K. 1985. The settlement of the Neolithic Szakálhát-group at Csanytelek-Újhalastó. *A Móra Ferenc Múzeum Évkönyve* 1982/83, 7–54.

Hegedűs, K. and Makkay, J. 1987. Vésztő-Mágor. In L. Tálas and P. Raczky (eds), *The Late Neolithic of the Tisza region*, 93–111. Budapest and Szolnok: Kossuth Kiadó.

Heide, B. 2001. *Das ältere Neolithikum im westlichen Kraichgau*. Rahden: Marie Leidorf.

Heintz, G.F. 1981. Tombe 'rubanée' fouillée en 1943 à Souffelweyersheim. *Cahiers Alsaciens d'Archéologie, d'Art et d'Histoire* 24, 11–13.

Heller, K. 2005. Das bandkeramische Gräberfeld von Inden-Altdorf. In H. Hellenkemper, H.G. Horn, G. Isenberg and J. Kunow (eds), *Von Anfang an: Archäologie in Nordrhein-Westfalen. Katalog-Handbuch zur Ausstellung 11.3.–28.8.2005 in Köln, Römisch-Germanisches Museum*, 336–7. Mainz: Philipp von Zabern.

Helliwell, C. 1996. Space and sociality in a Dayak longhouse. In M. Jackson (ed.), *Things as they are: new directions in phenomenological anthropology*, 128–48. Bloomington and Indianapolis: Indiana University Press.

Henderson, J. 1987. Factors determining the state of preservation of human remains. In A. Boddington, A.N. Garland and R.C. Janaway (eds), *Death, decay and reconstruction: approaches to archaeology and forensic science*, 43–54. Manchester: Manchester University Press.

Herren, B. 2003. *Die alt- und mittelneolithische Siedlung von Harting-Nord, Kr. Regensburg/Oberpfalz: Befunde und Keramik aus dem Übergangshorizont zwischen Linearbandkeramik und südostbayerischem Mittelneolithikum (SOB)*. Bonn: Habelt.

Herrmann, B., Grupe, G., Hummel, S., Piepenbrink, H. and Schutkowski, H. 1990. *Prähistorische Anthropologie: Leitfaden der Feld- und Labormethoden*. Heidelberg: Springer.

Hershkovitz, I., Bedford, L., Jellema, L.M. and Latimer, B. 1996. Injuries to the skeleton due to prolonged activity in hand-to-hand combat. *International Journal of Osteoarchaeology* 6, 167–78.

Hershkovitz, I., Donoghue, H.D., Minnikin, D.E., Besra, G.S., Lee, O.Y.C., Gernaey, A.M., Galili, E., Eshed, V., Greenblatt, C.L., Lemma, E., Bar-Gal, G.K. and Spigelman, M. 2008. Detection and molecular characterization of 9000-year-old Mycobacterium tuberculosis from a Neolithic settlement in the eastern Mediterranean. *PLoS ONE* 3, e3426.

Hertelendi, E., Kalicz, N., Horváth, F., Veres, M., Suingor, É., Futó, É. and Bartosiewicz, L. 1995. Re-evaluation of the Neolithic in eastern Hungary based on the calibrated radiocarbon dates. *Radiocarbon* 37, 239–45.

Hertelendi, E., Suingor, É., Raczky, P., Horváth, F., Futó, É., Bartosiewicz, L. and Molnár, M. 1998. Radiocarbon chronology of the Neolithic and timespan of tell settlements in eastern Hungary based on calibrated radiocarbon dates. In L. Kolto and L. Bartosiewicz (eds), *Archaeometrical research in Hungary II*, 61–9. Budapest, Kaposvár and Veszprém: Hungarian National Museum, Somogy Museum and Veszprém HAS.

Hill, J. 1970. *Broken K Pueblo: prehistoric social organization in the American Southwest*. Tucson: Anthropological Papers of the University of Arizona.

Hill, P.A. 1998. Bone remodeling. *British Journal of Orthodontics* 25, 101–7.

Hillemeyer, E.-M. 1989. Die linearbandkeramische Siedlung von Wang, Landkreis Freising, Oberbayern. *Das Archäologische Jahr in Bayern 1989*, 25–6.

Hillemeyer, E.-M. 2003. *Die Tonware der ältesten Bandkeramik in Wang, Landkreis Freising*. Bonn: Habelt.

Hillen, R.J., Burger, B.J., Pöll, R.G., Gast, A.D. and Robinson, C.M. 2010. Malunion after midshaft clavicle fractures in adults. *Acta Orthopaedica* 81, 273–9.

Hillson, S. 1996. *Dental anthropology*. Cambridge: Cambridge University Press.

Hillson, S. 2001. Recording dental caries in archaeological human remains. *International Journal of Osteoarchaeology* 11, 249–89.

Hillson, S. 2005. *Teeth*. Cambridge: Cambridge University Press.

Hirata, T., Tanoshima, M., Suga, A., Tanaka, Y.K., Nagata, Y., Shinohara, A. and Chiba, M. 2008. Isotopic analysis of calcium in blood plasma and bone from mouse samples by multiple collector-ICP-mass spectrometry. *Analytical Sciences* 24, 1501–7.

Hladilová, Š. 2002. Výsledky paleontologického studia ozdob z lokality Vedrovice (Ergebnisse paläontologischen Studiums der Verzierungen aus der Lokalität Vedrovice). In V. Podborský, *Dvě pohřebiště neolitického lidu s lineární keramikou ve Vedrovicích na Moravě*, 257–64. Brno: Ústav archeologie a muzeologie, Filozofická fakulta Masarykovy univerzity.

Ho, S.C., Leung, P.C., Swaminathan, R., Chan, C., Chan, S.S.G., Fan, Y.K. and Lindsay, R. 1994. Determinants of bone mass in Chinese women aged 21–40 years. II. Pattern of dietary calcium intake and association with bone mineral density. *Osteoporosis International* 4, 167–75.

Höckmann, O. 1982. Zur Verteilung von Männer- und Frauengräbern auf Gräberfeldern des Frühneolithikums und des älteren Mittelneolithikums. *Jahrbuch des Römisch-Germanischen Zentralmuseums Mainz* 29, 13–74.

Hodder, I. 1982. *Symbols in action: ethnoarchaeological studies of material culture*. Cambridge: Cambridge University Press.

Hodder, I. and Cessford, C. 2004. Daily practice and social memory at Çatalhöyük. *American Antiquity* 69, 17–40.

Högberg, P. 1997. Tansley Review No. 95: ^{15}N natural abundance in soil-plant systems. *New Phytologist* 137, 179–203.

Hoffmann, E. 1989. Die Anfänge des Brandritus – Versuch einer Deutung. In F. Schlette and D. Kaufmann (eds), *Religion und Kult in ur- und frühgeschichtlicher Zeit*, 99–110. Berlin: Akademie-Verlag.

Hofmann, D. 2006. *Being Neolithic: life, death and transformation in Neolithic Lower Bavaria*. Unpublished PhD thesis, Cardiff University.

Hofmann, D. 2009a. Cemetery and settlement burial in the Lower Bavarian LBK. In D. Hofmann and P. Bickle (eds), *Creating communities: new advances in central European Neolithic research*, 220–34. Oxford: Oxbow Books.

Hofmann, D. 2009b. Noch mehr Häuser für die Bandkeramik: neue Grabungen in Niederhummel und Wang, Landkreis Freising. In M. Chytráček, H. Gruber, J. Michálek, R. Sandner and K. Schmotz (eds), *Fines Transire 18*, 181–94. Rahden: Marie Leidorf.

Hofmann, D. 2010. Soziale Beziehungen und Verwandtschaft in der Bandkeramik: Struktur oder Flexibilität? In E. Claßen, T. Doppler and B. Ramminger (eds), *Familie – Verwandtschaft – Sozialstrukturen: Sozialarchäologische Forschungen zu neolithischen Befunden*, 31–42. Kerpen-Loogh: Welt und Erde.

Hofmann, D. forthcoming. *Longhouse people: life, death and transformation in the early Neolithic Linearbandkeramik culture of central Europe*. Oxford: Oxford University Press.

Hofmann, D. and Bickle, P. (eds) 2009. *Creating communities: new advances in central European Neolithic research.* Oxford: Oxbow Books.

Hofmann, D. and Bickle, P. 2011. Culture, tradition and the settlement burials of the *Linearbandkeramik* (LBK) culture. In B.W. Roberts and M. Vander Linden (eds), *Investigating archaeological cultures: material culture, variability, and transmission*, 183–200. New York: Springer.

Hofmann, D. and Orschiedt, J. forthcoming. Mortuary practices, bodies and persons in central Europe. In C. Fowler, J. Harding and D. Hofmann (eds), *The Oxford Handbook of Neolithic Europe*. Oxford: Oxford University Press.

Hofmann, D. and Whittle, A. 2008. Neolithic bodies. In A. Jones (ed.), *Prehistoric Europe: theory and practice*, 287–311. Oxford: Blackwell.

Hofmann, D. and Whittle, A. 2011. Häuser, Gruben, Bienenwachs: das tägliche Leben der ersten Bauern. Neue Untersuchungen in Niederhummel und Freising. *Archäologie im Landkreis Freising* 11, 45–64.

Hofmann, D., Bentley, A., Bickle, P., Bogaard, A., Crowther, J., Cullen, P., Fibiger, L., Grupe, G., Hamilton, J., Hedges, R.E.M., Macphail, R., Nowell, G., Pechtl, J., Salque, M., Schultz, M. and Whittle, A. 2012. Kinds of diversity and scales of analysis in the LBK. In S. Wolfram, H. Stäuble, M. Cladders and T. Tischendorf (eds), *Siedlungsstruktur und Kulturwandel in der Bandkeramik. Beiträge der internationalen Tagung "Neue Fragen zur Bandkeramik oder alles beim Alten?!" Leipzig, 23. bis 24. September 2010*, 107–17. Leipzig: Landesamt für Archäologie.

Hofmann, R. 1983/84. Die vegetabilischen vor- und frühgeschichtlichen Funde aus Niederbayern und der Oberpfalz südlich der Donau im Rahmen der Siedelgeschichte. Ein Beitrag zur Aussagefähigkeit der Paläo-Ethnobotanik. *Berichte der Bayerischen Bodendenkmalpflege* 24/25, 112–56.

Holden, C.J. 2002. Bantu language trees reflect the spread of farming across sub-Saharan Africa: a maximum-parsimony analysis. *Proceedings of the Royal Society B* 269, 793–9.

Holden, C. and Mace, R. 2003. Spread of cattle led to the loss of matrilineal descent in Africa: a coevolutionary analysis. *Proceedings of the Royal Society B* 270, 2425–33.

Holden, C.J., Sear, R. and Mace, R. 2003. Matriliny as daughter-biased investment. *Evolution and Human Behavior* 24, 99–112.

Holt, C. 1982. Inorganic constituents of milk. III. The colloidal calcium phosphate of cow's milk. *Journal of Dairy Research* 49, 29–38.

Horváth, F. 1989. A survey on the development of Neolithic settlement pattern and house types in the Tisza region. In S. Bökönyi (ed.), *Neolithic of southeastern Europe and its Near Eastern connections*, 85–96. Budapest: Akadémiai Kiadó.

Horváth, L. 2002. Neolithische Funde und Befunde in der Gemarkung von Dunakeszi. *Acta Archaeologica Academiae Scientiarum Hungaricae* 53, 1–40.

Horváth, L. 2004. Angaben zu den Haustypen des mittleren Neolithikums in Ungarn. *Antaeus* 27, 87–93.

Howland, M.R., Corr, L.T., Young, S.M.M., Jones, V., Jim, S., Van Der Merwe, N. J., Mitchell, A.D. and Evershed, R.P. 2003. Expression of the dietary isotope signal in the compound-specific $\delta^{13}C$ values of pig bone lipids and amino acids. *International Journal of Osteoarchaeology* 13, 54–65.

Hoyer, W. 2010. Das bandkeramische Gräberfeld Niedermerz 3 und die Siedlungen im mittleren Merzbachtal. In E. Claßen, T. Doppler and B. Ramminger (eds), *Familie–Verwandtschaft–Sozialstrukturen: sozialarchäologische Forschungen zu neolithischen Befunden*, 43–51. Kerpen-Loogh: Welt und Erde.

Hugh-Jones, C. 1996. Houses in the Neolithic imagination: an Amazonian example. In T. Darvill and J. Thomas (eds), *Neolithic houses in northwest Europe and beyond*, 185–93. Oxford: Oxbow Books.

Hugh-Jones, S. 1995. Inside-out and back-to-front: the androgynous house in northwest Amazonia. In J. Carsten and C. Hugh-Jones (eds), *About the house: Lévi-Strauss and beyond*, 226–52. Cambridge: Cambridge University Press.

Hrdy, S.B. 2009. *Mothers and others*. Cambridge, MA: Harvard University Press.

Hunt, H.V., van der Linden, M., Liu, X., Motuzaite-Matuzeviciute, G., Colledge, S. and Jones, M.K. 2008. Millets across Eurasia: chronology and context of early records of the genera *Panicum* and *Setaria* from archaeological sites in the Old World. *Vegetation History and Archaeobotany* 17, 5–18.

Hurrell, R.F., Reddy, M.B., Juillerat, M.A. and Cook, J.D. 2003. Degradation of phytic acid in cereal porridges improves iron absorption by human subjects. *American Journal of Clinical Nutrition* 77, 1213–19.

Husty, L. 1999. Ein außergewöhnliches Steinbeildepot aus der linearbandkeramischen Siedlung von Adldorf-Kreuzäcker, Gem. Eichendorf, Lkr. Dingolfing-Landau. *Jahrbuch des Historischen Vereins für Straubing und Umgebung* 101, 27–109.

Ilett, M. and Constantin, C. 1993. Rubané récent du Bassin parisien et Rubané récent du Haut-Rhin. In *Le Néolithique du Nord-Est de la France et ses relations avec les régions rhénanes et mosanes*, 94–9. Paris: Maison des Sciences de l'Homme.

Ilett, M., Constantin, C., Coudart, A. and Demoule, J.-P. 1982. The late Bandkeramik of the Aisne valley: environment and spatial organisation. *Analecta Praehistorica Leidensia* 15, 45–61.

Ihmig, M. 1971. Untersuchungen an einem bandkeramischen Gräberfeld bei Niedermerz, Kr. Jülich. *Germania* 49, 175–9.

Ingold, T. 1994. From trust to domination: an alternative history of human-animal relations. In A. Manning and J. Serpell (eds), *Animals and human society: changing perspectives*, 1–22. London: Routledge.

Ingold, T. (ed.) 1996a. *Key debates in anthropology*. London: Routledge.

Ingold, T. 1996b. Against the motion (1). In T. Ingold (ed.), *Key debates in anthropology*, 112–18. London: Routledge.

Ingold, T. 1996c. Hunting and gathering as ways of perceiving the environment. In R. Ellen and K. Fukui (eds), *Redefining nature: ecology, culture and domestication*, 117–55. Oxford: Berg.

Ingold, T. 2000. *The perception of the environment: essays in livelihood, dwelling and skill.* London: Routledge.

Ingold, T. 2011. *Being alive: essays on movement, knowledge and description.* London: Routledge.

Itan, Y., Powell, A., Beaumont, M.A., Burger, J. and Thomas, M.G. 2009. The origins of lactase persistence in Europe. *PLoS Computational Biology* 5, 1–13.

Jackes, M., Lubell, D. and Meiklejohn, C. 1997. Healthy but mortal: human biology and the first farmers of western Europe. *Antiquity* 71, 639–58.

Jacobi, F. and Engelbrecht, T. 2006. Eine ältestbandkeramische Siedlungsbestattung aus Friedberg-Bruchenbrücken. Anthropologische Untersuchung. *Hessen Archäologie 2006*, 19–22.

Jacomet, S. 2007. Neolithic plant economies in the northern Alpine Foreland from 5500–3500 cal BC. In S. Colledge and J. Conolly (eds), *The origins and spread of domestic plants in south-west Asia*, 221–58. Walnut Creek: Left Coast Press.

Jacomet, S. and Kreuz, A. 1999. *Archäobotanik: Aufgaben, Methoden und Ergebnisse vegetations- und agrargeschichtlicher Forschung*. Stuttgart: Ulmer.

Jankovich, B.D., Makkay, J. and Szőke, B.M. 1989. *Magyarország Régészeti Topográfiája: a Szarvasi járás IV/2*. Budapest: Akadémiai Kiadó.

Jankovich, B.D., Medgyesi, B.-P., Nikolin, E., Szatmári, I. and Torma, I. 1998. *Békés megye Régészeti Topográfiája. Békés és Békéscsaba környéke IV/3. Magyarország Régészeti Topográfiája 10*. Budapest: Akadémiai Kiadó.

Janz, H. and Vennemann, T.W. 2005. Isotopic composition (O, C, Sr, and Nd) and trace element ratios (Sr/Ca, Mg/Ca) of Miocene marine and brackish ostracods from North Alpine Foreland deposits (Germany and Austria) as indicators for palaeoclimate. *Palaeogeography, Palaeoclimatology, Palaeoecology* 225, 216–47.

Jarošová, I. 2008. Dietary inferences using buccal microwear analysis on the LBK population from Vedrovice, Czech Republic. *Anthropologie* 46, 175–84.

Jarošová, I. and Dočkalová, M. 2008. Dental remains from the Neolithic settlements in Moravia, Czech Republic. *Anthropologie* 46, 77–101.

Jelínek, J. 1975. Middle neolithic anthropological finds from Štúrovo, south Slovakia. *Anthropologie* 13, 183–92.

Jeunesse, C. 1980. Le peuplement rubané de la Basse-Alsace: aspects géographiques. In A. Thévenin and J.-P. Thévenot (eds), *Le Rubané d'Alsace et de Lorraine: état des recherches 1979*, 85–101. Strasbourg : Association d'Études Prehistoriques et Protohistoriques d'Alsace.

Jeunesse, C. 1986. Rapports avec le Néolithique ancien d'Alsace de la céramique danubienne de La Hoguette (à Fontenay-le-Marmion, Calvados). *Revue Archéologique de l'Ouest*, supplément 1, 41–50.

Jeunesse, C. 1987. La céramique de La Hoguette: un nouvel 'élément non-rubané' du Néolithique ancien de l'Europe du Nord-Ouest. *Cahiers Alsaciens d'Archéologie, d'Art et d'Histoire* 26, 5–33.

Jeunesse, C. 1990a. Habitats rubanés en grottes et abris-sous-roche. Contribution à l'étude des systèmes de subsistence de la Culture à Céramique Linéaire. In D. Cahen and M. Otte (eds), *Rubané et Cardial. Actes du colloque de Liège, novembre 1988*, 231–7. Liège: Université de Liège.

Jeunesse, C. 1990b. Le Néolithique alsacien et ses relations avec les régions voisines. In M. Höneisen (ed.), *Die ersten Bauern. Pfahlbaubefunde Europas. Band 2: Einführung, Balkan und angrenzende Regionen der Schweiz*, 177–94. Zürich: Schweizerisches Landesmuseum Zürich.

Jeunesse, C. 1991. Un nouvel habitat néolithique et protohistorique à Rosheim. *Cahiers de l'Association pour la Promotion de la Recherche Archéologique en Alsace* 7, 81–99.

Jeunesse, C. 1993. *Recherches sur le Néolithique danubien du sud de la plaine du Rhin supérieur et du nord de la Franche-Comté*. Unpublished PhD thesis, University of Strasbourg.

Jeunesse, C. 1995a. Les groupes régionaux occidentaux du Rubané (Rhin et Bassin parisien) à travers les pratiques funéraires. *Gallia Préhistoire* 37, 115–54.

Jeunesse, C. 1995b. Les rélations entre l'Alsace et le Bassin parisien au Néolithique ancien vues à travers l'étude des pratiques funéraires. *Revue Archéologique de l'Ouest*, supplément 7, 13–20.

Jeunesse, C. 1995c. Contribution à l'étude de la variabilité régionale au sein du Rubané: l'exemple du sud de la plaine du Rhin supérieur. *Cahiers de l'Association pour la Promotion de la Recherche Archéologique en Alsace* 11, 1–22.

Jeunesse, C. 1996. Variabilité des pratiques funéraires et différenciation sociale dans le Néolithique ancien danubien. *Gallia Préhistoire* 38, 249–86.

Jeunesse, C. 1997. *Pratiques funéraires au Néolithique ancien: sépultures et nécropoles danubiennes 5500–4900 av. J.-C.* Paris: Éditions Errance.

Jeunesse, C. 1998. La néolithisation de l'Europe occidentale (VIIe-VIe millénaires av. J.C.): nouvelles perspectives. In C. Cupillard and A. Richard (eds), *Les derniers chasseurs-cueilleurs du massif jurassien et de ses marges (13500–5500 avant Jésus-Christ)*, 208–17. Lons-le-Saunier: Centre Jurassien du Patrimoine.

Jeunesse, C. 1999. La sychronisation des séquences culturelles des bassins du Rhin, de la Meuse et de la Seine et la chronologie du Bassin parisien au Néolithique ancien et moyen (5200–4500 av. J. C.). *Bulletin de la Société Préhistorique Française* 20–1, 337–92.

Jeunesse, C. 2000a. Les composantes autochtones et danubiennes en Europe centrale et occidentale entre 5500 et 4000 av. J.-C.: contacts, transferts, acculturations. In A. Richard, C. Cupillard, H. Richard and A. Thévenin (eds), *Les derniers chasseurs-cueilleurs d'Europe occidentale (13000–5500 av. J.-C.): actes du colloque international de Besançon*, 361–78. Besançon: University of Besançon.

Jeunesse, C. 2000b. Ensembles mixtes et faciès de transition: contribution á la chronologie du Néolithique ancien du Bassin parisien. *Actes du Congrès National des Sociétés Historiques et Scientifiques* 125, 429–47.

Jeunesse, C. 2001. Les ensembles mixtes et la synchronisation des séquences régionales au sein du Néolithique danubien: la liaison Rhin-Bassin parisien. *Archeologické rozhledy* 54, 114–28.

Jeunesse, C. 2002a. Armatures asymétriques, régionalisation, acculturation: contribution à l'étude de la relation entre le Rubané et la composante autochtone dans l'ouest de la sphère danubienne. In M. Otte and J.K. Kozłowski (eds), *Préhistoire de la Grande Plaine du nord de l'Europe*, 147–65. Liège: ERAUL 99.

Jeunesse, C. 2002b. Tombes doubles, tombes symboliques et incinérations. In C. Jeunesse (ed.), *Vendenheim 'Le Haut du Coteau': une nécropole du Néolithique ancien. Document final de synthèse. Tome 1: texte*, 165–71. Strasbourg: Service Régional de l'Archéologie d'Alsace, unpublished document.

Jeunesse, C. 2002c. La coquille et la dent: parure de coquillage et évolution des systèmes symboliques dans le Néolithique danubien (5600–4500 BC). In J. Guilaine (ed.), *Matériaux, productions, circulations du Néolithique à l'Âge du Bronze*, 49–64. Paris: Éditions Errance.

Jeunesse, C. (ed.) 2002d. *Vendenheim 'Le Haut du Coteau': une nécropole du Néolithique ancien. Document final de synthèse. Tome 1: texte*, 141–2. Strasbourg: Service Régional de l'Archéologie d'Alsace, unpublished document.

Jeunesse, C. 2003a. Les pratiques funéraires du Néolithique ancien danubien et l'identité rubanée: découvertes récentes, nouvelles tendances de la recherche. In P. Chambon and J. Leclerc (eds), *Les pratiques funéraires néolithiques avant 3500 av. J.-C. en France et dans les régions limitrophes. Saint-Germain-en-Laye 15–17 juin 2001*, 19–32. Paris: Société Préhistorique Française.

Jeunesse, C. 2003b. Néolithique 'initial', Néolithique ancien et néolithisation dans l'espace centre-européen: une vision rénovée. *Revue d'Alsace* 129, 97–112.

Jeunesse, C. 2004. Les traditions funéraires du Néolithique moyen en Europe centrale dans le cadre du système funéraire danubien. *Cahiers de l'Association pour la Promotion de la Recherche Archéologique en Alsace* 20, 3–26.

Jeunesse, C. 2005. Nouvelles données sur la nécropole du Néolithique ancien de Quatzenheim (Bas-Rhin). *Cahiers Alsaciens d'Archéologie, d'Art et d'Histoire* 48, 5–30.

Jeunesse, C. 2006. Les traditions funéraires du Néolithique moyen en Europe centrale dans le cadre du système funéraire danubien. In K.W. Alt, R.-M. Arbogast, C. Jeunesse and S. van Willigen (eds), *Archéologie funéraire du Néolithique danubien: nouveaux enjeux, nouvelles approches. Actes de la table ronde de Fribourg-en-Brisgau, 17, 18 octobre 1998*, 3–26. Zimmersheim: Association pour la Promotion de la Recherche Archéologique en Alsace.

Jeunesse, C. 2009. Le front colonisation occidental (entre Rhin et Seine) et l'identité rubanée: réflexion sur les systèmes symboliques dans le Néolithique danubien. In J. Kozłowski (ed.), *Interactions between different models of neolithization north of the central European agro-ecological barrier*, 151–76. Krakow: Polska Akademia Umiejętności.

Jeunesse, C. and Lefranc, P. 1999. Rosheim 'Sainte-Odile'(Bas-Rhin), un habitat rubané avec fossé d'enceinte – première partie: les structures et la céramique. *Cahiers de l'Association pour la Promotion de la Recherche Archéologique en Alsace* 15, 1–111.

Jeunesse, C. and Sainty, J. 1991. Bischoffsheim 'le village' (Bas-Rhin). Un habitat rubané avec céramique de La Hoguette. *Cahiers de l'Association pour la Promotion de la Recherche Archéologique en Alsace* 7, 15–58.

Jeunesse, C. and Sainty, J. 1992. L'habitat néolithique ancien du site d'Ensisheim 'Ratfeld' (Haut-Rhin). Les structures, la céramique et la parure. *Cahiers de l'Association pour la Promotion de la Recherche Archéologique en Alsace* 8, 97–147.

Jeunesse, C. and van Willigen, S. 2010. Westmediterranes Frühneolithikum und westliche Linearbandkeramik: Impulse, Interaktionen, Mischkulturen. In D. Gronenborn and J. Petrasch (eds), *Die Neolithisierung Mitteleuropas (The spread of the Neolithic to central Europe)*, 569–604. Mainz: Römisch-Germanisches Zentralmuseum.

Jeunesse, C., Boës, E. and Mauvilly, M. 1996. *Rapport de fouille 1996 sur la nécropole rubanée d'Ensisheim 'Les Octrois' (Haut-Rhin)*. Strasbourg: Service Régional de l'Archéologie d'Alsace, unpublished document.

Jeunesse, C., Kirmann, C. and Lefranc, P. 2007b. Nouveaux tessons de céramique de La Hoguette à Rosheim (Bas-Rhin). *Cahiers de l'Association pour la Promotion de la Recherche Archéologique en Alsace* 17, 61–7.

Jeunesse, C., Lefranc, P. and van Willigen, S. 2009. Die pfälzische Bandkeramik: Definition und Periodisierung einer neuen Regionalgruppe der Linearbandkeramik. In A. Zeeb-Lanz (ed.), *Krisen – Kulturwandel – Kontinuitäten: zum Ende der Bandkeramik in Mitteleuropa*, 61–78. Rahden: Marie Leidorf.

Jeunesse, C., Wolf, J.J., Lefranc, P. and Schaltenbrand, K. 2007a. Rubané du Sud-Ouest et maisons trapéziformes: exemple de la maison 11 de Sierentz (Haut-Rhin). In O. Agogué, D. Leroy and C. Verjux (eds), *Camps, enceintes et structures d'habitat néolithiques en France septentrionale: actes du 24ème colloque interrégional sur le Néolithique, Orléans, 19–21 novembre 1999*, 39–54. Tours: Éditions RERACF.

Jim, S., Ambrose, S.H. and Evershed, R.P. 2004. Stable carbon isotopic evidence for differences in the dietary origin of bone cholesterol, collagen and apatite: implications for their use in palaeodietary reconstruction. *Geochimica et Cosmochimica Acta*, 68, 61–72.

Jim, S., Jones, V., Ambrose, S.H., and Evershed, R.P. 2007. Quantifying dietary macronutrient sources of carbon for bone collagen biosynthesis using natural abundance stable carbon isotope analysis. *British Journal of Nutrition* 95,1055–62.

Jochim, M. 1990. The late Mesolithic in southwest Germany: culture change or population decline? In P. Vermeersch and P. van Peer (eds), *Contributions to the Mesolithic in Europe: papers presented at the 4th international symposium 'The Mesolithic in Europe', Leuven 1990*, 183–91. Leuven: Leuven University Press.

Jochim, M. 1998. *A hunter-gatherer landscape: southwest Germany in the late Palaeolithic and Mesolithic*. New York: Plenum.

Jochim, M. 2006. Regional perspectives on Early Mesolithic land use in southwestern Germany. *Journal of Anthropological Archaeology* 25, 204–12.

Jochim, M. 2008. The Mesolithic of the Upper Danube and Upper Rhine. In G. Bailey and P. Spikins (eds), *Mesolithic Europe*, 203–20. Cambridge: Cambridge University Press.

Jochim, M., Glass, M., Fisher, L. and McCartney, P. 1998. Mapping the Stone Age: an interim report on the South German survey project. In N. Conrad and C. Kind (eds), *Aktuelle Forschungen zum Mesolithikum: current Mesolithic research*, 121–31. Tübingen: Mohr Vince.

John, J. 2005. Příspěvek ke struktuře prohřební výbavy v kultuře s volutovou keramikou. *Příspěvky k archaeologii* 2, 11–20.

John, J. 2011. Status of *Spondylus* artifacts within the LBK grave goods. In F. Ifantidis and M. Nikolaidou (eds), *Spondylus in prehistory: new data and approaches – contributions to the archaeology of shell technology*, 39–45. Oxford: Archaeopress.

Johnson, D.H. 1994. *Nuer prophets: a history of prophecy from the Upper Nile in the nineteenth and twentieth centuries*. Oxford: Clarendon Press.

Jones, A. 2005. Lives in fragments? Personhood and the European Neolithic. *Journal of Social Archaeology* 5, 193–224.

Jones, A. 2007. *Memory and material culture*. Cambridge: Cambridge University Press.

Jordan, P. and O'Neill, S.O. 2010. Untangling cultural inheritance: language diversity and long-house architecture on the Pacific northwest coast. *Philosophical Transactions of the Royal Society B* 365, 3875–88.

Jørkov, M.L.S., Heinemeier, J. and Lynnerup, N. 2007. Evaluating bone collagen extraction methods for stable isotope analysis in dietary studies. *Journal of Archaeological Science* 34, 1824–9.

Joyce, R.A. and Gillespie, S.D. (eds) 2000. *Beyond kinship: social and material reproduction in house societies*. Philadelphia: University of Pennsylvania Press.

Judd, M.A. and Roberts, C.A. 1999. Fracture trauma in a medieval British farming village. *American Journal of Physical Anthropology* 109, 229–43.

Kaczanowska, M. and Kozłowski, J.K. 2010. Chipped stone industry from Ibrány. In J.K. Kozłowski and P. Raczky (eds), *Neolithization of the Carpathian basin: northernmost distribution of the Starčevo/Körös culture*, 254–65. Kraków and Budapest: Polish Academy of Sciences and Institute of Archaeological Sciences of the Eötvös Loránd University.

Kaczanowska, M., Kozłowski, J.K. and Wasilewski, M. 2010. Lithic implements from Maroslele-Panahát. In J.K. Kozłowski and P. Raczky (eds), *Neolithization of the Carpathian basin: northernmost distribution of the Starčevo/Körös culture*, 305–24. Kraków and Budapest: Polish Academy of Sciences and Institute of Archaeological Sciences of the Eötvös Loránd University.

Kahlke, D. 1954. *Die Bestattungssitten des Donauländischen Kulturkreises der jüngeren Steinzeit. Teil 1: Linienbandkeramik*. Berlin: Rütten und Loening.

Kahlke, D. 1957. Neue Gräber mit Bandkeramik aus Thüringen. *Ausgrabungen und Funde* 2, 107–12.

Kahlke, D. 1958. Ein Gräberfeld mit Bandkeramik im Stadtgebiet von Sondershausen. *Ausgrabungen und Funde* 3, 181–2.

Kahlke, D. 2004. *Sondershausen und Bruchstedt: zwei Gräberfelder mit älterer Linienbandkeramik in Thüringen*. Weimar: Thüringisches Landesamt für Archäologische Denkmalpflege.

Kalicz, N. 1957. *A Tiszazug őskori települései*. Budapest: Magyar Nemzeti Múzeum.

Kalicz, N. 1978. Früh- und spätneolithische Funde in der Gemarkung des Ortes Lánycsók (Vorbericht). *Janus Pannonius Múzeum Évkönyve* 22, 137–56.

Kalicz, N. 1980a. 1. Becsehely I, Bükkaljai dűlő (Komitat Zala, Kreis Nagykanizsa). *Mitteilungen des Archäologischen Instituts der Ungarischen Akademie der Wissenschaften* 8/9, 201–3, Taf. 103–5.

Kalicz, N. 1980b. 2. Becsehely II, Homokos (Komitat Zala, Kreis Nagykanizsa). *Mitteilungen des Archäologischen Instituts der Ungarischen Akademie der Wissenschaften* 8/9, 203, Taf. 106.

Kalicz, N. 1980c. Funde der ältesten Phase der Linienbandkeramik in Südtransdanubien. *Mitteilungen des Archäologischen Instituts der Ungarischen Akademie der Wissenschaften* 8/9, 13–46, Taf. 1–14.

Kalicz, N. 1980d. Neue Forschungen über die Entstehung des Neolithikums in Ungarn. In J. Kozłowski and J. Machnik (eds), *Problèmes de la néolithisation dans certaines régions de l'Europe: actes du colloque international, Krakow-Mogilany 1979*, 97–122. Wrocław–Warszawa–Kraków–Gdańsk: Polska Akademia Nauk.

Kalicz, N. 1984. Die Körös-Starčevo-Kulturen und ihre Beziehungen zur Linearbandkeramik. *Nachrichten aus Niedersachsens Urgeschichte* 52, 91–130.

Kalicz, N. 1985. *Kőkori falu Aszódon (Neolithisches Dorf in Aszód)*. Aszód: Petőfi Múzeum.

Kalicz, N. 1990. *Frühneolithische Siedlungsfunde aus Südwestungarn: Quellenanalyse zur Geschichte der Starčevo-Kultur*. Budapest: Magyar Nemzeti Múzeum.

Kalicz, N. 1994. A Dunántúli (Közép-európai) vonaldíszes kerámia legidősebb leletei és a korai Vinča kultúra – Die Ältesten Funde der Transdanubischen (Mitteleuropäischen) Linienbandkeramik und die frühe Vinča-Kultur. In G. Lőrinczy (ed.), *A kőkortól a középkorig. Tanulmányok Trogmayer Ottó 60. Születésnapjára – Von der Steinzeit bis zum Mittelalter. Studien zum 60. Geburtstag von Ottó Trogmayer*, 67–84. Szeged: Csongrád Megyei Múzeumok Igazgatósága.

Kalicz, N. 1998. Die Linienbandkeramik im ungarischen Transdanubien. In J. Preuß, (ed.), *Das Neolithikum in Mitteleuropa. Kulturen – Wirtschaft – Umwelt vom 6. bis 3. Jahrtausend v.u.Z.*, 1/2, 263–7. Weissbach: Beier and Beran.

Kalicz, N. 2011. Forschung über die Starčevo-Kultur in Südtransdanubien (Ungarn). In M. Dizdar (ed.), *Panonski prpovijesni osviti. Zbornik radova posvećenih Korneliji Minichreiter uz 65. obljetnicu života*, 105–29. Zagreb: Institut za arheologiju.

Kalicz, N. and Kalicz-Schreiber, R. 2001. Die Verbreitungsgrenze der früneolithischen Kulturen in Transdanubien (Westungarn). *Preistoria Alpina* 37, 25–44.

Kalicz, N. and Koós, J. 1997a. Mezőkövesd-Mocsolyás. In P. Raczky, T. Kovács and A. Anders (eds), *Utak a múltba: az M3-as autópálya régészeti leletmentései*, 28–33. Budapest: Magyar Nemzeti Múzeum and Eötvös Loránd Tudományegyetem Régészettudományi Intézet.

Kalicz, N. and Koós, J. 1997b. Eine Siedlung mit ältestneolithischen Hausresten und Gräbern in Nordostungarn. In M. Lazić (ed.), *ANTIΔΩPON Dragoslavo Srejović*, 123–35. Belgrade: Centre for Archaeological Research, Faculty of Philosophy, University of Belgrade.

Kalicz, N. and Koós J. 2001. Eine Siedlung mit ältestneolithischen Gräbern in Nordostungarn. *Preistoria Alpina* 37, 45–79.

Kalicz, N. and Makkay, J. 1966. Die Probleme der Linearkeramik im Alföld. *Acta Antiqua et Archaeologica* 10, 35–47.

Kalicz, N. and Makkay, J. 1972a. Probleme des frühen Neolithikums der nördlichen Tiefebene. In J. Fitz and J. Makkay (eds), *Die aktuellen Fragen der Bandkeramik,* 77–92. Székesfehérvár: A Féjer Megyei Múzeumok Igazgatósága.

Kalicz, N. and Makkay, J. 1972b. Südliche Einflüsse im frühen und mittleren Neolithikum Transdanubiens. In J. Fitz and J. Makkay (eds), *Die aktuellen Fragen der Bandkeramik,* 93–105. Székesfehérvár: A Féjer Megyei Múzeumok Igazgatósága.

Kalicz, N. and Makkay, J. 1976. Frühneolithische Siedlung in Méhtelek–Nádas. *Mitteilungen des Archäologischen Instituts der Ungarischen Akademie der Wissenschaften* 6, 13–24, Taf. 1–8.

Kalicz, N. and Makkay, J. 1977. *Die Linienbandkeramik in der Großen Ungarischen Tiefebene.* Budapest: Akadémiai Kiadó.

Kalicz, N. and Raczky, P. 1987. The Late Neolithic of the Tisza region: a survey of recent archaeological research. In L. Tálas and P. Raczky (eds), *The late Neolithic of the Tisza region*, 11–30. Budapest and Szolnok: Kossuth Kiadó.

Kalis, A.J. and Meurers-Balke, J. 1998. Die 'Landam' Modelle von Iversen und Troels-Smith zur Neolithisierung des westlichen Ostseegebietes – ein Versuch ihrer Aktualisierung. *Prähistorische Zeitschrift* 73, 1–24.

Kalis, A.J. and Meurers-Balke, J. 2003. Zur pflanzensoziologischen Deutung archäobotanischer Befunde: zwei Pollendiagramme aus dem Wurmtal (Aldenhovener Platte). In J. Eckert, U. Eisenhauer and A. Zimmermann (eds), *Archäologische Perspektiven: Analysen und Interpretationen im Wandel. Festschrift für Jens Lüning zum 65. Geburtstag*, 251–77. Rahden: Marie Leidorf.

Kalis, A.J., Merkt, J. and Wunderlich, J. 2003. Environmental changes during the Holocene climatic optimum in central Europe – human impact and natural causes. *Quaternary Science Reviews* 22, 33–79.

Katzenberg, M.A. and Lovell, N.C. 1999. Stable isotope variation in pathological bone 1. *International Journal of Osteoarchaeology* 9, 316–24.

Kaufmann, D. 1989. Kultische Äußerungen im Frühneolithikum des Elbe-Saale-Gebietes. In F. Schlette and D. Kaufmann (eds),

Religion und Kult in ur- und frühgeschichtlicher Zeit, 113–39. Berlin: Akademie-Verlag.

Kaufmann, D. 2009. Anmerkungen zum Übergang von der Linien- zur Stichbandkeramik in Mitteldeutschland. In A. Zeeb-Lanz (ed.), *Krisen – Kulturwandel – Kontinuitäten: zum Ende der Bandkeramik in Mitteleuropa*, 267–82. Rahden: Marie Leidorf.

Kaulich, B. 1993. Rettungsgrabungen im Industriegebiet von Straubing-Sand III. Die Silexartefakte aus den Grabungskampagnen 1991–1994. *Historischer Verein für Straubing und Umgebung, Jahresbericht* 95, 11–37.

Kazdová, E. 2008. Těšetice-Kyjovice (okr. Znojmo). In Z. Čižmář (ed.), *Život a smrt v mladší době kamenné*, 88–101. Brno: Ústav archeologické památkové péče Brno.

Keaveney, E.M. and Reimer, P.J. 2012. Understanding the variability in freshwater radiocarbon reservoir offsets: a cautionary tale. *Journal of Archaeological Science* 39, 1306–16.

Kellner, C.M. and Schoeninger, M.J. 2007. A simple carbon isotope model for reconstructing prehistoric human diet. *American Journal of Physical Anthropology,* 133, 1112–27.

Kelly, J.F. 2000. Stable isotopes of carbon and nitrogen in the study of avian and mammalian trophic ecology. *Canadian Journal of Zoology* 78, 1–27.

Kerig, T. 2010. Grenzen ziehen: zur Chronologie regionaler und sozialer Unterschiede im hessischen Altneolithikum. In D. Gronenborn and J. Petrasch (eds), *Die Neolithisierung Mitteleuropas (The spread of the Neolithic to central Europe)*, 475–86. Mainz: Römisch-Germanisches Zentralmuseum.

Kertész, R. 1996. The Mesolithic in the Great Hungarian Plain. In L. Tálas (ed.), *At the fringes of three worlds: hunter-gatherers and farmers in the middle Tisza valley,* 5–34. Szolnok: Damjanich Museum.

Kertész, R. 2003. Mesolithic hunter-gatherers in the northwestern part of the Great Hungarian Plain. *Praehistoria* 3, 281–304.

Kertész, R. and Sümegi, P. 2001. Theories, critiques and a model: why did the expansion of the Körös-Starčevo culture stop in the centre of the Carpathian basin? In R. Kertész and J. Makkay (eds), *From the Mesolithic to the Neolithic*, 225–46. Budapest: Archaeolingua.

Kienlin, T.L. and Valde-Nowak, P. 2003. Neolithic transhumance in the Black Forest Mountains, south-west Germany. *Journal of Field Archaeology* 29, 29–44.

Kind, C.-J. 1989. *Ulm-Eggingen: die Ausgrabungen 1982 bis 1985 in der bandkeramischen Siedlung und der mittelalterlichen Wüstung*. Stuttgart: Theiss.

Kind, C.-J. 1992. Der Freilandfundplatz Henauhof Nord II am Federsee und die "Buchauer Gruppe" des Endmesolithikums. *Archäologisches Korrespondenzblatt* 22, 341–53.

Kind, C.-J. 1997. *Die letzen Wildbeuter: Henaufhof Nord II und das Endmesolithikum in Baden-Württemberg*. Stuttgart: Theiss.

Kind, C.-J. 1998. Komplexe Wildbeuter und frühe Ackerbauern: Bemerkungen zur Ausbreitung der Linearbandkeramik im südlichen Mitteleuropa. *Germania* 76, 1–24.

Kind, C.-J. 2006. Settlement and subsistence in the Mesolithic sites of Siebenlinden, southwest Germany. In C.-J. Kind (ed.), *After the Ice Age: settlements, subsistence and social development in the Mesolithic of central Europe*, 251–8. Stuttgart: Theiss.

Kind, C.-J. 2010. Diversity at the transition – a view from the Mesolithic. In D. Gronenborn and J. Petrasch (eds), *Die Neolithisierung Mitteleuropas (The spread of the Neolithic to central Europe)*, 449–60. Mainz: Römisch-Germanisches Zentralmuseum.

Kirchengast, S. and Winkler, E.-M. 1994. Die menschlichen Skelette der neolithischen und hallstattzeitlichen Gräberfelder von Rutzing in Oberösterreich: eine Revision der demographischen und metrischen Ergebnisse. *Jahrbuch des Oberösterreichischen Musealvereines* 139, 127–63.

Klassen, L. 2004. *Jade und Kupfer: Untersuchung zum Neolithisierungsprozess im westlichen Ostseeraum unter besonderer Berücksichtigung der Kulturentwicklung Europas 5500–3500 BC.* Åarhus: Åarhus University Press.

Klingner, S., Teegen, W.-R. and Schultz, M. 2007. Respiratory disease interactions in the early Neolithic Linear Pottery culture Wandersleben. *7. Kongress der deutschen Gesellschaft für Anthropologie e.V., Anthropologie – eine Wissenschaft in der Öffentlichkeit, 10.–14. September 2007, Freiburg im Breisgau, Abstracts,* 128.

Kloiber, Ä. and Kneidinger, J. 1968. Die neolithischen Siedlungen und die neolithischen Gräberfundplätze von Rutzing und Haid, Ortsgemeinde Hörsching, politischer Bezirk Linz-Land. Teil I. *Jahrbuch des Oberösterreichischen Musealvereins* 113, 9–58.

Kloiber, Ä. and Kneidinger, J. 1969. Die neolithischen Siedlungen und die neolithischen Gräberfundplätze von Rutzing und Haid, Ortsgemeinde Hörsching, politischer Bezirk Linz-Land. Teil II. *Jahrbuch des Oberösterreichischen Musealvereins* 114, 19–28.

Kloiber, Ä., Kneidinger, J. and Pertlwieser, M. 1971. Die neolithischen Siedlungen und die neolithischen Gräberfundplätze von Rutzing und Haid, Ortsgemeinde Hörsching, politischer Bezirk Linz-Land, Oberösterreich. Teil III. *Jahrbuch des Oberösterreichischen Musealvereins* 116, 23–50.

Kmoch, L. 1966. Eine Mesolithstation auf dem Bisamberg bei Wien. *Archaeologia Austriaca* 40, 13–24.

Knauft, B.M. 1993. *South coast New Guinea cultures: history, comparison, dialectic.* Cambridge: Cambridge University Press.

Knipper, C. 2004. Die Strontiumisotopenanalyse: eine naturwissenschaftliche Methode zur Erfassung von Mobilität in der Ur- und Frühgeschichte. *Jahrbuch des Römisch-Germanischen Zentralmuseums Mainz* 51, 589–685.

Knipper, C. 2009. Mobility in a sedentary society: insights from isotope analysis of LBK human and animal teeth. In D. Hofmann and P. Bickle (eds), *Creating communities: new advances in central European Research*, 142–58. Oxford: Oxbow Books.

Knipper, C. 2011. *Die räumliche Organisation der linearbandkeramischen Rinderhaltung: naturwissenschaftliche und archäologische Untersuchungen*. Oxford: Archaeopress.

Knipper, C. and Price, T.D. 2010. Individuelle Mobilität in der Linearbandkeramik: Strontiumisotopenanalysen vom Gräberfeld Stuttgart-Mühlhausen 'Viesenhäuser Hof'. In A. Krenn-Leeb, H.-J. Beier, E. Claßen, F. Falkenstein and S. Schwenzer (eds), *Varia Neolithica V: Mobilität, Migration und Kommunikation in Europa während des Neolithikums und der Bronzezeit*, 53–63. Halle: Beier und Beran.

Knipper, C., Harris, S., Fisher, L., Schreg, R., Giesler, J. and Nocerino, E. 2005. The Neolithic settlement landscape of the southeastern Swabian Alb (Germany). www.jungsteinSITE.de, 23 July 2005.

Knipping, M. 2001. Pollenanalytische Untersuchungen an einem Profil aus dem Ottmaringer Tal (südliche Frankenalb). *Quartär* 51/52, 211–27.

Knörzer, K.-H. 1967. Subfossile Pflanzenreste von bandkeramischen Fundstellen im Rheinland. *Archaeo-Physika* 2, 3–29.

Knudson, K.J. and Stojanowski, C.M. 2008. New directions in bioarchaeological research: recent contributions to the study of human social identities. *Journal of Archaeological Research* 16, 397–432.

Knudson, K.J., Williams, H.M., Buikstra, J.E.,Tomczak, P.D., Gordon, G.W. and Anbar, A.D. 2010. Introducing $\delta^{88/86}$Sr analysis in archaeology: a demonstration of the utility of strontium isotope fractionation in paleodietary studies. *Journal of Archaeological Science* 37, 2352–64.

Knüsel, C.J. 2000. Activity-related skeletal change. In V. Fiorato, A. Boylston and C. Knüsel (eds), *Blood red roses: the archaeology of a mass grave from the battle of Towton*, 103–18. Oxford: Oxbow Books.

Knüsel, C.J., Roberts, C.A. and Boyleston, A. 1996. Brief communication: when Adam delved. An activity-related lesion in three human skeletal populations. *American Journal of Physical Anthropology* 100, 427–33.

Koch, P.L., Tuross, N. and Fogel, M.L. 1997. The effects of sample treatment and diagenesis on the isotopic integrity of carbonate in biogenic hydroxylapatite. *Journal of Archaeological Science* 24, 417–29.

Kohl, M. (ed.) 1978. *Infanticide and the value of life*. Buffalo: Prometheus.

Kohl, P.L. and Pérez Gollán, J.A. 2002. Religion, politics and prehistory: reassessing the lingering legacy of Oswald Menghin. *Current Anthropology* 43, 561–86.

Kohler-Schneider, M. 2007. Early agriculture and subsistence in Austria: a review of Neolithic plant records. In S. Colledge and J. Conolly (eds), *The origins and spread of domestic plants in southwest Asia*, 209–20. Walnut Creek: Left Coast Press.

Kohler-Schneider, M. and Caneppele, A. 2010. Archäobotanische Analyse des Kultur- und Wildpflanzenspektrums der linearbandkeramischen Siedlung Mold, Niederösterreich. In E. Lenneis (ed.), *Die bandkeramische Siedlung von Mold bei Horn in Niederösterreich, Teil 1. Naturwissenschaftliche Untersuchungen und Einzelanalysen*, 209–39. Rahden: Marie Leidorf.

Kohler-Schneider, M., Caneppele, A. and Geihofer, A. 2009. Archäobotanische Analyse des Kultur- und Wildpflanzenspektrums der linearbandkeramischen Siedlung Mold, Niederösterreich (Archaeobotanical analysis of cultivated and wild plant remains from the Linear Pottery settlement Mold, Lower Austria). *Verhandlungen der Zoologisch-Botanischen-Gesellschaft in Österreich* 145, 113–37.

Kolhoff, C. 1999. *Die Keramik des bandkeramischen Fundplatzes Weisweiler 110*. Unpublished M.A. dissertation, Köln University.

Končelová, M. 2005. Struktura osídlení lidu s lineární keramikou ve východních Čechách (Linear Pottery settlement structure in East Bohemia). *Archeologické rozhledy* 57, 651–706.

Köppen, W. and Geiger, R. 1936. *Handbuch der Klimatologie in fünf Bänden*. Berlin: Gebrüder Bornträger.

Korek, J. 1960. Vonaldíszes kerámia kultúra elterjedése az Alföldön (Verbreitung der linearkeramischen Kultur aus dem Alföld). *A Móra Ferenc Múzeum Évkönyve* 1958/59, 19–52.

Korek, J. 1970. Nyiltszíni bükki telep és sírok Agyteleken (Eine Freilandstation und Gräber der Bükk-Kultur in Agytelek). *Archaeológiai Értesítő* 1970, 3–22.

Korek, J. and Patay, P. 1958. *A bükki kultúra elterjedése Magyarországon (Die Verbreitung der Bükk-Kultur in Ungarn). Régészeti Füzetek* Series II, 2. Budapest: Magyar Nemzeti Múzeum–Történeti Múzeum.

Körner, C., Farquhar, G.D. and Wong, S.C. 1991. Carbon isotope discrimination by plants follows latitudinal and altitudinal trends. *Oecologia* 88, 30–40.

Kortfunke, C. 1992. *Über die spät- und postglaziale Vegetationsgeschichte des Donaumooses und seiner Umgebung*. Berlin: Cramer.

Kossack, G. and Schmeidl, H. 1974/75. Vorneolithischer Getreideanbau im bayerischen Alpenvorland. *Jahresbericht der Bayerischen Bodendenkmalpflege* 15/16, 7–23.

Kosse, K. 1979. *Settlement ecology of the Körös and Linear Pottery cultures in Hungary*. Oxford: British Archaeological Reports.

Koštuřík, P. 1986. Mladší doba kamenná (Neolit). In P. Koštuřík, J. Kovárník, Z. Měřínský and M. Oliva, *Pravěk Třebíčska*, 57–79. Brno: Muzejní a vlastivědná společnost v Brně, and Západomoravské muzeum v Třebíči.

Kovács, Z.E., Gál, E. and Bartosiewicz, L. 2010. Early Neolithic animal bones from Ibrány-Nagyerdő, Hungary. In J.K. Kozłowski and P. Raczky (eds), *Neolithization of the Carpathian basin: northernmost distribution of the Starčevo/Körös culture*, 238–54. Kraków and Budapest: Polish Academy of Sciences and Institute of Archaeological Sciences of the Eötvös Loránd University.

Koval, K.J. and Zuckermann, J.D. 2006. *Handbook of fractures*. Philadelphia: Lippincott, Williams and Wilkins.

Kovárník, J. 2007. Osídlování nížin ve starším stupni kultury s lineární keramikou na jižní Moravě (Besiedlung der Tiefebenen in der älteren Stufe der Kultur mit Linearbandkeramik in Südmähren). *Sborník prací Filozofické fakulty brněnské univerzity* M8–9, 31–52.

Kovárník, J. 2008. K dějinám výzkumu neolitu (a zvláště moravské malované keramiky) (History of research on the Neolithic (especially Moravian Painted Pottery)). In Z. Čižmář (ed.), *Život a smrt v mladší době kamenné*, 4–11. Brno: Ústav archeologické památkové péče Brno.

Kowarik, K. 2003. Die Keramikfunde der Häuser 1–4 aus der bandkeramischen Siedlung von Mold in Niederösterreich. In E. Lenneis (ed.), *Die bandkeramische Siedlung von Mold bei Horn in Niederösterreich. Teil 1. Naturwissenschaftliche Untersuchungen und Einzelanalysen*, 33–168. Rahden: Marie Leidorf.

Kozłowski, J.K. 2005. Remarks on the Mesolithic in the northern part of the Carpathian Basin. In E. Gál, I. Juhász and P. Sümegi (eds), *Environmental archaeology in north-eastern Hungary*, 175–86. Budapest: Institute of Archaeology, Hungarian Academy of Sciences.

Kozłowski, J.K. and Nowak, M. (eds) 2007. *Mesolithic/Neolithic interactions in the Balkans and the middle Danube basin*. Oxford: Archaeopress.

Kozłowski, J.K. and Nowak, M. 2010. From Körös/Criş to the early Eastern Linear complex: multidirectional transitions in the north-eastern fringe of the Carpathian basin. In J.K. Kozłowski and P. Raczky (eds), *Neolithization of the Carpathian basin: northernmost distribution of the Starčevo/Körös culture*, 65–90. Kraków/Budapest: Polish Academy of Sciences/Institute of Archaeological Sciences of the Eötvös Loránd University Budapest.

Kozłowski, J.K. and Raczky, P. (eds) 2007. *The Lengyel, Polgár and related cultures in the Middle/Late Neolithic in central Europe*. Kraków: Polska Akademia Umiejetności.

Kozłowski, J.K. and Raczky, P. 2010. Concluding remarks. In J.K. Kozłowski and P. Raczky (eds), *Neolithization of the Carpathian basin: northernmost distribution of the Starčevo/Körös culture*, 349–60. Kraków/Budapest: Polish Academy of

Sciences/Institute of Archaeological Sciences of the Eötvös Loránd University Budapest.

Kozłowski, T. and Witas, H.W. 2012. Metabolic and endocrine diseases. In A.L. Grauer (ed.), *A companion to palaeopathology*, 401–19. Chichester: Wiley-Blackwell.

Kráčmarová, A., Bruchová, H., Černý, V. and Brdička, R. 2006. Podíl "paleolitických" versus "neolitických" haploskupin Y chromozomu u české populace (The contributions of 'Palaeolithic' and 'Neolithic' Y chromosome haplogroups in the Czech population). *Archeologické rozhledy* 58, 237–49.

Kraft, H.-P. 1977. *Linearbandkeramik aus dem Neckarmündungsgebiet und ihre chronologische Gliederung*. Bonn: Habelt.

Krahe, G. 1989. Alt- und mittelneolithische Siedlungen bei Nördlingen-Baldingen, Landkreis Donau-Ries, Schwaben. *Das Archäologische Jahr in Bayern 1988*, 29–31.

Krahn, C. 2003. Überlegungen zum Interaktionssystem der bandkeramischen Siedlungen auf der Aldenhovener Platte. In J. Eckert, U. Eisenhauer and A. Zimmermann (eds), *Archäologische Perspektiven: Analysen und Interpretationen im Wandel. Festschrift für Jens Lüning zum 65. Geburtstag*, 515–44. Rahden: Marie Leidorf.

Krahn-Schigiol, C. 2005. Regionale und überregionale Kommunikationsnetzwerke der bandkeramischen Siedlungen auf der Aldenhovener Platte. In J. Lüning, C. Frirdich and A. Zimmermann (eds), *Die Bandkeramik im 21. Jahrhundert. Symposium in der Abtei Brauweiler bei Köln vom 16.9.–19.9.2002*, Beilage 1. Rahden: Marie Leidorf.

Krause, R. 1997. Bandkeramische Grabenwerke im Neckarland: Überraschende neue Erkenntnisse durch Ausgrabungen in Vaihingen an der Enz, Kreis Ludwigsburg. In K. Schmotz (ed.), *Vorträge des 15. Niederbayerischen Archäologentages*, 89–118. Espelkamp: Marie Leidorf.

Krause, R. 1998. Die bandkeramischen Siedlungsspuren bei Vaihingen an der Enz, Kreis Ludwigsburg (Baden-Württemberg). Ein Vorbericht zu den Ausgrabungen von 1994–1997. *Bericht der Römisch-Germanischen Kommission* 79, 5–105.

Krause, R. 2003. Zum Abschluss der Grabungen 1994–2002 in der bandkeramischen Siedlung bei Vaihingen an der Enz, Kreis Ludwigsburg. *Archäologische Ausgrabungen in Baden-Württemberg 2002*, 34–9.

Kreiner, L. and Pscheidl, C. 2006. Ein bandkeramisches Grab mit Fischzähnen in Aufhausen, Gemeinde Eichendorf, Landkreis Dingolfing-Landau, Niederbayern. *Das Archäologische Jahr in Bayern 2005*, 15–17.

Kreuz, A. 1990. Die ersten Bauern Mitteleuropas – eine archäobotanische Untersuchung zu Umwelt und Landwirtschaft der ältesten Bandkeramik. *Analecta Praehistorica Leidensia* 23, 1–145.

Kreuz, A. 1992. Charcoal from ten early Neolithic settlements in central Europe and its interpretation in terms of woodland management and wildwood resources. *Bulletin de la Société Botanique de France, Actualités Botaniques* 139, 383–94.

Kreuz, A. 2007. Archaeobotanical perspectives on the beginning of agriculture north of the Alps. In S. Colledge and J. Conolly (eds), *The origins and spread of domestic plants in southwest Asia*, 259–94. Walnut Creek: Left Coast Press.

Kreuz, A. and Boenke, N. 2003. Zweikörniges Einkorn zur Zeit der Bandkeramik: Archäologisches Indiz oder Laune der Natur? In J. Eckert, U. Eisenhauer and A. Zimmermann (eds), *Archäologische Perspektiven: Analysen und Interpretationen im Wandel. Festschrift für Jens Lüning zum 65. Geburtstag*, 233–41. Rahden: Marie Leidorf.

Kreuz, A., Marinova, E., Schäfer, E. and Wiethold, J. 2005. A comparison of early Neolithic crop and weed assemblages from the Linearbandkeramik and the Bulgarian Neolithic cultures: differences and similarities. *Vegetation History and Archaeobotany* 14, 237–58.

Krippner, F. 1984. Fundstellen mit ältester Bandkeramik im Ries. *Bayerische Vorgeschichtsblätter* 49, 279–84.

Krippner, F. 1995. Siedlungskundliches aus dem Ries. *Bayerische Vorgeschichtsblätter* 60, 63–80.

Krippner, F. 2000. *Vom Inferno zur Kulturlandschaft: der prähistorische Mensch im Nördlinger Ries*. Nördlingen: Steinmeier.

Kristiansen, K. 2012. The Bronze Age expansion of Indo-European languages: an archaeological model. In C. Prescott and H. Glørstad (eds), *Becoming European: the transformation of third millennium Northern and Western Europe*, 165–81. Oxford: Oxbow Books.

Kruk, J. 1973. *Studia osadnicze nad neolitem wyzyn lessowych*. Wrocław: Ossolineum.

Kruk, J. 1980. *The Neolithic settlement of southern Poland*. Oxford: British Archaeological Reports.

Kuijt, I. 2000. Near Eastern Neolithic research: directions and trends. In I. Kuijt (ed.), *Life in Neolithic farming communities: social organization, identity, and differentiation*, 311–22. New York: Kluwer Academic/Plenum.

Kunkel, O. 1955. Die Jungfernhöhle bei Tiefenellern. Eine neolithische Kultstätte auf dem fränkischen Jura bei Bamberg. *Münchner Beiträge zur Ur- und Frühgeschichte* 5, 1–138.

Kunst, G.K. 2001. Archäozoologisches Fundmaterial. In K. Grömer (ed), *Jungsteinzeit im Großraum Linz: Siedlungs- und Grabfunde aus Leonding*, 116–34. Linz: Linzer Archäologische Forschungen.

Kuper, A. 1988. *The invention of primitive society: transformations of an illusion*. London: Routledge.

Kuper, A. 1999. *Culture: the anthropologists' account*. Cambridge, Massachusetts: Harvard University Press.

Kuper, R., Löhr, H., Lüning, J., Stehli, P. and Zimmermann, A. 1977. *Der bandkeramische Siedlungsplatz Langweiler 9, Gemeinde Aldenhoven, Kreis Düren*. Bonn: Habelt.

Kurz, G. 1994. Zum Abschluß der Ausgrabungen im Viesenhäuser Hof, Stuttgart-Mühlhausen. *Archäologische Ausgrabungen in Baden-Württemberg 1993*, 34–8.

Küster, H.-J. 1991. Pflanzenreste aus einer Siedlung der ältesten Linearbandkeramik von Langenbach/Niederhummel, Lkr. Freising. *Archäologie im Landkreis Freising* 2, 77–9.

Küster, H.-J. 1992. Kulturpflanzenbau in Südbayern seit der Jungsteinzeit. In B. Engelhardt and J. Prammer (eds), *Bauern in Bayern von den Anfängen bis zur Römerzeit*, 137–55. Straubing: Gäubodenmuseum.

Küster, H.-J. 1995. *Postglaziale Vegetationsgeschichte Südbayerns: geobotanische Studien zur prähistorischen Landschaftskunde*. Berlin: Akademie Verlag.

Küster, H.-J. 1997. The role of farming in the postglacial expansion of beech and hornbeam in the oak woodlands of central Europe. *The Holocene* 7, 239–42.

Kutzián, I. 1944. *A Körös kultúra. Dissertationes Pannonicae Ser. II, number 23*. Budapest: Péter Pázmány University.

Kutzián, I. 1946. Újabb neolithikus leletek a Magyar Történeti Múzeumban (Recent Neolithic acquisitions in the Hungarian National Museum). *Magyar Múzeum*, 45–54, 94.

Květina, P. 2004. Mocní muži a sociální identita jednotlivců – prostorová analýza pohřebiště LnK ve Vedrovicích. *Archeologické rozhledy* 56, 383–92.

Labes, S. 2003. Kulturpflanzenvielfalt bei den ersten Bauern in Bayern: Pflanzenfunde aus der bandkeramischen Siedlung

Aich, Gemeinde Altdorf, Landkreis Landshut, Niederbayern. *Das Archäologische Jahr in Bayern 2002*, 15–18.

Lacan, M., Keyser, C., Ricaut, F.-X., Brucato, N., Duranthon, F., Guilaine, J., Crubézy, E. and Ludes, B. 2011. Ancient DNA suggests the leading role played by men in the Neolithic dissemination. *Proceedings of the National Academy of Sciences of the United States of America* 108, 18255–9.

Lang, G. 1994. *Quartäre Vegetationsgeschichte Europas: Methoden und Ergebnisse*. New York: Fischer.

Lantermann, R. 1980. *Anthropologische Untersuchung an den Skeletten des bandkeramischen Gräberfeldes von Aiterhofen, Ldkr. Straubing-Bogen*. Unpublished Diplomarbeit, Johann Wolfgang Goethe-Universität, Frankfurt a. Main.

Larsen, C.S. 1997. *Bioarchaeology: interpreting behaviour from the human skeleton*. Cambridge: Cambridge University Press.

Larsen, C.S. 2002. Bioarchaeology: the lives and lifestyles of past people. *Journal of Archaeological Research* 10, 119–66.

Larsen, C.S., Shavit, R. and Griffin, M.C. 1991. Dental caries evidence for dietary change: an archaeological context. In M.A. Kelley and C.S. Larsen (eds), *Advances in dental anthropology*, 179–202. New York: Wiley-Liss.

Larson, G., Albarella, U., Dobney, K., Rowley-Conwy, P., Schibler, J., Tresset, A., Vigne, J.-D., Edwards, C.J., Schlumbaum, A., Dinu, A., Balacsescu, A., Dolman, G., Tagliacozzo, A., Manaseryan, N., Miracle, P., Van Wijngaarden-Bakker, L., Masseti, M., Bradley, D.G. and Cooper, A. 2007. Ancient DNA, pig domestication, and the spread of the Neolithic into Europe. *Proceedings of the National Academy of Sciences of the United States of America* 104, 15276–81.

Larson, G., Dobney, K., Albarella, U., Fang, M., Matisoo-Smith, E., Robins, J., Lowden, S., Finlayson, H., Brand, T., Willerslev, E., Rowley-Conwy, P., Andersson, L. and Cooper, A. 2005. Worldwide phylogeography of wild boar reveals multiple centers of pig domestication. *Science* 307, 1618–21.

Latkoczy, C., Prohaska, T., Stingeder, G. and Teschler-Nicola, M. 1998. Strontium isotope ratio measurements in prehistoric human bone samples by means of high-resolution inductively coupled plasma mass spectrometry (HR-ICP-MS). *Journal of Analytical Atomic Spectromtry* 13, 561–6.

Latour, B. 1993. *We have never been modern*. London: Harvester Wheatsheaf.

Laus, S. 2009. Foragers in the alpine Rhine valley: interpreting two Mesolithic rockshelters near Koblach in Vorarlberg, Austria. In S.B. McCartan, R. Schulting, G. Warren and P. Woodman (eds), *Mesolithic horizons: papers presented at the seventh international conference on the Mesolithic in Europe, Belfast 2005, Volume II*, 772–8. Oxford: Oxbow Books.

Leach, E. 1976. *Culture and communication: the logic by which symbols are connected*. Cambridge: Cambridge University Press.

Leach, S., Lewis, M., Chenery, C., Müldner, G. and Eckardt, H. 2009. Migration and diversity in Roman Britain: a multidisciplinary approach to the identification of immigrants in Roman York, England. *American Journal of Physical Anthropology* 140, 546–61.

Lebzelter, V. and Zimmerman, G. 1936. Neolithische Gräber aus Klein-Hadersdorf bei Poysdorf in Niederösterreich. *Mitteilungen der Anthropologischen Gesellschaft in Wien* 66, 1–16.

Lech, J. 1990. The organisation of siliceous rock supplies to the Danubian early farming communities (LBK): central European examples. In D. Cahen and M. Otte (eds), *Rubané et Cardial: actes du colloque de Liège, novembre 1988*, 51–9. Liège: Études et Recherches Archéologiques de l'Université de Liège 39.

Lecolle, P. 1985. The oxygen isotope composition of landsnail shells as a climatic indicator – applications to hydrogeology and paleoclimatology. *Chemical Geology* 58, 157–81.

Lee-Thorp, J.A., Sealy, J.C. and van der Merwe, N.J. 1989. Stable carbon isotope ratio differences between bone collagen and bone apatite, and their relationship to diet. *Journal of Archaeological Science* 16, 585–99.

Lefranc, P. 2001. La fin de la séquence rubanée en Haute-Alsace (Rubané récent et final) vue à travers l'évolution de la céramique décorée du site de Sierentz-Sandgrube et Tiergarten (Haut-Rhin). *Bulletin de la Société Préhistorique Française* 98, 253–9.

Lefranc, P. 2002. Les orientations. In C. Jeunesse (ed.), *Vendenheim 'Le Haut du Coteau': une nécropole du Néolithique ancien. Document final de synthèse. Tome 1: texte*, 37–47. Strasbourg: Service Régional de l'Archéologie d'Alsace, unpublished document.

Lefranc, P. 2007a. *La céramique du Rubané en Alsace*. Strasbourg: Université Marc-Bloch.

Lefranc, P. 2007b. Néolithique. *Bilan Scientifique Alsace*, 19–104.

Lefranc, P. 2007c. L'habitat rubané de Bischoffsheim 'AFUA' (Bas-Rhin, France): premiers résultats. In F. Le Brun-Ricalens, F. Valotteau and A. Hauzeur (eds), *Relations interrégionales au Néolithique entre Bassin parisien et Bassin rhénan*, 99–111. Luxembourg. Faber.

Lefranc, P. and Boës, E. 2009. Les restes humains manipulés du site rubané d'Ittenheim 'Complexe sportif' (Bas-Rhin). In A. Zeeb-Lanz (ed.), *Krisen – Kulturwandel – Kontinuitäten: zum Ende der Bandkeramik in Mitteleuropa*, 197–211. Rahden: Marie Leidorf.

Lefranc, P. and Denaire, A. 2000. Deux nouvelles maisons du Néolithique ancien rubané et une fosse de la culture Grossgartach à Sierentz-Tiergarten (Haut-Rhin). *Cahiers de l'Association pour la Promotion de la Recherche Archéologique en Alsace* 16, 17–36.

Lefranc, P., Arbogast, R.-M., Mauvilly, M. and van Willigen, S. 1998. L'habitat Rubané final de Westhouse-Ziegelhof (Bas-Rhin). *Cahiers de l'Association pour la Promotion de la Recherche Archéologique en Alsace* 14, 5–43.

Lefranc, P., Bakaj, B., Robert, F. and Zehner, M. 2004. *Bischoffsheim: AFUA du Stade*. Unpublished site report.

Lefranc, P., Denaire, A. and Boës, E. 2010. L'habitat néolithique ancien et moyen d'Ittenheim (Bas-Rhin). *Revue Archéologique de l'Est* 59, 65–97.

Lehmann, J. 2004. Die Keramik und Befunde des bandkeramischen Siedlungsplatzes Erkelenz-Kückhoven, Kr. Heinsberg (Grabungskampagnen 1989–1994). In H. Koschick (ed.), *Der bandkeramische Siedlungsplatz von Erkelenz-Kückhoven. I – Archäologie*, 1–364. Köln: Rheinland-Verlag.

Leitner, W. 1984. Zum Stand der Mesolithforschung in Österreich. *Preistoria Alpina* 19, 75–82.

Leitner, W. 2004. Eine mittelsteinzeitliche Fundstelle bei Riezlen im Kleinwalsertal (Vorbericht). *Jahrbuch des Vorarlberger Landesmuseumsvereins* 148, 15–20.

Lenneis, E. 1977. *Siedlungsfunde aus Poigen und Frauenhofen bei Horn: ein Beitrag zur Erforschung der Linear- und Stichbandkeramik in Niederösterreich*. Horn: Ferdinand Berger und Söhne.

Lenneis, E. 1982a. Die Siedlungsverteilung der Linearbandkeramik in Österreich. *Archaeologia Austriaca* 66, 1–19.

Lenneis, E. 1982b. Überblick über den derzeitigen Forschungsstand linearbandkeramischer Siedlungen in Österreich. In J. Pavúk (ed.), *Siedlungen der Kultur mit Linearkeramik in Europa: Internationales Kolloquium Nové Vozokany*, 107–23. Nitra: Archäologisches Institut der Slowakischen Akademie der Wissenschaften.

Lenneis, E. 1989. Zum Forschungsstand der ältesten Bandkeramik in Österreich. *Archäologisches Korrespondenzblatt* 19, 23–36.

Lenneis, E. 1990. La ceramique linéaire ancienne en Autriche: premiers résultats des recherches récentes. In D. Cahen and M. Otte (eds), *Rubané et Cardial: actes du colloque de Liège, novembre 1988*, 61–3. Liège: University of Liège.

Lenneis, E. 1991. Zu den ersten festen Wohnhäusern im Raume Österreichs. *Mitteilungen der Anthropologischen Gesellschaft in Wien* 121, 121–36.

Lenneis, E. 1992. Vorbericht über die Ausgrabungen 1988–1991 der Linearbandkeramischen Siedlung in Rosenburg im Kamptal, Niederösterreich. *Archaeologia Austriaca* 76, 19–37.

Lenneis, E. 1995. Altneolithikum: die Bandkeramik. In E. Lenneis, C. Neugebauer-Maresch and E. Ruttkay (eds), *Jungsteinzeit im Osten Österreichs*, 11–56. St. Pölten and Wien: Niederösterreichisches Pressehaus.

Lenneis, E. 1997. Houseforms of the central European Linear pottery culture and of the Balkan Early Neolithic – a comparison. *Poročilo o Raziskovanju Paleolitika, Neolitika in Eneolitika v Sloveniji* 24, 143–9.

Lenneis, E. 2000. Interkulturelle Gruppengrenzen – Überlegungen auf der Basis der Regionalisierung in der jüngeren Linearbandkeramik. In H.-J. Beier (ed.), *Varia Neolithica I, Beiträge zur Ur- und Frühgeschichte Mitteleuropas 22*, 77–80. Weissbach: Beier & Beran.

Lenneis, E. 2001. The beginning of the Neolithic in Austria – a report about recent and current investigations. *Documenta Praehistorica* 28, 99–116.

Lenneis, E. 2003. Die frühneolithische Besiedlung Österreichs in Bezug zur natürlichen Umwelt. In J. Eckert, U. Eisenhauer and A. Zimmermann (eds), *Archäologische Perspektiven: Analysen und Interpretationen im Wandel. Festschrift für Jens Lüning zum 65.Geburtstag*, 279–92. Rahden: Marie Leidorf.

Lenneis, E. 2004a. Architecture and settlement structure of the early Linear Pottery Culture in east central Europe. In A. Lukes and M. Zvelebil (eds), *LBK dialogues: studies in the formation of the Linear Pottery Culture*, 151–7. Oxford: Archaeopress.

Lenneis, E. 2004b. Erste Anzeichen der Regionalisierung sowie Nachweise von Fernkontakten in der älteren Linearbandkeramik. *Antaeus* 27, 47–60.

Lenneis, E. 2004c. Ein unvollendet (?) abgebranntes Haus der Linearbandkeramik aus Mold bei Horn. *Archäologie Österreichs* 15, 16–18.

Lenneis, E. 2004d. Ein bandkeramischer Großbau aus Mold bei Horn. In B. Hänsel and E. Studeniková (eds), *Zwischen Karpaten und Ägäis: Gedenkschrift für Viera Nemecková-Pavúková,* 379–94. Rahden: Marie Leidorf.

Lenneis, E. 2005. Die "Einheitlichkeit" der frühen Bandkeramik – Forschungsstand oder Realität? In J. Lüning, C. Frirdrich and A. Zimmermann (eds), *Die Bandkeramik im 21. Jahrhundert. Symposium in der Abtei Brauweiler bei Köln vom 16.9.–19.9.2002*, 75–9. Rahden: Marie Leidorf.

Lenneis, E. 2006. Die Bedeutung von Prellenkirchen für die Erforschung der älteren Linearbandkeramik in Österreich. *Archäologie Österreichs* 17, 13–20.

Lenneis, E. 2007. Mesolithic heritage in early Neolithic burial rituals and personal adornments. *Documenta Praehistorica* 34, 129–37.

Lenneis, E. 2008. Perspectives on the beginning of the earliest LBK in east-central Europe. In D. Bailey, A. Whittle and D. Hofmann (eds), *Living well together? Settlement and materiality in the Neolithic of south-east and central Europe*, 164–78. Oxford: Oxbow Books.

Lenneis, E. 2009. *Rosenburg im Kamptal, Niederösterreich: ein Sonderplatz der älteren Linearbandkeramik.* Bonn: Habelt.

Lenneis, E. (ed.) 2010a. *Die bandkeramische Siedlung von Mold bei Horn in Niederösterreich. Teil 1. Naturwissenschaftliche Untersuchungen und Einzelanalysen.* Rahden: Marie Leidorf.

Lenneis, E. 2010b. Zur Chronologie der älteren Linearbandkeramik in Österreich. In P. Kalábková, B. Kovár, P. Pavúk and J. Šuteková (eds), *PANTA RHEI: studies in chronology and cultural development of south-eastern and central Europe in earlier prehistory presented to Juraj Pavúk on the occasion of his 75th birthday*, 189–200. Bratislava: Comenius University.

Lenneis, E. 2010c. Empty graves in LBK cemeteries – indications of special burial practices. *Documenta Praehistorica* 37, 161–6.

Lenneis, E. 2010d. Kleine Schmuckschnecken in linearbandkeramischen Gräbern: ein Mosaikstein für unsere Vorstellung der Neolithisierung Mitteleuropas. In D. Gronenborn and J. Petrasch (eds), *Die Neolithisierung Mitteleuropas (The spread of the Neolithic to central Europe)*, 333–50. Mainz: Römisch-Germanisches Zentralmuseum.

Lenneis, E. and Kuijper, W.J. 1992. Vorbericht über die Ausgrabungen 1988–1991 der linearbandkeramischen Siedlung in Rosenburg im Kamptal, Niederösterreich. *Archaeologia Austriaca* 76, 19–37.

Lenneis, E. and Lüning, J. 2001. *Die altbandkeramischen Siedlungen von Neckenmarkt und Strögen.* Bonn: Habelt.

Lenneis, E. and Stadler, P. 2001. ^{14}C-Daten und Seriation altbandkeramischer Inventare. *Archeologické rozhledy* 54, 191–201.

Lenneis, E., Brinkkemper, O., Frank, C., Mateiciucová, I., Pieler, F., Schmitzberger, M. and Stadler, P. 2010. Soziale Organisation und Wirtschaftsstruktur früher bandkeramischer Siedlungen – erste Teilergebnisse eines Forschungsprojektes in Österreich. In E. Claßen, T. Doppler and B. Ramminger (eds), *Familie – Verwandtschaft – Sozialstrukturen: sozialarchäologische Forschungen zu neolithischen Befunden*, 81–9. Kerpen-Loogh: Welt und Erde.

Lenneis, E., Stadler, P. and Windl, H. 1996. Neue ^{14}C-Daten zum Frühneolithikum in Österreich. *Préhistoire Européene* 8, 97–116.

Leopold, M. Gannaway, E. and Völkel, J. 2011. Ans Licht gebracht – Magnetometer-Prospektion an einer der ältesten Siedlungen Bayerns in Niederhummel, Landkreis Freising. *Archäologie im Landkreis Freising* 11, 35–44.

Lévi-Strauss, C. 1979. *La voie des masques.* Paris: Plon.

Lévi-Strauss, C. 1982. *The way of the masks* (translated by Sylvia Modleski). Seattle: University of Washington Press.

Lévi-Strauss, C. 1987. *Anthropology and myth: lectures 1951–1982* (translated by Roy Willis). Oxford: Blackwell.

Lewis, M. 2007. *The bioarchaeology of children: perspectives from biological and forensic anthropology.* Cambridge: Cambridge University Press.

Liberson, F. 1937. Os acromiale – a contested anomaly. *Journal of Bone and Joint Surgery* 19, 683–9.

Lichardus, J. 1964. Beitrag zur Linearbandkeramik in der Ostslowakei. *Archeologické rozhledy* 16, 841–81.

Lichardus, J. 1972a. Beitrag zur chronologischen Stellung der östlichen Linearbandkeramik. In J. Fitz and J. Makkay (eds), *Die aktuellen Fragen der Bandkeramik*, 107–22. Székesfehérvár: A Fejér Megyei Múzeumok Igazgatósága.

Lichardus, J. 1972b. Zur Entstehung der Linearbandkeramik. *Germania* 50, 1–15.

Lichardus-Itten, M. 1980. *Die Gräberfelder der Großgartacher Gruppe im Elsaß*. Bonn: Habelt.

Lichardus-Itten, M. 1986. Premières influences méditerranéennes dans le Néolithique du Bassin parisien: contribution au débat. In J.-P. Demoule (ed.), *Le Néolithique de la France: hommage à Gérard Bailloud*, 147–60. Paris: Picard.

Lichardus-Itten, M. and Lichardus, J. 2004. Frühneolithische Häuser im balkano-karpatischen Raum als Grundlagen linearbandkeramischer Bauweise. In J. Bätora, V. Furmánek and L. Veliačik (eds), *Einflüsse und Kontakte alteuropäischer Kulturen: Festschrift für Jozef Vladár zum 70. Geburtstag*, 25–56. Nitra: Archäologisches Institut der Slowakischen Akademie der Wissenschaften.

Lichter, C. 2001. *Untersuchungen zu den Bestattungssitten des südosteuropäischen Neolithikums und Chalkolithikums*. Mainz: Philipp von Zabern.

Lienemann, J. 1998. Phosphatkartierungen in bandkeramischen Häusern. In R. Krause, 'Die bandkeramischen Siedlungsspuren bei Vaihingen an der Enz, Kreis Ludwigsburg (Baden-Württemberg). Ein Vorbericht zu den Ausgrabungen von 1994–1997'. *Bericht der Römisch-Germanischen Kommission* 79, 39–45.

Lightfoot, E. and Stevens, R.E. 2012. Stable isotope investigations of charred barley (*Hordeum vulgare*) and wheat (*Triticum spelta*) grains from Danebury hillfort: implications for palaeodietary reconstructions. *Journal of Archaeological Science* 39, 656–62.

Lightfoot, E., Boneva, B., Miracle, P.T., Slaus, M. and O'Connell, T.C. 2011. Exploring the Mesolithic and Neolithic transition in Croatia through isotopic investigations. *Antiquity* 85, 73–86.

Lillie, M. 2008. Vedrovice: demography and palaeopathology in an early farming population. *Anthropologie* 46, 135–52.

Lindig, S. 2002. *Das Früh- und Mittelneolithikum im Neckarmündungsgebiet*. Bonn: Habelt.

Lister, D.L., Thaw, S., Bower, M.A., Jones, H., Charles, M.P., Jones, G., Smith, L.M.J., Howe, C.J., Brown, T.A. and Jones, M.K. 2009. Latitudinal variation in a photoperiod response gene in European barley: insight into the dynamics of agricultural spread from 'historic' specimens. *Journal of Archaeological Science* 36, 1092–8.

Loewe, G. 1958. Zur Frage der Echtheit der jungsteinzeitlichen 'Wetterauer Brandgräber'. *Germania* 36, 421–36.

Longinelli, A. 1984. Oxygen isotopes in mammal bone phosphate: a new tool for palaeohydrological and palaeoclimatological research? *Geochimica et Cosmochimica Acta* 48, 385–90.

Louwe Kooijmans, L.P., van de Velde, P. and Kamermans, H. 2003. The early Bandkeramik settlement of Geleen-Janskamperveld: its intrasite structure and dynamics. In J. Eckert, U. Eisenhauer and A. Zimmermann (eds), *Archäologische Perspektiven: Analysen und Interpretationen im Wandel. Festschrift für Jens Lüning zum 65. Geburtstag*, 373–97. Rahden: Marie Leidorf.

Lovejoy, C.O., Meindl, R.S., Pryzbeck, T.R. and Mensforth, R.P. 1985. Chronological metamorphosis of the auricular surface of the ilium: a new method for the determination of age at death. *American Journal of Physical Anthropology* 68, 15–28.

Lovell, N.C. 1997. Trauma analysis in paleopathology. *Yearbook of Physical Anthropology* 104, 139–70.

Lowie, R.H. 1948. *Social organization*. New York: Rinehart.

Ludwig, H. and Strasser, K. 2001. Symptomatology of anemia. *Seminars in Oncology* 28, Supplement 8, 7–14.

Lukacs, J.R. 2008. Fertility and agriculture accentuate sex differences in dental caries rates. *Current Anthropology* 49, 901–14.

Lukacs, J.R. 2012. Oral health in past populations: context, concepts and controversies. In A.L. Grauer (ed.), *A companion to palaeopathology*, 530–81. Chichester: Wiley-Blackwell.

Lukacs, J.R. and Thompson, L.M. 2009. Dental caries prevalence by sex in prehistory: magnitude and meaning. In J.D. Irish and G.C. Nelson (eds), *Technique and application in dental anthropology*, 136–77. Cambridge: Cambridge University Press.

Lukes, A. 2004. Social perspectives on the constitution of the Linear Pottery culture (LBK). In A. Lukes and M. Zvelebil (eds), *LBK dialogues: studies in the formation of the Linear Pottery culture*, 13–33. Oxford: Archaeopress.

Lukes, A. and Zvelebil, M. (eds) 2004. *LBK dialogues: studies in the formation of the Linear Pottery culture*. Oxford: Archaeopress.

Lukes, A. and Zvelebil, M. 2008. Inter-generational transmission of culture and LBK origins: some indications from eastern-central Europe. In D. Bailey, A. Whittle and D. Hofmann (eds), *Living well together? Settlement and materiality in the Neolithic of south-east and central Europe*, 139–50. Oxford: Oxbow Books.

Lukes, A., Zvelebil, M. and Pettitt, P. 2008. Biological and cultural identity of the first farmers: introduction to the Vedrovice bioarchaeology project. *Anthropologie* 46, 117–24.

Lüning, J. 1979/1980. Bandkeramische Pflüge? *Fundberichte aus Hessen* 19/20, 55–68.

Lüning, J. 1982. Siedlung und Siedlungslandschaft in bandkeramischer und Rössener Zeit. *Offa* 39, 9–33.

Lüning, J. 1986a. Ausgrabungen zur ältesten Bandkeramik. *Das Archäologische Jahr in Bayern 1986*, 33–4.

Lüning, J. 1986b. Die Ausgrabungen zum Neolithikum in Schwanfeld, Ldkr. Schweinfurt. In L. Wamser (ed.), *Aus Frankens Frühzeit: Festgabe für Peter Endrich*, 9–16. Würzburg: Freunde Mainfränkischer Kunst und Geschichte.

Lüning, J. 1988a. Frühe Bauern in Mitteleuropa im 6. and 5. Jahrtausend v. Chr. *Jahrbuch des Römisch-Germanischen Zentralmuseums Mainz* 35, 27–93.

Lüning, J. 1988b. Ausgrabungen zur ältesten Bandkeramik im Nördlinger Ries. *Das Archäologische Jahr in Bayern 1987*, 32–4.

Lüning, J. 1997a. Anfänge und frühe Entwicklung der Landwirtschaft im Neolithikum (5500–2200 v. Chr.). In J. Lüning, A. Jockenhövel, H. Bender and T. Capelle (eds), *Deutsche Agrargeschichte: Vor-und Frühgeschichte*, 15–139. Stuttgart: Eugen Ullmer.

Lüning, J. 1997b. Wohin mit der Bandkeramik? Programmatische Bemerkungen zu einem allgemeinen Problem am Beispiel Hessens. In C. Becker, M.-L. Dunkelmann, C. Metzner-Nebelsick, H. Peter-Röcher, M. Roeder and B. Feržan (eds), *Chronos: Beiträge zur prähistorischen Archäologie zwischen Nord- und Südosteuropa. Festschrift für Bernhard Hänsel*, 21–57. Espelkamp: Marie Leidorf.

Lüning, J. 1998. L'organisation régionale des habitats rubanés: sites centraux et sites secondaires (groupement de sites). In N. Cauwe and P.-L. van Berg (eds), *Organisation néolithique de l'espace en Europe du Nord-Ouest*, 163–85. Bruxelles: Société Royale Belge d'Anthropologie.

Lüning, J. 2000. *Steinzeitliche Bauern in Deutschland. Die Landwirtschaft im Neolithikum.* Bonn: Habelt.

Lüning, J. 2005a. Bandkeramische Hofplätze und die absolute Chronologie der Bandkeramik. In J. Lüning, C. Frirdich and A. Zimmermann (eds), *Die Bandkeramik im 21. Jahrhundert. Symposium in der Abtei Brauweiler bei Köln vom 16.9.–19.9.2002*, 49–74. Rahden: Marie Leidorf.

Lüning, J. 2005b. Die Macht der Ahnen und ihrer Abbilder. Wer hatte das Sagen in der Gesellschaft? In J. Lüning (ed.), *Die Bandkeramiker: erste Steinzeitbauern in Deutschland. Bilder einer Ausstellung beim Hessentag in Heppenheim/Bergstraße im Juni 2004*, 272–84. Rahden: Marie Leidorf.

Lüning, J. 2009. Bandkeramische Kultanlagen. In A. Zeeb-Lanz (ed.), *Krisen – Kulturwandel – Kontinuitäten: zum Ende der Bandkeramik in Mitteleuropa*, 129–90. Rahden: Marie Leidorf.

Lüning, J. and Stehli, P. 1989. Die Bandkeramik in Mitteleuropa: von der Natur- zur Kulturlandschaft. In J. Lüning (ed.), *Siedlungen der Steinzeit: Haus, Festung und Kult,* 110–21. Heidelberg: Spektrum der Wissenschaften.

Lüning, J. and Stehli, P. (eds) 1994. *Die Bandkeramik im Merzbachtal auf der Aldenhovener Platte: Beiträge zur Besiedlung der Aldenhovener Platte V.* Köln: Rheinland Verlag.

Lüning, J., Frirdich, C. and Zimmermann, A. (eds) 2005. *Die Bandkeramik im 21. Jahrhundert. Symposium in der Abtei Brauweiler bei Köln vom 16.9.–19.9.2002.* Rahden: Marie Leidorf.

Lüning, J., Kloos, U. and Albert, S. 1989. Westliche Nachbarn der bandkeramischen Kultur: La Hoguette und Limburg. *Germania* 67, 355–420.

Luz, B. and Kolodny, Y. 1985. Oxygen isotope variations in phosphate of biogenic apatites, IV. Mammal teeth and bones. *Earth and Planetary Science Letters* 75, 29–36.

Lynch, A.H., Hamilton, J. and Hedges, R.E.M. 2008. Where the wild things are: aurochs and cattle in England. *Antiquity* 82, 1025–39.

Mace, C., Holden, C.J. and Shennan, S. (eds) 2005. *The evolution of cultural diversity: a phylogenetic approach.* London: University College London Press.

Magyari, A., Musitz, B., Csontos, L. and Van Vliet Lanoë, B. 2005. Quaternary neotectonics of the Somogy Hills, Hungary (part I): evidence from field observations. *Tectonophysics* 410, 43–62.

Mainland, I.L. 2007. A microwear analysis of selected sheep and goat mandibles. In A. Whittle (ed.), *The early Neolithic on the Great Hungarian Plain: investigations of the Körös culture site of Ecsegfalva 23, County Békés*, 343–8. Budapest: Institute of Archaeology, Hungarian Academy of Sciences.

Makkay, J. 1978. Excavations at Bicske. I. The early Neolithic – the earliest Linear Band Ceramic. *Alba Regia* 16, 9–60.

Makkay, J. 1982a. *A magyarországi neolithikum kutatásának új eredményei. Az időrend és népi azonosíás kérdései (New results in the research of the Hungarian Neolithic).* Budapest: Akadémiai Kiadó.

Makkay, J. 1982b. Some comments on the settlement patterns of the Alföld Linear Pottery. In J. Pavúk (ed.), *Siedlungen der Kultur mit Linearkeramik: Internationales Kolloquium Nové Vozokany 17–20. November 1981*, 157–66. Nitra: Archäologisches Institut der Slowakischen Akademie der Wissenschaften.

Makkay, J. 1992. Excavations at the Körös culture settlement of Endrőd-Öregszőlők 119 in 1986–1989. In S. Bökönyi (ed.), *Cultural and landscape changes in south-east Hungary*, 121–93. Budapest: Archaeolingua.

Makkay, J., Starnini, E. and Tulok, M. 1996. *Excavations at Bicske-Galagonyás (Part III). The Notenkopf and Sopot-Bicske cultural phases.* Trieste: Società per la Preistoria e Protostoria della Regione Friuli-Venezia Giulia.

Manen, C. and Mazurié de Keroualin, K. 2003. Les concepts 'La Hoguette' et 'Limburg': un bilan des données. In M. Besse, L.-I. Stahl Gretsch and P. Curdy (eds), *ConstellaSion: hommage à Alain Gallay*, 115–45. Lausanne: Cahiers d'Archéologie Romande 95.

Mant, A.K. 1987. Knowledge acquired from post-war exhumations: approaches to archaeology and forensic science. In A.K. Boddington, A.N. Garland and R.C. Janaway (eds), *Death, decay and reconstruction,* 65–80. Manchester: Manchester University Press.

Marciniak, A. 2005. *Placing animals in the Neolithic: social zooarchaeology of prehistoric farming communities.* London: Institute of Archaeology Publications, University College, London.

Marciniak, A. 2011. The Secondary Products Revolution: empirical evidence and its current zooarchaeological critique. *Journal of World Prehistory* 24, 117–30.

Mariotti, A. 1983. Atmospheric nitrogen is a reliable standard for natural ^{15}N measurements. *Nature* 303, 685–7.

Martin, D.L. and Frayer, D.W. (eds) 1997. *Troubled times: violence and warfare in the past.* Amsterdam: Gordon and Breach.

Marton, T. 2008. Development of pottery style on the LBK settlement of Balatonszárszó-Kis-erdei-dűlő in Hungary. *Acta Terrae Septemcastrensis* 7, 197–216.

Marton, T. and Oross, K. 2009. Reconstructing space in a familiar world: the formation of late LBK settlements in central Transdanubia. In J.K. Kozłowski (ed.), *Interactions between different models of Neolithization north of the central European agro-ecological barrier*, 51–73. Kraków: Polska Akademiai Umiejętności.

Marton, T. and Oross, K. 2012. Siedlungsforschung an linearbandkeramischen Fundorten in Zentral- und Südtransdanubien – Wiege, Peripherie oder beides? In S. Wolfram, H. Stäuble, M. Cladders and T. Tischendorf (eds), *Siedlungsstruktur und Kulturwandel in der Bandkeramik. Beiträge der internationalen Tagung "Neue Fragen zur Bandkeramik oder alles beim Alten?!" Leipzig, 23. bis 24. September 2010*, 220–39. Leipzig: Landesamt für Archäologie.

Masur, A. 2009. *Die Häuser der linearbandkeramischen Siedlung von Saladorf, Österrreich.* Saarbrücken: VDM Verlag Dr. Müller.

Mateiciucová, I. 2001. Silexindustrie in der ältesten Linearbandkeramik-Kultur in Mähren und Niederösterreich auf der Basis der Silexindustrie des Lokalmesolithikums. In R. Kertész and J. Makkay (eds), *From the Mesolithic to the Neolithic*, 283–300. Budapest: Archaeolingua.

Mateiciucová, I. 2002. Silexartefakte der ältesten und älteren Linearbandkeramik aus Brunn am Gebirge, Niederösterreich (Vorbericht). *Antaeus* 25, 169–88.

Mateiciucová, I. 2003. Mesolithische Traditionen und der Ursprung der Linearbandkeramik. *Archäologische Informationen* 26, 299–320.

Mateiciucová, I. 2007. Worked stone: obsidian and flint. In A. Whittle (ed.), *The Early Neolithic on the Great Hungarian Plain: investigations of the Körös culture site of Ecsegfalva*

23, Co. Békés, 677–726. Budapest: Institute of Archaeology, Hungarian Academy of Sciences.

Mateiciucová, I. 2008a. *Talking stones: the chipped stone industry in Lower Austria and Moravia and the beginnings of the Neolithic in central Europe (LBK), 5700–4900 BC*. Brno: Masarykova univerzita.

Mateiciucová, I. 2008b. Neolitizace Evropy a vznik kultury s lineární keramikou (The Neolithization of central Europe and the rise of the Linear Pottery culture). In Z. Čižmář (ed.), *Život a smrt v mladší době kamenné*, 30–7. Brno: Ústav archeologické památkové péče Brno.

Mateiciucová, I. 2010. The beginnings of the Neolithic and raw material distribution networks in eastern Central Europe: symbolic dimensions of the distribution of Szentgál radiolarite. In D. Gronenborn and J. Petrasch (eds), *Die Neolithisierung Mitteleuropas (The spread of the Neolithic to central Europe)*, 273–300. Mainz: Römisch-Germanisches Zentralmuseum.

Mateiciucová, I. and Trnka, G. 2004. Die Silexartefakte aus der Siedlung mit Kreisgrabenanlage von Kamegg, Niederösterreich. In E. Kazdová, Z. Měřínský and K. Šabatová (eds), *K poctě Vladimíru Podborskému: přátelé a žáci k sedmdesátým narozeninám*, 89–99. Brno: Masaryk University.

Mathieu, G. and Mathieu, M. 1993. La nécropole rubanée d'Ensisheim 'Les Octrois' (Haut-Rhin). Présentation générale des fouilles de 1984. *Cahiers de l'Association pour la Promotion de la Recherche Archéologique en Alsace* 9, 1–16.

Mattheußer, E. 1991. Die geographische Ausrichtung bandkeramischer Häuser. In J. Lüning (ed.), *Studien zur Siedlungsarchäologie 1*, 3–49. Bonn: Habelt.

Mattheußer, E. 2009. Ein mehrperiodiger Siedlungsplatz am 'Hirtenweg' in Herkheim, Stadt Nördlingen, Landkreis Donau-Ries, Schwaben. *Das Archäologische Jahr in Bayern 2008*, 19–21.

Maurer, H. and Jama, N. 2006. Linearbandkeramische Kultgefäße aus dem nördlichen Niederösterreich. *Archäologie Österreichs* 17, 18–20.

Mauvilly, M. 1997. L'industrie lithique de la culture à céramique linéaire de Haute et Basse Alsace: état des recherches et bilan provisoire. In C. Jeunesse (ed.), *Le Néolithique danubien et ses marges entre Rhin et Seine*, 327–58. Strasbourg: Cahiers de l'Association pour la Promotion de la Recherche Archéologique en Alsace.

Mauvilly, M. 2001. Le mobilier lithique du site rubané de Rosheim 'Lotissement Sainte-Odile' (Bas-Rhin) – deuxième partie: objets en roches tenaces. *Cahiers de l'Association pour la Promotion de la Recherche Archéologique en Alsace* 17, 35–59.

Mays, S. 1998. *The archaeology of human bones*. London: Routledge.

Mays, S. and Beavan, N. 2012. An investigation of diet in early Anglo-Saxon England using carbon and nitrogen stable isotope analysis of human bone collagen. *Journal of Archaeological Science* 39, 867–74.

Mays, S.A., Richards, M.P. and Fuller, B.T. 2002. Bone stable isotope evidence for infant feeding in mediaeval England. *Antiquity* 76, 654–6.

Mays, S., Taylor, G.M., Legge, A.J., Young, D.B. and Turner-Walker, G. 2001. Paleopathological and biomolecular study of tuberculosis in a medieval skeletal collection from England. *American Journal of Physical Anthropology* 114, 298–311.

McCutchan, J.H., Lewis, W.M., Kendall, C. and McGrath, C.C. 2003. Variation in trophic shift for stable isotope ratios of carbon, nitrogen, and sulfur. *Oikos* 102, 378–90.

McHugh, F. 1999. *Theoretical and quantitative approaches to the study of mortuary practice*. Oxford: British Archaeological Reports.

Meier-Arendt, W. 1966. *Die bandkeramische Kultur in Untermaingebiet*. Bonn: Habelt.

Meixner, G. 1998. Paläoböden und Siedlungsbefunde der Linearbandkeramik von Altdorf, Landkreis Landshut. In K. Schmotz (ed.), *Vorträge des 16. Niederbayerischen Archäologentages*, 13–40. Rahden: Marie Leidorf.

Menghin, O. 1931. *Weltgeschichte der Steinzeit*. Vienna: Anton Schroll.

Menke, M. 1978. Zum Frühneolithikum zwischen Jura und Alpenrand. *Germania* 56, 24–52.

Merbs, C.F. 1983. *Patterns of activity-induced pathology in a Canadian Inuit population*. Ottawa: National Museum of Man.

Metcalf, P. 2010. *The life of the longhouse: an archaeology of ethnicity*. Cambridge: Cambridge University Press.

Meurers-Balke, J. and Kalis, A.J. 2001. Früh-, alt- und jungneolithische Landnutzung – archäopalynologische Bearbeitung der Wilhelma-Travertine von Bad Cannstatt. In B. Gehlen, M. Heinen and A. Tillmann (eds), *Zeit-Räume: Gedenkschrift für Wolfgang Taute. Band 2*, 631–48. Bonn: Deutsche Gesellschaft für Ur- und Frühgeschichte/Habelt.

Meyer, M. 2003. Zur formalen Gliederung alt- und mittelneolithischer Einhegungen. In J. Eckert, U. Eisenhauer and A. Zimmermann (eds), *Archäologische Perspektiven: Analysen und Interpretationen im Wandel. Festschrift für Jens Lüning zum 65. Geburtstag*, 423–40. Rahden: Marie Leidorf.

Meyer, C. and Alt, K.W. 2010. An anthropological perspective of the Early and Middle Neolithic of the Upper Rhine valley: results of an osteometric study of postcranial skeletal elements. In D. Gronenborn and J. Petrasch (eds), *Die Neolithisierung Mitteleuropas (The spread of the Neolithic to Central Europe)*, 487–96. Mainz: Römisch-Germanisches Zentralmuseum.

Meyer, C., Kürbis, O. and Alt, K.W. 2004. Das Massengrab von Wiederstedt, Ldkr. Mansfelder Land. Auswertung und Gedanken zur Deutung im Kontext der Linienbandkeramik. *Jahresschrift für Mitteldeutsche Vorgeschichte* 88, 31–66.

Milisauskas, S. 1976. *Archaeological investigations on the Linear Culture village of Olszanica*. Wrocław: Zakład Narodowy Imienia Ossolińskich.

Milisauskas, S. 1986. *Early Neolithic settlement and society at Olszanica*. Ann Arbor: University of Michigan.

Milisauskas, S. and Kruk, J. 1989. Neolithic economy in central Europe. *Journal of World Prehistory* 4, 403–46.

Minagawa, M. and Wada, E. 1984. Stepwise enrichment of ^{15}N along food chains: further evidence and the relation between δ^{15}N and animal age. *Geochimica et Cosmochimica Acta* 48, 1135–40.

Minichreiter, K. 2001. The architecture of Early and Middle Neolithic settlements of the Starčevo culture in northern Croatia. *Documenta Praehistorica* 28, 199–214.

Mitchell, F.J.G. 2005. How open were European primeval forests? Hypothesis testing using palaeoecological data. *Journal of Ecology* 93, 168–77.

Modderman, P.J.R. 1970. Linearbandkeramik aus Elsloo und Stein. *Analecta Praehistorica Leidensia* 3, 1–217.

Modderman, P.J.R. 1972. Die Hausbauten und Siedlungen der Linienbandkeramik in ihrem westlichen Bereich. In H. Schwabedissen (ed.), *Die Anfänge des Neolithikums vom Orient bis Nordeuropa. Fundamenta A/3 Va*, 77–84. Köln and Wien: Böhlau.

Modderman, P.J.R. 1976. Abschwemmung und neolithische

Siedlungsplätze in Niederbayern. *Archäologisches Korrespondenzblatt* 6, 105–8.
Modderman, P.J.R. 1977. *Die neolithische Besiedlung bei Hienheim, Ldkr. Kelheim I: Die Ausgrabungen am Weinberg 1965 bis 1970. Materialhefte zur Bayerischen Vorgeschichte 33*. Kallmünz: Michael Lassleben.
Modderman, P.J.R. 1978. Eine jungsteinzeitliche Siedlung aus Meindling, Gemeinde Oberschneiding, Landkreis Straubing-Bogen. *Beiträge zur Geschichte Niederbayerns während der Jungsteinzeit I. Beilage zum amtlichen Schul-Anzeiger für den Regierungsbezirk Niederbayern Nr. 1*, 21–7.
Modderman, P.J.R. 1985. Die Bandkeramik im Graetheidegebiet, Niederländisch- Limburg. *Bericht der Römisch-Germanischen Kommission* 66, 25–121.
Modderman, P.J.R. 1986a. Die neolithische Besiedlung bei Hienheim, Ldkr. Kelheim. *Analecta Praehistorica Leidensia* 19, 1–187.
Modderman, P.J.R. 1986b. On the typology of the houseplans and their European setting. In I. Pavlů, J. Rulf and M. Zápotocká (eds), *Theses on the Neolithic site of Bylany. Památky archeologické* 77, 383–94.
Modderman, P.J.R. 1988. The Linear Pottery culture: diversity in uniformity. *Berichten van de Rijksdienst voor het Oudheidkundig Bodemonderzoek* 38, 63–139.
Modderman, P.J.R. 1992. Linearbandkeramik aus Meindling, Gem. Oberschneiding, Ldkr. Straubing-Bogen. *Analecta Praehistorica Leidensia* 25, 25–42.
Molnar, P. 2006. Tracing prehistoric activities: musculoskeletal stress marker analysis of a Stone-Age population on the island of Gotland in the Baltic Sea. *American Journal of Physical Anthropology* 129, 12–23.
Molnar, S., Barrett, M.J., Brian, L., Brace, C.L., Brose, D.S., Dewey, J.R., Frisch, J.E., Ganguly, P., Gejvall, N.-G., Greene, D.L., Kennedy, K.A.R., Poirier, F.E., Pourchet, M.J., Rhine, S., II, C.G.T., Valen, L.V., Koenigswald, G.H.R.V., Wilkinson, R.G., Wolpoff, M.H. and Wright, G.A. 1972. Tooth wear and culture: a survey of tooth functions among some prehistoric populations. *Current Anthropology* 13, 511–26.
Montgomery, J. 2010. Passports from the past: investigating human dispersals using strontium isotope analysis of tooth enamel. *Annals of Human Biology* 37, 325–46.
Montgomery, J., Evans, J.A. and Cooper, R.E. 2007. Resolving archaeological populations with Sr-isotope mixing diagrams. *Applied Geochemistry* 22, 1502–14.
Morgan, L.H. 1877. *Ancient society. Or researches in the lines of human progress from savagery through barbarism to civilization.* London: MacMillan and Co.
Morris, I. 1991. The archaeology of ancestors: the Saxe/Goldstein hypothesis revisited. *Cambridge Archaeological Journal* 1, 147–69.
Müldner, G. and Richards, M.P. 2007. Stable isotope evidence for 1500 years of human diet at the city of York, UK. *American Journal of Physical Anthropology* 133, 682–97.
Müldner, G., Chenery, C. and Eckardt, H. 2011. The 'Headless Romans': multi-isotope investigations of an unusual burial ground from Roman Britain. *Journal of Archaeological Science* 38, 280–90.
Müller, J. 1997. Neolitische und chalkolithische *Spondylus*-Artefakte. Anmerkungen zu Verbreitung, Tauschgebiet und sozialer Funktion. In C. Becker, M.-L. Dunkelmann, C. Metzner-Nebelsick, H. Peter-Röcher, M. Röder and B. Terzan (eds), *Chronos: Beiträge zur prähistorischen Archäologie zwischen Nord- und Südosteuropa. Festschrift für Bernhard Hänsel*, 91–106. Espelkamp: Marie Leidorf.
Müller, J. 2002. Zur Belegungsabfolge des Gräberfeldes von Trebur: Argumente der typologieunabhängigen Datierungen. www.jungsteinsite.de.
Müller, J. 2003. Zur Belegungsabfolge des Gräberfeldes von Trebur: Argumente der typologieunabhängigen Datierungen. *Prähistorische Zeitschrift* 77, 148–58.
Müller, J., Herrera, A. and Knossalla, N. 1996. Spondylus und Dechsel – zwei gegensätzliche Hinweise auf Prestige in der mitteleuropäischen Linearbandkeramik? In J. Müller and R. Bernbeck (eds), *Prestige – Prestigegüter – Sozialstrukturen: Beispiele aus dem europäischen und vorderasiatischen Neolithikum*, 81–96. Bonn: Holos.
Murdock, G.P. 1949. *Social structure*. New York: MacMillan.
Murdock, G.P. and White, D.R. 1969. Standard cross-cultural sample. *Ethnology* 8, 329–69.
Murphy, B.P. and Bowman, D.M.J.S. 2009. The carbon and nitrogen isotope composition of Australian grasses in relation to climate. *Functional Ecology* 23, 1040–9.
Mussi, M. 2001. *Earliest Italy: an overview of the Italian Paleolithic and Mesolithic*. New York: Springer.
Nadler, M. and Zeeb, A. 1994. Südbayern zwischen Linearbandkeramik und Altheim: ein neuer Gliederungsvorschlag (with contributions by K. Böhm, H. Brink-Kloke, K. Riedhammer, R. Ganslmeier, U. Poensgen, E. Riedmeier-Fischer, H. Spatz, M. Rind and F. Blaich). In H.-J. Beier (ed.), *Der Rössener Horizont in Mitteleuropa*, 127–89. Wilkau-Hasslau: Beier and Beran.
Nagy, E.G. 2005. *Adatok az alföldi vonaldíszes kerámia kultúrájának településtörténeti képéhez a Felső-Tisza-vidéken.* Unpublished PhD dissertation, Eötvös Loránd University, Budapest.
Nanci, A. and Ten Cate, A.R. 2008. *Ten Cate's oral histology: development, structure, and function.* St Louis: Mosby Elsevier.
Nehlich, O., Montgomery, J., Evans, J., Schade-Lindig, S., Pichler, S.L., Richards, M.P. and Alt, K.W. 2009. Mobility or migration: a case study from the Neolithic settlement of Nieder-Mörlen (Hessen, Germany). *Journal of Archaeological Science* 36, 1791–9.
Nelle, O. 2002. Zur holozänen Vegetations- und Waldnutzungsgeschichte des Vorderen Bayerischen Waldes anhand von Pollen- und Holzkohleanalysen. *Hoppea: Denkschriften der Regensburgischen Botanischen Gesellschaft* 63, 161–361.
Neth, A. 1999. *Eine Siedlung der frühen Bandkeramik in Gerling, Kreis Ludwigsburg*. Stuttgart: Theiss.
Neudert, C. 2005. Linienbandkeramische Funde aus einer Höhle bei Hemau, Lkr. Regensburg. *Beiträge zur Archäologie in der Oberpfalz und in Regensburg* 7, 17–30.
Neugebauer, J.-W. 1981a. Hainburg. *Fundberichte aus Österreich* 19, 336–8.
Neugebauer, J.-W. 1981b. Gnadendorf. *Fundberichte aus Österreich* 19, 334.
Neugebauer, J.-W. 1993. *Archäologie in Niederösterreich: Poysdorf und das Weinviertel*. Vienna: Niederösterreichisches Pressehaus.
Neugebauer-Maresch, C. 1983. Neolithische und urnenfelderzeitliche Siedlungsstelle bei Gnadendorf, VB Mistelbach. *Fundberichte aus Österreich* 21, 107–32.
Neugebauer-Maresch, C. 1992. Der bandkeramische Friedhof von Kleinhadersdorf bei Poysdorf, NÖ. *Archäologie Österreichs* 3, 5–11.
Neugebauer-Maresch, C. and Lenneis, E. forthcoming. *Das bandkeramische Gräberfeld von Kleinhadersdorf.*
Neugebauer-Maresch, C. and Neugebauer, J.-W. 1987.

Kleinhadersdorf. *Fundberichte aus Österreich* 26, 194.

Neugebauer-Maresch, C. and Neugebauer, J.-W. 1989. Kleinhadersdorf. *Fundberichte aus Österreich* 27, 265.

Neugebauer-Maresch, C. and Neugebauer, J.-W. 1990. Kleinhadersdorf. *Fundberichte aus Österreich* 29, 182.

Neugebauer-Maresch, C. and Neydharth, F. 1988. Wultendorf. *Fundberichte aus Österreich* 24/25, 220.

Neumair, E. 1991. Die ersten Siedler und Ackerbauern Mitteleuropas. *Archäologie im Landkreis Freising* 2, 9–42.

Neumair, E. 1994. Die bandkeramische Siedlung Murr. *Archäologie im Landkreis Freising* 4, 7–62.

Neumair, E. 2008. Das neue Bild der frühen Geschichte des Landkreises Freising als Ergebnis der 30-jährigen ehrenamtlichen Forschungsarbeit. *Archäologie im Landkreis Freising* 10, 101–19.

Neumann, G. and Wiegand, F. 1940. Ein bandkeramisches Gräberfeld von Arnstadt. *Der Spatenforscher* 5, 9–32.

Newell, R.R. 1970. The flint industry of the Dutch Linearbandkeramik. In P.J.R. Modderman, 'Linearbandkeramik aus Elsloo und Stein'. *Analecta Praehistorica Leidensia* 3, 144–83.

Nielsen, E. 1994. Bemerkungen zum schweizerischen Spätmesolithikum. *Archäologisches Korrespondenzblatt* 24, 145–55.

Nieszery, N. 1995. *Linearbandkeramische Gräberfelder in Bayern.* Espelkamp: Marie Leidorf.

Nitsch, E.K., Humphrey, L.T. and Hedges, R.E.M. 2010. The effect of parity status on $\delta^{15}N$: looking for the "pregnancy effect" in 18th and 19th century London. *Journal of Archaeological Science* 37, 3191–9.

Nockemann, G.A.W. 2008. Different types of economies within the LBK settlement Erkelenz-Kückhoven. In A. Posluschy, K. Lambers and I. Herzog (eds), *Layers of perception. Proceedings of the 35th international conference on computer applications and quantitive methods in archaeology (CAA), Berlin, Germany, April 2–6, 2007*, 373–81. Bonn: Habelt.

Novotný, B. 1958. *Slovensko v mladšej dobe kamennej (Die Slowakei in der jüngeren Steinzeit).* Bratislava: Vydavateľstvo Slovenskej akadémie vied.

Nowak, M. 2004. Is 'pot prehistory' real prehistory? The case of the early LBK. In A. Lukes and M. Zvelebil (eds), *LBK dialogues: studies in the formation of the Linear Pottery culture*, 7–15. Oxford: Archaeopress.

Nowell, G.M. and Horstwood, M.S.A. 2009. Comments on Richards *et al.*, *Journal of Archaeological Science* 35, 2008 'Strontium isotope evidence of Neanderthal mobility at the site of Lakonis, Greece, using laser-ablation PIMMS'. *Journal of Archaeological Science* 36, 1334–41.

Nystrom, P. 2008. Dental microwear signatures of an early LBK population from Vedrovice, Moravia, Czech Republic. *Anthropologie* 46, 161–73.

O'Brian, S.R., Mayewski, P.A., Meeker, L.D., Meese, D.A., Twickler, M.S. and Whitlow, S.I. 1995. Complexity of Holocene climate as reconstructed from a Greenland ice core. *Science* 270, 1962–64.

O'Connell, T.C. and Hedges, R.E.M. 1999. Isotopic comparison of hair and bone: archaeological analyses. *Journal of Archaeological Science* 26, 661–5.

Oelze, V.M., Siebert, A., Nicklisch, N., Meller, H., Dresely, V. and Alt, K.W. 2011. Early Neolithic diet and animal husbandry: stable isotope evidence from three Linearbandkeramik (LBK) sites in Central Germany. *Journal of Archaeological Science* 38, 270–9.

Ogden, A. 2008. Advances in the palaeopathology of teeth and jaws. In R. Pinhasi and S. Mays (eds), *Advances in human palaeopathology*, 283–307. Chichester: Wiley.

Ohio State University 2002. Global History of Health Project – European Module [Online]. Available: http://global.sbs.ohio-state.edu/

O'Leary, M.H. 1988. Carbon isotopes in photosynthesis. *BioScience* 38, 328–36.

O'Leary, M. 1995. Environmental effects on carbon isotope fractionation in terrestrial plants. In E. Wada, T. Yoneyama, M. Minegawa, T. Ando and B.D. Fry (eds), *Stable isotopes in the biosphere*, 78–91. Kyoto: Kyoto University Press.

Oliveira, H. 2008. Molecular biology and the human past: a theory of archaeogenetics. *Archaeological Review from Cambridge* 23, 109–26.

Ondruš, V. 2002. Dvě pohřebiště lidu s neolitickou lineární keramikou ve Vedrovicích (Zwei Gräberfelder des Volkes mit neolithischer Linearbandkeramik in Vedrovice). In V. Podborský, *Dvě pohřebiště neolitického lidu s lineární keramikou ve Vedrovicích na Moravě*, 9–130. Brno: Ústav archeologie a muzeologie, Filozofická fakulta Masarykovy univerzity.

Oravecz, H. 1998–1999. Middle Neolithic burials at Tiszaföldvár. Data to the burial customs and social relations of the Alföld Linearband Pottery Culture—Középső újkőkori temetkezések Tiszaföldváron. Adatok az Alföldi Vonaldíszes Kerámia Kultúra temetkezési szokásainak és társadalmi viszonyainak vizsgálatához. *Folia Archaeologica* 47, 43–62.

Oross, K. 2004. Das neolithische Dorf von Balatonszárszó (Forschungen zwischen 2000–2002). *Antaeus* 27, 61–80.

Oross, K. and Bánffy, E. 2009. Three successive waves of Neolithisation: LBK development in Transdanubia. *Documenta Praehistorica* 36, 175–89.

Oross, K. and Marton, T. 2012. Neolithic burials of the *Linearbandkeramik* settlement at Balatonszárszó and their European context. *Acta Archaeologica Academiae Scientiarum Hungaricae* 63, 257–300.

Oross, K., Marton, T. and Fábián, S. 2004. Balatonszárszó–Kis-erdei-dűlő középső neolit településének temetkezései. Előzetes jelentés (Bestattungen der mittelneolithischen Siedlung von Balatonszárszó–Kis-erdei-dűlő. Vorbericht). In G. Ilon (ed.), *ΜΩΜΟΣ 3. Őskoros kutatók III, Összejövetelének konferenciakötete*, 283–92. Szombathely: Vas Megyei Múzeumok Igazgatósága.

Oross, K., Marton, T., Whittle, A., Hedges, R.E.M. and Cramp, L.J.E. 2010. Die Siedlung der Balaton-Lasinja-Kultur in Balatonszárszó-Kis-erdei-dűlő. In P. Kalábková, B. Kovár, P. Pavúk and J. Šuteková (eds), *PANTA RHEI: studies in chronology and cultural development of south-eastern and central Europe in earlier prehistory presented to Juraj Pavúk on the occasion of his 75th birthday*, 381–407. Bratislava: Comenius University.

Orschiedt, J. 1997. Die Jungfernhöhle bei Tiefenellern. Neue Interpretation der menschlichen Skelettreste. *Bericht des Historischen Vereins Bamberg* 133, 185–98.

Orschiedt, J. 1998a. *Bandkeramische Siedlungsbestattungen in Südwestdeutschland: archäologische und anthropologische Befunde.* Rahden: Marie Leidorf.

Orschiedt, J. 1998b. Ergebnisse einer neuen Untersuchung der spätmesolithischen Kopfbestattungen aus Süddeutschland. In N.J. Conard and C.-J. Kind (eds), *Aktuelle Forschungen zum Mesolithikum/Current Mesolithic Research*, 147–60. Tübingen: Mo Vince.

Orschiedt, J. 1999. *Manipulationen an menschlichen Skelettresten: taphonomische Prozesse, Sekundärbestattungen oder Kannibalismus?* Tübingen: Mo Vince Verlag.

Orschiedt, J. 2002. Die Kopfbestattungen der Ofnet-Höhle: ein Beleg für kriegerische Auseinandersetzungen im Mesolithikum. *Archäologische Informationen* 24, 199–207.

Orschiedt, J. and Haidle, M.N. 2007. The LBK enclosure at Herxheim: theatre of war or ritual centre? References from osteoarchaeological investigations. In T. Pollard and I. Banks (eds), *War and sacrifice: studies in the archaeology of conflict*, 153–67. Leiden: Brill.

Orschiedt, J. and Haidle, M.N. 2009. Die menschlichen Skelettreste von Herxheim. In A. Zeeb-Lanz (ed.), *Krisen – Kulturwandel – Kontinuitäten: zum Ende der Bandkeramik in Mitteleuropa*, 41–52. Rahden: Marie Leidorf.

Orschiedt, J., Häußer, A., Haidle, M.N., Alt, K.W. and Buitrago-Téllez, C.H. 2003. Survival of a multiple skull trauma: the case of an early Neolithic individual from the LBK enclosure at Herxheim (Southwest Germany). *International Journal of Osteoarchaeology* 13, 375–83.

Ortner, D.J. 2003. *Identification of pathological conditions in human skeletal remains*. San Diego: Academic Press.

Ortner, D.J. 2008. Differential diagnosis of skeletal lesions in infectious disease. In R. Pinhasi and S. Mays (eds), *Advances in human palaeopathology*, 191–214. Chichester: Wiley.

Ortner, D.J. and Putschar, W.G.J. 1985. *Identification of pathological conditions in human skeletal remains*. Washington: Smithsonian.

Ortner, D.J., Butler, W., Cafarella, J. and Milligan, L. 2001. Evidence of probable scurvy in subadults from archeological sites in North America. *American Journal of Physical Anthropology* 114, 343–51.

Ortner, D.J., Kimmerle, E.H. and Diez, M. 1999. Probable evidence of scurvy in subadults from archeological sites in Peru. *American Journal of Physical Anthropology* 108, 321–31.

Otte, M. 1984. Interprétation générale de la Place Saint-Lambert à Liège 1. *Études et Recherches Archéologiques de l'Université de Liège* 18, 247–50.

Overing, J. and Passes, A. (eds) 2000. *The anthropology of love and anger: the aesthetics of conviviality in native Amazonia*. London: Routledge.

Paetzold, D. 1992. Bemerkungen zum Siedlungsverhalten neolithischer bis latènezeitlicher Bevölkerungen zwischen Regensburg und Deggendorf. Gab es Besiedlungsschwerpunkte in Abhängigkeit von naturräumlicher Gliederung und Bodenbeschaffenheit? *Bayerische Vorgeschichtsblätter* 57, 77–102.

Palliardi, J. 1914. Die relative Chronologie der jüngeren Steinzeit in Mähren. *Wiener Prähistorische Zeitschrift* 1, 256–77.

Paluch, T. 2007. The Körös culture graves. In J. Makkay, *The excavations of the early Neolithic sites of the Körös culture in the Körös valley, Hungary: the final report, Quaderno* 11, 247–56. Trieste: Società per la Preistoria e Protostoria della regione Friuli-Venezia Giulia.

Papathanasiou, A. 2005. Health status of the Neolithic population of Alepotrypa Cave, Greece. *American Journal of Physical Anthropology* 126, 377–90.

Pariat, J.-G. 2007. *Des morts sans tombe? Le cas des ossements humains en contexte non-sépulcral en Europe tempérée entre les 6ème et 3ème millénaires av. J. C.* Oxford: Archaeopress.

Pauketat, T.R. 2007. *Chiefdoms and other delusions*. Lanham: Altamira Press.

Pavlů, I. 1986. Ceramic chronology of the Linear Pottery Culture site. In I. Pavlů, J. Rulf and M. Zápotocká, 'Theses on the Neolithic site of Bylany'. *Památky archeologické* 77, 288–412.

Pavlů, I. 2000a. Dům kultury s lineární keramikou na Moravě (House of the Linear Pottery culture at Moravia). *Sborník prací filozofické fakulty brněnské univerzity* M4, 21–9.

Pavlů, I. 2000b. *Life on a Neolithic Site: Bylany – a situational analysis of artefacts*. Prague: Institute of Archaeology.

Pavlů, I. 2004. The origins of the early Linear Pottery culture in Bohemia. In A. Lukes and M. Zvelebil (eds), *LBK dialogues: studies in the formation of the Linear Pottery culture*, 83–90. Oxford: Archaeopress.

Pavlů, I. 2005a. Neolitizace střední Evropy (The neolithisation of central Europe). *Archeologické rozhledy* 57, 293–302.

Pavlů, I. 2005b. Regionalisierung der Kultur mit Linearbandkeramik. In J. Lüning, C. Frirdich and A. Zimmermann (eds), *Die Bandkeramik im 21. Jahrhundert. Symposium in der Abtei Brauweiler bei Köln vom 16.9.–19.9.2002*, 41–7. Rahden: Marie Leidorf.

Pavlů, I. 2010. *Činnosti na neolitickém sídlišti Bylany: prostorová analýza keramiky (Activities on a Neolithic site of Bylany: an intrasite spatial analysis of pottery)*. Praha: Vydal Archeologický ústav AV ČR.

Pavlů, I. and Květina, P. 2009. Die kulturelle Entwicklung in Böhmen am Ende des 6. Jahrhunderts v. Chr. In A. Zeeb-Lanz (ed.), *Krisen – Kulturwandel – Kontinuitäten: zum Ende der Bandkeramik in Mitteleuropa*, 283–302. Rahden: Marie Leidorf.

Pavlů, I. and Rulf, J. 1991. Stone industry from the Neolithic site of Bylany. *Památky archeologické* 82, 277–365.

Pavlů, I. and Zápotocká, M. 1979. Současný stav a úkoly studia neolitu v Čechách. *Památky archeologické* 50, 281–318.

Pavúk, J. 1969. Chronologie der Železovce-Gruppe. *Slovenská archeológia* 17, 269–367.

Pavúk, J. 1972a. Neolithisches Gräberfeld in Nitra. *Slovenská archeológia* 20, 5–105.

Pavúk, J. 1972b. Zum Problem der Gräberfelder mit der Linienbandkeramik. *Alba Regia* 12, 123–30.

Pavúk, J. 1978. Výskum neolitického sídliska v Blatnom. *Archeologické výskumy a nálezy na Slovensku 1977*, 192–5.

Pavúk, J. 1980a. Ältere Linearkeramik in der Slowakei. *Slovenská archeológia* 28, 7–90.

Pavúk, J. 1980b. Výskum neolitického sídliska v Blatnom. *Archeologické výskumy a nálezy na Slovensku 1978*, 206–11.

Pavúk, J. 1982a. Die Hauptzüge der neolithischen Besiedlung in der Slowakei in Bezug zu Naturbedingungen. *Metodologické problémy československé archeologie*, 40–8. Prague: Archeologický ústav ĆSAV.

Pavúk, J. 1982b. Vorbericht über die Ausgrabung der neolithischen Siedlung in Štúrovo. In J. Pavúk (ed.), *Siedlungen der Kultur mit Linearkeramik in Europa. Internationales Kolloquium Nové Vozokany 17.–20. November 1981*, 207–26. Nitra: Archäologisches Institut der Slowakischen Akademie der Wissenschaften.

Pavúk, J. 1986. Linearkeramische Großbauten aus Čataj. *Slovenská archeológia* 34, 365–82.

Pavúk, J. 1994. *Štúrovo: ein Siedlungsplatz der Kultur mit Linearkeramik und der Želiezovce-Gruppe*. Nitra: Archäologisches Institut der Slowakischen Akademie der Wissenschaften.

Pavúk, J. 2004. Early Linear Pottery culture in Slovakia and the neolithisation of central Europe. In A. Lukes and M. Zvelebil (eds), *LBK dialogues: studies in the formation of the Linear Pottery culture*, 71–82. Oxford: Archaeopress.

Pavúk, J. 2009. Die Entwicklung der Želiezovce-Gruppe und die Entstehung der Lengyel-Kultur. In A. Zeeb-Lanz (ed.), *Krisen – Kulturwandel – Kontinuitäten: zum Ende der Bandkeramik in Mitteleuropa*, 249–66. Rahden: Marie Leidorf.

Pavúk, J. 2012. Zur Frage des Anfangs der jungen Linienbandkeramik. In S. Wolfram, H. Stäuble, M. Cladders and T. Tischendorf (eds), *Siedlungsstruktur und Kulturwandel in der Bandkeramik. Beiträge der internationalen Tagung "Neue Fragen zur Bandkeramik oder alles beim Alten?!" Leipzig, 23. bis 24. September 2010*, 295–309. Leipzig: Landesamt für Archäologie.

Pavúk, J. and Šiška, S. 1971. Neolitické a eneolitické osídlenie Slovenska (Neolitische und äneolitische Besiedlung der Slowakei). *Slovenská archeológia* 19, 319–64.

Pavúk, J. and Šiška, S. 1980. Neolit a eneolit (Das Neolithikum und Äneolithikum). *Slovenská archeológia* 28, 137–58.

Pearce, A.I., Richards, R.G., Milz, S., Schneider, E. and Pearce, S.G. 2007. Animal models for implant biomaterial research in bone: a review. *European Cells and Materials* 13, 1–10.

Pechtl, J. 2008. Vom Euphrat zum Lech – Zur Ausbreitung der ersten Bauernkulturen. In U. Gruber, G. Mahnkopf, D. Meixner, J. Pechtl and L. Steguweit, *Steinzeit im Landkreis Augsburg: Jäger, Sammler, Ackerbauern*, 22–37. Friedberg: Likias.

Pechtl, J. 2009a. *Stephansposching und sein Umfeld: Studien zum Altneolithikum im bayerischen Donauraum*. Unpublished PhD dissertation, Heidelberg University.

Pechtl, J. 2009b. A monumental prestige patchwork. In D. Hofmann and P. Bickle (eds), *Creating communities: new advances in central European Neolithic research*, 186–201. Oxford: Oxbow Books.

Pechtl, J. 2009c. Überlegungen zur Historie der ältesten Linienbandkeramik (ÄLBK) im südlichen Bayern. In M. Chytráček, H. Gruber, J. Michálek, R. Sandner and K. Schmotz (eds), *Fines Transire 18*, 79–115. Rahden: Marie Leidorf.

Pechtl, J. 2010. Anmerkungen zum Kenntnisstand linienbandkeramischer Hausarchitektur in südöstlichen Bayern und zum Potenzial ihrer typologischen Auswertung. In M. Chytráček, H. Gruber, J. Michálek, R. Sandner and K. Schmotz (eds), *Fines Transire 19*, 35–51. Rahden: Marie Leidorf..

Pechtl, J. forthcoming. Linearbandkeramik pottery and society. In C. Fowler, J. Harding and D. Hofmann (eds), *The Oxford Handbook of Neolithic Europe*. Oxford: Oxford University Press.

Pechtl, J. and Eibl, F. 2011. Die neolithische Graphitnutzung in Südbayern. In K. Schmotz (ed.), *Vorträge des 29. Niederbayerischen Archäologentages*, 349–432. Rahden: Marie Leidorf.

Pécsi, M. 1970. *Geomorphological regions in Hungary*. Budapest: Academic Press.

Peel, M.C., Finlayson, B.L. and McMahon, T.A. 2007. Updated world map of the Köppen-Geiger climate classification. *Hydrology and Earth System Sciences* 11, 1633–44.

Pellet, C. 1978. La nécropole rubanée de 'l'Etang David' à Chichery (Yonne). *Révue Archéologique de l'Est et du Centre-Est* 29, 65–84.

Perrin, J. 2002. La fin du Mésolithique dans l'arc jurassien: approche statistique des industries lithiques taillées. *Bulletin de la Société Préhistorique Française* 99, 487–99.

Peschel, C. 1992. *Regel und Ausnahme: linearbandkeramische Bestattungssitten in Deutschland und angrenzenden Gebieten, unter besonderer Berücksichtigung der Sonderbestattungen*. Rahden: Marie Leidorf.

Peter-Röcher, H. 2007. *Gewalt und Krieg im prähistorischen Europa. Beiträge zur Konfliktforschung auf der Grundlage archäologischer, anthropologischer und ethnologischer Quellen*. Bonn: Rudolf Habelt.

Peters, M. 2004. Zum Stand der paläobotanischen Forschung zwischen Donau und Alpen (Südbayern). In K. Schmotz (ed.), *Vorträge des 20. Niederbayerischen Archäologentages*, 353–67. Rahden: Marie Leidorf.

Peterson, B.J. and Fry, B. 1987. Stable isotopes in ecosystem studies. *Annual Review of Ecology and Systematics* 18, 293–320.

Petrasch, J. 1986. Typologie und Funktion neolithischer Öfen in Mittel- und Südosteuropa. *Acta Praehistorica et Archaeologica* 18, 33–83.

Petrasch, J. 1999. Mord und Krieg in der Bandkeramik. *Archäologisches Korrespondenzblatt* 29, 505–16.

Petrasch, J. 2003. Zentrale Orte in der Bandkeramik? In J. Eckert, U. Eisenhauer and A. Zimmermann (eds), *Archäologische Perspektiven: Analysen und Interpretationen im Wandel. Festschrift für Jens Lüning zum 65. Geburtstag*, 505–13. Rahden: Marie Leidorf.

Petrasch, J. 2010. Demografischer Wandel während der Neolithisierung in Mitteleuropa. In D. Gronenborn and J. Petrasch (eds), *Die Neolithisierung Mitteleuropas (The spread of the Neolithic to central Europe)*, 351–63. Mainz: Römisch-Germanisches Zentralmuseum.

Pétrequin, P., Martineau, R., Nowicki, P., Gauthier, E. and Schaal, C. 2009. La poterie Hoguette de Choisey (Jura), les Champins: observations, techniques et insertion régionale. *Bulletin de la Société Préhistorique Française* 106, 491–515.

Pettitt, P. and Hedges, R. 2008. The age of the Vedrovice cemetery: the AMS radiocarbon dating programme. *Anthropologie* 46, 125–34.

Petzet, M., Schmotz, K. and Keller, E. 1991. Vorwort. *Das Archäologische Jahr in Bayern 1990*, 9–11.

Phillips, D.L., Newsome, S.D. and Gregg, J.W. 2005. Combining sources in stable isotope mixing models: alternative methods. *Oecologia* 144, 520–7.

Pieler, F. 2004. *Die bandkeramische Siedlung von Ratzersdorf bei St.Pölten (Niederösterreich)*. Bonn: Habelt.

Pieler, F. 2006. Eine Siedlung der Vornotenkopfkeramik aus Mörtersdorf, VB. Horn. *Archäologie Österreichs* 17, 21–30.

Pieler, F. 2010. *Die Bandkeramik im Horner Becken (Niederösterreich): Studien zur Struktur einer frühneolithischen Siedlungskammer*. Bonn: Habelt.

Pinhasi, R. and Mays, S.A. (eds) 2008. *Advances in human palaeopathology*. Chichester: Wiley.

Pittioni, R. 1953. Altweltliches Keramikum als historisches Problem. *Archaeologia Austriaca* 13, 105–16.

Pittioni, R. 1954. *Urgeschichte des österreichischen Raumes*. Vienna: Franz Deuticke.

Pittioni, R. 1980. *Urzeit – von etwa 80.000 bis 15 v. Chr. Anmerkungen und Exkurse mit einer Literaturübersicht über 25 Jahre Urgeschichtsforschung in Österreich 1954–1978*. Vienna: Österreichische Akademie der Wissenschaften.

Plesl, E. 1952. Pohřebiště lidu s volutovou keramikou v Mlynárcích na Slovensku. *Archeologické rozhledy* 4, 9–19.

Podborský, V. 1988. *Těšetice-Kyjovice 4: rondel osady lidu s moravskou malovanou kermikou*. Brno: Ústav archeologie a muzeologie, Filozofická fakulta Masarykovy univerzity.

Podborský, V. 1993. Nástup zemědělské civilizace (neolit). In V. Podborský (ed.), *Pravěké dějiny Moravy (Vlastivěda moravská. Země a lid, sv. 3)*, 71–152. Brno: Muzejní a vlastivědná společnost.

Podborský, V. (ed.) 1999. *Pravěká sociokultovní architektura na Moravě (Primeval socio-ritual architecture in Moravia)*. Brno: Ústav archeologie a muzeologie, Filozofická fakulta Masarykovy univerzity.

Podborský, V. (ed.) 2001. *50 let archeologických výzkumů Masarykovy univerzity na Znojemsku (50 Jahre archäologischer Forschungen der Masaryk-Universität im Gebiet von Znaim)*. Brno: Ústav archeologie a muzeologie, Filozofická fakulta Masarykovy univerzity.

Podborský, V. 2002a. Úvodem (Einleitung). In V. Podborský, *Dvě pohřebiště neolitického lidu s lineární keramikou ve Vedrovicích na Moravě*, 5–8. Brno: Ústav archeologie a muzeologie, Filozofická fakulta Masarykovy univerzity.

Podborský, V. 2002b. Vedrovická pohřebiště ve starším moravském a středoevropském neolitu (Die Gräberfelder von Vedrovice im älteren mährischen und mitteleuropäischen Neolithikum). In V. Podborský, *Dvě pohřebiště neolitického lidu s lineární keramikou ve Vedrovicích na Moravě*, 293–338. Brno: Ústav archeologie a muzeologie, Filozofická fakulta Masarykovy univerzity.

Podborský, V. 2002c. Spondylový šperk z vedrovických pohřebišť (Spondylusschmuck in den Gräbern des Volkes mit Linearbandkeramik in Vedrovice). In V. Podborský, *Dvě pohřebiště neolitického lidu s lineární keramikou ve Vedrovicích na Moravě*, 235–55. Brno: Ústav archeologie a muzeologie, Filozofická fakulta Masarykovy univerzity.

Podborský, V. and Vildomec, V. 1972. *Pravěk Znojemska (Die Urzeit des Gebietes von Znojmo)*. Brno: Musejní spolek v Brně, and Jihomoravské muzeum ve Znojmě.

Pollard, A.M. 2011.Isotopes and impact: a cautionary tale. *Antiquity* 85, 631–8.

Ponsard, S. and Averbuch, P. 1999. Should growing and adult animals fed on the same diet show different δ^{15}N values? *Rapid Communications in Mass Spectrometry* 13, 1305–10.

Potter, J.M. and Perry, E.M. 2011. Mortuary features and identity construction in an early village community in the American Southwest. *American Antiquity* 76, 529–46.

Prescott, C. and Glørstad, H. (eds) 2012. *Becoming European: the transformation of third millennium Northern and Western Europe*. Oxford: Oxbow Books.

Price, T.D. and Bentley, R.A. 2005. Human mobility in the Linearbandkeramik: an archaeometric approach. In J. Lüning, C. Frirdich and A. Zimmermann (eds), *Die Bandkeramik im 21. Jahrhundert: Symposium in der Abtei Brauweiler bei Köln vom 16.9–19.9.2002*, 203–15. Rahden: Marie Leidorf.

Price, T. D., Bentley, R.A., Lüning, J., Gronenborn, D. and Wahl, J. 2001. Prehistoric human migration in the Linearbandkeramik of Central Europe. *Antiquity* 75, 593–603.

Price, T.D., Burton, J. and Bentley, R.A. 2002. Characterization of biologically available strontium isotope ratios for the study of prehistoric migration. *Archaeometry* 44, 117–35.

Price, T.D., Frei, K.M., Tiesler, V. and Gestsdóttir, H. 2012. Isotopes and mobility: case studies with large samples. In E. Kaiser, J. Burger, and S. Wolfram (eds), *Population dynamics in prehistory and early history: new approaches using stable isotopes and genetics*, 311–21. Berlin: de Gruyter.

Price, T.D., Grupe, G. and Schröter, P. 1998. Migration and mobility in the Bell Beaker period in Central Europe. *Antiquity* 72, 405–11.

Price, T.D., Knipper, C., Grupe, G. and Smrcka, V. 2004. Strontium isotopes and prehistoric human migration: the Bell Beaker period in central Europe. *European Journal of Archaeology* 7, 9–40.

Price, T.D., Wahl, J. and Bentley, R.A. 2006. Isotopic evidence for mobility and group organization among Neolithic farmers at Talheim, Germany, 5000 BC. *European Journal of Archaeology* 9, 259–84.

Price, T.D., Wahl, J., Knipper, C., Burger-Heinrich, E., Kurz, G. and Bentley, R.A. 2003. Das bandkeramische Gräberfeld vom 'Viesenhäuser Hof' bei Stuttgart-Mühlhausen: neue Untersuchungsergebnisse zum Migrationsverhalten im frühen Neolithikum. *Fundberichte aus Baden-Württemberg* 27, 23–58.

Přichystal, A. 2002. Petrografický výzkum broušené a ostatní kamenné industrie z vedrovických pohřebišt (Petrographische Untersuchung geschliffener und übriger Steinindustrie aus den Vedrovice Gräberfeldern). In V. Podborský, *Dvě pohřebiště neolitického lidu s lineární keramikou ve Vedrovicích na Moravě*, 211–15. Brno: Ústav archeologie a muzeologie, Filozofická fakulta Masarykovy univerzity.

Přichystal, M. 2008. Brno (k. ú. Bohunice, Nový a Starý Lískovec, okr. Brno-město). In Z. Čižmář (ed.), *Život a smrt v mladší době kamenné*, 50–5. Brno: Ústav archeologické památkové péče Brno.

Prostředník, J., Šída, P., Šrein, V., Šreinerová, B. and Šťastný, M. 2005. Neolithic quarrying in the foothills of the Jizera Mountains and the dating thereof. *Archeologické rozhledy* 57, 477–92.

Pucher, E. 1987. Viehwirtschaft und Jagd zur Zeit der ältesten Linearbandkeramik von Neckenmarkt (Burgenland) und Strögen (Niederösterreich). *Mitteilungen der Anthropologischen Gesellschaft in Wien* 117, 141–55.

Pucher, E. 2001. Tierknochen. In E. Lenneis and J. Lüning, *Die altbandkeramischen Siedlungen von Neckenmarkt und Strögen*, 258–69. Bonn: Habelt.

Pyzel, J. 2009. Settlement history of the Linear Band Pottery culture in Kuyavia. In D. Hofmann and P. Bickle (eds), *Creating communities: new advances in central European Neolithic research*, 71–9. Oxford: Oxbow Books.

Quitta, H. 1960. Zur Frage der ältesten Bandkeramik in Mitteleuropa. *Prähistorische Zeitschrift* 38, 1–38, 153–88.

Quitta, H. 1964. Zur Herkunft des frühen Neolithikums in Mitteleuropa. In P. Grimm (ed.), *Varia Archaeologica: Wilhelm Unverzagt zum 70. Geburtstag dargebracht*, 14–24. Berlin: Deutsche Akademie der Wissenschaften zu Berlin.

Raczky, P. 1983. A korai neolitikumból a középső neolitikumba való átmenet kérdései a Közép- és Felső-Tiszavidéken (Questions of transition between the Early and Middle Neolithic in the Middle and Upper Tisza region). *Archaeologiai Értesítő* 110, 161–94.

Raczky, P. 1986. Megjegyzések az „alföldi vonaldíszes kerámia" kialakulásának kérdéséhez. *Régészeti tanulmányok Kelet-Magyarországról. Folklór és etnográfia* 24, 25–43.

Raczky, P. 1987. Öcsöd-Kováshalom: a settlement of the Tisza culture. In L. Tálas and P. Raczky (eds), *The Late Neolithic of the Tisza Region. A survey of recent excavations and their findings: Hódmezővásárhely-Gorzsa, Szegvár-Tűzköves, Öcsöd-Kováshalom, Vésztő-Mágor, Berettyóújfalu-Herpály*. 61–83. Budapest and Szolnok: Directorate of the Szolnok County Museums.

Raczky, P. 1988. *A Tisza-vidék kulturális és kronólogiai kapcsolatai a Balkánnal és az Égeikummal a neolitikum, rézkor időszakában: újabb kutatási eredmények és problémák*. Szolnok: Szolnok Megyei Múzeumok Igazgatósága/Eötvös Loránd Tudományegyetem Régészeti Tanszéke.

Raczky, P. 1989. Chronological framework of the Early and Middle Neolithic in the Tisza region. In S. Bökönyi (ed.), *Neolithic of southeastern Europe and its Near Eastern connections*, 233–51. Budapest: Akadémiai Kiadó.

Raczky, P. 2004. Polgár, Ferenci-hát. *Régészeti Kutatások Magyarországon (Archaeological Investigations in Hungary) 2002,* 257–8.

Raczky, P. and Anders, A. 2003. The internal relations of the Alföld Linear Pottery culture in Hungary and characteristics of human representation. In E. Jerem and P. Raczky (eds), *Morgenrot der Kulturen: frühe Etappen der Menscheitsgeschichte in Mittel- und Südosteuropa. Festschrift für Nándor Kalicz zum 75. Geburtstag*, 155–82. Budapest: Archaeolingua.

Raczky, P. and Anders, A. 2008. Late Neolithic spatial differentiation at Polgár-Csőszhalom, eastern Hungary. In D. Bailey, A. Whittle and D. Hofmann (eds), *Living well together? Settlement and materiality in the Neolithic of south-east and central Europe*, 35–53. Oxford: Oxbow Books.

Raczky, P. and Anders, A. 2009. Settlement history of the Middle Neolithic in the Polgár micro-region (the development of the Alföld Linearband Pottery in the upper Tisza region, Hungary). In J.K. Kozłowski (ed.), *Interactions between different models of Neolithization north of the central European agro-ecological barrier*, 31–50. Kraków: Polska Akademiai Umiejętności.

Raczky, P. and Anders, A. 2012. Neolithic enclosures in eastern Hungary and their survival into the Copper Age. In F. Bertemes, P.F. Biehl and H. Meller (eds), *Neolithische Kreisgrabenanlagen in Europa/Neolithic circular enclosures in Europe*, 271–309. Halle: Landesamtes für Archäologie/ Landesmuseum für Vorgeschichte, Sachsen-Anhalt.

Raczky, P., Sümegi, P., Bartosiewicz, L., Gál, E., Kaczanowska, M., Kozłowski, J.K. and Anders, A. 2010. Ecological barrier versus mental marginal zone? Problems of the northernmost Körös culture settlements in the Great Hungarian Plain. In D. Gronenborn and J. Petrasch (eds), *Die Neolithisierung Mitteleuropas (The spread of the Neolithic to central Europe)*, 147–73. Mainz: Römisch-Germanisches Zentralmuseum.

Ramminger, B. 2005. Die Viehzucht: viel Arbeit mit den Haustieren. In J. Lüning (ed.), *Die Bandkeramiker: erste Steinzeitbauern in Deutschland. Bilder einer Ausstellung beim Hessentag in Heppenheim/Bergstraße im Juni 2004*, 75–9. Rahden: Marie Leidorf.

Ramminger, B. 2007. *Wirtschaftsarchäologische Untersuchungen zu alt- und mittelneolithischen Felsgesteingeräten in Mittel- und Nordhessen: Archäologie und Rohmaterialversorgung*. Rahden: Marie Leidorf.

Ramminger, B. 2009. The exchange of LBK adze blades in central Europe: an example for economic investigations in archaeology. In D. Hofmann and P. Bickle (eds), *Creating communities: new advances in central European Neolithic research*, 80–94. Oxford: Oxbow Books.

Rasbash, J., Charlton, C., Browne, W.J., Healy, M. and Cameron, B. 2005. *MLwiN Version 2.02*. Bristol: Centre for Multilevel Modelling, University of Bristol.

Rasbash, J., Charlton, C., Browne, W.J., Healy, M. and Cameron, B. 2009a. *MLwiN Version 2.1*. Bristol: Centre for Multilevel Modelling, University of Bristol.

Rasbash, J., Steele, F., Browne, W.J. and Goldstein, H. 2009b. *A user's guide to MLwiN, v2.10*. Bristol: Centre for Multilevel Modelling, University of Bristol.

Rasbash, J., Charlton, C. and Pillinger, R. 2009c. *Manual supplement to MlwiN, v2.10*. Bristol: Centre for Multilevel Modelling, University of Bristol.

Raßhofer, G. 2001. Prähistorische Archäologie und Denkmalpflege in der Oberpfalz – eine Bilanz. In M. Chytrácek, J. Michálek and K. Schmotz (eds), *Archäologische Arbeitsgemeinschaft Ostbayern/West- und Südböhmen. 10. Treffen, 7.-10. Juni 2000 in Ceský Krumlov*, 27–42. Rahden: Marie Leidorf.

Rasteiro, R., Bouttier, P.-A., Sousa, V.C. and Chikhi, L. 2012. Investigating sex-biased migration during the Neolithic transition in Europe, using an explicit spatial simulation framework. *Proceedings of the Royal Society B* 279, 2409–16.

Reim, H. 1992. Ein Hausgrundriss in der ältestbandkeramischen Siedlung von Rottenburg am Neckar, Kreis Tübingen. *Archäologische Ausgrabungen in Baden-Württemberg 1992*, 56–60.

Reimer, P., Baillie, M., Bard, E., Bayliss, A., Beck, J., Blackwell, P., Bronk Ramsey, C., Buck, C., Burr, G., Edwards, R., Friedrich, M., Grootes, P., Guilderson, T., Hajdas, I., Heaton, T., Hogg, A., Hughen, K., Kaiser, K., Kromer, B., McCormac, F., Manning, S., Reimer, R., Richards, D., Southon, J., Talamo, S., Turney, C., van der Plicht, J. and Weyhenmeyer, C. 2009. IntCal 09 and Marine09 radiocarbon age calibration curves, 0–50,000 years cal BP. *Radiocarbon* 51, 1111–50.

Reinecke, K. 1978a. Linearbandkeramische Forschungen im unteren Aitrachtal. *Der Storchenturm. Geschichtsblätter für die Landkreise um Dingolfing, Landau und Vilsbiburg* 26, 49–83.

Reinecke, K. 1978b. Die Linearbandkeramik in Niederbayern. *Beiträge zur Geschichte Niederbayerns während der Jungsteinzeit I. Beilage zum amtlichen Schul-Anzeiger für den Regierungsbezirk Niederbayern Nr. 1*, 4–20.

Reinecke, K. 1982. Linearbandkeramische Siedlungen in Niederbayern. In J. Pavúk (ed.), *Siedlungen der Kultur mit Linearkeramik in Europa. Internationales Kolloquium Nové Vozokany 17–20 November 1981*, 239–46. Nitra: Archäologisches Institut der slovakischen Akademie der Wissenschaften.

Reinecke, K. 1983. Zwei Siedlungen der ältesten Linearbandkeramik aus dem Isartal. *Bayerische Vorgeschichtsblätter* 48, 31–62.

Reinecke, P. 1929. Die Stufe der neolithischen Spiralkeramik im rechtsrheinischen Bayern. *Bayerischer Vorgeschichtsfreund* 8, 1–13.

Renfrew, C. 1973. Monuments, mobilization and social organization in Neolithic Wessex. In C. Renfrew (ed.), *The explanation of culture change: models in prehistory*, 539–58. London: Duckworth.

Renfrew, C. 2000. Archaeogenetics: towards a population prehistory of Europe. In C. Renfrew and K. Boyle (eds), *Archaeogenetics: DNA and the population prehistory of Europe*, 3–12. Cambridge: McDonald Institute for Archaeological Research.

Renner, C. 1994. Die Bandkeramik von Nassenfels, Lkr. Eichstätt, Oberbayern. *Bayerische Vorgeschichtsblätter* 59, 19–37.

Rettenbacher, C. and Tichý, G. 1994. Ein frühmesolithisches Kindergrab aus der Zigeunerhöhle in Elsbethen bei Salzburg. *Mitteilungen der Gesellschaft Salzburger Landeskunde* 134, 625–42.

Reuter, E. 1991. *Die ältestbandkeramische Tonware aus Enkingen, Ldkr. Donau-Ries*. Unpublished M.A. dissertation, Frankfurt a.M. University.

Reuter, E. 1994. Eine Siedlung der 'Bandkeramiker' in Enkingen. *Rieser Kulturtage 9, Dokumentation*, 123–36. Nördlingen: Verlag Rieser Kulturtage.

Reynard, L.M., Henderson, G.M. and Hedges, R.E.M. 2010. Calcium isotope ratios in animal and human bone. *Geochimica et Cosmochimica Acta* 74, 3735–50.

Reynard, L.M., Henderson, G.M. and Hedges, R.E.M. 2011. Calcium isotopes in archaeological bones and their relationship to dairy consumption. *Journal of Archaeological Science* 38, 657–64.

Richards, M., Côrte-Real, H., Forster, P., Macaulay, V., Wilkinson-Herbots, H., Demaine, A., Papiha, S., Hedges, R.E.M., Bandelt, H.-J. and Sykes, B. 1996. Paleolithic and Neolithic lineages in the European mitochondrial gene pool. *American Journal of Human Genetics* 59, 185–203.

Richards, M.P., Hedges, R.E.M., Molleson, T.I. and Vogel, J.C. 1998. Stable isotope analysis reveals variations in human diet at the Poundbury Camp cemetery site. *Journal of Archaeological Science* 25, 1247–52.

Richards, M.P., Montgomery, J., Nehlich, O. and Grimes, V. 2008. Isotopic analysis of humans and animals from Vedrovice. *Anthropologie* 46, 185–94.

Richards, M.P., Pearson, J.A., Molleson, T.I., Russell, N. and Martin, L. 2003a. Stable isotope evidence of diet at Neolithic Çatalhöyük, Turkey. *Journal of Archaeological Science* 30, 67–76.

Richards, M.P., Schulting, R.J. and Hedges, R.E.M. 2003b. Sharp shift in diet at onset of Neolithic. *Nature* 425, 366.

Richter, I. 1969. Die bandkeramischen Gräber von Flomborn, Kreis Alzey, und vom Adlerberg bei Worms. *Mainzer Zeitschrift* 63/64, 158–79.

Richter, T. 2009. *Die Silexartefakte des mesolithischen Oberflächenfundplatzes Germering-Nebel, Lkr. Fürstenfeld-Bruck.* Unpublished M.A. dissertation, University of Cologne.

Rieder, K. and Tillmann, A. 1989. Steinzeitliche Fundhorizonte in der Wasserburg Nassenfels, Lkr. Eichstätt. In K. Rieder, A. Tillmann and J. Weining (eds), *Steinzeitliche Kulturen an Donau und Altmühl: Begleitheft zur Ausstellung im Stadtmuseum Ingolstadt*, 70–80. Ingolstadt: Bayerisches Landesamt für Denkmalpflege.

Rieder, K., Tillmann, A. and Weining, J. (eds) 1989. *Steinzeitliche Kulturen an Donau und Altmühl. Begleitheft zur Ausstellung im Stadtmuseum Ingolstadt.* Ingolstadt: Bayerisches Landesamt für Denkmalpflege.

Rind, M. 1994. Siedlungsspuren der Oberlauterbacher Gruppe in Wildenberg – ein Vorbericht. In M. Rind (ed.), *Scherben, Schädel, Schratzellöcher. Archäologie im Landkreis Kelheim Band 1 (1991–1993)*, 33–9. Regensburg: Buchverlag der Mittelbayerischen Zeitung.

Robb, J. 2007. *The early Mediterranean village: agency, material culture, and social change in Neolithic Italy.* Cambridge: Cambridge University Press.

Robb, J. and Miracle, P. 2007. Beyond 'migration' versus 'acculturation': new models for the spread of agriculture. In A. Whittle and V. Cummings (eds), *Going over: the Mesolithic-Neolithic transition in north-west Europe*, 99–115. Oxford: Oxford University Press for the British Academy.

Roberts, C.A. 2000. Trauma in biocultural perspective: past, present and future work in Britain. In M. Cox and S. Mays (eds), *Human osteology in archaeology and forensic science*, 337–56. London: Greenwich Medical Media.

Roberts, C.A. 2009. *Human remains in archaeology: a handbook.* York: Council for British Archaeology.

Roberts, C.A. and Buikstra, J.E. 2003. *The bioarchaeology of tuberculosis: a global view of a reemerging disease.* Gainesville: University of Florida Press.

Roberts, C.A. and Manchester, K. 2005. *The archaeology of disease.* Stroud: Sutton.

Robey, P.G. and Boskey, A.L. 2006. Extracellular matrix and biomineralization of bone. In M.J. Favus (ed.), *Primer on the metabolic bone diseases and disorders of mineral metabolism* (sixth edition), 12–19. Washington, DC: The American Society for Bone and Mineral Research.

Rosaldo, R. 1989. *Culture and truth: the remaking of social analysis.* Boston: Beacon Press.

Roth, G. 2008. *Geben und Nehmen: eine wirtschaftshistorische Studie zum neolithischen Hornsteinbergbau von Abensberg-Arnhofen, Kr. Kelheim (Niederbayern).* http://kups.ub-koeln.de/4176/.

Rötting, H. 1983. Das alt- und mittelneolithische Gräberfeld von Wittmar, Ldkr. Wolfenbüttel: eine Übersicht zu den Grabungsergebnissen. In R. Wegner (ed.), *Frühe Bauernkulturen in Niedersachsen: Linienbandkeramik, Stichbandkeramik, Rössener Kultur*, 135–57. Oldenburg: Staatliches Museum für Naturkunde und Vorgeschichte.

Rowley-Conwy, P. 1981. Slash and burn agriculture in the temperate European Neolithic. In R. Mercer (ed.), *Farming practice in British prehistory*, 85–96. Edinburgh: Edinburgh University Press.

Rück, O. 2001. Eine bandkeramische Siedlung bei Utzwingen, Gemeinde Maihingen, Landkreis Donau-Ries, Schwaben. *Das Archäologische Jahr in Bayern 2000*, 17–19.

Rück, O. 2007. *Neue Aspekte und Modelle in der Siedlungsforschung zur Bandkeramik: die Siedlung Weisweiler 111 auf der Aldenhovener Platte, Kreis Düren.* Rahden: Marie Leidorf.

Rück, O. 2009. New aspects and models for Bandkeramik settlement research. In D. Hofmann and P. Bickle (eds), *Creating communities: new advances in central European Neolithic research*, 159–85. Oxford: Oxbow Books.

Rulf, J. 1997. *Die Elbe-Provinz der Linearbandkeramik. Památky archeologické, Supplementum* 9. Prague: Institute of Archaeology.

Ruttkay, A. 1998. Šesť'desiat rokov od vzniku Archeologického ústavu na Slovensku (Sechzig Jahre seit der Entstehung des Archäologischen Institutes in der Slowakei). *Slovenská archeológia* 46, 137–40.

Ruttkay, E., Wessely, G. and Wolff, P. 1976. Eine Kulturschicht der ältesten Linearbandkeramik in Prellenkirchen, p.B. Bruck, NÖ. *Annalen Naturhistorisches Museum Wien* 80, 843–61.

Ruttner, I. 2003. Ur- und frühgeschichtliche Forschung in Oberösterreich: ein historischer Überblick. In J. Leskovar, C. Schwanzer and G. Winkler (eds), *Worauf wir stehen: Archäologie in Oberösterreich*, 11–22. Weitra: Bibliothek der Provinz.

Sachweh, M. and Enders, G. 1996. *Klimaatlas von Bayern.* Munich: BayFORKLIM.

Sahlins, M. 1974. *Stone Age economics.* Chicago: Aldine.

Sahlins, M. 1999. Two or three things that I know about culture. *Journal of the Royal Anthropological Institute* 5, 399–421.

Saile, T. 2010. Aspects of neolithisation in the Weser-Harz region. In D. Gronenborn and J. Petrasch (eds), *Die Neolithisierung Mitteleuropas (The spread of the Neolithic to central Europe)*, 439–47. Mainz: Römisch-Germanisches Zentralmuseum.

Sainty, J., Jeunesse, C. and Lambach, F. 1988. Sauvetage urgent sur le site de Wettolsheim 'Koenigsbreite' (Haut-Rhin) en 1986: contribution à l'étude du peuplement néolithique ancien dans le secteur de Colmar-sud. *Cahiers de l'Association pour la Promotion de la Recherche Archéologique en Alsace* 31, 5–16.

Sainty, J., Thévenin, A., Thévenin, C. and Piningre, J.-F. 1984. Le site rubané récent de Rouffach 'Gallbühl' (Haut-Rhin). *Revue Archéologique de l'Est et du Centre-Est* 35, 3–39.

Salque, M., Radi, G., Fabbri, C., Tagliacozzo, A., Pina Uria B., Wolfram, S., Hohle, I., Stäuble, H., Whittle, A., Hofmann, D., Pechtl, J., Schade-Lindig, S., Eisenhauer, U. and Evershed, R.P. 2012a. New insights into the early Neolithic economy and management of animals in southern and central Europe revealed using lipid residue analyses of pottery vessels. *Anthropozoologica* 47, 45–62.

Salque, M., Bogucki, P.I., Pyzel, J., Sobkowiak-Tabaka, I., Grygiel, R., Szmyt, M. and Evershed, R.P. 2012b. Earliest evidence for cheese making in the sixth millennium BC in northern Europe. *Nature Letter* 12 Dec. 2012.

Saxe, A.A. 1971. Social dimensions of mortuary practices in a Mesolithic population from Wadi Halfa, Sudan. In J.A. Brown (ed.), *Approaches to the social dimensions of mortuary practices*, 39–57. Washington: Society of American Anthropology.

Schade-Lindig, S. and Schade, C. 2010. Woher kommt Flomborn? Keramikimporte und Nachahmungen in der bandkeramischen Siedlung Bad Nauheim – Nieder-Mörlen auf dem Hempler. In D. Gronenborn and J. Petrasch (eds), *Die Neolithisierung Mitteleuropas (The spread of the Neolithic to central Europe)*, 461–74. Mainz: Römisch-Germanisches Zentralmuseum.

Schäfer, D. 1999. Untersuchungen zur mesolithischen Begehung in Tirol. In P. Della Casa (ed.), *Prehistoric Alpine environment, society and economy. Papers of the international colloquium PAESE, 1997*, 37–46. Bonn: Habelt.

Schäfer, D., Müller, H., Frizzi, U., Seeber-Kneußl, S., Brouček, B., Rastbichler-Zissernig, E. and Ullman, J. 1998. Untersuchungen zur mesolithischen Begehung des Fotschertales, nördl. Stubaier Alpen, Tirol. In N.J. Conard and C.-J. Kind (eds), *Aktuelle Forschungen zum Mesolithikum/Current Mesolithic Research*, 161–73. Tübingen: Mo Vince.

Schäfer, M. 2010. Viehzucht- und Jagdstrategien der ersten Bauern in Süddeutschland. In E. Claßen, T. Doppler and B. Ramminger (eds), *Familie – Verwandtschaft – Sozialstrukturen: Sozialarchäologische Forschungen zu neolithischen Befunden*, 107–18. Kerpen-Loogh: Welt und Erde.

Schafter, R.C. 1997. *Cranial/facial trauma*. La Grange: ACA Press.

Scheffler, H.W. 1966. Ancestor worship in anthropology: or, observations on descent and descent groups. *Current Anthropology* 7, 541–51.

Scheuer, L. and Black, S. 2000. *Developmental juvenile osteology*. London: Academic Press.

Schibler, J. 2001. Methodische Überlegungen zum Problem der Einschätzung der Bedeutung von Jagd und Viehwirtschaft im schweizerischen Neolithikum. In R.-M. Arbogast, C. Jeunesse and J. Schibler (eds), *Rôle et statut de la chasse dans le Néolithique ancien danubien (5500–4900 av. J.-C.). Premières rencontres danubiennes, Strasbourg 20 et 21 novembre 1996. Actes de la première table ronde*, 153–70. Rahden: Marie Leidorf.

Schieffelin, E. 1996. Comment in the debate. In T. Ingold (ed.), *Key debates in anthropology*, 136. London: Routledge.

Schier, W. 1985. Zur vorrömischen Besiedlung des Donautales südöstlich von Regensburg. *Bayerische Vorgeschichtsblätter* 50, 9–80.

Schiesberg, S. 2010. Von Häusern und Menschen. Das Beispiel Bandkeramik. In E. Claßen, T. Doppler and B. Ramminger (eds), *Familie – Verwandtschaft – Sozialstrukturen: sozialarchäologische Forschungen zu neolithischen Befunden*, 53–69. Kerpen-Loogh: Welt und Erde.

Schigiol, C. 2000. *Vier bandkeramische Siedlungen im Tal des Schlangengrabens auf der Aldenhovener Platte im Rheinland.* PhD thesis, Frankfurt a. M. University.

Schmidgen-Hager, E. 1992. Das bandkeramische Erdwerk von Heilbronn-Neckargartach. *Fundberichte aus Baden-Württemberg* 17, 173–291.

Schmidt, B. and Gruhle, W. 2003a. Niederschlagsschwankungen in Westeuropa während der letzten 8000 Jahre: Versuch einer Rekonstruktion mit Hilfe eines neuen dendrochronologischen Verfahrens (Grad der Wuchshomogenität). *Archäologisches Korrespondenzblatt* 33, 281–300.

Schmidt, B. and Gruhle, W. 2003b. Wuchshomogenität als ein neues Analyseverfahren zur Verbesserung der dendrochronologischen Datierungsmethode: die Hölzer der neolithischen Brunnen von Erkelenz-Kückhoven, Zwenkau und Mohelnice sowie vom Fundplatz Kaster. In J. Eckert, U. Eisenhauer and A. Zimmermann (eds), *Archäologische Perspektiven: Analysen und Interpretationen im Wandel. Festschrift für Jens Lüning zum 65. Geburtstag*, 49–60. Rahden: Marie Leidorf.

Schmidt, B., Gruhle, W. and Rück, O. 2004. Klimaextreme in bandkeramischer Zeit (5300 bis 5000 v. Chr.): Interpretation dendrochronologischer und archäologischer Befunde. *Archäologisches Korrespondenzblatt* 34, 303–7.

Schmidt, B., Gruhle, W., Rück, O. and Freckmann, K. 2005a. Zur Dauerhaftigkeit bandkeramischer Häuser im Rheinland (5300–4950 v. Chr.) – eine Interpretation dendrochronologischer und bauhistorischer Befunde. In D. Gronenborn (ed.), *Klimaveränderung und Kulturwandel in neolithischen Gesellschaften Mitteleuropas, 6700–2200 v. Chr.*, 151–70. Mainz: Römisch-Germanisches Zentralmuseum.

Schmidt, B., Gruhle, W., Zimmermann, A. and Fischer, T. 2005b. Mögliche Schwankungen von Getreideerträgen – Befunde zur rheinischen Linienbandkeramik und römischen Kaiserzeit. *Archäologisches Korrespondenzblatt* 3, 301–16.

Schmitzberger, M. 2009a. Tierknochen. In E. Lenneis, *Rosenburg im Kamptal, Niederösterreich: ein Sonderplatz der älteren Linearbandkeramik*, 110–23. Bonn: Habelt.

Schmitzberger, M. 2009b. *Haus- und Jagdtiere im Neolithikum des österreichischen Donauraumes*. Unpublished PhD thesis, University of Vienna.

Schmitzberger, M. 2010. Die linearbandkeramische Fauna von Mold bei Horn, Niederösterreich. In E. Lenneis (ed.), *Die bandkeramische Siedlung von Mold bei Horn in Niederösterreich. Teil 1. Naturwissenschaftliche Untersuchungen und Einzelanalysen*, 241–308. Rahden: Marie Leidorf.

Schmotz, K. 1989. *Die vorgeschichtliche Besiedlung im Isarmündungsgebiet. Materialhefte zur Bayerischen Vorgeschichte 58*. Kallmünz: Michael Lassleben.

Schmotz, K. 1992. *Das bandkeramische Gräberfeld von Stephansposching. Archäologische Denkmäler im Landkreis Deggendorf, Heft 7*. Deggendorf: Ebner.

Schmotz, K. 1994. Das altneolithische Siedlungsareal im Ortskern von Stephansposching, Lkr. Deggendorf. In K. Schmotz (ed.), *Vorträge des 12. Niederbayerischen Archäologentages*, 17–33. Buch am Erlbach: Marie Leidorf.

Schmotz, K. 1995. Perspektiven archäologischer Denkmalpflege und Forschung im Zeichen gewandelter Wertvorstellungen – Versuch einer Zustandsbeschreibung aus regionaler Sicht. In K. Schmotz (ed.), *Vorträge des 13. Niederbayerischen Archäologentages*, 13–19. Espelkamp: Marie Leidorf.

Schmotz, K. 1996. Fortschritte in der archäologischen Forschung und ihre Darstellung – ein Dilemma. In K. Schmotz (ed.), *Vorträge des 14. Niederbayerischen Archäologentages*, 13–16. Espelkamp: Marie Leidorf.

Schmotz, K. 1997. Altneolithische Grabenwerke in Niederbayern. Zum Stand der Kenntnis aufgrund Luftbildarchäologie, Magnetometerprospektion und archäologischer Ausgrabung. In K. Schmotz (ed.), *Vorträge des 15. Niederbayerischen Archäologentages*, 119–60. Espelkamp: Marie Leidorf.

Schmotz, K. 2001. Die altneolithische Siedlung von Otzing, Landkreis Deggendorf, Niederbayern. *Das Archäologische Jahr in Bayern 2000*, 14–17.

Schmotz, K. 2002a. Das Alt- und Mittelneolithikum. In K. Schmotz (ed.), *Vorträge des 20. Niederbayerischen Archäologentages*, 203–26. Rahden: Marie Leidorf.

Schmotz, K. 2002b. Bestattungsformen des 6. und 5. Jahrtausends im Landkreis Deggendorf (Niederbayern) – Erkenntnisse aus 20 Jahren kommunaler Denkmalpflege. *Archeologické rozhledy* 54, 264–78.

Schmotz, K. 2007a. Ein viertel Jahrhundert Niederbayerische Archäologentage. In K. Schmotz (ed.), *Vorträge des 25. Niederbayerischen Archäologentages*, 21–7. Rahden: Marie Leidorf.

Schmotz, K. 2007b. Kommunale Jubiläen in Niederbayern IV. In K. Schmotz (ed.), *Vorträge des 25. Niederbayerischen Archäologentages*, 29–41. Rahden: Marie Leidorf.

Schmotz, K. and Weber, W. 2000. Untersuchungen in der linienbandkeramischen Siedlung von Otzing, Lkr. Deggendorf. In K. Schmotz (ed.), *Vorträge des 18. Niederbayerischen Archäologentages*, 15–37. Rahden: Marie Leidorf.

Schneider, D. 1968. *American kinship: a cultural account*. Chicago: University of Chicago Press.

Schneikert, F. 2002. Architecture des fosses sépulchrales et localisation du squelette dans la fosse. In C. Jeunesse (ed.), *Vendenheim 'Le Haut du Coteau'. Une nécropole du Néolithique ancien. Document final de synthèse. Tome 1: texte*. 33–6. Strasbourg: Service Régional de l'Archéologie d'Alsace, unpublished document.

Schneikert, F. and Boës, E. 2002. La nécropole: présentation générale. In C. Jeunesse (ed.), *Vendenheim 'Le Haut du Coteau'. Une nécropole du Néolithique ancien. Document final de synthèse. Tome 1: texte*, 25–31. Strasbourg: Service Régional de l'Archéologie d'Alsace, unpublished document.

Schneikert, F. and Lasserre, M. 2002. Présentation générale. In C. Jeunesse (ed.), *Vendenheim 'Le Haut du Coteau'. Une nécropole du Néolithique ancien. Document final de synthèse. Tome 1: texte*, 1–5. Strasbourg: Service Régional de l'Archéologie d'Alsace, unpublished document.

Schoeninger, M. and DeNiro, M.J. 1984. Nitrogen and carbon isotopic composition of bone collagen from marine and terrestrial animals. *Geochimica et Cosmochimica Acta* 48, 625–39.

Schoeninger, M., DeNiro, M. and Tauber, H. 1983. Stable nitrogen isotope ratios of bone collagen reflect marine and terrestrial components of prehistoric human diet. *Science* 220, 1381–3.

Schönweiß, W. 1988. Die Ausgrabungen von Sarching-Friesheim im Rahmen des nordbayerischen Mesolithikums. In W. Schönweiß (ed.), *Mesolithische Fundplätze in Nordbayern*, 11–99. Fürth: Verlag Grafische Werkstätte Graf.

Schönweiß, W. and Werner, H.-J. 1974. Mesolithische Wohnanlagen von Sarching, Landkreis Regensburg. *Bayerische Vorgeschichtsblätter* 39, 1–29.

Schötz, M. 1984. Die neolithische Besiedlung der Flußtäler im niederbayerischen Hügelland südlich der Isar. *Historische Heimatblätter für die Stadt und den früheren Landkreis Landau a. d. Isar 1984*, 12–34.

Schötz, M. 1986. Die jungsteinzeitliche Besiedlung des Vilstals. Vorläufige Ergebnisse jahrelanger Flurbegehungen. In B. Engelhardt and K. Schmotz (eds), *Vorträge des 4. Niederbayerischen Archäologentages*, 37–44. Buch am Erlbach: Marie Leidorf.

Schötz, M. 1988. Zwei unterschiedliche Silexabsatzgebiete im Neolithikum des Vilstals. *Bayerische Vorgeschichtsblätter* 53, 1–15.

Schroeder, H., O'Connell, T.C., Evans, J.A., Shuler, K.A. and Hedges, R.E.M. 2009. Trans-Atlantic slavery: isotopic evidence for forced migration to Barbados. *American Journal of Physical Anthropology* 139, 547–57.

Schuchhardt, C. 1919. *Alteuropa in seiner Kultur- und Stilentwicklung*. Berlin: de Gruyter.

Schulting, R. 2007. Non-dietary occlusal grooves on anterior maxillary dentition in the Hungarian Neolithic. In A. Whittle (ed.), *The Early Neolithic on the Great Hungarian Plain. Investigations of the Körös culture site of Ecsegfalva 23, County Békés*, 469–80. Budapest: Institute of Archaeology, Hungarian Academy of Sciences.

Schulting, R. and Fibiger, L. (eds) 2012. *Sticks, stones, and broken bones: Neolithic violence in a European perspective*. Oxford: Oxford University Press.

Schulting, R.J. and Richards, M.P. 2002. The wet, the wild and the domesticated: the Mesolithic-Neolithic transition on the west coast of Scotland. *European Journal of Archaeology* 5, 147–89.

Schwarcz, H.P. and Schoeninger, M.J. 1991. Stable isotope analyses in human nutritional ecology. *American Journal of Physical Anthropology* 34, 283–321.

Schweissing, M.M. and Grupe, G. 2003. Stable strontium isotopes in human teeth and bone: a key to migration events of the late Roman period in Bavaria. *Journal of Archaeological Science* 30: 1373–83.

Schweitzer, J. 1971. Découverte de trois nouvelles sépultures dans la nécropole danubienne de Mulhouse-Est. *Bulletin du Musée Historique de Mulhouse* 79, 11–16.

Schweitzer, J. 1978. Le site néolithique d'Ensisheim premier bilan, campagne de 1977. *Bulletin du Musée Historique de Mulhouse* 85, 7–75.

Schweitzer, J. 1980. La céramique rubanée dans le sud du Haut-Rhin. In A. Thévenin and J.-P. Thévenot (eds), *Le Rubané d'Alsace et de Lorraine: état des recherches 1979*, 135–98. Strasbourg: Association d'Études Préhistoriques et Protohistoriques d'Alsace.

Schweitzer, R. and Schweitzer, J. 1977. La nécropole du Danubien moyen de Mulhouse-Est. *Bulletin du Musée Historique de Mulhouse* 84, 11–75.

Schweizer, A. 2003. Archäopalynologische Untersuchungen zur Neolithisierung der Wetterau (Hessen). In J. Eckert, U. Eisenhauer and A. Zimmermann (eds), *Archäologische Perspektiven: Analysen und Interpretationen im Wandel. Festschrift für Jens Lüning zum 65. Geburtstag*, 243–9. Rahden: Marie Leidorf.

Schweizer, A. 2005. Die Neolithisierung der Wetterau (Hessen) aus archäopalynologischer Sicht. In J. Lüning, C. Frirdich and A. Zimmermann (eds), *Die Bandkeramik im 21. Jahrhundert. Symposium in der Abtei Brauweiler bei Köln vom 16.9.–19.9.2002*, 289–97. Rahden: Marie Leidorf.

Schwerdtner, G. 2009. Zum Hausbau im frühen Neolithikum. *Archäologisches Korrespondenzblatt* 39, 21–37.

Scott, E. 1999. *The archaeology of infancy and infant death*. Oxford: British Archaeological Reports.

Scott, E., Cook, G. and Naysmith, P. 2010. The fifth international radiocarbon intercomparison (VIRI): an assessment of laboratory performance in stage 3. *Radiocarbon* 53, 859–65.

Sealy, J.C., Armstrong, R. and Schrire, C. 1995. Beyond lifetime averages: tracing life histories through isotopic analysis of different calcified tissues from archaeological human skeletons. *Antiquity* 69, 290–300.

Seewald, O. 1942. Ein jungsteinzeitlicher Grabfund mit Muschelschmuck aus Emmersdorf an der Donau. *Wiener Prähistorische Zeitschrift* 29, 1–18.

Séfériadès, M. 1995. *Spondylus gaederopus*: the earliest European long-distance exchange system. A symbolic and structural archaeological approach to Neolithic societies. *Poročilo o raziskovanju paleolitica, neolitika in eneolitika v Sloveniji* 22, 233–56.

Séfériadès, M.L. 2010. *Spondylus* and long-distance trade in prehistoric Europe. In D.W. Anthony with J.Y. Chi (eds), *The lost world of Old Europe: the Danube valley, 5000–3500 BC*, 178–90. New York/Princeton: Institute for the Study of the Old World/Princeton University Press.

Seghedi, I., Downes, H., Szakacs, A., Mason, P., Thirlwall, M., Rosu, E., Zoltan, P., Marton, E., Panaiotu, C. 2004. Neogene-Quaternary magmatism and geodynamics in the Carpathian-Pannonian region: a synthesis. *Lithos* 72, 117–46.

Seielstad, M.T., Minch E. and Cavalli-Sforza, L.L., 1998. Genetic evidence for a higher female migration rate in humans. *Nature Genetics* 20, 278–80.

Seregély, T. and Link, T. 2009. Urgeschichtliches Ritualgeschehen am Hohlen Stein bei Schwabthal, Stadt Bad Staffelstein, Landkreis Lichtenfels, Oberfranken. *Das Archäologische Jahr in Bayern 2008*, 15–17.

Service, E.R. 1962. *Primitive social organization: an evolutionary perspective*. New York: Random House.

Shennan, S. 2002. *Genes, memes and human history: Darwinian archaeology and cultural evolution*. London: Thames and Hudson.

Shennan, S.J. 2011. Property and wealth inequality as cultural niche construction. *Philosophical Transactions of the Royal Society B* 366, 918–26.

Shephard, J.P., Shapland, M., Pearce, N.X. and Scully, C. 1990. Pattern, severity and etiology of injuries in victims of assault. *Journal of the Royal Society of Medicine* 83, 75–8.

Sherratt, A.G. 1976. Resources, technology and trade: an essay in early European metallurgy. In G. de G. Sieveking, I.H. Longworth and K.E. Wilson (eds), *Problems in social and economic archaeology*, 557–81. London: Duckworth.

Sherratt, A.G. 1982a. The development of Neolithic and Copper Age settlement in the Great Hungarian Plain. Part 1: the regional setting. *Oxford Journal of Archaeology* 1, 287–316.

Sherratt, A. 1982b. Mobile resources: settlement and exchange in early agricultural Europe. In C. Renfrew and S. Shennan (eds), *Ranking, resource and exchange*, 13–26. Cambridge: Cambridge University Press.

Sherratt, A.G. 1983a. The development of Neolithic and Copper Age settlement in the Great Hungarian Plain. Part II: site survey and settlement dynamics. *Oxford Journal of Archaeology* 2, 13–41.

Sherratt, A.G. 1983b. Early agrarian settlement in the Körös region of the Great Hungarian Plain. *Acta Archaeologica Academiae Scientiarum Hungaricae* 35, 155–69.

Sherratt, A.G. 2004. Fractal farmers: patterns of Neolithic origin and dispersal. In J. Cherry, C. Scarre and S. Shennan (eds), *Explaining social change: studies in honour of Colin Renfrew*, 53–63. Cambridge: McDonald Institute for Archaeological Research.

Šída, P. 2006. Distribuční areály surovin v neolitu na území České republiky (Raw material distribution areas in the Neolithic in the area of the Czech Republic). *Archeologické rozhledy* 58, 407–26.

Sielmann, B. 1972. Die frühneolithische Besiedlung Mitteleuropas. In H. Schwabedissen (ed.), *Die Anfänge des Neolithikums vom Orient bis Nordeuropa. Va, Westliches Mitteleuropa*, 1–65. Köln: Böhlau.

Sielmann, B. 1976. Der Einfluß der geographischen Umwelt auf die linien- und stichbandkeramische Besiedlung des Mittelelbe-Saale-Gebietes. *Jahresschift für Mitteldeutsche Vorgeschichte* 60, 305–29.

Siemoneit, B. 1997. *Das Kind in der Linienbandkeramik: Befunde aus Gräberfeldern und Siedlungen in Mitteleuropa*. Rahden: Marie Leidorf.

Siklósi Z. and Csengeri, P. 2011. Reconsideration of *Spondylus* usage in the Middle and Late Neolithic of the Carpathian Basin. In F. Ifantidis and M. Nikolaidou (eds), *Spondylus in prehistory: new data and approaches: contributions to the archaeology of shell technologies*, 47–62. Oxford: Archaeopress.

Sillen, A., Hall, G., Richardson, S. and Armstrong, R. 1998. $^{87}Sr/^{86}Sr$ ratios in modern and fossil food-webs of the Sterkfontein Valley: implications for early hominid habitat preference. *Geochimica et Cosmochimica Acta* 62, 2463–73.

Simpson, I.A., Bol, R., Dockrill, S.J., Petzke, K.-J. and Evershed, R.P. 1998. Compound-specific $\delta^{15}N$ amino acid signals in palaeosols as indicators of early land use: a preliminary study. *Archaeological Prospect* 4, 147–52.

Šiška, S. 1989. *Kultúra s východnou lineárnou keramikou na Slovensku*. Bratislava: Slovak Academy of Sciences Press.

Šiška, S. 1998. Architektúra neolitickej osady v Šarišských Michaľanoch. *Slovenská archeológia* 46, 187–204.

Šiška, S. 2002. Náčrt neolitického a eneolitického osídlenia severozápadného Slovenska (Skizze der neolithischen und äneolithischen Besiedlung der Nordwestslowakei). *Slovenská archeológia* 50, 69–78.

Sklenář, K. 1993. *Archaeology in central Europe: the first 500 years*. Leicester: Leicester University Press.

Skulan, J. and DePaolo, D.J. 1999. Calcium isotope fractionation between soft and mineralized tissues as a monitor of calcium use in vertebrates. *Proceedings of the National Academy of Sciences of the United States of America*, 96, 13709–13.

Skulan, J., Bullen, T., Anbar, A.D., Puzas, J.E., Shackelford, L., LeBlanc, A. and Smith, S.M. 2007. Natural calcium isotopic composition of urine as a marker of bone mineral balance. *Clinical Chemistry* 53, 1155–8.

Skulan, J., DePaolo, D.J. and Owens, T.L. 1997. Biological control of calcium isotopic abundances in the global calcium cycle. *Geochimica et Cosmochimica Acta* 61, 2505–10.

Skutil, J. 1941. Linearkeramische Gräber in Mähren. *Wiener Prähistorische Zeitschrift* 28, 21–37.

Šmíd, M. 2008. Kralice na Hané (okr. Prostějov). In Z. Čižmář (ed.), *Život a smrt v mladší době kamenné*, 60–1. Brno: Ústav archeologické památkové péče Brno.

Smith, B.H. 1991. Standards of human tooth formation and dental age assessment. In M.A. Kelley and C.S. Larsen (eds), *Advances in dental anthropology*, 143–68. New York: Wiley-Liss.

Smrčka, V., Bůzek, F. and Zocová, J. 2008a. C and N stable isotopes in a set of 17 skeletons from the Vedrovice cemetery. *Anthropologie* 46, 227–31.

Smrčka, V., Bůzek, F., Erban, V., Berkovec, T., Dočkalová, M., Neumanová, K. and Nývltová-Fišáková, M. 2005. Carbon, nitrogen and strontium isotopes in the set of skeletons from the Neolithic settlement at Vedrovice (Czech Republic). *Anthropologie* 43, 315–23.

Smrčka, V., Erban, V., Hložek, M., Gregerová, M. and Dočkalová, M. 2008b. Reconstruction of mobility: comparison between the analysis of Sr isotopes in a set of Neolithic skeletons from the Vedrovice cemetery, and the petrographical analysis of pottery in graves. *Anthropologie* 46, 233–8.

Smrčka, V., Mihaljevic, M., Zocová, J., Šebek, O., Humpolová, A., Berkovec, T. and Dočkalová, M. 2008c. Trace-elemental analysis of skeletal remains of humans and animals at the Neolithic settlement in Vedrovice (Czech Republic). *Anthropologie* 46, 219–26.

Soják, M. 2000. Neolitické osídlenie Spiša (Die neolithische Besiedlung der Zips). *Slovenská archeológia* 48, 185–314.

Sommer, U. 2001. "Hear the instructions of thy father, and forsake not the law of thy mother": change and persistence in the European Early Neolithic. *Journal of Social Archaeology* 1, 244–70.

Sommerer, E. 2005. Der geographische Raum vom Unteren Traisental bis in das Tullner Becken. In Bundesdenkmalamt Wien (ed.), *Zeitschienen: vom Tullnerfeld ins Traisental. Archäologische Funde aus 20.000 Jahren*, 16–21. Horn: Ferdinand Berger and Söhne.

Soudský, B. 1969. Étude de la maison néolithique. *Slovenská archeológia* 17, 5–96.

Souvatzi, S. 2008. *A social archaeology of households in Neolithic Greece: an anthropological approach*. Cambridge: Cambridge University Press.

Spatz, H. 1997. La nécropole du Néolithique moyen (Hinkelstein, Grossgartach) de Trebur (Gross-Gerau, Hesse). In C. Jeunesse (ed.), *Le Néolithique danubien et ses marges entre Rhin et Seine*, 157–70. Strasbourg: Cahiers de l'Association pour la Promotion de la Recherche Archéologique en Alsace.

Sponheimer, M., Lee-Thorp, J.A., DeRuiter, D.J., Smith, J.M., Merwe, N.J.v.d., Reed, K., Grant, C.C., Ayliffe, L.K., Robinson, T.F., Heidelberger, C. and Marcus, W. 2003a. Diets of Southern African Bovidae: stable isotope evidence. *Journal of Mammalogy* 84, 471–9.

Sponheimer, M., Robinson, T., Ayliffe, L., Roeder, B., Hammer, J., Passey, B., West, A., Cerling, T., Dearing, D. and Ehleringer, J. 2003b. Nitrogen isotopes in mammalian herbivores: hair $\delta^{15}N$ values from a controlled feeding study. *International Journal of Osteoarchaeology* 13, 80–7.

Stadler, P. 2005. Settlement of the Early Linear ceramics culture at Brunn am Gebirge, Wolfholz site. *Documenta Praehistorica* 32, 269–78.

Stadler, P. 2010. Auswertung der C-Daten von Mold mittels Kombinationskalibrationen und Sequencing der durch Seriation ermittelten Hausabfolge. In E. Lenneis (ed.), *Die bandkeramische Siedlung von Mold bei Horn in Niederösterreich. Teil 1. Naturwissenschaftliche Untersuchungen und Einzelanalysen*, 23–9. Rahden: Marie Leidorf.

Stadler, P. and Kotova, N. 2010a. Early Neolithic settlement from Brunn Wolfholz in Lower Austria and the problem of the origin of (Western) LBK. In J.K. Kozłowski and P. Raczky (eds), *Neolithization of the Carpathian basin: northernmost distribution of the Starčevo/Körös culture*, 325–48. Kraków and Budapest: Polish Academy of Sciences and Institute of Archaeological Sciences of the Eötvös Loránd University.

Stadler, P. and Kotova, N. 2010b. The early Neolithic settlement from Brunn Wolfholz in Lower Austria and the problem of the typology and chronology of the low bowls with sharply curved wall. *Slovenská archeológia* 58, 207–28.

Stadler, P. and Lenneis, E. 2009.Verteilungsanalysen. In E. Lenneis, *Rosenburg im Kamptal, Niederösterreich: ein Sonderplatz der älteren Linearbandkeramik*, 163–79. Bonn: Habelt.

Stadler, P., Draxler, S., Friesinger, H., Kutschera, W., Priller, A., Rom, W., Steier, P. and Wild, E.M. 2000. *Status of the Austrian Science Fund Project P-12253-PHY: Absolute Chronology for Early Civilisations in Austria and Central Europe using ^{14}C Dating with Accelerator Mass Spectrometry*. Unpublished project report for the FWF.

Standaert, C.J. and Herring, S.A. 2000. Spondylolysis: a critical review. *British Journal of Sports Medicine* 34, 415–22.

Starkel, L. 1977. The paleogeography of mid- and east Europe during the last cold stage, with west European comparisons. *Philosophical Transactions of the Royal Society B* 280, 351–72.

Starnini, E. 2001. The Mesolithic/Neolithic transition in Hungary: the lithic perspective. In R. Kertész and J. Makkay (eds), *From the Mesolithic to the Neolithic*, 395–404. Budapest: Archaeolingua.

Stäuble, H. 1994. *Häuser und absolute Datierung der Ältesten Bandkeramik*. PhD thesis, Frankfurt a.M. University.

Stäuble, H. 1995. Radiocarbon dates of the earliest Neolithic in central Europe. *Radiocarbon* 37, 227–37.

Stäuble, H. 1997. Häuser, Gruben und Fundverteilung. In J. Lüning (ed.), *Ein Siedlungsplatz der ältesten Bandkeramik in Bruchenbrücken, Stadt Friedberg/Hessen*, 17–150. Bonn: Habelt.

Stäuble, H. 2005. *Häuser und absolute Chronologie der ältesten Bandkeramik*. Bonn: Habelt.

Stäuble, H. and Lüning, J. 1999. Phosphatanalysen in bandkeramischen Häusern. *Archäologisches Korrespondenzblatt* 29, 165–87.

Staude, K. 2007. Besonderheiten einer bandkeramischen Siedlung in Utzwingen, Gemeinde Maihingen, Landkreis Donau-Ries, Schwaben. *Das Archäologische Jahr in Bayern 2006*, 11–13.

Steele, F.A. 2008. *Module 5: Introduction to multilevel modelling (concepts)*. Bristol: ESRC National Centre for Research Methods, Learning Environment for Multilevel Methodology and Applications (http://www.cmm.bris.ac.uk/lemma/).

Stehli, P. 1973. Keramik. In J.-P. Farruggia, R. Kuper, J. Lüning and P. Stehli (eds), *Der bandkeramische Siedlungsplatz Langweiler 2, Gemeinde Aldenhoven, Kreis Düren*, 57–100. Bonn: Rheinland-Verlag.

Stehli, P. 1989a. Merzbachtal – Umwelt und Geschichte einer bandkeramischen Siedlungskammer. *Germania* 67, 51–76.

Stehli, P. 1989b. Zur relativen und absoluten Chronologie der Bandkeramik in Mitteleuropa. In J. Rulf (ed.), *Bylany Seminar 1987: collected papers*, 69–78. Prague: Archeologický Ústav CSAV.

Stehli, P. 1994. Chronologie der Bandkeramik im Merzbachtal. In J. Lüning and P. Stehli (eds), *Die Bandkeramik im Merzbachtal auf der Aldenhovener Platte: Beiträge zur Besiedlung der Aldenhovener Platte V*, 79–191. Köln: Rheinland-Verlag.

Steier, P. and Rom, W. 2000. The use of Bayesian statistics for ^{14}C dates of chronological ordered samples: a critical analysis. *Radiocarbon* 42, 183–98.

Stephan, E. 2005. Tierknochenfunde aus Rottenburg Fröbelweg, Kreis Tübingen: ein Beitrag zur Wirtschaftsweise in der Ältesten Bandkeramik. *Materialhefte zur Archäologie in Baden-Württemberg* 68, 323–83.

Stirland, A.J. 2000. *Raising the dead: the skeleton crew of King Henry VIII's great ship, the Mary Rose*. Chichester: Wiley.

Stöckl, H. 1992. Die Bandkeramik im nördlichen Kaiserstuhl

und dem angrenzenden Vorland. *Cahiers de l'Association pour la Promotion de la Recherche Archéologique en Alsace* 8, 1–42.

Stoll-Tucker, B. 1997. *Nacheiszeitliche Höhlennutzung am Beispiel des oberen Pegnitztales (nördliche Frankenalb): Arbeiten zur Archäologie Süddeutschlands 4*. Büchenbach: Dr. Faustus.

Storch, H.-P. 1984/85. Frühneolithische Bestattungssitten: ein Beitrag zur Urgeschichte des südlichen Oberrheins. *Acta Praehistorica et Archaeologica* 16–17, 23–53.

Street, M., Baales, M., Cziesla, E., Hartz, S., Heinen, M., Jöris, O., Koch, I., Pasda, C., Terberger, T. and Vollbrecht, J. 2002. Final Paleolithic and Mesolithic research in reunified Germany. *Journal of World Prehistory* 15, 365–453.

Strien, H.-C. 1993. Die Beziehungen der Südwestlichen Bandkeramik zur RRBP. In M. Willaume (ed.), *Le Néolithique du nord-est de la France et des régions limitrophes: actes du XIIIème colloque inter-régional sur le Néolithique*, 64–7. Paris: Éditions de la Maison des Sciences de l'Homme.

Strien, H.-C. 2000. *Untersuchungen zur Bandkeramik in Württemberg*. Bonn: Habelt.

Strien, H.-C. 2003. Zur Herkunft der mitteleuropäischen Elemente in der Bandkeramik des Pariser Beckens. In J. Eckert, U. Eisenhauer and A. Zimmermann (eds), *Archäologische Perspektiven: Analysen und Interpretationen im Wandel. Festschrift für Jens Lüning zum 65. Geburtstag*, 61–70. Rahden: Marie Leidorf.

Strien, H.-C. 2005. Familientraditionen in der bandkeramischen Siedlung bei Vaihingen/Enz. In J. Lüning, C. Frirdich and A. Zimmermann (eds), *Die Bandkeramik im 21. Jahrhundert. Symposium in der Abtei Brauweiler bei Köln vom 16.9.–19.9.2002*, 189–97. Rahden: Marie Leidorf.

Strien, H.-C. 2009. Die 'jüngerbandkeramische Gruppenbildung' – ein Requiem. In A. Zeeb-Lanz (ed.), *Krisen – Kulturwandel – Kontinuitäten: zum Ende der Bandkeramik in Mitteleuropa*, 213–17. Rahden: Marie Leidorf.

Strien, H.-C. 2010a. Mobilität in bandkeramischer Zeit im Spiegel der Fernimporte. In D. Gronenborn and J. Petrasch (eds), *Die Neolithisierung Mitteleuropas (The spread of the Neolithic to central Europe)*, 497–508. Mainz: Römisch-Germanisches Zentralmuseum.

Strien, H.-C. 2010b. Demographische und erbrechtliche Überlegungen zur bandkeramischen Familienstruktur. In E. Claßen, T. Doppler and B. Ramminger (eds), *Familie – Verwandtschaft – Sozialstrukturen: sozialarchäologische Forschungen zu neolithischen Befunden*, 71–80. Kerpen-Loogh: Welt und Erde.

Strien, H.-C. and Gronenborn, D. 2005. Klima- und Kulturwandel während des mitteleuropäischen Altneolithikums (58./57.–51./50. Jahrhundert v. Chr.). In D. Gronenborn (ed.), *Klimaveränderung und Kulturwandel in neolithischen Gesellschaften Mitteleuropas, 6700–2200 v. Chr. (Climate variability and culture change in Neolithic societies of central Europe 6700–2200 cal BC)*, 131–49. Mainz: Römisch-Germanisches Zentralmuseum.

Stuart-Macadam, P. 1991. Anaemia in Roman Britain: Poundbury Camp. In H. Bush and M. Zvelebil (eds), *Health in past societies: biocultural interpretations of human skeletal remains in archaeological contexts*, 101–13. Oxford: Archaeopress.

Stuart-Macadam, P. 1998. Iron deficiency anemia: exploring the difference. In A.L. Grauer and P. Stuart-Macadam (eds), *Sex and gender in paleopathological perspective*, 45–63. Cambridge: Cambridge University Press.

Stuiver, M. and Polach, H.A. 1977. Discussion, reporting of ^{14}C data. *Radiocarbon* 19, 355–63.

Stuiver, M. and Reimer, P.J. 1986. A computer program for radiocarbon age calculation. *Radiocarbon* 28, 1022–30.

Süß, L. 1954. Eine jungsteinzeitliche Siedlungsgrube beim Gradhof/Kösching, Landkreis Ingolstadt. *Sammelblatt des Historischen Vereins Ingolstadt* 63, 3–15.

Svoboda, J.A. 2008. The Mesolithic of the middle Danube and upper Elbe rivers. In G. Bailey and P. Spikins (eds), *Mesolithic Europe*, 221–37. Cambridge: Cambridge University Press.

Sykes, B. 1999. *The human inheritance: genes, language, and evolution*. Oxford: Oxford University Press.

Sykes, B. and Renfrew, C. 2000. Concepts in molecular genetics. In C. Renfrew and K. Boyle (eds), *Archaeogenetics: DNA and the population prehistory of Europe*, 13–21. Cambridge: McDonald Institute for Archaeological Research.

Taute, W. 1966. Das Felsdach Lautereck, eine mesolithisch-neolithisch-bronzezeitliche Stratigraphie an der oberen Donau. *Palaeohistoria* 12, 483–504.

Taute, W. (ed.) 1980. *Das Mesolithikum in Süddeutschland. Teil 2: Naturwissenschaftliche Untersuchungen*. Tübingen: Institut für Urgeschichte der Universität Tübingen.

Teschler-Nicola, M. 2006. Der Fundkomplex von Asparn/Schletz (Niederösterreich) und seine Bedeutung für den aktuellen Diskurs endlinearkeramischer Phänomene in Zentraleuropa. *Beiträge zur Ur- und Frühgeschichte Mecklenburg-Vorpommerns* 41, 1–16.

Teschler-Nicola, M. 2012. The Early Neolithic site Asparn/Schletz (Lower Austria): anthropological evidence of interpersonal violence. In R. Schulting and L. Fibiger (eds), *Sticks, stones, and broken bones: Neolithic violence in a European perspective*, 101–20. Oxford: Oxford University Press.

Teschler-Nicola, M., Gerold, F., Kanz, F., Lindenbauer, K. and Spannagl, M. 1996. Anthropologische Spurensicherung – die traumatischen und postmortalen Veränderungen an den linearbandkeramischen Skelettresten von Asparn/Schletz. In H. Windl, J. Steiner and N. Weigl (eds), *Rätsel um Gewalt und Tod vor 7000 Jahren: eine Spurensicherung*, 47–64. Wien: Amt der NÖ Landesregierung.

Teschler-Nicola, M., Gerold, F., Bujatti-Narbeshuber, M., Prohaska, T., Latkoczy, C., Stringeder, G. and Watkins, M. 1999. Evidence of genocide 7000 BP – Neolithic paradigm and geo-climatic reality. *Collegium Anthropologicum* 23, 437–50.

Teschler-Nicola, M., Prohaska, T. and Wild, E.M. 2005. Der Fundkomplex von Asparn/Schletz (Niederösterreich) und seine Bedeutung für den aktuellen Diskurs endlinearbandkeramischer Phänomene in Zentraleuropa. In J. Piek and T. Terberger (eds), *Frühe Spuren der Gewalt – Schädelverletzungen und Wundversorgung an prähistorischen Menschenresten aus interdisziplinärer Sicht. Workshop in Rostock-Warnemünde vom 28.–30. November 2003*, 61–76. Schwerin: Landesamt für Kultur und Denkmalpflege.

Thévenet, C. 2004. Une relecture des pratiques funéraires du Rubané récent et final du Bassin parisien: l'exemple des fosses sépulcrales dans la vallée de l'Aisne. *Bulletin de la Société Préhistorique Française* 101, 815–26.

Thévenet, C. 2009. Les sépultures rubanées du Bassin parisien: composition de l'échantillon funéraire et implantation sépulchrale. In A. Zeeb-Lanz (ed.), *Krisen – Kulturwandel – Kontinuitäten: zum Ende der Bandkeramik in Mitteleuropa*, 111–27. Rahden: Marie Leidorf.

Thévenin, A. 1980. Haut-Rhin: informations archéologiques (Sainte Croix en Plaine). *Gallia Préhistoire* 23, 322–36.

Thévenin, A. and Sainty, J. 1980. Nouveaux sites rubanés et données récentes sur la séquence chronologique Néolithique ancien/Néolithique moyen dans le Bas-Rhin. In A. Thévenin and J.-P. Thévenot (eds), *Le Rubané d'Alsace et de Lorraine: état des recherches 1979*, 22–79. Strasbourg: Association d'Études Préhistoriques et Protohistoriques d'Alsace.

Thévenin, A. and Thévenot, J.-P. (eds) 1980. *Le Rubané d'Alsace et de Lorraine: état des recherches 1979*. Strasbourg: Association d'Études Préhistoriques et Protohistoriques d'Alsace.

Thévenin, C. 1988. *Le Rubané du Haut-Rhin: étude typologique de la céramique fine et essai de chronologie*. Alsace: Société d'Histoire de la Hochkirch et de Haute-Alsace.

Thévenin, C. 1993. Origine et extension des groupes rubanés d'Alsace. In M. Willaume (ed.), *Le Néolithique du nord-est de la France et des régions limitrophes: actes du XIIIème colloque inter-régional sur le Néolithique*, 76–83. Paris: Éditions de la Maison des Sciences de l'Homme.

Thomas, J. forthcoming. *The birth of Neolithic Britain*. Oxford: Oxford University Press.

Thomas, N. 1999. Becoming undisciplined: anthropology and cultural studies. In H.L. Moore (ed.), *Anthropological theory today*, 262–79. Oxford: Polity.

Tichý, R. 1956. Neolitické sídliště v Mohelnici na Moravě. *Archeologické rozhledy* 8, 3–8.

Tichý, R. 1960. K nejstarší volutové keramice na Moravě (Zur ältesten Volutenkeramik in Mähren). *Památky archeologické* 51, 415–41.

Tichý, R. 1961. Einige Bemerkungen zum Neolithikum in der Tschechoslowakei, nach den Forschungsergebnissen seit 1945. *Archaeologia Austriaca* 29, 96–122.

Tichý, R. 1962a. Osídlení s volutovou keramikou na Moravě. *Památky archeologické* 53, 245–305.

Tichý, R. 1962b. Volutové nálezy z Mohelnice u Zábřeha. *Sborník Československé společnosti archeologické* 2, 201–4.

Tichý, R. 1972. XIII. Grabungssaison in Mohelnice (Bez. Šumperk). *Přehled výzkumů* 1971, 17–21.

Tichý, Rad. 2004. From the Mediterranean to central Europe: origins of the LBK. In A. Lukes and M. Zvelebil (eds), *LBK dialogues: studies in the formation of the Linear Pottery culture*, 109–26. Oxford: Archaeopress.

Tichý, Rad. 2007. Sídliště kultury s lineární keramikou v Mohelnici "u Cukrovaru": aktuální problém pro dataci neolitických sídlišť? (Siedlung der Kultur mit Linearbandkeramik in Mohelnice "u Cukrovaru": ein aktuelles Problem der Datierung neolithischer Siedlungen?). *Pravěk* 17, 5–26.

Tiefenböck, B. 2010. *Die krankhaften Veränderungen an den linearbandkeramischen Skelettresten von Kleinhadersdorf, NÖ – ein anthropologischer Beitrag zur Rekonstruktion der Lebensbedingung im Frühneolithikum*. Unpublished MA dissertation, University of Vienna.

Tieszen, L. and Fagre, T. 1993. Effect of diet quality and composition on the isotopic composition of respiratory CO_2, bone collagen, bioapatite, and soft tissues. In J. Lambert and G. Grupe (eds), *Prehistoric human bone: archaeology at the molecular* level, 121–55. Berlin: Springer.

Tilley, C. 1996. *An ethnography of the Neolithic: early prehistoric societies in southern Scandinavia*. Cambridge: Cambridge University Press.

Tilley, C. 1999. *Metaphor and material culture*. Oxford: Blackwell.

Tillmann, A. 1989. Die Lochschlaghöhle bei Obereichstätt, Lkr. Eichstätt. In K. Rieder, A. Tillmann and J. Weining (eds), *Steinzeitliche Kulturen an Donau und Altmühl. Begleitheft zur Ausstellung im Stadtmuseum Ingolstadt*, 108–13. Ingolstadt: Bayerisches Landesamt für Denkmalpflege.

Tillmann, A. 1993. Kontinuität oder Diskontinuität? Zur Frage einer bandkeramischen Landnahme im südlichen Mitteleuropa. *Archäologische Informationen* 16, 157–87.

Tinner, W. and Lotter, A. 2001. Central European vegetation response to abrupt climate change at 8.2 ka. *Geology* 29, 551–4.

Tinner, W., Nielsen, E.H. and Lotter, A.F. 2007. Mesolithic agriculture in Switzerland? A critical review of the evidence. *Quaternary Science Reviews* 26, 1416–31.

Tishkoff, S.A., Reed, F.A., Ranciaro, A., Voight, B.F., Babbitt, C.C., Silverman, J.S., Powell, K., Mortensen, H.M., Hirbo, J.B., Osman, M., Ibrahim, M., Omar, S.A., Lema, G., Nyambo, T.B., Ghori, J., Bumpstead, S., Pritchard, J.K., Wray, G.A. and Deloukas, P. 2006. Convergent adaptation of human lactase persistence in Africa and Europe. *Nature Genetics* 39, 31–40.

Tompa, F. 1929. *A szalagdíszes agyagművesség kultúrája Magyarországon. A Bükki és a Tiszai kultúra (Die Bandkeramik in Ungarn. Die Bükker- und die Theiss-Kultur)*. Budapest: Magyar Nemzeti Múzeum.

Tompa, F. 1937. 25 Jahre Urgeschichtsforschung in Ungarn 1912–1936. *Bericht der Römisch-Germanischen Kommission* 24–25, 27–127.

Torke, W. 1987. Urgeschichtliche Umwelt und Fischwaid am Beispiel der bandkeramischen Fundstelle Singen 'Scharmenseewadel'. *Archäologische Nachrichten aus Baden* 38/39, 18–19.

Trautmann, I. 2007. *The significance of cremations in Early Neolithic communities in central Europe*. PhD thesis, Eberhard-Karls-Universität, Tübingen. http://tobias-lib.uni-tuebingen.de/volltexte/2007/3005

Trautmann, I. and Wahl, J. 2005. Leichenbrände aus linearbandkeramischen Gräberfeldern Südwestdeutschlands – zum Bestattungsbrauch in Schwetzingen und Fellbach-Oeffingen. *Fundberichte aus Baden-Württemberg* 28, 7–18.

Tremaine, W.J., Newcomer, A.D., Riggs, B.L. and McGill, D.B. 1986. Calcium absorption from milk in lactase-deficient and lactase-sufficient adults. *Digestive Diseases and Sciences* 31, 376–8.

Tricca, A., Stille, P., Steinmann, M., Kiefel, B., Samuel, J. and Eikenberg, J. 1999. Rare earth elements and Sr and Nd isotopic compositions of dissolved and suspended loads from small river systems in the Vosges mountains (France), the river Rhine and the groundwater. *Chemical Geology* 160, 139–58.

Tringham, R. 1971. *Hunters, fishers and farmers of eastern Europe 6000–3000 B.C.* London: Hutchinson.

Trnka, G. 1980. Siedlungsreste der jüngeren Linearbandkeramik aus Pulkau, p.B. Hollabrunn, NÖ. *Archaeologia Austriaca* 64, 53–110.

Trnka, G. 1982. *Fenster zur Urzeit: Luftbildarchäologie in Niederösterreich*. Vienna: Amt der Niederösterreichischen Landesregierung.

Trogmayer, O. 1967. Bemerkungen zur Chronologie des Frühneolithikums auf dem Südalföld. *A Móra Ferenc Múzeum Évkönyve* 1966–67, 35–40.

Trogmayer, O. 1968. Die Hauptfragen des Neolithikums der ungarischen Südtiefebene. *A Móra Ferenc Múzeum Évkönyve* 1, 11–19.

Trogmayer, O. 1969. Die Bestattungen der Körös-Gruppe. *A Móra Ferenc Múzeum Évkönyve* 2, 5–15.

Trogmayer, O. 1972. Körös-Gruppe – Linienbandkeramik.

In J. Fitz and J. Makkay (eds), *Die aktuellen Fragen der Bandkeramik,* 71–6. Székesfehérvár: A Féjer Megyei Múzeumok Igazgatósága.

Trogmayer, O. 1982. Zur relativen Zeitstellung der älteren Linearbandkeramik. In J. Pavúk (ed.), *Siedlungen der Kultur mit Bandkeramik in Europa. Internationales Kolloquium Nové Vozokany 17.–20. November 1981*, 279–83. Nitra: Archäologisches Institut der Slovakischen Akademie der Wissenschaften.

Tung, T.A. and Knudson, K.J. 2010. Childhood lost: abductions, sacrifice, and trophy heads of children in the Wari Empire. *Latin American Antiquity* 22, 44–66.

Turck, R., Kober, B., Kontny, J., Haack, F. and Zeeb-Lanz, A. 2012. "Widely travelled" people at Herxheim? Sr isotopes as indicators of mobility. In E. Kaiser, J. Burger and S. Wolfram (eds), *Population dynamics in prehistory and early history: new approaches using stable isotopes and genetics*, 149–63. Berlin: de Gruyter.

Tylor, E.B. 1871. *Primitive culture: researches into the development of mythology, philosophy, religion, language, art and custom.* London: J. Murray.

Ubelaker, D.H. 1989. *Human skeletal remains: excavation, analysis, interpretation.* Washington, DC: Taraxacum.

Ubelaker, D.H., Buchholz, B.A. and Stewart, J.E.B. 2006. Analysis of radiocarbon in different skeletal and dental tissue types to evaluate date of death. *Journal of Forensic Science* 51, 484–8.

Uenze, H.-P. 1990. Das Neolithikum im bayerischen Raum. In M. Höneisen (ed.), *Die ersten Bauern. Pfahlbaubefunde Europas. Band 2: Einführung, Balkan und angrenzende Regionen der Schweiz*, 123–34. Zürich: Schweizerisches Landesmuseum.

Uerpmann, H.-P. 1979. *Probleme der Neolithisierung des Mittelmeerraums.* Wiesbaden: L. Reichert.

Uerpmann, M. 2001. Animaux sauvages et domestiques du Rubané 'le plus ancien' (LBK 1) en Allemagne. In R.-M. Arbogast, C. Jeunesse and J. Schibler (eds), *Rôle et statut de la chasse dans le Néolithique ancien danubien (5500–4900 av. J.-C.)/ Rolle und Bedeutung der Jagd während des Frühneolithikums Mitteleuropas (Linearbandkeramik 5500–4900 v. Chr.)*, 57–75. Rahden: Marie Leidorf.

Uerpmann, M. and Uerpmann, H.-P. 1997. Remarks on the faunal remains of some early farming communities in central Europe. *Anthropozoologica* 25/26, 571–8.

Ulrich, H. 1946. Quelques particularités intéressantes observées sur les crânes néolithiques de Hoenheim-Souffelweyersheim. *Cahiers d'Archeologie et d'Histoire d'Alsace* 127, 129–33.

Ulrich, H. 1952. Nouvelles du cimetière néolithique de Hoenheim-Souffelweyersheim. *Cahiers d'Archeologie et d'Histoire d'Alsace* 132, 41–2.

Ulrich, H. 1953. Le cimetière Néolithique a céramique rubanée de Hoenheim-Souffelweyersheim: bilan d'ensemble avec les nouvelles sépultures. *Cahiers d'Archeologie et d'Histoire d'Alsace* 133, 21–36.

Uno, K.T., Cerling, T.E., Harris, J.M., Kunimatsu, Y., Leakey, M.G., Nakatsukasa, M. and Nakaya, H. 2011. Late Miocene to Pliocene carbon isotope record of differential diet change among East African herbivores. *Proceedings of the National Academy of Sciences of the United States of America* 108, 6509–14.

Urban, O.H. 1996. 'Er war der Mann zwischen den Fronten': Oswald Menghin und das Urgeschichtliche Institut der Universität Wien während der Nazizeit. *Archaeologia Austrica* 80, 1–24.

Urban, O.H. 2004. Universität Wien: Institut für Ur- und Frühgeschichte. In H. Friesinger and S. Titschler (eds), *Archäologie in Österreich: Eckpunkte für Strukturplanung*, 37–49. Vienna: Österreichische Akademie der Wissenschaften.

Valde-Nowak, P. 2002. *Siedlungsarchäologische Untersuchungen zur neolithischen Nutzung der mitteleuropäischen Gebirgslandschaften.* Rahden: Marie Leidorf.

van Berg, P.-L. 1990. Céramique du Limburg et néolithisation en Europe de Nord-Ouest. In D. Cahen and M. Otte (eds), *Rubané et Cardial: actes du colloque de Liège, Novembre 1988*, 161–85. Liège: Université de Liège.

Van Klinken, G.J., van der Plicht, H. and Hedges, R.E.M. 1994. Bond $^{13}C/^{12}C$ ratios reflect (palaeo-)climatic variations. *Geophysical Research Letters* 21, 445–8.

van de Velde, P. 1979a. On Bandkeramik social structure. *Analecta Praehistorica Leidensia* 12, 1–242.

van de Velde, P. 1979b. The social anthropology of a Neolithic cemetery in the Netherlands. *Current Anthropology* 20, 37–58.

van de Velde, P. 1990. Bandkeramik social inequality – a case study. *Germania* 68, 19–38.

van de Velde, P. 1997. Much ado about nothing: Bandkeramik funerary ritual. *Analecta Praehistorica Leidensia* 29, 83–90.

van de Velde, P. (ed.) 2008. *Excavations at Geleen-Janskamperveld 1990/1991.* Leiden: Faculty of Archaeology, Leiden University.

Van Vleet, K.E. 2008. *Performing kinship: narrative, gender, and the intimacies of power in the Andes.* Austin: University of Texas.

Veit, U. 1993. Burials within settlements of the Linienbandkeramik and Stichbandkeramik cultures of central Europe: on the social construction of death in Early-Neolithic society. *Journal of European Archaeology* 1, 107–40.

Veit, U. 1996. *Studien zum Problem der Siedlungsbestattung im europäischen Neolithikum.* Münster: Waxmann.

Vera, F.W.M. 2000. *Grazing ecology and forest history.* Wallingford: CABI Publishing.

Vigne, J.-D. and Helmer, D. 2007. Was milk a "secondary product" in the Old World Neolithisation process? Its role in the domestication of cattle, sheep and goats. *Anthropozoologica* 42 (2), 9–40.

Virág, Z. 2009. The eastern periphery of the central European LPC in the region of Budapest (connections between the Transdanubian LPC and the Alföld LPC). In J.K. Kozłowski (ed.), *Interactions between different models of Neolithization north of the central European agro-ecological barrier*, 9–30. Kraków: Polska Akademiai Umiejętności.

Voegtlin, C., Mauvilly, M. and Jeunesse, C. 1988. 'Zimmerman Haeussleplatz', une fosse du Rubané final de Haute-Alsace. *Cahiers de l'Association pour la Promotion de la Recherche Archéologique en Alsace* 4, 1–38.

Völkel, J. 2006. Naturräumliche Charakteristika Bayerns. In Gesellschaft für Archäologie in Bayern (eds), *Archäologie: Fenster zur Vergangenheit in Bayern*, 24–31. Regensburg: Friedrich Pustet.

von den Driesch, A. 2004. Fortschritte der Archäozoologie in Niederbayern während der letzten beiden Dezennien. In K. Schmotz (ed.), *Vorträge des 22. Niederbayerischen Archäologentages*, 331–51. Rahden: Marie Leidorf.

Wagner, E. 1908. *Fundstätten und Funde aus vorgeschichtlicher, römischer und alamannisch-fränkischer Zeit im Großherzogtum Baden. 1, Das Badische Oberland: Kreise Konstanz, Villingen, Waldshut, Lorrach, Freiburg, Offenburg.* Tübingen: Mohr.

Wagner, E. 1911. *Fundstätten und Funde aus vorgeschichtlicher, römischer und alamannisch-fränkischer Zeit im Großherzogtum Baden. 2. Teil. Das badische Unterland.* Tübingen: Mohr.

Wahl, J. 1985. Ein neolithisches Massengrab bei Talheim, Landkreis Heilbronn. *Archäologische Ausgrabungen in Baden-Württemberg 1984*, 30–2.

Wahl, J. and König, H.G. 1987. Anthropologisch-traumatologische Untersuchung der menschlichen Skelettreste aus dem bandkeramischen Massengrab bei Talheim, Kreis Heilbronn. *Fundberichte aus Baden-Württemberg* 12, 65–193.

Wahl, J. and Trautmann, I. 2012. The Neolithic massacre at Talheim – a pivotal find in conflict archaeology. In R. Schulting and L. Fibiger (eds), *Sticks, stones, and broken bones: Neolithic violence in a European perspective*, 77–100. Oxford: Oxford University Press.

Walker, P.L. 2001. A bioarchaeological perspective on the history of violence. *Annual Review of Anthropology* 30, 573–96.

Walker, P.L. and Hewlett, B.S. 1990. Dental health, diet and social status among central African foragers and farmers. *American Anthropologist* 92, 383–98.

Walter, D. 1985. *Thüringer Höhlen und ihre holozänen Bodenaltertümer*. Weimar: Museum für Ur- und Frühgeschichte Thüringens.

Walther, W. and Schwedler, I. 1991. Sondierungsgrabung auf einem birituellen linienbandkeramischen Gräberfeld bei Niederdorla, Kr. Mühlhausen. *Ausgrabungen und Funde* 36, 203–11.

Ward, G.K. and Wilson, S.R. 1978. Procedures for comparing and combining radiocarbon age determinations: a critique. *Archaeometry* 20, 19–31.

Warinner, C. and Tuross, N. 2009. Alkaline cooking and stable isotope tissue-diet spacing in swine: archaeological implications. *Journal of Archaeological Science* 36, 1690–7.

Warrick, G. 1996. Evolution of the Iroquois longhouse. In G. Coupland and E.B. Banning (eds), *People who lived in big houses*, 11–26. Madison: Prehistory Press.

Waterson, R. 1990. *The living house: an anthropology of architecture in south-east Asia.* Oxford: Oxford University Press.

Waterson, R. 1995. Houses and hierarchies in island southeast Asia. In J. Carsten and C. Hugh-Jones (eds), *About the house: Lévi-Strauss and beyond*, 47–68. Cambridge: Cambridge University Press.

Waters-Rist, A.L. and Katzenberg, M.A. 2010. The effect of growth on stable nitrogen isotope ratios in subadult bone collagen. *International Journal of Osteoarchaeology* 20, 172–91.

Weiner, J. 2003. Profane Geräte oder Prunkstücke? Überlegungen zur Zweckbestimmung übergrosser Dechselklingen. In J. Eckert, U. Eisenhauer and A. Zimmermann (eds), *Archäologische Perspektiven. Analysen und Interpretationen im Wandel. Festschrift für Jens Lüning zum 65. Geburtstag*, 423–40. Rahden: Marie Leidorf.

Weißmüller, W. 1986. *Postmesolithische Funde aus Höhlen und Abris am Beispiel des südlichen Riesrandgebiets*. Oxford: British Archaeological Reports.

Weißmüller, W. 1991. Der Silexabbau von Flintsbach-Hardt – eine bedeutende Rohmateriallagerstätte für die Steinzeit Südost-Bayerns. In K. Schmotz (ed.), *Vorträge des 9. Niederbayerischen Archäologentages*, 11–39. Buch am Erlbach: Marie Leidorf.

Weißmüller, W. 2002. Alt- und Mittelsteinzeit am bayerischen Donaulauf zwischen Lech und Inn. Ein Überblick. In K. Schmotz (ed.), *Vorträge des 20. Niederbayerischen Archäologentages*, 165–201. Rahden: Marie Leidorf.

Weston, D.A. 2008. Investigating the specificity of periosteal reactions in pathology museum specimens. *American Journal of Physical Anthropology* 137, 48–59.

Weston, D. 2012. Nonspecific infection in palaeopathology: interpreting periosteal reactions. In A.L. Grauer (ed.), *A companion to palaeopathology*, 492–512. Chichester: Wiley-Blackwell.

White, C.D., Storey, R., Longstaffe, F.J. and Spence, M.W. 2004. Immigration, assimilation, and status in the ancient city of Teotihuacan: stable isotopic evidence from Tlajinga 33. *Latin American Antiquity* 15, 176–98.

Whitley, J. 2002. Too many ancestors. *Antiquity* 76, 119–26.

Whittle, A. 1988. *Problems in Neolithic archaeology.* Cambridge: Cambridge University Press.

Whittle, A. 1990. Radiocarbon dating of the Linear Pottery culture: the contribution of cereal and bone samples. *Antiquity* 64, 297–302.

Whittle, A. 1996. *Europe in the Neolithic: the creation of new worlds*. Cambridge: Cambridge University Press.

Whittle, A. 2003. *The archaeology of people: dimensions of Neolithic life*. London: Routledge.

Whittle, A. 2005. Lived experience in the Early Neolithic of the Great Hungarian Plain. In D. Bailey, A. Whittle and V. Cummings (eds), *(un)settling the Neolithic*, 64–70. Oxford: Oxbow Books.

Whittle, A. (ed.) 2007. *The Early Neolithic on the Great Hungarian Plain: investigations of the Körös culture site of Ecsegfalva 23, Co. Békés*. Budapest: Institute of Archaeology, Hungarian Academy of Sciences.

Whittle, A. 2009. The people who lived in longhouses: what's the big idea? In D. Hofmann and P. Bickle (eds), *Creating communities: new advances in Central European Neolithic research*, 249–63. Oxford: Oxbow Books.

Whittle, A. 2012. Being alive and being dead: house and grave in the LBK. In A.M. Jones, J. Pollard, M.J. Allen and J. Gardiner (eds), *Image, memory and monumentality: archaeological engagements with the material world (a celebration of the academic achievements of Professor Richard Bradley)*, 194–206. Oxford: Oxbow Books.

Whittle, A., Bartosiewicz, L., Borić, D., Pettitt, P. and Richards, M. 2002. In the beginning: new radiocarbon dates for the Early Neolithic in northern Serbia and south-east Hungary. *Antaeus* 25, 63–117.

Whittle, A., Healy, F. and Bayliss, A. 2011. *Gathering time: dating the early Neolithic enclosures of southern Britain and Ireland.* Oxford: Oxbow Books.

Wild, E.M., Stadler, P., Häußer, A., Kutschera, W., Steier, P., Teschler-Nicola, M., Wahl, J. and Windl, H. 2004. Neolithic massacres: local skirmishes or general warfare in Europe? *Radiocarbon* 46, 377–85.

Wilkins, J.F. and Marlowe, F.W. 2006. Sex-biased migration in humans: what should we expect from genetic data? *BioEssays* 28, 290–300.

Willerding, U. 1980. Zum Ackerbau der Bandkeramiker. In T. Krüger and H.-G. Stephan (eds), *Beiträge zur Archäologie Nordwestdeutschlands und Mitteleuropas*, 421–56. Hildesheim: Lax.

Willms, C. 2003. Löwe, Elch und Schildkröte: kein jungsteinzeitliches Märchen. In J. Eckert, U. Eisenhauer and A. Zimmermann (eds), *Archäologische Perspektiven: Analysen und Interpretationen im Wandel. Festschrift für Jens Lüning zum 65. Geburtstag*, 181–94. Rahden: Marie Leidorf.

Willms, E. 1985. Neolithischer Spondylusschmuck. Hundert Jahre Forschung. *Germania* 63, 331–43.

Wilshusen, R.H. and Potter, J.M. 2010. The emergence of early villages in the American Southwest: cultural issues and historical perspectives. In M.S. Bandy and J.R. Fox (eds), *Becoming villagers: comparing early village societies*, 165–83. Tucson: University of Arizona Press.

Windl, H.J. 1983. Asparn an der Zaya/Schletz. *Fundberichte aus Österreich* 22, 232.

Windl, H.J. 1990. Grabungen in einem Siedlungsareal der Linearbandkeramik in Asparn an der Zaya, BH Mistelbach, Niederösterreich. *Archäologische Konferenz Keszthely 1989, Zalai Muzeum 2*, 19–22.

Windl, H.J. 1994. 10 Jahre Grabung Schletz, VB. Mistelbach, Niederösterreich. *Archäologie Österreichs* 5, 11–18.

Windl, H.J. 1996. Archäologie einer Katastrophe und deren Vorgeschichte. In H. Windl, J. Steiner and N. Weigl (eds), *Rätsel um Gewalt und Tod vor 7000 Jahren: eine Spurensicherung*, 7–29. Wien: Amt der NÖ Landesregierung.

Windl, H.J. 2002. Schletz. *Fundberichte aus Österreich* 41, 573.

Windl, H.J. 2005. Asparn an der Zaya. *Fundberichte aus Österreich* 44, 453.

Windl, H.J. 2009. Zur Stratigraphie der bandkeramischen Grabenwerke von Asparn an der Zaya-Schletz. In A. Zeeb-Lanz (ed.), *Krisen – Kulturwandel – Kontinuitäten: zum Ende der Bandkeramik in Mitteleuropa*, 191–6. Rahden: Marie Leidorf.

Winghart, S. 1986, Vorgeschichtliche Deponate im ostbayerischen Grenzgebirge und im Schwarzwald. Zu Horten und Einzelfunden in Mittelgebirgslandschaften. *Bericht der Römisch-Germanischen Kommission* 67, 89–201.

Wirtz, K.W. and Lemmen, C. 2003. A global dynamic model for the Neolithic transition. *Climatic Change* 59, 333–67.

Wischenbarth, P. 1991. Das Neolithikum im Landkeris Neu-Ulm. Eine Fundübersicht. *Bayerische Vorgeschichtsblätter* 56, 63–98.

Wischenbarth, P. 1993. Die Verbreitung neolithischer Import-Kreidefeuersteinartefakte im süddeutschen Raum. *Bayerische Vorgeschichtsblätter* 58, 1–21.

Wischenbarth, P. 1995. Spätmesolithische und linearbandkeramische Funde der Riß-Lech-Platte und deren Interpretation. *Germania* 73, 1–40.

Wischenbarth, P. 1999. *Alt- und Mittelsteinzeit im westlichen Bayerisch-Schwaben. Berichte zur Archäologie im Landkreis Neu-Ulm und in den angrenzenden Gebieten*. Neu-Ulm: Kreisarchäologie.

Wischenbarth, P. 2000. Neue steinzeitliche Alpinfundstellen in Voralberg/Österreich. Ergebnisse mehrjähriger Geländebegehungen. *Germania* 78, 273–96.

Wittwer-Backofen, U. and Timo, N. 2008. From health to civilization stress? In search of traces of a health transition during the Early Neolithic in Europe. In J.-P. Bocquet-Appel and O. Bar-Yosef (eds), *The Neolithic demographic transition and its consequences*, 501–37. New York: Springer.

Wolf, E. 1982. *Europe and the people without history*. Berkeley: University of California Press.

Wolf, J.J. 1980. Contribution à l'étude du Rubané au sud du Haut-Rhin. In A. Thévenin and J.-P. Thévenot (eds), *Le Rubané d'Alsace et de Lorraine: état des recherches 1979*, 199–224. Strasbourg: Association d'Études Préhistoriques et Protohistoriques d'Alsace.

Wolf, J.J. and Viroulet, B. 1992. Un village du Néolithique rubané récent à Sierentz (Haut-Rhin). 1. Présentation générale et étude des structures. *Cahiers de l'Association pour la Promotion de la Recherche Archéologique en Alsace* 8, 43–94.

Wolf, J.J. and Viroulet, B. 1997. Sierentz (Haut-Rhin). Un habitat rubané de Haute-Alsace. In C. Jeunesse (ed.), *Le Néolithique danubien et ses marges entre Rhin et Seine*, 407–10. Strasbourg: Cahiers de l'Association pour la Promotion de la Recherche Archéologique en Alsace.

Wolff, P. 1980. Das Tierknochenmaterial von Pulkau. In G. Trnka, 'Siedlungsreste der jüngeren Linienbandkeramik aus Pulkau, p. B. Hollabrunn, Niederösterreich'. *Archaeologia Austriaca* 64, 106–7.

Wolfram, S., Stäuble, H., Cladders, M. and Tischendorf, T. (eds) 2012. *Siedlungsstruktur und Kulturwandel in der Bandkeramik. Beiträge der internationalen Tagung "Neue Fragen zur Bandkeramik oder alles beim Alten?!" Leipzig, 23. bis 24. September 2010*. Leipzig: Landesamt für Archäologie.

Yaeger, J. 2000. The social construction of communities in the Classic Maya countryside: strategies of affiliation in western Belize. In M.A. Canuto and J. Yaeger (eds), *The archaeology of communities: a New World perspective*, 123–42. London: Routledge.

Zalai-Gaál, I. 2009. *Zur Herkunft des Schädelkults im Neolithikum des Karpatenbeckens*. Budapest: Archaeolingua.

Zalai-Gaál, I., Gál, E., Köhler, K. and Osztás, A. 2011. "Ins Jenseits begleitend": Hundemitbestattungen der Lengyel-Kultur von Alsónyék-Bátaszék. *Acta Archaeologica Academiae Scientiarum Hungaricae* 62, 29–74.

Zalai-Gaál, I., Osztás, A. and Köhler, K. 2012. Totenbrett oder Totenhütte? Zur Struktur der Gräber der Lengyel-Kultur mit Pfostenstellung in Südtransdanubien. *Acta Archaeologica Academiae Scientiarum Hungaricae* 63, 69–116.

Zápotocká, M. 1998. Pohřební ritus českého neolitu – nálezový stav a možnosti interpretace (Burial rites of the Czech Neolithic: the state of finds and possible interpretation. *Archeologické rozhledy* 50, 801–21.

Zápotocká, M. 2002. Kontakte, Importe, Warenaustausch und mögliche Pässe und Wege zwischen Böhmen und Bayern im Neolithikum. In J. Michálek, G. Raßhofer, K. Schmotz and P. Weinzierl (eds), *Archäologische Arbeitsgemeinschaft Ostbayern/West- und Südböhmen 11. Tagung Obernzell 2001*, 35–41. Rahden: Marie Leidorf.

Zeeb, A. 1993. Vorgeschichtliche Siedlungsbefunde in Nördlingen, Landkreis Donau-Ries, Schwaben. *Das Archäologische Jahr in Bayern 1992*, 87–9.

Zeeb-Lanz, A. 2003. Das Ries und seine steinzeitlichen Bewohner. Beobachtungen zur neolithischen Siedlungsentwicklung in einer Mikroregion. In J. Eckert, U. Eisenhauer and A. Zimmermann (eds), *Archäologische Perspektiven: Analysen und Interpretationen im Wandel. Festschrift für Jens Lüning zum 65. Geburtstag*, 293–306. Rahden: Marie Leidorf.

Zeeb-Lanz, A. (ed.) 2009a. *Krisen – Kulturwandel – Kontinuitäten: zum Ende der Bandkeramik in Mitteleuropa*. Rahden: Marie Leidorf.

Zeeb-Lanz, A. 2009b. Gewaltszenarien oder Sinnkrise? Die Grubenanlage von Herxheim und das Ende der Bandkeramik. In A. Zeeb-Lanz (ed.), *Krisen – Kulturwandel – Kontinuitäten: zum Ende der Bandkeramik in Mitteleuropa*, 87–101. Rahden: Marie Leidorf.

Zeeb-Lanz, A., Arbogast, A., Haack, F., Haidle, M.N., Jeunesse, C., Orschiedt, J., Schimmelpfennig, D. and van Willigen, S. 2009. The LBK settlement with pit enclosure at Herxheim near Landau (Palatinate): first results. In D. Hofmann and P. Bickle (eds), *Creating communities: new advances in central European Neolithic research*, 202–19. Oxford: Oxbow Books.

Ziegler, R. 1985/1986. Neolithische Tierreste aus Straubing-

Lerchenhaid (Niederbayern). *Berichte der Bayerischen Bodendenkmalpflege* 26/27, 7–32.

Zimmermann, A. 1995. *Austauschsysteme von Silexartefakten in der Bandkeramik Mitteleuropas*. Bonn: Habelt.

Zimmermann, A. 2002. Landschaftarchäologie I: die Bandkeramik auf der Aldenhovenener Platte. *Bericht der Römisch-Germanischen Kommission* 83, 17–38.

Zimmermann, A. 2010. Migration oder Adaption? Zur Entwicklung vom Mesolithikum zur Bandkeramik im Rheinland. In D. Gronenborn and J. Petrasch (eds), *Die Neolithisierung Mitteleuropas (The spread of the Neolithic to central Europe)*, 509–15. Mainz: Verlag des Römisch-Germanischen Zentralmuseums.

Zimmermann, A., Wendt, K.P., Frank, T. and Hilpert, J. 2009. Landscape archaeology in central Europe. *Proceedings of the Prehistoric Society* 75, 1–53.

Zoffmann, Z.K. 2000. Anthropological sketch of the prehistoric population of the Carpathian Basin. *Acta Biologica Szegediensis* 44, 75–9.

Zoffmann, Z.K. 2012. Anthropological analysis of the burials from the LBK settlement at Balatonszárszó-Kis-erdei-dűlő. *Acta Archaeologica Academiae Scientiarum Hungaricae* 63, 301–16.

Züchner, C. 2006. Wildbeuter in Bayern – Paläo- und Mesolithikum (with contributions by M. Beck, S. Feldmann, B. Gehlen, B. Kaulich, T. Rathgeber and A. Tillmann). In Gesellschaft für Archäologie in Bayern (eds), *Archäologie: Fenster zur Vergangenheit in Bayern*, 32–53. Regensburg: Friedrich Pustet.

Zvelebil, M. 1994. Plant use in the Mesolithic and the implications for the transition to farming. *Proceedings of the Prehistoric Society* 60, 95–134.

Zvelebil, M. 1996. The agricultural frontier and the transition to farming in the circum-Baltic region. In D. Harris (ed.), *The origins and spread of agriculture and pastoralism in Eurasia*, 323–45. London: University College London Press.

Zvelebil, M. 2000. Les derniers chasseurs-collecteurs d'Europe tempérée. In A. Richard, C. Cupillard, H. Richard and A. Thévenin (eds), *Les derniers chasseurs-cueilleurs d'Europe occidentale (13000–5500 av. J.-C.): actes du colloque international de Besançon*, 379–406. Besançon: University of Besançon.

Zvelebil, M. 2004. The many origins of the LBK. In A. Lukes and M. Zvelebil (eds), *LBK dialogues: studies in the formation of the Linear Pottery Culture*, 183–205. Oxford: Archaeopress.

Zvelebil, M. and Dolukanov, P. 1991. Transition to farming in eastern and northern Europe. *Journal of World Prehistory* 5, 233–78.

Zvelebil, M. and Pettitt, P. 2006. Contribution of Palaeolithic and Neolithic Y-chromosome lineages to the modern Czech population. *Archeologické rozhledy* 58, 250–60.

Zvelebil, M. and Pettitt, P. 2008. Human condition, life, and death at an early Neolithic settlement: bioarchaeological analyses of the Vedrovice cemetery and their biosocial implications for the spread of agriculture in central Europe. *Anthropologie* 46, 195–218.

Zvelebil, M., Lillie, M., Montgomery, J., Lukes, A., Pettitt, P. and Richards, M.P. 2012. The emergence of the LBK: migration, memory and meaning at the transition to agriculture. In E. Kaiser, J. Burger, and S. Wolfram (eds), *Population dynamics in prehistory and early history: new approaches using stable isotopes and genetics*,133–48. Berlin: de Gruyter.

Zvelebil, M., Lukes, A. and Pettitt, P. 2010. The emergence of the LBK culture: search for the ancestors. In D. Gronenborn and J. Petrasch (eds), *Die Neolithisierung Mitteleuropas (The spread of the Neolithic to central Europe)*, 301–25. Mainz: Römisch-Germanisches Zentralmuseum.

Web resources

Internet ref. 1: Geschichte: Naturhistorisches Museum Wien http://www.nhm-wien.ac.at/forschung/anthropologie/geschichte last accessed 21st February 2011.

Internet ref. 2: Geschichte des Bayerischen Landesamts für Denkmalpflege. http://www.blfd.bayern.de/landesamt/geschichte/index.php last accessed 1st March 2011.

Internet ref.3: Geschichtliche Entwicklung der Denkmalpflege Baden-Württemberg http://www.denkmalpflege-bw.de/geschichte-auftrag-struktur last accessed 9th March 2012.

Internet ref. 4 International Water Management Institute Atlas http://wcatlas.iwmi.org last accessed 21st June 2012.

Internet ref. 5 Climatic Research Unit, University of East Anglia http://www.cru.uea.ac.uk/ last accessed 21st June 2012.

Index

Page numbers for principal passages relating to a topic are shown in **bold**, page numbers for illustrations relating to a topic are shown in *italics*